FROMMER'S
DOLLARWISE GUIDE
TO THE CARIBBEAN

by Darwin Porter
assisted by Danforth Prince

1988-89 Edition

Published by Prentice Hall Press
A Division of Simon & Schuster, Inc.
Gulf + Western Building
One Gulf + Western Plaza
New York, NY 10023

ISBN 0–13–217696–3

Manufactured in the United States of America

CONTENTS

MAPS

Acknowledgment

I wish to thank Margaret Foresman, New York, for her tireless editorial assistance.

WHAT THE SYMBOLS MEAN: Travelers to the Caribbean may at first be confused by classifications on rate sheets. I've used these same classifications in this guide. One of the most common rates is **MAP,** meaning "Modified American Plan." Simply put, that usually means room, breakfast, and dinner, unless the room rate has been quoted separately, and then it means only breakfast and dinner. **CP** means Continental Plan—that is, room and a light breakfast. **EP** is European Plan, which means room only, and **AP** (American Plan) is the most expensive rate of all, because it includes not only your room but three meals a day.

INFLATION ALERT: I don't have to tell you that inflation has hit the Caribbean as it has everywhere else. In researching this book I have made every effort to obtain up-to-the-minute prices, but even the most conscientious researcher cannot keep up with the current pace of inflation. As the guide goes to press, I believe I have obtained the most reliable data possible. Nonetheless, in the lifetime of this edition—particularly its second year (1989)—the wise traveler will add 15% to 20% to the prices quoted throughout these pages.

A DISCLAIMER: Although every effort was made to ensure the accuracy of the prices and travel information appearing in this book, it should be kept in mind that prices do fluctuate in the course of time, and that information does change under the impact of the varied and volatile factors that affect the travel industry.

Introduction

A DOLLARWISE GUIDE TO THE CARIBBEAN

ONE OF THE WORLD'S greatest travel oases, the Caribbean spins its own sunny web of enchantment.

The dream is real enough, and all but the unimaginative can picture themselves part of the lazy life of these striking, dramatic islands, often called the "eighth continent of the world."

In just a few hours by plane from the North American continent, you're submerged in lands that have absorbed the cultures of other continents, including America, Europe, and Africa.

On a white sandy beach, shaded by a row of palm trees, you've just returned from a swim in gin-clear waters and are lying in the tanning sun, listening to the murmur of the surf, cooled by trade-wind-fed breezes, waiting for your tall rum punch drink as a sundowner before you dine on a West Indian buffet and dance to a steel band as you look out upon a shimmering sea under moonlight.

Although this fantasy comes true often enough for dreamers and lovers, I do not suggest that the complex, often perplexing Caribbean region is just a romantic mirage, without its problems. Few single travel destinations pose such confusion and require such advance, detailed information—data you need to know not just when you get off the plane, but material to review in advance when you ask the important question, "Which island should I choose?"

Leading you through this maze of emerging nations and colonial outposts is the purpose of this guide.

DOLLARWISE—WHAT IT MEANS: In brief, this is a guidebook giving specific, practical details (including prices) about the hotels, restaurants, sightseeing attractions, and nightlife of the Caribbean. Establishments in *all* price ranges have been documented and described, from the classily elegant Round Hill on a 98-acre peninsula in Montego Bay, Jamaica (where everybody from Coward to Porter to Rodgers used to play the resident piano), to a "Mom and Pop"–run, informal inn in Tortola in the British Virgin Islands.

In all cases, establishments have been judged by the strict yardstick of value. If they "measured up," they were included in this book—regardless of the price classification. The uniqueness of the book, I think, lies in the fact it could be used by everybody from Jacqueline Kennedy Onassis to a free-wheeling, adventure-seeking

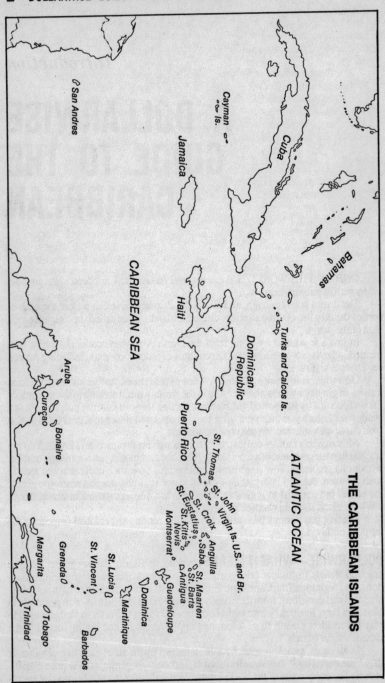

THE CARIBBEAN ISLANDS

ATLANTIC OCEAN

CARIBBEAN SEA

Cuba

Cayman Is.

Jamaica

San Andres

Bahamas

Turks and Caicos Is.

Haiti

Dominican Republic

Puerto Rico

St. Thomas St. John
Virgin Is. U.S. and Br.
St. Croix Anguilla
St. Eustatius Saba St. Maarten
St. Kitts St. Barts
Nevis Antigua
Montserrat
Guadeloupe
Dominica
Martinique
St. Lucia
St. Vincent Barbados
Grenada
Margarita Tobago
Trinidad

Aruba
Curaçao
Bonaire

collegian who seeks a different type of vacation—not just the sand and sea, but wants to learn something about other people and their lands, the intoxicating power of the Haitian Créole or the mystery of the Rastafarians who consider themselves Africans, not Jamaicans, and worship the late Emperor Haile Selassie I of Ethiopia as the Messiah.

But the major focus of the book is not centered either on the impecunious whose sole resources jingle in their pockets, or the affluent whose gold rests in numbered accounts in the Cayman Islands. Rather, my chief concern is the average, middle-income-bracket voyager who'd like to patronize some of the less documented hotels of the Caribbean, those places travel agents are sometimes reluctant to tell you about because the commission is not high.

AN INVITATION TO READERS: Like all its sister Dollarwise books, *Dollarwise Guide to the Caribbean* hopes to maintain a continuing dialogue between its author and its readers. All of us share a common aim—to travel as widely and as well as possible, at the best value for our money. And in achieving that goal, your comments and suggestions can be of tremendous help. Therefore, if you come across a particularly appealing hotel, restaurant, shop, even sightseeing attraction, please don't keep it to yourself. Remember too, the fact that a listing appears in this edition doesn't give it squatter's rights in future editions. If its services have deteriorated, its chef grown stale, its prices risen unfairly, these failings should be known. Or if you enjoyed every place and found every description accurate—that, too, can cheer many a gray day. Every letter will be read by me personally, although I find it well-nigh impossible to answer each and every one. Send your comments to Darwin Porter, c/o Prentice Hall Press, Gulf + Western Building, One Gulf + Western Plaza, New York, NY 10023.

TIME OUT FOR A COMMERCIAL: Many visitors erroneously consider The Bahamas part of the Caribbean, and may wonder why this world tourist mecca is not covered here. I do not mean to overlook The Bahamas. In fact, the publisher of this guide considers them important enough to create a companion volume, the 1988–1989 edition of *Frommer's Dollarwise Guide to Bermuda and The Bahamas,* which you may want to peruse in your search for an island hideaway.

The $25-A-Day Travel Club—How to Save Money on All Your Travels

In this book we'll be looking at how to get your money's worth in the Caribbean, but there is a "device" for saving money and determining value on *all* your trips. It's the popular, international $25-A-Day Travel Club, now in its 25th successful year of operation. The Club was formed at the urging of numerous readers of the $$$-A-Day and Dollarwise Guides, who felt that such an organization could provide continuing travel information and a sense of community to value-minded travelers in all parts of the world. And so it does!

In keeping with the budget concept, the annual membership fee is low and is immediately exceeded by the value of your benefits. Upon receipt of $18 (U.S. residents), or $20 U.S. by check drawn on a U.S. bank or via international postal money order in U.S. funds (Canadian, Mexican, and other foreign residents), to cover one year's membership, we will send all new members the following items.

(1) *Any two* of the following books
Please designate in your letter which two you wish to receive:

Frommer's $-A-Day Guides
Europe on $25 a Day
Australia on $25 a Day
Eastern Europe on $25 a Day
England on $35 a Day
Greece including Istanbul and Turkey's Aegean Coast on $25 a Day
Hawaii on $50 a Day
India on $15 & $25 a Day
Ireland on $30 a Day
Israel on $30 & $35 a Day
Mexico on $20 a Day (plus Belize and Guatemala)
New York on $45 a Day
New Zealand on $35 a Day
Scandinavia on $50 a Day
Scotland and Wales on $35 a Day
South America on $30 a Day
Spain and Morocco (plus the Canary Is.) on $40 a Day
Turkey on $25 a Day
Washington, D.C., on $40 a Day

Frommer's Dollarwise Guides
Dollarwise Guide to Austria and Hungary
Dollarwise Guide to Belgium, Holland, & Luxembourg
Dollarwise Guide to Bermuda and The Bahamas
Dollarwise Guide to Canada
Dollarwise Guide to the Caribbean
Dollarwise Guide to Egypt
Dollarwise Guide to England and Scotland
Dollarwise Guide to France
Dollarwise Guide to Germany
Dollarwise Guide to Italy
Dollarwise Guide to Japan and Hong Kong
Dollarwise Guide to Portugal, Madeira, and the Azores
Dollarwise Guide to the South Pacific
Dollarwise Guide to Switzerland and Liechtenstein
Dollarwise Guide to Alaska
Dollarwise Guide to California and Las Vegas
Dollarwise Guide to Florida
Dollarwise Guide to the Mid-Atlantic States
Dollarwise Guide to New England
Dollarwise Guide to New York State
Dollarwise Guide to the Northwest
Dollarwise Guide to Skiing USA—East
Dollarwise Guide to Skiing USA—West
Dollarwise Guide to the Southeast and New Orleans
Dollarwise Guide to the Southwest
Dollarwise Guide to Texas
(Dollarwise Guides discuss accommodations and facilities in all price ranges, with emphasis on the medium-priced.)

Frommer's Touring Guides
Egypt
Florence

London
Paris
Venice
(These new, color illustrated guides include walking tours, cultural and historic sites, and other vital travel information.)

A Shopper's Guide to Best Buys in England, Scotland, and Wales
(Describes in detail hundreds of places to shop—department stores, factory outlets, street markets, and craft centers—for great quality British bargains.)

A Shopper's Guide to the Caribbean
(Two experienced Caribbean hands guide you through this shopper's paradise, offering witty insights and helpful tips on the wares and emporia of more than 25 islands.)

Bed & Breakfast—North America
(This guide contains a directory of over 150 organizations that offer bed & breakfast referrals and reservations throughout North America. The scenic attractions, businesses, and major schools and universities near the homes of each are also listed.)

Dollarwise Guide to Cruises
(This complete guide covers all the basics of cruising—ports of call, costs, fly-cruise package bargains, cabin selection booking, embarkation and debarkation and describes in detail over 60 or so ships cruising the waters of Alaska, the Caribbean, Mexico, Hawaii, Panama, Canada, and the United States.)

Honeymoon Guide
(A special guide for that most romantic trip of your life, with full details on planning and choosing the destination that will be just right in the U.S. [California, New England, Hawaii, Florida, New York, South Carolina, etc.], Canada, Mexico, and the Caribbean.)

Dollarwise Guide to Skiing Europe
(Describes top ski resorts in Austria, France, Italy, and Switzerland. Illustrated with maps of each resort area plus full-color trail maps.)

Fast 'n' Easy Phrase Book
(French, German, Spanish, and Italian—all in one convenient, easy-to-use phrase guide.)

How to Beat the High Cost of Travel
(This practical guide details how to save money on absolutely all travel items—accommodations, transportation, dining, sightseeing, shopping, taxes, and more. Includes special budget information for seniors, students, singles, and families.)

Marilyn Wood's Wonderful Weekends
(This very selective guide covers the best mini-vacation destinations within a 175-mile radius of New York City. It describes special country inns and other accommodations, restaurants, picnic spots, sights, and activities—all the information needed for a two- or three-day stay.)

Motorist's Phrase Book
(A practical phrase book in French, German, and Spanish designed specifically for the English-speaking motorist touring abroad.)

Swap and Go—Home Exchanging Made Easy
(Two veteran home exchangers explain in detail all the money-saving benefits of a home exchange, and then describe precisely how to do it. Also includes information on home rentals and many tips on low-cost travel.)

The Candy Apple: New York for Kids
(A spirited guide to the wonders of the Big Apple by a savvy New York grandmother with a kid's-eye view to fun. Indispensable for visitors and residents alike.)

Travel Diary and Record Book
(A 96-page diary for personal travel notes plus a section for such vital data as passport and traveler's check numbers, itinerary, postcard list, special people and places to visit, and a reference section with temperature and conversion charts, and world maps with distance zones.)

Where to Stay USA
(By the Council on International Educational Exchange, this extraordinary guide is the first to list accommodations in all 50 states that cost anywhere from $3 to $30 per night.)

(2) A one-year subscription to *The Wonderful World of Budget Travel*

This quarterly eight-page tabloid newspaper keeps you up to date on fast-breaking developments in low-cost travel in all parts of the world bringing you the latest money-saving information—the kind of information you'd have to pay $25 a year to obtain elsewhere. This consumer-conscious publication also features columns of special interest to readers: **Hospitality Exchange** (members all over the world who are willing to provide hospitality to other members as they pass through their home cities); **Share-a-Trip** (offers and requests from members for travel companions who can share costs and help avoid the burdensome single supplement); and **Readers Ask . . . Readers Reply** (travel questions from members to which other members reply with authentic firsthand information).

(3) A copy of *Arthur Frommer's Guide to New York*

This is a pocket-size guide to hotels, restaurants, nightspots, and sightseeing attractions in all price ranges throughout the New York area.

(4) Your personal membership card

Membership entitles you to purchase through the Club all Arthur Frommer publications for a third to a half off their regular retail prices during the term of your membership.

So why not join this hardy band of international budgeteers and participate in its exchange of travel information and hospitality? Simply send your name and address, together with your annual membership fee of $18 (U.S. residents) or $20 U.S. (Canadian, Mexican, and other foreign residents), by check drawn on a U.S. bank or via international postal money order in U.S. funds to: $25-A-Day Travel Club, Inc., Frommer Books, Gulf + Western Building, One Gulf + Western Plaza, New York, NY 10023. And please remember to specify which *two* of the books in section (1) above you wish to receive in your initial package of members' benefits. Or, if you prefer, use the last page of this book, simply checking off the two books you select and enclosing $18 or $20 in U.S. currency.

Once you are a member, there is no obligation to buy additional books. No books will be mailed to you without your specific order.

PLANNING A TRIP

EACH ISLAND OF THE CARIBBEAN is unique, often reflecting a colonial past, especially British, French, Spanish, or Dutch. Regardless of individual histories, each island country, even the remote ones, has forged its own personality and identity. Therefore, even though they are about the same part of the world, each chapter in this guide is different, focusing on special food, characteristics, and attractions.

Because all of the islands of the West Indies share similarities of geography, however, I have packed this opening chapter with information you need to know when planning a holiday in the Caribbean. Many questions will come to mind, including temperature, summer versus winter travel, wardrobe, phones, or a hotel versus a guesthouse. Of course this section doesn't pretend to answer all the general questions you may have, so I'll follow with another chapter devoted to more background, including climate, geography, history, food, and drink.

From Miami to Trinidad at the southern tip of the Caribbean is a distance of some 1,800 miles. A lot of islands are strung out between Florida and the coast of South America. Someone once estimated that if you don't count the rocks sticking up in the Caribbean, there are some 7,000 islands. That's a lot of islands. Fortunately for the page count of this guide, most of them are not inhabited, and many of those that are inhabited don't have hotels. At least that simplifies our task a bit.

Nevertheless, the Caribbean is an overwhelming piece of geography, and making a choice of islands is one of the most formidable decisions you'll have to make. After all, none of the islands is remote anymore. Even the so-called remote ones can usually be reached after a change of planes, unless you live at an inconvenient transportation point in the United States.

One of the most serious suggestions of this guide is to recommend that you island-hop as never before, instead of locating in one spot for a week or more and perhaps getting bored after the fourth day. Transportation schedules have never been more convenient, and you can now experience a vastly different culture perhaps after just a 15-minute flight. For example, if you're visiting the island of St. Martin, you might consider flying to Saba, Statia, Anguilla, St. Kitts, Nevis, or St. Barts. Such island-hopping for not a lot more in transportation cost can lend much richness to a Caribbean vacation and can help avoid sterile stopovers.

I'll begin with the first point of consideration—that of getting there in the first place.

1. Getting There

FLYING SOUTH: From North America, it's easy to wing your way south to the Caribbean. In just a matter of hours you can flee the Arctic winds and be lying on the beach, sipping your rum punch.

Travel agents who keep up-to-the-minute schedules can inform you about special stopover privileges, as "island-hopping" is becoming an increasingly popular diversion for both a summer or winter holiday.

All the biggest islands have air links to the North American continent, with regularly scheduled service. The smaller islands are tied into this vast network through their own carriers, such as Prinair. For example to reach Montserrat, you fly, say, from New York to Antigua, where a smaller craft will take you the rest of the short distance.

For a specific description of how to reach each island in this guide by plane, refer to the individual "Getting There" sections.

TOURING BY PLANE: Chances are, you'll spend less than half a day flying from your point of embarkation in North America to your Caribbean island, and unless connecting links are impossible, that includes time lodged in waiting for inter-island flights. Obviously, the less time spent in getting there means more time on the beach. Direct flights from, say, New York, are possible to all major cities or islands of the Caribbean, including Antigua and Puerto Rico.

You face a choice of booking a seat on a regularly scheduled flight or else a charter plane, the latter being cheaper, of course. On a regular flight you can cancel your ticket without penalty. On a charter you do not have such leeway.

Charter Flights

Now open to the general public, charter flights allow you to travel at rates cheaper than on regularly scheduled flights. Many of the major carriers offer charter flights at rates that are sometimes 30% (or more) off the regular air fare.

There are some drawbacks to charter flights that you need to consider. Advance booking, for example, of up to 45 days or more may be required. You could lose most of the money you've advanced if an emergency should force you to cancel a flight. However, it is now possible to take out cancellation insurance against such an eventuality.

Unfortunately, on the charter flight you are forced to depart and return on a scheduled date. It will do no good to call the airline and tell them you're in Trinidad with yellow fever! If you're not on the plane, you can kiss your money good-bye.

Since charter flights are so complicated, it's best to go to a good travel agent and ask him or her to explain to you the problems, and advantages. Sometimes charters require ground arrangements, such as the prebooking of hotel rooms.

While there, ask about APEX fares, meaning advance purchase. These individual inclusive fares include land arrangements along with your excursion fare, and can represent a considerable savings to you.

TOURING BY CRUISE SHIP: If you'd like to sail the Caribbean, having a home with an ocean view, the cruise ship might be for you. It's slow and easy, and it's no longer to be enjoyed only by the idle rich who have months to spend away from home. Most cruises today appeal to the middle-income voyager who probably has no more than one or two weeks to spend cruising the Caribbean. Some 300 passenger ships sail the Caribbean all year, and in January and February that figure may go up another hundred or so. That's why it's impossible for me, given our space limitations, to recommend particular cruises to readers. You might want to pick up a copy of *Frommer's Dollarwise Guide to Cruises* for more detailed information.

Most cruise-ship operators suggest the concept of a "total vacation." Some promote activities "from sunup to sundown" while others suggest the possibility of "having absolutely nothing to do but lounge." Cruise ships are self-contained resorts, offering everything on board but actual sightseeing once you arrive in a port of call.

If you don't want to spend all your time at sea, some lines offer a fly-and-cruise vacation. Terms vary widely under this arrangement. You spend a week cruising the Caribbean, another week staying at an interesting hotel at reduced prices. These total packages cost less (or should) than if you'd purchased the cruise and air portions separately.

On yet another interpretation of "fly and cruise," you fly to meet the cruise and to leave it. Although multifarious in nature, most plans offer a package deal from the principal airport closest to your residence to the major airport nearest to the cruise departure point. Otherwise, you can purchase your air ticket on your own—say, from Kansas City to Fort Lauderdale—and book your cruise ticket separately as well, but you'll save money by combining the fares in a package deal.

Miami is the "cruise capital of the world," and vessels also leave from San Juan, New York, Port Everglades, Los Angeles, and other points of embarkation as well.

Most of the cruise ships prefer to do their traveling at night, arriving the next morning at the day's port of call, as anybody who has ever had a hotel room overlooking the water in St. Thomas can testify. In port, passengers can go ashore for sightseeing and shopping (it's also possible to have lunch at a restaurant of your choice to sample some of the island specialties and break the monotony of taking every meal aboard ship).

Prices vary so widely that I cannot possibly document them. Sometimes the same route, stopping at the identical ports of call, will carry different fares.

TOURING BY CHARTERED BOAT: There is perhaps no more dream-making way of having a holiday in the Caribbean than from the deck of your own yacht. An impossible dream? Not really. No one said you had to own that yacht. You can charter it or go on a prearranged cruise.

Experienced sailors and navigators, with a sea-wise crew, can charter "bareboat," a term meaning a rental with a fully equipped boat but with no captain or crew. You're on your own, and you'll have to prove you can handle it before you're allowed to go on such a craft. Even if you're your own skipper, you may want to take along an experienced yachtsman familiar with local waters, which may be tricky in some places. (The company that insures the craft will definitely want to know that the vessel in question is in safe hands.)

Of course, if you can afford it, the ideal way is to charter a boat with a skilled skipper and a fully competent crew. Four to six people, maybe more, often charter yachts varying from 50 to more than 100 feet. Sometimes a dozen people will go out; at other times, a more romantic twosome.

Both the U.S. and British Virgin Islands are good cruising grounds, as are the Leeward and Windward Islands, which stretch from Antigua to Grenada, taking in such jewels of the French West Indies as Martinique and Guadeloupe. St. Vincent and the satellite Grenadines are also beautiful cruising grounds.

Most yachts are rented on a weekly basis, with a fully stocked bar, plus equipment for fishing and water sports. More and more bareboat charters are learning that they can save money and select menus more suited to their tastes by doing their own provisioning, rather than relying on the yacht company that rented them the vessel.

Unless money is no problem to you, the immediate question the average sailor asks is "How much will it cost?" Depending on the type of boat and the facilities offered, one person can count on spending from $90 to $150 a day. That doesn't mean you can't go out for less, and you certainly can sail for a lot more. Perhaps in summer, when business might be slow, you might get some yacht companies to charter you a boat for four or five days instead of a week or longer.

Some of the best-known firms in the charter business include the following:

Stevens Yachts, 252 East Ave., East Norwalk, CT 06855 (tel. 203/866-8989 within Connecticut, or toll free 800/638-7044 elsewhere in the U.S.). This outfit specializes in yacht chartering from its bases in Tortola (the British Virgin Islands) and St. Lucia. Bareboat and crewed yachts between 39 and 56 feet are available from a well-maintained fleet of Sparkman and Stephens–designed sailing craft. Heidi Patty, the charter manager, suggests that four- to six-month advance bookings (which require a 50% deposit) are a good idea for locked-in dates. Clients whose schedules are more flexible need only about a month's reservations in advance. Insurance and full equipment are included in the rates.

Windjammer Barefoot Cruises, Ltd., P.O. Box 120, Miami Beach, FL 33119 (tel. 305/373-2090, or toll free 800/327-2600, 800/432-3364 in Florida), offers trips on large sailing ships through the Caribbean. Its *Flying Cloud* goes through the British Virgin Islands; its *Polynesia* sails the Leeward and Windward Islands; its *Yankee Clipper* sails from Antigua; and *Fantome,* from The Bahamas. The newest ship, *Mandalay,* makes 13-day cruises out of Grenada and Antigua. Rates start at $625. Air-sea package deals are offered. S/V *Fantome,* S/V *Polynesia,* and S/V *Yankee Clipper* are registered in the British Virgin Islands, and the *Flying Cloud* is registered in The Bahamas. All ships comply with international safety standards except 1966 fire safety standards.

Nicholson Yacht Charters, 9 Chauncy St., Cambridge, MA 02138 (tel. 617/661-8174, or toll free 800/662-6066), or write P.O. Box 103, St. John's, Antigua, West Indies. This company, one of the best in the business, handles charter yachts for use throughout the Caribbean basin, particularly the route between Dutch-held St. Maarten to Grenada, as well as the routes around the U.S. and British Virgin Islands. Specializing in boats of all sizes, they can arrange rentals of motor or sailing yachts of up to 164 feet long (in this case, a Hanse motor yacht), with a skipper and crew, or smaller boats accommodating anywhere from 2 to 12 people in private single or double cabins. Especially popular are arrangements where two or more yachts, each sleeping eight guests in four equal double cabins, race each other from island to island during the day, anchoring near each other in secluded coves or at berths in Caribbean capitals at night. Nicholson's offers a series of possibilities. An average package, according to the owners, costs approximately $1,000 per week.

It's also possible to cruise in the Caribbean on yachts that have set sailing dates. On this type of craft, depending on its size, of course, there might be anywhere from 6 to 50 passengers. You are in fact a cruise passenger.

PACKAGE TOURS: If you want everything done for you, plus want to save money as well, you might consider traveling the Caribbean on a package tour. General tours appealing to the average voyager are commonly offered, but many of the tours are very specific—tennis packages, golf packages, scuba and snorkeling packages, and, only for those who qualify, honeymooners' specials.

Economy and convenience are the chief advantage of a package tour in that the cost of transportation (usually an airplane fare), a hotel room, food (sometimes), and sightseeing (sometimes) are combined in one package, neatly tied up with a single price tag.

There are extras, of course, but in general you'll know in advance roughly what the cost of your vacation will be, and can budget accordingly.

If you booked your flight separately, likewise your hotel, you could not come out as cheaply as on a package tour—hence their immense and increasing appeal. There are disadvantages too. You may find yourself in a hotel you dislike immensely, yet you are virtually trapped there, as you've already paid for it.

Everybody from Idaho potato growers to birdwatchers of Alcatraz seemingly offers package tours to the Caribbean. Choosing the right one can be a bit of a problem. Your travel agent may offer one. Certainly all the major airline carriers will. It's best to go to a travel agent, tell him or her what island (or islands) you'd like to visit, and see what's currently offered.

These packages are available because tour operators can mass-book hotels and make volume purchases. You generally have to pay the cost of the total package in advance. Transfers between your hotel and the airport are often included, and this is more of a financial break than it sounds at first, as some airports are situated a $40 or more taxi ride from a resort. Many packages carry several options, including the possibility of low-cost car rentals.

The single traveler, regrettably, usually suffers, as nearly all tour packages are based on double occupancy.

2. A Traveler's Advisory

Will I be safe in the Caribbean? This is one of the questions most often asked by the first-time visitor, and it's one of the most difficult to answer. Can a guidebook writer safely recommend traveling to New York or any major American city? Are you, in fact, free from harm in your own home?

The "attitude toward the visitor" takes on a wide range of meaning depending on whose attitude you are talking about. The Caribbean is composed of many nations, some of whom have broken, at least on paper, from colonial powers that dominated their cultures for years; others, such as Montserrat, preferring to retain their safe links with the past. Some islands, such as Guadeloupe and Martinique, are actually part of France, while other Caribbean nations prefer to seek help anywhere else but from their former colonial masters.

That attitude I mentioned might mean friendliness and hospitality, or it could encompass everything from indifferent service in a hotel dining room to theft and perhaps violence.

Many tourist boards are increasingly sensitive to the treatment of visitors, because their fragile economies depend on how many people their islands attract. Rudeness, room burglaries, anything that results in unfavorable publicity can cause damage. As a result, many islands are taking steps to make their own people more aware of the importance of tourism, and to treat their guests as they themselves would want to be treated if traveling in a foreign land.

Of course, many of the problems have come from the tourists themselves. A white person arriving in a predominantly black society may feel threatened—or worse, superior—and that can create difficulties. The people of the Caribbean must be given their respect and dignity. A smile usually wins a smile.

In addition, many of the islanders are deeply religious, and are offended by tourists who wear bikinis on shopping expeditions in town. One West Indian woman who runs a small hotel in Antigua had rented rooms to a film crew making a pirate adventure. When the men on that crew started running drunk and nude on the beach, a sight witnessed by the woman's two teenage daughters, she was deeply shocked. She handled the situation by posting a sign—"Pirates Must Wear Bathing Suits on the Beach."

Don't leave valuables such as cameras and cash-stuffed purses lying unattended on the beach while you go for a swim. Would you be so careless of your possessions in any town or city in Europe or America? Caribbean tourist officials often warn visitors, "If you've got it, don't flaunt it."

Problems do exist, and tomorrow's headlines may carry the story of a Caribbean disaster. Let me point out, however, that trouble in, say, Kingston, Jamaica, doesn't mean trouble in Barbados, no more than a bombing in London means you should cancel your trip to Munich.

Know that most of the people in the West Indies are proud, very proper, and most respectable, and if you treat them like such, they will likely treat you the same way. Others—certainly the minority, but a visible minority—are downright antagonistic. Some, in fact, are skunks. But, then, any country on the globe has its share of that type.

Some islands are more hospitable to tourists than others. Your greeting in Montserrat is likely to be friendlier than it is in more jaded St. Thomas. But, then, Montserrat doesn't have five cruise ships a day docking at its harbor.

3. Traveling Year Round

More and more, the Caribbean is becoming a vacation goal for all seasons. Although they have more rain in the late spring and summer, the West Indies islands have so little variation in temperature that you can enjoy a visit there at any time. Installation of air conditioning in many accommodations, plus the swirling ceiling fans in almost every room you'll see, make for personal comfort everywhere. Sunshine is practically an everyday affair, even between the showers. So come on down!

IN WINTER: The so-called season in the Caribbean runs roughly from the middle of December to the middle of April. Hotels in the Caribbean charge their highest prices during the peak winter period when visitors fleeing from the cold north winds crowd into the islands. Winter is the dry season in the islands, and most of the days are invariably sunny.

During the winter months, make reservations two to three months in advance, and if you rely on writing directly to the hotels, know that the mails are unreliable and take a long time. At certain hotels it is almost impossible to secure accommodations at Christmas and in February. One hotel in particular, Caneel Bay Plantation in St. John, books its rooms in February about a year in advance. Instead of writing to reserve your own room, it's better to book through one of the many Stateside representatives all major and many minor hotels use, or else to deal directly through a travel agent. If you don't want to do that, you should telephone the hotel of your choice in the Caribbean, agree on terms, and rush a deposit to hold the room.

Air-conditioned by trade winds, the temperature variations in the Caribbean are surprisingly slight, ranging between 75° and 85° Fahrenheit in both winter and summer. In other words, it's like a perpetual June.

IS THE SUMMER TOO HOT? For many travelers the islands of the Caribbean simply do not exist except when fearsome winds beat around corners and ice and slush pile up on the sidewalks up north. Regrettably, because everybody wants to visit the islands at these times, "the season" developed. Knowing they had a hot item to sell—warm, sandy beaches when much of North America was hit by blizzards—hotel entrepreneurs charge the maximum for their accommodations in winter, "the maximum" meaning all that the traffic will bear.

When North America warms up, vacationers head for Cape Cod or the Jersey shore or the beaches of California, forgetting the islands in the sun, thinking perhaps that the Caribbean is a caldron. This is not the case. The fabled Caribbean weather is balmy all year, with temperatures varying little more than five degrees between winter and summer. The mid-80s prevail throughout most of the region, and trade winds make for comfortable days and nights, even in cheaper places that don't have air conditioning.

Truth is, you're better off in the West Indies most of the time than you are suffering through a roaring August heat wave in Chicago or New York.

Dollar for dollar, you'll save more money by renting a house or self-sufficient unit in the Caribbean than you would on Cape Cod, Fire Island, Laguna Beach, or the coast of Maine. Sailing and water sports are better too, because the West Indies is protected from the Atlantic on its western shores which border the calm Caribbean Sea.

In essence, because of the trade winds and the various ocean currents, the Caribbean is virtually "seasonless."

20% TO 60% REDUCTIONS: The off-season in the Caribbean—roughly from mid-April to mid-December (although this varies from hotel to hotel)—amounts to a summer sale. Except that summer in this context is eight months long, stretched out to include spring and autumn, often ideal times for travel.

In most cases, hotel rates are slashed a startling 20% to 60%, and these rate reductions are emphasized in this guide by being set in *italics*.

It's a bonanza for cost-conscious travelers, especially families who like to go on vacations together. Unbelievable, you say. You need proof.

In the chapters ahead, I'll spell out in dollars the specific amounts hotels charge during the off-season. In the meantime I'll cite percentages to back up my case. These percentages, incidentally, were tabulated by the Caribbean Tourism Association, and released to the press only after a careful screening for verification.

In the French island of Guadeloupe, which possesses some of the finest beaches in the Caribbean, and is covered with rain forests and topped by a sulfurous volcano, the PLM Arawak cuts its rates by 45% in the off-season. A skyscraper on the shore, it offers ten floors of "modern Créole rooms."

On the popular island of Barbados, the easternmost island in the West Indies, the Barbados Hilton cuts rates by about 33%. Built around a central court full of tropical gardens, right on the beach, it's a citadel of luxury living, Bajan style.

On the "spice island" of Grenada, southernmost island of the Windward Antilles, the Calabash, one of the finest hotels in the island country, slashes its rates by a whopping 57% on certain rooms.

On Nevis, once known for its sugarcane estates, the Nisbet Plantation Inn, a gracious estate house on a copra farm, the former home of Lord Nelson's bride, cuts tariffs by 43%.

In Tortola, the capital of the British Virgin Islands, Long Bay Hotel, a low-rise hotel complex set in a 50-acre estate with nearly a mile of white sand beach, cuts charges in summer by a big 55%.

Finally, the best for last. In the Dominican Republic, the Casa de Campo, the most fabulous resort in the West Indies, reduces its winter tariffs by 51% in the off-season, which makes it so reasonable that many middle-class Dominican families plan their holidays in this super-complete, luxurious resort dedicated to sports.

OTHER OFF-SEASON ADVANTAGES: In addition to price slashes at hotels, there are some other important reasons for visiting the Caribbean in spring, summer, and autumn.

- After the winter hordes have left, a less hurried way of life prevails. You'll have a better chance to appreciate the food, the culture, and the local customs.
- Swimming pools and beaches are less crowded—perhaps not crowded at all.
- Because summer business has grown, year-round resort facilities are offered, often at reduced rates. This is likely to include, among other activities, snorkeling, boating, and scuba-diving.
- To survive, resort boutiques often feature summer sales, hoping to clear the merchandise they didn't sell in February. They've ordered stock for the com-

ing winter, and must clean their shelves and clear their racks. Duty-free items in free-port shopping are draws all year too.

● You can often walk in unannounced at a top restaurant and get a seat for dinner, a seat that would have been denied you in winter unless you'd made reservations far in advance. When the waiters are less hurried, you'll get far better service too.

● The endless waiting game is over in the off-season. No waiting for a rented car (only to be told none is available). No long tee-up for golf. More immediate access to the tennis courts and water sports.

● The atmosphere is more cosmopolitan in the off-season than it is in winter, mainly because of the influx of Europeans. You'll no longer feel as if you're at a Canadian or American outpost. Also, the Antilleans themselves travel in the off-season, and our holiday becomes more of a people-to-people experience.

● Some package-tour fares are as much as 20% cheaper, and individual excursion fares are also reduced between 5% and 10%.

● All accommodations, including airline seats and hotel rooms, are much easier to obtain.

● Summer is the time for family travel, which is not possible during the winter season. Or else parents can travel while children are away at camp.

● Finally, the very best of wintertime attractions remain undiminished—sea, sand, sun, and surf.

4. Where to Stay

If deciding on the island or islands to visit seems complicated, selecting the place to live once you get there may be even more perplexing. Few travel destinations in the world offer such a wide range of accommodations: a tropical villa in St. Thomas, a millionaire's estate in Jamaica, a 17th-century great house in St. Kitts, a 200-year-old sugar warehouse in St. Vincent, or a beachfront apartel in Puerto Rico. You can even perch in a treehouse by the sea! In this guide, I've surveyed the widest possible range of accommodations, from deluxe citadels to simply furnished, low-cost cottages near the sea.

HOTELS AND RESORTS: One of the most galling occurrences is to run into someone from your hometown and learn that the couple next door are staying in the same hotel that you are, even enjoying an ocean view as opposed to your "mountain view," but are paying some $200 to $300 less per week than you are. That happens more often than you'd imagine.

A lot of it stems from a zeal among Caribbean hoteliers, especially during the slow months, to promote business. There are package deals galore, and though they have many disadvantages, they are always cheaper than rack rates (what an individual pays who literally walks in from the street). Therefore it's always good to go to a reliable travel agent to find out what is available in the way of a land-and-air package before booking into a particular property.

There is no rigid classification of Caribbean hotel properties. The word "deluxe" is often used—or misused—when "first class" might have been a more appropriate term. First class itself often isn't. For that and other reasons, I've presented fairly detailed descriptions of the properties, so that you'll get an idea of what to expect once you're there. However, even in the deluxe and first-class properties, don't expect top-rate service and efficiency. "Things," as they are called in the West Indies, don't seem to work as well in the tropics as they do in certain fancy resorts of California or Europe. Life in the tropics has its disadvantages. When you go to turn on the shower, sometimes you get water and sometimes you don't. You may even experience island power failures. To prepare yourself, read the Herman Wouk novel *Don't Stop the Carnival*, and go to the West Indies already armed with the information that a hotel operation might not work as well as it would back home.

Facilities often determine the choice of a hotel. For example, if golf is your passion, you may want to book into a hotel resort such as Casa de Campo in the Dominican Republic. If scuba-diving is your goal, then head, say, for the Cayman Islands and a "dive resort." Regardless of your particular interest, there is probably a hotel catering to your need.

THE WEST INDIAN GUESTHOUSE: An entirely different type of accommodation is the guesthouse, where most of the Antilleans themselves stay when they travel in the Caribbean. Some of these are surprisingly comfortable, often with swimming pools and private baths with each room. You may or may not have air conditioning. The rooms are sometimes cooled by ceiling fans or trade winds blowing through open windows at night. Of course, don't expect the luxuries of a fabulous resort, but for value the guesthouse can't be topped. Staying in a guesthouse, you can journey over to a big beach resort, using its seaside facilities for only a small charge, perhaps no more than $3.

Although bereft of frills, the guesthouses I've recommended are clean, decent, and safe for families or single women. Many of the cheapest ones are not places you'd like to live in all night and day too, because of their simple, modest furnishings.

However, many of today's new breed of travelers to the Caribbean don't want to spend more than eight hours in their rooms anyway. Otherwise, you'll find them on the beach, snorkeling or going scuba-diving, and at night patronizing the native taverns serving local food and just getting to know people. To this type of traveler a hotel is a mere convenience, to go to for sleep after an activity-filled day and a nightlife-packed evening.

Dressing up for dinner and otherwise practicing a routine familiar at American country clubs may not appeal to many of today's more adventurous travelers, who often arrive in the West Indies with a bikini, a T-shirt, and a pair of jeans.

In the Caribbean, the term "guesthouse" can mean anything. Sometimes so-called guesthouses are really like simple motels built around swimming pools. Others are small individual cottages, with their own kitchenettes, constructed around a main building in which you'll often find a bar and a restaurant serving local food.

SELF-CATERING HOLIDAYS: Particularly if you're a family or friendly group, a housekeeping holiday can be one of the least expensive ways of vacationing in the Caribbean. These types of accommodations are now available on nearly all the islands previewed. Sometimes you can rent individual cottages; others are housed in one building. Some are private homes rented when the owners are away. All have small kitchens or kitchenettes where you can do your home-cooking, shopping for groceries, and whenever possible, buying freshly caught fish and some Caribbean lobster.

A housekeeping holiday, however, doesn't always mean you'll have to do maid's work. Most of the self-catering places have maid service included in the rental, and you're given fresh linen as well.

Cooking most of your meals yourself and dining out on occasion, such as when a neighboring big hotel has a beachside barbecue with entertainment, is the surest way of keeping holiday costs at a minimum.

FOR SINGLE TRAVELERS: If you've ever read bargain-travel advertisements, you'll sometimes see an asterisk, indicating below (in fine print) that the tempting deal being presented is based on "double occupancy." If you're a lone wolf or without a traveling companion, you'll often get hit with a painful supplement called a "surcharge" that can be at least 35% and perhaps a lot more. The hotelier in the Caribbean, of course, likes to shelter at least two in a room, and sometimes they crowd in three or four. It's the same room, and two to three persons spend a lot more on drinks, water sports, and food.

In addition to the cruises for singles that have gained mass popularity in the past few years, there is another way to keep costs bone-trimmed and take advantage of some of the package tours, cruises, and cut-rate hotel deals. But it means you may have to join a club.

One of the most successful such groups is **Gramercy's Singleworld,** 444 Madison Ave., New York, NY 10022 (tel. 212/758-2433), which for some 30 years has catered to single and unattached persons—the never-married, the separated, divorced, widowed, and those traveling alone. They have no age limits, although most of their club members are under 35. Certain cruise and tour departures are designated for people of all ages or under 35.

Anyone who is single or traveling alone is eligible for membership. The membership fee is $18 (nonrefundable). However, it is effective from the date of a departure for one full year. Singleworld emphasizes that they are *not* a lonely-hearts club, *not* a matrimonial bureau, and do *not* guarantee equal numbers of men and women in their groups.

Because Singleworld offers more than 500 departures a year, the prices offered for the cruise and tour departures are competitive. In addition, you can avoid the extra expense of a single-room accommodation by sharing a unit with another member.

5. Family Vacations

The islands of the Caribbean contend for top position on the world list of places for vacations for the entire family. The smallest toddlers can spend blissful hours on sandy beaches and in the shallow sea water or pools constructed with them in mind. There's no end to the fascinating pursuits offered for older children too, ranging from boat rides to shell collecting to horseback riding, hiking, even discoing. Perhaps yours are old enough to learn to snorkel and explore the wonderland of the underwater Caribbean.

There are places where such skills are taught as weaving hats of coconut-palm fronds, learning circus performance skills, swimming, windsurfing, and a variety of other activities unique to the islands.

There are important pointers to keep in mind when you're planning a family vacation anywhere in the Caribbean so that your trip is fun for all with a minimum of worries. Most resort hotels will advise you as to what there is in the way of fun for all ages, and many have play directors and supervised activities for the young of various age groups. However, there are some tips for making the trip a success which parents should attend to in advance so that when the family finds itself in the sunny paradise, nobody will think they've gone the wrong direction.

Take along a "security blanket" for your child. This might be a pacifier, a favorite toy, or books the child likes especially—something to make him or her feel at home. An older offspring might take along a treasure such as a baseball cap, a favorite T-shirt (even though there'll be plenty to buy down there), or some special trinket or good-luck piece.

Take protection from the sun. For tiny tots, this should include a sun umbrella, while the whole family will need sunburn or tanning preparations, plus sunglasses.

Take along anti-insect lotions and sprays. You'll probably need these both to repel such little unwanted island denizens as mosquitoes and sand fleas as well as to ease the itching and possible other after-effects of insect bites.

Arrange ahead for such necessities as a crib, bottle warmer, and car seat (if you're driving anywhere) for the very young, as well as for cots in your room for larger children. Find out if the place you're staying stocks baby food, and if not, take it with you.

Draw up rules for your family to follow during your holiday. These should be flexible, of course—after all, this trip is for fun. But guidelines on bedtime, eating, keeping tidy, being in the sun, even shopping and spending, can help make everybody's vacation more enjoyable.

Babysitters can be found for you by most hotels, but you should insist that yours knows at least rudimentary English in order to avoid traumatic experiences for young children. Talk with the sitter yourself, and introduce him or her to those to be cared for before you leave the hotel room or nursery.

In addition to fundamentals that you should take along whenever you travel with children—such as a thermometer, basic first-aid supplies, and medications your doctor may suggest—don't forget swimsuits, beach and pool toys, waterwings for tiny mites, flip-flops for everybody, and terrycloth robes.

5. Some Practical Facts

Because of the variety of backgrounds, language, and other factors found in the Caribbean islands, most of the information I have collected to make your visit more enjoyable will be found in the chapters dealing with each island or group of islands. However, there are a few matters that are general enough to be included here.

TELEPHONING: While the area code for most of the Eastern Caribbean is 809, for many locations it is not possible to place a direct-dialed long-distance call from North America. (In fact, in some of the places I have listed, telephoning is not possible!) If you want to call ahead in the Caribbean, the Bell System has suggested that you call information for the area (dial 809/555-1212) and the operator will tell you the procedure for direct dialing.

However, to call station to station to one of the French-held islands, such as Guadeloupe, Martinique, St. Barts, or St. Martin, dial 011-596, then the local number.

The Dutch-held islands of Aruba, Bonaire, and Curaçao also have a different system. To call Aruba station to station, dial the international code 011, followed by the prefix 5998, then the local number. To reach Bonaire, dial 011/5997, followed by the local number; and to call Curaçao, dial 011/5999, then the local number. Dutch-held St. Maarten is reached by calling 011/596, followed by the local number. To reach little Saba, dial 011/5994 and the local number. Finally, for St. Eustatius, call 011/5993 and the local number.

Even within the 809 international access code, there are prefix numbers which must be dialed before the local number. Each island has its own. The procedure is to dial 809 first, then the island prefix, then the local number.

The various prefix codes for the islands, *in each case following the 809 number, and coming before the local number,* are as follows:

Anguilla (497); Antigua (46); Barbados (42); the British Virgin Islands (49); the Cayman Islands (94); Dominica (445); Montserrat (491); St. Kitts (465); Nevis (also 465); St. Lucia (455); St. Vincent, Trinidad and Tobago (45).

You can dial Jamaica, Puerto Rico, the U.S. Virgins, and the Dominican Republic by dialing 809, then the local seven-digit number.

Haiti is a special case. Dial 1/509, followed by the local number in Haiti.

WHAT TO WEAR: In this day when dress is such a personal statement, I can no longer present checklists of what to pack. Many beachcombers arrive in the Caribbean with the jeans they're wearing, a toothbrush, and a bikini (perhaps!). Most travelers today are aware of clothing needed in subtropical or tropical climates. You'll want to dress casually to stay cool, and you'll want to select apparel that is easy to clean, of course.

If you're living at deluxe and first-class hotels, women should be prepared for at least an evening cocktail party. Some restaurants and hotels—and admittedly it's a hopeless battle—still require men to wear a jacket and tie in the evening.

Treading the balance between a personal statement in apparel and a concern for others, clothing in the Caribbean ultimately becomes a matter of taste. Some resorts that used to have dress codes—that is, men required to wear jackets after 6 p.m.—have, in despair, posted signs that dress should be "casual but chic." You are allowed to interpret that according to your wishes. I have attempted to give clues in individual writeups when hotels have set particular standards of dress.

Obviously, you should take coordinated clothing so that you can travel lightly.

Chapter II

WHAT IS THE CARIBBEAN?

1. Geography and Climate
2. Before the Europeans
3. History Since the Discoveries
4. The Caribbean Today

THE QUESTION—What is the Caribbean?—is a legitimate one. The bewildering variety of islands in the sun sowed confusion in its first tourist, Christopher Columbus, back in 1492. To Isabella back home in Spain, he wrote in a rapturous letter, "I saw so many islands that I could hardly decide which to visit first." As far as decisions go, things haven't changed that much for today's southbound, sunseeking tourist.

As diverse in mood as they are in number, the islands of the Caribbean are each gifted with a distinctive sparkle and style, even when part of the same nation. The short trip from St. Kitts to Nevis, when the plane goes up merely to set down again, has taken you not just to a sister state, but a nostalgic island, of decaying, once-flourishing plantations, remarkably unlike the place you left only ten minutes ago.

First, some basic orientation. The Caribbean Sea is ringed by the Greater Antilles in the north (Cuba, Jamaica, Hispaniola, and Puerto Rico), the Lesser Antilles on the east, the coasts of Venezuela, Colombia, and Panama on the south (once referred to as the Spanish Main), and the countries of Central America and the Mexican Yucatán peninsula on the west. Its total area is somewhat over one million square miles!

For the purposes of this book, I've concentrated on the West Indies, which form the border between the chilly Atlantic and the warm, calm Caribbean Sea. The West Indies begin with Cuba, curving south to Trinidad, lying between the peninsula of Florida and the northern coast of South America. The Dutch Leewards, often called the "ABC Islands," lie off the coast of the Spanish Main or what is today Venezuela.

The question of a specific destination depends largely on who you are and what your vacation goals are—to sunbathe in the buff on the nudist beaches of Guadeloupe; to snorkel and scuba-dive off Bonaire; to scale a volcanic crater in Saba; to sail as Lord Nelson did from English Harbour in Antigua more than 200 years ago; to take a donkey ride in Haiti to the Citadelle (one of the seven man-made wonders of the world); to explore Santo Domingo, the oldest city in the Americas; or to shop the winding alleys in the merchandise-loaded bazaars of St. Thomas and St. Croix in the U.S. Virgin Islands.

1. Geography and Climate

The islands of the Caribbean lie around the Caribbean Sea, which is divided into three main parts: the Cayman Sea in the northwest, the Venezuelan Basin in the southeast, and the Columbian Basin in the southwest and center. The amazing variety of form and structure of these islands—which stretch from 10° north of the Equator almost to the Tropic of Cancer—is shown in size, topography, and depths of the sea around them, but all are tropical and fascinating to vacationers, historians, sociologists, geologists, mariners, fishermen, a host of people with all sorts of interests.

The islands and island groups are referred to by different names, which since the time of Columbus has caused confusion. Are you going to the West Indies? the Windward Islands? the Leewards? Hispaniola? or to the Greater or Lesser Antilles? perhaps the Caribees?

The name "West Indies" has had a number of meanings since Columbus first called his discoveries Las Indies Occidentales (the West Indies), thinking he had reached Asia, but the name is now fairly widely taken to include the groups of islands once called the Greater Antilles and the Lesser Antilles. A medieval legend placed an island called Antilia someplace in the Atlantic Ocean, supposed to have been a refuge for Christians fleeing Portugal and Spain when the Moors invaded. (The Azores were once called Antilia.) In the 15th and 16th centuries the name Antilles was given to the tropical islands ringing the Caribbean.

Cuba (once known as the "Pearl of the Antilles"), Jamaica, Hispaniola (the island comprised of Haiti and the Dominican Republic), Puerto Rico, and the Cayman Islands lie in the Greater Antilles. The title Lesser Antilles was given to the remainder of the chain of islands forming the eastern perimeter of the Caribbean Sea, an arc of islands also widely known as the Caribbees. Included are the Leeward Islands, curving from Anguilla in the north to Dominica in the south, and the Windward Islands, from Martinique to Grenada, but not including Barbados (although it's also a Caribbean island). There is also a little island chain paralleling the South American coast embracing three of the six islands today called the Netherlands Antilles.

Oddly, the Leeward Islands lie more to the windward than do the Windwards. All this had something to do with the accuracy of mariners who originally named the parts of the archipelago, and it can be quite confusing when you realize that three of the Netherlands Antilles islands—Sint Maarten, Sint Eustatius, and Saba—are the Dutch Windwards, but they lie in the Leeward Islands. On the other hand, the other three islands of the Netherlands Antilles—Aruba, Bonaire, and Curaçao—lying off the coast of South America, are called the Dutch Leewards.

However, you needn't let this varied nomenclature be a worry so far as a visit to the Caribbean is concerned—unless, of course, you're going by your own boat. Whatever they're called, all the Caribbean islands enjoy the warm waters of the sea lapping their shores, the movement of the trade winds and the sea breezes, and almost constant sunshine. A rainy season usually lasts from around May or June through October, but winter is known as the dry season. Such weather conditions as hurricanes, which sometimes come in summer and fall, need not create the fear those seasons once did, because constant watch is kept and warnings issued early enough for safety to be fairly certain. Rather cool weather is likely to visit the highland areas of some of the islands, but the only cold zones are found at altitudes reached by some mountain peaks, such as the 7,402-foot Blue Mountain in Jamaica and a 10,417-foot peak in Haiti. In all the hill sections, you can expect cool nights at most times of year.

2. Before the Europeans

Many pictures have been painted of the landing of Columbus and later Spanish expeditions on islands of the West Indies, with the unsuspecting Indian inhabitants showing little fear of the strange, overdressed (for the climate) beings from across the big water. The age of innocence for these islanders came to an abrupt end—and, in the sweep of history, so did their very existence.

The people indigenous to the Greater Antilles, The Bahamas, and some of the Lesser Antilles were related, all speaking forms of the Arawak language. They are thought to have come originally from South America's Amazon basin, risking their lives in oar-propelled dugout canoes to find better, safer places to live as fiercer South American Indians disrupted their home territories. There were various tribes of these people linked through their Arawak-tongue background, one of the strongest being the Taínos. Some traces of this tribe have been found in Cuba and Puerto Rico, while a few artifacts from other tribes have been unearthed in Haiti, the Dominican Republic, and Jamaica. It is believed that the route of the Taínos, which probably took several centuries, was from South America to Puerto Rico and on to Hispaniola and Cuba. There were surely many stops lasting years at a time in islands of the Antilles, and it is known that some tribes even made their way as far north as the southern Bahamas.

Much of the travel of the Arawak indigenous peoples was in flight from the blood-thirsty Caribs, another group from South America, who took control of some of the Lesser Antilles and Hispaniola.

It didn't take the Spaniards long to wipe out the American Indian population throughout the West Indies. The *conquistadores* inflicted unspeakable cruelties on the natives, enslaving the survivors of small battles and using them as tools to dig precious metals from the ground, dive for pearls, and perform constant back-breaking labor for the new masters. The Caribs, being warlike, lasted a little longer than did any of the Arawak tribes, but it was only about a century after Spanish claims were established before the Indians were almost entirely annihilated from the Caribbean islands.

About the only places where traces of Arawak blood may still exist are Cuba and the Dominican Republic, where you sometimes see white people with Indian facial characteristics. The stronger Caribs have left their mark in Dominica and St. Vincent, where there are little groups of people called "black Caribs," of mixed Negro and West Indian blood. Also, on Aruba you'll meet many *mestizos*, whose blood is mixed Indian and white, but their ancestors probably came much later from South America than did the Arawaks and Caribs.

3. History Since the Discoveries

All the Caribbean islands, which today have a wide variation of governmental structures, belonged to Spain in the late 15th and 16th centuries. Their discovery by Columbus and other explorers who claimed the widespread area for Spain was soon followed by seizure of some islands and initial landings by representatives of other European countries. Britain, France, and the Netherlands established Caribbean/West Indian colonies in competition with Spain. Other governments followed suit, and by the 18th century Denmark, Sweden, and the now-defunct German principalities of Brandenburg and Courland once counted Caribbean possessions among their assets.

In the beginning, Spain, hungry for gold and with the support of the Catholic church, laid claim to everything in sight—and to a lot of lands only rumored to be in the area. On his four voyages Columbus discovered Cuba, Hispaniola (the whole island then being called Haiti, or High Land, by the inhabitants), Dominica, Guadeloupe in the Lesser Antilles, Puerto Rico, the Cayman Islands, Jamaica, and Trinidad, as well as Central and South American territories. From the early 16th century the Spaniards' quest for gold and silver led to some colonization of towns at the good natural harbors, but they were not really settlers in these new lands. The harbors served as ports on favorable sea lanes among the islands along which treasures were sent back to Spain. The newcomers spread their religion and their communicable diseases to the indigenous inhabitants, who died off rapidly as they were enslaved and brutalized by the Spaniards.

The treasures of the Antilles proved too tempting for other Europeans to pass up, and by the middle of the 16th century sea-going plunderers from various European nations were preying on the galleons bearing rich cargoes from the New World to fill the coffers of Spain. The Dutch, French, British—called variously corsairs, freebooters, pirates, privateers, filibusters, and buccaneers—prowled the seas, leaving their legacy of blood-spattered romance.

From the middle of the 17th century assorted peoples from Western Europe began to settle in the new lands, which changed flags frequently as first this nation and then that claimed ownership. The British, French, Danes, and Dutch were chief among the claimants, as Spain was forced out of the running with its decline as ruler of the waves. The Dutch held Curaçao and the French kept Martinique, although the claims were long disputed. By 1670 Britain had seized Jamaica, its colonial government being recognized by the ousted Spanish. The French government, following in the footsteps of freebooters, took over all of Hispaniola, which was renamed Saint-Domingue.

As colonization took hold, the new landowners established sugar plantations, first in the Lesser Antilles and then on islands of the Greater Antilles. With the plantations came the slave trade—the importation of blacks from Africa as the labor force of the West Indies.

In 1763, after years of conflict (particularly between Britain and France) over the fortune-generating islands, the treaty ending the Seven Years' War in Europe gave Britain the upper hand in many areas of the Caribbean, but it did not end the strife. Everybody wanted a piece of the rich sugar pie. Britain seized Guadeloupe. Major turmoil erupted in Hispaniola: as the 19th century dawned, the long discontent of blacks and mulattoes boiled up in revolt; the sons and daughters of Africa took eastern Hispaniola from Spain but were soon forced to relinquish the prize. However, they threw off their chains of slavery and succeeded also in throwing off the yoke of French sovereignty in the western third of the island, establishing a republic and naming it Haiti.

Following the Napoleonic wars, treaties distributed the Caribbean islands as follows: France had only Martinique and Guadeloupe (and satellite islands) in the Lesser Antilles; the Netherlands finally got a clear claim to Curaçao; Britain held Jamaica, the Cayman Islands, and most of the Lesser Antilles (except for the French colonies and some small island possessions of the Danes and the Dutch); and Spain kept Puerto Rico, Cuba, and eastern Hispaniola, by now called Santo Domingo. The tribulations of Haiti were not over, although it was considered independent of European rule. The new republic kept trying to include eastern Hispaniola under its flag, but by the middle of the 19th century that part of the island had achieved independence from both Spain and Haiti, and the Dominican Republic had been set up. Hispaniola was henceforth an island of two separate republics.

During these years slavery was coming to an end from island to island as the various controlling nations abolished the trade, but by then blacks and persons of mixed blood whose ancestors were imported from Africa were deeply rooted in the West Indies.

The United States became a presence in the Caribbean in 1898, not through colonization but by military and monetary power. Spain lost Cuba and Puerto Rico to the big neighbor to the north in the Spanish-American War. The U.S. occupied Haiti from 1915 to 1934 because of a bloody power struggle in the island republic between blacks and mulattoes, performing the same service for the Dominican Republic from 1916 to 1924, this time to protect U.S. interests. The people of Puerto Rico became U.S. citizens in 1917 and were granted limited self-government. In that same year the Danish Virgin Islands were bought by the United States and became territories of the new owners, known as the U.S. Virgin Islands. The people there are U.S. citizens, but they cannot vote in federal elections. In 1952 the internally self-governing Commonwealth of Puerto Rico was established, and the island may eventually become one of the United States of America.

The 20th century has seen the end of colonialism in most of the Caribbean. The Netherlands Antilles now have internal self-government. Martinique and Guadeloupe were made overseas départements of France. Some of the former British colonies now have various forms of their own government. There are constitutional states, independent states, one presidential republic, one independent republic, and one British Associated State, all within the British Commonwealth. The British monarch is still head of state (represented by a governor) for the British Virgin Islands, the Caymans, and Montserrat, which are designated as Crown Colonies.

4. The Caribbean Today

Discoverers, fortune-hunters, pirates, planters, shipwrecked sailors, slaves, and free men have all splashed their colorful swatches across the canvas of the Caribbean. From the day Christopher Columbus dropped anchor at an island he named San Salvador in The Bahamas until today, the mystique of the Caribbean and its exotic islands endures.

THE PEOPLE: After the indigenous population of the West Indies had been almost annihilated, the population of the numerous bits of land took on a variegated hue. Colonists brought European culture, customs, and languages of several nations, many of which imports still exist, although inevitably they have been influenced by the tropical ambience. As the colonists came, particularly the big planters, they needed a vast labor force, and as mentioned earlier, this need was met by bringing in black slaves from Africa by the hundreds of thousands. These reluctant immigrants, although they were forcibly "converted" to Christianity, retained many superstitions, beliefs, and tribal customs of their native lands. This is seen in the mixture of pagan and Christian religious rites as observed by the *voodoo* followers in Haiti, *santería* in Cuba, and *xango* (shango) in Trinidad. The basic beliefs and rituals from Africa have been fitted in comfortably with Roman Catholic worship forms and figures, and Protestant faiths as followed in predominantly black and mulatto sections are also strongly affected by the African heritage.

Abolition of slavery ended the importation of blacks, but already they were a large part of the population, and today by far the majority of the islanders are descended from those African slaves (of which, more below).

When the white colonials were no longer allowed to augment their possessions by bringing in African blacks, the British and French turned to a system of importing indentured servants from India, and some Chinese and Lebanese also came to the West Indies. These have added to the mixed bloodlines of the Caribbean populace, although some have maintained their ethnic purity, culture, religion, and customs through the years. Blacks predominate in most of the islands, especially where vast numbers were imported to work the sugar plantations, but there are also many mulattoes in these areas whose skin color ranges from very light to dark—an outcome that makes it nearly impossible to fix any certain population breakdown along these lines.

It is estimated that in the former British and French colonies, the colored population (descendants of former slaves, with or without other ancestry) tops 90%. In the islands settled by Spain (Puerto Rico and Cuba), on the other hand, the white ancestry strongly predominates (less strongly in the Dominican Republic, which was affected by being twice made a part of black Haiti). There were fewer blacks in those islands in the colonial period because the plantation system did not develop there in the early days. By the time it did, slavery was no longer permitted, and the labor force for the Spanish-held islands came from the mother country and from the Canary Islands.

As to the East Indian population, it is mainly found in former British and French colonies. Especially on Trinidad and Tobago you'll find that Asians make up some 40% of the count, and they are found in lesser numbers in Barbados, Curaçao, Grenada, Guadeloupe, Martinique, St. Lucia, St. Vincent, St. Kitts, Nevis, and a smattering in Haiti and Jamaica—and probably elsewhere.

Class distinctions throughout the islands were once based on race and color as well as wealth, a system which is undergoing change. Instead a small, mostly white, rich upper class and a large, poor, largely black, mulatto, or otherwise mixed lower class, today a middle class is developing as a result of industrialization and other economic changes and improved education.

LANGUAGES: With such a mélange of backgrounds, it's not surprising to find a linguistic mixture also. The language of former colonial overlords is the official tongue of each island, even Haiti. There, the form is French, but the common speech is a French Créole. In fact the speech you'll hear when you travel in rural areas of many of the countries is heavily dependent on local dialects and patois, some with many phrases of African origin.

Official languages of the islands are:

English—the Caymans, Jamaica, the U.S. and British Virgin Islands, Antigua, Barbuda, Montserrat, St. Kitts, Nevis, Anguilla, Dominica, St. Lucia, Barbados, Grenada, St. Vincent, the Grenadines, Trinidad, and Tobago.

Spanish—the Dominican Republic and Puerto Rico (where English is a second language), and Cuba.

French—Haiti, St. Martin, St. Barthélemy, Martinique, and Guadeloupe.

Dutch—Sint Maarten, Sint Eustatius, Saba, Aruba, Bonaire, and Curaçao.

CULTURE: The ethnic heritage of the islands has enriched the cultural life of the Caribbean islands. Multinational influences are seen in architecture (places of worship, plantation great houses, villages, and huts), fine arts, and entertainment. Afro-Caribbean music, dancing, and island (especially Haitian) painting are the most widely known of fine-arts aspects of the islands, but there have also been literary efforts and other expressions of cultural interest displayed.

Music and Dancing

Calypso, reggae, the beat of voodoo drums in the faraway mountains—these terms spring to mind when the music of the Caribbean is mentioned. And rightly so, because these are the sounds of the islands which long ago drowned out the tinkling harpsichord notes drifting through the great houses of plantations. The gutsy, aggressive beat and soul of African music was brought in with the cargoes of slave ships, shaped and augmented by the misery and the joys of generations of blacks and mulattoes, fused with the melodies of Spain and certain structure and harmony from other countries. The result was the music of the Caribbean.

The **calypso** music, which originated with the blacks in Trinidad, is such a mixture—basically African but with Afro-Spanish rhythms, English verses, and traces of French structure. The words to calypso tunes were originally (and sometimes still are) spontaneous improvisations, based on all sorts of subjects—love, sex, politics, whatever. Of more recent origin is **reggae,** which originated in Jamaica and is closely linked with the Rastafarian religious cult (whose messiah is Haile Selassie, the Promised Land being Ethiopia). Reggae, developing out of an old form of folk music in Jamaica, embraces elements of music from Africa most strongly, but also uses ideas from Europe and India, calypso, the rumba, and the limbo. Reggae verses tend to accentuate views on politics, religion, social change, and, unfortunately, anti-white feelings.

A basic source of Afro-Caribbean music is the percussion instrument, which is seen and heard in several forms, ranging from the tom-toms used in Haitian voodoo rites, African in shape and decoration, to conga, mambo, and the more modern steel drums that originated in Antigua but really came into popularity in Trinidad in the 1940s. Other instruments of African inspiration are marimbas and banjos, while from Spain comes the infusion of guitar and wind instruments. To the conventional brass, woodwinds, and strings, the blacks, mulattoes, and people of the Spanish peasant ancestry have added other sources of sound as they came to hand: gourds, pots and pans, bamboo sticks, garbage cans and lids, cowbells, saws, even the jawbones of asses and horses and the trunks of trees. The making of music on old oil drums has become an art in itself when done by the steel bands of the islands.

African dances, like the music, were mainly brought to the West Indies by slaves who had been born into the cultures of Dahomey and the Ashanti in what is now Ghana, along the Upper Guinea coast, and Nigerian Yoruba. Even today in Africa, especially in Ghana, the same kind of extempore verses are sung to the same rhythms as you'll hear in the calypso of the Caribbean. The **limbo** dance of the islands is a descendant of ancient tribal rites of Africa. Another dance form, seen mainly in Haiti, is the **merengue,** a dance ballad similar to calypso but usually more erotic in nature.

Spanish and Afro-Spanish influences are reflected in such dances as the **rumba, tango,** and **samba,** closely related to the Afro-French **calenda,** a dance whose movements were considered too suggestive by slave-owners in Martinique and Guadeloupe so that it was banned. Outlawing the calenda didn't entirely kill it, however, and it even played a part in development of the **béguine** in those islands.

The best way to see the music and dancing of the Caribbean is at **carnival** time. In islands with strong Roman Catholic ties this is similar to Mardi Gras in New Orleans, with several days and nights of celebration and parades. For some islands, carnival (*carnaval*, where French is the official language) lasts from Epiphany (January 6) to Ash Wednesday, with parades and dancing in the streets especially on each Sunday before Lent. On other islands, festivals, fiestas, and special days, many held in summer, take the place of carnival. For example, Barbados holds a Crop-Over Festival in June/July celebrating the end of the sugarcane harvest.

The carnivals and festivals are marked by flamboyant masqueraders parading and dancing to the pervasive island music, together with feasting on the foods common to the area. People of each island present folklore in song and dance at these events. If you can't be there for carnival, you may still have a chance to enjoy this bright facet of island life, as many hotels and nightclubs present abbreviated versions by folkloric groups as part of the entertainment program.

Art

Other Caribbean islands have followed the lead of Haiti in producing—and selling—the primitive art of the people. The best of this Haitian primitive (or naïve) painting, almost unknown before the 1940s, is highly stylized, done in bold colors and using or centered on Haitian subjects. You can see the work of the top artists, whose paintings command high prices, at galleries on a number of the islands, but you may be able to acquire a good and characteristic painting at a street show or even off the walls of some little café. Keep looking.

Woodcarvings are interesting art objects of the islands. They range from rough animal and human figures to fierce masks to smoothly finished statuary of mahogany and other native woods.

Literature

Much has been written about the West Indies since their discovery, but it was not until this century that what is known as "the literature of négritude" developed in Africa and the West Indies. Missionary priests wrote about various aspects of the Caribbean islands. History, poetry, drama, and a few novels were written by people born in Guadeloupe, Martinique, Puerto Rico, the Dominican Republic, and Haiti during the 17th, 18th, and 19th centuries. This early literary output, whether in English, French, or Spanish, had little originality of thought or form, and in some cases the writers even sought to distance themselves from their island roots by seeking recognition in the capitals of the colonial empire rather than on the home scene. The lack of literary progress among the nonwhite islanders was largely due to the lack of any education even after the abolition of slavery.

During the present century a literature has developed in the Caribbean (and in Africa) in which individuality of expression and originality of subject matter have come to the fore. Because of the African heredity it was natural for the new literature to be written using African expression patterns and to be based on African traditions. This "literature of négritude" has played an important role in strengthening the racial pride and independence of thought and feeling among the people of African ancestry. That the natural literature of the islands is in its nascency is attested by a statement by George Lamming, novelist from Barbados, in 1960: "The West Indian novel, by which I mean the novel written by the West Indian about the West Indian reality, is hardly 20 years old."

There were a few leaders in the field of "the literature of négritude" working before and after Lamming's 1940 watershed date. Among them are Jamaican Claude McKay, poet and first professional Caribbean novelist; Jacques Roumain, essayist, poet, and novelist of Haiti; St. Lucia–born Trinidad-dweller Derek Walcott, playwright and poet; John Hearne, Canada-born Jamaican novelist; and Roger Mais, Jamaican short-story writer, poet, and novelist.

Perhaps the spirit of the writers of the West Indies today was best voiced by Aimé Césaire, a poet born in 1913 in Martinique of poor peasants from Africa. He described his négritude by saying, "I want to rediscover the secret of great speech and of great burning . . . The man who couldn't understand me couldn't understand the roaring of a tiger."

FOOD AND DRINK: Throughout the Caribbean, hotel chefs prepare a presentable American and continental cuisine, dishes usually familiar to most visitors from Canada and the United States. However, in recent years hotels have placed a greater emphasis on local dishes, everything from curried goat stew to lambi (conch meat). Even so, it's still better to order a $15 meal at a local native restaurant than it is to have a $50 dinner in a so-called gourmet restaurant of some deluxe resort.

Many recipes in the West Indies date back to the days of the Arawak and Carib Indians, the original settlers. Since they weren't able to enjoy chateaubriand airlifted from Miami, they relied on what was available locally. Then came the conquerors from Europe and variations began to appear in the cuisine, not only French, but Dutch, English, Spanish, and of course African, the latter because of the slave trade. Even later influences would include Hindu, Chinese, and Indonesian dishes, such as a rijsttafel, or rice table, so popular in Aruba and Curaçao.

The abundance of fruit in the islands is naturally reflected in the cuisine, which you'll see first at breakfast, usually on a platter freshly sliced. Coconut, for example, is used in everything from breads to soups. Naturally, it's most popular as an ingredient in desserts, but can also appear in a main course, perhaps mixed with chicken. Soursop ice cream appears on some menus, and the guava might turn up in anything from juice to cheese. Papaya is called "paw paw," and it will most often be your melon choice at breakfast. Native cooks also use it in many other ingenious ways, including preparing it as one would squash fritters. Mango is ubiquitous, used in chutney, but also in drinks and desserts. But it's never better than when fresh, ripe, and unadorned. The avocado, most often called "pears," is used in fresh seafood salads and often stuffed with fresh crabmeat.

By now most visitors know that plantain (which is similar to a banana but red in color) is not eaten raw. These are served most often as a cooked side dish, the way we might present french fries. Puerto Ricans eat dried plantains, called tostones, from cellophane bags in lieu of potato chips. Plantains can also be served mashed or boiled, and they turn up in many desserts, especially when mixed with coconut and pineapple.

Two staples of the Caribbean islands have always been rice and pigeon peas. Balls of cornmeal, called fungi, have also long been a staple of the West Indian diet. They often accompany a salt pork main dish known as "mauffay." Sometimes these cornmeal concoctions will appear on the menus of native restaurants as coo coo. Roast suckling pig is nowhere better than in Puerto Rico and the Dominican Republic. Everything that appears unattractive and less desirable in the pig usually turns up in "souse," most often the head, tail, and feet. Souse is usually served with black pudding.

One of the most common vegetables in the islands is christophene (sometimes called foo foo), which is green and prickly and tastes somewhat like zucchini. Breadfruit, introduced to the islands by Captain Bligh (of *Bounty* fame) is green and ball shaped. It is used by the West Indians much as we use potatoes. Often it's simply boiled and served with salt, pepper, and butter. When a chef gets fancy, he'll concoct something like a breadfruit soufflé or vichyssoise. Potatoes and yams are also local favorites. The leaf-like callaloo (regardless of how it's spelled) is one of the best-known vegetables in the West Indies. It's like spinach and is often served with crab, salt pork, and fresh fish with floating fungi as a garnish. You might call it the Caribbean version of bouillabaisse.

Throughout the islands, lobster is the king of the sea and the most sought-after—and most expensive—main course to order. Many readers might take pot luck and order the "catch of the day," which is most likely to be red snapper or grouper but could also be shark or barracuda.

In a truly native restaurant in the Caribbean, you'll see hot peppers placed on the table. Be sparing. A selection of these hot pepper pastes is called sambal.

As you travel from island to island, you'll find many variations on Créole cookery. For example, on Dominica and Montserrat, "mountain chicken"—sometimes known as crapaud—is a delicacy. It's not chicken at all, but large frog's legs. The national dish of the Dominican Republic is sancocho, which is a soupy stew made with seven different kinds of meat.

In Puerto Rico the cuisine even today reflects the former inhabitants, ranging from the peaceful Taíno Indians to the Spanish conquerors. The most popular dish is sopa de frijoles negros, or black bean soup. Arroz con pollo, or chicken with rice, long ago traveled north of the border. Asopao is a thick rice-based soup to which seafood has been added, and mofongo is a baseball-sized patty made with plantains, pork rind, and lots of garlic.

Martinique and Guadeloupe are said to have the best food in the Caribbean. Of course, Mother France is the main influence, and all the classic French dishes, such as duck in orange sauce and beef bourguignon, are served on both islands. Native cooks have created their own unique recipes, however. The most popular dishes include crabes farcis (stuffed land crabs), colombo de poulet (a spicy chicken curry), and acrats de morue (salt codfish fritters).

The truly adventurous diner in the Caribbean will always be searching for unusual dishes—perhaps iguana stew. One recipe in a Montserrat cookbook rather chauvinistically calls for only "fat female iguanas," please.

Your best bet when traveling through the islands is to sample what Bajans call a "Cohoblopot," or a medley of "the best of it all."

Drink in the Islands

Since the late 16th century rum has been a legend, involved with slavery, Yankee traders, pirates, and rum bootlegging. A whole series of rum barons arose, with names that became famous around the world: Bacardí, González, Myers, and Barceló, to name only a few. "Kill-devil" (rum), as it was once called, is of course the established drink of the islands.

Distilled in a not-very-complicated process from sugarcane, rum has played a major role in the history of the West Indies, as the greatest naval powers of Europe struggled for supremacy. It can be argued that even slavery existed to service the flourishing sister industries of sugar, molasses, and rum. Today the rusted machinery and tumbledown ruins of distilleries (once an almost certain source of pleasure and prosperity) are considered tourist stopovers on dozens of Caribbean islands. Be sure to note the names of whatever foundry cast the original mechanisms. In the best traditions of the industrial revolution, many of the machines were imported from Glasgow.

The enormous crushing devices were powered, depending on the natural circumstances, by wind, water, or steam. The resulting mash was fermented in open vats and then distilled through long lengths of copper tubing. Conditions were far from sanitary, as everything from bat dung to spiders to crumbled leaves would routinely fall into the bubbling, foul-smelling mash.

Today the rum that adds zest to your piña colada will probably have been made in modern distilleries using methods vastly more sanitary than those adopted by the colonials of a century ago. Each island seems to turn out a variety of rum which its inhabitants claim is their particular favorite. However, when masked with the layers of fruit, syrup, and sugar that usually are included in a rum-based drink, it's difficult to tell the difference. Planter's punch in its many variations is the most popular drink in the islands.

The average bar in the Caribbean is likely to offer a bewildering array of rum-based drinks. Available in all the hues of the spectrum, they might contain just about anything. However, should you be concerned with morning-after hangovers, diabetic overdoses, or high caloric intake, you'd better stick to scotch or vodka.

About beer, don't think that the only brew you'll be able to find will be imported from Milwaukee or Holland. Of course, Heineken is ubiquitous, as is Amstel, especially in the Dutch islands. Many, many islands have their local favorites. Red Stripe from Jamaica is the most famous.

A word of caution: The innocent-looking pastel-colored drinks that taste so yummy and look so pretty can make neophytes lethally drunk on very short notice. Partly because of their elevated sugar content, and partly because of the almost blinding heat of the Caribbean, be alert to your limits, especially if you're driving on unfamiliar roads. Be assured that if you've had one too many, about half of your fellow motorists are in the same predicament, which leads to fatal motor accidents.

You can always drink water. But, then, should you? Water is generally safe throughout the islands, but many tourists get sick from drinking it. Sometimes that's simply because it's different from the water you're accustomed to. If available, it's better to order bottled water which will be easier on your stomach.

Chapter III

THE CAYMAN ISLANDS

COLUMBUS FIRST SIGHTED the Cayman Islands in 1503, calling them "Las Tortugas," or the turtles. The Name "Cayman" comes from an Indian name for a species of lizard. The first inhabitants consisted of a motley crew—buccaneers, beach-combers, bands of shipwrecked sailors. Rollicking Sir Henry Morgan once lived here, but in time Scottish fishermen arrived to forge a quiet, peaceful, God-fearing chain of islands that is an oasis of tranquility at the western edge of the Caribbean.

Don't go to the Cayman Islands expecting the fast-paced excitement of some of the Caribbean islands to the south. The world of the Cayman Islands centers around the sea. Snorkelers find it a paradise, as do beach buffs who are attracted to the powdery sands of West Bay Beach, renamed Seven Mile Beach with the opening of the Holiday Inn.

The Cayman Islands, 480 miles due south of Miami, consist of three islands—the pretentiously named Grand Cayman, Cayman Brac, and Little Cayman. Despite its name, Grand Cayman is only 22 miles long and 8 miles across at its widest point. The other islands are considerably smaller, of course, containing very limited tourist facilities. In contrast, Grand Cayman has become well developed just in the past decade or so.

These islands were once a dependency of Jamaica. But when that island opted for independence in 1962, the Cayman Islands preferred to remain a British Crown Colony, a land where there is no income tax.

Unlike the rest of the Caribbean, the population of the Cayman Islands is predominantly mixed. Essentially, the islanders are a self-reliant people who for years have enjoyed their unspoiled natural beauty in isolation, but at long last are inviting the world to come and share it with them.

Appointed by Queen Elizabeth II, a governor heads the local government, and English is the official language of the islands, although often spoken like an English slur mixed with the American southern drawl and finished off with a lilting Welsh accent.

George Town on Grand Cayman is the capital, the hub of government, banking, and shopping. Money rests here in more than 400 banks, free of the tax bite.

GETTING THERE: Currently, only two airlines service the routes from the United States to the Cayman Islands: **Cayman Airways** and a more recent arrival, the well-respected **Northwest Orient.** Cayman Airways operates regularly scheduled flights from only two North American gateways, Miami and Houston. Round-trip flights go three times a week from Houston and daily from Miami. On Grand Cayman are connections to Cayman Brac (daily except Tuesday) and Little Cayman (three times a week).

Oddly, midsummer is considered high season for passengers in Houston but low season for passengers in Miami. The least expensive fares are available at preselected times of the year when Cayman Airways offers reasonable midwinter round-trip fares of $249 from Houston and $159 from Miami. Restrictions include a two-day minimum stopover and a 14-day advance reservation period. The price of the ticket is nonrefundable but changes can be made in the traveling schedule without additional payment if the proposed new dates fall within the period of the promotional offer.

The Minneapolis-based Northwest Orient acquired the air routes of Republic Airways during its takeover. Northwest Orient offers more daily flights (two) from Miami than even the national carrier. A ticket on Northwest Orient can be booked at any time before departure. It requires no minimum stay, but a maximum of three weeks is the limit.

Some passengers resist the idea of a change of aircraft in Houston or Miami. For residents of New York, Detroit, and Chicago, a charter company offers nonstop service for passengers wishing to remain in the Cayman Islands for at least a week. Called **Cayman Express,** it's a Tennessee-based charter company which flies Cayman Airways aircraft on weekly departures from Chicago and Detroit and twice-weekly departures from New York. Currently only winter flights are available, but check with a travel agent. For more information and reservations, call Cayman Express (tel. 901/767-0140 in Tennessee, or toll free 800/247-9900).

GETTING AROUND: All arriving flights are met by **taxis,** and the rates are fixed by the director of civil aviation (tel. 949-2275). A typical one-way fare from the airport to George Town is $6.25. However, to the Holiday Inn on Seven Mile Beach, the fare is $10. If you've booked a room at Rum Point on the North Shore, the fare is about $35. Taxis also transport visitors on around-the-island tours. Five people can ride in the same cab.

Between George Town and West Bay, there is **bus** service approximately hourly. Many visitors use the much cheaper buses when shopping or dining in George Town, where you can catch buses at Panton Avenue, near the By-Rite Super Market.

Several **car-rental companies** operate on the island, where the competition is keen. These include such familiar U.S.-based contenders as **Avis, Hertz, National,** and **Budget.** Each will issue the mandatory Cayman Island driving permit, priced at $3 U.S. Each requires between 24 and 36 hours' advance reservation to qualify for the most economical rates. In high season cars begin at around $25 per day, coming to slightly less if you rent a vehicle on unlimited mileage for a full week. If possible, ask for a car with air conditioning. For more information or reservations, call each of the companies at their toll-free U.S. numbers: Avis at 800/331-2112 (locally it's 949-2468), Hertz at 800/654-3001 (locally, 949-2280), National at 800/328-4567 (locally, 949-4790), and Budget, which tends to offer slightly cheaper rates, at 800/527-0700 (locally, 949-4808). If you're interested in a local contender, try **Coconut Car Rentals** (tel. 949-4037).

Remember to *drive on the left* and to reserve your car as early as possible, especially in midwinter. You can return your car to the airport when you leave the island, but because of the local taxi drivers' union, you can't pick it up at the airport. Rather, take a taxi to your hotel and phone for your car.

Another increasingly popular means of transport is a Honda, rented from **Caribbean Motors,** opposite Burger King (tel. 949-4051) and opposite the Holiday Inn (tel. 947-4466), for $12 to $20 per day. These motorcycles can carry two persons. The same outfit also rents Mopeds from C.I. $9.60 ($11.40) a day.

PRACTICAL FACTS: In **currency,** the legal tender is the Cayman Islands dollar, its value based on the U.S. dollar. At prevailing exchange rates, one Cayman dollar equals about $1.19 in U.S. currency. Or one U.S. dollar brings about C.I. 84¢. Canadian, U.S., and British currencies are readily acceptable throughout the Cayman Islands. Most hotels quote rates in U.S. dollars. However, many restaurants quote prices in Cayman Islands dollars, leading you to think that food is much cheaper. Unless otherwise noted, quotations in this chapter are in U.S. dollars. The cost of living is about 20% higher than in the U.S.

The best time to go is from mid-November to March, as violent rains often lash these islands in summer. Mosquitoes, once the scourge of the islands, are now kept under control through a government program.

Documents: No passports are required for U.S. or Canadian citizens. However, proof of citizenship is (voter registration card, birth certificate). Your return ticket is also required. A departure tax of $7.50 (U.S.) is collected when you leave the island.

Telephone: A modern automatic telephone system links the islands to the world via a submarine coaxial cable. Automatic-switching links in Jamaica enable the Cayman operators to dial numbers worldwide as a 24-hour service. International direct dialing was introduced in 1984.

Telegraph and Telex: The Cable and Wireless handling these is open from 8 a.m. to 5 p.m. weekdays, to 1 p.m. on Saturday, and to 11 a.m. on Sunday.

Time: Eastern Standard Time is in effect all year. Daylight Saving Time is not observed. Therefore, when Miami is on Daylight Saving Time and it's noon there, it's still 11 a.m. in the nearby Cayman Islands.

Banks: That most important part of Cayman Island life, the bank (or banks) is open from 9 a.m. to 2:30 p.m. Monday to Thursday and from 9 a.m. to 1 p.m. and 2:30 to 4:30 on Friday.

Drugs: The Cayman Islands have very severe laws on the use of marijuana and other drugs. Large fines and prison terms are given out to offenders.

Post Office: In Grand Cayman at George Town, the post office is open from 8:30 a.m. to 3:30 p.m. Monday to Friday and 8:30 to 11:30 a.m. on Saturday. It also has a Philatelic Bureau.

Electricity: It is 110 volts, 60 cycles—therefore American appliances will need no adapters.

Taxes: A government tourist tax of 6% is added to your hotel bill.

Tipping: Many restaurants add a 10% to 15% charge in lieu of tipping.

1. Where to Stay

The true dollarwise hotel shopper will rent an apartment or condominium (most often shared with friends or families), as in my opinion these units offer the best value. As they're furnished with kitchenettes, you can cut costs considerably by cooking your own breakfast, perhaps preparing a light lunch, then dining out for only one main meal of the day. Divers are often attracted to hotels or small resorts that include a half day's dive in their tariffs. I'll lead off with the most expensive choices—and the best properties—along Seven Mile Beach, then follow with the moderate range and what few bargains there are. After that, I'll preview a selection of the best values in condominium living on Grand Cayman.

HOTELS AND RESORTS: If you're willing to pay the price, Grand Cayman has some of the finest resort living in the Caribbean, as reflected by the recommendations outlined below.

The Upper Bracket

The **Hyatt Regency Grand Cayman,** P.O. Box 1698, Seven Mile Beach (tel. 949-7440), part of the new Britannia Golf and Beach Resort, is in a $50-million, 235-room luxury complex made up of the hotel, the Jack Nicklaus championship golf course, a free-form pool occupying half an acre, condominium villas, and a beach club. It's just two miles from town and three miles from the international airport and can be reached by road or by canal. Boat docking adjacent to the hotel makes it convenient for guests to go snorkeling, fishing, and diving. Besides the golf course, there are two tennis courts and the huge freshwater pool with a swim-up bar and a Jacuzzi, plus a beachfront pool at the beach club right on Seven Mile Beach.

Designed in traditional British-colonial style with an open-air lobby and a lush tropical courtyard, the hotel consists of seven low-rise buildings, two of which house the 43 rooms of the Regency Club, Hyatt's VIP-level accommodations with concierge service. There are 11 suites in the hotel, and some villa units will be available for rental among the 400 luxury condominium villas being built along the golf course and canal. Rooms have both ceiling fans and air conditioning, and the furnishings add to the airy, tropical feeling. EP single or double rooms cost $175 to $205 in winter; suites of course are higher. *In summer, EP singles or doubles are rented for $115 to $145 daily.* Restaurants include an open-air café and lobby bar in the hotel, a restaurant and lounge with dancing at the beach club, and a golf course clubhouse terrace for casual dining.

Grand Pavilion Hotel and Beach Club, P.O. Box 69, West Bay Road (tel. 947-4666). Just before the completion of one of Grand Cayman's most prestigious office complexes, its developers, Transnational Enterprises, decided to devote about half of the floor space to a luxury hotel. Today, nestled amid banks and insurance companies on an airy stretch of land three miles west of George Town, you'll spot the quadruplicate square columns of its pseudo-Georgian façade. Inside what almost became a se-

GRAND CAYMAN

Conch Point

Water Point

Great Bluff

George Town

Bodden Town

Half Moon Bay

CARIBBEAN SEA

ries of private offices are lushly upholstered interiors which duplicate some of the most prestigious hotels of France and England. Near the lobby lies the entrance to one of the island's best restaurants, le Diplomat (see the dining section). Within the glass-covered interior is a splashing Tahiti-style fountain cluster, a small swimming pool, palm and date trees, a thatch-covered bar (where employees of the adjoining companies often enjoy the mid-afternoon music and happy hour), and a sprawling garden restaurant.

Each of the 60 well-decorated, air-conditioned bedrooms, including four suites, contains Louis XV–style furniture in bleached or pickled oak, thick carpeting, French fabrics, cable TV, and air conditioning. Furnishings for each unit cost $10,000. Depending on the accommodation, winter prices for singles or doubles cost between $190 and $430, the latter the price of a suite. *Summer prices for two persons begin at $125 for the standard rooms, with a continental breakfast included.*

Caribbean Club, P.O. Box 504, Seven Mile Beach (tel. 947-4099), is an exclusive compound of 18 luxuriously furnished one- and two-bedroom villas, each with a full-size living room, dining area, patio, and kitchen. When the owners are away these villas are rented to guests who prefer the style, taste, and discrimination of a self-contained retreat. The club is actually a cluster of pink villas, either on or just off the beach. Oceanfront villas are always more expensive, of course. In winter, a one-bedroom villa ranges from $155 to $175 as a single, $195 to $215 as a double. *In summer, a one-bedroom villa costs $95 to $130 in a single, $125 to $160 in a double.* All tariffs are on the EP. The winter season requires casually elegant wear in the evening, either in the Green Turtle Lounge or in the dining room. At the core of the colony is the club center, rising two stories with tall, graceful arches and picture windows. On the grounds is an abundance of foliage—many palm trees and flowering shrubbery—and there's a professional tennis court as well.

West Indian Club, P.O. Box 703, Seven Mile Beach (tel. 949-2494), true to its name, is like a small private club, right on the white sands. It offers some of the poshest comfort on the entire island, with nine individually decorated one- and two-bedroom housekeeping apartments. Each apartment, furnished in a tropical idiom, has a large living room with patio or balcony overlooking the beach. Best of all, a full-time maid comes with each apartment. She will not only cook, clean, and do your laundry, but she can prepare native foods and is also trained in the standard American cuisine. Her hours are 8:30 a.m. to 3:30 p.m. (never on Sunday). This imitation Tara, painted in salmon pink, is reached by an entrance drive lined with stately royal palms. Rates in winter are $185 per day for two persons in a one-bedroom unit and $240 per day for four in a two-bedroom apartment. *In summer, these tariffs drop to $135 and $170 per day.* There is also an efficiency unit available for two persons, costing $110 in winter, *$95 in summer.* An extra person is charged $15 per day. Bedrooms are air-conditioned, and all have ceiling fans and phones. Local calls are free. Children of guests must be age 8 or older, and a stay of at least a week in winter and three days in summer is requested.

Holiday Inn Grand Cayman, P.O. Box 904, Seven Mile Beach (tel. 947-4444), is an all-purpose, all-inclusive resort three miles from George Town and five miles from the airport. The location is along a prominent stretch of Seven Mile Beach. This is a modern, 213-room beachfront hotel. Bedrooms have a bright, tropical flair, with floral prints. Most of them have sitting areas, and all have baths with dressing rooms, plus air conditioning, but, alas, no TV. Each unit has a glistening southern-style balcony whose white balustrades overlook a garden courtyard planted with palms and shrubs. Ocean-view and oceanfront rooms are more expensive, of course, than island-view units. Depending on the accommodation, one person in winter pays $114 to $184 per day; two persons, $118 to $188 per day. There is no extra charge for a third or fourth person. *In summer, these tariffs are reduced to $92 to $122 per day for one person, $96 to $126 per day for two persons.*

There is a theatrically designed swimming pool, lagoon-like with arched bridges and surrounding areas for sunbathing and entertainment. You can order tall rum punches beside the pool. Bars include the Corsair's Wharf, poolside, and the Wreck of the Ten Sails, for evening entertainment with a live band. At the Corsair's Wharf the bar is set into the shell of a wooden boat and sheltered from the sun with a high roof from which swing symbolic hangman's nooses from a re-created ship's yardarm. There is a fully equipped dive shop on the premises, and sailboats, waterskiing, and deep-sea fishing are available. Tennis is played on the inn's four courts (lit at night).

Moderately Priced Choices

Coral Apartments Ltd., P.O. Box 1093, West Bay Road (tel. 949-4054), is the name of the management company that maintains a trio of interconnected resort hotels located between West Bay Road and Seven Mile Beach. The oldest, yet still very comfortable, accommodations are contained within the **Coral Wing Hotel,** whose crescent-shaped exterior encompasses three sides of a seaside garden with palms and sea grapes. Originally established as one of the first hotels on the island, it offers accommodations noted for their wide expanses of glass windows which slide open directly into the large garden.

Next door, occupying an equally valuable expanse of beachfront, is the **Royal Palms Hotel.** Built in the mid-1970s, it is best known for its array of water sports facilities and its rustically inviting bar. From the premises, an employee of Don Foster's Dive Shop escorts divers on seafaring excursions aboard one of four specially equipped boats. The Royal Palm boasts an attractive swimming pool which is, of course, accessible to residents of its sister hotels. Brian Shields, the Scotland-born general manager of the complex, quotes *summer rates at these two properties at $72 to $115 in a single, $85 to $128 in a double, and $100 to $140 in a triple.* In winter, singles cost $110 to $160, doubles are $128 to $180, and triples run $135 to $200. The best accommodations are those with private patios or balconies overlooking the beach. Standard rooms are in the main building.

Also on the grounds of this sprawling complex is the **Coral Caymanian** in an Iberian-style building whose stucco walls and wrought-iron balustrades shelter 11 fully equipped apartments. Each contains a kitchenette, living room, and between one and three comfortable bedrooms. Completed in the early 1980s, the building doesn't occupy a beachside site, but instead sits in a garden within earshot, but not within view, of the waves. In winter, condo rates are $150 daily for two guests in a one-bedroom, rising to $185 in a two-bedroom/two-bath apartment, and $225 in a three-bedroom/three-bath apartment. *In summer, condo rates are $130 for two guests in a one-bedroom, $145 in a two-bedroom/two-bath apartment, and $165 in a three-bedroom/three-bath unit.*

Tortuga Club, P.O. Box 496, East End (tel. 947-7551), is a group of long, low buildings set in a grove of coconut trees. The windows open to the sea breezes. The club is small, only 14 rooms with air conditioning and ceiling fans. The dining room is built of rugged stone, with Spanish elm beams, flagstone floors, and a water view. The spacious bedrooms have indoor/outdoor life with wall-wide glass doors opening onto a terrace with white furniture. Everything is homemade—conch pie, turtle steak, lobster, whatever. One morning one guest ordered beer pancakes—and got them! In winter a single person can stay here on the MAP for $115 daily, the cost going up to $159 for two, $195 for three. A fourth person sharing a room is charged $60 daily for half board. *From April 15 to mid-December a MAP single rents for $80 daily, $115 for two.* Scuba packages are also offered. Snorkeling and deep-sea fishing are available.

The Best Bargains

The Cayman Islander, P.O. Box 509, West Bay Road (tel. 949-5533), is one of the best buys in George Town if you don't ask for a lot of fancy resort amenities. Its location near a string of high-priced condos might suggest that this unpretentious motel is more expensive than it is. However, it's reasonable in price for its buff-colored units. Built in 1978, the hotel offers 67 basic but comfortable accommodations, each with air conditioning, TV, phone, twin beds, and plenty of easy parking. *Each unit, suitable for two persons, costs $63 daily in summer,* rising to $99 in winter. To reach the beach, you cross West Bay Road and walk through a grove of sea grapes. There is a pool on the grounds if you don't wish to go that far. The hotel also owns one of the island's best-known nightclubs.

Cayman Diving Lodge, P.O. Box 11, East End (tel. 947-7555), is primarily for divers. The location is 25 miles from George Town, 20 miles from the airport. It was taken over in late 1984 by Ron Kipp, owner of Bob Soto's Diving, Ltd., the biggest dive operator on the island. The lodge is a two-story half-timbered building set against a backdrop of tropical trees on a private beachfront. Ocean-view rooms are modern, pleasant, simple, and air-conditioned. In the southeast corner of the island, the lodge is on a coral sand beach with a live coral barrier reef just offshore. Meals are prepared by native Caymanian chefs who serve abundant portions. The accent is on fish. In summer or winter the single MAP rate is $115 daily, rising to $180 in a double. This tariff includes not only room and half board, but also one two-tank dive daily, unlimited shore diving, and one night dive on five- and seven-day packages. Diving on the day of arrival and departure is not included. Nondivers deduct $20 per person nightly.

Villa Caribe Resort, P.O. Box 1410, North Side (tel. 947-9636), is an isolated 14-room resort about 22 miles from the airport and some 25½ miles from George Town on the relatively undeveloped north shore. Periwinkles flank the entrance of this stucco-sided angular exterior erected in 1984 between a sandy beach and the road. James Terry, a former police officer, built the place, much of it with his own hands. Each accommodation is air-conditioned, with big sun-flooded windows and home-like bedrooms filled with cozy touches. With breakfast included, winter prices are $95 to $120 daily in a single, $100 to $125 in a double. *In summer, singles cost $68 to $85 daily, and doubles run $73 to $90,* depending on the exposure.

One of the best parts about this place is the ground-floor bar and restaurant where Norma Terry prepares such island specialties as ham with pineapple, cracked conch, turtle steak, and house-style lobster. Full dinners cost from $14 each. During the day drinks are served on a seaside terrace whose only barrier from the surf is a row of formal balustrades. The Terry family exudes a kindly charm, making a vacation here one of the most personable experiences on the island.

Spanish Cove, P.O. Box 1014, Spanish Bay (tel. 949-3765), is a resort for divers located on a remote, rugged beach on the northern tip of the island, which offers good scuba-diving. A dining room and bar is constructed out of coral rock and natural wood. There are 46 rooms, pleasantly designed with ceramic tile floors and rough wood trim. The restaurant is outstanding on the island. The food is well prepared, with luncheon served buffet style. The dining room is at beach level with a large outdoor patio and barbecue. The bar and lounge are on the second floor overlooking the water. There is a pool on the premises. All rooms have two queen-size beds, air conditioning, and ceiling fans. Four rooms are suitable for families or small groups. The double rate is $130 in winter, *$95 in summer*. Spanish Cove is a full-service dive resort and that means a NAUI/PADI training facility. Facilities include a sheltered three-boat slipway, two outstanding dive boats, and the latest in rental equipment.

To make reservations in the U.S., call 305/948-8003, or toll free 800/231-4610.

Windsor House Apartment, P.O. Box 487 (tel. 949-2604), is one of the least expensive accommodations on the island. The owner, Mrs. Bernard St. Aubyn, rents out a self-contained apartment, separated from her own private residence by a breezeway, ensuring complete privacy. In the best residential area, with a fine view of the harbor, the house stands in a well-kept garden with plenty of flowering shrubs, trees, and birds. The Windsor is about ten minutes by car from Seven Mile Beach and a mile from a small sandy cove in the opposite direction. Each bedroom (there are two) contains twin beds, making the apartment suitable for four persons. The kitchen is fully equipped, and a large living room opens onto an enclosed veranda. Mrs. St. Aubyn says, "Don't be put off by our low rates. We want repeat business." *In summer, the tariffs are $35 per day for two persons,* increasing to around $45 in winter. An extra person pays $5. The apartment is not air-conditioned, but there is a large standing fan and an attic fan. Guests are on their own as far as maid service is concerned.

Condo Living

Tamarind Bay, P.O. Box 1595 (tel. 949-6485), built in 1980 is one of the most luxurious and pleasant condominium complexes on the island. It occupies a dramatic stretch of Seven Mile Beach about 1½ miles west of George Town on West Bay Road. It was designed a bit like an interconnected series of modernized Tuscan villas, with zigzagging paths linking the curved walls of the swimming pool with privacy barriers of crotons, ferns, boxwood, miniature date palms, bougainvillea, and mahogany trees. A pair of feathery casuarinas shade the frond-covered beachside gazebos and surfside hammocks from the sun. The Ecuador-born manager, Mrs. Connolly, welcomes visitors with a sunny smile and well-timed doses of charm. Accommodations in the privately owned villas are beautifully furnished, flooded with sunlight, and impeccably maintained. Each contains two bedrooms, two baths, central air conditioning, ceiling fans, cable TV, and a private screened-in patio overlooking the sea, along with a fully equipped kitchen and hotel-style maid service. *For single or double occupancy, units rent for $165 in summer,* $200 in winter. *For three to four persons, each unit costs $185 in summer,* $235 in winter.

Pan-Cayman House, P.O. Box 440 (tel. 947-4002). The Georgian-style beachfront façade of this popular choice was attractively altered to suit its Caribbean setting. Only ten apartments are contained within this long, two-story building. Each has its own fully equipped kitchen, air conditioning, a private balcony or patio with an unrestricted view of the sea, and comfortable summer-type furniture. Hotel-type maid service is provided as part of the rental of these two- and three-bedroom apartments. Rates vary with the season and according to the number of persons staying in an accommodation. In high season, two-bedroom apartments rent for $190 to $225 daily, while a three-bedroom unit, holding up to six persons, costs $290. *In summer, two-bedroom apartments rent for $95 to $150 daily, while three-bedroom accommodations go for $170 to $210.* A service charge of 5% is added. This place tends to be so popular that it's sometimes fully booked long in advance of the winter season.

Villas Pappagallo, P.O. Box 952, Barkers (tel. 949-3568, or toll free 800/232-1034 in the continental U.S.). Its Mediterranean-style red tile roofs and white stucco walls are arranged symmetrically around formally landscaped semitropical gardens. One end opens onto a stretch of white sandy beach while the other is exposed to an isolated road about eight miles west of George Town. Nestled between groves of palms and bougainvillea, the waters of a two-tiered swimming pool cascade into splashing layers of froth. On the grounds is a tennis court. Built in 1980, the establishment contains 44 one- or two-bedroom privately owned units, about 15 of which are usually available for rentals. *One-bedroom units for two persons cost $170 in summer, and two-bedroom apartments, suitable for up to four persons, go for $200 off-season.* In winter, a one-bedroom unit for two costs $200, and a two-bedroom apartment for up to four guests, $260 a day. An extra guest is charged another $20 per person.

Victoria House, P.O. Box 636, Seven Mile Beach (tel. 947-4233), is an apartment complex standing at the north end of the beach. It's an expanded and modernized version of the colonial plantation style of architecture, with a U-shaped garden encompassing palmettos and palms. Hammocks lure you to a quiet perch near the beachfront. The management is among the friendliest and most helpful on the island.

Twenty-five studio, and one- and two-bedroom apartments are rented, each with an open, airy feeling, furnished tastefully, generally in white bamboo with colorful fabrics. Kitchens are not only equipped with dishes and cutlery, but have a stylish appearance, and the dining area is in the living room. In high season, December 1 to April 30, two persons pay $102 to $126 daily in either a studio or one-bedroom apartment; and four persons are charged from $162 in a two-bedroom unit up to $178 in a penthouse. *Off-season, for these same units, two persons are charged $78 to $95; four persons, $120 to $130.* Daily hotel-type maid service is included, but not tax and service. Between swims, string hammocks are strung up between the trees for naps, and a professional tennis court is nearby.

Silver Sands, P.O. Box 952, Seven Mile Beach (tel. 949-3343), is a modern, eight-building complex arranged horseshoe fashion directly on the beach, taking up to 550 feet of frontage. A row of date palms separates the two-tone buildings of painted concrete from the road. After breakfast on their private sea-view balcony, guests hit the sands for a morning constitutional and a swim. The air-conditioned apartments are grouped around a rectangular freshwater pool. The eight apartment blocks contain either two-bedroom/two-bath, or three-bedroom/three-bath units. Kitchens are fully equipped, and hotel-type maid service is offered. The resident manager will point out the twin tennis courts and two utility rooms with washer-dryers. In the winter season, two persons rent a two-bedroom apartment for $175 daily, the cost going up to $215 for three to four persons. Six persons are given a three-bedroom unit at a cost of $240 daily. *Rates are greatly lowered off-season—from $145 daily for two in a two-bedroom to $155 daily for three to four persons in the same apartment. The three-bedroom units cost from $190 daily, and six guests are sheltered for that tariff.*

Harbour Heights, P.O. Box 688, West Bay Beach (tel. 947-4295), is a beachfront condominium, where you can stay in style and comfort by the day, week, or month. You're "on your own" for meals, but there's a good-size recreation area and a large free-form swimming pool with a surrounding tile terrace (filled with white lounge furniture). The gardens are planted with palms and subtropical shrubbery. Apartments are of generous size, each having a living room and dinette, an attractive and complete kitchen, two bedrooms, two baths, and ample closet space. Each apartment has its own balcony or patio; furnishings are all in white tropical designs with decorative fabrics and accent rugs. Daily maid service is included. It's a short distance into George Town for shopping or restaurants. In the high season, a two-bedroom/two-bath apartment rents for $175 for one to four persons, with each additional person charged another $15 daily. A minimum stay of five days is required year round. *In the off-season, mid-April to mid-December, that same apartment costs $100 for one to four persons.*

2. Eating Out

American and continental dishes predominate, although there is also a cuisine known as Caymanian, featuring specialties made from turtle, even turtleburgers, certainly turtle soups and steaks. Fresh fish is the star, and conch is used in many ways. Native lobster is in season from late summer through January. While most visitors dine at their hotels, many of my recommendations are apartments or villas, which do not always serve meals, allowing you to sample some of the island's many restaurants. Since most dining places have to rely on imported ingredients, prices tend to be high.

THE UPPER BRACKET: Chef Tell's Grand Old House, Petra Plantation, South Church Street (tel. 949-2020), is a beautiful white-walled mansion, a former plantation house built at the turn of the century by a Bostonian coconut merchant, lying amid venerable trees about five minute's drive south of George Town. Built on bedrock near the edge of the sea, it stands on 129 ironwood posts supporting the main house and a bevy of gazebo-like satellites. Converted into a restaurant in 1969, it was purchased in

1986 by the German-born chef, Erhardt Tell, as a showcase for culinary specialties which have been widely publicized throughout Europe and the United States.

Amid burnished wooden floors, flickering candles, airy latticework, and tropical embellishments, you can enjoy full lunches for around C.I. $9 ($10.75) and full dinners, wine not included, for around C.I. $35 ($41.75) per person. Maître d' Ed Burns (a native of Philadelphia) recommends such specialties as steak tartare, pasta du jour, conch fritters, layered fish terrine with essence of tomato, a Teutonic recipe for peppered pork (schweinepfeffer) with spaetzle, turtle steak, sautéed loin of pork with pear and gorgonzola, and mesquite-grilled filet of local fish. Reservations are a good idea at dinner. Go between noon and 2:30 p.m. and 6 and 10 p.m. daily.

Ristorante Pappagallo, West Bay (tel. 949-1119), is one of the most whimsically amusing and memorable restaurants on the island, set in isolated grandeur on the western edge of the island, eight miles from George Town, at the end of a series of winding roads that traverse many of the island's residential neighborhoods. Its designers incorporated both Caymanian and Aztec weaving techniques in its thatched roof, whose soaring heights top leaded-glass doors, black marble, polished brass, mixing a kind of Edwardian opulence into an otherwise Tahitian decor. As you dine, a fountain shoots water skyward from the saltwater pond outside. Canadian-born owner Peter Fedele serves dinner from 6:30 p.m. till midnight every day except Monday in summer.

For around C.I. $32 ($38) and up, they offer an array of northern Italian dishes which include such specialties as lobster cocktail, shrimp bisque with cognac, fettuccine in cream sauce with mushrooms and parmesan cheese, spaghetti with fresh seafood, an array of fresh fish dishes, carpaccio, grilled or flambéed steaks, and Italian-style veal and chicken dishes. Lunches, costing around C.I. $16 ($19) and including wahoo steak, fresh tuna, grills, and salads, are served only in winter, every day except Monday. Don't overlook this place as a location for a nightcap, where you'll select from a wide choice of fruited drinks.

Caribbean Club, West Bay Road, Seven Mile Beach (tel. 947-4099), already recommended for its accommodations, is one of the best places for dining in Grand Cayman. A popular luncheon stopover, it offers such hot dishes as Cayman turtle Stroganoff, served with rice and coleslaw. For an appetizer, I suggest the marinated conch. A selection of sandwiches is also available. Each day a special is featured. Lunch begins at $15. In the Governor's Dining Room, the setting is elegant and guests dine by candlelight. The chef prepares excellent international dishes. The appetizers are tempting, ranging from something continental like escargots bourguignonnes, to something local, like conch fritters. The specialty of the house is tournedos (two small filets, wrapped in bacon and topped with mushrooms and a light madeira sauce). The deep-fried crab claws are also superb. Main dishes are likely to include broiled lamb chops with garlic butter, broiled lobster, and boneless quail with almond stuffing. A dinner here can easily run around $35 or more. Reservations are required in the evening. Lunch is served from noon to 2 p.m. and dinner from 7 to 9:30 p.m.

The **Periwinkle Restaurant,** West Bay Road (tel. 949-2927), named after the flowers that flank its concrete foundations, is a pleasantly unpretentious bungalow offering some of the best Italian/Caribbean cuisine in town. You'll find it about three miles from the center of George Town, beside the road that parallels Seven Mile Beach. Owned and operated by the Anglo-Austrian alliance of Johann Guschelbauer, Mervin Cumber, and Clemens Gutter, the establishment offers an al fresco terrace, a cedar-lined bar with some of the best piña coladas on the island, a Caymanian thatch roof, and a pleasantly sun-flooded dining room where full dinners cost around $28. Specialties include steamed lobster Créole, catch of the day meunière, curried seafood, linguine with clams, scaloppine marsala, mixed frittare misto di mare, and piccata milanese. Dinners, which usually require a reservation, are served daily from 6 to 10 p.m. Lunches, served Monday to Friday only between noon and 2:30 p.m., cost around $13. Less formal than dinners, they feature such dishes as shrimp, crab, and mushroom quiche, roast beef sandwiches on French bread, cold seafood salad, and homemade chowders.

Lobster Pot, North Church Street (tel. 949-2736), is one of the island's best-known restaurants, overlooking the water from its simple, second-floor perch right outside George Town. True to its name, it offers lobster prepared in many different ways: Cayman style, bisque, salad, or a lobster potpourri with conch, tuna, and shrimp also included. Conch schnitzel and seafood curry are on the menu, together with the increasingly rare turtle steak. The place is also known for its prime steaks. For lunch, served from 11 a.m. to 2:30 p.m., you might like the English-style fish and chips or perhaps a seafood basket of fried oysters and shrimp. The midday meal costs around $15. Dinner is served from 6 to 10 p.m. in the restaurant, a complete repast costing $25 and up. A pleasant place for a drink is the Lobster Pot's pub, with its attractive oak booths. Try their fresh banana daiquiri. You may find someone to challenge to a game of darts while you enjoy an English ale. The restaurant lies at the western perimeter of George Town.

The **Cayman Arms,** Harbour Drive (tel. 949-2661), overlooks the water and is a long-established gathering point for an expatriate colony—that is, a number of outside business people and bankers who find the Cayman Islands an ideal place in which to carry on international transactions. Therefore, it gets very crowded at lunchtime. The food is good, as is the service. At lunch you can order such appetizers as marinated Cayman conch or escargots in garlic butter, followed by such main-dish selections as "mushrooms Cayman Arms," a casserole and onion dish with a loyal following. At dinner, appetizers include the mushrooms ordered in a smaller portion before your main course. Among the recommended main dishes are turtle in garlic butter, English fish and chips, and oysters Cayman Arms. Desserts include homemade pies and cakes. Count on spending around $15 for lunch, $25 to $30 for dinner. The restaurant is closed for Sunday at lunch and on Monday evening.

MODERATE TO BUDGET DINING: **Captain Bryan's,** North Church Street (tel. 949-6163), isn't the most glamorous restaurant on the island, yet many visitors quickly adopt it as their preferred hideaway for a candlelit meal. It sits on a stony plot of land at the edge of the sea, a short distance from the heart of George Town. You might enjoy a before-dinner drink or two at the spacious and friendly bar where the walls are sheathed with pine planks and fish nets, and where the woman bartender is likely to wear a flowered Hawaiian shirt. Afterward you can select a dimly illuminated table near the sea, either on a veranda or on a pier jutting out above the waves. Cooperative waitresses serve full meals which cost from around C.I. $20 ($23.75) each. They could include fried plantains, seafood chowder, turtle steak, stewed conch, coconut-flavored grouper, catch of the day, and such "land fare" as curried chicken, grilled steak, prime rib of beef, and teriyaki steak. Dessert might be a slice of key lime or coconut pie or a heady brew of West Indian liqueur with Blue Mountain coffee. Because of its popularity, reservations are suggested. It's open daily: for lunch from noon to 2:30 p.m., and for dinner from 7 to 9:30 p.m.

Benjamin's Roof, Coconut Place, West Bay Road (tel. 947-4080), occupies the uppermost floor of a three-story building whose severe angles form one side of a shopping and restaurant compound near the Holiday Inn. The cascades of philodendron and bougainvillea that twine around the balustrades are just a hint of the greenhouse motif you'll find upstairs. There, as many readers have discovered, you'll find a bevy of warm-hearted waitresses who do their best to make you feel welcome. It's rumored by visitors who have encountered their fair share of daiquiris around the Caribbean that the fruity 16-ounce libations at this place are the best on the island. They're made with a secret ingredient known only to Dudley Yates, the gregarious bartender.

Carlin Brown, the U.S.-born owner, offers full meals which cost from C.I. $17 ($20.25) each. Written in multicolored chalk on a duet of blackboards and prepared with finesse by the long-standing cook, Bently, they include listings of the best hamburgers on the island, native turtle steak (pan-fried with Worcestershire sauce, soy sauce, and peppers), conch chowder, black bean soup, a spicy version of marinated conch, a Créole version of blackened fish, and a beef, sweet pepper, and onion dish borrowed from Mexico called "almost fajitas." It's open from 6 to 11:30 p.m. Monday to Saturday.

The Cracked Conch, Selkirk Plaza, West Bay Road (tel. 949-5717), invites you to eat as "Caymanians eat." After that, the menu lists what they mean: conch in every known way, ranging from conch burgers to conch fritters, from cream-style conch chowder to Manhattan conch chowder, not to mention marinated conch and cracked conch, as well as conch stewed in coconut milk. If you don't like conch, a turtle sticks its head out and becomes turtle burger, turtle Cordon Bleu, turtle steak, and turtle schnitzel. If any of that is too exotic for you, order vichyssoise, followed by lobster tails or the fish of the day. Stuffed shrimp, filets, and chicken Cordon Bleu round out the selections. Lunch and dinner are served daily: from 11:30 a.m. to 4:30 p.m. for lunch and dinner from 6 to 10:30 p.m. You'll spend $10 to $25 for a meal. Closed Sunday. The location is about a five-minute drive from George Town. The restaurant, staffed by Caymanians, is a family operation.

FAVORITE LOCAL HANGOUTS: Morgan's Harbour, Batabano, West Bay (tel. 949-3948), offers dinner from 5 to 10 p.m. in the unpretentious main restaurant every day except Tuesday and during September. The distantly related partners, Eugene and Leonard Ebanks, serve a full array of island specialties, with full meals costing from C.I. $11 ($13). Menu items, always prepared from fresh ingredients, include conch chowder, shrimp cocktail, conch fritters, shrimp Créole, turtle steak, conch stew, and several lobster dishes. Before dinner, and throughout the day, you can rub elbows with the islanders at the veranda-style plank-sided bar, whose wood frame is supported by a pier stretching out above the water. Service is friendly, with clients coming from the adjacent marina, where saltwater aficionados always seem to be repairing one of the dozens of securely moored vessels. If you stop in for lunch, you can order sandwiches, hamburgers, and salads from the nearby snackbar, whose cabaña-style design occupies an isolated position near the water. Its hours are 7:30 a.m. to 5 p.m. daily.

Welly's Cool Spot, North Sound Road (tel. 949-2541), is the place to go for native dishes. The emphasis is on those old reliable friends, the conch and the turtle. The owner, E. M. Wellington, also does lobster superbly, and in fact offers different specials every night. If you give him advance notice, Welly will do something special —maybe curried goat. Meals cost from $12. Isolated in a parking lot, the place is a bungalow of pink-painted cinder blocks, with as simple a decor as metal chairs will allow. It's open Monday to Friday from 9 a.m. to 1 a.m., on Saturday to midnight, and on Sunday from 1 p.m. to midnight. In the evening, you should call ahead for a reservation.

3. The Sporting Life

What they lack in nightlife, the Caymans make up in water sports—fishing, swimming, waterskiing, and diving are among the finest in the Caribbean.

DIVING AND OTHER WATER SPORTS: *Skin Diver* magazine wrote, "Grand Cayman has become the largest single island in the Caribbean for dive tourism." There is lots of marine life, a large variety, and many coral formations. There are plenty of boats and scuba facilities. Coral reefs encircle the islands, and these reefs are filled with marine life. However, the government bans scuba-divers from taking any form of marine life. It's easy to dive close to shore—therefore, boats aren't necessary.

But for certain excursions I recommend a trip with a qualified divemaster. For rentals, the island maintains many "dive shops." Hotels also rent in-house facilities as well; however, a dive shop will not rent scuba gear or supply air to a diver unless he or she has a card from one of the national diving schools, such as NAUI or PADI. Hotels arrange snorkeling and scuba-diving trips.

Established in 1957, the largest dive operation in the Cayman Islands is **Bob Soto's Diving Ltd.,** P.O. Box 1801, Grand Cayman (tel. 949-2022). Owned by Ron Kipp, the operation has grown to include full-service dive shops at the Holiday Inn, Cayman Islander, Grand Pavillion, Scuba Centre, and Soto's Coconut, in addition to its headquarters below the Lobster Pot restaurant. Nondivers can take advantage of the glass-bottom boat and daily snorkel trips. Besides a wide range of scuba gear, underwater cameras with free film and snorkeling gear can be rented at reasonable rates. At Bob Soto's, people are friendly, helpful, and highly professional. They can arrange for small-boat rentals, costing from $25 to $100 per day.

Surfside Watersports, Ltd., P.O. Box 891 (tel. 947-4224), which Joseph P. Donahue operates out of Le Club Cayman on Seven Mile Beach, is the island's most complete water-sports center, offering much more than just diving. A morning two-tank dive costs $40 and an afternoon one-tank trip goes for $25. Various diving courses are offered, and gear can be rented. Besides snorkel trips ($12.50) and beach lunch trips ($30 per person), the following are for rent: Hobie Cats, day sailers, jet skis, windsurfers, and Aqua Trikes. Daytime glass-bottom-boat trips cost $15 and a night-time trip is $20. Additionally, Surfside is the only operation at Grand Cayman offering parasailing ($30 per ride).

FISHING: Grouper and snapper are most plentiful for those who bottom fish along the reef. Deeper waters turn up barracuda and bonito. The flats on Little Cayman are said to offer the best bonefishing in the world. Sports people from all over the world come to the Caymans for the big ones—tuna, wahoo, marlin. Most hotels can make arrangements for charter boats. Experienced guides are also available.

At **Tortuga Club Ltd.,** P.O. Box 496, Grand Cayman (tel. 947-7551), an experienced local guide will escort anglers seeking blue-water action from marlin, wahoo, dolphin, and a variety of tuna, for $150 per half day (up to four passengers), bait and tackle included.

BEACHES: About the finest in the Caribbean. Grand Cayman's **Seven Mile Beach** has sparkling white sands with Australian pines in the background. In addition, beaches on the east coast and north coast are also fine, as they are protected by an offshore barrier reef. In winter the average water temperature is 80°, rising to 85° in summer.

SUBMERSIBLES: For a once-in-a-lifetime experience, you can take a deep dive in a submarine during your visit to the Cayman Islands, even choosing between a submersible vessel that can go to a depth of 150 feet and others that can plunge downward to as deep as 800 feet below the surface.

Research Submersibles Ltd., P.O. Box 1719, Grand Cayman (tel. 949-2896), operates the *Deep Explorer 3* and the *Deep Explorer 8* research submarines, each carrying a pilot and two passengers on four dives a day, going as deep as 780 to 800 feet. Grand Cayman is the top of an underwater mountain, the side of which is known as the Cayman Wall, which has a 500-foot sheer drop down its side before becoming a steep slope falling away for 6,000 feet to the bottom of the ocean. The *Deep Explorers*, in their 1½-hour trips, allow passengers to see the variety of sea life at different levels of the dive. Weather permitting, each trip goes down to the wreck of the *Kirk Pride*, a cargo ship that sank off George Town Harbour in 1976 and was lodged on a rock ledge of the wall at 780 feet. The submarines are dry and at one atmosphere pressure, so no previous experience is necessary. Each passenger receives a certificate of the dive and a sub crew T-shirt. It's possible to take pictures with 400 ASA film in your camera.

The *Deep Explorer* trips cost $200 per passenger, and they're open to everyone over the age of 8. Reservations should be made at least a week in advance.

More shallow dives, but nonetheless thrilling, are made by the **Atlantis,** a 50-foot submarine with a capacity of 28 passengers and two crew members. It submerges 90 to 150 feet. The *Atlantis* provides air-conditioned comfort and good visibility of the underwater world. The sealed hull ensures a normal atmospheric pressure inside. Day dives cost $45 and night dives go for $55. Children under 12 pay half price; those under 4 are not accepted. Early reservations are advised. The *Atlantis* docks at George Town Harbour (tel. 949-7700). For further information get in touch with the Cayman Islands Department of Tourism, 420 Lexington Ave., Suite 2312, New York, NY 10170 (tel. 212/682-5582).

GOLF: The **Britannia Golf Course,** Seven Mile Beach, Grand Cayman (tel. 949-7440; or toll free 800/527-7882 for reservations and information), is the only golf course in the Cayman Islands, the first of its type in the world. It can be played either as a championship course or the Cayman course. Designed and built by the Jack Nicklaus organization, the course is part of the Hyatt Regency complex. The innovation known as the Cayman course is played with the Cayman ball, which travels about half as far as an ordinary golf ball.

4. Exploring the Island

The capital, **George Town,** can easily be explored in an afternoon. It is principally a place to visit for its restaurants and shops (or banks!)—not sightseeing. It does offer a clock monument to King George V and the oldest government building in use today, the post office on Edward Street, where stamps sold there are an avid prize to collectors.

Elsewhere on the island, you might go to **Hell!** That's at the north end of West Bay Beach, a jagged piece of rock named Hell by a former commissioner. There the postmistress, Mrs. Mary Ebanks, will stamp Hell, Grand Cayman, on your postcard to send back to the States.

Cayman Turtle Farm, at Northwest Point (tel. 949-3894), houses giant turtles and is in fact the world's only sea turtle farm, with thousands of turtles on view ranging in weight from six ounces to 600 pounds. Admission is $5 for adults and $2.50 for children. There is a gift shop. Hours are 9 a.m. to 5 p.m. daily.

At **Botabano,** on the North Sound, fishermen tie up with their catch, much to the delight of photographers. If you've got your own kitchenette, you can buy lobster (in season), fresh fish, even conch and turtle meat, from these fishermen. A large barrier reef protects the sound, which is surrounded on three sides by the island, a mecca for divers and sports fishermen.

If you're driving, you might want to go along **South Sound Road,** lined with pines and, in places, old wooden Cayman Island houses. After leaving the houses, including many modern ones, behind, you'll find good spots for a picnic.

Pedro's Castle is reached by going along Old Prospect Road to Bodden Town. A few miles from there, you turn right at the crossroads at Savannah. Originally called St. James Castle, Pedro's is the oldest standing building in the Caymans. Erected by slave labor, today it houses a restaurant.

Also, just outside Savannah, on Spots Bay, is the island's best-known cave, **Bat Cave.** Frankly, I recommend this attraction to cave buffs only. Backtracking from Pedro's Castle, you go just beyond the speed restriction sign, as if heading back to George Town. On your left (the sea side of the road), you'll see a dirt road. Follow it to the end. Once you reach the sea, turn left. Walking along the cliff edge for some 30 yards, you'll reach a sandy beach. After climbing down ten feet, you'll spot the cave's low mouth. The cave is explored on your hands and knees (thankfully, the floor is sandy). The bats will squeak loudly at your entrance but they're harmless.

On the road again, you reach **Bodden Town,** which was once the largest settlement on the island. At Gun Square, two cannons commanded the channel through the reef. They are now stuck muzzle-first into the ground.

On the way to the **East End,** just before Old Isaac Village you'll see the onshore sprays of water shooting up like geysers, their sound like the roar of a lion. These are called "blowholes."

Later, you'll spot the fluke of an anchor sticking up from the ocean floor. As the story goes, this is a relic of the famous "Wreck of the Ten Sails" in 1788. A modern wreck can also be seen—the *Ridgefield,* a 7,500-ton Liberty ship from New England which struck the reef in 1943.

Old Man Bay is reached by a new road that opened in 1983. Head back to town along the cross-island road through savannah country, where royal palms sway in the breeze and the appearance is veldt-like. You might even spot the green Cayman parrot. At Old Man Bay, you can travel along the north shore of the island to **Rum Point,** with its lovely beach, which is as good a place as any to end the tour.

An annual event, **Cayman Islands Pirates' Week** is held in late October, a national festival with cutlass-bearing pirates and sassy wenches storming George Town, capturing the governor, thronging the streets, and staging a colorful costume parade. The celebration, which is held throughout the islands, pays tribute to the nation's past and its cultural heritage. For information as to the dates of the festival each year, get in touch with Pirates Week Festival Administration, P.O. Box 51, Grand Cayman.

5. Free-Port Shopping

This is not the most compelling reason to take a vacation in Grand Cayman. However, having said that, it should be noted that there is free-port shopping, with merchandise from all over the world available in the stores of George Town. Often you'll find bargains in silver, china, crystal, Irish linen, French perfumes, British woolen goods, and such native crafts as black coral jewelry and thatch-woven baskets. However, you should know the prices prevailing in U.S. stores. I have found them to be the same on many items.

Don't purchase turtle products. They cannot be brought into the U.S.

In George Town, my recommendations follow:

Caribe Island Jewelry, North West Point, West Bay (tel. 949-1077), offers locally made jewelry from black coral, caymanite, whelk, and conch. The jewelry is produced in many forms, including necklaces, bracelets, and earrings. The store is on the way to the turtle farm.

Viking Gallery, Harbour Drive on the waterfront (tel. 949-4090), offers two floors of handcrafts, as well as hand-painted skirts and tops, a calypso boutique, native bolt material, and local and Caribbean paintings. They also sell pewter, crystal, black coral, fine jewelry, porcelain, and bank tax-haven books.

Bridget's Fashions and Fragrances, Harbour Drive, Freeport Plaza (tel. 949-2699), opposite the cruise-ship passenger landing, offers a selection of fashions from around the world. These include Gottex swimwear from Israel, handcrafted batik from Bangkok, Irish linen, Cayman map wall hangings, special design (woven) turtle ties for men, and Cayman coat-of-arms ties, along with sportswear for men.

Caymandicraft, South Church Street (tel. 949-2405), a short distance from the center of George Town, imports 4711 colognes, soap, and powder, cashmere scarves, kilts, mohair stoles, and blankets from Scotland, Irish linen, and a wide range of Liberty of London fabrics.

English Shoppe, Church Street, on the seafront (tel. 949-2457), stocks duty-free perfumes, along with a fine collection of watches and other fine jewelry. They also carry Irish Belleek china, Irish crystal, and collectors' items. All prices are quoted in U.S. dollars.

The **Jewellery Factory,** Fort Street (tel. 949-2719), is one of the most popular jewelry shops on Grand Cayman. Gold jewelry is sold by weight, according to the London bullion price the day you make your purchase. You can also purchase black coral items and gold-framed doubloons.

Black Coral and . . . , Fort Street (tel. 949-4949), is where you can see and purchase some of the fine handcrafted black coral pieces designed by Bernard Passman, the renowned sculptor who introduced the black coral art medium to the world. Some of the sculptures and jewelry in the shop are done with gold and gems. Passman designed and executed the wedding gifts of the Cayman Islands people to Prince Charles and Lady Diana—a 97-piece cutlery set of black coral and gold.

Coral Arts Collections, Old Fort Building, on the waterfront (tel. 949-3951), offers a wide selection of jewelry, much of it designed "by Mitzi" (owner Mitzi Mercedes Ebanks). She uses many types of coral—black, pink, angelskin, oxblood, apple, gold, tiger, and blue—all crafted in 14-karat and 18-karat gold.

Kirk Freeport Plaza, Cardinal Avenue (tel. 949-7477), has a treasure trove of gold jewelry, Greenfire emeralds, gems, colognes, perfumes, and watches. Because of its proximity to South America, Grand Cayman is a good outlet for the fine emeralds and other stones mined in Colombia and other countries. You can see these fine gems at the plaza.

6. Caymanian Nightlife

PUBS: Because of its links with Britain, nightlife in the Caymans has a decidedly English tilt. Your options might include a sampling of rum-based drinks beneath swaying coconut palms, but you'll probably order it from a paneled bar whose accessories resemble those of a roadside pub. Here's a survey of the action.

Wreck of the Ten Sails Lounge, Holiday Inn (tel. 947-4444). In spite of its location in one of Grand Cayman's largest hotels, many residents of the island drop in at regular intervals. There they enjoy the large murals of swashbuckling pirates above smallish tables raised on platforms. The elongated bar with its adjacent floor is usually a good place for a conversation, especially as the evening wears on. Open nightly except Sunday from 8:30 p.m. to 12:45 a.m., it has as its drawing card live music presented by the island's most vivid musical personality, "Barefoot Man" and his band. There's a cover charge of $5 for nonresidents of Holiday Inn. Once inside, hard liquor begins at $3 a drink. The barman's specialty is a Cayman Mama, made with coconut, rum, and banana liqueur.

Cayman Islander Nightclub, off West Bay Road (tel. 949-7603), is the leading nightlife complex on the island. It's owned by the Cayman Islander Hotel, previously recommended. Guests of the hotel get in free; otherwise, you'll pay an entrance fee of C.I. $5 ($6), plus another C.I. $3 ($3.50) once you're inside for drinks. Live music, including island floor shows, have been presented here in the past, but check its current status before going. There's usually plenty of disco action as well. It's closed on Sunday and Monday but open otherwise from 9 p.m. to 1 a.m.

Lord Nelson Pub, Trafalgar Place, West Bay Road (tel. 947-4595). The Caribbean sunlight streams through leaded-glass windows, but the interior is fashioned after thousands of pubs found in the English countryside. Beneath blackened ceiling beams and polished saddle brasses, you can enjoy pub grub, foamy mugs of English ale, and the animated conversation of some of the island's British expatriates. A pint of ale costs around C.I. $3.50 ($4.25) and might be accompanied by steak-and-kidney pie, fish and chips, and meat-stuffed pastries. The establishment is open daily between noon and 3 p.m. Weekdays it reopens between 5 p.m. and 1 a.m. (on weekends between 5 p.m. and midnight). Dinner is served nightly between 6 and 10 p.m.

The **Lone Star Bar & Grill,** West Bay Road (tel. 949-5575), is really just a little corner of the Texas Panhandle transported to some of the most gilt-edged real estate in the Caribbean. You can enjoy some of the juiciest hamburgers in the Caymans beneath the heavy trusses of the smoke-filled dining room, unless you prefer to head to the satellite bar in back. There, beneath murals of Lone Star beauties lassoing rattlesnake-entwined bottles of tequila, you can watch replays of some of last season's best football games. The house specialty drink is a banana split (that's right—it's pulverized with rum, banana liqueur, and ice cream). A huge plate of nachos is C.I. $5 ($6), and most guests go whole-hog for three kinds of fajitas, chicken-fried steak, Texas-style cheese steak (hot chili peppers cost extra), and tacos. Full meals cost from C.I. $10 ($12). You can order a cup of chili as well. It once won the "best chili contest" on the island.

THEATER: The **Cayman National Theatre Company,** P.O. Box 1684 (tel. 949-5477), presents a varied program of productions ranging from Cayman drama to *Macbeth,* as well as West Indian musicals and Broadway revues. Some presentations are at Harquail Cultural Center on West Bay Road. The box office is on North Church Street, Grand Cayman. The theater season is from October to June.

7. Cayman Brac

The "middle sister" of the three Cayman Islands is Cayman Brac, a piece of limestone and coral-based land 12 miles long and a mile wide, about 89 miles east-northeast of Grand Cayman. It was given the name Brac (Gaelic for bluff) by 17th-century Scottish fishermen who settled here. The bluff for which the island was named is a towering limestone plateau rising to 140 feet above the sea, covering the eastern half of Cayman Brac. Caymanians refer to the island simply as Brac, and its 1,200 inhabitants are called Brackers, friendly and hospitable people, as folk with seafaring backgrounds tend to be.

In earlier years, when Brac was a shipbuilding island (which ended with World War II), extremely hard wood used as the ribs for sailing ships came from the bluff, and there were little vegetable garden plots in pockets of fertile soil there. Today, with the need for home-produced vegetables no longer pressing, the thick vegetation of the bluff is a winter home or stopover for migratory birds. Frangipani, century plants, and oleanders burgeon on the heights.

The big attraction of the bluff today isn't something new. There are more than 170 caves honeycombing its limestone height. In the early 18th century the Caymans were in the hands of pirates, and Edward Teach, the infamous Blackbeard, is supposed to have spent quite a bit of time around Cayman Brac, lurking in protected coves. What could be more natural than for him to have hidden some of his loot in one or more of the bluff's caverns, a lure for treasure-hunters? (They haven't found any yet.) Some of the caves are at the bluff's foot while others can be reached only by climbing over jagged limestone rock. One of the biggest of them is Great Cave, with a number of chambers. Harmless fruit bats cling to the roofs of the caverns.

On the south side of the bluff, you won't see many people, and the only sounds are the sea crashing against the lava-like shore. The island's herons and wild green parrots are seen here.

Now to the inhabited north side of Cayman Brac: Most of the Brackers live here, many in traditional wooden seaside cottages, some built by the island's pioneers. One of the most popular attractions is the home and gift shop of **Eddie Scott,** industrial art teacher who obviously likes to work with wood. Around his yard you'll see such hand-made articles as a sailboat, a weathervane with a turtle logo, a sundial, and inviting love seats. Of special interest is a beautifully carved miniature tanker. The house has intricately worked balconies, and Scott has turned out little wooden trains, planes, and trucks which children love.

The islanders must all have green thumbs, as attested by the variety of flowers, shrubs, and fruit trees in many of the yards. On Cayman Brac you'll see all sorts of vegetation: poinciana trees, bougainvillea, Cayman orchids, croton, hibiscus, aloe, sea grapes, cactus, and of course coconut and cabbage palms. The gardeners grow cassava, pumpkins, breadfruit, yams, and sweet potatoes.

There are no actual towns on the island—only settlements such as **Stake Bay** (the "capital"), **Spot Bay, The Creek, Tibbitt's Turn, The Bight,** and **West End,** where the airport is located.

The **Brack Museum,** in the former Government Administration Building, has an interesting collection of Caymanian antiques, including pieces rescued after shipwrecks. The museum is open daily. Admission is free.

Of course, the biggest lure to Cayman Brac is the variety of water sports—swimming, fishing, snorkeling, and some of the world's best diving and exploration of coral reefs. There are undersea walls on both the north and south sides of the island, with stunning specimens lining their sides. All the hotels offer the services of Brac Aquatics or Dive Tiara, which provide a variety of diving excursions.

Cayman Airways operates direct jet flights several times a week from Miami, Houston, Tampa, Atlanta, and Grand Cayman. There is also daily commuter service from Grand Cayman aboard the 17-passenger turbo-prop Islander of Cayman Airways.

WHERE TO STAY: My favorite resort on the island is **Brac Reef Beach Resort** (tel. 948-7323, or toll free 800/327-3835, 800/233-8880 in Florida), occupying a sandy plot of land on the south shore, near some of the best snorkeling in the region. Run by Fran and Ken Morris, the resort contains 40 motel-like units, each comfortably furnished and outfitted with air conditioning, carpeting, ceiling fans, and modern well-lit bathrooms. Once the location was little more than a maze of sea grapes, a few of whose venerable trunks still rise amid the picnic tables, hammocks, and boardwalks of this pleasant and well-maintained resort.

You'll pay for your drinks with doubloons, which one of the smiling receptionists will sell to you in a blue velvet bag. A hideaway no guest should miss is the thatch-roofed two-story bar whose stout wooden columns rise from above the surf. Perfect for a moonlit tryst, it has a breeze-filled interior where nightcaps are served to the occupants of boats moored alongside. Laundry, maid service, and meals appear from one of the well-mannered staff members. Lunches are informal affairs accented with sunlight and water, while dinners are most often served buffet style in copious quantities under the stars. On the premises are a sapphire-like pool, a Jacuzzi, a water-sports facility, and the rusted remains of a Russian lighthouse tower which was retrieved several years ago from a Cuban-made trawler.

Most guests who stay here opt for one of the all-inclusive packages. Otherwise, singles in winter rent for $100 daily; doubles, $110. *In summer, doubles go for $75 daily; singles, $70.* Breakfast and dinner are another $35 per person daily.

Tiara Beach Hotel (tel. 948-7313), part of the Divi Divi hotel chain, attracts divers and honeymooners. The location is about two miles from the airport. Many newcomers respond immediately to the landscaping, incorporating retaining walls of porous stone with fences of croton, bougainvillea, palms, and giant rubber trees. Each of the 33 air-conditioned accommodations is in two-story motel-like outbuildings, many of which offer a view of the surf, the outlying reef, and an array of palm-thatched outbuildings. A square swimming pool is raised above a white sand beach whose boardwalks run beneath groves of swaying palm trees. On piers jutting down into the water is a Tahitian-style thatch-roofed bar where drinkers can gaze out to the sea. Management "intentionally keeps the real world from clouding our minds" by banishing all TVs, radios, and phones. However, there is twice-weekly entertainment. On the premises is a full dive operation. In winter singles range from $100 to $120 daily; doubles, $110 to $130. *In summer, singles pay $65 to $75 daily; doubles, $70 to $80.* However, ask about one of their many special package plans, which are the best bargains.

A DIVE OPERATION: At **Brac Aquatics** (tel. 948-7429, or toll free 800/327-3835, 800/233-8880 in Florida), the island's authorities on the outlying reefs and underwater features of Cayman Brac are Winston and Denise McDermot. From a position a few steps from the Brac Reef Beach Resort, boats negotiate a narrow channel through the reef into the open sea beyond it. Scuba and snorkeling lessons and equipment are available on a per-day basis. Most seriously dedicated scuba-divers, however, negotiate a combined hotel-meal-dive package with the Morrises, the managers of the hotel. The inclusive deal offers better value.

8. Little Cayman

Smallest of the Cayman Islands is Little Cayman, measuring about nine miles long by two miles at its widest point, lying about 75 miles northeast of Grand Cayman. This cigar-shaped island, which today has only about 20 or so permanent inhabitants, was first settled in the 17th century by European adventurers. However, they soon became the target of pirate raids and the little island was abandoned. With the stifling of pirate enterprise, settlers from Grand Cayman moved to Little Cayman in 1833, and it has been home to a few people ever since, although economic endeavors, including turtling and coconut growing, were not successful.

The island seems to have come into its own now that fishing and diving have been recognized as its main resources. This is a near-perfect place for such pursuits. The waters around the little island were hailed by the late Phillipe Cousteau as one of the three finest diving spots in the world.

The islands of the Caymans are mountaintops of the long-submerged Sierra Maestra Range which runs north under the sea and into Cuba. The peaks were slowly built on by living corals after the drowning of the mountains, forming the islands of today and leaving subsea walls down the mountain precipices on which coral and other marine life grew for centuries, unseen and undisturbed. Little Cayman's Bloody Bay offers one of the walls nearest the surface, a stunning sight for snorkelers and scuba-divers.

Fine bonefishing is available just offshore, and an inland brackish pool can be fished for tarpon. Even if you don't dive or fish, you can row 200 yards off Little Cayman to isolated and uninhabited Owen Island where you can swim from the sandy beach and picnic by a blue lagoon.

Blossom Village, the island's "capital," is on the southwest coast. There are no shops on Little Cayman and only two private phones and one pay phone.

Cayman Airways offers two flights four days a week from Cayman Brac to Little Cayman.

FOOD AND LODGING: The **Pirates Point Resort Ltd.** (tel. 948-4210) offers a family environment with gourmet cooking. The new owner and manager, Gladys Howard, is a graduate of Cordon Bleu in Paris. The place has six newly remodeled and comfortably furnished rooms with private baths, rented for occupancy by one to four persons. The charge is $145 per person per day, for the same hospitality offered in the resort's package holidays. A package includes the room, three excellent meals per day with appropriate wines, two-tank boat dives daily featuring the Bloody Bay Wall, the Cayman trench, and Jackson Reef, plus unlimited beach diving and a special happy hour with hors d'oeuvres and free spirits daily. Nondiving activities include snorkeling, birdwatching, bonefishing, tarpon fishing, an Owen Island picnic, and exploring.

Southern Cross Club (tel. 948-3255, or 317/636-9501 in Indiana) is a ten-unit resort on a natural lagoon. Hosts are Mike and Donna Emmanuel. Scuba-diving and spin, fly, and deep-sea fishing are among the attractions. Guides are available. A double room with three meals per day costs *$90 per person from May to November,* $110 per person per day from December to April.

Chapter IV

PUERTO RICO

IT WAS ON COLUMBUS's second voyage to the New World in 1493 that he discovered the island of San Juan (St. John the Baptist), later renamed Puerto Rico. The island's government has undergone many changes since the days of its first governor, Ponce de León, to its present status as an American Commonwealth.

However, the beauty and charm have remained since the first navigators set foot on Puerto Rican soil. They called it "the island of enchantment."

Even though the island is in the "torrid zone," found between the Tropics of Capricorn and Cancer, it enjoys a lower temperature than that typical of the region. Trade winds blow in from the northeast toward the southwest of the island, acting as a gigantic fan, cooling and protecting the island from excessive heat. The sea, land, and mountain breezes further contribute to maintaining the temperature at a comfortable level.

Puerto Rico's climate, one of the best in the Caribbean, is fairly stable all year, with an average temperature of 76° Fahrenheit. The only variants are found in the mountain regions, where the average temperature fluctuates between 66° and 76° Fahrenheit, and on the north coast, where the temperature goes from 70° to 80°.

It may date from the discovery of the New World, but Puerto Rico, at least in San Juan, its capital, is as modern as tomorrow. The "bootstrap" island is remaking itself and holding out much promise for a bright future. It is no longer called "the poorhouse of the Caribbean."

Lush, verdant Puerto Rico is only half the size of New Jersey, roughly speaking. Its location is some 1,000 miles southeast of the tip of Florida. As such, it is at the hub of the Caribbean chain of islands, and you'll probably fly in and out of San Juan at least once if you're doing much touring in the area.

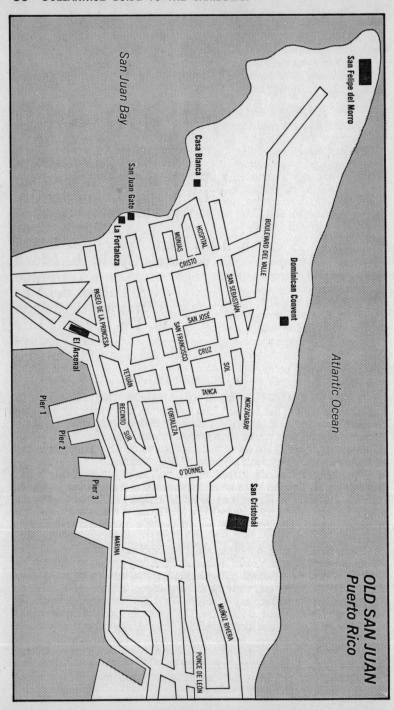

San Juan Bay

San Felipe del Morro

Casa Blanca

San Juan Gate

La Fortaleza

Atlantic Ocean

MONJAS

HOSPITAL

CRISTO

SAN SEBASTIAN

BOULEVARD DEL VALLE

Dominican Convent

PASEO DE LA PRINCESA

SAN JOSÉ

SAN FRANCISCO

CRUZ

SOL

El Arsenal

TETUAN

TANCA

Pier 1

RECINTO SUR

FORTALEZA

MORZAGARAY

Pier 2

O'DONNEL

San Cristobal

Pier 3

MARINA

MUÑOZ RIVERA

PONCE DE LEÓN

OLD SAN JUAN
Puerto Rico

After a slump in the mid-'70s and early '80s, tourism has improved. Now you'll find some of the best golf and tennis in the Caribbean at such posh resorts as the Hyatt Dorado Beach and Palmas del Mar. Accommodations have also greatly improved at out-on-the-island cities such as Mayagüez with its Hilton. Paradores—government-sponsored inns—are sprinkled across the country for visitors who want a deeper look at the island than that provided by the posh hotels and gambling casinos of San Juan, with their Las Vegas–type shows.

GETTING THERE: For frequency of flights and convenience of service to Puerto Rico, **American Airlines** is the most efficient carrier. American offers no fewer than five nonstop flights to San Juan from New York's Kennedy Airport, two daily nonstop flights from Newark Airport, a daily nonstop from Boston, three daily nonstops from Miami, and a daily nonstop from both Chicago and Dallas. Travelers find that the sheer volume of American's flights make connections through major cities in the West, Southwest, and Central states to be almost always efficient. Part of this massive volume is the result of a $35-million investment in 1986–1987 in a glistening hub in San Juan. Designed to funnel air traffic from North America through the Caribbean Basin, it's the most up-to-date terminal in the Caribbean. Ranking as the airline's fifth-largest hub (after Dallas, Chicago, Nashville, and Durham), it has a daily volume that already rivals that of many medium-sized airports on the U.S. mainland.

From San Juan, **American Eagle** (American's commuter carrier partner) takes off dozens of times throughout the day to other destinations within the Caribbean, usually on smaller planes suitable for between 19 and 49 passengers. Frequent travelers have learned that the shortest point from anywhere in the Caribbean to either North or South America is often through San Juan.

The cheapest air fares are usually those a travel agent or American's tour desk will arrange in conjunction with a hotel booking. Known as the "Get Carried Away" vacations, they usually offer substantial savings over the price you'd pay if you booked hotel and air fare separately. Excluding that, the least expensive time to fly is between Monday and Friday, since air fares often rise for weekend travel. Inexpensive bookings, as low as $239 round trip in high season (at press time) are available, usually if you book and pay for your ticket at least seven days in advance and wait for between 3 and 30 days before using the return portion of your ticket. For perhaps the biggest savings of all, try to take your Puerto Rican vacation between April 16 and December 16, when low-season fares apply. For more information, call American or your travel agent.

Another possibility is the service offered by a relative newcomer on the Caribbean scene, although a world-class heavyweight in the airline business. **TWA** offers two daily nonstop flights to San Juan from New York's JFK and two daily flights from Newark. Prices are competitive, with takeoffs scheduled for convenient connections for TWA's passengers from other areas of the country.

Passengers from the Southeast sometimes try the services of **Delta,** which offers daily nonstop service to San Juan from its hub of Atlanta, where easy connections from the rest of Delta's network are usually possible.

GETTING AROUND: After you land at **Isla Verde International Airport** in San Juan, your first problem is to get to your hotel. Less expensive than taxis, **limousines** run to various parts of the city beginning at $1.25 per person. Stops are made en route, and you share the ride. On the way back to the airport, however, you'll have to take a taxi, as limousines aren't allowed hotel pickups.

Public Transportation

Taxis are metered in San Juan, and the meter handle should be up when you get in, down as the taxi pulls out. Rates begin at 80¢, going up 10¢ for each additional mile. Each suitcase carries a supplement of 50¢, and tipping is very much allowed. Waiting time costs $8 per hour.

Públicos are cars or minibuses which provide low-cost transportation and are designated with the letters "P" or "PD" following the numbers on their license plates. They run to all the main towns of Puerto Rico. Passengers are either let off or picked up along the way. Rates are set by the Public Service Commission. Públicos usually operate during daylight hours, departing from the main plaza (central square) of a town.

Buses run both day and night and operate on a fixed-fare system. Some are air-conditioned. City terminals are on the Plaza Colón and at Pier One. The **Puerto Rico Motor Coach,** 327 Recinto Sur in Old San Juan (tel. 725-2460), runs daily service between San Juan and Mayagüez, a one-way fare costing $6.

Car Rentals

Car rentals are readily available, and some local agencies may tempt you with special slashed prices. But if you're planning to tour out on the island, you won't find any local branches should you run into car trouble. Also, some of the agencies widely advertising low-cost deals don't take credit cards and want cash paid in advance. If you plan to do much touring, it's better to stick with one of the reliables, including **Avis** (tel. 721-8605) and **Hertz** (tel. 791-0840).

For my latest trek across Puerto Rico, I tried out the services of **Budget Rent-a-Car** (tel. 791-3685), which operates two offices in San Juan and a well-maintained fleet of late-model cars. As soon as visitors pick up their luggage, they can head for the Budget kiosk near the airport's busy taxi stand. An employee will arrange for a mini-van to transport arrivals to the agency's main office at Km. 187, 12 Isla Verde Road, near El San Juan Hotel. (Another, smaller, office is at La Concha Hotel on Ashford Avenue in the hotel zone of the Condado.) An advance reservation, which can be made by calling toll free 800/527-0700 from anywhere in the U.S., usually guarantees a less expensive rate. The agency's hours are from 6 a.m. to 11 p.m. Considered by Budget to be one of their best branches in the Caribbean, its prices are sometimes a bit cheaper than those of its two major competitors.

Added security comes from the antitheft double-locking mechanisms that have been installed on most of the agency's cars. The inventory consists mainly of Japanese-made Datsuns which perform well on the narrow roads. There is also a fleet of American-made cars, such as four-door Chevrolet Cavaliers.

As an indication of prices, the Cavalier with unlimited mileage included costs $51 for a one-day rental, or $306 for the week. Most visitors, however, will settle for a less expensive model, a peppy Mitsubishi Mirage with manual transmission. A daily rental costs from $34; a weekly contract, from $215. Unlimited mileage is included.

Renting a car in Puerto Rico is easy. Motorists should remember that distances are often posted in kilometers rather than miles, but speed limits are in miles! Drivers on the island must be at least 21 years old. Drivers between the age of 21 and 25 pay an additional surcharge of $3 per day for insurance. Drivers who don't purchase collision damage waivers (around $8 per day) are responsible for the first $3,000 worth of damage to their vehicles in case of an accident. I strongly recommend purchasing the extra insurance. I always do.

Reader Sylvia Dick of Roxbury, Mass., points out (accurately, I feel) that driving conditions in Puerto Rico are less than desirable. She writes: "Many of the roads you mention are barely one lane in either direction and take tortuous paths through the mountains. Roads are sometimes poorly or incorrectly labeled. People drive *fast* and rarely resort to using their horns. The quality of roads varies greatly, and looking at a map is not reliable."

Sightseeing Tours

Sightseeing bus tours are convenient for people who don't want to drive. **Borinquen Tours, Inc.,** 868 Ashford Ave., Condado (tel. 725-4990), operates some of the best tours. You can arrange to be picked up at your hotel for a tour which can usually be booked at the hotel desk.

One of the most popular half-day tours, leaving at 1 p.m. daily (at 9 a.m. on Sunday), lasting four hours and costing $12.50 per person, goes along the northeastern part of the island to El Yunque rain forest, then making a stop at Luquillo Beach.

A city tour of Old and New San Juan departs at 9 a.m. daily, and at 9 a.m. and 1:30 p.m. on Saturday, Sunday, and holidays. The 2½-hour trip costs $9 per person. Another tour within Old San Juan takes you on a sightseeing jaunt and then to Bacardi's Rum Distillery, where you're treated to a complimentary rum drink. The tour, lasting three hours and costing $10 per person, leaves from hotels at 1:30 p.m. daily except Saturday, Sunday, and holidays.

Borinquen has offices at the Caribe Hilton Hotel, El Gran Convento Hotel, Howard Johnson Hotel, and Condado Beach La Concha.

For a sea excursion, **Capt. Jack Becker** (tel. 749-0162) invites you to go out aboard his 40-foot catamaran, *Spread Eagle*, at a cost of $30 per person, including a buffet lunch and snorkel gear. It ties up at the Villa Marina Yacht Harbour in Fajardo, about an hour's drive east from San Juan. Departures for Icacos Island are at 10 a.m. Once there, you can swim, beachcomb, snorkel, or whatever. The *Spread Eagle* sails back at 2:30 p.m., the trip taking about an hour. To make reservations, telephone Captain Jack from 7 a.m. to 10 p.m. Transportation is available from metro San Juan for $10 round trip. Some 60% of the passengers on the *Spread Eagle* are repeats or referrals. For information, write P.O. Box 445, Puerto Real, PR 00740.

PRACTICAL FACTS: To get into Puerto Rico, American citizens do not have to have a passport or visa. Canadians, however, should carry some form of identification, such as a birth certificate.

As mentioned, Puerto Rico has Commonwealth status with the United States, even though thousands of local citizens want to break away and be an independent nation. However, Puerto Rico is vitally linked financially to the United States, and many citizens want statehood. The country elects its own governor, who serves a term of four years.

The Yankee **dollar** is the coin of the realm. All major U.S. **banks** are located in San Juan, and hours are 9 a.m. to 2:30 p.m. Monday to Friday. Canadian currency will be accepted in some big hotels in San Juan, although reluctantly.

English is understood at the big resorts and in most of San Juan. Out in the island, the **language** of Spain is still *numero uno*.

To dial Puerto Rico from the U.S., the **telephone area code** is 809. In an emergency, call the local **police** (tel. 343-2020), **fire department** (tel. 343-2330), **ambulance** (tel. 343-2550), and **medical emergency** number (tel. 754-3535).

The **electric current** is 110 volts, 60 cycles, as it is in the continental U.S. and Canada.

Puerto Rico operates on **Atlantic Standard Time,** which is one hour earlier than Eastern Standard Time. However, when the eastern part of the U.S. goes on Daylight Saving Time, Puerto Rico does *not* change its time.

Puerto Rico has a large number of **public holidays** when stores, offices, and schools are closed. They include New Year's Day, January 6 (Three Kings' Day), Washington's Birthday, Good Friday, Memorial Day, July 4, Labor Day, Thanksgiving, Veterans' Day, and Christmas, plus local holidays such as July 25 (Constitution Day) and November 19 (Discovery Day).

There is no airport departure tax.

As you arrive at Isla Verde International Airport, outside San Juan, you'll find a

tourist information center. However, if you're seeking more details, you can visit the head office at 301 San Justo in the old town (tel. 721-2400). Out on the island, it's best to go to the local city hall for tourist data. Ask for a copy of *Qué Pasa*, the official visitors' guide which contains much helpful information.

The **English-language newspaper,** the *San Juan Star,* is published daily.

Some hotels add a 10% **service charge** to your bill in addition to the government tax. If they don't, you are expected to tip for services rendered. **Tip** as you would in the U.S.

If you need **information** before leaving North America, there are several Puerto Rican tourist offices to help you. They include: 1920 Avenue of the Americas, New York, NY 10104 (tel. 212/541-6630); 3575 W. Cahuenga Blvd., Los Angeles, CA 90068 (tel. 213/874-5991); 11 E. Adams St., Chicago, IL 60603 (tel. 312/922-9701); 2995 LBJ Freeway, Dallas, TX 75234 (tel. 214/243-3737); 200 SE 1st St., Miami, FL 33131 (tel. 305/381-8915); and 10 King St. East, Toronto, Ontario M5C 1C3 (tel. 416/367-0190).

SAN JUAN

The capital of Puerto Rico is today an urban sprawl, one municipality flowing into another to form a great metropolitan area. San Juan introduces you to Puerto Rico, and the look of this old city ranges from decaying ruins that recall the Spanish empire to modern, beachfront hotels that evoke Miami Beach.

The city roughly breaks down into general divisions, including the old walled city on San Juan Island (see "What to See in San Juan"); the city center on San Juan Island containing the Capitol building; Santurce, on a larger peninsula, which is reached by causeway bridges from San Juan Island (the lagoonfront section here is called Miramar); and Condado, the narrow peninsula that stretches from San Juan Island to Santurce.

The Condado strip of beachfront hotels, restaurants, casinos, and nightclubs is separated from Miramar by a lagoon. Isla Verde is in the vicinity of the airport, which is detached from the rest of San Juan by an isthmus.

1. Where to Stay in San Juan

From a guesthouse directly on the beach to a restored convent in Old San Juan, the choice of accommodations in the Puerto Rican capital is wide ranging, as are the tariff sheets. It's easy to spend $200 a day here, or else get by for $35. There are package deals galore, and you may want to check with a travel agent to see if one fills your needs.

Most of the hotels lie in Condado and Isla Verde, out by the airport. Both these sections border the beach. However, I'll also have other choices for those who prefer to live in sectors such as Ocean Park. I'll start where San Juan started, even though you'll find fewer accommodations in the old town than anywhere else.

Note: All hotel rooms in Puerto Rico are subject to a 6% tax.

IN OLD SAN JUAN: Considered by many as the "Grand Hotel of Puerto Rico," **El Convento,** 100 Cristo St., San Juan, PR 00901 (tel. 809/723-9020), is an authentically restored, 300-year-old Carmelite convent boasting of a solid Spanish brick and limestone structure. It stands directly across the street from a building which was the original city hall in 1521 (during the Spanish colonial period) and a few steps from the cathedral where the remains of Juan Ponce de León are buried. Most of the historical landmarks of the colonial walled city are within walking distance. Some of the rooms, furnished in a Spanish style of heavy wood, have a view of either the old town square (Little Plaza of the Nuns) or of San Juan Bay, where one can spot modern ships and island schooners go past the ancient fortress of El Morro. Because of its location there are no beach facilities, but the pool in the downstairs patio will serve you daily buffets. *In summer, singles range in price from $85 to $100 daily, while doubles go for $90 to $130*. In high season, a single costs $95 to $145 daily; doubles begin at $105, climbing to $145.

PUERTA DE TIERRA: A complete resort, the **Caribe Hilton,** San Jeronimo Street, PR 00901 (tel. 809/721-0303), stands near the old Fort San Jeronimo, which has been incorporated into its complex. With Old San Juan at its doorstep and San Juan Bay at its backyard, the Caribe Hilton can be called the gateway to the walled city of San Juan. Near what was once the ultra-exclusive Escambrón Beach Club, it is the only major luxury hotel in the Old San Juan sector. There are times when tourists to the island arrive at the airport, go directly to the Caribe Hilton, and stay within the hotel confines and in Old San Juan for the duration of their vacation. The main reason for this is that the hotel has so much to offer that, according to the less adventurous visitor, there is no need to venture farther inland or anywhere else. Built in 1949, the Caribe Hilton was a new breed of resort, offering total entertainment and luxury. It still offers all that and more. Set in a 17-acre tropical park, the 667-room hotel has a private palm-shaded beach and swimming cove. One can walk to the 16th-century fort or spend the day on a tour of Old San Juan, then come back to either of two freshwater swimming pools, work out at the health club, play a tennis match (day or night), swim at the beach, or simply lie on the white sand under a palm tree.

Some of the rooms are in the 20-story tower added in 1972. The Garden Wing units are decorated in tropical fashion. On the family plan, there is no charge for children regardless of age, if they stay in the same room as their parents. *In summer, guests on the MAP pay $157 to $205 daily, with doubles going for $205 to $253*. In winter, two persons can stay here on the MAP paying $273 to $323; singles on the same plan pay $211 to $261. The Terrace restaurant complex of the hotel features cuisine of the world, with a different menu each night of the week on its Dine-Around Plan. For only $39 you can take dinner on the Terrace, at El Café, or at El Batey restaurant, and for dessert, go to the Fiesta Club Caribe show in the elegant nightclub. In addition to the special nights, each of the restaurants serves regular menus. Another eating facility at the hotel is La Rôtisserie (see my dining recommendations). The Club Caribe, which features headline entertainment, is previewed in "After Dark in San Juan." One of San Juan's leading discos, Juliana's, is also on the premises.

CONDADO: Condado used to be an exclusive residential section near the beach, but it isn't anymore. Over the years private villas have been torn down to make way for high-rise hotel blocks, restaurants, and nightclubs, many with a kinky bent. Old San Juan has a lot of action at night, and Condado does too, regardless of your sexual persuasion. There are good bus connections into the old town, or you can take the taxis that are usually available. Attempts are made periodically to clean up the beach area, but many readers have written complaining about "the broken glass and dogwalkers." Watch your step!

If you like a Caribbean Coney Island by the sea, then the Condado area might be for you, especially if you're gay. Condado has now become the homosexual stamping ground of the Caribbean. There's plenty of straight action too, much of it for sale.

The Leading Hotels

Condado Plaza Hotel & Casino, 999 Ashford Ave., San Juan, PR 00907 (tel. 809/721-1000), is a two-in-one hotel complex, an original oceanfront structure linked by an elevated passageway across Ashford to its Laguna section. It now ranks as the city's second-largest hotel, containing 580 units. Just as the Caribe Hilton is the gateway to Old San Juan, so is the Condado Plaza the gateway to San Juan's Condado area.

Every room is air-conditioned and has a private terrace. Units have king-size and double beds. The management claims to have the largest casino on the island, and when your gambling fever won't come down, there are slot machines as well. If the San Juan temperature becomes unbearable, take a dip in any of the four swimming pools or the beach at the back entrance of the hotel. In the cool of the evening, stroll over to the Copa Room which features a Latin-style revue. Or else patronize Isadora, a disco (see my nightlife suggestions). The hotel has some of the finest dining choices—in several price ranges—of any hotel in Puerto Rico. Besides the Lotus Flower, the finest Chinese restaurant on the island, right next door there's the Renaissance, an elegant continental dining room. The Capriccio has Italian seafood and homemade pastas, and also a collection of classic Italian dishes. La Cantina is an attractive bar—cozy, dark, intimate—and La Posada, a 24-hour café, with its Spanish-style decor is known for its prime western beef. The ground-floor La Fiesta also has live entertainment and Latin rhythms.

The deluxe part of the hotel is the Plaza Club, which covers two floors, a total of 72 units with five suites. A stairway connects the two floors, and a VIP lounge is reserved for guests. Accommodations have cable TV, and there is a special keyed elevator so that members can avoid the crowds in the other sections of the hotel. The least expensive rooms are labeled Ashford, and the higher-priced units are either laguna view or oceanfront. From December 1 to the end of April, singles range from $170 to $250 daily; two persons pay $185 to $270. *Summer tariffs (room only) range from $115 to $195 daily in a single, from $125 to $205 in a double,* plus another $20 charged for an extra person sharing a unit. While at the beach and at poolside, the chaises longues and towels are provided free. There are two tennis courts (lit at night) and water sports are featured in the lagoon (at no cost) right behind the hotel. Make arrangements at the front desk for the use of any sport facility and equipment.

Condado Beach Hotel, 1071 Ashford Ave., San Juan, PR 00907 (tel. 809/721-6090). Formerly connected to its neighbor, the La Concha Hotel, the austere façade of this hotel now stands alone in dignified grandeur. Its jutting eaves, formal garden, and Spanish colonial design evoke the feeling of an archbishop's palace. Built as the first hotel (in 1919) along what is now the heavily congested Condado, its interior has been upgraded and modernized many times. The lobby is dominated by a grand double staircase whose summit leads to a wrap-around gallery and a high vaulted ceiling painted in shades of pink and white.

Many of the almost 250 bedrooms are within a rambling modern wing (invisible from the street) whose red-tile roof mimics the detailing of the original core. During the day many visitors ignore the nearby beach in favor of the wind-sheltered pool area, where a double-tiered waterfall ringed with miniature palms evokes a jungle retreat. On the premises is a handful of relaxing bars, including the Trade Winds, whose low-slung wicker chairs could lull you to sleep. The El Gobernador, a formal restaurant whose blue-and-white decor matches the views of the sea, offers fresh seafood, among other dishes, and courteous service. Each room has its own balcony, overlooking the seacoast or the hotel's pool. In winter, singles range between $145 and $200 daily; doubles, $155 to $210. *In summer, singles cost $100 to $145 daily; doubles, $115 and $155.*

Hotel La Concha, Ashford Avenue, San Juan, PR 00907 (tel. 809/722-4343). Built in 1956, and named after its gracefully curved roof which resembles a section of a large sea shell, this comfortable hotel was once connected to its more prestigious neighbor, the Condado Beach Hotel. Now independent and thriving because of its proximity to one of the island's large convention centers, the hotel offers 250 renovated bedrooms and a cluster of drinking and dining facilities. You register in a sun-flooded marble-floored lobby where plaster bas-reliefs cast striking images. On the premises is San Juan's "disco of the moment," Club Mykonos, plus a pleasant restaurant, the Ocean Patio Terrace, open to the breezes that sweep in from the adjacent beach to the enclosed swimming pool. Naturally, the exterior of the complex is painted the same rosy coral color as a mature seashell.

Most of the 250 accommodations are within a more modern wing running beside the beach, and a handful of the more expensive suites are built town-house style along the swimming pool. Most of the accommodations have private balconies facing the sea and cable color TV. In winter, singles cost $130 to $180; doubles, $140 to $200. *In summer, singles go for $85 to $130; doubles, $95 to $150.* MAP can be arranged for another $35 per person daily.

First-Class Hotels at Condado

Dutch Inn & Tower, corner of Condado and Ashford Avenues, San Juan, PR 00907 (tel. 809/721-0810, or toll free 800/468-2014). In spite of its name, this is a very Latin hotel, drawing not only foreigners but many islanders visiting San Juan as well. It consists of twin buildings, one on the Condado, with a reception area on a side street. Each unit has a light-blue balcony. One building contains a series of suites; the other, standard hotel units. Every room has a TV set with cable TV and a radio. The air conditioning is individually controlled (this is a convenience since most of the hotels featuring air conditioning control it from a central unit which may not provide sufficient cooling, or may freeze you out of your room). *In summer, singles range in price from $60 to $65 daily; doubles, from $65 to $70; and suites, $95.* Winter rates are $85 to $100 for singles, from $90 to $105 for doubles, and $130 for suites. For MAP, add $30 daily per person to the room rates. An extra adult in a room costs $15 or more. The rates are subject to a government tax.

For lunch or dinner, you can choose the Greenhouse sidewalk café opening onto the sea with its intimate Galleria, open until 5 a.m. For dinner, you can also go to the Roof Garden restaurant, Il Giardino. Drinks are enjoyed in the Cocolobo Lobby Bar. The hotel has no beach facilities, but the Condado beach is just steps away. There is also an invigorating freshwater pool, and a casino has been added to the inn's facilities.

Ramada San Juan Hotel and Casino, 1045 Ashford Ave., San Juan, PR 00907 (tel. 809/724-5657), is an intimate 96-room first-class hotel right on the beach in the heart of the Condado section. The facilities and services anticipate the needs of all their guests whether on vacation or business trips. You can bask in the sun by the pool or on the sandy beach, have lunch or drinks on the sundeck, and dance the night away in the Polo Lounge to live music alternating between Latin rhythms and soft romantic melodies. The intimate Polo Restaurant serves local specialties or continental fare. The hotel's casino is open daily from noon to 4 a.m. In addition, shopping, sights, and island nightlife are within walking distance or only a short ride away. Rooms are classified as standard, superior, and deluxe. *In summer, singles pay from $85 to $125 daily; doubles, $95 to $135.* In winter, singles range from $145 to $175 daily, while doubles go for $155 to $185.

A Budget Hotel at Condado

Condado Lagoon Hotel, 6 Clemenceau St. (P.O. Box 13145), San Juan, PR 00907 (tel. 809/721-0170), in Santurce at the corner of Joffre, boasts of its smallness and the fact that because it is not a gigantic, cavernous hotel, one can get friendly, personal service. If you are booking from the States, allow plenty of time (two to three weeks will do) since the lodge has only 49 rooms, which go very fast both in and off-season. The suitably furnished rooms all have TVs and refrigerators. The Tabarin cocktail lounge offers no entertainment other than a piano-bar atmosphere in the evening. There are no beach facilities—one has to walk to the sands (nearby)—but there is a swimming pool. The hotel is one block from the main drag of Condado where entertainment, casinos, and restaurants are all a short walk away. There is parking available at no extra charge. Year round, singles rent for $70 daily, going up to $80 in a double. An extra person is charged $15. Tariffs include use not only of the swimming pool but also the gym. There is a mini-market on the premises.

Condado Guesthouses

El Canario Inn, 1317 Ashford Ave., San Juan, PR 00907 (tel. 809/724-2793), offers one of the best bed-and-breakfast values in San Juan. You'll recognize the building by its arched veranda and the porte-cochère which covers a side yard filled with plants. Keith and Jude Olson are the accommodating owners. The hotel consists of a main house and two nearby sets of servants' quarters, all linked by a terrace. There's a small, exquisite pool designed like a jungle pond, where water splashes down a stone wall into the bathing area. On the premises is an outdoor breakfast bar and lots of quiet corners for conversation. The 25 bedrooms are air-conditioned, with private baths and unpretentious furnishings. There's a communal kitchen if guests feel like cooking. There are rooms with two double beds, with twin beds, and with one double bed. A few have kitchens. *In low season, singles cost $35 and doubles run $65.* High-season rates are $55 in a single, $65 in a double. An additional person pays $10 per night. Efficiency units rent for $90. All tariffs include a continental breakfast.

Casa Blanca, 57 Calle Caribe, San Juan, PR 00907 (tel. 809/722-7139). Despite its self-image as an informal guesthouse, it occupies a valuable plot of land just a few paces from the Condado and some of the glitziest hotels in the Caribbean. Originally built as a guesthouse in the 1940s, it was expanded by a former resident of Massachusetts, Alex Leighton, and his wife, Suzanne, formerly a well-paid model in New York. You'll find it behind a wrap-around veranda, a wall, and a garden across Ashford Avenue. Inside, a total of seven small and simple rooms usually have a ceiling fan and copies of movie posters from the golden age of Hollywood. An honor bar is open throughout the day, turning the front porch into a social center for guests. You shouldn't expect the Ritz if you select this place, but you'll probably benefit from the culmulative advice that the Leightons have assembled during their sojourn on the Condado. Year-round prices range from $40 to $45 daily in a single, from $50 to $55 in a double. In winter only, a continental breakfast is served on the front veranda and included in the price of the room.

HOTELS IN MIRAMAR: Miramar, a quiet, residential sector, is very much a part of

metropolitan San Juan, and a long brisk walk will take you where the action is. The beach, regrettably, is at least half a mile away.

Quality Royale & Casino, 600 Avenida Fernandez Juncos, San Juan, PR 00907 (tel. 809/541-6630). Soaring above a commercial and residential district, this glistening 27-story hotel is the tallest skyscraper in the Caribbean. Its lobby and many of its public rooms are sheathed in marble. Near the reception desk a splashing fountain sustains clusters of plants. There's a swimming pool in back and a long cylindrical tunnel leading to a pleasant restaurant. The angled windows of its uppermost story contain a busy nightclub, Windows of the Caribbean, which evokes something you might encounter in South America. Each of the accommodations of this restored and redecorated hotel offers TV, phone, air conditioning, and a color scheme of stylish cream and pastels. In winter, singles rent for $115 daily, and doubles go for $125. *In summer, singles cost $85 daily; doubles, $100.*

Hotel Excelsior, 801 Ponce de León Ave., San Juan, PR 00907 (tel. 809/721-7400), is a 140-room facility which offers handsome accommodations and good service. Built in 1966, the hotel has a recently added, elegant lobby graced by four sculptures especially commissioned. The bedrooms have been completely refurbished, with cotton pastel fabrics from Denmark and Holland. Many have fully equipped kitchenettes, and all are air-conditioned and have color TV and bathrooms. The corridors of all ten guest-room floors have fine woolen carpets. Color schemes are melon, off-white, and brown. *Summer rentals are $56 to $78 single and $66 to $77 double.* Winter tariffs are $78 to $98 in single units, $89 to $109 in doubles. Use of the swimming pool, complimentary daily coffee, a newspaper, shoe shines, and transportation, as well as parking in either the underground garage or the adjacent parking lot, are included in the rates, which are subject to a 6% government tax. Children under age 10 are allowed to share a room with two adults free, and there is no charge for a crib. The Excelsior's Ali Oli Restaurant operates El Gazebo, a new pyramid-shaped wooden structure at poolside where guests can order a full American breakfast. A cocktail lounge, gift shop, and beauty shop complete the hotel's facilities. This hotel is known for its excellent maintenance and meticulous housekeeping.

A GUESTHOUSE AT OCEAN PARK:
The former private residence of the Spanish consul is now **La Condesa Inn**, 2071 Calle Cacique, San Juan, PR 00911 (tel. 809/727-3698). You're about a five-minute drive from most of the casinos, restaurants, and entertainment centers. Because La Condesa is limited to just 20 accommodations, I recommend that you book and plan accordingly. It is in the residential Ocean Park–Condado area, just 60 yards from San Juan's most spacious beach. All but the upstairs suites have their own private entrances. Some rooms contain complete individual kitchens and dining bars. There is also a pool restaurant. *In the off-season, a single rents for $35 and a double goes for $42.* In winter, regular singles cost $50 and doubles are $57. *In summer, a third person in a room pays only $12 extra.* A 15% service charge is levied, plus a $3-a-day energy surcharge.

A GUESTHOUSE AT PUNTA LAS MARIAS:
So many readers have praised **Tres Palmas Guest House**, 2212 Park Blvd., San Juan, PR 00913 (tel. 809/727-4617) that I went to investigate it myself. The guesthouse is ten minutes from the airport, midway between Isla Verde and Condado, lying on the ocean between Parque Barbosa and Punta Las Marias. Benjamin Lawlor and Catherine Lawlor Nadeau, owners of the Old Village Inn in Ogunquit, Maine, are the innkeepers who purchased Tres Palmas in 1985. They have renovated the comfortable bedrooms with decorative wall-to-wall mirrors, bright paint, and shiny floors. Screened windows and ceiling fans allow tropic breezes to flow through without resorting to use of the air conditioners. Some of the bedrooms have color TV. Sheets, towels, beach towels, whatever, are always sparkling clean. The seven units rent for $55 to $70 for one or two persons in winter, *for $35 to $50 off-season.* A continental breakfast, usually with homemade muffins, which you can enjoy at tile patio tables with umbrellas and benches, is included in the rates. The tropic mini-pool is refreshing after a day at the beach or sunning on the rooftop deck. The living area of the main house became like a private den back home, where guests relax, read, watch HBO, or just enjoy chatting. At night the rooftop deck provides a private gateway to the sunset and stars. The managers are friendly, as you learn immediately on arrival when they give you a free piña colada. In my opinion, this guesthouse is one of the best bargains on the island.

ISLA VERDE:
Beach-bordering Isla Verde is closer to the airport than the other sections of San Juan. Hotels here lie farther from the old town than do those considered in Miramar, Condado, and Ocean Park. If you don't mind the isolation and want access to the fairly good beaches, then you might consider one of the following hotels.

Deluxe Living

El San Juan Hotel and Casino, Route 187 (P.O. Box 2872), San Juan, PR 00903 (tel. 809/791-1000, or toll free 800/468-2818). For dozens of reasons which involve more than its spectacular physical plant, this is considered the best hotel in Puerto Rico, and some say the best in the entire Caribbean basin. Built in the 1950s, and graced with much handcrafted detailing, it fell into sad neglect. But in 1985, with the infusion of $45 million and the enlightened guidance of a sophisticated manager, Klaus Reincke, the hotel entered a renaissance. It appears from the exterior like one of the dozens of other high-rise towers lining the Isla Verde section of San Juan's seacoast, but the hotel is surrounded by 350 palms, century-old banyans, and lavish gardens designed by Edward Durrell Stone. The hotel's sandy beach with its almond trees is probably the finest in the San Juan area, visibly wider and less violent than the beaches that flank some of the older hotels of the Condado. Socially the hotel has skyrocketed into prominence and is known for its glamorous functions filling its banqueting halls and conference rooms.

The hotel has a lobby that is perhaps the most opulent and memorable in the Caribbean. Entirely sheathed in russet-colored marble and hand-carved mahogany paneling, the public rooms stretch on almost endlessly. The in-house casino is an important attraction, and it's open daily from noon to 4 a.m. Gamblers and gourmets alike work out their energy in the rooftop health club or promenade down a re-creation of a waterfront street in Hong Kong to a Chinese restaurant.

The opulent accommodations have intriguing touches of hi-tech. Each makes maximum use of irregular spaces to include such amenities as dressing rooms, three different phones, air conditioning, video-linked TV, and ceiling fans. A few feature Jacuzzis. Each benefits from a harmonious color scheme of restful but stimulating Caribbean colors. About 150 of the 400 accommodations are within the outer reaches of the garden. Each is designed as a rustic but comfortable bungalow. Known as casitas, they include the accessories that most honeymooners fantasize about, including Roman tubs, atrium showers, and access to the fern-lined paths of a tropical jungle a few steps away. In winter, singles and doubles rent for $190 to $290 daily. *In summer, singles or doubles go for $155 to $250.* The hotel is near the airport, about a five-minute drive away.

El San Juan Towers, Rte. 187 (P.O. Box S3445), Isla Verde, San Juan, PR 00913 (tel. 809/791-5151, or toll free 800/468-2026), offers the closest thing a vacationer can get to apartment living. About a third of the 451 units are privately owned and occupied year round, while the rest are rented for at least part of the year as hotel accommodations. Each accommodation is completely air-conditioned, with a fully equipped kitchen, cable color TV, and a private balcony. *Off-season rates range from $135 daily in a minimum studio or efficiency for two, rising to $160 in a deluxe. A one-bedroom unit costs from $200 minumum to $270 daily, and two- and three-bedroom accommodations are also available.* In winter, studios and efficiencies for two range from $160 to $260 daily, while one-bedroom units cost anywhere from $270 to $335 daily. While at the hotel, you have access to the well-equipped private health club, with separate facilities for men and women. An outdoor playground and an indoor nursery for children are both supervised. The ground-floor restaurant, the Happy Apple, is open for breakfast and lunch, closing just before dinnertime. In a bar and lounge, the Mano-a-Mano, you can dance to low-key disco music after doing your shopping at the lobbyside mini-market. A car wash and laundry are on the premises.

A First-Class Choice

Carib-Inn of San Juan, Rte. 187, San Juan, PR 00913 (tel. 809/791-3535), is a complete tropical resort and casino just eight minutes from the airport. The 225 high-ceilinged bedrooms and the cabanas, many with balconies, have outside views. Most overlook a giant racquet-shaped swimming pool, with a generous sunning and refreshment terrace, plus a Bohio Bar. The rooms are traditionally furnished, most having two double beds. Rooms are graded moderate, superior, and deluxe. *Summer tariffs are: singles $68; doubles $70*. In winter, prices are: singles, $85 to $110; doubles, $110 to $130. Meal plans are available for a seven-day stay. Action is lively at night, particularly in the intimate casino. La Tinajita Restaurant serves local and international cuisine, and Cousin Ho's, a Chinese eatery, is one of the best restaurants in town. La Tinajita lobby bar often provides live entertainment and dancing until the early hours. Tennis is taken seriously here, with eight professional Laykold-surfaced courts, of which four are lit for night games. The largest tennis facility in the San Juan area, the Carib-Inn features a group of tennis professionals at your command to sharpen your game. A ball-throwing machine and a large tennis club membership always ensure an opportunity to play. There's a health center for men and women, including a gym, steam room, and sauna.

On a Budget in Isla Verde

Green Isle Inn / Casa Mathiesen, 36 Calle Uno Este Villamar Urb, San Juan, PR 00913 (tel. 809/726-4330). Benefiting from a combined ownership by an entrepreneurial management, these twin establishments are set within a one-minute walk of each other. Both inns were originally built as private homes in the 1950s and later converted into guesthouses. They lie behind a screen of palms in a subdivision near El San Juan Hotel. Some regular and longtime habitués have returned for more than 20 years. What makes this place especially inviting is the presence of equipped kitchens in 29 of the 35 units (those without such facilities contain at least a refrigerator). One of the island's most charming owners, Pat Campbell, directs her guests to the array of meat markets, produce stands, and bakeries that lie within a few blocks. Both inns are sheathed in the same green-and-white color scheme, but reception formalities are conducted in the better-established Green Isle Inn. The Alabama-born co-owner, James Wilson, extends a warm form of hospitality. Each inn has its own sheltered rectangular swimming pools. Many of the guest rooms offer built-in mahogany closets, and each unit is air-conditioned, with a ceiling fan and private bathroom. Laundry facilities are on the premises, along with transportation to and from the nearby airport in the hotel's 14-passenger mini-van. Rates at these establishments are a real bargain. In rooms suitable for either one or two guests, accommodations with kitchens cost $60 daily in winter, *$46 in summer*. Units without kitchens go for $53 daily in winter for one or two persons, *$39 daily in summer*.

La Playa, 6 Amapola St., San Juan, PR 00913 (tel. 809/791-1115), is a true bargain. Its situation and atmosphere make it a persuasive choice. It's a two-story, L-shaped hotel, directly on the water, with rooms overlooking a courtyard crowded with lush, semitropical trees and shrubbery. The second-floor bedrooms, with long balconies, are preferred. Across from the front entrance lies the beginning of a two-mile-long beach. Each of the 16 well-furnished bedrooms has a private bath and a bright ambience. Bold-patterned draperies match the bedspreads. *In summer, doubles cost from $50; singles, from $40*. Tariffs go up to $60 in a double in winter, $50 in a single. All units have private bath and air conditioning. The hotel's waterfront bar is one of the most popular on the island (see my nighttime suggestions).

The Duffys', 9 Isla Verde Rd., San Juan, PR 00913 (tel. 809/726-1415). Built as a private home in the 1930s, but converted into a guesthouse in 1946, it resembles a secluded California bungalow compound hidden by flowering trees. There's a parking area where you can leave your car before heading in to meet the Rochester-born owner, Madeline Weihe. Everything is a bit time-worn, but that is perhaps what makes the place so low-key and mellow. Each of the 14 accommodations has air conditioning, a ceiling fan, cable TV, and a view of the vegetation outside. They lie in a motel-like conversion of an older house a few steps away. None has a phone. Winter rates cost $55 daily in a single, $65 in a double. *Summer tariffs are $50 daily in a single, $55 in a* *double*. Discounts are offered off-season to prepaying guests who remain seven days or longer. Guests congregate and socialize in a rear compound ringed with a wall in an area known as Duffys' Restaurant. Full dinners, costing $20 each, include grilled pork chops and chicken Cordon Bleu.

Don Pedro Hotel, 4 Rosa St., San Juan, PR 00913 (tel. 809/791-2838), was created in the old Spanish style, with its L-shaped room block overlooking a courtyard, a swimming pool, and an adjoining garden restaurant. It's quite informal, the tone set by the youthful staff. Each of the bedrooms has tile floors, basic furnishings, with good-size closets and a tile bath. The furnishings are hit and miss, with older chests, maybe a vintage rocker, simple beds—in all, good for sleeping, and most important, clean. Each room is air-conditioned, and some have tiny kitchenettes opening onto a bed-sitting room. In winter, a single costs $46 daily, and a double goes for $54. *In summer, singles cost only $36, with doubles going for $42.* Rates include a continental breakfast.

2. Dining Out in Puerto Rico

In recent years San Juan restaurants have returned to a greater appreciation of Puerto Rican cooking. Now many of the leading restaurants, although they still offer Stateside dishes, also feature a selection of local specialties as well. Even big hotels such as the Caribe Hilton are in on the act. While Puerto Rican cookery has similarities to both Spanish and Mexican cuisine, it is quite different.

Of course, out on the island ask for any fresh fish dish and chances are you'll be pleased. Finish your meal with Puerto Rican coffee, which is strong, black, aromatic. Perhaps you'll have only a small cup. Rum is the national drink, and you can buy it in almost any shade. In Puerto Rico it's quite proper to order a cold beer before one even looks at the menu. Popular among the locals is India, brewed in Mayagüez, famous for its pure water.

MEALS IN OLD SAN JUAN: Old Spain is recaptured at **La Zaragozana,** 356 San Francisco (tel. 723-5103), with its white adobe walls, rough-hewn beams, slate and terracotta floors, as well as antiques, murals, brass lamps, and wine racks. In the beamed bodega, you can enjoy a before-dinner drink. The restaurant, which specializes in Spanish, Cuban, and Puerto Rican cuisine, is run by the much-awarded Wilberto Alejandro. On my most recent rounds I was served my finest meal in Old San Juan in this restaurant. The top specialty is called "The Chef's," a filet of beef tenderloin stuffed with Spanish ham and cheese in a burgundy wine sauce with mushrooms. The kitchen has long been known for its classic black-bean soup, but other kettles are likely to contain gazpacho, caldo gallego, garlic, or fish soup. Other temptations in-

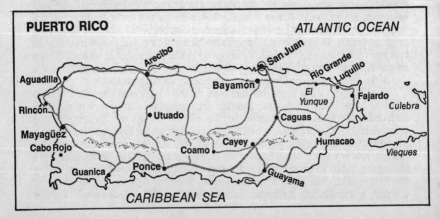

clude snails Zaragozana, beef Stroganoff, Valencian paella, a zarzuela of seafood, or perhaps lobster Créole. Puerto Rican dishes include filet of pork Old San Juan, followed by "custard from heaven." Count on parting with $30. The restaurant is open daily from 11:30 a.m. to 1 a.m., and reservations are important.

Los Galanes, 65 San Francisco (tel. 722-4008), links Old Seville with Old San Juan. It's a 16th-century setting on a one-way street, an easy walk down from El Convento. As you enter, on your right is a small bar for a before-dinner drink (it's fashionable to order a dry sherry). The maître d' and his staff are courtesy oriented. The familiar selection of international appetizers is presented on the elaborate scroll of the parchment menu, including gazpacho, homemade pâté, and escargots bouguignonnes. The main courses are usually good and sometimes excellent—filet of sole meunière, shrimp in garlic sauce, veal marsala, filet mignon, and chicken Cordon Bleu. Another specialty is paella, prepared for two or more. For dessert, most diners seem to prefer the chocolate cheesecake. For a complete dinner here, expect to spend from $25. The restaurant is open from 7 to 11 p.m. for dinner only, and reservations are imperative. It is closed Sunday and Monday.

Restaurant Amadeus, 106 Calle San Sebastian (tel. 722-8635). An abstract watercolor portrait of a young Mozart decorates the wall near the entrance of this restaurant where lovers of music and fine food feel at home. The other paintings, many by emerging Puerto Rican artists, change as rapidly as the menu items which emerge from the kitchen. Formerly a cafeteria, this old building was adapted (and supplemented with just a hint of hi-tech) by architect José Ramirez and his brother, Ramón, a biologist. The charming Patricia Wilson assists José in the kitchen, where Caribbean ingredients are given a nouvelle twist. You might enjoy an appetizer of fried green plantains with caviar and fish mousse, fried dumplings in guava sauce, ceviche, a cassoulet of shrimp with black beans and sausages, marlin, shark in white wine sauce, and rabbit with prunes and red wine sauce. Full meals cost from $17 at dinner, from $12 at lunch. Lunch is served Tuesday through Friday from noon to 2:30 p.m.; dinner, daily except Monday from 6:30 p.m. to 12:30 a.m. The bar remains open until 2:30 a.m. The establishment lies in the heart of the old city, across from the side of the Church of San José.

El Patio de Sam, 102 San Sebastian (tel. 724-9254), stands across from the San José Church, the oldest building on the island, and faces the statue of Ponce de León, the island's first governor. This popular place is a gathering spot for American expatriates, newspeople, and shopkeepers in the old town. It's known for having the best hamburgers in San Juan. Even though the dining room is not on the outside, it has been transformed into a patio. The illusion is so credible you'll swear you're dining al fresco. Every table is strategically placed near a cluster of potted, outdoor plants, and the canvas panels and awnings covering the skylight give the dining area the feeling of being outside (rain or shine). For a cooling and satisfying lunch, ideal after you've strolled through the streets of the old town, try the black-bean soup, followed by the cold meat platter, and topped with a key lime tart. Other main dishes include various steaks, barbecued ribs, filet of sole stuffed with crab, and fish and chips. At lunch, expect to pay around $10, the tab rising to $15 and up for dinner. It is open from 11 a.m. to 2 a.m. Sunday through Thursday, from 11 a.m. to 4:30 a.m. on Friday and Saturday. The kitchen is open until 1:30 a.m. Sunday through Thursday and until 3:30 a.m. on Friday and Saturday.

Casa Paco, 256 San Justo (tel. 723-7830), is considered one of the most charming restaurants in the old town, mainly because of the sensitive and dedicated intentions of its owners, Carmen Ramos and Alicia Palerm. It lies behind a white façade which shelters a high-ceilinged re-creation of a Spanish colonial inn. Ceiling fans whirl above terracotta floors, pink walls, and a sun-flooded atrium supported by arches of exposed brick. Full meals cost from $30 and include an array of such specialties as house-style clams in a creamy garlic sauce, baked oysters provençale, lobster with

Armagnac, grouper terrine with green pepper sauce, a seafood zarzuela in a spicy Créole sauce, and cognac-laced lobster bisque. The Toulouse-born chef, Jean-Pierre Denys, is an award-winning expert dedicated to his art. There's a friendly bar near the entrance where you can get a drink during meal hours and throughout the afternoon. Lunch is served every weekday between 11:30 a.m. and 3 p.m. and almost continuously every Sunday from 1 to 8 p.m. Dinner on other days is between 6 and 11 p.m.

La Mallorquina, 207 San Justo (tel. 722-3261), is San Juan's oldest restaurant, founded in 1848. A bit of Old Spain transplanted to the New World, the restaurant is in a three-story, glassed-in courtyard with arches and antique wall clocks. Even if you've already eaten and are shopping in the old town, you might want to visit just to perch at the old-fashioned wooden bar which runs the length of the left wall as you enter. The waiters appear as if they've been hired by central casting, and they slip in the back to eat the food too. The chef specializes in the most typical Puerto Rican rice dish—asopao. You can have it with either chicken, shrimp, or lobster and shrimp (if you're feeling extravagant). Arroz con pollo is almost as popular. I suggest you get your dinner rolling by ordering garlic soup. If that frightens you, gazpacho is served also. Among other recommended main dishes are grilled pork chop with fried plantain, and beef tenderloin, Puerto Rican style. Imaginatively prepared, the assorted seafood stewed in wine is good. Lunch is busy, and dinners are sometimes quiet. A full dinner should cost somewhere between $15 and $25. It's best to go between noon and 2 p.m. and 8 and 10 p.m. It is closed Sunday.

El Meson Vasco, 47 Cristo St., corner of San Sebastian (tel. 725-7819), serves savory Basque specialties right in the old town, near the more popular El Patio de Sam. A corner building, the restaurant opens directly onto the Plaza de San José. Even if you prowl the streets of Seville, you couldn't find a more Spanish restaurant. High arched windows and a beamed ceiling add the right architectural details, and as you sit on raffia-covered chairs you can check out the paintings and woodcarvings. The very leisurely service is from 11:30 a.m. to midnight. I've seen visitors stroll in here and order a hamburger, but it's better to stick to the chef's specialties--garlic chicken, codfish Bilbaina, Spanish hake in green sauce, trout molinera, eggs Bilbaina. Every time I'm in San Juan I journey here for an order of the small white beans, Basque style (with sausages), a meal in themselves. Soups are good, especially the porrusalda (potato and leek). If you eat here, expect a tab ranging from $18.

La Chaumière, 367 Tétuan (tel. 722-3330), is decorated like an inn in provincial France, with heavy ceiling beams, black and white checkerboard floors, large rows of wine racks, and half-timbered walls. Menu items include beef Wellington, a surprise in a French restaurant, rack of lamb for two, chateaubriand for two, pheasant flambéed with Calvados, onion soup, vichyssoise, pâté maison made with pork, chicken, and duck liver, and daily specials, such as fish soup. Full meals range upward from $40. It's open daily except Sunday from 6 p.m. to midnight. Upstairs is La Crêperie, a French pancake house.

The **Butterfly People,** 152 Fortaleza (tel. 725-0756), has gossamer wings. This butterfly venture (see my shopping recommendations) is the special world of Drakir Purington and his wife, Attendaire. He was a Harvard graduate and she a Jordanian translator at the United Nations before opening this second-floor café in a restored mansion in Old San Juan. Next to the world's largest gallery devoted to butterflies, you can dine in the Palm Court Café, opening to a patio. It is mainly a bar, with 15 tables serving drinks and lunch from 11 a.m. to 6 p.m. Monday to Saturday. The café specializes in tropical and light European fare utilizing only the freshest ingredients. You might begin with gazpacho or vichyssoise, follow with quiche or one of the daily specials, and top it all off with chocolate mousse or the tantalizing raspberry chiffon pie with fresh raspberry sauce. A full bar offers tropical specialties featuring piña coladas, fresh-squeezed Puerto Rican orange juice, and Fantasias—a frappé of seven fresh fruits. Wherever you look, framed butterflies will delight you. At times, especially the afternoons when cruise-ship passengers aren't visiting, the place has a private-club atmosphere, where the customers play chess and backgammon. Drakir himself is quite an attraction as he goes about the premises. With his long gray hair, he is almost mystical in demeanor. The clothes he wears are as striking as he is, but then one must work hard to compete in a room full of butterflies.

Maria's, 204 Calle Cristo (no phone). Every time I get off the plane in San Juan, I head for this narrow little bar with back tables in the old part of town. There, perched on a stool, you'll be served some of the coolest and most refreshingly original drinks in the capital—a banana frost, a pineapple frost, an orange freeze, a papaya freeze, a chocolate frost, a lime freeze, a mixed fruit frappé. Two drinks generally cost $6. The students, TV personalities, writers, and models who gather here also enjoy Mexican dishes such as chili with cheese, a taco, or an enchilada. If that sounds too heavy on a hot day, then I suggest the fruit salad. Count on spending from $6 up for a drink and a snack. The blender continues to whir from 11 a.m. until 2 a.m. seven days a week.

PUERTA DE TIERRA: One of the most elegant—and best—restaurants in Puerto Rico is **La Rôtisserie,** in the Caribe Hilton (tel. 721-0303). The chef, August Schreiner, has won many awards for his outstanding international cuisine. The restaurant is tastefully appointed, located on the second floor of the deluxe hotel next to the casino. Fashion shows are presented at lunchtime on Tuesday and Thursday. Reservations are necessary, and in the evening men are requested to wear a jacket and tie. Meals usually average around $35. For that, you are likely to be tempted with roast prime rib of beef, two succulent double lamb chops, perhaps duckling with wild rice. There is always fresh fish, such as red snapper, as well as the ever-popular steak Diane. The chef shows his imagination in such dishes as medallions of veal and lobster flavored with tarragon. For an unusual opener, if featured, try the pumpkin bisque with lobster flavored with coriander. The Caesar salad is always spectacular, and you might want to conclude with a hot chocolate soufflé. It's best to go between 8 and 10 p.m.

CONDADO: One of the best restaurants on the island, the **Charthouse,** Ashford Avenue (tel. 728-0110), is also one of the most popular bars in the Caribbean. The lattice-trimmed villa, built in 1910 and once the home of the German consul, attracts on any night literally hundreds of sociable local residents, mostly aged 18 to 40, to its long bar in what used to be a spacious salon. Today the heavy ceiling beams have been exposed, track lighting installed, and paintings added to create a warm ambience. The large ground-floor salon contains an almost endless Victorian-style series of shelves, complete with Corinthian columns and beveled mirrors.

The food here is beautifully prepared. The prime rib dishes may be the best in the entire Caribbean. You can enjoy New England clam chowder, the copious salad that comes with all main courses, blue marlin, fresh broccoli, top sirloin, shrimp teriyaki, one-tail Australian lobster, Hawaiian chicken, and a dessert affectionately known by the staff (most of whom are Californians) as "mud pie." Full meals here are often less expensive than those at less desirable restaurants in San Juan. They begin at around $30, although if you drink a lot (and that's part of the fun here) you can spend a lot more. The Charthouse is part of a chain of ambience-filled restaurants scattered across the American West, based in California. The bar is open from 5 p.m. to 1 a.m. Meals are served daily: from 6 to 11 p.m. on weekdays, until midnight on Friday and Saturday. Reservations are imperative.

Lotus Flower, 999 Ashford Ave., Laguna Wing of the Condado Plaza Hotel and Casino (tel. 721-1000, ext. 1950), on Condado Beach, is one of the finest Chinese restaurants in the Caribbean. Overlooking the Condado Lagoon, the restaurant serves dishes that are a wonderful medley of flavors. It's open Monday to Friday from noon to 3 p.m. and 6 to 11:30 p.m. On Saturday it is open only from 6 to 11:30 p.m., and on Sunday from 1 to 11:30 p.m. The decor is a sophisticated blend of colors such as sea green and terracotta. Hanging plants, tilework, and bamboo accessories make for pleasant dining, along with the immaculate napery. The chef is equally at home in turning out Hunan, Szechuan, or Cantonese cookery. He'll even do a Peking duck if you order it far enough in advance. Specialties include lemon chicken, beef with scallops and shrimp in a hot sauce, and Szechuan Phoenix, made with prime beef and chicken in a hot sauce. Open your meal with the noodles in sesame sauce, a delectable dish. Count on spending around $30, but you can do it for less.

Don Pelayo, 71 Calle Luisa (tel. 724-1812), serves some of the best Spanish and international cuisine in the city. The hosts and proprietors are the Cueto brothers, who extend a warm welcome. They have created a cozy ambience that suggests some corner of Segovia, Spain, with hanging hams and armor displays, along with tiles. Ceramic plates are also exhibited. You might begin with one of the excellently prepared appetizers or soups, including shrimp in garlic sauce, sweetbreads in sherry, a Galician broth, or a Castilian garlic soup. The house salad is an array of such ingredients as asparagus, hearts of palm, artichoke hearts, ham, tomato, lettuce, and pimento. Many diners come here just to enjoy a heaping plate of paella in the Valencian style. The seafood is outstanding, especially the seabass Basque style and the broiled lobster. The meat and poultry dishes are equally as good, including chicken in garlic sauce and several versions of steak. The service is excellent: sometimes fresh fish is boned right at your table. Expect to spend from $30 per person for a satisfying meal. The restaurant is open Monday to Saturday from 11:30 a.m. to 3:30 p.m. and 6 to 11:30 p.m., on Sunday from 11:30 a.m. to 11:30 p.m.

L'Escargot, 1106 Magdalena Ave. (tel. 722-2436), is one of the best and most reasonably priced French restaurants in San Juan. Open Monday through Saturday, it's housed in a building that evokes a private hacienda, with red awnings and a tile roof. When guests at one of the hotels flanking the Convention Center hear about this place, they often head here and are rarely disappointed. The price is right too: from $25 for dinner. Try to arrive between noon and 2 p.m. or 8 and 10 p.m. My most recent meal began with a potage du jour and was followed by a delectable roast veal. My dining companion ordered filet of red snapper in escargot butter. Each night a different dessert maison is offered. The wine list is limited but well chosen.

SANTURCE: Operation of the **Swiss Chalet**, Hotel Pierre, De Diego (tel. 721-2233), has continued successfully for more than 30 years. The menu is large, with a host of cheese dishes and other Swiss specialties, including everything from sauerbraten to minced veal in white wine sauce with mushrooms, a favorite in Zurich. Hors d'oeuvres offered are a dozen escargots du Jura maison and soups such as French onion, green pea, and vichyssoise. The main dishes are well prepared, and you can enjoy a Swiss-style bratwurst with onion sauce or roast rack of lamb provençale. Fish and seafood are good too. Try the Mexican Gulf shrimp sautéed in garlic and herb butter. Among the desserts, I like Bavarois au kirsch with raspberry sauce. Meals average around $25. The management suggests that you dress "elegantly casual." Hours are daily from noon to 10:30 p.m.

MIRAMAR: An interesting choice is **Restaurant Ali Oli**, Hotel Excelsior, 801 Ponce de León Ave. (tel. 721-7400). Is it Japanese or is it minimalist hi-tech with touches of Latin bravado? The decor, like the food, is interesting if a bit of an enigma. The neutral gray walls highlight the starkly modern arrangements of flowers, the big windows with a pool view, and the abstract paintings. It's a bit as if the setting were designed to showcase the unusual, even bizarre, combinations of ingredients comprising the cuisine. Full meals, costing from $30, include a cassoulet of local roots with fish, crayfish, and clams, quails stuffed with Puerto Rican chestnuts and madeira sauce, poached salmon with passion fruit and coriander sauce, banana mousse with escargots, and fried plantain casing with octopus. Some of the dishes, frankly, are more successful than others, but it's an avant-garde culinary experience and worth a try. Reservations are necessary. Lunch is served weekdays between noon and 3 p.m.; dinner is weekdays and Saturday from 7 to 10:30 p.m. No lunch is served on Saturday, and the place is closed Sunday.

La Fragua, in the Capitol Hotel, 800 Ponce de León Ave. (tel. 722-4699), is one of my favorite restaurants in and around San Juan. Go here for their fresh-tasting and well-prepared fish dishes, along with impeccable service. Sea bass is a specialty (it appears on the menu as mero). Don't go here for the decor. The restaurant is vaguely Spanish, and the average meal is priced at $25. The waiters are helpful in explaining what's available on a particular day. Many professionals, such as lawyers, in the San Juan community patronize this establishment, considering it their ''secret'' address. It's open Monday to Friday from noon to 3:30 p.m. and 6:30 to 11 p.m., on Saturday from 6:30 to 11 p.m. only.

ISLA VERDE: One of the best choices in San Juan for a taste of the good life, **Dar Tiffany,** in the Hotel El San Juan, Rte. 187 (tel. 791-1000), is usually jammed, especially on weekends, with the island's resident literati, glitterati, and beautiful people. On the ground floor of Puerto Rico's most glamorous hotel, it provides considerate service. You dine within a labyrinth of etched glass whose palm-leaf motifs mimic the plants growing outside. A few steps away, just on the other side of the translucent walls, you'll glimpse the whirling ceiling fans of one of the hotel's more popular tropical bars. Dar Tiffany is actually a very upscale steakhouse, where Larry Sweeney is enthusiastically involved in each of the details that make this a special place. Drinks, especially the martinis, are full-fisted libations made the way you like them. The wine list is actually more extensive than the food menu, which offers such carefully aged and seasoned specialties as prime rib, filet mignon, veal chops, jumbo lobster, sea scallops, and filet of fresh Norwegian salmon. A Caesar salad and a temptingly caloric dessert might be the appropriate beginning and ending for a meal here. Dinners, served between 6:30 p.m. and midnight seven days a week, cost from $35, and reservations are recommended.

Back Street Hong Kong, Hotel El San Juan, Rte. 187 (tel. 791-1224). To reach it, you promenade down a disconcertingly realistic re-creation of a backwater street in Hong Kong. Disassembled from its original home at the 1964 New York's World Fair, it was purchased and rebuilt, with the exposed electrical meters and lopsided façades of its original design intact. A few steps later, you enter the immaculate interior of one of the best Chinese restaurants in the Caribbean. Beneath a soaring redwood ceiling, and ringed with teakwood lattices, iron filigree, and formally dressed employees, you can enjoy meals for around $30. The Mandarin/Szechuan/Hunan menu includes pineapple fried rice served in a real pineapple, a superb version of scallops with orange sauce, Szechuan-style beef with chicken, steamed fish, sizzling three delicacies (beef, shrimp, and scallops), and a dragon and phoenix (lobster mixed with shrimp). Seasonal specialties include asparagus sautéed with beef, shrimp, or chicken and soft-shell crabs sautéed with scallops. No lunch is served, and dinner lasts from 6 p.m. to midnight seven days a week.

FOOD ON THE ISLAND: In your tour out on the island, you'll find few well-known restaurants, except those in the major hotels. However, there are plenty of roadside places and simple taverns. The most popular restaurant outside of San Juan follows:

El Yunque Restaurant, at El Yunque (tel. 790-4237), has been in business since 1936 right in the heart of the island's exotic rain forest. You can dine on some of the most authentic Puerto Rican specialties offered on the island. On the narrow ledge of a mountain road, this chalet restaurant is made of wood, with a stone fireplace at each end. The side of the dining room with the best view has an all-glass wall. The atmosphere is rustic, and at some time during your meal it will definitely rain—I can guarantee that! You park your car on the road above, walking down a covered staircase to this seemingly remote spot. The soups, served in pewter bowls, are excellent and homemade, ranging from a regional garlic version to the classic caldo gallego. The specialty is asopao, that soupy Puerto Rican rice dish, prepared here with everything from land crab to squid. The best, I think, is the asopao paella, a really big meal. Also good are white turtle-meat steak, land crab prepared native style, and a casserole of shrimp and lobster in wine sauce. First-timers might be attracted to the yuquiyu. This is half a pineapple shell filled with turtle meat and Spanish sausage, pigeon peas, and crushed fresh pineapple. If you don't want such heavy food for lunch, try a native fruit salad, followed by custard. A full repast will cost from $22 per person. Hours are daily from 9 a.m. to 6 p.m.

Heading west from San Juan along the northern coast, you reach Vega Baja. There I suggest dining at **Dino's Steak House,** Rte. 2, no. 12, in the Jardines de Vega Baja (tel. 858-1100). It's an Italian steakhouse and seafood oasis right off Rte. 2 in Vega Baja. If you're headed toward the west coast, a stopover here for a meal would be in order. Dino is the gregarious owner, and some of his cuisine reflects his parental influence (his mother was from Genoa, his father from the Basque country). The ambience is friendly and relaxed, and musical entertainment is offered at dinner on weekends when the mood is informal. The most expensive steak is a 14-ounce prime, and the menu includes a variety of local seafood dishes, depending on what's available. Try the lobster salad suprème. Dino brings in fine ingredients whenever necessary: for example, prime meat from New Zealand or Nebraska, red snapper from Hong Kong, and shrimp from Australia. Most dishes include side orders of spaghetti, with a savory Italian sauce to which only Dino has the recipe, and he's not talking! Meals cost from $20. Hours are Tuesday, Wednesday, and Thursday from noon to p.m., on Friday and Saturday from noon to 11 p.m., and on Sunday from 11 a.m. to 11 p.m.; closed Monday.

3. What to See in San Juan

The streets are narrow and teeming with traffic, but a walk through Old San Juan —in Spanish, El Viejo San Juan—is like a stroll through five centuries of history. You can do it in less than a day. In a historic landmark seven-square-block area in the westernmost part of the city, you can see on foot many of Puerto Rico's chief historical sightseeing attractions, and when you tire of monuments, you can combine your tour with some shopping along the way. Many of the museums in Old San Juan close at 11:45 a.m. for lunch and don't reopen until 2 p.m.

The Spanish moved to Old San Juan in 1521, and the city founded there was to play an important role as Spain's bastion of defense in the Caribbean. Once the city was called Puerto Rico (Rich Port), as the name San Juan was given to the whole island.

I'll begin our tour at the northeast corner of Old San Juan. On Calle Norzagaray stands the 1783 **Fort San Cristobal,** which was built to defend San Juan against attacks by land, as well as to form backup support for El Morro if that fort were attacked from the sea. Composed of six independent units, the fort is connected to a central structure by means of tunnels and dry moats. You'll get the idea if you look at a scale model on display. On a site of 27 acres, the fort is overseen by the National Park Service. Be sure to see the Garita del Diablo, or the Devil's Sentry Box. The devil himself, it is said, would snatch away soldiers on guard duty at the box. Free guided tours are offered daily at 9:30 and 11 a.m. and at 2 and 3:30 p.m.

The **Tapia Theater,** Avenida Ponce de León, was paid for by taxes on bread and imported liquor. Standing across from the Plaza de Colón, it is one of the oldest theaters in the western hemisphere, built about 1832. In 1976 a restoration returned the theater to its original look. Much of Puerto Rican theater history is connected with Tapia. It's named after the island's first prominent playwright, Alejandro Tapia y Rivera (1826–1882), and Adelina Patti (1843–1919), the most popular and highly paid singer of her day, made her operatic debut here when she was barely 14.

Before you leave, pause to look at the **Plaza de Colón.** Once named the Plaza de Santiago, it had its name changed to honor Columbus on November 19, 1893, the 400th anniversary of the island's discovery. In the center of the square is a statue of Columbus, and at its base are plaques tracing incidents in his globe-trotting life.

La Casa del Callejon, Calle San Francisco (tel. 725-5250), run by the Institute of Culture, houses two museums. On the first floor of this 18th-century house, the Museum of Colonial Architecture has scale models of El Morro and La Fortaleza which may give you some perspective before you see the real thing. Exhibits of iron and woodwork, along with ceramic tiles, can also be seen. I find the second-floor Museum of the Puerto Rican Family much more interesting, as it gives you a glimpse into the life of how these island people lived in the 19th century. The rooms are small, and the life, as depicted here, was definitely middle class. Hours are 9 a.m. to noon and 1 to 4:30 p.m. Admission is free. Guided tours are conducted Tuesday through Saturday at 9 a.m. and again at 4:30 p.m.

El Arsenal, La Puntilla (tel. 725-5584). The Spaniards used a shallow craft to patrol lagoons and mangroves in and around San Juan. Needing a base for these vessels, they constructed El Arsenal at the turn of the century, and it was at this same base that they, so to speak, staged their last stand, flying the Spanish colors until the final Spaniard was removed in 1898, at the end of the Spanish-American War.

Cristo Chapel, on Calle Cristo, was built to commemorate what legend says was a miracle. Horse racing down Cristo Street was the highlight of the fiestas on St. John's Day, the patron saint of the city. In 1753 a young rider lost control of his horse and plunged over the precipice. Moved by the accident, a spectator, the secretary of the city, Don Mateo Pratts, invoked Christ to save the youth. He had the chapel built that same year. Today it is a landmark in the old city and one of its best-known historical monuments. The Campèche paintings and gold and silver altar can be seen through its glass doors.

La Casa de Libro, 255 Calle Cristo (tel. 723-0354), is a restored 18th-century house sheltering a library devoted to the arts of printing and bookmaking, with examples of fine printing from the 15th century to the present, as well as some medieval illuminated manuscripts. Special exhibits are usually shown on the first floor, open from 11 a.m. to 4:30 p.m. except weekends and holidays.

La Fortaleza, at the west end of Calle Fortaleza overlooking the San Juan Harbor (tel. 721-7000, ext. 2323), is the office and residence of the governor of Puerto Rico. The oldest executive mansion in continuous use in the western hemisphere, it has served as the island's seat of government for more than three centuries. Yet its history goes back even further, to 1533, when construction began for a fortress (*fortaleza*) to protect San Juan's settlers during raids by cannibalistic Caribs. The original medieval towers remain, but as the edifice was subsequently enlarged into a palace, other modes of architecture and ornamentation were also incorporated, including baroque, Gothic, neoclassical, and Arabian. La Fortaleza has been designated a National Historic Site of the U.S. government. Tours in English are conducted every hour on weekdays from 9 a.m. until 4 p.m.—but don't show up in your bikini.

San Juan Gate, Calle San Francisco and Calle Recinto Oeste, built around 1635, just north of La Fortaleza, was the main gate and entry point into San Juan—that is, if you came by ship in the 18th century. The gate is the only one remaining of the several entries to the old walled city.

The **City Hall,** Calle San Francisco, was ordered built in 1604, but work suffered many delays because of lack of money. Rebuilt twice in the 18th century, it was finally ready to be occupied in 1789. The clock in the tower was installed in 1889. Guided tours are given Monday through Friday, except holidays, from 8 a.m. to 4:15 p.m.

San Juan Cathedral, Calle Cristo and Caleta San Juan, was begun in 1540. Since that time it's had a rough life. Restoration today has been extensive, so it hardly resembles the thatch-roofed structure that had stood there until 1529 when it was wiped out by a hurricane. Hampered by lack of funds, the cathedral slowly added a circular staircase and two adjoining vaulted Gothic chambers. But along came the Earl of Cumberland in 1598 to loot it, and a hurricane in 1615 to blow off its roof. In 1908 the body of Ponce de León was brought here. After he'd died from an arrow wound in Florida, his body had originally been taken to San José Church. The cathedral faces the Plaza de las Monjas (or the Nuns' Square), a tree-shaded old town spot where you can rest and cool off.

Plazuela de la Rogativa, Caleta de las Monjas, basks in legend. In 1797 the British across San Juan Bay at Santurce held the old town under siege. However, that same year they mysteriously sailed away. Later, the commander claimed he feared the enemy was well prepared behind those walls, apparently seeing many lights and thinking them to be reinforcements. Some people believe those lights were torches carried by women in a rogativa, or religious procession, as they followed their bishop. A handsome statue of a bishop, trailed by a trio of torch-bearing women, was donated to the city on its 450th anniversary.

Casa Blanca, 1 Calle San Sebastian (tel. 724-4102). Ponce de León never lived here, although construction of the house (built in 1523) sometimes is attributed to him. The house was erected two years after the explorer's death, and work was ordered by his son-in-law, Juan Garcia Troche. The parcel of land was given to Ponce de León as a reward for services rendered to the Crown. Descendants of the explorer lived in the house for about 2½ centuries until the Spanish government took it over in 1779 for use as a resident for military commanders. The U.S. government as well used it as a home for army commanders. Today it's a museum, showing how Puerto Ricans lived in the 16th and 17th centuries. Guided tours are Tuesday through Saturday at 9 a.m. and 4:30 p.m. On Sunday it can be visited from 9 a.m. to noon and 1 to 4:30 p.m.

Back on Calle Cristo, **San José Church** is centered in San José Plaza, right next to the Dominican monastery. Initial plans were drawn in 1523 and work, supervised by Dominican friars, began in 1532. Before going into the church, look for the statue of Ponce de León on the adjoining plaza. It was made from British cannons captured during Sir Ralph Abercromby's unsuccessful attack on San Juan in 1797.

Both the church and its monastery were closed by decree in 1838, the property confiscated by the royal treasury. Later, the Crown turned the convent into a military barracks. The Jesuits restored the badly damaged church. The church was the place of worship for Ponce de León's descendants, who are buried there under the family's coat-of-arms. The conquistador was interred there until his removal to the cathedral in 1908.

Although badly looted, the church still has some treasures, including *Christ of the Ponces,* a carved crucifix presented to Ponce de León. Packed in a crate, the image survived a terrible shipwreck outside San Juan Harbor. The church has four oils by José Campèche and two large works by Francisco Oller. Many miracles have been attributed to a painting in the Chapel of Belém. It's a 15th-century Flemish work called *Virgin of Bethlehem.*

Adjacent to the church, at the corner of the square, the **Pablo Casals Museum** (tel. 723-9185) is devoted to the memorabilia left by the artist to the people of Puerto Rico. Born in 1876, Casals of course achieved fame as a cellist, and also won renown as a conductor and composer of symphonies and symphonic poems. Later in Puerto Rico, his "Casals Festivals" drew worldwide interest, attracting some of the greatest performing artists. The maestro's cello is here, along with a library of videotapes, played on request, of some of the festival concerts. This small, 18th-century house also contains manuscripts and photographs of Casals. It is open daily: from 9 a.m. to 5 p.m. Monday through Saturday, and from 1 to 5 p.m. on Sunday.

The **Casa de los Contrafuertes** (House of the Buttresses) stands adjacent to the Pablo Casals Museum at Calle San Sebastian. The building with its thick buttresses is believed to be the oldest residence remaining in El Viejo San Juan, and it's open from 9 a.m. to noon and 1 to 4:30 p.m. Wednesday through Sunday. This is a three-in-one museum, containing a Pharmacy Museum, which existed in the 19th century in the town of Cayey. Even more interesting is its Museo de Santos (saints carved in native woods). Both of these museums are on the ground floor. If you go upstairs, you'll find a Graphic Arts Museum, displaying an exhibition of watercolors, prints, and paintings by local artists.

Dominican Convent, Calle Norzagaray (tel. 725-5584), was started by Dominican friars in 1523, shortly after the city itself was founded. It was the first convent in Puerto Rico, and women and children often hid out here during Carib Indian attacks. The friars lived here until 1838 when the Crown closed down the monasteries, turning the building into an army barracks. The American army used it as its headquarters until 1966. Today it is the center of the Institute of Puerto Rican Culture. The institute promotes cultural events all over the island. On the ground floor is a permanent display of treasures, featuring a medieval altar piece. Gregorian chants help re-create the long-ago atmosphere. It is open daily from 8 a.m. to 4:30 p.m.

The **City Walls,** Calle Norzagaray, around San Juan were built in 1630 to protect the town against both European invaders and Caribbean pirates. The width of the walls averages from 20 feet at the base to 12 feet at the top, with an average height of 40 feet. Between San Cristobal and El Morro, bastions were erected at frequent intervals. You can start seeing the walls from your approach from San Cristobal on your way to El Morro.

The **San Juan Cemetery,** Calle Norzagaray, officially opened in 1814 and has since been the final resting place for many prominent Puerto Rican families. The circular chapel is dedicated to Saint Magdalene of Pazzis and was built in the 1860s. Necrophiles can wander through marble monuments, mausoleums, and statues, marvelous examples of Victorian funereal statuary. However, there are no trees or any form of shade in the cemetery, so don't go wandering in the noonday sun.

Museo del Niño is a museum devoted to children and sheltered in an 18th-century powder house, within the grounds of El Morro. It deals with arts and sciences, concentrating on exhibits that can be touched. Displays are devoted to sun, earth, and family. Hours are daily, except Monday and Thursday, from 9 a.m. to noon and 1 to 4:30 p.m.

El Morro, Calle Norzagaray (tel. 724-1978), stands on a rocky promontory, dominating San Juan Bay. Called the Castillo San Felipe del Morro, it was ordered built in 1539 and construction started the following year. The original fort was a round tower which can still be seen inside the main bastion of the castle. More walls were added, a line of batteries installed. By 1787 the structure reached its present stage. Sir Francis Drake was turned away in 1595. The fort is run and administered by the U.S. National Park Service. As one of the loftiest points in the old town, it is a labyrinth of dungeons, barracks, outposts, and ramps. Free guided tours are offered daily at 9:30 and 11 a.m., and at 2 and 3:30 p.m. Slide shows in English and Spanish are also free.

Unless you've grown weary of forts, there's one more. **Fort San Jeronimo,** or what's left of it, stands east of the Caribe Hilton at the entrance to Condado Bay. Completed in 1788, it was badly damaged in the English assault of 1797. Reconstructed in the closing year of the 18th century, it has now been taken over by the Institute of Puerto Rican Culture. A museum has been lodged there, with life-size mannequins wearing military uniforms. Ship's models and charts are also displayed. Charging no admission, the museum is open from 8 a.m. to 5 p.m.

The **Museum of the University of Puerto Rico,** Recinto de Río Piedras, has good collections of paintings by Puerto Rican artists, including Francisco Oller and José Campèche, the first important artist of the country (18th century). There is also a large collection of pre-Columbian Puerto Rican Indian artifacts from the Ingeri, sub-Taíno, and Taíno civilizations. In the museum's temporary exhibition hall, you can see such attractions as the work of contemporary Puerto Rican artists, retrospectives of important aspects of Puerto Rican art, and exhibits of the work of Puerto Rican and United States artists. Admission to the museum is free. It's open Monday to Friday from 9 a.m. to 9 p.m. and on Saturday and Sunday from 9 a.m. to 3 p.m.

A WALKING TOUR OF OLD SAN JUAN: For a sweeping view of the 200-acre city

of Old San Juan, climb to the top of **El Morro,** the formidable fortress rising 140 feet above the ocean. From that lofty spot you can get your bearings and, at the bottom, begin your walking tour of the old city. **Plaza de San José,** a favorite meeting place, is just two short blocks from the fort's exit. Look for the statue of Ponce de León, Puerto Rico's first governor, built from bronze cannons captured from the British. The **San José Church** where the coat-of-arms of the conquistador hangs above the altar is facing the plaza. The church, started by the Dominicans in 1523, is said to be one of the oldest Christian places of worship in the New World. The **Pablo Casals Museum** stands at the corner of the plaza adjacent to the church. Across the street is the **San Juan Museum of Art and History,** built as a marketplace but restored in 1985 to house galleries displaying Puerto Rican art, with a big patio for concerts and cultural events.

Adjacent to the Pablo Casals Museum on the corner of Calle San Sebastian is **Casa de los Contrafuertes** (House of the Buttresses), an 18th-century structure thought to be the oldest civilian building on the island. Between San José Church and Calle Norzagaray is the **Dominican Convent,** built in 1523, which houses the Institute of Puerto Rican culture. Head west on Calle San Sebastian toward San Juan Bay to see **Casa Blanca** (White House), built for Ponce de León by his son-in-law although the conquistador never lived there. This structure, started in 1521, is supposed to be the oldest continuously inhabited residence site in the New World.

From Calle del Sol, just south of Casa Blanca, past streets that are actually stone stairways, turn right and continue downhill on Calle del Cristo until you reach **San Juan Cathedral.** Recent renovations and restoration have brought the famed house of worship back to its original beauty. As you leave the cathedral, face the square on the right where you'll see an imposing building, **El Convento,** a 17th-century convent with great wooden doors.

From El Convento, you can explore more of Old San Juan's colorful past by following Caleta de las Monjas (Little Street of the Nuns) downhill to the **Plaza de la Rogativa** at the city wall. You'll see a statue of a bishop and three women, commemorating the time in 1797 when British soldiers mistook a religious procession for the arrival of Spanish reinforcements and fled.

Turn left off Calle Recinto Oeste at the west end of Caleta de las Monjas, and walk downhill past San Juan Gate to **La Fortaleza,** the oldest executive mansion in the western hemisphere, home to some 170 governors of Puerto Rico. It was built in 1533 as a fort and enlarged to its present state in 1846. Proceed east along Calle Fortaleza and turn right onto Calle del Cristo. At the end of this street is **Parque de las Palomas,** named for its resident pigeons. The park is a good place to sit and rest, while viewing the cluster of ancient buildings including tiny **Cristo Chapel** with its silver altar visible through glass doors. Along Calle del Cristo is **La Casa del Libro,** a small 18th-century museum dedicated to books, and also the **Museum of Puerto Rican Art,** with collections ranging from pre-Columbian to contemporary, displayed in a beautiful example of 18th-century Spanish architecture.

If you're not worn out yet, follow the wall east one block to **Bastion de las Pal-**

mas, a defense emplacement that is now a park with a magnificent view of San Juan Bay and the mountains beyond. Turn north on Calle San José and walk two blocks to the **Plaza de Armas,** faced on the west by the neoclassic Indendencia, which houses some State Department offices, and on the north by City Hall, where a Tourist Information Center is to be found near the main entrance.

Follow either Calle San Francisco or Calle Fortaleza to **Plaza de Colón,** with its statue of Christopher Columbus erected in 1893 to commemorate the 400th anniversary of the discovery of Puerto Rico, and the **Tapia Theater,** recently restored to its original 19th-century elegance. Proceed one block west of the plaza on Calle Fortaleza, and you'll come to the **Museum of Colonial Architecture** that features scale models of El Morro, La Fortaleza, and some private houses—a good place to conclude your walking tour of Old San Juan.

4. A Shopping Tour

Puerto Rico has the same tariff barriers as the U.S. mainland. That's why you don't pay duty on items brought back to the United States. That means you don't walk away with great bargains, either. Nevertheless, there are a number of boutiques and specialized stores—especially in the old town—that may tempt you into a purchase.

Native handcrafts can be good buys. Look for "santos," hand-carved wooden religious figures, needlework (women no longer get 3¢ an hour for it!), straw work, ceramics, hammocks, guayabera shirts for men, papier-mâché fruit and vegetables, and paintings and sculptures by Puerto Rican artists.

IN OLD SAN JUAN: You might begin your shopping tour as you emerge from El Convento onto Cristo Street.

Galería Botello, 208 Cristo St. (tel. 723-2879), is almost a museum or art gallery. It's a living tribute to the fiery success story of Angel Botello, now considered one of the most outstanding artists working in Puerto Rico. He was born in a small village in Galicia, Spain, although he fled after the Spanish Civil War to the Dominican Republic. Then there was a 12-year period in the dynamic, art-conscious country of Haiti. His paintings and metal sculpture, while to the knowing eye evocative of his colorful background, have a style very much his own. This galería is his former home, and he did the restoration on the colonial mansion himself. Today it's an appropriate setting to display his paintings and sculpture. Most of the salons open onto courtyards. The gallery offers a large collection of Puerto Rican antique santos, which are small, carved wooden figures of saints, and it carries the work of some of Puerto Rico's leading artists. You'll also find colorful posters.

José E. Alegria & Associates, 152-154 Cristo St. (tel. 721-8091), opposite El Convento, is housed in an impressive old Spanish-style building dating from 1523 with rooms opening onto patios and courtyards. It displays antique furniture and paintings, its collection considered the finest in San Juan. Intermingled are the paintings of contemporary artists who live in Puerto Rico. Prices are not low, but the quality is very high. There is a wine boutique in the old cellars.

Casa Cavanagh, 202 Cristo St. (mailing address: P.O. Box 3282, San Juan, PR 00936; tel. 725-3520), about half a block from El Convento, is famous. For more than 30 years the owners have traveled around the globe on purchasing trips to buy the exotic and different. Fine gifts of china and crystal imported from England, France, and Italy are featured, as well as an array of items made by Puerto Rican artisans. Accessories for decorating your home or office include bronzes, porcelain, lacquerware, and more from the markets of India, Singapore, Thailand, Latin America, and Sri Lanka. Casa Cavanagh also has stores in Plaza las Americas, Puerta de Tierra, and several major hotels.

Don Roberto, 205 Cristo St. (tel. 724-0194), is one of the oldest and most established shops in Old San Juan. It's owned by Tom Catlett, who seems to know everything there is to know about unusual sources for gifts. His taste is excellent, his prices realistic. The collection is eclectic. He offers a superb collection of soft leather items imported from Bogotá, Colombia, at prices sometimes half those of the U.S. Another hard-to-find item is antique santos (saints), and he has a fine collection of ceramics, molas, tapestries, hammocks, and swings. You'll find an intriguing collection of "gold" jewelry (actually pewter, gold plated, and replicas of jewelry) from Bogotá. You may be tempted by the replicas of coquí, the tree frog that sounds like a bird.

Reinhold, 201 Cristo St. (tel. 725-6878), is perhaps the most distinguished jewelry store in Old San Juan. It's family owned, and has its own diamond mines to make a stunning collection of jewelry. Look at the display case on your right as you enter. The collection of glittering semiprecious and precious rings will fascinate you. Reinhold's occupies the entire two-story colonial building, a minute's walk from El Convento.

The **Butterfly People,** 152 Fortaleza (tel. 723-2432). Once Drakir Purington used to sell his butterflies in the snow outside the Seagram Building in New York. And again, on the beach in St. Thomas. But now he has a café and museum of his own in a handsomely restored building in Old San Juan. There he and his wife, Attendaire, along with their assistants, have artfully arranged butterflies in Lucite boxes. The cost could range from $20 for a single butterfly to as much as $70,000 for a swarm. What began as a decorating scheme for the room of their coming child has turned into a successful business. Their butterflies come from farms in New Guinea and South America, among other places. The butterfly bodies are preserved by a secret formula, and the color is forever. The dimensional artwork is sold in limited editions, and the gallery ships boxes worldwide.

Puerto Rican Art and Crafts, 204 Fortaleza (tel. 725-5596), is a large, high-ceilinged brick room loaded with handmade products from around the country. Owned and operated by the Amador family, the shop offers vividly painted papier-mâché carnival masks which leer down at visitors with macabre grins. Other items include pottery, textiles, serigraphs and original artworks, batiks, woodcarvings, hand-knotted hammocks, ceramic jewelry, and a colorful series of posters.

Olé, 105 Fortaleza (tel. 724-2445), is the kind of store where even if you don't buy anything, you can still learn a lot about the crafts displayed. Practically everything here that wasn't made in Puerto Rico came from a different part of South America, all artistically displayed in a high-ceilinged room decorated clear to the top. If you want a straw hat from Ecuador, hand-beaten Chilean silver, Peruvian woodcarvings, or Puerto Rican santos, this is the place to buy them. Olé is open daily except Sunday.

Hathaway Factory Outlet, 203 Cristo St. (tel. 723-8946). The selection of dress shirts, known for their "Red H," may vary widely in this factory outlet, but if you happen to be there shortly after stock is replenished, you can stock up at bargain prices on shirts that could easily cost twice as much back home. Most items are top-quality dress and knit shirts from the Hathaway factories in Waterville, Maine, and while you shop, a video will play over and over again a story about how the shirts are sewn. Most items, including articles by Chaps, Ralph Lauren, or Christian Dior, are reduced by 30% to 50%. Service is efficient and friendly, and if you need shirts, you might walk out with a full year's supply.

Carmen's Watch and Gem Center, 204 San José (tel. 725-2284), carries a full selection of jewelry, watches, and chains, each of which will be shown by an attractive saleswoman whose smile seems genuinely friendly.

200 Fortaleza, 200 Fortaleza St., corner of Cruz Street (mailing address: P.O. Box 607, San Juan, PR 00936; tel. 723-1989), is known as a leading place to buy fine jewelry in Old San Juan. It has famous-name watches, and you can purchase 14- and 18-karat gold chains, which are measured, fitted, and sold by the weight, priced accordingly to the gold market. You can buy your initial in diamonds set in 14-karat white and yellow gold for $90, or even a 14-karat gold ring set with a diamond for $135.

La Plazoleta del Puerto, Marina Street in front of Pier 3 (tel. 722-3053), is one of the most important achievements of San Juan's municipal government: the first Puerto Rican crafts market. Once a depressed waterfront building, the structure has been restored by city hall to simulate a typical street of Old San Juan. It attracts local visitors as well as tourists. The artisans' shops are open between 9 a.m. and 6 p.m. daily. Folk art is displayed in various forms, including the work of ceramists, doll-makers, needle-workers, and other craftspeople.

ON THE CONDADO: You'll find a well-stocked gift shop, **Ambiance,** Condado Beach Arcade, Ashford Avenue (tel. 724-6426), near the Ramada Inn, selling a wide selection of porcelain, crystal, jewelry, and china. It's considered by many to be the finest store in the Caribbean, and a quick look at its stock will tell you why. If you want products from Lladro to Lalique, from Aynsley to Wedgwood, Ambiance will probably have them in dozens of patterns. They also sell watches. Don't ignore the second floor if you're interested in china, since there is a considerable display upstairs as well. The store is open from 9 a.m. to 6 p.m. daily except Sunday, when it is open from noon to 5 p.m.

PLAZA LAS AMERICAS: The biggest and most up-to-date shopping plaza in the Caribbean Basin is Plaza Las Americas, which lies in the financial district of Hato Rey, right off the Las Americas Expressway. The complex, with its fountains and advanced architecture, has a total of 200 shops, most of them upmarket. Hours are 9:30 a.m. to 6 p.m. Monday to Saturday. Friday is for late-night shopping—that is, until 9:30 p.m.

5. After Dark Around the Island

Puerto Rico has the most varied nightlife in the Caribbean.

CASINOS: These are one of the island's biggest draws. Many visitors come here on package deals, staying at one of Condado's plush hotels, with just one intent—to gamble at games ranging from blackjack to baccarat.

The biggest, splashiest game room is at **El Centro,** the Hilton-operated, government-owned complex that connects the Condado Beach and La Concha Hotels, reviewed earlier.

All the other game rooms are in hotels, the plush ones certainly. Therefore you can try your luck at the **Caribe Hilton** (one of the better ones), the **El San Juan,** way out in Isla Verde, and the **Condado Plaza Hotel & Casino** (largest on the island). There are no passports to flash, admissions to pay, or whatever, as there often is in European gambling casinos.

The best casinos "out in the island" are those at the **Hyatt Regency, Cerromar Beach** and **Hyatt Dorado Beach.** In fact, you can easily drive to either of these hotels from San Juan to enjoy their nighttime diversions. There is also a casino at Palmas del Mar.

Drinking, incidentally, is not permitted at the tables. Most casinos open between 1 and 4 p.m., and again from around 8 p.m. to 4 a.m. Jackets and ties for men are often requested, as the Commonwealth is trying to keep a "dignified, refined atmosphere."

SHOWS AT HOTELS: For after-dark amusements, the resort hotels have the most beautiful, swank (and expensive) meccas, ranging from Las Vegas–type shows (everybody from Liza Minnelli to Sammy Davis, Jr.) to discos.

Tropicoro Supper Club, Hotel El San Juan, Isla Verde (tel. 791-1000), is the premier nightclub attraction of the premier hotel of Puerto Rico. It engages big stars to entertain, including Rita Moreno, Peter Allen, and Suzanne Somers. The acts change frequently, so you'd be well advised to call before your arrival, not only to find out who's playing, but to make a reservation and find out what times shows are presented.

You sit beneath garlands of tropical vines stretched thickly over a glistening lattice, while flamenco and dance music fills the space between the major acts. Two drinks are included in the cover charge of $25 per person when big stars are booked. On other nights, when local bands play, there's a cover charge of only $10.

The Caribe Hilton at Puerta de Tierra (tel. 721-0303) contains one of the most complete entertainment complexes on the island, drawing thousands of visitors into its nightlife facilities every season. The most prominent is the **Club Caribe,** where the live music from some of the western hemisphere's biggest entertainers—as well as a promising crop of newcomers—sometimes wafts down to the customers at the surrounding bars and restaurants. Some of the big names who have appeared at the Club Caribe include Chita Rivera, Robert Goulet, and Diahann Carroll. You need not eat dinner to enjoy the show, but if you do, à la carte evening meals cost $28 to $40. The music begins between 10 and 10:30 p.m., and if you just want to enjoy the show, you'll be charged around $20 to enter Sunday to Thursday, around $25 on Friday and Saturday. A two-drink minimum, costing around $10 per person, is required. Men must wear jackets and ties. Service and taxes are not included in these prices. One of the popular weekend pastimes in San Juan is to attend the Club Caribe's international buffet, held from 6:30 to 9:30 p.m. every Sunday. The price is around $28 per person and includes all you can eat from the well-stocked tables.

The hotel has a **casino,** of course, offering all the glitter and excitement of money changing hands, with row on row of flashing lights and excited clusters of players gathered around tables devoted to craps, 21, or roulette. Jackets and ties are required for men. Cold nonalcoholic drinks or coffee will be served to your gaming table free. It is open daily from 12:30 p.m. to 4 a.m.

There's always something happening at the **Condado Plaza Hotel & Casino,** 999 Ashford Ave. (tel. 721-1000). It bills itself quite rightly as "San Juan's entertainment center." There is continuous live music nightly in the La Fiesta lobby bar. But for the best of international revues, head for the Copa Room, where your cover charge and two-drink minimum is settled for $25. Show time in the Copa Room is 10 p.m. except Tuesday and Wednesday when two presentations are given, at 9:15 and 11:15 p.m. Closed Monday.

One of the best flamenco shows in town is presented at **El Convento,** 100 Cristo St. (tel. 723-9020), in the heart of the old town. The cost is about $5 per person if guests are registered at the hotel and if they plan to dine there. Otherwise, nondining outsiders pay around $10. Shows are most often presented around 9 p.m. on Thursday, Friday, and Saturday.

DISCO FEVER: At the Caribe Hilton in the Puerta de Tierra section is **Juliana's** (tel. 725-0303), affiliated with Juliana's of London. It's a private disco club at this deluxe hotel, drawing some of the most sophisticated of San Juaneros along with visitors every night from 9 p.m. till 4 a.m. It's considered "the right sound and the right place." You may prance to every beat from merengue to salsa to a waltz. It's even considered possible to converse because of discreet sound engineering. It is built arena style, with bamboo and rattan seating and graceful art nouveau lighting. Singles drink at a bar on the upper ledge. There are two kinds of prices (guests of the hotel are admitted free). Nonguests on Friday and Saturday pay a $20 cover with a two-drink minimum (at $4 per drink). On weekdays and Sunday the cover charge is lowered to $14. It opens earlier, but the action doesn't get under way until 10:30 p.m. or later.

Amadeus Disco, El San Juan Hotel, Isla Verde (tel. 791-1000). Its conservative art deco interior welcomes a widely divergent collection of the rich and beautiful, the merely rich, and the gaggle of onlookers pretending to be both. It's contained within the most exciting hotel in San Juan (see my hotel recommendation), so a visit here would at least offer the possibility of examining the adjacent casino and the best-decorated lobby in Puerto Rico. The cover charge of $20 is politely called a guest membership. After paying it, you'll be admitted to a duplex area with one of the best sound systems in the Caribbean. Don't overlook the more sedate piano bar on the upper floor.

Club Mykonos, Hotel La Concha, Ashford Avenue (tel. 722-4343). Considered to be the "disco of the moment," this place dazzles with a decor that might be described as futuristic Pharonaic. It's on the lobby level of La Concha Hotel. Don't come here expecting to be admitted in sloppy clothes, since the owner, Juan Santoni, has set a precedent for relative stylishness. Be sure to notice the frescoes near the entrance and above the bar and the hi-tech versions of Hellenistic columns whose summits flash strobes of multicolored lights. The $25 cover charge entitles you to two free drinks, after which a libation costs $4.50 each. In time-honored Latin style, the fashion is to go late—that is, after 11 p.m.

Isadora's, Condado Plaza Hotel & Casino, 999 Ashford Ave. (tel. 721-1000), is one of the most elegant discos and after-dark rendezvous points in Puerto Rico. This strobe-lit jungle garden is named after the legendary dancer. Sometimes you get music from the '50s—or what John Lennon's son, Sean, called "the old stuff from the '70s." The interior is in shades of russet and peach, with etched glass, mirrors, and padded corners. The $15 minimum includes the first two drinks, and the club opens daily at 9:30 p.m. and closes at 4 a.m.

FLAMENCO: In La Rada Building in Condado, the **Copacabana,** 1020 Ashford Ave. (tel. 723-0691), features flamenco entertainment nightly, with typical Spanish food in the true Spanish fashion and tradition. Entrees include paella valenciana as well as lobster and beefsteak. You can also order highy seasoned red snapper filet. Dinner and show usually run as little as $18 per person. Check at the lobby at La Rada for announcements of who is currently appearing.

BAR HOPPING: In the previously recommended Quality Royale Hotel & Casino, **Windows of the Caribbean,** 600 Avenida Fernandez Juncos (tel. 541-6630), lies on the top floor of the tallest skyscraper in the Caribbean. Set in the Miramar district, the establishment, which sometimes has a live band, offers a sweeping view over the seacoast and of the city of San Juan. Happy hour lasts from 5 to 8 p.m., when two drinks go for the price of one. In winter the club is open daily from 5 p.m. until very, very late. In summer it's open only on Friday and Saturday. After 8 p.m. there's a two-drink minimum, of $4 per drink.

Café 1897, 105 Cristo in Old San Juan (tel. 725-7761). The original well inside this former private home, still filled with water, has been transformed into a wishing well into which poets, politicians, and trysting lovers toss coins. As any Puerto Rican knows, 1897 was the last year of the Spanish occupation of the island, but the Spanish provincial flavor has been re-created at this café/bar. You enter through a long hallway, past a formal green and white façade, to reach the accommodating and friendly bar. Table-sitters may prefer a place in the inner room, below a skylit ceiling. Some guests are likely to be registered at the Hotel El Convento just across the street. Many will savor the house drink, "Sweet Love," containing "43" liquor, vanilla liqueur, coconut cream, orange juice, and grenadine. This libation costs about $4. Beer is $2.50, and there's a cover charge of $2.50 whenever there's live music. This is usually Wednesday to Saturday. The bar opens daily at 5 p.m. and stays open as late as 4 a.m. on weekends.

Tiffany's, 213 Cristo in Old San Juan (tel. 725-0380). Many young guests have wandered in here expecting a quick piña colada or daiquiri, only to stay all evening. The drawing card is the video rock concerts and occasional full-length movies which the bartender shows on a big screen behind the hanging Tiffany-style lamps and the dark-wood bar. If you order beer, it will probably be served in the can. Tropical drinks and frappés (chocolate-peanut is a favorite) are also popular. To add to the electronic ambience, you'll find a collection of video games off to the side of the movie screen. The establishment, lying behind a wooden façade and a big window on one of the main streets of Old San Juan, is open from 11:30 a.m. to 2 a.m. On Friday and Saturday, it closes at 3 a.m. The bar is closed on Sunday.

SUNSET WATCHING: A busy nightspot at **Hotel La Playa**, 6 Amapola St., Isla Verde (tel. 791-1115), is built out over the water in back. It's a disco bar, and although no one might actually be dancing, it's still one of the hottest places in town every night during and after happy hour, weeknights from 4 to 7 p.m. The boat-shaped bar is open to the breezes from the ocean, and colored lights hang from the beamed ceiling, illuminating everyone from athletes to artists to bona fide tourists. There's live Latin music on Wednesday and Saturday from 8 to 11 p.m. Free drinks are given to women for a one-hour period on Wednesday and to men for a similar period on Thursday.

An adjoining restaurant, in addition to the bar, serves hamburgers, chili, and roast chicken. Drinks costs from $1.75. The restaurant is open from 8 a.m. to 11 p.m., and the bar from 11 p.m. till 2 a.m., seven days a week.

CULTURAL EVENTS: Built in 1981, the **Performing Arts Center** (tel. 724-4747) is in the heart of Santurce, a six-minute taxi jaunt from most of the hotels on Condado Beach. Costing $18 million (relatively modest for such a complex), the center contains 1,883 seats in the Festival Hall, 760 in the Drama Hall, and 210 in the Experimental Theater. Some of the events here will be of interest only to Spanish-speaking readers, while others attract an international audience. When the Puerto Rico Symphonic Orchestra performs, seats generally sell for $12 up to $50.

LE LO LAI FESTIVAL: This is a year-round vacation package that has many savings for the visitor who plans to stay in Puerto Rico at least a few days. Le Lo Lai is a name created by the island people to express their love of song and dance and a cultural heritage that comes from Spanish, Indian, and African traditions. The government-sponsored Le Lo Lai Festival welcomes visitors to a complimentary week-long celebration, with the pre-purchase, at several participating San Juan hotels, of a seven-night stay from December 15 to April 14 and a five-night stay from April 15 to December 14.

A 26-page discount booklet offers additional sightseeing suggestions and cents-off coupons to many of the island's boutiques and shops. There are admission tickets to several folkloric shows which will entitle the holder to a free souvenir upon presentation at the event. In 1987 the package included car rental and Paradores Puertorriqueños (country inns) special offers, and museum and theme park admissions, all outside San Juan city limits. The package of tickets is sold in San Juan at authorized travel agencies for those visitors who do not qualify for them on a free basis. The selling price is $8 for adults, $6 for children.

For further information, write to the **Le Lo Lai Festival**, P.O. Box 4195, San Juan, PR 00905, or call 723-3135. If in Puerto Rico, you can drop in at the Le Lo Lai Festival office at the street level of the Convention Center in the Condado area.

OUT IN THE ISLAND

The Puerto Rico Company of Tourism (a government agency) has been quite successful in its efforts to have Puerto Rico known as "The Complete Island." Tourism promoters in the island agree with this concept and add that since it is the complete island, why then stay in only one place and say that one has seen Puerto Rico?

After seeing and enjoying San Juan, there is a lot more yet to see, do, and enjoy in the rest of the island. It's amazing how many visitors return home unaware of the many attractions and places they could have visited beyond the San Juan area. There are 79 towns and cities, each having its unique charm and flavor. Puerto Rico has a rich countryside with many panoramas, centuries-old coffee plantations, sugar estates still in use, foreboding caves and enormous boulders with mysterious petroglyphs carved by the Taíno Indians (original settlers of the island), colorful but often narrow and steep roads, and meandering mountain trails leading out to tropical settings.

6. Hotels Out in the Island

Until recently, this other Puerto Rico was thought of as "too far out" for the fast-moving visitor. Because of the efforts of Paradores Puertorriqueños, a chain of privately owned and operated inns under the auspices and supervision of the Commonwealth Development Company, today everyone can enjoy the Puerto Rican countryside.

THE PARADORES: These hostelries are easily identified by a Taíno grass hut in the signs and the logo of each inn. There are three categories of paradores scattered throughout the island:

Hotel—where you have full-service facilities very much like the tourist hotels of the big cities, but set in a coastal or countryside setting.

Guesthouse—having all the basic large hotel facilities except dining facilities. Breakfast menus are available at most.

Villa or lodge—here you find the minimum tourist facilities in a rural setting. These paradores are composed of individual cottages or units centered around a main building where all the basic services, dining facilities, and entertainment take place. In this type of parador you are expected to do your basic housekeeping and cooking.

My survey of the paradores of Puerto Rico follows. For yet another parador, refer to the section on San German.

Parador Baños de Coamo, P.O. Box 540, Coamo, PR 00640 (tel. 809/825-2186). Legend has it that the hot springs of Baños de Coamo were the fountain of youth sought by Ponce de León. It is believed the Taíno Indians, during pre-Columbian times, held rituals and pilgrimages here as they sought health and well-being. For more than 100 years (1847 to 1958) the site was a center for rest and relaxation where many Puerto Ricans as well as others had enjoyable stays, some on their honeymoon, others in search of the curative powers of the thermal springs, which lie about a five-minute walk from the hotel. The spa is now a parador offering hospitality in the Puerto Rican tradition. Even so, the place has a somewhat Mexican atmosphere. Buildings range from a lattice-adorned, two-story motel-style unit with wooden verandas, to a Spanish colonial pink stucco building housing the restaurant. The cuisine is both Créole and international, and the coffee Baños style is a special treat. All 48 units are air-conditioned and roomy. The decor has been restored to its original 19th-century style. All year the parador charges the same rates—$45 daily in a room with twin beds, $40 in a single.

Coamo is inland on the south coast, about two hours from San Juan, and swimming is limited to an angular pool, but one can always drive to a nearby public beach. Horseback riding is unique at Baños de Coamo—here you can ride Paso Fino horses. This beautiful breed of Arabians is the pride of Puerto Rico's equestrian breeders. The Baños lists many notables among its past visitors, including F. D. Roosevelt in 1933, as well as Frank Lloyd Wright. Alexander Graham Bell and Thomas Edison were also visitors.

Parador Hacienda Gripiñas, Rte. 527, km. 2.5 (P.O. Box 387), Jayuya, PR 00664 (tel. 809/721-2884), is a former coffee plantation in the very heart of the Central Mountain Range, reached by a long, narrow, and curvy road. This home-turned-inn is a delightful blend of hacienda of days gone by and the modern conveniences of today. The plantation's ambience is found everywhere—ceiling fans, splendid gardens, hammocks on a porch gallery, and more than 20 acres of coffee-bearing bushes. You'll taste the home-grown product when you order the inn's aromatic brew. You can swim in the pool (away from the main building), soak up the sun, or go and enjoy the nearby sights such as the Indian Ceremonial Park at Utuado or the Pool of the Petroglyphs. Boating and plenty of fishing are just 30 minutes away at Lake Caonillas.

The restaurant of the parador, reached from San Juan in about 2½ hours, features a Puerto Rican and international cuisine. Complete meals can range from as little as $8 to a high of $25, depending on your selection. Each of their 19 rooms has a private bath, and most come with ceiling fans. Rates are modest: $35 in a double and $30 in a single. These are in effect year round.

Parador Martorell, 6A Ocean Dr., Luquillo, PR 00673 (tel. 809/889-2710). Back in 1800 the Martorell family came to Puerto Rico from Spain and fell in love with the island. Today their descendants own and manage the Parador Martorell in Luquillo, in the vicinity of the most impressive beach in all of Puerto Rico. The Martorells think of themselves as pioneers, having opened their parador in 1966, before the government began its program, and keep this feeling alive by blending modern household furnishings with the simplicity of Spanish decor. When you arrive at the parador, you will enter an open courtyard by a tropical garden. *Off-season rates are $25 in a single and $34 to $35 in a double.* In high season, tariffs are $35 in a single, $40 to $50 in a double.

Meals in the patio of the guesthouse come with fragrant flowers, the elusive hummingbirds, and the occasional music of the coquí, the tiny Puerto Rican tree frog that very few people are privileged to see. Breakfast at the Martorell is a surprise. The buffet-style breakfast always features plenty of freshly picked fruit and baskets full of homemade breads and compotes. While at the parador, you must include the rain forest in your itinerary. At day's end you can come back to the parador, where guests often gather on the patio to swap anecdotes and taste the homemade "Ponche María" as an apéritif. The main reason for staying at the Martorell is Luquillo Beach, with its shady palm groves, crescent beaches, coral reefs for snorkeling and scuba-diving, and the surfing area.

Parador Hacienda Juanita, Rte. 105, km. 23.5 (Apartado 838), Maricao, PR 00706 (tel. 809/838-2550). Right at the foot of the state forest in the mountain region where the Taíno Indians offered their final resistance to the Spanish conquistadores, the Hacienda Juanita has preserved intact the flavor of an old coffee plantation. Every room has a private bath. There is a bar featuring a balcony from which you get a magnificent view of the country greenery surrounding the parador. For relaxation, the swimming pool is always available. There is always a volleyball or basketball game in progress. Near the former plantation house, the new rooms are pleasantly furnished, containing private baths. In all, 21 units are rented out. Despite their modernity, the accommodations still have a traditional feeling. The same rates are charged all year— $25 daily in a single, $30 in a double. Children under 12 are sheltered free, and a third adult in the room pays $6. For MAP (breakfast and dinner), add another $15 per person daily. The hearty cuisine includes many regional dishes, and every single plate served you is enough for two.

From the parador, you can visit the only fish hatchery that supplies the lakes and rivers of Puerto Rico with native fish, tour the town's grotto dedicated to its patron saint, John the Baptist, visit a colonial cemetery, trek through the state forest, and explore the town of Maricao, one of the smallest in the island (pop. 3,000), which still retains many of its colonial traditions. Mayagüez is only 12 miles away.

Parador El Guajataca, Rte. 2, km. 103.8 (P.O. Box H), Quebradillas, PR 00742 (tel. 809/895-3070), lies along the north coast 60 miles west of San Juan. Service, hospitality, and the natural beauty surrounding El Guajataca—all this, plus modern conveniences and a family atmosphere, add up to a good visit. The parador is set on a rolling hillside which reaches down to the surf-beaten beach. Each of the 38 air-conditioned rooms is like a private villa with its own entrance and private balcony opening onto the turbulent Atlantic. All year, prices are the same—$57 to $65 daily in a single, $60 to $65 in a double. On the grounds are two swimming pools, one for adults, another for children, and there are two tennis courts free to guests, plus a playground for children.

For breakfast, you're served eggs and fresh fruit tasting as if they were brought directly from the farm to your table. Room service is available, but meals are more enjoyable in the glassed-in dining room where all the windows face the sea. Dinner is an experience, with a cuisine that is a mixture of Créole and international specialties. A local musical group plays for dining and dancing on weekend evenings. On Sunday there is a traditional buffet dinner from noon to 3 p.m. The native bar is open daily from 11 a.m. to 10 p.m. (until 1 a.m. on weekends). Friday is Créole night, when the chef pulls out all the stops with an array of Puerto Rican dishes, buffet style. For the shell and fossil collectors, early-morning jaunts along the beach and along the cliffs where the ocean and mountains meet may turn up some interesting finds.

Parador Montemar, Rte. 111, Aguadilla, PR 00603 (tel. 809/891-5959), offers a total of 40 pleasantly furnished accommodations, most of which open onto views of the Atlantic. Rates, in effect year round, are $45 in a single and $55 in a double, plus tax and an energy charge. Each unit is air-conditioned. Only minutes from the Punta Borinquen Golf Course, the hotel was built on a site above the Mona Passage. It's also near one of the finest surfing beaches in Puerto Rico at Rincón, but you have to drive to it. On weekends live groups are brought to the parador to entertain guests, who can enjoy their pools, one for small children and one for adults. Even if you're not staying at Montemar, you might want to visit for lunch or dinner, enjoying a meal in one of the two restaurants. Local dishes and dark Puerto Rican coffee are served. Sunday's international buffet is the parador's specialty.

Parador Villa Parguera, Rte. 273, La Parguera, Lajas, PR 00667 (tel. 809/721-2884 in San Juan and 899-3975 in La Parguera). Although the water in the bay alongside this hotel is too polluted for swimming, guests still benefit from a view of the water, a swimming pool, and a pleasantly isolated kind of peacefulness. This parador is known for its seafood dinners, the air-conditioned comfort of most of the rooms, and its location beside the glistening phosphorescent waters of one of the coast's best-known bays. The establishment is set behind a white wall on a quiet street. The reception area is in an alcove off the screened-in dining room, where ceiling fans supplement the sea breezes. Each of the 50 rooms contains a private or semiprivate bath. Prices year round are $60 in either a single or double room with air conditioning. Units without that amenity cost $55. The dining room offers daily specials, plus chef's favorites including filet of fish stuffed with lobster and shrimp as well as several other dishes.

Parador Vistamar, P.O. Box T-38, Quebradillas, PR 00742 (tel. 809/895-2065). High atop a mountain, overlooking greenery and a seascape in the Guajataca area, this parador sits like a sentinel surveying the scene. There are gardens and intricate paths carved into the side of the mountain where you can stroll while you take in the fragrance of the tropical flowers that grow in the area. Or you may choose to search for the calcified fossils which abound on the carved mountainside. For a unique experience, visitors can try their hand at freshwater fishing in the only river in Puerto Rico with green waters, just down the hill from the hotel. Flocks of rare tropical birds are frequently seen in the nearby mangroves. Whether you are a seasoned professional photographer or just like to tote an Instamatic about with you, you're sure to get some pictures.

A short drive from the hotel will bring you to the popular Punta Borinquen Golf Course. Tennis courts are just down the hill from the inn itself. Sightseeing trips to the nearby Ionospheric Observatory in Arecibo, with the largest radiotelescope in the world, and to Monte Calvario (a replica of Mount Calvary), are side trips available. Another popular visit is to the plaza in the town of Quebradillas, where you can tour the town in a horse-driven coach. Back at the hotel, prepare yourself for a typical Puerto

Rican dinner, or choose from the international menu, in the dining room with its view of the ocean. Rates are in effect all year—$35 daily in a single, $45 in a double. Children under 12 in the same room stay here free (a maximum of two).

Parador Boquemar, Rte. 101 (P. O. Box 133), Cabo Rojo, PR 00623 (tel. 809/851-2158), lies near Boquerón Beach in the southwest corner of Puerto Rico, between Mayagüez and Ponce. The beach at Boquerón is considered one of the best bathing beaches on the island. The hotel is not right on the beach, but it's just a short walk away. There is also a swimming pool—popular with Puerto Rican families—in back of the hotel. The Boquemar rents out 41 rooms, all air-conditioned. Refrigerators are small but serve the purpose. Year-round rates are $36 in a single, $46 to $52 in a double. There is a communal TV set in the lobby, and for dining, several seafood restaurants are in the vicinity.

PONCE: A description of the sightseeing possibilities of Ponce is carried in the following section ("Touring the Island"). However, those not going back to San Juan will find good accommodations in Puerto Rico's second city:

Meliá, 2 Cristina St., Ponce, PR 00731 (tel. 809/842-0260), offers southern hospitality. A city hotel, often attracting business people, it has no connection with other hotels in the world bearing the same name. The location is a few steps away from Our Lady of Guadalupe Cathedral and from the famous Parque de Bombas (the red-and-black firehouse). The lobby floor and all stairs are covered with Spanish tiles of Moorish design. The desk clerks, oftentimes family members, are well versed in English, and in their charming and courteous way will attend you. Once you have checked in and parked your car in the lot nearby, a very pleasant surprise awaits you when you open your room door. The central air conditioning is turned on just right for comfort, every room has a television set, and most have a balcony facing either busy Cristina Street or the old plaza. The rooms are comfortably furnished, pleasant enough. Year-round rates are $55 daily in a single, $65 in a double. Breakfast is served on a rooftop terrace with a good view of Ponce, and the hotel's dining room serves some of the best cuisine in town.

MAYAGÜEZ: Overnighting in Puerto Rico's "third city" has this interesting possibility:

Hilton International Mayagüez (tel. 809/834-7575) is a country club–style hotel set on 20 acres of lushly planted tropical gardens. Reasonable in price, it is nevertheless the finest hotel to be found in western Puerto Rico. Its grounds have been designated as an adjunct to the nearby Mayagüez Institute of Tropical Agriculture by the U.S. Department of Agriculture. There are no fewer than five species of palm trees, including the royal palm (native to Puerto Rico), eight kinds of bougainvillea, and numerous species of rare flora. If you want to get deep into botany, the nearby Mayagüez Institute of Tropical Agriculture has the largest collection of tropical plants in the western hemisphere. The hotel stands at the edge of the city, and can be reached from San Juan after a scenic 2½-hour drive. Or else it's a half-hour flight aboard either Eastern Metro or CrownAir. It's also possible to take a Capitol Airlines flight from San Juan to Borinquen Field (the Hilton is a 30-minute limousine drive away).

Built in 1964, the hotel has been completely refurbished, and in fact is better than ever. Some 150 well-appointed rooms open onto an Olympic-size swimming pool. Many units contain private balconies. Year-round rates in effect depend on whether you take a standard, superior, or a deluxe accommodation. Singles cost $114 to $137; doubles, $137 to $164. MAP is another $40 per person daily. The hotel is very sports oriented. Not only does it offer excellent courts, but there are also physical fitness trails. Near the hotel is a small, well-stocked lake filled with Congo perch. It's possible, if enough time is allowed, that the chef might prepare your catch for the evening. Deep-sea fishing can also be arranged, as can skindiving, surfing, and scuba-diving.

An 18-hole golf course lies at Borinquen Field, a former SAC airbase, about 30 minutes from the Hilton. Of course, some of the most beautiful beaches on the island can be reached in an easy drive. Boquerón, for example, is a four-mile stretch adorned with palms.

The elegant Rôtisserie Dining Room turns out the best food on the west coast of Puerto Rico. The food is a blend of Puerto Rican and international specialties. There is even a section called flambé fireworks which features "El Pescador," fresh lobster and jumbo shrimp sautéed with local herbs. Freshly caught fish of the day is also a specialty. The chef also prepares international beef recipes featured in sister Hilton hotels around the world. The Hilton is also the entertainment center of the city. On Saturday, a Mexican Night buffet is offered. The cost is only $15 per person ($8 for children). Otherwise, there is always something happening in the Cacique Lounge, including such events as a merengue contest. One night a week is ladies' night, when women don't pay.

GUESTHOUSES: That hidden little guesthouse "out in the island" may appeal to a certain type of traveler interested in a more offbeat experience. If so, I have a few recommendations:

Caribe Playa Resort, Rte. 3, km. 112, Guardarraya, Patillas, PR 00723 (no phone), in the southern edge of Puerto Rico, appeals to nature lovers and environmentalists. The 26-unit resort is sheltered in tropical greenery (45 acres) with a coconut farm, just 75 feet from a crescent-shaped Caribbean beach. The reefs at this beach make it a good spot for snorkeling, scuba-diving, surf fishing, or just swimming. Walking along the shore in a spot nicknamed "Scrounge Point," you can collect numerous shapes of seashells and odd-shaped colored glass and stone formations washed ashore. To get to the Caribe Playa Resort, you must either rent a car (a 1½-hour drive from San Juan), use a publico, or make arrangements with the management. However you choose to get there, your visit, with some of the most beautiful and interesting scenery on the island, will be well worth the trip.

Accommodations are in three modern two-level breezeway-style concrete buildings. The interior-room units are large and well appointed, with private toilets and showers. Up to four persons can be accommodated in each of these units. Outdoor patios and balconies come with each rental. Seabeach rooms cost $49 nightly, whether occupied by one or two persons. For seabeach efficiencies, however, the charge is $59 for one or two persons, $71 for three guests, and $83 for quartets. Children under 6 sharing a room stay free. Rates apply year round. These rates do not include government tax and service. Call 212/988-1801 in New York City for Stateside information. Telephone service in Guardarraya is presently limited to three phones, and these can be used for emergency situations only, so the resort has no phone.

Posada Porlamar, Rte. 304 (P.O. Box 405), La Parguera, Lajas, PR 00667 (tel. 809/899-4015), offers life in a simple, informal fishing village where you can enjoy the restful tempo of the Caribbean. That and all the modern conveniences you want in a vacation are what you find at the Posada Porlamar (Guest House by the Sea), in the Parguera section of Lajas in the southwestern part of the island. The area is famous for its Phosphorescent Bay and good fishing, especially snapper. The guesthouse is near several fishing villages and other points of interest. If you like to collect seashells, you can beachcomb. Other collectors' items found here are fossilized crustacea and marine plants. If you prefer fishing, you can rent boats at the nearby villages, and even bring your catch back to the guesthouse, where you can prepare it in your own kitchenette. The drive to Lajas is several hours from San Juan, but if you prefer, you can fly from San Juan to Mayagüez and then take the much shorter drive to Lajas. Porlamar has only 18 rooms, so early reservations are necessary to ensure a booking. All the rooms are air-conditioned and include kitchen facilities. All year, rates are the same: $36 daily in a single, $45 in a double.

Villa Antonio, Rte. 115, km. 12.3 (P.O. Box 68), Rincón, PR 00743 (tel. 809/823-2645), offers air-conditioned cottages and apartments by the sea with sand at your doorstep, privacy, and tropical beauty around you. On the westernmost point of the island, Rincón has one of the most exotic beaches on the island, drawing surfers from around the world. The most sensible way to get there is by way of Mayagüez airport, just 15 minutes by car from Villa Antonio. Facilities at this guest complex include a children's playground, two tennis courts, and a swimming pool. Surfing and fishing can be done just outside your front door. And you can bring your catch right into your cottage and prepare a fresh seafood dinner in your own kitchenette. All year, the rates charged by the hosts, Ilia and Hector Ruíz, are the same, with two-bedroom units renting for $58 to $74 daily (the latter for the beachfront properties) for up to four persons. A one-bedroom apartment with kitchenette rents for $42.50 daily for two persons, $45 for three. A single with kitchenette costs $34 daily. The beachfront one-bedroom apartments cost $53 for one or two persons, $58 for three persons, and $7 each for additional persons.

7. Dorado

The name itself evokes a kind of magic. Along the north shore of Puerto Rico, about a 40-minute drive west of the capital, a world of luxury resorts and villa complexes unfolds. The big properties of the Hyatt Dorado Beach Hotel and Hyatt Regency Cerromar Beach Hotel, occupy choice real estate in this section of Puerto Rico, enjoying white sandy beaches.

Many clients book into either of these hotels directly, stopping off in San Juan only to arrive and leave by plane. Others, particularly first-timers, may want to spend a day or so sightseeing and shopping in San Juan before heading for one of these complete resort properties, since, chances are, once there they'll never leave the grounds. The hotels are self-contained, with beach, swimming, golf, tennis, dining, and nightlife possibilities.

The site was originally purchased in 1905 by Dr. Alfred T. Livingston, a Jamestown, N.Y., physician, who had it developed as a grapefruit and coconut plantation of 1,000 acres. Previously, the finca (farm) had been used as pastureland and as a source of lumber. The grapefruit plantation at one time had as many as 35 to 40 families living in homes furnished by Dr. Livingston. He also provided what amounted to a large free clinic and fostered the first school (named in his honor) in the area about 45 years ago. Dr. Livingston's daughter, Clara, widely known in aviation circles and a friend of the late Amelia Earhart, owned and operated the plantation after her father's death. It was she who built the airstrip here. The building housing Su Casa Restaurant, previewed below, was for many years the plantation home of the Livingstons.

Reservations can be made through travel agents or by calling the Hyatt Worldwide Reservation Center toll free at 800/228-9000 or directly to the hotels.

Hyatt Dorado Beach Hotel (tel. 796-1600) sprawls across the plantation, filled with palms, pine trees, and purple bougainvillea, and a two-mile stretch of sandy ocean beach. It's 20 miles west of San Juan. Two side-by-side 18-hole championship golf courses, designed by Robert Trent Jones, are its big draw (see "The Sporting Life," below). Tennis buffs find seven all-weather courts, and there are the expected swimming pools, as well as a private airfield and a casino. The place is so large, in fact, that during the day guests can bicycle all over the grounds. The present hotel, originally a Rockefeller playground, opened in 1958, and many repeat guests have been going back ever since that time. After several owners, Hyatt Hotels Corporation is in charge. Hyatt has spent more than $30 million on its first resorts in the Caribbean, and an added $10 million is allotted for future improvements.

The 300 bedrooms all are totally renovated and newly furnished, with marble baths, spacious mirrors, and exceptional lighting. The flooring throughout is terracotta. Rooms are available on the beach or in villas tucked in and around the lushly planted grounds. The villas bordering the golf course fairways are concealed by foliage. All prices quoted are for MAP. In winter, standard singles rent for $290 daily, going up to $380 for deluxe units. Doubles range from $330 to $420, with triples renting for an additional $65 for the extra person. Casitas, private beach houses, cost $440 daily in a single, $480 in a double. *In summer, guests can stay here for $95 to $115 per person, with casitas costing $130 per person.* Breakfast can be taken on your private balcony and lunch on an outdoor ocean terrace. Dinner is served in a three-tiered main dining room where you can watch the surf. Hyatt Dorado chefs have won many awards, and the food at the hotel restaurants and Su Casa Restaurant (not included in the MAP) is considered among the finest in the Caribbean.

The **Hyatt Regency Cerromar Beach Hotel** (tel. 796-1010) stands near its elegant sister, the Hyatt Dorado Beach Hotel, although occupying its own sandy crescent beach. Cerromar is a combination of two words—*cerro* (mountain) and *mar* (sea)—and true to its name, you're surrounded by mountains and ocean. Approximately 22 miles west of San Juan, Cerromar shares the 1,000-acre former Livingston estate with the Dorado, enjoying the Robert Trent Jones golf courses. Guests of Cerromar have the use of the facilities at the next-door hotel. A shuttle bus runs back and forth between the two resorts every half hour. Like its sister resort, this hotel was acquired by the Hyatt Hotels Corporation in 1985.

Every room or suite has a sweeping ocean view. The rooms have luxury appointments and are well maintained. Naturally, they are air-conditioned and contain private baths. *In summer, attractive package deals are offered (ask your travel agent). Otherwise, you pay $95 daily in a standard single or double, June 1 to October 1. Shoulder-season tariffs are quoted too—that is, from April 26 to May 31 and October 1 to December 19: $145 to $200 daily in a single or double; extra persons pay $25 in each triple or quad. MAP is an additional $40 per person daily.* In winter, guests on the EP pay $200 to $260 in a single or double. The hotel has a total of 506 rooms, of which 19 are suites. The seven-story facility is designed in a double Y-wing configuration, with guest accommodations on one side of the corridors, providing a view of the sea from each room. The majority of units have private balconies. Most of the totally renovated and refurnished rooms are spacious, with marble baths, three-way mirrors, and excellent lighting. Floors throughout are tile and furnishings are casual tropical, in soft colors and pastels. All rooms have honor bars and in-room safes.

The outdoor Garden Terrace is triple level with a dramatic staircase. Some tables are at the edge of a lake, complete with swans and flamingos, paralleling the hotel's swimming pool. The Orchid Pavilion is a new restaurant, named for the profusion of the flowers. The Flamingo bar offers a wide, open-air expanse overlooking a swimming pool water-playground and the sea. The water playground contains the world's longest freshwater swimming pool—a 1,776-foot-long fantasy pool inaugurated in 1986, with a current like a river because of differing heights in five connected free-form pools. It takes 15 minutes to float from one end of the pool to the other. There are 14 waterfalls, tropical landscaping, subterranean Jacuzzis, water slides, walks, bridges, and a children's pool.

A variety of other lounges is offered, with entertainment and restaurants. In addition to 14 tennis courts, there is a children's day camp for guests aged 5 through 13, open from mid-June to Labor Day, at Christmas, and at Easter. While the children are at play, grownups can enjoy the beach, bicycle riding, or just plain sunning. Snorkeling and scuba equipment are available for a reasonable rental. Guests from both the Hyatt Regency Cerromar Beach and the Hyatt Dorado Beach hotels may interchange dining and recreation facilities.

Su Casa, in the Hyatt Dorado Beach Hotel (tel. 796-1600), the Livingston family plantation home on the resort property, has been extensively renovated by the Hyatt Hotels Corporation to resume a place of eminence as one of the area's most outstanding and inviting restaurants. The Spanish colonial building with tile courtyards has been a favorite dining place for the rich and famous since the Rockefellers entertained guests at their posh Dorado Beach hideaway, and today persons of international prominence still frequent the fine restaurant. Diners sit at candlelit tables and enjoy the serenade of strolling entertainers as they partake of gourmet Puerto Rican and classical European dishes. The Austrian-born chef, Wilhelm Pirngruber, who has had experience in both the United States and Latin America, produces an innovative cuisine, using Puerto Rican fruits and vegetables whenever possible. These include plantain, spinach, eggplant, and other island-grown ingredients. I recommend his cucumber-shrimp soup, which I like to follow up with roast veal tenderloin and tomatillo sauce, a tender and tasty main dish.

Don't plan to rush through a meal at Su Casa, but allow yourself time enough to enjoy the quality of your dinner in this relaxed tropical setting. It's best to show up at 8 p.m., and reservations are mandatory. Expect to pay from $40 for a dinner.

Puerto Rico's liveliest club is **El Coquí,** at the Hyatt Regency Cerromar Beach Hotel (tel. 796-1010). Because of the effective sound system here, you can actually talk if you don't want to dance. Favored perches are the basket couches. Glass-etched coquís, those singing tree frogs, are lit in the corners. There's action from 9:30 p.m. to 4 a.m., and don't count on spending less than $15. The entrance fee is $18 for men, $9 for women, including the first two drinks. In winter it's closed on Monday and Tuesday; off-season it's likely to be open only on Friday and Saturday.

8. Palmas del Mar

It's called a "new American Riviera" in the making. The resort residential community of Palmas del Mar lies on the island's southeastern shore, 45 miles from San Juan, outside the town of Humacao, about an hour's drive from the San Juan airport. It's also possible to fly in from San Juan.

Once there, you'll find the place so vast you'll need a rental car to reach your friends staying somewhere else on the grounds. Hiking on the resort's grounds is another favorite activity. There is a forest preserve with giant ferns, orchids, and hanging vines.

The resort also has one of the most action-packed sports programs in the Caribbean (refer to "The Sporting Life" section, coming up, for more details).

The New York sales and reservations office for the Puerto Rican resort of Palmas del Mar and its Candelero Hotel and Villas and the Palmas Inn is at 350 Park Ave., 12th Floor, New York, NY 10022 (tel. 212/935-3200, or toll free 800/221-4874).

ACCOMMODATIONS: Lying on 2,700 acres, **Palmas del Mar,** P.O. Box 2020, Humacao, PR 00661 (tel. 809/852-6000), is a former sugar plantation including a stretch of the Caribbean coastline. Guests are housed in villas built around a marina, a tennis complex, and a championship golf course. You have a choice of either rooms or villas, depending on your space needs. Within the same complex are some privately owned condominium homes which the landlords make available to guests when they're not living in them. In addition to the villas, guests can stay at the luxurious Palmas Inn or the Candelero Hotel.

The **Palmas Inn** is a gem, containing only 23 deluxe junior suites, each with a panoramic vista of sea and mountains. The inn also shelters Paolo's Restaurant and La Galería lounge, previewed below. Accommodations are decorated in a Spanish antique style, and baths are designed so that you can sit in the tub while drinking in a view of the Caribbean. Your continental breakfast is left on a service counter in the entrance hall. The inn's decor evokes that of a Mediterranean villa, with a spacious, airy feeling. Most rooms are rented as doubles, costing from $210 EP, in winter, *dropping to around $145 daily in summer*. Singles, however, are accepted at $190 daily in winter, *falling to $125 in summer*. For breakfast and dinner, add $35 per person.

At the **Candelero Hotel,** rooms come in a variety of sizes, some with king-size beds. High cathedral ceilings accentuate the roominess which is further extended by patios on the ground floor. Room colors are light—pastels offset by strong colors on bedspreads—with original watercolors decorating the walls. The Candelero lobby, in common with that of the Palmas Inn, has a very open feeling. All around, the rattan furniture is of Puerto Rican make, the same style and quality that has marked the Palmas Inn since it opened in 1974. In all, there are 102 rooms and mini-suites. Its main dining spot is Las Garzas restaurant, previewed below. Many of the units have private balconies, with views of the sea. The beach and golf course are near at hand. The hotel doesn't have the charm of the Palmas Inn, but many of its units are cheaper. In winter, a single rents for $140 to $180 daily, while a double goes for $160 to $200. MAP is another $35 per person. *Summer tariffs are lowered to $80 to $115 daily in a single, from $100 to $135 in a double.*

Candelero Villas, adjacent to the hotel, might be more suitable if you're a group. The management rents out one-, two-, and three-bedroom villas, each handsomely furnished and well equipped. Accommodations are in attached houses, and these villas are privately owned. However, when the owners are away, villas are rented out to transient guests. Villas overlook the beach, the golf course, or else are built on a hillside overlooking the tennis courts. Those called "Harborside," naturally, open onto the waterfront. In winter, a one-bedroom villa for up to two persons costs $240 daily; two bedrooms, $330 for four persons; and three bedrooms, $400, the last suitable for up to six persons. *In summer, rates go down; a one-bedroom costs $160; two bedrooms, $235; and three bedrooms, $300.* Rates quoted are individual tariffs. However, most guests at Palmas del Mar book in here on a package plan, perhaps taking one of the sports options such as golf. Most packages are for seven days and six nights.

WHERE TO DINE: Moods for dining come in a wide variety, depending on which "village" you're staying in. Paolo's Ristorante Italiano is arguably the best, serving northern Italian food, but the choice is vast. If management continues its policy of a dine-around plan, MAP guests need not be bored. On my most recent visit, MAP guests could select from a choice of six specialty restaurants on the grounds, as well as five restaurants off the property. They could also enjoy five theme nights, including a Western night and a Mexican night.

To reach restaurants below for which I have listed only an extension number, call 852-6000, then ask for the individual extension.

Paolo's Ristorante Italiano, at the Palmas del Mar complex at Humacao (ext. 2417), serves strictly northern Italian cuisine at the Palmas Inn. It is a venture for tennis entrepreneur and former Italian Davis Cup star Paolo Bodo. Bodo claims that his is the only Puerto Rico restaurant serving *real* northern Italian food. "The Italian restaurants in San Juan are all southern Italian, overlaid with U.S.–Puerto Rican flavors." The restaurant opens at 6:30 p.m. and stays open until 11 p.m. A complete meal will easily cost from $30, plus your wine. The kitchen makes its own pastas, such as ravioli, tortellini, or spaghetti carbonara. You might follow with such dishes as red snapper, eggplant parmigiana, filet of sole, jumbo shrimp, and veal cutlet Valdostana. The setting is elegant. You dine on blue-and-white tiles, with the sea on your side, in an enclosed courtyard. It's chic and airy.

Adjoining the restaurant (actually a part of it) is **Avo's Piano Bar,** where Avo Uvezian entertains nightly from 8 o'clock.

Las Garzas (ext. 2010) is the outstanding restaurant in the Candelero Hotel. Cooled by trade winds, it overlooks a courtyard and swimming pool, and is an ideal choice for either breakfast, lunch, or dinner. Hours are 7 to 11 a.m., noon to 3 p.m., and 6 to 10:30 p.m. Lunches cost $12 and up and are likely to include sandwiches and burgers galore. If you want heartier fare, you can ask for the Puerto Rican specialty of the day, perhaps red snapper in garlic butter, preceded by black-bean soup. Dinner is more elaborate, costing from $25. Perhaps you'll begin with ceviche, following with two center-cut pork chops seasoned with "a dobo" or a nine-ounce churrasco served with "the salad bowl" and a baked potato. The chef always prepares the catch of the day, and you can invariably count on a good filet mignon. Saturday is Steak and Wine Night when you can feast on steaks and salads from 6:30 to 10:30 p.m.

Chez Daniel, The Marina (ext. 4785). It's French, it's nautical, it's fun, and it's the preferred dining area for the occupants of the yachts that moor at its adjacent pier. You'll find it in its own little pocket of chic beneath an inclined ceiling, within walls where only a suggestion of lattices keep out the cooling harborside breezes. Owned and operated by Daniel and Lucy Vasse (who come from the north and south of France, respectively), the establishment offers an alluring combination of traditional French food which sometimes veers perceptibly toward nouvelle cuisine. You can enjoy a filet of sole stuffed with pulverized crabmeat, a grouper-based bouillabaisse, salmon in green sauce with a tarragon soufflé, breast of chicken with lemon sauce, steamed salmon in herbs, a pungently flavored skewer of fish, lobster with calvados, asparagus mousseline, shrimp salad with orange vinaigrette, and a changing array of daily specials. Full meals cost from $25 and are served daily from noon to 3 p.m. and 7 to 10:30 p.m.

Le Bistroquet (tel. 852-8474) in Montesol, close to the tennis courts, is done in typical French-bistro style in the atmosphere of the 1930s. Here Martine and Robert Gaffori serve French food in air-conditioned comfort, with dinners costing from $30 per person. You might choose as your main dish coq au vin, entrecôte bordelaise, escargots, or lobster bisque. Only dinner is served, seven days a week from November to the end of April, Tuesday to Saturday the remainder of the year. Hours are 7 to 11 p.m.

Polynesian Restaurant (ext. 2503). Directed by Hong Kong-born Stanley Yau and his wife, Adele, this restaurant serves Chinese food and the kind of frothy mai tais you find in Hawaii. You dine in a lattice-framed pavilion whose translucent ceiling creates a greenhouse effect of dappled shadows between the Sun Fun Hut and the sea. Lunches are relatively simple, but spicy and flavorful, with a limited menu of Oriental-Polynesian dishes costing $8 for a full meal. Dinners are more elaborate, from $10 to $12.50 for a fixed-price menu, rising to $25 for a full-fledged luau-style spread. Specialties include shrimp Bora Bora, sizzling Honolulu steak, lobster aloha, and Peking-style duck. Lunch is served daily between 11:30 a.m. and 3:30 p.m., and dinner from 6 to 11 p.m.

The **Café de la Pace** evokes Old Spain. It occupies a village square setting in the evening to serve its buffets. Here, families bring their children to enjoy hamburgers, crêpes, and spaghetti, dinners costing from $15. Each night a different Puerto Rican specialty is featured. Open from noon to 10 p.m.

This has been only a preview of the dining possibilities. You will discover several more on your own. All the restaurants are open during the winter season; however, in summer, only three or four may be fully functioning.

WELLNESS CENTER: Palmas del Mar has installed a Wellness Center which uses the newest techniques of fitness analysis and exercise. It is equipped with state-of-the-art Hydra-Fitness exercise apparatus with hydraulic action for resistance, providing the ultimate training program for all fitness levels from the novice to the professional athlete. You can have a full workout in about 30 minutes, burning more calories than you would in the same time spent jogging. The center also uses the Medi-Fit Health Assessment System, which provides a choice of the newest and most reliable medically approved computerized evaluations. The nine-category fitness assessment covers areas from blood pressure to muscular endurance, an analysis of body composition with exercise and weight-loss recommendations, and a nutritional evaluation.

A basic exercise program includes classes in aerobics, aqua-aerobics, yoga, and stretching. Free weight-training supervision is also offered. Lifestyle management programs have been designed to help you manage stress, stop smoking, lose weight, and eat right. There are also special activities such as prenatal fitness classes, programs for toddlers and their mothers, and sports programs in tennis, running, cycling, skiing, basketball, and other fields.

The Wellness Center staff is made up of experts in the various program areas, all specialists in their sphere of activity. For information, get in touch with the Palmas del Mar offices in New York (cited above).

AFTER DARK: The most romantic spot in Palmas del Mar is **La Galería,** a lounge bar where guests can drink and dance to live music five nights a week, Wednesday through Sunday, from 8 p.m. to 2 a.m. The $8 minimum includes your first drink.

The **casino** in the Palmas del Mar complex, near the Palmas Inn, is in the Culebra Room on the second floor of the building that houses La Galería bar. The casino has nine blackjack tables, two roulette wheels, a craps table, and dozens of slot machines. The place is open from 6 p.m. to 2 a.m. daily. Under Puerto Rican law drinks cannot be served in a casino, and men must wear jackets after 8 p.m. You can have a drink in the lounge adjoining the gaming room or in La Galería downstairs.

9. Touring the Island

Even though Puerto Rico is an island barely 100 miles long by 35 miles wide, it offers a variety of scenery, from the rain forests and lush mountains of El Yunque to the lime deposits of the north and the arid areas of the south shore, where irrigation is a necessity and the cactus grows wild. In Puerto Rico you will find some of the most complicated geological formations in the world.

While driving on the mountain roads of Puerto Rico, blow your horn before every turn, contrary to urban zone regulations. Commercial road signs are forbidden, so make sure you take along a map and this guide to inform you of restaurants, hotels, and possible points of interest. The kilometer information refers to the roadside markers painted on a white background with black letters telling you the kilometer and hectometer.

Puerto Rico is a subtropical country, yet you can see seasonal changes. In November the sugarcane fields are in bloom, and in January and February the flowering trees along the roads are covered with red and orange blossoms.

When spring comes, the Puerto Rican oak is covered with delicate pink flowers and the African tulip tree is ablaze with its deep-red blossoms. Summer is the glorious flamboyant time when the roadsides seem as if on fire.

A HALF-DAY TRIP AROUND SAN JUAN: I'll suggest a number of itineraries, beginning with a half-day trip around the metropolitan San Juan area up to a rum distillery, Isla de Cobras, Loiza Aldea, and Boca de Cangrejos.

From San Juan, take Rte. 2 up to km. 6.4. To the right you will see a small park containing the ruins of the house erected in 1509 by Juan Ponce de León in Caparra, the first Spanish settlement in Puerto Rico.

Continue on Rte. 2 until you reach Bayamón. Facing the town plaza you have the old church, built in 1877, an excellent example of period architecture.

Afterward, you can then continue on Rte. 167 toward Cantano, turning left at km. 5.2. Within a short distance you will find yourself in the **Barrilito Rum Distillery.** To the left you will see a 200-year-old mansion with grand outdoor staircases leading to the second-floor galleries. This is the original mansion of the Santa Ana plantation (which once covered 2,400 acres) and is still occupied by members of the family, owners of the distillery. There's an office on the right, near a tower which was originally a windmill from which the entire valley and bay could be seen.

Back on Rte. 167, drive until you reach Catano, then take Rte. 165 going west and turning left (hugging the shoreline) until you reach **Isla de Cabras.** From this point, you can see the entire bay of San Juan. At the end of the road in Isla de Cabras you will come upon Fort Canuelo, erected in 1610 and reconstructed in 1625 after the Dutch attack on Puerto Rico. Originally built on what was then a tiny islet, the fort seemed to be emerging from the water. Today, however, because of modern landfill techniques it is connected to Isla de Cabras. Picnic facilities are available. Here, the breezes are cool and you have a good view of San Juan Bay and El Morro, built in 1539.

On the way back, drive toward Catano where you can take a short ferry ride to Old San Juan. Boats leave every 15 minutes, taking the same time to cross each way. The fare is 20¢ per person, round trip. A more extensive tour of the bay is offered by the Port Authority, leaving from the San Juan Terminal only on Sunday and holidays at 2:30 and 4:30 p.m. The tour takes you near the Coast Guard base, and you have a view of the governor's palace, the San Juan Door (Puerta de San Juan), and El Morro. The trip lasts 1½ hours and the price is $1.50 for adults and $1 for children.

From Catano, continue on Rte. 24 until the Caparra intersection on Rte. 20; then take Rte. 20 to Guaynabo until you reach Rte. 21. After going past the psychiatric hospital, the medical center, and the state penitentiary, continue until the Río Piedras intersection, turning left toward Carolina by way of Avenida 65 de Infantería (Rte. 3), from which you can see El Yunque. When you reach km. 18.3, turn onto the bridge and stay to the left to reach **Loiza Aldea.** If you are in Puerto Rico between July 19 and 29, the trip to Loiza Aldea will be quite an experience. This is when the whole town comes out to celebrate the feast day of its patron saint (Santiago Apostol). The festivities are unusual and bizarre, a mixture of pagan Afro-Caribbean and Christian elements forming part of the celebration and carnival.

The Church of San Patricio (St. Patrick), dating from 1645, in Loiza Aldea is in front of the road that leads you to the barge for crossing the Río Grande de Loiza. It's a bit of a thrill to cross this river (with your car) on a barge propelled by a man with ropes. Continue for half an hour on a sandy (but hard) road lined with coconut palms and shady trees until you reach the Nautical Club, then on to Santurce and San Juan.

RAIN FORESTS AND BEACHES:
From San Juan, if you have two days to explore, you can take the following itineraries, going on the first day to Trujillo Alto, Gurabo, El Yunque (rain forest), Luquillo Beach, and Fajardo. Perhaps you'll find the makings of a picnic lunch at one of the thatched stands along the road, eating it at El Yunque (there is also a restaurant in the rain forest—see "Dining Out in Puerto Rico"). On the second day you can explore Fajardo, Naguabo, Humacao, Yabucoa, Patillas, and Caguas, returning to San Juan in the late afternoon.

Water is considered one of Puerto Rico's most important resources; the other is its fertile soil. During the period of a year, 400 billion cubic feet of rain falls on the island. The Spaniards nicknamed the island "The Land of Rivers." To harness this water for public consumption, many dams were built, creating lakes which can be visited.

From San Juan, go to Río Piedras and take Rte. 3 (Avenida 65 de Infantería, named after the Puerto Rican regiment which battled in World War II and in Korea). Turn, heading south on Rte. 181 toward Trujillo Alto, then take Rte. 851 up to Rte. 941. At the end of the valley you can spot the **Lake of Loiza.** Houses can be seen nestled on the surrounding hills. You can even see local farmers (jibaros) riding their horses laden with produce, on the way to and from the marketplace. The lake is surrounded by mountains.

Your next stop is the town of **Gurabo.** This is tobacco country and you'll know you are nearing the town from the sweet aroma enveloping it (tobacco smells sweet before it's harvested). Part of the town of Gurabo is set on the side of a mountain, and the streets are made up of steps. One street has as many as 128 steps.

You will leave the town by way of Rte. 30. Then get on Rte. 185 north, then Rte. 186 south. This road has views of the ocean beyond the valleys. You will at this stage be driving on the lower section of the **Caribe Experimental Forest;** the vegetation is dense and you'll be surrounded by giant ferns. The brooks descending from El Yunque become small waterfalls on both sides of the road. If you have plans to have lunch at El Yunque, turn to go up on Rte. 191.

At about 25 miles east of San Juan, **El Yunque** consists of about 28,000 acres and is the only tropical forest in the U.S. National Forest system. It is said to contain some 240 different tree species native to the area (only half a dozen of these are actually found on the mainland). In this world of cedars and satinwood (draped in tangles of vines), you'll hear chirping birds, see wild orchids, and perhaps hear the song of the tree frog, the coquí. The entire forest is a bird sanctuary, and may be the last retreat of the rare Puerto Rican parrot.

El Yunque is 3,493 feet high, and the peak of El Toro rises 3,526 feet. You know you'll be showered upon, as more than 100 billion gallons of rain fall annually. However, the showers are brief, and there are many shelters.

You might go first to the Visitor Center, at km. 11.6. It's open daily from 9 a.m. to 5:30 p.m., and guides here will give lectures and show slides. Groups, if arranged in advance, can go on guided hikes.

To make your way back, head north along Rte. 191, connecting with Rte. 3. If you drive east for five miles, you will reach **Luquillo Beach,** lying about 30 miles east of San Juan. Edged by a vast coconut grove, this crescent-shaped beach is not only the best in Puerto Rico, it's one of the finest in the Caribbean. You pay to enter with your car, and you're allowed to rent a locker, take a shower, and have a place to change into your bathing suit or bikini. Luquillo gets very crowded on weekends, and if possible go on a weekday when you'll have more sand to yourself. Picnic tables are available as well.

The beach is open from 9 a.m. to 6 p.m. daily. It is closed on Monday, however. If Monday is a holiday, then the beach will shut down on Tuesday that week. Before entering the beach, you may want to stop at one of the roadside thatched huts, selling Puerto Rican snacks, the makings for your picnic.

Continuing east, Rte. 3 leads to **Fajardo,** a fishing port hotly contested in the Spanish-American War. Fishermen and sailors are attracted to its shores and to nearby **Las Croabas,** which has a lot of native fish restaurants. Puerto Ricans are fond of giving nicknames to people and places. For many years the residents of Fajardo have been called *cariduros* ("the hard-faced ones"). However, don't be misled by that. The people here are very friendly.

At Fajardo you can also rent boats or take the ferry ride to the islands of Vieques and Culebra.

On the second day, you can continue south on Rte. 3, following the Caribbean coastline. At **Cayo Lobos,** not far from the Fajardo port, the Atlantic meets the Caribbean. Here, the vivid colors of the Caribbean seem subdued compared to those of the ocean.

Go across the town of Ceiba, near the Roosevelt Navy Base, to reach **Naguabo Beach,** where you can have coffee and "pastelillos de chapin," pastry turnovers used as tax payments in Spanish colonial days. At km. 70.9, briefly detour to Naguabo and enjoy the scented shady laurel trees from India in the town's plaza.

Continue on Rte. 3, going through **Humacao** and its sugarcane fields. When the cane blooms around November and December, the tops of the fields change colors according to the time of day. Humacao is of little interest, but it has a balneario-equipped beach. From here you can detour to the 2,800-acre resort, Palmas del Mar, already described.

After the stopover, you can continue until the town of Yabucoa, nestled among hills. The road suddenly opens up through **Cerro** (mountain) **La Pandura,** giving you some of the most spectacular sights in Puerto Rico. Take note of the giant boulders, beyond which you will see the Caribbean.

After passing the town of Maunabo along Rte. 181 (a tree-lined road which runs next to Lake Patillas), stay on the highway until you reach San Lorenzo, across the mountains. You then take Rte. 183 to reach Caguas, then Rte. 1 back into San Juan.

PINEAPPLES AND COFFEE PLANTATIONS: The trip outlined below takes two days, as you cross an extraordinary limestone region. However, the itinerary can be cut down to one day if you eliminate a stay at the coffee plantation.

The trip takes you across the famous "Karst" district in Puerto Rico, one of the most developed regions of this type in the world. This area was formed by the wearing down of limestone by acids in the water, leaving a maze of deep fissures and mounds. Some of the depressions in the area are 400 feet across and as deep as 160 feet. The radiotelescope in nearby Arecibo is built inside one of these craters, more than 300 feet deep and 1,300 feet wide. Underground rivers are sometimes formed in this type of geological environment. An example of this is the Tanama River, which emerges and disappears at five different places.

From San Juan, take Rte. 2 heading west toward Manati, after which you will pass the pineapple region. At km. 57.9, turn onto Rte. 140 south to Florida. At km. 25.5 you will find a coffee cooperative where during harvest time the beans are processed, ground, and packed. At km. 30.7, turn right toward Hacienda Rosas. A coffee plantation is interesting at all times, but especially around harvest time (from September to December, sometimes as late as January) when the pickers, gathered in groups, walk under the bushes and pick the crimson beans while other workers process the already-picked yield.

Continuing, take Rte. 141 to Jayuya, where you can stay at the Parador Gripiñas (refer to "Hotels Out in the Island").

After a restful day there, take Rte. 141 north until you are back on Rte. 140. Head west on Rte. 140 until you pass Caonillas Lake. There, turn onto Rte. 111 west, go across the town of Utuado, and continue to km. 12.5. Here you will find the **Taíno Indian Ceremonial Ball Park.** Archeological clues date this site to approximately two centuries before the discovery of the New World. It is believed that Indian Chief Guarionex gathered his subjects on this site to celebrate rituals and practice sports. Set on a 13-acre field surrounded by trees are some 14 vertical monoliths with colorful petroglyphs, all arranged around a central sacrificial stone monument. The ball complex also includes a museum, open from 9 a.m. to 5 p.m., charging no admission. There is also a gallery, Herencia Indígena, where visitors can purchase Indian relics at very reasonable prices, including the sought-after Cemi (Taíno Indian idols) and the famous little frog, the coquí.

Continue next on Rte. 111 up to Rte. 129 north and head toward Arecibo (going across the Karst region) until you reach km. 13.6. Take Rte. 489 south to La Cueva de la Luz (Cave of Light).

Next, follow Rte. 489 until the Barrio Aibonito, Pagan sector. If you have any doubts, ask anyone for **"La Cueva de Pagan Pagan"** (Pagan Pagan's cave). A narrow road will lead you, only to end at a general store where anyone will find Pagan for you. Only the agile and those who like to explore should venture inside the cave. The cave is lit by daylight, but the floor is rough and irregular. Women should wear slacks and possibly sneakers or rubbersoles. There are no bats in the cave. Inside, a stone vessel contains fresh water which some believe has rejuvenating qualities. Other caves in this area have not been explored fully, but Indian relics have been found. Return by way of Rte. 489 to Rte. 129 north, to Arecibo.

The **Arecibo Observatory,** referred to earlier, is a 35-minute drive south from the commercial city of Arecibo. Take Rtes. 129, 134, 635, and 625. This is the largest radar-radiotelescope on earth. The grounds are open to the public on Sunday only from 1 to 4:30 p.m. Guided tours are given Tuesday through Friday at 10:30 a.m. and 2 p.m. The observatory and grounds are closed to the public on Monday, Saturday, and public holidays. There is a souvenir shop on the grounds. The 20-acre reflector is a curving expanse of some 40,000 aluminum panels which have been installed over a sinkhole 300 feet deep and 1,000 feet wide. The observatory is operated by Cornell University for the National Science Foundation and carries out research in the fields of astronomy and atmospheric science. For more information, write to Cornell University, P.O. Box 995, Arecibo, PR 00613.

After you return to Arecibo, you can take Rte. 2 east back to San Juan.

A FOUR-DAY TRIP: More ambitious than the itineraries considered so far, this next trip takes you to the west coast and south on the island:

On the first day, follow Rte. 2 from San Juan west up to **Guajataca.** Just before you reach km. 103.4, you will spot a sign for the Guajataca recreation area. Make a right turn and stay on the road to the parking area.

Go back to Rte. 2 and to the Guajataca Beach. It is so fine a beach you may want to stay there for at least one more day. (The Parador Guajataca is just above the hill from the beach.)

When you decide to continue, take Rte. 2 up to km. 91 and turn toward the south, across the Karst region (see the previous tour) until you reach man-made Guajataca Lake. Follow the lake's shoreline for about 2½ miles and turn left at km. 19 to Rte. 455 until you reach a bridge spanning the Guajataca River, which runs through the lush mountainside.

Return by way of Rte. 119 and continue toward San Sebastian and to Rte. 109 across coffee plantations to Anasco. Turn onto Rte. 2 and head for Mayagüez.

Mayagüez

On your second day you can explore what Puerto Ricans have nicknamed "The Sultan of the West." This busy port city, not architecturally remarkable, is the third largest on the island. Once considered the needlework capital of the island, it still has women who do fine embroidery and drawn-thread work. Some of the older downtown shops sell it, and the clever shopper will seek out some good buys.

Mayagüez dates from the mid-18th century. It was built to control the location of the Mona Passage, a vital trade route for the Spanish empire. Queen Isabel II of Spain recognized its status as a town in 1836. Her son, Alfonso XII, granted it a city charter in 1877.

Mayagüez is the honeymoon capital of Puerto Rico. The tradition dates from the 16th century, when, it is said, local fathers kidnapped young Spanish sailors who stopped for provisions there en route to South America. Because of the scarcity of eligible young men, they needed husbands for their daughters.

The major industry is tuna packing, representing about 60% of all U.S. tuna consumption.

The chief sight is the **Tropical Agriculture Research Station.** At the administration office, ask for a free map of the tropical gardens, which contain one of the largest collections of tropical species useful to people, including cacao, fruit trees, spices, timbers, and ornamentals.

The location is on Rte. 65, between Post Street and Rte. 108, adjacent to the University of Puerto Rico at Mayagüez campus and across the street from the **Parque de los Próceres** or patriots' park. The grounds are open Monday through Friday from 7:30 a.m. to noon and 1 to 4:30 p.m., charging no admission. For more information, call 834-2435.

The **Puerto Rico Zoological Garden,** Rte. 108 (tel. 834-8110), at Mayagüez, exhibits birds, reptiles, and mammals, plus a South American exhibit, all contained in a lush tropical environment. Hours year round are 9 a.m. to 5 p.m. Tuesday through Sunday, and admission is $1 for adults, 50¢ for children, and $1 for parking.

Mayagüez might also be the jumping-off point for a visit to **Mona Island,** which enjoys many legends of pirate treasure and is known for its white sand beaches and marine life. Accessible only by private boat or plane, the island is virtually uninhabited, except for two policemen and a director of the institute of natural resources. The island attracts hunters seeking pigs, iguanas, and wild goats, along with big-game fishermen. But mostly it is intriguing to anyone who wants to escape civilization. Playa Sardinera on Mona Island was a nesting ground of pirates. On one side of the island, Playa de Pajaros, there are caves where the Taíno Indians left their mysterious hieroglyphs.

After touring Mayagüez, you can pick up the tour by taking Rte. 105 up to Rte. 120 as far as **Maricao.** The town is colorful and rather small. On the outskirts look for a sign that reads "Los Viveros" **(The Hatcheries);** then take Rte. 410. Here, the Commonwealth Department of Agriculture hatches as many as 25,000 fish for stocking the Puerto Rican freshwater lakes and streams.

Go back to Maricao to Rte. 120 south up to km. 13.8 until you reach the **Maricao State Forest** picnic area at a height of 2,900 feet above sea level. The observation tower provides a splendid view across the green mountain range up to the coastal plains. Continue on Rte. 120 across the forest to the town of Sabana Grande (Great Plain). Rte. 2 will then take you to San German.

San German

This town is a little museum piece. It was founded in 1512, although destroyed by the French in 1528. Rebuilt in 1570, it was named after Dona Germana de Foix, King Ferdinand of Spain's second wife. Once it rivaled San Juan in importance, although it has now settled into slumber, a living example of Spanish colonization. Gracious old-world buildings line the streets, and flowers brighten the patios as they do in Seville. Also as in a small Spanish town, the population turns out to stroll in the plaza in the early evening.

On a knoll at one end of the town stands the chapel of **Porta Coeli** (Gate of Heaven), dating from the 17th century, oldest in the New World. Restored by the Institute of Puerto Rican Culture, it contains a museum of religious art which is open (admission free) Tuesday to Sunday from 9 a.m. to noon and 2 to 4:30 p.m. The museum has a collection of ancient santos, carved holy figures and saints. Guided tours are offered Wednesday through Sunday. For more information, call 892-5845.

It's possible to spend the night in comfort in the town at the **Parador Oasis,** 72 Luna St., San German, PR 00753 (tel. 809/892-1175), housed within a 200-year-old building. Originally this parador was a fashionable private home and later a winery. It was also a small family-run hotel. Today it offers the same ornate verandas and decorative latticeworks—called *soles truncos*—that it used to, except everything has been considerably restored. Here visitors will see examples of *mediopunto*, a decorative room divider usually made of fine wooded lacework, highly characteristic of architecture in Puerto Rico between 1890 and 1940. Below are underground tunnels once believed used for contraband. All the pleasantly furnished rooms are air-conditioned. Units contain private baths, and some face the inner patio, which is a gathering place for both guests and local patrons. Year round, rates in the old building are $42 single, $52 double. In the new part of the parador, rents are $48 in a single, $54 in a double. Each additional adult in a room is charged $10, but children (maximum two) stay free when accompanied by an adult. Government tax and a $2 energy charge are not included in the quoted rates. Good regional food is served in the 18th-century dining room, known for its frescoes. The Parador has an elegant and contemporary disco, the Club Elite, and a convention center. Ask about their honeymoon package.

From San German, take Rte. 320 to Rte. 101, then on to Lajas where Rte. 116 will lead to Rte. 304 which will take you to La Parguera where you can visit the **Phosphorescent Bay** (best on a moonless night). A boat leaves Villa Parguera pier nightly at 7:30 p.m. ($4 per person). The experience of seeing fish jump out of the water and emit a luminous streak on the surface and watching the water ripples created by the boat glimmer in the dark is unique. Phosphorescent Bay is near the fishing village of Paraguera. The phenomenon, incidentally, is caused by a big colony of dinoflagellates, a small form of marine life. They produce these sparks of chemical light when their nesting is disturbed.

On the third day, take Rte. 104 up to Rte. 116 to Enseñada. From there you can continue on Rte. 116 to Guánica Bay. Or you could turn off on Rte. 333 to Cana Gorda Beach, to have a swim or lunch at the already-previewed Copamarina Hotel. While there, look for the species of cacti typical of the region. Continue on Rte. 2 to Yauco, then take Rte. 132 and head for—

Ponce

Puerto Rico's second-largest city, Ponce—called "The Pearl of the South"—was named after Ponce de León. Founded in 1692, it is today Puerto Rico's principal shipping port on the Caribbean. The city is well kept and attractive, as reflected by its many plazas, parks, and public buildings. There is something in its lingering air that suggests a provincial Mediterranean town. Look for the rejas, or framed balconies of the handsome colonial mansions.

Any of the Ponceños will direct you to their **Museum of Art,** at Las Americas Avenue (tel. 848-0505). This excellent museum was donated to the people of Puerto Rico by Luís A. Ferré, a former governor. The building in which the museum is housed was designed by Edward Durell Stone (the designer of New York's Museum of Modern Art), and it's been called "The Parthenon of the Caribbean." In spite of such a fanciful label, its collection represents principal schools of American and European Art of the past five centuries. Hours are 10 a.m. to noon and 1 to 4 p.m. Monday through Friday, 10 a.m. to 4 p.m. on Saturday, to 5 p.m. on Sunday and holidays. The museum is closed on Tuesday. Adults pay $1.50; children under 12, 75¢.

All visitors as well head for the **Parque de Bombas,** on the main plaza of Ponce. This old firehouse is fantastic—painted black, red, green, and yellow. It was built for a fair in 1883, and is today the headquarters for the government tourism agency's Ponce Information Office.

Around from the firehouse, the trail will lead to the **Cathedral of Our Lady of Guadalupe.** The church rises between two plazas.

The marketplace at Atocha and Castillo Streets is colorful, the Perla Theater historic, and the Serralles rum distillery is worth a visit. Or perhaps you'll want to just sit at the plaza, watching the Ponceños at their favorite pastime, strolling in the plaza.

The oldest cemetery in the Antilles, excavated in 1975, is on Rte. 503, km. 2.7. The **Tibes Indian Ceremonial Center** (tel. 840-2255) contains some 186 skeletons, dating from A.D. 300, as well as pre-Taíno plazas from A.D. 700. Bordered by the Portugués River, the museum is open daily except Monday from 9 a.m. to 4:30 p.m. Admission is $1 for adults and 50¢ for children. Guided tours in English and Spanish are conducted through the grounds (for more information, call 844-5575). Shaded by such trees as the calabash, seven rectangular ballcourts and two dance grounds can be viewed. The arrangement of stone points on the dance grounds, in line with the solstices and equinoxes, suggest a pre-Columbian Stonehenge. A re-created Taíno village includes not only the museum but an exhibition hall which shows a documentary about Tibes, a cafeteria where you can find refreshments, and a souvenir shop.

On the fourth and final day, leave Ponce by Rte. 1. As vast sugarcane fields fade from view, take Rte. 3 to **Guayama,** one of the handsomest towns in Puerto Rico. There, find Rte. 15, going north. If you travel this road in either spring or summer, you'll be surrounded by the brilliant colors of flowering trees.

At km. 17.1, in Jajome, you can see the governor's summer palace, an ancient, now restored and enlarged roadside inn. Continue on Rte. 15; then get on Rte. 1 which leads directly back to San Juan.

BEACHES ALONG THE ATLANTIC: An interesting scenic trip to the beaches between San Juan and Arecibo follows. Allow at least 5½ hours, not counting beach time.

The ever-changing colors of the Atlantic make this trip a memorable experience. Start at Rte. 2 to the Caparra intersection, where you turn onto Rte. 24 to Catano; then continue west on Rte. 165. El Morro and Old San Juan can be seen across the bay.

After passing a dense coconut grove, you will reach Levittown City (a housing development). The sea turns a blue-green shade at this spot. Continue up to the river and the town of **Dorado** by way of Rte. 690 north. Within a short distance, you will reach **Cerro Gordo Beach.** Watch your time, for you might be mesmerized by the natural beauty of this beach and stay longer than planned.

If you can break away from Cerro Gordo, take Rte. 688 back to Rte. 2 headed toward **Vega Baja** (founded in 1776). The residents of Vega Baja are nicknamed "melao-melao" ("molasses-molasses") because of the large amount of molasses produced in the town.

Route 676 north takes you to a spectacular beach in the west, where the water turns jade green with touches of purple and lots of white foam. Over to the east of this beach the water is less turbulent, held back by a giant rocky barrier where the waves crash thunderously. This beach is dotted with cabins and cabañas belonging to the local residents. Continue on Rte. 686 until you reach Rte. 648, which will take you to **Mar Chiquita,** where the high rocks enclose an oval lagoon perfect for swimming.

Return by way of Rte. 648 to Rte. 685, which will lead you to Rte. 2. Head north on Rte. 2 to Rte. 140 until you get to Barceloneta; then take Rte. 681 up to the Plazuela sugar mill and go through cane fields edged with almond trees.

Continue toward the beach and look for a sign which reads **"La Cueva del Indio"** (The Indian Cave). Many Indian symbols can be seen on the cave walls.

Leave the area by way of Rte. 681 up to where it meets Rte. 2 in Arecibo. Route 2 east will take you back to San Juan through cane fields and perfumed pineapple plantations.

10. The Sporting Life

Dorado Beach, Cerromar Beach, and Palmas del Mar are the chief centers for those seeking the golf, tennis, and beach life. Hotels on the Condado/Isla Verde coast also have, for the most part, complete water sports.

BEACHES: Beaches in Puerto Rico are open to the public, although you will be charged for parking and for use of balneario facilities, such as lockers and showers. The public beaches on the north shore of San Juan at Ocean Park and Park Barbosa are good, and can be reached by bus. Luquillo, on the north coast, some 30 miles east of San Juan, is discussed separately in the touring section. Also refer to the touring section for more tips on beaches west from San Juan. Public beaches shut down on Monday. If Monday is a holiday, the beaches are open then but close the next day, Tuesday. In winter, beach hours are 9 a.m. to 5 p.m., to 6 p.m. in summer.

Along the coastal roads of Rte. 2, to the north of Mayagüez, lie what are reputed to be the best surfing beaches in the Caribbean. Surfers from as far away as New Zealand are attracted to these beaches. The most outstanding of all, comparable to the finest surfing spots in the world, according to competitors in the 1968 World Surfing Championship held there, is at Punta Higuero, on Rte. 413 near the town of Rincón. In the winter months especially, uninterrupted Atlantic swells with perfectly formed waves averaging five to six feet in height roll shoreward and rideable swells sometimes reach 15 to 25 feet.

SNORKELING AND SCUBA: The coral reefs and cays around Puerto Rico make it ideal snorkeling country. Most major hotel water-sports offices also offer scuba-diving instructions. All the major hotels have water sports, but one of the most professional outfits is **Caribe Aquatic Adventures** (tel. 721-0303, ext. 447), at the Caribe Hilton on Puerta de Tierra in San Juan. Karen Vega, the president of the resort division, is a NAUI-PADI certified instructor. She's helped by her husband, Tony, a NAUI dive-master. Their shop is a NAUI Pro facility. The best dive sites in San Juan are off the Hilton's beach. Deserted island sailing trips are also available, costing $60 for non-divers, $85 for divers. Day or weekend charters are available on the 60-foot dive boat *San António*.

A nearby competitor of the Hilton, the **Condado Plaza Hotel & Casino**, 999 Ashford Ave. (tel. 721-1000), operates a full dive shop on its premises also. Capt. Bill Conway, a certified NAUI instructor, directs scuba facilities. Programs are available for everyone from novices to advanced divers. A half-day program, which includes classroom, pool, and underwater work, costs around $60 for a complete introduction to scuba. Once a beginner has completed this, he or she can qualify for one of the most comprehensive expeditions on the Condado, the Island Safari Tour. Depending on the weather at any one of several dive spots along Puerto Rico's east coast, Captain Conway or a member of his staff will lead selected groups for a full day of picnicking, sightseeing, skindiving, and exploring. An hour's minibus ride takes participants through the rain forest to a boat called the *Innovation*. All equipment is included, as well as the services of a guide.

Palmas del Mar Aquatics (tel. 852-6000, ext. 4701) has been set up by Coral Head Divers, Puerto Rico's largest scuba-diving operation, at the resort's marina. The new operation, supervised by Jim Abbott, owner of Coral Head Divers, offers diving, snorkeling, coastal cruising, and wing sailing. It carries a range of equipment for rent, including canoes, kayaks, boogie boards, floats, and fishing rods and reels, as well as underwater photographic equipment. Abbott, a member of NAUI and PADI, and his staff do research and commercial diving work as well as resort diving and diver training at all levels.

DEEP-SEA FISHING: It's top-notch. Allison tuna, white marlin, sailfish, wahoo, dolphin, mackerel, and tarpon are some of the fish that can be caught in Puerto Rican waters where 30 world records have been broken.

It is said in Puerto Rico that **Capt. Mike Benitez** sets the standards by which to judge other captains. He is especially praised by marlin fishermen. You can write him directly at P.O. Box 5141, Puerta de Tierra, San Juan, PR 00906 (call 723-2292 daily to 9 p.m.), or else get in touch with him at Caribe Aquatic Adventures in the Hilton Dive Shop (tel. 721-0303, ext. 447). The captain has chartered out of San Juan for 35 years. He takes his clients out on his 45-foot, air-conditioned, deluxe Hatteras, *Sea Born*. Fishing tours cost $285 for a half day, $490 for a full day, and take up to six sportsmen.

You can also go out with **Capt. Jorge L. Torruella,** the owner of the *Gin Pole,* a 41-foot Hatteras sportfisherman which is fully equipped and diesel powered. A half-day tour costs $240 to $270. It's cheaper to go on a split charter, which costs only $80 per angler. A maximum of six passengers is taken out. For more information, write Captain Torruella, Apt. 204, Condado Gardens, 1436 Estrella St., Santurce, PR 00907 (tel. 725-0998).

Some of the best year-round fishing in the Caribbean is found in the waters just off Palmas del Mar, the resort complex on the southeast coast of Puerto Rico (tel. 850-7442 after 6 p.m.). There **Capt. Bill Burleson** operates charters out of Palmas's harbor. His 44-foot customized sportsfishing boat *Karolette* is the second-largest charter fishing vessel operating out of Puerto Rico. He has fished the Caribbean for more than 20 years. Burleson prefers to take visiting fishermen to Grappler Banks, 18 nautical miles away. The banks are two sea mounts, rising to about 240 feet below the surface and surrounded by deeps of 6,000 to 8,000 feet. They lie in the migratory paths of wahoo, tuna, and marlin. Reservations can be made at Palmas del Mar's Candelero Hotel, at the guest service desk. The cost is $625 per day; maximum is six persons.

SAILING: In Humacao, the **Palmas del Mar Sailing Center** (tel. 852-8114) offers a satisfying collection of wind-related water sports every day from 9 a.m. to 5 p.m. From a kiosk on a flat sandy area of scrub grass, a mini-van ride from the resort's lodging facilities, Capt. Carol Fernandez and Doug Smith, two American-born entrepreneurs, maintain a full and complete sailing school. Spearheads of the Copa de Palmas races, which occur here every Labor Day weekend, they offer for rental (with a captain) sailboats which range from between 27 and 46 feet in length. On a less grand scale, a wintersurfer rents for $15 per hour, and a two-hour lesson costs $30. Sunfish and paddleboats cost the same price, while waterskiing is $15 for a 15-minute ride. The couple offers a junior sailing school at prearranged sessions every June and July, where teenagers learn basic sailing and seamanship, eventually participating in an end-of-the-season regatta.

The **Condado Plaza Hotel & Casino,** 999 Ashford Ave. (tel. 721-1000), offers a wide selection of boats for rent to visitors who want to sail in the sheltered lagoon near the heart of town. A 35-foot Pierson, holding a maximum of six passengers, can be chartered for a half-day excursion, costing around $350. On a less grand scale, Sunfish can be rented for $18 an hour. Aquacycles can also be rented, for $10 per half hour.

GOLF: A golfer's dream, Puerto Rico has some splendid courses, too many for me to document here. The **Hyatt Dorado Beach** (tel. 796-1600) and the **Hyatt Regency Cerromar Beach** (tel. 796-1010), with 72 holes of golf, constitute the greatest concentration of the sport in the Caribbean. The course at Dorado Beach is rated as one of the finest anywhere. These side-by-side 18-hole courses were designed by Robert Trent Jones.

The **Club de Golf,** at Palmas del Mar in Humacao (tel. 852-6000, ext. 2526), is one of the leading courses for golf in Puerto Rico. On Puerto Rico's southeast coast, it has a par-72, 6,690-yard layout designed by Gary Player. It's under the direction of club professional Seth Bull.

The Mayagüez Hilton makes arrangements for guests to play at a nine-hole course at a nearby country club. Punta Borinquen, at Aguadilla, the former Ramey Air Force Base, has an 18-hole public golf course which is open daily.

TENNIS: Again, the sister resorts of Dorado and Cerromar (tel. 796-1010) have the monopoly on this game, a total of 21 courts between them. The charge is $12 an hour. Take your racquet and tennis outfit along (attire and equipment are often available in shops, but prices are high, the selection minimal). If your backhand is a bit rusty or your game needs a few pointers, take advantage of the professional tennis clinic. Lessons cost $32 per hour.

In San Juan, the Caribe Hilton, the Condado Plaza, Carib Inn, and the Condado Beach and La Concha have tennis courts. Also in the San Juan area there's a public court at the old navy base, Isla Grande, Miramar. The entrance is from Fernandez Juncos Avenue at Stop 11.

The Tennis Center at Palmas del Mar in Humacao, run by All American Sports, features 20 courts (5 Hartru, 15 Tenneflex). Court fees are $12 per hour for doubles in daylight, $16 at night. Call 852-3450, ext. 2527, to reserve court time.

HORSE RACING: Great thoroughbreds and outstanding jockeys compete all year at **El Comandante,** Rte. 3, km. 15.3 at Canóvanas (tel. 724-6060), a modern track. Races are held Wednesday, Friday, Sunday, and holidays at 2:30 p.m. Admission to the clubhouse is $3, and you pay only $1 for the grandstand. An air-conditioned terrace dining room opens at 12:30 p.m. on each race day. Telephone 724-6060 for luncheon reservations. Most credit cards are accepted.

COCKFIGHTING: Puerto Ricans are tremendously fond of this sport, as is most of Latin America. The **Club Gallistico,** Rte. 187, km. 1.5, Isla Verde (tel. 791-1557), is air-conditioned, complete with restaurant and cocktail lounge. General admission is $8; ringside admission, $15. Fights are on Saturday at 2 p.m.

HORSEBACK RIDING: The equestrian center at **Palmas del Mar,** under the direction of Fernando Salgado, a riding instructor of international experience, has 42 horses, including English hunters for jumping, plus a variety of trail rides and instruction on all levels of ability. The land set aside for equestrian pursuits abuts the resort's airstrip and is bounded on one side by a stream. Trail rides skirt this creek, following paths through the coconut plantation and jungle and swinging along the beach.

11. Vieques

About six miles east of the big island of Puerto Rico lies Vieques (pronounced Bee-*ay*-kase), an island about twice the size of Manhattan with some 8,000 inhabitants and scores of palm-lined white sand beaches. Since World War II some two-thirds of the 21-mile-long island has belonged to the United States military forces. Much of the government-owned land is now leased for cattle grazing, and when there are no military maneuvers the public can visit the beaches, sometimes restricted. Being allowed use of the land does not, however, totally cover local discontent and protest at the presence of the navy and Marine Corps personnel on the island.

The Spanish conquistadores didn't think much of Vieques. They came here in the 16th century but didn't stay long, reporting that the island and neighboring bits of land held no gold and were therefore "Las Islas Inutiles" (useless islands). The name Vieques comes from an Indian word for small island, *bieques*. Later Spanish occupation is attested to by the main town, **Isabel Segunda,** on the northern shore. The last Spanish fort in the New World was started around 1843 under the reign of the second Queen Isabella, for whom the town was named. The fort was never completed and is not of any special interest. The **Punta Mula lighthouse** north of Isabel Segunda provides panoramic views of the land and sea. The island fishermen and farmers conduct much of their business in Isabel Segunda.

On the south coast, **Esperanza,** once a center for the island's sugarcane industry, now a pretty little fishing village, lies near **Sun Bay** (Sombe) **public beach.** Sun Bay is a government-run, magnificent crescent of sand. The fenced area has picnic tables, a bathhouse, and a parking lot. Admission is $1 per car. A recently built resort and marina, and other facilities, add to the lure of the many scalloped stretches of sandy waterfront along the south coast.

Few of the island's 40-some beaches have even been named, but most have their loyal supporters—loyal, that is, until too many people learn about them, in which case the devotees can always find another good spot. The U.S. Navy named some of the strands, such as **Green Beach,** a beautiful clean stretch at the island's west end. **Red and Blue Beaches,** also with navy nomenclature, are great jumping-off points for snorkelers. Other popular beaches are **Navia, Half Moon, Orchid,** and **Silver,** but if you continue along the water, you may find your own nameless secluded cove with a fine strip of sand. **Mosquito Bay,** which glows with phosphorescence on moonless nights, is a short way east of Esperanza. (This inlet is sometimes called Phosphorescent Bay, probably to discourage ideas of being the target of mosquitoes.) Less well known than the handful of other phosphorescent bays scattered throughout the Caribbean, the one at Vieques is in some ways the most vivid. The luminosity filling its waters is a function of millions of microorganisms—technically known as Dinoflagelata—which thrive on the roots of red mangrove trees.

The best way to see this amazing light show is to head for the Esperanza Hotel every night for the 7 and 9 p.m. tours, leaving from the hotel's dock. Costing $8 per person, and including two beers or soft drinks per person, the tour usually lasts 1½ hours. Transportation is on a 32-foot motor launch, owned and operated by the hotel. You stand a better chance of seeing the glowing waters if you phone the hotel in advance (tel. 741-8675) to find out any last-minute changes. Those who decide to swim off the side of the boat are amazed at the way the whorls of churning water created by their moving bodies seem to come alive with the glow of an eerie kind of phosphorescence.

GETTING THERE: Small **planes** fly to Vieques from Isla Grande Airport in San Juan, a 15-minute cab ride from San Juan International Airport. After a 30-minute flight, costing about $25, your plane lands at the airstrip about 15 minutes from Esperanza.

Ferryboats ply the waters between Vieques and the port of Fajardo on the east side of Puerto Rico, making the voyage in about 1½ hours for about $2 per trip each way.

GETTING AROUND: Públicos transport people around the island.

Esperanza Rental Cars, Parador Villa Esperanza, Esperanza (tel. 741-8675). Other car rentals exist on the island, but most of them seem to be located at someone's private house somewhere in Isabela Segunda. On my most recent trip to Vieques I had the feeling that I had rented a not-very-well-maintained private car of a local family and deprived them of a long-awaited outing. You might be more secure heading for the Parador Villa Esperanza, where owner Ramón Ruíz-Cox will rent you a late-model Mitsubishi, suitable for up to five passengers, for $40 a day. Motorscooters are also available for $28 per day.

WHERE TO DIVE: Vieques Divers, P.O. Box 1001, Esperanza (tel. 741-8600), is open seven days a week in high season, but closed every Tuesday off-season.

WHERE TO STAY: Established in 1985 on the site of an abandoned sugar plantation, whose sandy boundaries encompass a fine beach and a 900-acre national park, the **Parador Villa Esperanza Beach Club & Marina,** Esperanza, PR 00765 (tel. 809/741-8675), is the most interesting and best-managed hotel on the island. You register between the massive brick walls and the soaring ceiling of a 19th-century Spanish warehouse. This was converted into the lobby of the hotel by former real estate broker Ramón Ruíz-Cox (Moncho, to his friends). The massive space is pleasingly bedecked with wicker furniture and plants. Scattered amid the outbuildings of the parador's 30 acres are the 19th-century remains of the wood-burning steam-powered locomotives which used to haul sugarcane to the refinery. The 50 simple but stylish accommodations are contained within Caribbean adaptations of alpine chalets which lie scattered over the surrounding lawns. Each contains large windows, private bathrooms, whirling ceiling fans, and lots of sun-flooded space. Year round rates in a single range from $53 to $63 daily, while doubles run $61 to $81; children under 11 stay in a double room free with their parents.

On the premises is a swimming pool, copses of well-placed mahogany trees, a handful of century-old banyans, two tennis courts, and a 550-foot concrete dock stretching out toward a pair of uninhabited islands known throughout the region for their excellent offshore snorkeling. Some guests spend at least part of their afternoons sipping piña coladas beneath the shade of a thatch-roofed outdoor bar, where comfortable chairs and cooling breezes make the sea even more beautiful. The hotel's fine restaurant, Las Marinas, is reviewed separately. Mr. Ruíz-Cox, one of the most charming hoteliers in Puerto Rico, grew up in New York where his father was a professor at the Juilliard School of Music. An experienced sailor, he served as the coach for Puerto Rico's Olympic sailing team for many years. He's happy to show guests an adjoining building used in 1962 by a film crew shooting *Lord of the Flies*.

La Casa del Frances, Barrio Esperanza, Vieques, PR 00765 (tel. 809/741-3751). Set in a field near the southern coastline, its columns and imposing façade rise from the lush landscape surrounding it. It was completed in 1905 by a retired French general as the headquarters for his working sugar plantation. In the 1950s it was acquired by W. F. Woolworth, who installed a swimming pool and transformed it into an oasis for the R&R of his executives. In the 1970s a retired optometrist from Boston, Irving Greenblatt, transformed 19 of its high-ceilinged bedrooms into pleasantly old-fashioned hotel accommodations. Each contains a private bath, and many enjoy access to the sweeping two-story verandas ringing the white façade. With MAP included, doubles rent for $110 per night throughout the year.

Scattered throughout the dozen acres attached to the main house are century-old tropical trees and a glass-fronted shrine to the Virgin. The estate's architectural highlight is the two-story interior courtyard whose center is lush with bamboo, palms, philodendron, and well-chosen examples of Haitian art. The fixed-price dinners, costing $12 each, are attended by many island residents who enjoy the changing array of Italian, barbecue, or Puerto Rican buffets which the staff presents with flair beneath a 200-year-old mahogany tree. The location is about a 15-minute drive southeast of Isabela Segunda, just north of the center of Esperanza.

Bananas, Barrio Esperanza, Vieques, PR 00765 (tel. 809/741-8700). During the 1986 filming of the film *Heartbreak Ridge,* the actors and crew transformed this establishment's windswept porch into their second home. Better known for its bar and restaurant than for its rooms, this guesthouse nonetheless contains nine simple but comfortable bedrooms scattered off either end of a high-ceilinged and narrow corridor in back. Each has a private bath and ceiling fan, and about half of them are air-conditioned. Year-round rates range from $40 to $45 daily in a single or double. The real heart of the place, however, is contained within owner Tom Lugrin's pleasant veranda restaurant. In 1981, having left a career in Boston as a computer marketer, he set up this guesthouse with his wife, Debra, in what had been a private home. Open every day in high season between 7:30 a.m. and midnight, the establishment serves meals and potent rum punches to anyone who arrives. You can have deli sandwiches, three different versions of lobster, such local fish as grouper and snapper, Nebraska-bred steaks, and ice cream. Lunches cost $3 to $10; dinners, $5 to $15. Off-season, the place closes between one and two days a week.

The **Trade Winds Guesthouse,** Barrio Esperanza, Vieques, PR 00765 (tel. 809/741-8666). Beside the road on the south side of the island, in the fishing village of Esperanza, this pleasant guesthouse offers nine bedrooms and three apartments. Housed in an angular complex of comfortably decorated buildings, the establishment is well known for its veranda restaurant (see below). Each of the simple rooms has a ceiling fan, and three offer private terraces. High-season prices run $40 daily in a single, $50 in a double. Rooms with terraces, suitable for one or two persons, go for $55 each. A continental breakfast is included in these winter tariffs. *In summer, each accommodation rents for $5 less per night,* but breakfast is not included.

Posada Vistamar, Esperanza, Vieques, PR 00765 (tel. 809/741-8716), is very simple but its convenience to the beach at Sun Bay is an asset. Each of the half dozen bedrooms is in a low-lying motel-like building adjacent to the establishment's restaurant. Each unit has a private bath with twin beds and a ceiling fan. Year round, single or double rooms rent for $25 per night. Astor Luís Benitez and Olga Ortiz are the kindly owners.

WHERE TO DINE: La Campesina (The Country Place), La Hueca (no phone). Consciously designed to look like an Indian shack, this unusual (and excellent) restaurant was built in the forest a few steps from one of the richest archeological deposits of Taíno Indian artifacts in the Caribbean. The location is about six miles southwest of Isabela Segunda in the untrammeled fishing village of La Hueca. The establishment is the creation of a charming Stateside entrepreneur, Stacie Notine, whom newcomers sometimes compare to Sissy Spacek. In a decor lined with baskets and weavings (many by Stacie herself), amid trailing vines and flickering candles, you can enjoy the culinary art of chef Sally Brown. Born in New York, Ms. Brown is beginning to enjoy a wide reputation for her expertise in nouvelle Caribbean cuisine.

Only dinner is served, between 7 and 9:30 p.m. every evening from mid-November to early May. Full meals, priced at from $12, might include lobster ravioli, yellowtail snapper en papillotte, chowders, pungently seasoned shrimp broths, avocado or black-bean soup, chocolate mousse, sorbets, and occasional homemade ice creams. Occasionally a potent form of cocktail is available, including a muleta (made with rum and local fruits) or a billi made with local quenepa, rum, and cognac. The place has no phone, but Ms. Notine's friends at Tradewinds (tel. 741-8666) will arrange reservations and (if it's available) a pickup at your hotel in a mini-van.

Restaurant La Marina, Parador Villa Esperanza, Esperanza (tel. 741-8675), is contained in an octagonal building which the best hotel on the island uses as a dining room. Most guests select a table on the wrap-around veranda, but there's a pleasant wood-sheathed interior if you prefer to dine indoors. Full dinners cost between $13 and $20, and luncheon buffets, held in high season only, go for $10 for all you can eat. Lunch is served from noon to 2:30 p.m. and dinner from 8 to 11 p.m., seven days a week. The well-prepared meals might include shrimp with garlic, conch salad, a spicy and thick version of lobster soup (asopao de langosta), many versions of fresh fish, several different steaks and filet mignon, and thick overstuffed lunchtime sandwiches. The in-house piña coladas are creamy, but after your second or third you may want to switch to a tamaringo (tamarind juice with rum) or a guayacol (guava juice with rum).

The Tradewinds, Barrio Esperanza (tel. 741-8368), is an attractively raffish kind of restaurant where you can enjoy a drink on the veranda bar before moving to the upper sundeck for your meal. The club is open only four days a week, even in high season. Only dinner is served, between 6:30 and 9 p.m. Thursday through Sunday. Menu items which might tempt you include surf and turf, several shrimp dishes, chicken teriyaki, steak Christina (with mushrooms, sour cream, and spices), chicken with lemon and sour-cream sauce, and pompano or grouper en papillotte. Full meals cost from $15 each.

Restaurant El Quenepo, Barrio Esperanza (tel. 741-8541). Named after a large fruit tree growing between it and the nearby coastal road, this open-air pavilion is the year-round domain of Mario Abreu and his wife, Carmen. You dine beneath a raftered ceiling where revolving fans stir up a bit of the indolent air. Natives of Vieques, the Abreus prepare the specialties for which the island is best known: lobster and conch or an octopus salad, certainly a thick and deliciously spicy lobster soup (asopao), many varieties of locally caught fish, and several kinds of chicken. Difficult-to-find local land crabs, when available, are a favorite of many residents, who sometimes spend long weekends in or around this place. Full meals cost $9 to $20 each and are served daily except Tuesday from 9 a.m. to 7 p.m.

Richard's Café, Calle Antonio Mellado, Isabel Segunda (tel. 741-5242). Its oil-cloth decor and low-slung façade might remind you of an unpretentious coffeeshop, but this is actually a substantial restaurant. The location is beside the road near the entrance to town. It's considered one of the most popular and reliable of the inexpensive restaurants on the island. Its outgoing owner, Richard Rivera, is a native-born Viequan. He serves an impressive array of sandwiches (including one with roast pork and cheese known as a "Cubano"). You can order a snail or octopus salad, a T-bone steak, pork chops, and a savory version of asopao made from well-spiced hunks of lobster or shrimp. Full meals cost from $10 each, but one of the sandwiches, averaging around $3, makes an ample repast. The establishment is open daily except Sunday from 11 a.m. to 2:30 p.m. and from 6:30 to 11 p.m.

12. Culebra

A tranquil little island, Culebra lies in a mini-archipelago of 24 chunks of land, rocks, and cays in the sea, halfway between Puerto Rico and St. Thomas, U.S. Virgin Islands. Seven miles long and three miles wide, with nearly 2,000 residents, the inviting little island is in U.S. territorial waters belonging to Puerto Rico, 18 miles away. This little-known, year-round vacation spot in what was once called the Spanish Virgin Islands was settled as a Spanish colony in 1886, but like Puerto Rico and Vieques, it became part of the U.S. after the Spanish-American War in 1898. In fact Culebra's only town, **Dewey,** was named for Adm. George Dewey, American hero of that war, although the locals call the fishing village **Puebla.**

For a long time, beginning in 1909, Culebra was used by the U.S. Navy as a gunnery range, even becoming a practice bomb site in World War II. In 1975, after years of protest over military abuse of the island's environment, the navy withdrew from Culebra, with the understanding that the island be kept as a nature preserve and habitat for the many rare species of birds, turtles, and fish that abound there. The four tracts of the Culebra Wildlife Refuge, plus 23 other offshore islands, are managed by the U.S. Fish and Wildlife Service. Culebra is one of the most important turtle-nesting sites in the Caribbean. Large seabird colonies, notably terns and boobies, are seen.

Today vacationers and boating people can explore the island's beauties, both on land and in the sea. Culebra's white sand beaches—especially Flamenco Beach—the clear waters, and long coral reefs invite swimmers, snorkelers, and scuba-divers. The landscape ranges from scrub and cactus to poincianas, frangipanis, and coconut palms.

Culebrita, a mile-long coral isle satellite of Culebra, has a hilltop lighthouse and crescent beaches.

GETTING THERE: As with Vieques, you can take a small plane or a ferry to Culebra from Puerto Rico. A flight from San Juan's Isla Grande Airport takes about 40 minutes and costs around $35. The ferry trips from Fajardo last about an hour and three-quarters and cost $2.25. You can also fly from St. Thomas, U.S.V.I., to Culebra for around $35.

WATER SPORTS AND SAILING: Increasing numbers of divers have recognized Culebra as a treasure trove of marine zoology. The best and most experienced dive operation there is **CUDA, Culebra Underwater Diving Association** (tel. 742-3839). It was created by an Ohio-born entrepreneur, Jim Kneaskern. After escaping from his engineer's job in Cleveland, he adopted as a full-time career his hobby of exploring an underwater world.

Culebra School of Sailing (tel. 742-3839) is owned and operated by Hugh and Diane Callum, who hail from Indiana and Québec, respectively. Daily sails cost $25 per hour. At their disposal is a regatta of five sailboats which vary between 27 and 48 feet in length. Currently this is the only sailing school on the island. It operates out of the Callums' home on a 42-foot sailboat moored off Enseñada Honda.

WHERE TO STAY: The **Club Seabourne,** P.O. Box 357, Culebra, PR 00645 (tel. 809/742-3169), one of the newest hotels on the island, sits across the road from an inlet of the sea about an eight-minute drive from the center of town. You'll find a pink-and-white clapboard building prefaced with an oval pool and a well-built terrace out of which sprouts a tree. The establishment's communal area is beneath a cathedral ceiling, off which lie the eight elegantly simple bedrooms. Most of these are found in chalet-style outbuildings for additional privacy. However, the conviviality of the poolside restaurant is never far away. Year-round rates range from $75 to $100 nightly for two persons. This place is within a garden of crotons and palms, lying at the mouth of one of the island's best harbors, Enseñada Honda. The owners are also the managers of a sailboat-chartering business in case you want to rent a boat.

Flamenco Resort and Fishing Club, P.O. Box 241, Culebra, PR 00645 (tel. 809/721-0695), is the only guesthouse or hotel which lies close to the white sands of one of the best beaches in the region, Flamenco Beach. Its location, coupled with the grace and charm of the friendly owners, Rafael and Yvette Mena, sometimes produce a special, albeit isolated, kind of vacation. The establishment's concrete walls jut abruptly above a flat sandy lawn, planted with palms and almond trees. It contains only eight rooms, though not all have a private bath. Each unit has access to a communal kitchen. The place would really be ideal for a cluster of friends or an extended family since the accommodations are arranged around spacious sitting rooms much like those in an informal beach house. Per-person rates year round cost $35 daily in a single, $20 in a double, $16 in a triple, and $14 in a quad. The Menas operate a small store on the premises where guests can stock up on food staples, but most meals are consumed in a simple windswept oceanside terrace where soaring sea grapes rising overhead create an atmosphere a bit like that of a gazebo. An array of supplemental diversions includes day trips on a sailboat to one of the nearby islands, snorkeling, and fishing expeditions.

Punta Aloe, P.O. Box 207, Culebra, PR 00645 (tel. 809/742-3167), is a series of waterfront homes on Culebra's beautiful Enseñada Honda (bay). Each villa has a large deck overlooking the bay and/or the sea, two bedrooms (one with a queen-size bed and one with two singles), two baths, a living room/kitchen, and two additional sofas for sitting or sleeping. Kitchens are fully equipped. Rates year round are from $295 per week for a couple at the guesthouse to $495 per week for a villa accommodating up to six guests. Free use of a washing machine and of windsurfers and snorkeling gear is provided, and cars and boats are available for rental by guests. Your hosts are Tania and Dick Hayes.

Villa Boheme, Enseñada Honda (P.O. Box 218), Culebra, PR 00645 (tel. 809/742-3508). Trade winds blow through the five bedrooms and one apartment offered for by-the-week rental by former Maine resident Renée Coolman, who maintains what's become almost a mini-marina, where access to the many craft bobbing in the harbor is made easier by the on-site wharf extending into the bay from the backyard of the guesthouse. The units are arranged in a split-level format, each with its own private entrance, a view of the harbor, a king-size bed, a table or ceiling fan, windows protected by metal louvers, and a private bath. No meals are served, but there are two communal kitchens where guests can prepare their own meals. Also, several restaurants are within walking distance. The apartment includes a full kitchen and rents for $485 per week year round, although it is usually left vacant in summer. The five rooms cost $360 a week in winter and *$310 in summer,* single or double occupancy.

Villa Fulladoza, P.O. Box 162, Culebra, PR 00645 (tel. 809/742-3576). Built as a three-unit apartment house in 1982 by a Culebra-born sailor, Carlos Feliciano, and his wife, Norma, this place is unpretentious, clean, and pleasant. Its small, sandy backyard abuts the harbor, where you can admire the marine activity of the moored boats. Each of the trio of units contains its own bathroom, kitchenette, ceiling fan, and TV. My favorite is on the upper floor, a room which benefits from access to the building's pebble-decorated upper veranda. Accommodations cost $200 for a seven-day rental or $38 per day for two persons. The location is about a quarter mile east of town and a five-minute walk from a grocery store. It remains open all year.

Coral Island Guest House, P.O. Box 396, Culebra, PR 00645 (tel. 809/742-3177). Until Colorado-born Chuck Bickley took over, this four-room guesthouse stood in serious danger of falling into total disrepair. Even today it's probably the most raffish little accommodation alongside the port, with dormitory-style bedrooms which most often share a bath. Despite its lack of glamour, you're almost certain to meet an array of nautically minded residents who quickly fall under the spell of the urbane and genteel owner who is considered the best piano player on the island. Each pair of rooms shares a common bathroom, and two communal kitchens are at the disposal of guests. Rooms are scattered over two floors of a concrete building, and each has its own ceiling fan. Year-round rates are $25 daily in a single, $35 in a double.

WHERE TO EAT: Located behind a low-slung façade near the port, across the street from the Town Hall, **El Pescador,** 14 Pedro Margúez (tel. 742-3175), offers the best food and some of the most carefully planned ambience on the island. Virtually every yachtsman visiting Culebra, including members of the Yachting Club of Austria, enjoys at least one drink around the copious bar in the anteroom. Born in New York, Chuck Licci is the capable owner and bartender of this place. Having met a woman from Culebra in New York, he married her and moved to the island of her parents in 1981. Today the kitchen specializes in fresh seafood, including seafood salad, sautéed shrimp, breaded shrimp, conch salad, eggplant parmesan, and the catch of the day. You can also enjoy hearty chunks of such steaks as New York strip with onions, stuffed peppers, or such pasta dishes as lasagne or ziti. Full meals cost from $12, and the average price for one of the thick sandwiches served at the bar is only $2. Full meals are served only in the evening from 6 to 10 p.m. seven days a week in summer. In winter El Pescador is closed on Tuesday.

    Tina's (El Caobo Restaurant), Calle Muñoz Marín, Sector Clark (tel. 742-3235). Except for the friendly welcome offered by the owner, this would be little more than an open veranda with a tin ceiling, slightly rickety tables, and floor fans. The location is in a poor residential neighborhood within a seven-minute walk north of the center of town. Andres Abreo named his friendly restaurant after his wife, Tina. It opens early every morning, keeping no set hours, as it melds breakfast, lunch, and dinner into one long socializing session. Full dinners cost from $10 and might include lobster, octopus, fish fries, rice with beans, meat pies, and various kinds of beefsteak. Lunchtime sandwiches cost $2 each, and a full breakfast goes for only $1.75. Any of these meals is washed down, local style, with a can of cold beer which everyone on the island seems to fetch for himself from the frost-dappled refrigerator in back.

    El Batey (tel. 742-3828) across from the harbor, is a large, clean place which maintains a full bar as well as an array of deli-style sandwiches, costing around $4.50. Coffee and doughnuts are served every morning. Beer is a popular drink, and the pool tables make the place lively, especially on weekends when many locals throng in. Weekdays, it's much calmer. The owners, Digna Feliciano and Tomás Ayala, are friendly and have many fans on the island. Breezes from the harbor cool the place. Service is from 10 a.m. to 10 p.m. Closed Monday.

Chapter V

THE U.S. VIRGIN ISLANDS

1. St. Thomas
2. St. John
3. St. Croix

SEPARATING THE ATLANTIC from the Caribbean, the U.S. Virgin Islands —St. Thomas, St. John, and St. Croix—enjoy one of the most perfect year-round climates in the world. They lie directly in the belt of the subtropical, easterly trade winds. At the eastern end of the Greater Antilles and the northern tip of the Lesser Antilles, the U.S. Virgins are some 40 miles east of Puerto Rico, 1,400 miles southeast of New York City, and 1,000 miles east-southeast of Miami. Some of their sugar-white beaches, experts cite, are among the most beautiful on the globe.

Christopher Columbus (there's that name again) discovered the Virgin Islands on his second voyage to the New World, in 1493. He anchored at Salt River on St. Croix, naming the islands for St. Ursula and her 10,999 virgins martyred by the Huns at Cologne in the Middle Ages.

In 1666 the Danes took formal possession of St. Thomas, changing the name of its capital to Charlotte Amalie in 1691. St. Thomas was divided into plantations, and an attempt was also made to colonize the island with convicts and prostitutes.

To help guard the Panama Canal, the United States purchased the islands in 1917 at a cost of $25 million, a price considered scandalously high at the time. Of course, the Americans feared German U-boat flotillas. These American outposts in the Caribbean today have territorial status, governed by an elected 15-member legislature and a governor.

GETTING TO ST. THOMAS AND ST. CROIX: Travelers living in the northeast quadrant of the United States will probably find that **American Airlines** offers the easiest link to and from the two Virgin Islands. Two flights leave within 90 minutes of one another from New York's JFK Airport every morning. Both planes fly nonstop to St. Thomas, where passengers transfer on to St. Croix, often on another aircraft. Passengers bound for St. Croix usually choose the second of American's daily flights because the connection in St. Thomas is more efficient. Travelers can arrange to have their luggage routed directly to their final destination. In the afternoon, both flights return to New York, both originating in St. Thomas and then touching down briefly to pick up passengers in St. Croix before continuing on nonstop to New York. American makes its flights convenient for Boston-based travelers, since the airline offers excellent connections to and from that city for persons traveling to or from the Virgin Islands.

Bargain-seeking passengers can always call American and ask to be connected with the tour desk. There, someone can arrange discount air passage if a hotel reservation is made through American at the same time. A wide array of accommodations and flight dates is available, although the options are so varied and complicated that only an airline staff member (or a travel agent) can describe them in detail. Most travelers, however, opt for a cost-conscious APEX ticket, whose simple restrictions don't usually present any hardship. It requires a seven-day advance purchase and a delay of 3 to 30 days before you can use the return half of your ticket. If you change any detail of your passage before departure from North America, American will impose a $50 penalty. Changes in the date, but not in the routing of your return, are permitted without any penalty once you arrive at the farthest point of your itinerary. As with any airline, American's APEX fares vary with the season, and travel in both directions on a weekday usually qualifies a passenger for a slightly reduced fare.

For passengers whose schedules don't permit a seven-day advance purchase and a stopover of 3 to 30 days, it still pays to reserve and pay for a ticket as far in advance as possible. For promotional purposes, American keeps a controlled inventory of coach-class seats on each of its flights which cost less than the regular coach-class fares. If your schedule is flexible and you're looking for one-way passage, ask an American Airlines reservations clerk for his or her advice about the cheapest way to travel. American uses wide-body DC-10s and stretch 727s for the longest legs of the New York–U.S. Virgin Islands route, which usually lasts around 3½ hours. The flight between St. Thomas and St. Croix takes about 20 minutes.

Hint: A flight to the U.S. Virgin Islands is sometimes less expensive if you request a change of aircraft at American's glistening new hub in nearby Puerto Rico. The airline's service from many parts of North America changes aircraft there before being rechanneled to scattered parts of the Caribbean basin on smaller planes. These are usually owned by American's partner, **American Eagle.** This routing, which may or may not have an efficient connection depending on many factors, might save you around $65 over the APEX fare on a nonstop flight from new York.

If you're coming from Miami, you'll find that **Eastern Airlines** has nonstop jet service from Miami to St. Thomas / St. Croix. Eastern also provides connections from many cities throughout the north and the southeast to its flights from Miami to the U.S. Virgins.

To compare prices and routings, be sure to check the **Pan American** daily nonstop service from New York to St. Thomas. As with American, Pan Am's flights touch down first on St. Thomas before continuing on to St. Croix. Pan Am routes Middle Atlantic and midwestern passengers through Miami. A daily nonstop flight departs Miami every day at 5:40 p.m., leaving plenty of time to hook up with connections from the rest of the country before continuing nonstop to St. Croix.

For information on getting to St. John, refer to Section 2 in this chapter.

PRACTICAL FACTS: Since the Stars and Stripes fly over these islands with their old-world Danish towns, you don't have a language barrier and you don't have to exchange the Yankee dollar for some other currency.

Of course, the big attraction of St. Croix and St. Thomas, in addition to serving as a winter playpen and an increasing summer destination, is that every U.S. resident can bring home $800 worth of duty-free purchases, including a gallon of alcoholic beverages per adult. In addition, you can mail home an unlimited amount in gifts valued at up to $100 each. (At other spots in the Caribbean, U.S. citizens are limited to $400 worth of merchandise and a single bottle.)

Whatever appliances you use on the mainland (hair dryer, etc.), should work for you in St. Thomas. The **electrical current** in the Virgin Islands is the same as on the mainland: 120 volts, 60 cycles, A. C. No adapter or converter is necessary.

As for **time,** when it's 6 a.m. in Charlotte Amalie, it's still 5 a.m. in Miami. The U.S. Virgins are on Atlantic Time, which places the islands an hour ahead of Eastern Standard Time. When the east coast goes on Daylight Saving Time, Virgin Island clocks and those on the mainland record the same time.

Several major **banks** are represented in St. Thomas, and they are usually open from 9 a.m. to 2:30 p.m. Monday to Thursday. Friday hours are different: 9 a.m. to 2 p.m. and 3:30 to 5 p.m.

Since the Virgin Islands are part of the U.S. Postal System, postage rates are the same as on the mainland.

Remember to drive on the left, a carryover from Danish rule, and obey speed laws, which are 20 mph in town, 35 mph outside.

Virgin Islanders celebrate a total of 24 legal **holidays**! In addition to the standard ones, they observe the following: January 6 (Three Kings' Day); January 15 (Martin Luther King's birthday); March 31 (Transfer Day—transfer of the Danish Virgin Islands to the Americans); April 29 (Children's Carnival Parade); April 30 (Grand Carnival Parade); June 20 (Organic Act Day—in lieu of a constitution, they have an "Organic Act"); July 3 (Emancipation Day, commemorating the freeing of the slaves by the Danes in 1848); July 25 (hurricane supplication day); October 17 (hurricane thanksgiving day); November 1 (Liberty Day); and December 26 (Boxing Day).

For a local call at a **telephone** booth, place 25¢ into the meter. From many points on the mainland you can dial direct to the Virgin Islands (or vice versa). Cable service is available as well.

Daily newspapers from the mainland are flown in to St. Thomas and St. Croix every day, and local papers such as the *Virgin Island Daily News* on both islands also carry the latest news.

St. Thomas receives both cable and commercial TV stations. Radio weather reports can be heard at 7:30 p.m. and 8:30 a.m. on 99.5 FM.

In **hospitals,** St. Thomas has the 200-bed Knud Hansen Memorial (tel. 774-9000), with an emergency room open 24 hours a day. There is also the St. Thomas Hospital and Community Center (tel. 776-8311).

In St. John there is the DeCastro Clinic (tel. 776-6461) in Cruz Bay and the more recent St. John Hospital and Community Center at Centerline (tel. 776-6400).

St. Croix is well equipped with hospitals, including the Charles Harwood Memorial (tel. 773-2099) and the St. Croix Hospital (tel. 773-8311), both at Christiansted, and Ingerborg Nesbitt Clinic at Frederiksted (tel. 772-0260).

As a general **tipping** rule, it is customary to tip 15%. Some hotels add a 10% to 15% surcharge to cover service. When in doubt, ask.

There is ample water for showers and bathing in the Virgin Islands, but you are asked to conserve. Hotels will supply you with all your water for drinking.

1. St. Thomas

The busiest cruise-ship harbor in the West Indies, St. Thomas is the second largest of the U.S. Virgins, lying about 40 miles north of St. Croix, which is larger. St. Thomas, with its capital at **Charlotte Amalie,** is about 12 miles long and 3 miles wide. The capital is also the shopping center of the Caribbean (refer to the section on what to buy).

Hotels on the north side of St. Thomas look out onto the Atlantic, and those on the south side front the calmer Caribbean. It's possible for the sun to shine in the south as the north experiences showers.

January and February are the coolest period, recording lows around 60° Fahrenheit, but highs in the 80s. August is the hottest time, with daily peaks in the high 80s. The temperature drops to the 70s at night.

Holiday makers discovered St. Thomas right after World War II, and they've been flocking back ever since in increasing numbers. Shopping, sights, and sun prove a potent lure. Tourism has raised the standard of living here until it is one of the highest in the Caribbean. Condominium apartments have grown up over the debris of bull-dozed shacks.

In all honesty, I must point out that St. Thomas is not paradise for all our visitors. Many readers have written in to make the same point: "It's strictly for cruise ship passengers in town to shop." There have been many complaints about hostility to visitors, and the area around the waterfront and the little alleyways shooting off from Back street are not considered safe at night. Be duly warned.

If you're visiting in August, make sure you carry along mosquito repellent.

GETTING AROUND: The chief means of transport is the **taxi,** which is unmetered. Therefore it is important to agree with the driver *before* you get into the car. Actually, taxi fares are controlled and are widely posted, perhaps at your hotel desk. In St. Thomas cabs are plentiful. Most trips cost only $3.50 to $7. For example, a transfer from the airport to Bolongo Bay is about $7 for the first passenger. Surcharges, ranging from $1 to $1.50, are added on after midnight. If you rent a taxi and a driver (who just may serve as a guide) for the day, the cost is about $25 for two persons for two hours of sightseeing. Each additional passenger pays another $12.

St. Thomas has what they call an *open air "taxi bus."* Departures are from Red Hook dock on the hour from 7:15 a.m. to 6:15 p.m. They also depart from the Market Place for Red Hook on the hour from 8:15 a.m. to 5:15 p.m., costing $2 for a one-way ticket.

Manassah Country Bus goes between Charlotte Amalie and Red Hook nearly every hour. Service starts at 6 a.m. from Charlotte Amalie, ending at the last run at 8 p.m. from Red Hook, all for a one-way ticket cost of 75¢. Throughout the day, other buses depart from the Market Place in Charlotte Amalie, heading across St. Thomas as far west as Bordeaux, a one-way passage going for 75¢. For information about exact schedules, telephone 774-5678.

A **Safari Bus,** which goes from Market Square to Red Hook, departs hourly on the quarter hour at a one-way cost of $2 per passenger.

Car Rentals

St. Thomas has a lot of cars to rent and a lot of agencies, and rates, I feel, are pretty steep. Naturally, the big names, such as **Hertz** (tel. 774-1897) and **Avis** (tel. 774-1468), are here, as is **National** (tel. 774-6220). You'll find these companies operating out of expensive kiosks at the airport.

On a recent trip, I used **Budget Rent-a-Car** and found that their high-season rates, including insurance, were slightly less than those charged at Hertz or Avis. This is still true, but circumstances could change by the time of your visit. To find out, you can call Avis toll free at 800/331-1212 or Hertz toll free at 00/654-3131. Budget's toll-free reservations service is 800/527-0700. Budget maintains offices at the St. Thomas airport (tel. 774-5774) and at the St. Thomas Sub Base (tel. 776-5774). Most travelers use the airport branch, which is in the arrivals hall.

All but the cheapest vehicles rented by Budget in St. Thomas come with automatic transmission and air conditioning as standard features. The least expensive car in high season is a Chevy Sprint, which seats four persons in comfort, with space for luggage. Weekly rentals without air conditioning but with unlimited mileage included cost $220 per week or $32 per day. With air conditioning, the cost goes up to $270 per week or $39 per day. These are all high-season tariffs, which are lowered in summer. To qualify for the rates listed, you must reserve a vehicle at least two business days in advance by calling Budget's toll-free number given above. Vehicles are well-maintained, clean, and late models, and I found the staff to be courteous.

All of St. Thomas's major rental companies require that in the event of an accident, the driver must pay for the first many hundred dollars of the repair cost unless additional insurance is arranged. If the driver does not purchase the added insurance, he or she is obligated to pay up to the first $1,500 worth of damage should a mishap occur with a Budget car. At both Hertz and Avis, uninsured drivers are responsible for up to $3,000 worth of collision damage. All three agencies charge about $8 per day for this extra insurance. Additional personal accident insurance is available at all agencies for $2.50 per day.

Sightseeing Tours

American Sightseeing International is headquartered at Travel Services, Inc., in the Red Hook Shopping Center, Upper Level (tel. 775-9035), and can provide visitors with a private car and driver. The air-conditioned vans are $40 per hour and can seat up to ten passengers. The tour of the island generally takes two hours, three hours if Coral World is included.

Local Air Services

If you'd like to hop over to St. Croix or perhaps Tortola (the capital of the British Virgin Islands), call on **Virgin Islands Seaplane Shuttle.** For reservations, telephone 773-1776. The seaplane also flies to St. John in case you don't want to take the ferryboat.

HOTELS: There are more hotels in the Virgin Islands than anywhere else in the Caribbean. Nearly every beach has its own hostelry. You're faced with a choice of staying in the capital, Charlotte Amalie, or at any of the far points of St. Thomas. Perhaps St. Thomas has more inns of character than anyplace else in the Caribbean. I've included a wide-ranging survey, hoping to find the one place that will meet your needs. Rates are subject to a 7½% government tax.

Luxury Leaders

Bluebeard's Castle, P.O. Box 7480, Charlotte Amalie, VI 00801 (tel. 809/744-1600, or toll free 800/524-6599), is almost a monument in St. Thomas, a popular, all-around resort lying on one side of the bay overlooking Charlotte Amalie. The history of this spot is long, as it dates from 1665. The U.S. government turned what had been a private home into a hotel in the 1930s, on one occasion attracting Franklin D. Roosevelt. Over the years, Bluebeard's has had many additions and extensions to accommodate the ever-increasing throng of holiday makers. When cruise ships are in the harbor, groups of tourists arrive by the busload, swarming through the buildings with their well-tended gardens, old trees, and flowery shrubbery. But, in time, they go back to their vessels, and you have the 20-acre site to yourself, along with your fellow guests. Not for beach buffs, the hotel has a freshwater swimming pool and two whirlpools, but the guests are also provided free transportation to famous Magens Bay Beach. Championship tennis courts are on the premises.

Bedchambers come in a wide variety of shapes and sizes—110 units in all, pleasantly decorated and air-conditioned. You may find the best way to stay here is on a package deal (ask your travel agent what is currently offered). Otherwise, winter rates in a single range from $165 to $195 daily and from $170 to $198 in a double. Add $42 per person extra per day for breakfast and dinner. *In summer, tariffs are lowered. Singles pay $122 to $172 daily and two persons $125 to $175*. More expensive suites, some with parlors, are also available. The Terrace Restaurant commands a breathtaking view and offers many American and Caribbean specialties as well as West Indian cookery, open-air brunching, lunching, or late-night dining.

Stouffer Grand Beach Resort, P.O. Box 8267, Charlotte Amalie, VI 00801 (tel. 809/775-1510). Perched on a steep hillside above a narrow beach, this dramatic

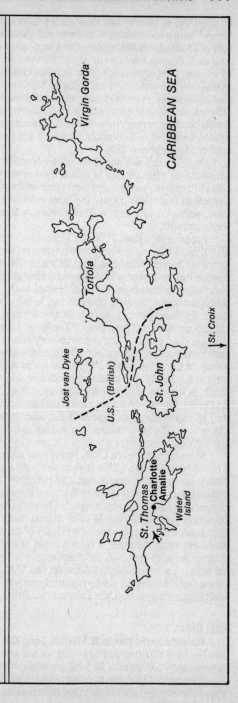

THE VIRGIN ISLANDS

hotel proved so alluring that its original builder duplicated it later on St. John. It's derived from a combination of futuristic and classical models, including Palladian. A total of 13 shingle-roofed buildings are interconnected by steeply inclined roads which an armada of open-sided cars navigate. After you register, you are driven to your room by a friendly employee. Each of the accommodations is stylishly and plushly outfitted in shades of rose and mauve and encircled with a conglomeration of acute angles, fan-shaped windows, open balconies, and sophisticated lighting. Each of the suites has Jacuzzis, and all units contain color TV, mini-bar, and phone. Winter rates, single or double occupancy, range from $250 to $340 per night. *Summer tariffs, either single or double, cost $190 to $230 daily, plus taxis and services.* MAP can be arranged for another $45 per person daily.

On the premises is one of the most innovative swimming pools in St. Thomas, whose zigzag edges create a hi-tech version of an Aztec ritual bath, plus an alluring collection of boutiques, a water-sports desk where you can rent sailboats or snorkeling equipment, and tennis courts. The hotel restaurant offers good food and entertainment, perhaps a jazz harpist. Bruce Hearn, a former naval aviator, is the capable young manager.

Frenchman's Reef, P.O. Box 7100, Charlotte Amalie, VI 00801 (tel. 809/776-8500), has a winning southern position on a projection of land overlooking both the harbor at Charlotte Amalie and the Caribbean. The hotel stands in such a conspicuous position that the traveler with the worst possible sense of direction can't help but find it. Everywhere you look are facilities devoted to the good life—two giant swimming pools, suntanning areas, a poolside bar, tennis courts, every kind of water sports (snorkeling, scuba-diving, sailing, deep-sea fishing). Whatever your holiday needs, chances are you'll find them met at "The Reef." To reach the private beach, you take a glass-enclosed elevator. The bedrooms vary greatly, but in general are furnished in a traditional manner, with various color groups and quite good taste. In winter, except during the Christmas season when prices are increased, singles or doubles range from $208 to $268 daily. For breakfast and dinner, add about $42 per person to the room tariffs. *In summer, singles or doubles cost $158 to $218 daily.* Good food is served in the Gazebo Room, which has a view of the harbor, and you can also get simple meals at the Lighthouse Bar, once an actual lighthouse. In the evening, the Top of the Reef, a supper club, offers entertainment, or you can go to La Terraza lounge. The Lighthouse Bar is another possibility.

Morning Star Beach Club, Frenchman's Reef Beach Resort, Charlotte Amalie VI 00802 (tel. 809/776-8500). Both its public areas and its plushly outfitted accommodations are among the most desirable on the island. They were built on the landscaped flatlands near the beach of the well-known Frenchman's Reef Beach Resort, as the elegant twin sister of the older hotel. The resort has five cruciform buildings, each containing between 16 and 24 units. Guests have the amenities and attractions of a large hotel nearby, yet maintain the privacy of an exclusive enclave. Each accommodation has rattan furniture, a color scheme of lilac, plum, and red mahogany, and views of the garden or beach. In winter, singles or doubles cost between $300 and $350 per night. *In summer, singles or doubles run $220 daily.* MAP costs another $40 per person daily. Swimming can be supplemented with a wide array of water sports. The establishment's restaurant, the Tavern on the Beach, is recommended separately.

First Class

Ramada Yacht Haven & Marina, Long Bay Road (P.O. Box 7970), Charlotte Amalie, VI 00801 (tel. 809/774-9700, or toll free 800/2-RAMADA). In 1982 this large property underwent a $2.5-million renovation and later was endorsed by Ramada as a member of its chain. Its centerpiece is a trio of interconnected swimming pools whose core is belted with a footbridge and a handful of splashing waterfalls. You enter a pink-toned lobby, whose large blue-and-white murals are illuminated by a soaring wall of tiny-paned windows. Some of the accommodations have been sold as private vacationers' apartments, but 150 of them ring the gardens where footpaths pass beside shrubbery and gazebos capped with cedar shingles. Each room contains large twin or king-size beds, air conditioning, tile bathrooms, radio, and color TV with satellite reception. Single or double rooms rent for $125 to $180 daily in winter, *from $100 to $135 daily in summer,* depending on size and exposure. MAP can be arranged for another $35 per person daily, plus tax and service. One of my preferred spots is in the breeze-filled restaurant, where you sit on a modern version of a Victorian veranda, within view of the docks and moorings of one of the biggest marinas in the Caribbean.

Pavilions & Pools, Rte. 6, Charlotte Amalie, VI 00802 (tel. 809/775-6110), is ideal for either a honeymoon or an off-the-record weekend. It seems the ultimate in small-scale luxury—your own air-conditioned villa, with floor-to-ceiling glass doors opening directly onto your own private swimming pool. The resort is a string of condominium units, built and furnished with good taste. After checking in and following a wooden pathway to your attached villa, you don't have to see another soul until you check out, if that is your desire. The fence and gate are high, and your space opens into tropical greenery. Around your own swimming pool is an encircling deck. Inside, a high room divider screens a full, well-equipped kitchen. Each bedroom has its own style, with plenty of closets behind louvered doors. the bath may intrigue you, as it has a garden shower where you can bathe surrounded by greenery, yet are protected from Peeping Toms. Inquire about honeymoon packages if that's what you're on. Otherwise, in winter expect to pay $183 to $193 daily in a double. *Two persons in summer pay $119 to $129 daily.* A small bar and barbecue area is set against a wall on the reception terrace, and here rum parties and cookouts are staged. There's also an informal dining room. Occasionally a musician or singer will entertain. There's free use of snorkeling gear, and you also can play on adjacent tennis courts. The resort adjoins Sapphire Bay with its good beach.

Limetree Beach Hotel, P.O. Box 7307, Charlotte Amalie, VI 00801 (tel. 809/776-4770, or toll free 800/524-2007), nestled on Frenchman's Cove, is a very private, very pleasant collection of well-built three-story bungalows set on a hillside above the sea. After registering in the comfortably airy public rooms, guests move into their simple but attractive units, each of which is air-conditioned and contains a phone, TV, and a private bath, and lies only a few steps from the white sands of the palm-fringed beach. On the premises are two floodlit tennis courts and an amply proportioned swimming pool shaped like a modified boomerang. The cheerful staff presents live entertainment every night, which is likely to include a King Voodoo show. Snorkeling, scuba, and sailing can be arranged upon request. Charlotte Amalie is only a ten-minute drive away, but because of the resort's southern shore seclusion, you'd think it was far more distant. In winter, singles range from $175 to $190, while double cost $190 to $205. Each additional person pays an extra $40. *In summer, singles range from $110 to $120 and doubles go for $120 to $145. Triples cost $140 to $170, while quads are $170 to $190.* All tariffs include a full breakfast. Refrigerators can be rented for an additional $6 a day.

Inns of Character

Hotel 1829, Kongens Gade (Danish for Kings Street; P.O. Box 1567), Charlotte Amalie, VI 00802 (tel. 809/774-1829), is my favorite nest in St. Thomas. After a major renaissance, this once-decaying historical site has become one of the leading small hotels of character in the Caribbean. Right in the heart of town, it stands about three minutes from Government House, built on a hillside with many levels and many steps (no elevator). It is reached by a climb. The hotel is the prize possession of Vernon and Eva Ball. He's from Ohio—and known as the ''Bobby Fisher of backgammon''—

and she's from the enchanting little German village of Dinkelsbuhl. The Baron and Baroness Ball (he purchased the title from an Italian nobleman) have wisely selected a considerate, thoughtful staff, many of them virtually in the "family retainer" category. The 1829 has actually been a hotel since the 19th century, entertaining such celebrated guests as King Carol of Rumania (and his mistress, Madame Lupescu), Suzy Parker, Edna St. Vincent Millay, and Mikhail Baryshnikov.

Amid a cascade of flowering bougainvillea, you can reach the upper rooms which overlook a central courtyard with a miniature swimming pool. The units, some of which are small, are beautifully designed, comfortable, and attractive, but don't expect phones, TVs, or room service. In the restoration, the old was preserved whenever possible. In high season, the cheapest and smallest double rents for $80 daily, a single for $70. All have baths and air conditioning. However, superior and deluxe doubles range in price from $110 to $165 daily; singles in that category cost $105 to $165. A few special suites cost $230 to $335 for two persons. There are only a dozen rooms in all, most of which face the sea. A few have antiques such as four-poster beds. *In summer, singles range from $55 to $110 daily, with doubles costing $65 to $120. Two persons can rent a suite for $155.* The hotel cannot take children under 12.

Harbor View, Frenchman's Hill (P.O. Box 1975), Charlotte Amalie, VI 00801 (tel. 809/774-2651), was a once-scandalous *maison de tolerance,* built in the 1700s by French Huguenot political refugees at the western edge of Charlotte Amalie. After a remarkable transformation by two cosmopolitan American women, Arlene Lockwood and Lenore Wolfe, it became not only one of the finest restaurants in St. Thomas (see my dining recommendations) but an inn, often touted as "the most sophisticated small hotel in the West Indies." The women visited the hotel when it was a wreck. When word reached them in New York that it was for sale, they flew here and bought it, creating a small wonder and opening it in the early 1960s. They brought individuality and chic to the ten air-conditioned bedrooms, which contain many four-poster beds, old chests, dressing tables, mellow paintings, flower prints, and, of course, coordinated fabrics at the windows and on the beds. Guests have access to the garden living room and a swimming pool combined. It's like a classic terraced garden in Portofino; *Harper's Bazaar* called it "very Tennessee Williams." Winter rates, in effect from November 1 to May 1, are $90 in a double and $75 in a single. *In the off-season, lasting from May 1 to Labor Day, prices go down: $60 daily in a double and $40 in a single.* Rates include a continental breakfast, and a full breakfast is available at an extra charge. Lunch is available to house guests, except on Tuesday.

Galleon House, P.O. Box 6577, Charlotte Amalie, VI 00801 (tel. 809/774-6952, or toll free 800/524-2052). You walk up a long flight of stairs past a neighboring restaurant's veranda to reach the concrete terrace that doubles as this hotel's reception area. The ten rooms are scattered in several hillside buildings, and each contains a ceiling fan or air conditioning. There's even a small pool on the grounds. The main attraction of this place is its location, set next to the Hotel 1829 on Government Hill about one block from the main shopping section of St. Thomas. Cordell and Elise Tittle are the directors of this bed-and-breakfast house, having rebuilt it after a disastrous fire which closed an older establishment on the same premises. Winter rates for singles range from $40 to $70, while doubles cost $45 to $95. *Summer prices go down to $35 to $55 in a single, $40 to $70 in a double.* A third person in any double costs an additional $10 per day. A continental breakfast is included in the tariffs.

Blackbeard's Castle, P.O. Box 6041, Charlotte Amalie, VI 00801 (tel. 809/776-1234), required the inspiration of an Illinois businessman to transform what had been a private residence into a genuinely charming five-room inn. It enjoys one of the finest views of Charlotte Amalie and its harbor, thanks to its perch high on a hillside above town. The owner, Bob Harrington, wasn't alone in his appreciation of this location. In 1679 the Danish governor erected a soaring tower of chiseled stone as a lookout for unfriendly ships. Legend says that Blackbeard himself lived in the tower half a century later. Today the Brazilian-born co-owner, Henrique Konzen, contributed to the design ideas that flavor the bedrooms. Each has some kind of semi-secluded lattice-enclosed veranda, a flat-weave Turkish kilim, air conditioning, cable TV, terracotta floors, and consciously simple furniture, along with private baths. *In summer, singles or doubles cost $100 to $125 daily*, rising in winter to $125 to $160, plus tax. A continental breakfast is included. Guests enjoy use of a swimming pool whose waters almost lap the edge of the famous tower. The establishment's social center is within the stylish bar and restaurant, which is covered later.

Small, Special Resorts

Secret Harbour Beach Hotel, P.O. Box 7576, Charlotte Amalie, VI 00801 (tel. 809/775-1010, or toll free 800/524-2250), directly on the beach at Nazareth Bay, built in a contemporary style on the south coast, about a 15-minute ride from Charlotte Amalie. At first you'll think you've arrived at a South Seas island beach resort, set apart from civilization. Spread out in a setting of tall palm trees is a row of air-conditioned accommodations. Dating from 1969, it was the first condominium apartment complex to open in St. Thomas. Each suite or bedroom has its own private veranda, and the rooms have a distinct charm, as they are decorated to the taste of each individual owner. There are three kinds of accommodations: studio apartments with a bed-sitting room, patio, and bath, as well as a dressing room; one-bedroom suites with a living/dining area, a separate bedroom and bath, plus a sun gallery; and the most luxurious—a two-bedroom suite with two baths. Accommodations have fully equipped kitchens. *In summer, a studio apartment for two persons costs $98 daily, going up to $115 for a one-bedroom apartment and peaking at $175 for a two-bedroom unit suitable for four guests.* In winter, a two-person studio apartment costs $155 daily, rising to $198 for a one-bedroom apartment, and peaking at $295 for a two-bedroom apartment suitable for four guests. Certain shoulder-season reductions are granted, usually from mid-November to right before Christmas and for most of the month of April. All rates are subject to a 7½% tax and 10% service charge. The Bird of Paradise restaurant, previewed later, offers lunch on an outdoor terrace in a setting on the beach. Or else you can dine inside. Before that, you may want to go to the Beach Bar or Gazebo for drinks. There's a full water-sports center on the beach, and two new championship tennis courts.

Bolongo Bay Beach Hotel and Tennis Club, P.O. Box 7337, Charlotte Amalie, VI 00801 (tel. 809/775-1800). Its ten beachside acres, about six miles east of Charlotte Amalie, are among the best places to swim on St. Thomas. Owners Dick and Joyce Doumeng take advantage of its popularity to sponsor a dive center, among the best equipped on the island. The establishment's 77 accommodations are contained in three separate sections whose square concrete angles jut up from shelterbelts of palm and sea grape. On the premises are four tennis courts, a pleasant restaurant, and a thatch-roofed bar which perches regally above a half-moon-shaped pool. Each unit contains its own kitchenette, a fact appreciated by cost-conscious vacationers who purchase supplies at local grocery stores. Each contains air conditioning, a ceiling fan, cable color TV, phone, and simple modern furniture. All but a dozen rooms offer views of the water. An array of package deals is offered by the hotel. Most clients, however, select daily rates in winter of $195 to $210 in a double, $180 to $200 in a single. *In summer, singles pay $125 to $140 daily and doubles run $140 to $155*, with a continental breakfast, an introductory scuba lesson, free tennis, snorkeling equipment, and use of sailboats included. Bolongo, by the way, means "beautiful" in Congolese.

Magens Point Hotel, Magens Bay Road, Charlotte Amalie, VI 00802 (tel. 809/775-5500, or toll free 800/524-2031), has a personality and charm of its own. On the northern shoreline, an eight-minute ride from downtown, it lies on a hillcrest overlooking Magens Bay with its beach that the *National Geographic* called "one of the ten best in the world." Naturally, there's regularly scheduled transportation to and from the beach and the adjacent Mahogany Run Golf Course as well as to the downtown free-port shopping. The hotel is small enough to retain its individuality, yet large enough to provide excellent holiday facilities. The main building is constructed with taste in native stone, with two rows of view balconies and a shingled town-house style of roofing. There's a wide, tree-shaded terrace with in- and outdoor dining. Buffets are often set out on long tables decorated with hibiscus bushes. On a cliff, the swimming pool is set in the midst of rough stones, giving it a rain forest look, with a sunbathing ledge on one side.

Bedrooms are air-conditioned, each with color TV and telephone, framed watercolors, and Caribbean-style furnishings. From every unit there's a generously proportioned veranda. A single in winter, on the EP, rents for $125 to $135 daily, going up to $135 to $145 in a double. *In summer, these same singles cost $76 to $83 daily; doubles, $83 to $94.* Inquire about special honeymoon packages. For your use are several tennis courts, lit at night, and you can also make arrangements for golf, scuba-diving, deep-sea diving, and sailing. Overlooking the sea is the popular restaurant, the Green Parrot. Unfortunately, a condominium blocks the view of the bay at sunset. Sometimes entertainment is provided. If you don't stay here, call before striking out from Charlotte Amalie or wherever.

Point Pleasant Resort, Estate Smith Bay No. 4, Charlotte Amalie, VI 00802 (tel. 809/775-7200, or toll free 800/645-5306), is a very private, unique resort on Water Bay, on the far northeastern tip of St. Thomas, remote enough to connect you with the sea and islands. From your living room gallery, you look out on a Virgin collection—Tortola, St. John, and Jost Van Dyke. The hotel complex is set on a bluff with flowering shrubbery, century plants, frangipani trees, secluded trails, old rock formations, and lookout points. Hummingbirds share your breakfast. An open-air restaurant offers elegant dining.

Living arrangements are varied, and all units (except the bedrooms) feature fully equipped kitchens and private galleries facing that view. Guests are always close to the three freshwater swimming pools. You'll have a choice of living in a two-bedroom suite with two or three baths, a one-bedroom villa with two baths, a studio, an efficiency, or a bedroom. The studio is approximately 800 square feet with a bedroom closed off by louvered doors. The efficiency of about 500 square feet has a sleep-living room. The regular bedrooms have a full bath and are hotel size, with a balcony or sunken garden. The furnishings are light and airy, mostly rattan with floral fabrics. *On the EP, one person in summer pays $700 to $850 a week, and two persons pay $735 to $1,260 weekly, the latter for a villa. Four persons can occupy a studio in summer for $1,295 weekly, a villa for $1,540 a week.* In winter, the rates go up. Then a single on the EP ranges from $870 weekly in a bedroom to $1,260 for a villa. Two persons pay $910 for a bedroom, $1,855 for a villa. Up to seven persons can stay in a suite for $3,080 per week. A 7½% government tax and an energy surcharge are added to all bills. Many free offerings tip the scale. There is use of tennis courts, snorkeling equipment, and Sunfish sailboats. Free use of a car for four hours daily is allowed on a sign-out basis. You're also given free introductory scuba or windsurfing lessons.

Villa Olga Harbor Hotel, P.O. Box 4976, Charlotte Amalie, VI 00801 (tel. 809/774-1376). Set on an isolated peninsula in Frenchtown, behind a screen of palms, this hotel appears secluded, yet it's only a short ride to Charlotte Amalie. You can watch seaplanes land as you sip your daiquiri on the establishment's front porch, which is a heavily restored remnant of a Danish West Indian–style gingerbread house. Guests climb a steep hill to reach the eight comfortably simple accommodations, each of which shares a rambling veranda whose view encompasses nearby Hassel Island. Along the way you'll pass the cramped but inviting sapphire of the establishment's swimming pool, whose flowering borders were terraced into the slope. Each unit is air-conditioned, with a private bathroom, in winter costing $95 daily in a single, $110 in a double, plus tax. *In summer, singles pay $60 daily; doubles, $70.*

Budget Inns and Guesthouses

Miller Manor, Princess Gade (P.O. Box 1570), Charlotte Amalie, VI 00801 (tel. 809/774-1535), has been around for a long time, but it wasn't always a guesthouse. This is a 150-year-old Danish town house/villa, built on a bluff up in the residential section on Frenchman's Hill, about five minutes from downtown Charlotte Amalie. The owner-manager, Aida Miller, has lived here since she was seven years old. The house has a heavy collection of antiques, mixed with modern pieces. You enter through wrought-iron gates into a small courtyard with flowering bushes. The two lounges have crystal chandeliers, island antiques, and adjoining is a covered dining terrace with a view of the bay. The bedrooms are on four levels, each with its own style and furnishings. Many have tropical bamboo, ornate headboards, brass chandeliers, and a few have exposed-brick walls. There are 22 rooms in all, each with private bath and some with ceiling fans, others with air conditioning. *In summer, a single with bath costs $32; a double, also with bath, goes for $36 and $39.* In winter, singles range in price from $38 to $42 and doubles pay $46 to $49.

Maison Greaux Guest House, 23 Solberg Rd. (P.O. Box 1856), Charlotte Amalie, VI 00801 (tel. 809/774-0063), is an immaculate three-story white building with orange trim, surrounded by palms, bougainvillea, poinciana (flamboyant) trees, and other tropical vegetation. It's perched on a bluff above Frenchtown. A panoramic view of the harbor from Yacht Haven through Hassel and Water Islands and the submarine base is provided from the upper terrace where breakfast is served, reached by an outdoor staircase. The terrace is also a favorite place to enjoy cocktails at sunset and on into the night, with the view of the harbor lights. The guesthouse has ten rooms on its three levels, and there's a second-floor terrace for special privacy. Some of the rooms have private baths, while occupants of others share spotless facilities with fellow guests. Most units are air-conditioned, though a few are cooled by the trade winds. *In summer, singles rent for $28 to $32 and doubles go for $36 to $40.* Winter rates are $40 to $45 in a single, $48 to $55 in a double. Reader Steve Kralick, a writer who makes his home on St. Thomas, says that "most of the repeat clientele at Maison Greaux prefers to idle away the hours at the honor bar on the windswept terrace, where sounds of calypso strains sift softly up the steep mountainside which is a pleasant 5°-plus cooler than below." At the guesthouse you're only minutes from downtown Charlotte Amalie and the many excellent restaurants. It's an easy walk down, Mr. Kralick warns, but "take a cab back up!"

Island View, P.O. Box 1903, Charlotte Amalie, VI 00801 (tel. 809/774-4270, or toll free 800/524-2023), is a nine-room guesthouse 545 feet up Crown Mountain overlooking St. Thomas harbor and the town of Charlotte Amalie. You enter onto a large gallery with this breathtaking view. The Island View is moderately priced for the budget-minded guest. Poolside rooms and one suite have private baths. Of the four main-floor rooms, two have private baths and two share hall baths. All bedrooms are cooled by natural breezes and fans. The freshwater pool provides a view of the town and harbor. Tropical fruits and flowers abound. In winter, on the main floor singles pay $45 daily, the rate going up to $50 at poolside with a private bath. Doubles pay $50 on the main floor, $60 for a poolside room, $68 for a suite. *In summer, these rates are lowered to $33 in a single, $38 in a double.* All rates include a continental breakfast, with a full breakfast available. The self-service, open-air bar on the gallery is run on the honor system.

Bunkers' Hill View Guest House, Bunkers' Hill, 9 Commandant Gade, Charlotte Amalie, VI 00802 (tel. 809/774-8056), is a clean and centrally situated guest lodge that would be suitable for students and others on an economy budget who don't want to sacrifice comfort and safety. Hubert V. Rawlins, the owner and manager, operates this establishment, renting pleasant rooms, most of which contain air conditioning and TV. Bunkers' Hill View lies right in the heart of town, just a short walk from the Main Street and all the major restaurants of Charlotte Amalie. Daily rates in winter are from $45 in a single, going up to $55 or more in a double. *Summer tariffs are $40 daily in a single, $50 in a double.* Rates include breakfast and limousine service to the airport. A kitchenette is provided if you want to prepare your own meals, and a laundromat stands about 25 yards from the guesthouse.

DINING OUT: The restaurants in St. Thomas have a cuisine that puts them among the top in quality in the entire West Indies. Prices, unfortunately, are high, and many of the best spots can only be reached by taxi. With a few exceptions, the finest and most charming restaurants aren't in Charlotte Amalie but out on the island.

Dining in Charlotte Amalie

Hotel 1829, Government Hill (tel. 774-1829), has some of the finest food in St. Thomas. The building is graceful, and historic too (see the previous hotel recommendations). For carefully prepared food and drink, with a distinctive European flavor, guests walk up the hill and climb the stairs of this old structure, heading for the attractive bar for a before-dinner drink. Dining is on a terrace or in the main room whose walls are made from ships' ballast and whose cooling is by ceiling fans. The floor is made of Moroccan tiles, two centuries old. Baron and Baroness Ball are your hosts. The bartender specializes in frozen daiquiris, including coconut and strawberry. For an appetizer, you might select the escargots maître d'hôtel or perhaps one of the velvety-smooth soups such as cold cucumber. Try also the lobster bisque, which is made here fresh daily. Fish and meat dishes are usually excellent. Among the favorite dishes are piccata of veal, shrimps imperial, tournedos of venison with chanterelles, and rack of baby spring lamb, along with many grill dishes. The specialty of the house is one of the award-winning soufflés such as chocolate, amaretto, or raspberry. If you plan to dine here, expect to spend from $40 per person. Dinner is from 5 to 11 p.m., and reservations are requested. Closed Sunday.

L'Escargot, 3 Creques Alley (tel. 774-8880), has the same good food as its sister "Snail" (see below), but its menu is nowhere near as extensive. For the downtown shopper seeking some Gallic specialties, it offers good food, reasonable prices, and fine service. The location is in the Royal Dane Mall in a restored Danish building which is air-conditioned. Lunch is served from 11:30 a.m. to 3 p.m. and dinner from 6 to 10 p.m., except Sunday. Lunch has a range of well-chosen appetizers, including the namesake escargots. Soups are especially good, especially lobster bisque and onion soup au gratin. You help yourself to the salad bar. Prime rib is a specialty, and roast duck with orange sauce is another winner. Count on spending about $20 per person for lunch or dinner.

Yesterdays, 1 Commandant Gade (tel. 774-3088), begins where Back Street ends. Cooled by ceiling fans, it's a casual place, a favorite with the locals who gravitate to the relaxed atmosphere. You can select a table outside on the veranda fronting the street, or else one covered with a gingham cloth resting under ceiling fans. Wood floors, a good-size bar (with the coldest beer in town), a dart game, paintings on driftwood for sale—you get the picture. All patrons seem to know each other. Table hopping is commonplace. Sandwiches, a lunch in themselves, are served on pita or french bread. The chef's special is a hamburger seasoned with sweet vermouth. But that's only one of many hamburgers from around the world that are served, ranging from Texas to Japan. You can also order the baby back ribs in the evening, the chef's specialty. You might begin with a banana daiquiri, arguably the best on the island. The typical meal will cost from $15. One of the oldest bars on the island, Yesterdays is behind the Chase Manhattan Bank. For amusement, you can watch rock concerts on the video screen. Service is until around midnight.

Blackbeard's Castle (tel. 776-1234) lies within the previously recommended five-room hotel. This elegant and ambitious dining room presents seafood and nouvelle American cuisine. Awarded a trio of gold, silver, and bronze medals in local culinary contests, owners Bob Harrington and Henrique Konzen serve lunch every weekday between 11:30 a.m. to 2:30 p.m., Sunday brunch with live music between 11 a.m. and 3 p.m., and musical dinners nightly between 6:30 and 10:30 p.m. Full dinners, costing from $25, include such frequently changing specials as sautéed duck with Madagascar sauce, roast stuffed pork, grilled rib-eye steak, and shrimp and scallop curry. Pastas are available in half portions as appetizers. Lunches are slightly less elaborate and about half the price, featuring salads, delicately seasoned platters, and frothy rum-based drinks. Reservations are suggested for dinner. Don't miss the elaborately ornate cast-iron chandelier hanging in the anteroom of the bar. The laughing cherubs decorating its many arms were found in a Danish manor house and installed in their new home overlooking one of the best harbor views on the island.

On Frenchman's Hill

Harbour View, Frenchman's Hill (tel. 774-2651). Two very sophisticated American women, Arlene Lockwood and Lenore Wolfe, have welcomed guests to their gracious 19th-century Danish manor house for some 25 years. When magazines such as *Mademoiselle, Cosmopolitan,* and *Harper's Bazaar* started publishing reports of their imaginative cuisine—true creative cookery—the world came to their doorstep. Countless diners return again and again, and have become friends of the management.

The setting alone is dramatic (described in part in the hotel recommendations). You enter to the sounds of a tinkling concert grand piano. One of the staff shows you to a terrace with a spectacular view of Charlotte Amalie and the harbor. While you sip your apéritif, menu selections are made. Later you are shown through a montage of sweeping brick arches to your shimmering candlelit table, a polished mahogany set with a pewter service. One of the three dining rooms is in the original kitchen. Forget the expense for one night, and sit back to enjoy fine food, a Mediterranean cuisine, and impeccable service.

Recommended appetizers include West Indian meat "pattes" (beef) and a cassolette of fresh mushrooms prepared with sour cream and herbs. The chef is noted for his classic gazpacho, but one should also inquire about the soup du jour (I recently enjoyed the best carrot soup I've ever had). Main dishes are served with salad greens and a choice of potato soufflé or a side order of pasta. My favorite orders include a delightfully delicate dish of sautéed shrimp and cream sauce embellished with grated cheese and dry sherry, scaloppina maison (thin slices of veal stuffed with cheese and served with a fresh mushroom sauce), steak pizzaiola (filet mignon cooked to order and prepared with an herbed tomato sauce), and spanaki tou fournou (Greek-style spinach casserole baked with a creamy blend of cheeses). Each day the cooks bake good-tasting pies from their collection of house recipes.

Dinner is served nightly, except Tuesday, and reservations are imperative. Count on spending $35 or more for a complete dinner, served from 7 to 10:30 p.m. On certain nights in season it seems that half the denizens of St. Thomas drive up the narrow, wiggly road from the marketplace to this hillside-hugging gastronomic retreat. I suggest you join them. The restaurant is open year round except for a vacation period just after the Labor Day weekend.

At Compass Point

Raffles, Compass Point (tel. 775-6004), named after the legendary hotel in Singapore, is an establishment filled with tropical accents more evocative of the South Pacific than of the Caribbean. No one will mind if women wear flowers in their hair or if men dress in sports clothes for dinner on the outdoor terrace. The furnishings include peacock chairs, lots of wicker, ceiling fans, and the kind of bar where you may want to toss off a few rounds before dinner, perhaps sampling the daiquiris which are known throughout the island. Dinner is served daily except Sunday from 6:30 to 10:30 p.m. A pianist, Gray-Gray-Gray, plays Gershwin and Porter during dinner, and showtime is at 10:30 p.m.—a little risqué, with Noël Coward renditions, but its lots of fun. You can choose from dishes which are organized on the menu into categories, including beef, veal, lamb, chicken, and shrimp. The fish of the day is freshly caught and well prepared, with various tasty sauces. You may also enjoy coconut shrimp, "two-day duck," steak Raffles prepared at your table, veal tsaritsa, a mixed English grill, or chicken Rangoon. Full meals range from $25 upward. You'll find this place outside the lagoon at Compass Point, a few miles east of Charlotte Amalie.

The **Windjammer Restaurant,** Compass Point Seaport (tel. 775-2275). Much of the paneling and the smoothly finished bar of this pleasant place are crafted from thick slabs of island mahogany, which is illuminated by light streaming in from the open windows looking out onto the nearby marina. Uwe Dedekind, the German-born owner, lived in Bremen and later in Costa Rica before opening this nautical-style hideaway. Dinner is served seven days a week from 6:30 to 10 p.m. Of course, no one will mind if you want to join the drinkers at the commodious bar for a round or two before tucking into a few of the house specialties. The selection of house drinks ranges from a "Shiver Me Timbers" to the "Half Hitch" to the "Drunken Sailor." On the menu is a wide selection of seafood, such as queen triggerfish, a Caribbean delicacy locally referred to as "whole ole wife," five different shrimp dishes, a Teutonic rahmschnitzel (veal cutlets with spices in a heady cream sauce), snapper and dolphin prepared in many different ways, some of them stuffed with lobster, a well-prepared wienerschnitzel, and a fisherman's platter. Full meals cost from $15 up.

For the Birds, Scott Beach (tel. 775-6431). Set in a low-slung bungalow whose green roof matches the growth around it, this pleasant restaurant offers reasonably priced, well-prepared food in gargantuan helpings. It's the home of several varieties of birds, both live and replicas. A few steps from the restaurant's big windows, the surf and a sandy beach beckon. Lunch is served only on Sunday, when live jazz artists perform between noon and 4 p.m. Other than Sunday, the establishment opens daily at 3:30 p.m., serving until midnight. You can eat for $15 and up, selecting from such spicy tempers as a dinner platter smothered with heaps of nachos or an entire loaf of deep-fried onion rings, a plate of the best baby back ribs on the island, beef brisket, West Indian grouper, chicken au gratin, filet mignon, and southern fried catfish. There's also a selection of such Mexican specialties as beef or chicken enchiladas, chimichangas (tortillas with spicy beef, guacamole, and sour cream), and burritos.

At Frenchtown

The **Café Normandie,** rue de St. Barthélemy, at Frenchtown (tel. 774-1622), is my favorite dining nook in this colorful section of St. Thomas. It also offers one of the best dining values on the island. From 6:30 to 10 p.m. daily except Monday you can order a table d'hôte menu for just $20, which might begin with hors d'oeuvres, perhaps made with seafood, plus soup, perhaps French onion. You're served not only a salad and sherbet (to clear your palate), but are allowed to choose from a selection of main-dish specialties ranging from langouste to beef Wellington (an odd name for a French restaurant), or hasenpfeffer (pieces of hare, bacon, and steak in a rich, savory sauce). The dessert special (not featured on the set meal) is their original chocolate fudge pie. All the food writers from such magazines as *Food and Wine* and *Gourmet* have so far been unsuccessful in getting the chef to part with the secret recipe. The restaurant is air-conditioned, and the glow of candlelight makes it quite elegant. It's beautifully run, and the service is excellent. There is a relaxed informality about the dress code, but you shouldn't show up in a bikini. Reservations are absolutely mandatory, and if you're dining there from mid-December to May 1 you may need to call several days in advance.

Alexander's, Frenchtown (tel. 774-4349), will warmly accommodate you. Its walls are painted a pale shade of gray, while the thick mahogany bar is lined with a moveable collection of stools, which, of course, change positions as different crowds of drinkers come and go. This is especially true during the happy hour, 4 to 6 p.m., when your second drink costs only $1.25. In addition to serving drinks—a brandy Café Alexander is a favorite—the place is a well-run restaurant as well. There are only ten tables, but on them, Austrian specialties are served with flair. A few seafood dishes are offered, among them a conch schnitzel, but most of the others are strictly Middle European. They include a mouthwatering wienerschnitzel, Nürnburger röstbraten, goulash, breaded mushrooms, schweinebraten with dumplings and sauerkraut, and homemade pâté. For dessert, you might try the homemade strudel, either apple or cheese, or else the richly caloric Schwartzwald torte. A full dinner, served from 6:30 to 10 p.m. seven days a week, costs from $25. Lunches, served from noon to 3 p.m., are considerably cheaper, around $12. Midday meals consist of a variety of crêpes, quiches, and a daily chef's special. You'll find this place on the waterfront overlooking the harbor.

Barbary Coast, Frenchtown (tel. 774-8354). Chianti bottles hang from the walls of this dimly lit restaurant which serves the best Italian food on the island. The ambience is informal and can be a lot of fun, especially around the large bar in the outer room which many patrons abandon only reluctantly to head inside to dinner. This light-hearted establishment is owned by three young partners, Mike, Rick, and Randy, who work hard to keep it going seven days a week. If you want a touch of the Caribbean, you might try the conch parmigiana. Otherwise, you'll have to stick to savory dishes such as veal served either piccata, marsala, or parmigiana, eggplant parmigiana, many versions of pasta, homemade minestrone, and a fresh fish dish of the day, which might be grouper served four different ways. Other choices are scampi, filet mignon, New York strip steak, fresh garlic bread, mozzarella sticks, and shrimp cocktail. Fresh homemade desserts are a specialty. Wine is sold by the bottle or by the glass. The restaurant is closed for lunch. The bar opens daily at 5 p.m., staying open till around 4 a.m. Full meals cost from $20.

Gregerie East, 17 Crown Bay (tel. 774-2432). Named after the East Gregerie Channel, at the side of which it sits, this restaurant is a good choice for a quiet afternoon of boat watching. Guests anchor in at the mahogany bar beneath mulberry-colored ceiling beams and swirling fans in a breezy pavilion whose minimum of walls are sheathed in diagonal strips of varnished pine. You can head here for a drink throughout the day (and often late into the night), but meals are served only from 11:30 a.m. to 3 p.m. and 6 to 10 p.m. Sunday brunch lasts from 10:30 a.m. to 3 p.m. Lunch is seven days a week, costing from $10 and likely to include a choice of deli sandwiches, veal piccata, coq au vin, Texas shrimp in a beer batter, soup, and omelets. Dinner is served nightly except Monday, costing from $22 and featuring such dishes as sautéed snails in an anchovy-and-caper sauce, shrimp Pernod, lobster, poached filet of red snapper with mushroom sauce, lamb chops with rosemary and a chutney-curry sauce, and pepper steak.

Red Hook

Piccola Marina, at Red Hook (tel. 775-6350), has an open veranda offering a closeup view of the boats moored at this popular marina. Lunch is served between 11 a.m. and 3 p.m., costing from $12. The bill of fare might include fried potato skins, sandwiches, antipasta primavera, charcoal-broiled burgers, homemade pastas, and rare roast beef. Sunday brunches, often accompanied by tropical rum-based drinks, go for $10. Dinner, served between 6:30 and 10 p.m., costing from $12. The bill of fare might include fried potato skins, sandwiches, antipasta primavera, charcoal-broiled burgers, homemade pastas, and rare roast beef. Sunday brunches, often accompanied by tropical rum-based drinks, go for $10. Dinner, served between 6:30 and 10 p.m., might include specialties for a mesquite grill, seafood brochette, shrimp, catch of the day, a selection of piccola pastas (including carbonara and with pesto sauce), and Szechuan-style chicken. Dinners cost from $20 each. The restaurant is open daily in high season, but closed Monday off-season. A bar, pasta shop, and charcuterie do a thriving business on the premises.

Scattered Choices

Au Bon Vivant (tel. 774-2158), atop Government Hill, is known for its superb view of Charlotte Amalie and the lights in the harbor. It is also known for its classic French cookery, carefully supervised by José Chevrotée, the owner and chef. You may order French champagne by the glass while choosing from an extensive selection of fine dishes. Hot hors d'oeuvres are likely to include an onion tart or escargots de Bourgogne. Soups are imaginative and include cream of watercress and fresh fish flavors. The chef also takes care with his salads, avoiding the iceberg lettuce monotony by using endive, fresh mushrooms, and romaine lettuce, each served with a different dressing. Main-dish specialties include a rack of lamb aux herbes and fish normande. You might also select the filet mignon with Madagascar pepper, Dover sole stuffed with fish mousse, or baby veal sautéed and steamed with plums and flamed with champagne. The chef also prepares chicken breast with lime and coconut. Dinner, from $30, is served Monday to Saturday from 6:30 to 10 p.m. Reservations are necessary.

Fiddle Leaf, Watergate Villas (tel. 775-2810). Airy, open, and sophisticated, this imaginative restaurant offers some of the most deliciously creative food on the island. Nestled in a well-heeled condo complex near the Frenchman's Reef Hotel, it offers a slick, trendy decor, suggesting a tropical Manhattan. Carefully aimed pin lighting, lattices, and ficus trees enhance the Haitian metal sculptures and framed posters. The motivating force behind all this is the diminutive but dynamic Patricia La Corte, who was reared in the U.S. by French parents who were totally enamored of fine food. Her menu rotates every week, making maximum use of fresh ingredients flown in from the U.S. Known for her pastas, Ms. La Corte prepares fettuccine with mushrooms, pesto, and olives, and many other varieties as ingredients come into season. Other specialties are likely to include beef tournedos stuffed with brie, filet mignon with wild mushrooms, breast of chicken with coriander and dried tomatoes, kiwi sorbet, Linzertorte, and chocolate pâté with raspberry sauce. The restaurant is open only for dinner, every night (except Monday in low season) between 7 and 10 p.m. Reservations are strongly advised.

Chart House Restaurant, at the Villa Olga Harbor Hotel (see above) in Frenchtown (tel. 774-4262), was the site of the Russian consulate in the 19th century. The restaurant is on the same property but is run separately from the hotel. You may want to journey out past Frenchtown Village for lunch or dinner in this tranquil spot. The restaurant is in the rebuilt Victorian villa. In the bar area you can listen to divers' "bull sessions." The dining gallery is a large open terrace fronting the sea.

Dinner at the Chart House is served Monday through Thursday from 5:30 to 10 p.m. and Friday through Sunday from 5:30 to 11 p.m. Cocktail service starts at 5 p.m. seven days a week, and the bartender will make you his special drink called a Bailey's colada. The restaurant features the best salad bar on the island, with a choice of 30 to 40 items, which comes with dinner. Dinners begin at $13, going up to $25, and menu choices range from chicken to Alaskan king crab. Of course, this chain is known for serving the finest cut of prime rib anywhere, and here it comes loading down a plate at 22 ounces. For dessert, you can order the famous Chart House "mud pie," which, in spite of its name, is a shockingly calorie-laden ice-cream concoction. You don't make a reservation. Seating is on a first-come, first-served basis, so just arrive and hope you'll get a table. If you get here before sunset, you can watch the seaplanes land directly in front of the restaurant.

Royal Rum Barrel, Government Hill (tel. 776-1854), occupies a charming, secluded nook in an 1854 house. Tables for food and drink are set up in one of the most tucked-away little courtyards in St. Thomas, with a waterfall and enclosing stone walls. If you find your way here to this Government Hill spot, you'll be served sandwiches and salad plates at lunch, and such tempting dinner fare as conch native style and steak in a Dijon mustard sauce, along with "regal coffees" and a new dessert every evening. Full meals cost from $9 up. Refreshing island drinks are served 12 hours a day, till midnight. The restaurant is a short walk from downtown.

Eunice's Terrace, 67 Smith Bay (tel. 775-3975). This unpretentious plank-covered building welcomes a hard-fisted collection of Stateside construction workers, West Indian locals, and an occasional tourist into its confines for savory platters of island food served in generous portions. The number of tables (about seven) is so limited that many diners wait at the bar with a drink before eventually seating themselves. A popular concoction called a Queen Mary (a combination of tropical fruits laced with dark rum) is a favorite. Eunice Best, formerly of Charleston, South Carolina, set up this restaurant years ago after marrying a resident of St. Thomas. She spends her days as a guidance counselor in a public school, sometimes leaving the lunch crowd in the capable hands of Mrs. Thelma Small, although in the evening, Mrs. Best is likely to be on hand. The establishment is open from 9 a.m. to 10 p.m. seven days a week. You'll find it just east of the Coral World turnoff. Dinner specialties include conch fritters, boiled or fried fish, especially dolphin, sweet potato pie, and a number of chalkboard specials which are usually served with fungi, rice, or plantain. Full dinners cost from $10 and lunches, $6. On the lunch menu are fishburgers, sandwiches, and such daily specials as Virgin Islands doved pork or mutton. Key lime pie is a favorite dessert. Reservations are a good idea at dinnertime.

WHAT TO SEE: The color and charm of a real Caribbean waterfront town vividly come to life in the capital of St. Thomas, Charlotte Amalie, where most visitors begin their sightseeing exploration of the small island. In days of yore seafarers and adventure seekers from all over the world, including the prostitutes who kept them amused, flocked to this old-world Danish town, as have pirates, slaves, and members of the Confederacy using the port during the American Civil War. St. Thomas was the biggest slave market in the world.

The old warehouses, once used for storing pirate goods, still stand, for the most part housing the merchandise I'll preview in the shopping expedition. Cruise-ship passengers have taken the place of Captain Kidd and Blackbeard the pirate, walking the same old streets, called "gade" here in honor of their Danish heritage.

The main streets of town are now a virtual shopping mall, and are usually packed. Sandwiched among these shops are a few historic buildings, most of which can be covered on foot in about two hours.

Before starting your tour, you might stop off in the so-called **Grand Hotel.** Mercifully, it's no longer a hotel, for which its last tenants can be grateful. Along with shops, it also contains a Visitors' Bureau, near tiny **Emancipation Park** where a proclamation freeing the slaves was read on July 3, 1848. The architectural relic was built in 1841.

West of the park, and across the street, the **Central Post Office** displays WPA-type murals by Stephen Dohanos, who later became famous as a *Saturday Evening Post* cover artist.

Next, you can climb a steep street, Kongens (Danish for "king") Gade, passing the entrance to the historic **Hotel 1829,** which has already been previewed in both the hotel and restaurant sections.

Continue past the hotel until you reach **Government House,** the administrative headquarters for all the Virgin Islands. It's been the center of official life in the islands since it was built around the time of the American Civil War. Visitors are allowed on the first two floors, weekdays from 8 a.m. to noon and from 1 to 5 p.m. Some paintings by former resident Camille Pissarro are on display, plus works by other St. Thomian artists.

Nearby is one of the few remaining streets of the old Danish town. Called the **99 Steps,** it was erected in the early 1700s.

After climbing the stairs, you can see the façade of **Crown House,** built in the mid-18th century, a stately home which was the residence of two of the past governors of the Virgin Islands. Here the rich and privileged lived in the 18th century, surrounded by Chinese wall hangings, a crystal chandelier from Versailles, and carved West Indian furniture. It was once the home of von Scholten, the Danish ruler who freed the slaves in the 1848 proclamation.

Southeast of Emancipation Park stands **Fort Christian,** dating from 1672. Named after the Danish king Christian V, the structure has been everything from a governor's official residence to a jail. Many pirates, it is said, were hanged in the courtyard. In some cells the Virgin Islands Museum has been installed, displaying some minor Indian artifacts. Admission free, it is open Monday to Friday from 8 a.m. to 5 p.m. and on Saturday from 1 to 5 p.m.

The oldest **synagogue** building in continuous use under the American flag still maintains the tradition of sand on the floor, commemorating the exodus from Egypt. It stands on Crystal Gade, and is reached by a steep walk up from Main Street. Not as old as the synagogue in Curaçao, this one was erected in 1833 by Sephardic Jews. It marked its 150th anniversary in 1983. The synagogue was built of native stone, along with brick from Denmark and mortar made of molasses and sand. It's open from 9 a.m. to 4 p.m. Monday to Friday for visitors, and conducts its religious school for children on Saturday morning from September through May.

At the point where Main Street intersects Strand Gade, **Market Square,** or "de market" as it is known locally, was the center of a large slave-trading market before the emancipation was proclaimed. Roofed over, it is an open-air fruit and vegetable market today, selling, among other items, genips (you break open the skin and suck the pulp off a pit). The wrought-iron roof came from Europe, and at the turn of the century covered a railway station. It's open every day but Sunday, reaching the peak of its activity on Saturday.

If the genip didn't satisfy you, you can take Strand Gade down to the waterfront. There you can purchase a fresh coconut, getting the vendor to whack off the top with his machete. Then you can drink the sweet milk from its hull.

After finishing your tour in Charlotte Amalie, head west on Main Street until you connect with Hardwood Hwy. Turn off at the Villa Olga sign to visit "Cha-Cha Town," or **Frenchtown** as it's called. The French people who settled here—named for the "cha-chas" or straw hats made and worn here—are descendants of immigrants from the French islands, speaking an unusual patois. The colorful little town, most of whose residents seem to be engaged in fishing, contains some interesting restaurants and taverns.

Later, you can strike out for **Mountain Top,** the traditional stopping-off point for a banana daiquiri.

To cap your tour, locate **Drake's Seat** on a good map and head there for the most spectacular view in St. Thomas. According to legend (and not really to be believed), Sir Francis Drake sat there charting the channels and passages of the Virgin Islands. Nevertheless, you have spread at your feet the entire sweep of almost 100 Virgin Islands, both U.S. and British.

St. Thomas's most popular attraction is **Coral World,** Rte. 6 (tel. 775-1555), a marine complex that includes a three-story underwater observation tower 100 feet offshore. Through windows large and clear you get to see sponges, deep-sea flowers, fish, and coral—underwater life in its natural state. In the Marine Gardens Aquarium, 21 saltwater tanks display everything from seahorses to urchins. The entire complex is at Coki Beach on the northeastern shore, 15 minutes from downtown, and is open seven days a week from 9 a.m. to 6 p.m. Adults pay $8; children, $6. Shark and fish feeding is at 11 a.m. Shuttle service is available from downtown and major hotels. The shuttle departure is from the Gray Line Tour office at the Grand Hotel in Charlotte Amalie. Departures are daily excepting Sunday at 9:30 a.m. and again at 12:30 p.m. A one-way ticket costs $3.50 for each passenger.

West of the center of Charlotte Amalie, on the campus of the College of the Virgin Islands, the **Reichhold Center** (tel. 774-8475) is one of the major cultural centers in the Caribbean. Frequent art exhibits of local artists are staged here at this Japanese-inspired amphitheater set in a natural valley. About 1,200 spectators are accommodated here, and big-time cultural entertainment has arrived in St. Thomas. Ask about possible events during your visit. You might see, perhaps, the Joffrey Ballet. The smell of gardenias will only add to the evening's pleasure. If no event is being sponsored, you can still take a guided tour of the center Monday through Friday by calling the number given above.

A Side Trip to Water Island

The fourth largest of the U.S. Virgins, Water Island is only half a mile long and about a half to one mile wide. At its nearest point, it comes about three-eighths of a mile from St. Thomas. Visitors go there to spend the day on Honeymoon Beach where they swim, snorkel, sail, waterski, or just sunbathe while they relax under the palm-shaded beach, ordering lunch or a drink from the beach bar. The highest elevation is only 300 feet above sea level, and the Arawak Indians were the first to inhabit it. Originally the island had freshwater ponds to which sailing vessels came to replenish their casks. The army used Fort Segarra as a base in World War I.

It's possible to go on your own. A ferry runs between Water Island Dock and the Sub Base at St. Thomas, a seven-minute ride costing $5 for a round-trip ticket, $3.50 one way. Service is from 7 a.m. to midnight.

SHOPPING: The $800 duty-free allowance makes every purchase a double bargain. Often well-known brand names are presented at savings of up to 60% off Stateside prices. However, that's likely to be an exceptional purchase. I don't want to paint too optimistic a picture. To find true value, you often have to plow through a lot of junk. Many items offered for sale—binoculars, stereos, watches, cameras—can be matched in price at your hometown discount store. Therefore, you need to know the price of the item involved back home to determine if you are in fact making a savings. Having sounded that warning, I'll survey some St. Thomas shops where I have personally found good buys. Know that there are lots more you can discover on your own.

Most of the shops, some of which occupy former pirate warehouses, are open from 9 a.m. to 5 p.m., regular business hours, and some stay open later. Nearly all stores close on Sunday and major holidays—that is, unless a cruise ship is in port. Few shopkeepers can stand the prospect of dozens of potential customers, their purses full, wandering by their padlocked doors. Therefore those gates are likely to swing open, at least for half a day on Sunday. Friday is the biggest cruise-ship visiting day at Charlotte Amalie (one day I counted eight at one time)—so try to avoid shopping then.

Cardow Jewelers, 39 Dronningens Gade (tel. 774-1140), often called the Tiffany's of the Caribbean, is the first store on Main Street. It boasts the largest selection of fine jewelry shown in the world. This fabulous shop, where there are more than 6,000 rings displayed, offers enormous savings because of its worldwide direct buying, large turnover, and duty-free prices. Unusual and traditional designs are offered in diamonds, emeralds, rubies, sapphires, and Brazilian stones, as well as pearls and coral. Cardow has a whole wall of Indian gold chains at savings of 40% and 50%. Also featured are antique coin jewelry and Piaget watches. The Treasure Cove has case after case of gold jewelry.

A. H. Riise Gifts, 37 Main St. at A. H. Riise Alley (tel. 776-2303), offers the

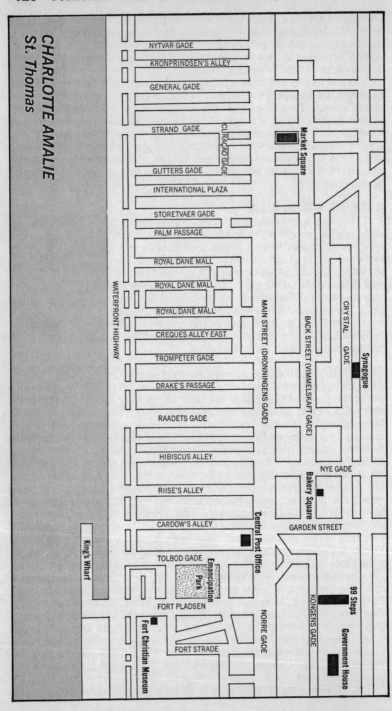

CHARLOTTE AMALIE
St. Thomas

NYTVAR GADE
KRONPRINDSEN'S ALLEY
GENERAL GADE
STRAND GADE
CURAÇAO GADE
GUTTERS GADE
INTERNATIONAL PLAZA
STORETVAER GADE
PALM PASSAGE
ROYAL DANE MALL
ROYAL DANE MALL
ROYAL DANE MALL
CREQUES ALLEY EAST
TROMPETER GADE
DRAKE'S PASSAGE
RAADETS GADE
HIBISCUS ALLEY
RIISE'S ALLEY
CARDOW'S ALLEY
TOLBOD GADE
FORT PLADSEN
FORT STRADE

WATERFRONT HIGHWAY

MAIN STREET (DRONNINGENS GADE)

BACK STREET (VIMMELSKAFT GADE)

CRYSTAL GADE

Synagogue

Market Square

NYE GADE
Bakery Square
GARDEN STREET

Central Post Office

Emancipation Park

King's Wharf

Fort Christian Museum

NORRE GADE

KONGENS GADE

99 Steps

Government House

customer a memorable shopping experience. Displayed in a restored 18th-century Danish warehouse that extends from Main Street to the waterfront is an unusually wide and fine selection of quality imported merchandise. Special attention is given to the collection of fine jewelry and watches from Europe's leading craftspeople, including Patek Philippe, the most prestigious watch in the world, Ebel, Concord, and many others. Waterford, Lalique, Daum, Baccarat, Wedgwood, Royal Crown Derby, Royal Doulton, Royal Copenhagen, and Lladro are but a few of the internationally known names found in the crystal and china departments. The perfume and cosmetics are found in one of the largest parfumeries in the Caribbean, all at duty-free prices of up to 50% less than Stateside. Specialties also include Crabtree & Evelyn, Liberty of London, and Hilda Icelandic Woolens boutiques, as well as a complete duty-free art gallery featuring original Caribbean art. Toll-free shop-by-phone service is available by calling 800/524-2037 from the U.S. Call for a free brochure.

Tropicana Perfumes Shoppes, 2 Dronningens Gade (tel. 774-0010), stand at the beginning of Main Street near the Central Post Office. They are the exclusive agents of Yendi by Capucci. The first of these two shops is billed as the largest perfumerie in the world. Behind its rose-and-white façade, it offers all the famous names in perfumes, colognes, as well as cosmetics and toilet water, including Poison, Diva, and Perry Ellis for men and women. Men will find Europe's best colognes and aftershave lotions.

Little Switzerland, 5 Dronningens Gade (tel. 776-2010), with three stores in downtown Charlotte Amalie and one on the dock at Havensight Mall, sells fine watches, a wide selection of jewelry, and the best in crystal and china. The watches are priced as they are in Switzerland, which is a good saving on such name brands as Rolex, Ebel, Girard-Perregaux, Vacheron & Constanin, Concord, and many more. Incidentally, the owners employ Swiss watchmakers to ensure that every watch is properly adjusted. Names in chinaware and crystal such as Baccarat, Lalique, Rosenthal, Aynsley, Royal Doulton, Wedgwood, and many more are here. This is also the official Hummel and Lladro shop, as well as being the largest Waterford crystal importer in the West Indies.

H. Stern Jewellers (tel. 776-1939) offers trendy, colorful gem and jewel creations at five locations in St. Thomas—two on Main Street, in Havensight Shopping Mall, and branches at Bluebeard's Castle and Frenchman's Reef Hotel—as well as in a store at Sint Maarten, Netherlands Antilles. Every shop has the same duty-free prices, a considerable savings for visiting shoppers. Stern gives worldwide guaranteed service, including a one-year exchange privilege.

If you want to combine a little history with shopping, you might go into the courtyard of the old **Pissarro Building,** entered through an archway off Main Street. The celebrated impressionist painter lived here as a child. The old apartments have been turned into a warren of interesting shops.

The Leather Shop, Inc., Main Street and Havensight Mall (tel. 776-3995), has a good selection from Italian designers. Many handbags are from chic Italian boutiques: Fendi, Bottega Veneta, and Il Bisonte. You'll find a wide assortment of belts, sized to order with your choice of buckle. There are many styles of wallets, briefcases, and attaché cases, as well as all-leather luggage from Land.

Sweet Passion (tel. 774-2990), close by the fountain, across from L'Escargot Restaurant in the Royal Dane Mall, facing the square, sells antique jewelry, with many items from the Georgian and early Victorian periods. On these items—that is, anything more than a century old—there is no duty. The shopkeepers will also show you jewelry of a later design, including art nouveau and 1920s deco. The shop also carries a line of luxury gifts in sterling and crystal as well as a fun line of early plastic and paste "fashion" jewelry.

The Straw Factory, 24 Garden St. (tel. 774-4849), a stroll up from Post Office Square, has the island's largest selection of straw hats, from classic Panamas to beachcomber bargains, as well as handcrafted wares. Be sure to check out the modestly priced Haitian terracotta figurines and the wide selection of all-cotton sportswear. There are shopping bags with embroidered flowers, but most of the shop is filled with one-of-a-kind items, both decorative and useful. Stop at the counter outside for an ice-cream cone and eat it seated in the shade of the Straw Factory patio.

The wafting aroma of spices will lead you to **Down Island Traders,** 9 C Contant (tel. 774-3419). It has an attractive array of spices, teas, seasonings, jams, and condiments, most of which are packaged from natural Caribbean products. Look also for its nuts, candies, and jellies—it's an original native market. The owner also carries a line of local cookbooks, as well as silkscreened island designs on T-shirts, scarves, and bags.

Blue Carib Gems and Rocks (tel. 774-8525), the Bakery Shopping Square, is perched behind Little Switzerland on Back Street. For a decade the owners prospected for gemstones in the Caribbean, and these stones have been brought direct from the mine to you. The raw stones are cut and polished and then fashioned into jewelry by the lost-wax process. On one side of the premises you can see the craftspeople at work, and on the other side view their finished products, including such handsomely set stones as larimar, the sea/sky-blue–patterned variety of pectolite found only in the Caribbean. A lifetime guarantee is given on all handcrafted jewelry. Since the items are locally made, they are duty free and not included in the $800 exemption. Incidentally, this establishment also provides emergency eyeglass repair.

The **Royal Caribbean,** 33 Main St. and Havensight Mall (tel. 776-4110), is one of the largest camera and electronic stores in the Caribbean. Since 1977 it has offered good values in cameras and electronic equipment, including all accessories. The store also has good buys in linen.

Sheela's Jewel Palace, 23 Main St. (tel. 776-5449), under the same ownership as the Royal Caribbean, carries a complete range of fine jewelry and a full collection of watches from all over the world.

Irmela's Jewel Studio, in the Old Grand Hotel at the beginning of Main Street (tel. 774-5875, or toll free 800/524-2047), has made a name for itself in the highly competitive jewelry business in St. Thomas. Here the jewelry is unique, custom designed by Irmela and handmade by her studio or imported from around the world. Irmela has the largest selection of cultured pearls in the Caribbean, including freshwater Biwa and South Sea pearls. Choose from hundreds of clasps and pearl shorteners. Irmela has a large selection of unset stones, such as rubies, sapphires, emeralds, and unusual ones including tanzanite and alexandrite. Diamonds range from pear-shaped to emerald cut, marquis, even heart-shaped, in sizes from tiny two pointers to several carats.

Java Wraps (tel. 774-3700), in Palm Passage on the waterfront in Charlotte Amalie, is all white tiles with traditional Javanese matting decorated with exotic Balinese woodcarvings on the walls. Locals and tourists alike buy the hand-batiked resortwear line specializing in shorts, shirts, sundresses, and children's clothing. Java Wraps is known for its sarong pieces and demonstrates the tying of them in at least 15 different ways.

The **Linen House** is considered one of the best stores for linens in the West Indies. It has two locations, one at 7A Royal Dane Mall (tel. 774-8117) and another at Palm Passage (tel. 774-8405). You'll find a wide selection of placemats, decorative tablecloths, and many hand-embroidered goods. There are many high-fashion styles.

The **Cloth Horse,** Bakery Square (tel. 774-4761), sells the celebrated Marimekko of Finland fabric as well as the French Oulivado fabric from Provence, both at a 40% saving over Stateside prices. You can also buy ready-made items such as scarves, handbags, and pillow covers. The Caribbean products carried here are natural cotton bedspreads, wall tapestries, placemats, baskets, and mahogany plates from Haiti.

At **Al Cohen's** big warehouse at Havensight, 18A Estate Thomas (tel. 774-

3690), across from the West Indian Company dock, where cruise-ship passengers come in, you can purchase discount liquor, fragrances, T-shirts, and souvenirs. Your purchases are delivered free to the airport or your ship.

A visit to the boutique, art gallery, and craft studios of **Jim Tillett,** Tillett Gardens, Tutu (tel. 775-1405), is like a combined shopping and sightseeing expedition. The Tillett compound was converted from a Danish farm called "Tutu." The Tillett name conjures up high-fashion silkscreen printing by the famous Tillett brothers, who for years have had their exquisite fabrics used by top designers and featured in such magazines as *Vogue* and *Harper's Bazaar*. Jim Tillett settled in St. Thomas, after creating a big splash in Mexico, where his work was featured in *Life* magazine. At his compound you can casually visit the adjoining workshops, where you can see silkscreening in progress. Mr. Tillett and his staff produce about 40,000 yards a year. He's daring in his color consciousness, and as you enter the shop, operated by his wife, Rhoda, you're struck by the power of the colors used. The boutique is stocked with fabric sold by the yard, costing from $10 (silk starts at $20). Out of this fabric, resort wear has been fashioned, including dresses and caftans from $45; scarves, from $5. If you don't see what you want, just ask—it'll be made up for you. Bargain hunters might also want to ask Mrs. Tillett or one of the staff "about some special sale stuff" which is usually available.

Adjoining the boutique is an art gallery which has an abundance of maps, paintings, and graphics made by Mr. Tillett himself. He's created a series of maps on fine cotton canvas which have been bestselling items. Silkscreened maps of St. Thomas on canvas start at $25. *Shopping tip:* Buy a square of florid Tillett fabric and frame it when you return. It can make a vivid wall hanging.

Arts Alive Fairs are held in the Tillett Gardens three times a year—in autumn, spring, and summer. These fairs give local artists a showcase for their work and offer crafts demonstrations and such special features as puppet shows for children; folkloric dancers; other dancing such as tap, ballet, and modern; steel bands; calypso music; and other activities.

THE SPORTING LIFE: Chances are, your hotel will be right on the beach, or very close to one, and this is where you'll anchor for most of your stay, perhaps occasionally going out in a Sailfish or Hobie Cat. All the beaches in the Virgin Islands are public, incidentally.

Beaches

Most of the beaches lie anywhere from two to five miles from Charlotte Amalie. I've already extolled the glory of **Magens Bay,** three miles from the capital, which charges 50¢ for adults and 25¢ for children. Dressing rooms are provided, and snorkeling equipment and small sailboats can be rented. There is also a restaurant.

Others include **Morning Star Beach,** about two miles outside Charlotte Amalie, which also has dressing rooms and a restaurant, charging adults an admission of $2 (children under 12 are admitted free). **Lindberg Beach,** adjacent to the airport, is another favorite, as is **Coki Point** at Coral World (at the latter you can rent snorkeling gear).

Boating

The biggest charter business in the Caribbean is done by Virgin Islanders. In St. Thomas most of the business centers around the Red Hook and Yacht Haven marinas.

Perhaps the easiest way to go out to sea is to charter "your yacht for a day," from **Yacht** *Nightwind,* Red Hook (tel. 776-1110), for only $50 per person. You're granted a full-day sail with a champagne tropical lunch and open bar, aboard the 50-foot yawl *Nightwind*. You're also given free snorkeling equipment and instruction. For reservations, call between 8 a.m. and 9 p.m. daily. Stephen and June Marsh, operators of the service, natives of New Jersey, offer special attractions such as the "Bumperoo" show with the most photographed dog in the Caribbean and a break-dancing finale.

My Way is a 35-foot Pearson sloop which sails to the uninhabited island of Hans Lollick for $50 per person (call 776-9547 for reservations). Snorkeling equipment and instruction are provided, and there's an all-day bar. You take lunch on a deserted beach. Everything is included. Sailings leave from the north side of St. Thomas.

True Love is a sleek Malabar schooner, used during the filming of *High Society* starring Bing Crosby and Grace Kelly. It gave its name to the Cole Porter duet they sang. At 54 feet in length, it sails at 9:15 a.m. from Red Hook into Pillsbury Sound. Bill and Sue Beer have sailed it since 1965. You can join one of Bill's snorkeling classes and later enjoy one of Sue's gourmet lunches with champagne. Call 775-6547 for reservations. The cost is $50 per person.

The half-day sail to Buck Island on the 53-foot catamaran *Ho-Tei* is a bargain at $30. You'll have time to explore the sandy beaches too. Ask your hotel travel desk to book it for you, or else telephone 776-3139 for reservations.

Of course, if you want something more elaborate, you can go bareboating. That may suggest nudity, but it means renting a craft where you're the captain. However, you must prove you're able to handle the craft before you're allowed to go out in it alone. If you'd like everything done for you, a fully crewed yacht with the captain and crew at your service is the way to go on a charter plan. This type of charter rental is available through **Avery's Boathouse** (tel. 776-0113).

Deep-Sea Fishing

It's very good in the U.S. Virgins. Nineteen world records have been set in recent years (eight for blue marlin). Sports fishing is offered on the *Fish Hawk*. Al Petrosky of New Jersey sails from Fish Hawk Marina Lagoon at the East End on his 43-foot diesel-powered craft, which is fully equipped with rods and reels. Telephone 775-9058 for information.

Tennis

Many courts are lit for night play, and St. Thomas has a lot of them. Outstanding ones are at the **Bolongo Bay Beach and Tennis Club** (tel. 775-2489), which has four courts, two of which are lit until 11 p.m. It caters to members and hotel guests only, except for lessons which cost $14 per half hour.

At **Frenchman's Reef Tennis Courts** (tel. 774-8500, ext. 350), four courts are available and those not hotel guests are charged $6 a half hour per court. Lights stay on until 10 p.m.

There are also two courts at the **Virgin Isle Hotel** (tel. 774-1500), which charges $4 per hour during the day, $6 per hour at night.

Scuba and Snorkeling

With 30 spectacular reefs just off St. Thomas, the U.S. Virgins are rated as one of the "most beautiful areas in the world" by *Skin Diver* magazine. Since 1960 your best place for dive operations is **Joe Vogel Diving Co.**, 12B Mandahl Rd., Rte. 42, a one-minute drive east of the Mahogany Run Resort. It's run by ex-U.S. Navy frogman and company founder, Joe Vogel, and his wife, Debby Powers-Vogel. Joe still personally conducts all dives and limits each group to six or seven divers for your greater safety and enjoyment. Debby is company manager and an established underwater photographer. Scuba portraits by Debby cost $50 for 36 professional-quality color prints of your dive with them. For details on their NAUI certification-checkout dive service, courses, and other information, write P.O. Box 7322, St. Thomas, VI 00801, or call 809/775-7610 between 9 a.m. and 5 p.m. Monday through Saturday.

St. Thomas Diving Club, Bolongo Bay Beach and Tennis Resort (tel. 775-1800). Set in a wood-sided building on the beach of the Bolongo Bay Hotel, this well-equipped establishment offers everything a scuba enthusiast could want. Courses are organized for both beginners and experienced divers.

AFTER DARK: There are no casinos, no supper Las Vegas–type shows. However, there's some action. You just have to look for it:

Frenchman's Reef (tel. 776-8500) has the most nightlife, and enjoys a deserved reputation as "the entertainment center of St. Thomas." Occasionally top acts are imported to perform at the stage show at its **Top of the Reef Supper Club,** Monday through Saturday, with dancing offered not only before the show but until the early hours of the morning. Most people go for dinner, at which time they can order the chef's specialties, meals costing from $30. Dinner is from 8 to 10 p.m. If you go just for the show, you pay an $11.50 cover charge, which includes your first drink.

In addition, the hotel also offers **La Terrazza,** where a steel band plays and a limbo show is staged on Monday. Pop music and country and western are sometimes added to the evening's entertainment. Check at the desk for what's on. Dance music by top-flight entertainers is played from 9 p.m. to 2 a.m. except Monday. No minimum is charged, and drinks cost $3.50.

Bluebeard's Castle Hotel (tel. 774-1600) is another entertainment center. Call and see what's playing. Overlooking the pool and yacht harbor, the Dungeon Bar offers piano bar–type entertainment nightly except Thursday. You can dance, too. On Thursday and Friday nights there's a lively steel band. On Saturday night you can dance the night away to the music of one of the island's great combos. There is continuous entertainment until 1 a.m. All drink specialties are named after Bluebeard himself —Bluebeard's wench, cooler, and ghost. Most drinks cost from $2.50, although some specialty drinks are priced from $3. The Dungeon Bar is a popular gathering spot for both residents and visitors.

The **Carib Beach Hotel** (tel. 774-2525) is another lively spot. Perhaps you'll journey out here on Friday night for their West Indian buffet with a steel band and limbo show. You'll see a little fire-eating, walking on broken glass, stuff like that. Count on spending from $25 per person. Always call to make sure that Friday night is *the* night. St. Thomas hotels are known for switching the dates of their entertainment activities.

In town, I like the **Greenhouse,** Waterfront (tel. 774-7998), which enjoys a harbor view and features rock-'n-roll entertainment Tuesday to Sunday. At this restaurant-lounge, the chef offers a full breakfast from 7 to 11 a.m. and a lunch menu with a native special. There are also eight kinds of hamburgers. Dinner is served every night, costing from $10. The lounge features live entertainment seven nights a week, usually from 9:30 p.m. to 2 a.m. A friendly, breezy waterfront oasis, the Greenhouse will answer your questions about specials and entertainment if you give them a ring.

The **Ritz Cabaret,** on Dronningens Gade, popularly known as Back Street (tel. 774-6597), is clustered among a colony of nightlife places, outside of which it's sometimes dangerous to walk alone. Once you get inside the whimsically decorated, high-ceilinged interior of what used to be a warehouse, you'll forget any problems about the neighborhood and concentrate on one of the most glamorous urban-inspired milieus in Charlotte Amalie. Geraldine Ferraro dropped in here for a strawberry daiquiri after the 1984 presidential election, although few of the staff recognized her.

A New York City artist painted a huge mural of jazz musicians on one of the walls. Ceiling fans whir, mirrors glisten, and, during lunchtime, daily from 10 a.m. to 4 p.m., a cabaret-style pianist tickles the ivories as diners enjoy generous salads, sandwiches, or summer avocados or pineapples stuffed with various fillings.

Later in the day, the establishment's bar does a thriving business. Movies are sometimes shown between 7 and 9 p.m., after which the place becomes a disco. Guests, many of whom don't leave until around 4 a.m., pay $3.50 for a mixed drink and $3 for a beer. On Sunday the place is open only as a disco, from 9:30 p.m. to 4 a.m.

Walter's Living Room, 14 Kongens Gade (tel. 776-3880), at the foot of Government Hill, corner of Roosevelt Park, draws a lively crowd, often native Virgin Islanders. Sometimes live jazz groups appear at this old Danish cottage, and when they do there's a $3 minimum. The host who invites you into his "living room" is Walter Springette, a veteran of some 25 years in the nightclub business. The Living Room has a tropical atmosphere. Open Monday to Saturday from 11 a.m. to 4 a.m.

There is also **Walter's Living Room II,** on Back Street in front of Fat City (tel. 774-5025). This popular local disco is open from 11 a.m. to 4 a.m. (from 6:30 p.m. to 4 a.m. on Sunday). The second version of Walter's is housed in a restored early 20th-century wooden town house. It, too, has a lively ambience. You're never sure at which club Walter will turn up.

Jimmy'z, 41 Contant (tel. 776-4655), is a European-style disco where you can also enjoy northern Italian cuisine, presented by a chef from Turin, with proper Italian ingredients brought in by air. The nightclub, open from 10 p.m., levies no cover charge if you also have dinner. Otherwise it costs $10 just for the disco. The restaurant is open Monday to Saturday for lunch and dinner as well as for Sunday brunch. Dinner costs around $70, and drinks, about $4.50. Jimmy'z is a Regine's franchise, lying between the airport and the center of town, overlooking Crown Bay.

In Charlotte Amalie, a popular nighttime diversion is to patronize one of the local pubs along "Back Street," which is literally in back of the shopping malls fronting the waterfront. However, this street can be extremely dangerous at night—so don't go alone.

Along this row, I prefer **Chaps Western Saloon,** 11 Dronningens Gade (tel. 774-6597), which is a westernized pub with wide plank floors and food inspired by Texas and Mexico, rib-sticking fare like chili con carne, big beefburgers, and tacos. Drinks are generous, and the cost is low, around $15 for an evening with plenty of beer. Electronic games are the rage, and the place stays open late.

Rosie O'Grady's, on Dronningens Gade (tel. 774-0099). The original owners of this very old brick-walled bar were Irish, as you might guess from the name. Before retiring, they decorated the walls with memorabilia from the Emerald Isle and encouraged guests to sing whenever the spirit moved them. Today the spontaneous singing has been replaced with recorded music, although there's still a Gaelic kind of charm in the attitude of the friendly barmaids (yes, they're still called that here) and an occasional rowdiness worthy even of a pub in Killarney. No food is served here, so no one minds if you bring it in from the pizzeria across the street. Beer costs $2.50 to $3.25. Every day except Sunday the establishment opens for business at 10:30 a.m.; on Sunday it opens at 6 p.m. Closing is between 1 and 2 a.m.

2. St. John

About two miles east of St. Thomas, little St. John lies just across Pillsbury Sound. It is about seven miles long and three miles wide, with a total land area of some 19 square miles.

The smallest and least populated of the three main U.S. Virgins, St. John has more than one half of its land mass, as well as its shoreline waters, set aside as the Virgin Islands National Park, dedicated in 1956.

Once it was slated for big development when it was under Danish control, but a slave rebellion and a decline of the sugarcane plantations signaled the end of many a man's dream. For that reason St. John has remained truly virginal, unlike some other U.S. Virgins.

GETTING THERE AND AROUND: Among the many methods of reaching the island, the easiest and most frequented is by **ferryboat,** leaving from Red Hook landing on St. Thomas, the trip taking about 20 minutes. Beginning at 6:30 a.m., except weekends and holidays, boats depart every hour. The last ferry back heads out of the harbor at St. John at 10 p.m.

Because of such frequent departures, even cruise-ship passengers, anchored in Charlotte Amalie for only a short time, can visit St. John for a quickie island tour, perhaps a picnic and a swim at one of its fine sandy beaches, returning in time for dinner. The one-way fare is $2 per adult, $1 for children.

Should you ever get stranded, water-taxi service is available 24 hours a day for about $35 for two persons.

To reach the ferry, you can take an open-air shuttle which departs from the Market Square in Charlotte Amalie. It will take you on weekdays (not on Sunday) to the ferry dock at Red Hook. The fare is $2 per person each way. It's also possible to board a boat directly at the Charlotte Amalie waterfront for a cost of $5 one way, the ride taking 45 minutes. Boats depart St. Thomas at 9 a.m., 11 a.m., 3 p.m., 5:30 p.m., and 7 p.m., and they leave Cruz Bay on St. John at 7:15 a.m., 9:15 a.m., 1:15 p.m., 3:45 p.m., and finally at 5:15 p.m. (the last departure from the National Park Dock).

Also, a launch service leaves from the dock at Caneel Bay at St. John heading for the National Park Dock at Red Hook on St. Thomas. This one-way fare, however, costs $9 per person.

In addition, **Virgin Islands Seaplane Shuttle** will take you from either St. Thomas or St. Croix on either Tuesday or Thursday. For reservations, telephone 773-1776.

Getting Around

Once on St. John, there are several methods of getting around, the most popular of which is by **surrey-style taxi.** If you just want to go from the ferry landing dock to Trunk Bay, for example, the cost is about $6 for two passengers. Between midnight and 6 a.m., fares are increased by 40%.

The **St. John Taxi Association** (tel. 776-6060) also conducts a historical tour of St. John, including swimming at Trunk Bay and a visit to the Caneel Bay resort, at a cost of $18 for one or two persons. Tours depart Cruz Bay seven days a week at 9:45 a.m., 10:45 a.m., and 11:45 a.m.

It's also possible to use the **bus** service running from Cruz Bay to Maho Bay, stopping at Caneel and Cinnamon Bays. The one-way bus fare costs $3.50 for adults.

Varlack Ventures, P.O. Box 300, St. John, VI 00830 (tel. 809/776-6412). Many visitors feel that the real beauty of St. John lies away from Cruz Bay, along some of the relatively inaccessible coastline. Should you wish to reach such places, a Jeep might be the best means of getting there. Rentals of these four-wheel drives cost $45 per day, with $5 per day for insurance. Renters are required to post a $45 deposit and must be between the ages of 25 and 65. Gas is not provided, although there's usually just enough in the Jeep to get you to one of the two gas stations on the island. It's never a good idea to drive around St. John with an almost-empty tank. Varlack, about a block from the ferryboat pier, also rents a limited number of air-conditioned cars, priced at $40 per day.

Many newcomers to St. John hope to explore at least a part of the island, yet are frustrated because of the poorly marked, sometimes barely passable roads. You can always rent a four-wheel-drive vehicle, but even then you'll lack the guidance of a leader who knows the charming hidden inlets and the most panoramic vistas. Margie Brown-Boynes, who used to work for the mayor's office in Philadelphia, might offer a solution. Her company, **B&B Photo Tours** (tel. 776-6979), has created a choice of unusual ways to while away your hours on St. John. Photographers appreciate the dozens of stops which a guide makes for perfect picture-postcard mementos. A tour of the land and waters ringing St. John, in surprisingly posh circumstances, costs $25 per person. For more information, get in touch with Ms. Brown-Boynes.

WHERE TO STAY: From a tropical retreat, one of the most spectacular in the Caribbean, to a campsite, the choice of accommodations in St. John is limited, and that's how most people would like to keep it.

Upper-Bracket Living

Caneel Bay, Inc., Caneel Bay, Cruz Bay, VI 00830 (tel. 809/776-6111), grew out of a dream of an idealistic man, Laurance S. Rockefeller, and it's a remarkable achievement. Now owned by a Virginia corporation, it's a super-luxurious resort placed on a 170-acre portion of St. John, built on the site of a mid-1700s sugar plantation directly on the bay, with a choice of seven beaches. Resort owners throughout the Caribbean speak of Caneel Bay with supreme respect. It's still operated by Rockresorts. The retreat of many an industrialist and government leader, the hotel caters to people with full purses who know their needs can be met with style. The main buildings are strung along the bays, with a Caribbean lounge and dining room at its core. Other, separate units—really bedroom villas—stand along the beaches, so all you have to do is step from your private veranda onto the sands.

Not all of the 170 rooms, however, are on the beaches. Some are set back on low cliffs or headlands. AP rates in winter range from $305 to $465 daily in a single, from $335 to $495 daily in a double. *In summer, daily AP rates in a single go from $175 to $315, from $205 to $345 in a double*. But if you're coming down for the summer, you should ask about one of the special packages likely to be offered, everything from honeymoon to boating to one that combines a visit at Caneel Bay with a stay at Little Dix Bay in the British Virgins. The most loyal devotees of Caneel Bay book their favorite room in winter a year in advance, and February is almost always sold out.

The buildings have a quiet understatement in decor, and I suspect the habitués of the place would rebel if the management tried to change the dark bamboo. The choice spot at Caneel Bay is the Turtle Bay Estate House, part of the 18th-century Dutch sugar plantation, serving now as one of a trio of dining locations (for the most part, only guests dine here; the other dining facilities are described in the "Where to Eat" section, which follows the hotel recommendations). Surrounding all buildings is a skillfully planted garden, filled with sea grape, brilliant-red flamboyant, the geranium tree, the golden shower tree, poinsettias, hibiscus, oleander, the red ixora, and of course plenty of bougainvillea that washes everything with color. When man has intruded architecturally, it is generally with natural elements such as wood and native stone.

There are many, many scheduled activities per week, ranging from a fishing trip to a walk through the ruin of the old sugar mill. Of course, in addition to its beaches, the plantation also opens onto an undersea world, as there are endless inlets and secret reefs to explore. Snorkeling lessons are given free each day, and divers can go on trips to the many historic shipwrecks. A fleet of boats awaits your command, and there is complimentary use of the resort's sailboards for windsurfers. Perhaps the pursuit of the elusive wahoo will send you on a deep-sea fishing trip. In the evening you can listen to calypso music, dance, perhaps enjoy a steel band.

The **Virgin Grand Beach Hotel,** Great Cruz Bay, VI 00830 (tel. 809/776-7171, 212/661-4540 in New York City, or toll free 800/223-1588 in the U.S., 800/531-6767 in Canada), is the newest, splashiest, and best-designed hotel in St. John. Frequently confused with the Wyndham Grand in St. Thomas, it was built by the same Ohio-based contractor, who used most of the design ideas he'd already used in St. Thomas. Despite the aggressively independent management of the two rivals, there are striking similarities of architecture and color. However, the St. John property occupies a better natural site and is probably built on a more lavish scale than its competitor in St. Thomas. It sits on 34 acres of what used to be scrub forest on the southeast side of the island. Its design is filled with ziggurat-shaped angles, soaring ceilings, large windows, and an overall style that seems inspired by Aztec, Egyptian, or neocolonial models.

A total of 13 cedar-roofed buildings contain the 264 bedrooms and the handful of stylish restaurants and bars. Herringbone-patterned brick walkways interconnect the gardens (where 400 palms were imported from Puerto Rico) with the beach and the zigzag borders of the most unusual swimming pool in the Virgin Islands. Tennis courts, a sandy beach, an array of water sports, and an enthusiastic staff make this place memorable. Each of the stylish accommodations contains fan-shaped windows, curved ceilings, unusual but pleasing dimensions, and a softly vibrant color scheme of rose and mauve. James St. John III, the Texas-born manager, charges winter rates of $300 to $450 in a single, $350 to $550 in a double, with full board. *Expect to spend at least 30% less in summer*. Guests from North America use the hotel's special waiting lounge at the St. Thomas airport, where connections are made for transportation to St. John.

Campgrounds

Maho Bay, P.O. Box 310, Cruz Bay, St. John, VI 00830 (tel. 809/776-6240). What I like most about this place is that there is a help-yourself center where groceries, books, and magazines are left by departing campers for new arrivals to take. That sets the tone for this interesting concept in ecology vacationing, where you get about as close to nature as you can, but with considerable comfort. Maho Bay is a deluxe campground set in the heart of the National Park Reserve, seemingly inspired by Fire Island (New York) where the technique of running wooden walkways through vegetation was advanced. Utility lines and pipes are hidden underneath.

You stay in a tent-like cottage made of canvas. Each unit has a choice of a double bed or two built-in single beds, a couch that converts into a double bed, electric lamps and outlets, a round dining table, chairs, a propane stove, and an ice chest (cooler). That's not all—you're furnished linen, towels, dinner service, and utensils. There's a store where you can buy (expensive) supplies. You do your own housekeeping and cooking, although you can eat at the camp's outdoor restaurant. Guests share a community bathhouse. Each unit is cantilevered over a thickly wooded area, providing a view of the sea, sky, and beach. *From mid-April to mid-December, no minimum stay is required and cottages (limited to two adults) rent for $45 per day. Children under age 7 pay $7 per night per person; over 7, $10 each*. In season, the minimum stay is seven nights, and the cost is $60 per cottage, occupancy by two persons. Others sharing a cottage pay from $10 per person nightly.

Maho Bay has a community center, housing a restaurant which serves breakfast every morning for $3 to $5. This includes juice, eggs or french toast, and coffee. There is no charge for extra juice or coffee. For dinner, they have asked some of the best cooks on St. John to cater. Menus are posted and people who are interested sign up in advance. Typical meals are fresh fish or chicken, goat stew, whelk stew, conch stew, quiche, and lasagne. Prices range from $7 to $10 for a full dinner. This allows guests to meet the local people who function as entrepreneurs rather than staff, and also to taste local cooking. The islanders, by making the food preparation a family endeavor, can offer a good meal much cheaper than the camp could. Meals are served on a covered patio which overlooks the water. This same patio functions as an amphitheater where they have nature lectures, concerts of folk music, scuba and sailing movies, and lectures by park rangers. The bathhouse which services the community center is testing the Clivus Multrum composting toilets which use no water at all. So far, the word is that they are a miracle.

The camp attracts an interesting array of guests, everybody from honeymoon couples to botanists to college students. Don't expect a bar or entertainment. It's a camp for people who love the sounds, smells, textures, and visual splendor of a beautiful preserve. The location is an eight-mile drive from Cruz Bay, and there's regularly scheduled bus service. The camp also has the best program of water sports on the island (see below).

Cinnamon Bay Campground, P.O. Box 720, Cruz Bay, VI 00830 (tel. 809/

776-6330), established by the National Park Service in 1964, is the most complete campground in the Caribbean. The site is directly on the beach, and thousands of acres of tropical vegetation surround you, an opportunity to get insect-repellent close to nature. Life is simple here, and you have a choice of three different ways of sleeping—tents, cottages, and bare sites. In winter, a cottage rents for $59 a day for two persons, a tent for $49, and a bare site for $10. *In the off-season, cottages cost $33 to $48 per day for two persons; tents $26 to $39; and bare sites, from $10.*

At the bare campsites, nothing is provided except general facilities. Canvas tents are 10 by 14 feet with floor, and a number of facilities are offered, including all cooking equipment. Even your linen is changed weekly. Cottages are 15 by 15 feet, a screened room with two concrete walls and two screen walls. They consist of four twin beds, and two cots can be added. Cooking facilities are also supplied. Lavatories and showers are in separate buildings nearby. Camping is limited to a two-week period in any given year. Near the road is a camp center office, with a grocer and a cafeteria (serving $8 dinners).

Management is handled by Rockresorts, and reservations can be made at 30 Rockefeller Plaza, Room 5400, New York, NY 10112 (tel. 212/586-4459 in New York City, or toll free 800/223-7637, 800/442-8198 in New York state).

Housekeeping Holidays

Gallows Point, P.O. Box 58, Cruz Bay, VI 00830 (tel. 809/776-6434), is a cluster of appealing cottages whose villa-style architecture assures privacy. Nestled into a carefully cultivated garden, they were patterned after 18th-century Danish manor houses. The clapboards, the latticework, the fan-shaped windows, the panoramic porches, and the louvered French doors are stained a shade of putty. Each villa contains four separate units, the most desirable being on the top floor. These have massive exposed beams of Canadian cedar, yards and yards of planking, sleeping lofts, and comfortable tropical furniture. The ground-floor (garden) units have sunken living rooms, wooden decks facing the water, and bathrooms full of greenery. Each has its own fully equipped kitchenette. In winter, a garden suite costs $225 per night; a loft suite, around $250. *In summer, a garden suite rents for around $130; a loft unit, around $150.* Prices are reduced for stays of five nights or longer. The management will accept collect phone calls for reservations. You'll notice this complex of stylish buildings from the ferryboat as it enters the mouth of Cruz Bay, because of its sentinel position above the yachts bobbing below.

Carla's Cottages, Estate Bethany (P.O. Box 432), Cruz Bay, VI 00830 (tel. 809/776-6133), one of the intimate inns of St. John, is charming and small enough to permit guests to make friends with the attractive owner, Carla Corkins. Formerly of Cincinnati, she purchased a small estate in 1978 and enlarged the facilities, opening for business three years later. The establishment is set at one of the highest points of the island, with a view of both the Atlantic and the Caribbean. Three well-built cottages, with comfortable furniture and lots of exposed planking, have two separate accommodations each. Continental breakfast, included in the rates, is served every morning on the panoramic veranda of Carla's private house, and other meals can be arranged in advance. Double rooms cost $125 to $250 in winter, *$80 to $145 in summer,* the price depending on the accommodation. The cottages' social center revolves around the spacious living room and front veranda of Carla's house, a few steps from the bubbling turquoise waters of a Jacuzzi and the most beautifully situated swimming pool on the island.

Estate Zootenvaal, Hurricane Hole, St. John, VI 00830 (tel. 809/776-6321, 216/861-5337 in the U.S.), lies within the boundaries of the U.S. National Park at the edge of a horseshoe-shaped bay which local mariners know is usually safe from even the most violent hurricane. It's a good choice for escapees from urban areas who want the minimum of interference they might find at a large hotel. Consisting of five cement-sided villas, each sporting exterior walls of vivid turquoise, it sits within earshot of the waves on the grounds of what used to be a private estate called Zootenvaal. Each villa is clean, comfortably furnished with tasteful simplicity, and exceptionally quiet. Each has a fully equipped kitchen. A few have housed novelists holing up to complete a manuscript. Maid service can be arranged for an extra cost, on an as-needed basis. In winter, two persons can live here for around $150 per day or $840 per week. An extra person in a unit pays $25 per day. *In summer, two persons pay around $120 per day or $670 per week.*

Best for the Budget

Raintree Inn, P.O. Box 566, Cruz Bay, VI 00830 (tel. 809/776-7449), with rambling wooden verandas and consciously simple decor, is reminiscent of a place you might have camped out in during a rock concert in the 1960s. There are only some 11 bedrooms, three with kitchenettes. Each has a high ceiling and one or two ceiling fans, lots of latticework, and arched windows. Cantilevered above a lush valley, near the Catholic church just above the center of town, the establishment charges winter prices of $55 for a double without kitchen, $85 for one with a kitchen. *The rest of the year, from mid-April to mid-December, rooms without kitchen cost $55 for two persons, and units with kitchens go for around $75.* An extra person in a room is charged $14 per day. Prices are slightly reduced for rentals of a week or more.

WHERE TO EAT: Visitors over just for the day generally like to have lunch at the **Sugar Mill Kitchen** on the grounds of Caneel Bay (tel. 776-6111). From 11:30 a.m. to 3 p.m. it offers grilled items, salads, and sandwiches. Up until 3 p.m. you can order good-tasting tropical drinks, such as a plantation punch or a peach daiquiri. From the restaurant there is a panoramic view overlooking St. Thomas and its surrounding cays. Diners are seated on a "horse-mill" platform (when the wind was insufficient to turn the mills in the old days, beasts of burden such as one-eyed donkeys were used). Lunch specialties include lobster salad, ginger barbecued chicken, and broiled chopped sirloin. There is always a cake of the day. Guests come here for sundowners at 6:30 p.m. For about $40 you can enjoy a buffet dinner served nightly except Sunday on a reservation-only basis. Featured are a choice of grilled entrees, a salad bar, and a dessert table. Dining is only from 7 to 8:30 p.m. Dress is informal, but no shorts are permitted in the evening unless worn with knee socks.

Before someone has settled into St. John, he or she has been told about the buffets served overlooking the water at the **Caneel Bay Beach Terrace Dining Room** (tel. 776-6111), on the grounds of the Caneel Bay Hotel, right below the Sugar Mill. The $20 buffet luncheon is one of the best in the Virgin Islands. It is always necessary to make a reservation. After you're assigned an open-air table overlooking the beach and the water, and you've given your drink order, you proceed to the buffet counter. I suggest a visit first to a side counter where freshly cut tropical fruit such as pineapple is spread around a bowl of cold soup (my recent bisque of almond sent me rushing back to the chef for the recipe). After soup and fruit, you can proceed to the tempting array of salads (usually one made of avocado) and cold meats. As an elegant touch, fresh mushrooms are sliced, awaiting your favorite dressing. Corn chutney, smoked oysters, and many other plates await your selection. If, after all that, you still have room for hot dishes, you'll find those followed by a big table of desserts, including such delectable pies as blueberry cheese. Drinks are extra.

In the evening, if you return for dinner from 7 to 8:30 p.m., you should make a reservation, and men are required to wear jackets from November to May. At that time you can have a complete dinner for $40 per person. Appetizers might include papaya with prosciutto, followed by excellently prepared soups (perhaps potato leek, maybe cold strawberry tapioca). Salads are invariably good, including the marinated green bean or the tossed garden greens mimosa. Main dishes are likely to include baked filet of red snapper (with onions, tomatoes, and green peppers), beef tenderloin à la Stroganoff, or roast prime rib of blue-ribbon beef carved to order with natural juices. There are always some calorie-loaded desserts such as strawberry cheesecake or Boston cream pie. Menus are changed nightly. On Sunday the chef offers a sumptuous buffet of West Indian, continental, and American dishes between 7 and 9 p.m.

Ellington's, Gallows Point, Cruz Bay (tel. 776-7166), is by far the most stylish and exciting independent restaurant on St. John. Set near the neocolonial villas of Gallows Point, its putty-colored exterior has the same kind of double staircase, fan windows, louvers, and low-slung hip roof found in an 18th-century Danish manor house. Inside is a surprising collection of tropical hardwoods, fashioned into generous sheaths which envelop bar tops, tabletops, stair treads, and the floor. The slabs of red locust, Brazilian angelique, purpleheart, and mahogany were chosen by New Jersey–born Ed Gilroy. Drop in for a drink on the panoramic upper deck where a view of Cruz Bay unfolds. The establishment is named after a local radio announcer ("The Fat Man"), raconteur, and mystery writer whose real estate developments helped transform St. John into a stylish enclave for the American literati of the 1950s and '60s. Named Richard "Duke" Ellington (not to be confused with the great musician), he entertained his friends, martini in hand, around a frequently photographed table painted with a map of St. John. The tabletop today hangs in the Ellington's dining room.

Breakfast is served daily from 8 to 10 a.m., followed by lunch, costing from $12 and served from 11:30 a.m. to 2:30 p.m. The menu might include crab salad sandwiches, hot Italian steak sandwiches, crisp salads, and New England–style conch chowder. Dinners are elegant, elaborate, and lighthearted affairs. Specialties include mushrooms stuffed with crabmeat, conch fritters, Tahitian-style fish salads, coconut-laced chicken, surf and turf, and shrimp with scallops dijonaise. Costing from $30 each, dinners are served nightly from 6 to 10 p.m.

The Upper Deck, Cruz Bay (tel. 776-6318), has the best view and the most atmospheric location of any restaurant on St. John, outside of Caneel Bay. Reached by a bumpy Jeep ride, it's a honey. The bar opens at 5 p.m. and I recommend that you go then for your sundowner, enjoying that view while it's still daylight. You don't need a reservation—just arrive, but only Wednesday through Sunday. No luncheons are served, only dinner, anytime between 6:30 and 9 p.m. The decor is casual and rustic, like an overscale mountain cabin. Tables, lit by candlelight, are placed on an open deck. The location is about five minutes from Cruz Bay dock.

Your hosts are Clarence and Sis Thomas, both Americans. He worked for an advertising agency in New York, producing TV shows, before finding his little oasis on St. John. Sis never went to cooking school, and she has no pretensions in that direction: "At 16 I learned to cook for hungry farmers in Pennsylvania." She offers plain, ordinary cookery, and it's good. Each day she makes a pot of soup such as New England clam chowder. Many of her dishes come from the charcoal grill, including lamb chops, sirloin steak, and pork chops. These dishes are served with a choice of tossed salad or coleslaw. Each night she offers a special, perhaps spareribs or chicken à la king. From the sea, a nightly fish special with accompaniments is served. Try also her fried scallops followed by one of her homemade desserts. An average repast here is likely to cost from $15 per person.

The restaurant is on the same premises as the Bethany Condominiums, also managed by Sis Thomas. High on a breezy hill in a park-like setting, the nine studio apartments (one single and four doubles) are equipped for housekeeping and have sleeping facilities for two or four persons as well as sweeping views of the Caribbean Sea and adjacent islands. Rents are $50 to $55 per day for two persons year round, with each extra person charged $10.

Mongoose Restaurant, Café, and Bar, Mongoose Junction (tel. 776-7586). Some visitors compare its soaring interior design to a large Japanese birdcage because of the strong vertical lines and its 25-foot ceiling. Set among trees and built above a stream, it's a lot like a structure you'd come across in Marin County in northern California. Many guests create a perch for themselves at the bar for a drink and sandwich; other possibilities for seating lie on an adjacent deck where a canopy of trees filters the tropical sunlight. The establishment is open daily on weekdays for breakfast, continuing without interruption until around midnight. The bar offers more than 20 varieties of frothy island-inspired libations. Lunches, served weekdays only, cost from $12 and include well-stuffed sandwiches, salad platters, and main courses such as seafood Creole, island fishcakes, and vegetable stir-fries. Dinners include more of the same but are slightly more expensive, from $18 each. The salad bar is served in an old-fashioned boat. A Friday-night buffet ranges from $10 to $19, depending on whether you select lobster as a main course. An especially popular Saturday and Sunday brunch, lasting between 9 a.m. and 3 p.m. every weekend, costs $10 per person.

Café Roma, Cruz Bay (tel. 776-6443), is the only Italian restaurant and pizza parlor on St. John. Diners climb a long flight of concrete exterior steps before reaching the pleasantly rustic domain of the McGinnis family. Open daily for dinner only, between 5 and 10 p.m., the establishment charges around $15 for a full meal. You might begin with a strawberry colada, then enjoy one of four kinds of spaghetti, lasagne, fettuccine Alfredo, chicken cacciatore (or else francese, marsala, or romano), or five different kinds of veal. Italian wines are sold by the bottle or glass, any one of which could be followed by a cup of chocolate-flavored espresso.

The **Lime Inn,** Lemon Tree Center, Cruz Bay (tel. 776-6425), pleasant and airy, and sheathed with glowing strips of well-finished pine, is the perfect choice for a well-prepared meal and a suitably frothy drink. It's in a labyrinth of boutiques and shops in the center of Cruz Bay, decorated with lattices and plants and crowned by a solidly trussed tin roof. This is the domain of a New Jersey–born couple, Richard and Christine Meyer, who offer live music (calypso and rock and roll) most nights in high season. Lunch is served daily except Saturday from 11:30 a.m. to 5:30 p.m. Dinner is daily except Sunday from 5:30 to 10 p.m. An island event is the all-you-can-eat shrimp dinner, every Wednesday, costing $15 per person. Other nights, the menu items include filet mignon stuffed with bleu cheese and brie, smoked marlin salad, quiche du jour, caesar salad, steaks, and three kinds of shrimp. Full meals go for $17 per person.

Redbeard's Saloon, Coral Bay (tel. 776-9214). It's fun, it's friendly, and it's one of the best places on the island for doses of humor and goodwill. It was established in 1982 when Ted (Redbeard) and Barbara Johnson quit their jobs in New York as an advertising agent and graphic artist to move to St. John. Dubbing their rustic saloon "Redbeard's Saloon Day Care Center and Animal Shelter," they then proceeded to welcome friends and clients (many of whom are one and the same) into their bar. It's contained in a breeze-filled building from the 1940s with a pleasant courtyard in back overlooking Coral Harbor. Murals line many of the walls, both inside and out, many showing tropical themes. You can always come here just to drink (and many do), although breakfast, lunch, and dinner are served every day of the week. Full dinners cost around $12; lunches, about half that. Blackboard specials are likely to include baked red snapper, spaghetti carbonara, and steaks. Because a country store and a gift shop are on the premises, the place opens for breakfast and remains so until every client has gone home later that night.

Shipwreck Landing, Coral Bay (tel. 776-6253). Its location eight miles east of Cruz Bay, in an isolated position at the edge of Coral Bay, qualifies it as an attractive destination after an island sightseeing tour. You dine near palms and old trees, on a deliberately rustic veranda of a raffish and rakish island house. Tom Meacham, the owner, came here from New Jersey in the 1960s to hunt treasure, and decided to stay. He built many of the tables that grace the deck, along with much of the interior finish work of the cramped and deliberately intimate bar. Open daily for food and drink between 10 a.m. and 10 p.m., the place serves a potent cocktail called a "Shipwreck," made with four kinds of rum and a deceptively bland fruited base. Menu items include grilled dolphin, swordfish, steaks, the catch of the day, roast beef, lasagne, and barbecued ribs. Full meals cost from $15; however, many clients come here just to order a sandwich, from $4.50. The landing lies on the road between Cruz Bay and Salt Pond Beach.

Shady Grove Restaurant, 265 Great Cruz Bay (tel. 776-7630), cantilevered on stilts above a steeply sloping, scrub-covered hillside, is one of the most casual places at which to eat on the entire island. Canopies of trees which rise above its terrace create a cool oasis for the guests who drop in. You order whatever you want from a deli-like counter inside, then carry it to your seat at a picnic table. Elvis, the owner, offers beef, hamburgers, sandwiches, fried chicken, fried eggs, french fries, and steaks. Sandwiches cost $2.50; a steak, $7. Breakfast is also available, for $4.50. The restaurant is open daily except Sunday from 8:30 a.m. to 6 p.m.

Vie's Snack Shack, East End (tel. 776-6486), looks like little more than a plywood-sided hut on the island's East End, about 12½ miles from Cruz Bay. Nonetheless, its charming and gregarious owner is known as one of the best local chefs in St. John. After living in both Texas and Germany, Vie decided that what St. John needed was an infusion of her own special recipes. Her garlic-flavored chicken is considered the best on the island, and you can also order johnny cakes, conch fritters, and fresh fish when it's available. Full meals cost from $8 each. Most weekdays she's open for business between 9 or 10 in the morning until around 7 p.m., but she's been known to remain open until around midnight. As she says, "Some days we might not be there at all." So you'd better call before heading out.

WHAT TO SEE: I personally like to spend lots of time at Cruz Bay, where the ferry docks. In this West Indian village there are interesting bars, restaurants, boutiques, and pastel-painted houses. It's pretty sleepy, but amusing to some after the fast pace of St. Thomas. The museum at Cruz Bay isn't big, but it does contain some local artifacts and will teach you something about the history of the island. It's at the public library, and can be visited from 9 a.m. to 5 p.m. Monday through Friday.

Most cruise-ship passengers seem to dart through Cruz Bay, heading for the island's biggest attraction, the **Virgin Islands National Park.**

Before going to the park, you may want to stop at the Visitor's Center at Cruz Bay, which is open daily from 8 a.m. to 4:30 p.m. There you'll see some exhibits and learn more about what you'll be viewing. Regular briefings are given.

By 1981 the size of the park totaled 12,624 acres, including submerged lands and waters adjacent to St. John, and since 1956 a trail system of 20 miles has been developed. This is the only national park in the Caribbean area.

In 1952 Laurance S. Rockefeller purchased a small resort here and developed it, eventually donating it to the nonprofit Jackson Hole Preserve, an organization founded and supported by the Rockefeller family. Jackson Hole, in turn, after purchasing more than 5,000 acres of St. John, about half the island, donated the land to the U.S. government.

If time is very limited, try a visit to the **Annaberg Ruins,** where the Danes launched sugar-mill plantation life in 1718. On Tuesday, Wednesday, and Friday from 10 a.m. to 1 p.m., St. John islanders show you their own style of native cookery and explain basketweaving.

Trunk Bay is considered by those who know such things as "one of the world's most beautiful beaches." The beach is also the site of one of the world's first marked underwater trails.

Park rangers conduct **national park tours** of St. John. You can explore a three-mile trail which goes by the petroglyphs, figures (still undeciphered) carved on boulders by mysterious people of the past. You'll also pass by the ruins of sugar mills and a great house. You must make a reservation for all tours by calling 776-6201. A bus tour leaves on Monday. To catch up with it, you must be on the 8 a.m. ferry from Red

Hook. Once on St. John, you board a special bus for $10 per passenger, leaving from the National Park Visitor's Center at 9 a.m. The tour lasts three hours.

Every Friday the rangers conduct a Reef Bay hike at 9 a.m. This time, it is necessary to take the 9 a.m. ferry from Red Hook in St. Thomas. The bus ride, costing $2, leaves from the National Park Visitor's Center at 10 a.m. A special boat, costing $5 per passenger, takes you back to Cruz Bay at 3:30 p.m. when you can catch another ferry to St. Thomas. Bring your own food and beverage.

Fort Berg (called Fortsberg) at Coral Bay dates from 1717 and played a disastrous role in history in the 1733 slave revolt that devastated the economy of St. John. The fort may be restored as a historic monument.

THE SPORTING LIFE: Don't visit here expecting to play golf. Rather, anticipate some of the best snorkeling, scuba-diving, swimming, fishing, hiking, sailing, and underwater photography in the Caribbean. The island is known for its coral-sand beaches, winding mountain roads, trails past decaying, bushcover sugarcane plantations, and hidden coves.

Water Sports

The most complete line of water sports available on St. John is offered at the **Cinnamon Bay Watersports Center** on Cinnamon Bay Beach (tel. 776-6458). Specializing in sailing and sailboat rentals, the staff will charge you $40 for a full day's outing ($25 for a half day) aboard the yacht *Gloria*. Snorkeling equipment and stopoffs at secluded reefs and uninhabited islands provide some of the most vivid underwater viewing in the region. Beer, sodas, and snorkeling equipment are covered by the cost of the trip, but you must bring your own picnic lunch. A less rigorous (and more romantic) cruise, costing $17 per person, departs every Thursday at 5 p.m. for sunset viewing, returning 1½ hours later. Rum punch is included in the price. An introductory scuba-diving course, recommended for strong swimmers only, includes a lecture, a pool dive, and a one-tank shallow-reef dive.

If you're only interested in snorkeling, you can make trips on the M/V *Cinnamon Bay*, which circumnavigates St. John every Wednesday, leaving at 9 a.m. and stopping frequently for snorkelers to explore little-visited reefs. The cost is $25 per person.

Windsurfing here is some of the best to be found anywhere. You can rent a board for $12 per hour, $30 for half a day. A 90-minute lesson costs around $30.

Swimming

Trunk Bay is the word. It's the biggest attraction on St. John and a beach collector's find. To miss its great white sweep would be like going to Europe and skipping Paris. As mentioned, **Caneel Bay** fronts seven beautiful beaches, and the camps at **Cinnamon** and **Maho Bay** have their own beaches where forest rangers constantly have to remind visitors to put their swimming suits back on, if they have any.

Hiking

It's the big thing here, and a network of trails covers the national park. However, I suggest a tour by Jeep first, just to get your bearings. At the Visitor's Center at Cruz Bay, ask for a free trail map of the park. It's best to set out with someone experienced in the mysteries of the island. Both Maho and Cinnamon Bays conduct nature walks.

Tennis

Caneel Bay Plantation monopolizes the game, with seven courts and a pro shop. However, these courts aren't lit at night, and are likely to be used almost exclusively by guests. There are two public courts at Cruz Bay, however.

SHOPPING: Compared to St. Thomas, it isn't much, but what there is in interesting.

The **Caneel Bay Boutique** is the place to go for island resort wear—no contest. The style here is casual but sophisticated, and the prices are high.

The boutiques and shops of Cruz Bay are individualized and quite special. Most of the shops are clustered at **Mongoose Junction**, in a woodsy area beside the road-way, about a fast five-minute walk from the ferry dock. I've already endorsed dining in this avant-garde complex, and it also contains shops of merit.

Donald Schnell Studio (tel. 776-6420) is a working studio and gallery at Mongoose Junction on St. John. Mr. Schnell and his assistants feature one of the finest collections of handmade pottery, sculpture, and blown glass in the Caribbean. They can be seen producing daily and are especially noted for their rough-textured coral work. Water fountains are a specialty item, as are house signs. The complete six-piece coral pottery dinnerware is unique and popular. The studio will mail works all over the world. Go in and discuss any particular design you may have in mind. They enjoy designing to please customers.

The **Canvas Factory,** Cruz Bay (tel. 776-6196), produces its own handmade, rugged, and colorful canvas bags in the "factory" in Mongoose Junction. They also specialize in well-made, practical, 100% canvas clothing.

Virgin Canvas and Crafts, Cruz Bay (tel. 776-6223), offers canvas bags and fine gifts, consisting of locally made jewelry, baskets, hats, clothes, and hammocks, along with an array of canvas bags and luggage manufactured on the premises. Marine canvas work is a specialty. The establishment is one block west of the Chase Bank.

The **Clothing Studio,** Mongoose Junction (tel. 776-6585), is the Caribbean's oldest hand-painted-clothing studio, in operation since 1978. You can watch talented artists create original designs on fine tropical clothing, including swimwear, daytime and evening clothing, and articles for babies, children, men, and women. The shop studio will create custom designs just for you.

You'll find some exciting fabrics at **Fabric Mill** (tel. 776-6194), another Mongoose Junction shopping attraction. Specializing in silkscreened and batik prints from around the world, Fabric Mill also carries locally silkscreened fabric displaying island motifs. Interesting accessories, soft sculptures, and unique gift items are also made in this studio shop.

R and I Patton Goldsmithing (tel. 776-6548), by the entrance to Mongoose Junction, has a large selection of Rudy and Irene Pattons' island-designed jewelry in sterling, gold, and precious stones.

D. Knight & Company, Cruz Bay (tel. 776-7958), is an establishment of interest only to a limited handful of readers who are interested in fine cabinetry and tropical hardwoods. In an industrial building just east of Cruz Bay on Rte. 104 you'll find one of the finest collections of exotic woods in the Caribbean. Mr. Knight's inventory includes beautifully striated Brazilian angelique, red locust from Dominica, honey-colored samaan, Burmese teak, ebony, black jacaranda, brown heart, green heart, purple heart, and rosewood. Unless you plan to buy massive quantities of the stuff, shipping it home will be a problem, but if you're just looking for a few boards for the top of something you're rebuilding in your workshop, Mr. Knight can arrange shipping through the mail.

3. St. Croix

The largest of the U.S. Virgin Islands, 84 square miles of real estate, St. Croix was discovered by Columbus on November 14, 1493, but the reception committee of Carib Indians was far from friendly. He anchored his ship off Salt River Point, on the north shore of St. Croix, before the Indians drove him away. However, before leaving he named the island Santa Cruz (Spanish for Holy Cross). Those cannibalistic Indians made later colonizing parties less than eager to settle in St. Croix.

However, the Dutch arrived, as did the English, and for a short time St. Croix was owned by the Knights of Malta, no great pioneers. The Spanish drove the British out, only to be driven out themselves by the French, and so the familiar story of Caribbean colonization went. It wasn't until 1650 that the French laid claim to the island, later abandoning their attempts at colonization.

The Danes purchased St. Croix in 1773, attracted to the island because of its slave labor and sugarcane fields. This marked the golden era of St. Croix, as both planters and pirates grew wealthy. However, the sugar boom ended, with eventual slave uprisings, the introduction of the sugar beet in Europe, and the emancipation of 1848. Even though seven different flags have flown over St. Croix, it is the nearly 2½ centuries of Danish influence that still permeates the island and its architecture.

St. Croix has some of the best beaches in the Virgin Islands, and ideal weather. It doesn't have the sophisticated nightlife of St. Thomas, nor would its permanent residents want that.

African tulips are just some of the flowers that add a splash of color to the landscape, and stately towers that once supported grinding mills are but lonely ghosts on moonlit nights.

At the east end of St. Croix, which, incidentally, is the easternmost point of the United States, the terrain is rocky, arid, with cacti growing, evoking in some memories of parts of Arizona. However, the west end is lusher, with a rain forest of mango and mahogany, tree ferns, and dangling lianas. Rolling hills and upland pastures characterize the area lying between the two extremes.

GETTING THERE: For a description of the air transportation offered by **American, Pan American,** and **Eastern,** refer to the "Getting There" section at the beginning of this chapter.

GETTING AROUND: At the airport you'll find official taxi rates posted. Per-person rates require a minimum of two passengers. One person would be double the fares listed below. Expect to pay about $4 per person from the airport to Christiansted and about $3.25 per person from the airport to Frederiksted. As the cabs are unmetered, you'll want to agree on the rate before getting in. The **St. Croix Taxicab Association,** offering door-to-door service, can be reached by calling 773-5220 or 778-1088.

Buses

Fares are cheap, the rates depending on the distance you go. The main route is between the towns of Christiansted and Frederiksted.

Car Rentals

This is a suitable means of exploring for some, but know that if you're going into "bush country," the roads are often disastrous. Sometimes the government smooths them out before the big season begins.

Three of North America's major car-rental companies maintain popular branches at the St. Croix airport. After reviewing the prices of all the "Big Three," I concluded that **Budget Rent-a-Car** (tel. 778-9636 locally in St. Croix) maintains the most consistently inexpensive rentals. Any of its fleet can be reserved by calling toll free 800/527-0700 at least two business days in advance. But, as any dollarwise shopper should do, you might also compare up-to-the-minute prices at **Hertz** (tel. toll free 800/654-3131) or at **Avis** (tel. toll free 800/331-1212).

High-season prices at Avis and Budget are about the same. However, more of Budget's cars offer air conditioning than similarly priced vehicles at Avis. On the other hand, tariffs for most of the cars at Hertz were almost always higher than either of its two major competitors. Keep in mind, of course, that Hertz at any time could initiate a series of promotional fares.

On my most recent visit, insurance premiums tended to buy more coverage at Budget than at either Hertz or Avis, and the number of days of advance booking at Budget is usually less than that required for rentals at Hertz and Avis. All the major car-rental companies usually announce off-season reductions after April 15.

All of Budget's rental vehicles come with automatic transmission as a standard feature. Its least expensive rental is a peppy four-door Mitsubishi capable of holding four passengers in air-conditioned comfort. A similarly priced Isuzu at Avis did not offer air conditioning. Budget's Mitsubishi Mirage rents for $216 a week, with unlimited mileage included. Day-long rentals of this car cost $38 with unlimited mileage included. Budget also offers a wide range of other well-built Japanese cars in ascending price order. If you're looking for a more substantial vehicle, Budget offers a solid Mitsubishi Galant with automatic transmission and air conditioning for $320 a week or $53 a day, including unlimited mileage.

Drivers at Budget's St. Croix subsidiary must be between the ages of 25 and 70. For more information about insurance costs, refer to the section on "Car Rentals" in St. Thomas, since basically the same insurance situation applies to Hertz, Avis, and Budget on both islands.

Taxi Tours

Many prefer to see St. Croix this way, resting at their hotel or shopping for the rest of their stay after a strenuous day's outing which, for a party of two, will cost from $20 for two hours. This fare is to be negotiated and definitely agreed upon in advance.

Scooter Rentals

To rent a motorized two-wheel vehicle to ride around the island, go to **R. J. Scooter Rentals,** 3 Hospital St., in Christiansted (tel. 778-8822). It's about 50 yards from the Old Fort. Between 9 a.m. and 5 p.m. daily you can rent a vehicle by the hour, half day, day, or week.

Local Air Services

The **Virgin Islands Seaplane Shuttle, Inc.,** Seaplane Ramp (tel. 809/773-1776, or toll free 800/524-2050), offers scheduled downtown-to-downtown flights to St. Thomas, St. Croix, and St. John in the U.S. Virgin Islands, Tortola in the British Virgin Islands, and San Juan, Puerto Rico.

WHERE TO STAY: You can stay at one of the many charming waterfront inns at Christiansted, or at one of the resorts, plantations, or condominium units scattered throughout the island, many at beachside perches. Tariffs for the most part are steep, and all rooms are subject to a 7½% hotel room tax.

The Luxury Leaders

Carambola Beach Resort and Golf Club, Davis Bay (tel. 809/778-3800, 212/586-4459 in New York City, or toll free 800/223-7637, 800/442-8198 in New York state), is one of the newest resorts in the U.S. Virgin Islands. After its completion, sometime in the future, its 4,000 acres will include entire communities and additional golf courses. The dreams and ideals sound extravagant, but since the developer is Rockresorts, the concept perhaps isn't so far-fetched. What you'll see today includes the finest golf course in the region and almost 160 luxurious accommodations arranged in isolated clusters of well-decorated villas. The Danish colonial buildings containing the accommodations are separated from their neighbors with screens of hibiscus and palms. Each unit offers the best possible view of the sea, lots of stucco and exposed wood, both ceiling fans and air conditioning, fine reproduction antique furniture, a refrigerator, and a West Indian motif of louvered doors and plenty of sunlight. With all meals included, high-season rates are $350 daily for a single, $410 for a double, $520 for a triple, and $610 for a quad, all plus tax and service. *Expect reductions of around 30% in low season*. The establishment's specialty dining area is the Mahogany Room. Many guests check in here just for the palm-dotted 18-hole championship golf course, designed by Robert Trent Jones. There are four all-weather tennis courts, a complete list of water-related activities, two Jacuzzis, and a many-angled swimming pool near the wide sandy beach.

The **Buccaneer,** P.O. Box 218, Christiansted, VI 00820 (tel. 809/773-2100), is a big, fancy resort. Among other offerings, it opens onto a trio of the island's best beaches. With its hilltop perch and its beachside sites, it is almost two resorts rolled into one. The location is about a four-mile drive from Christiansted, in a sweeping, rolling landscape. Once the Buccaneer was a sugar plantation, and its first estate house, dating from the mid-17th century, stands near the freshwater swimming pool. The Buccaneer's present history as a resort hotel dates from the postwar era when it was opened by the Armstrong family. The Armstrongs are still going strong at the Buccaneer. Robert D. Armstrong is the owner and general manager. Pink and patrician, the hotel offers you a choice of rooms in its main building or in one of its beachside properties. The baronially arched main building has a lobby opening toward drinking or viewing terraces, with a sea vista on two sides. The architecture is inspired by the Danish custom of free use of arched colonnades. Throughout the estate are units of varying sizes with this architectural theme.

The interiors of the suites and rooms effectively use slanted wood ceilings, chalk-white walls, and all-white furniture to create a fresh, uncluttered look. Rooms are categorized as deluxe, sea-view, and standard. *In the off-season, single EP rates range from $80 to $120 daily, with doubles going for $90 to $130*. For breakfast and dinner, add another $35 per person. However, in winter double occupancy costs $145 to $270 daily. Prices quoted are on the EP, but there are many choices for meals. Most guests lunch lightly in the sun at the Grotto, tanning as they enjoy juicy hamburgers or hot dogs. Lunch is also served at the Little Mermaid Restaurant, the beach, and in the Terrace Dining Room of the main hotel. Cocktails and dinner are available at the Mermaid and the Terrace. Entertainment nightly, with a variety of music ranging from Jimmy Hamilton's jazz to island steel drums, is a feature at the Terrace. One of the most elegant places to dine is the resort's Brass Parrot Restaurant (see the recommendations to follow).

The resort has the best sports program in St. Croix—eight championship tennis courts, two lit at night, and an 18-hole golf course, as well as sports fishing, scuba-diving, and snorkeling available from its own dock. Excursions are arranged to Buck Island's reef.

For reservations, get in touch with Ralph Locke, 315 E. 72nd St., New York, NY 10021 (tel. 212/586-3070, or toll free 800/223-1108).

First-Class Hotels

Cormorant Beach Club, 108 LaGrande Princesse, Christiansted, VI 00820 (tel. 809/778-8920, 212/696-1323 in New York City, or toll free 800/372-1323), is set amid a colony of king palms, about three miles west of Christiansted on Pelican Cove. Occupying the site of an older property, it was radically improved by its dynamic owners who describe themselves as "professional consumers who became professional hoteliers." Walter Bregman, formerly an executive with the Playtex corporation, came with his charming wife, Robbi, from their home in Westport, Connecticut, bringing the experience they accumulated from years of dedicated resort-watching to their cedar-sheathed haven. Long Reef, one of the better-known zoological playgrounds of the Caribbean, lies a few hundred feet from the hotel's sandy beachfront. Its social center revolves around a wood-sheathed and high-ceilinged clubhouse, whose walls were removed for a firsthand taste of the salty air. Radiating out from its central core is a well-stocked library (the books came from the Bregmans' private home), the largest freshwater pool on St. Croix, and a tastefully airy dining room, where half a dozen large fan-shaped windows encompass a view of the beach.

Accommodations lie in well-maintained outbuildings. Each contains a spacious shower lined with coral blocks, a tastefully stylish and clean decor of pleasing colors, cane and wicker furniture from the Dominican Republic, and bouquets of seasonal flowers. Units are priced on a basis used nowhere else in St. Croix. Dubbed the CBC Plan (Cormorant Beach Club Plan), it includes breakfast, lunch, and all drinks until 5 p.m., tennis, snorkeling, daily aerobic classes, special golf rates, and use of the fitness trail. In winter, with these features included, singles cost $140 to $300 daily, and doubles run $175 to $325, depending on the date. *In the off-season, singles cost $175, while doubles go for $210, plus tax and service, on the same plan.* Dinners, served à la carte, are elegantly lighthearted affairs, costing about $25 per person and including such island cuisine as shellfish, steaks, and chicken, often grilled over a kashawood fire. Very young children are not welcome—a fact that many vacationers appreciate— and children under 16 are politely discouraged in the peak midwinter season. The hotel is closed between mid-June and early November.

The **Hotel on the Cay,** on Protestant Cay in Christiansted Harbor (P.O. Box 4020), Christiansted, VI 00820 (tel. 809/524-2035), is an isolated resort, just a one-minute ferry ride from Christiansted to its dockside. The hotel offers ferry service to its guests and visitors from 6 a.m. to 1:45 a.m. daily. The establishment has the only beach in Christiansted, as well as a clean freshwater pool. For guests who wish to dip more extensively in the world of water sports, a complete program is offered, with on-property experts to teach, guide, and recommend activities for everyone, from the novice to the more experienced. For the tennis lover, the Cay has three fine, well-kept courts. Play is complimentary to guests. Continental and West Indian fare are offered in the hotel's main dining room and tropical terrace, with a less formal beach barbecue on Tuesday night and a steak-and-lobster beach party on Saturday. Island entertainment accompanies dinner on most evenings, followed by dancing. The 55 clean, air-conditioned rooms are decorated in good taste, with cypress and fine ceramic tile. All units have either a sea view or overlook the gardens and waterfalls. *Accommodations are available in summer at $78 to $85 single occupancy, $85 to $95 double occupancy.* In winter, singles range from $125 to $130; doubles, $149 to $159. Breakfast and dinner may be included for an additional $32 per person daily.

The Special Inns of Christiansted

Club Comanche, 1 Strand, Christiansted, VI 00820 (tel. 809/773-0210), lives up to my idea of what a West Indian inn should really be like. Right on the Christiansted waterfront, it's the domain of its friendly innkeepers, Dick Boehm and Ted Dale. The main house is old, but has been completely adapted to modern tastes in its remodeling. At every turning, you come upon a charming setting. Take the open iron-cage elevator, where you expect Katharine Hepburn to descend in *Suddenly Last Summer.* Some of the bedrooms have slanted ceilings with handsomely carved four-poster beds, old chests, and mahogany mirrors. Reached by a glassed-in covered bridge, the newer addition passes over the colorful shopping street to the waterside. Other rooms, more recently constructed, are the poolside and harborfront buildings. One row of bedroom units is stretched along the swimming pool area, edged by a stone balustrade and flowering shrubbery. A honeymoon suite is a re-creation of an old sugar mill, sitting on the wharf, perhaps the cutest accommodation in town. It boasts a downstairs salon and a king-size bed upstairs. At one side is a waterfront refreshment bar where you can order drinks and watch yachts come into dock. On the EP, four different sets of rates are offered. The highest prices are charged from December 15 to mid-April: doubles for $65 to $130, daily; singles, $45 to $85. *From mid-April to December 14, doubles go for $50 to $90; singles, $40 to $53.* The club is also one of the leading choices for dining in town.

Anchor Inn, 58A King St., Christiansted, VI 00820 (tel. 809/773-4000, or toll free 800/524-2030), is one of the few hotels lodged directly on the waterfront, in a quiet courtyard close to such historic buildings as Government House and the Old Danish Customs House. Of course, it's right in the heart of the shopping belt as well. The space is so compact and intimate you might not believe it holds 30 units, each with twin beds, small refrigerator, radio, telephone, cable color TV, bath, and a balcony. Air conditioning is individually controlled. A few suites have double beds, no balconies. *In the off-season, EP singles rent for $54 to $60 daily; doubles, $66 to $72; and triples, $79 to $85.* In winter, tariffs go up: $83 to $94 daily in a single, $98 to $109 in a double, and $113 to $124 in a triple, all EP. Furnishings for the rooms are warmly conventional, with good color combinations used. Lon Southerland "anchored" here more than a decade ago, and he has a seasoned local staff to ease your adjustment into Christiansted. (The Anchor Inn restaurant, under separate management, is recommended in the "Where to Dine" section, following.) Directly on the waterfront is a sundeck and small swimming pool, as well as the Anchor Inn's own boardwalk, where catamarans and glass-bottom boats operate daily to Buck Island. There are also deep-sea fishing boats, a scuba-dive shop, and honeymoon and family package tours.

Pink Fancy, 27 Prince St., Christiansted, VI 00820 (tel. 809/773-8460), is my favorite hotel on the island. Sam Dillon, your host, has restored this small, unique private hotel in downtown Christiansted, offering 13 efficiency rooms in four buildings. Units are furnished in a Caribbean motif, with ceiling fans and color TV. *In summer, the rate is only $75 daily, either single or double occupancy,* rising to $160 daily in winter. The location is one block from the Annapolis Sailing School and the V.I. Seaplane Shuttle.

The oldest part of the four-building complex is a 1780 Danish town house, now one of the historic places of St. Croix. Years ago the building was a private club for wealthy planters. Fame came when Jane Gottlieb, the Ziegfeld Follies star, opened it as a hotel in 1948. In the '50s the hotel became a mecca for writers and artists, attracting among others, Noël Coward. To date its present owner, Mr. Dillon, has spent some $1 million in restoration. Before Pink Fancy, he was an orchard owner, a navy vet, a legislator from Maryland, and a former newspaper owner. He also served for a time in the State Department. Built on different levels, the units are clustered around the swimming pool and a monkey puzzle tree. At the free bar there, guests easily get acquainted. A complimentary continental breakfast is served every morning; otherwise, you're on your own for meals. Units are known by estate names such as "Sweet Bottom." If that's too suggestive a selection for you, ask instead for, say, "Upper Love."

King Christian Hotel, King's Wharf (P.O. Box 3619), Christiansted, VI 00820 (tel. 809/773-2285), is Betty Sperber's own special place, and she's one of the finest innkeepers on the island. The location is right in the heart of everything, directly on the waterfront, within walking distance of the duty-free shops, major restaurants, and water-sports activities. All its front rooms have two double beds, cable color TV, refrigerator, room safe, and private balconies overlooking the harbor. However, the "no frills" economy wing has rooms with two single beds or one double bed, but no view or balconies. All units are air-conditioned and contain private bath. Winter EP tariffs range from $60 daily in a single for the "no frills" room up to $90, with doubles costing from $70 to $98. *In summer, it's a real bargain: no-frills singles cost only $50, going up to $55 in a double. The superior units rent for $70 in a single, $80 in a double.* The staff will also make arrangements for golf, tennis, horseback riding, and sightseeing tours. You can relax on the sun deck, shaded patio, or freshwater pool.

There's a beach just a few hundred yards across the harbor, reached by ferry. On the premises is the Chart House, one of the best restaurants in St. Croix (it's noted for its salad bar).

King's Alley Hotel, 55 King St., Christiansted, VI 00820 (tel. 809/773-0103, or toll free 800/843-3574), stands at water's edge, surveying Christiansted Harbor's yacht basin. The hotel, a series of air-conditioned bedrooms, is furnished with a distinct Mediterranean flair. Many of its units overlook a swimming pool terrace, with its oval pool surrounded by tropical plants. The galleries opening off the bedrooms are almost spacious enough for entertaining. *The meticulously cared for rooms rent for $60 to $95 per day double occupancy, in summer; $50 to $85 per day for single occupancy.* All the rooms, incidentally, are twin-bedded or king-size. In winter, singles cost $70 to $115; doubles, $80 to $125. The Marina Bar features nightly entertainment by the pool. Right outside your door you'll find boutiques and restaurants.

Hotel Caravelle, Queen Cross Street, Christiansted, VI 00820 (tel. 809/773-0687, or toll free 800/524-0410). The façade of this sprawling hostelry is painted a dark Mediterranean pink and pierced with high, arched windows which illuminate the pleasant accommodations. This establishment, biggest of the downtown hotels, usually caters to a clientele of international business people who prefer to be near the center of town. There's an Andalusian-style tile fountain splashing near the rectangular bar in the middle of the ground-floor reception area. One of the most dramatically located restaurants in town, the Binnacle (see "Where to Dine," below), is a few steps away. Many resort activities, such as sailing, deep-sea fishing, snorkeling, scuba, golf, and tennis, can be arranged from the reception desk. A swimming pool and sun deck face the water, a health club is on the premises, and all the shopping and activities of the town are close at hand. Accommodations, each with color TV, air conditioning, a phone, and a private bath, are priced according to their views. In winter, singles go from $74 to $98 daily, while doubles cost $90 to $110. *In summer, singles are priced at $62 to $85 daily, while doubles range from $65 to $95.* An additional person staying in any double is charged an extra $15 a day.

Holger Danske Hotel, 1 King Cross St., Christiansted, VI 00820 (tel. 809/773-3600), named after World War II's Danish resistance movement, is a pleasant garden-style hotel stretching along a concrete walkway leading from the outlying reception area. The feeling here is a lot like that in a suburban apartment complex in the Sunbelt. A restaurant and a pool are on the premises. The decor of each of the 44 accommodations is unfussy, spacious, and comfortable, and most have a simple kitchen, a patio or veranda, air conditioning, TV, a phone, and a radio. Best Western, the management company, charges winter rates of $70 to $80 daily in a single, $80 to $93 in a double, and $18 for each additional person lodged in a double room. *In summer, single rates range from $50 to $65 daily, doubles run $65 to $75, and additional occupants in double rooms pay $12 per day.*

Small, Select Hotels

The Lodge, 43A Queen Cross St., Christiansted, VI 00820 (tel. 809/773-1535), is a charming blend of the old and the new in the heart of Christiansted, run by English-born brothers Simon Marks and John Pickles. The hotel has been completely renovated inside and out, and redecorated, often in rattan. Bedrooms surround an old Danish courtyard shaded by a flourishing mango tree, and all are decorated with ornate white Victorian chairs. All 15 of the units have private bath, TV, refrigerator, phone, and air conditioning. *Double rates off-season are $50 to $60, while singles go for $45 to $55.* In winter, double charges range from $58 to $65 and singles run $52 to $60, with an extra person paying $10 year round. The hotel's Moonraker Lounge on the second floor is a favorite rendezvous of tourists and locals alike. Live entertainment is offered nightly in season. The Lodge is close to the waterfront, free-port shopping, excellent dining, and nightlife.

Charte House Hotel, 2 Company St., Christiansted, VI 00820 (tel. 809/773-1377), is built around an old Danish courtyard and a freshwater pool right in the heart of Christiansted. It's a compound that combines the very old and the very new. The hotel was erected on the site of a Danish West Indies Company's counting house. An L-shaped three-story addition stands in the rear, with spacious, air-conditioned rooms with encircling balconies and private baths. All units overlook an intimate courtyard, dominated by an ancient mahogany tree. The entrance to the courtyard is through old arches. *The owner charges $45 to $55 daily in a single in summer, $55 to $65 daily in a double*. Tariffs rise in winter to $55 to $65 daily in a single, $65 to $75 in a double. These charges include morning coffee. There is occasional entertainment in the bar, Two's Company, a tropical lounge.

The Waves at Cane Bay, P.O. Box 1749, Kingshill, VI 00850 (tel. 809/778-1805), is an intimate and tasteful property run by John and Betty Silander. The location is about eight miles from the airport, midway between the island's two biggest towns, on a well-landscaped plot of oceanfront property, which is somewhat like you'd find on the coast of southern Italy. Accommodations rise in angular two-story units with screened-in verandas. The Silanders welcome their guests as part of their extended family, hosting twice-weekly cocktail parties in their private quarters, opening their private library to their guests, and adding many home-like touches to their accommodations. Each of these is high-ceilinged, with fresh flowers, well-stocked kitchens, comfortable and tasteful furnishings, and thick towels. In winter, units rent for $85 to $100, single or double occupancy, with a continental breakfast included. *In summer, singles cost between $45 and $55 daily; doubles, $50 to $60*. In any season, another person can be housed for $25 a night. The establishment's social center is the beachside bar, ringed with local stone. Mr. Silander was a salesman of restaurant equipment in Chicago for many years, and his wife, Betty, is a gifted painter. The concierge, Frances Breeze, enjoyed a career as an operatic mezzo-soprano in New York. Don't overlook the possibility of a game of golf or tennis at the nearby Rockresort course, Carambola.

Cathy's Fancy Beach Hotel, P.O. Box 1668, Christiansted, VI 00820 (tel. 809/773-5595, or toll free 800/524-2026), advertises itself accurately as "the Caribbean the way it used to be." This 21-unit hotel lies three miles west of Christiansted on a sandy four-acre plot of beachfront property covered with palm trees, where hammocks have been strung. Mary Frances and Paul Kruse, the charming owners of the place, renovated the 1960s-era ruin into a more stylish format with Haitian paintings and many amenities. However, they don't have phones or TV, a deliberate policy. Each unit has a ceiling fan, veranda, comfortable tropical furniture, and a "barefoot on the beach" kind of feeling. Accommodations are named after tropical flowers, containing kitchens for self-catering (supplies can be bought nearby). *In summer, prices are reduced to $60 to $85 daily for two to four persons*. In winter, these same studios and one- or two-bedroom accommodations rent for $95 to $135 daily for up to four persons. A 15% surcharge for tax and service is added. There is no formal restaurant, but snacks and drinks, including succulent versions of papaya daiquiris, are sold near the beach.

Chenay Bay Colony, P.O. Box T, Christiansted, VI 00820 (tel. 809/773-2918). The 20 cottages of this complex rest amid a 14-acre grove of gray-barked gnipes trees, about four miles east of Christiansted. Each cottage is a few steps from a sandy beach, and has vertical cedar siding, louvered-glass windows, peaked ceilings, ceiling fans, and self-contained kitchens. It's a good choice for a reasonably priced and relaxing holiday. The resort is the creative expression of Vienna-born George Hindels, who "had a dream that only a crazy dentist would follow up on." After discovering a suitable plot of semi-forested land, whose focal point was the ruins of an 18th-century sugar mill, he commissioned the construction. It's powered with solar energy and the goodwill of resident managers, Pam and Michael Colleary. Depending on the location of your bungalow (on the beach or on the forested hillside several yards away), units rent in winter for $220 to $335 per person weekly, double occupancy. *In summer, bungalows cost $180 to $190 per person weekly, double occupancy*. Windsurfing and scuba instructions can be arranged at moderate prices, and a handful of boats are available to rent.

The Special Inns of Frederiksted

The **King Frederik on the Beach**, P.O. Box 1908, Frederiksted, VI 00840 (tel. 809/772-1205, or toll free 800/524-2018), has many recommendable assets. For those who'd like to stay near Frederiksted, it's within walking distance of the town, with its own beach and private swimming pool. Hidden behind a high stone façade wall is a cluster of apartments opening onto gardens. You enter through a reception patio, with its Italian-tile floor apartments and efficiencies. At the end of the pathway is the small pool area with its rustic beverage bar. Next comes the sea, with a gentle surf. Each of the apartments has a good view, as they are built in a staggered fashion so that one unit doesn't block the other's vista. The complex is owned by a California educator, William Owens, who is very helpful to new arrivals. His (also helpful) assistant manager is Reba McCain Finley, a former school secretary from Los Angeles.

The apartments have a veranda and covered gallery where you can dine. The living rooms have a clean-cut decor, furnished in part with reed and bamboo. The bedrooms contain one double and one twin bed, and the baths are equipped with closets. It's possible to prepare a full meal in the walk-in kitchen. The efficiencies have the same concept, but there are no bedrooms. Maid service is provided. All units, even the lowest priced, have air conditioning and kitchens (except for the beachfront homes). *In the off-season, singles rent for $29 to $60 daily, with doubles going for $34 to $75*. In season, singles cost $54 to $85 daily; doubles, $59 to $95. Mr. Owens has two large beachfront homes, on both sides of his hotel. Each home has two bedrooms, two baths, a large kitchen and living area, and a private dining patio with a sea view. It's ideal for couples or families traveling together. *The off-season rate for four persons is $90 daily*, going up to $145 in season. He's also added six efficiency units directly across the street from the main building. *Rates off-season are $40 in a single, $48 in a double*. In season, tariffs go up to $74 daily in a single or double. Rates include coffee, juice, and rolls every morning.

The hotel provides gas grills on the beach patio where you can grill your dinner while watching the sunset. It's both inexpensive and romantic. A daily morning shuttle service is provided to the large Sunshine Supermarket for shopping. Also, several restaurants in Frederiksted provide free round-trip transportation if you wish to eat out.

Frederiksted Hotel, 20 Strand, Frederiksted, VI 00840 (tel. 809/772-0500, or toll free 800/524-2036). If you don't demand a location right on the beach, this interesting and charming little hotel is a pleasant and attractive offbeat choice. It sits on the harborfront of Frederiksted, a few feet from the retaining wall whose concrete is battered by the surf. In 1976, when Denmark's Queen Margrethe II and her prince occupied a yacht offshore, much of her contingent stayed at the hotel. The hotel's four-story façade of stippled stucco opens onto an interior courtyard, where a small pool and bar/restaurant provides a social center. There is no formal dinner service, but the owners, Bostonian Ed Staats and Syracuse-born Jim Byrne, draw on their extensive travels in Spain to offer cocktail hours with flavorful tapas. Lauchland Tonge, the genteel manager, sees to the welfare of his guests. Each of the 40 accommodations contains air conditioning, phone, cable color TV, and a walk-around wet bar with its own refrigerator. In winter, singles cost $130 daily; doubles, $150; and triples, $170. *In summer, the single rate is $80; the double, $90; and the triple, $115 daily*.

The **Royal Dane Hotel**, 13 Strand, Frederiksted, VI 00840 (tel. 809/772-2780). Visitors to the harbor at Frederiksted have always noticed the 200-year-old house with the sweeping stone staircase angled against the building's side, deploring its apparent abandonment for a number of years. However, late in 1984 it was reopened as a sophisticated and charming 15-room hotel operated by partners Warren Singer and Michael Zullo. Built of local bricks, thick stone blocks, and clapboards, the structure is capped with an upper story done with latticework and open verandas. It's about half a mile from some of the best beaches on the island, expeditions to which are made convenient through the frequent free transportation that the hotel arranges for guests, who also have free access to transport to a nearby tennis club. Each of the air-conditioned accommodations is an imaginatively decorated refuge with unusual prints, framed posters, and comfortable furnishings. No children under 14 are admitted to the hotel. In winter, singles range from $40 to $75 per day, while doubles cost about $5 more per night per room. *In summer, singles cost $30 to $60 daily, with doubles ranging from $35 to $65, depending on the week and the accommodation.* These prices include a continental breakfast, daily maid service, and a welcoming drink. A 10% energy surcharge is added to the rates. An extra person can be housed in any double for $10 to $15 per night, depending on the season. The restaurant serves West Indian and continental dinners, which cost from $20. Lunches are less expensive, costing from $12.

Plantation Life

The **Sprat Hall Plantation**, Rte. 63 (P.O. Box 695), Frederiksted, VI 00840 (tel. 809/772-0305, or toll free 800/834-3584), one mile north of Frederiksted, can never be duplicated. It's the oldest plantation great house on St. Croix, dating back to the French occupation of 1650–1690, and set on 20 acres of grounds, with private white sandy beaches. The co-owner of Sprat Hall, Joyce Hurd, was born here, and she'll show you the four-poster bed where that happy event took place, as she guides you through her home. For generations and generations this has been the family home. She is ably assisted by her husband, Jim Hurd. Joyce, a rosy-faced, cherubic, but dynamic-looking woman of natural charm, still operates the plantation, growing most of the food she serves guests or people who drop in (see my dining recommendations). She seems to take delight in every visitor who finds himself or herself at her doorstep, right near the ruins of the original sugar mill and rum factory. Of course, only arrive on the threshold of this ancestral manor if you want to experience the casual life of yesterday. It's totally wrong for you if you want to be pampered. On my most recent visit, she rushed to bring me a cool glass of pure rainwater and huge slice of papaya she'd grown herself. If you wash up in the hall bath, you'll find the soap resting on fresh green leaves. That's a telltale clue as to how natural this place is.

Guests keep returning and sending their friends. I hope you'll stay in the main house, furnished with a helter-skelter collection of antiques, including many old mahogany pieces dating from the various eras of occupation. Some units are converted slave quarters on the grounds, and for those who want to get away from everything, Joyce will rent you one of her Arawak cottages, air-conditioned and equipped only in a basic way, for families who like to rough it. *In summer, rooms at the house rent for $60 daily in a single, $80 in a double, and $100 in triple.* In winter, the single rate is $80 daily; double, $100 to $110; and triple, $120—all EP. *The cottages in summer range in price from $90 for one to $130 daily for a two-bedroom unit suitable for four persons.* In winter, the single or double tariff is $120 and the four-person charge, $200. On the grounds is the best equestrian stable in the Caribbean. At the beach the Hurds offer skin- and scuba-diving, Sunfish sailing, waterskiing, and deep-sea fishing.

Self-Sufficient Units

If St. Croix's high hotel tariffs deflate your budget too severely, there is an alternative. In general, condominiums are rented at half or a third the going hotel rates. Particularly in the Frederiksted area, you'll find some excellent bargains. And if you wait until after April 15, prices are often half what they are in high season. My recommendations follow.

Tamarind Reef Beach Club, P.O. Box 1112 (tel. 809/773-0463), named after the lace-leafed tamarind trees growing on the property, sits behind a hedge of allamanda on the north coast of the island, between the beach and one of the fastest-growing marinas in the Caribbean. Accommodations are clustered on flat, sandy ground, in semiprivate cabañas and low-lying bungalows, partially sheltered by trees and flowering shrubs. Each of the 16 units has a TV, kitchenette, computerized safe, ceiling fan, and comfortable but spartan furniture. In winter, depending on the week and the size of the unit, prices range from $125 daily in a single to $135 in a double. *In the off-season, they cost from $75 daily in a single, $85 in a double.*

There's a swimming pool on the premises, and a nearby tropical bar, The Deep End, is often peopled with escapees from Christiansted who enjoy the all-day happy hour (two drinks for the price of one) stretching from 11 a.m. to 9 p.m. Children are welcome here and can enjoy spending most of their day on the half-moon-shaped beach which has a view of an uninhabited cay just across the water. There's no restaurant on the property, but light meals and snacks are served beside the pool. Clients can use the club's Sunfish, snorkeling gear, pedalboat, and rowing dinghy free. General managers Henry Nelson and Dorothy Flash take special efforts to make a vacation here pleasant, distributing information packets that advise about local activities and safety precautions.

Sugar Beach Condominiums, Golden Rock Estate, Christiansted, VI 00820 (tel. 809/773-5345, or toll free 800/524-2049), is a row of modernized, stylized one-, two-, and three-bedroom apartments strung along the famous white Sugar Beach. When you tire of its white sands, you can swim in the curvy freshwater swimming pool nestled beside a sugar mill where Virgin Islands rum was made three centuries ago. Under red-tile roofs, the apartments are staggered, with patios set back to provide privacy. The units, opening toward the sea, are complete with kitchens and are tastefully furnished. In winter, a studio costs $110 daily, ranging upward to $190 for a two-bedroom unit. *In summer, studios go for $65 daily, two-bedroom villas for $100.* Maid service costs extra, but the charge is nominal. The property has two lit tennis courts with Laykold playing surfaces. The Fountain Valley Golf Course is only a short drive away.

Colony Cove, 221A Estate Golden Rock, Christiansted, VI 00820 (tel. 809/773-1965, or toll free 800/524-2025). Of all the condo complexes of St. Croix, this one is perhaps the most like a full-fledged hotel, lying about a mile west of Christiansted. It's composed of a quartet of buff-colored three-story buildings whose angular façades ring a kidney-shaped swimming pool. Its well-landscaped gardens, ripe with semitropical plants, lie within earshot of the surf. Behind a barrier of shrub-like cactus you'll find a palm-dotted beach. Each unit contains its own clothes washer and dryer (rare for St. Croix), a kitchen, cable color TV, enclosed veranda or gallery, floors layered with cool rows of ceramic tiles, two air-conditioned bedrooms, and a pair of bathrooms. Winter rates, based on double occupancy, are $170 daily. A third or fourth person sharing pays an extra $20 each. *Summer rates, double occupancy, run $110 daily, a third or fourth party paying $15 each.*

Cane Bay Reef Club, P.O. Box 1407, Kingshill, VI 00850 (tel. 809/778-2966). Nine suites overlook the surf, each with a fully equipped kitchen, bedroom, living room, bath, and balcony where you can dine out. The suites have been painted white, carpeted, and redecorated. The living room couches make into two single beds, so one suite can become a family accommodation, suitable for five guests. From your own private balcony you'll have a view of the surf of the Caribbean. *In summer, one person pays from $40 daily or $280 weekly; two persons, $50 daily or $350 weekly.* In winter, only weekly rentals are accepted, costing $455 for two persons, each additional person paying $15 daily. When you want to leave your own private retreat, you'll surely meet the hosts, Dulcy and Carl Seiffer, who always seem to be about, keeping a smooth control. When you tire of nearby beaches or their own 40-foot swimming pool, they'll direct you to the island's restaurants and nightspots. Or perhaps you'll stick around, joining other guests in an outdoor barbecue. The hotel lies within walking distance of Cane Bay Plantation, where you can dine if you make a reservation. According to *Skin Diver* magazine, the club is one of the ten best dive spots in the Caribbean. It's also the closest resort to the famed Fountain Valley championship golf course.

WHERE TO DINE: Don't limit yourself to the mainly continental places in Christiansted, but head also for Frederiksted, not just for food but for what might be called "dining adventures" in establishments reeking with character.

In Christiansted

Top Hat Restaurant, opposite Market Square on Company Street (tel. 773-2346), represents the culinary adventure of two Scandinavians, Bent and Hanne Rasmussen, who sought the sun and wanted to make an income-producing, creative statement while in that pursuit. Mr. Rasmussen was a photographer in Copenhagen where he married his blonde and beautiful wife. They took this second-floor space over an arcade, creating the aura of a Danish kro (inn). Mrs. Rasmussen has suspended a series of cloud-like large white paper balloon lights from the old beamed ceiling. Only dinner is served, offered Monday through Saturday from 6 to 10 p.m. from November 1 to May 1. I find theirs the best place among St. Croix eateries.

Appetizers range from smoked eel to cheese croquettes, as well as small Ping-Pong meatballs so popular in Denmark. My favorite soup is the homemade split pea. From the sea you might try filet of plaice Hanne (served with a white wine sauce). I'd also suggest the crêpes stuffed with shrimp from Greenland and topped with a white wine sauce. The inevitable frikadeller (Danish meatballs with red cabbage) is here, and the Copenhagen steak (tenderloin topped with onions). You can also order a herring platter, steak tartare, roast duck, wienerschnitzel, and tournedos béarnaise. A good selection of desserts is offered, or else you might finish with their Viking coffee. Dinners begin at $30 per person.

Perhaps the finest and most authentic smörgåsbord in the Caribbean is served on Sunday, costing about $25 per person and drawing such longtime smörgåsbord devotees as local resident Victor Borge. You are presented with an array of at least 20 delectable dishes, including homemade herring in wine sauce, fried filets of plaice, boiled beef tongue slices, and curried codfish balls, along with a salad of those small Greenland shrimp. Naturally, the drink to order is Danish aquavit, followed by a frosty Carlsberg beer.

Comanche, 1 Strand St. (tel. 773-2664), is one of the best-liked restaurants on the island. You can dine in the older part of this inn, or at a newer covered deck added on the water side of the premises. An original Surinam war canoe hangs under the beamed ceiling of the dining room. The size, openness, hanging plants, and rattan chairs create a real West Indian aura, and the welcome by Dick and Mary Boehm (or Vernon) is really superb. Even though relaxed, it is quietly elegant in its own way. It's a very busy place, and you'll really need a reservation. Lunch is served from 11:30 a.m. to 2:30 p.m. and dinner from 6 to 10 p.m. The menu of West Indian and continental specialties is eclectic—an assortment of mouthwatering delicacies likely to include everything from fish and conch chowder to Cantonese shrimp balls. In the evening, most people seek the roast prime ribs of beef, sweetbreads, barbecued baby back ribs, duckling in orange sauce, the lime-broiled chicken, or the fresh island fish, steamed and broiled, or served with a Créole sauce. Each night a different special is featured (mine was roast chicken with an oyster stuffing). Desserts include a bread pudding with rum sauce. Dinner tabs average around $30 per head.

Donn's Anchor Inn Restaurant, 58A King St. (tel. 773-0263), is downtown in Christiansted, right on King's Wharf, but it reminds some diners of a Sausalito bistro.

Guests who live elsewhere keep drifting in for an occasional meal. It's on the second floor, so from your dining perch you can see the boats in the harbor. Run by Glenn L. Hesselgrave, Jr., of California, the restaurant occupies a simple covered terrace. It's the perfect place to meet your friends for a late breakfast, enjoying their custardy french toast topped with sliced ripe bananas covered in real whipped cream. The cost is $5. You might also try their beer buttermilk pancakes. "Creative" omelets, 14 in all, are quite good too. At lunch the menu is predictable—burgers, chef's salad, and soups. At dinner the menu improves considerably. You might order conch fritters as an appetizer. I'd suggest a variety of fresh island fish, such as lobster and conch, which are brought in almost daily from the local charter boats and fishermen. The catch of the day is usually prepared West Indian style (sautéed in butter, then stewed with fresh onions, green peppers, tomatoes, and spices). Donn always manages to have a continuing supply of fresh local lobster. Count on spending from $18 to $25 for dinner. It's open seven days a week. It's best to go from 8 to 10 a.m. for breakfast, noon to 2 p.m. for lunch, and 7 to 10 p.m. for dinner.

Golden China, 28 King Cross St. (tel. 773-8181), serves food as fine as that enjoyed in the Chinatowns of New York or San Francisco. The best experience is to get a group of six couples and arrange for the special Chinese banquet. You'll hardly believe it. If you don't know that many people, you can still enjoy many specialties, including those from the Hunan and Szechuan kitchens. Each dish is prepared to order, and only the finest-quality ingredients are used. Of course, from time to time certain ingredients may not be available because of the vagaries of supply in St. Croix. Dinner is likely to run around $22 per person. However, lunches, served Monday to Saturday from 11:30 a.m. to 2:30 p.m., go for only about $8.

Kendricks, 52 King St. (tel. 773-9199), is a second-floor restaurant with a warm ambience, serving some of the finest continental cuisine in Christiansted. It's reached after a climb up brick stairs. You might begin your meal with an elegant cold soup such as tomato, basil, and walnut. A house specialty is "angel chair" with sun-dried tomatoes. Try also the grilled New York strip steak, roast pecan-crusted pork loin, or grilled chicken with a tomato and black olive vinaigrette. There is a daily selection of homemade desserts. Meals cost from $25 and are served at lunch, from 11:30 a.m. to 2:30 p.m. Monday to Friday, and at dinner, nightly from 6 to 10:30 p.m.

Tivoli Gardens, upstairs over the Pan Am Pavilion (tel. 773-6782), is a favorite local rendezvous, run by Gary Thomson. From this large second-floor porch festooned in lights you get the same view of Christiansted Harbor that a sea captain might. White beams hold up the porch, and trellises and hanging plants help to evoke its namesake, the pleasure gardens of Copenhagen. The owner was a Wall Street executive before heading for St. Croix, and he often plays the guitar and entertains his guests with time-tested favorite songs. The menu is international, everything from gazpacho to pâté, to a country terrine, to a quiche made with snails, to a goulash inspired by a recipe concocted in the day of the Austro-Hungarian Empire. When available, lobster is featured, along with fresh fish and kebabs. Chicken, shrimp, and steak are given imaginative touches, and for dessert, those in the know order a wicked, calorie-heavy chocolate velvet cake. Save room for it, and count on spending from $25 to dine here or $12 for lunch, served from 11:30 a.m. to 2:30 p.m. Dinner hours are 6 to 9:30 p.m. Often there is live dancing from 7 p.m., when reservations are advised. The Sunday brunch, served between 10:30 a.m. and 2:30 p.m., is one of the most popular in town.

The **Chart House,** 59 King's Wharf (tel. 773-7718). This nautically decorated waterfront restaurant opens onto the waterfront in Christiansted. It has a classy look of Oriental carpets and wicker chairs. Normally I don't like chain restaurants. However, when I'm on an island such as St. Thomas or Puerto Rico, I always head for a Chart House, knowing that I am likely to get one of my finest meals. The Chart House in St. Croix lives up to the well-deserved reputation of this U.S.-based chain. To begin with, it has the best salad bar on the island, and many come here just for that. However, I always order their celebrated prime rib, which is a huge slab of meat. You might prefer instead their lobster, shrimp teriyaki, fresh local fish, swordfish, or barbecued beef ribs. Regardless, try their baked potato: it's a palate-pleaser. The kitchen always takes care to turn out fresh steamed vegetables, and, for dessert, the mud pie is justly renowned. Telephone for a reservation and visit only for dinner, seven nights a week from 6 to 10 p.m. Meals cost from $15 to $25.

Bombay Club, 5A King St. (tel. 773-1838). Its plant-encircled ambience is concealed from the street by the foundations of an 18th-century building that is only partially extant today. Many diners linger at the dimly intimate bar beneath the brick vaulting inside, eventually going to their tables within the sheltered courtyard. The food, while not overly fancy, is some of the best in Christiansted and reasonable in price: full dinners cost from $25. Menu items include the catch of the day, chicken Bombay, New York strip steak, beef ribs, and sautés of shrimp, beef, or chicken. Dining is best from noon to 2 p.m. and 8 to 10 p.m.

Frank's, 1 Queen Cross St. (tel. 773-0090), is one of the most attractively amusing places in town, serving well-prepared Italian meals with lots of atmosphere. When you enter the 300-year-old house, you'll be faced with a stone-walled bar where every painting or photograph on it depicts a different version of cigar-chomping Frank Gullace, the owner. Whether shown as Bismarck, the subject of a portrait by Velásquez, Harpo Marx, or a flame-bearing Statue of Liberty, he is the most omnipresent figure among the assembled extroverts who make up the clientele of this sprawling restaurant. There's an inner room, formerly part of a Danish colonial house, filled with elegant tables and a graveled courtyard such as you might find in southern France, except for the dozens of director's chairs, each emblazoned with the word "Frank." Try for a garden table if you can. Entertainer Jacques Vilmain plays piano and sings nightly.

In many ways, this is one of the most "dollarwise" restaurants in Christiansted. You get good value for your money, and the food is well prepared and served in plentiful portions. Among the dishes from the Italian kitchen, the veal is handled particularly nicely. Many boating types drop in here for the relatively inexpensive pasta dishes, not only spaghetti, but fettuccine, lasagne, and other combinations. The chef knows how to make a rib-sticking minestrone, and you can also order good seafood, including fresh dolphin (the fish, not the mammal). When available, lobster is broiled and served with drawn butter, and the steaks are big and juicy, prepared as you like them. Either way, you'll end up paying around $25 for a complete meal, unless you ordered only a pasta, salad, and glass of wine. Only dinner is served, and since the place is a beehive of activity, it's best to reserve a table. Hours are from 5:30 to 10 p.m.

Ritz Café, Bar, and Deli, Queen Cross Street (tel. 773-2985), is a neighborhood enclave of friendly locals, owing its success to New York–born Mike Harris. Its beamed ceiling and brick walls were originally part of an 18th-century great house. Today the warmly intimate ambience is like a warm-weather version of everyone's favorite Manhattan bar. The wahoo, served in well-prepared portions, was often caught that very day by Mr. Harris's deep-sea expeditions. Lunches, costing around $8, might include shrimp salad, lobster salad, and Black Forest cake. A fixed-price steak dinner is served nightly for about $12. Sandwiches, cold cuts, and drinks are readily available. Breakfast is a daily ritual as well. The café is open without interruption Monday through Saturday from 7:30 a.m. to 10 p.m., on Sunday from 4 to 10 p.m.

Kings Alley Café, 55 King St. (tel. 773-0468), is a popular place to eat right in the very heart of Christiansted activity. In a breezy, open-air setting, you'll have a view of the harbor from one of its tables. If you wish, you can patronize only the bar which specializes in calypso daiquiris. Many of these are consumed at happy hour from 4 to 7 p.m. Actually the place opens for breakfast at 7:30 a.m., serving until 11 a.m.; it also presents a Sunday brunch from 8 a.m. to 2 p.m. Otherwise, lunch and dinner are served continuously from 11:30 a.m. to 10 p.m. During the day guests order from the extensive menu of sandwiches and burgers, paying from $10 for a light meal. At night they usually sample more elaborate fare, such as one of the barbecue dishes (ribs or chicken), or the catch of the day. Buttered conch is a local favorite. Some Mexican dishes are presented, including enchiladas, and you can also get chicken or steak teriyaki. Dinners cost $15 and up.

Around the Island

The **Brass Parrot** is at the Buccaneer Hotel (tel. 773-2100), which was already previewed as the leading resort on the island. It also comes up with one of the fanciest —and best—dining choices. Most of the diners are guests at this star resort on 240 hilly acres, but if you call to make a reservation, the air-conditioned Brass Parrot is open to nonresidents as well. Men should wear a jacket, and women should appear in their most chic resort wear. The restaurant has been completely redone and installed in the "Great House" of the Buccaneer, a pink stucco building. Views of the hills are framed by large windows. Piano music plays softly in the background—in all, a romantic, candlelit evening. Bamboo furniture and thick pile carpeting add to the atmosphere of elegance. Decor aside, the reason people come here is for the food. French cuisine and West Indian dishes are the chef's specialties. The kitchen is known for such delicacies as rack of lamb, chateaubriand for two, Caribbean lobster, and veal langoustina. All this glamour comes with a price: expect to spend from $35 per person. Go between 7 and 9 p.m.

Dining at Frederiksted

Swashbuckler, Prince Philip's Passage (tel. 772-1773), is in a modern hip-roofed structure finished with cedar shingles. It's one of the most tastefully designed modern buildings along the harbor, and the bar within serves arguably the best piña coladas in town. Guests enter through a wooden arch set near the road and climb to the second floor. The view is of an uninterrupted 180° horizon visible from your perch on a bar stool. The Neville family makes a point of giving the best tables to dinner guests rather than to bar clients. If you choose to dine here, the menu includes a conch and seafood jambalaya, New York sirloin, roast rack of lamb, fish baked Cruzan style, sautéed calves' liver with onions, several chicken dishes, sweetbreads, prime ribs, coq au vin with mushrooms, seafood chowder, and barbecued Canadian ribs. Full dinners cost from $18, although less elaborate lunches go for only $10. Lunch is served from 11:30 a.m. to 3 p.m., and dinner from 6:30 to 10 p.m.

Outside of Frederiksted, one mile to the north on Rte. 63, stands **Sprat Hall Plantation** (tel. 772-0305), which I have endorsed with enthusiasm as a place to stay. However, if that isn't possible, you might want to call the co-owner of Sprat Hall, Joyce Hurd, and tell her you'd like to come by for dinner. (Try to get there at 7 p.m.) That won't fluster her a bit. She and her West Indian cooks have been feeding guests for years, and they've won their own kind of fame on the island for dining in what is the oldest plantation great house in St. Croix. She runs everything in the kitchen, dashing out to see if everybody's pleased. I even dropped in once for a good country breakfast, costing $6. The dinners here, going for around $18, are recommended by *Gourmet* magazine. Chances are, the vegetables you'll be served came right from the plantation gardens. Each night you face a choice of main dishes. It might be lobster, conch, duck, turkey, or lamb. The roast beef is a winner. And you get "as much as you want to eat." Joyce will have made some soursop ice cream ("I think I invented it"). Dinners are served every night. "We never close," Joyce said. "People have to eat, don't they?" Yes, they do, and they eat very well at Joyce's table.

WHAT TO SEE: The picture-book harbor town of the Caribbean, **Christiansted** is an old Danish port, handsomely restored (or at least in the process of being restored). On the northeastern shore of the island, on a coral-bound bay, it is filled with Danish buildings, usually erected by prosperous merchants in the booming 18th century. These red-roofed structures are often washed in pink, ochre, or yellow. A blaze of bougain-villea will add yet another color splash. Built of solid stone, these 18th-century build-ings have such thick walls they form their own kind of air conditioning. Arcades over the sidewalks make ideal shaded colonnades for shoppers. To maintain what Christian-sted had, Government House—in fact, the whole area around the harborfront—has been designated as a historical site, and is looked after by the National Park Service.

You might begin your tour at the russet-red **Fort Christiansvaern,** the best pre-served of the five remaining Danish forts in the U.S. Virgins. Cannons, dungeons, an officer's kitchen, and bastions from its old defensive days are displayed. The fort saw many additions in the 19th century, as the Danish army garrisoned here until 1878. For the most part the fort was built of tough yellow bricks brought from Denmark as bal-last.

As you leave the fort, walk through a park to Company Street, stopping at **Steeple Building,** which was once the Lutheran Church of the Lord of Sabaoth. This was the first church built by the Danes after they colonized the island in 1734. The steeple, for which it was named, was added around 1794.

Today it is the U.S. Post Office and Customs House, but the **Danish West India and Guinea Company,** also on Company Street, dates from 1749. Once it was a mili-tary depot.

In the old days, the customs house was **Scalehouse,** near the bandstand at the Wharf. Built in 1835, it was the office of the Danish weighmaster. Troops were also housed here; today the premises are occupied by a Visitors' Bureau.

In the Steeple Building and the Scalehouse, exhibits develop important facets of West Indian history. Choice examples of pre-Columbian Indian artifacts depict the life of these early inhabitants of the West Indies. European discovery and colonization, with special emphasis on the rise and decline of the plantation sugar economy, are graphically re-created. A special exhibit on the particular Danish colonial architecture developed on this island also displays restoration techniques. A focus on black history acknowledges the important contributions these citizens have played in the life of the island. Hours are 9 a.m. to 4 p.m. Monday through Friday.

Government House, on King Street, was finished in 1747, and this cream-colored and white residence housed the Danish governor-general before America pur-chased St. Croix. You can still see the tiny red guardhouse at the foot of the staircase going up from the patio to the big ballrooms with crystal chandeliers. These chande-liers and mirrors were a gift of the Danish government in 1966, replacing the originals. This house was joined with another house built in 1794 for a wealthy planter merchant named Adam Sobotker.

The original **Alexander Hamilton House** was built at the end of 1750, and it is said that Hamilton worked here when he was a clerk. The present house is a recon-struction, the original having burned in the 1960s.

Finally, try to visit the **marketplace,** where fruit and vegetables are sold. It's open every day, reaching its peak activity on Saturday morning.

The next day, or that afternoon, you might go on a walking tour of **Frederiksted.** Set by recently freed slaves, a fire in 1879 swept over this harbor town. The denizens later rebuilt, using wood construction on top of the old Danish stone and yellow-brick foundations. In the reconstruction, Victorian gingerbread embellished the stone arches that remained, forming an elaborate jigsaw pattern. The old Danish town lies at the western end of the island, about 17 miles from Christiansted. This is a sleepy port town, very old-world looking, which comes to life only when a cruise ship docks at its shoreline.

Most visitors begin their tour at **Fort Frederik,** considered the first fort to sound a foreign salute to the U.S. flag, in 1776. (St. Eustatius in the Dutch Windwards makes a convincing rival claim.) It was here on July 3, 1848, that Governor-General Peter von

Scholten emancipated the slaves in the Danish West Indies. The fort has been restored to its 1840 look, and you can explore the courtyard and stables. The location is at the northern end of Frederiksted. An exhibit area has been installed in what was once the Garrison Room.

Just south of the fort, the **Customs House** is an 18th-century building which has a two-story gallery built in the 19th century. Here you can go into the Visitors' Bureau and pick up a free map of the town.

Nearby, privately owned **Victoria House** is a gingerbread structure built after the fire that swept over the town. In the rebuilding, some of the original 1803 structure was preserved.

Along the waterfront Strand Street, you reach the **Bellhouse,** the old Frederiksted Public Library. One of its owners, G. A. Bell, ornamented the steps with bells. The house today is an arts and crafts center and a nursery. Sometimes a local theater group presents dramas here.

Other buildings of interest include the **Danish School,** giving way in the 1830s to a building designed by Hingelberg, a well-known Danish architect. Today it's the police station and Welfare Department.

Two churches are of interest. One is **St. Paul's Episcopal Church,** founded outside the port in the late 18th century. However, the present building dates from 1812. **St. Patrick's Catholic Church,** on Prince Street, began in the 1840s.

Finally, the **marketplace,** on Market Street, is also from the early days, the mid-18th century, and is lively on both weekdays and Sunday.

North of Frederiksted you can drop in at **Sprat Hall,** the island's oldest plantation (see my hotel and dining recommendations), or else continue along to the **rain forest,** covering about 15 acres, including the **Creque Dam.** Mahogany trees and yellow cedar grow in profusion, as do wild lilies. The dam is 150 feet high. As you travel through the terrain, which is private property incidentally, you'll hear the call of the mountain dove. The owner graciously lets visitors go inside to explore.

Most people want to see **Salt River,** but there isn't much to see. That's where Columbus landed for a brief moment, sending a boat out to a village filled with naked natives. These inhabitants turned out to be Arawaks, peaceful Indians captured by the militant Caribs. On their return, one of the Spanish leaders captured a "very beautiful Carib girl" from a native canoe, later writing that she "seemed to have been raised in a school of harlots." Columbus himself didn't actually set foot on ground.

The **St. George Village Botanical Garden,** just north of Centerline Road, four miles east of Frederiksted, at Estate St. George, is a veritable Eden of tropical trees, shrubs, vines, and flowers. Built around the ruins of a 19th-century sugarcane workers' village, the garden is a feast for the eye and the camera, from the entrance drive bordered by royal palms and bougainvillea to the towering kapok and tamarind trees, the multicolored hibiscus and frangipani, and the vast poinsettia bed—almost a quarter acre of red and white blooms from December to March. Restoration of the ruins is a continuing project. Two sets of workers' cottages provide space for a gift shop, rest rooms, a kitchen, and offices. These have been joined together with a Great Hall which is used by the St. Croix community for various functions. Other completed projects include the superintendent's house, the blacksmith's shop, and various smaller buildings used for a library, a plant nursery, workshops, and storehouses. Visitors are welcome from early morning until late afternoon; however, maps are available at the Great Hall. The gift shop is open Monday through Saturday from 9 a.m. to 3 p.m.; and the nursery on Tuesday, Thursday, and Saturday from 9 a.m. to noon. Admission is free, but donations toward the continued development of the garden are welcome.

Out on West Airport Road, the **Cruzan Rum Factory** makes the famous Virgin Islands rum. Guided tours depart daily from the visitors' pavilion Monday through Friday from 8:30 to 11:15 a.m. and 1 to 4:15 p.m. For reservations and information, telephone 772-0799.

The best for last, **Estate Whim Plantation Museum** (tel. 772-0598), a restoration of the St. Croix Landmarks Society, is one of the most intriguing of the West Indian plantation houses. The house was built soon after its Danish owner, a life-long bachelor of great wealth, took over in 1794. It's actually small, with only a trio of rooms in the main section. The location is on Centerline Road, about two miles east of Frederiksted, and hours are 10 a.m. to 5 p.m. daily. Admission is $3 for adults and $1 for children. Some of the antiques in the main house are from old Cruzan homes. Around the perimeter is a dry moat. The house has semicircular ends, and walls three feet thick held together in part with molasses. On the grounds are restored mills for grinding sugarcane, one powered by wind and the other animal powered. Exhibits display how the artisans of the day created everything from nails to fine mahogany furniture, and how the townspeople lived. There is a gift shop whose proceeds support the society's preservation efforts.

SHOPPING IN CHRISTIANSTED: In Christiansted, where the core of my shopping recommendations are found, the emphasis is on hole-in-the-wall boutiques, selling one-of-a-kind merchandise. Handmade items are strong. Of course the same duty-free stipulations, as outlined earlier, apply to your shopping selections in St. Croix.

Knowing it can't compete with Charlotte Amalie, Christiansted has forged its own creative statement in its shops, and by reputation it has now become the "chic spot for merchandise" in the Caribbean. All the shops are easily compressed into half a mile or so, so on a day's tour (or half day) you'll be able to inspect much merchandise before making your purchases.

Little Switzerland, King Street (tel. 773-1976), is the unquestioned elite shop on the island for prestige watches, jewelry, china, and crystal. Only the finest watches are sold here, only the best crystal. The watches are priced exactly as they are in Switzerland—which is quite a saving on such name brands as Rolex, Concord, Ebel, Girard-Perregaux, Rado, Vacheron & Constantin, and many others. Incidentally, the owners employ Swiss watchmakers to see that every watch is in perfect adjustment. It's validated for you. Names in chinaware—Rosenthal, Aynsley, Royal Doulton, and Wedgwood—are here. This is also the official Hummel and Lladro shop. In addition, the shop is the largest Waterford importer in the West Indies.

Casa Carlota, 13A Caravelle Arcade (tel. 778-8940), is a boutique owned by Jill Yohn, who, with her husband, Michael (formerly in the diplomatic service in Mexico City), works to make the establishment a success. She specializes in high-quality cotton garments for women, presenting a distinctive collection of lightweight fashions that feature fine fabrics, meticulous craftsmanship, and outstanding styling. Included are Anokhi hand-blocked prints from Jaipur, India. You can view the colorful and creative collection in air-conditioned comfort in the shop.

Nini of Scandinavia, 16AB Church St. (tel. 773-2269), is home base for Nini Cohn, who has at least two dozen of the outstanding clothing and accessory sources of Scandinavia lined up. She has rolls of designer fabrics from Sweden and Denmark to decorate your condo, villa, or home. You can select fashions from top name-brand houses of Scandinavia, including Marimekko of Finland. Nini imports lots of ready-to-wear apparel, offering at least 2,000 dresses at all times. In stock is a large swimwear and sportswear selection, plus avant-garde jewelry from Denmark. As Nini rightly says, "It's mainly the people who have traveled the world who know the bargains here."

Finesse Boutique, Company Street (tel. 773-5711), is owned by Mrs. Juan Luís, wife of the governor. It's one of the best places in Christiansted to go for perfume, offering such designer fragrances as Oscar de la Renta, Van Cleef and Arpel. Maria Nela runs the perfume department and also operates the store, which has a tasteful, elegant selection of designer dresses.

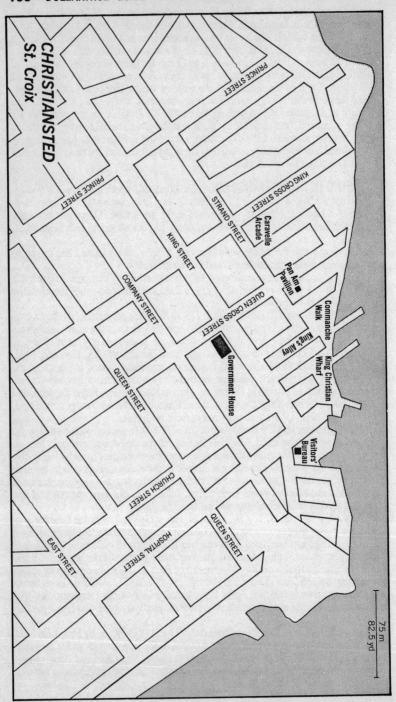

CHRISTIANSTED
St. Croix

PRINCE STREET
PRINCE STREET
PRINCE STREET
KING CROSS STREET
STRAND STREET
KING STREET
COMPANY STREET
QUEEN CROSS STREET
QUEEN STREET
QUEEN CROSS STREET
CHURCH STREET
QUEEN STREET
HOSPITAL STREET
EAST STREET

Caravelle
Arcade
Pan Am
Pavilion
Commanche
Walk
King's Alley
King Christian
Wharf
Government House
Visitors'
Bureau

75 m
82.5 yd

Java Wraps, Pan Am Pavilion (tel. 773-3700), on the corner of Strand Street, sells what is perhaps the most avant-garde fashion in the Caribbean. The dedicated owner is Twila Wilson, originally from Colorado, who spends six months of the year in Java and Bali overseeing the production of her resort designs made of hand-batiked prints. It's made in the classical traditional manner. Twila, who naturally wears a slinky sarong herself, says her "designs and fabrics emphasize cool, easy-to-wear, clean good-looking things." Her shop on Strand Street is a perfect setting, with Haitian floor matting, straw fan-back chairs, and potted palms. You'll find kimonos, rompers, bikinis, shorts sets, sun dresses, and shirts for men and boys. But the bestseller is the one-size sarong. If you purchase it, you're given a sheet of instructions on how to wear it. Her antique Dorothy Lamour sarongs sell for $250 and up, and new sarongs are as low as $30. She also has a collection of children's wear.

The Compass Rose, 5 Company St. (tel. 773-0444), has been firmly entrenched on the island since 1957. It is an authorized Seiko dealer, but, in addition, offers an array of well-selected items from the Orient, including pearls, jade, and coral. They also sell tablecloths from China.

Violette Boutique, 38 Strand St., Caravelle Arcade (tel. 773-2148), is a small department store with many boutique areas carrying exclusive lines known worldwide. Besides the largest perfume inventory in St. Croix, you'll also find the latest in Cartier, Seiko, Yves St. Laurent, and Pulsar watches, all at duty-free prices. Clarins and Lancôme cosmetics have a private salon area. Upstairs, Gucci handbags and the finest in women's fashions are shown year round. This treasure house is done in gold and silver.

The Spanish Main, Pan Am Pavilion (tel. 773-0711), off the Strand, is for those who favor handcrafted fabrics with style and integrity. The owner of this shop puts it most accurately when she says she offers "memories by the yard." You'll find bolts of hand-screened island prints on fabric that is 65% polyester, 35% cotton. The subjects are happy ones—a garden of native flowers, sails against the water, or flying birds against the sky. You can make your own apparel. Ready-to-wear dresses and evening wear are intriguing buys.

Pegasus, 58 Company St. (tel. 773-6926), is both the retail outlet and workshop of three jewelers, including Laura T. Leblow, a certified gemologist. They specialize in diamonds, gold, and gemstones, and can be trusted. In their undulating showcase they offer earrings, pendants, bracelets, and many one-of-a-kind pieces. Tariffs are based on the fluctuating price of gold. They also have a varied selection of handcrafted black coral, pink coral, and pearl jewelry.

Many Hands, Pan Am Pavilion (tel. 773-1990), is devoted exclusively to Virgin Islands handcrafts. There is also a collection of local paintings. You're invited to see their year-round "Christmas tree." Children get a lot of attention here, as there's an assortment of custom-made dresses and suits, along with stuffed toys. West Indian spices and teas are also sold, as are shellwork, stained glass, hand-painted china, and ceramic switch plates, as well as other ceramic objects and handmade jewelry.

Happiness Is, Pan Am Pavilion (tel. 778-8833). I was drawn to this shop by its catchy name. Inside, you'll find a collection of island-made handcrafts, along with a selection of jewelry, including some made out of black coral. There is also a collection of resort-style clothing. Ask for Jean.

Grog and Spirits Liquor Store, 56 Kings Wharf (tel. 778-8400), in the King Christian Hotel building, is the place to go for choice beverages and snack foods. Larry S. Willett, a ten-year resident of St. Croix, can advise you on how much you can take back home with you in the liquor, liqueur, wine, and champagne line. Many times the prices here are so low in comparison with those charged in the States that you will be well off to buy here and pay duty if you go over the U.S. Customs limit. If you're making a trip to Buck Island from the dock next to the grog shop, you can purchase grocery items for a picnic, as well as beer and soda. Cigarettes are also sold here. You can have everything packed in easy-to-carry boxes and delivered to your hotel ready for you to take home.

Land of Oz, Kings Alley (tel. 773-4610), is the most enchanting store for children in the Caribbean. Daniel W. Furman runs it "somewhat like a hobby." You name it—if it's for children, the store stocks it. Everything is here from dinosaur replicas to witches' hats. Naturally, there are toys and dolls galore, but many surprising items as well, such as the *Newlyweds' Guide to Sex on the First Night*. A former nuclear physicist, Mr. Furman was always amazed at the "creativity of toys," and he collects them from all over the world. As a "gadget person," he is fascinated by the ingenuity that goes into the craft and likes to share his enthusiasm with others.

SHOPPING AROUND THE ISLAND: In your visit to the Estate Whim Plantation Museum, east of Frederiksted on Centerline Road, you might also want to browse through the **Whim Gift Shop.** Offering a good selection of gifts, appealing to a wide age spectrum, it has many imported items, but also many that are Cruzan made. Some were personally made for the Whim shop. And as any member of the staff will point out, if you buy something, it all goes to a worthy cause: the upkeep of the museum and the grounds.

On your tour of the island, especially if you're in western St. Croix in the vicinity of Frederiksted, you might want to stop off at the following offbeat shopping recommendations:

St. Croix Leap, Mahogany Road, Rte. 76 (tel. 772-0421), is a fascinating adventure. You can visit the open-air shop, where you can see stacks of rare and beautiful wood being fashioned into tasteful objects. It is a St. Croix Life and Environmental Arts Project, dedicated to the natural environment through manual work, conversation, and self-development. The end result is a fine collection of Cruzan mahogany serving boards, tables, wall hangings, clocks, and sections of unusual pieces crafted into functional objects. They become a form of naturalistic art. St. Croix Leap is two miles up Mahogany Road from the beach north of Frederiksted. Large mahogany signs and sculptures flank the driveway. Visitors should bear to the right to reach the woodworking area and gift shop. For inquiries, write to Leap, P.O. Box 245, Frederiksted, VI 00840.

The **Tradewinds Shop,** 320 King St. (tel. 772-0939), at the corner of Market Street, is the best-stocked store in Frederiksted. Housed in a series of high-ceilinged, spacious rooms, variously devoted to jewelry and watches, liquor, cigarettes, and clothing, the place is hard to miss during a shopping expedition. Purchases will be delivered to the airport, although if you buy a watch or perfume, you may want to carry it with you. The store is open from 8:30 a.m. to 5:30 p.m. daily except Sunday.

THE SPORTING LIFE: Beaches are the big attraction. The drawback is that getting to them from Christiansted, center of most of the hotels, isn't always easy. It can also be expensive, especially if you want to go back and forth during every day of your stay. Of course, you can always rent one of those housekeeping condominiums right on the water.

In Christiansted, if you want to beach it, head for the **Hotel on the Cay.** You'll have to take a ferry to this palm-shaded island.

Cramer Park, at the northeast end of the island, is a special public park operated by the Department of Agriculture. Lined with sea grape trees, the beach also has a picnic area, a restaurant, and a bar.

I highly recommended **Davis Bay** and **Cane Bay** as the type of beaches you'd expect to find on a Caribbean island—that is, palms, white sand, good swimming, and great snorkeling.

If you'd like to enjoy nude bathing, then head for **Isaac's Bay.**

Snorkeling and Scuba

Spectacular sponge life, black-coral trees (considered the finest in the West Indies), and steep dropoffs into water near the shoreline have made St. Croix a diver's goal.

Buck Island, with a visibility of more than 100 feet, is the site of the nature trail of the Underwater National Park, and it's the major diving target. All the minor and major agencies offer scuba and snorkeling tours to Buck Island. Divers also like to go to **Pillar Coral,** with its columns of coral spiraling up to 25 feet; **North Cut,** one of the tallest, largest coral pinnacles in the West Indies; and **Salt River Dropoff,** plunging to well over 1,000 feet deep, as well as **Davis Bay Dropoff,** with its unique coral and rock mound structures in grotesque shapes.

Your best bet in Christiansted is **Caribbean Sea Adventures,** Kings Wharf (tel. 773-6011). Write to them at P.O. Box 3015, Christiansted, VI 00820. They have guided snorkeling tours. You can sail aboard a 40-foot catamaran for a full day, costing $30 for adults, $22 for children, or a half day at $25 for adults, $18 for children. The same trip by a 36-foot trimaran costs $35 for adults and $25 for children for a full day, $25 for adults and $20 for children for a half day. If you prefer to go by motorboat, both M/V *Deliverance* and M/V *Scorpio* make trips from 9:30 a.m. to 1 p.m. and 2 to 5:30 p.m., costing $20 for adults and $15 for children. Courses for divers are also offered, at prices ranging from $40 for a novice resort course to $300 for a 14-dive package.

St. Croix's most complete diving and training facility is **Dive Experience** (tel. 773-3307), at Club Comanche Hotel in Christiansted.

Sea Shadows, Cane Bay (tel. 778-3850), offers complete scuba programs as well as equipment for all purposes, plus snorkeling sets to rent. Tours go to the spectacular dropoff walls of the north shore of St. Croix. Libby and Steve, the friendly owners of Sea Shadows, are familiar with the diving aims of their customers and provide all they need for successful experiences.

Tennis

It's best at the **Caribbean Tennis Club** (tel. 773-7285), with its fully stocked pro shop. The charge here is $6 per person. In addition, **Hotel on the Cay** offers four Laykold courts, charging $4 per hour (there's a pro shop).

Golf

St. Croix has the best in the U.S. Virgins. In fact, guests at Caneel Bay Plantation on St. John, or visitors from St. Thomas, often fly over for a day's round.

On the island are two 18-hole golf courses. **Carambola Golf Course** (tel. 778-0747), formerly the Fountain Valley Course, designed by Robert Trent Jones, is on the northwest side of St. Croix. The site of "Shell's Wonderful World of Golf," Carambola's course record of 69 was set by "Chi-Chi" Rodriguez. The other course is at the **Buccaneer Hotel** (tel. 773-2100).

Horseback Riding

Jill's Equestrian Stables (tel. 772-2880) is found on the sprawling grounds of Sprat Hall Plantation, operated by Jill Hurd, daughter of the dynamic Joyce Hurd, who runs the fine plantation hotel and restaurant. Jill's stables are known throughout the Caribbean for excellent horses and beautiful trail rides through the rain forest, past sugarmill ruins to the tops of the scenic hills of St. Croix. Beginners are offered reining and cantering instructions along the ride. Jill points out the massive kapok and baobab trees, mongooses, and fascinating termite nests. In season, riders get to sample the unique tropical fruits that grow in the area: sugar apple, soursop, mango, guava, tamarind, limeberry, and genep (Spanish limes). Reservations must be made for rides at least a day in advance. Guests staying at Sprat Hall are given a discount on the prices.

Fishing

The fishing grounds at **Lang Bank** are about ten miles from St. Croix. Here you'll find kingfish, wahoo, and dolphin. On light-tackle boats gliding along the reef, the catch is likely to turn up jack or bone fish. At Clover Crest, in Frederiksted, Cruzan anglers fish right from the rocks.

Jim Hurd, fishing guide, takes his hotel guests from Sprat Hall Plantation deep-sea fishing for $150 per day for two persons. He will also act as a bonefishing and snook fishing guide for hotel guests for $100 per day. Guests should bring their own light fishing tackle and gear. See my hotel recommendation for Sprat Hall for phone numbers and other information.

You can try your luck against such gamefish as marlin, wahoo, dolphin, tuna, and kingfish when you go out deep-sea sportfishing aboard the *Ritz Café* (tel. 778-8862), departing from the Anchor Inn Boardwalk in Christiansted. All fishing gear is provided, and if you catch an edible species, you can have it for dinner that night at the Ritz Café Restaurant. For a half-day charter, costing $300 (which can be shared with other anglers), beverages are included, and on a full-day trip, costing $495, lunch is also provided. For information, call the restaurant (tel. 773-2985).

Boating

Most boats move out to Buck Island. St. Croix has many boats for hire at widely varying rates, depending on the craft. **Llewellyn's Charter, Inc.** (tel. 773-5037), rents a 36-foot trimaran for sailing, fishing, and diving.

Windsurfing

The best place for this increasingly popular sport is the **Tradewindsurfing Water Sports Center** (tel. 773-2035). They give lessons too, and are open from 10 a.m. to 6 p.m. daily.

AFTER DARK: To find the action, you might have to hotel or bar-hop: nightlife in St. Croix is like a floating game of craps.

If he's playing, the one man to seek out is Jimmy Hamilton, Duke Ellington's "Mr. Sax." He and his quartet are a regular feature of St. Croix nightlife. Ask at your hotel to learn if he is appearing locally at the time of your visit.

The big treat of St. Croix is the **Quadrille Dancers.** Try to catch a performance if you can. You have to check at your hotel as to where you are likely to see one of their dances, little changed since plantation days. The women wear long dresses, white gloves, and turbans; and the men are attired in flamboyant shirts, sashes, and tight black trousers. When you've learned their steps, you're invited to join the dancers on the floor.

Bombay Club, 5A King St. (tel. 773-1838). Owners Jeff Seroogy and Tom Rodenhaver have managed to squeeze much miscellany into what is one of the most popular jazz clubs on the island. A large photograph of John Lennon greets visitors near the entrance. Other ornaments include original paintings, posters, and an array of tropical plants. You enter through a low stone tunnel and eventually find yourself near a collection of bars and a courtyard garden with tables and chairs. Live jazz is presented three nights a week. You can lunch here five days a week and enjoy dinner seven nights. Menu choices include fresh local seafood, prime rib, shrimp scampi, various sautéed dishes, steaks, and sandwiches. Dinners begin at $25, but if you just want a sandwich to go with your beer, it will be less.

I've also spent many a pleasant evening at the **Moonraker Lounge,** which often has some very good guitar music. The location is on the balcony upstairs at The Lodge on Queen Cross Street (tel. 773-1535). Drinks cost from $1.50. Open nightly from 8, Moonraker presents entertainment beginning at 8:30 p.m.

Bogart's, Pan Am Shopping Center (tel. 773-1559). At the water's edge, at the most distant end of the city's shopping centers, this horseshoe-shaped bar is little more than a celebration of the open air and the balmy climate. Many of the sightlines focus on a big TV screen. Drinks are strong and frothy. It's open daily from 11 a.m. to midnight (on Sunday from 5 p.m. to midnight).

Rumors, 54B Company St. (tel. 773-6602), can be a lot of fun on a good night, since there's live entertainment occasionally. Otherwise, it's rock video. Surrounded by bentwood chairs, hanging fans, potted plants, and raftered pink ceilings, you can see locals watching video near the bar or observe a romance blossoming in a corner. Beer costs $2. The place is open nightly.

BUCK ISLAND: The crystal-clear water and the white coral sand of Buck Island, a

satellite of St. Croix, are legendary. Now the National Park Service has marked an underwater snorkeling trail. The park covers about 850 acres, including the land area, which has a sandy beach with picnic tables set out and pits for having your own barbe-cues. There are two major underwater trails for snorkeling on the reef, plus many other labyrinths and grottos for more serious divers.

Slithering through its undergrowth of days of yore, you were likely to run into Morgan, LaFitte, Blackbeard, or even Captain Kidd.

A barrier reef of elkhorn coral, the calm waters of Buck Island shelter many reef fish, including the queen angelfish and the smooth trunkfish. Buck Island lies only 1½ miles off the northeast coast of St. Croix. Uninhabited, it is only a third of a mile wide and a mile long.

Now a parkland, the island was inhabited for a long time, since the 1750s in fact. It's been a place of residence and a garden for growing crops. It's also been used for pasturage, and its timbers have been cut to build houses on St. Croix. It became a park in 1948, and the goats were eliminated in the 1950s. The attempt was to return Buck Island to nature, and it's been successful. Even the endangered brown pelicans are producing young here.

Small boats run between St. Croix and Buck Island, charging from $20 to $30, and snorkeling equipment is furnished. You head out in the morning, and nearly all charters allow an hour and a half of snorkeling and swimming.

One company well versed in transporting nature lovers to the Buck Island under-water trail is **Mile Mark Charters,** King Christian Hotel, 59 King's Wharf, in Christ-iansted (tel. 773-2285). Owned and operated by Miles and Mark Sperber, the company offers full-day snorkeling tours lasting from 9 a.m. to 3 p.m. and half-day tours from 9 a.m. to 1 p.m. and from 1 to 5 p.m.

Captain Llewellyn (tel. 773-9027) has been sailing to Buck Island for more than 20 years, and he'll take you there on *Charis,* a 36-foot trimaran, which is the only charter boat sailing from the east end. Both half-day and full-day sails are arranged, as are sunset sails.

Captain Heinz (tel. 773-3161 or 773-4041) is another skipper with some 20 years of sailing experience. His trimaran, *Teroro II,* leaves Green Cay Marina "H" Dock at 9 a.m. and 2:30 p.m., usually filled with small groups, never more than 11 passengers. All gear and safety equipment are provided. The captain sailed the first *Teroro* across the Atlantic, and he's not only a skilled sailor, but a very considerate and concerned host while you're aboard. He will even take you around the *outer* reef, which the other guides do not, for an unforgettable underwater experience.

The easiest, smoothest, and most popular way to get to Buck Island is aboard the glass-bottom boat *Reef Queen,* which sails daily at 9:45 a.m. and again at 1:45 p.m. It's the only boat that stops at "Scotch Bank." It offers a four-hour snorkel cruise or glass-bottom viewing. There's a changing room as well as a complete sit-down bar. For reservations, call 773-0754.

On the island, you can take a hiking trail through the tropical vegetation that covers the island. There are rest rooms, plus a small changing room for visitors.

Chapter VI

THE BRITISH VIRGIN ISLANDS

1. Anegada
2. Jost Van Dyke
3. Marina Cay
4. Peter Island
5. Tortola
6. Virgin Gorda
7. Mosquito Island
8. Guana Island

WITH ITS SMALL BAYS and hidden coves, once havens for pirates, the British Virgin Islands are considered among the world's loveliest cruising grounds by the yachting set.

Strung over the northeast corner of the Caribbean are some 40 islands, although skeptics might consider many of these rocks, perhaps cays, and in some cases, "spits of land." Only a trio of the British Virgins are of any significant size, including Virgin Gorda (the "fat virgin") and Tortola ("dove of peace"), as well as Jost Van Dyke.

The islands have such names as Fallen Jerusalem and Ginger. Norman Island is said to have been the prototype for Robert Louis Stevenson's *Treasure Island*. On Deadman Bay, a rocky cay, Blackbeard marooned 15 pirates and a bottle of rum, which gave rise to the ditty.

Columbus came this way in 1493, gazing upon beautiful harbors and green hills, but the British Virgins apparently made little impression on him. Sir Francis Drake sailed into the channel in 1595, seeking Spanish treasure ships. Drake's arrival here was commemorated by having the channel named after him. Less than a generation later the British claimed the island, and the Spanish and Dutch contested it. Tortola was officially annexed by the English in 1672.

The British Virgin chain lies some 60 miles east of Puerto Rico. These islands, craggy and volcanic in origin, are just 15 "air minutes" from St. Thomas. There is regularly scheduled ferry service between St. Thomas and Tortola as well.

The vegetation is varied. In some parts of the British Virgins palms and mangoes grow in profusion, while other places are arid and studded with cactus. Everything depends on the rainfall.

The islands are a British colony, with their own elected government and a population of about 11,000, mainly black. English is the tongue of the realm, and the Yankee dollar is the coin, much to the surprise of arriving Britishers who find no one willing to accept their pounds ("but this is a British colony," they protest to no avail). The islands, covering about 59 square miles, have a perfect year-round climate, with temperatures averaging between 77° and 85° Fahrenheit.

Note: All prices in this chapter are given in U.S. dollars.

Even though there are predictions that mass tourism is on the way, the British Virgins are still a paradise for escapists. The British Home Office, according to a report I once read, listed them as "the least important place in the British Empire."

GETTING THERE: There are no direct flights from New York to Tortola, but you can make good connections through San Juan, St. Thomas, or St. Croix, each of which is serviced by such major carriers as **American, Pan American,** and **Eastern.**

Air BVI is your best bet from San Juan. It has flights not only from there to Tortola, but on to Virgin Gorda as well. The little carrier also has service from St. Thomas to Tortola, as well as from St. Maarten, St. Kitts, and Antigua.

CrownAir also flies from San Juan to Tortola and from St. Thomas to Tortola. It has flights as well from San Juan to Virgin Gorda and from St. Thomas to Virgin Gorda.

From Canada it's best to fly to a U.S. city, such as Miami, and make a connecting flight to San Juan.

Passengers arriving from Europe can best make connections through Antigua. Antigua is serviced directly from London on **British Airways.** In Antigua, as mentioned, BVI takes over from there.

You can also go from Charlotte Amalie (St. Thomas) by **public ferry** to West End and Road Town on Tortola, a quiet, 45-minute voyage along Drake's Channel through the islands. Ferries shuttle between Road Town and Peter Island seven times a day, and there are also daily trips connecting Road Town, Tortola, and Spanish Town on Virgin Gorda.

PRACTICAL FACTS: U.S. and Canadian citizens need produce only an authenticated birth certificate or a voter registration card to enter the British Virgin Islands. On that evidence, they are welcome for a stay of up to six months, but must possess return or ongoing tickets and show evidence of adequate means of support and prearranged accommodations during their stay. Upon leaving, the BVI levies a $5 **departure tax** for those leaving by air or $3 for those leaving by sea.

Another government **tax**—this one to the tune of 5%—is imposed on all hotel rooms. However, there is no sales tax.

The **temperature** is about 75° to 80° Fahrenheit, and the prevailing trade winds keep the islands from being too humid. Rainfall is infrequent, but even during the rainy season, precipitation is generally heavy for only about 10 or 15 minutes and stops just as abruptly as it began.

Watch your clock. The island operates on **Atlantic Standard Time.** In the peak winter season, when it's 6 a.m. in the British Virgins, it's only 5 a.m. in Miami. However, when Miami and the rest of the east coast goes on Daylight Saving Time, the clocks are the same in both places.

Ten **doctors** practice in Tortola, and there is a hospital with X-ray and laboratory facilities. One doctor practices on Virgin Gorda. Your hotel will put you in touch with the BVI's medical staff.

Unlike some parts of the Caribbean, nudity is an offense punishable by law in the BVI. Drugs, their use or sale, are also strictly prohibited.

Your U.S.-made appliances can be used here, as the **electrical current** is 110 volts, 60 cycles.

1. Anegada

The most northerly and isolated of the British Virgins, 30 miles east of Tortola, Anegada has more than 500 wrecks lying off its notorious Horseshoe Reef. It's different from the other British Virgins in that it's a coral and limestone atoll, flat with a 2,500-foot airstrip.

At its highest point its land mass reaches a height of 28 feet, and hardly appears on the horizon if you're sailing to it. At the northern and western ends of the island are some good beaches, which might be your only reason for coming here.

The population numbers about 250, many of whom have looked for (but not found) the legendary hidden treasure on such sunken ships as the *Paramatta,* which has been at rest for a century. If you decide to come here, know that you're at a remote little corner of the Caribbean: don't expect one frill and be prepared to put up with some hardships, such as mosquitoes.

The only major accommodation on the island is the **Reef Hotel** (tel. 494-3425 Marine Operator and ask for Anegada Reef). As the saying goes, it isn't for everyone. It's one of the most remote little places recommended in this guide, and guests who stay here are in effect "hiding out." It's not for first-time visitors to the Caribbean either, and attracts those who can settle for its barebone life in one of 12 motel-like rooms with only the simplest of amenities. The beach is not that desirable but it's still a favorite of the yachting set, who like to stop off here to enjoy hospitality provided by Vivian and Lowell Wheatley.

Naturally in such an isolated place guests book in here on the American plan, paying $115 daily in a single and $170 in a double in winter. *Off-season tariffs on the AP are $95 daily in a single, $145 in a double.* Fishing, both inshore and deep sea, along with diving, snorkeling, and of course swimming, are possible, even a little beachcombing. On party nights the Wheatleys bring in a fungi band, or they might stage a barbecue right on the beach with tall rum punches. If you're going over just for the day, you can order lunch at the beach bar. The cook specializes in conch fritters. At night, barbecued lobster is a favorite at dinner. In addition to lobster you'll find fresh fish, beef, and poultry, along with the inevitable conch. If you're over touring for the day and want to dine at the Reef, drop in early and make a reservation.

While on the island, you may want to visit **Neptune's Treasure,** a seaside restaurant run by the Soares family, who serve fresh fish and fresh lobster that they catch themselves. One reader writes, "I had my first dogfish shark at this restaurant, and it was great!" Meals cost from $15 per person, and the people are friendly and helpful in explaining to you how to explore their island. To get in touch with them, their radio contact in the BVI is on Tortola Radio (tel. 494-3425).

The family also rents tents with single or double air mattresses if you'd like to stay on the island—and don't mind roughing it a bit. You can take a taxi to one of their sandy beaches and go snorkeling along their reefs.

2. Jost Van Dyke

This rugged island, on the seaward side of Tortola, was probably named for some Dutch pirate. About 130 people live in four square miles. On the south shore of this mountainous island are some good beaches at White Bay and Great Harbour.

In the 1700s a Quaker colony settled here to develop sugarcane plantations. One of the colonists, William Thornton, won a worldwide competition to design the Capitol in Washington, D.C.

Smaller islands surround the place, including Little Jost Van Dyke, the birthplace of Dr. John Lettsome, founder of the London Medical Society.

The island has only a handful of places to stay but several dining choices, as it's a popular stopping-over point for the yachting set.

WHERE TO STAY: A perfect retreat for escapists, the **Sandcastle,** White Bay (tel. 494-2462), is a four-villa colony with cottages built in an octagonal style and surrounded by flowering shrubbery and bougainvillea. Nestled among the palms, these individual cottages take advantage of the tropical breezes and gain every inch of the view. This is a small, personalized place, catering to only a handful of guests. You're allowed to mix your own drinks at the beachside bar, the Soggy Dollar, but you'll also have to keep your own tab. Visiting yachting people often drop in here for a while, enjoying the beachside informality and ordering a drink called a "Painkiller." In the guest book you'll find this quotation: "I thought places like this only existed in the movies." Billy and Lisa Hawkins, former yachties who have dropped anchor in White Bay, are your hosts. In winter, two persons can stay here on the full-board plan at a cost of $215 per day; a single person pays $175. *Also on the full-board plan, a couple in summer need pay only $190 per day, and a single, $165.* Tax and service are added to all tariffs. The owners will pick up guests at West End in Tortola. Fly to Beef Island and take a taxi from there. Or else you can take the ferry from St. Thomas, which goes to the West End three times a day. There's a $75 transportation charge for stays of less than six nights. For information, write to the Hawkinses, P.O. Box 9997, St. Thomas, VI 00801.

Sandy Ground, Box 594, West End, Tortola (tel. 494-3391), offers eight villas with self-sufficient housekeeping units of the type you might see along Spain's Costa del Sol. The estates, as it is called, is built on a 17-acre hill site on the eastern part of Jost Van Dyke. The colony rents out two- and three-bedroom villas. One of my favorites was constructed on a cliff that seems to hang about 60 or so feet over a good beach. If you've come all this way to reach this tiny outpost you might as well stay a week, which are the rates quoted. In winter, two persons are charged $850 weekly, each additional person paying another $100. *However, in summer, the charge is lowered to $700 for two persons weekly, with each additional person paying only $85.* Sandy Ground was created by John Eastman, who once headed an art school in Maine. The airy villas are each privately owned, and each unit is fully equipped with such necessities as refrigerators and stoves. They have their own electric generator. Bob and Billie Grunzinger, formerly of New York state, do a good job of running the property for the absentee owners. They'll help guests with boat rentals and water sports.

WHERE TO EAT: Explorers on Jost Van Dyke don't have to bring a packed lunch before heading out. The previously recommended **Sandcastle** on White Bay (tel. 494-2462), has good food, but it does require a reservation and a set time to be agreed upon, as supplies in the kitchen are limited. You dine right on the beach, taking breakfast, lunch, or dinner. Naturally, attire is casual. Lunch costs from $8, and dinner, featuring fresh fish when available, is from $20.

Yachtsmen like to drop in at **Ira's-by-the-Sea,** at Little Harbour (no phone). Perhaps that's because a free welcoming drink awaits the captain. If you're a passenger or one of the crew, you have to pay. The food is simply prepared and inexpensive. Conch is always available, prepared in several ways. A fish dinner of whelks is more expensive. A catch of the day is always featured, and it might even be lobster. Then, the price "depends." Otherwise count on spending around $20 with drinks. Lunch is served from noon to 3 p.m.; dinner, from 7 to 9:30 p.m. Ira's is open seven days a week.

Abe's by the Sea is a native bar and restaurant on Little Harbour where the cook knows how to please the sailors with a menu of fish, lobster, conch, and chicken. Prices are low too. Most diners escape for around $20, money well spent, especially when a fungi band entertains you with its music and plays for dancing. For the price of the main course, you get peas and rice, along with coleslaw and beans, plus dessert. Sometimes Abe's has a pig roast, and these turn out to be festive nights. Approaching the harbor, you'll see Abe's restaurant on your right. Seven days a week, lunch is served from noon to 3 p.m. and dinner from 7 to 9:30 p.m. For reservations, call Abe's on Channel 16 Marine Radio.

3. Marina Cay

Near Beef Island, Marina Cay is a tiny islet of six acres. Its only claim to fame was as the setting of the Robb White book *Our Virgin Island*, which was filmed with Sidney Poitier and John Cassavetes. The island lies only five minutes away by launch from the Beef Island dock.

The reason I'm mentioning such a tiny cay is because it's the site of a cottage hotel, previewed below:

Marina Cay Hotel (write to P.O. Box 76, Road Town, Tortola; tel. 494-2174). This cottage colony run by Chris and Maria Tilling is spread over the whole island, offering 16 pleasant A-frame cottages, consisting of two units each. Built along the water, they were among the earliest resort structures to open in the British Virgins. Subsequently, newer ones were added. A one-bedroom apartment costs $1,000 per week for two persons, and a two-bedroom unit rents for $1,400 per week for four persons. Rates, in effect all year, are EP. The hotel shuts down in September and October.

You of course have the use of a private beach, guaranteed not to be crowded. Sailing, fishing, and scuba-diving can be arranged, and use of Sunfish as well as snorkeling gear is included in the rates. At the beach bar and restaurant, both lunch and dinner are offered, with menus changed daily. As you'd expect, fresh fish such as grouper and snapper is the best item to order. A lobster farm is built into their dock. That doesn't mean you can't also enjoy Virginia ham and New York steaks. For dessert, try the banana paradise pie. You can show up here in sports attire, providing you've let them know you're coming over to eat. The decor of the pavilion keeps everything nautical with driftwood, turtleshell lamps, and conch shells.

4. Peter Island

Half of the 1,050-acre island, with its good marina and docking facilities, is devoted to the yacht club described below. A ferry makes the run across Sir Francis Drake Channel to Peter Island. Leaving from the CSY Dock, the craft takes from 20 minutes to half an hour. The CSY Dock is approached before you reach Road Town on the road from Beef Island Airport. Beach facilities are found at palm-fringed Deadman Bay, which faces the Atlantic but is protected by a reef.

The island is so private that except for an occasional mason at work and the endless vegetation, about the only creature a guest will encounter is an iguana or a wild cat whose ancestors were abandoned generations ago by shippers (they are said to have virtually eliminated the rodent population).

Peter Island Hotel and Yacht Harbour (tel. 494-2561, or toll free 800/346-4451; for reservations, write Peter Island, 220 Lyon St., Grand Rapids, MI 49503) is a maritime village resort on a 675-acre site created by Peter Smedvig, the Norwegian shipowner and now owned by Amway of Michigan. In eight harborfront units, 32 air-conditioned rooms are rented. The upper-floor units have front and rear balconies, and the lower-floor rooms have private patios, each with a view. The deft design of the intimate cottage colony set in a charming cove is a great success. Special touches include built-in refrigerators, his-and-hers washbasins, and pull-out magnifying mirrors. To add to the room count, 20 units were constructed overlooking Deadman Bay. In all, there are five beachfront villas, each with four rooms. All of these open onto beautiful views, and the interiors are in a tropical motif. Broad louvered wooden doors across the front of each unit open to balconies on the second floor and patios at beach level. The villas were built from locally quarried stones in blues, sand-bleached grays, taupes, and browns.

The beach-house units, on the MAP, cost from $425 for two persons. It's cheaper for two guests to stay at one of the harborfront units. There MAP rates are $350 daily. *In summer, MAP tariffs are reduced: two persons pay $245 to $285 daily.* Special package plans are also offered. The Crow's Nest, overlooking Deadman Bay, crowns the peak above the hotel. This four-bedroom villa, with its own saltwater swimming pool, is rented for $1,640 for up to eight persons per day. In addition, Peter Island offers Sprat Bay villa, on the water's edge. It has three bedrooms, two baths a kitchen, terrace, and living room, plus a rustic wooden interior. The daily EP rate for Spray Bay is $600 for up to six persons. For two meals a day, cottage occupants can add another $45 per person.

Naturally, there is a main swimming pool, and the club's marina facilities are considered among the best equipped in the Virgin Islands. Horseback riding, tennis, and sailing are easily arranged, as are such water sports as scuba-diving, snorkeling, and skiing. Scotland-born Jim Davidson, the general manager, is the kind of experienced hotelier who anticipates in advance the problems and needs of his international clientele, which has included actors Nick Nolte, Robert Shaw, and Jacqueline Bisset, who stayed there during the filming of *The Deep.*

For dining, the **Peter Island Hotel and Yacht Harbour** (tel. 494-2561) serves food that is considered among the best in the British Virgins. Even if you aren't staying in one of the previously recommended accommodations, you can go over just for the cuisine. Boats depart from CSY Baughers Bay at 10 a.m. and noon for lunch and at 6:30 p.m. for dinner (reservations are required). Barbecue lunches and dinners are featured on the beach, or you can eat in the main dining room decorated in a nautical motif. The prix-fixe dinner, served nightly except Saturday, costs $30, plus service. Both European and local chefs prepare specialties. On Saturday evening, a big smörgåsbord is prepared, the accent on local seafood. Meat or grilled fish is served from the rôtisserie. A prime rib is carved right at your table, and you can enjoy one of the best and most varied wine lists in the Virgin Islands, with some rare clarets. In season a jacket is required in the main dining room.

5. Tortola

On the southern shore of this 42-square-mile island, **Road Town** is more like a village. Still, it's the capital of the British Virgin Islands, the seat of Government House and other administrative buildings. The landfill at Wickhams Cay, a 70-acre town center development and marina in the harbor, has brought in a massive yacht-chartering business and has transformed the sleepy capital into more of a bustling, sophisticated center.

On the same southern coast as Road Town, Tortola is characterized by rugged mountain peaks which contain yellow cedar and frangipani, among other foliage. On the northern coast, however, are white sandy beaches, banana trees, mangoes, and clusters of palms.

No visit to Tortola is complete without a trip to **Mount Sage,** a national park rising 1,780 feet. Here on its slopes you'll not only find traces of a primeval rain forest, but you can enjoy a picnic, overlooking neighboring islets and cays. The mountain is reached by heading west from Road Town.

Also west from Road Town for about 4½ miles, you come to **"The Dungeon,"** the island's oldest fort, erected by the Dutch in 1640. Botanists should look for the rare wild West Indian cherry tree growing on the unkempt grounds.

Nearby you can view the ruins (and I mean ruins) of **Thornton Great House.** Here lived Dr. William Thornton, the Quaker I've mentioned previously who won the competition to design the Capitol in Washington, D.C.

Close to Tortola's eastern end, **Beef Island** is the site of the main airport for passengers arriving in the British Virgins. The airstrip is 3,600 feet long and can accommodate the Avro 748 turbo-jet 48-seaters.

The tiny island is connected to Tortola by the Queen Elizabeth Bridge, which the queen herself dedicated in 1966. The one-lane bridge spans the 300-foot channel which divides the little island from its bigger sister, Tortola. On the north shore of Beef Island is a good beach, Long Bay.

GETTING AROUND: In this remote part of the Caribbean, getting around can be a bit of a problem. However, there are **taxis,** which meet every arriving flight. Your hotel can also call up a taxi, and one will soon arrive at your doorstep. Only problem is, forget about the "official" taxi rates—they are generally ignored, as they're completely out of date. You negotiate your own fare.

Car Rentals

Driving in the BVI is only for those who like hairpin turns on a Coney Island Cyclone terrain. You'll need a Canadian or American driver's license, and in addition, you must pay $5 at police headquarters for a temporary British Virgins driving permit, good for about a month.

Both **Budget Rent-a-Car** and **Avis** operate out of Road Town on Tortola, offering cars for $25 to $40 per day, or $150 to $240 per week. Budget is at 11 Wickhams Cay (tel. 494-2639), and Avis has its offices opposite Prospect Reef Resort (tel. 494-2832).

Driving is on the left, as I'd like to remind the policeman who nearly killed me recently as he came speeding down the pike on the right!

Local Air Services

CrownAir will fly you to Virgin Gorda and on to San Juan or St. Thomas. For reservations, telephone 495-2548 in Tortola (actually Beef Island) or 495-5555 in Virgin Gorda.

Air BVI also flies from Beef Island (Tortola) to Virgin Gorda several times a day. For flight information and reservations, telephone 494-2777 in Tortola.

Sightseeing Tours

This is probably your best bet for taking a look at Tortola. **Travel Plan Tours** (tel. 494-2348) will pick you up at your hotel (a minimum of four persons required) and take you on a 2½-hour tour of the island, for $25 per person. At night you can call 494-2154 and arrange for a morning tour.

Bicycle Rentals

If you can handle the rugged terrain, you'll find single and tandem bicycles for rent at **Hero's Rental** (tel. 494-3536) in Road Town in Tortola. Rates start at $4 per hour.

WHERE TO STAY: Most of the places are small—"mom and pop" operations—and informality is the keynote at these inns. My favorites follow:

Frenchman's Cay Hotel & Yacht Club, P.O. Box 1054 (tel. 495-4844), is the newest luxury resort in the British Virgin Islands, on the windward side of the little island of Frenchman's Cay that is connected to Tortola by a bridge. Its location provides it with year-round cooling breezes and panoramic views of the Sir Francis Drake Channel and the outer Virgins. The hotel, set in 12 acres of handsomely landscaped waterfront land, has one- and two-bedroom detached villas, elegantly furnished, each with a shady terrace, a full kitchen, a dining room, and a sitting room with a queen-size sofa bed suitable for two persons. The two-bedroom units have two full baths. One-bedroom villas rent for $100 for single occupancy, $110 for use as a double in winter. Three persons in a two-bedroom unit are charged $135 per day; four occupants pay

$160 per day. Additional guests using the queen-size sofa beds are billed at the rate of $10 per person per day. *In summer, a 30% discount is made on all rates.* Service and tax are added to your bill.

The Clubhouse restaurant and lounge bar, overlooking the freshwater pool, is between the beach and the tennis court. It's a true island structure, with a distinctive open-beam roof. Brunch is served from 11 a.m. to 2:30 p.m. and dinner from 6:30 to 9 p.m. You can enjoy a drink while you watch the chef prepare one of the barbecue specialties of the restaurant. The hotel offers snorkeling, windsurfing, sailing, scuba-diving, fishing, and horseback riding. Island tours and car rentals can be arranged, as well as boat charters.

For reservations or information, get in touch with E and M Associates, 45 W. 45th St., New York, NY 10036 (tel. 212/719-4898, or toll-free 800/223-9832).

Long Bay Hotel, P.O. Box 433 (tel. 495-4252), on the north shore, about ten minutes from the West End, is a low-rise hotel complex set in a 50-acre estate with nearly a mile of white sand beach. It is the first port of entry to Tortola. Escapists who want a far-away corner of a half-forgotten island come here. Units are available in a wide range of styles, shapes, and sizes. Suites, including regular and superior, as well as cottages are scattered up the side of a hill planted with such flowery shrubbery as hibiscus. Cottages come with two bedrooms, a bath and shower, a kitchen, and a living room overlooking the ocean. Some elevated beachfront rooms are set at the edge of the white sands, with twin beds, a bathroom, and a kitchenette, as well as a deck overlooking the ocean with a patio at beach level. In winter on the EP, these rent for $140 double, $110 single. *In summer, rates go down quite a bit, to $66 double, $55 single.* Service and tax are added to all rates. In winter, suites range in price from $90 to $120 for double occupancy, EP. Cottages housing four persons peak at $172 daily, *this rate being lowered to $80 in summer. Doubles can book a suite here in summer at tariffs ranging from $50 to $70; singles, $40 to $60.* Suites, called hillside studios, are air-conditioned and have a dressing area with vanity.

The beach restaurant serves breakfast and luncheon and, in the winter, informal à la carte suppers. The Garden Restaurant serves dinner by reservation only, and the food is of excellent quality. Boats can also be rented for sailing, diving, and exploring the out islands. If the surf is too rough for you, an oceanside saltwater swimming pool adjoins the beach house (which was once a distillery, incidentally). If you write the director, Terence M. Ford will be helpful in responding to your inquiries.

The Sugar Mill, P.O. Box 425, Apple Bay (tel. 495-4355), is set in lush foliage, on the north side of Tortola, a long $20 haul from the airport. Built on the site of a 300-year-old sugar mill, the cottage colony sweeps down the hillside to its own little beach, with jasmine, oleander, hibiscus, avocados, plantains, citrus trees, gardenias, bougainvillea, mangoes, bananas, pineapples, and sugar apples brightening the grounds. The estate is owned by Jeff and Jinx Morgan, formerly of San Francisco, who are travel, food, and wine writers. They provide a warm greeting and atmosphere, and make one feel immediately welcome.

Comfortable apartments climb up the hillside. At the center is a circular swimming pool for those who don't want to go down to the beach. Accommodations are contemporary and beautifully thought out, ranging from suites and cottages to studio apartments, all self-contained with kitchenettes and private terraces with views. In winter, two persons (EP) pay from $100 to $120 daily, and *tariffs are lowered off-season to anywhere from $60 to $80 for two,* plus $27.50 per person extra for breakfast and dinner. The four suites rented are each suitable for four family members. Ceilings are sloped, made of native lumber, and to keep the sea breezes moving, you can turn on a ceiling fan. Lunch is served down by the beach, and dinner in the old Sugar Mill Room, its stone walls decorated with Haitian paintings (see my dining recommendations). Breakfast is on the terrace. The bars are on the honor system, and snorkeling equipment is loaned free. The estate is usually closed in August and September.

Treasure Isle Hotel, P.O. Box 68, Road Town (tel. 494-2501), is the most complete and central resort on Tortola, built at the edge of the capital, on 15 acres of hillside overlooking a marina. The late Herbert Showering of Harvey's sherry spent time, money, and energy transforming the hotel. The general manager, Peter W. S. Wimbush, keeps the British traditions alive today and runs a fine "isle." The core of the hotel is a rather splashy and colorful lounge and swimming pool area. Adjoining it is an open-air dining room (covered), also overlooking the harbor. The cuisine is respected here, with such delights from the barbecue as fresh grouper or snapper when available or a plump, tasty chicken with hot sauce. Every Friday and Sunday evening there's a barbecue. At the hotel's Caribbean evening on Wednesday, you get tasty native dishes, including local conch in a spicy liquor, callaloo soup, curried local beef, and a mango fool or pumpkin pie for dessert.

Along hillside terraces are more than two dozen hotel rooms on one level, more than a dozen efficiencies on another, and higher still, ten condominiums. Winter rates are $105 daily in a double, $100 in a single. For MAP, add $30 per person extra per day. *In summer, a number of low-cost package tours are offered. Otherwise, singles cost $70 daily; doubles, $78.* The atmosphere in each room is striking, with high bamboo beds, tile floors, and white walls forming a fine background for the large framed Jim Tillett silkscreen prints. While most guests stay here for the water-sports activities, there are two tennis courts and another for squash. The hotel's own marina has facilities for visiting yachting people. The big treat here is to go on a day trip to the hotel's own beach club at nearby Cooper Island. The hotel's powerboat runs three times a week to Cooper Island for lunch, swimming, and snorkeling. This tour must be booked through Treasure Isle. The hotel also has a fully equipped dive facility, handling beginning instruction and ranging upward to full certification courses. The hotel's also the "home" in the Caribbean for an offshore sailing school.

Prospect Reef Resort, P.O. Box 104, Road Town (tel. 494-3311), is British-owned, managed by Graham Sedgwick, the largest and most up-to-date resort in the British Virgins. From this village built on a coral reef, panoramic views of Sir Francis Drake Channel unfold. Attractively modern buildings have been set tastefully on landscaped grounds of 38 acres, opening onto a bustling little private harbor. Built as condominiums, rental units consist of suites, town houses, villas, and apartments. Appointments are modern and colorful, in a Caribbean motif. In winter, guests on the EP are charged $98 to $158 in a single or double. A two-bedroom villa costs $398 daily for four persons. Breakfast and dinner carry a supplement of $39 per person daily. *In the off-season, EP singles or doubles cost $59 to $95. Two-bedroom villas suitable for four persons go for $235 daily.* Accommodations include private balconies or patios, private baths or shower, good-size living and dining areas, plus separate bedrooms or sleeping lofts.

There's a pool to swim in, another to dive in, plus sea pools for snorkeling or just fish watching. Six tennis courts with lights are available to buffs. There's also a pitch-and-putt course. Food at the Prospect Restaurant, a combination of continental specialties and island favorites, was praised by *Gourmet* magazine. Diners usually begin their meals with an apéritif at the Drop Inn Bar by Prospect Harbour. The chef's specialties include duckling in orange sauce, steak au poivre, and lobster in champagne. Count on spending about $25 at dinner, if you don't order lobster. The water-sports desk can fill you in on what's available in day sailing, dinghy rental, snorkeling, scuba-diving, or sports fishing.

The Moorings/Mariner Inn, P.O. Box 139, Road Harbour (tel. 494-2332), is the Caribbean's only complete yachting resort, outfitted with 100 sailing yachts, some worth around $500,000. On an eight-acre resort, the inn was obviously designed with the yachting crowd in mind. Charlie and Ginny Cary, a couple from New Orleans who started the British Virgins' first charter service, manage it. They originally came to the Virgins in 1969 to "get away from the cold weather." Not only do yachting people find support facilities and service, but shoreside accommodations as well: lanai hotel rooms, a dockside restaurant, Mariner Bar, a swimming pool, a tennis court, a beach club, a gift shop, and a dive shop. Some 40 units are rented on the EP in winter at a rate of $115 daily in a double, $90 in a single. *Off-season, doubles are lowered to $75 daily, and singles go for $65.* Rooms are spacious, decorated in a light Caribbean motif. All have kitchenettes.

WHERE TO EAT: Most guests dine at their hotels, but if you want to break the monotony of that, I have a few suggestions.

Sugar Mill Room, Apple Bay (tel. 495-4440). You dine in an informal room which was transformed from a three-centuries-old sugar mill (see my hotel recommendations). Your hosts are Jeff and Jinx Morgan, formerly of San Francisco. They know much about food and wine. Together they write a monthly column, "Cooking for Two," in *Bon Appétit,* and she is contributing editor for food and dining for *American Way,* the American Airlines in-flight magazine. Their most recent book is called *Two Cooks in One Kitchen.* Works by Haitian painters have been hung on the old stone walls of the dining room, forming a museum of primitive art. Big copper basins, once used as mortar cisterns, have been planted with tropical flowers. Before going to the dining room, once part of the old boiling house, I suggest a visit to the charming little bar, everything open air in the true West Indian fashion.

Jinx Morgan supervises the dining room and is an imaginative cook herself. One of their most popular creations, published in *Bon Appétit,* is a curried banana soup. They are likely to prepare delectable chicken breasts in a number of ways, seafood soufflé, black-bean soup, herb pasta with hearts of palm sauce, lobster Créole, and a cold rum soufflé. That's just an opening repertoire. The next time around, you might try their breadfruit vichyssoise, conch ceviche with coconut cream, and homemade rum-raisin ice cream. Everything here is homemade, including many island specialties. You're asked to help yourself from a crisp salad bar, like those good ones found in New York. Try to arrive for lunch around 1 p.m.; for dinner, about 8 p.m. At dinner, the cost is around $22, and you must call for a reservation.

The **Cloud Room** (tel. 494-2821) provides a unique dining experience in Tortola. This restaurant and bar sits at the top of Butu Mountain, overlooking Road Town. When weather permits, which is practically every day of the year, the roof slides back, allowing you to dine under the stars. The catch is that the road there is bad (and there's no place to park), so the owner, Paul Wattley, prefers to arrange to pick you up when you make your reservation for dinner, served nightly from 7:30 to 10 p.m. For anywhere from $20 to $30, including wine, you'll get a selection of juicy sirloin steaks, filet mignon, lobster (if available), king crab, fresh fish in season, shish kebab (the house specialty), and shrimp in Créole sauce. At the West Indian buffet every Tuesday night, you'll find such native dishes as curried shrimp, pineapple spareribs, stewed mutton, or curried veal.

Brandywine Bay Restaurant (tel. 495-2301). Marti and Ben Brown over the years have developed quite a few fans in the Virgin Islands. You'll find them in a garden-like atmosphere on the south shore of Tortola, overlooking Drake's Channel, about ten minutes by taxi from Road Town. This is an elite hideaway, attracting the yachting crowd whenever they want to get their feet on solid ground. The setting may be romantic, but it is mainly the food that attracts the patrons. Very fresh ingredients are used, and the menu is both West Indian and continental. That is, you might prefer cracked conch Bahamian style, but you can also get a perfect wienerschnitzel or a veal piccata. Their Sunday brunch from 11 a.m. to 2:30 p.m. is quickly becoming a legend on the island. If the caviar crêpes don't tempt you, perhaps the chicken Kiev will. For dessert, you might try key lime pie or the coco-banana crêpe. Meals cost from $25, and are served nightly except Monday from 6:30 to 9:30 p.m. Always make a reservation.

If you're staying in one of the efficiency apartments on Tortola and don't want to cook, I suggest you go over to **Carib Casseroles,** on Main Street, near the post office in Road Town (tel. 494-3271). Even the *New York Times* praised its "excellent frozen meals," which are called "Meals on Keels." Persons aboard yachts who don't want to be galley slaves drop in here, selecting from a choice of 30 international dishes, including such West Indian specialties as beef and green banana curry, red snapper in fresh lime butter, shrimp with garlic, and Cuban picadillo. Meals begin at $15. Very popular are the rotis (the celebrated Trinidadian taco stuffed with spicy curried meat or shellfish). These wonderful dishes are the creation of Canada-born Roslyn Griffiths, whose recipes were featured in *Cuisine* magazine. You can purchase these fast-food pouches which you cook by dropping in hot water. If you're in town for lunch or dinner, you can go over to her little garden restaurant and "splice the mainbrace" with her ROZmatazz rum punch. You can enjoy her memorable soups, including Créole fisherman's stew, tomato and eggplant, peanut Créole, and pumpkin. For dessert, try the sugar Bum Bum pie (with custard and cream). The garden restaurant is likely to be closed for two months beginning in August. Otherwise, hours are 11 a.m. to 3 p.m. and 7 to 10 p.m. daily except Sunday.

The Pub (tel. 494-2608) stands at water's edge, and locals on Tortola like to go here for a sundowner. It's a British-style pub in the Fort Burt Marina complex, with a good view of the sailing scene. Boat owners like to visit at opening time, 10:30 a.m., for drinks, and a few might make it to the 1 a.m. curfew, depending on how thirsty they are or how long at sea. Lunches are simply prepared and inexpensive, featuring dishes such as chicken and chips, fish and chips, hamburgers, sandwiches, and a special of the day. At dinner there is more of a choice, with shrimp, chicken, chicken Kiev, and prime ribs flown in from Puerto Rico on Thursday. Meals cost $5 to $15. The atmosphere of the Pub is friendly and relaxed, dress is casual, and reservations are not required. On Friday and Saturday nights entertainment is provided all year, and there is a dartboard for daily use.

EXCURSIONS FOR THE DAY: If you've decided to risk everything and navigate the roller-coaster hills of the BVI, then you need a destination. **Cane Garden Bay** is one of the choicest pieces of real estate on the island, long discovered by the sailing crowd. Its white sandy beach is a cliché of Caribbean charm, with sheltering palms. It is nearly always semi-deserted. No one crowds you here.

Rhymer's (tel. 495-4639) is the place to go for food and entertainment at Cane Garden Bay. The success of the place depends very much on James E. Rhymer himself, who, to judge from the size of him, likes his own food a lot. Skippers of any kind of craft are likely to stock up on supplies here; but you can also order cold beer and refreshing rum drinks. Turtle, conch, and whelk show up regularly on the bill of fare, and, when available, Caribbean langouste. If you're tired of fish, maybe James will make you some of his barbecued spareribs. You might also try the mutton stew with peppers and herbs or the honey-dipped chicken. The beach bar and restaurant is open seven days a week from 8 a.m., serving not only breakfast, but lunch and dinner, which costs from $18 up. On some nights a steel drum band will entertain the mariners, and maybe the host himself will show you what a limbo dance is all about! Ice and freshwater showers are available (there are towels to rent as well), and you can ask about renting Sunfish and windsurfers.

Skyworld, Ridge Road (tel. 494-3567), is all the rage, certainly the worthiest excursion on the island. At one of the loftiest peaks on the island, a breezy 1,337 feet, it offers views of both the American and Britannia Virgins. An enterprising Yank, Warren McKenna, who's been a longtime Tortola resident, created this bit of whimsy. Obviously he was taken with the view, but decided to create good food to go along with it. Guests come here for his seafood, such as fresh lobster served simply but superbly with drawn butter, and his beef dishes. He doesn't neglect his side dishes either;

in fact his french fries and onion rings have been praised by *Gourmet* magazine. If you're here at sundowner time, order some of his conch fritters, which are considered the best on the island. They're served with mayonnaise laced with basil. A house specialty is chicken in a coconut shell. Meals cost from $12 to $25. The place opens for lunch (go anytime from noon on), stays open for afternoon tea, and even remains so for sundowners around 6 p.m. However, should you want dinner, it's by reservation only, the time and menu to be discussed with Mr. McKenna.

THE SPORTING LIFE: Tortola boasts the largest fleet of bareboat sailing charter boats in the world, and is also one of the finest diving areas anywhere.

Snorkeling and Scuba

Marina Cay is known for its good snorkeling beach, and the one at Cooper Island (see the Treasure Isle Hotel recommendation) is another honey. Divers are attracted to Anegada Reef, which is the site of many shipwrecks, including the *Paramatta* and the *Astrea*. However, the one dive site in the British Virgins that lures them over from St. Thomas is the wreckage of the R.M.S. *Rhone,* near the western point of Salt Island. *SkinDiver* magazine called this "the world's most fantastic ship wreck dive." It teems with beautiful marine life and coral formations, and was featured in the motion picture *The Deep*.

Aquatic Centers, P.O. Box 108, Road Town (tel. 494-2858). For a good swimmer interested in taking his or her first dive under careful supervision, this well-equipped outfit is the best choice in Tortola. Owned and operated by U.S. citizen Alan Baskin and his wife, Eva Cope, the establishment offers a resort course for beginners which includes lessons in a pool and a one-tank reef dive lasting a full afternoon. The cost is $75. The Baskins provide expeditions to many dive sites, including the R.M.S. *Rhone* which sank in 1867, and have a solid working knowledge of the best offshore dive sites.

Boating

The best for this is Charlie and Ginny Cary's **The Moorings,** P.O. Box 139, Road Town (tel. 494-2332), whose eight-acre waterside resort I've already previewed as a dockside hotel recommendation. This place, along with others, makes the British Virgins the cruising capital of the world. The Carys started the first charter service in the British Virgins. From their beautiful fleet of sailing craft, you can choose your own design, including a Moorings 50 and a Morgan 46, considered the queens of the Caribbean charter fleet. They can accommodate three couples in comfort and style. Arrangements can be made for bareboating or going out with a skipper.

They have a staff of some 60 mechanics, electricians, riggers, and cleaners. In addition, if you're going out on your own, you'll get a thorough briefing session about Virgin Island waters and anchorages. Tariffs are generally from $1,500 per person per week. To make reservations in the U.S., call 800/535-7289, toll free.

The *Shadowfax,* Treasure Isle Hotel Jetty, Tortola (tel. 494-2175), is a catamaran whose double-hulled construction permits smooth sailing even in rough seas, with an experienced crew taking the boat out for a day of snorkeling off reefs rich in marine life. Snorkel equipment, a buffet lunch, and an open bar are covered by the fee of $60 per person. The highlight of the outing is a tour through weirdly angled granite formations of Virgin Gorda "Baths." These shelter tidal pools, massive tree roots, exotic fish, and hidden catches of soft white sand. Considered haunted by the native Indians, these massive boulders offer one of the most bizarre and colorful expeditions in the islands.

AFTER DARK: There isn't much nightlife. Your best bet is to ask around and find out which hotel might have entertainment on any given evening. Fungi and scratch bands appear regularly. Nonresidents are usually welcome, but call first.

WHERE TO SHOP: Most of the shops are on Main Street, Road Town, on Tortola, but know that the British Virgins have no duty-free-port shopping. British goods are imported without duty, and the wise shopper will be able to find some good buys among these imported items, especially in English china.

The **Cockle Shop** carries jewelry handmade in the British Virgins, including many gifts and souvenir items, even pieces of Wedgwood.

Go to **Past and Presents** to see china and pewter, as well as a collection of antique silver. They sell books too.

The **Shipwreck Shop,** depending on what "washed up" on its premises, usually has a collection of West Indian handcrafts, including placemats, sandals, grass rugs, straw bags, shell jewelry, and wooden bowls, all for sale in one of the more traditional structures in Road Town.

Pusser's Company Store (tel. 494-2467) is equally divided between a long, mahogany-trimmed bar accented with many fine nautical artifacts and a souvenir store selling T-shirts, postcards, and upmarket gift items. Pusser's Rum is one of the best-selling items here, or perhaps you'd prefer polished brass mementoes of your visit. The place is open from 9:30 a.m. to 5 p.m. daily except Sunday.

Sunny Caribbee Spice Company, Main Street in Road Town (tel. 494-2178), in a lovely old West Indian building which was the first hotel on Tortola, specializes in Caribbean spices, seasonings, teas, condiments, and handcrafts. Most of the products are blended and packaged on the island. You can buy two world-famous specialties here: West Indian hangover cure and Arawak love potion.

6. Virgin Gorda

The second-largest island in the cluster of British Virgins, Virgin Gorda (Fat Virgin) remains truly virginal. However, seen from the sea, it doesn't look virginal at all—rather, like a pregnant woman lying on her back.

Virgin Gorda is ten miles long and two miles wide, with a population of some 1,100. It lies 12 miles east of Road Town, and is reached by frequent flights from Beef Island off the shores of Tortola. Virgin Gorda is also frequently visited from St. Thomas, which lies only 26 miles away. Speedy's Fantasy (tel. 495-5240) operates a ferry service between Road Town and Virgin Gorda, the trip taking only half an hour. The ferry makes several trips daily, but does not operate on Sunday.

The northern side of Virgin Gorda is mountainous, a peak reaching 1,370 feet. However, the southern half is flat, with large boulders appearing at every turn. The best beaches are at Spring Bay, Trunk Bay, and Devil's Bay.

Among the places of interest, **Coppermine Point** is the site of an abandoned copper mine and smelter. Because of loose rock formations, it can be dangerous to explore and caution should be used if you're going there. Legend has it that the Spanish worked these mines in the 1600s. However, the only authenticated document reveals that the English sank the shafts in 1838 to mine copper.

The Baths are on every visitor's list to Virgin Gorda. These are a phenomenon of tranquil pools and caves formed by gigantic house-sized boulders. As these boulders toppled over one another, they formed saltwater grottos, suitable for exploring.

The best way to see the island if you're over for a day trip is to call Andy Flax at Fischers Cove Beach Hotel (tel. 495-5252). He runs **Virgin Gorda Tours Assoc.,** which will give you a tour of the island for about $30 per person. The tour is operated twice daily from the hotel's parking lot.

Kilbride's Underwater Tours, Saba Rock (tel. 494-2746), is run by the Kilbride clan. Among them they have been diving for more than a century. The Kilbride family members have done everything from spending two weeks under the sea as "aquanauts" to underwater demolition work. They'll take you on underwater tours of the dive sites in the area, ranging from coral forests and wall-to-wall fish to wrecks (the *Rhone* among others). A one-tank dive costs $40; two-tank dive, $60. A half day's snorkeling costs $25 per person. Saba Rock is an island on the eastern end of Gorda Sound.

THE RESORT HOTELS: An embodiment of understatement in luxury is **Little Dix Bay,** P.O. Box 70 (tel. 495-5555; 212/586-4459 in New York City, or toll free 800/ 223-7637, 800/442-8198 in New York State), an 84-room resort discreetly scattered along a crescent-shaped private bay on a 500-acre preserve. Millions of dollars after the discovery of the site by Laurance Rockefeller, this resort opened in 1964 on the northwest corner of the "Fat Virgin," in the Sir Francis Drake Channel, where pirates once prowled. It has the same quiet elegance as its fellow Rockresort, Caneel Bay Plantation on St. John in the U.S. Virgins.

All rooms, built in woods of purpleheart, mahogany, locust, and ash, have private terraces, with a view of the sea or of gardens. Some units are two-story rondavels raised on stilts to form their own relaxing breezeways. On the outside they may appear like South Seas huts, but on the inside intelligent decorating has brought a sophisticated contemporary styling with all the conveniences. They are often characterized by rough stone walls, open beamed ceilings, hanging basket lamps, wicker chests, and Toledo-red fabrics. *From mid-April until mid-May and from November 1 through December 19, singles rent for $300 and doubles $320, the prices including three meals daily. From mid-May until the end of October, the single rate is $280 daily, $300 in a double. Special plans, such as tennis specials, honeymoon packages, whatever, are also offered in summer.* In winter, full AP rates are $465 daily for two persons, $445 in a single, $565 in a triple. Trade winds come through louvres and walls of screens, the air mixture further cooled by ceiling fans. In the rondavels, hammocks swing from the stilts.

At the Pavilion, with its peaked roofs, you can dine in the open, or else enjoy meals in the Sugar Mill Restaurant with its adjoining bar. If you're coming over for lunch at Sugar Mill, you can order such light fare as an Antilles fresh fruit salad with coconut sherbert or sandwiches. Figure on spending $19 for lunch and $39 for dinner, all prix fixe. Little Dix offers many extras. Guests have the use of Sunfish, floats, and snorkeling gear. They also have Boston whalers that take you to the beach of your choice with a picnic lunch, and horseback riding is also available (extra). On Thursday all the guests at Little Dix are transported by car or Boston whaler to Spring Bay for a barbecue luncheon with a steel band.

Biras Creek, P.O. Box 54 (tel. 494-3555), is a magnificent resort lying at the northern end of Virgin Gorda. It stands like a hilltop-crowning fortress, not to keep away pirates, but to welcome the sun and views. On a 150-acre estate with its own marina, it occupies a narrow neck of land, flanking the sea on three sides. To create their Caribbean hideaway, Norwegian shipping interests carved out this resort in a wilderness, but wisely protected the natural terrain. The estate is well planted with flowering trees and bushes, and there is a greenhouse on the grounds to keep the estate supplied in foliage and flowers. Along the walks laid out, you can inspect diddle doe cactus, golden-barked turpentine trees, tamarind, frangipani, white cedar, and wild nutmeg. Looking like a prehistoric monster, a timid iguana may run across your path. Along the way, you might also see iridescent hummingbirds and the friendly little bananaquit.

Scattered along the shore, 16 cottages and 32 suites shelter guests. Cooled by ceiling fans, suites have well-furnished bedrooms and divan beds with a sitting room and private patio, plus a refrigerator. You can open your windows to enjoy the sea breezes. There are three sets of rates. *The cheapest is during the summer period from June 1 lasting until November 15. At that time, double AP rates are $250 a day.*

Shoulder-season rates for the spring and part of the fall are slightly higher. Highest tariffs are charged from mid-December until early April: from $330 daily in a single, from $370 in a double, both AP. Tax and service are added to all bills. These tariffs include three meals a day, plus use of facilities and equipment, such as a pool, snorkeling gear, Sunfishes, paddleboards, and tennis courts. Also provided are free trips to nearby islands and beach barbecues twice a week. Special honeymoon packages are also offered off-season.

The food has won high praise. You never know what you're going to be served. Take the soups—it might be gazpacho, perhaps clam chowder, maybe cucumber, or even curried apple or grapefruit soup. Grouper baked in a shell, chicken Kiev prepared just right, filet of pork with apricot sauce, moussaka with banana bread, and pheasant flown in from the British Isles are just some of the dishes you are likely to be served during your stay. The wine cellar is also good. At the peaked-roof hilltop main house, the dining room and its connecting drinking lounge are quietly elegant, with heavy hewn beams and a ceramic tile mural. There's always a table with a view. A barbecued lunch is served on the beach on Monday and Friday. A buffet lunch from 1 to 2 p.m. is served Tuesday, Thursday, and Sunday, and a curry dish—a Malayan rice specialty—is offered for Sunday brunch. Dinner, from 7 to 9 p.m., is priced from $30. Guests arriving in Virgin Gorda can be met by a taxi and taken to the hotel's motor launch for a speedy trip to Biras Creek.

Bitter End Yacht Club, P.O. Box 46, John O'Point, North Sound (tel. 494-2746), is a rendezvous point for the yachting set cruising through the British Virgins. Bitter End offers an informal life, guests taking one of the well-appointed beachfront and hillside villas overlooking the sound and yachts at anchor. If you're not a sailor, the helpful staff gives free on-the-beach instruction to get you started. Formal lessons are also available. A sailboat practically comes with your room, as rates include unlimited use of the club's fleet of Lasers, Sunfish, Rhodes 19s, and J-24s, as well as windsurfers and outboard skiffs. Or you can charter a CAL 2-27 for an overnight trip. There are great sheltered-water sailing, reef snorkeling as you hunt for that doomed Spanish galleon, expeditions to neighboring cays, shelling, endless beachcombing possibilities, marine science participation, whatever, all included in the rates.

For something novel, you can stay aboard one of the 27-foot yachts, yours to sail, with dockage including daily maid service, meals in the Yacht Club dining room, and overnight provisions. On the AP *in summer, yacht live-aboards pay $120 daily in a single, $160 for two persons. Villa rooms are $150 to $210 in a single, $180 to $260 for two persons daily. For two adults with two, three, or four children under 16, a family plan includes a second room free on the eight-day/seven-night Admiral's package. The summer package also provides for deep-sea fishing, lobster/champagne beach party, night snorkeling with lights, children's sailing classes, and a dinner sail on the world's largest catamaran. A ten-day/nine-night private yacht/villa package in summer is $675 per person. In the fall, daily yacht live-aboards pay $165 single, $195 for two persons; and villa rooms cost $195 to $250 single, $225 to $280 for two persons.* In winter, AP yacht live-aboards pay $245 single daily, $275 for two persons. Villa rooms are $285 to $335 daily in a single, $315 to $365 for two persons. *In spring, AP yacht live-aboards pay $185 daily for a single, $215 for two persons, while villa rooms go for $215 to $270 daily in a single, $245 to $300 for two persons.* New marina rooms are the same rates as live-aboard yachts, a good saving. Furnishings are a Caribbean motif—a grass rug from Dominica, a hand-printed bedcover from the French West Indies.

The social hub of the place is the bar where you're likely to find everybody from the publisher of *Yachting* magazine to the sun-streaked Flying Dutchman and the Barefoot Contessa. At dinner you'll find fresh native fish, lobster, and steak, and every manner of burgee hanging gaily along the walls. Yachting people arrive for the buffet breakfast, costing $9, or the lunch, $12. Dinner, from 6 p.m., is by reservation only, and the cost ranges from $28. All meals are included for club guests. There are boat races, plus a special lunch on Sunday.

For reservations, call 312/944-5855 (collect), or write to Bitter End Yacht Club, 875 N. Michigan Ave., Chicago, IL 60611.

The **Tradewinds Resort**, P.O. Box 64 (tel. 494-3151), is a holiday mecca for active people, offering activities for both experienced participants and novices in such pursuits as sailing, snorkeling, swimming, and boardsailing, plus tennis and sunbathing. Guests have free use of boardsailers and 12- and 14-foot Holder daysailers. For an additional charge you can go scuba-diving, waterskiing, deep-sea fishing, sailing on a 26-foot boat, and making excursions aboard chartered vessels. The resort has a secluded beach of its own, or you can go to neighboring sandy strips along the sea. Each of the 38 spacious guest rooms is light, airy, and furnished with two queen-size beds, comfortable chairs, and a corner table for drinks or games. A balcony overlooking the North Sound and a refrigerator complete each of the attractive accommodations. In winter, single occupancy costs $205 to $255 daily on the MAP, rising to $240 to $300 daily for double occupancy. *Summer rates are $175 single, $200 double.* Taxes and service are added to all bills. Children under 5 are not accepted. Ask about their "summer splash" packages. Complimentary round-trip transfers are given to and from Virgin Gorda airport on stays of seven nights or longer. Meals are served in the open-air dining room. Coverups are required in the dining room and main bar, where casually elegant dress is called for, and men are asked to wear slacks at dinner. The Beach Bar serves light lunches, snacks, and cold drinks.

Olde Yard Inn, P.O. Box 26, The Valley (tel. 495-5544), is a charmer. It's got a lot going for it, namely its owner, Carol Kaufman, a New Yorker in the restaurant business in Fort Lauderdale, Florida, for 13 years before coming here. This little 11-room Caribbean inn is beautifully run, with good food, good beds, and hospitality that ranks among the best in the British Virgins. Near the main house are two long bungalows with small but adequate bedrooms, each with its own bath and Haitian bedspreads. Scattered about are a few antiques and special accessories. On the MAP in winter, guests pay $185 daily in a double, $105 in a single. *From mid-April to mid-May, and again from mid-November to mid-December, MAP bookings are accepted at $125 daily in a double, $85 in a single. The EP charge is $45 per person. However, from mid-May until mid-November, you can stay here for $45 daily in a single, $65 in a double, and $85 in a triple, including a buffet-style breakfast.*

When you arrive you'll be asked about your interests. Perhaps you'll find a saddled horse waiting for a before-breakfast or a moonlight ride. Or you'll go for a sail on a yacht or a snorkeling adventure at one of 16 beaches, with a picnic lunch provided (perhaps lobster, pâté, champagne, or peanut butter sandwiches). Under a banana-leaf thatched roof, the meals served here are one of the reasons for coming over. You might begin with snails or coquilles, and follow with local fish or lobster. Steaks cut at the inn are from the finest fresh sirloin. Meals have a decided French accent. If you're just visiting for the day, you can enjoy a lunch from noon to 2 p.m., costing from $10. Dinners, from 7 to 9 p.m., begin at $15 but could run up to $30 if you want lobster. Movies are shown at 9 p.m. daily in the library, and there is live entertainment twice a week in the dining room. On the premises is a small boutique full of bright, intriguing items such as local silkscreened clothes, arts and crafts, painting and sculpture, as well as other fun items such as Chinese and American kites in silk, nylon, cotton, and paper.

Fischers Cove Beach Hotel, P.O. Box 60 (tel. 495-5252), is a group of cottages nestled near the beach of St. Thomas Bay, with swimming at your doorstep. Erected of native stone, each house is self-contained, with one- or two-bedroom units having a combination living and dining room with a kitchenette. The design is attractive, with open pitched ceilings accented by dark-wood beams. At a food store near the grounds, you can stock up on your provisions if you're doing your own cooking. A two-story unit (12 rooms) has been added to the resort. These are pleasant but simple rooms, offering a view of Drake Channel. Each has its own private bath (hot and cold showers) and private balcony.

The place was started in 1962 as a small bar by Andy Flax, who always wears his baseball hat and bears a faint resemblance to Reggie Jackson. His grandfather gave him the land. In winter, he rents one-bedroom cottages for $130 daily, and a two-bedroom cottage goes for $210. *In summer, one- and two-bedroom cottages are in the $100 to $185 daily range*. The hotel rooms are rented for $190 daily in a double and $140 in a single, both MAP tariffs. *In summer, the MAP tariffs are $105 in a double and $80 in a single in the hotel units*. The cottages are rented on the EP and the rooms on the MAP.

Andy's wife, Norma, is from Antigua, and she's known as one of the best cooks on the island. Lunch, from noon to 2 p.m., costs around $10 and up, and dinner, from 7 to 10:30 p.m., ranges from $22. A resident steel band provides entertainment most nights, and periodically a local scratch band plays. In whatever form, something nice is always happening here.

Guavaberry Spring Bay Vacation Homes (tel. 495-5227) are clusters of hexagonal redwood, white-roofed houses built on stilts and available for daily or weekly rentals. It's like living in a treehouse, with screened and louvered walls open to let in sea breezes. Each home has one or two bedrooms, and all have private baths, with a small kitchenette and dining area. The friendly hosts are Betty Roy and Tina and Ludwig Goschler, her daughter and son-in-law. They'll show you to one of their unique vacation homes, each with its own elevated sundeck overlooking Sir Francis Drake Passage. Two persons in winter pay $95 daily for a one-bedroom house, the rate rising to $145 per day for four persons in a two-bedroom house, plus service and tax. An extra person pays $15 per day. *In summer, a one-bedroom house costs $65 per day; the two-bedroom house, $93 per day, also plus tax and service*. Within a few minutes of the cottage colony is the beach at Spring Bay. It's also possible to explore the "Baths" nearby. The owners provide a complete commissary for guests, and such tropical fruits as tamarind and soursop can be picked in season or else bought at local shops. They will make arrangements for day charters for scuba-diving or fishing, and will also arrange for island Jeep tours and saddle horses.

7. Mosquito Island

The sandy, 125-acre Mosquito Island just north of Virgin Gorda wasn't named for those pesky insects we all know and few if any love. It took its name from the Mosquito (or Moskito) Indians, who were the only known inhabitants of the small land mass before the arrival of the Spanish conquistadors in the 15th century. Archeological relics of these peaceful Indians and their agricultural pursuits have been found here.

Today the privately owned island is uninhabited except for **Drake's Anchorage,** P.O. Box 2510, North Sound, Virgin Gorda (tel. 494-2254, or toll free 800/624-6651), which many repeat patrons consider their favorite retreat in the British Virgins. The hotel offers only ten comfortable rooms and two villas. All the accommodations are decorated with Haitian art, and each contains a private bath and sea-view veranda. The villas have private kitchens. Units at this idyllic oasis are managed by Peter and Jamy Faust. In winter, charges are $265 daily for a double room, $190 for a single, and $80 for a third person lodged in a double, all AP. *Summer rates are $190 in a double, $140 in a single, with a third person in a double paying $65 daily, AP*.

The resort provides free use of windsurfers, snorkeling equipment, and bicycles. For additional fees, you can go scuba-diving, take boat trips to a nearby deserted island or to the "Baths" at Virgin Gorda, go deep-sea fishing, make day sails, go horseback riding, or try your skill at waterskiing. The snorkeling and scuba here are considered so good that members of the Cousteau Society spend one month each year exploring local waters. There are four beaches on Mosquito Island, each with different wave and water conditions, so guests can choose what suits them. The resort's restaurant is attractively tropical in design and conscious of both French and Caribbean culinary styles. It faces the water and offers a superb cuisine which features local and continental dishes, lobster, a fresh fish of the day, and a weekly pig roast, with a live band for entertainment.

Getting here requires taking a plane to the Virgin Gorda airport and Speedy's Taxi from there to the Leverick Bay Dock. The taxi driver will "radio" ahead, and a boat will be sent from Drake's Anchorage to take you on the five-minute ride from the dock to the resort. The fare is complimentary if you stay at least seven nights. Otherwise, it will be added to your room bill upon checkout.

8. Guana Island

This 850-acre island, a nature sanctuary, is one of the most private hideaways in the Caribbean. Don't go here seeking resort action, but if you want to retreat from the world, to envelop yourself in a natural setting where intrusion by people has been wisely controlled, then Guana Island might be for you. It lies right off the coast of Tortola. To reach it, the **Guana Island Club**, P.O. Box 32, Road Town, Tortola (tel. 4-2354), will send a boatman to meet arriving guests at Beef Island airport. Of course, you must give the club fair warning of your arrival. You should advise their office in New York of your arrival. For reservations, write or call Guana Island Club, Timber Trail, Rye, NY 10580 (tel. 914/967-6050).

After your arrival on Guana Island, a Nissan Patrol with an open surrey top will transport you up one of the most scenic hills in the region. You arrive at a cluster of whitewalled cottages that were built as a private club in the 1930s on the foundations of a Quaker homestead. The stone-trimmed bungalows never hold more than a total of 30 guests. Since the dwellings are staggered along a flower-dotted hillside, the sense of privacy is almost absolute. The panoramic sweep from the terraces is spectacular, particularly at sunset. When guests hunger for company, they'll find a friendly atmosphere at the rattan-furnished clubhouse. Dinners by candlelight are served family style on the veranda, with menus which include home-grown vegetables and continental and Stateside specialties. Dinner is a casually elegant sit-down affair, whereas lunch is served buffet style every day. The bars are self-service, and the hotel bills clients according to the honor system.

Each guest cottage, complete with shower (but don't use too much water), has an individual charm. The interiors are fairly rustic, with wood beams. Cottages are named after such islands as Grenada. In high season, two persons pay $325 daily and a single is charged $255. *In the off-season, tariffs in a double range from $205 to $230 daily, with singles paying $150 to $175*. Tariffs include all meals, but service and tax are extra, as is the $20-per-person round-trip boat transfer. If you'd like to round up 30 of your friends, you can rent the whole island! Paula Selby is the thoughtful hostess here, directing a pleasant staff. Sports lovers and/or beachcombers will find seven beaches, some of which require a boat to reach. There's also a clay tennis court, all water sports including fishing and snorkeling, a fleet of small sailing craft, and a network of nature trails.

HAITI

SIGHTS, SOUNDS, TASTES, and smells come together uniquely in the oldest black republic in the western hemisphere. In the heart of the Caribbean, Haiti is the size of the state of Maryland and shaped like the claw of a large Maine lobster. Bizarrely exotic, inescapably moving, it is the most flamboyant island in the Caribbean, a French-speaking land with a pure African cast.

These warm people, who extend a *bienvenue* to visitors, speak their special Créole tongue and maintain the songs and dances of their African past. They still very much practice voodoo with its richly symbolic ceremonies.

Haiti occupies the western port of the island of Hispaniola, lying some 643 air miles southeast of Miami, and even though it's on the same island, it bears almost no resemblance to the Spanish-speaking Dominican Republic.

A primitive rhythm seems to pulsate through Haiti, this teeming, turbulent land of stark contrasts and subtle blending. Its poverty is often masked in the blossoms of the flamboyant tree and the bougainvillea vine.

Just how poor is Haiti? To illustrate, one family lives in a tin-roofed hovel, only seven feet square, some of its rotting wooden boards missing. The family members, seven in all, sleep huddled together on a bed made of banana leaves. Yet they are considered rich enough to employ a servant.

The landscape is dominated by a trio of mountain ranges, the major ones of which are the Cibao Mountains and the Cordillera Central, their peaks climbing to 8,000 to 9,000 feet above sea level.

Some six million people live in Haiti, about 90% are black. In addition to a scattering of whites, many of the remaining 10% are mulattoes, Haitian Créoles, descendants of the early French colonists who mixed with Africans.

GETTING THERE: Haiti's international airport at Port-au-Prince is served by several major airlines, all offering good-quality service and usually prompt arrivals. For most passengers living in the northeastern part of the United States (especially in the New York area), the most attractive routing is on one of the **American Airlines** streamlined stretch 747s from JFK Airport to Port-au-Prince. American Airlines, in fact, is the only carrier to fly nonstop from New York to Haiti, departing every day for the approximately 3½-hour flight to the Haitian capital. Other airlines such as **Eastern** and **Pan Am** have nonstop flights to Haiti leaving daily from Miami.

A wide variety of ticket options is available on American, the prices varying with the time of year, the day of the week, and whether or not a passenger opts for a complete travel and hotel package. These sometimes represent impressive bargains when purchased simultaneously from a representative of American's tour department.

The cheapest ticket that is *not* a part of a package is an excursion ticket. This ticket usually requires no advance purchase, but you must delay using the return half for 3 to 30 days. Depending on the day of your flights, high-season round-trip fares range from $407 to $420, while low-season round trips cost as little as $355 to $367, depending on the day of your departure.

More information about schedules, exact prices, tour options, and connections from the dozens of cities that the airline serves can be obtained by calling American Airlines on one of their local or toll-free numbers, available from your local telephone company's directory and directory assistance.

If you're in Miami or San Juan, you can take an **Air France** jet to Port-au-Prince. Connections from San Juan to the Haitian capital are also possible on **Prinair.** For Canadians, a popular routing is an **Air Canada** flight from Montréal. If you're resort-hopping, you'll find that **Air Jamaica** wings into Port-au-Prince from both Kingston and Montego Bay. It's also possible to take a **Bahamasair** flight from Nassau.

GETTING AROUND: After you've gone through a thorough Customs inspection, you emerge from the crowded bustle of the airport into the bright sunshine where, waiting for you, will be some—

Taxis

Drivers hang out in front of airports, major nightspots, and restaurants. But don't be surprised if, after they've gotten you in the back seat, the vehicle breaks down on your way to your hotel. The cars, often in bad condition, aren't metered, so rates will have to be negotiated.

I will quote typical rates, but they are likely to be out of date by the time of your arrival in Port-au-Prince. For example, from Port-au-Prince to Pétionville, the most frequented route, costs $16 per person, while from the airport to the Holiday Inn downtown costs about $12. It will cost $30 to $45 or more to go from the airport to a hotel on the beach! At that rate, you won't want to make a lot of trips between the beaches and Port-au-Prince. Rates for all vehicles are government controlled. For information, call 2-0330.

Taxi Tours

The best way to go on a shopping or sightseeing expedition is by taxi. Navigating through the teeming streets of Port-au-Prince, where denizens casually run in front of cars, is for the adventuresome only. Of course, taxi drivers will try to take you to shops where owners have promised them commissions on every purchase. They'll tell you that the shop or gallery you wanted to visit "just burned down" or is a "tourist trap." Both are a possibility, but don't necessarily believe what you're told, and be firm in what you want to see.

In hiring a car or a driver, it's best to have your hotel make the arrangements rather than doing it yourself. The people at your hotel desk are likely to know the most reliable people and make the best deal for you. You can rent a taxi for three hours for around $35.

Publiques

These public cars or jitneys are such an offbeat mode of transportation that I hesitate to suggest them to first-time or fastidious visitors. The fare is only one Haitian gourde or 15¢ and there is no cheaper method other than walking if you want to get around Port-au-Prince inexpensively. However, if the driver enters the grounds of your hotel, he is legally entitled to charge you more. You'll recognize the publique by the red kerchief or ribbon dangling from the rear-view mirror. Drivers rarely speak English and they stop wherever they choose, picking up whomever or however many passengers they want to.

Camionettes

These are bus-like vehicles, usually Peugeot station wagons, charging one Haitian gourde or 15¢ on most runs. If you stop off the scheduled route, however, you'll have to negotiate the fare. Literally "little trucks," camionettes run between Port-au-Prince and Pétionville Square. Camionettes that take you to other places besides Pétionville are trucks with wooden benches in the back. They are canopied and painted like circus wagons, each with a name such as "La Petite Fleur" (The Little Flower).

Tap-Taps

These gaily decorated station wagons, charging a gourde or 15¢ a ride, are like a circus carousel on wheels. The subject of countless paintings, the tap-tap has no springs, and your bad back will be in rotten shape after bouncing along the rough streets of Port-au-Prince. The government says "tap-taps are more often photographed by tourists than used by them for transportation." That's good advice, unless you like crowding in with a few chickens or maybe a live pig on the way to market!

Car Rentals

Roads are unmarked, and out in the country often rutted. In exploring the hinterlands I've often had to ford a stream when the road just gave out.

In overpopulated Haiti, people don't seem car conscious. In Port-au-Prince, in particular, you're often trapped in a mass of people and cars, a cacophony of shouts and horns. Women with half-naked children march in front of your moving car with seemingly reckless abandon for their own safety, much less their child's. As they're often colorfully clad in flaming reds, lime greens, and sunflower yellows, they're at least easy to spot.

But if you're willing to run the risk, and want to save the cost of a driver, you'd better stick to one of the bigger international car-rental firms. Over the years, I've encountered major problems with some local companies.

Hertz (tel. 6-0700) is well represented in Haiti by Dynamic Car Rentals S.A., with a fleet of Mitsubishis, all with four doors and air conditioning. They have Colts, Lancers, and the famous 4WD-Pajeros. The Haiti operation maintains a desk at the airport (tel. 6-2048). For toll-free information call 800/654-3131.

I have also used **Avis** (tel. 6-4161) satisfactorily in the past. They rent rear-engine Volkswagen Beetles as their low-priced entry and higher-priced Datsuns for those who want more luxury and comfort.

For the purposes of updating this guide, I used the services of **Budget Rent-a-Car** (tel. 6-2324). My comments about certain of their policies, such as insurance, will pertain to all car-rentals in Haiti in general. Budget has an exceptional and friendly staff in Haiti, and they seem eager to help with problems, which are likely to occur. The inventory at Budget emphasizes peppy Nipponese cars well suited to the winding roads and steep inclines of Haiti.

You must have a valid driver's license, a major credit card (or else a cash deposit), and be between the ages of 25 and 65. Budget charges $4 per day for a collision damage waiver which, nonetheless, will mean that a driver must be responsible for the first $250 in damage costs in the event of an accident. Without the waiver, a driver is responsible for the *full* price of repairs to the vehicle. A local driver, if hired, must also be registered on the policy.

Budget's cheapest car is a Pony or a Daihatsu Charade with manual transmission and a seating capacity of four persons. Rentals of three days or less cost $30 per day. Rentals in this category for a full week, with unlimited mileage included, are $175. Automatic transmission vehicles cost $32 per day or $192 per week with unlimited mileage. From the top-category listing of vehicles, there is a manual transmission Honda Civic with air conditioning. Rentals with unlimited mileage cost $35 per day or $250 per week.

These rates require an advance reservation of two business days through Budget's reservation center in Dallas (tel. 800/527-0700).

Bus Tours

All the companies in Port-au-Prince offer the same tours at similar prices. **Chatelain Tours and Travel Service,** rue Geffrard (tel. 2-4469), is the representative for Gray Line tours in Port-au-Prince. In minibuses or limousines they operate both large- and small-group excursions, not only to the sights within the periphery of Port-au-Prince, but to Cap-Haitien as well. Rates are very steep if only one person goes on the tour. However, they are considerably reduced if two or more persons go along. The most popular tour is the three-hour one previewing the highlights of Port-au-Prince, including the Iron Market, at $13 per person. The three-hour Kenscoff Mountain Drive at $15 per person visits the Jane Barbancourt Rum Castle.

PRACTICAL FACTS: The official **currency** of the country is the Haitian gourde. One U.S. dollar presently is exchanged for 6.25 Haitian gourdes. There is usually no problem in paying with U.S. dollars, except perhaps in some remote places. In fact, some places quote their prices *only* in U.S. dollars. However, Canadian dollars are not freely exchanged and therefore should be converted into Haitian gourdes. In general, banks are open from 9 a.m. to 1 p.m. except Saturday and Sunday. *Unless otherwise stated, prices quoted in this chapter are in U.S. dollars.*

English is commonly spoken in all tourist centers (not in the country), but French is the **official language.** Créole is the unofficial second language, and it's filled with wonderful proverbs, such as "When a cockroach is giving a dance, he never invites a chicken."

Entering Haiti is rarely a problem if you're a U.S. or Canadian citizen. A **passport,** either current or expired, is accepted, or else a voter registration card or birth certificate. You'll also need to produce an ongoing or return ticket, a requirement common in the Caribbean. The tourist card issued is valid for a month (it can be extended upon application), and upon departing Haiti, you'll be charged a $15 departure tax. However, the new government may change entry requirements during the lifetime of this edition. Therefore it's best to check with your travel agent.

In **electric current,** Haiti uses 110 volts, 60 cycles, so therefore most U.S. appliances do not need a converter.

Haiti operates on **Eastern Standard Time.** The mainland and Haiti keep the same time for most of the year, except when the conversion in the U.S. comes to Daylight Savings Time. Then the clocks of Haiti are one hour behind those of, say, New York or Miami.

All hotels in Haiti have a **doctor** on call, and more often than not he speaks English. Port-au-Prince has four hospitals, none particularly distinguished.

Someone once said that a shop in Haiti will open any time you want to buy something. This is an exaggeration, of course, but might be true for certain art galleries. In general, **store hours** are 8 a.m. to 5 p.m. weekdays. Many owners take a long lunch break, from noon to 2 p.m., and often close on Saturday at 1 p.m. Nearly all shops close on Sunday.

Haiti observes the usual **holidays,** but has some unique ones as well: January 2 (The Day of the Forefathers); April 14 (Pan Am Day); May 1 (Workers Day); May 18 (Flag and University); May 22 (in honor of sovereignty); August 15 (Assumption); October 17 (honors anniversary of death of liberator Dessaline); October 24 (honors the U.N.); November 1 (All Saints); December 5 (day Columbus discovered Haiti); along with Carnival or Mardi Gras, previewed in a separate section.

Driving is on the right, and to rent a car (see below) you'll need an international driver's license or else a valid U.S. or Canadian one.

As for **tipping,** 10% for service is added to most hotels and restaurant tabs; otherwise, tip from 10% to 15%.

Hotels add a 5% government occupancy tax:

In Port-au-Prince, the **Tourist Office** is at Avenue Marie Jeanne, Cité de l'Exposition (tel. 2-1720), open from 8 a.m. to 2 p.m. Monday to Friday.

A VIOLENT PAST: The first tourist, the Haitians say, was Columbus, who discovered the island of Hispaniola on his maiden voyage to the New World on December 5, 1492. In time, Spain was to conquer the island, killing nearly one million peaceful Arawak Indians who made up the native population.

Under Spanish rule, a decree called for the importation of African blacks as slaves. When Spain failed to colonize the entire island, French buccaneers, from their base in Tortuga off the northwest coast, moved into what is now Haiti. Eventually they

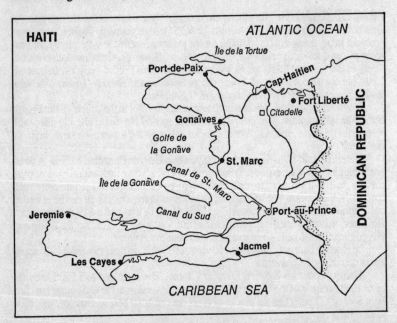

took control in the western part of Hispaniola, a move legalized by treaty in 1697. Spain officially ceded the territory to France.

In May 1801 a former slave and coachman, Toussaint L'Ouverture, was elected governor. Considering this secession, Napoleon ordered the rebellion quelled. Defeating the Haitians, the French took L'Ouverture prisoner.

However, revolutionists led by Jean-Jacques Dessalines and Alexandre Pétion, two Haitian generals, eventually defeated the French army, whose troops returned to Paris in 1803. Dessalines proclaimed Haitian independence on January 1, 1804. He also proclaimed himself emperor, a title he held until his death in 1806.

Henri Christophe, the prototype of Eugene O'Neill's *Emperor Jones,* was named as first president of the republic. But he proclaimed himself king. Pétion was to succeed him. However, Christophe's action divided the nation, and the north and west were ruled as an empire until the self-proclaimed king shot himself in 1820.

At the overthrow of Haitian president Guillaume Sam in 1915, the Americans, fearing a German invasion, occupied the country and didn't leave until 1934. After much turmoil and many leaders, Dr. François Duvalier ("Papa Doc") was elected president in 1957, launching an iron-fisted dictatorship until his death in 1971. He was succeeded by his less militant son, Jean-Claude ("Baby Doc") Duvalier, as "president-for-life." However, the title was a misnomer. The pudgy dictator, along with his wife and family, fled Haiti in February of 1986 to a life of exile in Europe. Unfortunately, he and his wife looted much of the treasury. A period of unrest and upheaval followed in the wake of their departure. The present Haitian government faces an uncertain future.

NOTES ON CARNAVAL: If you can arrange your trip to Haiti during the time between Epiphany, January 6, and Mardi Gras on Shrove Tuesday, you will be treated each Sunday to a true Haitian folk spectacle, **carnaval.**

In Port-au-Prince and all other towns of any size, groups parade through the streets, costumed in burlap bags or other outré garb, singing and making noise with any implement they can find. One popular "instrument" is the leaves from old automobile springs, which are cut to varying lengths to give off different sounds when beaten together or pounded with a metal knife. They also use bongo drums, tambourines, washboards, saws, and cowbells. Some of the costumed people powder or paint their faces a ghostly white, while others wear masks that look like bulls' heads, with horns.

In the capital, groups of five or six start out in various parts of the city and are rapidly joined by happy Haitians (and sometimes by tourists) as they proceed. They serenade guests at the hotels close in. This all may begin sometime in the late morning, but the marching and chanting go on all day. Toward evening, all celebrants converge on the heart of the city and throng the streets, writhing in abandon in their serpentine march until late at night.

In other large towns, the celebration may start a little later in the day, but by nightfall the main streets are alive with a singing, whistling, shouting mass of humanity. In Cap-Haitien, a real steam calliope is mounted on a high, flatbed truck with dancers capering around it on the truck as it inches its way through the main part of town. If a highway passes through a town, you might as well stop and watch the fun if you are there during carnaval, because the highway is where it all goes on, so that your passage is blocked by hundreds of moving bodies. However, the festivities conclude earlier in the outlying towns than in the capital, so you won't be stuck all night and be a prey to zombies.

With all this lead-up, you can be sure that Mardi Gras itself is a hysterically festive occasion, not highly organized with floats and masked balls and all that, like New Orleans, but nevertheless an unforgettable occurrence.

Fortified with some background, you can now plunge into the bustling capital. But don't come here for a quiet vacation. Go instead for an experience.

PORT-AU-PRINCE

Framed by mountains, the capital of Haiti, founded in 1704, is a jumble of bonbon-colored gingerbread houses, art galleries full of vivid, primitive paintings, and streets filled with vendors. If you're wearing a pair of shoes, you're prosperous looking enough to be approached by somebody selling something—perhaps a chandelier made of Pet Milk cans. In Haiti, everything is used. Even old tires are made into sandals.

A bastion of American and French culture, uniquely mixed, Port-au-Prince is a kaleidoscope of brilliant, flashing colors, such as frangipani blossoms. The very heart of this magic country, the capital happily blends the Christian with the pagan. Modernity coexists with the past, a voodoo shop standing next door to a unisex beauty salon. European-style hotels—lush, sensual—often lie in some of the worst poverty belts in the western hemisphere.

Rich in sights by day, vivid in color and texture, Port-au-Prince comes alive at night, in mesmerizing enticement, with the blood-pounding beat of the merengue. And in the distant hills, you hear the beating of drums.

Home to some 700,000 residents, Port-au-Prince rises from the Gulf of Gonâve to the cool slopes of the resort of Pétionville. Many people may want to stay in Pétionville, leaving the city with its teeming markets and the scents of fresh spices. The route up is shaded in part by a canopy of poinciana trees. From Pétionville, Port-au-Prince 1,500 feet below doesn't look as intimidating.

1. Hotels of Port-au-Prince

Perhaps the nicest thing about the hotels of Haiti is that the maids will still iron a shirt or sew on a button. The hotels of Haiti are among the most charming in the Caribbean, special inns, many converted from once-palatial mansions.

You have a choice of a mountain-cooled villa high in the hills or a modern hostelry right in the bustling heart of Port-au-Prince. Most of these are scattered on the eastern outskirts of the capital or in the suburban foothills of Pétionville.

THE UPPER BRACKET: At Pétionville, **El Rancho**, P.O. Box 71 (tel. 7-2080), is a leading Haitian resort hotel owned by Marvin Ornstein and Allan Mirchin. It's a lavishly designed extravaganza of curved surfaces, dramatic passageways, and hacienda-style decor, as well as a series of interconnected entertainment facilities. Built in the 1950s, El Rancho contains wings of rooms filled with mahogany furniture, some hand-carved native sculpture, dramatically contrasting Italian marble floors, and primitive island paintings. The first thing visitors see is a zigzag zebra-stripe tile walk capped with a curved cement awning and two splashing fountains. In the center of the patio garden is a key-shaped Jacuzzi, and near the sundeck is a whirlpool. The swimming pool is two separate bodies of water, both gracefully curved into their settings, divided and traversed by an arched walkway reminiscent of something you might find in a Japanese garden. At the top of a flight of stairs, there's a piano bar sheltered from the sun, with a view over all the comings and goings of the hotel.

On the grounds are tennis courts, plus a gymnasium and a sauna. As you sit on the terrace, strolling guitarists may serenade you. Later, you can enjoy music and dancing in the nightclub, L'Epicure. There's also one of the city's two casinos in a cabaña-shaped building near the swimming pool. On some nights, barbecues are held, accompanied by a Haitian revue and folklore show, one of the best-known attractions in the Port-au-Prince nightlife scene.

In summer, singles range in price from $49 to $79 daily, while doubles cost $69 to $119. In winter, singles range from $75 to $115, and doubles go for $99 to $140. A third person in a unit is assessed an additional $25 a day, while MAP costs a $20 supplement per person per day. Service and taxes are extra. You'll find TV, a radio, and a phone in each accommodation.

Splendid, P.O. Box 1214 (tel. 5-0116), is one of Haiti's oldest hotels and one of the few Relais et Châteaux hotels in the Caribbean. Built at the turn of the century as a family mansion, it was transformed beautifully into a hotel many years ago, entertaining as a grande dame in the country's early days of tourism. The architecture is a combination of Victorian and Mediterranean. The Splendid is one mile from Port-au-Prince, four miles from the airport. It's within walking distance of both of Haiti's cultural centers, the Centre d'Art and the Musée d'Art Haitien du College St-Pierre. Formal entry steps lead up to a long, open loggia with classic columns and potted palms. Set out for your pleasure is a row of handmade Haitian rockers. The hallway leads to a drawing room with antiques, cretonne armchairs, and gilt mirrors, making for a restrained gentility. A central staircase goes up to a few of the handsomely furnished bedrooms. White walls form a good backdrop for the Haitian bedspreads and matching draperies. French doors open onto balustraded balconies.

The director, Wolfgang Wagner, offers all air-conditioned guest rooms, including seven in the original mansion, but most are in newer sections, built around a filtered freshwater swimming pool with a courtyard feeling. The hotel has its own well, 240 feet below the ground. Therefore even the tap water is safe for drinking. All year, the same tariffs are charged: $60 to $75 daily in a single, $70 to $85 in a twin, and $80 to $95 in a triple, plus tax and service.

The hotel has a restaurant, Gala. You are likely to be served Créole dishes along with international fare, perhaps lobster Thermidor. Dishes are usually accompanied by Haitian white rice with fresh vegetables from Kenscoff. Fresh fruits in season are the traditional dessert offering. Expect to spend from $25 for a meal, which is served from 11 a.m. to 4 p.m. and 7 to 10 p.m. Nonguests of the hotel should call for a reservation.

THE MIDDLE BRACKET: One of Haiti's leading all-around resorts, **Ibo Lele,** P.O. Box 1237, Pétionville (tel. 7-0845), is nestled high up in the hills. Named for a voodoo god, it has its own private beach on Cacique Island which you reach after a 20-mile, 30-minute ride from Pétionville to the site of a motor launch which in five minutes takes you to the island. At Pétionville, modern buildings are spread over acres of terraced gardens, centered around an old mansion with its pool plaza, the social center of the hotel. Jacques and Conchita Baussan welcome you to their dramatic perch, 1,575 feet above sea level. Much of the architectural harmony of Ibo Lele was achieved by its late president, Robert Baussan, a well-known local architect.

Accommodations are in 50 well-furnished rooms or 18 suites, all with private bath, color TV, and a terrace where you can take in that view. In winter, singles range in price from $65 to $90 daily; doubles, $80 to $125; and triples, $110 to $135. All these rates include breakfast. *In summer, also with breakfast, the single tariff ranges from $60 to $85 daily; the double, from $70 to $115; and the triple, from $90 to $135.* French, Haitian, and seafood specialties are served in the hotel's restaurant, and guests can later enjoy the exotic Shango nightclub, which has voodoo shows. Friday is the big night. In the lounge is a good collection of Haitian art.

Villa Créole, P.O. Box 126, Pétionville (tel. 7-1570), is a restored hilltop Spanish-style mansion that has seen graceful additions over the years. Now there are 72 bedrooms, all with private bath, color TV, phone, and air conditioning, plus a deluxe wing which opened in 1977. Private balconies open off many of the units. The transformation is a result of the labor of one of the country's most distinguished personalities, Dr. Reindall A. Assad, and his daughters, Alicia Assad and Ariel Dunwell. They keep an atmosphere of pure Haitiana alive here. The walls have a vibrant collection of Rousseau-like primitive paintings, including murals by Dorcelly, who studied with Picasso. Each of the bedrooms is in a restrained contemporary style, with louvered doors and a painting by a local artist. In winter, singles range from $55 to $85 daily, while doubles cost $70 to $100. A third person in a room is an additional $25. *In summer, singles range from $55 to $80, while doubles go for $65 to $90, depending on* *the accommodations*. American breakfasts are included in the prices, but service and taxes are not. Full MAP is an extra $15 per day per person.

The long terrace adjoining the big house has tables set under a pillared arbor. Dining in Villa Belle is by candlelight with a view of the free-form pool, which reaches the hillside terrace where there is an almond tree with widespread branches. Breakfast starts with freshly picked fruit, accompanied by the aromatic Haitian coffee. The cuisine is French Créole, the chef specializing in such dishes as Haitian rice with black mushrooms and lambi (conch) Créole. Monday night is barbecue night with fresh lobster on charcoal. Thursday night is a Créole buffet time, and on Monday and Thursday evening the bar by the pool features a one-man show with an organist. There are two Plexipave all-weather tennis courts, one lit for night play.

Hotel Castelhaiti, P.O. Box 446 (tel. 2-0624; 212/840-6636 in New York City, or toll free 800/223-9815), sits imposingly near the top of a forested hill high above the city. Built in a pleasantly airy 1950s style of geometrically angled balconies, curved walls, and large expanses of glass, it was designed to capture as much of the view as possible. To reach the hotel, your car or taxi will have to shift into low gear while negotiating one of the steepest cobblestone roads in town. Visitors sitting in the dining room's breezeway enjoy the aroma from the flowering vines entwined around the balcony as well as a view of the boomerang-shaped pool, the sprawling city, and the ocean in the distance. The lobby is an open-air arrangement washed with breezes and filled with rich colors, vivid Haitian murals, and plants. The staff is pleasant at this monumental hotel which is capable of accepting large conventions as well as individuals.

Winter rates range from $52 to $84 daily in a single, from $59 to $90 in a double. *Summer rates go from $36 to $60 in a single, from $42 to $66 in a double*. Service and taxes are added to the tab.

Holiday Inn–Le Plaza, 10 rue Capois, P.O. Box 1429 (tel. 2-3722), faces the city park. It is entered from a public square. You'll see a well-cultivated courtyard centered around an open-air pool, surrounded by the open balconies of this business people's hotel in the center of town. The bedrooms are simple, comfortable, and air-conditioned, all outfitted in typical Holiday Inn style, with TV, radio, and phone. On the premises are a bar and a restaurant, both filled most of the time with vacationing families and commercial travelers relaxing after a day of business. *In summer, single rooms, depending on the accommodation, range from $50 to $70, while doubles rent for $60 to $75*. Singles cost $65 to $80 in winter, with doubles or twins going for $75 to $90 and suites costing more. All rooms include a full American breakfast for each occupant. A third person in any room must pay an additional $10 per night. Teens and younger children stay at no charge when occupying the same room as their parents. Service and taxes are extra, and the hotel adds a 25% surcharge during carnival week.

Royal Haitian Hotel and Casino, P.O. Box 2075 (tel. 4-0258), is one of the best-landscaped and most spacious hotels in the country as well as containing one of the biggest casinos in Haiti. Standing just outside the heart of the city, and hard to reach because of traffic, surrounded by a well and ringed with palms, the Royal Haitian, built in 1975, boasts many of the facilities of a resort, with the exception of a beach. If that isn't a top priority for you, or if you don't mind traveling outside Port-au-Prince to the beach resorts, you'll appreciate the splashing fountain connecting two swimming pools, the cultivated planting, and the restaurant set to the side, all in 16 acres of land which include the casino. The reception area is reached by crossing a roofed terrace open on three sides and bedecked with singing birds in ornate cages and life-size Haitian sculptures of figures blowing conch shells or mending nets. The simple, sunny rooms are air-conditioned, and each has a private tile bath. The 90-room units are clustered in compact groupings around the grounds, providing a feeling of lots of space around the living quarters. There are two tennis courts as well. *From June to October the single rate is $30 per day, rising to $35 in a double*. The rest of the year the hotel charges $45 for a double, $40 for a single. Suites are available.

Kinam Hotel, Place St-Pierre (P.O. Box 324), Pétionville (tel. 7-6525), is probably the best-designed and most charming new hotel to be built in Haiti in a decade. It required the creative inspiration of Richard Buteau and his lovely wife, Johanna, to bring it to its current position as a favorite stopover for business people, although it deserves recognition as a tourist hotel too. Sitting across from a rambling lawn near the casino in the center of Pétionville, the hotel was built around the 19th-century core of a private house. Above the concrete substructure of its expanded perimeter, the building is totally sheathed in lacy neo-Victorian gingerbread, with rambling latticed verandas. The hotel is designed around front and back courtyards with fountains and a pleasant swimming pool.

You negotiate stairs and a re-creation of breeze-cooled corridors clinging to the building's sides before seeing your comfortable bedrooms. Each of these has air conditioning, a private bath, Haitian paintings, color TV, radio, and phone. The Victorian theme is enhanced by pink and mauve color schemes, and sunlight filtering through elaborate copies of 19th-century window blinds. In winter, singles cost $50 to $95 daily; doubles, $60 to $105. *In summer, singles range from $45 to $85; doubles, from $55 to $95*. The charming in-house restaurant is recommended separately.

BEST FOR THE BUDGET: Between Port-au-Prince and Pétionville, **Montana,** P.O. Box 523 (tel. 7-1920), is estate-like, surrounded by a hillside garden with well-tended flowers growing in a setting of palm trees and bougainvillea. Even the dining room, La Palmeraie, has a tropical look with palm trees and latticework. Those seeking a good buy like it here, enjoying the pool which avoids that sterile resort look by being surrounded by flowers and a sundeck area. A pair of sisters is the force behind the recent improvements to this well-managed hotel. Nadine Cardozo Riedl and Garthe Cardozo Stephens have made this place a favorite with visiting business people and vacationing Europeans. It lies midway between town and country on a hillside just outside Port-au-Prince in the lower region of the suburb of Pétionville.

The rooms, 76 in all, are decorated with native mahogany contrasted with bold, strong colors used in draperies and bedspreads. Each unit has a private bath and air conditioning, as well as color TV and a balcony. The charge in winter is $46 to $64 for a double, $35 to $52 in a single; another $18 is charged for a third person in a double room. *In summer, CP rates range from $32 to $6 daily in a single and from $42 to $56 in a double*. The cuisine, a mixture of French and Haitian, is good, and on Sunday, a Créole buffet is featured. The hotel provides a beach bus for a minimum fare three times a week.

Prince Hotel, P.O. Box 2151 (tel. 5-2765), was once an elaborate private mansion with a French colonial façade, standing in a residential area only minutes from the commercial heart of Port-au-Prince and next to the Gallery Issa. Its owner, Raymond Chancy, has adapted it to its present function, filling its high-ceilinged public room with Haitian paintings and sculpture, and adding a modern wing which is reached through a labyrinthine series of internal and exterior staircases. The long, narrow dining room has high-backed wooden chairs, a wall sculpture, and a large window opening onto a screen of greenery. Several tables are set up in the courtyard if you find the interior claustrophobic (some people do), where you find a West Indian cuisine with continental overtones is served, sometimes to the accompaniment of live music. On the way to the backyard pool you'll pass a grotto bar whose serpentine banquettes offer a hideaway from both direct sunlight and other guests.

This attractive, Haitian-owned hotel offers 24 rooms, plus nine studio apartments. They range from the high-ceilinged and old-fashioned (number 12 is a favorite in this category) to a comfortably contemporary format which at its best matches much more expensive accommodations in Port-au-Prince hotels. Each of the units is air-conditioned, and they vary in size and treatment from standard to deluxe. All have bath and phone, and several contain old-style furniture ranging from art deco to hand-carved Haitian. In winter, the rates range from $36 to $55 in a single, from $46 to $68 in a double. *Summer rates range from $30 to $35 daily in a single and from $40 to $45 in a double.*

Marabou Hotel, rue Archer, Parc de Pétionville, P.O. Box 99 (tel. 7-1934), set behind a high white wall in a good neighborhood of Pétionville, is a hotel still serving also as a private home. It belongs to Odette Gerard Wiener, a Haitian choreographer who, with her polite staff, is very much a creative force. You enter a brick-floored courtyard, above which rise gingerbreaded rooflines. She has a scattering of island antiques, a particularly lovely dining room, a well-maintained collection of plants, and 14 comfortable bedrooms. Depending on their size and the quality of their furnishings, they rent for $20 to $45 for two persons throughout the year. My favorite is Room 1, whose Haitian paintings and a massive bed are impressive. The more expensive accommodations are air-conditioned. There's a swimming pool on the premises. The place has an intriguing air of faded colonial splendor.

In the rear of the inn, overlooking a swimming pool, a few guests gather in the dining room. Around the walls of the lounge is a permanent art exhibit. The food is pure Créole. The location is convenient to the well-known restaurant, Chez Gerard.

2. The Beach Hotels

THE BEACH LIFE: The beaches are a long haul from the capital, involving expensive taxi commutes. Those tourists who come to Haiti "just for the beach" will do better by seeking out other islands in the Caribbean, such as the Cayman Islands or Antigua. However, those who'd like a holiday in Haiti with some beach life "thrown in" will do all right here if they don't mind coping with some transportation problems.

Ibo Beach on reef-rimmed Cacique Island is about a 35-minute taxi ride from the capital, and a ten-minute motor launch from there. There, tiny huts and lockers can be rented for the day, and you have a choice of water sports.

About ten minutes beyond the Ibo Beach turnoff is Kyona Beach, where, besides swimming and dining, you can negotiate for a native sloop and captain to take you on a sail to the Arcadins islands or a shorter sail along the coast. If you go to Kyona early in the morning, you can rent a horse for a ride in the hills or along the abandoned railroad track bed to the nearby fishing village of Luly. This little village is one of the major fishing ports and the leading lobster port. You can also get there by going out of Port-au-Prince on Hwy. 1, taking the dirt road on the left where you see a little hand-painted sign saying "Luly." The road winds down to the sea, past little clusters of thatch-roofed houses, many with new lobster traps in the front yards. Turn left at the water's edge and on the beach you'll see men building fishing boats and repairing lobster traps. If you're early enough you might see lobsters being brought in. For a low price, you can perhaps get one of the fishermen to take you out to see a trap he set.

Just beyond Kyona is Kaliko Beach, which offers all kinds of water sports and is headquarters for scuba-diving. The next beach, not far beyond Kaliko, is the newest one, Jolly Beach. Besides the beach, you have a splendid view of the sea and mountains from the large, open dining room and bar. Shortly past Jolly Beach is Ouanga Bay, also with a fine beach and a dining room.

One of the loveliest and most unique places to visit is the Moulin Sur Mer (more about this later). This beautifully restored colonial sugar plantation is a short distance beyond Montrouis. A day at Moulin Sur Mer includes a tour, lunch, use of the game room (which has a billiard table among other games), and swimming in the pool or at the nearby beach.

THE HOTELS: Part of the well-known chain, this **Club Med,** Point de Montrouis (tel. 2-4400; 212/750-1670 in New York City, or toll free 800/CLUB-MED), often caters to those who never see Haiti at all, but enjoy this popular holiday-in-the-sun club. Guests are picked up at the airport and transported to this Club Med, occupying 120 acres some 46 miles north of Port-au-Prince, about a 75-minute ride (or longer if too many pedestrians and roosters are on the road). At its peak some 600 members can check in here in one of the double occupancy bungalows, furnished with rattan pieces and overlooking the sea. Perhaps to honor the color of Haiti itself, the houses are flamboyantly painted, and all are air-conditioned with a private bathroom (shower, no tub). The clusters of one-, two-, and three-story casitas with peaked roofs are built along the garden and good beach. Reopened in the winter of 1986, the hotel charges between $470 and $690 per person weekly for land arrangements. The cost rises to $890 per person weekly between Christmas and New Year's. *In summer, prices are $490 to $550 per person per week.*

In typical Club Med fashion, activities revolve around a combined bar/dance floor and a theater complex facing a large pool and the beach. You have a choice of dining possibilities. The restaurants offer many Haitian specialties, along with fresh grilled fish and clubhouse buffets. It wouldn't be a Club Med without a lot of sports, and these include windsurfing, sailing, waterskiing, snorkeling to sponge beds, swimming, archery, yoga, basketball, and tennis (played on 14 courts, 6 of which are lit for night games).

Ibo Beach Hotel, P.O. Box 1237 (tel. 7-1200), is one of the most complete beach hotels in Haiti. It's owned and run by the same Baussan family who manage the Ibo Lele in Pétionville, which has exchange privileges with their spot on Cacique Island. The club occupies several acres dominated on one side by the sea and on the other by the surrounding mountains. This is the closest beach resort on the north side of Port-au-Prince. On its grounds, visitors discover one of the most complete marinas in Haiti, highly popular with yachtsmen. If you don't have a yacht, park your car near a small shed beside a pier about three-tenths of a mile from the resort. Someone will telephone to have a boat come for you through islet-strewn shallow water. The social center of the resort—the various parts of which are interconnected with cement jogging paths, covered breezeways, and scattered voodoo designs set mosaic-style into the pathways—is the bar/restaurant. This, filled with Haitian metal sculptures, woodcarvings, and sea breezes, leads up to a pair of swimming pools. Surrounded by cultivated foliage, the complex contains a private sandy beach. There are also tennis courts and a separate series of restaurant facilities serving the marina.

Throughout the flat spaces and palms of this scrub-covered coral island stand some 70 A-frame bungalows, with voodoo or Indian designs, private baths, and porches. Some are large enough to accommodate up to six persons. Natural wood has been used extensively, and units are decorated with pierced tin lanterns and ceiling fans. In winter, singles cost $84, while doubles rent for $90, triples for $102, and quads for $120. *In summer, prices are $72 in a single, $84 in a double, $96 in a triple, and $110 in a quad.* These prices include breakfast. If you choose to stay here on the MAP, figure on spending $14 additional per day per person. At the hotel, a full program of water sports is offered.

Moulin Sur Mer, Rte. Nationale No. 1, km. 77, Montrouis (tel. 2-1844), lies about 45 miles north of Port-au-Prince along the beachfront. This unusual hotel evokes Provence in the south of France. It's housed within the enormous masonry walls of what used to be a sugar mill. Its soaring arches and flagstone floors were built before Henri Christophe's revolution in 1803, but it required six years of patient labor, huge expenditures of money, and the enlightened guidance of one of Haiti's best-known architects, Gerard Fombrun, to restore them and incorporate them in this fine hotel. An aqueduct built on a scale like that of ancient Rome still arches over the driveway. The hotel has two restaurants, both recommended separately. The elegant evening dinner spot, l'Espadon, is near the reception desk and the less formal Les Boucaniers is on the beachfront, about a five-minute stroll away.

You have to be driven to your accommodation in an electric cart. Vaguely Norman units accented with gingerbread lie close to the beachfront, edge to edge against a garden. Inside are fine fabrics of roughly textured Haitian cotton, copies of Empire furniture, metal sculpture, private baths, and air conditioning. *With MAP, a week's low-season stay costs $450 for a single, $350 per person for a double.* A week's high-season stay, with MAP included, costs $550 in a single, $415 per person in a double. On the premises is an attractive swimming pool and gingerbread-laden poolhouse, along with 36 acres whose duck ponds, century-old machinery (now displayed as art), ancient trees, and modern sculpture make it a landscape architect's dream. There's also a tennis court, plus rentable sailboats, and a sandy beach with its own Victorian gazebo built on piers above the surf.

For reservations, the hotel maintains offices at 7 Ruelle St-Cyr in Port-au-Prince (tel. 2-1844). Dominique Carvonis, the genteel daughter of the owner, will take your reservation.

Kyona Beach Club, P.O. Box 1647 (tel. 2-6788), lies about an hour's drive north of the Port-au-Prince airport. A pleasant resort, this can be the focus of either a day's outing in the sun or a hospitable place to spend an entire low-key vacation. If you're up just for the day, there's an entry charge of $2.50 to come in and use the beach facilities. The white sand is well raked and has unusual trees, thatched bungalows, and chairs clustered beneath coconut palms. The accommodations, scattered over a flat, grassy expanse, are constructed with cement and stucco walls, big glass windows, and thatched roofs, and have an unpretentious decor of summertime furniture, ceiling fans, iron headboards, and carved Haitian art. This is a place for the simple beach life. The social center of the resort is a circular bar area with a thatched roof.

The friendly manager is Jean Hervé. The hotel is owned by the American interior designer Muriel Martin, from New York, who's considered one of the founders of modern Haitian tourism. Her resort is the best established and the oldest along the coast. Many clients, especially Europeans, return year after year. *The 20 rooms rent for $55 daily in a single and $65 for a double in summer.* Winter rates are around $65 single and $75 double, and an additional person in any unit pays an extra $30 in all seasons. Breakfast is included in the prices, but service and taxes are not. Clients wishing to stay here on the MAP pay an additional $15 per person per day. Children under 12 stay free with their parents but pay extra for meals.

3. Dining Out in the Capital

Hotels and restaurants throughout Haiti offer a French Créole cuisine among the finest and most imaginative served in the entire Caribbean. Local snails from the mountains end up on your plate swimming in garlic butter, chicken is offered flavored with cashew nuts, a velvety-smooth ice cream is made with coconut, whatever—the cuisine delights with surprises, happy ones. You can dine in expensive French restaurants in Pétionville or on simple native food. Everybody in Haiti seemingly knows how to cook.

Créole cookery is spicy, but not overly so. Tassot, an old Indian recipe, is a specialty. In its classic method of preparation, pork, beef, or fowl (often turkey) is dried on a hot tin roof all day, facing the burning sun before it's marinated in a highly seasoned lime juice, then grilled. Conch is called "lambi" here, and it's prepared in an infinite number of ways. Cabrit (goat) is barbecued in the ground (that is, under leaves) and marinated à la Créole. A spicy, homemade peanut butter is known as "mamba," and it appears with a number of dishes.

Street food, incidentally, although readily available and plentiful, is only for the courageous or those with cast-iron stomachs, definitely not for delicate digestive systems. If you've survived Mexico, then you might be ready for a streetside snack called "griot," charcoal-roasted pork with a hot sauce.

La Cascade, corner of rue Oge and rue Clerveau in Pétionville (tel. 7-6704), the best place for French food, is a family-owned establishment named for a small artificial waterfall (cascade) which splashes across a rock wall just inside the entrance to what used to be a private home. The owners, Guy Augier and his English-speaking wife, Sylvie, originally from Grasse in the south of France, had owned or managed five restaurants before setting up this one, an airy place with especially constructed stone walls. Patrons can enjoy a drink seated on one of the low-slung canvas-covered couches in the tropical bar, whose raised platform is open to the hillside breezes. Next, they'll be seated on one of the Empire cane-bottom chairs in the dining room, where, accompanied by the scent of flowers and the occasional sound of live music, they can enjoy full meals costing from around $30. Specialties include conch with Noilly Prat and saffron, lobster flan, fresh filet of fish with scallions or sorrel, several kinds of lobster, roquefort filet, tagliatelle with cognac (homemade pasta with tomatoes, crème fraiche, garlic, Provençale herbs, and cognac), smoked trout, and filet of sole à la persillade. The dessert everyone seems to order is lightly caramelized cherries gratinée au chantilly. The restaurant is closed Sunday. The rest of the week it's open for dinner only, from 6 to around 11:30 p.m.

La Lanterne, 41 rue Borno (tel. 7-0479), in Pétionville, is generally conceded to be the finest deluxe restaurant in Haiti. It's owned by Budapest-born George Kenn de Balinthazy and his wife, Edwige, who is a seventh-generation Haitian. Guests, everybody from Mike Wallace to Walter Cronkite, dine (or have) around a swimming pool. Along with antiques and objects of art from his native Hungary, the owner displays an outstanding collection of Haitian paintings and sculptures. Guests enjoy an apéritif in the cocktail bar and are allowed to inspect the aquarium. Delectable dishes, served with fine wines, are offered for dinner from 6 p.m. to midnight, every day except Monday. Call for a reservation. I suggest that you ask the chef to prepare you a cold avocado soup. The menu is international, as reflected by the spaghetti with snails and garlic, the beef Stroganoff, the fried frogs' legs, the filet of pike à la Lanterne, and the shrimp curry. I'm also fond of the fondue bourguignonne, the spring chicken à la Bruno (marinated in coconut juice and spices, sautéed and served with mustard butter), and the sliced pork marengo with steamed shrimp. A luscious dessert is the iced Grand Marnier soufflé, and you can top it off with a "zombie coffee." A complete meal costs from $30 per person. Closed Monday.

Chez Gerard, 17 rue Pinchinal (tel. 7-1949), is a stone structure, in a delightful garden setting, providing a panoramic view of Port-au-Prince at night. Before dinner, have an apéritif in the little bar to your left as you enter. Tables are placed on an open-air veranda or in an inside dining room with a timbered ceiling, formal chairs, and dozens of botanical prints elegantly framed in gold. The taste of the decor is high, as is the skill behind the essentially French cookery. In a quiet, relaxed ambience, you feel much as you would dining in a private home—that is, until you get the bill. The restaurant was created by its owner-chef, Gerard, an adventure-seeking Frenchman and a seafarer of great skill. Before his stunning Créole wife, Louison, drew him here, he'd founded the well-known Chez Gerard in Martinique.

If it flies, crawls, swims, creeps, or hops, the chef is likely to have it on the menu at some point during the year. The appetizers always intrigue me, especially the snails done in the Burgundy style or the clams with garlic. Four kinds of terrine are usually offered. Among the most recommendable main courses, I suggest frogs' legs, poached red snapper in a wine sauce, wild duck with peaches, and guinea hen with black mushrooms. If none of the above tempts you, surely the chicken chasseur will. Desserts are spectacular—flambéed bananas or baked Alaska. Dinner is likely to cost around $60 for two persons. Add 10% for service. Hours are noon to 3 p.m. and 7 to 10:30 p.m.; closed Sunday.

La Belle Époque, 23 rue Grégoire (tel. 7-0984), has a pleasant dining room, reached by an ornate flight of stairs on the exterior of the building. There's a popular bar on the ground floor, with a terrace extending under one of the upper parapets. You dine in a simple, high-ceilinged room where the vertical dado molding is white. Shadows of the gingerbread of the Victorian structure housing the bar and restaurant sometimes play across the immaculate white tablecloths. Beneath the swirling ceiling fans, you can enjoy such specialties as baby back spareribs, sole Belle Époque, pot roast, Italian dishes such as lasagne, baked fish in cheese sauce, pepper steak, chicken in black mushrooms, duck in orange sauce, Kenscoff snails in garlic butter, and conch chowder. Your meal might be followed by a heady concoction called zombie coffee, bringing the grand total per person to around $30. A Haitian buffet is usually featured every Saturday night. The restaurant is open only at dinnertime, daily from 4 to 11:30 p.m.

Le Recif, 430 rue de Delmas (tel. 6-2605), is the first seafood restaurant of any size in Haiti. Whatever is found in the deep waters of the Caribbean is likely to turn up here on your plate—lobster, octopus, conch, blue crab, red snapper, scallops, "monster" shrimps, sea turtle, hawksbill turtle, and sea urchins. A two-level, rustic restaurant, it has a pitched beamed ceiling, with rugged stone walls. There's also an outdoor terrace with bougainvillea. One of the most native seafood dishes is a pimentade de lambi (conch). At luncheon the lobster salad is preferred. If you'd like a little bit of everything, order the assiette de fruits de mer. I'm partial to rice Le Recif (with lobster, conch, oysters, and other denizens of the deep). Try also spaghetti Le Recif, with about the same mixture of sea creatures. There's a large barbecue pit for "buccaneer style" brochettes that come in a wide range. The house specialty, with a mixture of seafood, is brochette Le Recif, or you may prefer to stick to one taste sensation, perhaps the turtle-steak brochette. Pan-fried turtle steak is also good. The menu features photographs of the dishes so you'll have some idea of what you're ordering. Incidentally, I find the king crab here tastier than Florida's stone crab. If you don't want fish, you can order "Rocky Mountain oysters," which the French call Jean Jolle. The restaurant is open from noon to 3 p.m. and 7 p.m. to midnight, offering meals for about $25 per person. Closed Sunday.

Restaurant Le Rond Point, Avenue Marie-Jeanne (tel. 2-0621), has a pleasantly furnished and spacious interior. Owner Max Buteau directs a large staff of uniformed waiters, who serve inexpensive and well-prepared island specialties between the large windows and paneling of the interior. Full meals, costing from around $18, might include lobster Créole, conch in sauce, brochette of seafood, guinea hen with black mushrooms, grilled steak with anchovy butter, and many versions of shrimp and chicken. The establishment, at a traffic circle not far from the Iron Market, is open from 8 a.m. to midnight daily.

Kinam Hotel Restaurant, Place St-Pierre (tel. 7-6525), is on the back veranda of this previously recommended hotel. Guests enjoy a drink at the bar, which sits in the quadrangle created by four soaring brick arches of the hotel's original 19th-century core. A few steps away, beneath neo-Victorian moldings and lattices, you can enjoy some of the best food in Pétionville. The establishment offers both French and Créole cuisine in full meals costing from $18 each. Specialties include lobster bisque, pâté de foie gras, watercress soup, duck à l'orange, beef Stroganoff, Créole lobster and shrimp, grilled goat, several different turkey dishes, and red snapper in butter sauce. The sophisticated manager, Richard Buteau (the product of a Haitian family of hoteliers), and his wife, Johanna, are graduates of Cornell's School of Hotel Administration. Meals are served daily from noon to 3 p.m. and 6 to 11 p.m.

La Voile, 32 rue Rigaud (tel. 7-4561), is considered a high-quality outpost of Gallic cuisine. Housed in a pleasant room sheathed with cedar, filled with mahogany tables, and lit by candles, it serves French-inspired meals daily except Monday from noon to 3 p.m. and 6 to 11 p.m. An overseas branch of the world-famous Paris delicatessen, Fauchon, lies immediately adjacent to the restaurant's entrance. Full meals with wine cost $20 per person for the well-prepared food. Your meal might include fish or onion soup, grilled filet steak with barbecue sauce, brochette of fish, grilled fish or lobster, fish filet with peppercorns, or three varieties of pasta, topped off by a peach Melba. The restaurant is owned by the Augier family whose more formal restaurant, the previously recommended La Cascade, is more elaborate and more expensive.

Le Steak Inn, 37 rue Magny (tel. 7-2153), is in a palatial stone-trimmed villa that looks like the kind of prosperous dwelling sometimes built in expensive American suburbs in the 1940s. It stands in the upper regions of Pétionville, on a quiet residential street lined with similar buildings. Known for its low-key charm and its juicy steaks, the restaurant has attracted some of Haiti's finest families over the past decade. Lunch is served in the garden, beneath the thatch-roofed simple outdoor pavilion in the shadow of palms and poinsettias. Dinner is a more glamorous meal here. Before entering the arched dining room, you might have a drink in the elegantly modern, darkly intimate bar, near a musician and his piano. You dine amid plants, elegant accessories, candlelight, and riveting paintings. You can choose from seven different cuts of steak, charcoal-grilled chicken, gratinée of seafood, and such desserts as lime crêpes and crêpes Suzette. Meals cost from $30 per person, and a reservation is required. Lunch is offered from noon to 3 p.m. daily except Sunday, and dinner is served from 7 p.m. to midnight seven days a week.

Le Végediète 32 Avenue Christophe (no phone). The architecture of this vegetarian restaurant gives a hint as to what a private, upper-class Haitian home used to look like. At the corner of the rue Saint-Cyr, the restaurant extends from a high-ceilinged, very simple interior onto the sprawling verandas that are visible from the far end of the walled courtyard. Paule Duncan, the Haitian director, may suggest an initial island tonic called Maby, whose essence comes from several kinds of local tree barks. This might be followed by home-style vegetable pâté, rice with black mushrooms, breadfruit and tomato cake, potato omelet, salad of avocado and green peppers, a selection of fruit juices (including soursop), and colonial pudding made with cassava and native fruits. The establishment, open for lunch and dinner daily except Sunday, serves a complete meal for around $12. Hours are 8 a.m. to 9 p.m. daily; closed Sunday.

4. Dining Along the Beachfront

L'Espadon, Moulin Sur Mer, Rte. Nationale No. 1, km. 77, Montrouis (tel. 2-1844), near the elegant reception area of the previously recommended Moulin Sur Mer Hotel, is the establishment's formal evening restaurant. Containing a scattering of antiques, a polished slate floor, heavy ceiling beams, and a view of the terraced garden, it's one of the most alluring dining spots along the north coast. A meal might consist of shrimp in Créole sauce, a house preparation of lobster tails, catch of the day meunière, gratin of conch brochettes or conch with a hot sauce, steak studded with three different peppers, or grilled filet steak with béarnaise sauce. Desserts might be flambéed figs. Full dinners cost from $25 each, and are served from 7 to 10 p.m. daily. Reservations are suggested.

Les Boucaniers, Moulin Sur Mer, Rte. Nationale No. 1, km. 77, Montrouis (tel. 2-1844), is the amusing and lighthearted beachside restaurant of the Moulin Sur Mer Hotel. To reach it, you have to drive (or be driven in an electric cart) across some of the resort's 36 acres before arriving at the restaurant parking lot. Les Boucaniers is in a cluster of neo-Victorian pavilions rising on stout beams or columns above an open-air deck. Waiters in brightly colored 18th-century costumes bring you complete lunches costing from $20. These might include conch salad with spinach, chiffonade of herring, crayfish brochette, hamburgers, crayfish tails with garlic and tarragon, and an array of barbecued meats. The restaurant is open only at lunchtime, from 11:30 a.m. to

4 p.m. When I was last here, a trio of Haitian musicians added spice to the zesty Créole food. If you show up for dinner, you'll be directed to Moulin Sur Mer's more formal evening restaurant, the separately recommended l'Espadon.

Kyona Beach Club, (tel. 2-6788) is one of the truly pleasant dining spots along the Haitian Riviera. Its restaurant is little more than a terrace with a high-ceilinged parapet on stilts, but the food is well prepared, the view gorgeous, and the staff accommodating. The restaurant and the resort surrounding it were two of the first such places set up in the entire region. Muriel Martin, the astute and experienced owner, welcomes an array of friends. Either before or after your meal, you can stroll down to the palm-fringed sands of the nearby beach for a swim. Meals are served in one continuous stretch, lasting from 8:30 a.m. to 10:30 p.m. It's a good idea, but not absolutely essential, to telephone before your intended arrival so that the friendly manager, Jean Hervé, can plan ahead, perhaps greeting you with a drink. Full meals cost $15 to $25 each, and might include the house fish soup, five different preparations of lobster, a choice of five shrimp dishes, or brochettes of seafood, fish, or beef. You can also order just a sandwich or a hamburger, if you want one. Plan to spend at least part of the afternoon here, and be sure to order one of the house special rum punches.

5. Sights, Galleries, and Markets

Haiti itself is a sightseeing adventure. A walk down any street in Port-au-Prince is a look at life and excitement, but you may want to give more definition to your tour through the capital. If so, seek out the following specific targets:

SIGHTS: The **Cathédrale de la Sainte Trinité,** at the intersection of rue Pavée and rue Msgr-Guilloux, about two blocks north of the Champ de Mars, has its walls covered with naïve biblical mural paintings, and is considered Haiti's finest showcase of regional art. Begun in 1951, the murals represent the turning point in the country's art. Started in some unpromising beginnings it reached a full blossom. The apse and transepts of this Episcopal church are done in tempera by some of the country's best-known artists, and as such it forms a fine and proper introduction to Haitian art before your visit to specific galleries.

In the wake of charges of "paganism," Bishop Voegeli agreed to have the murals painted, admitting that it "pays to be somewhat crazy at times." Called away, he returned only when the charcoal sketches had been completed. His comment? "Praise the Lord! They painted Haitians!"

Look for the *Marriage Feast at Cana,* on the south transept wall. It was painted by Wilson Bigaud, then only 22 years old. In 1947 at the age of 14 he'd been discovered by Hector Hyppolite, a voodoo priest and artist. The critic Selden Rodman considers Bigaud the Haitian Brueghel, "the most brilliant and technically advanced of the self-taught artists" of Haiti.

Other Haitian masters who painted murals include Rigaud Benoit (a former taxi driver), Castera Bazile (a former busboy), and Cap-Haitien-born Philomé Obin (who died in 1986). Obin painted Christ without the traditional beard. Bazille painted his characters so that their fingers and toes were exposed flat. Gabriel Leveque did the murals overhead, placing his angels upside down. Incidentally, in *The Last Supper,* a black Christ is betrayed by a Judas in white face!

Le Musée d'Art Haitien du College St-Pierre, Place des Héros (also called Champ de Mars; tel. 2-2510), is often known as the "modern museum." It is a major museum of painting and sculpture, from its beginning postwar years to its present renaissance. Many of the paintings are from the DeWitt Peters collection, the founder of the Centre d'Art who discovered and popularized the creativity of Haitian artists in the late 1940s. Others are pieces of art sponsored by Bishop Voegeli of Sainte Trinité Episcopal cathedral.

The collection at the museum of art is an ever-changing one, as many paintings are in storage and others have been lent to museums throughout the world. As you enter, look straight ahead at the large canvas by Antonio Joseph, a protégé of the late Mr. Peters. While not primitive in subject, it portrays gentle yet powerful forces in a contemporary style. Other paintings often on display include works by Hector Hyppolite, as well as Wilson Bigaud and Philomé Obin, who did some of the murals at the cathedral. Displayed also are paintings and sculpture by such well-known artists as Jasmin Joseph and Georges Liautaud, and black iron pieces which usually depict voodoo symbols. At the rear of the museum is a boutique of handcrafts (see my shopping recommendations).

Hours, likely to vary, are Monday through Friday from 9 a.m. to 1 p.m.; on Monday, Wednesday, and Friday from 4 to 6 p.m.; and on Saturday and Sunday from 9 a.m. to noon. This museum is really underfinanced, and it thrives only on public help (you'll see the little box at the entrance).

La Maison Defly stands next door to the Musée d'Art Haitien du College St-Pierre, right off the Place des Héros. Here in this Haitian museum you have a chance to see what the inside of a Haitian army house looked like in 1898. General Defly was the commander of the Haitian army, and he lived here. The house is rich in gingerbread details. A tall four-sided wooden tower with a peaked roof dominates the façade. Surrounding half of the front portion is a wide veranda. A hostess will guide you through the house, telling you about the uses of the various rooms and pointing out authentic furnishings. The museum is open daily except Sunday from 10 a.m. to 1 p.m., charging $1 per visitor.

The **Musée du Panthéon National Haitien** (tel. 2-4560), the national shrine honoring the heroes of Haitian independence, is now in the center of Port-au-Prince on the Champ de Mars in a handsome building designed by French architect Alexander Guichard. Constructed to blend perfectly with the surrounding gardens, the museum is seen from outside as seven blue mosaic cones, arranged in a circle around a larger central cone of white marble. Inside, there are three circular sections. In the first and central part is the marble sarcophagus in which are kept the remains of the forefathers of Haiti—Toussaint L'Ouverture, Jean-Jacques Dessalines, Henri Christophe, and Alexandre Pétion.

The museum also has mementos of these men. For example, there is the gold pocketwatch said to have been the property of Toussaint L'Ouverture, who fought against the troops of General Leclerc, brother-in-law of Napoleon Bonaparte. L'Ouverture was arrested, deported, and imprisoned in a French prison, Fort de Joux, where he died in 1803. In the showroom is the silver pistol used by Henri Christophe to kill himself. Also displayed is some silverware that belonged to one of his secretaries, Baron Alexis Dupuy. A permanent historical display in the second arc-like section shows life of the Haitian people from pre-Columbian times to the present. In this section can be seen, among other historical relics, the towering anchor from Columbus's flagship, the *Santa Maria,* wrecked during his first voyage along the northern coast of Hispaniola in 1492. The splendid gold crown of Faustin I focuses attention on the 19th-century imperial state of Faustin Soulouque. A third section of the museum is used to present both visiting and Haitian art shows. The museum is open Monday to Saturday from 10 a.m. to 4 p.m. Admission is $1.

Le Centre d'Art, 58 rue Roy (tel. 2-2018), is housed in a splendid old mansion with a garden. This art center is listed below under "Where to Buy Art," but it is also an important sightseeing attraction. The gallery grew out of the inspiration of an American, DeWitt Peters, a painter of the Hudson River School, who founded it back in 1944. Even before that, Mr. Peters had discovered the excitement of Haitian art when he came to Port-au-Prince in the early 1940s to teach English. A young man named Philomé Obin came to him with a painting, and immediately Mr. Peters sensed the vitality of the country's art. Obin, of course, is now collected by art patrons around the world. He died in 1986. Mr. Peters met a voodoo priest, Hector Hyppolite, discovering his explosive talent, and there were others—enough so that he decided to devote his life to developing and encouraging the artists of Haiti. He didn't show them how to paint, or even what to paint. Rather, he taught them how to apply their ideas to canvas, wood, beaverboard, or whatever backdrop they could find. Eventually he set up a government showcase for their works. He persuaded Bishop Voegeli and a wealthy patrician octogenarian, Mrs. Ann Kennedy, to assist the artists morally and financially. Mr. Peters was later assisted by Selden Rodman, the poet, author, and art critic who now runs a superb museum in Jacmel.

The Centre d'Art has some of the best collections of important artists in Haiti, and should be considered as a museum in itself. The lovely director, Francine Murat, will assist you, pointing out paintings of exceptional interest. They display works by Haiti's three great sculptors, George Liautaud, Murat Brierre, and Jasmin Joseph. Of course, the works of Benoit are found here. Hours are Monday to Friday from 9 a.m. to 4 p.m., on Saturday from 9 a.m. to noon. It's closed on Sunday.

The so-called "President for Life," Jean-Claude ("Baby Doc") Duvalier, son of the dictator, Dr. François Duvalier, lived in the **National Palace** until 1986. It is gleaming white, now the official center of the black republic, standing next to the barracks of the army. You can look through the grounds at this palace—the nerve center of the "new Haiti"—but you can't go inside without an invitation.

It opens onto the **Place des Héros de l'Independence** which is more popularly known as the Champ de Mars. This "Square of the Heroes of Independence" contains statues of Jean-Jacques Dessalines, who is considered the father of his country (Haiti's first emperor in 1804), as well as the ill-fated Henri Christophe, whose silver bullet ended his life, and Alexandre Pétion, for whom Pétionville was named. Look for the well-known bronze statue of the Unknown Marron blowing a call to liberty on a conch shell.

Adjoining the square is the Place Toussaint L'Ouverture, named after the popular hero. The Haitian sculptor, Normil Ulysee Charles, created the statue that stands there of his ill-fated hero.

WHERE TO BUY ART: Art is Haiti's fourth-biggest export. The country has seen such self-taught contemporary grand masters as Hector Hyppolite, Philomé Obin, Wilson Bigaud, and Rigaud Benoit. It also, quite frankly, hawks and exports some of the worst primitive art of any nation on earth.

Ever since the 1940s when Haitian art began to bloom, there has been such an increase in painting that even the average Haitian, talented or not, has gotten on the bandwagon. As long as tourists will buy, Haitians will sell. Every hotel lobby, every shop, practically every street corner will be hustling primitive art.

Unfortunately, even some of the galleries I'm recommending display bad art. That's not why I'm recommending them, however. The galleries set forth below display the works of many good artists. You must know, however, what you're looking for.

The market, frankly, is filled with fraud. Obin never saw many of the paintings on which his name was shamelessly signed by others. So unless you're an expert, don't expect to find a winner among the unknowns. Of course, if you have a genuine Obin, a Georges Liautaud, a Rigaud Benoit, or a Gerard Valcin, you can't go wrong, but you'll pay a high price for these. Therefore, a Haitian painting should be purchased if it fulfills your emotional needs. Don't count on buying cheap and reselling at a high price.

Le Centre d'Art, 58 rue Roy (tel. 2-2018), is housed in a former mansion with gardens. Established originally in another location, the Centre d'Art was the birthplace of Haitian art (see the previous sightseeing attractions). It still remains the most trustworthy place to buy Haitian art, but only if you're interested in top-quality paintings or sculpture in iron. For example, some of the prestigious paintings sell for

$10,000. However, you might pick up a Bigaud beginning at $800. Antonio Joseph, another well-known artist, has smaller paintings that sell here from $1,000 (you might also consider some of his serigraphs for $50 to $60). Some of the iron sculptures are by Haiti's leading artist in the medium, Georges Liautaud, and these go for $200 to $1,000. Some pieces by lesser-known artists are in the $250 to $500 range. I'm also enthusiastic about a number of handcrafted articles, all with a strong Haitian accent. A stool-size cedar-lined storage box, brightly decorated, will be yours for around $20, although some cost as much as $250. The art center is open Monday to Friday from 9 a.m. to 4 p.m., on Saturday to 12:30 p.m.

Galerie Marassa, 17 rue Lamarre (tel. 7-5424), is one of the most important galleries in Port-au-Prince, with an impressive representation of famous Haitian artists. If you see a particular painting you can't live without, you won't see it duplicated anywhere else. If you're interested in a bargain, however, you might be well advised to do a bit of comparison-shopping before you buy. The gallery's articulate owner, Michele Frisch, is an authority on Haitian art. Don't ignore the interesting collection of handmade art objects here, a few of which are priced at only a few dollars. Particularly tasteful are the hand-painted boxes covered in vivid jungle scenes.

Galerie Issa, 9 rue Bonne-Foi (tel. 2-8522), gets a recommendation for fair play, decent art, and handcraft work. A Haitian dealer, Issa El Saieh, runs this air-conditioned gallery. He's an oldtimer in Haiti and once owned the first department store in the country, along with his older brother. He gave it up in 1957 to open Galerie Issa. He seems to know everyone, certainly all the established, good, or even promising painters. His gallery is more a way of life than a place to buy. Artists often frequent the place, making it their second home. It's the kind of gallery where no deals are made with taxi drivers, and unlike the rest of Haiti, no one bargains. The price asked is the price Issa expects you to pay. He keeps his tariffs low, and therefore his profits are only marginal.

Even though a merchant of art, he's hooked on believing in artists, which means he often has to come to their financial aid. A soft-spoken, low-key individual, he will share his knowledge of Haitian art willingly with customers. If you insist, he'll show you a few small paintings, although he won't pretend they represent great art. They are merely decorative, to be enjoyed if you like a whimsy. Issa has backed many talented artists who went on to win fame. André Pierre is one such painter, as is Gerard Valcin. André Normil paints in the finest tradition of Haitian art. Pierre is a voodoo priest, and you'll find his religious symbols used significantly in his works. You might also ask Issa to see some of his new favorites.

The **Gallery of Aubelin Jolicoeur** (also called Claire's), 9 rue 3 (tel. 2-4752), is a very special place owned by one of the most colorful characters in the West Indies. He reputedly was the model for Petit Pierre in Graham Greene's *The Comedians*. A natty dresser, he is often called "The Butterfly" by Haitians. He is also known, quite simply, as "Mr. Haiti." A most unforgettable person, he is a man of wit and wisdom, as he prances around with his cane. When he meets a woman, he bows and kisses her hand. He has assembled a remarkable collection of paintings, some of which could begin at $10,000 and go up. He also handles talented but lesser-known artists, some of whose works begin at $400. His gallery is also his home, and every room, even the garage, is filled with his paintings. André Malraux called the house "a museum of art."

Nader's Art Gallery, 92 rue du Magasin de l'État (tel. 2-0033), is operated by an enterprising merchant who is set to take over the mass art business in Haiti. Nader's is the largest and most varied center for paintings, sculpture, and art books in Port-au-Prince. Georges Nader's energy is amazing, and it has made his store the best all-around place for purchases. He even has a collection at his home at 4 Croix des Prez (tel. 5-4524), where he keeps his finest paintings. He handles the works of such prestigious artists as Gerard Valcin, Philomé Obin, Prefete DuFaut, André Pierre, Joseph Jean-Gilles, Lyonel Laurenceau, and others. At the other end of the canvas are tourist "cheapies," for as little as $20. In the middle-price bracket are many fine works in the $200 to $500 range. Nader has collected some excellent metal sculptures and mahogany carvings as well. This is the best place in Haiti to purchase books on the country's art.

Olivier Studio Gallery, 124 Avenue Christophe (tel. 2-6982), is the only gallery in Haiti managed by a Haitian master painter, Raymond Olivier, whose works have a modern flavor rather than being in the old naïve style. His gallery, one of Haiti's largest, is much visited by art collectors and art lovers, museum director, art critics, and art dealers. You can select from fine paintings by many of the country's top artists, all originals. Sculptures and mahogany articles are also available here. The gallery is open daily from 8:30 a.m. to 6 p.m. (to noon on Sunday).

MARKETS, HANDCRAFTS, AND OTHER ITEMS: Shopping in Haiti is different from any other island in the Caribbean. On the big "shopping islands," visitors head for free-port areas, where merchandise is imported, usually Europe, and sold at prices often comparable to the land of its origin.

In Haiti you buy items actually made in the country. No islanders turn out as many handcrafts as do the Haitians—and not just paintings or mahogany carvings, although these items predominate. Seek out handmade furniture, baskets, sandals; hand-loomed fabrics for upholstery and draperies; and jewelry, articles of mahogany, sisal products, even stuffed voodoo dolls. Officials at the airport are now blasé about seeing visitors checking in with bulky packages.

The **Iron Market** is considered one of the leading attractions of Port-au-Prince, and true to its name, it's built of lacy ironwork, a block square open on all sides, right in the center of the city. It has a definite Haitian style and flavor.

Vendors have one or more stalls, and near the entrances everybody from gourdeless women to nagging children will accost you, urging you to buy. It's not unlike a Tower of Babel, with churning noises and a nerve-wracking pace. To shop here can be exciting and stimulating; it can also be exasperating. Hardened shoppers will learn to ignore the hands, the faces, the voices that besiege you at every turn. Yet you have to keep your eyes open to find the purchase you might want. Some visitors engage a local youth as their guide, and I'd endorse that. To earn his gourdes, he'll ward off intruders or overly enthusiastic vendors.

Frankly, many readers are intimidated by this outdoor emporium, which is probably the most competitive market in the western hemisphere. Stalls crowded one upon the other, with merchandise sometimes wired in suspension, are bewildering. Try a systematic tour, going up one aisle, down the other. Almost no booth has a monopoly on one kind of merchandise.

Passing a stall with straw hats, a vendor asks $4. Your guide says, "Pay no more than $1.50." Bargaining is essential here. Everybody expects it. Ask the price, then offer half the amount quoted. Chances are, you'll get away with it.

The inevitable $10 bad primitives show up here, and you'll find cedar-lined coral boxes and every style of basket to be imagined. There are placemats, sandals, mahogany statues, some good mahogany plates, bowls, and masks. However, I suggest you consider fumigating these products to remove wood-craving beasties which might infest your house when you get back home.

Articles made of tin interest many shoppers, including the pierced lanterns. The iron plaques with voodoo motifs are, in my opinion, the best buys.

The **Boutique of the Musée d'Art Haitien du College St-Pierre,** at the Place des Héros, Champ de Mars (tel. 2-2510), was already previewed as a museum. In the back of a boutique, displaying one of the best collections of handcrafted objects in

Haiti. The work of only the finest artisans is sold here. After all, this is a museum, and must be concerned with its reputation.

New and unusual wood plaques depicting Haitian scenes are carved in hard, unvarnished wood. These are in such contrast to the highly varnished mahogany figures hawked on every street corner. The ones at the boutique sell for $20 to $80. Seek out also the unusual voodoo flags, about three feet square with designs made of sequins in various colors, in the $80 to $150 price bracket. There's also a fine selection of iron plaques, some utilizing voodoo and folkloric symbols. The subjects are different—Adam and Eve, crabs, a bull. Eye-catching and outrageous papier-mâché figures are sold, as are carnaval masks, in the $20 to $75 range. Another enchanting collection is of Haitian gingerbread and lacy houses, made of paper and selling for as little as $60. However, you'll have to carry these back in the airplane on your lap, I fear. These houses appear only at Christmas but are available for several months afterward. The boutique also sells boxes of all shapes and sizes, painted with Haitian jungle scenes. The curator, or one of the staff, will be there to aid and assist.

Caribbean Hand Craft Mahogany, 19 Lamartinnière, Bois Verna (tel. 5-5820), sells every object made of mahogany. The place is an old, Haitian frame shop, and it's stuffed with wooden merchandise. Nearby, under the big trees, workmen chisel, saw, file, sand, and polish the items sold in the front building. The list of merchandise is extensive, including salad plates, bowls, stemware. The craftsmen will also make furniture to order. The owner and manager of Caribbean Hand Craft Mahogany is Philip R. Khawly. Hours are daily except Sunday from 7:30 a.m. to 4 p.m.

Ambiance, 17 Ave. M (tel. 5-2494), featured in *Town and Country,* was started by Nancy Chenet, who, along with her husband, also has a place in Jacmel. In a gingerbread house, you can select from Haitian crafts and imported goods from around the world specializing in home furnishings shown in a home environment. They also have a fashion line consisting of hand-painted tropical dresses made in Haiti.

Traditions, corner of rue Chavannes and rue Geffrard, Pétionville (tel. 7-2167), is in a mid-19th-century house surrounded by a lawn; and one of the most charming residences in the capital. Today it houses a collection of Haitian antiques assembled by a gracious newcomer to the business, Guylène Bouchereau. She scours the countryside for her treasures, which are kept in mint condition by an energetic employee armed with a dustcloth. One of the rooms is reserved for antique toys, lace dresses, and accessories. Mme Bouchereau will arrange for shipment of any of the larger pieces you want.

Carlos, Cité de l'Exposition, 1 rue Eden (tel. 2-0349), has perhaps the most complete inventory of handcrafted Haitian souvenirs in town. It stands across the street from the tourist office near the post office. A friendly staff will explain the origin of many of the goods, which include hewn salad bowls, naïve paintings, papier-mâché sculptures, jewelry, clothing, and rough-textured furniture.

La Maison de l'Artisanat, Office National de l'Artisanat, 81 rue Montarlais (no phone), is the handcrafts outlet of the Haitian government. It isn't by any means the best-stocked or the most imaginative handcrafts store in Haiti, but it nonetheless displays a sampling of the merchandise created in some of the outlying regions of the country.

Mimi d'Haiti (formerly the Haiti Perfume Factory), 21 rue Panaméricaine (tel. 7-1304), in Pétionville, is owned by folk artist Mimi Beckett. The colorful, flower-painted cottage carries aloe vera cosmetic products, including a good selection of suntan preparations for your visits to Haitian beaches or local hotel pools. Visitors have the chance to watch as many exotic tropical perfumes are prepared, blended, and bottled in a glassed-in area at the rear of the shop. The perfume counter is covered with testers of all of the fragrances so you can choose your favorites from among frangipani, jasmin, vetíver, and many others. An interesting selection of other gift items and home decorator pieces is also offered. The shop is eager to serve you from 9 a.m. to 6 p.m. daily except Sunday and holidays. Jean-Marie Louis-Charles is the charming bilingual manager.

Jules Gay and his sons operate **Gay Pottery,** off 11 Delmas (no phone). There's a sign on the corner of 11 Delmas and another one a block away that tells you to turn right, and the pottery is straight ahead. There's no other sign, but you'll see people and cars in front of a two-story building. Inside, you can see men working at the potter's wheel making bowls, vases, and plates, while others put on the different designs. Some of the workers are sculpturing miniature Haitian scenes, such as a woman at a sewing machine, a merchant, a man with a soda cart or shining shoes, cockfights, and countless other scenes. In the yard at the back are the supply of raw clay to be prepared for working and the large kiln where the pieces are fired. Jules Gay was a teacher of ceramics for the Ministry of Education for 30 years before starting his own business a number of years ago. He or one of his sons is always there to explain the various stages and to take you to the showroom upstairs.

6. Water Sports

Port-au-Prince is not blessed with superior beaches, so on weekends many of the sunworshippers who can afford it head north to Cacique Island and the **Ibo Beach Club** (see my previous hotel recommendation). There, in addition to a 100-ship marina, are restaurants, bars, sandy beaches, and a wide range of water-sports facilities. Deep-sea fishing is also available, or you can charter a boat. There's even a boat excursion offered, costing around $55 per person, going to Gonâve Island. Requiring about three hours each way, the trip comprises a full day in the sun, with feasting on lobster, steak, fish, rum punches, beer, and wine. Snorkeling expeditions to the Arcadins, lasting half a day and including snacks, soft drinks, and snorkeling gear, cost around $30 per person.

7. Voodoo and Nightlife

Voodoo is not the dark, secret society it's often depicted to be. It certainly isn't "black magic" or "snake worship," as some have labeled it; and it isn't just fun and folklore games staged for tourists either. However, know that many Haitians are willing to put on a voodoo show for you if you'll pay them.

First of all, voodoo is a vitally alive religion, with a dominant African heritage. It is frowned upon but tolerated by the Catholic hierarchy in Haiti, who apparently have recognized that it's here to stay. Millions of Haitians who call themselves Catholics also practice voodoo. Incidentally, there are many spellings of the word. In Haiti, you'll often see it written as "vaudou."

Count yourself lucky if while you're in Haiti a show is staged at **Le Peristyle de Mariani** (tel. 4-2818), which lies about a 30-minute trek outside the capital on the principal highway to Jacmel and the south of Haiti, beyond Carrefour. Once there, you'll be enthralled at Max Beauvoir, the hougan-proprietor and his "vaudou" ceremony. This may not be authentic voodoo, but you'll leave with a greater understanding of the often-baffling ritual.

Before the entertainment Mr. Beauvoir gives a thorough introduction in English. The actual vaudou ceremony takes you through invocation, vevers, followed by dancing and drumming. You'll see a vaudou possession—that is, when the possessed one speaks in strange tongues, assuming the character of the divinity invoked. One is possessed, so to speak, when "mounted" by the loa, achieving communication with the gods.

To achieve this possession, hounsis are chosen who are considered most susceptible to trance. On many a night this ceremony, staged for tourists, has been known to produce an inadvertent trance in a member of the audience. On some evenings the vaudou ceremony is staged across the highway in a jungle-like setting where a

Grecian-style amphitheater has been erected. Admission is usually $12 per person. Ask at your hotel if a show will be staged during your visit.

Several of the leading hotels, such as El Rancho, have occasional live entertainment. Shows start after dinner, and some of the best talent of Haiti and other islands is presented, usually consisting of folkloric groups, colorfully costumed in the garb of their native areas. Your hotel desk will know where the action is on any given night. However, with the drop-off in tourism, these shows are increasingly rare to find.

CASINO ACTION: There are three major casinos in Port-au-Prince. When business is flourishing in the country, they are both often filled with excited gamblers, onlookers, and people-watchers, but otherwise they can be quite dull. The one at the **Royal Haitian Hotel** (tel. 4-0258) in Port-au-Prince features a paneled decor with shades of scarlet. Players will find the ubiquitous rows of slot machines, as well as roulette, baccarat, and 21 tables. Drinks are free, even to small-stakes gamblers. The casino is open nightly from 9 until the early hours of the morning, depending on business. There is no cover charge.

Haiti's second major casino is at **El Rancho Hotel,** in Pétionville (tel. 7-2080), where the roulette wheels begin to spin every night at 8:30. The casino is like a cabaña, reached via a gently arched bridge leading over a section of the swimming pool. Visitors might also appreciate the hotel's nightclub, the Epicure, which occasionally offers live music and the chance to leave the gaming tables for a dancing break.

The latest casino on the scene is **McLaney's Casino Choucoune,** Place St-Pierre, in Pétionvile (tel. 7-5138).

OUTSIDE THE CAPITAL

If you haven't time to go north to Cap-Haitien or south to Jacmel, you'll find some intriguing sights right on the doorstep of Port-au-Prince, except you'll have to head up in the hills to see them. On a hot day, that isn't a bad idea, as it's much cooler in the hills.

8. Day Trips from the Capital

KENSCOFF: When you go from the heart of Port-au-Prince at barely above sea level to Pétionville at 1,500 feet, the change of climate is noticeable, as I've mentioned. Then, if you continue on the road for ten miles to Kenscoff at 6,000 feet, you'll again be astonished that in such a short time you can pass through various climatic strata. Going to Kenscoff is an adventure, whether in a self-drive rental car or with a Haitian driver and car which you can engage by the hour or the day.

The drive to Kenscoff and back is breathtaking, both because of the frequent splendid panoramic views of the Cul-de-Sac, of Port-au-Prince, of the wide bay, deep valleys, and barren mountainsides; and because of the Haitian drivers' taking horseshoe curves and blind corners with a blithe insouciance.

Taking it from the top, Kenscoff is a select spot so far as climate goes, and a number of well-to-do Haitians have built summer homes in the area. Reputedly named for a French count who owned a beautiful estate there when France governed the country, the tiny town is mainly noted today because of the market held on Tuesday and Friday, when the street and the rocky hillside are alive with people, animals, and fowl, walking, standing, sitting, squatting—most of them hawking wares which range from fruit, vegetables, flowers, chunks of meat to items of clothing, goatskins, and baskets. The air is heavy with the aroma from tiny charcoal braziers and less pleasing odors exuded by unrefrigerated meat and decaying food scraps, as the day wears on.

Despite the sad squalor of much of the scene and a few beggars who may dog your footsteps but will be easily appeased by the gift of a dime or a quarter, any visitor must be impressed with the sheer lushness of vegetables and fruits in season—evidence that there is a great potential for productivity in this place. There are raspberries, strawberries, all types of root vegetables, mangoes, corn, beans, many kinds of squash, artichokes, avocadoes, and bananas to name a few, most of which can be had at any time of year because of the variation of belts of climate. Beautiful flowers are offered for sale here and along the roadside, ranging from tropical blossoms to daisies. Much of the year, all along the road from Pétionville to Kenscoff, you see vibrant flamboyant trees (poincianas) and tall poinsettia plants like small trees, bearing masses of bright blooms.

Also on the road you will see many Haitian women and girls strutting along (only a fortunate few travel by donkey), making their way from the high country around Kenscoff and other more remote areas, their heads laden with baskets, produce, eggs, chickens, or whatever, going all the way to the Port-au-Prince Iron Market and then walking all the way home again. A Haiti visitor reports seeing one woman making this trek with 16 large baskets tied together and somehow balanced on her head.

Many Haitians have been kept alive, well, and educated through continuing missionary efforts by various churches. On the road between Pétionville and Kenscoff, on the right going up the mountain, is the **Baptist Mission's Mountain Maid Self-Help Project,** with a school and a shop where you can purchase at low prices items, such as a woman's string macramé bag, made by the Haitian students and their families. Men's shirts, patchwork skirts, wooden plates and bowls, and many other gift items are sold inexpensively. The mission also sells farm produce at a stand.

At the Baptist Mission, you'll be served what one enthusiastic newspaper reporter calls "one of the biggest, thickest, and juiciest grilled ham and cheese sandwiches anywhere." The cost is only $3. A cup of hot tea is complimentary.

If you're truly adventurous, you can turn off the road between the Baptist Mission and Kenscoff, to the left as you ascend, onto a rocky, unpaved road which leads to the ruins of **Fort Jacque** and **Fort Alexander.** You're sure to be offered small cannon balls which the Haitians find in the ruins and sell as souvenirs for a small price.

RHUM-LIQUEUR BY THE BARBANCOURT FAMILY: Another trip upward from Pétionville will take you to the **Jane Barbancourt "castle,"** at Laboule 12 (tel. 7-0589), about five miles from Kenscoff, where for free you can sample the rums (rhums) bottled by the Barbancourt family to your heart's content, although if you work your way through all 23 flavors your head may rebel. If you're driving yourself, it's best to ask directions at the square in Pétionville to be sure of taking the proper route.

The castle is a tongue-in-cheek re-creation of a German fortress, constructed whimsically over the past 30 years by Rudolf Linge, the charming and articulate German-Jewish husband of Jane Barbancourt. The de Barbancourt family, incidentally, began its Haitian history after receiving a land grant here from the governor of Bordeaux in 1736. They've been distilling rum since the 1760s, adding exotic and highly successful versions of the spirit based on the knowledge Rudolf gained while concocting perfumes in the south of France before World War II. The coconut rum, in particular, is worth writing home about.

At the castle you'll be shown to a terrace which overlooks a deep valley with steep hillsides dotted here and there with color when the jacarandas and poinsettias are in bloom, or you can be comfortable in the barrel-stooled sampling room. It's recommended that you sit outdoors if possible, where you relax in the peaceful quiet, broken rarely with a complaint from a goat somewhere down the mountain, while you taste the varied rums the Barbancourt distillery produced from sugarcane. They range from light, liqueur-like drinks to the dark five-star rum that is more like a brandy. Flavors include hibiscus, coconut, coffee, orange, and chocolate, among others. You can sample them all, from glasses, and they'll keep pouring as long as you want to keep tasting, even allowing repeats on any flavor you like and wish to be sure of. It's a heady experience, and you don't have to purchase anything at all, although you're sure to want to. Bottles of the drinks are available at low cost (about $5 a fifth) if you wish.

LEOGANE: Less somnolent than Jacmel, less frantic than Port-au-Prince, Leogane, on the south coast of the bay, a few miles west of the capital city, was once Haiti's capital, and you can still see traces of its hauteur in stately but too often dilapidated wooden houses that have withstood the devastating forces of nature and of man. Efforts at establishing a boat-building industry there, on a small scale, are evident. This town was once called Yagunana, having been an ancient Indian settlement known for its heroic Queen Anacaona. Spanish invaders captured the Indian Caonabo here.

A large soccer field in the center of the town is the scene of much action and can provide a matchless opportunity to see Haitians at play. It attracts crowds from the capital.

The road west from Port-au-Prince to Leogane was paved many years ago and maintained in fair condition to permit the constant passage of *camions* laden with goods and people to and from the capital, together with people on donkeys, people walking, people on bicycles, and people just standing to watch the passing parade. Just outside the town is the road leading south to Jacmel.

There's a tiny black sand beach not presently recommended for swimming or sunning, but a place to get a close look at this unique sand found here and there in the Caribbean and reminding that once volcanoes were a part of the hazards of life in this area of the world.

9. North to Cap-Haitien

Years ago, the only recommendable way to travel between the capital city and Cap-Haitien was by plane, as the only road was a nightmare of broken pavement, washed out in many places, requiring detours through streambeds and around boulders. If you were lucky and had a valiant driver, you might make the trip in 12 hours. Today, thanks to the engineering and financial aid of France, a fine, two-lane, blacktop highway permits you to make the 155-mile trip in about five to seven hours. It's a worthwhile journey, giving a view of scenic mountains, verdant valleys, desert sections, little towns, and a glimpse of Africa.

THE DRIVE NORTH: You observe, as you drive along, that the people all through the Artibonite Valley seem to feel that the highway is their personal mall. Literally hordes of them flock the road, especially on weekends, sauntering along or just standing or squatting. Drivers honk their horns, and with the utmost nonchalance the Haitians, their goats, dogs, and chickens, move slowly out of the way.

Through the valleys, it is startling to see many little villages of **cailles,** one-room thatched huts of wattle and daub with dirt floors, exact replicas of such villages in remote areas of Africa. You learn that when the slaves were brought to Hispaniola to work in the cane fields and on the estates of the French settlers, they were obliged to erect their own shelters, and the only construction they knew was the one they had learned in their African homeland.

When the French were ousted and the independent nation of Haiti instituted at the beginning of the 19th century, time stood still for the tiny country villages, and they look today just as they did then, some sitting close beside the modern highway. They have no electricity, no telephones, no waterlines.

The cailles vary slightly in different villages, some of those closer to the capital no longer using thatching for the roofs. Some villages may have cailles with a higher roof line, a different arrangement of the one door and small window, because the original Africans who were placed in the different areas came from diverse tribes and followed their own heritage, as knowledgeable anthropologists attest. Some have shutters and doors painted in bright colors—blue, pink, yellow, or green—and overall they look like little houses drawn by a child in the early grades of school—frequently lopsided.

As you look into the open doors, you may see a table, which is usually the only piece of furniture, but the whole family sleeps in the hut, on thick straw mats spread on the dirt floor and rolled up and stacked along a wall in the daytime. The little windows, usually only one to a house, have no glass, but each has wooden slat shutters. At night when the family goes to bed, all shutters are closed and barred, as is the door, to keep out the stray spirits that most Haitians believe to be constantly roaming.

Cooking and eating are done outside, where the mother or grandmother squats beside a tiny charcoal fire, stirring the family's dinner in an iron pot.

Whatever you may be told, the belief in voodoo is still strong, particularly among the country people, and each village or group of villages still has its houngan, who is the leader of the community and skilled at curing ills, besides playing the lead role in the religious ceremonies which are still held in outlying areas as serious events, not as tourist attractions.

When you leave the valley and go into the mountains, now and then you will see a little hut standing alone, an orange tree laden with fruit, or a small herd of goats nibbling the vegetation by the roadside. Not many people are usually to be seen in this high country, possibly for reasons of superstition. A driver once told me that if the car broke down in the mountains late in the day, we must stay in the car, roll up the windows, and wait until the sun rose the next day to find help, because zombies who lurk in the forests would find us otherwise.

Miles and miles of sugarcane fields are still in use south of Cap-Haitien, the source of wealth for their owners even today, although not to the extent that they were in the days of slavery. The habitations of the Haitians who are born, live, work, and die in the humid mist of the cane fields are variations of the cailles found elsewhere in the country.

CAP-HAITIEN: After your drive from Port-au-Prince—with perhaps a few stops along the way—you arrive at the old colonial gate marking the entrance to the city on the north coast of Haiti. A policeman may register your entry into Cap-Haitien, and he'll probably give you a free map of the city if you ask. All streets here parallel to the ocean are lettered, from A to Q. Streets perpendicular to the Atlantic are numbered, from 0 to 29. Be cautious driving in Cap-Haitien, as you may be mistaken if you think you have the right of way at a corner.

If you're in too much of a hurry to take the drive from Port-au-Prince to Cap-Haitien, it's sometimes possible to fly, about a 30-minute trip. As of this writing, there is no regular air service, so I suggest you call the Port-au-Prince reservation number, 2-7764, for the latest information.

Selden Rodman, poet, anthologist, and art critic who has encouraged artists who have become internationally renowned, calls Cap-Haitien "the most subtly beautiful city in the West Indies." It was a favorite and stronghold of the French before their expulsion following the insurrection led by L'Ouverture and Dessalines in the last years of the 18th century and the beginning of the 19th. In 1802 King Henri Christophe, self-proclaimed ruler of northern Haiti, burned the city, so that of some 2,000 houses, only about 60 survived.

Today, Cap-Haitien, a city of more than 30,000 people, is slowly awakening from a long sleep. Miles of fine beaches stretch out "to either side of the town. Not too far away, to the west, lies Île de la Tortue, or Tortuga Island, about ten miles off the northern coast of Haiti, off which Columbus's flagship, the *Santa Maria*, sank. Efforts are mounted with increasing frequency to find and recover the remains of this historic vessel.

"Le Cap," as Haitians call it, is today a mixture of structures which look as if they have been there forever, built from or on the ruins of the buildings Christophe destroyed, and painted in shades of blue, pink, and earth tones. Many are built of bricks retrieved from the ruins, bricks that were brought to the island as ballast for the French ships that came to take away loads of sugar produced in the cane fields, which still survive.

Among the giants of Haitian art the name Obin looms high. Cap-Haitien is the place of origin of the Obins. The uncontested leader of the Haitian school was Philomé Obin. The grand master, born in 1892 and dead at a ripe old age in 1986, was once a barber. He first painted Franklin D. Roosevelt, who arrived in Cap-Haitien to end the U.S. occupation of the country. There are at least eight Obins who are highly valued by collectors, in addition to the late Philomé. These artists, both living and dead, include Sénèque, Antoine, Télèmaque, Henri-Claude, Michaëlle, Michel, Othon, and Jean-Marie. Many works allegedly signed by them are forgeries. One cruise-ship passenger recently told me that she acquired an "original" by Philomé Obin for $20!

Seeing the Town

Haitians are friendly and gentle people. They like foreigners, and you can **walk** anytime, day or night, in Cap-Haitien without fear for your safety. If you'd like, you can get a boy to guide you on your walk who will probably know a little English. Tip him at your discretion ($2 will do). Carry small change with you at all times.

Taxis are unreliable, and you should ask how much the charge to your destination will be before you enter the vehicle. Current rates are posted at the airport, the pier, and your hotel. Ask at your hotel about a taxi to take you on a sightseeing tour.

The Beaches

Cap-Haitien has two fine beaches, **Cormier** and **Labadee,** both about five miles out of town. The Cormier Beach Hotel has facilities such as changing rooms, a bar, a restaurant, and a speedboat and diving equipment for rent. The other, Labadee (formerly Labadie), actually has five separate beach areas, with such names as Columbus Cove, Nellie's, Barefoot, Hideaway, and Dragon Tail. Snorkeling is possible at some, but not all, of these beaches, and swimming, windsurfing, and other water sports are offered at some of them.

Labadee has been developed by the Royal Caribbean Cruise Line, and on cruise-ship days (Monday, Tuesday, and Thursday) a native market is open, selling Haitian crafts and paintings. There are also shops in the area. Hotel Mont-Joli offers all-day excursions to Labadee, with lunch included in the $20 fee. On days when no cruise ships are in, you have 50 acres of beaches pretty well all to yourself. Entrance is only $3.

The little town of Labadie took its name from the 17th-century owner of the land and harbor for provision ships, the Marquis de La'Badie. Labadie town includes several villages: Meran-n, Labadie, Boute Roche, and Cap-Pierre. Authentic voodoo ceremonies are held here. The people are friendly and interested in visitors, and all forms of begging are forbidden by the city council.

Sans Souci

In spite of his anger and vengeance wreaked on Cap-Haitien, King Henri Christophe obviously liked the general area on or near the north coast, because it was at Milot, a tiny village nearby, that he built his Sans Souci palace, nestling in splendor at the base of the 3,000-foot mountain on which he had constructed the towering fortress known as the Citadel, called one of the Seven Wonders of the Modern World. To reach Milot, you go about 15 miles inland from Cap-Haitien.

A reminder of the past is afforded by the sight here and there of huge decorated stone gateposts and massive brick chimneys which are all that is left of the palatial homes and great estates of the early French overlords.

Sans Souci, completed in 1813, is now in ruins, but plans call for its restoration.

What remains is part of the massive façade, some of the mosaic marble floors, staircases, and Christophe's domed chapel, which you can visit with the permission of the nuns who have an adjacent school. The dome is a restoration, but a good one. You can roam through the remainder of the ruins at will, and I advise doing so *before* making the trek up to the Citadel.

Built of stuccoed brick, four stories high, the palace complex covered 20 acres of ground in the valley. In what was surely Christophe's effort to outdo Versailles, the palace boasted conduits carrying a cold mountain stream under the floors and numerous bathrooms.

It was here that Christophe, as legend has it, shot himself through the head with a silver bullet. He'd suffered a stroke months earlier and had become increasingly incapacitated.

The Citadel

To ascend to the dizzying heights of the fortress, you go to Milot, where, technically, you should stop at the kiosk lying opposite the neoclassical, imposingly domed cathedral. This is the **Bureau de l'Information,** Place de la Cathédral, Milot, where a uniformed tourist official will sell you a ticket costing $1.25 per person for the right to ascend the mountain. (If you can't find the official, or if you forget, no one will mind if you pay at the kiosk after your descent.) The mechanics of an ascent to the Citadel are one of the most free-floating crap games in Haiti, with policies that change frequently.

If you're in a vehicle tough enough to ascend to the uppermost parking lot, you can afford to ignore at this level the entreaties of the horsemen who whip their little mountain horses (with here and there a sturdier mule) into a gallop to follow your ascending car. You'll probably spot two or three cars that couldn't make the steep climb and were forced to stop along the way. At numerous points along the way you will be offered mounts for the ascent, sometimes at very inflated prices. At times the energy expended on getting your attention is almost chaotic. If your car actually deposits you at the road's highest point, there's nothing to prevent you from walking the 20-minute uphill climb to the base of the fortress. Many animal respecters fear that their weight will be too much for the often-overworked small mountain horses to bear, so they opt for the walk.

If you want a horse, the official price is $1 for the man who leads the animal by its tether and $1.25 for the man who follows behind keeping the animal moving by beating it with a switch, or worse, with a stick. When it's time to pay the piper, hordes of "helpers" may suddenly appear to claim that they helped to encourage your horse up the hill. If you want to avoid all this frenzy, wear good hiking shoes and walk unaided from the uppermost parking lot.

Whatever your experiences getting there, the Citadel is magnificent, the most eerily fascinating spectacle in the Caribbean—and perhaps in the western hemisphere.

Henri Christophe had the mountain fastness built, at ghastly expense in blood, sweat, and lives, rising nearly 200 feet from the peak, to be an impregnable fortress from which any attack forces by land or sea could be seen. The walls are 20 to 30 feet thick, of brick, mortar, and stone, and the **Citadelle La Ferrière,** as it was named, could house 15,000 troops. You can tour through, but walk carefully, as there are no guard rails around the top to protect you from the 200-foot plunge. Also, some of the stone steps down below are moss-encrusted and may be damp and slippery.

The fort held a 40-room section for Christophe and his family and staff, plus ammunition storerooms, a hospital area, dungeons, and treasure chambers. Giant cannons of English, French, and Spanish origin that you will see lying about were dragged up the steep mountain trail by manpower alone, a monumental undertaking. There's a whole, immense storeroom full of cannonballs left as they were when Christophe died. He is believed to have been interred in a quicklime pit somewhere within the fort.

Preservation of the Citadel, Sans Souci Palace, and the nearby fortified site of

Ramiers and restoration of the buildings as part of a National Historic Park (Parc National Historique) started in 1979, through efforts of the Institut de Sauvegarde du Patrimoine National (ISPAN), a government agency, and UNESCO. The National Historic Park covers an area embracing the monuments built by King Henry Christophe at the beginning of the 19th century. The United Nations Development Program has also taken part in the tremendous restoration project in connection with its interest in preservation of historical monuments which form an integral part of Western society and culture. Much work, particularly on the Citadel, has already been accomplished.

Food and Lodging

When you arrive at **Hotel Mont-Joli,** P.O. Box 12 (tel. 2-0300, or toll free 800/ 223-6510), about five minutes from the center of town, Walter Bussenius will make you welcome. The ambience at this first-class hotel is provided by the best features of Haiti—colorful fabrics, art and craftwork, pleasing music, and the soft voices of the Haitian staff, blending to let you know this is a special place. You can enjoy drinks at the bar or on the deck overlooking the pool, as the mysterious Haitian night falls. Standing tall on a hill with vine-covered terraces, Mont-Joli was originally a private home that grew into the present popular inn, opening onto view of sea and mountain. It became a hotel in 1956, and since then it has been expanded with a terraced collection of wings and outbuildings, ringing a handsome swimming pool. Each of the rooms is air-conditioned, finished with a trim of mahogany or tropical oak, and filled with antiques from those Yvette Bussenius, the matriarch of the family, has collected over the decades. Many of the rooms have balconies, and all have private baths, lots of comfortably furnished space, and modern desks and chairs crafted from island hardwoods, mingling with the antiques. All year, singles on the MAP pay from $60 to $65 daily; doubles, $85 to $90 daily. Ask for one of the older rooms (which I prefer), as you'll likely find century-old French colonial beds and lots of mahogany antiques.

Good-tasting Créole, French, and American food is served in the ground-floor dining room by polite waiters. The hotel kitchen will pack a lunch for you to take along if you're going to the Citadel, and Mr. Bussenius will organize a Jeep ride to the beautiful beach at Labadee, about a half hour's ride from the hotel, where you can snorkel and spearfish or just lounge around. A short stroll from the hotel will take you to almost anyplace in town.

Hotel Beck, Bel Air, P.O. Box 48 (tel. 2-0001), is housed in a cluster of similar veranda-fronted buildings on a mountainside richly planted with mango trees. Kurt Beck, born in Haiti but educated in Germany, is the owner. He designed the strong angles of his hotel in the 1950s along neo-Bauhaus lines. The air-conditioned, stone-trimmed bedrooms are scattered among a trio of buildings. Most contain mahogany furniture made from trees originally chopped down on the property. Year-round rates are $40 to $50 in a single, $62 to $75 in a double, and $80 to $90 in a triple, on the MAP. Guests enjoy the hotel's terraced, spring-fed swimming pool, and they sometimes climb up the hillside for a view of the 36-acre mango plantation, the fruit of which is shipped to the United States. The hotel also makes arrangements for guests to visit its private beach, Cormier Plage, several miles away.

One of the most inviting spots of the property is the wide veranda of the hotel's bar and restaurant. Mahogany rocking chairs, low-slung tables, and a view over the densely forested hillside make the spot perfect for a before-dinner drink. If you're a nonresident dropping in for a meal, lunch is served from noon to 2 p.m. daily; dinner, from 7 to 9 p.m. Meals cost from $8. Menu specialties include selections from German, Créole, French, and American cuisine.

Roi Christophe Hotel, rue 24B, P.O. Box 34 (tel. 2-0414), built in 1724, was the home of the French governor, and later used by General Leclerc and Pauline Bonaparte. When Henri Christophe placed prisoners there, the appointments were so sumptuous the natives called it the "Golden Jail." Patios, arcades, rambling old gardens, and courtyards festooned with flowering vines recapture the charm of yesterday, although the hotel has been considerably modernized for today's visitors. Accommodations come in a variety of styles and sizes, the most elaborate being the Pauline Bonaparte suite, perhaps the largest and most opulently furnished hotel room in town. Boasting a magnificent armoire and a bathroom larger than most bedrooms, it has a wide veranda furnished like a private living room. Units rated superior are air-conditioned and have small terraces. With breakfast, single rooms rent for $29 to $46 year round, with doubles costing $39 to $56, and triples, $56 to $66. Service and tax are added to the bill. The hotel's thick-walled dining room, Iberian in decor, draws restaurant business from nonresidents. Lunch is served from noon to 3 p.m., and dinner, from 7 to 9 p.m. daily. Full meals, costing from around $12, include a wide choice of seafood, fried frogs' legs in Créole sauce, fish kebabs, soup of the day, seafood crêpes, T-bone steak, and a selection of snacks and sandwiches for lunch.

Cormier Plage Hotel & Restaurant, P.O. Box 70 (tel. 2-1000), derives its name from cormier, a tropical hardwood known for its durability and a word used to describe early French colonists in Haiti. The resort sits on a sandy acreage beloved of the dozens of tropical birds that make the place their home. As you dine in one of the two restaurants here, uncaged parakeets, finches, and cockatoos lend color to the ambience with their plumage. The resort is the product of the inspiration of Kathy Dicquemare, who is capably assisted by her dynamic France-born husband, Jean-Claude. (From the hotel, Jean-Claude runs a scuba-diving company, described below.) Accommodations stretch along the seafront behind a screen of century-old tropical trees. Each of the 30 clean and comfortable units contains a scattering of island antiques, big windows for a view of the landscaping, ceiling fans, and private baths. Year-round rates, MAP, range from $60 to $70 daily in a single, $80 to $95 in a double, and $105 to $115 in a triple.

The lunch and dinner restaurants sit at opposite ends of the resort, in buildings with high, mahogany-trussed ceilings and sides open to receive the incoming sea breezes. The more formal evening dining spot is a rounded peristyle, not unlike the theater Haitians use for voodoo ceremonies. Meals are casually elegant and good tasting. A grilled filet of sarthe with beurre blanc sauce was one of the best fish dishes I've ever had. The menu lists multiple choices of fresh fish, chicken, lobster, and imported beef. Specialties are fish soup, rice with seafood, Créole shrimp, and frogs' legs provençale. Lunch is served daily from noon to 3:30 p.m.; dinner, from 7:30 to 9:30 p.m. Full meals cost from $15 at lunch, from $20 at dinner. Reservations are suggested for nonresidents of the hotel. This inviting resort lies about four miles west of Cap-Haitien in a combined land- and seascape.

Scuba at Cormier Plage

Cormier Plage Dive Shop, P.O. Box 70 (tel. 2-1000), in a kiosk on the grounds of the previously recommended Cormier Plage Hotel, is run by the dashing co-owner of the resort, Jean-Claude Dicquemare. He once dived with Jean-Jacques Cousteau during six months of research off the coast of Sri Lanka. He teaches beginners to dive and takes experienced divers to some of the interesting reefs and wrecks off the north coast of Haiti. An introductory resort course costs $50 per person. If you're already a certified diver, a one-tank dive costs $30. Rental of snorkeling equipment is $4 per day; windsurfing, $4 per hour.

Where to Shop

Galerie de Trois Visages, rue 5 Boulevard, P.O. Box 100 (tel. 2-0938), represents a list of Haitian painters that reads like a who's who of the Caribbean art world. This is probably the best gallery in the whole north of Haiti and certainly one of the best in the entire country. If you're even tempted to buy a picture by a famous artist, you might do well to delay your purchase until you reach Cap-Haitien because of the substantially lower prices asked here on work similar to paintings sold in Port-au-Prince. The gallery's heart and soul is the driving creative power of the charming entrepreneur, owner Jacinthe Zephir. This is a woman to watch. Her contacts in circles of the nation's painters are already making her a woman of influence in the international art world. Mme Zephir maintains a branch of her excellent gallery at the Labadie cruise-ship terminal and is usually there on the days of a major cruise-ship docking. If you want to be absolutely sure of finding her, phone her gallery in advance of your arrival. Her collection of one brilliant Haitian artist, Jean Baptiste, is among the best in the world.

Les Ateliers Taggart (tel. 2-1931) offers the roughly textured weavings and textiles that are among north Haiti's most famous artistic products. The prototypes are usually created by Haitian entrepreneur Ginette Taggart and then copied by a battalion of studio employees. Examples of her work are on display at the Labadie cruise-ship terminal, but if you want more direct exposure to her creative process, you can visit the atelier. There you'll find shell-encrusted lampshades, bumpy-surfaced rugs, made-on-the-site metal sculptures, and some unusual table accessories. Some of the most dramatic pieces cost as much as $5,000. My favorite is a wall hanging showing cascades of wheat being poured from a huge receptacle. Other items on sale, such as a pastel placemat, cost only $1.50 each. The raw materials for these products are among the most common in Haiti—sisal, palm fronds, horsehair, banana bark, sansevieria, and vétiver.

10. South to Jacmel

Since 1977 a good two-lane blacktop highway has been in use, leading from Port-au-Prince westward and south. Shortly past Leogane the well-graded road, built with financial and engineering assistance from the government of France, branches off south toward Jacmel, about a two-hour drive through beautiful high country, probably less time if you hire a Haitian driver.

If you follow the highway west past the Jacmel turnoff, there are interesting stops to make before setting out on your trip to the south coast. Both Petit Goâve and Miragoane have points of interest to the visitor. I suggest going directly to Miragoane, then stopping at Petit Goâve as you return to the Jacmel highway.

MIRAGOANE: The little town stretches along the hills leading down to the harbor, about two hours from the nation's capital. As you start to descend into the downtown area, stop at the old cathedral overlooking the harbor. From this historic ecclesiastical landmark, one of several being restored in Haiti, continue down the hill and drive along the waterfront past colorful buildings that once were centers for coffee and sisal exporting. When you return to the place where you entered the town, ask directions to the Reynolds Mines. A decent road winds up high above the town, with views around each bend. It leads to the forest of pine trees planted by the Reynolds Company over the years. This is a good place to relax, perhaps have a picnic.

PETIT GOÂVE: If you go early enough to Miragoane, stop on the way back in Petit Goâve at the **Relais de l'Empereur,** a small hotel across from the town square. Check in Port-au-Prince on its status before heading there. The hotel is housed in the former residence of the Haitian emperor, Faustin I, who ruled the land from 1849 to 1856. He was eventually exiled to Jamaica, but Haitian authorities in power allowed him to return here to die. His burial place is within five minutes of the village. Faustin constructed his home in a grandly arched format of red brick that had come into the country from France as ships' ballast. The building, one of the oldest in town, has been completely renovated, and the hotel's stunning interior is filled with antiques and objets d'art.

About three or four blocks from there is the **U.N. artisan project,** where you can watch workers at their looms weaving materials used in making articles sold in many Port-au-Prince boutiques. The work stops at 2 p.m., so plan accordingly if you'd like to see the artisans at their tasks. One of the treasures of Petit Goâve is the old crucifix dating from Spanish times, one of the oldest in the country. You find it next to the old road that goes out of town.

In Petit Goâve you can see women carrying bundles on their heads, men with machetes, and the whole richly varied street life of a rural Haitian village.

Cocoyer Beach

A private launch will take you from Petit Goâve to Cocoyer Beach, lying just offshore, one of the best beaches in Haiti. It is popular with the Haitians, the women going into the water topless and looking as though they stepped out of a photograph in *National Geographic*. Hammocks and straw couches abound along the beach, and in addition to a 150-foot swimming pool, you'll find a croquet field, barbecue, equipment for water sports, and marina facilities.

JACMEL: For many years this once-thriving coffee export "capital" was difficult to visit from other parts of Haiti, lying as it does 50 miles from Port-au-Prince on the south shore of the republic. It was accessible only by boat, by airplane, or for the truly adventurous, by a so-called road which followed the rocky route of a shallow stream, requiring frequent crossings at fords and sometimes making use of the streambed itself as a road. This was called the Route de l'Amitié. Today's travelers find the interesting trip south considerably more comfortable, thanks to the good road described above.

Jacmel is a quiet little sun-drenched town with a strong French flavor, shown in its public buildings and three-storied balconied homes, now in various stages of disrepair. A walk through its narrow streets will take you past coffee warehouses, most now unused but still redolent of the lush shipments of other days. Women who sit under porticos use the centuries-old hand method of sorting and sizing huge piles of coffee beans for export. Down at the docks you can see bags of coffee for shipment overseas.

An **Iron Market,** facing the cathedral, is a smaller version of the vast market in Port-au-Prince, with the same sights, sounds, smells, and sales items.

Selden Rodman, poet, anthologist, and art critic, has a gallery, **Renaissance II,** rue du Commerce, which is open to visitors, with a good exhibition of Haitian art selectively displayed, so you are not overwhelmed. Also, you are not pressured to purchase. Rodman has a patio behind the gallery and his living quarters are above. The people of Jacmel treat him and his gallery as showpieces.

Ask at your hotel about making the horseback ride to the legendary **Blue Pool** ("Bassin Bleu" in French) in the nearby hills. *Warning:* This is a rough journey, involving taking a trail along a steep chasm, walking up and down hills, and fording streams. Figure on spending most of the day. Water nymphs, according to the natives of Jacmel, live here in three mountain grottoes. The goddess is said to sit on a rock on Palm Lake, combing her hair but disappearing at the sound of mortal footsteps. According to legend, if you find her golden comb, you'll become as rich as a king.

The Beaches

As you drive into Jacmel, turn left at the Texaco station and follow a dirt road (generally in good condition) until you come to the sign letting you know you've reached **Cyvadier Beach,** a short distance in from the road on a little cove, where there's also a small hotel. The beach is about ten minutes from Jacmel.

Another ten minutes along the road is **Raymond Beach.** It was once lined with tall palm trees, but many were ripped out by a hurricane. The beach is a huge expanse of sand, where you may see children playing, soccer games in progress, or perhaps only a few other people walking along the shore. If you continue along the road, you come to **Ti-Mouillage,** a good beach on a small harbor. At any of these places, you can usually get fresh lobster and have it cooked right there.

Food and Lodging

A hotel on the beach, **La Jacmelienne,** P.O. Box 916 (tel. 2-4899), is partly the result of the love affair between Erick Danies and his wife, Marlene, who met in New York while she was an art director for RCA and he was marketing pharmaceuticals. Deciding to return to an enchanted corner of Mr. Danies's homeland, Haiti, in 1972, they commissioned the innovative design of this hotel from a Canadian architect and set up business in what had been a grove of coconut palms on the water. Although this is technically a beach resort, it benefits from an ideal location close to the center of the gingerbread town, within sight of a parade of colorfully dressed women carrying food on their heads, field workers carrying machetes, and fishermen mending their nets, all using the street as a passage between their tiny nearby village and the center of Jacmel.

You'll enter the hotel through a covered breezeway flanked with soaring palms, the leaves of which shade the upper-level dining room. The sound of the surf is heard in the attractive bedrooms, each of which contains a covered balcony screened with wooden louvers, wicker furniture, and a view over the palm grove, the pool, and the black sand beach. The attractive and helpful staff is dressed in colonial-style garb of gracefully draped cotton, complete with headdress, all designed by Marlene and worn with a shy kind of style by the girls. The cuisine is derived from Haitian recipes of long ago, with a scattering of French-inspired dishes. Elegant lunches, served on the palm terrace, cost around $12, while dinners go for around $18 apiece. Year-round MAP packages cost about $64 in a single, $94 in a double, and $132 in a triple. The Danieses offer a special package of $250 a week per person, MAP, for guests who want to really explore Jacmel.

Pension Craft, P.O. Box 916 (tel. 8-3331), stands on the north side of the town square, a pleasant place to stay only a short walk from the local Iron Market. The Jacmel-born proprietor is one of the kindest and most interesting persons in town. She is Adeline Danies (sister of Erick Danies, owner of La Jacmelienne), and by all accounts, she's the premier chef of Jacmel. Even if you're just passing through town, you can feel safe about leaving the menu up to her. Often (if she has it) she'll prepare fresh lobster, as well as Haitian bouillon, a vegetable soup with spinach, beans, and potatoes. Other specialties include pisquet (the caviar of Jacmel), crab with eggplant, Haitian chicken from the nearby mountains (reputed to be stronger and more flavorful than its lowland cousins), lambi (conch) with lima beans and rice, pumpkin soup, guinea hen with cabbage, Haitian turkey, leeks gratinée, and what is reputed to be the best goat meat in Jacmel. Meals are served in the high-ceilinged, simply decorated dining room or on the adjoining veranda.

The original house on this spot was rebuilt in 1860 after a disastrous fire wiped out much of the town. The new building was constructed mainly with materials from France, following techniques in use in Europe at the time. Adeline, in her time as operator of the Craft, has hosted dignitaries ranging from the late "Papa Doc" to Mike Wallace, to culinary historians eager to record her folkloric recipes as part of the popular history of Haiti.

The building's grandly proportioned stairwell is lined with portraits representing all branches of Adeline's family: she is by descent part Italian, part English, part Jewish, and part Haitian. At the top of the stairs, visitors can find wood-walled bedrooms that have been subdivided from the original chambers of the spaciously elegant house. The units today are functional, simple, and modern—solid, no-frills accommodations. The dozen rooms rent all year for $42 in a double, breakfast included. Dinner costs an additional $9. Ten of the 12 units have private bath.

Le Manoir Alexandra, 36 rue d'Orléans, P.O. Box 916 (tel. 8-2711), is a handsome, tiered mansion one block down from the town square, looking out on the Bay of

Jacmel, with steps leading from floor to floor outside and down to the street below, through well-kept gardens. Meals are served on the bougainvillea-framed, top-floor porch which provides a view of the bay and the mountains in the distance. When it was built some 70 years ago, it was the private family home of one of the most important merchants in the region. French antiques are used in many parts of the hotel, and some of the main rooms have ornate ceilings.

Enjoyment of the Créole and French cuisine is heightened by the sound of a donkey braying in the distance, laundry women chattering in the island patois in the courtyard three stories below, and the rustle of fronds at eye level topping tall palm trees growing in the lower garden. Most of the comfortable, clean rooms, only six in all (none with private bath), have good views. The owner of the hotel is Mme Alexandre Vital. She charges $30 per person daily, with breakfast and dinner included, plus tax and service. If you visit just for a meal, the cost is $12.

Nightlife

If you're adventurous, you can ask at your hotel to attend a voodoo ceremony. You're likely to be taken up a dusty hill road at night, lined with primitive little huts. You arrive at a tin-roofed "temple of voodoo." To the beat of conga drums, the high priestess (called *hougoun* locally) chants and rings a little bell. The devout undulate. Perhaps it's all staged just for tourists. Perhaps no.

THE DOMINICAN REPUBLIC

FIVE CENTURIES OF CULTURE and tradition converge in the mountainous country of the Dominican Republic, which has been called "the best-kept secret in the Caribbean." The 54-mile-wide Mona Passage separates the Dominican Republic from Puerto Rico. In the Dominican interior, the fertile Valley of the Cibao (this is rich sugarcane country) ends its upward sweep at the Pico Duarte, formerly Pico Trujillo, the highest mountain peak in the West Indies, soaring to a height of 10,417 feet.

Nestled amid Cuba, Jamaica, and Puerto Rico, the island of Hispaniola (Little Spain) consists of both Haiti (which takes up the westernmost third of the island), and the Dominican Republic, which has a lush land mass equal to that of Vermont and New Hampshire combined.

Columbus sighted the coral-edged Caribbean coastline on his first voyage to the New World—"There is no more beautiful island in the world." The first permanent European settlement in the New World was founded on November 7, 1493, the ruins still remaining near Montecristi in the northeast. Primitive Indian tribes had called the island Quisqueya, "mother earth," before the arrival of the Spaniards to butcher them.

Much of what Columbus first sighted still remains in a natural, unspoiled condition, but that may change. The country is building and expanding rapidly, launching itself in the Caribbean resort race as fast as time and money will allow. The Dominican Republic is becoming a fast-growing tourist destination.

Gulf + Western created and subsequently sold a fabulous resort on the southeastern coast of La Romana; and the northern shore, centered around Puerto Plata and

Sosua, is still a vast sweep of shimmering surf and sand, and is itself currently the scene of heavy resort development.

In the heart of the Caribbean archipelago, the country has an 870-mile coastline, about a third of which is given to magnificent beach. The average temperature is 77° Fahrenheit. August is the warmest month and January the coolest period, although even then it is still warm enough to swim at the beaches and enjoy the tropical sun.

That being so, you may ask why the Dominican Republic has been relatively undiscovered by visitors. The answer is largely political. The country has been steeped in misery and bloodshed almost from the beginning, climaxed by the infamous reign of Rafael Trujillo and the civil wars that followed.

The seeds of trouble were sown early. Hispaniola is divided today largely because a 1697 treaty with Spain granted the western part of the island to France. In 1795 another treaty between France and Spain granted the eastern part to France too.

But the French weren't in control for long. Their possession gave rise to the War for Reconquest in which the French colonials were defeated, the country returning to Spanish domination. José Nuñez de Caceres in 1821 proclaimed the "Ephemeral Independence," but after that Charles Boyer, the Haitian president, declared the Dominican Republic a part of Haiti, an occupation that lasted for nearly a quarter of a century.

It wasn't until February 27, 1844, that "La Trinitaria" was founded. This freedom movement, begun by Juan Duarte, made him the father of the Dominican Republic.

The country's problems weren't solved easily, as it once more became a pawn in the colonial possession game. The Spanish claimed the country until they were ousted.

In 1916 the United States established a military occupation which lasted until July 12, 1924. After their departure, Rafael Trujillo eventually overthrew the elected president in 1930, gaining power and dominating the country until his assassination in 1961. He wanted to be known as "El Benefactor," but more often his oppressed people called him "The Goat," because of his revolting excesses.

Now, with much of their often notorious past a subject of history books, the Dominicans are rapidly rebuilding and restoring their country. It does offer the visitor a chance to enjoy the sun and sea as well as an opportunity to learn something historically or even politically if the problems of a developing society should interest you.

GETTING THERE: A nonstop once-a-day morning flight is offered by **American Airlines** from New York's Kennedy Airport to Santo Domingo, with continuing service to Puerto Plata. It leaves enough time after your arrival for a leisurely afternoon on the beach. During periods of peak demand, American also offers at least one (and sometimes two) additional nonstop flights from JFK, which tend to depart after 10:30 p.m. for very late arrivals.

The lowest fares on American's DC-10s are usually offered between Monday and Friday (weekend departures and returns are usually a bit more expensive) between early March and late June and between early September and late November. Special promotion fares at the time of this writing for the periods listed above were as low as $299 round trip, if certain restrictions were observed. These special fares require an advance purchase of at least seven days and a wait of between 3 and 30 days before using the return half of your ticket. American's service from other North American cities tends to be routed through the airline's glistening hub in San Juan.

Pan American offers 11 weekly flights from New York's La Guardia Airport to Santo Domingo, four of which continue to Puerto Plata. For New Yorkers, these flights touch down briefly in Miami. However, travelers connecting from cities in the American South or Southwest might find this connection very convenient.

If you wish to fly on a local carrier, you can always opt for one of the **Air Dominicana** daily flights from New York, or one of its frequent flights from Miami or San Juan, to Santo Domingo or Puerto Plata.

For up-to-date prices and departure schedules, contact one of the airlines or your travel agent.

GETTING AROUND: This is not always easy if your hotel is remotely perched. The most convenient means of transport is provided by:

Taxis

Taxis aren't metered, and determining the cost in advance (which you should do) may be difficult if you and your driver have a language problem. Taxis can be hailed in the streets, and you'll definitely find them stationed outside the major hotels, most definitely outside the airport as you emerge from Customs.

Car Rentals

The best way to see the Dominican Republic is by car, particularly since intra-island transport by bus tends to be erratic. Rail transport is virtually nonexistent. Several car-rental companies maintain agencies here, among them **Budget** and **Hertz.** All offer attractive rates and relatively well-maintained cars.

Two of Budget Rent-a-Car's best Caribbean agencies are in Santo Domingo and in Puerto Plata. Cars are mainly Daihatsus, Isuzus, and Hondas. If you're between the ages of 25 and 70, the cheapest rates are available by reserving a car at least 36 business hours before your arrival and keeping it for at least five days. The least expensive car begins at around $245 per week, with unlimited mileage and no tax. If you plan to arrive at either airport late at night, your reservation can be guaranteed by giving the number of your American Express card to a phone clerk at Budget's phone reservations (tel. toll free 800/527-0700) when you call for information and current prices.

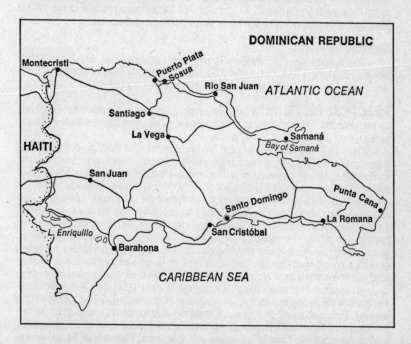

Whether you travel inexpensively or in first-class luxury, Budget has a wide selection of cars in many price categories. These range from a peppy Daihatsu 550 with manual transmission to a miniature bus capable of carrying up to 15 passengers in air-conditioned comfort. In Santo Domingo, Budget is at the corner of John F. Kennedy and Lope de Vega (tel. 562-7211). In Puerto Plata, the office is on Carretera Luperón, km. 1, in front of the baseball stadium (tel. 586-2685). The agencies maintain branches at the airports of both Santo Domingo and Puerto Plata.

Finally, Hertz maintains a single office at Santo Domingo, with a branch at the airport. It has a fleet of mostly Japanese cars also, although its cheapest model, a Lada, is made in Eastern Europe. Call Hertz's international booking desk (tel. toll free 800/651-3001) for information.

Driving requirements include a valid Canadian or American driver's license. Unlike many places in the Caribbean, you drive on the right side of the road.

Public Transportation

Cars which transport the public in Santo Domingo, as well as elsewhere in the Dominican Republic, are called **públicos.** They are a kind of multipassenger taxis that travel on main thoroughfares, stopping to pick up persons waving from the side of the street, motioning the direction they want to go. You must tell the driver your destination when he stops to pick you up. If he doesn't go to the place you are headed, he'll let you know, and you can wait for another público. Watch for cars with a white seal on the car's front door. Fares range from 30 centavos (11¢) to 50 centavos (18¢), depending on your destination.

Public buses, called **guaguas,** provide the same service as públicos, but you're likely to be somewhat more crowded in the buses, as conductors hang out the side and hop off to try to get riders for their vehicles in competition with the públicos. In the towns the guagua fare is usually 20 centavos (7¢). Larger buses provide service outside the towns, charging around RD $1 (one peso) (35¢), depending on how far you go.

Sightseeing Tours

Tour operators include: **Fantasy Tours,** Hotel Embajador (tel. 533-2131); **Prieto Tours,** 125 Francia Ave. (tel. 685-0101); **Metro Tours,** Winston Churchill Avenue (tel. 567-3138); and **Turinter,** 4 Leopoldo Navarro St. (tel. 685-4020).

PRACTICAL FACTS: The official **language,** of course, is Spanish, but English is making inroads. Even if they can't understand you (too often the case with waiters in hotels), they'll give you a friendly smile.

Since 1947 the **Dominican peso** has been on par with the U.S. dollar, at least theoretically, and price quotations in this chapter appear sometimes in American and sometimes in Dominican **currency.** The latter is identified by the prefix RD $. As of this writing, you get about RD $2.85 to $1 U.S. (RD $1 equals about 35¢ U.S.), but this rate will probably fluctuate many times during the lifetime of this guide. You should always check with your bank or the tourist office before planning your budget for the Dominican Republic. At the international airports and major hotels, there are bank booths where you can get your American currency converted into Dominican pesos at the rate of exchange prevailing in the free market. This rate is established periodically and therefore fluctuates. You will be given a receipt for the amount of foreign currency you have exchanged. If you don't spend all your Dominican currency, you can present the receipt with the remaining pesos (RD $s) at the Banco de Reservas booth at the airport and receive the equivalent in American dollars to take out of the country. Payments by credit card are charged to you at the rate of exchange of the free market. In the Dominican Republic, exchange banks (bancos de cambio) can convert foreign currency into Dominican money and vice versa. Commercial banks can exchange dollars for pesos but not the reverse.

Note: All currency quotations in this chapter are in U.S. dollars unless RD $ is specifically designated.

Upon your arrival at the airport, you must purchase a **tourist card** for $5 in U.S. currency. To enter, citizens of the U.S. and Canada need only proof of citizenship such as a passport or an original birth certificate, although U.S. citizens may have trouble returning home without a passport. A reproduced birth certificate is not acceptable. In addition, upon leaving the Dominican Republic, a **departure tax** of $20 (U.S.) is assessed. This must be paid in U.S. currency.

It's **Atlantic Standard Time** throughout the country. When New York and Miami are on Eastern Standard Time, and it's 6 a.m. in either city, it is 7 a.m. in Santo Domingo. However, during Daylight Saving Time, when it's noon on the east coast mainland, it is the same time in Santo Domingo.

In most **restaurants and hotels,** a 10% service charge is added to your check to include service. Most well-bred citizens of the country usually add from 5% to 10% more, especially if the service has been good. The government imposes an 11% tax on hotel rooms, 6% on food and beverages.

The Dominican Republic celebrates the usual **holidays,** such as Christmas and New Year's, but also has some of its own. They include January 21 (Our Lady of La Altagracia); January 26 (Duarte's Birthday); February 27 (National Independence Day); Movable feast (60 days after Good Friday, a Corpus Christi holiday), August 16 (Restoration Day); and September 24 (Our Lady of Las Mercedes).

In Santo Domingo, the **U.S. Embassy** is on César Nicolas Penson Street (tel. 682-2171).

The country has the same **electricity** as the U.S.—that is, 110 volts AC, 60 cycles—so adapters are not necessary.

Once the hassle of Customs (you get a very thorough check!) is over, some four million Dominicans extend a *bienvenido.*

SANTO DOMINGO

Bartholomew Columbus, brother of the discoverer, founded the city of New Isabella on August 4, 1496, later renamed Santo Domingo. That makes it the oldest city in the New World, a haven for history buffs, built on the banks of the Ozama River.

On the southeastern Caribbean coast, Santo Domingo—known as Ciudad Trujillo from 1936 to 1961—is, of course, the capital of the Dominican Republic. It has had a long, sometimes glorious, more often sad, history. At the peak of its power, Diego de Valásquez sailed from here to settle Cuba; Ponce de León went forth to discover and settle Puerto Rico and Florida; and Cortés was launched in the direction of Mexico.

The city today still reflects its long history—French, Haitian, and especially Spanish.

I'll first review its modern (for the most part) hotels and restaurants before picking up the sightseeing trail.

1. Hotels in Santo Domingo

Hotel Santo Domingo, Avenida Independencia (tel. 532-1511), run by Premier Hotels, has a tasteful extravagance, the designs of William Cox, and the styling of the famed Dominican haute couturier, Oscar de la Renta. Their flair has made this ochre stucco structure, 15 minutes from the downtown area, the most prestigious—and best —hotel in Santo Domingo, often attracting presidents of other Latin American countries. Opening into the sea, the deluxe hotel stands on 14 acres of landscaped ground of tropical planting, some of which forms a pleasing backdrop for an Olympic-size swimming pool area.

Air-conditioned rooms are spread out in two structures, three stories tall, these framing latticework loggias, one dedicated to orange trees. Most of the rooms open onto views of the water, but some face the garden, which isn't bad either. A fine collection of antiques, marble, wicker and bamboo pieces, and color—lots of color—set a high level of style that borrows at times from both the Moroccans and the Aztecs. Mr. de la Renta had local artists produce bold, primitive paintings for the bedrooms. A superior room—that is, extra-large with two double beds—rents for $110 in winter, going up to $120 in a deluxe unit with a balcony overlooking the Caribbean. Rates are for either double or single occupancy. *In summer, these rates are reduced to $74 and $81 daily.* Add 15% for tax and service.

Just off the lobby, guests gather for drinks at La Cabuya, enjoying dinner at El Alcazar (see my dining recommendations). At a fountain is the informal restaurant El Cafetal, and you can also enjoy a poolside lunch at Las Brisas. The piano bar, Las Palmas, draws a lively crowd at night. Of the hotel's three professional tennis courts, two are lit for night games.

Hotel Santo Domingo North Hispaniola, Avenida Independencia (tel. 533-7111), has done an amazing Cinderella act. It was practically rebuilt and completely transformed. The location is across from its sister establishment, the deluxe Hotel Santo Domingo, already recommended. The designs of William Cox and the color and fabrics of Oscar de la Renta have transformed the hotel into a resort. On ten beautifully landscaped acres, it is a six-story structure, with an attractive swimming pool and a thatched coffeehouse (a bohío), where you can order breakfast, lunches, or drinks.

The top-floor rooms, which are preferable, offer seaside views. The rooms reflect Dominican styling, and it is the fabric as well as the colors that give them excitement. I feel the designer wisely allowed the 1950s-style baths to remain as they are, a comment on an era. A standard room with balcony costs $65 daily in winter, and there are more than a dozen garden rooms going for $78 daily, either single or double occupancy, plus 15% for service and taxes. *In summer, these tariffs are considerably reduced, a standard unit going for only $42 daily, a garden room for $48, either single or double occupancy.*

The hotel's restaurant, Vivero, serves international specialties, as you sit on locally made ladderback chairs. The evening hot spot is the disco Neon 2002, attracting a great deal of local trade. Guests at the Hispaniola are entitled to use the facilities at the Hotel Santo Domingo, including its professional tennis courts, for which there is a charge.

Santo Domingo Sheraton, 365 Avenida George Washington (tel. 685-5151), is a high-rise right on the Malecón, with a splashy, dramatic entrance, along a boutique-lined drive that passes a waterfall, arriving at a vast lobby that is really a solarium. Vibrant colors and handsomely styled bamboo and rattan furnishings greet you, setting the taste and tone of the hotel. The bedrooms have personal Sheraton flair, traditional with Caribbean overtones (such as bamboo headboards), a small refrigerator for drinks, and room to lounge a bit. Beds are large, and music is piped in. There are 260 rooms, all doubles, plus 18 suites. *In summer the single rate ranges from $75 daily, and doubles go for $80. Suites are more expensive.* In winter, singles or doubles rent for $130 to $140. A third person in a room pays $20 extra. Units are equipped with color TV showing free English movies. A Casino is also within the building.

At the plant-filled Petit Café, overlooking the lobby, you can enjoy a sundowner before heading for Yarey's Lounge, a piano bar with good entertainment. Dining is at Antoine's (see the recommendations to follow), an elegant continental place. Breakfast or lunch is taken at La Terraza coffeehouse, which opens onto a poolside terrace. Try the tropical fruit salad served in a fresh pineapple. Other additions to the hotel are La Canasta, a restaurant featuring Dominican food, and the Omni Disco. The hotel is a good bet for the commercial traveler, as it offers direct-dial phones, 24-hour room service, babysitters, laundry and dry-cleaning services, secretarial and translation services, and mail and telegram service, as well as an Avis car rental on the premises.

Dominican Concorde, Avenida Anacaona, Mirador del Sur (tel. 562-8344), is a complete resort with a casino outside the city, about half an hour's drive from the airport. The Paseo de los Indios is a five-mile park right outside the hotel's grounds. The only ingredient missing at the Dominicana is a beach. Instead it places emphasis on its geometrically designed swimming pool with its lavish surroundings, including a bar jutting out into the pool with underwater seats. The main building is a high-rise, with many built-in playground facilities. The pool is placed adjacent to eight tennis courts, which are lit at night. The bedrooms, 310 in all, utilize island colors and furnishings, and each has a double bed, refrigerator, radio, an intimate sitting area, plus private balconies where you can see clearly a view of faraway mountains or the nearby sea. In winter, singles or doubles cost $66. *Off-season, singles or doubles go for $56 daily.* Service and taxes are added to all bills. Even more expensive suites are available.

The lobby is in colorful warm hues, and the most advanced design is El Mercado coffeeshop, which uses wooden packing cases and baskets of island-grown produce such as bananas. You can order everything from such Stateside specialties as a hamburger to such local delicacies as pumpkin bisque. A luncheon buffet is featured. The main dining room, La Casa, was decorated to evoke a colonial Dominican mansion. Both seafood and international dishes are offered here, including lobster Thermidor. The rooftop lounge, L'Azotea, offers a magnificent view at night. You'll want to have at least a drink here. Other facilities include eight lit tennis courts, basketball, volleyball, a health club, and a sauna.

Hostal Nicolas de Ovando, 53 Calle las Damas (tel. 687-3101), stands in the Atarazana, created from two 15th-century mansions, a brilliant restoration that makes it one of the most charming inns in the Caribbean. Once it was the home of the governor of Hispaniola, from 1502 to 1509 (the hostal is named after him), and is an example of a fortified house, with its own mirador or observation tower overlooking the Ozama River. The spearhead of the restoration program in the historic city, the hostal will serve you a good dinner in its restaurant (see the Extramadura, under "Where to Dine"), even if you can't stay here. The public rooms are gracious, furnished in part with heraldic tapestries and bronze mirrors. The furniture, produced in Spain, is typical of the colonial era, and you might see some interesting Isabeline Gothic ornamentations. Bedrooms are furnished with good reproductions of antique spoolbeds. Baths contain hand-painted tiles from Talavera. In winter, a single costs $75; a double, $85. *In summer, a single goes for RD $85 ($29.75), and a double runs RD $95 ($33.25),* plus 21% tax. Inside, the original patios with arched colonnades have been returned to their former glory. There's always a vista of the water-splashing central fountain. In the Caceres Bar you can enjoy an apéritif before dinner, and in the heat of the day, you can refresh yourself in a swimming pool set in a tropical garden.

El Embajador Hotel Casino, Avenida Sarasota (tel. 533-2131), was created by Trujillo as a concrete-and-glass deluxe hotel with a luxury penthouse for his own use. It was built at the western outskirts of the city on the grounds of a horse-racing track, but today modern high-rise buildings have made inroads on the land where, in the Trujillo era, playboy Porfirio Rubirosa and El Jefe's son, Ramfis Trujillo, once played polo. Perhaps no hotel in Santo Domingo has undergone such a metamorphosis in spirit as this place. The Oriental owners, however, have given it a major refurbishing. The seven-story modern building has 309 air-conditioned bedrooms, French provincial in style, with both king- and queen-size beds, walk-in closets, color TV via satellite, and private terraces. Singles range in price during winter from RD $180 ($63) daily; doubles, from RD $210 ($73.50). For breakfast and dinner, guests pay an additional charge of $25 per person daily. *In summer, a single ranges from RD $145 ($50.75) daily; doubles, from RD $175 ($61.25).*

Among the best restaurants in Santo Domingo are the Jade Garden, featuring Chinese cuisine, and the Embassy Club, the deluxe restaurant with an international cuisine, which is known for its flambé dishes. You can drink and dance in La Fontana lounge. On the grounds are tennis courts and an undulating swimming pool with a waterside terrace for refreshments. Its casino is previewed in the After Dark section.

Hotel Lina, Avenidas Maximo Gomez and 27 de Febrero (tel. 689-5185), is the modern, six-story outgrowth of the restaurant that was begun by Lina Aguado, a Spanish woman who came to Santo Domingo to cook for Trujillo. The restaurant has grown into one of the best known in the Caribbean (see my dining recommendations to follow). The hotel, one of the most famous in the Dominican Republic, has attracted everybody from Julio Iglesias to David Rockefeller to Latin American presidents to "The Incredible Hulk." Under the direction of Angel Montero, the hotel is better than ever. After a much-needed renovation, its facilities have been considerably upgraded, including a gym for both men and women, along with a sauna and whirlpool. There is also a piano bar, a Kiosko Bar, and a gambling casino. There are also a swimming pool and tennis courts. The hotel offers 217 well-furnished rooms, each with private bath and air conditioning. *On the EP, singles or doubles in summer cost from RD $175 ($61.25).* Even more expensive suites are available. Another 21% is added for service and tax. In winter, singles or doubles cost RD $280 ($98).

Hotel Continental, 16 Avenida Maximo Gomez (tel. 689-1151), is one of the best buys in Santo Domingo, a 100-room hotel facing the Palace of the Fine Arts, with pleasantly styled bedrooms, each with private bath and air conditioning. Fabrics in bold, primitive colors have been coordinated in the bedrooms, and sliding glass doors open onto private balconies. Year-round rates in a single range from $42 to $59, and doubles cost $47 to $65, plus 21%. For breakfast and dinner, add $14, plus another 16% for service and taxes. Off the street-floor lounge is an intimate free-form swimming pool, giving the Continental a resort touch. The main lounge is traditionally designed with ornate tile walls and wood paneling. The coffeeshop has been given a contemporary tropical look, with wood trim and terracotta pots of greenery. The bar has an angular wood-paneled ceiling, comfortable stools, and a "sit-down" drinking area. You can dine in the hotel's French restaurant, Le Jardin, later dancing nightly in the disco.

Hotel El Napolitano, Avenida George Washington (tel. 687-1131), is a safe haven—and a good bargain—along the Malecón, which is usually lively until the wee hours. Popular with Dominicans, as is the Naco, El Napolitano rents out 72 comfortably furnished units, many of which are family rooms. There is a swimming pool on the second floor. The units have central air conditioning, and most rooms are equipped with two double beds. Year round, the charge is RD $125 ($43.75) for one person, going up to RD $143 ($50) for two. All accommodations open onto the sea. The café is open 24 hours a day, and the hotel also has a good restaurant, specializing in seafood, especially lobsters (kept in a tank). There is also a disco and a piano bar, with both live and recorded music. If you like crowds, lots of action, and informality, El Napolitano may be for you.

2. Where to Dine

In Santo Domingo, guests are not forced to dine every night in their hotels. The city has a host of restaurants serving good food. Dining rooms offering European cuisine, especially Italian, abound. Most of the restaurants stretch along the seaside-bordering Avenida George Washington, popularly known as the Malecón. Unless otherwise specified, lunch is served from noon to 3 p.m., and dinner, from 7 to 11 p.m.

The national dish is sancocho, a thick stew made with meats (maybe seven different ones), vegetables, and herbs, especially marjoram. Another national favorite is chicharrones de pollo, pieces of fried chicken and fried green bananas flavored with pungent spices.

Everything tastes better with a good local beer known as El Presidente. Wines, under strict and limited control by Customs, are imported, and the prices tend to run high. Dominican coffee is compared favorably with that of Colombia and Brazil.

Lina, in the Hotel Lina, Avenida Maximo Gomez (tel. 689-5185). Spanish-born Lina Aguado originally came to Santo Domingo when it was Ciudad Trujillo. Her culinary fame was so great in Madrid that she'd been hired as the personal *chef de rang* of the dictator Trujillo. She served El Jefe well until she left to open her own fonda. It was a small place, but the restaurant grew in international renown, and she became the number one restauratrice of the Dominican Republic. Today her nephew, Armando Alvarez, runs this modern hotel and restaurant, and it has nothing to do with the old place, except that Dona Lina taught the cooks her secret recipes. Four master chefs now rule in the kitchen. Mr. Alvarez is considered a gastronomic expert and a connoisseur of the finest wines. He offers one of the best Spanish, French, and Dominican cuisines on the island, and he's not at all disappointed if you tell him Lina is "one of the world's greatest eating places."

The place is known for its paella Valencian style and its paella with seafood. Seabass is prepared in two different ways, both good—one flambéed with brandy, another in Lina's familiar Basque style. I'm also fond of the tempting mixed seafood au Pernod cooked in a casserole. Tender steak is also prepared in three different ways: roquefort, pepper, and mustard. Appetizers are large in number and unusual, more than just your regular shrimp cocktail. For example, I recently ordered a pâté of wild boar's head. Naturally, the chefs will prepare a cold Andalusian gazpacho. One good main dish you might like is stewed lima beans, Asturian style. The menu is vast, and you may give up and order something before you finish reading it. For dessert, you can ask for flaming apples with Cointreau. Other classic desserts are also rewarding. The prices are among the highest in the capital, from $25 for dinner, but the food is deserving. Reservations are suggested. Food is served daily from noon to 3 p.m. and 6:30 p.m. to 1 a.m.

El Alcazar, in the Hotel Santo Domingo, Avenida Independencia (tel. 532-1511), was created by Dominican designer Oscar de la Renta in a Moroccan motif, with aged mother-of-pearl, small mirrors, and lots of fabric. All of this forms a setting to show off the culinary skills of the restaurant's chef. Perhaps here you'll enjoy your most elegant evening in Santo Domingo, and you should save it for your final night. The preparation of dishes from the extensive international menu is always acceptable, and sometimes excellent. Good materials are used, and well-made sauces add further zest to dining. The presentation of the food, as well as the service from a well-trained staff, provides yet another reason to dine here. Appetizers include onion soup and lobster bisque. The kitchen is known for its steaks and grills, such as filet mignon with béarnaise sauce. There is also a good selection of seafood, including grilled shellfish. Dinner, served nightly from 7 to 11 p.m., costs from RD $75 ($26.25). Lunch, from noon to 3 p.m., features international buffets: one day it might be Chinese; another day, Italian. These cost from RD $18 ($6.30) and provide one of the best food buys in the city. Call for a reservation.

Antoine's, 361 Avenida George Washington, in the Santo Domingo Sheraton (tel. 685-5151), is the place where the well-dressed Dominican family goes to celebrate a special occasion. Of course, the well-run restaurant in this deluxe hotel also draws an international crowd among the guests staying at the Sheraton. Elegantly decorated, the restaurant also offers entertainment from the piano bar. The cookery is international, and the service is among the finest in the capital. Unusual appetizers include squid in garlic dressing. I am very fond of the black-bean soup and also of the baked garlic soup with egg. The waiters often suggest the lobster Thermidor, but I've found the red snapper Basque style more interesting, and it costs less. If you don't want fish, perhaps the tournedos Rossini will intrigue you. One night I asked the chef to suggest something, and he told me I'd like his Madras hot pot of stewed beef, pork, and crab—and I did. While I was assured that his stewed seafood imperial is even better, that will have to wait until next time. For dessert, I happily settle for Spanish coffee, but the next table on my most recent visit preferred baked Alaska. Tabs tend to be wide-ranging here, but count on at least RD $50 ($17.50). Dinner is served from 7 p.m. to 1 a.m.

Vesuvio I, 521 Avenida George Washington (tel. 689-2141), is the most famous Italian restaurant in the Dominican Republic, possibly Santo Domingo's most heavily patronized dining facility. Both visitors and local business people crowd in here for tasty, reasonably priced Italian fare, about every dish you can think of from that country's vast culinary repertoire. On the way to your table you can inspect the display counter of antipasti. In the hot months guests seem to stay inside in air-conditioned comfort, but in winter they may prefer to dine under the canopy outside. White-jacketed waiters are efficient, maybe too much so, and by the time you've read the menu your meal has arrived. If you have the time between courses, you can contemplate the colorful paintings placed on the walls.

What to order? That is always a problem here, as the Neopolitan owners, the Bonarelli family, have worked since 1954 to perfect and enlarge their menu. Their homemade soups are excellent. I prefer either the seafood soup or the clam soup (in season only), but you may go for spiedini alla romana, a homemade mozzarella cheese and bread deep-fried and topped with anchovy and butter sauce. From the north coast the restaurant receives such fresh fish as red snapper, sea bass, and oysters, and prepares them in imaginative and interesting ways. The crowfish is one of their specialties, one variety being à la Vesuvio—grilled crowfish topped with garlic and bacon. The broiled seafood platter is a sample of all their seafood. The veal comes from the Bonarellis' own herd. I recommend the pink gorgonzola veal or a rolled-up veal stuffed with homemade ricotta cheese and zucchini, and of course, being an Italian restaurant, Vesuvio I has one of the largest homemade pasta menus in the Caribbean. A favorite dessert is tortelloni al vodka, but you may prefer a recent creation, choccolat fettuccini à la parra, a real chocolate pasta, only instead of sugar they've added salt. An average meal begins at RD $35 ($12.25). The restaurant is open daily all year from noon to 2 a.m., and you don't need a reservation as it's run on a first-come, first-served basis.

The owner of Vesuvio claims to be the pioneer of pizza in the Dominican Republic. He makes a unique one next door in **Pizzeria Vesuvio**—a yard-long pizza pie! If you want to try another Italian place, go to **Vesuvio II,** 17 Tiradentes (tel. 565-9797).

Il Buco, 152-A Arzobispo Meriño (tel. 685-0884), is one of the most popular dining choices in the capital, drawing haut Santo Domingo to its precincts, where they are served an array of countrywide Italian and international specialties. Giuseppe Storniolo is the guiding light behind this successful enterprise in a restored 16th-century house accented with brick, stucco, and flowered tablecloths. All in-the-know diners request his antipasti, an array of both hot and cold Italian-style hors d'oeuvres. Follow with a pasta if you have the appetite, as it's homemade and likely to be served in a savory sauce. Fresh seafood, including bass and lobster, are served as well, depending on what looked good that day at the market. Award-winning dishes include green lasagne, risotto with four cheeses, stuffed crayfish, stuffed chicken breast, and stuffed veal rollatine. The waiters are polite and efficient, and often there is entertainment, all of which makes for a romantic dining choice. On Friday and Saturday nights the restaurant is likely to be crowded, so it's prudent to call for a reservation. Count on spending around $20 or more for one of your finest meals in the capital. Open noon to midnight.

Juan Carlos, 7 Gustavo Mejía Ricart (tel. 562-6444), is a top-quality restaurant, handsomely decorated in pinks and mauves. Local paintings add to the attractiveness of the place. But it is the food that attracts the repeat clientele, mostly Dominicans. Several years ago the restaurant with a bodega was opened by Carlos Gil from Valencia, Spain. His specialties include tripe in the Madrid style, guinea hen in madeira, rabbit in a wine sauce, a seafood paella (prepared for at least two persons), roast lamb, and a seafood casserole. You can also order quail stew and seabass in orange sauce.

Count on spending from RD $50 ($17.50) and up. The restaurant is open from noon to 3 p.m. and 7 to midnight seven days a week.

La Fromagerie, Plaza Criolla (tel. 567-9430), has a regional tavern-style decor, and it's one of the most attractive restaurants in Santo Domingo. It's air-conditioned inside, but you also have a choice of outside tables as well. The staff is accommodating, and the list of dishes is international, including Dominican specialties. At lunch, you may prefer to sample one of the crêpes, stuffed with a variety of fillings. Classic dishes include stuffed pot roast, duckling in an orange sauce, and bouillabaisse. More unusual fare is likely to feature a shellfish fondue, frogs' legs in a champagne sauce, and crabmeat in a red sauce. Meals cost from RD $40 ($14). Reservations are rarely needed. Open noon to midnight seven days a week.

Fonda La Atarazana, La Atarazana Street (tel. 689-2900). For native food in a colonial atmosphere, with night music for dancing as well, this patio restaurant often has forkloric festivals. Just across from the Alcázar, the restored structure can easily be visited as you're shopping and sightseeing in the old city. This friendly place retains plenty of character, without being deliberately self-conscious about it. A cheap, good dish is chicharrones de pollo, which is tasty fried bits of Dominican chicken. Otherwise, you might try curried goat in a sherry sauce. Sometimes the chef cooks guinea fowl in wine. I also like the Spanish-style seabass. If you don't mind waiting half an hour, you can order the sopa de ajo (garlic soup). The pork dishes attract many fans, who come here especially for the fricassé pork chops. An average repast will cost $15 to $20.

Extremadura, in the Hostal Nicolas de Ovando, 53 Calle las Damas (tel. 687-0450). In the most enchanting old-world hotel in Santo Domingo, you get good dishes, well prepared and served in a typically Iberian ambience of terracotta floors, soaring timbered ceilings, leather-bottomed wooden chairs, gilded chandeliers, and an imposing grandeur. The restaurant presents a long menu of favorite foods that borrow from many of Spain's provincial kitchens, from Castile to Valencia, from the province of Asturias to Andalusia. As an appetizer, you might like the snails Ovando bourguignonne style or a cup of either garlic soup or onion soup. Main dishes include a pottery casserole of seafood flambéed in rum, roast chicken or rabbit in garlic sauce, two types of paella, and stewed lobster. For dessert, you might choose caramel custard or flambéed bananas for two persons. Most meals range from RD $45 ($15.75). Waiters wear uniforms of bandarilleros from the province of Extremadura in Spain, from which the restaurant takes its name. Hours are noon to 3 p.m. and 5:30 p.m. to midnight.

Café San Michel, 24 Avenida de Lope de Vega (tel. 562-4141), on a traffic-clogged street in a section of town called Naco, is a popular restaurant which may have its finest hour daily at lunchtime, when local business people come here with their friends, lovers, and clients. The wood-trimmed façade opens into an interior of light-grained wood, stone trim, and a curved black-accented bar which is open daily from noon to midnight. Menu items include many different kinds of beefsteak, seabass, red snapper, shrimp, lobster prepared in several ways, caesar salad, spinach lasagne, soufflés of shrimp or spinach, cream of pumpkin soup, gazpacho, and a series of flavorful chicken breast dishes, each stuffed in a different way. A dessert spectacular is soufflé Grand Marnier. Full meals here cost around RD $40 ($14.50) per person.

Restaurant/Bar Jai-Alai, 411 Avenida Independencia, corner of José Joaquin Pérez (tel. 685-2409). The original owner of this cosmopolitan restaurant left his home in Bilbao, Spain, when he was 18. After running a successful eatery in Lima, Peru, he came to Santo Domingo, where he set up this restaurant named after the favorite sport of his Basque ancestors. The establishment is housed in what used to be a wealthy private home. It's decorated like an informal gathering place in a Spanish plantation house, with lime-green tile floors, dark-wood accents, and a rather dark dining area set behind thick walls. Today the restaurant is directed by the founder's son, Luís Llaque Gordillo, and his wife, Goyi, who welcomes guests with a smile and a fluency in several languages. Shellfish is famous here, with such offerings as lobster créole, shrimp Jai-Alai, seafood casserole, and oysters in red sauce. Other dishes include octopus créole, garlic soup, Spanish-style pork chops, rabbit in garlic sauce, and seabass, both Basque and Breton style. As a before-dinner drink you might enjoy a glass of the Peruvian pick-me-up called *pisco*. Full meals cost from RD $50 ($17.50). The restaurant, which you'll find just back of the Sheraton Hotel, is open for lunch and dinner daily from 11:30 a.m. to 4 p.m. and 6:30 p.m. to midnight.

Restaurante Café-Concierto El Bodegón, 152 Arzobispo Meriño (tel. 682-6864), occupies several elegant rooms in the heart of the oldest part of the city, immediately opposite the cathedral. The building is a house whose oldest parts date from the 15th century, all of it decorated with heavy ceiling timbers, massive wrought-iron chandeliers, old furniture, and scores of pictures by well-known Dominican artists. Many of the artists are friends of the owner, Frank Salcedo, whose cuisine has won gastronomic awards and whose devotees include luminaries. The bar has received an international award for the house special, a rum caña. Full meals, costing from around RD $35 ($12.25), can include international dishes such as zarzuela de mariscos (fish and shellfish in a casserole), tripe with ham and Spanish sausage, paella valenciana, seabass with shrimp and clams, rabbit in a special sauce, gazpacho, garlic soup, or a special cassoulet made with lamb, pork stew, sausage, and beans. For dessert you might like to try the pineapple custard. Meals are served daily except Sunday from noon to 3:30 p.m. and 7 p.m. to midnight.

De Ciro, 38 Avenida Independencia (tel. 689-6046). As you approach this well-known rendezvous point, you may imagine you're arriving at an embassy rather than at a restaurant. This feeling is engendered by the fact that the ochre-colored villa was originally intended to house the Dominican/American cultural center before it became a restaurant in 1971. Guests usually enjoy a drink in the warmly paneled Piccolo Bar before entering the light-blue dining room. Full meals usually cost from RD $40 ($14) and may include such specialties as spaghetti with red or white clam sauce, a full array of pasta dishes, chateaubriand, chicken cacciatore, grilled lobster, deviled shrimp, Sicilian-style seabass, minestrone, or stracciatella—in all, a wide selection of Italian foods. The restaurant is open daily except Tuesday for lunch and dinner. Service is from noon to 3 p.m. and 7 to 11 p.m.

Restaurant Aubergine, Plaza México Edificio, Alma Mater Avenue, corner of México (tel. 566-6622). This is one of the smallest restaurants in Santo Domingo, with no more than eight tables, yet it offers 150 different dishes, many of which are inspired by German-Swiss recipes. Simple but stylish, it contains tones of pink, violet, and red, with hanging straw lamps and enlarged photos of Germany. The music might be a Strauss melody about the Blue Danube. The location is in a residential neighborhood on the ground floor of a tall building. Full dinners, prepared by the owner-chef, Harald Mossle, cost from RD $55 ($19.25). These might include veal Zurich style, beef filet in a roquefort sauce, sauerkraut with sausage and pork chops, seabass with almonds, chicken breasts with asparagus, and snails with cabbage-flavored butter. For dessert, try a slice of the Black Forest cake. Open daily except Sunday, the establishment serves from noon to 3 p.m. and 7 p.m. to midnight. Reservations are important.

La Bahia, 1 Avenida George Washington (tel. 682-4022), is an unprepossessing type of place right on the Malecón. You'd never know that it serves some of the best, and freshest, seafood in the Dominican Republic. One predawn morning as I passed by, early-rising fishermen were waiting outside to sell the chef their latest catch. Rarely in the Caribbean will you find a restaurant with such a diversity of seafood offerings. For your appetizer, you might prefer ceviche, seabass marinated in lime juice, or lobster cocktail. Soups come from the sea and are likely to contain big chunks of lobster as well as shrimp. See if any of these specialties tempt you—kingfish in coconut sauce, seabass Ukrainian style (a specialty—how did they get the recipe?), baked red snapper, and seafood in the pot. A lot of unusual offerings show up on the menu. Conch is a special favorite with the chef, who knows how to prepare it in many ways. After a big seafood dinner here, costing from RD $35 ($12.25), desserts are superfluous. No reservations are needed. Service is from 9 a.m. until the last customer departs for home in the early hours of the morning.

Jade Garden, Hotel Embajador, Avenida Sarasota (tel. 533-2131), is clearly in the front rank in Chinese cookery in Santo Domingo. The management even sent its cooks to Hong Kong to learn some of the secret methods of Peking and northern Chinese cookery, and they returned to please customers with an array of specialties, including such delectables as minced pigeon, soya-bean chicken, sweet-corn soup (superb), lemon duck (even better!), sweet-and-sour pork, deep-fried fish, and fortune chicken, finished off with a toffee banana. The pièce de résistance is the Peking duck, which the chef roasts in an open-fire stove. Before peeling it with a special knife, it is presented to the diners who ordered it. Most of Jade Garden's ducks come from Tientsin, China, where they are well fed and restricted from movement to give their meat a special texture. Depending on what dinner you select, your tab might be as little as RD $25 ($8.75), going up to RD $40 ($14). Luncheons are great buys, one set meal costing from RD $15 ($5.25), another from RD $20 ($7). Hours are noon to 3 p.m. and 7:30 to 11:30 p.m.

Ananda, 7 Casimiro de Moya, corner of Pasteur (tel. 682-4465), is a vegetarian restaurant where you can enjoy good food in an informal, cozy room with Oriental or classical music supplying the background effect. The menu here, under the direction of Cristina Rosario de Pérez, includes a dish of the day as well as other foods all combining natural products. You can feast on a salad made of cucumber, tomato, celery, and spinach, black beans and rice with vegetables, white rice cooked in Chinese or Hindu style with fruits or vegetables, or even a "grilled steak"—actually made of glutin and served with a tasty sauce. Try the ripe plantain pudding for dessert with a local flavor, or perhaps you'd like the peanut or whole-bread pudding. All the desserts at Ananda are made with brown sugar or honey. A meal will cost from RD $25 ($8.75) at this health-oriented restaurant. Open noon to 10 p.m.

La Canasta, in the Santo Domingo Sheraton, 365 Avenida George Washington (tel. 685-5151), is the best late-night dining spot in the capital. Between the Omni Casino and the Omni Disco (both recommended separately in the nightlife section), the restaurant is not only economical, but it serves until 6 a.m. If you're an early diner, you can also drop in. The best news is that the restaurant serves the most popular Dominican dishes, culled from favorite recipes throughout the country. A complete meal costs RD $20 ($7) and up. Among the favorite local offerings are sancocho, a typical stew with a variety of meats and yucca, and mondongo (tripe cooked with tomatoes and peppers). Unusual offerings include goatmeat braised in a rum sauce and beefsteak Créole style. One section of the menu is labeled the "Dominican inflation fighter" and includes such offerings as crunchy chicken wings. You can also order soups such as fish or black bean and a selection from the sandwich basket.

3. Exploring the Capital

Santo Domingo, a treasure trove, is part of a major government-sponsored restoration. The old town is still partially enclosed by remnants of its original city wall. Its narrow streets, old stone buildings, and forts are like nothing else in the Caribbean. The only thing missing is the clank of the armor of the conquistadores.

Old and modern Santo Domingo meet at the **Parque Independencia,** a big city square whose most prominent feature is its Altar de la Patria, a shrine dedicated to the three fathers of the country, Duarte, Sanchez, and Mella, all of whom are buried here. These men led the country's fight for freedom from Haiti in 1844. As in provincial Spanish cities, the square is a popular gathering point for families on Sunday afternoon. Old men sit in the sun and play dominoes. El Conde Gate stands at the entrance to the plaza. It was named in 1955 for Count (El Conde) de Penalva, the governor who resisted the forces of Admiral Penn, the leader of a British invasion. It was also the site of the March for Independence in 1844, and holds a special place in the hearts of Dominicans.

Heading east along El Conde Street—a microcosm of Dominican life—you reach Columbus Square, with a large bronze statue honoring the discoverer. The statue was made in 1882 by a French sculptor. On the south side of the plaza, the **Cathedral of Santa Maria la Menor** (tel. 689-1920) is the oldest cathedral in the Americas, begun in 1514 and completed in 1540. Characterized by a gold coral limestone façade, it is a stunning example of the Spanish Renaissance style, with elements of Gothic and baroque. In the 472-year-old nave, a neo-Gothic marble mausoleum supports a bronze sarcophagus believed to contain the remains of Columbus. (It must be pointed out that several other locations make this same claim.) The cathedral was visited by Pope John Paul II in 1979 and again in 1984, at which time he was shown work in progress for celebration of the 500th anniversary of the Discovery of America to be marked in 1992. The cathedral will be the axis of the celebration. An excellent art collection of retables, ancient woodcarvings, furnishings, funerary monuments, and silver and jewelry of the so-called Treasure of the Cathedral can be seen.

The most outstanding structure in the old city is the **Alcázar,** the palace built for the son of Columbus, Diego, and his wife, the niece of Ferdinand, king of Spain. Diego became the colony's governor in 1509, and Santo Domingo rose as the hub of Spanish commerce and culture in America. Constructed of native coral limestone, it stands on the bluffs of the Ozama River. For more than 60 years it was the center of the Spanish court, entertaining such distinguished visitors as Cortés, Ponce de León, and Balboa. After its heyday, it fell on bad days, or rather two disastrous centuries, as invaders pillaged it. By 1835 it lay in virtual ruins; and it wasn't until 1957, in Trujillo's day, that the Dominican government finally restored it to its former splendor. Its nearly two dozen rooms and open-air loggias are decorated with paintings and period tapestries, as well as 16th-century antiques. It is open from 9 a.m. to noon and 2:30 to 5:30 p.m. daily, except Tuesday, charging 75¢ admission for adults, 25¢ for children. The same ticket entitles you to visit the **Museu Virreinal** or Museum of the Viceroys, adjacent to the Alcázar. It houses period furnishings and tapestries, as well as paintings dating from the colonial period.

The **Casa del Cordon,** or ''Cord House,'' stands near the Alcázar at the corner of Calles Emiliano Tejera and Isabel la Católica. It was named for the cord of the Franciscan order which is carved above the door. Francisco de Garay, who came to Hispaniola with Columbus, built the casa in 1503–1504, making it the oldest stone house in the western hemisphere. Among important events that took place within the walls of the Casa del Cordon was the time it lodged the first Royal Audience of the New World which performed as the Supreme Court of Justice in the island and the rest of the West Indies. On another occasion, in January 1586, as a memorable gesture, the noble ladies of Santo Domingo gathered here to donate their jewelry as ransom demanded by Sir Francis Drake in return for his promise to leave the city. The restoration of this historical manor was financed by the Banco Popular Dominicano, where its executive offices are found.

Also in the shadow of the Alcázar, **La Atarazana** is a fully restored section which centered around one of the New World's first arsenals, serving the conquistadores. It extends for a city block, catacombed with merchandise-loaded shops, art galleries (both Haitian and Dominican paintings), and boutiques, as well as some good native and international restaurants, some of which have been recommended previously.

Just behind river moorings, the oldest street in the New World is called **Calle las Damas,** or ''Street of the Ladies.'' Some visitors assume this was a bordello district. Actually it wasn't. Rather, the elegant ladies of the viceregal court used to promenade there in the evening. It is lined with colonial buildings, including the government-owned and already-recommended Hostal Nicolas de Ovando.

Across the street, the **National Pantheon**—a fine example of Spanish American colonial architecture—was originally a Jesuit monastery in 1714, although it was later used as a warehouse for storing tobacco. Once it was a theater as well, and its massive size is characterized by austere lines. Trujillo had restored it in 1955, projecting it as his burial place, but instead one chapel preserves the ashes of the martyrs of June 14, 1959, who tried vainly to overthrow the dictator. Admission free, it can be visited Monday through Saturday.

From here you can walk a few steps north to visit the chapel of **Our Lady of Remedies,** where the first inhabitants of the city used to attend Mass before the cathedral was erected.

The **Museo de las Casas Reales,** or Museum of the Royal Houses, also stands on the Calle las Damas (tel. 682-4202). Originally it was the Palace of the Royal Audencia and Indias Chancery and the Palace of Governors and Captain Generals. Through artifacts, tapestries, maps, and re-created halls, including a courtroom, it traces Santo Domingo's history from 1492 to 1821. Gilded, elegant furniture, arms and armor, and other colonial artifacts, all inspected by King Juan Carlos of Spain in 1976, make it the most interesting of all museums of Old Santo Domingo. It contains replicas of the three ships commanded by Columbus, and one exhibit is said to hold part of the ashes of the famed explorer. You can see, in addition to pre-Columbian art, the main artifacts of two galleons sunk in 1724 on their way from Spain to Mexico, along with remnants of another Spanish ship, the *Concepción* (18th century). Hours are daily except Monday from 9 a.m. to 5 p.m., and admission is 50¢ for adults, 25¢ for children.

On Padre Billini, formerly University Street, at the corner of Arzobispo Meriño, is the **Casa de Tostado** (Tostado House) whose beautiful Gothic double window (geminated window) is the only one existing today in the New World. The house was first owned by the scribe Francisco Tostado, and inherited by his son of the same name, a professor, writer, and poet who was the victim in 1586 of a shot fired during Drake's bombardment of Santo Domingo. The Casa de Tostado, which at one time was the archbishop's palace, now houses the **Museum of the Dominican Family,** showing how life was in the 19th century for a well-to-do household. It can be visited daily except Monday from 9 a.m. to 5:30 p.m. Admission is 50¢ for adults, 25¢ for children.

Museo del Hombre Dominicano, Plaza de la Cultura, Calle Pedro Henríquez Ureña (tel. 687-3622), houses the most important collection in the world of artifacts made by the Taíno Indians, who greeted Columbus in 1492. Thousands of magnificently sculptured ceramic, stone, bone, and shell works are on display. Daily, except Monday, hours are 10 a.m. to 5 p.m., and admission is 50¢.

If time remains, try also to see the **Puerta de la Misericordia.** Part of the original city wall, this "Gate of Mercy" was once a refuge for colonists fleeing hurricanes and earthquakes.

The **Monastery of San Francisco** is but a mere ruin, lit at night. That any part of it still is standing must be counted as a miracle. It was destroyed by earthquakes, pillaged by Drake, bombarded by French artillery.

In total contrast to the colonial city, modern Santo Domingo dates from the Trujillo era. A city of broad, palm-shaded avenues, its seaside drive is called **Avenida George Washington,** more popularly known as the **Malecón.** This boulevard is filled with restaurants, as well as hotels and nightclubs.

In downtown Santo Domingo, it is now possible to visit the **National Palace,** the three-story, domed structure ordered built by President Trujillo in 1939 and used as the seat of government since its inauguration in 1947. The edifice, considered an architectural triumph in the Dominican Republic, was designed by Italian architect Guido D'Alessandro. It stands in landscaped gardens, where concerts are sometimes held. Because the first floor is mainly occupied by staff offices, visits start on the second floor, where you'll see the Gallery of Presidents. Paintings of the Dominican coat-of-arms from the first design to the one now in use are also displayed. In this room too are the velvet-upholstered, carved mahogany chair used by Trujillo and a mammoth conference table. Of particular interest is the Hall of Caryatides on the third floor, surrounded by 44 marble columns topped by carvings of female figures, separated by mirrors. A presidential suite on this floor is used to house visiting dignitaries. Visitors are sure to be impressed by the extensive use of marble throughout the palace, most of it the country's own product. For a guided tour of the palace, call 689-1131, ext. 211. Admission is free.

The **Museum of History and Geography,** Calle Pedro Henríquez Ureña, near the National Library, contains personal belongings of Trujillo, such as clothing, handkerchiefs, French perfume, uniforms, combs, briefcases, and medals from Argentina, Spain, and Japan, as well as personal documents. A series of photographs traces the career of the former ruler. Also on exhibit at the museum are artifacts of the conquistadores, the early colonists under Spanish rule, the Haitian invasion of the Dominican Republic, and other highlights of the nation's history. Admission is $1, and English-speaking guides are available.

The former site of the Trujillo mansion, the **Plaza de la Cultura** has been turned into a large, attractive park, containing the National Library and the National Theater, which sponsors folkloric dances, opera, outdoor jazz concerts, traveling art exhibits, classical ballet, and music concerts. Also in the center, the Gallery of Modern Art has an exhibition of national and international paintings (the emphasis on native-born artists), as well as antiques.

I'd also suggest a visit to the **Paseo de los Indios,** that sprawling five-mile park with a restaurant, fountain displays, and a lake.

About a 20-minute drive from the heart of the city is **Los Tres Ojos** or "three eyes," which stare at you across the Ozama River from Old Santo Domingo. There is a trio of lagoons set in scenic caverns, with lots of stalactites and stalagmites. One lagoon is 40 feet deep, another 20 feet, and yet a third—known as "Ladies Bath"—only 5 feet deep. A Dominican Tarzan will sometimes dive off the walls of the cavern into the deepest lagoon. The area is equipped with walkways. The location is off the Autopista de las Americas on the way to the airport and the beach at Boca Chica.

In the northern sector of Santo Domingo, the **Botanical Gardens** at Arroyo Hondo are the biggest in all of Latin America. In 1.8 million square meters, flowers and lush vegetation of the Dominican Republic can be seen anytime from 9 a.m. to noon and 2 to 6 p.m., and admission is 50¢ for adults, 25¢ for children. Seek out, in particular, the Japanese Park, the Great Ravine, and the floral clock. You can also tour the grounds by horse carriage or else take a boat. The gardens are closed Monday.

4. Sports, Shopping, Nightlife

Typical of Latin cities, Santo Domingo has a pulsating life both day and night. I'll preview some of the action in the sections ahead, beginning with—

THE SPORTING LIFE: The Dominican Republic may have some great beaches, but they aren't in Santo Domingo. The principal beach resort in the area of the capital is at **Boca Chica,** less than 2 miles east of the international airport and about 19 miles from Santo Domingo. Clear, shallow blue water laves the fine white sand beach and a natural coral reef that protects the area from big fish. The east side of the beach, known as "St. Tropez," is popular with Europeans. The great beaches are at **Puerto Plata,** but that's a rough, three-hour drive from the capital, and at **La Romana,** a two-hour drive to the east. Most of the major Santo Domingo hotels have swimming pools.

For other descriptions of sporting activities, refer to the sections on La Romana and Puerto Plata.

Snorkeling and Scuba

Divers rate the Dominican Republic high for its so-called virgin coral reefs, where you can explore ancient shipwrecks and undersea gardens with an endless variety of marine life.

Mundo Submarino, 99 Gustavo Mejía Ricart (tel. 682-3466), is the best in Santo Domingo. It offers a snorkel tour from 9 a.m. to 1:30 p.m. from the beach or a secluded cove. A minimum of four divers is required, paying $25 per head. Advanced scuba tours are featured at the same time—daily diving by boat, in both a shallow and a deep reef with steep walls. The possibilities for photography are excellent. All equipment is included at a cost of $25 for one dive.

Golf

Serious golfers head for **La Romana** or the course that Robert Trent Jones designed at **Playa Dorada,** in the vicinity of Puerto Plata. Golf is also available in the capital at the **Santo Domingo Country Club,** an 18-hole course which grants privileges to guests of most of the major hotels. The rule here is members first, which means it's impossible for weekend games.

Tennis

The major hotels have very good courts, especially at the **Hotel Santo Domingo** (three courts, two lit for night play), **Santo Domingo Sheraton, Embajador, Lina,** and the **Dominican Concorde** (eight championship courts). The cost is usually RD $15 ($5.25) per hour during the day, RD $18 ($6.25) per hour at night. Some of these courts are lit for night games.

Polo

Made so famous during Trujillo's day, polo is still a popular sport. Polo fields are in Santo Domingo at **Sierra Prieta,** with games played on weekends.

Baseball

As in America, the most popular spectator sport is baseball, and many of the country's native-born sons have gone on to the major leagues. From October through February, games are played at stadiums in Santo Domingo. Check the local newspaper for schedules and locations of the nearest game.

Horse Racing

Santo Domingo's race track, **Perla Antillana,** schedules races on Tuesday, Wednesday, Thursday, and Saturday. You can make it a day here, having lunch at the track's restaurant.

Cockfighting

Dominicans like this brutal "sport," but it offends many foreign visitors. However, if you want to see a cockfight, go to the **Santo Domingo Cockfighting Coliseum,** Avenida Luperton (tel. 565-3844), across from the Alas del Caribe Airport. This is a modern installation, and you'll see the spectators reach fever excitement. Stakes are high, and the cocks are well trained. The action is followed on closed-circuit TV, as guests sit in air conditioning on comfortable seats.

SHOPPING: The best buys are in handcrafted native items, especially amber jewelry, the national gem, a petrified fossil resin millions of years old. The pine from which the resin came disappeared from the earth long ago. The origins of amber were a mystery until the beginning of the 19th century when scientists determined the source of the gem.

Look for pieces of amber with trapped objects such as insects and spiders inside the enveloping material. Colors range from a bright yellow to black, but most of the gems are golden in tone. Amber deposits in the Dominican Republic were only discovered in the past three decades. Fine-quality amber jewelry is sold throughout the country.

A semiprecious stone of light blue (sometimes a dark-blue color), larimar is the Dominican turquoise. It often makes striking jewelry, and is sometimes mounted with wild boar's teeth, but you may prefer to make a less obvious statement with silver.

Ever since the Dominicans presented John F. Kennedy with what became his favorite rocker, visitors have wanted to take home a rocking chair, a piece of furniture popular throughout the country. To simplify transport, these rockers are often sold unassembled (you put them together when you get home).

Other good buys include Dominican rum, hand-knit articles, macramé, ceramics, and crafts in native mahogany. Always haggle over the price, particularly in the open-air markets. No stallkeeper expects you to pay the first price asked. The best shopping streets are El Conde, the oldest and most traditional shop-flanked avenue, and Avenida Mella.

In the colonial section, **La Atarazana** is filled with galleries and gift and jewelry stores, charging inflated prices. Duty-free shops are found at the airport, in the capital at the **Centro de los Heroes,** and at both the Hotel Santo Domingo and the Hotel Embajador. Shopping hours are generally from 9 a.m. to 12:30 p.m. and from 2 to 5 p.m., Monday through Saturday.

Head first for the **Mercado Modelo,** the National Market, on the Avenida Mella, filled with stall after stall of craft products. Of course, this is a workaday market, catering to the needs of the capital's citizens, so it also overflows with spices, fruits, and vegetables. The merchants will be most eager to sell, and you can easily get lost in the crunch. Remember to bargain for any item that strikes your fancy. You'll see a lot of tortoise-shell work here, but exercise caution, since many species, especially the hawksbill, are on the endangered-species list and could be impounded by U.S. Customs if discovered in your luggage. The already-mentioned rockers are for sale here, as are mahogany ware, sandals, baskets, hats, clay braziers for grilling fish, whatever.

If you're worried that that piece of amber you like may be plastic (and you don't want to strike a match to it in front of the stallkeeper), then you can be assured of the real thing at **Ambar Marie,** 9 Caonabo (tel. 682-7539). At this small shop, you can even design your own setting for your choice gem. Look especially for the tear-drop earrings. The shop is in the house of its owner, Marie Louise Taule, who had a Dominican mother and a French father. In a residential area, the shop is open at regular business hours Monday to Friday (closed weekends).

Novo Atarazana, 21 La Atarazana (tel. 689-0582). Although its name would imply that it's new, this is actually one of the best-established shops in town. Inside you can purchase pieces of amber, black coral, tortoise shell, leather goods, woodcarvings, and even rocking chairs. It's open seven days a week.

Ambar Tres, 3 La Atarazana (tel. 688-0474), lies in the colonial section of the old city. This shop sells jewelry made from coconut shells, cow-horn earrings, mahogany carvings, watercolors, oil paintings, and tortoise shell. The shop is open seven days a week, but it closes at noon on Sunday.

Galería de Arte Nader, 9 La Atarazana (tel. 688-0969), in the center of the most historical section of town, is a well-known gallery that sells so many Dominican and Haitian paintings that they're sometimes stacked in rows against the walls. There's an ancient courtyard in back if you want a glimpse of how things looked in the Spanish colonies hundreds of years ago. The gallery is open daily except Sunday from 10 a.m. to 1 p.m. and 4 to 7 p.m.

The **Plaza Criolla** is a modern shopping complex, with a distinguished design theme. A complex of shops is set in gardens with tropical shrubbery and flowers, facing the Olympic Center on 27 de Febrero. The architecture makes generous use of natural woods, and a covered wooden walkway links the stalls together.

NIGHTLIFE: From a hectic night of merengue to gambling casinos to disco dancing, Santo Domingo has some of the most varied nightlife in the Caribbean.

Nightclubs

Meson de la Cava, Avenida Mirador del Sur (tel. 533-2818), is a charming restaurant and nightclub built in a natural cave 50 feet under the ground, providing live music for dancing. Shows with merengue music are offered. To reach it, you descend a perilous open-backed iron stairway. At first I thought this was a mere gimmicky club until I sampled the food, finding it among the best in the capital. Waiters bring in one good-tasting platter after another, placing them on your table perched under stalagmites and stalactites if you've been sent to the grottoes. For an appetizer you're faced with the usual selection—shrimp cocktail, onion soup, or gazpacho. Instead of those, however, you may go for the bisque of seafood or red snapper chowder. Among the main-course selections, you'll find "gourmet" beefsteak, fresh seabass in red sauce, tournedos, and coq au vin. You can finish off with a sorbet. Meals begin at RD $40 ($14) per person, plus the cost of your drinks. Hot food is served daily from noon to 4 p.m. and 6 p.m. to midnight. If you go just for the music and dancing, and many do, you'll be charged an entrance fee of RD $3 ($1) per person. After midnight, the waiters present a show of their own. The place is open every day.

José, 555 Avenida George Washington (tel. 688-8242), is one of the leading nightclubs in town, costing from RD $10 ($3.50) to enter. A different show (usually Vegas style) is presented at 9:30 and 11:30 p.m. and again at 2:30 a.m. There is music for disco dancing when the show isn't on. The club closes at 5 a.m., and is also closed on Tuesday.

Pubs and Bars

Two of the leading rendezvous points of Santo Domingo are close to one another, in the oldest section of the city. The **Village Pub,** 350 Calle Hostos (tel. 689-5408), is my favorite nightlife spot in town, and if you appreciate lively places, you may like it too. At this sprawling complex, you can talk quietly in the tropical garden below one of the soaring trees or enjoy watching the oversize video screen where films of the world's greatest rock stars compete for attention with the crowds jostling at the stand-up bar. Just off the entrance vestibule you'll discover what looks like someone's elegant private living room, complete with unusual busts and old musical instruments. The place is open daily from 5 p.m. Most drinks cost around $2.50.

When you're ready for a change, you can drop into **Raffles,** next door at 352 Calle Hostos. You'll be greeted by a John Lennon collage near the entrance. You may have to hunt around for a table somewhere in the series of high-ceilinged Spanish-style rooms with heavy beams, masses of plants, soothing candlelight, dimly lit Indian art, and textured baskets hanging beneath staircases leading to nowhere. Any lone woman who ventures in here will probably be approached whether she's looking for it or not. The bar opens at 7 p.m. daily except Sunday. You'll pay $2.50 for most drinks.

Piano Bars

Most of the "chic stops" are in the big hotels. **Las Palmas,** at the Hotel Santo Domingo, Avenida Independencia (tel. 532-1511), was decorated by the country's best-known designer, Oscar de la Renta. Under a high-vaulted ceiling, mirrored walls are painted with palm fronds. This is the best piano bar in town. A terrace, open to the sea, adjoins the bar. Music starts at 6 p.m., the "happy hour," when hors d'oeuvres are free. Romantic music is often played, and you can hear, on occasion, jazz, samba, and the bossa nova. Dancing music is played on certain nights. There is never a cover charge, and hard liquor costs from RD $7.50 ($2.65). Waitresses wear Dominican colonial dress.

The **Fontana Bar** of El Embajador hotel, Avenida Sarasota (tel. 533-2131), is a place to enjoy good music whether it's by the piano player and vocalist early in the evening or the orchestra later, with a variety of tunes for listening or dancing. The rhythms range from Dominican folk songs to samba to the highly popular merengue. The bar, which faces the front door of the hotel's lobby, is inviting, with rattan chairs and wooden tables, plus cozy candlelit corners in the evening. The Fontana also looks out on a patio leading to a swimming pool. Drinks cost from RD $8 ($2.80).

Disco Action

Disco-hopping in the Dominican Republic is an after-dinner ritual, although many couples postpone their almost-obligatory visits until after the end of a movie or whatever. At that time, even the most dedicated career woman may don sequins and other alluring garments for an evening out at such places as—

The **Neon Discothèque,** Hotel Santo Domingo North/Hispaniola, Avenida Independencia (tel. 533-7111), is one of the town's best-established discos. It offers Latin jazz with different guest stars each week, although disco dancing under flashing lights is one of the main reasons for its popularity. The clientele tends to be somewhat formal compared to that of other nightclubs of Santo Domingo. For example, men should wear jackets. You might see Oscar de la Renta and some of his friends among the well-dressed patrons, most of whom seem to be over 30. The decor is done in purple, blue, and red, contributing a colorful note to the sensuous merengue music and dancing. The Neon has a cover charge of around RD $9 ($3.15) on weekends, RD $7 ($2.45) the rest of the week. The place is closed on Monday. Otherwise, it opens at 8 a.m. and stays open until very late, depending on the crowd.

The **Omni Disco** at the Sheraton Santo Domingo, 365 Avenida George Washington (tel. 685-5151), is popular with tourists and some of the sons and daughters of the country's most prestigious families, who come here to drink and dance. The setting is plush. The cover charge is RD $5 ($1.75) on weeknights, rising to RD $15 ($5.25) on weekends. Drinks cost from RD $8 ($2.80). The club opens at 8 p.m. and stays so until 2 a.m., perhaps later, depending on the crowd.

L'Azotea, Dominican Concorde Hotel, Avenida Anacaona, Mirador del Sur (tel. 532-2531), has the most dramatic premises of any disco in town. On the top floor of this first-class hotel, it is one of the most attractive after-dark rendezvous points in Santo Domingo, with stunning views. Occasionally, live entertainment is featured, and there is always recorded music. The entrance ranges from RD $2 (70¢) to RD $10 ($3.50), depending on what act is booked. The club is open nightly except on Monday and Tuesday from 9 p.m. to 1 a.m.

Casinos

Santo Domingo has several major gambling casinos. The largest is **El Embadajor Casino,** Avenida Sarasota (tel. 533-2131), where you'll hear the whirr and clicks from the gaming tables. The popular games of blackjack, craps, and roulette are offered from 3 p.m. to 4 a.m. In between gaming sessions, you can spend an intimate moment at La Fontana, their casual bar where hors d'oeuvres are served.

Hotel Naco Casino, 22 Avenida Tiradentes (tel. 562-6191), also offers roulette, craps, and blackjack. The doors open at 4 p.m., shutting again at 4 a.m.

One of the most stylish casinos is at the Sheraton Santo Domingo, 365 Avenida George Washington (tel. 685-5151). Called the **Omni Casino,** it has a bilingual staff offering blackjack, craps, baccarat, and keno, among other popular games. It's open daily from 3 p.m. to 4 a.m., and players get free cigarettes and drinks.

Yet another casino, a bit far from the heart of the city for my taste, is the **Dominican Concorde Casino,** Avenida Anacaona, Mirador del Sur (tel. 532-2531), which is about half an hour's drive from the airport, bordering the Paseo de los Indios. If you're a high roller, you'll find that it has the highest limits in the city. The most popular games are wheel of fortune and keno, along with blackjack, baccarat, and roulette.

5. East to La Romana

On the southeast coast of the Dominican Republic, about a two-hour drive east of Santo Domingo, lies this rich sugarcane and cattle-raising country that was turned into a tropical paradise resort of refinement and luxury living by Gulf + Western (which later sold it). A typical Dominican town, La Romana itself contains one of the largest sugar mills in the world.

THE ULTIMATE RESORT: Translated as "House in the Country," **Casa de Campo** (tel. 682-2111, or toll free 800/223-6620; in Florida, 305/856-5405 collect) offers the greatest resort in the entire Caribbean area—and the competition is stiff. It brings a whole new dimension to a holiday. Gulf + Western took a vast hunk of coastal land, more than 7,000 acres in all, allowing enough breathing space for everyone, and carved out this stunningly chic resort, which today is operated by Premier Hotels. The hotel attracts many celebrities as well as titans of industry. Some have built private homes on the grounds, including Oscar de la Renta. The ubiquitous Miami architect, William Cox, helped create it, and de la Renta provided the style and flair in some of the interiors, even designing the long, white flowing gowns, with pink bows and turbans, the waitresses wear when they serve you a piña colada. Most of the buildings are one or two stories high, and they never go beyond three. Built of native stone, they are finished in stucco, with red corrugated roofs and local mahogany. Tiles, Dominican paintings, and louvered doors, as well as those flamboyant de la Renta patterned fabrics, characterize most of the interiors. The main buildings form a network, constructed of native-grown unpainted wood, each connected by walkways and sheltered by roofs, a combination of naturalism and the late Frank Lloyd Wright. Gardens blossom with flowering shrubbery and scenic vistas confront you in every direction.

Red-roofed casitas are two-story structures around the main building, and these are the least expensive accommodations. *In summer, charges are only $95 to $110, based on either single or double occupancy. Suites rent from $145 up.* In the high season these same accommodations rent for $170 to $190, either single or double occupancy, and from $305 in a suite. Villas cluster along the golf course, using the broad Bermuda fairways as common lawns; and there are more villas built along the sea. The tennis village cluster of villas at **La Terraza** is perched high on the hills, looking out across the cane, fairway, and meadows to the Caribbean. Villas, furnished with a kind of rustic Dominican elegance, come with bath and shower, a large living room, kitchen, refrigerator, and balcony. Mr. Cox designed each villa so that it offers either a private terrace or veranda overlooking some land or sea vista. *In summer, a two-bedroom villa for four rents for $160.* In winter, these golf and tennis villas go up in price, costing from $400 for one bedroom.

At the core of everything is a wonderland swimming pool—three, in fact—each on a different level, with thatch huts on stilts to provide beverages and light meals. Perched over the pool is La Caña, the two-level bar and lounge, with a thatched roof but no walls. Dinner is on a rustic roofed terrace. The food is among the best in the

Dominican Republic, and the chefs always make it interesting. Perhaps they'll throw a roast suckling pig barbecue right on the beach. Most of the beef used is grown right on the plains of La Romana.

Dining at Casa de Campo

To reach any of the dining spots recommended below by telephone, call the Casa de Campo resort complex number, 682-2111, and then the four-digit extension number given for each of the restaurants listed.

Tropicana (ext. 3000) is the most glamorous restaurant at the complex. It's a breeze-filled pavilion known for its innovative seafood market, where diners leave their tables to browse through some of the freshest seafood in the region. Displayed on ice near sizzling woks and smoking grills, the offerings are described by a polite maître d'. Any one of 20 or so spices can be used in the way you decide. When I was last there, I ordered a steak of seabass sautéed in garlic, and it was superb. Other choices depend on whatever was fresh at the sea market. Lobster and giant shrimps are always available. Your meal might begin with selections from a salad bar whose ingredients are displayed beneath the dragon-shaped prow of a fantasy version of a war canoe. If you prefer meat or chicken, a mouthwatering choice of tempura, Szechuan, and Polynesian specialties are offered. Full meals cost from RD $110 ($38.50) and are served daily from 7 to 11 p.m. Reservations are necessary.

El Patio (ext. 2265). Originally designed as a disco, this high-ceilinged room now contains a shield of lattices, banks of plants, checkerboard tablecloths, and a pleasantly familiar battalion of enthusiastic waiters. Technically, its format is that of a glamorized coffeeshop, but you can order some substantial platters from a list of daily specials. Full meals, costing from RD $35 ($12.25), include ceviche, Cuban-style black-bean soup, sandwiches, salad bowls, sirloin steaks, and several pasta dishes. Full meals are served from 6 a.m. to midnight daily.

Lago Grill (ext. 2266). Whether or not you enjoy its favors later in the day, this place is ideal for breakfast. It has one of the best-stocked morning buffets in the country. It's so popular that residents of the resort's dozens of secluded villas sometimes break their self-imposed code of privacy to come here to sample its offerings. Your view is of a lake, a sloping meadow, and the resort's private airport, with the sea in the distance. Serve yourself from a fresh juice bar, where a Dominican employee in colonial costume will extract juices from one of 25 different tropical fruits in any combination you prefer. Then select your ingredients for an omelet from several overflowing bowls, give them to a man in a toque, and he'll whip them into an omelet as you wait. The fixed-price breakfast costs RD $22 ($7.70), and is served daily from 7 to 11 a.m. Lunch is from noon to 3 p.m., costs RD $28 ($9.80), and includes sandwiches, burgers, sancocho (the famous Dominican stew), and fresh conch chowder, along with cold avocado soup in a half pineapple. There is also a well-stocked salad bar.

SPORTS: At La Romana, on 7,000 acres of lush tropical turf, you'll find two Pete Dye golf courses, a stable of horses with twice-weekly polo, a private marina with deep-sea and river trips, snorkeling on live reefs, skeet and trap ranges, plus 17 tennis courts.

Golf

The **Casa de Campo** courses are known to dedicated golfers everywhere—in fact, *Golf* magazine called it "the finest golf resort in the world." The course, Teeth of the Dog, has also been called "a thing of almighty beauty," and it is. The site of the "Eisenhower Cup" World Amateur Tournament in 1974, it is a ruggedly natural terrain, with seven holes skirting the ocean. Opened in 1977, the Links is the inland course, built on sandy soil away from the beach. Québec-born Gilles Gagnon, the head golf professional, will answer your questions (call him at 692-6956, ext. 3115). Hours are 7 a.m. to 7 p.m.

Beaches

Bayahibe is a large, palm-fringed sandy crescent reached by a 20-minute launch trip or else by road, a 30-minute drive from La Romana. In addition, **La Minitas** is tiny, but nice, an immaculate little beach and lagoon. Free transportation is by horse-drawn buckboard, leaving from Casa de Campo every hour.

Tennis

A total of 13 clay and four hard-surface courts at Casa de Campo, the best on the island, are lit for night play. Tennis pro Paco Hernandez of Beverly Hills and his assistant, Emilio Vasquez, are available for lessons and frequently arrange some of the biggest tennis tournaments in the Caribbean. The courts are available seven days a week from 8 a.m. to 10 p.m., and an hour of daylight net time costs RD $35 ($12.25), while 60 minutes of nighttime play is RD $45 ($15.75).

Water Sports and Fishing

The **Casa de Campo Yachting and Beach Club** (tel. 682-2111) is one of the most complete water-sports facilities anywhere in the Dominican Republic. Reservations and information on any seaside activity can be arranged through the resort's concierge. A sampling of what's available includes the following:

You can charter a boat for a cruise to snorkel or go deep-sea fishing. The resort maintains eight charter vessels, with a minimum of eight persons required per outing. Only four can fish at a time. A half-day cruise costs RD $750 ($262.50); a full day, RD $1,050 ($367.50).

Patrons interested in river fishing on the Chavón can arrange trips there through the hotel as well. Some of the biggest snook ever recorded have been caught here. Half-day trips, lasting from 8 a.m. to noon or noon to 4 p.m., cost RD $50 ($17.50) per person. This is a more private form of activity, as only two persons are permitted in any single boat.

If you only want a look at the famous river which gave Altos de Chavón its name, Casa de Campo arranges river tours from 5 to 7 p.m. daily, costing RD $55 ($19.25) per person. Each boat holds a maximum of four.

If all you're looking for is a secluded beach with everything from palm trees to sailboats for rent, you'll appreciate the club's Minitas Beach, where the following rental items are available: snorkeling gear, sunfloats, canoe, Sunfish sailboats, windsurfers, and Hobie Cats. Windsurfing costs RD $30 ($10.50), and snorkeling is RD $750 ($2.65) per hour. Sunfish and paddleboats can be rented for anywhere from RD $40 ($14) to RD $50 ($21) per hour. The center can be reached by calling extension 2293, and it's open from 9 a.m. to 5 p.m. daily. The resort offers free transportation to the beach by horse-drawn buckboard every hour.

There are no on-site arrangements for scuba-diving, but the hotel will put interested clients in touch with a nearby place which leads such trips.

Polo and Horseback Riding

Ever since the grand days when Dominican playboy Porfirio Rubirosa mounted some of the finest horses in the world, the Dominican Republic has prided itself on its prowess as a polo-playing mecca. The Casa de Campo has always prided itself on the polo traditions it has kept alive since it was first established. For many years the resort employed a nephew of the Maharajah of Jodhpur, Jabar Singh, whose pupils included Ramfis Trujillo, son of the former dictator.

Today the Casa de Campo is the best place in the Caribbean for playing, learning, and watching the fabled sport of kings and princes. On the premises are two full-size polo fields, a polo-pony breeding farm, and scores of polo ponies, as well as a small army of veterinarians, grooms, and polo-related employees. If during your visit you hear that a polo match will be played, by all means go.

The man who spearheads this reverence for polo-related traditions is a former brigadier-general in the British army, Arthur Douglas-Nugent. Rarely will a man combine sophisticated charm and polo-playing skill the way Mr. Douglas-Nugent does, attracting devotees from South and North America and Europe. As equally gifted at the social arts is Mr. Douglas-Nugent's charming and stylish wife, Diana.

Most serious polo players arrive with their own equipment, but beginners learn by watching more experienced players and participating in trail rides (which last from one to three hours), as well as riding lessons at the resort's dude ranch. These cost RD $40 ($14) each.

Fitness Center

The Casa de Campo operates one of the most complete fitness centers in the country. It also has one of the very few squash courts in the Dominican Republic, costing RD $30 ($10.50) per hour. Aerobics sessions cost RD $5 ($1.75) per class, and there is also a collection of weights and exercise machines which are free. A whirlpool and sauna bath costs RD $25 ($8.75) for 30 minutes. The place is best known for its masseuses, who will massage away your tensions for RD $40 ($14) an hour.

ALTOS DE CHAVÓN: Again under the daring guiding eye—and purse—of Gulf +

Western, an international arts center known as Altos de Chavón was created at a point six miles from La Romana and three miles east of Casa de Campo. At the edge of its acreage, on the high banks of the Chavón River, an entire hamlet was built to house artisans, both local and international, who come here on a rotating basis, teaching sculpture, pottery, silkscreen printing, weaving, dance, and music, among other artistic pursuits.

Here they can work in their craft shops and display their finished wares for sale. The construction was under the energetic guidance of an Italian builder, who was seemingly inspired by a hill town in the Tuscan countryside. He did a stunning job of creating an old-world village. To many, the village already looks as if it has stood there for centuries. It almost suggests a Hollywood movie set, except that everything here is real.

In the center is the red-tile Church of St. Stanislaus. Surrounding it are "old" houses, along with restaurants on the main plaza, an inn, and other buildings, all overlooking the valley with its river. Arcaded shops sell merchandise, and stairways lead to studio apartments for the artisans and their private loggias.

Frank Sinatra inaugurated the 5,000-seat auditorium, an ampitheater modeled after the Greek antiquity at Epidaurus. Local and international artists appear here frequently. "Sunset performances" are usually on Friday and Sunday evening.

In addition, the museum, **Museo Arqueologico Regional,** open from 9 a.m. to 9 p.m., is devoted to the legacy of the vanished Taíno Indian, displaying artifacts found along the banks of the river.

A narrow walk leads down over a small arched bridge, wending its way to the river below. Before you arrive at the village, there's a large parking area. A bus runs between the Casa de Campo and Altos de Chavón every hour.

Accomplished professional artists compete for 20 three-month residencies here each year. Representing many countries and artistic disciplines, the residents live and work in the village and hold exhibitions throughout the year.

Where to Stay

La Posada (tel. 682-9656, ext. 2312) is a charming, ten-room, regional-style inn, evoking something that might have been known to El Greco in Toledo, but with far more refined touches, including modern plumbing facilities. The air-conditioned inn has rustic stucco and massive ceiling beams. The location is near a parapet overlooking the gorge. It might be hard to get in here, as many artisans like to book these accommodations, so reservations are absolutely essential. *Summer tariffs are only $60 daily for a room, either single or double occupancy.* This rate rises in winter to $120 daily, either single or double occupancy. For your dining, you have a choice of all the little restaurants in Altos de Chavón (see below).

Where to Dine

Casa del Río (tel. 682-1596) is the most glamorous and interesting restaurant at Altos de Chavón. It occupies the basement of a re-creation of an Iberian house whose towers, turrets, tiles, and massive stairs are gracefully entwined with strands of bougainvillea. Inside, artfully textured brick arches support oversize chandeliers, suspended racing sculls, and wine racks filled with bottles of champagne. Music from the kind of strolling minstrel you'd expect to find in Budapest might accompany your meal. This could include such nouvelle cuisine specialties as sautéed shrimp with an orange-and-pistachio sauce, a red-beet taglionlini, duck soup laced with vodka and broccoli ravioli, red snapper in pink peppercorn sauce, duckling in bourbon (with pine nuts, zucchini, and prunes), or perhaps veal medallions in a walnut cream sauce or a ragoût of lobster in dill sauce. Dessert might be a chocolate mousse with green figs and blueberry sauce or a soufflé du jour. Full meals cost from RD $100 ($35) and are served only at dinner after 7 p.m. Reservations are essential.

La Piazzetta (tel. 682-1239) snuggles happily within the 16th-century-style "village" set high above the Chavón River. Well-prepared Italian dinners are served here. The decor is regional, with colorful tiles, high ceilings, and timbers. You might begin with an antipasto misto, following with filet of seabass pizzaiola or rib steak in the Florentine style. Chicken saltimbocca, with sage and prosciutto, is also popular. Your fellow diners are likely to be guests from the deluxe Casa de Campo nearby, enjoying a respite from living in Eden. You'll spend $25 and up for dinner, but this tab could rise much higher if you order a costly wine. Dinner is served daily except Monday from 7 to 11 p.m.

La Fonda (tel. 682-2111, ext. 2350) styles its cookery as "Créole," but what you get is a lovely array of some Dominican dishes not readily available in most of the major resort hotels. By that, I don't mean just rice-and-bean dishes either. Beef and fresh seafood appear regularly on the menu, and vegetables are interesting, including, when available, fried cazabe (a kind of bread made of a root called yuca). Count yourself lucky if you're here on a night the chef prepares sancocho, a thick goat stew, the national dish of the Dominican Republic. You can also order lobster Dominican style and conch Créole. Or perhaps you'd prefer seabass in coconut sauce, filet medallions in Créole sauce, shrimp in Dominican sauce, or grilled chicken, all served with vegetables. Fixed-price meals cost $8 and $12.65, and include salad, dessert, coffee, and a glass of wine, beer, rum, or soft drinks. The decor is regional, including examples of Dominican pottery. There are ceiling fans and stucco walls, and dining is partially al fresco. À la carte, depending on what you order of course, dinner will likely begin at $12, going up to around $22 with wine. La Fonda serves daily except Monday from 11 a.m. to 11 p.m.

Café de Sol (tel. 682-2346). If you want a refreshing snack after your exploration of the mosaic-dotted plaza near the church, you'll probably enjoy this stone-floored indoor/outdoor café. To reach it, you climb a graciously proportioned flight of exterior stone steps to the rooftop of a building whose ground floor houses a jewelry shop. This is the only true outdoor café in the village, and it's so popular that you may encounter most of the executive staff and many of the artists and students who make Altos de Chavón a full-time residence. The outdoor area is ringed with flowers, shaded with an arbor, and accented with unusual masonry that merits a close examination. Open from

7 a.m. to 9:30 p.m., the café serves simple and appetizing meals with warm-weather specialties including two kinds of salad, croissant sandwiches, three kinds of pizza, Texas-style chili, and burgers. Meals cost from RD $25 ($8.75).

El Sombrero (tel. 682-2353) occupies a thick-walled colonial-style building whose jutting hand-hewn timbers and roughly textured plaster evoke a corner of old Mexico. There's a scattering of dark, heavy furniture and an occasional genuine antique, but the main allure comes from the friendly service and spicy Mexican cuisine. Most guests dine outside on the covered patio, within earshot of a group of wandering minstrels whose sombreros accentuate their romantic lyrics. A marguerita, laced with salt and tequila, is an appropriate accompaniment to the tortillas, nachos, enchiladas, and burritos that are the house specialties. Grilled steaks and brochettes are also popular. Full meals cost from RD $45 ($15.75) and are served at dinner only, every night of the week between 7 and 11 p.m. Because of its popularity, reservations are a good idea.

Shopping

Oscar de la Renta/Freya Boutique (tel. 565-6300, ext. 2359). Other than an outlet in Miami, this boutique is reputed to sell the creations of Sr. de la Renta less expensively than anywhere else. Some dresses begin as cheaply as $150, but rise to hundreds of dollars for the more lavish designs. Also for sale is a striking collection of purses and boxes cunningly fashioned from tortoiseshell, bone, and cowhorn. Visitors are welcome daily except Sunday from 10 a.m. to 6 p.m.

Everett Designs (tel. 682-2331). Its designs are so original that many visitors mistake this place for a museum. Each piece of jewelry is handcrafted in a minifactory at the rear of the shop. Minnesota-born Bill Everett is the inspirational force for many of these pieces, which include Dominican larimar and amber, hematite from Germany, and polished silver and gold. Prices begin at RD $125 ($43.75). The shop is open from 10 a.m. to 9 p.m. daily.

Bugambilia (tel. 682-2355). A staff of sales clerks will explain the origins of dozens of ceramic figures on display. Sculpted in positions ranging from bearing water to carrying flowers to posing as brides, the female figures are crafted in the industrial city of Santiago as part of a long tradition of presenting peasant women without faces. Look, however, for an expression of dignity in the bodies of the figurines. The largest pieces sell for $60 and are packed but not shipped. The store also has a winning collection of amusingly grotesque papier-mâché carnival masks. It's open daily from 9 a.m. to 9 p.m.

After Dark

Genesis Disco (tel. 682-2340) features just about every kind of music at least once each evening. Clients are wide-ranging in tastes, from the most avant-garde artists to relatively conservative visitors from the corporate world. In any event, if you've always wanted to dance your way through the gamut from rock, blues, salsa, merengue, to a good dose of romantic "music for lovers," this is the place for you. The illuminated and translucent dance floor is studded with multicolored pieces of coral. Open at 9 each night, the disco levies a cover charge ranging from RD $8 ($2.80) to RD $12 ($4.20). It is closed on Sunday in summer.

Legends (Bill's Bar) (tel. 682-2380). To the right of the cathedral (as you face its front entrance), this is the premier gathering place for the assembled artists, masons, literati, and students of Altos de Chavón. Owned and managed by American-born Bill Bakas, it's an alluringly simple milieu of framed art posters, exposed wood, and animated conversation. Only drinks are served, averaging RD $6 ($2.10). The bar is open seven days a week between 4 p.m. and 2 a.m. (and often much later).

PUNTA CAÑA: At the far eastern tip of the island of Hispaniola, this Club Med opened in 1981. The village lies along a reef-protected white beach, said to have some of the best diving areas in the island. It was here that the crews of the *Pinta, Niña,* and *Santa Maria* put ashore. The crew of Columbus wouldn't recognize the place. Some 600 rooms fill three-story clusters of bungalows strung along the beach. Units contain twin beds and open either on the sea or onto a coconut grove. Each is air-conditioned with red-tile floors and a private shower/bathroom. Rates vary throughout the year, and there's a $25 membership fee that must be paid if you haven't joined before. Club Med–Punta Caña offers direct air service via Presidential/Key Airlines into the Punta Caña Airport, five minutes from the village. Land and air packages utilizing this service depart from Boston, New York, Atlanta, Washington, D.C., Chicago, Detroit, Houston, and Miami. All flights connect in Miami with the club's flight on a British Aerospace 146 aircraft, to make a 2½-hour trip to Club Med.

Depending on the week selected, the combined land-and-air package—per person per week—is $799 to $1,340 from New York; $799 to $1,285 from Miami; $920 to $1,390 from Boston, Washington, and Atlanta; $899 to $1,390 from Chicago; $1,005 to $1,475 from Houston; and $990 to $1,390 from Detroit. The land/air package includes air fare, transfers, double-occupancy accommodations, meals (all you can eat), use of sports facilities, and nightly entertainment. The land-only cost for one week is $450 to $920 per person. *Warning:* Tariffs go up during the Christmas and New Year's weeks. During Christmas and New Year's, when air space is the tightest, Club Med (at least in the past) has had its own charter flights to Punta Caña. *Rates in summer, including air fare, are around $799 to $910 per week for everything.*

Sports include sailing, windsurfing, snorkeling, waterskiing, swimming, archery, and tennis on ten courts (four of which are lit for night games). You get the usual Club Med activities: picnics, boat rides, nightly dancing, shows, and optional excursions. There's even a computer workshop with 14 Atari computers. Activities spin around a combined dining room/bar/dance floor and theater complex facing the sea in the center of the village. In front of this beehive of activity is a big swimming pool; a small restaurant and disco, nearby, are built beside the sea. Club Med–Punta Caña has a Mini-Club for juniors, highlighting circus training, computer workshops, and other activities. This is a separate area in the village with activities from 9 a.m. to 9 p.m. for the younger set, plus supervised lunches and dinners.

For reservations and information in New York, call 212/750-1670; otherwise, dial toll free 800/CLUB-MED nationwide.

6. North to Puerto Plata

Originally it was Columbus's intention to found America's first city at Puerto Plata, naming it La Isabela. But a tempest detained him, and it wasn't until 1502 that Nicolas de Ovando founded Puerto Plata, or "port of silver," lying 130 miles northwest of Santo Domingo. The port in time became the last stop for ships going back to Europe, their holds laden with treasures taken from the New World.

From Santo Domingo, the 3½-hour drive directly north passes through the lush Cibao Valley, home of the tobacco industry and Bermudez rum. You pass through Santiago, the second-largest city in the country, 90 miles north of Santo Domingo. The longest airport landing strip in the Dominican Republic is in operation at Puerto Plata. Most of the hotels are not in Puerto Plata itself but in a special tourist zone called **Playa Dorada.** The airport is actually not in Puerto Plata but lies east of Playa Dorada on the road to Sosua.

Puerto Plata shows signs of offering a broad-based appeal to a market which may shun more expensive resorts, with some hotels boasting a nearly full occupancy rate almost all year. It is already casting a shadow on business at longer-established resorts throughout the Caribbean, especially in Puerto Rico.

The backers of this sun-drenched spot have poured vast amounts of money into a flat area between a pond and the curved and verdant shoreline. Major hotels have been constructed, as well as a scattering of secluded condominiums and villas and a Robert Trent Jones–designed golf course, plus a riding stable with a complement of horses for each of the major properties.

Fort San Felipe, considered to be the oldest fort in the New World, is a popular attraction. Philip II of Spain ordered its construction in 1564, a task that took 33 years to complete. Built with eight-foot-thick walls, the fort was virtually impenetrable, and the moat surrounding it was treacherous. The Spaniards sharpened swords and embedded them in coral below the surface of the water to discourage use of the moat for entrance or exit purposes. The doors of the fort are only four feet high, another deterrent to swift passage. During Trujillo's rule Fort San Felipe was used as a prison. Standing at the end of the Malecón, the fort was restored in the early 1970s. On cruise-ship days, usually Tuesday and Thursday, it's likely to be overcrowded. The entrance fee is RD $1 (35¢).

Isabel de Torres, a tower with a fort built when Trujillo was in power, affords a magnificent view of the Amber Coast from a point near the top, 2,565 feet above sea level. You reach the observation point by cable car *(teleférico)*, a seven-minute ascent. Once there, you are also treated to seven square acres of botanical gardens. The round trip costs RD $2 (70¢). The aerial ride is operated daily except Monday and Wednesday from 8 a.m. to 6 p.m. Be warned: There is often a long wait in line for the cable car.

You can see a fascinating collection of rare amber specimens at the **Museum of Dominican Amber,** 61 Duarte St. (tel. 586-2848), owned and operated by Didi and Aldo Costa. The museum, open Monday to Saturday from 9 a.m. to 5 p.m., is near Puerto Plata's Central Park. Guided tours in English are offered. Admission is $1.

GETTING AROUND: If you prefer to be free to come and go as you wish, you may choose to rent a **car.** For information on this, see the discussion of car rentals in the Santo Domingo introduction. You might even find that a **motor scooter** will be suitable for transportation in Puerto Plata or Sosua.

If you take a **taxi,** make an agreement with the driver on the fare before your trip starts, as the vehicles are not metered. You'll find taxis in Central Park. At night it's wise to establish your cab ride on a round-trip basis. If you go in the daytime by taxi to any of the other beach resorts or villages, check on reserving a vehicle for your return trip.

For a much cheaper ride, take a **público,** a multipassenger taxi that travels on the main road. If you take one from Central Park, be sure it's really a público and not a regular taxi. You can also flag down these vehicles on the highway, but you have to wave at all cars as the públicos are not designated on the outside. If it is one, and has room for another passenger, it will stop for you.

Guaguas are public buses which you can take to the gate of Playa Dorada about every 20 minutes as well as to other destinations in the area. You can catch a guagua on the main street corners in Puerto Plata, a ride costing less than 10¢. Buses run from 7 a.m. to 7 p.m. daily.

WHERE TO STAY: The combined Aztec and Moorish design of **Eurotel,** P.O. Box 337, Playa Dorada (tel. 586-3663), makes this property the most imaginative and stylish on the coast. It sits on a flat, sun-washed plot of land in the hotel zone, amid a garden of flowering plants, flagstone walkways, and a roughly textured rock wall from which a dozen artificial springs send cascades of water into a contemplative pool. Under the soaring ceiling of the open-sided reception area, you'll find a stage setting combining decorative elements from Europe, Africa, and South America. Each of the outbuildings is dotted with repetitively rhythmic triangular roofs which, when combined with the citrus-inspired colors, give a futuristic twist to the breezy colonial theme. Each of the comfortable and stylish bedrooms has its own Spanish-style *mira-*

dor (sheltered balcony) and the aura of a comfortable private apartment. Outside, if you follow the swiftly flowing tropical stream (which empties the pool), you reach a palm-thatched beachside entertainment center with its own bubbling whirlpool, an offering of water sports, a music platform for live entertainment, and a cluster of dining and drinking facilities. Depending on the accommodation, winter rates run from $100 in a single, from $110 in a double. *In summer, tariffs are reduced to $50 in a single, from $60 in a double.*

Playa Dorada Hotel, P.O. Box 272 (tel. 586-3988), a dramatically designed Holiday Inn, set new standards for the Puerto Plata community when it opened in 1983. It is one of the few hotels in all the Caribbean which can boast nearly full occupancy during most of the year. The resort is designed in a style that might be called "Aztec Modern," arranged in massive blocks of coral-colored stucco, some with angled walls, soaring stairways, and greenery where the outdoors frequently blends pleasingly with the interior. It offers one of the biggest swimming pools in Puerto Plata, around which the hotel management hosts barbecues, buffet suppers, and weekly entertainment which includes singers and dancers known throughout the Spanish-speaking world. The reception area is an air-conditioned oasis of Victorian-style latticework set whimsically beneath the soaring ceiling.

The 253 bedrooms are arranged along rambling corridors which, at the end of a long day on the beach, may seem almost endless. Once you reach your room, however, you'll enjoy well-upholstered surroundings with up-to-date colors. More than two-thirds of the hotel's units are set into red-roofed wings which face the sands of the 1½-mile beach. Not including taxes and service, winter single rates run $115 to $135 daily; doubles, from $130 to $150. *In summer, a single ranges from $65 to $85; a double, from $75 to $95.* MAP is available for an additional $23 per person per day. A sports package is included in all tariffs. The hotel also has specially designed rooms for handicapped patrons.

In addition to La Palma restaurant and the many bars and entertainment facilities, guests have access to a full range of boating, water sports, and golf activities (see "Sports," below). Three tennis courts are lit for night games. There's a cocktail lounge, Las Olas, where live entertainment is presented every night, as well as one of the hottest discos in town on the premises. Among the amenities are a babysitting service, laundry and valet service, and video movies. Resident manager Manuel Domenech is excellent as master of ceremonies at his weekly entertainment extravaganzas.

Puerto Plata Beach Club, Malecón (tel. 586-4243), stands on the most remote stretch of the seaside promenade which local residents call the Malecón, behind a high wall and a security guard who protects the gardens. Accommodations lie within a series of neo-Moorish, neo-Victorian buildings which cluster at the edges of a well-planted courtyard filled with gazebos and flowering plants. In winter, singles or doubles cost $95 to $125 per night. *In summer, tariffs are $60 to $90 for singles or doubles,* plus service and taxes. Children under 12 stay free in their parents' room. The establishment's social center is within the sheltering wings of a semi-secluded pool area. There, a two-story building, ringed with elaborate gingerbread and glistening lattices, serves drinks and meals, as well as showcases the live musicians who sometimes perform after dinner. On the premises are two restaurants, a poolside grill, and a cafeteria.

Montemar, Avenida Circunvalación del Norte, P.O. Box 382 (tel. 586-2800), is a glistening hotel complex that plays a double role: it's one of the pioneer resorts in the area, and it houses the local hotel school. Its buff-colored stucco façade is pierced by rows of brick-lined windows angled to catch the sunlight. Near Long Beach, the Montemar's rear entrance faces a copy of Michelangelo's *David,* set near the popular beach filled with residents of the town. The lobby is one of the most distinctive in the area. Enormous bamboo chandeliers illuminate the upholstery, where images of birds flit across the comfortable couches and the naturalistic mural behind the reception desk. Your needs will be cared for by a battalion of students. A lounge nearby engages a merengue band which plays every night beside the illuminated palms. The hotel offers a total of 96 attractively decorated units, most with views of palms and the sea, and all with fresh colors and plush fabrics. *During low season, single rooms cost RD $67 ($23.50), while doubles rent for RD $79 ($27.75).* Rates in winter range from RD $90 ($31.50) in a single and from RD $100 ($35) in a double. The on-the-premises restaurant, La Isabella (see my dining recommendation) is one of the best decorated and most sophisticated restaurants in town. There are three tennis courts in the hotel complex.

The **Villas Doradas,** Playa Dorada (tel. 586-3000), is a pleasant collection of town houses arranged in landscaped clusters, usually around a courtyard. There's no beachfront here. Rather, part of your experience will be almost a community feeling, with neighbors all around in the groups of small villages set up around a series of green areas. The complex is within walking distance of sand beaches and golf facilities. A focal point of the resort is the restaurant, Las Garzas, where a musical trio entertains guests every evening beneath the soaring pine ceiling. The management also features barbecues around the kidney-shaped pool area, where a net is sometimes set up for volleyball games. Of course, it would be tempting never to leave the shade of the cone-shaped thatch-roofed pool bar, which is one of the most attractive and popular parts of the whole resort.

Many guests choose to cook in their villas for at least part of their daily meals, since kitchenettes are a part of each accommodation. Each unit is pleasantly furnished and attractively unpretentious, with louvered doors and windows to make your temporary home either open or closed to the outside world. There's a TV in each villa. *In summer, singles or doubles cost RD $130 ($45.50), while one-bedroom suites go for RD $180 ($63).* In winter, the prices go up to RD $230 ($80.50) for a single or double, RD $285 ($99.75) in a one-bedroom suite, all rates plus 21% tax.

Jack Tar Village, Playa Dorada (tel. 586-3800, or toll free 800/527-9299). Purchased by an investment group from Texas, this all-inclusive resort may represent the shape of things to come. Set at the edge of the sea and clustered around an L-shaped pool, the facility offers drinks, all meals, most water sports, and entertainment within its compound, so that you need never leave the grounds. In the central, cement-covered core of the resort, you'll find dozens of vacationing adults and children playing shuffleboard, cards, Ping-Pong, or volleyball, or just whiling away the time. If you simply prefer to linger beside one of the indoor/outdoor bars, where everything is free (even cigarettes), you'll have plenty of company. If you're more energetic, many water and land sports are offered, most of them included in the overall price of your accommodation in one of the white-walled villas. The 240 units rent for $150 per person double occupancy in high season, for $180 single occupancy. *In low season, the charge is $128 per person for double occupancy, $160 for single occupancy.* One child age 2 to 12 may stay in the parents' double room for $30 in either season. Four nights a week, dinners are sit-down affairs in the high-ceilinged dining room, with waiter service and frequent musical entertainment. The rest of the time, and often at lunch, meals are buffet style.

When **Dorado Naco,** P.O. Box 162 (tel. 596-2019), was built in 1982, there was only one other hotel in the entire Playa Dorada area. It's designed almost like a suburban apartment complex in the American sunbelt, yet at night when the merengue bands begin, the flavor is wholly Latin. A flight of exterior wooden stairs passes under a portico and into a monochromatic lobby whose soaring ceiling is trussed with laminated pine beams. After registering, you'll be ushered past the poolside bar and restaurant complex, down a series of flowered walkways into one of the 150 units. A wide range of sports and entertainment is available to guests. A beach bar and grill lie a short walk from every room. The hotel has live music every night and live shows Thursday through Sunday. On Wednesday the manager hosts a cocktail party, and on Thursday night there's a beach party, complete with a bonfire, when you can dance on a raised floor. Throughout the week in season, guests find a full range of planned activities emanating from the social director. A nightly buffet is served under a portico near the pool, and à la carte meals are available in a covered dining room. A snackbar also does a brisk business.

Each unit contains comfortable furniture, a kitchen, and a creative arrangement of interior space. Many guests choose to spend some of their evenings *en famille*, cooking at home, although a popular weekly meal plan includes seven breakfasts and four dinners for around $60 in high season. Many of the units are clustered along parapets or around well-planted atriums, and some of the larger ones include duplex floor plans and about as much spacious luxury as a vacationer could hope for. *In summer, the price is $100 in a one-bedroom suite for one to two persons. A one-bedroom penthouse suite, housing up to four persons, costs $130 daily, and a two-bedroom suite, also suitable for four, goes for the same price.* In winter, a one-bedroom suite for one or two persons rents for $140, the cost rising to $190 for up to four persons in either a one-bedroom penthouse suite or a two-bedroom suite.

Costambar Beach Resort, P.O. Box 547 (tel. 586-3828, or 718/507-6770 in New York City), has more land connected to it—almost three square miles—than any other hotel property in the country. The section closest to the beach contains 50 low-lying villas, each pleasantly furnished in summertime colors and functional furniture. Many of the units belong to absentee investors, but the only rental arrangements that the average visitor will make are with the charming Dominican/Yugoslav partnership of Cecilia Ochoa and her husband, Jovan. Each of the 50 villas comes with a kitchenette, daily maid service, and access to the nearby Costambar Country Club. Visitors will find both a supermarket and an 18-hole golf course within easy reach, and there's a freshwater pond nearby. Babysitters are readily available. The various units contain from one to three bedrooms, complete with housekeeping accessories which include linens and kitchen utensils. Daily winter rates range from $66 for a one-bedroom apartment, $110 for a two-bedroom villa, and $135 for a three-bedroom apartment. *Summer prices are $55 in a single, $90 in a double. They also offer special package in summer. Call for the latest quotation.* Government tax and a service charge are not included in the prices. To help assure the tranquility of the guests, there are no phones in any of the units, but calls can be placed and received at the reception area.

WHERE TO DINE: One of the loveliest buildings in downtown Puerto Plata, **Jimmy's,** 72 Calle Beller (tel. 586-4325), is an alluring establishment, serving some of the best food. It lies behind lacy rows of cast-iron balustrades in a century-old building whose thick walls were originally constructed as a private house. Inside, beneath ornate high ceilings, you'll find a neo-Victorian bar filled with hardwoods and tones of pink and mauve, mahogany doors, and leaded-glass windows. Full meals are priced from RD $55 ($19.25) and are served daily between noon and 3 p.m. and between 6:30 and 10:30 p.m. The internationally inspired menu includes lobster "Jimmy's style" which is flambéed at your table with cream sauce, along with such steaks as tournedos, chateaubriand, and filet mignon. The kitchen turns out a delectable version of a local cream of fish soup called sopita, along with several versions of chicken (including one with lemon) and such dramatic desserts as bananas flambé and crêpes suzette.

Valter's, Las Hermanas Mirabel Boulevard (tel. 586-2329). Its low-slung Victorian porch, with its adjacent garden, seems like the ideal place for a romantic candlelit dinner. Built about a century ago as a private home, it has ring-around gingerbread painted in vivid shades of lime green, an oversize veranda laden with dozens of tables, and a neo-Victorian bar occupying a high-ceilinged, sparsely furnished front parlor. Open seven days a week between 11 a.m. and 3 p.m. and 6 and 11 p.m., it serves meals from RD $65 ($22.75). Surf and turf is the house specialty, and you'll also find an array of classic pasta dishes. The owner, Victor Tapparo, is from Vicenza, Italy. Other preparations include chop suey, veal and beef dishes, five different versions of lobster, and grilled shrimp. Reservations are necessary, particularly on weekends when many local residents make dining a special event.

Jade Garden, Villas Doradas, Playa Dorada (tel. 586-3000). Contained on the grounds of the previously recommended Villas Doradas in the hotel zone, this is a high-ceilinged and airily modern restaurant specializing in Chinese food. Amid a decor of large windows, exposed pine, and stone and lacquered-wood tables, you can enjoy a special businessman's lunch for RD $15 ($5.25). Set evening meals for two persons cost between RD $55 ($19.25) and RD $75 ($26.25), with à la carte dinners going for RD $30 ($10.50) per person. Typical menu items include barbecued Peking duck, sautéed diced chicken in chili sauce, whole "beggar's chicken," beef curry rolls, and fried crab claws. The restaurant is open seven days a week from noon to 3 p.m. and 6 to 11 p.m.

Porto Fino, Hermanas Mirabel Boulevard (tel. 586-2858), is a good Italian restaurant just across from the entrance of the Hotel Montemar. You can dine in the bright, lively dining room, which is trimmed in lime green, or in the garden at a secluded table on a covered terrace surrounded by shrubbery. The owner's Italian dishes have made this place popular in the Puerto Plata area. Parmesan breast of chicken, eggplant parmesan, spaghetti, ravioli, and pizzas are served in generous helpings. Expect to pay from RD $25 ($8.75) for a complete meal, although you'll get off much cheaper if you only order pizza. The restaurant is open daily from 11 a.m. to 11 p.m.

Los Pinos Restaurant/Bar La Chispa, Hermanas Mirabel Boulevard (tel. 586-3222). Within the rough-hewn walls of this intimate retreat lies a warmly decorated restaurant created by a pair of expatriate Québecois, Helen Bourke and Monique Leveiller. Styled a bit like something you'd come across in the South Seas, it's a convenient perch for daiquiri drinkers; however, many customers prefer the comfortable banquettes ringing the tables looking out over the forest. You can extend your stay by selecting a dining spot for a leisurely dinner. In clement weather you can choose a chair near the open-air grill, in the shadow of a giant Australian pine. Another option is a seat in the shed-like dining room, where a battalion of polite waiters serve within sight of a sepia-toned collection of antique photographs. Lunch is from noon to 2:30 p.m. and dinner from 5 to 11:30 p.m. Meals, costing from RD $50 ($17.50), include seafood paella, pepper steak, pastas, cream of garlic soup, roast goat, seabass, wine-baked chicken, and grilled lamb chops.

Restaurant La Isabella, Hotel Montemar (tel. 586-2800). Because many of the staff of this restaurant are students at the adjoining hotel school, the service is probably better than at places where the help has become jaded. The decor is one of the most elegant in Puerto Plata. You enter a spacious, split-level room with subtle lighting, where the combined effect is like a page from an avant-garde fashion magazine. The carpets, walls, and upholstery are patterned in muted shades of dusty rose, turquoise, and white, with insertions of chrome at just the right places. One of the focal points is a quilted wall hanging whose patterns emphasize the art nouveau design of curved chairs and table settings. Only dinner is served here, from 7 to 11 p.m., with a polite staff of uniformed waiters looking after you. The food items are likely to change, but throughout the year feature such dishes as a paella for two persons, oysters, veal kidneys Beefeater style, and a chicken suprême in a cream sauce.

Roma II, Beller Street at Emilio Prud'homme (tel. 586-3904). It's an open-air street-corner pavilion, ringed with neo-Victorian gingerbread, where diners can enjoy what might be the best vantage point for the city's sometimes vivid street life. Open daily from 11 a.m. to midnight, it is staffed by an engaging crew of well-mannered young employees, who work hard to converse in English. A specialty is the 13 varieties of pizza beginning at RD $5 ($1.75), including tempting combinations of cheese, shrimp, and garlic. Full meals cost from RD $50 ($17.50), including a full array of seafood such as paella, seafood casserole, several preparations of lobster, seabass, and octopus prepared Créole style or with vinaigrette. Beef dishes include Stroganoff or tenderloin. Only the roar of an occasional motorcycle will drown out the animated chatter of your fellow diners.

WHERE TO SHOP: The best place in town to purchase fairly priced samples of the two stones for which the Dominican Republic is noted is the **Factory Gift Shop,** 23 Duarte St. (tel. 586-3834). Amber from the island's north shore and larimar turquoise from the south shore are sold in a wide and attractive variety, or you can buy black coral, bull's horn, or Dominican pictures. Ramón Ortiz and his pleasant family will show you their workshop, where they polish different grades of their raw material into cunningly shaped figures, representing everything from frogs to rabbits. Some of the rare (and expensive) pieces contain well-preserved insects, and one even has in it a (petrified) lizard. Anything you buy can be mounted in silver or gold. The store is open daily from 8 a.m. to 6 p.m.

Tourist Bazaar Boutique, 61 Calle Duarte (tel. 586-2848), is a neoclassical house sheltering the Amber Museum, but it also contains the densest collection of boutiques in Puerta Plata. Merchandise is literally packed into seven competing establishments. A generous percentage of the paintings is from neighboring Haiti, but the amber, larimar, and mahogany woodcarving are from the Dominican Republic. On the premises is a patio bar. The boutiques are open daily except Sunday between 9 a.m. and 6 p.m.

Centro Artesanal, 3 Calle Kennedy (tel. 586-3724). This is a nonprofit school for the training of future Dominican crafts people, and it's also a promotion center for local crafts and jewelry. Selected student projects are for sale. The establishment is open weekdays from 8 a.m. to noon and 2 to 5 p.m.

SPORTS: Because of the location of Puerto Plata and Playa Dorada on the Atlantic Ocean, this is not the best spot in the Caribbean for water sports. At times, the sea tends to be rough.

Formal training in **scuba-diving and water sports** is therefore underdeveloped in Puerto Plata, requiring many aficionados to search out the facilities in the large resorts. A kiosk at Jack Tar Village (tel. 586-3800, ext. 7700) offers a half-day snorkeling trip for RD $45 ($15.75) per person, scuba-diving for RD $80 ($28) per half day, and deep-sea fishing for $325 for a half day (up to six fishermen at one time). Nonresidents of Jack Tar should phone in advance, because the resort's policy about accepting nonresidents seems to change with the number of clients in residence.

Tennis, on the other hand, is a popular pastime at such hotels as Playa Dorada (tel. 586-3988, ext. 7277), where it costs RD $12 ($4.20) per hour for nonresidents.

Robert Trent Jones, Jr., designed the par-72, 18-hole **Playa Dorada championship golf course** which surrounds the resorts and runs along the coast. Even nongolfers can stop at the clubhouse for a drink or a snack to enjoy the views. Instead of trying to call the course, it's best to make arrangements at the activities desk of your hotel.

You'll find superb **beaches** to the east and west of Puerto Plata. Among the better known are Playa Dorada, Sosua, Long Beach, Cofresi, Jack Tar, and Cabarete.

AFTER DARK: A heavily patronized disco is **Vivaldi's,** corner of Hermanas Mirabel Boulevard and the Malecón (tel. 586-3752). Many non-Dominicans wouldn't think of coming back to Puerto Plata without rendezvousing with their acquaintances here. There's a restaurant on the upper floor, but most of the people who stream in head immediately for the ground-floor disco, where a combination of everything from salsa to reggae to New York City's recent dance releases is played practically all night. The interior is ringed with what you might call wrap-around neon. If you want a breath of cool air, there's a little-used terrace in front. There's a cover charge of RD $5 ($1.75) to RD $10 ($3.50), depending on the night of the week.

The disco at the **Playa Dorada Hotel** is among the most animated nightspots in Puerto Plata. Head for the central core of the hotel on the ground level and pass through the orchid-colored lobby to reach it. The entrance fee is RD $10 ($3.50) on Friday and Saturday night; otherwise it's free. Once inside, you're faced with a dance floor (which is usually packed by the end of the evening) and lots of banquette seating, tiny tables, and flashing lights.

7. Sosua

About 15 miles east of Puerto Plata lies one of the finest beaches in the Dominican Republic, Sosua Beach, a strip of white sand more than half a mile wide in a cove sheltered by coral cliffs. The beach connects two communities, which together make up the town known as Sosua.

At one end of the beach is **El Batey,** an area with quiet residential streets, gardens, restaurants, shops, and hotels that can be visited by those who can tear themselves away from the beach. Real estate transactions have been booming in El Batey and its environs, where many streets have been paved, and fine villas with manicured lawns are maintained by eminent Dominicans.

At the other end of Sosua Beach lies **Los Charamicos,** a sharp contrast to El Batey. Here you'll find tin-roofed shacks, vegetable stands, chickens scrabbling in the rubbish, and warm, friendly people. This community is a typical Latin American village, recognizable through the smells, sights, and sounds in the narrow, rambling streets. All this may be changed even by the time you visit, however, as developers are eyeing the entire Sosua area.

Sosua isn't very old, as history records time. It was founded in 1940 by European Jews seeking refuge from the growing destruction of their race by Adolf Hitler. Trujillo invited 100,000 Jews to settle in his country, where they would escape Nazi terror on a banana plantation. One of the reasons behind the offer was allegedly to "whiten the blood of the islanders." Actually, only 600 or so Jews were allowed to immigrate, and of those, only about a dozen or so remain. However, there are some 20 Jewish families living in Sosua. For the most part they are engaged in the dairy and smoked-meat industry which the refugees began during the war. Nowadays, with the dwindling Jewish population, many German expatriates are found in the town. There is a local one-room synagogue, rescued from the termites, where biweekly services are held. Many of the Jews intermarried with Dominicans, and the town has taken on an increasingly Spanish flavor. Women of the town are often seen wearing both the Star of David and the Virgin de Alta Gracia.

Taxis, charter buses, and públicos from Puerto Plata and Playa Dorada let passengers off at the stairs leading down to Sosua Beach from the highway.

WHERE TO STAY: One of the newest and most pleasant places to stay is **Hotel Yaroa,** El Batey (tel. 571-2651). It was named after a long-ago Indian village, within whose boundaries many of the hotel's staff still live. Opened in 1986, it encompasses views of dozens of leafy trees that ring its foundations. Inside are such decorative touches as an atrium illuminated by a skylight shaped like a Star of David, lots of exposed wood and stone, and a well-designed garden ringing a sheltered swimming pool. Each of the two dozen bedrooms has a Spanish-style mirador with a planter filled with local ferns, pine louvers for privacy, terracotta floors, lots of airy space, and a private bathroom. Two of the accommodations are designed like private cabañas at poolside. Only breakfast and light lunches are served in the wood- and lattice-sheathed dining room. Single or double rooms cost $37 in winter, *$30 in summer*. Joe Benjamin and his wife, Virginia Jackson, are the owners.

Hotel Sosua, El Batey (tel. 571-2683), is an aquamarine-colored hotel in the suburban community about two minutes by car from the center of town. Its simple and attractive layout includes a reception area designed to conceal a flagstone-rimmed pool from the quiet residential street outside. The bedrooms are strung along a wing extending beside the pool. Amid an unpretentious decor of sea-green accessories, the rooms contain air conditioning, ceiling fans, and an occasional pine balcony. *In summer, the 37 double rooms rent for $25, the three apartments going for $30.* In winter, the cost is $30 in a double, $35 in an apartment.

Auberge du Village Inn, 8 Dr. Rosen, El Batey (tel. 571-2569). Low slung, low-key, and unpretentious, this pleasant country inn was purchased late in 1985 by a Swedish-born couple, Ninni and Hans Magnusson. Formerly a professor of modern and classical dance in Gothenburg, Sweden, Ninni is an avid horsewoman and spends part of her day running a nearby horse-breeding farm. You pass beneath a grape arbor to reach the concrete walls of the reception area, which encircles an almost oval swimming pool. Only breakfast is served here, but drinks and snacks are available throughout the day at the poolside veranda. Each of the seven accommodations has its own ceiling fan and private bathroom and angular furniture. Single or double rooms cost $35 daily in winter, *$25 in summer.* The establishment lies about a five-minute walk from the beach.

WHERE TO DINE: The best and arguably the most pleasant restaurant in town is **El Coral,** El Batey (tel. 571-2645). It's in a Spanish-style building roofed with red tiles and set at the bottom of the cultivated garden near the end of Sosua Beach. As you approach it from the front the place looks smaller than it actually is, but as soon as you pass through the heavy doors you are in a spacious area with terracotta tiles, wooden accents, and stark white walls opening onto a panoramic view of the ocean. If you look out over the rear garden from one of the flowered terraces or through one of the big windows, you see an elliptical pool midway down the hill leading to the ocean. There's a bar in a room adjoining the dining room, covered with slickly modern brass accents and vertical metallic lines, each reflecting the spinning motion of the wicker ceiling fans. The specialties include lobster cocktail, grilled seabass, conch Créole style, pork chops with pineapple, lobster Thermidor, octopus Créole style, shrimps with garlic, filet mignon, and flan. Full meals begin at around RD $30 ($10.50). It opens for breakfast at 7:45 a.m. and serves dinner till 11 p.m.

La Roca, El Batey (tel. 571-2216), is a banana warehouse when it was built 85 years ago, and it later became a general store. That was before two German expatriates and Rene Kirchheimer, the son of one of Sosua's original settlers, decided to transform it into the leading nightlife choice of Sosua. The architect wisely chose to retain many of the massive structural beams and the darkly stained planks of the interior, achieving an exotic touch in the decor. Many guests opt for dinner on the breeze-cooled terrace, which stretches to the side of the disco and interior bar. Full meals cost from around RD $30 ($10.50) and might include seafood chowder, an array of tropical salads, curried chicken, and a filet of fish, facetiously named after the United Fruit Company, with banana and pineapple. They also serve a number of pasta dishes. The restaurant serves from 11 a.m. to 11 p.m. daily. Also on the premises is the most popular disco in Sosua, open daily from 9 p.m. to 2 a.m. The entrance is free to diners of the restaurant. The disco has a high ceiling and a DJ cage in a lofty perch above the floor. The bar is both indoor and outdoor, with Haitian carvings.

Café Mama Juana, El Batey (no phone), is so well known, and so tied in with the social life of Sosua, that any local will be able to direct you to the entrance. Built virtually without walls, under a makeshift kind of ceiling, it offers seating on cedarwood picnic tables behind a screen of tropical plants, a few steps from the commercial center of town. Swedish-born Michel Magnusson, whose parents maintain the previously recommended Auberge du Village Inn, long ago memorized the recipes for the dozens of tropical drinks he dispenses with an almost Latin flair to his many admiring friends. Open nonstop between 8 a.m. and midnight seven days a week, this establishment serves breakfast for RD $7 ($2.45) between 8 a.m. and 2 p.m. Sandwich platters are also available, and a specialty is octopus salad. More filling meals cost from RD $40 ($14) and include lobster, crayfish, king crab, four different versions of grouper, and such desserts as a Mama Juana flambé (bananas with ice cream and fruit). As the night wears on, you might want one of the special coffees heavily laced with several kinds of rum and tropical liqueurs.

Restaurant Morua Mai, El Batey (tel. 571-2541). Its patio, facing a popular intersection, is the closest thing to a European sidewalk café in town. Inside, where occasional live entertainment is an important attraction, is a high-ceilinged, double-decked, and stylish space filled with touches of neo-Victorian gingerbread, upholstered banquettes, and wicker furniture. Don't overlook the possibility of a sun-washed drink or cup of afternoon tea in this establishment's side courtyard where a cabaña bar serves drinks from beneath a palm-thatched roof. The café is open throughout the day, and lunch is served between 11:30 a.m. and 3 p.m., dinner is on from 7 to 11 p.m. daily. Pizzas, sandwiches, and light meals at lunch cost from RD $18 ($6.30), while full dinners go for RD $28 ($9.80). Menu specialties include charcoal-grilled lobster, fish platters (with oysters, octopus, conch, and seabass), paella, and daily specials such as grilled chicken with orange sauce.

8. Río San Juan

The best reason for going to this sleepy town is to explore the Laguna Gri-gri (see below), requiring a 1½-hour drive from Puerto Plata. If you decide to spend the night or even a few relaxing days, the **Hotel Río San Juan** (tel. 589-2379) is a simple and attractive hostelry which usually caters to a Dominican clientele. The various sections of the structure are connected by catwalks and breezeways, most of which are raised above a series of cultivated gardens. The building is outfitted in a modern interpretation of a plantation style and contains a piano bar. Here, amid a color scheme with red accents and exposed wood, the management hosts Friday- and Saturday-night combo entertainment. Each of the 38 rooms has a private bath, painted cinderblock walls, mahogany trim, wall-to-wall carpeting, and air conditioning. In winter, tariffs are RD $90 ($31.50) in a single, rising to RD $100 ($35) in a double. *In summer, the charge is RD $65 ($22.75) for a single, RD $76 ($26.60) for a double, all plus 21% tax.*

LAGUNA GRI-GRI: Lots of people dream about embarking (safely, of course) on a tour of a prehistoric swamp, but few realize that in the Dominican Republic the opportunity exists for one of the most exotically beautiful trips anywhere in the Caribbean. Near the spot where the waters of the Arroyo Grande feed into the ocean, a wilderness of mangrove swampland has thrived in isolation for centuries.

Today, almost completely unspoiled, it's a refuge for hundreds of tropical and migrant birds, with surprisingly few insects in residence. At a well-marked departure point in Río San Juan, you can negotiate for the services of a motorboat and its crew for between one and ten persons. The well-maintained, wide-bottomed boats embark on tours of an area that is reminiscent of the most secluded sections of the Florida Everglades.

You might suggest that the end point of your tour be **La Cueva de las Galondrinas,** which lies beyond the mouth of the river several miles along the rocky coastline. The cost will be around RD $40 ($14) per boatload. Along the way, note the soaring gri-gri trees, whose roots descend like tentacles into the water, plus the bizarre rock formations along the coast. Their forms include everything from natural arches to configurations resembling skulls. The end point of the tour, the cave of the galondrinas, was formed by a rockslide in 1846. Today the grotto takes its name from the bird, the galondrina, resembling the swallow, which migrates to South America in winter. If the water isn't too rough, a boat can be navigated right into the azure waters of the eerily echoing grotto, which some visitors say is just as blue as, and much less crowded than, anything along the Neapolitan coast of Italy.

9. Samaná

Lying on Samaná Peninsula, about 27 miles on eastward around the oceanfront from Puerto Plata and 12 miles from Sosua, Samaná overlooks a large bay surrounded by outstanding natural beauty. The little town was founded in 1756 by Canary Islanders sent here by the Spanish government, which was seeking to protect the area from seizure by French pirates. France had its eye on the place as a site for a projected Fort Napoleon, showcase for France's New World colonies. The Gallic bubble burst, and the Spanish colonists kept their foothold in Samaná. They were joined by slaves from America who had fled the cotton plantations of the south. The U.S. government had designs on Samaná Bay and its harbor in the late 19th century and tried to lease the area. This effort was thwarted by the somewhat shaky Dominican Republic.

The beauty of this part of the country is made up of high hills sloping gently to the ocean, tree- and shrub-covered valleys, and little harbors and coves with white sand beaches. The seaside fishing village of Samaná was targeted for development by the government in the mid-'70s, but construction of a large resort hotel failed to bring tourists flocking to the place instantly. However, an upswing in the tourist industry is hoped for.

There are beautiful beaches around the bay, some of which can be reached only by boat. Many activities are possible here, among them scuba-diving, snorkeling, swimming, sailing, deep-sea fishing, and hiking.

WHERE TO STAY: Simple living for independent types is found at **El Portillo Beach Club,** Las Terrenas, a tranquil and unspoiled place with a setting of rustic charm. The club has 75 rooms with views from private verandas, either a condo-style building or in a one- or two-bedroom cottage. Each of the cottages has a kitchen, private bath, and ample space. All the rooms have ceiling fans and are furnished with native fabrics and natural woods. In winter, when the place is likely to be filled with charter packages, rates are $75 in a standard single room, $57.50 per person in a standard double, $63 per person in a cottage double, and $58 per person in a two-bedroom cottage for four persons. *In summer, the standard single price is $56, with a standard double going for $43 per person, a cottage double for $47 per person, and a two-bedroom cottage for four persons for $45 per person.* The rates include service charge, taxes, full board, unlimited drinks at the beach bar, terrace, restaurant, and disco/tavern, plus all sports activities, which include snorkeling, sailing, horseback riding, volleyball, tennis, paddleboating, and windsurfing. The price also covers entertainment, cigarettes, games, and the daily program of activities. Information and reservations are available from Prieto Tours, 125 Francia Ave. in Santo Domingo (tel. 585-0102) or in New York (tel. 718/457-9628).

Hostal Cotubanama (tel. 538-2558), overlooking Samaná Bay, is for self-sufficient types who will settle mainly for sand and sea. The 14 simply furnished double rooms, cooled by fans, cost RD $50 ($17.50) for a single, and RD $65 ($22.75) for a double that will accommodate up to three persons. Breakfast is included in the rates, but taxes are extra. The hostal has a restaurant.

Chapter IX

BRITISH LEEWARD ISLANDS

1. Antigua and Barbuda
2. Montserrat
3. St. Kitts
4. Nevis
5. Anguilla

ONCE A BRITISH COLONY, the Leeward Islands, except for Montserrat, have moved into more independent seas.

An aviator once said that these islands look like "a fleet of cockleshells set afloat in the sea." Between French-controlled Guadeloupe and the U.S. Virgins, at a bend of an archipelago, the British Leewards consist of Antigua (in association with isolated Barbuda), Montserrat, the twin state of St. Kitts and Nevis, and little Anguilla. Of them all, Antigua with its many beaches and resort hotels is the best equipped for mass tourism.

Once only Antigua and St. Kitts were visited by tourists, except for some curious, adventurous voyagers. However, the opening of more hotels and the providing of modern tourist facilities now draw thousands to Montserrat, Nevis, and to more remote Anguilla.

U.S. and Canadian citizens do not have to have a visa, but they will be asked for some means of identification such as a birth certificate or voter registration card. An outbound ticket for transportation is also required. Antigua makes a good base for going almost anywhere in the West Indies.

All the islands in this chapter use the Eastern Caribbean dollar (EC$), also called the "Bee Wee." However, no one faints if you give them a U.S. dollar. Nearly all hotels bill you in U.S. dollars. Only certain tiny restaurants present their prices in EC dollars. Make sure you know which dollars are referred to when you inquire about the price of something. The "Bee Wee" is worth about 37¢ in U.S. currency (EC$2.70 to $1 U.S.). Unless otherwise specified, rates quoted in this chapter are given in U.S. dollars.

1. Antigua and Barbuda

Antigua boasts a different beach for every day of the year—365 of them! Most of these beaches are protected by coral reefs, and the color of the sand is often sugar-white.

Antigua, Barbuda, and Redonda form the State of Antigua, an associated state within the British Commonwealth. (Redonda is an uninhabited rocky islet of less than one square mile, located 20 miles southwest of Antigua; and sparsely populated Barbuda is previewed at the end of this section.)

From a poverty-stricken sugar island, Antigua has risen to the position of a 20th-century vacation haven. Yankee millionaires seeking British serenity under a tropical sun turned Antigua into a citadel of elegance around the exclusive Mill Reef Club. The island has now developed a broader base of tourism—attracting not just the rich, but the middle-, even lower-income voyager.

Rolling, rustic Antigua (pronounced An-*tee*-ga) has as its highest point Babby Peak, 1,360 feet above sea level. Stone towers, once sugar mills, dot the landscape; but in inland scenery Antigua isn't as dramatic as some of the British Leewards such as St. Kitts. But, oh, those beaches!

Discovered by Columbus on his second voyage in 1493, Antigua has a population of about 75,000 and an area of 108 square miles. The average all-year temperature ranges from 75° to 85° Fahrenheit.

Independence has come, but Antigua is still British in many of its traditions. English planters settled Antigua in 1623. In 1666 the French occupied the island, but Antigua was ceded to England the following year by the Treaty of Breda.

The summer carnival takes place on the first Monday and Tuesday in August and the preceding week. Included in this festival of fun and spectacle are a beauty competition, as well as calypso and steel-band competitions. Carnival envelops the streets in exotic costumes that recall the people's African heritage. The spring highlight is Antigua's annual sailing week in April.

The capital is **St. John's,** a neatly laid-out large town, six miles from the airport and less than a mile from the deep-water Harbour Terminal. The port is the focal point of commerce and industry, as well as the seat of government and tourist shopping.

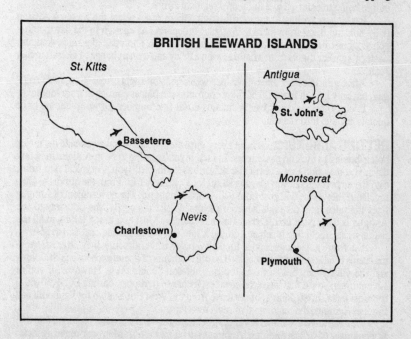

BRITISH LEEWARD ISLANDS

St. Kitts

Antigua

● St. John's

● Basseterre

Montserrat

Nevis

Charlestown ●

Plymouth ●

Trade winds keep the streets fairly cool, as they were built wide just for that purpose. Protected in the throat of a narrow bay, the port city consists of cobblestone sidewalks, weather-beaten wooden houses (painted or not), corrugated iron roofs, and louvered West Indian verandas.

GETTING THERE: Because of its role as a hub of transport to several other islands, Antigua is considered an important air link. Most passengers in the Northeast opt for the **American Airlines** nonstop service to Antigua from New York's JFK. Departing every day around 9:20 a.m., it leaves late enough for passengers from Boston, Providence, Hartford, and other cities to make early-morning connections. Winging in to Antigua at 2:15 p.m., the flight lands in time for passengers to enjoy a late-afternoon sunbath.

American's rate structure is cheaper when a Caribbean-bound vacationer books his or her hotel reservation simultaneously with air transport. Many of the hotels that an American Airlines reservation clerk will propose are reviewed in this guide. If, however, you prefer to book your hotel independently, American's cheapest travel option requires no advance booking, though a delay of 3 to 21 days is required before flying back to the point of origin. Best of all, there's no cancellation penalty imposed if you decide to change the dates of your travel after paying for your ticket. Currently, high-season fares cost $539 to $573 per person, depending on the day of the week.

Traffic from other North American cities is often funneled through American's hubs of Chicago, Miami, or San Juan. A telephone reservations clerk will work with a complicated array of flight patterns to ensure the quickest, most efficient, and least expensive connections.

Pan American offers routings to Antigua, but passengers originating in New York are required to wait for as much as four hours in either St. Maarten or Miami before being transferred to a flight on a regional airline.

Passengers willing to transfer through Miami often select the **Eastern Airline** daily nonstop flight from there to Antigua. It departs late enough in the day to allow connections from the West Coast, but it lands after dark, around 9:15 p.m. in Antigua. Eastern's earlier flights from Miami require a delay and then a change of aircraft in San Juan.

Air Canada offers three-times-per-week nonstop flights from Toronto to Antigua, but only in high season. The flight connects with planes coming in from Montréal.

Each of the major airlines maintains a toll-free number for reservations, tariff quotations, and information.

GETTING AROUND: Taxis meet every airplane, and drivers wait outside the major hotels hoping to pick up passengers. In fact, if you're going to be in Antigua for a few days, you may find that a particular driver has "adopted" you. A typical fare from, say, the airport to Halcyon Cove is $8.50 for a one-way trip. From the airport to Curtain Bluff, however, will cost from $20, as it's a long run. The government of Antigua fixes the rates, and the taxis have no meters. While it's costly, the best way to see Antigua is by private taxi. Drivers are also guides. Most taxi tours, taking in all the major sights, including lunch at Admiral's Inn, last 3½ hours and cost $50 to $60.

Buses are not recommended for the average visitor, although they do exist. Service seems erratic and undependable. The official hours of operation between St. John's and the villages are 5:30 a.m. to 6 p.m., but don't count on it. However, if you're adventurous, you'll find buses the cheapest means of transport, costing EC$1.60 (60¢) for most fares. In St. John's, buses leave from the West Bus Station for Falmouth and English Harbour, the major goal of most travelers.

Car Rentals: A self-drive car may be more practical for some visitors. Note that as a holdover of British tradition, Antiguans *drive on the left*. Many car-rental agencies operate in Antigua. However, there is one important requirement. You must obtain a driver's license, costing $12. To obtain one, you must produce a valid U.S. or Canadian license. It is no longer necessary to go to the police station to obtain this license. Most car-rental firms are authorized to issue it to you in exchange for a fee. Car-rental firms in Antigua are local operations, although two or three are affiliated with major car-rental firms in the United States. **Avis** is represented by a local firm with a different name, and you also have a choice of some very local and often small operations (one of which I recommend). However, several local firms rent cars that aren't in the best of condition, and with the pot-holed roads of Antigua you need the best-maintained vehicle you can get.

Operating under its own banner, **Budget Rent-a-Car** maintains a local office in Antigua at the corner of American and Factory Road (tel. 46-22544). When you arrive at the Coolidge Airport, a Budget representative will see that you are delivered to Budget's island headquarters.

There, the cheapest car available is usually a manual-transmission Toyota Starlet without air conditioning. In high season, it rents for $200 per week, with each additional day costing $31. However, you must notify Budget at least two business days in advance to get this rate. You must also be at least 22 years old.

If you're looking for a car with air conditioning and automatic transmission (either two- or four-door, seating four passengers comfortably), the charge for a Nissan Sunny with these options is $240 weekly, with each additional day costing $40.

Budget charges $10 per day for a collision damage waiver, which in case of an accident will void your financial responsibility for repairs. Without that waiver, the renter is responsible for the first $250 worth of damage to the vehicle. These rates may change during the lifetime of this edition. Before making your travel plans, you can call Budget toll free at 800/527-0700.

Carib Car Rentals, P.O. Box 1258, Hodge's Bay (tel. 46-22062), will pick you up and deliver you anywhere on Antigua. It rents vehicles that are clean, modern, and reliable. For one day expect to pay from $38, with a free choice of automatic or stick shift. If you keep the car from two to six days, it costs $35 per day, and after seven days, the charge is lowered to only $32 per day. Hours are 8 a.m. to 5 p.m. seven days a week.

PRACTICAL FACTS: Arriving passengers are allowed 200 cigarettes and one quart of liquor, plus six ounces of perfume. Upon departing, a **departure tax** of EC$10 ($3.70) is imposed.

In addition, the government imposes a 6% **government tax,** which is added to all hotel bills. There is also a 10% service charge added by most hotels.

Most of the island's **electricity** is 220 volts AC, 60 cycles. However, the Hodges Bay area and some hotels are supplied with 110 volts, 60 cycles.

Holberton Hospital (tel. 46-20251) on Queen Elizabeth Hwy. is the principal **medical facility** on Antigua. Water is desalinated and therefore safe to drink.

Antigua falls within the **Atlantic Time Zone,** placing it one hour ahead of the east coast of the U.S. However, both Antigua and the U.S. East Coast keep the same time when the U.S. goes on Daylight Saving Time.

For emergencies, the **U.S. Embassy** is on Redcliffe Street, St. John's (tel. 46-23511).

Bank hours are usually Monday to Wednesday from 8 a.m. to 2 p.m., on Thursday to 1 p.m. and on Friday from 8 a.m. to 1 p.m. and 3 to 5 p.m.

HOTELS: Antigua's hotels are among the best and most plentiful in the eastern Caribbean, and generally they are small—a 100-room hotel is rare on the island. Check summer closings, which often depend on the caprice of the owners who will decide to shut down if business isn't good. Incidentally, air conditioning, except in first-class hotels, isn't as plentiful as some visitors think it should be. Chances are, your hotel will be on a beach. You can also rent an apartment or cottage if you want to cook for yourself.

The Leaders in Luxury

Curtain Bluff, Old Road, P.O. Box 288 (tel. 46-31115; 212/289-8888, in New York City), lies in southwest Antigua, the most tropical-looking section of the resort-studded island. A world set apart on a finger of land, it was built on Curtain Bluff Peninsula, with two beaches, about 14 miles from the airport. The setting is like a subtropical forest, with sky-high coconut trees off each of its leeward and windward beaches. I'd rate Curtain Bluff as the outstanding hotel on the island, where competition is stiff. The chairman, Howard Hulford, once a pilot for Texaco, and the managing director, Edward Sheerin, demand and get the best staff on the island, maintaining a private-club atmosphere that appeals to everybody from Herman Wouk to *The Sensuous Woman*. Architecturally, the resort's buildings are original, suggesting the South Seas. Guests meet for drinks in the round bar, inspired by the early stone sugar mills. Ship models are set against the stone walls, and the round ceiling is beamed. Low modern sofas make it easy to while away the hours.

The peaked-roof bedrooms and the suites on the bluff, only 60 units in all, have open, covered verandas where you can take your breakfast. The white bamboo furnishings set the right taste tone. With its own secluded balcony and private bath, each unit faces the sea and is cooled by the breezes. The tariffs are expensive, but you get a lot of extras for your money, including Sunfish sailboats, waterskiing from a fiberglass speedboat, skindiving (masks, snorkels, and flippers furnished), Aqualungs (complete equipment except regulators, for certified divers), boating (guided trips to Cades Reef), tennis (championship courts, three Laykold and one Astroturf), and golf (a putting green). From mid-December to mid-April, a double room is $340 to $360 daily on the MAP; a single goes for $295 to $315, and a one-bedroom suite for $520. *Off-season rates are reduced by $100 per night.* After dining (men should wear a jacket and tie after 7 p.m.), there's entertainment. It might be a steel band or calypso music for dancing. Beach parties are staged weekly. A European chef, Ruedi Portmann, prepares a very good continental cuisine, his menu backed up by a well-chosen and extensive wine cellar. Be sure to try his deep-fried ice cream! The hotel is closed from June 1 to mid-October.

The **St. James's Club**, P.O. Box 63, St. John's (tel. 46-31430; 212/309-3330 in New York City, or toll free 800/235-3505, 800/268-9051 in Canada), a luxurious resort on Mamora Bay, offers an example of how $30 million, careful planning and construction, and international management expertise with a heavy European emphasis can establish a lovely, relaxing, and much sought-after resort in just two years. The 100-acre setting, which today blossoms with hundreds of tropical plants and trees, is on a sun-drenched peninsula jutting into the Caribbean. The pedigrees of the resort, a branch of the fashionable St. James's Clubs in London and Paris, and the owner, Peter de Savary, are impeccable.

In a deep harbor dug out of what had been a shallow cove, the builders constructed a full-service yacht marina with permanent berths for 20 yachts and good anchorage for up to 50 vessels. The club offers two secluded palm-lined beaches, Mamora and Coco Bay, topped with white sand from neighboring Barbuda. As the club is surrounded by the ocean on three sides, there are, of course, water sports galore: sailing, waterskiing, surf jetting, windsurfing, snorkeling, scuba-diving at the St. James's Club Scuba School, glass-bottom-boat excursions, and deep-sea fishing on the club's sport fishing boat. The club has its own full-size swimming pool with a surrounding sundeck, and individual sundecks are positioned throughout the property at the water's edge. In addition to beach activities, there are seven floodlit all-weather tennis courts with an All American Sports professional tennis clinic. The St. James's stables house about a dozen Texas quarterhorses which guests can ride along woodland and hillside trails carved out of the surrounding landscape. The club has a complete Nautilus-equipped gymnasium, a Jacuzzi overlooking the ocean boutiques, and a hair and beauty salon run by Leonards of London.

Each accommodation looks like a page out of a decorator's magazine. Comfortable club rooms, elegant deluxe rooms, handsome suites, and beautiful villas are done in imaginative pastels intertwined with Dominican paintings, furnished with wicker and bentwood pieces and commodious canopied beds, and have sweeping views of the seascapes. All rooms are equipped with Hunter fans, and most are air-conditioned. Villas are supplied with cable TV and 24-hour delivery service. Other units have 24-hour room service. With MAP, *double-occupancy rates range from $235 in low season* to a maximum of $385 in high season for club room accommodation. *Lodgings in suites go from $450 per couple, with MAP, off-season*, to $600 with MAP in winter. For single guests, the club deducts $50 per day from the rate charged in a double. Government tax and service are added to the bills.

There are three eating spots for guests. The Rainbow Garden overlooking the ocean contains a soaring white ceiling, a dinnertime pianist perched on a platform eyrie high above the floor, and a "rebuilt" tree which the designers reassembled from a nearby forest and festooned with iridescent crystals. The Docksider Café overlooking Mamora Beach provides al fresco dining by candlelight, a setting for the steel band and strolling calypso singers. For real fun, guests can try the hillside trattoria. The Jacaranda nightclub is a "see and be seen" kind of place, offering an end to an evening for the more active guests. Many enjoy gambling in the high-ceilinged in-house small European-style casino whose walls are covered in a combination of Italian art deco columns and vertical stripes.

Jumby Bay, P.O. Box 243 (tel. 46-32176), is an exclusive little island resort, 300 acres in all, lying off the eastern coast of Antigua and reached after a 12-minute motor launch ride. The site was selected for its powdery white sandy beaches, along a coastline protected by coral reefs. In gin-clear waters, guests can snorkel, go scuba-diving, or swim when they're not playing tennis, going fishing or sailing, or perhaps waterskiing. The grounds have been handsomely landscaped in part with loblolly and white cedar trees. The resort at its peak can accommodate about 56 guests, and with such a low house-count the place often takes on a house-party atmosphere. The hotel is on the site of what had been the private home of a plantation owner who grew sugarcane. In the 200-year-old vastly restored estate house, there is now a lounge, a library and games room. Dinner is served here, often attracting the yachting crowd who put into the 750-foot dock. The food is excellent, and picnic lunches can be arranged.

Pampered guests are housed in one of a dozen cottage rooms, each with a large master bedroom and its own patio overlooking the water, or else in one of 16 guest units fronting the ocean on Jumby Bay Beach. These latter units have a living and sitting area as well as a wet bar. Some of them even have a private "no curtains" shower courtyard which can provide entertainment to your roommate if you've kept your figure in shape. From November 1 to April 30, two persons can stay here on the AP at rates ranging from $425 to $525 daily. *Off-season is from the first of April to the end of May, when two persons are charged $300 daily, AP, and from the first of June until the first of September when tariffs are $260, AP, for two guests.* The hotel is closed in September and October.

For reservations, consult your travel agent or get in touch with Jumby Bay, U.S.A., 1111 Cedar Swamp Rd., Old Brookville, NY 11545 (tel. 516/626-9200, 718/895-9868 in New York City, or toll free 800/437-0049).

First-Class Hotels

Halcyon Cove Beach Resort and Casino, P.O. Box 251, Dickenson Bay (tel. 46-20256), is a total resort with plenty of glamour and a casino. There, in the midst of waterfront gardens, are clusters of two-story buildings overlooking either the sea or well-tended grounds spread out around the swimming pool area. There are 150 stylish bedrooms, equipped for discerning guests. The decorating has authority, usually fine furnishings and coordinated fabrics. You have your own furnished private veranda; however, if you're on the ground floor you may get a lot of inspection from fellow guests, providing you are interesting enough. In winter, rooms (either single or double occupancy) rent for anywhere from $200 to $250 daily, *dropping to $105 to $130 from mid-April to mid-December*.

The Arawak Terrace, the hotel's main dining room, is open for breakfast and dinner. You can also lunch or dine on the elongated Warri Pier, standing on stilts 200 feet from the shore. It's reached by a boardwalk over the sea. You dine and drink under a thatched and shingled open-air café. There seems nearly half a mile of beach, and at one end is one of the major centers of Antigua's water-sports program. Often there are buffet dinners. Other activities include playing tennis on the hotel's own courts and horseback riding. The hotel is on an elevation, and it's but a three-minute walk down to the beach. Deck chairs and umbrellas are placed around a bar built right at the freshwater swimming pool, and a large airy dining room has a view of the sea. The hotel also has an ice-cream-parlor/coffeeshop as well as a cocktail lounge that occasionally has entertainment. Tennis players will find three courts lit for night play. In season, the management brings in a steel band to provide poolside entertainment on Sunday. The location is 1½ miles from the airport and 7 miles from St. John's, about a 15-minute taxi ride.

Blue Waters, P.O. Box 256, Soldier Bay (tel. 46-20292), curves around a private sandy beach, where you can lie in a hammock as a waiter serves you a strawberry-red rum punch. The location is four miles (about a 15-minute ride) from St. John's, to which the management provides a shuttle service at $3 per person. Hamish Datson manages this thoroughly refined little Caribbean inn where all rooms are beachfront and air-conditioned, surrounded by luxurious flowers and shrubs with coconut palms and shade trees in the extensive grounds. The property was extensively renovated in 1986, and eight two- and three-bedroom villas were built. In winter, doubles pay from $240 to $330, MAP, daily. The resort is likely to be closed from mid-May to mid-July. *Otherwise, the single rate off-season ranges $70 to $115, going up to $82 to $150 in a double, plus another $36 per person for MAP*. The Sunday brunch is deservedly praised. A lavish buffet table, decorated with coconuts and bougainvillea, is spread before you; and on Tuesday and Friday, outdoor barbecues with continental and West Indian dishes, among the best in Antigua, attract a lively crowd. In season, you can dance to combos, steel bands, or disco music, and every Saturday night the management throws a house party featuring crab racing. Water sports, tennis, sailing, and fishing are all complimentary, or you may prefer just to relax in the clear freshwater pool or enjoy a sundowner from the gazebo. Deep-sea fishing and coastal trips to nearby islands are available.

The Anchorage, P.O. Box 147, Dickenson Bay (tel. 46-20267), is a special retreat and compound right on the beach, with modern, airy, and stylish reception areas. Guests face a choice of staying in a large, well-furnished room or a tropical thatch-roofed rondavel, with a private patio overlooking the sea. The cheapest way to stay here is to take one of the air-conditioned cottage rooms, costing $180 daily in season, either single or double occupancy. *These cottages drop to only $95 daily in summer, either single or double*. The most luxurious way to live here is in one of the air-conditioned deluxe beach rooms and rondavels. They rent for $220 daily in winter, *dropping to only $125 in summer*, either single or double occupancy. For breakfast and dinner, add another $38 per person daily. Many thoughtful extras go into making the Anchorage one of the best-run hotels on the island. For example, the maid comes around twice a day. The beachfront setting is in a coconut grove, and there's a wide assortment of water sports, plus three championship tennis courts. The chef can also accommodate special diets. Native bands and special guest performers are brought in to entertain in season, and down the beach you can enjoy casino action at the Halcyon Cove Hotel.

Pineapple Beach Club, P.O. Box 54, St. John's (tel. 46-32006, 212/840-6636 in New York City, or toll free 800/223-9815, 800/468-0023 in Québec and Ontario), is one of the Antigua's newest hotels, having opened late in 1986. It also offers all-inclusive meals, sports, and drinks as part of its total price structure. The older and smaller hotel that stood on this spot was gutted and rebuilt. The property lies on 45 acres of forested land, sloping down to a beach and a peninsula. Each unit is privately owned, and a management team is charged with maintaining the grounds, the buildings, and the rental of the accommodations in the owners' absence. Many of the present accommodations are outfitted in shades of pink and green, with a collection of woven cane furniture from the Dominican Republic. Units contain two large beds and a private bath. In high season, one person pays $150 per night, *the rate lowered to $125 per person in summer*, again an all-inclusive tariff. Additional units are planned. On the premises are tennis courts, two bars, a restaurant, a freshwater pool, and a windsurfing school.

Small, Special Inns

The **Copper and Lumber Store,** P.O. Box, Nelson's Dockyard, English Harbour (tel. 46-31058), is an 18th-century building originally occupied by purveyors of wood and sheet copper for the construction and/or repair of sailing ships of the British fleet plying the waters of the Caribbean. Today the louvered and shuttered windows of its dignified Georgian façade look out on increasing numbers of guests who recognize that in many ways this is the most understatedly elegant hotel in Antigua. The store and its adjacent harbor structures were built of brick brought from England in the holds of ships as ballast, to be replaced on return voyages by sugar, rum, and other rich products of the West Indies. These bricks imbue the building with 18th-century English charm and sometimes serve to conceal its necessary modern amenities. Gillian Gutteridge and her husband, a former British navy commander, worked for years to restore and preserve the weathered charm of the place.

Each of the 14 brick-lined period accommodations has its own design and is named after one of the ships that fought at the battle of Trafalgar. Each is a well-proportioned study in high-quality 18th-century decorating. They're filled with fine Chippendale and Queen Anne reproductions, antiques, gleaming brass chandeliers, hardwood paneling, and hand-stenciled floors, all with a curator's eye for detail. Even the showers look like cabinetry in a sailing vessel, being lined with thick paneled slabs of mahogany accented with polished brass fittings, then carefully shielded with many coats of waterproofing. The hotel has four one-level rooms and ten duplexes, each with a self-contained kitchen if you're interested in self-catering. Most have wide-angle views over the harbor where boats come and go much as they did 200 years ago. Maid service is included in the price of the rooms, which in winter cost $150 in a studio sleeping up to three persons and $215 in a one-bedroom suite which sleeps up to four. *In summer, the rates go down to $75 in a studio, $110 in a one-bedroom suite*. These tariffs are for double occupancy. Extra persons cost an additional $20 to $30 per day, depending on the season and the accommodation. The hotel also has comfortable and charming contemporary accommodations as well. While not awash in the Georgian authenticity of the period rooms, they represent a reasonable investment at $85 for a studio and $125 for a one-bedroom suite (double occupancy) in winter. *Summer rates, double occupancy, are $50 in a studio and $70 in a one-bedroom suite*.

The **Admiral's Inn,** P.O. Box 713, English Harbour (tel. 46-31027), as a building, was planned in 1785, the year Nelson sailed into the harbor as captain of the H.M.S. *Boreas*. Completed in 1788, the building's ground floor was used to store lead, turpentine, and pitch, with offices for dockyard engineers upstairs. Today it has been converted into one of the most atmospheric inns in Antigua. In the heart of Nelson's Dockyard, and loaded with West Indian charm, the hostelry is constructed of weathered brick brought from England as ships' ballast. The façade is eye-captivating, with white shutters, dormers, and a terrace opening onto a centuries-old garden. The look is that of a small manor house, and it's also a hangout for the yachting set. The ground floor, with its brick walls, giant ship beams, and island-made furniture, has a tavern atmosphere, with decorative copper, boat lanterns, and old oil paintings, everything lit at night by wrought-iron chandeliers.

Antilles ambience collectors will find that whatever room they're assigned will be full of character. There are three types of accommodations. Highest tariffs are charged for some ground-floor rooms in a tiny brick building—on the site of a provisional warehouse for Nelson's troops—across the pillared courtyard from the main structure. Each of these rooms has a little patio and a garden entry. Ceiling fans and optional air conditioning keep these spacious rooms cool. The same superior rate applies to front rooms on the first floor above the ground floor of the main building, with a view out over the lawn and harbor. A medium rate applies to the back rooms on this floor, all of which have air conditioning. The least expensive rate is for smaller chambers on the top floor, which may get warm during the day in summer but are quiet, with dormer-window views over the yacht-filled harbor. All rooms have ceiling fans and private baths and showers. Only 14 twin-bedded rooms are rented out, so reservations are imperative. One bedchamber has a four-poster bed, but it didn't belong to Nelson or even Lady Hamilton. The manager, Ethelyn Philip, who has been with the inn for some 20 years, will welcome you and see to your needs. *In summer, singles on the EP stay here at rates that range from $44 to $50 daily; doubles, $48 to $56.* In winter, EP rates go up—$55 to $66 for a single, $68 to $78 for a double. The inn is closed in September. Rates entitle you to use the inn's snorkeling equipment and Sunfish craft. Free transportation is also provided to two nearby beaches. On Saturday night a steel band plays. For the inn's restaurant, refer to the section on where to dine.

Galley Bay Surf Club, P.O. Box 305, Five Islands (tel. 46-20302). When she created this place west of St. John's, Edee Holbert had a fantasy of Gauguin and Polynesia—grass roofs and lily ponds. The world beat a path to her door, including Greta Garbo, who was caught unaware by a nosy magazine photographer who snapped her photograph in the nude on the beach. All that was a long time ago and the Galley Bay has now become part of Caribbean legend. It's still around, still offering its "just for fun" accommodations, but the fickle "big names" have gone elsewhere.

Horses suitable even for beginning riders are available—"on the house." Also included free are hard-surface tennis courts, snorkeling (a sunken schooner is nearby), and a dinghy for fishing. In season, dancing is nightly to West Indian bands, particularly at the barbecues. The food is especially good, and *Gourmet* magazine has published some of the recipes. Outstanding are the Caribbean fish chowder, flambé desserts, roast duckling with banana stuffing, paper-thin crêpes, callaloo soup, coq au vin, and lobster Thermidor.

A variety of accommodations is offered. For tranquility seekers, the Gauguin Village, with 12 units, is 150 feet off the beach, built around a salt pond under a leafy coconut grove. Each of these units consists of two villas—one with a spacious bedroom, the other with a good-sized bath and dressing room. Furnishings are in rattan, the wall hangings from Haiti. Directly on the beach, advertised as "four seconds from bed to sea," are a dozen beach rooms with a South Seas decor of white walls, including a sunken tub in the bathroom and private lanai and hand-woven palm leaf shutters. In addition, a quartet of executive beach rooms are also on the beach. These are big double rooms, decorated with style and imagination, including a private lounge, private bar, dining porch, and kitchen. The price depends not only on the season, but the accommodation you select. In winter, a single in a beach room pays $180 daily; a double, $190. Double occupancy of an executive beach room is $220 daily, but only $160 in a Gauguin villa. *In summer, a single can rent a beach room for $115 daily, a double costing $125. Two persons pay $145 daily in an executive beach room, but only $115 in a Gauguin villa.* All these are EP tariffs. For MAP, add another $35 per person daily. A five-day minimum stay is required at Christmas and in February.

The Inn, P.O. Box 187, English Harbour (tel. 46-31014), is one of my favorite nooks, and I enjoy sharing it with others. Owned by Peter and Ann Deeth, it stands in a corner of Freeman's Bay. Guests have a choice of pleasingly furnished hillside studios and suites, or else beachfront units, the latter naturally costing more money. In winter, hillside singles on the MAP rent for $225 daily, rising to $245 to $275 on the beach. A MAP double on the hillside goes for $260, increasing to anywhere from $280 to $310 daily on the beach. In summer, hillside units are shut down. *However, regular off-season rates for the beachfront rooms with kitchenette, either single or double occupancy, range from $85 to $95 and up daily.* The Inn has one of the finest sites in Antigua, with views over Nelson's Dockyard and English Harbour from its terrace. Have a before-dinner drink in the old-style English Bar, with its stone walls and low-overhead beams. Lunch is served both at the beach house and in the main dining room, and the Inn is known for the quality of its cookery. The hotel also has its own waterski boat, Sailfish, and a yacht for sailing; other activities on the agenda include tennis, horseback riding, swimming, and snorkeling. Tennis and golf are nearby.

Long Bay Hotel, P.O. Box 442 (tel. 46-32005, or toll free 800/223-9868), is dramatically situated on a spit of land between the open sea and a sheltered lagoon, on the eastern shore, beyond the hamlet of Willikie's. It has been owned and operated by the Lafaurie family since 1966. Many repeat visitors consider it more of an inn than a large-scale hotel. It features 20 breeze-filled rooms as well as five furnished cottages for more reclusive guests. High-season rates range from $95 to $145 per person double occupancy on the EP. *However, from mid-October to December 20 and from mid-April to mid-June, tariffs go from $80 to $105 per person on the EP, based on double occupancy.* The service charge is added to your bill. The hotel is closed from mid-June to mid-October. The resort is centered around a hip-roofed clubhouse whose stone-walled dining room and artifact-dotted bar provide a relaxing environment. There's a championship tennis court, plus complete scuba facilities and a full array of rental sailboats on the premises. Golf is nearby. Babysitters are available when needed, and there is a special dinner sitting just for children. The hotel has a library and games room, a separate building for the dining room, and a beach house restaurant and bar.

Lord Nelson Club, P.O. Box 155 (tel. 46-23094), is a self-contained resort about a mile from the airport, some five miles from St. John's. The club occupies 19 acres, opening onto its own private sandy beach. The pink-walled hotel may look a bit ramshackle in places, but it has a lot of character. Expatriates, both English and American, flock here. The inn has American owners, the Fuller family. One of its members, Nick, was a former U.S. consul. Rooms vary widely, and I prefer the pleasantly decorated twin-bedded rooms, each with a private tile bath and a terrace with a view of the water. The trade winds keep it cool at night. In season, two persons can stay here on the MAP for $120 daily, a single person paying $85 daily. *From mid-April to mid-December, reductions are granted: $95 for two on the MAP, $65 for one person, plus tax and service.* The hotel is closed in September and October. The old-fashioned dining room offers a cuisine that includes some of the island specialties, as well as the partial hull of a beached dinghy set up in its center as a serving station. The stone-walled bar, shaped like a cabaña, contains hanging fish nets and a portrait which looks like Lord Nelson above the serving area. Set directly on the sand, the bar is ready to serve you a tropical drink at your request. The lounge and bar have a few decorative antiques to add zest. The beach is fringed with tropical trees and shrubbery.

Best for the Budget

Barrymore, just off Fort Road (P.O. Box 244), Runaway Bay, St. John's (tel. 46-21055), has its own special niche in resort-crowded Antigua. First, it's a good bargain. Second, it's Antiguan, run by the LaBarries, and offers an inexpensive holiday in an unpretentious setting. A small bungalow colony with a freshwater swimming pool, it stands on three acres of private grounds, about a mile from the nearest beach and the capital. Free transportation is provided to the beach. Waterskiing, horseback riding, and windsurfing facilities are available. The place does a good family business, and children are free to romp on the lawn planted with poinsettia bushes. Rooms and efficiencies are in blue-and-white modern bungalows scattered about the grounds, bordered by flowering shrubbery. Bedrooms have modern appointments motel style, private baths, and patios. Some, not all, contain air conditioning. In winter, singles on the EP range from $58 to $66 daily; doubles, $76 to $84. *Off-season, singles are charged from $46 to $54; doubles, $60 to $68 daily.* The LaBarries enjoy a good reputation on the island for serving West Indian dishes, especially Antiguan lobster, at their popular restaurant, Dubarry's (see "Where to Eat," below). You can dine inside or out on the porch, enjoying the breezes if there are any. The LaBarrie family is descended from Madame du Barry, and their French heritage is evident in the charm and grace with which they run their cozy restaurant.

Spanish Main, East Street (P.O. Box 655), St. John's (tel. 46-20660), is a restored governor's residence facing St. John's Park, the center of sporting events and the annual carnival. Architecturally it reflects a romantic past, with twin gables and an upper and lower balcony. Its restaurant alone has won honorable mention from *Gourmet* magazine (see my dining recommendations). There are 15 bedrooms, furnished in the main with rattan, all consistently appealing. At this small, intimate inn, you pay $30 in a single, $45 in a double, plus service and taxes. No meals are included for that, just a room and a bath. The owners, Bob and Janice Branker, are gentle, sweet, low-key people who have lived in New York and have won many friends, whom they welcome back again and again to their charming little place, one of the most delightful inns on the island. They preside over their garden-level bar and restaurant, always taking time out for some friendly gossip over a tall rum drink.

Self-Sufficient Accommodations

Antigua Village, P.O. Box 649, Dickenson Bay (tel. 46-24299), set on a peninsula stretching into the turquoise waters around it, is more of a self-contained condominium community than a holiday resort. The road leading to it winds through hilly country until it eventually passes through large groves of palm trees scattered on both sides of a seaside area that is ringed with white sandy beaches. A freshwater pool, a restaurant, a bar, and a mini-market are on the premises, with a casino and more restaurants within walking distance. You can use the neighboring tennis court, and there's an 18-hole golf course nearby. Water sports are free. The Village has studio apartments and villas, all of which have kitchenettes, patios or balconies, twin beds in the bedrooms, and sofa beds in the living rooms. One-bedroom apartments in winter cost $170 to $220 daily, depending on the number of occupants, the accommodation's design, and its location (beside the sea or the pool). Studios in winter cost $140 to $160 for two persons, and two-bedroom villas cost $290 to $380. *In summer, one-bedroom villas cost $95 to $135, studios go for $75 to $90 for two persons, and two-bedroom units are priced at $145 to $190.* Service and tax are added to your bill.

Siboney Beach Club, P.O. Box 222, St. John's (tel. 46-23356). Its Australian-born owner, Tony Johnson, passed through Antigua in 1959 and never left. His hotel, named after an Indian tribe believed to have predated even the Arawaks, is set into a well-landscaped acre of beachfront land. It's shielded on the inland side by what might be the tallest and most verdant hedge on the island. Its social center is within the separately recommended Lobster Pot restaurant. The dozen suites comprising the comfortable accommodations are contained in a two-story motel-like unit draped with bougainvillea and vines. None has a phone, air conditioning, or TV, but each has a separate bedroom, living room, and balcony or patio, plus a tiny kitchen behind movable shutters. Each of the units has big windows for natural cooling and spinning ceiling fans. In winter, singles range from $135 to $200 daily, and doubles go for $195 to $250. *In summer, singles go for $95 to $155 daily, while doubles run $95 to $150, plus service and tax.* MAP can be arranged for another $38 per person daily.

Hodges Bay Club, P.O. Box 1237 (tel. 46-22300). Set beside a well-managed restaurant, the Pelican Club, this neo-Mediterranean town-house complex lies between the seaside road and the beach. Technically, each unit is owned by an absentee investor, but an on-the-premises management company arranges their rentals when the accommodations are not in use. Although decorated differently, each is stylish and attractively personalized, with a fully equipped kitchen, daily maid service, two balconies, ceiling fans, and (in the bedrooms) air conditioning. Some have high cathedral ceilings, and all lie a few steps from a stretch of sandy beachfront where the snorkeling is said to be particularly good. In winter, a one-bedroom villa for two persons rents for $230, *dropping to only $125 in summer.* In winter, a two-bedroom villa for four persons ranges from $270 to $340 daily, *reduced to $140 to $175 daily in summer,* plus tax and service.

Dian Bay Resort, P.O. Box 231 (tel. 46-32003). Set on a sun-washed hilltop in an area filled with expensive private villas and flowering shrubs, this is a remote hideaway. Completed in 1985, it contains 24 units, 19 of which are suites. Each has a lattice-trimmed veranda, a fully equipped kitchenette, ceiling fans, and an easy-to-live-with decor of beige tiles and tan walls. Only two of the units are air-conditioned, but no one seems to mind because of the cooling trade winds. In winter, one-bedroom suites, suitable for two persons, cost $100 to $110 daily, and two-bedroom suites for up to four persons go for $185 a night. *In summer, one-bedroom suites go for $70 to $85 daily; two-bedroom suites, $140.* Children under 12, staying with paying adults, are housed free. A mini-market on the premises, managed by the articulate English-born manager, Gillian Wightman, provides food staples for those interested in cooking within their units. The in-house restaurant is recommended separately. A labyrinth of masonry walkways leads past a swimming pool to a sheltered lagoon, where windsurfing and snorkeling equipment is provided free to guests. The establishment lies on the windswept eastern end of the island.

Barrymore Beach Apartments, Runaway Bay (P.O. Box 244), St. John's (tel. 46-24101). Designed and built by a Scottish architect, these are probably the most pleasantly finished and furnished apartments in the area. They're managed by one of the charming co-owners of the nearby Barrymore Hotel, Linda Gordon, who decorated the on-premises restaurant, the Satay Hut (see "Where to Eat," below), with Indonesian art she collected in the Far East. There are 20 one- and two-bedroom apartments within this sun-drenched resort, where Linda, her husband, Brian, and the friendly staff do everything they can to create a "kick off your shoes" kind of ambience. The apartments are clustered within a handful of contemporary buildings whose cruciform design makes them look vaguely like Eastern Orthodox churches pierced with large windows. The apartments contain kitchenettes, which Linda stocks with breakfast items before the arrival of guests, and sea-view terraces, original paintings, and collections of rattan and bentwood furnishings. In winter, a standard room for two with bath costs $95 daily, one-bedroom apartments are $135 to $175, and two-bedroom units, suitable for four, run $185 to $235. *In summer, a double with bath costs from $60 daily, a one-bedroom apartment runs $75 to $90, and a two-bedroom accommodation for four goes for $100 to $120,* plus service.

Galleon Beach Club and Hotel, P.O. Box 1003, English Harbour (tel. 46-31024), is built on a flat sandy area dotted with palms, only a few feet above the level of the nearby harbor. Accommodations are in a handful of low-slung cottages with big verandas and large plate-glass windows. The decor includes louvered shutters, tile floors, vertical slats of varnished pine paneling, and bentwood or rattan chairs and tables in natural colors. Because of the isolated position of some of the cottages, you should never leave valuables in your room. In winter, one-bedroom studios cost $140 daily; one-bedroom cottages, $180; and two-bedroom cottages, $220. Two-bedroom deluxe villas go for $320. *In summer, one-bedroom studios are $85, one-bedroom cottages run $110, two-bedroom cottages cost $130, and two-bedroom deluxe villas, $180.* Service and tax are extra. Guests socialize on the veranda of the on-site Colombo's Restaurant (see "Where to Eat," below).

WHERE TO EAT: Traditionally, hotels were the answer if you wanted to dine out in Antigua. That is no longer true. In addition to the hotel facilities, many independently operated restaurants have opened in and around St. John's, serving West Indian food not readily available in the hotel dining rooms. Many dishes, especially the curries, show an East Indian influence. Lobster is a specialty. In the 1980s "gourmet" restaurants, charging inflated prices in some cases, started sprouting up on the island. Several of these are previewed in the section called "Elsewhere on the Island."

In and Around St. John's

Spanish Main Inn, East Street, P.O. Box 655 (tel. 46-20660), looks like a Tennessee Williams setting, a relaxed atmosphere combined with an old-world elegance. Bordering the park, it serves some of the best food in town, with a heavy emphasis on local specialties, including those from the neighboring island of Barbuda. For example, as an appetizer you can order stuffed crab back, perhaps shark puffs, or a clams casino Bee Wee. Their fish is always delivered fresh daily, so certain selections may not be available. However, if available I'd recommend Barbuda lobster. Try also the conch Barbuda style or the chef's special shark. Janice and Bob Branker once lived in New York—Janice working in an office, Bob digging for Con Edison. But they headed south after that with only $500 in savings and high hopes. They purchased this shingled house on Newgate Street, painting it white with red shutters. Gradually, because of their food and hospitality, the world came to their door.

In honor of their New York years, they still feature kosher knockwurst with sauerkraut. In season, they offer two rare delicacies—Barbuda guinea fowl and Barbuda venison. You might begin your meal with one of their good-tasting soups, such as goat water, red bean, clam or fish chowder. Their vegetables, a wide selection, are also tasty, composed, as they are, mainly of fresh home-grown produce. For dessert, I suggest Antigua Black Diamond pineapple. At lunch, hot dishes such as salisbury steak are served, or you may prefer a cheeseburger. Their club sandwiches are New York style. Expect to spend from $12 for lunch, $22 for dinner. Hours are noon to 3 p.m. and 7 to 9:30 p.m.

Brother B's, Long Street and Soul Alley (tel. 46-20616), is preferred for West Indian food, attracting a faithful crowd as well as a scattering of visitors. You can dine out on the patio, enjoying lobster caught fresh daily, plus fresh vegetables from Antiguan farms. The restaurant opens early (8 a.m.), remaining so until 11 p.m. Antiguan specials, prepared from recipes known for a century or two by oldtime island cooks, are served daily. For example, on Monday you might enjoy dumplings and mackerel, or pepperpot and fungi the following day, perhaps ducana (like a dumpling, made with sweet potatoes) and saltfish, or curried conch. At night, hot plates include grilled lobster, baked chicken legs, and breaded pork chops, Antiguan style. Bottles of Susie's hot sauce (and Susie means that!) are placed on every table. Expect to spend from $18 up. Sometimes a little jazz band plays on weekends.

The Victory, Redcliffe Street (tel. 46-24317), stands near the shopping center of Redcliffe Quay. The owners invite you to "come lime with us." This big restaurant, open to the breezes, is an especially good choice if you're in town on a shopping expedition. Lunches, costing from EC$30 ($11.10), feature sandwiches and fresh salad plates of lobster or tuna. At dinner, costing from EC$75 ($27.75), the fare is more elaborate, offering black Angus steak, T-bones, pan-fried snapper, and Antiguan lobster. The old stone-and-timber building also has a popular bar. It's open Monday to Saturday from 8 a.m. to 6 p.m., serving food and drink throughout the day. Dinner is nightly from 6:30 p.m. "until."

18 Carat, Church Street, St. John's (tel. 46-24219). The sign above the broken pavement outside is hard to see, but this is nonetheless one of the best lunchtime stopovers in town. Its location is in the center, under a lattice-trimmed parapet which the owners have built at the edge of an attractive sheltered garden. The blackboard menu appeals to a wide array of local residents. The kitchen produces flavorful versions of chicken and corn chowder, club sandwiches, liver and bacon, cheeseburgers and hamburgers, seafood platters, and chicken-stuffed baked potatoes. Full meals cost EC$40 ($14.80) and are served only at lunchtime, noon to 3 p.m. In the evening, the garden becomes a conversation area for one of the most popular discos in town. It's closed Sunday all year and also closed Saturday during off-season.

Cockleshell Inn, Lower Fort Road (tel. 46-20471), may be hard to find, but it's one of the most economical and best dining spots on the island. Its chef-owner, Winston Derrick, who once lived in Canada, uses the produce of Antigua—potatoes, eggplant, papaya, pineapple, but mainly freshly caught fish. His rolls are homemade: "You've got to cook for people so they come back." A complete dinner costs around $15, although up this to $25 if you want lobster. Red snapper is often featured. The inn is open daily from 6 p.m. until midnight.

Golden Peanut, High Street (tel. 46-21415), is a carousel-like place in the heart of town, the domain of Rolston Anthony, who was "born and bred on this island." His restaurant is unpretentious, and you might not imagine at first that its specialty is lobster Thermidor, which the chef prepares better than anyone else on the island. The lobster salad is also tempting, particularly at lunch. Mr. Anthony gets the finest of fresh lobster from his brother, a local fisherman, and that seems to be part of his secret. Every day he offers two local specials, perhaps mutton stew, pepperpot, or curried goat, each a typical West Indian dish. If you're dropping in for lunch during a shopping expedition, you can also ask for sandwiches. The Peanut opens early—at 8 a.m.—for breakfast. In addition, grill specialties such as lamb chops are also a feature. Your final tab will come to anywhere from $15 to $20. The Peanut snaps shut at 11 p.m.

Country Pond Restaurant, Upper Nevis Street, St. John's (tel. 46-24508). When Liz Mellor entered the scene, this pink colonial town house needed virtually all of the interior floors and walls replaced. Built in 1796, it housed various merchant families until, in greatly reduced circumstances, it served as the run-down office of a local doctor. Today the refurbished structure welcomes residents and visitors alike into its interior with its high, white ceiling. It's only a few steps away from a freshwater pond on the edge of the commercial center of town. If you're on a shopping expedition in St. John's, this might be the ideal place for you to have a light lunch. There's a terrace for al fresco dining, although the interior is kept cool by the slowly turning ceiling fans. Open daily except Sunday, the restaurant serves from 11 to 3 p.m. and 6 to 11 p.m. À la carte meals range upward from EC$25 ($9.25) and include red snapper, steak au poivre, veal piccata, chicken Kiev, shrimp and conch salad, and a full array of hamburgers and pizza.

The Yard, Upper Long Street (tel. 46-21856), gives you the feeling of dining in a living, growing garden. The tranquility demands that you relax. There is no decor added. The food is first rate. For lunch, the stuffed crab back is a specialty. There is a sumptuous Sunday brunch with a traditional local breakfast including fungi and shark. Dinner is from a well-chosen menu, costing from $18. A first-timer to the Yard should dine on the most delectable garlic shrimp in the region. Lunch is from noon to 2 p.m., and dinner, from 6 to 11 p.m. (on Sunday, go only for dinner).

Elsewhere on the Island

L'Aventure, Dian Bay (tel. 46-32003). Set within a graciously proportioned room whose greenheart floor glows after years of polishing, this is the former living room of a private house. At the core of the Dian Bay Resort, it curves around a vine-covered outdoor terrace whose panorama overlooks Indian Town Creek and a turquoise-colored lagoon. Lunch costs from EC$40 ($14.80) and is served from noon to 4 p.m. Stuffed croissant sandwiches, lobster bisque, a crab-and-shrimp rarebit, and seafood quiche are lunchtime specialties. Dinner, at EC$80 ($29.60) and up, is served from 5 to 9 p.m. nightly. Dinner specialties include steak au poivre, crab in mornay sauce topped with cheese, crabmeat crêpe with cream sauce, herring in sour cream, chicken Wellington with spinach sauce, boned rack of lamb in a pastry shell, and several preparations of Antiguan lobster. The adjacent bar is open from 11 a.m. till at least 11 p.m. seven days a week. Annual closing is during a six-week period sometime in early summer.

The **Pelican Club,** Hodge's Bay (tel. 46-22300), has been well recommended for its cuisine since its takeover by a trio of enthusiastic young Americans. It lies behind a low, white wall on a sloping plot of land between the road and the sea. Its interior is filled with modern country-style touches, including stone columns, brass ceiling fans, angled wooden ceilings of varnished pine, and a big-windowed view of the sea. Chefs Mark French and Gerard Allen concoct a sophisticated and creative cuisine drawing on many different culinary traditions. Jane French, Mark's attractive wife and the establishment's maître d', might suggest a meal that includes lobster bisque laced with aged cognac, medallions of veal with lobster covered with a béarnaise sauce, baby lamb cutlets with a herb-flavored soufflé stuffing, a ragoût of Créole-style seafood, and a filet of grouper wrapped in banana leaves and baked with a lime-butter and rum sauce. Desserts are sumptuous, including such delicacies as a gratin of kiwis with a pineapple-and-sabayon sauce, dark-chocolate mousse with a Grand Marnier sauce and orange segments, and a special banana-and-cinnamon frozen soufflé with an apricot sauce. Any of these dishes can be served without sauce for diet-conscious clients. Dinner usually requires a reservation and is served daily in high season from 6:30 to 9:30 p.m. (closes Tuesday in off-season). Lunches are less elaborate, offered from 11:30 a.m. to 2:30 p.m., costing from $15. The bill of fare is likely to include pan-fried red snapper, thick club sandwiches, and an array of pasta and curried salads. If you're in the neighborhood for breakfast, between 7 and 10:30 a.m., you'll get a full array of American-inspired eye-openers for $7 and up per person.

L'Auberge de Paris, Trade Winds, above Dickenson Bay (tel. 46-21223). Among all the restaurants of Antigua, this one offers the most sophisticated decor. It's reminiscent of a trendy bistro in the south of France, although both the accents and the attitude of the staff are pure Parisian. There is a glossy collection of cocktail tables, low-slung sofas, and soft lights of the bar area, where a pianist (sometimes imported from Paris) creates music until late in the evening. Most guests enjoy a cocktail in the bar before heading for the slope-ceilinged dining room, where the view is that of an ornamental swimming pool gracefully set between several wings of outlying buildings. Meals, costing from $50, are likely to include grilled lamb chops with onions and herbs, T-bone steak with herb butter, medallions of veal with fruit and curry, and grilled lobster with cocktail sauce. You might begin with snails in garlic butter, finishing with a champagne sorbet. It's open only for dinner, which is served nightly except Sunday from 7 to 11:30 p.m. It's on a hillside on the extreme northern end of the island, not far from the Halcyon Cove Hotel.

Lathefield Restaurant, Hodges Bay (tel. 46-22560). Personal, intimate, and charming, this unusual restaurant occupies a yellow-and-white Victorian house about eight miles northeast of St. John's. Set on 11 acres of what used to be a cotton planta-tion, the house was for several years the home of a Moravian bishop. It contains only 13 tables, each of which is freshly set with immaculate napery and often a clutch of seasonal flowers. From the old-fashioned windows you can admire copses of century-old mahogany trees. The focus of attention is on the creative specialties emerging from the sophisticated kitchen. Prepared by American-born Paul Corroon, and served by his wife, Lief, the fare might include char-broiled strips of filet mignon, chicken Ches-apeake (stuffed with lobster, green onions, and mushrooms and served with spinach), beef Wellington with pâté and a bordelaise sauce, seafood kebabs, lobster Newburg, chicken Cordon Bleu (stuffed with ham and cheese), and red snapper New Orleans style (with lobster chunks and béchamel sauce). A house specialty is California ciop-pino, a delectable fish stew whose recipe originated in San Francisco. Full meals cost from EC$85 ($31.50) and are served only at dinner from 7 to 11 p.m. every night except Wednesday and during late June and late October. Reservations are suggested in high season, and jackets and ties are discouraged. The restaurant is occasionally patronized by guests of the ultra-exclusive Mill Reef Club.

The **Lobster Pot,** Siboney Beach Club (P.O. Box 222), St. John's (tel. 46-23356), is contained within the pleasant confines of this previously recommended hotel. Guests dine at simple tables set on a flagstone floor beneath a thatched roof, near a long pinewood bar evocative of Tahiti. Nonresidents of the hotel are welcome throughout the day for drinks, meals, and snacks. Breakfast, from 7:30 to 11 a.m., costs from $7 (U.S.) for a filling American-inspired repast. Lunch, from EC$25 ($9.25), includes steaks, sandwiches, salads, and such English fare as sausages with eggs and baked beans. The fixed-price dinners, from EC$60 ($22.20) per person, fea-ture fresh seafood, grouper meunière, homemade lasagna, and grilled lobster with an-chovy butter.

Dubarry's, Barrymore Hotel (P.O. Box 244), Runaway Bay, St. John's (tel. 46-21055), is one of the best restaurants in town. In a modern, low-slung building adjacent to the Barrymore Hotel, it's divided into two distinctly different dining rooms and a pleasant paneled bar dotted with Indonesian art. On a chilly evening you'll be seated inside in an elegant modern room capped with a well-finished ceiling of Doug-las fir and pitch pine. In warm weather and during informal lunches, diners are seated behind an iron railing on an al fresco terrace overlooking the blue rectangle of an out-door pool. Strictly local vegetables are used as accompaniments to the specialties served by candlelight. They include seafood-stuffed tomatoes, lobster bouchées, quiche maison, seafood bisque, spicy pumpkin or red-bean soup, fresh salads, and main dishes such as potatoes stuffed with kingfish, fish and lobster mornay, deviled egg and shrimp casserole, curried coconut chicken served in coconut shells, spicy Ma-laysian lamb, and four different recipes for lobster, including a Créole-style "Fra Di-avolo." For dessert, you may want to try the chocolate-fudge-sundae pie, which the chef considers his signature. Other dessert choices include a collection of homemade ice creams and coconut meringue pudding. Pub lunches are served, but the real em-phasis is on the dinner menu, which is offered every day except Sunday from 7:30 to 10 p.m. Full meals range from EC$85 ($31.50), if you don't order expensive lobster. Reservations are suggested.

Colombo's Restaurant, Galleon Beach Club (P.O. Box 1003), English Harbour (tel. 46-31450), is a Polynesian-style open-air terrace sheltered from the sun and rain by a ceiling crafted from woven palm fronds suspended on top of vertical posts. It's only a few steps across the flat sands to the water. Lunches in this sprawling place cost EC$50 ($18.50) and might include spaghetti marinara, lobster salad, and sandwiches. Dinners are more elaborate, around EC$100 ($37), and include daily specials from a classic Italian inventory of veal scaloppine, red snapper, tagliatelle Colombo, veal piz-zaiola, and lobster mornay. These can be accompanied by a wide assortment of French or Italian wines. Lunch and dinner are offered daily, except for the annual vacation between early September and early October. Lunch is served from 12:30 to 2:30 p.m., and dinner from 7 to 10 p.m. On Sunday there's a special buffet, costing EC$35 ($13), offered from noon to 2:30 p.m.

Admiral's Inn (tel. 46-31027) has already been previewed in the hotel selections, a historic building in Nelson's Dockyard. If you're touring the southern coast, as most visitors do, it also makes an intriguing and pleasant stopover for lunch. In a 17th-century setting, lobster, seafood, and steaks are served, a lunch costing $9 to $13, the price rising to about $22 for a full dinner, plus service and tax. To get you started, the chef is likely to tempt you with anything from pumpkin soup to shrimp cocktail. For your main course, you're usually given four or five choices daily—perhaps lobster Thermidor, roast duckling, broiled kingfish, or lamb chops with mint sauce. If coconut custard pudding is on the menu, I'd recommend it highly. Before dinner, have a drink in the bar. There you can read the names of sailors carved in wood more than a century ago. The service is friendly and agreeable, and the setting is heavy on atmosphere. In season, you should make a reservation for dinner. It's open seven days a week, serving breakfast from 7:30 to 10 a.m., lunch from noon to 2:30 p.m., and dinner from 7:30 to 9:30 p.m. It's closed during all of September.

Shirley Heights Lookout, Shirley Heights (tel. 46-31274). In the 1790s this was the lookout station for advance warning of unfriendly ships heading toward English Harbour. To strengthen Britain's position in this strategic spot, Nelson ordered the construction of a powder magazine which, by the time Russell Hodge leased the heights from the government, had fallen into almost total ruin. Today the panoramic spot is one of the most romantic in Antigua. Mr. Hodge, who is also a commercial pilot, is the dedicated restaurateur who directs the ground-floor pub and the elegant, breezy upstairs dining room which he leases on a long-term basis. This is my favorite lookout point in the Caribbean. If visitors want to bring a picnic onto the stone battlements below the restaurant, they're welcome to sit in the shade of the palm-thatch-covered parasols.

A far more desirable experience to me is to dine under the angled rafters of the upstairs restaurant, where large, old-fashioned windows surround the room on all sides. Specialties include pumpkin soup, grilled lobster in lime butter, garlic-flavored shrimp, and good desserts, such as banana flambé and carrot cake. Full meals range from EC$80 ($29.50), although less expensive hamburgers and sandwiches are available from the pub downstairs. A Sunday-afternoon tradition with many of the area's residents are the steel-band concerts beginning at 3 p.m., accompanying the "end of the week" barbecues. The establishment is open from 10 a.m. to 10 p.m. daily. It never has a water shortage—part of Mr. Hodge's renovation included revamping the 200-year-old cistern.

Crabbs Pier 5, Crabbs Slipway & Marina (tel. 46-32144). Interesting for anyone who enjoys evaluating the attributes of boats, this pleasant open-air restaurant sits at the edge of a particularly opulent marina. You can drink at the thick mahogany bartop and then dine in a simple modern room whose menu is written on a blackboard. Full lunches, costing from EC$50 ($18.50), include hamburgers, salads, and grilled fish along with less expensive snacks. Dinners from EC$75 ($27.75) include more elaborate fare such as veal Cordon Bleu, pan-fried snapper, pumpkin soup, leek soup, and the catch of the day, along with Antiguan lobster. Breakfast is served daily (often to residents of the moored yachts) from 9 to 11:30 a.m., lunch from 11:30 a.m. to 3 p.m., and dinner from 7:30 p.m. until "late." The location is in the center of a sun-flooded marina complex on the windswept eastern coast of the island.

Jean Michel's Seafood Restaurant, Dickenson Bay, Antigua Village Hotel (tel. 46-24158). Set on the beach, on an airy veranda flooded with sea breezes and sunlight, this is considered one of the best French restaurants on the island. Nestling in the premises of this hotel, it lies between a row of hedges and the open sea. French-born Jean Michel and his English partner, Tony Sayer, serve three meals a day, seven days a week, within the casually elegant confines whose ambience might have been inspired by an afternoon in St. Tropez. Breakfast, costing from $7 per person, lasts from 8 to 11:30 a.m. and includes such eye-opening concoctions as eggs Benedict and an array of crêpes. Simple lunches, from 11:30 a.m. to 5:30 p.m., cost from $14 and include salads, pizzas, homemade soups, and pastas. It's only at night, between 6:30 and 10:30 p.m., that the true culinary skill of this team becomes obvious. Full dinners, costing from $30, usually require a reservation and include such specialties as the catch of the day, lobster Thermidor, chilled orange-and-melon soup, veal medallions, grilled red snapper (which is then flambéed with Pernod), mushroom duxelle vol-au-vent, and stuffed cannelloni with crabmeat, plus a full wine list.

The **Satay Hut,** Runaway Bay, St. John's (tel. 46-24101), is a simple and friend-ly restaurant which could serve as the focal point for a day at the beach. It sits directly on the sands of Runaway Bay, with breezes and the tropical drinks served by a smiling waitress keeping you cool. The interior is filled with Indonesian art which owner Linda Gordon picked up during her years in Jakarta. No one will mind if you just come here for a drink. Piña coladas and rum punch cost $1.50 (U.S.) each during happy hour, held during a part of every afternoon. If you want a nourishing and good-tasting lunch or dinner, complete meals begin at around EC$40 ($14.75). Specials are Indian curry, Antiguan lobster, and several different red snapper dishes. In keeping with the decor, the restaurant specializes in Indonesian satay, made with shrimp or skewered pork, chicken, and beef, served with nasi goreng (fried rice), peanut sauce, and pickled veg-etables. Less exotic and less expensive fare includes several kinds of hamburgers, cheeseburgers, club sandwiches, and chili dogs. It's open for lunch and dinner daily from noon to 2:30 p.m. and 7 to 9 p.m. The setting is informal, a fact appreciated by guests at the adjacent Barrymore Hotel.

EXPLORING ANTIGUA: In the southern part of St. John's, the **market** is colorful and interesting, especially on Saturday morning. Hucksters busy selling their fruits and vegetables bargain and gossip. The semi-open-air market lies at the lower end of Market Street. Scenery is provided by both dress and food.

Also in town, **St. John's Cathedral,** the Anglican cathedral, has had a disastrous history. Originally built in 1683, it was replaced by a stone building in 1745. That, however, was destroyed by an earthquake in 1843. The present pitch-pine interior, dating from 1847, shores up the stone walls against earthquakes. The interior was being restored when, in 1973, the twin towers and structure were badly damaged by an earthquake. The towers and the southern section have been restored, but restoring the northern part is estimated to cost thousands of dollars, for which contributions are gratefully received. At the entrance, iron gates were erected by the vestry in 1789. The figures of St. John the Baptist and St. John the Divine, at the south gate, were said to have been taken from one of the Napoleonic ships and brought to Antigua by a British man-of-war. The cathedral is between Long and Newgate Streets at Church Lane.

After leaving St. John's, the average visitor heads for one of the biggest attrac-tions in the eastern Caribbean, **Nelson's Dockyard.** It's open seven days a week from 8 a.m. to 6 p.m., charging an admission of EC$2 (75¢).

One of the safest landlocked harbors in the world, the restored dockyard was used by Admirals Nelson, Rodney, and Hood. It was the home of the British fleet at the time of the Napoleonic wars. From 1784 Nelson was the commander of the British navy in the Leeward Islands, having his headquarters at English Harbour. English ships used the harbor as early as 1671, finding it a refuge from hurricanes. The era of privateers, pirates, and great sea battles in the 18th century revolved around the dockyard.

Restored by the Friends of English Harbour, the dockyard is sometimes known as a Caribbean Williamsburg. Its colonial-style naval buildings stand now as they did when Nelson was there (1784–1787). However, Nelson never lived at the Admiral's House, as it was built in 1855. It does contain what may have been his bed, a four-poster of gilded ivory-colored wood. The house has been turned into a museum of nautical memorabilia. (For accommodations at English Harbour, refer to my earlier recommendations.)

A footpath leads to **Fort Barclay,** the fort at the entrance to English Harbour. The path starts just outside the dockyard gate and it's about half a mile away. The fort is interesting, a fine specimen of oldtime military engineering.

If you're at English Harbour at sunset, head for **Shirley Heights,** named after General Shirley, governor of the Leeward Islands in 1781. He fortified the hills guarding the harbor. Standing are Palladian arches, once part of the barracks. The Block House, one of the main buildings, was put up as a stronghold in case of siege. The nearby Victorian cemetery contains an obelisk to the officers and men of the 54th Regiment.

On a low hill overlooking Nelson's Dockyard, **Clarence House** was built by English stonemasons to accommodate Prince William Henry, later known as the Duke of Clarence (even later he became King William IV). The future king stayed here when he was in command of the *Pegasus* in 1787. At present, it is the country home of the governor of Antigua, and is open to visitors when His Excellency is not in residence. A caretaker will show you through (it's customary to tip him, of course), and you'll see many pieces of furniture on loan from the National Trust. In days of yore, Princess Margaret and Lord Snowdon stayed here on their honeymoon.

On the way back, take **Fig Tree Drive,** a 20-some-mile circular drive across the main mountain range. It passes through lush tropical hills and fishing villages along the southern coast. You can pick up the road just outside Liberta, north of Falmouth. Winding through a rain forest, it passes thatched villages, and every village has a church with lots of goats and children running about. However, don't expect fig trees. Fig is an Antiguan name for bananas.

About half a mile before reaching St. John's you come to **Fort James,** which was begun in 1704 as a main lookout post for the port. It was named after James II in whose reign efforts were made to build the fort on the point known as St. John's.

Other places on the island worth seeking out include the following:

Parkham Church: The origin of this church is unknown. However, a church stood on this spot in 1755. The church, overlooking Parkham Town, was destroyed by fire, and the present structure was erected in 1840 in the Italian style. Richly adorned with stucco work, it was damaged by an earthquake in 1843. Much of the ceiling was destroyed and very little of the stucco work remains, but the octagonal structure is still worth a visit.

Potsworks Dam: This is the largest man-made lake in Antigua, surrounded by an area of natural beauty. The dam has a capacity of a billion gallons of water, protection for Antigua in case of a drought.

Indian Town: One of Antigua's national parks, Indian Town is at a northeastern point on the island. Over the centuries Atlantic breakers have lashed against the rocks, carving a natural bridge known as Devil's Bridge. It's surrounded by numerous blowholes spouting surf.

Megaliths: At Greencastle Hill, a long climb will reveal these megaliths, said to have been set up by human hands for the worship of a sun god and a moon goddess. Some experts, however, believe that the arrangement is an unusual geological formation, a volcanic rockfall.

Antigua Rum Distillery: This production plant at Rat Island turns out two fine rums, Cavalier and Old Mill. Check at the tourist office about arranging a visit. Established in 1932, the plant is next to Deep Water Harbour. Its annual production rate is in excess of 250,000 imperial-proof gallons.

SHOPPING: Most of the shops are clustered on St. Mary's Street or High Street in St. John's. Some shops are open from 8:30 a.m. to noon and 1 to 4 p.m., but this rule varies greatly from store to store. Antiguan shopkeepers are an independent lot. Many of them close at noon on Thursday.

There are many duty-free items for sale, including English woolens and linens, and you can also purchase several specialized items made in Antigua. These include original pottery, local straw work, Antigua rum, and silkscreened, hand-printed local designs on fabrics, as well as mammy bags, floppy foldable hats, and shell curios.

Sea island cotton products are good buys, and some of the best are found at the **West Indian Sea Island Cotton Shop,** St. Mary's Street (tel. 46-22972). The shop is an outlet for the Romney Manor workshop on St. Kitts. The Caribelle label consists of batik and tie-dye, offering beach wraps, swimwear, and head ties.

The **Studio,** Cross Street, opposite Government House (tel. 46-21034). Heike Petersen came to Antigua in 1964, restoring this lovely old town house. When it was finished, the designer was ready to show off a collection of island fashions. The clothes are island-inspired originals, and Heike designs all of them herself, using fabrics from all over the world. The originals are hand-finished and styled in Antigua, however. Beach fashions are displayed, along with striking day wear, even evening gowns and coordinated accessories. The style is that of casual elegance. Heike is also available for consultation and custom designing.

The **Industrial School for the Blind,** All Saints Road (no phone), stands next to the public market. Here the government helps the handicapped in training programs. On sale are the results of some of their work—pieces of straw work, including floor-mats, baskets, chairs, mats, hats, and other small household items. You'll also see the craftspeople at work.

Coco Shop, the "brown house on St. Mary's Street" (tel. 46-21128), is one of the best-equipped marts in town. It's a West Indian beach and shore fashion center, utilizing sea island cottons, even prints from Liberty of London. You can purchase these fabrics either made up or by the yard. Men's shirts have a tropical flair, and some of the carefree clothes are hand-embroidered. Men, women, and children will find a selection of shirts, dresses, blouses, and bikinis. Placed on the counters are hand-crafted ceramics, all made in Antigua. The most popular are the famous steel bands-men. Ask for Antiguan Frangipani Perfume. There are Coco Shop branches at the airport and Deep Water Harbour.

Bay Boutique, St. Mary's Street (tel. 46-22183), is for women who are offered a choice line of ready-made clothes for sale. Hostess gowns are well styled, and there are both long and short skirts, and blouses. All of the items were sewn on the island from imported fabrics. Lots of English flowery fabrics were in evidence on my most recent rounds.

Sugar Mill Boutique, St. Mary's Street (tel. 46-24523), set amid a collection of other clothing stores and shops, sells garments whose fabrics have been silkscreened by local artist Ruth Clarage. The designs tend to include depictions of birds, fish, flowers, and shells indigenous to the region. The store sells a wide array of vibrantly colorful swimwear, evening wear, and casual clothes for men and women. Everything sold here is advertised as hand-washable.

Quin Farara's Liquor Store, Long Street and Corn Alley (tel. 46-20463). Antigua has some of the lowest liquor prices in the Caribbean, and this shop has one of the largest collections of wines and liquors on the island. Often you'll save up to 50% on what you'd pay in the States. The staff will show you how to take home a "gallon," pay the duty, and still save. Don Diego (originally Cuban) cigars are also on sale.

Shoul's Chief Store, on St. Mary's Street opposite Barcklays Bank (tel. 46-21139), is an Ali Baba's cave of treasures for visitors to Antigua. The store is new, having recently been redesigned and rebuilt at a cost of more than $1 million. Now the most modern store in St. John's, it is managed by well-known businessman Ian Shoul, the authorized Singer Sewing Machine dealer here. In addition to household items and appliances, a wide range of local and imported souvenirs, Antigua T-shirts, and fab-

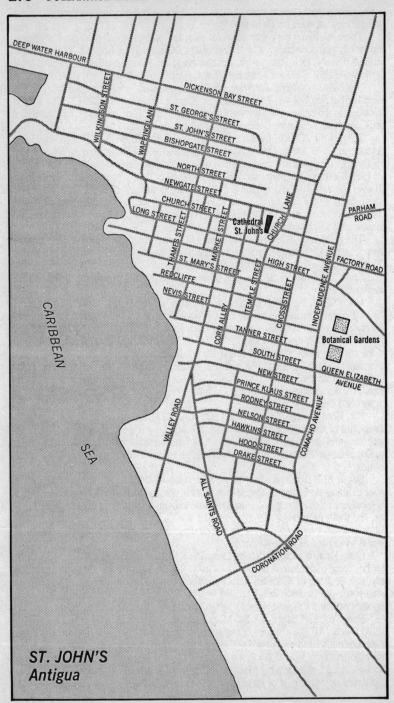

DEEP WATER HARBOUR

DICKENSON BAY STREET

WILKINGSON STREET

WAPPING LANE

ST. GEORGE'S STREET

ST. JOHN'S STREET

BISHOPGATE STREET

NORTH STREET

NEWGATE STREET

CHURCH STREET

LONG STREET

THAMES STREET

MARKET STREET

CHURCH LANE

PARHAM ROAD

Cathedral
St. John's

ST. MARY'S STREET

HIGH STREET

INDEPENDENCE AVENUE

FACTORY ROAD

REDCLIFFE

TEMPLE STREET

CROSS STREET

NEVIS STREET

CORN ALLEY

TANNER STREET

Botanical Gardens

SOUTH STREET

NEW STREET

QUEEN ELIZABETH
AVENUE

PRINCE KLAUS STREET

RODNEY STREET

NELSON STREET

HAWKINS STREET

COMACHO AVENUE

HOOD STREET

DRAKE STREET

VALLEY ROAD

CARIBBEAN

SEA

ALL SAINTS ROAD

CORONATION ROAD

ST. JOHN'S
Antigua

rics of all colors, designs, and textures will be shown to you by the helpful and friendly staff.

Shipwreck Shops Ltd. (tel. 46-21322) has four convenient locations: St. Mary's Street at Kensington Court, and at Jardine Court, the Jolly Beach Hotel, and the Halcyon Cove Hotel. Their walls, ceilings, and counters are loaded with merchandise either from Antigua or some neighboring island. They carry everything from A to Z—T-shirts, coverups, swim suits, dresses, photo supplies, beach accessories, jewelery, wooden bowls, figurines of wood and ceramic, glassware, hats, bags, postcards, and more. They also have daily newspapers, magazines, and many paperback books.

Custom Made Garment, Inc., Vivian Richards Street (no phone), features Jim Tillet silkscreen prints, plus other materials, in either ready- or custom-made garments. Doris George designs and makes clothing for you, as well as helping make sure the fit is right on ready-made clothing.

Serendipity, Redcliffe Quay (tel. 46-22026), sells merchandise from England, Scotland, and Ireland, including handmade Scottish teddy bears, crofter's hand-woven lambswool blankets and shawls, scrimshaw, and a small selection of Irish pewter.

The Galley Boutique, 7 Redcliffe Quay (tel. 46-24220), is considered one of the best of the unusual stores in the shopping labyrinth of Redcliffe Quay. Specializing in casual sportswear, usually for women, it also has a limited selection for men and children. A few of the garments are hand-blocked and batiked in tropical colors and designs, and are often made in Antigua.

A Thousand Flowers, Redcliffe Street (tel. 46-24264), sells Indonesian batiks, crafted on the island into sundresses, knock-'em-dead shirts, sarongs, rompers, and swimwear. Many of the garments are designed into a one-size-fits-all motif of knots and flowing expanses of cloth appropriate for the tropics.

The **Specialty Shop,** St. Mary's Street (tel. 46-21198), is the finest emporium of European porcelain, silver, and crystal on the island. The friendly sales personnel wear pink-and-white uniforms that match the color schemes of several of the Aynsley patterns.

The **Halcyon Cove Hotel boutique** at Dickenson Bay (tel. 46-20256) always has 100 or so casual dresses on hangers. There is a vast selection of attractive floral prints. For the most part the dresses are full length and strapless, some with spaghetti straps.

Kel-Print, Coolidge Airport and also St. Mary's Street in St. John's (tel. 46-22189), offers silkscreened, hand-print fabrics and T-shirts. Some children's wear is also sold.

If you want an island-made bead necklace, don't bother to go to any shop. Just lie on the beach—anywhere—and some ''bead lady'' will find you.

NIGHTLIFE: Most nightlife revolves around the hotels, unless you want to roam Antigua at night looking for that ''hot native club.'' If you're going out for the night, make arrangements to have a taxi pick you up—otherwise you could be stranded in the wilds somewhere. Antigua has some of the best steel bands in the Caribbean.

18 Carat, Church Street, St. John's (tel. 46-24219). Although it serves well-prepared lunches, this place's real identity comes from its function as a disco. Guests go through a pleasant garden, past a lattice-trimmed arbor, and then enter the cozy building at the garden's far end. The club's ambience is heightened by its small dimensions. There's occasionally a live singer in the disco, but most of the time the crowd seems to prefer to dance the night away to the sounds of the recorded music. The disco opens at 9 p.m. Wednesday through Sunday, charging an entrance fee of EC$6 ($2.20). In summer, it's open only on Friday and Saturday.

After dinner, you might also want to patronize the **Halcyon Cove Casino** (tel. 46-20256). It offers all the games of chance, giving you an opportunity to try your luck at roulette, blackjack, American craps, and super-jackpot slots.

Flamingo Antigua Hotel and Casino, on Michael's Mount (tel. 46-21266), is a gambling complex that's part of the hotel of the same name, about half a mile from the center. It offers blackjack and craps tables, plus a large assortment of slot machines and roulette.

THE SPORTING LIFE: Beaches, beaches, and more beaches—Antigua has, as mentioned, some 365 of them. Some are superior. There's a lovely beach at Pigeon Point, in Falmouth Harbour, about a four-minute drive from the Admiral's Inn. The beach at **Dickenson Bay,** near the Halcyon Cove Hotel, is also superior, and for a break, you can enjoy meals and drinks on the hotel's Warri Pier, built on stilts in the water (this beach is also a center for water sports). Chances are, however, you'll swim at your own hotel.

Golf

In golf, Antigua doesn't have the facilities of some of the other islands such as Puerto Rico. But what it has is good. The 18-hole **Cedar Valley Golf Club** (tel. 46-20161) is three miles out of St. John's, near the airport. It has been improved and expanded in recent years.

The other course of note is the one at **Half Moon Bay** (tel. 46-22726), on the southeast corner of Antigua. It's a nine-holer. In season, guests of the hotel are guaranteed a space—and you may not be.

Horseback Riding

It may no longer be prudent to ride a horse along the beach (there have been problems in the past), but this sport is still popular, costing $12 per hour. Riding is possible at the **Galley Bay Surf Club** (tel. 46-20302), 15 minutes from St. John's by taxi.

Tennis

Tennis buffs will find courts at most of the major hotels. Some are lit for night games. I don't recommend playing tennis at noon in Antigua unless you're a "mad dog or an Englishman." It's just too hot! If your hotel doesn't have a court, you'll find them available at the **Halcyon Cove, Anchorage, Half Moon Bay, Cedar Valley Golf Club,** and **Curtain Bluff.** If you're not a guest, you'll have to book a court, paying about $4 per hour, a price which can vary from hotel to hotel. Some hotels require a $25 deposit for the rental of balls and racquets, but the full amount is refunded if the equipment is returned.

Fishing

Deep-sea fishing can usually be arranged at your hotel desk. If you want to negotiate on your own, check out **Long Bay Hotel** (tel. 46-32005), which offers a half-day inshore fishing at $25 per person if there are two or more in your party. For deep-sea fishing, including guide, bait, and tackle, the cost is $125 per half-day trip.

Windsurfing

The **Blue Waters Beach Hotel,** Soldier Bay (tel. 46-20290), claims that nearly everybody can learn this sport. It's one of the leading facilities on the island for windsurfing, giving an introductory lesson for $35 for 1½ hours. If you already know how to windsurf, the cost is $12 per hour (complimentary to resident guests).

Water Sports

Snorkeling and scuba-diving are best arranged through **Dive Antigua,** at the Halcyon Cove Beach Resort and Casino on Dickenson Bay (tel. 46-20256), and at the Jolly Beach Hotel on Morris Bay (tel. 46-20061, ext. 111).

Long Bay Hotel (tel. 46-32005), on the northeastern coast of the island at Long

Bay, is another good location for water sports—swimming, sailing, waterskiing, deep-sea fishing, windsurfing, and scuba-diving. The hotel has complete scuba facilities. Both beginning snorkelers and experienced divers are welcomed. You're taken on snorkel trips by boat to Green Island at a cost of $10 per person (if there are two or more) and to Great Bird Island for $15 per person (again if there are two or more). The shallow side of the double reef across Long Bay is ideal for the neophyte, and the whole area on the northeastern tip has many reefs of varying depths.

The **Blue Waters Beach Hotel,** Soldier Bay (tel. 46-20290), has one of the best water-sports programs on the island. Waterskiing is available at about $10 per ski per person. In addition, they offer snorkeling gear free to their guests.

Parasailing

This sport is gaining in popularity in Antigua. Facilities are available during the day (except Sunday) on the beach at Dickenson Bay (tel. 461-0945).

Sailing

Since Admiral Nelson's day, sailing has been popular in Antigua. I prefer the **Servabo Fun Cruise** taken in a character-type vessel, the last constructed of a British sailing fishing trawler popular from 1750 to 1927. Based off the shores of Dickenson Bay, the 64-ton *Servabo* celebrated her 50th anniversary some time back. She even appeared before the cameras, in the Omar Sharif film *The Mysterious Island*. The vessel's barbecue cruise costs $40 per person. Out at sea you're given barbecued steak and lobster, and you're gone from 10 a.m. to 4 p.m. The cruise departs from Antigua Village. The day is filled with calypso music, snorkeling, and rum punches. Telephone 46-21581 for reservations.

All major hotel desks can book you on a day cruise on the 108-foot "pirate ship," the *Jolly Roger*. For $35, you are taken sightseeing on a fun-filled day, with drinks and a barbecue steak lunch. The *Jolly Roger* is the largest sailing ship in Antiguan waters. Lunch is combined with a snorkel trip. Dancing is on the poop deck, and members of the crew teach passengers how to dance calypso. Everything's a little corny, but most passengers love it. If you want to make reservations on your own, telephone 46-22064. There are daily sailings from Dickenson Bay.

BARBUDA: Known by the Spanish as Dulcina, sparsely populated Barbuda, part of an associated state with Antigua, was discovered by Columbus in 1493. The island lies 28 miles to the north of Antigua, and is about 15 miles long by 5 miles wide with a population of some 1,200 hardy souls, most of whom live around the unattractive village of Codrington.

Don't come here seeking lush, tropical scenery, as flat Barbuda consists of coral rock. Yet it is the flatness that gives the island some fine beaches that stretch for miles on both the leeward and the windward coasts.

Hunters, fishermen, and just plain beachcombers are attracted to the island, as it has some fallow deer, guinea fowl, pigeon, and wild pig. Barbuda also has a few deer. Those interested in fishing negotiate with the owners of small boats which hire them out. Bonefish and tarpon are frequently caught.

The main town is named after Christopher Codrington, who was once the governor of the Leeward Islands. He is believed to have deliberately wrecked ships on the reefs circling Barbuda. What is known is that he used the island, which he'd received in 1691 from the Crown, for the purposes of breeding slaves. He was given the island in return for "one fat pig per year, if asked."

Barbuda has a temperature that seldom falls below an average of 75° Fahrenheit.

The island is reached after a ten-minute flight from Antigua's Coolidge Airport. It has two airfields, one at Codrington, the other a private facility, "Kelly Field," at

Coco Point. Both are served by Leeward Islands Air Transport (LIAT) on both a scheduled and charter service.

The **Earl's Complex Barbuda Day Tour,** offered for a minimum of four persons, is a round-trip package taking you from Antigua to Barbuda. The tour takes passengers on a tour of the frigate bird sanctuary by boat and a short tour of the island. A barbecue is served on the beach, and drinks are included in the price. The charge is $98.50 per person. Reservations must be made at least 48 hours before you plan to make the trip, through Claudia Richards, P.O. Box 57, St. John's, Antigua (tel. 46-24489).

Paradise Tours, High Street, St. John's (tel. 46-24786), also conducts a round-trip tour to Barbuda for the day, including a picnic lunch. Prices are subject to variation, but count on spending some $100 for the day tour, including air flight.

Those trippers over just for the day usually head for **Wa'Omoni Beach Park,** where they can visit a frigate bird sanctuary, snorkel for lobster, and eat barbecue.

Curiosities of the island include a "**Dividing Wall,**" which once separated the Codringtons from the black people, and the **Martello Tower,** which predates the known history of the island. Tours also cover interesting underground caves on the island. Stamp collectors might want to call at the **Philatelic Bureau** in Codrington.

Where to Stay

Coco Point Lodge (tel. 212/696-4750 in New York City for reservations) is like a private club, occupying a 164-acre peninsula with more than 2½ miles of white sandy beach at the southern tip of Barbuda. Guests are housed either in the main building or in one of the newer cottages such as Spanish Point, Martello Tower, or Sea Crescent, a total of 32 accommodations with beachfront patios. Coco Point caters to everybody from a small-town banker to titans of industry or actresses who want to escape from it all, even Princess Margaret. A lot of wicker is used, making the lodge evoke a summer home in the Hamptons. The designer did the exclusive Mill Reef Club on Antigua. The inn is definitely understated, and that's how its clients like it. The social hub is the clubhouse. The lodge receives only from November 15 to May 1. Usually there are rarely more than 50 guests at one time, perhaps 60 at the very most, and it's estimated that some three-quarters of them are repeat customers. Dress is casual, and ties and jackets are certainly not required.

On the full-board plan, single peak-season rates range from $350 to $550 daily, with doubles costing $400 to $600 on the same plan. An additional person in a room is another $140. At least the booze is included in the rate. The food is flown in from Miami, except some fresh produce which may be shipped in from Dominica and St. Kitts. The venison is left for the natives to live on. Their seafood and homemade bisques are superb.

About 40% of the guests come here to enjoy the good fishing. A 43-foot motor sailer is placed at the disposal of guests. Guests who land on the lodge's own 3,000-foot strip are picked up quickly, and 15 minutes later are found sitting on the beach with a rum punch. Included in the rate is air transportation from Coolidge Airport in Antigua. Other facilities include waterskiing and two very fine all-weather tennis courts. The owner is Bill Kelly, who once lived next door to the Kennedys in Hyannis Port. His son, Patrick, is now in charge. His most helpful on-the-spot managers are Martin and Caroline Price. Frankly, Mr. Kelly prefers to keep the crowds out. After all, this is an exclusive resort. Therefore if you're planning to drop in for a drink or a meal, forget it, unless you're a paying guest. Many a visiting yachtsman has been turned away disappointed. At the rates charged, Coco Point guests demand—and get —their privacy.

Le Village Soleil, P.O. Box 1104, St. John's, Antigua (tel. 46-23147 in Antigua). If you've ever wanted to practice your French in as remote an environment as possible, you might enjoy this isolated guesthouse whose charming owners come from

Québec. André Cloutier and his attractive wife, Danie, maintain this tiny resort on Barbuda as if it were an extension of their private home. Of course, they speak English too. Most of the accommodations contain large bedrooms, verandas, private baths, thatched roofs, and rustic ceilings. Between mid-December and the end of April, single units cost $135 to $150 and doubles run $230 to $245. All meals are included in the tariffs, with an unlimited bar and water sports, including snorkeling equipment, Sunfish sailboat, and windsurfer. A 10% service charge is added to all bills. The public rooms revolve around a steep-roofed, cedar-sided bar and restaurant open to a sweeping view of the wide, curved beach of white clear sand. Meals are usually eaten at long tables with the other guests, where nightfall parties feast on the French and Caribbean cuisine. Since there are no telephones, television, or newspapers, most guests succumb to the temptation of simply relaxing. There's room for only 16 guests at this congenial establishment, most of whom are Americans. The hotel is not open in summer, at which time inquiries should be sent to P.O. Box 72, Roberval, Québec G8H 2N4, Canada (tel. 418/275-3861).

2. Montserrat

To see "the way the Caribbean used to be," a good choice for a visit is Montserrat. Vacationers often visit the volcanic island just for the day and later are sorry they hadn't booked more time. Called tritely "The Emerald Isle of the Caribbean," Montserrat is some 27 miles southwest of Antigua, lying between Guadeloupe and Nevis. The pear-shaped island is mountainous with lush green forests, much tropical vegetation, and some licorice beaches of volcanic sand that are powdery but black as midnight.

Montserrat was discovered by the ubiquitous Columbus in 1493 and named after the famous sawtoothed mountain near Barcelona. However, it wasn't until 1632 that Irish settlers colonized the island, when Oliver Cromwell, it is believed, shipped out a band of reluctant colonists who'd been captured after a rebellion. Sending the unwilling band to the ruggedly beautiful island was Cromwell's way of getting rid of them. Montserrat also became home to Irish settlers who fled their new homes on St. Kitts because of religious persecution. The Irish influence is shown in names of places on the island and in the surnames of present-day residents.

The flag of Montserrat is the British Union Jack, but the official badge is the very Irish "Lady with the Harp." The shamrock can be seen on the center gable of Government House, which can be visited, and it's also on the stamp with which Montserrat immigration people stamp your passport. The island even marks March 17 as a public holiday, but this is because the slaves in the early days staged a rebellion on St. Patrick's Day. By 1648 there were more than 1,000 Irish families living on Montserrat, a place that had become known as a sanctuary from religious persecution.

Today Montserrat's more than 15,000 hard-working, friendly people, most of whom were descended from African slaves, often speak with an Irish brogue as a heritage left by those early settlers.

The island was captured by the French in 1644, restored to England in 1668, and retaken by the French in 1782, who ceded it to Britain in 1783. Popular as a retiree resort, the island has political stability, its officials having elected to remain a British Crown Colony, as they don't have the financial independence to go it alone. The capital, **Plymouth,** is reputed to be one of the cleanest in the Caribbean. It's best viewed on Saturday market day, when gossip is traded along with fruit.

The mean temperature of Montserrat ranges from a high of 86.5° to a low of 73.5° Fahrenheit.

George Martin, best known as the producer of the Beatles, has launched a contemporary electronic studio in a Belham Valley estate, and he uses Olveston House, the residence of an early lime-juice magnate, as a private residence for the Aire recording company (tel. 491-5656). Therefore don't be surprised if, when exploring Montserrat, you encounter such artists as Paul McCartney or Elton John, both of whom have been known to come here for weeks at a time to record music and to "wind down." Among celebrities who have stayed on the island in years past have been Ringo Starr, Jimmy Buffet, and Stevie Wonder.

GETTING THERE: Antigua is the "gateway" to Montserrat. The government of Montserrat purchased two planes from LIAT (Leeward Islands Air Transport), calling their new airline the **Montserrat Air Service** (MAS for short). MAS still uses LIAT's ticketing facilities. In other words, a passenger might fly MAS and still think he or she was doing business with LIAT. There are several morning and afternoon flights every day of the week. The round-trip passage between Antigua and Montserrat is EC$134 ($49.50).

GETTING AROUND: There are 130 miles of surfaced roads, and taxis and buses are the most popular means of transport. **Taxi** drivers meet every plane. Typical fares from the airport to Vue Pointe are EC$35 ($13) one way, EC$26 ($9.50) from the airport to Montserrat Springs Hotel. Sightseeing tours cost about $10 per hour. Motor **buses** run between Plymouth and most areas at fees ranging from $1 to $2.

If you don't mind driving on the left, you can rent a car in Montserrat, although you must go to the police station where you'll be given a temporary driver's license upon presentation of a valid U.S. or Canadian license and payment of EC$7.50 ($2.80). Rental cars, ranging in price from $28 to $40 per day, unlimited mileage, are generally booked at your hotel, or you can get in touch with **Pauline's Car Rental** at Amersham (tel. 491-2345) or **Jefferson Car Rental** at Dagenham (tel. 491-2126). Incidentally, car rentals aren't allowed to operate out of the airport, so one must board a taxi for the cross-island trip to Plymouth. It's important to bear in mind that there are only two gasoline stations (they call it petrol here) in Montserrat. One is the Texaco station, north of Old Towne, and the other is opposite the public market.

PRACTICAL FACTS: Montserrat is on **Atlantic Standard Time.** When it's 6 a.m. in Plymouth, it's 5 a.m. in New York or Miami. However, island clocks match those of the mainland when the East Coast goes on Daylight Saving Time.

You'll need an electrical adapter for all U.S.-made appliances, as the island has 220–230 volts, 60 cycles, AC.

Most hotels add a 10% surcharge to your final tab to cover **tips.** If they don't, it's customary to tip from 10% to 15%.

As you leave Montserrat, the government will impose a $5 **departure tax.** They also charge a government **hotel tax** of 7%.

For information and assistance, see the **Montserrat Tourist Board,** in Plymouth (tel. 491-2230).

HOTELS: Montserrat has a very limited range of accommodations and these are wide-ranging in style, from plantation-style guesthouses to modest inns to condominium colonies. The trade winds, more than air conditioning, will keep you cool. Extreme informality is the keynote.

Vue Pointe Hotel, P.O. Box 65, Old Towne (tel. 491-5211), is a family-run cottage colony of 28 hexagonal, shingle-roofed villas, plus a dozen interconnected town houses. They're set on five acres of sloping land near a black sand beach. Most of the accommodations are constructed with natural lumber, having open-beamed ceilings, and they're furnished with sleekly modern pieces. Each has a private bath, a sitting room area, and twin beds. Your host is Cedric R. Osborne, a bright, charming West Indian aristocrat who welcomes guests with his customary style and grace, and does what he can to keep you from becoming bored, even though Montserrat is supposed to be "sleepy." His father built Vue Point, and he's assisted by Carole, his wife. If it's your second visit, he welcomes you as "part of the family." Mr. Osborne has selected what is the finest staff on the island, with Augustus Cruickshank as manager. They are unobtrusive, but so well trained they seem to anticipate your needs. When they can, they offer music and dancing to a steel-band beat. They'll even show movies.

In winter, two persons pay $185 daily in a cottage, while a single person is charged only $140, all on the MAP. A double room, also on the MAP, rents for $150 daily, a single for $110. *In summer, tariffs are lowered, with two persons on the MAP paying from $60 daily; a single, from $50.* A natural breeze sweeps through accommodations in lieu of air conditioning. Besides the freshwater swimming pool, there are two tennis courts, lit for evening games. The cuisine is the best on the island, and as proof of that, everybody seems to show up for the West Indian barbecue on Wednesday night. Food is served family style, which means that no one faints if you ask for second helpings. However, the first helpings are usually generous enough to suffice. There are two attractive bars, one at the rambling main house, the other, called the Nest, at water's edge.

The location is just 11 miles from the Montserrat airport and about two minutes from the challenging seaside Montserrat Golf Club. The staff will arrange for fishing, sailing, and snorkeling. Dress is informal, except on Monday and Saturday nights in season, when custom dictates that the men spruce up a bit.

Montserrat Springs Hotel, P.O. Box 259, Richmond (tel. 491-2481), is a 29-room inn nestled on a hillside, with a superb view of Plymouth, a mile away. The manager runs a quiet, subdued, small hotel, welcoming you into a split-level house with its trade-wind-swept, open-air terrace built around a swimming pool that juts out on the hill. Guest rooms extend down a breezy corridor. Your room has a picture window with a small patio. Baths are big and tiled. Rooms have air conditioning. The hotel has a Jacuzzi and a hot-water mineral bath. In the open-air lounge, you can enjoy a before-dinner drink before walking up to the mezzanine for a big, hearty West Indian dinner. In winter, singles on the EP pay $80 daily. Doubles are $90. *Off-season, singles are $55, while doubles cost $65.* A third adult in a room pays $20, but there is no charge for children up to 12 sharing a room with adults. The beach is 100 yards away. On some nights there is live music and entertainment, perhaps crab racing.

Coconut Hill Hotel, P.O. Box 337 (tel. 491-2144), in the residential suburbs half a mile outside Plymouth, once belonged to an English surgeon and plantation owner who settled in Montserrat at the time of the American Civil War. This antique Montserratian mansion has roots deep in the soil of the island. The son of the original owner converted the property into a hotel way back in 1908, adding rooms on the top floor. Other renovations have been carried out to improve the facilities. This is a very casual West Indian guesthouse, surrounded by park-like grounds. It's also classic in style—the façade has remained the same over the years, with a long upper and lower balcony across the front. Across the rear of the building, a dining room, serving island-style meals, offers an unmarred view. The furnishings are unusually fine, with a generous collection of Caribbean antiques. All but one of the nine bedrooms have private baths, and are furnished with a mixture of the old and new. Each room also has a phone, but don't expect air conditioning. However, you may sleep blissfully in a four-poster bed. In winter, guests on the MAP are charged $75 daily in a single, $92 in a double. *Off-season reductions drop the prices to $65 daily in a single, $85 in a double, both MAP tariffs.*

Flora Fountain Hotel, Lower Dagenham Road, P.O. Box 373 (tel. 491-2533), is popular with business travelers who appreciate its central location in Plymouth. This hotel is built around a circular courtyard centered on a fountain whose illumination is computerized. Each of its 18 bedrooms is concealed behind mahogany doors. There isn't much of a view, but each unit has its own balcony nonetheless. Rooms have private baths and air conditioning. In winter, singles cost $55 daily, and doubles run $75, with breakfast included. *In summer, singles rent for $45 daily and doubles go for $56, with breakfast included.* The hotel offers a fixed-price lunch from 11 a.m. to 2:30 p.m., costing only EC$11 ($4) per person.

SELF-SUFFICIENT VACATIONS: A condominium hillside colony, **Shamrock Villas,** P.O. Box 180, Plymouth (tel. 491-2434), suggests an Iberian village of white, balcony-studded houses. Owners have arranged for their villas to be rented in their absence. The interiors are decorated in the taste of their owners. You might, for example, find a style that is imaginative, with high walls of rugged stone, lofty ceilings with open beams, and furnishings that combine bamboo with locally made mahogany and cedar pieces. From all villas there are views of the sea, the black sandy beaches, and Plymouth. Up for rent are one- and two-bedroom apartments as well as penthouses. In season (December to April), the rates for one-bedroom/one-bath apartments are $70 per night for two persons, or $400 weekly. A two-bedroom unit, suitable for four, costs $80 nightly or $500 weekly. *In off-season, a one-bedroom unit for two persons is only $55 nightly, or $300 weekly. A two-bedroom accommodation for four persons rents for $70 per night, or $400 weekly.* Linen and cutlery are included, even for short-term rentals. Maid service is available at an extra cost. Services are close by. Bread comes fresh from the baker, and at the local market you can sample the produce grown on the island, especially the abundant tomatoes, carrots, and pineapples. A beach and tennis court are adjacent.

    Lime Court Apartments, P.O. Box 250, Plymouth (tel. 491-3656), is an apartment colony right in the center of town, a short walk from the beach, shops, and restaurants. The property is walled in, making the gardens private. Fully furnished one- and two-bedroom apartments are available with well-equipped kitchens and electric cooking. Each unit has a hot-water shower for the bedroom, and all utilities and maid service are included in the tariffs. The most luxurious unit is No. 9, a penthouse apartment offering a magnificent view of the harbor; it's well furnished, and has a private patio. This rents for $225 weekly year round. Four one-bedroom accommodations with private patio cost $150 weekly. Some two-bedroom units with private patios cost $215. The manager, Neville Bradshaw, advises that in winter all bookings should be made at least two months in advance.

    The **Belham Valley Hotel,** P.O. Box 420 (tel. 491-5553), is a series of cottages rented out by Chris and Barbara Crowe, two British expatriates. The cottages stand on a hillside overlooking the Belham Valley and its river. The entrance to the Montserrat Golf Course is directly below the property. The beach is about a seven-minute walk, and you can also stroll over for an evening at the already-previewed Vue Pointe Hotel. The Crowes call the Frangipani studio cottage their "showpiece," as it's surrounded by tropical shrubs and coconut palms. It consists of a large bed-sitting room, fully equipped kitchen, private bath, and balcony. *In low season, it rents for $205 weekly,* increasing to $285 weekly in high season. The Jasmine studio apartment, adjacent to their restaurant, the leading one on the island, consists of a large bed-sitting room, a small dinette area, a private bath, and a completely stocked kitchen. There is also a private patio for viewing the sea or the mountains in the distance. *It rents for only $145 weekly, in low season.* In winter, prices rise to $210 weekly. A newer apartment, the Mignonette, contains two bedrooms, a bath, and a living area with a fully equipped kitchen. Its large patio faces the golf course and the sea. *You can stay here for $260 weekly off-season,* $390 weekly in season.

WHERE TO EAT: Some of the best fruit and vegetables in the Caribbean are grown in the rich, volcanic soil of Montserrat. The island is known for its tomatoes, carrots, and mangoes; and "goat water" (a mutton stew) is the best-known local dish. Another island specialty is "mountain chicken," as locally caught frogs' legs are called.

The **Belham Valley Restaurant,** near the Vue Pointe Hotel (tel. 491-5553), is the premier restaurant of Montserrat. Britishers Chris and Barbara Crowe are most hospitable hosts, and they cater well to their diners. Naturally, they have to alter their menu a lot, as their biggest headache (the problem of the island itself) is the availability of supplies. But they're very inventive in the kitchen, and you'll probably not only get a good meal but have a good time, especially if Valerie is still around at the piano. Among their island dishes, you might enjoy chilled breadfruit vichyssoise, or a Créole crab-and-callaloo soup. However, they do the classic ones as well, including French onion with cheese and croutons. They generally have a steak on the grill, served with garlic butter or their own mushroom and red wine sauce. You might enjoy a seafood feast, a pepper steak, or a "mini-meal" of nut pie, quiche, or shrimp. Among the unusual items that might appear is fresh baby shark steak. Fondue bourguignonne is regularly featured, and occasionally that ubiquitous Montserrat "mountain chicken" or frogs' legs, a staple of the island. Their desserts are luscious, including fresh coco-nut pie, banana flambé, or a Belham super sundae. Calypso coffee is served, but true to heritage, an Irish coffee as well. The ice creams are a special feature, as they are homemade and come in such unusual flavors as soursop and guava. Meals average around EC$75 ($27.75).

The setting is tropical romantic, and the location is in a former private home, standing on a hillside overlooking the Belham River and its valley. It's also convenient for guests at the Montserrat Golf Course. The restaurant is open only in the evening and preferably by reservation. Go between 7 and 9 p.m. In winter it's open every night except Monday. During the summer it's open four nights a week: Thursday, Friday, Saturday, and Sunday. It's usually closed for three weeks in September.

Vue Pointe Restaurant, Vue Pointe Hotel (tel. 491-5211). Graciously elegant and surrounded with lawns and shrubbery of this previously recommended hotel, this is one of the best-directed restaurants on the island. You can enjoy a drink, served by a polite red-jacketed waiter, at a mahogany bar before heading for the high-ceilinged candlelit dining room. Fixed-price dinners cost from EC$60 ($9), and are served nightly from 7 to 9:30 p.m. The Wednesday-night barbecue is an island event, the evening enlivened by a steel band. The kitchen turns out such fare as roast prime rib of U.S. beef with corn fritters, "mountain chicken," filet of kingfish, chicken parma-giana, chicken Maryland, beef Wellington, Créole-style red snapper, roast leg of pork with apple compote, West Indian curried chicken with condiments, and filet of sole caprice. Dessert might be a slice of lime cheesecake, soursop mousse, or a tropical fruit salad. Reservations are suggested if you're a nonresident.

The Gallery, in Wapping (tel. 491-2579), across from the Yacht Club, opened in 1985. Matt Hawthorne and Bruce Munroe of Toronto came over from Antigua on a day trip and fell in love with Montserrat. They stuck around to open this place, where some readers have found what they claim is "the best pizza in the Caribbean." The friendly hosts also prepare an array of other dishes, including escargots, fried oysters, lamb chops, snapper stuffed with crab, and beef cooked in beer. There's always a spe-cial of the day as well. Lunch costs from EC$12 ($4.45), and dinner runs from EC$25 ($9.25). In season, the restaurant serves lunch daily from noon to 2 p.m. and dinner from 7 to 10 p.m. Happy hour is from 6 to 7 p.m. In off-season, they're closed on Tuesday and Wednesday. Sunday hours are from 6 p.m. "until." The decor is attract-ive in tones of pink and gray, and guests can dine outside, enjoying the breeze. Live bands are occasionally brought in for dancing on weekends.

Sugar Daddy's, at Wapping (tel. 491-3354), is a black-and-white building set beside the sea. Its origins go back to 1652, and it was once used as a fortification. The restaurant is run by Joan Rice and George "Sugar Daddy" Morgan. They have no printed menu, but offer different dishes every night, including kingfish, lobster, and shrimp. Sugar Daddy is keen on local cuisine, and you can count on such items as goat water, souse, salt fish (only on Friday), and the inevitable "mountain chicken." At lunch you can enjoy such simple fare as sandwiches and hamburgers along with one hot special, costing from EC$20 ($7.40). Go between 11:30 a.m. and 2:30 p.m. Dinner, served from 7:30 to 10:30 p.m., costs between EC$30 ($11.10) and EC$50 ($18.50). The restaurant is closed on Sunday and Monday.

Village Place, Salem (tel. 491-5202). If you weren't looking for it, you might think its encircling hedges and thatch fences concealed a private house. Local lore says that Elton John proposed marriage to his future wife at one of the outdoor tables. Other clients have included Eric Clapton and members of Sting and Dire Straits. The organizer and owner of the place is Andy Lawrence, a former disc jockey, who is aided by his softly humorous wife, Sonia. You can stand beneath the white cedar beams of the indoor bar admiring the musical memorabilia, or you can claim a table in the courtyard and listen to tree frogs. A three-course fixed-price meal costs from EC$30 ($11.10) and might include chicken, an array of salads, pumpkin or callaloo soup. If you just want a snack, then order some of the most delectable barbecued chicken wings in the West Indies. In high season the place is open from noon to midnight. In the off-season it opens at 5 p.m., closing "whenever guests decide to leave."

Blue Dolphin Restaurant, Parsons (tel. 491-3263). A meal within its painted concrete walls offers the advantage of contact with a friendly and kind-hearted staff, whose spokesperson is Richard Skirrey. The Blue Dolphin sits on the side of a steep hillside near the medical school amid a lush landscape of plants. You dine in an air-conditioned blue-sided dining room or on a breeze-cooled veranda sheltered from the rain by an overhang. In theory, lunch is from noon to 2 p.m., and dinner's on from 5 to 9 p.m. seven days a week. But if you don't call in advance, it's possible the restaurant will not be open to receive you. Full meals, costing from EC$30 ($11.10), include pumpkin soup, lobster, kingfish, "mountain chicken," pork chops, and breaded boneless breast of chicken, followed by coconut cream pie with ice cream.

The Pantry / The Attic, Marine Drive (tel. 491-2008), in Plymouth, occupy the same three-story cement building. On the second floor, the Pantry is open from 8 a.m. to 3 p.m. daily except Sunday. Breakfast is popular here, patronized by business travelers and office workers. Amid a simple West Indian decor with almost no ornamentation, you can enjoy ham and eggs, then stick around for lunch, at EC$17 ($6.30), which includes chicken or beef rôti, fish and chips, chicken or beef pot pie, sandwiches, and snacks, followed by such desserts as lemon meringue pie. On the third floor, the Attic is open nightly except Sunday from 6 to 10 p.m. You sit beneath a palm-thatched sun screen, surrounded by plants and open to the breeze. Full dinners, ranging from EC$35 ($13), include tenderloin steak, spareribs, red snapper or grouper, stuffed chicken leg, Carib bread pudding, and quesadilla (a dough envelope stuffed with shrimp, vegetables, or chicken, then doused with cheese).

The Iguana, Wapping (tel. 491-3637). Set in a tropical garden near a cluster of other restaurants, this establishment serves some of the most creative cuisine in the neighborhood. Its core was originally built 200 years ago as a cotton mill, but today its dark stone-walled interior contains a nautical, somewhat spartan bar where you can have a before-dinner drink. Guests dine beneath a palm-thatched sun screen in the back garden. The establishment remains open Wednesday through Sunday from 11 a.m. to 10 p.m. Lunch, costing from EC$30 ($11.10), includes a local version of lobster salad, fettuccine Alfredo, and pasta with clam sauce. Dinners are more elaborate, at EC$60 ($22.20), and require a reservation. Specialties include "mountain chicken," lobster mousse, seafood chowder, curried pumpkin soup, fresh tuna, kingfish Créole, red snapper, and sautéed chicken breast. Dessert is likely to be a freshly made batch of homemade ice cream. The bartenders, owners, chefs, and welcoming committee are Sophie and Michael Bishop, who used to live in Larchmont, New York.

Yacht Club Bar & Restaurant, Wapping (tel. 491-2237). Its stucco-sided premises could hardly be less pretentious, but some of the most famous musical groups of Britain—including Sting, the Police, and Boy George—have swilled their beer on its oceanside veranda. Eddie Edgecombe is the kind-hearted owner of this popular place near the sands, across from the Gallery Bar and Restaurant. In addition to drinks, lunches are served from 11 a.m. to 2 p.m. Tuesday to Friday. There's no lunch on Saturday and Sunday (only members are admitted then). Dinner is nightly except Sunday from 7 to 10 p.m. Lunch, costing from EC$14 ($5.20), includes lasagne, boiled fish, kingfish, hamburgers, salads, and sandwiches. Dinner, from EC$38 ($14) features such items as breaded shrimp, lobster, roast beef with Yorkshire pudding, sautéed frogs' legs with fried rice, and several kinds of chicken.

The Oasis, Wapping Road, Plymouth (tel. 491-2328), is nestled on the ground floor of an 18th-century stone house, and separated from the sea by a road and a copse of sea grape. The sound of the surf permeates the wide front veranda. If you select a table inside, you'll be ringed with stone walls craftsmen assembled more than 200 years ago. It's open weekdays from 9 a.m. to 8 p.m. and on Saturday from 3 p.m. until late at night. Dinner, however, is served only from 4:30 to 8 p.m., and reservations should be made. The cuisine is simple but full of flavor. Depending on the night of the week, you might be served boneless breast of chicken in a light batter and accompanied by "Oasis sauce," or a filet mignon wrapped in bacon, perhaps red snapper sautéed with lime-flavored butter. Meals cost from EC$35 ($13). Paul Coughlan, the owner, keeps everything low-key and laid-back.

EXPLORING MONTSERRAT:
The island is small, only 11 miles long and 7 miles across at its widest point. Its gently rolling hills and mountains reach their zenith at **Chances Peak,** rising to 3,000 feet. From its vantage point, a panoramic vista of the island unfolds. To climb the mountain, serious hikers need a guide, which your hotel can arrange. Near the airport the mountain can be hazardous, and it's best to have an experienced hand along.

Galway's Soufrière, in the south-central region of the island, is a crater which bubbles and steams with sulfur smoke. A journey of exploration here is recommended for nature lovers. The government has a shortcut path, allowing you to drive up to within a 15-minute walk of the vents. The crater is a natural wonder, and it's reached by a mountain road lined with tree ferns. Look also for the exotic incense tree. Yellow sulfur spills over the side in stark contrast to the green of the forest. Again, you should have your hotel arrange a mountain guide, who will boil an egg in the hot sulfur.

On the way there, you can stop to explore **Galway's Plantation,** an archeological project directed by the Montserrat National Trust. In the 1660s David Galway, an Irishman from Cork, settled the land with Irish indentured servants who were later replaced by African slaves. He established a sugar plantation which reached its peak a century later; however, the plantation declined after the slaves were freed. The ruins remain today, including the old sugar boiling house and the sugar mill.

Another natural wonder, the **Great Alps Waterfall,** is reached by first taking a 15-minute taxi ride south from Plymouth. After the driver lets you off, the waterfall lies a leisurely hour's walk through a lush interior. You come upon a horseshoe-shaped formation with crystal water plunging some 70 feet into a mountain pool. The noonday sun turns the mist into rainbow colors, reflecting the shadows of the rich surrounding foliage, a mystical effect of great beauty and worth the trek.

On the outskirts of Plymouth, **St. Anthony's Church**—the main Anglican church on the island—was built between 1632 and 1666, then rebuilt in 1730. Freed slaves, upon their emancipation, donated two beautiful silver chalices, on display. Next to the church is a gnarled tamarind tree two centuries old.

About a 15-minute drive from town, the ruined **Fort St. George** dates from the 18th century, and from it a magnificent panorama unfolds. The fort is 1,184 feet above sea level. Another ruin is **Fort Barrington,** also built in the 18th century.

At yet another fortification, **Bransby Point,** you can see restored cannons. The early earthworks date from 1640 to 1660. In 1693 a gun battery was built on this site, but it was destroyed by the French in 1712. In 1734 the British constructed a gun platform. By 1983 the restoration had been completed after 200 years of destruction.

The **Montserrat Museum,** in Plymouth, is housed in an old sugar mill at Richmond Hill. Here is displayed a collection of Montserratian artifacts, including pictures of island life at the turn of the century. Some of the artifacts relate to the island's pre-Columbian history. The featured exhibit is a small replica of a wind-driven sugar mill. Admission is free, but donations maintain the museum. Hours are 2:30 to 5 p.m. on Wednesday and Sunday. Curator Edward Laroussini will answer your questions. He can be reached at his home phone (tel. 491-5443).

Government House is one of the most interesting buildings on the island. Constructed in the 1700s, but with many changes over the years, the house can be viewed only on Wednesday from 10:30 a.m. to noon. However, it's possible to tour the grounds from 10:30 a.m. to noon on Monday, Tuesday, Thursday, and Friday.

THE SPORTING LIFE: There are many isolated areas for **swimming** and sunning; and perhaps you'll like black sand. Most hotels have pools and lounging areas, however.

People interested in **fishing** should ask at their hotel about the availability of small boats for rent.

Tennis buffs will find asphalt courts at the Vue Pointe Hotel. There are also two courts at Montserrat Springs, which are lit for night games. Residents play free, but nonresidents are charged EC$10 ($3.70) for daytime play, EC$16 ($5.90) for night games.

The **Montserrat Golf Club,** while only nine holes, is considered one of the finest in the eastern Caribbean. Even though it has only 11 greens, a full round of 18 holes can be played, by doubling up. The second hole, the best known, is about 600 yards across two branches of the Belham River. It covers an area of some 100 acres.

Shamrock Watersports, Vue Pointe Hotel (tel. 491-5211). After Danny Sweeney taught the British rock star Sting to windsurf, Sting used Danny's name in the lyrics of one of his hit songs. Today Danny still teaches windsurfing techniques from a kiosk on the black sand crescent of the Vue Pointe Hotel's beach. Windsurfers rent for $10 per hour, an introductory lesson costing only $2. You can rent Sunfish at $10 per hour, or a day's snorkeling equipment for $5.

SHOPPING: There is no duty-free shopping, but some interesting locally made handcrafts are for sale. Straw goods and small ceramic souvenirs predominate, along with sea island cotton fabrics. Most shops are open weekdays from 8 a.m. to noon and 1 to 4 p.m. They usually observe early closing on Wednesday, shutting down at 12:30 p.m.

The **Montserrat Sea Island Cotton Company** sales outlet, at the corner of George and Strand Streets (tel. 491-2557), offers exclusive hand-woven sea island cotton products and such souvenir items as leather goods and ceramics. The outlet is open from 8 a.m., closing at 4 p.m. on Monday, Tuesday, Thursday, and Friday, and at noon on Wednesday and Saturday.

Outside of town, the government-owned and -operated **Montserrat Leather Craft** (tel. 491-2378) is in an actual leathercraft shop at the Groves. There, artistic handcrafted leather goods are offered for sale. All items—belts, wallets, handbags, sandals, purses—are made from locally tanned genuine leather. See in particular the batik belts. The factory is closed on Saturday and Sunday.

The **Spinning Plant** (tel. 491-2825) and **Hand-Weaving Studio** (tel. 491-2915), both owned and operated by the government, are at sites on the Industrial Estate. Sea island cotton yarn and roving (a step in turning fiber into soft yarn), manufactured by the plant, are hand-woven into a variety of end products. Clara Davidson, who came from Nova Scotia, founded the Hand-Weaving Studio, teaching the young women of

Montserrat the craft. The products are unique, and the spun cotton is locally grown. Various designs of placemats, tablecloths, skirt-length material, clutch bags, stoles, scarves, baby blankets, and belts are offered for sale.

The **John Bull Shop,** over the bridge in Wapping just outside Plymouth (tel. 491-2520), has dress and decorating fabrics. Robert and Marilyn Townsend, formerly of Connecticut, have operated the shop since 1980. They design "Tapestries of Montserrat," fine handcrafted rugs and wall hangings.

Carol's Corner, Vue Pointe Hotel (tel. 491-5211), lies in a high-ceilinged public room of this previously recommended hotel. This shop offers one of the most concentrated collections of Montserrat-related memorabilia on the island. They sell the famous stamps of Montserrat and copies of the difficult-to-obtain flag. There's a version of a Montserrat cookbook, *Goatwater,* which describes "how to skin and clean a fat female iguana." There's also a collection of roadmaps, summery dresses of sea island cotton, and a selection of local jams and honey. If you forgot your toothbrush, there are simple cosmetics and sundries as well.

Dutcher's Studio (tel. 491-5253) is a glass and ceramic studio in Olveston just outside Plymouth. Items are made of hand-cut and hand-painted glass, with many signed and collectors' pieces. Featured are wind chimes made of bottles, hand-painted dishes, mobiles, dolls, and ceramic works of art, all made on Montserrat. Studio hours are 8:30 a.m. to 2:30 p.m. Monday to Friday. If you wish to go there on Saturday, Sunday, or holidays, you must call for an appointment. The studio is near the Vue Pointe Hotel and Salem.

AFTER DARK: Montserrat may be sleepy during the day, but it gets even quieter at night. The most activity is at the **Vue Pointe Hotel,** Old Towne (tel. 491-5210), where a steel band plays every Wednesday night, and there is nightly entertainment by local musicians in season. At the Wednesday-night bash, a barbecue dinner is cooked, costing EC$55 ($20.35) per person.

If you've never seen a West Indian disco, attracting just the local crowd, then you can drop in at **La Cave,** Evergreen Drive (no phone). In Plymouth, it is a modest little place, playing records for dancers. Some of the local dancers are very talented. The disco charges an entrance fee of EC$5 ($1.85).

The Plantation, Wapping Road, Plymouth (no phone). Much less formal and a bit more raucous than its neighbor, the previously recommended Oasis downstairs, this establishment occupies the upper story of a 200-year-old stone-walled house. It's one of the most popular bars for visiting musicians and local medical students. Only a bar, with no food service, it's open from 7:30 p.m. until very late. Video movies are sometimes shown as an accompaniment to the beer and rum drinks.

3. St. Kitts

The volcanic central island of the British Leewards is not really a resort mecca in the way Antigua is. Its major crop is sugar, and has been since the mid-17th century.

At some point in your visit you'll want to eat sugar directly from the cane. Any St. Kitts farmer will sell you a huge stalk, and there are sugarcane plantations all over the island. Just ask your taxi driver to take you to one. You strip off the hard exterior of the stalk and bite into it, chewing on the tasty reeds and swallowing the juice. It's best with a side glass of rum.

The Caribs, the early settlers, called St. Kitts "Liamuiga," or "fertile isle." Its mountain ranges reach up to nearly 4,000 feet, and in its interior are virgin rain forests, alive with the sound of hummingbirds and the chatter of wild green vervet monkeys. The monkeys were brought in as pets by the early French settlers and turned loose in the forests when the island became British in 1783. The native African animals have proliferated and can perhaps best be seen at the Estridge Estate Behavioral Research Institute. Another import, this one British, is the mongoose, brought in from India as an enemy of rats in the sugarcane fields. The people of the island say the only trouble with that plan is that the mongooses and rats operate on different time cycles, the rats committing their depredations while the mongooses sleep. Wild deer are found in the St. Kitts mountains.

Sugarcane climbs right up the slopes, and there are palm-lined beaches around the island as well. As you travel around St. Kitts, you'll notice ruins of old mills and plantation houses. You'll also see an island rich in trees and vegetation—frangipani, bougainvillea, hibiscus, and flamboyant trees (the treasured poinciana was first cultivated in the Caribbean by Count de Poincy).

St. Kitts is 33 miles long and 6½ miles wide, riding the crest of that arc of islands known as the northerly Leeward group of the Lesser Antilles. It is separated from its sister state of Nevis by a two-mile-wide strait. Its administrative capital is Basseterre.

In 1967 St. Kitts was given internal self-government and, along with Nevis, became a state in association with Britain (Anguilla broke away).

On his second voyage in 1493, Columbus spotted St. Kitts, naming it Saint Christopher, but the English later changed that to St. Kitts. In 1623 the Europeans colonized St. Kitts when Sir Thomas Warner landed with his wife and son, and a party of 14 farmers. This settlement made St. Kitts the oldest British colony in the West Indies. When the island later sent out parties of settlers to neighboring islands, St. Kitts became known as "the mother colony of the West Indies."

Shortly after their arrival, the English were joined by the French. In 1627 they divided the island between them and, united, they withstood attacks from the Caribs and the Spanish. But in time the British and French fought among themselves, and the island changed hands several times until it was finally given to the British by the Treaty of Versailles.

The capital, **Basseterre,** an 18th-century-print port with its waterfront intact, lies on the Caribbean shore near the southern end of the island, about a mile from Golden Rock Airport, where you will land. With its white-painted colonial houses with toothpick balconies and wide, palm-lined streets, it looks like a Hollywood version of a West Indian port.

The bustling harbor is filled with schooners from Antigua, St. Martin, and Nevis which carry the rich produce to St. Kitts to neighboring islands. You'll also spot freighters from the U.S. and Canada. The men of St. Kitts are known as good sailors, and it's interesting to see them in action, skillfully handling their boats.

This British colonial town is built around a so-called Circus, the town's round square. A tall green Victorian clock tower stands in the center of the Circus. In the old days, wealthy plantation owners and their families used to promenade here.

At some point, try to visit the marketplace. There, country women bring baskets brimming with mangoes, guavas, soursop, mammy apples, and wild strawberries and cherries just picked in the fields. You can see the vegetables you may eat later in the day—yams, breadfruit, hearts of palm, pumpkins, christophines. Tropical flowers abound.

Another major square is called Pall Mall, once a thriving slave market. It is surrounded by private homes of Georgian architecture.

GETTING THERE: St. Kitts is 2,000 miles southeast of New York or four hours by direct jet flight. Miami is 1,300 miles away, about three hours direct flight time. **BWIA** offers one nonstop flight per week (on Friday) from New York's JFK Airport to St. Kitts. Flights in any season return from St. Kitts to New York, also on Friday. If you want to go there any other day, BWIA connects with **LIAT** in Antigua. LIAT makes a three-hour wait in Antigua. From Miami, BWIA flies to Antigua, where it connects with LIAT for the flight on to St. Kitts.

You can fly from Boston, Chicago, Miami, New Orleans, New York, Philadelphia, Baltimore, or Washington to San Juan, St. Thomas, St. Croix, St. Maarten, or

Antigua on **American Airlines, Eastern Airlines, Pan Am, Capitol Air,** or **Delta.**
You then connect with LIAT to fly to St. Kitts or Nevis.

In addition, consult your travel agent for direct charter flights to St. Kitts from
New York and other major U.S. cities.

From Montréal or Toronto you can go to St. Kitts via San Juan or Antigua on **Air
Canada** and BWIA.

GETTING AROUND: A good road encircles the island. I'll preview the major means
of transport.

Car Rentals

Delisle Walwyn & Co. Ltd., Liverpool Row (tel. 465-2631), operates Economy
Car Rental, with cars and scooter bikes available. Suzuki sedans cost $28 per day,
$170 weekly; Mazda standard vehicles run $32 daily, $196 weekly; and Mazda auto-
matics go for $35 per day, $210 per week. A scooter bike rents for $14 daily, $84
weekly. The minimum age for car rental is 25. A valid St. Kitts and Nevis driver's
license is necessary, but this can easily be obtained at the police station. Rental rates
include public liability, property damage, and fire and theft insurance. If the car is
involved in a collision, the renter's responsibility for damage will be up to $400. This
responsibility will be waived if you elect to pay $5 per day. There is no extra charge for
leaving your vehicle at the airport or at your hotel if you notify the company in advance.

Taxis

Since most taxi drivers are also guides, this is the best means of getting around.
You don't even have to find a driver at the airport (one will find you). Drivers also wait
outside the major hotels, so getting around is fairly easy. Before heading out on an
expedition, however, you must agree on the price—taxis aren't metered. Also, ask if
the rates quoted to you are in U.S. dollars or the EC dollar. Taxi rates may have risen
considerably by the time you read this, so check the fares. At the time of writing, you
could go from the airport to, say, Frigate Bay for EC$18 ($6.65), or all the way to
Sandy Point for EC$29 ($10.75).

Sightseeing Tours

You can negotiate with a taxi driver to take you on a tour of the island for about
$45. Most drivers are well versed in the lore of the island, and all of them of course
speak English. Lunch can be arranged either at the Rawlins Plantation Inn or the Gold-
en Lemon.

Inter-Island Ferries

Most visitors to St. Kitts or Nevis like to spend at least one day on the sister island, and the government passenger ferry M.V. *Caribe Queen* provides such an opportunity. The schedule permits departures from either island between the hours of
7:30 and 8:30 a.m. daily except Thursday and Sunday, returning at 4 and 6 p.m. (check
the time at your hotel or the tourist office). The cost is EC$10 ($3.70) one way. Passengers are allowed one hand package free, with a minimal fee for additional pieces.

Local Air Service

LIAT (Leeward Islands Air Transport) provides daily morning and afternoon
flights to and from Nevis at a cost of $15 per person. Make reservations at the LIAT
office on Fort Street in Basseterre (tel. 465-2286) instead of at the airport.

PRACTICAL FACTS: Entry requirements, money, and language were previewed in
the introductory section to this chapter.

St. Kitts is on **Atlantic Standard Time,** and its clocks never change all year. That means that in winter when it's 6 a.m. in Basseterre, it's 5 a.m. in Miami or New York. When the U.S. goes on Daylight Saving Time, Basseterre and the East Coast mainland keep the same time.

St. Kitts lies in the tropics, its warm **climate** tempered by the trade winds. The average air temperature is 79° Fahrenheit and the average water temperature is 80°. Average rainfall is 55 inches. Dry, mild weather is usually experienced from November to April; May through October are hotter and rainier.

The water supply of the island is good and safe for drinking. However, since its **electricity** is 230 volts, 60 cycles, AC, you'll need an adapter for U.S.-made appliances.

Customs allows you in duty free with personal belongings.

Again, reflecting British tradition, *driving is on the left!* However, you'll need a local driver's license, which can be obtained at the Traffic Department in Basseterre for EC$30 ($11.10).

If you want to exchange your dollars into Eastern Caribbean currency, you'll find **banks** open Monday to Friday from 8 a.m. till noon (also on Friday from 3 to 5 p.m.).

Most hotels add a service charge of 10% to cover **tipping.** If not, tip from 10% to 15%.

The government also imposes a 7% tax on rooms and meals, plus another EC$13.50 ($5) airport departure tax (but not to go to Nevis).

In case of **emergency,** telephone 99 from Basseterre main exchanges and 999 from all other exchanges.

Telegrams and **Telexes** can be sent from Cable & Wireless, Cayon Street, Basseterre (tel. 465-2219), from 8 a.m. to 6 p.m. weekdays, 8 a.m. to 2 p.m. on Saturday, and 6 to 8 p.m. on Sunday and public holidays. International **telephone** calls, including collect calls, can also be made from the cable office.

Tourist information can be obtained from the **Tourist Board,** P.O. Box 132, Basseterre (tel. 465-2620), and from the **St. Kitts-Nevis Tourist Board** Stateside office, 414 E. 75th St., New York, NY 10021 (tel. 212/535-1234).

HOTELS: This is no resort-studded island like Antigua. Rather, the island has hotels of character, small and special, ranging from plantation-style living to retreats so remote they're accessible only by a bumpy boat ride.

Ocean Terrace Inn, P.O. Box 65 (tel. 465-2380), is affectionately known as the O.T.I. If you want to be near Basseterre, it's the best hotel around the port (it also has an excellent cuisine and is the chief center for water sports, all detailed in the section to follow). The O.T.I. commands a view of the harbor and the capital, with oceanfront verandas. With its many terraces and different levels, it's so compact that a stay here is like a house party on a great liner. Terraced into a well-landscaped hillside above the edge of Basseterre, the hotel has particularly beautiful gardens and grounds. Ringed with a picket fence, the compound is graced with neo-Victorian gazebos, hedges of flowering shrubs, and a fountain with a pool.

All the handsomely decorated, air-conditioned bedrooms overlook the "great open-air living room"—that is, a well-planted terrace with a flagstone-edged swimming pool (which has a row of underwater stools where you'll be served well-made drinks while still immersed). My favorite bar is in the shadow of an elaborate aviary. The furnishings are color coordinated, with a light, tropical feeling. In winter, singles on the MAP range from $75 to $135 daily, while doubles cost $110 to $200. *Off-season MAP rates range from $63 to $100 in a single, from $100 to $145 in a double.* Some more expensive suites are available, and guests can stay here on the EP if they wish, for somewhat lower prices. A third person in a room on the MAP costs $50 year round.

In addition to its stylish rooms in the hillside buildings, the hotel offers the Fisherman's Wharf and Village, a few steps from the nearby harbor. These wooden units are filled with most of the comforts of home. In winter, two persons can rent a one-bedroom apartment for $160 daily, and a two-bedroom apartment for four persons for $240, EP. *In summer, a one-bedroom apartment rents for $110 daily for two persons, a two-bedroom unit for four guests costing $150 daily, EP rates.* Colin Pereira, who is a Kittitian is your host at Ocean Terrace, and he runs a tight ship.

Fairview Inn, P.O. Box 212 (tel. 465-2472), was originally the 18th-century great house of a wealthy French plantation owner. Set on the rise of a hill, and surrounded by tropical flowers and blooming flamboyant trees, it is only five miles from the jetport and three miles west of the city, about a ten-minute run by taxi. It has its own swimming pool and sundeck, and there is a secluded beach just a 12-minute walk from the inn. Prince Charles danced the carnival queen around the pool. The manor house has plenty of character, with its lacy front verandas, louvered windows, and long, covered loggia. Some of the bedrooms are in the main building, and others are in cottages in the rear garden where the plantation outbuildings of yesteryear used to stand. Each of the 30 twin-bedded rooms has a private bath as well as its own patio. You can ask for air conditioning (available in some of the rooms), but trade winds usually suffice. I prefer the bedrooms that have been converted from stone stables. Natural-stone walls have been incorporated into the scheme. The rooms are clean and comfortable. In winter, for about four nights a week a calypso band will come in to entertain. In season, singles rent for $70 to $80 daily on the EP; doubles, from $80 to $90. *Off-season, a single pays only $50 to $60; two persons, $60 to $70.* Breakfast and dinner carry an additional daily supplement of $28 per person. In my opinion, the Fairview Inn is one of the best tourist buys in the Caribbean.

What makes Fairview Inn such a success, drawing repeat visitors, is its ownership. A Trinidadian, Freddy Lam, and his wife, Betty (she's from St. Kitts), extend old-fashioned hospitality. Betty's island background is reflected in her cuisine. For example, she grows her own papaya, making green papaya pie to delight her diners. The Lams also grow their own vegetables and pineapples, and often use breadfruit as well as making a superb callaloo soup.

Jack Tar Village Royal St. Kitts Resort & Casino, P.O. Box 406, Frigate Bay (tel. 465-8651, 214/670-9888, or toll free 800/527-9299), is the largest-scale hotel on St. Kitts and is certainly the showcase hotel of the much-touted Frigate Bay development. Set on a flat sandy isthmus between the sea and a saltwater lagoon, this is a lot like a private country club. It's popular with charter and tour groups, many of which originate in the home state of the Jack Tar chain, Texas. The resort is almost completely self-contained, with a built-in incentive never to leave its perimeter. It has the island's only casino and a helpful scattering of signposts indicating the direction to the dozens of sports-related activities. Thoughtful touches include the designation of one swimming pool area for quiet reading, another for such active sports as volleyball. Four tennis courts are illuminated for nighttime play, and a golf course is nearby.

The resort has no fewer than four restaurants, a number of bars, and a rate structure that includes everything (meals, drinks, and golf) in one all-inclusive price. *Single rooms cost $145 daily in summer, and doubles go for $260.* In winter, singles are $180; doubles, $290. Accommodations are separated into two groupings, one at either end of the resort. Each of the almost 300 units has individually controlled air conditioning, a patio or balcony, and tropical furniture. Most visitors prefer the second-floor rooms because of their higher ceilings. When you check in, I.D. tags are usually issued in an effort to help you get acquainted with your fellow guests quickly. Throughout the day an enthusiastic staff will keep anyone who's interested hopping from one organized activity to another. These include everything from Scrabble and shuffleboard tournaments to scuba lessons to toga ("it's time to get crazy") contests.

Golden Lemon, Dieppe Bay (tel. 465-7260), was created by Arthur Leaman, onetime decorating editor of *House & Garden* magazine. With his taste and background, he has formed a tiny oasis that is a citadel of charm in the British Leewards, in a place that was once a busy French shipping port named for a more famous bay in its home country. Mr. Leaman found this then-ramshackle 17th-century house, set back from a coconut grove and a black volcanic sand beach on the northwest coast of St. Kitts. The original French manor house has a Georgian upper story added in the 18th century. The two-story building, with its covered galleries looks like pictures from *House & Garden*. The high-ceilinged bedrooms are spacious and filled with rare antiques. Most units (there are 18, including five suites with private pools), have graceful canopy beds. Everywhere you look the Golden Lemon is swathed in color. Even the baths are often furnished with one-of-a-kind pieces. Overhead, slow-turning ceiling fans keep the air moving. Before retiring, you can place your breakfast order, having it served on your own gallery or in your bedroom. The rooms always contain fresh flowers, and you are waited on by a well-trained staff. "Sophisticated" and "elegant" are words most often used to describe the Golden Lemon and its clientele.

A minimum stay of four nights is required in season. Surprisingly, Mr. Leaman limits guests to a maximum stay of two weeks, fearing (and I'm guessing) that they might get restless even in Paradise. In winter, the MAP rates, including afternoon tea and laundry, are $160 daily in a single, $250 to $285 for a superior or deluxe double/twin, and $300 to $330 in one-bedroom suites with pool. *Off-season, on the MAP, singles are $130 daily, superior doubles and twins cost $185, deluxe doubles go for $210, and suites rent for $250 to $275.*

Fort Thomas Hotel, P.O. Box 407 (tel. 465-2695), has a sweeping view of the sea from its position above the town, across the street from its more exclusive neighbor, the Ocean Terrace Inn. Designed like a collection of rectangular solids stacked on top of one another, this is the most modern and dramatic hotel in the capital. Built in 1970 with government assistance, the hotel has 62 accommodations, half facing the ocean and half looking toward the hills. Each of the simple and predictably furnished rooms is air-conditioned with a private terrace or balcony. In winter, singles are charged $75 daily, and doubles pay $95. *Summer rates are $45 daily in a single, $52 in a double.* All tariffs are subject to tax and service charge. The hotel has a lovely pool terrace, a pleasant paneled restaurant named with the ancient Carib name for St. Kitts, Liamuiga, and a collection of trees planted on the site of a former burial ground. Tennis and free transportation to Frigate Beach can be arranged at the front desk.

Rawlins Plantation, P.O. Box 340, Mount Pleasant (tel. 465-6221), is a small, family-owned hotel, set on a former plantation among the remains of a muscovado sugar factory. The original great house burned in 1790, but was replaced by the present Walwyn family in 1970, who have turned it into an English country-home-type place. (Incidentally, the first Walwyn arrived in Nevis in 1677, moving his family to St. Kitts and founding the Rawlins Plantation in 1790.) Near Dieppe Bay on the northeast coast, the former plantation is 350 feet above sea level, enjoying cooling breezes from both ocean and mountains. Behind the grounds the land rises to a rain forest and Mount Misery. Rawlins is unique on St. Kitts, evoking certain plantation hotels on neighboring Nevis. A 17th-century windmill has become converted into a charming suite, complete with private bath and sitting room; and the boiling houses, formerly a caldron of molasses, have been turned into a cool courtyard where guests dine, enjoying the flowers and tropical birds. Accommodations are rented in the main house, as well as pleasantly decorated cottages which have been equipped with modern facilities. The plantation is run by Mr. and Mrs. Philip Walwyn, who graciously let you swim in their pool (fed from their own mountain spring), or eat at their table, offering peace and tranquility for the discriminating few who find their way to their door. Vegetables usually come from their own gardens. *On the MAP, singles are welcomed off-season for $130 daily; doubles, $190.* In winter, prices rise to $210 in a single, $275 in a double, all on the MAP. In season, a minimum stay of four days is required. You can also go for a sail on Philip's 45-foot catamaran on Sunday.

Frigate Bay Beach Hotel, P.O. Box 137, Frigate Bay (tel. 465-8935), is set on a verdant hillside above a point where English settlers used to watch the passing frigates. Accommodations are in white condominiums administered as hotel units for their absentee owners. The villas housing these "second homes" have alternating red and yellow tile roofs. The central core of the resort contains a pair of round swimming pools and a cabaña bar where you can enjoy a drink while partially immersed if you choose. Green hills rise up behind the hotel, while on either side are beaches lined with rugged cliffs. An 18-hole golf course and tennis courts are within easy walking distance. Units are nicely furnished to the taste of the owner and painted in an array of pastel colors. They have cool tile floors, ceiling fans, sliding glass doors leading onto verandas, private baths, and air conditioning. Winter rates are $95 to $120 daily for a double, $200 for a one-bedroom suite suitable for two persons, and $310 for a two-bedroom suite for up to four persons. *In summer, doubles go for $60 per day, a one-bedroom suite for $90, and a two-bedroom suite for $150.* Service is added to all bills. MAP is available for an additional $28 per day per person.

OTI Banana Bay Beach Resort, P.O. Box 65 (tel. 465-2754), is a secluded gem accessible only by boat. Guests are met at the airport and taken to OTI Pelican Cove Marina where the M.V. *Banana Peel* waits to take them on the scenic cruise to Banana Bay. The creativity put into the physical side of this ten-room hideaway is evident immediately from use of colors and attention to details capturing the perfect setting for a Caribbean vacation. The spiritual side is no less a factor, for the accent is on nothingness, allowing one to walk quietly along sandy beaches and absorb the beauty of surrounding landscape. Activity focuses on the beach. Snorkeling, windsurfing, or Sailfish sailing is complimentary. If you wish, you can take the hotel's regular boat service to the Ocean Terrace Inn's Pelican Cove Marina where an island tour of St. Kitts or shopping in downtown Basseterre can be arranged. Reading and good conversation have priorities, or just laze away the day in a hammock slung between palm trees, sipping an exotic elixir of tropical flavors from the Booby Bird Beach Bar. The food is excellent, served without fanfare, providing a good balance of fresh local seafood and continental dishes. MAP rates, including the cost of transportation on arrival and departure, are $145 in a single and $195 in a double from mid-December to mid-April. *Summer MAP rates, from mid-April to mid-December, are $110 in a single, $150 in a double.*

Leeward Cove Condominium Hotel, P.O. Box 123, Frigate Bay (tel. 465-8030), in addition to providing clean, well-maintained apartments for temporary vacation-oriented visitors, also offers condominiums for sale. The white-sided, two-story buildings are nestled into a lawn on the main road winding through Frigate Bay. Crotons and hedges of sea grapes add an emerald green allure. The hard-working manager, Mrs. Perta, will rent one of the units without meals in winter at $160 for a one-bedroom apartment suitable for two persons and $250 for a two-bedroom accommodation suitable for four persons. *In summer, a one-bedroom apartment rents for $100 daily for two persons, and a two-bedroom unit goes for $135 for four persons.*

Island Paradise Beach Village, P.O. Box 139, Frigate Bay (tel. 465-8035), is on a flat and sandy lawn, a few steps from one of the beaches of St. Kitts's fastest-developing resort communities, one of the island's first (and most important) condominium concepts. Each of the hip-roofed, motel-like buildings housing the comfortable accommodations has rows of verandas and patios, with no more than three units. The individually furnished apartments are available for rent when the absentee investors are not in residence. Each contains a kitchen, air conditioning, and one or two bedrooms. In any season, a one-bedroom unit for two rents for $700 to $850 per week, and a two-bedroom apartment costs $1,000 to $1,350 for the same time period. The restaurant and nightlife facilities of such neighboring hotels as the Jack Tar Village are available for residents, and an 18-hole golf course is nearby.

WHERE TO DINE: Most guests eat at their hotels; however, St. Kitts has a scattering of good restaurants where you are likely to have turtle stews, spiny lobster, crab back, pepperpot, breadfruit, and curried conch.

I'd recommend that you dine with a local family at least once. That way, you'll get to meet Kittitians in their homes as well as enjoy a good local cuisine. Your hotel will often make such arrangements.

The **Georgian House,** South Square Street (tel. 465-4049), fronts Independence Square. As the name suggests, this is a restored Georgian manor, decorated with Queen Anne reproductions, and said to be the oldest habitable building in St. Kitts. Long, long before its present reincarnation as the leading restaurant on the island, it was the exclusive Planters' Club. New Yorker Georgiana Bowers, the owner and chef, offers a well-prepared and sophisticated menu that changes nightly. You may be there on the night peanut soup is served, but you also might settle happily for chilled cucumber soup. Main courses are likely to include roast leg of lamb, chicken breasts in garlic, and lobster Thermidor. Desserts are luscious here. Maybe it'll be Tía Maria mousse. If not, then coconut cream pie or most definitely guava ice cream. The menu is à la carte. With a drink or two, count on spending around $25 per person. Hours are 11 a.m. to 2 p.m. and 6:30 to 9 p.m., except Sunday. Dinner is served in the beautifully restored dining room, and lunch is presented in a large walled garden. Lunch, of course, is much simpler, the price beginning at $12. You're given a choice of two soups and four main courses, along with a couple of desserts. Lobster salad is a favorite, and so is the chicken salad. Perhaps a club sandwich would tempt you. Each of these luncheon orders is accompanied by potato salad, lettuce, and tomato. The restaurant shuts down in summer when business in St. Kitts is at a minimum.

In Basseterre, some of the finest cuisine is found at the **Ocean Terrace Inn** (tel. 465-2754). It also offers the best view, especially at night when you can sit and watch the lights in the harbor. Native food is featured every night, and standard dishes from the international repertoire are invariably included as well. My most recent dinner, costing EC$50 ($18.50), began with curried chicken broth, followed by sliced hard-boiled eggs in a mushroom sauce served on the half shell. Then came an order of tasty fish cakes, accompanied by breaded carrot slices, creamed spinach, a stuffed potato, johnny cake, a cornmeal dumpling, and a green banana in a lime butter sauce, topped off by a tropical fruit pie and coffee! Dining is on an open-air veranda. On some nights the main dish might be a large breadfruit stuffed with chicken. On Sunday there's a chicken luncheon barbecue around the pool, costing EC$18 ($6.65). Lunch is served from 11 a.m. to 2 p.m. and dinner from 6 p.m. "until."

Fisherman's Wharf Seafood Restaurant and Bar (tel. 465-2380) is between the sea and the white picket fence surrounding its neighbor, the Ocean Terrace Inn. Its heart and soul lies near the busy buffet grill, where a quartet of hard-working chefs prepare fresh seafood in an organized and rapid-fire clockwork manner. The grill and picnic tables around the grill are supported by the stout planks of a seaside wharf. An employee hovers to take your drink order, but food orders should be requested personally at the buffet grill. Specialties (usually cooked at the grill while you stand and watch) are grilled lobster, shrimp in garlic sauce, shark steak with local herbs and spices, barbecued tuna steak, stuffed and baked shellfish, and grilled catch of the day. The cream-based conch chowder, served in flexible plastic cups, was some of the best I've ever had. Full meals go for $20 per person and up. Lunch is served only on weekdays, from noon to 2 p.m. You can dine seven days a week from 7 until at least 10:30 p.m. On Wednesday and Friday there's a Calypso seafood all-you-can-eat buffet costing a reasonable $18 per person, with live entertainment.

Jong's, Conaree Beach (tel. 465-2062), is an Oriental restaurant combined with Cisco's Hideaway Bar. It serves the best Oriental food in St. Kitts, the dishes well prepared, the service friendly and efficient. Main courses include chicken, beef, lobster, or shrimp chop sueys, curry beef, conch in garlic butter sauce, and ginger chicken along with spareribs and spicy pork. A complete meal costs about $20. The bar opens at 11 a.m., remaining so until midnight. Lunch is from noon to 2:30 p.m., and dinner from 6:30 to 10 p.m. It's important that you call and make a reservation. Closed Monday.

For West Indian food, you might try **Avondale House,** George Street (tel. 465-2487), a 200-year-old wood-frame house with an accommodating and well-used veranda. Its interior could hardly be simpler, having as a focal point a sturdy bar and clusters of rickety tables. Edmund Sheriff, the owner, serves meals every day except Sunday from 10 a.m. to 10 p.m. (on Sunday, usually from 2 to 10 p.m.). Only about half a dozen dishes are offered, written in block letters above the bar. Items include cheeseburgers, chicken and chips, chicken and rice, fish and rice, and fish and corn. A simple meal costs around EC$20 ($7.40).

Victor's, Stainforth Street (tel. 465-2518), is a friendly West Indian, totally Kittitian, neighborhood restaurant owned and operated by Victor and Florine (Vic and Flo) Gumbs. Set in concrete-sided quarters behind Basseterre's Church of the Immaculate Conception, it serves lunch from 11:30 a.m. to 2:30 p.m. and dinner from 7 to 9:30 p.m. every day except Sunday. Full meals cost from around EC$45 ($16.65) and might include curried goat stew, deep-fried fish with Spanish sauce, snapper, stewed lobster with a mild curry sauce, conch chowder, chicken, boneless beef, and mutton dishes. Coffee and tea are taken from serve-yourself dispensers near the bar.

If you're touring St. Kitts, the best luncheon stop is at the **Golden Lemon,** Dieppe Bay (tel. 465-7260), the 17th-century house converted into a hotel by Arthur Leaman, former decorating editor of *House & Garden* magazine (see the description above). Always call in advance for a reservation. Before dining, you may want to enjoy a Bloody Mary, rum punch, or piña colada at poolside. Lunch is in a lush tropical setting of ferns, bougainvillea, and ginger under a breadfruit tree. The food is very good, and the service is polite. A complete luncheon costs around $15, and special drinks are priced at $3.50. Dinner costs from $20 to $30, table d'hôte, and is served in an elegant, candlelit dining room. The cuisine features Créole, continental, and American dishes, with locally grown produce, and the menu changes daily. Dress is casual chic. Lunch is served from noon to 3 p.m.; dinner, from 7 to 10 p.m.

Ballahoo Restaurant, The Circus (tel. 465-4197), is about a block from the sea on the second story of a wood-frame Victorian building with lots of gingerbread. Its wide veranda is one of the coolest places in town on a hot afternoon, thanks to the sea breezes and the high ceiling. They serve such specialties as chicken kebab, "blue parrot" fish filets, beef Stroganoff, lobster Thermidor, chicken pie, and curried conch. It's open every day except Sunday from 10 a.m. to 11 p.m. As you dine, you can admire the dome of the nearby Treasury Building.

The Patio, Frigate Bay (tel. 465-8666), is at the private home of a likeable Kittitian family, the Peter Mallalieus. Only dinner is served, daily from 7:15 to 11 p.m. Because each dish is prepared to order, it is imperative that you phone ahead to announce your arrival. Cocktails are served in the lush flower garden just a few feet from the rear terrace of the house. The family's high-ceilinged modern living room is transformed with tablecloths and kerosene lanterns into a dining room. Meals cost around $35 per person, and they include home-grown vegetables and a fresh seafood menu that changes nightly. If you have any special menu requests, Mr. Mallalieu will probably follow them.

The Anchorage, Frigate Bay (tel. 465-8235), is an isolated beachfront restaurant on the rolling acres of Frigate Bay, in the shadow of an enormous leafy tree. The restaurant's many-peaked roof shelters its concrete-slab floor from sudden showers. Pansy and Ewart Martin (who come from Nevis and Bermuda respectively) prepare rum-based drinks and seafood every day of the week from 8 a.m. to midnight. The menu offers four different salads, broiled or Thermidor lobster, steak, pork or lamb chops, hamburgers, 13 kinds of sandwiches, fresh fish, and ice cream. Full meals cost

EC$35 ($13) to EC$60 ($22.25). If you're looking for an unspoiled beach with a casual restaurant nearby, this may be a good selection for you.

EXPLORING ST. KITTS: The chief sight is **Brimstone Hill,** which was once known as the "Gibraltar of the West Indies." In size, this 18th-century fortress rivaled the pyramids of Egypt. A car can be driven up the winding road, almost to the top. When your driver lets you out, you have to climb stairs to the main fortifications. A bronze plaque, unveiled by Queen Elizabeth II on a visit here, proclaims the citadel a national park. There's a $2 admission fee. Brimstone Hill is open daily from 9:30 a.m. to 5:30 p.m. (on Thursday and Sunday from 2 to 5:30 p.m.). The history of St. Kitts from the Stone Age is traced in a small museum.

In 1782 the fort was besieged and captured by the French, but Britain regained it the following year. Although the hurricanes of 1834 and 1852 brought great damage, the citadel has been partially reconstructed, its guns remounted. Today you can see the ruins of the officers' quarters, barracks, the ordinance store, a cemetery, and the redoubts.

Thousands of slaves worked for more than a century to complete this fortress. From its precincts there is a magnificent view with a radius of 70 miles. You can see Saba and St. Eustatius to the northwest, St. Barts and St. Maarten to the north, and Montserrat and Nevis to the southeast. The fortress dominates the southwest of St. Kitts.

Rugged visitors also make the eight-hour excursion to **Mount Misery** (at least you'll get a lot of exercise). A Land Rover will take you part of the way, and you should hire a guide. After that, it's a long, steady climb to the lip of the crater at 2,600 feet (the peak is 3,792 feet). Hikers can descend into the crater, clinging to vines and roots.

At the hamlet of **Half-Way Tree,** a large tamarind marked the boundary in the old days between the British-held sector and the French half.

It was near the hamlet of **Old Road Town** that Sir Thomas Warner landed with the first band of settlers, establishing the first permanent colony, to the northwest at Sandy Point. Sir Thomas's grave is in the cemetery of St. Thomas Church.

A sign in the middle of Old Road Town points the way to **Carib Rock Drawings,** all the evidence that remains of the former inhabitants. The markings are on black boulders, the pictographs dating back to prehistoric days.

Two commercial tours interest visitors. Get your driver to take you to the **Sugar Factory,** which is best seen from February through July, when the cane is ground. You don't need a reservation, and you'll see the process from when the raw cane enters the factory until it emerges as bulk sugar.

Guests are also allowed to visit the **Carib Beer Plant,** an English larger beer-processing house. Carib Beer is considered the best in the West Indies, if sales are any indication. At the end of the tour through the plant, visitors are given cold Carib in the lounge. The plant doesn't always operate, so check before heading there to see if it's open.

SHOPPING: The good buys here are in local handcrafts, including leather items made from goatskin, baskets, ceramic figurines, and coconut shells (the natives know how to make almost anything from these items). Some good values are also to be found in clothing and fabrics, especially sea island cottons. Store hours are 8 a.m. to noon and 1 to 4 p.m. except Sunday, although this is likely to vary greatly, depending on the individual shopkeeper.

Caribelle Batik, at Romney Manor (tel. 465-6253), qualifies as a sightseeing attraction as well as a shopping expedition. Its workroom and sales showrooms are in the most romantic setting of any shopping recommendation in this guide—the entire

Romney Manor, a plantation established in the 17th century. You'll need a car, as it's reached via a short, steep road off the coast. It's right off Old Road, in the shade of a flamboyant tree. On the way to the manor, ask your driver to show you the Carib petroglyphs carved on stones (right near Old Road Town).

In the showroom a chart explains the batik process. You can watch as island workers apply different layers of molten wax and color, both required in the printing process. Also there are facilities for tie-dye fabrics. Items include wall hangings made of West Indian sea island cotton. Take your time and you'll usually find someone willing to explain the process to you. The shop offers beautiful caftans, T-shirts (preshrunk), and batik pictures. U.S. citizens may make duty-free purchases here. If you want to create your own ensemble, you can do so by purchasing lengths of fabric. Visiting hours are Monday to Friday from 8 a.m. to 4 p.m.

Losada's Antiques and Things, Wigley Avenue, Fortlands (tel. 465-2564), near the Ocean Terrace Inn and the Fort Thomas Hotel, is a cozy "antiques and everything" shop in premises with access to a flower and shrub garden. It's owned by Mrs. Ghislaine Cramer, who keeps her eye on anything on the island that could be classified as an antique. She's at every estate sale and knows value. Her boutique has a collection of old gold watches, silver service, antique and contemporary jewelry in gold and silver, decanters, and teapots. She always has some antiques on consignment, and also offers local craftware such as bamboo fans and fabric hats. She encourages young, talented craftspeople on St. Kitts to sell their creations at her store.

You'll find the **Spencer Cameron Art Gallery** (tel. 465-4047) by the Circus, with its entrance on Bay Road. Here, a British woman, Rosey Cameron-Smith, produces watercolors and limited-edition prints of Kittitian and Nevian scenes. She arrived here about eight years ago and was captivated by the island's charms. She made an effort to reproduce in art some of the essence of true West Indian life, particularly the humor that sneaks into all its aspects. Rosey is well known on the island for her paintings of Kittitian Carnival clowns, showing all the color and excitement of this old island tradition. Exclusive Spencer Cameron designs form another facet of the gallery interest with a range of T-shirts and dresses silkscreened by hand in the gallery's workshop. The wide selection of artwork ranges from small prints for $5, large ones for around $15, and hand-colored prints for $35 to original paintings ranging from $40 to $300. Rosey also produces a variety of greeting cards, postcards, and calendars.

For the most luxurious shopping at affordable prices, I suggest **A Slice of the Lemon,** all white, carpeted, and mirrored inside. In 1979 Martin Kreiner opened a duty-free shop at the already-previewed Golden Lemon. However, the main store is in the Palms Arcade (tel. 465-2889) at the Circus in Basseterre, offering duty-free perfumes, watches, jewelry, and crystal.

Palmcrafts, on Princes Street, Basseterre (no phone), is one of several shops in the Palms Arcade. It sells locally produced jams, jellies, and chutneys, all made from natural ingredients; skin oils and lotions made from coconut oils scented with cinnamon, lemon, frangipani, and other essential components; spices, herb teas, and condiments from Sunny Caribbee; Spice Island fragrances; straw items; island postcards; local handcrafts; clothes handmade in Nevis from Southern Cross; the famous Caribbee Clothes; books on the Caribbean; tropical animals and fruits; and Haitian wall hangings.

Craftshouse (tel. 465-3241), is an outlet for the handcrafts of St. Kitts and Nevis made by craftsmen working through the National Handicraft and Cottage Industries Development Board. They offer items in copper, wood, coir, and coconut as well as furniture. You'll find Craftshouse shops at the Golden Rock International Airport; Ponds Pasture Industrial Site, Bay Road, Basseterre; the Treasury Pier, Bay Road; and the Deep Water Port. Shops are open during normal business hours.

Stamp collectors interested in what is essentially a new stamp-issuing country can find distinctive stamps bearing the name of St. Kitts at the **St. Kitts Philatelic Bureau,** Social Security Building, Bay Road, Basseterre (tel. 465-2874). When St. Kitts and Nevis formed their own government, they had independent stamp bureaus established on both islands.

The **Medic's Pharmacy,** corner of Cayone and Fort Streets, Basseterre (tel. 465-2228, 465-2810 after closing), is a place you can get prescriptions filled and find all the regular drugstore merchandise you need. It's open weekdays, from 8 a.m. to 6 p.m. (to 1 p.m. on Thursday) and 8 a.m. to 8 p.m. on Saturday.

THE SPORTING LIFE: Sporting activities aren't as developed on St. Kitts as they are on more tourist-oriented islands, but the outlook is improving. Beaches are the primary concern of most visitors, who find the swimming best at Conaree Beach (two miles from Basseterre), Frigate Bay, and Friar's Bay. The narrow peninsula in the southeast that contains the island's salt ponds also boasts its best beaches.

Water Sports

A variety of activities is offered by **Dive St. Kitts,** Pelican Cove Marina Ltd., Ocean Terrace Inn (tel. 465-2754). From Fisherman's Wharf, you can swim, sail, float, paddle, or go on scuba-diving and snorkeling expeditions.

Scuba trips, including all gear and guided dive trips by boat, cost $30 for one tank per person, $50 for two tanks per person per day, and $170 for eight tanks per person over four days. Total training in theories and practical applications to safe and enjoyable scuba-diving are offered in a full certification course, including all gear, text, and certification. The cost for this course is $200.

Snorkel trips, in a safety-equipped boat with an experienced boatman, take you to good spots to see the underwater life around St. Kitts. Mask, fins, and snorkel are included in the cost of $25 per person per half day for a minimum of two persons. A trip to Cockleshell or Banana Bay takes you down the uninhabited southern peninsula of St. Kitts, past the Nag's Head to the Banana Bay Beach Hotel or the Cockleshell Hotel. You can have a lazy lunch, hunt seashells, and explore the clear water. All snorkeling gear is included. The price of this full-day excursion is $35 per person, with a minimum of two persons required. Another snorkeling expedition is a beach picnic. You're taken on a scenic ride to the southern peninsula, where the beaches are inviting to swimmers and snorkelers. A camp-style lunch of freshly caught fish or lobster, plus white wine, is served. You leave the dock at 10 a.m., returning at 4 p.m. The charge is $40 per person, with a minimum of four persons required.

Waterskiing and windsurfing are also provided by Dive St. Kitts. Instruction in waterskiing is available for novices, and you can also be taught the fundamentals of windsurfing. Waterskiing prices are $30 per half hour, $50 per hour, while windsurfing costs $10 per hour. However, if you need instruction in this latter sport, the charge is $15 per hour.

Deep-Sea Fishing

Again, you must turn to Dive St. Kitts at the Ocean Terrace Inn (tel. 465-2754). If six persons want to go out, he can arrange a half-day fishing jaunt at a cost of $50 per half day, tackle and bait included.

Golfing

At **Frigate Bay** there is an 18-hole championship golf course, and there's a nine-hole course at **Golden Rock.** Robert Trent Jones designed the course at the Jack Tar at Frigate Bay. Greens fees are $20 for 18 holes, $12 for 9 holes. Caddies get $8 per 18 holes.

Tennis

The **Olympic Club**, just around the corner from the Ocean Terrace Hotel, has tennis courts on which visitors can play. Also downtown, at the **St. Kitts Lawn Tennis Club** you can arrange for a temporary membership. Call 465-2754 for details.

NIGHTLIFE: There isn't much. A moonlight cruise, offered by **Dive St. Kitts,** Pelican Cove Marina Ltd., Ocean Terrace Inn (tel. 465-2754), takes you from Fisherman's Wharf at about 6:30 p.m. You can enjoy rum punch, beer, and soft drinks as you relax under the moon. The cruise costs $25 per person, with a minimum of four persons required.

If you're in the mood to gamble, St. Kitts's only **casino** is at the Jack Tar Village, Frigate Bay (tel. 465-8651). It's open to all visitors, who can try their luck at roulette, blackjack, craps, and slot machines. The casino opens at 8 p.m. There is no entrance fee.

The best all-around place for entertainment is the **Ocean Terrace Inn** (tel. 465-2754), which has entertainment two nights weekly off-season and more frequently in season. There's no cover charge, and guests pay EC$3.75 ($1.40) per drink. Who knows what's likely to be happening on any given night? Often you dance to live bands. Perhaps you'll hear a West Indian group or watch an African dance. On several occasions carnival queens model batik bathing suits. And it's always a good idea to introduce yourself to the longtime bartender, Marcus Payne, who'll show you the aviary and aquarium behind the bar. Watch the "love birds." Also consider attending the Wednesday- or Friday-night buffets at the previously recommended Fisherman's Wharf, which lies on the waterfront down from the Ocean Terrace.

If you decide to venture into one of the local bars around the island, you just might be served a concoction known as "Halfway Three." It's made of bootleg and white lightning, along with moonshine, and is to be drunk at your own risk!

4. Nevis

Two miles south of St. Kitts, Nevis (pronounced *Nee*-vis) was discovered by Columbus in 1493. He called it Las Nieves, Spanish for "snows," because its cloud-capped mountains reminded him of the snow-capped range in the Pyrenees. The island, almost circular, appears like a perfect cone when viewed from St. Kitts, its sister state. The cone rises gradually to a height of 3,596 feet. A saddle joins the mountain to two smaller peaks, Saddle Hill (1,432 feet) in the south, and Hurricane Hill (1,192 feet) in the north. Coral reefs rim the shoreline, and there is mile after mile of palm-shaded white sandy beaches.

Columbus may have discovered the island, but it was settled by the British in 1628. The volcanic island is famous as the birthplace of Alexander Hamilton, drafter of the U.S. Constitution. It was also at Nevis that Admiral Nelson harbored his fleet in Napoleonic days, marrying a rich, young widow, Frances Nisbet. His best man was the Duke of Clarence, later King William IV of England.

In the 18th century Nevis, "The Queen of the Caribees," was the leading spa of the West Indies, made so by its hot mineral springs.

Once Nevis was peppered with prosperous sugarcane estates, which are gone now (many converted into some of the most intriguing character hotels in the Caribbean). Sea island cotton is the chief crop today.

As you drive around the nostalgic island, going through tiny villages such as Gingerland (named for the spice it used to export), you'll reach the heavily wooded slopes of Nevis Peak. From that vantage point there are magnificent views of the neighboring islands. Nevis is an island of exceptional beauty and has remained unspoiled. Its people, in the main, are black descendants of slaves. Nevis is usually approached by ferry boat or air from **St. Kitts.**

On the Caribbean side, **Charlestown,** the capital of Nevis, was very fashionable in the 18th century, as sugar planters were carried around in carriages and sedan chairs. Houses are of locally quarried volcanic stone, often supporting a clapboard second story, encircled by West Indian fretted verandas. A town of wide, quiet streets, this port only gets busy when its major link to the world, the ferry from St. Kitts, docks at the harbor. Then it becomes a cascade of activity.

GETTING THERE: You can fly to Nevis on **LIAT** (tel. 469-5238) on scheduled service from St. Kitts, Antigua, or Montserrat. No flight takes more than 25 minutes. There is direct service from St. Croix, St. Barts, and Anguilla. **Carib Aviation** is available for charters and will fly two to five passengers. The trip by air from St. Kitts takes only five minutes. The cost for a charter is $50 per person. For information, call 469-5295 in Nevis.

You can also use the **inter-island ferry** service from St. Kitts aboard the government passenger ferry M.V. *Caribe Queen*. For information on this service, see the section on St. Kitts, under "Getting Around."

GETTING AROUND: Your ten-seater plane arrives at the airport a half mile from Newcastle in the north of the island. Or if you're coming by ferryboat from St. Kitts, you'll be delivered right to the heart of the capital, Charlestown.

Rental Cars

If you're prepared to face the rocky, pot-holed roads of Nevis, you can arrange for a rental car from **Budget** before going there (call toll free at 800/527-0700). Avis and Hertz maintain no offices in Nevis. The Budget office is on Main Street in Charlestown (tel. 465-5390). This particular subsidiary of Budget requires a customer to take a taxi from the airport or from his or her hotel to the car-rental headquarters to pick up a vehicle.

The cheapest car is a Dodge Colt with automatic transmission. The cost is $150 per week with unlimited mileage. Drivers must be at least 25 years old. It's advisable to take out a collision damage waiver. This costs around $5 per day. Even if you buy it, you'll still be responsible for the first $200 worth of collision damage in the event of an accident. If you don't buy it, you'll be financially responsible for any and all damages to your car.

Taxis

You can also rent a taxi with a driver (who also doubles as a guide). You'll find them waiting at the airport at the arrival of every plane. As an example of fares charged: a taxi ride between Charlestown and Newcastle Airport costs $20; between Charlestown and Old Manor, $15; and from Charlestown to Pinney's Beach, $5. You can hire a taxi to or from Charlestown Pier and Bath Hotel or Bath Village for $5. To take a sightseeing tour around the island, a 3½-hour excursion, you'll pay $90. Between 10 p.m. and 6 a.m., 10% is added to the prices for Charlestown trips. The average taxi holds up to four persons, so when the cost is sliced per passenger, it's a reasonable investment. No sightseeing bus companies operate on Nevis.

PRACTICAL FACTS: Language, currency, and entry requirements have already been discussed in this chapter's introductory section. Most visitors will clear Customs in St. Kitts, so arrival in Nevis should not be complicated.

In case of **emergency**, telephone 999 from all Nevis exchanges.

Telegrams and **Telexes** can be sent from Cable & Wireless offices, Main Street, Charlestown (tel. 469-5294). International **telephone** calls, including collect calls, can also be sent from the cable office. Hours are 8 a.m. to 6 p.m. weekdays, 8 a.m. to 2 p.m. on Saturday, and 6 to 8 p.m. on Sunday and public holidays.

As in St. Kitts, an **electrical** transformer will be needed for most U.S. and Canadian appliances. The current is 230 volts, 60 cycles.

The **water** supply is good and safe to drink.

To **drive** in Nevis, you must obtain a permit from the Traffic Department, costing about EC$30 ($11.10) and valid for three months. Remember, all the vehicles must be driven on the *left-hand side of the road.*

The **post office** is open from 8 a.m. to 3 p.m. daily, except Thursday when it closes at 11:30 a.m.

Banking hours are 8 a.m. to noon daily except Saturday and Sunday. However, most banks reopen from 3:30 to 5:30 p.m. on Friday.

Normal **business hours** are 8 a.m. to noon and 1 to 4 p.m., except on Thursday.

The **Tourist Bureau** is on Chapel Street in Charlestown (tel. 469-5494). The St. Kitts–Nevis Tourist Board in the U.S. is at 414 E. 75th St., New York, NY 10021 (tel. 212/535-1234).

As in St. Kitts, Nevis is on **Atlantic Standard Time,** which means it's usually one hour ahead of the U.S. East Coast, except when the mainland goes on Daylight Saving Time. Then clocks are the same.

The information given in "Practical Facts" for St. Kitts regarding climate is also true for Nevis.

A 10% **service charge** is added to your hotel bill. In restaurants, it is customary to **tip** from 10% to 15% of the tab.

The government imposes a 7% **tax** on hotel bills, plus a departure tax of EC$13.50 ($5) per person. You don't have to pay this tax in Nevis if you're returning to St. Kitts, since Nevis and St. Kitts are the same country. However, if you're flying from either Nevis or St. Kitts to some other destination in the Caribbean, the tax will be assessed.

HOTELS: Several of the inns of Nevis have been adapted from long-decayed sugar plantations. The style and amenities may transport you back to a bygone era. In addition, there are a scattering of air-conditioned motel-type accommodations for those who prefer that.

Croney's Old Manor Estate, P.O. Box 70, Gingerland (tel. 465-5445, 212/840-6636 in New York City, or toll free 800/223-9815, 800/468-0023 in Canada), has an old-world kind of grace that makes it the most desirable hotel on Nevis and one of the most unusual and delightful hostelries in the entire Caribbean. When Nevis was settled in the 17th century, the forested plot of land on which the hotel sits was granted to the Croney family in 1690 by the King of England. Construction of a plantation whose main house, now in ruins, has been dubbed "the best example of Georgian domestic architecture in the Caribbean" continued in a gradual expansion throughout the 18th and 19th centuries. Until 1936 the estate was a working sugar plantation. On the grounds you can see the rusted flywheels of cane-crushing machines whose bases are engraved "Glasgow—1859–1861." For a dark and better-forgotten period of its history, this burgeoning plantation served as a stud farm for the breeding of slaves. When the last of the Croney line, Bertie, died in 1967, he left vacant the longest continually lived-in great house in the West Indies.

The entire complex, including the main house and stone outbuildings, sits at a cool and comfortable elevation of 800 feet. In 1981 a spunky, competent, and gracious Ohio widow, Vicki Knorr, purchased the property and embarked on its restoration. Everything about her regime has encouraged a nonplastic, solidly grounded foundation in architectural and culinary excellence. Mrs. Knorr has a creative and professional relationship with her hard-working and talented son, Greg. Living on the premises, he handles long-range administrative planning as easily as he tends bar. Although rehabilitation of the great house will require years of patient labor, the hotel occupies a trio of stone outbuildings that are almost as beautiful as the house. The estate workers' clapboard huts were replaced by the kind of structures sometimes seen on 800-year-old estates in the south of France. Gracefully proportioned stone stairs are flanked by ancient trees and vines, giving the place a dignified, colonial ambience of filtered sunlight. The former smokehouse and jail were replaced by a rambling villa called the Overseer's Building.

Each of the accommodations contains wide-plank floors of such tropical hardwoods as greenheart, plushly comfortable colonial-reproduction furniture, and high-ceilinged space. In high season, with MAP, singles cost $150 daily, and doubles go for $215. *In low season, singles on the MAP rent for $110 daily, and doubles run $160.* The resort is not recommended for children under 12. A big part of the success of Croney's is the culinary inspiration of Mrs. Knorr. Her Cooperage dining room, recommended separately, is the finest on the island. Breakfast is served every day in guests' bedrooms. Lunch is in the raftered dining room or beside the most unusual swimming pool on Nevis. Chiseled from fitted blocks of volcanic rock, it was crafted from a 150-year-old cistern. You serve yourself from a buffet table and a century-old grill in the plantation's colonial kitchens. Every Friday night, the natural stone amphitheater near the kitchen serves as the perfect acoustical setting for some of the best-attended parties on the island.

Nisbet Plantation Inn, New Castle (tel. 469-5325), is a gracious estate house on a coconut plantation where gentility and a respect for fine living prevail. This is the former home of Frances Nisbet, who married Lord Nelson at the age of 22. (Enamored of Miss Nisbet at the time, he later fell in love with Lady Hamilton, and Frances Nisbet died a bitter old woman in England, one of history's pathetic figures.) The present main building on the 30-acre plantation was rebuilt on the foundations of the original 18th-century great house. The ruins of a circular sugar mill stand at the entrance, covered with cassia, frangipani, hibiscus, and poinciana. Set in the palm grove are the guest cottages with covered verandas, all with private bathrooms with showers and two with ornate four-poster beds. On the MAP, winter rates are $240 to $300 in a double, $175 to $200 in a single. *In summer, the rates in a double are $150 to $200, and in a single, $85 to $110, also on the MAP.* These rates are for standard and superior rooms.

Breakfast is served on a veranda with a view down a wide grassy lawn lined with sentinel palm trees which leads to a half-mile-long sandy beach, one of the best in Nevis. Two neighboring bays combine to make a total of three miles for beachcombing and shelling. An offshore reef protects the swimming area, providing good snorkeling, with spearfishing and snorkeling equipment available free at the hotel. At the end of the day a tranquil evening meal is served in the dining room of the main house, furnished with English antiques. Local fish and lobster as well as continental and American cuisine are featured, and Créole dishes are offered on occasion. Complimentary wine is served at dinner. This is always a social event: the guests gather first on the veranda for "sundowners," then are seated at tables for four to six persons (if you want a different arrangement, ask in advance). Sunday is barbecue time on the beach, enjoyed to the accompaniment of a steel band. If visitors drop in, they are charged $25. The managers are easy-going and hospitable, and with the assistance of their well-trained staff, they see to your needs. There is a library in the main house, but if you want more energetic pursuits, horseback riding can be arranged, and you'll find a hard court for tennis near the main house. Racquets and balls are provided. Fishing, sailing, and surf-jetting are available about five miles from the hotel and can be arranged through the management. Car rentals are provided at the inn.

All reservations for stays here are taken in the Duluth, Minnesota, area office (tel. 218/722-5059).

Zetland Plantation, P.O. Box 448, Gingerland (tel. 469-5454), originally a sugar plantation, was converted into an exceptional hotel, occupying a 750-acre site with good views of both the Atlantic and the Caribbean Sea. The former plantation lies 1,000 feet up on the slopes of Mount Nevis, from which you can view Antigua and Montserrat. Its name is derived from Scotland's Shetland Islands. Today Zetland is more like a country-club lodge. More than a dozen plantation suites (square one-story houses) are rented, containing spacious lounges and bedrooms. Hotel-type maid service is included in the tariffs. Scattered about the grounds, all rental units are within easy walking distance of the main complex. Because of its mountain perch, trade-wind breezes keep the plantation cooled. *In summer, a single room rents for $80 daily on the MAP, going up to $120* daily in a double, also on the MAP. In winter, singles are charged $120 on the MAP, and two persons pay $150 daily. Some of the newer units, really mountainside suites, have their own plunge pools. Rates include wake-up coffee and transportation to the hotel beach hut. When making reservations, inquire about package rates and family plans. The Sugar Mill has been transformed into a family unit, housing up to six persons.

As only 44 guests can be accommodated at a time, everybody quickly gets to know everybody else. The manager, Nigel Adams, and his wife, Marion, have had experience in restaurant and tourist enterprises in England. They'll outline the sports program to you, including hikes through tropical forest, tennis, horseback riding, or swimming at the plantation pool. Or you can drive to Zetland's beach for ocean swimming. A place for the discriminating traveler, Zetland also serves good food. Most of it is grown on the plantation. People staying here on EP rates are charged extra for gas for cooking in their units.

The **Hermitage Plantation,** St. John Figtree Parish (tel. 465-5477), a much-photographed, frequently copied historians' delight, is said to be the oldest all-wood house in the Antilles, built amid the high-altitude plantations of Gingerland in 1740. It probably wouldn't offer the bucketloads of meticulously researched charm of today without the careful supervision of a former Philadelphia investment banker, Richard Lupinacci. He and his wife, Maureen (who maintains a sense of humor even in the most trying of circumstances), have assembled one of the best collections of antiques on Nevis. Each piece corresponds with taste and flair to the wide-plank floors, intricate latticework, and high ceilings of this beautiful hotel. The ten accommodations are in five glamorous outbuildings designed like small plantation houses. Many contain huge four-poster beds, antique accessories, and colonial louvered windows. With MAP, winter rates are $150 daily in a single, $170 in a double. *In summer, rooms with MAP are $120 daily in a single, $140 in a double.* Laundry service is one of this place's many fringe benefits. The property is protected by parallel rows of dry retaining walls. In the center, amid stands of very old mahogany trees, is a pleasant rectangular swimming pool.

Cliffdwellers, Tamarind Bay (tel. 465-5262), derives its name from its location on top of one of the steepest hills on Nevis. If you're afraid your car will stall on the incredibly steep access road, don't despair. A thatch-covered funicular, similar to the small trains the Swiss use to scale the Alps, climbs on rails up the bougainvillea-covered slope. Once you're on top, you'll enjoy sweeping views of the hills and harbors of the island's jagged western coastline. The 14 accommodations are in cedar-sided buildings whose rooflines are curved like the prows of Viking ships. Each unit is angled so that its balcony has the maximum benefit of the view. The large, almost square rooms have canopied king-size or twin beds, private baths, and tastefully informal wicker furniture. In winter, single rooms cost $175 daily; doubles go for $235, and triples for $300. *In summer, singles rent for $95 daily, doubles for $140, and triples for $180.* All tariffs include MAP, but tax and service are added. On the premises is a long swimming pool, plus a tennis court. Horseback riding on the sandy beach can be arranged. If you want to spend a day at sea, the hotel has its own 20-foot day-sailer more or less permanently moored at the bottom of the hill. The in-house restaurant is recommended separately.

Golden Rock Estate, P.O. Box 493, Gingerland (tel. 469-5346), a sugar estate built in 1815, high in the hills of Nevis, has been converted into one of the most charming and atmospheric inns in the Caribbean. You walk through a 25-acre garden in a tropical setting of about 150 acres, lush and lovely. The original windmill, a stone tower, has been turned into a duplex honeymoon retreat (or else accommodations for a family of four or five), with an elaborate four-poster bed. The inn has 15 double rooms in all, spread about the garden, shaded by hibiscus and allamanda, yet within a minute's walk of the freshwater swimming pool and shady terrace where tropical rum punches are served.

Each villa has been decorated with flair, and the king-size beds are four-posters made of bamboo. The fabrics used are island made, with tropical flower designs. Everything seems handsome and personal. In addition, the rooms have large porches for relaxing, reading, or just looking out at the sea. In winter, a single rents for $100 daily, and a double goes for $140, plus another $25 per person for breakfast and dinner. *In summer (April 1 to December 20), a single costs only $50 daily, a double renting for $80, plus $25 if you also want breakfast and dinner*. Children under age 2 stay free. Wine is included at dinner, which is likely to be a West Indian meal (ever had stuffed pumpkin?) served at the 175-year-old "long house." Before dinner you can enjoy a tall drink in the hotel's bar. A new facility at famous Pinney's Beach, the Carousel Bar, serves lobster, shrimp, grilled fish, and hamburgers with coconut-husk flavor. It's open daily except Sunday during the winter season. Otherwise you can have a picnic lunch prepared in the hotel's kitchen. To find the beach bar, turn at the sign of the hand-carved horse's head.

The manager, Pam Barry, came to Nevis on a project involving tanning of sheepskin and goatskin. She fell in love with the island, and her enthusiasm is contagious. She will show you to the tennis court or start you on a hike through a rain forest, where you might spot a wild monkey. The hotel's bus takes guests to one of Golden Rock's beaches every day at no extra cost. The estate owns one beach on the leeward side, part of Pinney's Beach, and another on the windward side where you can surf. The shuttle runs round trip to both beaches, with a shopping stop in Charlestown if you want it. In addition, a 20-foot fiberglass day-sailer and a 16-foot Boston whaler are offered for waterskiing, light offshore fishing, and snorkel and scuba-diving. Scuba is available to accredited divers only. Two windsurfers can be used free by guests (lessons cost extra). A private car, either a Mini-Moke or a Volkswagen, is available for one or two couples, including insurance and mileage. After dark, there might be a string band for your amusement.

Montpelier Plantation Inn, P.O. Box 474, Montpelier (tel. 469-5462), 700 feet up the slopes of Mount Nevis, is owned by the Milnes Gaskell family from Yorkshire. Sixteen rooms with private terraces and baths are in modern cottages and are kept cool and fresh by the almost-constant light breeze. Other portions were set on the foundations of the ruins of the great Montpelier estate. Much use has been made of local stonework and traditional architectural styles. The magnificent and extensive gardens have, at their center, the 18th-century sugar mill, a mammoth swimming pool and pool bar, and at the periphery a hard tennis court. The year 1986 saw renovations and complete redecoration. The atmosphere is of informal West Indian grandeur. The hotel concentrates on the quality of its food, using when possible fresh local produce. Winter rates on the MAP are $155 daily in a single and $210 daily in a double. *Off-season, MAP rates are $80 daily in a single and $120 in a double*. The inn has its own speedboat, a 17-foot Boston whaler with 85-hp outboard engine for waterskiing and snorkeling. Horseback riding, sailing, and deep-sea fishing can be arranged. In season, several nights a week there are dances at nearby establishments. Montpelier occasionally has a grand affair, featuring the Honey Bees Scratch Band.

Pinney's Beach Hotel, P.O. Box 61, Charlestown (tel. 469-5207), is the only hotel on one of the most spectacular beaches in Nevis. A miniature resort, it is a bungalow colony, 48 double rooms, including six family-type units, clustered around a waterside patio where you can have cooling drinks, lunch, or take a dip. The decor is traditional, with a certain amount of clutter, but guests seem to like such informality. Rooms are modestly equipped, yet supplied with the basic necessities. Some are airconditioned. Each unit comes with a private bath and a patio, and a view of the palmfringed coastline is thrown in as well. The cheaper bungalows are set back a bit, overlooking an inner flower garden, while the others have their own direct entrance onto the beach. In winter, double rooms rent for $95 to $130 daily on the MAP, and singles go for $65 to $85. *In summer, the manager reduces the tariffs to $50 to $60 daily in a single, $75 to $95 in a double, all MAP*. Horseback riding, sailing, and deep-sea fishing can be arranged by the hotel, and there's a tennis club about 50 yards from Pinney's. Many business people from the town come here for lunch, as the hotel is only a seven-minute walk into Charlestown (about a 15-minute drive from the airport).

Rest Haven Inn, P.O. Box 209, Old Hospital Road in Charlestown (tel. 469-5208), is a collection of bungalows standing on 2½ acres of grounds. I prefer the newer units which the soft-spoken owner, Almon Nisbett (with two Ts, no relation to Frances), has built at water's edge. Each with a private patio opening onto the Caribbean, these are his deluxe units—spacious, air-conditioned, containing twin-size and single beds. For these, of course, he charges his highest tariffs. The older rooms containing twin beds are set back a bit, located within the pool and dining area compound, facing each other with private patios. Some of these have simple efficiency units for light cooking. *Summer rates, depending on the accommodation, range from $25 to $65 daily in a single, from $40 to $80 in a double, EP*. In winter, EP tariffs are $45 to $80 daily in a single, from $60 to $100 in a double. For half board, add $20 per person daily. The hospitality is what counts here, not the grand surroundings, and you are close to Charlestown, a five-minute walk away. The location is also near Pinney's Beach, where you'll surely want to spend your days. Mr. Nisbett has a reputation for serving good-tasting island dishes, and if you want to go hiking, one of his staff will pack a picnic lunch for you. There is also a snackbar, where light lunches, including lobster, are served daily to those who don't want to leave the grounds. Tennis is available on the hotel's own courts.

WHERE TO DINE: When you can get it, the native food is good. If you request sea urchin, the chef won't be surprised. Good local dishes include not only that but turtle specialties as well (stew, steak, or pie). Suckling pig and pixilated pork are both roasted with many spices, and eggplant is used in a number of tasty ways, as is the avocado. Most people dine at their hotel. To break what could be monotony, many guests "hotel-hop," taking their lunch or dinner at one of the other hotels on the island.

If you find yourself Charlestown at midday, you might do better gathering the makings for your own picnic lunch. One way to do this is to go to the **market-place,** buying fresh fruit, such as mangoes, from the stallkeepers. Then head for the **Nevis Bakery,** where you can order coconut tarts, and fresh-baked bread. The friendly people at **Main Street Grocery Store** will provide the rest of the makings for your lunch, including canned pâté.

The Cooperage, Croney's Old Manor Estate, Gingerland (tel. 465-5445), is the previously recommended hotel's dining room, in a reconstructed building where coopers once made barrels for the sugar mill. Built in the 17th century, it had a tilted floor so that the coopers could roll their completed barrels from the enormous forge to a storage area at the building's opposite end. The floor has been leveled, but the colonial aura has been retained under the sophisticated guidance of Ohio-born Vicki Knorr. Dinner is served under the high, raftered ceiling surrounded by thick walls of local stone. In addition to having a fascinating history, the Cooperage is also the best restaurant on an island where there's plenty of stiff competition.

A few of the recipes used, particularly the one for Mrs. Knorr's superb version of cream of green pepper soup, are closely guarded secrets. Lunch, served daily from noon to 3 p.m., includes such light-textured specialties as spinach salad, stuffed Caribbean lobster, cream of broccoli soup, seafood crêpes, and fruit desserts. The cost is from $8. Dinner, with wine included, costs from $25, and you can choose from a changing list of specialties based on the daily availability of ingredients. Examples are shrimp with coconut served on spinach, an array of soups, curried chicken breasts "Old Manor style" with homemade noodles, dolphin, kingfish, wahoo, snapper bought fresh each morning from local fishermen, and a succulent variety of local shrimp caught off the coast of St. Kitts. Reservations are suggested, especially for nonresidents. Dinner is served from 7 to 9:30 p.m. daily.

The **Hermitage Plantation,** St. John Figtree Parish (tel. 465-5477), is a place to combine an excellent dinner with a visit to the oldest house on Nevis, now one of the island's most unusual hotels, recommended previously. Meals are served on the latticed porch of the main house, amid candles, immaculate napery, and good cheer. Maureen Lupinacci, who runs the place with her husband, Richard, is the skillful chef who combines continental recipes with local ingredients. Menu specialties include snapper steamed in banana leaves, lobster with Pernod, chicken baked with mushrooms, cream, and white papaya, plus carrot and tarragon soup, brown bread, ice cream, and a delectable version of rum soufflé. Full dinners with wine and drinks cost around $35 per person. Dinner is served daily at 8 p.m., but first you must have a before-dinner drink in the colonial-style living room of the Lupinacci family. Nonresidents are accepted as dinner guests.

Cliffdwellers, Tamarind Bay (tel. 465-5262), in the previously recommended hotel, offers one of the best spots on Nevis for a panoramic view with your before-dinner drink. If you can possibly get here before sunset, the spectrum of colors in the sky just before the dinner hour is worth the trip. Meals are served in a room decorated with wicker, hanging plants, exposed planking, and large windows. Menu items include lobster Thermidor, turtle steak, lemon chicken, fish in white wine sauce, fish Créole, pumpkin soup, eggplant-and-tomato casserole, lamb curry with mango chutney, Cornish game hen in a cognac-flavored cream sauce, and mango-chutney chicken. A preferred dessert, if available, is the pineapple-and-coconut mousse. Lunch, served daily from 1 to 2 p.m., costs from $10. Dinner, costing from $20 with wine included, is offered daily from 8 to 9:30 p.m. Reservations for dinner are suggested, as there is only one seating. Helen Kidd, the charming Scottish-born manager, is an absolute whiz on Trivial Pursuit and checkers.

Montpelier Plantation Inn, at Montpelier (tel. 469-5462), was previously recommended as a hotel, but it offers some of the finest dining on the island as well, and will accept nonresidents who make a reservation. At this grand old West Indian mansion, you can dine on the veranda, enjoying a three-course table d'hôte dinner for $25, plus wine and drinks. For that, you're given an appetizer, main course, and dessert. The owner, James Milnes Gaskell, likes to make use of local produce whenever available. Lobster and fish such as red snapper are served the day the catch comes in. The menu is eclectic, and sometimes you'll find roast beef and Yorkshire pudding on the menu. The candlelit dinner has an 8 p.m. seating, so try to show up on time. A buffet lunch, costing $12, is offered daily from 1 to 2 p.m. One of the local bands comes in to entertain about every ten days.

Gillies Husavik, Jones Bay (tel. 469-5291), stands on the western (leeward) side of the island. Translated from the Icelandic, *husavik* means "small house on the bay." The small house and the beach that adjoins it are the hibiscus-studded domain of a Canadian couple of Icelandic origin, Laurie and Lloyd Gillies. During the day the establishment's activity revolves around the hexagonal cabaña bar. Many visitors bring their beach paraphernalia and spend the day sipping rum punches and enjoying the surf. If you want to stay for a sunny lunch, shaved-ham or shaved-roast-beef sandwiches are served as part of meals costing $7 each. Technically, lunch lasts from noon to 2:30 p.m., but the cabaña is open for snacks and drinks throughout the day.

In the evening more substantial meals are served in the low-slung Gillies dwelling house, within earshot of the surf. At candlelit tables covered with blue napery, you can choose from a menu offering marinated barbecued steaks, locally grown spinach with yogurt dressing, fresh seafood, flambéed tarts, and fruit crêpes. Expect to spend about $30 for dinner. Because this is very much a private home, reservations are essential for the evening meal, which begins at 7 p.m.

EXPLORING NEVIS: When you arrive at the airport, it's best to negotiate with a taxi driver to take you around Nevis. The distance is only 20 miles. You may find yourself taking much longer if you stop to see specific sights. The people are friendly and will often engage you in conversation.

The major attraction is the **Birthplace of Alexander Hamilton,** on Main Street overlooking the bay. Mr. Hamilton was born illegitimate in 1755, the son of a Scotsman, James Hamilton, and a Créole, Rachael Fawcett. The family left the island in 1782 and never returned to Nevis, but Alexander went to the United States as a young man and entered the pages of history. The lava-stone house by the shore has been restored and a modest museum opened. In it are period furnishings, Hamilton memorabilia, and a library. Also displayed are exhibits of island history. The museum is open from 10 a.m. to 5 p.m. Monday to Friday. No admission is charged, but donations are requested. Hamilton Estate, above the town, was once the property of Alexander Hamilton's father.

At Bath Village, about half a mile from Charlestown, stands the **Bath Hotel,** in serious disrepair, and its **Bath House,** which has been restored to use. The hotel was built in 1778 by John Huggins to accommodate some 50 guests, mostly wealthy planters in the West Indies who were afflicted with rheumatism and gout. The hotel had five hot baths built in which temperatures ranged up to 108° Fahrenheit. It shut down in 1870. Intermittently through the years since, efforts were made to restore the complex to use, but mainly, for more than a century, the hotel, patched and proud, has stood as a reminder of Nevis's heyday, but with goats treading the tired verandas instead of fancy, if ailing, gentlemen who strolled about with their ladies when young Alexander Hamilton was making his name known in the American colonies. Both the hotel and the Bath House were acquired by the Nevis Island government in 1983, and the Bath House has been renovated and reopened for use under the management of the Ministry of Tourism, quickly becoming popular with both islanders and tourists. A feasibility study has been authorized with a view to restoration of the Bath Hotel, with the aim of using it for the promotion of industrial development and tourism.

Nearby, **St. John's Church** stands in the midst of a sprawling graveyard in Fig Tree Village. It is said to have been the parish church of Lady Nelson, wife of Horatio Lord Nelson. A church of gray stone, dating from the 18th century, it contains the record of Nelson's marriage to Frances Nisbet in the church register.

At Morning Star Plantation nearby, the **Nelson** contains a large collection of Nelson memorabilia gathered by Robert D. Abrahams, a Philadelphia lawyer. The museum can be visited free. Among other items displayed is a faded letter written by Nelson with his left hand, after he lost his right one. Also displayed are paintings depicting Nelson's romance with Lady Hamilton, plus dining chairs from the admiral's flagship, the *Victory.* See also a grandfather clock that was deliberately (and permanently) stopped the moment Queen Elizabeth entered the museum on February 22, 1966, the most recent big event that has happened on Nevis. The museum is open daily from 9:30 a.m. to 1 p.m.

Ashby Fort is now overgrown, but it was once used by Lord Nelson to guard his ships in Nevis while they took on fresh water and supplies. Nearby is **Nelson's Spring,** near Cotton Ground Village. In the 18th century, Nelson is said to have watered his ships here before they left to fight in the American Revolution. The fort, in bad ruin, overlooks the site of **Jamestown,** an early settlement that was devastated by a 1680 tidal wave.

The **Eden Brown Estate** lies about a mile and a half from New River and it's said to be haunted. Once it was the home of a wealthy planter, whose daughter was to be married, but her husband-to-be was killed in a duel at the prenuptial feast. The mansion was then closed forever and left to the ravages of nature. A gray solid stone still stands, and only the most adventurous go here on a moonlit night.

Outside the center of Charlestown, the **Jewish Cemetery** was restored in part by an American, Robert D. Abrahams, the Philadelphia lawyer already mentioned. At the lower end of Government Road, this necropolis was the resting place of many of the early shopkeepers of Nevis. At one time Sephardic Jews coming from Brazil made up a quarter of the population. It is believed that Jews introduced sugar production into the Leewards. Most of the tombstones date from between 1690 and 1710.

SHOPPING: Everybody, including Prince Charles, heads for **Eva Wilkins' Studio** on the grounds of the old sugar mill plantation her father owned. She is the most famous artist of Nevis, and invites visitors to come by her studio and home during the day, except from noon to 3 p.m. "when I need rest." A spry, elderly lady who doesn't "understand modern ways," she displays both black-and-white and color prints. Her studio is at Clay Ghaut Estate near Montpelier in Gingerland. She paints island people (using real models), local flowers and scenes. On the grounds near her house is a miniature reproduction of the original sugar factory. Ask your driver if she's in residence before starting out. Everybody knows when Miss Wilkins is on the island.

For one of the most bizarre shopping expeditions in this book, head for the home of **Mrs. Jones,** the last house on the right going east out of New Castle, a tumbledown old village near the airport. Mrs. Jones doesn't put out a sign "because I don't need one." She candidly admits, "I'm known all over the world, but I've been no place from Nevis." An elderly peanut farmer, she turns out unglazed pottery: "I make every creature but man, and only God can put life into him." Her specialty is terracotta birds, and she also makes oversize clay pots.

The **Sand-Box Tree** on Chapel Street (tel. 469-5540), offers silkscreened fabric, designed and printed on Nevis, made up in a ready-to-wear line of clothing and in soft crafts, such as tablemats, napkins, purses, ties, hats, and eyeglass cases, among other items. The fabric also is available by the yard and is suitable for garments, slipcovers, and curtains. All the fabric is 100% cotton and tropical in design and color. Custom-made clothing is also available, and you can order any type of garment for men or women, made to measure. Place your order one day and it will be ready the next. The shop also has a wide range of clothing for men, women, and children imported from many places, as well as Nevis-crafted furniture, which can be ordered for export. There are also many gift items, guidebooks, postcards, and jewelry. Also at the Chapel Street store is *Nevis Happenings,* an up-to-date bulletin board with notices of what's going on on the island, such as special nights at hotels, houses for rent, babysitting services, and information on where to get what. You can also make reservations here for a few day and long-term charter sailboats.

The **Nevis Handicraft Cooperative Society,** Lower Happy Hill Alley (no phone), is a stone building about 200 feet from the wharf. Near the colorful marketplace (visit on Tuesday, Thursday, and Saturday mornings), the handcraft shop contains locally made gift items, including unusual objects of goatskin.

Heading up Government Road, you reach the **School for the Blind** (no phone), where the Nevisians make handcrafts for sale. Visiting hours are 9 a.m. to noon and 1 to 4 p.m. Monday through Wednesday (9 a.m. to noon on Saturday). Go only if you want to buy something, as it seems cruel to disturb these unfortunate people who have very little money and few prospects.

The National Handicraft and Cottage Industries Development Board has a branch of its **Craftshouse** sales outlets, offering a variety of handcrafted articles, at Pinneys Industrial Site, Charlestown (tel. 469-5505).

Persons interested in stamp collecting can go to the **Nevis Philatelic Bureau,** Head Post Office, Market Street, Charlestown (tel. 469-5388), to purchase the colorful issues of the island.

The best for last—**Caribee Clothes,** on Main Street (tel. 469-5217), features hand-embroidered styles. It's run by R. V. W. Todd, who will sometimes grant customers permission to visit the factory. Nevis themes often form the motif in the patterns. Resort-type shirts and skirts are sold, and they're quite beautiful—and expensive. The little industry provides work for many craftspeople on the island, and Caribee Clothes are sold in many fine West Indian boutiques and in America.

THE SPORTING LIFE: The best beach on Nevis—in fact, one of the best beaches in the Caribbean—is the reef-protected **Pinney's Beach,** with its clear water and gradual slope. Just north of Charlestown, you'll have three miles of sand (often virtually to yourself), culminating in a sleepy lagoon that evokes a scene south of Pago-Pago.

In sports equipment, it's best to bring your own. However, hotels are stocked with limited gear (but equipment may often be in use by other guests).

Snorkeling

Again, head for Pinney's Beach. You might also try the waters of Fort Ashby, where the settlement of Jamestown is said to have slid into the sea, and legend has it that the church bells can still be heard and the undersea town can still be seen when conditions are just right. So far, no diver, to my knowledge, has ever found the conditions "just right."

Your best bet is the **Oualie Beach Pub** (tel. 469-5329), at Mosquito Bay, which has snorkeling trips at a cost of $20 per person (minimum of two required).

Deep-Sea Fishing

The fishing is excellent, not only for snapper and grouper, but for bonita and king-fish as well. The best hotel for making boating arrangements is the **Golden Rock** (tel. 469-5346). It has its own 20-foot fiberglass day-sailer, and a 16-foot Boston whaler for waterskiing, light offshore fishing, and snorkel and scuba-diving. Most trips cost $90 per half day for the boat. You can catch dolphin (the fish), wahoo, and Spanish mackerel.

Boating

The best arrangements are made at the **Golden Rock** (see above).

Oualie Beach Pub (tel. 469-5329), at Mosquito Bay, will rent you Sunfish, windsurfers and a Hobie Cat at costs ranging from $10 to $15 per hour. A daily sail and a picnic will cost $35 per person (a minimum of two required).

Waterskiing

Check with **Oualie Beach Pub** (tel. 465-5329), at Mosquito Bay, where the cost is $10 for every 15 minutes.

Tennis

Most of the major hotels have courts.

Golf

Addicts of this sport are invited to go to St. Kitts, a 45-minute boat ride or a 10-minute air hop, for a game.

Mountain Climbing

This is strenuous, recommended only to the stout of heart. Ask first at your hotel for a picnic lunch, and also the desk, to arrange a guide for you (he'll probably request about $20). Hikers climb Mount Nevis, 3,500 feet up to the volcanic (extinct) crater and enjoy a hike to the rain forest to watch for wild monkeys.

Horseback Riding

Rare in the Caribbean, horseback riding is available at the **Nisbet Plantation** (tel. 469-5325), previewed earlier. Naturally, you ride English saddle. The cost is $15 per person for one hour, $10 for each hour to follow. With a guide, you are taken along mountain trails, and along the way you visit the site of long-forgotten plantations.

5. Anguilla

The most northerly of the Leeward Islands in the eastern Caribbean, Anguilla, known as "Eel Island" because of its shape, is only 16 miles long and a maximum of 3 miles wide. This little nation has a population of 7,019 people, predominantly of African descent but mixed with European ancestry, particularly Irish. Anguilla lies five miles north of St. Martin. Flat as a pancake, long, slender Anguilla has very little rainfall. The soil is unproductive, with mainly low foliage and scrub vegetation.

Vegetation may be sparse, but the beaches of white coral sand around Anguilla are outstanding. Incidentally, these strips of sand are nearly deserted, as Anguilla attracts few tourists compared to an island such as Antigua.

Once Anguilla was part of a federation with St. Kitts and Nevis, but it declared its independence in 1967. Breaking away from that associated state, it is now a British dependency, and English, of course, is the official language. Most of the men on the island work in the tourist industry or as lobster fishermen or at the government-owned Salt Pond.

Columbus may have spotted the island, calling it Anguilla, Spanish for "eel." The island was first colonized by the British, in 1650. The colony was subjected to sporadic raids from Irish and French freebooters. In 1745 a French expedition of two frigates and some 700 soldiers launched an attack, but were repulsed by the governor and his militia. The French invaders landed again in 1796, an attack bravely resisted by heroic Anguillans who fed their cannons with lead balls from their sprat nets. The invasion failed and Anguilla went back to sleep under Britain's protection. It is said that the sea island cotton seed which spread to Georgia and the Carolinas in 1889 came originally from Anguilla.

One of the most popular beaches is Road Bay, framed by the crescent-shaped village of Sandy Ground and a large salt pond. There you can negotiate with one of the local fishermen to take you to **Sandy Island,** studded with palms, just 20 minutes from port. You can also go farther out to Prickly Pear Cay, stretching like a sweeping arc all the way to a sand spit populated by sea birds and rusty brown pelicans. The bay boasts some of Anguilla's best coral gardens, inhabited by small fish with iridescent markings.

Other good beaches include Shoal Bay, which apart from its silver sands boasts some of Anguilla's best coral gardens, the habitat of hundreds of tiny fish with iridescent, brilliantly colored markings. Crocus Bay is a long, golden beach, where a fisherman might take you out in search of snapper or grouper, or ferry you to such wee islands as Little Scrub.

At Island Harbour's horseshoe bay, fishermen bring in the lobster catch. On the beach they caulk colorful boats and mend their nets. You'll want to take plenty of pictures. Schooners are built on the shore at this hamlet, which lies at the east end of the island.

Boat trips can also be arranged to **Sombrero Island,** 38 miles northwest of Anguilla. This mysterious island, with its lone lighthouse, is 400 yards wide at its broadest point, three-quarters of a mile in length. Phosphate miners abandoned it in 1890; and limestone rocks, now eroded, rise in cliffs around the island. The treeless, water-less terrain evokes a moonscape. Once an 1869 lighthouse which stood here served the ships of the world. An old schooner, *Warspite,* leaves Anguilla twice a month (ask at the tourist office), taking mail and supplies to the hearty souls who inhabit the rock. The boat leaves at night, arriving at Sombrero Island at dawn, the rough trip taking four hours. This trip is recommended only to the stout of heart, more for travelers than tourists, as absolutely no comfort is provided.

In all, Anguilla is for the adventuresome explorer. Its limited nightlife will bore many visitors, although it is that very unspoiled nature that attracts those who decide to visit it. With the opening of some super-deluxe—and super-expensive—hotels, Anguilla in the past few years has become one of the chicest targets in the Caribbean. And it is its very isolation that attracts them.

One of Anguilla's most festive, and certainly most colorful, annual festivals is **Carnival,** held jointly under the auspices of the Ministries of Culture and of Tourism. The island's people display the culture, drama, creativity, and love of their land in a burst of color and fun. The festival begins on the Friday before the first Monday in August, lasting one week. Carnival harks back to Emancipation Day, or August Mon-day as it's called, when all enslaved Africans were freed.

GETTING THERE: The nearest jet airports to Anguilla are St. Maarten, St. Kitts, Antigua, St. Thomas, and San Juan. All these destinations offer direct scheduled air service to Anguilla. From St. Maarten, **Windward Island Airway** makes three scheduled flights daily. **LIAT** has three flights weekly from St. Kitts, two flights week-ly from Antigua. From St. Thomas, **Crown Air, AIR BVI,** and **WINAIR** all have scheduled flights, five weekly, three weekly, and one daily, respectively. AIR BVI and Crown Air provide three and five weekly flights from San Juan. From New York or Miami, you can make connections via San Juan or St. Maarten.

Air Anguilla and **Tyden Air** are air-taxi services offering several daily flights to and from St. Maarten, St. Thomas, Tortola, and St. Kitts. Charters are available on both carriers.

If you'd prefer to arrive in Anguilla by sea, a **ferry** called *Cheers* (tel. 497-2853) operates between Marigot on St. Martin and Anguilla. She was the first of the sleek, modern type, and the company has been in business since 1982. The Anguilla–Marigot run takes about 15 minutes and is made seven days a week, seven round trips a day. The charge is $12 per round trip. Reservations are not necessary.

GETTING AROUND: A **taxi** tour is the best way to see the island. In about two hours, one of the local drivers (all of them are guides) will show you everything. A driver costs about $40 for the day. If you're visiting just for the day (as most sightseers do), you can be let off at your favorite beach after a look around, then picked up and returned to the airport in time to catch your flight back to wherever.

To explore the island, it's best to **rent a car.** There are many rental agencies on the island which can issue temporary drivers' licenses. These are also issued at police headquarters in the Valley and at ports of entry, costing $6. To qualify for this local driver's license, you must possess a valid license from your home country. The tempo-rary license is good for three months. *Remember to drive on the left.*

Many visitors prefer the independence that only their own car can bring. **Budget Rent-a-Car** might be the best bet for a trouble-free car rental. You can make an ad-vance reservation from North America before you leave home (tel. toll free 800/527-0700). Rentals are available by the day, although they usually work out to be less expensive if you keep the car for a full week. Local taxi unions prevent any car-rental company from maintaining an office at the airport, so you'll have to take a taxi to Budget's headquarters in a concrete building at the Quarter (tel. 497-2217).

Drivers must be at least 25 years old to rent a car, and they must present a valid U.S. driver's license and either a credit card or a cash deposit. More adventurous drivers consider a Mini-Moke as the most dashing possibility, with its powerful engine and open body not unlike an army Jeep. They rent for $176 per week, with unlimited mileage. More conservative cars, with sides, such as a Hyundai Pony with manual transmission, rent for about $146 per week. The same car with air conditioning costs only $12 more weekly. Rental of any of Budget's cars carries the understanding that you'll pay the first $300 if there's any damage to the vehicle. To avoid responsibility, you can purchase an insurance policy (known as a collision damage waiver) that eliminates your financial responsibility if there's an accident. It costs around $5 per day.

If you'd prefer, you can rent an automatic- or standard-shift car from **Connor's Car Rental**, P.O. Box 65, South Hill (tel. 497-2433). Daily rates are $30 to $40 (the more expensive tariff is for air conditioning). Mileage is unlimited, but gas is extra. For reservations, write to Maurice Connor at the address given. Don't be surprised to find a vintage Japanese car waiting, as Connor's 57 cars are Toyotas, Hondas, and Isuzus.

PRACTICAL FACTS: Visitors to Anguilla require a valid **passport** or other form of identification bearing a photograph. All visitors must have an onward or return ticket.

Customs duties are levied on goods imported into the island at varying rates: from 5% on foodstuffs to 30% on luxury goods, wines, and liquors.

The Eastern Caribean dollar is the offical **currency** of Anguilla, although U.S. dollars are widely circulated. There are four banks in Anguilla, and the official exchange rate is EC$2.70 to $1 (U.S.), or 37¢ to EC$1.

The hottest months in Anguilla are from July to October; the coolest, from December to February. The mean monthly temperature is about 80° Fahrenheit.

In **time,** Anguilla is four hours behind Greenwich Mean Time and one hour ahead of Eastern Standard Time.

The main **post office** (tel. 497-2528) is in the Valley. Collectors consider Anguilla's stamps valuable, and the post office there also operates a philatelic bureau. Hours are 8 a.m. to noon and 1 to 3:30 p.m. Monday through Friday, and 8 a.m. to noon on Saturday. Hotel owners on Anguilla have told me that mail directed to them often ends up (for reasons known only to postal authorities) in either Bombay, India, or Sydney, Australia.

Crime is not a problem in Anguilla. If you do need to call the **police,** however, telephone police headquarters in the Valley (tel. 497-2333) or the substation at Sandy Ground (tel. 497-2354).

Telephone, cable, and Telex services are offered by Cable and Wireless (W.1) Ltd. Calls can be placed direct from the U.S. (dial 809/497 plus four digits) and may be made 24 hours a day. The company's hours are 7:30 a.m. to 10:30 p.m. weekdays, from 10 a.m. to 8 p.m. Sunday.

Electricity, except in the Valley area, is provided by privately owned generators. Current is 110/220 volts.

In medical services, there is a **Cottage Hospital,** The Valley (tel. 497-2551), plus several district clinics.

A daily broadcast service is provided by **Radio Anguilla,** which operates on a frequency of 1505 kHz (200 meters) with a power of 1,000 watts.

Special **holidays** include Anguilla Day (May 30), August Monday (the first Monday in August), August Thursday (the Thursday after August Monday), Constitution Day, (the Friday after August Monday), and Separation Day (December 19).

The government collects a departure **tax** of EC$3 ($1.10) and an 8% tax on rooms.

Tourist information is available at the Anguilla Department of Tourism, The Valley (tel. 497-2759).

ACCOMMODATIONS: Sleepy Anguilla has awakened to tourism, but the island still has a long way to go. In fact, it definitely doesn't want to become another St. Maarten. Development is being controlled, and it is emerging slowly. Some of the resorts recommended below are still under construction. Villas and cottages are being added, but no one seems in a hurry. Most of the operations are small, friendly, and informal, and there's a "touch of class" as well, as reflected by the elegant and expensive resorts I'll lead off with.

The Deluxe Hotels

Malliouhana, Maid's Bay (tel. 497-2111), is named for the Carib Indian word for Anguilla, but that's all that is primitive about this deluxe and glamorous hotel. A surprise in "sleepy" Anguilla, this is one of the few places in the Caribbean basin where you will be coddled in such splendor and comfort—for a price, of course. It was designed in a nostalgically semi-Andalusian format of terracotta roofs, reflecting fountains such as you find in the gardens of the Taj Mahal, and rows of arched and louvered windows. Everywhere you go, you see burnished mahogany, enough that it probably required the destruction of a small forest to provide. The many examples of sophisticated Haitian art were chosen by the famed "Boston Brahmin" decorator, Lawrence Carleton Peabody II. Some of my favorites are the oversize triptychs by a Haiti-born artist named Brésil. One of the most beautiful public areas is the one that leads to a memorable strip of lagoon-shape pools. Filled with artifacts from medieval Spain and Amerindian weavings, the effect is both mysterious, indescribably, and profoundly elegant.

The hotel has 20 bedrooms in the main buildings and seven outlying villas. They're set in the center of 25 arid acres and two miles of white sand beaches. Each room has expanses of closets crafted from Brazilian walnut and mahogany, spacious bathrooms of marble, tropical furnishings, and wide private verandas. Each of the villas can be rented as a single unit or subdivided into three comfortable accommodations. Now the bad news: You must pay the piper. In high season, rooms rent for $350 daily, single or double occupancy. Suites for two begin at $550 per day, stretching up to as much as $1,300 per day for an entire villa. *In the off-season, singles or doubles rent for $250 daily, with suites for two beginning at $350 per day.* These prices are EP. Taxes and service add another 18% to the total. There's a water-sports center, plus three tennis courts too. The food is appropriately good and described separately.

Cinnamon Reef Beach Club, Little Harbour (tel. 497-2727, 212/249-6840 in New York City, or toll free 800/223-1108), is one of the most sophisticated resorts in the British Leewards. No detail was overlooked in its design, from the uniforms of the friendly staff to the exquisite table settings that complement the culinary achievements of an experienced chef. Built slowly over many years, this resort officially opened in the autumn of 1984. Ringed with plants, its architectural style is a combination of ultramodern lines with a vaguely Moorish motif. Accommodations are contained in white stucco villas, the porticos of which are pierced by enormous portholes and large archways leading onto private terraces. Inside the units, guests climb several steps to reach the well-appointed bedrooms and dressing rooms, which look down on a spacious living room filled with comfortable furniture. Ample quantities of water—both hot and cold—are available, since the Hauser family included a giant cistern as part of the property. Since there are only 14 accommodations (garden suites, beach suites, and villas), guests have the feeling of being in a wealthy private home, a feeling enhanced by the ministrations of the manager, New York–born Scott Hauser, the son of the owner. Winter rates on the EP range from $200 per couple in a garden suite to $250 per couple in a villa. *Summer prices per couple run $80 to $120, EP, and November 1 to mid-December, couples pay $140 to $180.* The supplement for MAP is $40 per person. Children under 12 are not accepted at the club.

The dining room and bar areas are the focal points of this glamorous retreat, which has already attracted celebrities. The views over the veranda are of the reef-sheltered harbor where boats ride at anchor. The music greeting guests ranges from early Mozart or Vivaldi at breakfast to discreet dinner music. Some form of live entertainment and occasional dancing is offered at night. On the premises is a freshwater rectangular pool big enough to swim laps in, two championship tennis courts, free sailboats, paddleboats, snorkeling equipment, windsurfers, and fishing equipment for the use of guests. Scuba-diving can also be arranged. The beach, sheltered by a reef, has tons and tons of fine coral sand which marine geologists pumped in over many seasons.

First-Class Selections

The Mariners, Sandy Ground (tel. 497-2671), is the kind of place a vacationer might be tempted to return to again and again. It occupies a flat sandy area beside an isolated beach whose access road winds between flowering shrubs and hillocks. The only two-story building on the entire property is a clapboard house where someone will register you. Other structures are delightfully embellished one-story cottages with patterns of gingerbread. Glistening in the sun, their homey verandas face groves and a nearby beach. Each has window screens, ceiling fans, a modern tile bath, and decor reminiscent of 1930s shingled summer cottages in New England. Singles cost $135 to $155 daily in winter, doubles cost $170 to $180, and one-bedroom suites, suitable for up to four persons, run $270. *In summer, the price of singles is $120 to $125, doubles cost $115 to $120, and suites rent for $210.* MAP is an additional $45 per person per day. The resort's restaurant is recommended separately. For information and reservations, contact the Mariners Reservation Office, P.O. Box 756, Lewisville, AR 71845 (tel. toll free 800/223-0079; in Arkansas or Alaska, 501/921-4237.

Cul de Sac, Blowing Point (tel. 497-2461), advertises itself as a place for those who seek "sun, sea, and tranquility." You get all that and a lot more around here. There are six handsomely appointed and beautifully decorated studio apartments perched on the Caribbean at Blowing Point overlooking the mountains of St. Maarten. Each apartment has a bedroom/sitting room, bathroom, and kitchen/dining room with a large terrace opening onto the sea. In the winter, a studio cottage rents for $120 daily, EP; *the tariff drops to $60 daily for two persons in summer*. There is full maid service. A swimming pool opens onto those mountains of St. Maarten already referred to. There is, as well, a private beach with a jetty, known for its snorkeling possibilities. Guests at Cul de Sac can spend a lazy morning in the swimming pool placed in a garden setting, later enjoying a champagne and lobster picnic at one of the offshore cays. The food at Cul de Sac (your meals are extra) is among the best on the island (see below). It is also the entertainment center of Anguilla (more about that later too). An added advantage is that guests of Cul de Sac are entitled to enjoy the same benefits as the pampered residents of Malliouhana.

Coral Bay Resort Hotel, P.O. Box 250, Corito (tel. 497-2151), is a ten-unit facility on a four-acre plot of oceanfront property with an excellent view of French St. Martin, Flat Island, and St. Bartholomew. Accommodations include two self-contained two-bedroom cottages, one two-bedroom suite, and 19 one-bedroom units. All have microwave ovens, office-size refrigerators, and basic eating utensils. Some rooms have color TV. The living, dining, bath, and bedrooms of each apartment are separate private rooms. The apartments open onto large patios, and the furniture is mostly rattan. Winter rates range from $100 per night in singles to $250 per night in the two-bedroom cottages. On a weekly basis, the seventh night is free. *Summer prices go from $75 in a single to $160 per night in a two-bedroom cottage, the seventh night also being free*. The two-bedroom cottages are suitable for four persons.

La Santé, P.O. Box 104, Barnes Bay (tel. 495-2871, 212/840-6636, or toll free 800/223-9815, 800/468-0023 in Ontario and Québec), plays a dual role: resort and spa. Many guests who check into this seaside place aren't interested in hydrotherapy and spa facilities, but for those guests who are, an array of Austrian massages and mineral baths is available at extra cost. The resort's headquarters is below a soaring cathedral ceiling of varnished pine. The 40 villas sit on coral cliffs above the sea, angled for a superior view of sunsets. The hotel pool is especially attractive. Villas are stippled stucco, white-roofed, and large, with twin-level duplex design. Each is air-conditioned, with ceilings of varnished pine and lots of privacy. In winter, a villa for single occupancy costs $250 per day, with each additional person up to a total of four paying $20. *In summer, a villa rents for $150 for single occupancy, and the cost for each additional person is also $20.* MAP can be arranged for another $40 per person per day. Service and taxes are added to all bills. The resort has a trio of interesting restaurants, my favorite being the one appropriately named Lobster Pot. As you dine on a travertine terrace, you can watch lobsters crawling at the bottom of a huge retaining pool. You select the one that takes your fancy, and it's caught and prepared for your dinner.

The Moderate Range

Coyaba Beach Club (formerly Merrywing), Cove Bay (tel. 497-2752), consists of several modern units, part of a much larger vacation resort on 49 acres of choice property fronting a beachfront of 850 feet. The first condo units to sprout up contain two-bedroom apartments with two baths and four one-bedroom units with bath. Fully equipped kitchens contain service for up to six persons and a large dining and living room area leading to a private terrace. Ceiling fans circulate trade winds in lieu of air conditioning. *In summer, a one-bedroom condo rents for $50 daily, $315 weekly, for two persons. This goes up to $90 daily and $600 weekly for a two-bedroom apartment for four persons. A three-bedroom villa for six persons rents for $135 daily, $875 weekly.* In the winter season, the same one-bedroom condo costs $90 daily, $600 weekly; a two-bedroom apartment, $175 daily or $1,200 weekly; and a three-bedroom villa, $280 daily, $1,750 weekly. No meals are included in the rates quoted. Reservations for Anguilla's first condominium community can be made through Villa Vacations of Anguilla, 444 E. 52nd St., Suite 7F, New York, NY 10022 (tel. 212/753-1133).

Rendezvous Bay Hotel, Rendezvous Bay (tel. 497-2549), surrounded by a buffer of its own 60 coconut-covered acres, is an unpretentious resort offering the closest thing to complete privacy on the island. It sits on one of the most beautiful bays in the Caribbean, its sweep of shoreline having hardly any indentations or protrusions as seen from the hotel's concrete jetty. French cannons, retrieved from their watery graves occupied since the 17th-century battle of Rendezvous Bay, dot the surrounding garden. The 20 accommodations are in the cement motel-like annexes set amid a forest of tropical trees. Rooms are consciously spartan and not air-conditioned. On the MAP, singles cost around $90 in winter, when doubles are priced at $125. *Summer prices are $70 in a single, $100 in a double, all on the MAP.* Taxes and service are extra. When you're ready to socialize, head for the deep and wide porch in front of the dining room. Its pink concrete overhang is supported by stout columns that barely interrupt the almost constant breeze. Filled with rickety furniture, this porch is the preferred hangout of Jeremiah Gumbs, the patriarch-proprietor.

Apartments / Villas / Cottages

Sunshine Villas in Anguilla, P.O. Box 142 (tel. 497-2149, or 215/565-3462 in the U.S.), is a widely scattered collection of elegant villas organized into one rental pool by the entrepreneurial skill of a team of Canadian expatriates, Jim and Judy Henderson. Experienced realtors and rental agents, the Hendersons are probably the most articulate people in Anguilla to communicate with anyone interested in a nonhotel rental experience. Currently they have keys and access to 16 houses, each of which has a set of its own particular virtues. If you write to them, the Hendersons will send detailed information and sometimes photos, even a videotape, advertising special features of this villa or that. Each comes with daily maid service. Daily rentals for two range from $70 to $240, depending on the size and location.

The Seahorse, P.O. Box 17 (tel. 497-2751), between Shaddick Point and Rendezvous Bay, features four one-bedroom apartments. Each unit is spacious, fully equipped, and well furnished, with bath and private gallery where you can view the sunset. The apartments are on the water on a small but ideal beach. At water's edge is a barbecue area for outdoor cooking or enjoying a drink. *The weekly rate in summer is $350 for two persons,* going up to $425 in winter. Included in that is maid service, as well as the use of the Seahorse's windsurfer and Sunfish.

Loblolly Apartments, Sandy Hill (tel. 497-4250), was created by Capt. and Mrs. J. L. Wigley as a retirement retreat (he had been a London barrister). The apartments stand in the midst of tropical greenery, with an old smugglers' path leading down to a private beach. The apartments, along with a private residence, stand on a six-acre piece of property on a hill 100 feet above Sandy Hill Bay. The Wigleys offer two apartments, each with a double bedroom, kitchen, and bath. One has a dining room, the other a dinette. The apartments are ideal for two persons or else can be rented together to accommodate a family. Mahogany chests, fine chairs, and crystal chandeliers are in evidence. You can hire a cook, if needed, who will do your shopping, serving, and dish washing three times a day. In season, an apartment rents for $450 weekly, *dropping in summer to $350 weekly,* all prices plus tax.

Easy Corner Villas, P.O. Box 65, South Hill (tel. 497-2433), are owned by Maurice E. Connor, the same man who rents out most of the cars on the island. The 12 one-, two-, and three-bedroom units are in landscaped settings with sunset views from the private porches, and you can also watch sailboats and beach frolickers. All units have full kitchens, combination living-dining rooms, porches, large and airy rooms, ceiling fans, bright and light rattan furniture, and TV. Children over the age of 2 are welcome, and daily maid service is available at an extra charge. *In summer, one-bedroom accommodations cost $90 daily, two-bedroom units go for $120 to $150, and three-bedroom cottages for $160.* In winter, one-bedroom facilities cost $125 daily; two-bedroom units, $165 to $190; and three-bedroom accommodations, $205. Taxes and service are additional.

WHERE TO DINE: Order spiny lobster if you can get it. It's very good here and invariably fresh (many of the neighboring islands get their lobster from the fishermen of Anguilla). Home-grown vegetables, such as christophines and yams, accompany most dinners, with the inevitable rice.

Malliouhana Restaurant, Maids Bay (tel. 497-2111). Who would ever expect the celebrated Jo Rostang to turn up in such a remote outpost as Anguilla? Monsieur Rostang runs that deluxe citadel of haute cuisine, La Bonne Auberge, at Antibes on the French Riviera. The restaurant's nouvelle cuisine served there is ranked among the best along the Riviera. Mr. Rostang also operates the restaurant at Malliouhana, and his younger son runs it. Admittedly, not all the same ingredients from France are available to the Rostangs. Nevertheless their cuisine is still very French, but they also provide a Caribbean flair, making use of local ingredients not likely to be found in France. What they do with Anguillan fish, particularly red snapper, is amazing. They also have a French pastry chef who is among the finest in the Caribbean. You get good food, ideal service, and glamorous surroundings. Meals can easily cost $50 and up, particularly with wine. The wine cellar has at least 30,000 carefully selected bottles from which you can make your choice. Reservations are imperative. Plan to make an evening of it. Hours are 12:30 to 3 p.m. and 7:30 to 10 p.m.

The Mariners, Sandy Ground (tel. 497-2671), in one of the neo-Victorian outbuildings of the previously recommended hotel, is a wood-sided restaurant offering a comfortable indoor bar and a naturally ventilated outdoor veranda for dining. Full dinners might include Anguilla fish soup with rouille, Mariners pepperpot soup, filet of snapper with cream-and-chive sauce, chicken calypso, filet of beef with peppercorn sauce, and fresh lime cheescake with cinnamon and coconut crust. Lunches, served daily from noon to 2:30 p.m., cost $15 and up. Dinner, costing from $30, is offered from 7:30 to 9:30 p.m.

Lucy's Harbour View, South Hill (tel. 497-2253), not only has the most attractive view on the island, but offers imaginatively prepared food. What makes it special is its owner, Lucy Halley, who lived in the French part of St. Martin, learning many secrets of the cuisine there. With a ring on every finger, she has the figure of a high-fashion model. She features both French and West Indian cookery, and her place is open seven days a week for lunch and dinner (she closes it when "the last person is served"). The visiting French are fond of the place, placed like a converted home on a cliff, overlooking the salt ponds, with a view of three islands. Lucy has renovated and added to her place so that her 40-seat dining room offers everyone a spectacular view of Sandy Ground and Road Bay. When you call or just arrive, ask Lucy what she has in the larder, or tell her what kind of food you like. If the catch is right, she'll make a lobster stew. She serves fish filet, grilled lobster, Créole and curry dishes, conch, shrimp, goat meat, and pork or lamb chops. Meals cost from $15 up. Live entertainment is often presented. Lunch is served from 11:30 a.m. to 3 p.m. and dinner from 6:30 p.m. "until."

Barrel Stay Beach Bar & Restaurant, Sandy Ground (tel. 497-2831), is open all day, and full meals are served from 11 a.m. to 3 p.m. and 6:30 to 10 p.m., costing $15 and up. A favorite is the fish soup served in the French fashion. The chef is noted for his fresh Anguilla seafood, including lobster, crayfish, red snapper, yellowtail, and conch. You can also order prime steaks, smoked ham, and chicken brochette. All dishes are served with a variety of fresh local West Indian vegetables. Desserts include homemade chocolate mousse and French ice cream. A selection of French wines is offered at reasonable prices.

The Fish Trap, Island Harbour (tel. 497-4488), in a thatch-covered open-air cabaña with a wide-angle view of the sea, is the fish and lobster capital of the island. The owners are Thierry Van Dyck, formerly a horse trainer in his native Belgium, and his wife, Patricia, also Belgian, who was a chef's assistant. Their establishment is on the eastern edge of the island. Among menu items are duckling, pepper steak, snails, tomato pie, lobster bisque, snapper steamed in white butter, stuffed crab, and snapper in rock salt. Lunch is served from noon to 3 p.m. and dinner from 7 to 10:30 p.m.; full meals cost from $30. Reservations are usually a good idea, especially for dining after dark.

Trader Vic's Beach Bar and Restaurant, Shoal Bay (no phone), is a breeze-cooled restaurant beside the sands of one of the island's northern beaches, designed somewhat like a big gazebo. Fritz Smith, the friendly owner, opens for the breakfast crowd daily at 7 a.m., remaining open until midnight. You can always drink and snack in the gazebo, which many guests wouldn't think of abandoning in favor of a more formal dining room. However, there is a dining room in a concrete structure, available for more formal meals during the flexible lunch and dinner hours. Menu items include char-broiled lobster, conch sautéed with garlic and onions, chicken cooked by several recipes, ribs, and hamburgers. Full meals cost $25 to $30. The house lobster is usually caught by Fritz. Live entertainment is presented on the beach on Thursday, Friday, and Sunday from 2 to 5 p.m.

Roy's Place, Crocas Bay (tel. 497-2470), has absolutely no chic or elitist characteristics. What you'll find is an extension of the kind of pub you might find in Yorkshire or Devon. Owners Roy and Mandy Bossoms come from those two counties of England, so the similarity is only natural. There's an indoor dining room plus an ocean-view rear veranda with plastic tables and indestructible chairs. The bar near the entrance has a constantly busy trade whether the restaurant is full or not. Meals cost around $25 and include lobster soup, fish and chips, conch Créole, and tenderloin steak. Not all dishes listed on the menu will be available on the day of your visit. Lunch is served from noon to 2:30 p.m.; dinner, from 6 to 10 p.m.

Happy Jack's Restaurant, Shoal Bay Villas (tel. 497-4250), on a pure-white sand beach, has buildings hidden behind a screen of palms and aloe plants. On the premises is a thatch-covered water-sports center where instruction is offered in windsurfing, scuba, snorkeling, and Sunfish sailing. At the edge of the sand, a cabaña-style thatch-roofed restaurant and bar with wooden tables sits on a cement slab. Open from 8:30 a.m. to 5 p.m. in low season, from 7:30 a.m. to 10 p.m. in high season, it serves lobster, fish, and conch dinners for $25 each. Lunch costs about half that much.

The Old House (tel. 497-2228), is a pleasant restaurant with a reputation for good food and polite service, occupying a white-fronted plantation-style house overlooking the airport. Built in the 1950s as a private vacation home, the building is today the domain of a dedicated Rotarian and restaurateur, Kenneth Rogers. The place opens for the breakfast trade at 7 a.m. daily, closing its doors at 11 p.m. after a full day spent catering to lunch and dinner crowds. Lunch costs from around $10 and includes fresh preparations of fish Créole, London broil, chef's salad, freshly caught Anguillan pot fish, fish on a bun, and home-style barbecued beef. Dinner, costing from $18, might have among its offerings native lobster, West Indian breast of capon, fresh conch, barbecued steaks, and a limited selection of wine.

THE SPORTING LIFE: The major activity is swimming and lying on one of Anguilla's magnificent beaches (see the introduction). When you tire of that, the following are recommended:

Water Sports

Most of the coastline of Anguilla is fringed by coral reefs, and the island's waters are rich in marine life. Off the shore are sunken coral gardens and brilliantly colored fish. Fish include the torpedo-headed wrasse, the striped squirrelfish, and the sleek garfish. Conditions for scuba-diving and snorkeling on the island are ideal.

Tamariain Watersports Ltd., P.O. Box 247 (tel. 497-2798), has a shop at Mariners Hotel and its own base shop at Sandy Ground beach. It's a PADI training facility offering the complete line of PADI scuba-diving classes and certification courses. Waterskiing is also available.

Fishing

Fishing excursions can be made with the local fishermen. Your hotel can make the arrangements for you. You should bring your own tackle. Absolutely agree on the cost, however, before setting out, as some misunderstandings have been reported.

A more organized form of this activity is available at **Tamariain Watersports,** P.O. Box 247, at the Cul de Sac (tel. 497-2798). Here, deep-sea fishing trips can be arranged.

Malliouhana, Maids Bay (tel. 497-2741), can also make arrangements for guests to go deep-sea fishing. They also go on day trips to neighboring islands. The deluxe hotel has its own 34-foot cruiser, plus a sailing yacht at its disposal.

Tennis

Malliouhana, Maids Bay (tel. 497-2111), has three championship Laykold tennis courts with a tennis pro and shop. Guests have the latest in video training techniques and a ball machine.

There are also two courts at **Cinnamon Reef,** Little Harbour (tel. 497-2727). The cost to nonresidents is a steep $20 per hour.

Boat Cruises

The yacht *Baccarat,* a 52-foot yawl, goes out on day charters during the winter season. **Marc and Allison Hodder** (tel. 497-2470) arrange trips departing from Road Bay, Anguilla, for a leisurely sail to the Prickly Pear Cay, one of Anguilla's satellite islands. They anchor at a sandy lagoon so that guests can swim, snorkel, or just be lazy in the sun. Lunch is accompanied by wine and fruit juices, served aboard. The price is $50 per person, which includes lunch, an open bar, and use of the yacht's equipment. Passengers on the voyage meet at Johnos Beach Bar at 9 a.m., returning at 4:30 p.m.

SHOPPING: Efforts have been made in recent years to develop handcrafts among the islanders.

The best known is the **Local Gift Shop** in the Quarter (no phone), a tiny little place where every item is homemade. Gifts made of shells are displayed, along with wooden dolls. The hand-crocheted mats are quite beautiful, and tablecloths and bedspreads are woven into spidery lace designs, requiring awesome patience; but many of these are grabbed up by shops on neighboring islands and sold there at high prices. Baskets and mats are made from stripped corn husks and sisal rope. Model schooners and small pond boats are also for sale. Anguillan handcrafts are simple, an emerging industry deserving support.

Judy Henderson's **Sunshine Shop** (tel. 497-2149), co-owned by the already-mentioned Maurice E. Connor, is in South Hill opposite Connor's Car Rental agency. Judy stocks fine cotton wear, including dresses, coverups, shirts, and shorts from Thailand and sea island cotton pareos from St. Kitts. She also has an assortment of beachwear, as well as hand-painted wooden items from Haiti. You'll also find an assortment of interesting and ingenious silkscreened items and lithographs of island houses, ready to frame when you return Stateside. Look for the large color photographs of the island's famous ''Butterfly Wing'' boats, postcards, and note cards of island homes. The shop's full of many worthwhile carry-home items and contain a few hidden surprises.

La Romana, at Malliouhana Hotel (tel. 497-2111), is a showcase of the best European fashion and jewelry designers, whose products are offered at duty-free prices. Names such as Misani from Milan, La Nouvelle Bague from Florence, Carlo Weingrill, Petochi, and Jolanda Marini are among the fabulous jewelry designers represented. Women's and men's fashions are by Armani, La Perla, Fendi, Chanel, Byblos, and other top figures in the world. The shop is open daily from 9 a.m. to 1 p.m. and 4 to 8 p.m.

Stamp collectors will head for the already-mentioned **Valley Post Office,** The Valley (tel. 497-2528), if they want to acquire unusual stamps from Anguilla.

NIGHTLIFE: There isn't much. The best of what there is centers around the hotels in season only. The major hotel for entertainment is **Cul de Sac,** Blowing Point (tel. 497-2461), where, in season, there is something going on at least six nights a week. A performance of the Mayoumba Folkloric Theatre is presented every Thursday and Saturday night.

Chapter X

DUTCH WINDWARDS IN THE LEEWARDS

1. St. Maarten
2. St. Eustatius
3. Saba

THE DUTCH WINDWARDS have the same orientation to the northeast trades as do the British Leewards, documented in the previous chapter. However, the islands of St. Maarten, St. Eustatius (called "Statia"), and Saba—no more than dots in the Antilles—are called "The Dutch Windwards." This is confusing to the visitor, but it makes sense in the Netherlands. The Dutch-held islands of Aruba, Bonaire, and Curaçao, lying off the coast of South America, go by the name of "The Dutch Leewards."

The Windwards, which are actually in the Leewards, were once inhabited by the fierce Carib Indians who believed that one acquired and assimilated the strength of his slain enemy by eating his flesh!

Columbus, on his second voyage to America, is said to have sighted the group of small islands on the name day of San Martino (St. Martin of Tours), hence, the present name of Sint (St.) Maarten.

Cooled by trade winds, the Windwards are comfortable to visit at any time of the year. The three Windward Islands, along with Aruba, Bonaire, and Curaçao, form the Netherlands Antilles.

In currency, the legal tender is the NAf (guilder), and the official rate at which the banks accept U.S. dollars is 1.92 NAf equals $1. Regardless, U.S. dollars are easily, willingly, and often eagerly accepted in the Dutch Windwards, especially St. Maarten. *Note:* Prices in this chapter are given in U.S. currency unless otherwise designated.

Even though the language is officially Dutch, most people speak English.

1. St. Maarten

It's small, only 37 square miles, about half the area of the District of Columbia. A split-personality island, St. Maarten is half Dutch, half French (who call their part St. Martin).

The divided island is considered the smallest territory in the world shared by two sovereign states (for a preview of St. Martin, refer to Chapter XII on the French West Indies). The only way you know you're crossing an international border is when you see the sign—*"Bienvenue, Partie Française,"* a monument which commemorates the peaceful coexistence between the two nations.

The island was divided in 1648, and visitors still ascend Mount Concordia, near the border, where agreement was reached. Even so, St. Maarten was to change hands 16 times before becoming permanently Dutch.

Legend has it that a gin-drinking Dutchman and a wine-guzzling Frenchman walked around the island to see how much territory each could earmark for his side in one day. The Frenchman outwalked the Dutchman, but the canny Dutchman got the more valuable piece of property.

Northernmost of the Netherlands Antilles, St. Maarten lies some 150 miles southeast of Puerto Rico. A lush island, rimmed with bays and beaches, it has a year-round temperature of 80° Fahrenheit.

In addition to some 36 beaches—long, languorous coral strands—duty-free shopping and gambling casinos draw visitors to St. Maarten where there has been a rush of hotel building in the past few years.

The Dutch capital, **Philipsburg,** curves like a toy village along Great Bay. The town lies on a narrow sand isthmus separating Great Bay and Great Salt Pond. The capital was founded in 1763 by Commander John Philips, a Scot in Dutch employ. To protect Great Bay, Fort Amsterdam was built in 1737.

The town still retains some of its unique shingled architecture. The main thoroughfare is the traffic-clogged Front Street, stretching for about a mile. It's lined with stores selling international merchandise, such as French designer fashions and Swedish crystal. If you don't find what you want, you can take one of the little lanes, known as *steegijes,* that connect Front Street with Back Street, running parallel to it. Back Street is another shoppers' mart.

GETTING THERE: The large number of visitors who either fly to St. Maarten as a destination unto itself or use it as a jumping-off point for reaching neighboring islands has made its airport the second busiest in the Caribbean after San Juan's. Landing facilities have been improved in recent years as well as airline service.

Possibly the best connections are on **Pan American Airlines** from New York if you live in that area. Pan Am offers daily flights from New York's JFK to St. Maarten, leaving at 9:50 a.m., late enough to catch connecting flights from Washington, D.C., Philadelphia, Boston, upstate New York, Toronto, and Montréal. Pan Am's widebody Airbuses arrive after about three hours of flying time, enough to catch a late-afternoon sunbath before a Caribbean dinner.

If you plan to stay for 3 to 21 days, your fare will be slightly less expensive than if you opt for just a two-day weekend fling. In high season, a round-trip ticket costs $517 if you fly both legs of your trip on a weekday, about $32 more if you fly in both directions on a weekend. Most cost-conscious travelers, however, get in touch with a travel agent or a well-informed tour operator at Pan Am. Both hotel accommodations and air fare are slightly reduced when a traveler books both arrangements in one transaction. Fare options, of course, depend on seasonal availability of hotel space.

Some visitors, especially those from the West, Southwest, and Midwest, find it more convenient to connect to St. Maarten in Dallas/Fort Worth. **American Airlines** considers this city one of its most important hubs. It offers a daily flight departing

Dallas at 1:10 p.m., stopping in San Juan before continuing to St. Maarten, landing at 9 p.m. local time.

Other passengers fly from Florida. In that case, **Eastern** offers a nonstop flight from Miami, departing there at 5:20 p.m., in enough time to connect with dozens of flights from other areas of the country.

It's always best to confirm last-minute schedules and fares with the airlines or a travel agent. Most maintain toll-free numbers staffed day and night.

GETTING AROUND: Transportation is not difficult, with a variety of methods available.

Taxis

Taxis are unmetered, but St. Maarten law requires drivers to have a list which details fares for major targets on the island. Typical fares, say, from Juliana Airport to the Mullet Bay Resort and Casino are $4; from Philipsburg to Juliana Airport, $8. There are minimum fares for two passengers, and each additional passenger pays another $1. Passengers are entitled to two pieces of luggage free, and each additional piece is assessed 50¢ extra. Fares are higher by 25% between 10 p.m. and midnight, and 50% higher between midnight and 6 a.m. Even if you're renting a car, taxi regulations require you to take a cab to your hotel, where your car will be delivered.

Buses

This is a reasonable means of transport in St. Maarten if you don't mind inconveniences, and at times overcrowding. The fare is only 85¢, and buses run between 7 a.m. and midnight, serving most of the major locations in St. Maarten. The most popular run is from Philipsburg to Marigot on the French side. In Philipsburg, catch the bus in front of the Record Shop.

Car Rentals

Unlike some of the islands in the Caribbean, car rentals are a practical means of transport in St. Maarten, particularly if you're staying out near Oyster Pond Marina.

Budget Rent-a-Car maintains a booth at the airport, although because of local regulations the cars are kept at a different place. When you arrive by plane, a counter attendant will help you with the necessary forms and will arrange for a car to be delivered to your hotel. If your arrival is late at night, a phone call next day to Budget's local office, 95 Cole Bay, Philipsburg (tel. 44274; airport desk, 44308), will set things moving.

Drivers must be between 21 and 70 and must present a valid driver's license and a major credit card in lieu of a cash deposit. Clients who do not arrange for additional insurance at the time of rental will be fully responsible for the first $5,000 worth of damage to their car in the event of an accident.

Clients should reserve a vehicle through Budget's reservation center at least three days in advance. In the United States, a toll-free number is 800/527-0700. The least expensive car is a peppy Toyota Starlet, suitable for up to four persons. The weekly rate in high season, with unlimited mileage, is $175 per week, or $25 per day. In this rental, as in all others, a 5% tax is added to the bill. If your comfort is a priority, Budget will rent you a Toyota Corolla, with either manual or automatic transmission and air conditioning, for $245 per week, unlimited mileage included, with each additional day costing an extra $35.

Avis and **Hertz** are also represented in St. Maarten, although when I investigated their prices, I found that each charged more for their least expensive car than Budget was charging. Of course, any dollarwise shopper should compare last-minute Avis and

Hertz rates before embarking on a trip. You can call toll free: Hertz at 800/654-3131 and Avis at 800/331-1212.

Sightseeing Taxi Tours

If you don't want to drive, you can negotiate with a taxi driver who will also serve as your guide. One or two passengers are charged $30 for a 2½-hour tour, and an additional passenger pays around $5.

PRACTICAL FACTS: To enter the Dutch-held side of St. Maarten, U.S. citizens should have **proof of citizenship** in the form of a passport (preferably valid but not more than five years expired), or else an original birth certificate with a raised seal or a photocopy with a notary seal, or, finally, a voter's registration card. Naturalized citizens may show their naturalization certificate, and resident aliens must provide the alien registration "green" card or a temporary card which allows them to leave and reenter the U.S. All visitors must have a confirmed room reservation before their arrival on the island. A return or ongoing ticket must also be shown. When leaving, a $5 departure tax is charged.

In general, hotels add a 10% to 15% **service charge,** plus a 5% government **tax.** Unless service has not been added (unlikely), it is customary to **tip** around 15% in restaurants.

St. Maarten is on **Atlantic Standard Time.** In winter, when the U.S. is on Eastern Standard Time, it will be 6 a.m. in Philipsburg when it's only 5 a.m. in New York. During Daylight Saving Time, the island keeps the same time as the U.S. East Coast.

Traffic moves *on the right,* and international road signs are observed.

The Dutch side of the island operates on 110 volts AC (60 cycles) of **electricity,** and chances are, you won't need an adapter (unless you're staying on the French side).

Hotels serve desalinated **water,** and the water is safe to drink.

Emergency telephone numbers include the police at 2299 and an ambulance at 2299 also.

If you need **medical assistance,** ask at your hotel. There is one hospital (tel. 22300) on the Dutch side and another on the French side.

Most **banks** are open from 8:30 a.m. to 1 p.m. Monday to Friday, except on Friday they reopen between 4 and 5 p.m.

From Dutch St. Maarten, if you want **to call French St. Martin,** dial 06 plus the French number.

If you want information on any of the Dutch islands before you go, you can ask at the **St. Maarten, Saba, and St. Eustatius Tourist Office,** 275 Seventh Ave., 19th Floor, New York, NY 10001 (tel. 212/989-0000).

HOTELS: Hotels in St. Maarten run the gamut—from big-time resort hotels, some with tennis courts and gambling casinos, to motel-like efficiency units where guests prepare their own meals, to simple West Indian guesthouses. (For my selection of inns and hotels on St. Martin, refer to Chapter XII.)

Inns of Character

Oyster Pond Yacht Club, P.O. Box 239 (tel. 22206), is splendidly chic, a Caribbean Shangri-La, eight miles from Philipsburg, reached by a twisting, scenic road. On the windward side of the island, a circular harbor on the eastern shore near the French border, the fortress-like structure stands guard over a 35-acre protected marina. Catering to a select clientele, it is not unlike a small parador in southern Spain, unflawed in architecture and decoration. With its own harbor for yachts, it also has a private half-moon sandy beach reached by passing along beautiful landscaped grounds. Its central courtyard is open to the skies, and the living room, also al fresco, has an elegant touch, with wicker, fine paintings, an understatement of good taste. Off the courtyard, and opening onto the sea, is a bar/lounge, as warm and comfortable as one's private home. The dining room is exceptional, the chef turning out a well-prepared continental cuisine intermixed with some Créole dishes. The service is superb, and the tables are set with the finest of china and linen. All dining is à la carte. After dinner, guests sip coffee on the outer terrace under palm trees, watching the sea and listening to the waves crash against the cliff.

The hotel is furnished in part with nautical antiques, mostly white wicker, like a great country house. It offers only 20 rooms, and these are accommodations of character. Some are duplexes, and the decoration is often in the West Indian buccaneer style. Bedrooms open onto arches with a wooden balustraded balcony overlooking the pond or sea. In winter, two persons can stay here in units ranging from standard to deluxe at prices going from $270 to $290 daily. The most elegant accommodations are the tower suites, costing $310 daily. *In the off-season, two persons are charged $160 to $180 daily, with tower suites dropping to $200.*

Mary's Fancy, P.O. Box 420, Dutch Cul-de-Sac (tel. 22665), is the most exotic, treasure-filled retreat on the island. Here, on five acres of lush tropical gardens is a guesthouse and top restaurant, occupying what was once a sugar plantation great house. One of the early rich settlers, Mary Van Ramondt, was given her choice of any spot on the island to build her plantation home 250 years ago, and she chose this valley property between two mountains, only a 15-minute drive to Philipsburg or the nearest beach. When asked why she settled here, she replied, "I just fancied it!" Later it became the governor's mansion, where every famed visitor on the island made an appearance, with many staying as guests. A wooden bridge over an ancient slave wall cuts through a green meadow to the free-form swimming pool and sun patio. The main house, with its special rooms for before-dinner drinks, has one exceptionally furnished dining room after another. The service is gold, the linen the finest, and only fine china is used for your gourmet meal. On the veranda there must be 60 tall natural rattan peacock chairs for in- and outdoor dining, with candles flickering softly.

Ten individualized and pastel-painted cottages have been built in the garden, making superb one-of-a-kind suites. There is also a quartet of rooms in the main house. The abundant foliage provides complete privacy. The cottages (too humble a name, I feel) are really glamorous studios, with cathedral beamed ceilings, turn-of-the-century fans, each having its own color theme and style of decorating, hand-quilted bedspreads, and macramé lamps. One may have a Tudor four-poster bed with a lounge area of wicker, a bath and kitchen. Another may have a Chinese theme, with a red-and-white scroll dominating the bed, which is red bamboo. Another has a Victorian high headboard. There is one with a Bali theme, with a wall hanging to carry out the concept. Still another has a stone wall, a pair of Edwardian brass beds, and a large living room area. The cottages sleep two to four comfortably. They stand amid huge oaks, sandbox trees, a 200-year-old silk cotton tree, grounds lushly planted with frangipani, oleander, monkey-no-climb, pope's cap cactus, rubber trees, kapok, and cashew, as well as solid mahogany, with gently curving walks bordered by flowers leading through a meadow to a free-form swimming pool. In winter, the rate in a single or double ranges from $110 daily, going up to $130 to $150 daily in a junior suite. A room with a kitchen costs from $170 daily, and a one- to three-bedroom house is rented for $220 to $390 nightly. *In summer, rates are slashed by about 50%.*

The **Caravanserai,** P.O. Box 113, Maho Bay (tel. 44214), is an elegant oasis on its private coral promontory close to the airport, six miles west of Philipsburg. An occasional jet lands or takes off, but otherwise it's quiet around here. Its design concept, both original and tasteful, makes it special, and its many amenities cause it to rank as one of the finest resorts on the island. It was the creation of an exiled New Yorker, Dave Crane, who turned it into one of the most urbane inns in the West Indies. Both Juliana and Beatrix, from the Dutch royal family, have stayed here. The architecture utilizes natural woods and stone, with moorish arches, wooden frame octagonal structures, all decorated with tropical furnishings such as peacock bamboo and rattan chairs. Many potted palms and primitive paintings add a further decorative touch. There are two tennis courts, every kind of water sport, a private beach, and two swimming pools. Golf can be played at the Caravanserai's sister hotel, the Mullet Bay Resort and Casino (see below). The larger pool opens onto a long, arched loggia, where you can have an American-style breakfast or an evening meal with wine. The cuisine is international, and most memorable are the Wednesday Caribbean buffet with a complimentary glass of wine, the Friday seafood feast (again a complimentary glass of wine), and the Sunday brunch with complimentary champagne from 11 a.m. to 2:30 p.m. The octagonal peak-roofed Ocean View bar is on the tip of the promontory.

Accommodations come in a wide range—one-bedroom apartments and studios facing the Caribbean, 15 superior rooms also facing the sea, and 5 standards opening onto the courtyard, plus a quartet of villas, ideal for lovers. In winter, rooms range in price from $200 daily, based on either single or double occupancy. Apartments rent for anywhere from $300 to $350 daily. *In summer, rates, either double or single occupancy, are $90 in a standard bedroom, $110 in a studio, and $130 in a one-bedroom suite*. You can stay here on the full-board plan at an additional cost of $38 per person daily.

Mary's Boon, P.O. Box 278, Simpson Bay (tel. 44235), really a small casual inn, is a string of 12 oversize apartments with kitchenettes designed as private villas, with personalized style, directly on a three-mile sandy beach, just south of the Juliana Airport and 15 minutes from Philipsburg. It's near the airport, but big planes are rare, and when they do land, they do so only in the daytime. Gingerbread trim on the main building is garlanded with flowering bushes, and the grounds are planted with sea grape, coconut palms, and alamander. Reached by a long private road, Mary's Boon is set back from the sea, all pinky-beige with brown wooden balconies and stairs. The interior is imaginative, with peaked beamed cathedral ceilings and eclectic furnishings (English mahogany, ornate bamboo chairs and tables), plus a collection of Haitian paintings, tropical-style sofas, and a grand piano, which dominates the reception lounge. There's a dining gallery fronting Simpson Bay in case you decide to take the half-board arrangement, with punctured tin cones covering the overhead lights at the table, which gives a candlelit dinner atmosphere. The cuisine is Dutch/French West Indian. In the bar you fix your own drinks on the honor system. The rooms are done in rattan and wicker, louvered windows open to sea breezes, and there is an occasional tile and flagstone antique floor. Most of the rooms are in separate cottages, but there are two units in the main house. The efficiencies have ceiling fans. *On the EP, two persons are charged $60 daily in summer, with a third person paying another $15*. Rates go up in winter to $110 daily in a double, plus another $25 for a third party sharing. No children under 16 are allowed. Service and tax are added to the tariffs.

Pasanggrahan, P.O. Box 151, Front Street (tel. 23588), is the Indonesian word for guesthouse, and this one maintains a clientele which favors old-style West Indian living. It's a marvelous bargain in high-priced St. Maarten. A small, charming, informal guesthouse, it's right on the busy, narrow main street of Philipsburg. It's set back under tall trees, with a building-wide white wooden veranda. The interior still has many old features, such as peacock bamboo chairs, a pair of Indian spool tables, and a gilt-framed oil portrait of Queen Wilhelmina. In fact, so many guests asked to see the bedroom where the queen and her daughter, Juliana, stayed in World War II that the management turned it into the Sydney Greenstreet Bar. Set among the wild jungle of overgrown knep trees, coconut palms, and flowering shrubbery, is the dining area, Seaside by Candlelight. You reach the private beach, only 50 feet away, through the jungle filled with hummingbirds, yellowbirds, and mockingbirds. There are 26 newly renovated bedrooms with king-size beds and beautiful Mexican bedspreads, each with a private bath, some in the main building, others in an adjoining annex. All accommodations have ceiling fans, and air conditioning is available. *In summer, singles and* *doubles range in price from $54 to $72.* In winter, tariffs range from $79 to $110 daily in a single or double, plus tax and service.

Resort Hotels

Maho Beach Hotel & Casino, Maho Bay (tel. 42115, 718/917-8222 in New York City, or toll free 800/223-0757), opened in a vitally renovated format late in 1985, after more than $15 million had been lavished on its stylish interior. It's set about half a mile from the airport in a greenbelt which seems to showcase its pink-and-white façade. Inside the soaring lobby, a series of gracefully curved laminated beams peak pagoda style into a refreshingly airy summit. This will probably grow into one of the foremost resorts on the island. Its second-floor casino is red, brassy, and filled with repetitive geometric patterns and lots of glitter. A hexagonal pool nestles into a black-and-white-tile deck whose panorama soars over Maho Bay. A pleasant crescent of sandy beach, with water sports, lies at the bottom of the hill. On the premises are a trio of stylish restaurants, one of which, the Café de Paris, evokes a semitropical version of a café of the Edwardian age. About a third of the 247 rooms contain kitchenettes, and each has wicker furniture, air conditioning, TV, phone, Italian tiles, and plush upholstery. A few are in a separate cluster near the resort's tennis courts. In winter, depending on the accommodation, singles cost $155 to $200 daily; doubles, $165 to $215. *In low season, depending on the time of year, singles are $80 to $155 daily; doubles, $100 to $180.* Service and tax add an additional 20%.

Pelican Resort and Casino, P.O. Box 431, Simpson Bay (tel. 42503, 212/840-6636 in New York City, or toll free 800/223-9815), is a seaside resort whose architectural styles are about as varied as its clientele. The village-style sections are well separated with buffers of bougainvillea and hibiscus. The largest cluster contains only 20 units and, like all the others, is tucked into a hillside, with a sweeping view of the sea. Paths connecting the various elements are sometimes flanked by small waterways channeled into disciplined beds. Scattered among the 12 acres are a lily pond, an orchid garden, a Jacuzzi, tennis courts, a swimming pool, 1,400 feet of oceanfront, and a marina. Guests can arrange water sports through the hotel or outside agencies. There's a convenience deli on the premises to make shopping easy, and a casino and restaurant, the Suisse Chalet, add to vacationing pleasure.

All accommodations are privately owned and leased through the hotel management to vacationing guests. Each has one or two bedrooms, a kitchen, a 24-hour color TV with satellite reception, a phone, and a cassette tape player. Rates for the accommodations vary widely with the season and the exposure. Guests are required to remain for a minimum of seven nights during the most popular periods of the winter season. In winter, studios rent for $150 to $170 daily, one-bedroom units for $170 to $200, and two-bedroom quarters for $300 to $420. Additional persons in any unit are charged $30 each. *In summer, the daily rentals are: studios, $65; one-bedroom facilities, $85; and two-bedroom units, $140 to $230. An additional person pays $15.*

The **Belair Beach Hotel,** P.O. Box 140, Little Bay (tel. 23362). One of the most surprising things about this breezy oceanfront hotel is the size of the accommodations. Checking in is like renting your own apartment home in the tropics, especially if you stay in one of the seaside rooms whose arched patios sit only a few paces from the white sandy beach. Each of the 72 units contains two bedrooms, two full baths, a fully equipped kitchen, satellite-beamed color TV, a 21-foot patio or veranda with a sweeping view of the sea, two phones, and full air conditioning. This handsome hotel is perfect for relaxing in the most convenient circumstances, particularly since the comfortable circumstances provide for an elegant, well-upholstered retreat. For vacationers who want the activities of a resort, the Little Bay Beach Resort and Casino, just a short walk down the beach, offers a full array of facilities (see below).

Keith D. Franca is the general manager of the Belair. With his staff, he provides many extras, such as a nightly turn-down of the beds and fresh-daily beach towels. EP rates in winter begin at $195 daily in a single or double, rising to $325 during the peak visiting periods in February and around Christmas. Triples range in price from a low of $215 daily to a high of $355. *In the off-season, the single rate goes from $125 to $150 daily; the double tariff, for $125 to $165; and the triple rate, $140 to $180.* Service and tax are added to all bills. The hotel has two restaurants: the Sugarbird Café, serving breakfast, lunch, and dinner in a casual atmosphere; and Le Grenouille Restaurant, serving French cuisine at lunch and dinner. Grocery, gift, and clothing shops are on the premises, and there are desks for car rentals and water-sports arrangements.

Great Bay Beach Hotel & Casino, P.O. Box 310, Voorstraat (tel. 22446), is a complete modern resort at the southwestern corner of the Great Bay of downtown Philipsburg. In fact, all the shops and restaurants of the old town are walkable from the hotel. Its five floors of cellular rooms—225 air-conditioned, suitably furnished units— have walk-in closets and tile baths, each with a balcony and view of either the sea or hills. On the grounds are abundant facilities. Near the main building is a terracotta sun terrace, surrounded by palm trees and lounge furniture. At one end set in among the shrubbery is a poolside refreshment area. The main dining room has water-view windows, and features local foods in addition to Stateside cooking plus continental specialties from Great Bay's chef. *Summer EP rates in a single or double range from $75 to $115 daily.* In winter, guests are accepted on the EP, for $130 to $175 daily in a single, from $140 to $195 for two persons. Naturally, suites are more expensive. Service and tax are added to all bills. Below the swimming pool terrace is a wide sandy beach, and skiing boats can be had at your request. Across the road are tennis courts. There is also a water-sports center on the premises. Evenings are enlivened by a steel band, with calypso entertainment. Many gamblers flock here to one of the important casinos on the island, which has one-arm bandits in addition to roulette and baccarat.

Smaller Resort Hotels

Dawn Beach Hotel, P.O. Box 389 (tel. 22929), stands on the Atlantic side of the island, near the Dutch-French border. It cuddles next to a tall mountain at Oyster Pond. The location is about eight miles from Philipsburg, reached by a scenic but twisting road. Each of the 155 individual villas along the beach and on the mountain offers a choice of air conditioning or ceiling fans. *Summer EP rates range from $90 to $125 daily in a double,* going up in winter to $195 to $250. It's really villa condo living, and the owners of this resort complex have emphasized luxury and style. Beds are big enough to stretch out in and units are equipped with small kitchenettes. A large Bali-style restaurant, capped by a pagoda roof, is a potent lure, serving good meals. There is also a bar on the premises. The Oriental gardens use such Japanese-like touches as a bridge over the swimming pool. Sprawling sea grape trees provide cover from the sun, as do umbrellas around the freshwater pool with a cascading waterfall. The hotel has made many improvements, including two composition tennis courts lit for night play. A water-sports desk will make arrangements for cruising, windsurfing, waterskiing, snorkeling, and sailing, including all-day charters to St. Bart, Saba, and Anguilla. A shuttle to and from Philipsburg operates three times a day.

Little Bay Resort and Casino, P.O. Box 61, Little Bay (tel. 22333), the first of the island's resort hotels, is a very complete resort, with its private 1,000-foot beach, within a short distance of the shops and restaurants of Philipsburg. The hotel opened in 1955 with only 20 rooms, and Queen Juliana, and her husband, Prince Bernhard, were the first guests. Princess Margaret came here on her honeymoon. Other royalty has visited as well, including Queen Beatrix, whose latest scheduled visit was in early 1987. You'll find everything you might need on the premises, whether it's water sports, a beauty parlor, a Las Vegas-style casino, or a freshwater pool. There are three tennis courts, plus regular local entertainment. At a beach bar, you can order those long, cool, intoxicating drinks, and a deluxe snackbar is appealing for a light lunch. Continental dishes, Stateside favorites, and authentic Dutch and West Indian specialties are served in the historic Peter Stuyvesant Lounge opposite the casino. Diners enjoy a candlelit atmosphere with light music for listening or dancing. Guests gather at Le Café to enjoy the disco bar. A late-night coffeeshop, La Primavera, is open from 6 p.m. to 1 a.m. The decor of the bedrooms is warm and inviting, with private bath and terrace or balcony, as well as air conditioning and wall-to-wall carpeting. The best rooms are the beachfront accommodations. *In summer, singles range in price from $87 to $107 daily, with doubles going for $97 to $117,* plus another $35 per person charged year round for breakfast and dinner. Winter prices jump to $175 to $200 daily in a single, $185 to $210 in a double, the higher tariff, both single and double, for beach-level accommodation.

   Cupecoy Beach Resort, P.O. Box 14 (tel. 44297). One end of this imaginatively designed resort stands on a rocky bluff above a beach whose edges are dotted with caves. Other accommodations lie across a busy road and stretch up a hillside ablaze with bougainvillea. The resort's focal point is a piazza whose wrap-around arcade evokes a city in southern Europe. In the center, a splashing fountain sets the tone for the Treasure Island casino (more about this later). The resort's most expensive units lie, of course, near the beach in stylish buildings with sloping roofs. Each of the units contains Caribbean colors of blue and white, wicker furniture, cable color TV, private bathrooms, and private terraces. The 300 accommodations rent in winter for $150 to $300 daily for two persons. *In summer, accommodations range from $75 to $210 daily for two.* On the premises are tennis courts, a trio of swimming pools (one near the beach and two on the hillside), and a concierge and staff who can help arrange various water sports and outside excursions.

   Summit Resort Hotel, P.O. Box 456, Simpson Bay Lagoon (tel. 42270), north of the airport near the French border, is a delightful miniature resort, small enough to be personal, yet avoiding the confusion often found in a larger establishment. Rooms are in one- and two-story cottages, built like a little chalet village, Tudoresque in style, with decorative beams. The units are interconnected by walks through lush foliage and tall trees. Each unit is an individually owned condo, and some are for sale. With an 180° view, it sits on the side of a hill, facing Simpson Bay Lagoon, with an all-weather tennis court and swimming pool complex with a tiny informal bar and intimate restaurant. Each of the air-conditioned chalets has a combined living room/bedroom with two double beds, a full private bath, and either a balcony or terrace running the full length of the chalet. Each also has its private entrance. The receptionist can arrange for deep-sea fishing, sailing, snorkeling, and free use of a beach buggy. If gambling is your interest, the management can provide free transportation to two of the island's largest casinos less than five minutes away. In winter, standard rooms cost from $120 daily for two persons, the cost going up to $145 in a superior room, plus 20% extra for tax and service. Both are EP tariffs. *Rates are dramatically slashed off-season, ranging in price from $75 to $90 daily for two persons, plus tax and service. Singles are usually $10 cheaper in either unit.* Children under 12 are allowed to share a room with their parents. You might also ask a travel agent about special package rates offered at the Summit.

   Holland House, P.O. Box 393, Front Street (tel. 22572), shares the beach and water-sports center with the St. Maarten Beach Club, to which you also retire when you want some casino action. It rents 60 cozy apartments decorated with furnishings from the Netherlands. Each unit contains a very tiny kitchenette, ideal for cooking an omelet but not a big dinner. You're right on the beach, where you can order drinks at the bar. An open-air dining terrace fronts Great Bay. Some people like it, and maybe you will too. You're certainly near everything, including all the major restaurants and shops of Philipsburg. EP rates in a double in winter range from $135 to $155 daily. *Tariffs drop in summer to $75 to $85 daily for a double room, EP.* Even if you're not staying here, you might want to call and reserve a table for dinner. This is one of the few hotels that serves authentic Dutch specialties.

Seaview Beach Hotel, P.O. Box 65, Front Street (tel. 22323), is a 46-room modest but fine, waterfront hotel right in the shopping and restaurant section of Philipsburg, with half of its rooms overlooking Great Bay and its beach. In this three-story stucco building, each room has furnishings with a Caribbean theme, and each comes with a ceiling fan and private bath. If you stay here on a plan to include dinners, you can enjoy the Saturday-night barbecue (chicken, beef, and pork—whatever you want). You are given free use of beach chairs and umbrellas when a guest. Winter EP rates range from $85 to $105 in a single, from $105 to $130 in a double. *In summer, a single rents for $52 to $58; a double, for $60 to $70.* A casino, Rouge et Noir, operates at Seaview.

Efficiency Units and Guesthouses

The **Horny Toad Guest House,** Butterfish Road (P.O. Box 397), Elizabeth (tel. 44323), was once an island governor's residence. The present owners, Betty and Earle Vaughan, continue the tradition of hospitality found there in former days: hosts and guests are soon on a first-name basis. What you get here for your money makes it very desirable, as it opens directly onto the beach at Simpson Bay. The second floor of their white frame building has an encircling covered West Indies balcony, and all of their efficiency units have kitchen areas and private baths. Two have separate bedrooms housing three guests per unit. Daily maid service is included. The furnishings are "family style" with a plentiful use of colorful floral fabrics, rattan chairs, hanging lamps, and wood-paneled walls. Everything is casual and congenial. *In summer season, the efficiencies are $85 daily, EP, double occupancy;* in winter, $150. An extra person is charged $28 per day year round. Three of the units will accommodate a family of four. Sports activities are informal: nightly surfing, and for a modest fee a fully equipped fishing and diving boat. *Note:* The guesthouse is near the airfield, and does have noisy moments. To make reservations before traveling to the island, get in touch with Betty and Dave Harvey, 7 Warren St., Winchester, MA 01890 (tel. 617/729-3171).

The **Town House,** 175 Front St., P.O. Box 347 (tel. 22989), is a group of ten two-story apartments at the edge of the restaurant and shopping district of Philipsburg. At your doorstep is Great Bay Beach, dotted with palms—it's all shut off from the main street by a rugged stone wall and a wrought-iron gate. The town houses are handsome, rather formal with slanted shingled mansard roofs, and set-in second-floor windows. Each apartment has two large bedrooms and two bathrooms; the second-floor ones have a shower. There's a completely equipped kitchen, plus raised dining area in the long and well-furnished living room. Wide glass doors open onto a private terrace with lounge chairs. Whether dining or having conversation in the living room or drinks on your terrace, you can enjoy a view of the bay. To make it a holiday, a cook can also be provided inexpensively. *In summer, two persons pay $100 daily; three or four persons, $125.* In winter, up to four persons can rent one of these units for $250 per day.

The **Naked Boy,** P.O. Box 252, Philipsburg (tel. 22789, or 516/692-7878 in New York for information), is a small, modern two-story apartment house standing in a garden of trees, with covered balconies overlooking Great Bay. Here there is no surf, and the bathing is gentle. Each unit has an adequately furnished living room with two sofa beds, studio style, plus a fully equipped kitchenette. A bedroom has either singles or a king-size bed, a dressing room area, and a shower in the bath. Units are air-conditioned, and maid service is included. Within walking distance are shops for groceries and restaurants. If your apartment faces the sea, the rate is slightly higher. In winter, two persons pay from $85 daily for a unit, the tariff going up to $95 to $100 if oceanfront. Each additional person is assessed $15 per day. *In the off-season, the daily tab is $55 to $65 for two persons, depending on the room's location.* Special weekly rates are quoted. Tax and service are added to all bills. There's a modest surcharge for use of air conditioning.

RESTAURANTS: Half-Dutch, half-French St. Maarten/St. Martin has dozens of good international restaurants, and visitors on each side must decide each night if they want to "cross the border" to dine. Specialties range from Créole through continental, with a decided French accent. Dutch cooking is harder to come by.

Le Bec Fin, 119 Front St. (tel. 22976), is considered one of the best restaurants in St. Maarten, either on the French or the Dutch side of the island. Reims-born Pascal Petit is a chef still in his 20s, but his nouvelle cuisine has already been the recipient of many awards, not only in his native France but also in St. Maarten. Try his burgundy snails, his beef tenderloin in a pepper sauce, his veal scaloppine with morels, his fresh "salmon cucumbers," his lobster en croûte with a spinach mousse, finishing with a raspberry soufflé with apricot sauce that is among the best I've ever had, all for about $35 or so. Reservations are essential, as there are only about a dozen tables. Lunch is served daily from 11 a.m. to 2:30 p.m. and dinner from 7 to 10:30 or 11 p.m. It is closed on Sunday. To get to Le Bec Fin, you enter through La Coupole, a small café built on a patio, walk across the courtyard, and ascend a flight of stairs. At La Coupole you can enjoy breakfast, and if you linger long enough over coffee, you may choose to have lunch here also. This enclave of French gastronomy dates back to the mid-19th century. Try the croissants fresh from the oven, as well as French pastries and home-made ice cream.

Bilboquet, Pointe Blanche (no phone). For specialties unique in the Caribbean, this private house provides cookery that is imaginative and prepared with flair. With devotion to service and cuisine, Bill Ahlstrom and Bob Donn, former language teachers from Minnesota and New York, have opened this place providing two prix-fixe dinners for about $40 nightly. The five-course meals are served from 7:30 to 8:30 p.m., except Monday. The trick is, you must visit the place first to make a reservation (24 hours in advance). Perhaps that proves you can find it at night. Follow the road to Pointe Blanche, turning left at the Pot Rum factory, then taking another left at Vinomar. It's the first uphill left turn from that point. Once there, you write your name on a waiting list. Their cuisine is completely international, and they can travel from Thailand to Greece with little problem in translation (after all, they are language experts). For example, one meal might begin with a Cuban black-bean soup or callaloo soup with crabmeat, follow with scampi fritti, then a Greek moussaka with a green salad, topped off by a southern pecan pie. You'll like it so well you might come back the following evening, enjoying a lemon-zested shrimp soup or green papaya vichyssoise (a first for me), followed by seafood on the half shell, East or West Indian curries, stuffed eggplants, cucumber salad, and a rum and bourbon pudding. The view is of St. Barts.

L'Escargot, 84 Front St. (tel. 22483), is my favorite French bistro, right in the heart of Philipsburg where the competition is keen. It's perched in a gaily decorated 100-year-old Antillean house, with a red tin roof, celebrating its namesake by serving snails in pâté à choux, with mushrooms, in omelets, or in the more traditional escargots à la Provençale. For good-tasting *bonne cuisine française,* and some of the nicest, friendliest people around, you'll do well here, and the prices, although not cheap, seem reasonable to most diners. The personable Joel Morand established this much-awarded restaurant in 1970. If you arrive before your reservation, you can relax in the bar to your left before being shown to your candlelit table. Not one bit of space is undecorated, and the decor may appear too gimmicky to some. But that shouldn't make you suspicious of the food. It's first rate—caviar blinis, duck in a pineapple and banana sauce, quail with raisin sauce, lobster Thermidor, coq au vin. If you can handle it, the waiter will serve you a chocolate mousse to finish your repast, which should cost from $43, maybe a lot more. In season, reservations are absolutely necessary. It is open daily from 11:30 a.m. to 2:30 p.m. and 6:30 p.m. to "very late," perhaps 11:30 p.m. in season.

The Café Royal (tel. 23443), in the atrium of the Royal Palm Plaza, a few blocks from the Main Square in Philipsburg, is a local favorite. You can order lunch, dinner, and lavishly packed picnic baskets. You can eat for about $15 to $20. French pâtés and pastries, Dutch hams and cheeses, the local Caribbean spiny langouste, and fresh fruits such as papayas, mangoes, pineapple, and avocados, along with American favorites, including hamburgers and cheesecake, make up the regular fare. Rene Florijn is the owner of the café. He opens for breakfast at 8 a.m., serving until 11 a.m. In fact, it's the best place along Front Street for breakfast if you don't eat at your hotel. You can order a simple continental or a "millionaire's breakfast." The kitchen quickly prepares for lunch, serving it from 11 a.m. to 4 p.m., offering shrimp, herring, lobster, soups, salads. Happy hour is from 5 to 6 p.m. Dinner, offered from 6 to 11 p.m., is candlelit, and guests are offered a choice of a fixed-price meal or à la carte. On the set menu you're offered a selection of four appetizers, four main courses, and four desserts, along with garlic bread and a salad.

In the rear section of the Café Royal you'll discover a gourmet shop, "Eat Royal." This small shop is brimful of local and international delicacies, and has had many a satisfied customer, including Princess Margaret. If given notice, you'll be prepared an elegant picnic basket for two, costing $30. In addition to gift items, most of them packable, you'll be tempted with smoked salmon, pâté, caviar, lobster, and fresh croissants.

Antoine's, Front Street (tel. 22964), offers *la belle cuisine* in an atmospheric building next to the Little Pier in the center of Philipsburg. Wear your casual-chic resort wear here at night, enjoying the view of Great Bay from the sea-fronting terrace. You can also dine inside where the glow of candles makes everything more romantic. Be sure to make a reservation in season. The entrance is through a breezeway alive with greenery. You can enjoy an apéritif in the cocktail bar. If the crowd is right (usually in winter), Antoine's takes on worldly sophistication, and the staff will prove that you don't have to cross the border for impressive wines, top-quality service, and a long list of Gallic specialties. Fresh local fish is always available, but well-sauced beef and chicken dishes are also served, at a cost of around $40 for dinner, perhaps $20 for lunch. Every restaurant owner seems to specialize in the increasingly hard-to-get lobster, and Antoine's is no exception. The spiny Caribbean langouste is regularly featured, and prepared very well indeed. Hours are daily from 11:30 a.m. to 4 p.m. and 6:30 to 11 p.m.

Grenouille, Belair Beach Hotel, Little Bay (tel. 22269), has been around for a long time, having survived when many of its Gallic competitors bit the dust. However, it's moved from the heart of town to a new location in this previously recommended hotel. Surrounded by glass and arched windows on four sides, it encompasses views of the sea. It has a surprisingly informal decor of tile floors, wicker chairs, and a prominent bar. Reached by going through the lobby of the hotel, Grenouille serves lunch for $20 and up from noon to 2 p.m., and dinner, costing from $30, from 6:30 to 10 p.m. Fresh local fish and Caribbean spiny lobster are regularly featured, along with such delectable main dishes as pepper steak flambéed in cognac and Dover sole. In season, live oysters are flown in from Brittany. Guests should dress up a bit for dinner.

Felix Restaurant, Pelican Key (tel. 42797), is one of the island's best choices for an al fresco meal with a view of the sea. Because of its location a few paces from the white sands of a popular beach, many guests turn their outings here into full afternoon excursions. Chaises longues are available from the owners, Margaret and Richard (Felix) Ducrot, who describe their cuisine as "typically French." Felix's grandfather owns the well-known Felix's in Cannes. This place is at its most romantic during candlelit dinners when seating choices range from intimately sheltered booths to outdoor tables set within sight and sound of the sea. Many of the seafood specialties come from the lobster tank whose waters bubble at ground level near the lounge. Full dinners can total $40 per person and might include chateaubriand for two, rack of lamb, fish caught locally that day and sometimes served with an exquisite sorrel-flavored hollandaise, a wide selection of lobster dishes, and a Felix salad. Lunch is served only on request. Open daily except Tuesday from November 1 to May 1, the restaurant serves dinner from 7 to 10 p.m.

Spartaco, Almond Grove Plantation Estate (tel. 45379), lies in a residential suburb midway between Philipsburg and the airport. Its limestone walls were originally built in 1803 as part of the West Indian manor house, but the decor today includes strong doses of 1930s art deco and some hi-tech design. Guests sit in the main dining room with its discreet lighting or on a breeze-filled wrap-around veranda. The restaurant is the creation of an Italian entrepreneur from Siena, Spartaco Sagantoni, who is assisted by a handful of Milanese chefs. They offer one of the most sophisticated menus on the island, with full meals costing from $50 per person. Only dinner is served, nightly between 6:30 and 10 p.m. (closed Monday), and reservations are suggested. Specialties include fresh black tagliolini (angel-hair pasta flavored with squid ink, served with shrimp, parsley, and garlic sauce). The chef also prepares fresh green gnocchi with gorgonzola cheese. Among the main dishes, you might sample baked swordfish with a pink peppercorn sauce and rosemary or veal scaloppine with lemon sauce. The house antipasto makes a fine beginning.

Sitar, 4 Front St. (tel. 25294). Set on the main street of town, near the harbor, this is considered the best Indian restaurant on the island. Not only is the spicy food savory, it's also a bargain. At lunch you can order various platters of food, washed down with tea, plus a salad, an appetizer, and Indian bread, for $7 to $10. Go between 11 a.m. and 3 p.m. Dinner is more formal, and perhaps more intriguing, costing from $20 per person. Diners discover the most imaginative and extensive vegetarian menu on the island, along with an array of lamb and tenderloin dishes named after Mogul emperors. This exotic restaurant, the creative statement of the Kukreja family, is filled with art from the Jaipur and Rajastan regions in northwest India. You dine in air-conditioned comfort near a central gazebo of garden lattices and colorful ornaments.

Paradise Café, Maho Village (tel. 42842). Set at the top of a hill close to the airport, across from the Maho Beach Hotel, this has become a chic enclave. Near the bar, an elegant swimming pool is fed by a source splashing out of a terracotta urn. Visitors select a large peacock chair which, along with the caged birds and mahogany sheathing, create an aura much like you'd find in a colonial outpost of France. Lunch is served daily except Monday between noon and 4 p.m. Dinner is from 6 p.m. to midnight in high season and from 6:30 to 11 p.m. in off-season. The menu features occasional "creative outbursts from the chef," as well as always available Mexican specialties, T-bone steaks, banana flambé, and frothy tropical drinks. A separate listing includes those dishes temptingly grilled over mesquite wood, including kingfish steak, catch of the day, salmon, shrimp, chicken, and beef dishes. Full meals, costing from $30, might conclude with one of the specialty coffees.

Le Pavillon, Simpson Bay Village (tel. 44254), is one of the tiniest French restaurants in St. Maarten, providing just the right kind of intimacy and some of the best and most carefully prepared French food on the island. The owner-chef, Max Petit, runs everything, supervising the service and personally shopping for the fresh ingredients which he shapes into gourmet meals, costing around $25 and up for dinner. Monsieur Petit learned his culinary skills in his native Guadeloupe and picked up gastronomic secrets when he worked in the provinces of France as well as in Paris. His French and Créole repertoire includes lobster and crab omelets, cold platters, escargots, pepper steaks, crisp salad, and his specialties, a tasty duckling with pineapple sauce and assiete Tricoloure (lobster, shrimp, and snapper topped with three sauces). For dessert, ask him for his bananas flambé. You can enjoy a before-dinner drink at the bar or on the terrace. Reservations are advised. Dining is best between 7 and 9 p.m. (watch for those off-season closings).

A place to go if you have an insatiable sweet tooth is **Etna Gardens** (tel. 23424), set in a palm-shaded courtyard at the end of a fern-draped passageway a few steps from the Main Square in Philipsburg. Here you can dip into such frosty concoctions as banana, amaretto, or marron glacé ice creams, and lemon, mango, soursop, and pineapple sherbets. Owners Paolo and Betty Smiraldo make the confections right on the premises, using natural ingredients such as fresh fruit. And while Paolo is turning out the frozen items on the menu, Betty is busy in the kitchen, baking cookies and macaroons that are as light as a tropical breeze. The six cozy tables and the minuscule counter are always crowded with on- and off-islanders continuing the time-honored tradition of "cooling out," as they call it locally. The minimum tab is around $3. For a recommendation of the original Etna Shop, at Port La Royale, Marigot, refer to the St. Martin section in Chapter XII on the French West Indies. Your ice-cream passions can be satisfied from 9 a.m. to midnight weekdays (on Sunday, from noon to 6 p.m.).

Ristorante Da Livio, Front Street (tel. 22690), is the place to go for the classic Italian cuisine. The best of its kind in St. Maarten, it is run by Livio Bergamasco, who was the maître d' of the Great Bay Beach Resort before going into business for himself. A traditional dinner here might include linguine alle vongole (clams) or perhaps saltimbocco alla romana, a popular Roman specialty that literally means "jump in your mouth." It's made with ham and veal. The pasta specialty, fettuccine alla Livio, is prepared right at your table. Another one of Mr. Bergamasco's dishes, for which he is known, is fresh snapper, which I most recently enjoyed. For dessert, save room for the spumone salsa cioccolato, followed by café stravagante. He also has a good wine selection. Expect to spend from $30 for dinner, served from 7 to 10 p.m., and in season a reservation would be wise. Lunch, noon to 2 p.m., is also served, costing around $18. You can dine al fresco, overlooking Great Bay.

Pinocchio, Italian Village, Front Street (tel. 22166), has other entrances, but the preferred way to go in is through an authentically restored tunnel-shaped cistern leading into the Italian patio. In the heart of town, it can also be entered from the beach, luring diners to its terrace swept by trade winds and its al fresco patio bar, which is known for its frozen fruit daiquiris. The intricate latticework in the dining room frames the harbor, and you take a seat at a large community table. Most guests seem to prefer pasta, but you can also order many other Italian specialties, as well as fresh local fish and lobster. Try the curried conch, cold mango soup, or one of the veal dishes. Dinner costs from $18. You can also visit for lunch, even breakfast (it opens at 9 a.m.). The luncheon offering includes the usual array of burgers, sandwiches, and salads, along with tropical fruit drinks. Naturally, you can order a café espresso, and children's specials are also offered. This place usually stays active until 2 a.m. with live entertainment.

Chesterfields, Great Bay Marina, Pointe Blanche Road (tel. 23484), has a special attraction other than its good food—which, incidentally, is among the best served on the Dutch side. It offers pierside dining with a view of the harbor, on a trade-wind-swept veranda right close to Great Bay Marina. When the yachting set gathers here (everybody seems to know everybody else), the atmosphere becomes almost like that of your friendly "local." The setting and the dress are both casual, and you dine on several international specialties, with fresh seafood and French-inspired cookery a highlight. Dinners average around $25. In season there's always some lively activity going on, including champagne brunches on Sunday, "happy hours," or whatever. It's been an enduring favorite because it gives good service, and the staff makes you feel welcome. It's open Monday to Sunday from 7:30 a.m. to midnight, serving dinner from 6:30 p.m. On Sunday it offers brunch from 11 a.m.

Sam's Place (tel. 22989), at the end of Front Street, is where Bogie might land if he were alive and in St. Maarten today. Locals and tourists alike use Sam's "front porch" as a rendezvous point, practically at any time of the day. Boatmen come in here at breakfast ordering steak and eggs, vacationing southerners like the pancakes in syrup, and homesick New Yorkers ask for a toasted bagel with cream cheese. At lunch the item to order is one of the locally well-known "Samburgers." Dinner on the upper deck turns to heartier fare, such as charcoal-broiled steak. When available, try the fresh local fish or the Caribbean spiny langouste. The place is inexpensive: you can get by for around $18 unless you order the expensive lobster or steak. The open-air bar serves hors d'oeuvres at happy hour. It's open from 8:30 a.m. to 2 a.m. There's live entertainment nightly.

West Indian Tavern, at the "head" of Front Street (tel. 22965), is like a primitive island painting, exploding with vibrant colors such as turkey red and lime green. A buccaneerish place, it was built from local cedar early in the 1800s on the site of a Jewish synagogue. An Irishman, Stephen Thompson, runs this place where, after 5 p.m., everybody in St. Maarten seems to gather for a sundowner. The place has plenty of atmosphere—bamboo and rattan chairs, big potted ferns, tropical plants, slow-turning overhead fans, and old-world nautical prints. If conversation slackens, a noisy parrot keeps it lively. The chef specializes in fresh local lobster, which he does in six different ways, all a treat. Some of his other good-tasting dishes include fresh local grouper sautéed with bacon, hazelnuts, and served in a cream sauce; yellowtail with medallions of lobster in a mornay sauce; and fisherman's pie (lobster, crab, shrimp, and snapper in champagne). I'm also fond of the black Javanese pepper steak. The dessert specialty is real key lime pie. An average meal will cost about $18, unless you order lobster—then count on dinner going for $30 or more. You dine in a garden patio, shaded by tamarind, frangipani, and lime trees. Dinner is from 6 p.m. to midnight. Backgammon is played until 2 in the morning, and there is live entertainment on most nights.

Calypso Restaurant, Airport Road, Simpson Bay (tel. 44233), lies just east of the airport, and don't be deceived by its dusty parking lot and concrete façade. The place serves excellent Créole food in a blue-and-white setting which is airy. Melford Hazel and a polite staff offer meals any time you want them from 11 a.m. to midnight seven days a week. Lunch starts at $12, including pizzas, sandwiches, a calypso salad (with peppers, avocados, pineapple, cheese, and hard-boiled egg), and five different local dishes. These include spicy versions of fish, chicken, mutton, lobster, and conch. Dinners are more elaborate, costing from $23. Featured are crab backs, conch fritters, fish soup, bullfoot soup, broiled lobster, and flambé custard with brandy. There's usually a steel band playing every Wednesday night. The specialty drink of the house is a Calypso Treat, concocted from Galliano, apricot brandy, coconut cream, and rum.

The Greenhouse, Veterans Drive, Bobby's Marina (tel. 22941), open to a view of the harbor, is filled with plants and decorated in pleasing shades of pink and white. It's the best restaurant in the marina area, and probably one of the finest in its price category. As you dine, breezes filter through the dozens of lattices separating its perimeter from the waterfront outside. Lunch is served daily from 11 a.m. to 4 p.m., and dinner from 5 to 10 p.m. Live entertainment is offered nightly from 10 p.m., when the copious rectangular bar fills up. Lunches, costing from $12, include the catch of the day, a wide selection of burgers, icy gazpacho, a chef's salad, hot and cold sandwiches, and frittatas. Dinners, from $25, might feature Jamaican pepper steak, whole local red snapper, coconut scampi, assorted fried fish, chicken curry, escargots with garlic bread, homemade chili, and heaping platters of nachos.

The Wajang Doll, 125 Front St. (tel. 22687), housed in a wood-fronted West Indian building on the main street of town, is considered one of the best Indonesian restaurants in the Caribbean. There's a low-slung front porch where you can watch the pedestrian traffic outside, and big windows in back overlooking the sea. The restaurant is best known for the way a waiter will bring 20 little dishes to your table, the combined total of which is known as a rijsttafel. The cuisine varies from Bali to Java, and each dish carries the distinctive culinary touch of the restaurant's owner, Edu Joedhosawarno. He crushes his spices every day for maximum pungency, according to an ancient craft. A meal costs $35 per person, and specialties in addition to the rijsttafel include fried snapper in a chili sauce, marinated pork on a bamboo stick, and Javanese chicken. The restaurant is open for dinner only, every night except Sunday, from 6:45 to 10 p.m. Reservations are suggested.

Captain Oliver's, Oyster Pond (tel. 873000). Because its access road sometimes requires a four-wheel-drive vehicle to reach it, most diners approach it more leisurely by boat—a vessel departs from the pier at the Oyster Pond Yacht Club (phone the restaurant before your arrival and the staff will tell a boatman to come and fetch you). The restaurant is built partially on piers above the bay, with a cedar-shingled roof, a parasol-dotted waterside deck, and a breezy interior. Lunch is served daily except Monday from noon to 3 p.m., and dinner from 7 to 10 p.m. Simple lunches in the sun cost from $10, with more elaborate dinners going for $20 and up. You might enjoy raw marinated tuna as an hors d'oeuvre, then grilled lobster, steak tartare, pepper steak, or the catch of the day.

SHOPPING: St. Maarten is not only a free port, but there are no local taxes. Prices are sometimes lower than anywhere else in the Caribbean. However, the problem is that you must know what you're looking for—what is actually a bargain. Too many cruise-ship passengers have returned home to find the same Japanese camera selling for less in their local discount store! Many well-known shops in Curaçao offer branches here, in case you're not going on to the ABC islands.

Except for the boutiques at resort hotels, the main shopping center is in downtown Philipsburg. Most of the shops are on two leading streets, Front Street (called Voorstraat in Dutch), which is closer to the bay, and Back Street (Achterstraat), which runs parallel. Shopping hours in general are from 8 a.m. to noon and 2 to 6 p.m. weekdays. If a cruise ship is in port, many shops open even on Sunday.

I'll only mention a few shops to get you started, as nearly every building in Philipsburg seems to be a store ready to sell.

Shipwreck Shop, Front Street (tel. 22962), is a West Indian store selling hammocks, colorful beach towels, steak plates and salad bowls, baskets, handmade jewelry, T-shirts, postcards, stamps, books, and much more. It's the home of Caribelle Batik and Lord & Hunter seasalt, cane sugar, and spices.

Java Wraps has a new location at Mullet Bay Hotel Shopping Arcade (tel. 42801, ext. 2789). The store is all white with Javanese straw matting on the walls and decorated with exotic Balinese woodcarvings. Locals and tourists alike buy the hand-batiked resortwear line, specializing in shorts, shirts, sundresses, and children's clothing. Java Wraps is known for its sarongs. You can have a demonstration of how to tie them in at least 15 different ways.

The New Amsterdam Store, Front Street (tel. 22787), offers novelty items, T-shirts, and costume jewelry, hand-embroidered blouses for women, and porcelain figurines from Italy and Spain. They also feature St. Maarten's largest linen department. Beachwear for women is also on display, including on my latest rounds Gottex and Oberson swimwear from Israel. They sell men's and women's elegant sportswear from leading French and Italian designers, as well as accessories and shoes. You'll find everything from jogging suits to watches to 14- and 18-karat gold and silver jewelry.

Gulmohar's, Front Street (tel. 22956), could save you a shopping trip to the Orient. It's a real bazaar. On display are linen and drip-dry tablecloths, batik dresses and shirts, silk blouses, Japanese kimonos, and elegantly beaded handbags. Look for meerschaum pipes, musical jewel boxes, fine silk scarves, souvenirs, and, of course, liquor at duty-free prices.

Spritzer & Fuhrmann, "The jewelers of the Caribbean," offering jewelry, watches, china, crystal, and giftware, have two shops on St. Maarten: in the shopping arcade at the Mullet Bay Resort (tel. 44381) and at the Juliana Airport. They provide a wide range of elegant creations in a wide range of prices.

La Romana, Royal Palm Plaza (tel. 22181), is arguably the chicest international

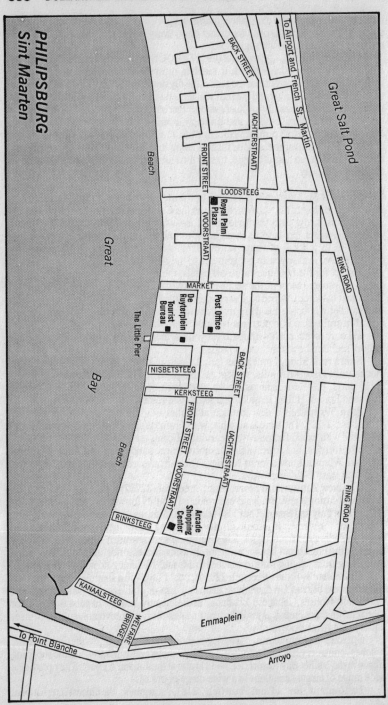

PHILIPSBURG
Sint Maarten

Great Salt Pond

To Airport and French St. Martin

BACK STREET
(ACHTERSTRAAT)

RING ROAD

FRONT STREET
(VOORSTRAAT)

Beach

Great

Bay

LOODSTEEG

Royal Palm
Plaza

MARKET

The Little Pier

De
Ruyterplein

Tourist
Bureau

Post Office

BACK STREET

NISBETSTEEG

KERKSTEEG

(ACHTERSTRAAT)

FRONT STREET
(VOORSTRAAT)

Beach

RING ROAD

Arcade
Shopping
Center

RINKSTEEG

KANAALSTEEG

WELFARE BRIDGE

Emmaplein

To Point Blanche

Arroyo

boutique in St. Maarten. On two floors, you'll find a display of designer wares, including Italian sportswear and beach outfits. Their shoe salon, for both men and women, is superb. Name designers such as Giorgio Armani are regularly featured here with merchandise that is often 25% lower than it is in the United States. La Romana has three other shops on St. Maarten: 61 Front St., Philipsburg; Mullet Bay Resort; and Porsche Design, Juliana Airport.

Oro de Sol Jewelers, Front Street (tel. 22602), is a well-stocked store offering one of the most imaginative selections in St. Maarten. Included in the inventory is an array of gold watches, as well as high-fashion jewelry studded with precious stones. The establishment also has a branch on the rue de la République in Marigot, which carries perfumes and fragrances as well as jewelry. The Rosell family—Donna and Jacques—buy their inventory from around the world, often offering discounts of up to 50% over Stateside prices.

Yellow House (Casa Amarilla), Wilhelminastraat (tel. 23438). Residents of the Dutch-speaking islands know this place as the branch of a century-old establishment in Curaçao. All kinds of perfumes and luxury items are sold here, including fine porcelain dishes and figurines. Everything is sold at duty-free prices, so it's easy to find bargains.

Thimbles & Things, Back Street (tel. 22898), north of the post office, is for noteworthy needlework with flair. Housed in a little pink home, it features West Indian batiks, as well as pillows that are appliquéed or hand-embroidered. If it's something made by hand, with fine needlework, you'll surely be drawn to the items here. Take special note of hand-painted island scenes in needlepoint made by Nusza. The shop also sells Dutch kits for do-it-yourself needlepoint.

Leda of Venice, 96 Front St. (tel. 23441), carries fine Italian fashions by such top designers as Valentino, Missoni, Missoni Uomo, Carrano, and others. You can shop here for clothes, shoes, swimsuits, handbags, belts, costume jewelry, and fashion accessories.

H. Stern Jewellers, 56 Front St. (tel. 23328), is the Philipsburg branch of a worldwide firm that engages in mining, designing, manufacturing, exporting, and retailing jewelry for all occasions and in all price ranges. They use precious gems to create pieces in contemporary and traditional designs.

Little Switzerland, Front Street (tel. 23530), offers fine-quality European imports made even more attractive by the prices charged in Philipsburg. Elegant and finely crafted watches, china, crystal, and jewelry are on display. Watches include Rolex, Chopard, Baume & Mercier, Ebel, and Audemars Piguet, and other famous names. You can purchase Aynsley, Royal Doulton, Wedgwood, what have you, from the stock of fine china, or add crystal pieces by Lalique, Waterford, Daum, Baccarat, and Orrefors to your collection.

Colombian Emeralds International has a store on Front Street (tel. 22438), where you can find stones from collector to investment quality. Unmounted duty-free emeralds from the rich mines of Colombia, as well as emerald, gold, diamond, ruby, and sapphire jewelry, will tempt your eye and pocketbook.

Around the Bend, 17 Front St. (tel. 22290). The 18th-century stone house containing this shop is almost as interesting as the merchandise inside. This is the sophisticated domain of Jean MacBeth, who came to St. Maarten many years ago. Her specialty is a selection of hand-painted beach coverups usually crafted on the island and an array of Gottex bathing suits. There's also a collection of amusing locally made dolls. Sharing the premises with her in friendly competition is **Sergio Moreto** (no phone), whose Italian imports for women are noteworthy.

Danielle Boutique, 106 Front St. (tel. 22343), is a sophisticated shop carrying one of the most imaginative selections possible for French-designed fashion sportswear, whimsical accessories, Italian handbags, and reasonably priced jewelry. The boutique is just across from the previously recommended restaurant, Le Bec Fin, in a Créole house.

As you're leaving, you might drop in at **Antillean Liquors,** at Juliana Airport (tel. 44267). This duty-free shop which attracts the last-minute shopper is open seven days a week, 365 days a year, from 8 a.m. until the last plane has left. It has a complete assortment of all the leading brands of liquor and liqueurs, as well as cigarettes and cigars.

THE SPORTING LIFE: Regardless of what hotel you select in St. Maarten, you're never far from the water. On the Dutch side you'll find a magnificent collection of white sandy beaches, perhaps your own hidden cove. If you're a beach-sampler, you can often use the changing facilities at some of the bigger resorts for a fee of about $3. (Nudists should head for the French side of the island, although the Dutch side is getting more liberal about those who prefer to take their sand sans attire.)

Windsurfing and jet-skiing are especially popular on St. Maarten. The unruffled waters of Simpson Bay Lagoon, the largest in the West Indies, are ideal for these sports, as well as for the more traditional waterskiing. For the truly daring, parasailing is also available.

Snorkeling and Scuba

Both the serious snorkeler and the scuba-diver are attracted to St. Maarten's crystal-clear bays and the countless coves that honeycomb the island. Underwater visibility reportedly runs from 75 to 125 feet. The biggest attraction for scuba-divers is the 1801 British man-o-war, H.M.S. *Proselyte,* which came to a watery grave on a reef a mile off the coast. Divers today can see her cannons and anchors. Most of the big resort hotels have facilities for scuba-diving, and someone on the staff will provide information about underwater tours, for photography as well as night diving.

One of the major water-sports centers is **Maho Watersports** on the beach at Mullet Bay Resort (tel. 44387). The dive center provides scuba lessons. Dive packages are available on request. For snorkelers, there are half-day coral-reef trips to Pinel Island, including an island tour, a short boat ride, instruction, all equipment (life jackets and beach umbrellas included), soft drinks, rum punch, and the sea. You can rent snorkel equipment and other dive items. Owned and operated by Adrienne Gonia and Mike Myers, Maho Watersports is open seven days a week from 8:30 a.m. to 5 p.m.

Sint Maarten Divers, at the Great Bay Hotel (tel. 22446), provides a good dive service. The owner, Pierre DeCelles, is a French-Canadian who knows some exciting and colorful spots to dive among reefs, wrecks, and a maze of tunnels and coral valleys. He also makes interesting night-dive trips.

Windsurfing

Windsurfing is available at the following water-sports centers at a cost of about $15 to $20 per hour: **Little Bay Beach Hotel Watersports Center** (tel. 22333); **Maho Watersports,** Mullet Bay Resort and Casino (tel. 44387); **Red Ensign Watersports,** Oyster Pond (tel. 22929 for information); and **St. Maarten Beach Club** (tel. 23434).

Parasailing

Lagoon Cruises & Watersports N.V., on the lagoon at Mullet Bay Resort (tel. 45304, ext. 337), offers a parasailing thrill—a 20-minute flight for about $25 per person. Combining the lift of a kite with the drag of a parachute, parasailing gives you a view of the island from above on closer terms than you get from an airplane. No experience is required, and Lagoon Cruises is open daily.

Waterskiing

At **Red Ensign Watersports,** Oyster Pond (tel. 22929 for information), you can take to the water on skis. The cost is $22.50 per person for a 15-minute run, and they allow the time to be shared between two people. A half-hour trip costs $37.50, and hardy souls can waterski for an hour for $70.

Deep-Sea Fishing

St. Maarten offers several possibilities for deep-sea fishing, as anglers pursue such game fish as bonito, red snapper, marlin, and albacore. One of the best-equipped centers is the **Blue Water Sport Fishing Charters,** run by the Maho Beach Hotel (tel. 42020) from a location near Mullet Pond. George Shetter, originally from Virginia, operates a 28-foot Bertram with a flybridge. All equipment is included on quarter-day excursions costing $220; a half day is $330, and full day runs $650.

You should compare prices and equipment with those of another company before you commit yourself. A group of boatmen headed by Larry George operates from **Bobby's Marina** in Philipsburg (tel. 22366). There, anglers rent an open-hulled Boston whaler for $160 per day or a larger boat such as *Sweet Cynthia* or *Pamela* for roughly the same price as those offered by Blue Water.

Tennis

You can try the courts at any of the large hotels. **Mullet Bay Resort and Casino** (tel. 42801) takes tennis more seriously than anyplace else on the island, but if you're not a guest there you will have to book a court, paying about $5 per hour. A trio of Mullet Bay's courts are lit at night.

Great Bay Beach Hotel and Casino (tel. 22447) has one court. Night play costs $5 per hour. There is no pro or pro shop. Guests are allowed to use the court free.

Little Bay Beach Hotel (tel. 22333) and **Belair Beach Hotel** (tel. 23560) each has three asphalt courts, some of them available for night play, at a charge of $5. A pro to give instruction, a pro shop, and a tennis clinic are among the amenities. Guests of the hotels are allowed free court time.

Golf

Mullet Bay Resort and Casino (tel. 42801) has an 18-hole course, one of the most challenging in the Caribbean, designed by Joseph Lee. The greens stretch along Mullet Pond and Simson Bay Lagoon, providing both beauty and hazards. Carts and clubs can be rented, and there are pros to help you improve your game. Residents of the resort get the first chance at starting times.

Sailing

Red Ensign Watersports, at Oyster Pond (call 22929, at the Dawn Beach Hotel, for information), rents Sunfish and Hobie Cats for your sailing pleasure. You can take sailing instructions daily at 4:30 p.m. for $25 per hour for a maximum of two persons with the skipper. Sunfish cost $10 per hour, while Hobie Cats go for $17.50 per hour (maximum two persons). Sunset sails are also offered daily.

Picnic Sails

One of the most popular fair-weather pastimes for vacationers to St. Maarten is to sign on for a day of picnicking, sailing, snorkeling, and sightseeing aboard one of several boats providing this service. The sleek sailboats usually pack large wicker hampers full of vituals and stretch tarpaulins over sections of the deck to protect sun-shy visitors.

A 60-foot schooner, the *Gandalf,* at Bobby's Marina, sails daily to the island of Tintamarre (Flat Island), where for 30 years beginning in 1902 the locally dubbed

"King of Tintamarre" and his 100 workers operated a cotton plantation. Swimming and snorkeling are good here, benefiting from the outlying reef which keeps the waters calm and full of sea life. Luncheon on the *Gandalf* includes a barbecue, with shish kebab, spareribs, hearty salads, and fresh-baked bread. Snorkeling equipment is provided. The cost is $55 per person.

Another picnic sail is offered on the *Gabrielle,* which also sails from Bobby's Marina, leaving at 9 a.m. and returning at 5 p.m. year round. The *Gabrielle* is a 46-foot ketch, with a spacious cockpit and large decks. Its $55-per-person price includes lunch, beer, French wine, and use of all equipment. You're taken to a secluded cove on a small island where you can sunbathe, swim, and snorkel. Boston-born Jerry Rosen is your skipper. Call 23170 after 6 p.m., 22366 during the day.

In most cases you can make reservations for any of these cruises at the activities desk of your hotel.

Sailing to Other Island Countries

Vacationers to St. Maarten have the opportunity to visit other inhabited Caribbean islands on day trips. Experienced skippers make voyages to St. Barts in the French West Indies and to Saba, another of the islands comprising the Dutch Windwards in the Leewards, stopping long enough for passengers to familiarize themselves with the island ports, to shop, and to have lunch if they wish, returning to St. Maarten the same day. The trips are available several times each week, costing $45 plus port taxes unless otherwise stated.

The *Quicksilver,* a 61-foot motor-sailing catamaran, leaves from the charter-boat dock at Bobby's Marina daily at 9 a.m., returning around 4:45 p.m. It makes a two-hour run to the French island of St. Barts, where you can visit the little capital, Gustavia, shop, and tour the island at your leisure. The fare includes an open bar. A $3 departure tax is required. You can visit the *Quicksilver* at the dock before or after a cruise.

On the power yacht *Maison Maru,* passengers sail along the shoreline while the captain, Larry Berkowitz, points out landmarks and regales his listeners with amusing tales of island life. During a day-long excursion, lunch with wine is served. An hour's layover in Marigot allows time for shopping and sightseeing on the French side of the island. You can even go swimming and snorkeling in secluded coves. The 57-foot *Maison Maru* (tel. 22188) departs from the Little Pier in Philipsburg at 9:30 a.m.

The *Eagle,* one of the most beautiful catamarans home-ported in Philipsburg, sails for St. Barts daily except Friday and Sunday at 9:30 a.m., returning to St. Maarten at 5 p.m. The boat, with double hulls painted black with gold trim and propelled by a billowing spinnaker, takes passengers on the cruise which includes snacks, open bar, use of snorkeling gear, and spectacular views. The *Eagle* makes an excursion to Saba once a week, on Friday, leaving at 8 a.m. and returning at around 5:30 p.m. Snacks, open bar, a lunch at a restaurant on Saba, and a bus tour of the island are all included in the $80-per-person charge. The *Eagle* docks at Bobby's Marina.

The *White Octopus,* an 80-foot motor-driven catamaran, offers spacious upper and lower decks for passengers going from St. Maarten to St. Barts, a trip lasting 1½ hours. The boat leaves Philipsburg every Tuesday through Saturday at 9:15 a.m., returning at 5 p.m.

For a voyage to deserted Sandy Island near the British island of Anguilla, you can embark on either Frik's *Bluebeard I* or *Bluebeard II,* leaving from Marigot small dock at 9 a.m. daily and returning at around 5:30 p.m. The two 50-foot catamarans supply snorkeling gear, and the captain and crew provide instruction for novices. A barbecue lunch is served on Sandy Island, and you can enjoy drinks from the island bar. For information and reservations for the trip, costing $55 per person, phone 2801, ext. 337.

El Tigre, a 60-foot catamaran, sails daily from Great Bay Marina at 9:30 a.m., cruising to St. Barts where you can spend the day touring, shopping, and going to the beach. *El Tigre* arrives back on St. Maarten around 5:30 p.m. The fare includes an open bar.

Sunset Island Cruise

The luxury yacht *Catcall*, a 51-foot catamaran, will provide a happy signoff to your day's activities by taking you on a two-hour sunset sail along the coast of St. Maarten to the tune of Caribbean music and unlimited drinks, costing $25 per person. The vessel leaves from Chesterfield's at Great Bay Marina at 4 p.m., returning at 6 p.m. For reservations, phone 22167.

Horseback Riding

Crazy Acres, Wathey Estate, Cole Bay (tel. 22503, ext. 201). Riding expeditions here invariably end on an isolated beach where the horses, with or without their riders, enjoy the cool waters in an after-ride romp. Two experienced escorts accompany eight-person outings which begin at 9 a.m. every weekday, returning about noon. The price is $40 per person. Riders of all levels of experience are welcome, with the single provision that they wear bathing suits under their jeans for a grand finale on the beach. It's recommended that reservations for any activity be made at least two days in advance. On weekends, families wishing to picnic together can arrange horseback outings *en famille* through the stable.

NIGHTLIFE: On the Dutch side of St. Maarten, there are few real nightclubs. After-dark activities begin early here, as guests select their favorite nook for a sundowner, perhaps the veranda of the **West Indian Tavern** or the beautiful garden patio of **Pasanggrahan,** both of these establishments having been previously recommended.

A favorite spot for sunset watching is at the **Caravanserai,** a luxury hotel also previously recommended. An airy octagonal gazebo caps a rocky outcropping at Burgeaux Bay. From here, guests watch for the legendary "green flash," an atmospheric phenomenon written about by Hemingway that sometimes occurs in these latitudes just as the sun drops below the horizon. Each evening guests wait expectantly, and have been known to break into a round of applause at a particularly spectacular sunset.

Most of the combos and **gambling casinos** as well are in the big hotels such as the **Mullet Bay Resort and Casino,** the **Maho Reef Beach Resort, Little Bay, Great Bay,** the **Seaview Beach Hotel,** and the **St. Maarten Beach Club** (refer to the previous recommendations for descriptions and locations). Casino action is usually from 8 p.m. till 3 a.m., but the casino at the St. Maarten Beach Club opens at 1 in the afternoon. A newer casino is at the **Pelican Resort** (tel. 42503), built to a Swiss design incorporating a panoramic view of Simpson Bay. It features Las Vegas rules.

Treasure Island Casino, Cupecoy Beach Hotel (tel. 44297), is one of the most imaginative and lighthearted casinos in the Caribbean. Its gaming tables and sharp-eyed staff are everything you'd expect them to be, and 17th-century figures ring the trompe l'oeil gallery on the ceiling. Peering down (presumably into your cards) is a cast of raffish and humorous characters. There's no cover charge to enter.

The big hotels, and some of the smaller ones too, sponsor **beachside barbecues** (particularly in season), bringing in steel bands and offering native music and folk dancing. Outsiders are welcomed at most of these events, but call ahead to see if it's a private catered affair.

Hemingway's, Front Street (tel. 22976), is the most unusual club on the island. At the top of a sweeping flight of steps, you'll see nostalgic Hollywood photos, a panoramic sweep of ocean, and an international collection of guests. The club combines chic with ribald comedy presented in its mini-theater at 11 p.m. by female impersonators portraying such stars as Bette Davis, Gloria Swanson, Josephine Baker, and Marlene Dietrich. Some of the performers come from as far away as Zurich. Occasionally one of them will really be a woman born. In addition to the wide assortment of drinks, full dinners are served, costing from $35, featuring an international cuisine. Hemingway's is open from 11 a.m. to 3 a.m. Reservations for the 11 p.m. show as well as for dinner are a good idea.

Many hotels have discos as well. One is **Le Club,** at the Mullet Bay Resort and Casino (tel. 42801). Drinks cost from $3.50.

Studio Seven Nightclub and Disco, Maho Beach Hotel (tel. 42115). Glittering, electronic, and contemporary, this disco is just above the lobby level of this previously recommended hotel. Open from 10 p.m. to 5 a.m. nightly, it offers a water view, changeable lighting, danceable music, and a pair of video screens showing unusual films. There's no cover charge on weeknights, but on Friday and Saturday a $6 door charge is assessed.

2. St. Eustatius

Called "Statia," this Dutch-held island is just an eight-square-mile pinpoint in the Netherlands Antilles, still basking in its 18th-century heritage as the "Golden Rock." One of the true backwaters of the West Indies, it is just awakening to tourism. The location is 150 miles east of Puerto Rico, 90 miles east of St. Croix, 38 miles due south of St. Maarten, and 17 miles southeast of Saba.

Two extinct volcanoes, the Quill and "Little Mountain," are linked by a sloping agricultural plain, growing yams and sweet potatoes, forming the topography of Statia. The valley is known as De Cultuurvlakte.

Overlooking the Caribbean on the western edge of the plain, Oranjestad (Orange City) is the capital and the only village, consisting of both an Upper and Lower Town, connected by stone-paved, dogleg Fort Road.

Statia was sighted by Columbus in 1493, on his second voyage, and the island was claimed for Holland by Jan Snouck in 1640. The island's history was turbulent before it settled down to peaceful slumber under Dutch protection. From 1650 to 1816, Statia changed flags 22 times!

Once the trading hub of the Caribbean, Statia was a thriving market, both for goods and for slaves. Benjamin Franklin directed his mail to Europe through Statia.

Before the American Revolution, the population of Statia did not exceed 1,200, most of whom were slaves engaged in raising sugarcane. When war came and Britain blockaded the North American coast, Europe's trade was diverted to the West Indies. Dutch neutrality lured many traders, which led to the construction of a mile and a half of warehouses in Lower Town. The Americans obtained gunpowder and ammunition shipped through Statia.

Statia's historical links are strong with the United States. Its Fort Oranje was the first fortress to salute the Stars and Stripes, flying from the 14-gun brigantine *Andrew Doria*. The date was November 16, 1776. Statia paid for such early recognition of a revolutionary government. In reprisal, in 1781 Great Britain's Admiral Rodney seized and sacked Statia, luring unsuspecting vessels into anchorage by continuing to fly the Dutch flag. It is estimated that when Rodney sailed away, he carried from $15 to $20 million of booty from Statia.

Contrary to legend, Statia was not destroyed by Rodney. After his forces left, the island bounced back to reach the pinnacle of its prosperity in 1790, with a population put at 8,125 persons. Its gradual decay came about when it was no longer needed as a transit port for the American colonies. Also it was bled by the exorbitant demands of interim French and English governments. Its unprotected warehouses eventually tumbled into the sea, and only their barest shells and raw foundations remain, skeletal stone walls that one historian dubbed "the Pompeii of the Caribbean."

GETTING THERE: St. Eustatius can be reached from St. Maarten's Juliana Airport via **Windward Islands Airways** (called Winair). The flight, leaving both in the morning and the afternoon, takes only 30 minutes. Connections can be made on Statia for either Saba or St. Kitts. Telephone 34210 or 34237 for schedules. There are often as many as four flights per day.

GETTING AROUND: Taxis are your best bet. They meet all incoming flights and will drive from there to your hotel. On the way to the hotel, I assure you that your driver will offer himself as a guide during your stay on the island. Taxi rates are inexpensive, probably no more than a $3 ride to your hotel from the airport. If you book a 3½-hour tour later in the day (and in that time you should be able to cover all the sights on Statia), the cost is about $35 per vehicle.

Avis Rent-a-Car is represented through a local dealer, **Rouse Enterprises** at 1 Lampeweg (tel. 32311). It's your best bet if you're preplanning your trip and want to reserve a car in advance. The cheapest vehicle is a Daihatsu Cuore, which, with unlimited mileage included, costs $36 per day. Drivers must be 21 years old to rent a car. For more information, call toll-free anywhere in the U.S. by dialing 800/331-1212.

PRACTICAL FACTS: Dutch is the official **language,** but English is commonly spoken. The official unit of **currency** is the Netherlands Antilles guilder (NAf), but nearly all places will quote you prices in U.S. dollars.

Arrival is at **Franklin Delano Roosevelt Airport,** where there is no Customs (the island is a free port). U.S. and Canadian citizens need **proof of citizenship,** such as a passport, voter registration card, or a birth certificate, along with an ongoing ticket.

There is no **departure tax** if you are returning to the Dutch-held islands of St. Maarten or Saba. If going elsewhere, you'll be charged $5.

Once on the island, visitors find a **climate** with an average daytime temperature of 78° to 82° F. The annual rainfall is only 45 inches.

The **time** is the same as Eastern Daylight Saving Time. **Electricity** is 110 volts AC, 60 cycles, the same as the U.S.

The **water** is considered safe to drink.

At the **Princess Beatrix Hospital,** 25 Prinsesweg (tel. 32211), in Oranjestad, a licensed physician is on duty.

Tipping is at the visitor's discretion, and most hotels, guesthouses, and restaurants include a 10% service charge.

Ask at your hotel if you need to send a cable. St. Eustatius maintains a 24-hour-a-day **telephone service** to the world, and sometimes it takes about that much time to get a call through!

The **Banco Popular Antiliano** is open from 8:30 a.m. to 1 p.m. Monday to Friday and also from 4 to 5 p.m. on Friday.

The **Tourist Bureau** is at 3 Fort Oranjestraat (tel. 32209). Hours are 8 a.m. to noon and 1 to 5 p.m. Monday to Friday.

Finally, this is a place in the world where crime is almost nonexistent. If there is any trouble at all, it is likely to be caused by your fellow tourists, not by the locals.

HOTELS: Don't expect deluxe hotels or high-rises. Statia is strictly for escapists. Sometimes guests are placed in private homes. There are, as well, some small guesthouses on the island.

The Old Gin House, Bay Road (P.O. Box 172), Lower Town (tel. 32319), is a two-in-one hotel, with half a dozen rooms facing the beach in Oranjestad, the other 14 built across the street and opening onto a pool. What used to be known as the ''Mooshay Bay Public House''—the hotel set back from the beach—is of more recent vintage than the Old Gin House. However, it was built on the ruins of 18th-century warehouses once used to store molasses.

It is run by John May and Marty Scofield, two expatriate Americans. Before coming to the island, Mr. Scofield was an art director for J. Walter Thompson in New York, and Mr. May taught art classes in Greenwich, Connecticut. In their inn, they have mixed antiques with practical and well-chosen pieces. They have shown a healthy respect for the past but were not trapped by it, remembering that this was an inn to be used and enjoyed by modern-day travelers. From a decaying cistern a small pool was shaped, and an old cannon was discovered while digging the swimming hole. It's been retired to a peaceful nook. The rooms at the Publick House are set in a brick building with a double row of balconies. An overseer's gallery has been turned into a library and backgammon room. Cooled by overhead fans and sea breezes, each accommodation has sophisticated touches, including paintings and wrought-iron wall hangings from Haiti. The floral lightness evokes a touch of Matisse. Terracotta plaques were imported from New Orleans for the brick walls, and flowering plants cascade from terraces and large ceramic urns.

Across the street, the Old Gin House originally began as a hot-dog stand in 1972, and like Topsy it just grew and grew, becoming a six-room inn of character, small but special. On the ruins of an old cotton gin, the house was designed by Mr. May, who with the help of his partner has made it a comfortable haven. He used red brick brought to Statia as ballast from Holland.

The decision to build grew out of a response from clients who came here to eat and stayed around looking for a place to stay. Antiques "gathered from all over" are scattered about the place—a wooden candelabrum came from Louisiana, a rare 18th-century Bristol clock "from wherever." A two-story unit faces the sea, the rooms cooled by breezes. The ceilings are high, and balconies open onto the waterfront from which you can see Statia's fishermen leaving early in the morning. In winter, the oceanfront deluxe double accommodations rent for $130. *Single or double occupancy in summer is $100 daily.* For breakfast and dinner (with complimentary wine), there is an additional charge of $32 per person daily, plus tax and service.

La Maison sur la Plage, Zeelandia Bay (tel. 32256), is set along the eastern edge of the island, above a long and lonely beach whose surf crashes violently against the sand. Owned and operated by French-born entrepreneur Michelle Greca, it contains only ten bedrooms, a pleasant swimming pool, and a restaurant which is recommended separately. The hotel's collection of green-and-white outbuildings and its sloping lawn are set near the hollow of a verdant and rocky glen. Because of the mists, the grazing cows (and the goats), along with the hills, it evokes a landscape like you might find in a warm-weather version of Scotland. The rooms are angular and a bit spartan, and residents use their private front verandas for reading and talking. Each unit contains a private bathroom and a fan, renting for $85 daily, either single or double, in winter. *In summer, single or double units cost $65 daily.* The social center, where you'll get a glimpse of island life, is a long and comfortable bar where the sound of the sea is never far away.

Golden Era Hotel, Lower Town (tel. 32345). Set directly on the water, this modern 20-room hotel is clean and serviceable. Less elegant than its next-door neighbor, the Old Gin House, it is sincere in its welcome and is air-conditioned and comfortable. It and its simply decorated bar and dining room are owned and operated by Hubert Lyfrock, a local entrepreneur. Eight of the accommodations don't have a water view, but the remaining dozen offer a full or partial exposure to the sea. Tasteful and spacious, these units rent for $80 daily in a single, $90 in a double, and $120 in a triple in winter. *Summer tariffs are $70 single, $80 double, and $100 triple.* Service and tax are extra. Nonresidents of the hotel who want a meal should phone for a reservation at least 30 minutes before their arrival. Lunch is from noon to 2 p.m. and costs $15 per person. Dinner, from 7 to 9 p.m. daily, costs from $20 per person and is likely to include stewed fish, curried lobster, beef steak, lamb chops, sandwiches, and ice creams such as passion fruit and mango. The fruit punch, with or without rum, is delectable.

WHERE TO DINE: Overlooking the beach, the **Old Gin House and Mooshay Public House,** Lower Town (tel. 32319), provides a nostalgic atmosphere where guests at lunch can enjoy the shady treillage terrace. Perhaps you'll begin with a soursop or strawberry daiquiri. If featured, I'd suggest the peanut soup (so good its recipe was published in *Gourmet* magazine). The secret is dry-roasted peanuts and a dollop or so of *ketjap bentang*. You might also order conch chowder. Recipes are the creation of American expatriate Marty Scofield. He's an inspired cook, depending on his own inventiveness: "I certainly didn't learn from my mother, who always served boiled peas and carrots." Some of his luncheon specialties include lobster Antillean, skewered chicken with peanut sauce, and red snapper mousse. I'm also fond of the chicken and coconut salad or the beef crêpes, although you can also order a hamburger if you're so inclined. Fresh pineapple is the preferred dessert. Expect to spend $15 to $20, depending on your selection. For dinner all you have to do is walk across the street.

Try to arrive before the dinner setting, so you can enjoy a drink in the pub, a structure of wooden beams and old ship-ballast bricks. The chefs are likely to feature a delicate quiche niçoise with a light, flaky crust, or perhaps fish chowder—"I can't make it unless the catch is good." Specialties (among a wide-ranging repertoire) include the bisque de homard with rouille, made with lobster legs, perfectly balanced with Mediterranean spicing. Perhaps he'll offer snapper mousse with broccoli. Service is on pewter trenchers and Spode china, and the staff is friendly and smiling. Complimentary wine is included, and the total cost is $30, well-spent money. In homage to the 18th century, Delft and pewter are used generously. Dining is by candlelight in either of two rooms, connected by brick arches with an eclectic collection of ship models, old clocks, and primitive paintings. The owners went to Haiti to order the hardwood chairs with rush seats. But everything is just a showcase of Mr. Scofield's creative cookery. Lunch is from noon to 2 p.m., and dinner from 6 to 9 p.m.

La Maison sur la Plage, Zeelandia Bay (tel. 32256), is contained in a greenhouse-style wing of the previously recommended hotel. On immaculate napery, beneath a high ceiling whose walls are open to the wind, you enjoy full meals, costing 35 NAf ($18.20) at lunch, 60 NAf ($31.20) at dinner. These are served from noon to 2 p.m. and 7 to 9 p.m. daily, except in September. Lunch might consist of fish soup, lobster salad (served in a shell), and marinated fish Tahiti style. Dinner is more elaborate, featuring such choices as fish mousse with chives, French onion soup, lobster with basil and cream sauce, beef filet with mustard sauce, stuffed chicken, and lamb with tomatoes, mushrooms, and thyme. French-born Michelle Greca is your host, imbuing her cuisine with Gallic flair.

Talk of the Town, Golden Rock (tel. 32236), offers the largest menu on the island, but don't expect all the dishes listed to be available. However, the cook, Melvina Nias, if given sufficient notice can prepare an international array of dishes that ranges from Dutch favorites to Créole cookery, with side trips to the Orient. Anyone who's eaten in the airport restaurant in Aruba may find the menu vaguely familiar. Ms. Nias used to cook there at the 7 Nations restaurant, and when she returned to her native Statia, she brought back with her the secrets she'd learned. She's taken me on a tour of her well-stocked freezers in back. Bulging with food, her larder has an unbelievable array of foodstuffs, but as most of it's frozen, you've got to call her in time to allow her to thaw it out.

To get you started, she might offer shark-fin soup or perhaps her own native fish soup. I prefer her Dutch green-pea soup, really good. Among her main dishes, I'd recommend any of her curry concoctions, her soy-sauce duck (which is served with an orange-flavored Curaçao sauce), her Caribbean red snapper with a Spanish sauce, or her beef Stroganoff. You might also enjoy her spaghetti bolognese, her nasi-goreng special, her Chinese rice (a meal in itself), or her pepper steak with oyster sauce. Another special, which she secretly labels "Happy Family," is her self-styled Chinese concoction. Meals begin at $18 per head. Although she doesn't like to say she's the best native cook on the island, some refer to her as such; she modestly admits, "I try." Drop in for lunch or dinner any time between 9 a.m. and 10 p.m.

L'Etoile, 6 Van Rheeweg (tel. 32299), is a second-floor native restaurant with a few simple tables. Eric and Caren Henriquez have had this place for some time, and they are well known in Statia for their local cuisine, but you don't run into too many tourists here. In fact, it's one of the few places on the island that quotes menu prices in Netherland Antillean guilders. Favored and recommended main dishes include the ubiquitous "goat water" (a stew), fried liver and onions, stuffed crab backs, stewed whelks, as well as tasty spareribs. Caren is also known for her pastechis, deep-fried turnovers stuffed with meat. Expect to pay from $18 for a complete and very filling meal. Lunch is from noon to 2 p.m.; dinner, 7 to 10 p.m. (on Sunday, from 8 a.m. to 6 p.m.).

SEEING THE SIGHTS: The capital, **Oranjestad,** stands on a cliff looking out upon a beach and the island's calm anchorage, where in the 18th century you might have seen 200 vessels offshore. **Fort Oranje** was built in 1636 and restored in honor of the U.S. Bicentennial celebration of 1976. Today it is perched like one of the island's seabirds atop the cliffs. Its terraced rampart is lined with old cannons. You'll see a bronze plaque honoring the fact that "Here the sovereignty of the United States of America was first formally acknowledged to a national vessel by a foreign official." The plaque was presented by Franklin D. Roosevelt. The fort is now used for government offices.

One of the island's most attractive buildings stands across from the square. Once this house belonged to Johannes de Graaff, Statia's most famous governor. It was de Graaff who ordered the salute to the Stars and Stripes. The plundering Rodney also stayed here in 1781. Today **Statia Museum,** Doncker de Graaff House, Upper Town (no phone), the island's most impressive museum, is contained inside the 17th-century walls of the governor's house. It lies in the center of town, amid a dusty garden, with a 20th-century wing crafted from mahogany. Open weekdays from 9 a.m. to 5 p.m. and weekends from 1 to 4 p.m., it charges an entrance fee of $1 for adults, 50¢ for children. Exhibits demonstrate the process of sugar refining, archeological artifacts from the precolonial period, and a pair of elegantly beautiful reproductions of 18th-century rooms. On the upper floor is a massive piece of needlework by an American, Catherine Mary Williams, showing the flowers of Statia.

A few steps away, a cluster of 18th-century buildings is called **Three Widows' Corner,** surrounding a quiet courtyard.

Nearby are the ruins of the first **Dutch Reformed church.** To reach it, turn west from Three Widows' Corner onto Kerkweg. Tilting headstones record the names of the characters in the island's past. The St. Eustatius Historical Foundation recently completed restoration of the church. Visitors may climb to the top level of the tower and see the bay as lookouts did many years before.

In the center, **Honen Dalim,** a Jewish synagogue, the second in the western hemisphere, can be explored, although it is in ruins. Once Statia had a large Jewish colony of traders. This house of prayer was begun about 1740 and was damaged by a hurricane in 1772. It fell into disuse at the dawn of the 19th century. The synagogue stands beside Synagogpad, a narrow lane whose entrance faces Madam Theatre on the square.

The walls of a ritual mikvah rise beside the **Jewish burial ground** on the edge of town. The oldest stone in the cemetery is that of Abraham Hisquiau de la Motta, who died in 1742. The inscription is in both Portuguese and Hebrew. The most recent marker is that of Moses Waag, who died February 25, 1825. Most poignant is the memorial of David Haim Hezeciah de Lion, who died in 1760 at the age of "2 years, 8 months, 26 days." Carved into the baroque surface is an angel releasing a tiny songbird from its cage.

In addition, a short ride from Oranjestad takes you to the road's end at White Wall. There on your left is **Sugarloaf,** a mini-replica of Rio's famed cone. On the right is a panoramic view of **St. Kitts.**

At the base of the pink-gray cliff beneath Fort Oranje, **Lower Town** was the mercantile center of Statia in the 18th century. Bulging with sugar, rum, and tobacco, Lower Town was once filled with row upon row of brick warehouses. Part of the rich cargo of some of these warehouses was human, slaves held in bondage awaiting shipment to other islands in the Caribbean. You can wander at leisure through the ruins, stopping later at the Old Gin House for a drink.

The Quill is an extinct volcano, called "the most perfect" in the Caribbean, sheltering a lush tropical rain forest, a botanical wonderland, in its deep wide crater. The Quill rises to 1,960 feet on the southern edge of the island. Hikers climb it. Birdwatchers come here for a glimpse of the blue pigeon, a rare bird known to frequent the breadfruit and cottonwood trees in the mountains.

SHOPPING: Merchandise is very limited, but you may want to pick up a local item or two as a reminder of a pleasant stay. Most shops, what few there are, are open from 8 a.m. to noon and 1:30 to 5:30 p.m. weekdays, from 10 a.m. to noon and 2:30 to 5:30 p.m. on Saturday. Of course, this could vary widely.

Mazinga Giftshop, Upper Town (tel. 32245), sells an array of souvenirs of the island, T-shirts, liquor, costume jewelry, handbags, Delft from Holland, and paperback romances. You may have seen more exciting stores in your life, but this is without parallel the best Statia offers.

THE SPORTING LIFE: There are few organized sports activities. Life here is casual.

Water Sports

On the Atlantic side of the island, at Concordia Bay, surfing possibilities are best. However, there is no lifeguard protection.

Snorkeling tours through the Caribbean Sea to explore the remnants of an 18th-century man-of-war and the walls of warehouses, taverns, and shops that sank below the surface of Oranje Bay more than 200 years ago are available.

Surfside Statia, a fully equipped diving center, lures underwater adventurers to its location in a former warehouse next to the Old Gin House. Surfside's professional instructors guide divers of all levels of experience to the historic shipwrecks and ruins of 18th-century seaports sitting on the ocean bottom. Scores of rare fish and gardens of coral formations can be seen. The establishment offers two-tank morning and one-tank afternoon dives daily, with night dives available on request. Certification courses and underwater photography gear are offered for rent. For reservations and information on Surfside Statia, get in touch with Surfside Watersports, 1838-40 N. Main Ave., Scranton, PA 18508 (tel. 717/346-6382, or toll free 800/468-1708 outside Pennsylvania).

Tennis

Tennis can be played at Madam Estate at the **Community Center.** The court has a concrete surface and is lit for night play. Changing facilities are also available. It should cost about $2 or less to use the court. The center and the tennis facilities were dedicated on Statia-American Day, November 16. Bring your own equipment.

Crab Catching

I'm perfectly serious. If you're interested in this sport, you can join Statians in a crab hunt. The Quill's crater is the breeding ground for these large crustaceans. At night they emerge from their holes to forage, and that's when they're caught. Men, either with flashlights or else relying on moonlight, climb the Quill, catch a crab, and take the local delicacy back to their favorite cooks on the island who prepare stuffed crab back.

Hiking

Perhaps this is the most popular sporting activity. Those with the stamina can climb the slopes of the Quill. Hikers make their way through a lush rain forest which grew when volcanic activity died down. The trip takes about half a day, and you can ask the tourist office to arrange for a guide for you. He'll expect at least $15.

Swimming

On the southwestern shore of Statia are the best volcanic beaches for swimming. Any taxi driver can take you to what he or she thinks is the best spot.

3. Saba

An extinct volcano, exotic, cone-shaped Saba is five square miles of rock carpeted in lush foliage such as orchids (which grow in profusion), giant elephant ear, and Eucharist lilies. At its zenith it reaches a height of 2,900 feet at Mount Scenery, which the locals call simply "The Mountain." The Dutch settled it in the mid-17th century, and out of such an unusual piece of jagged geography they created an experiment in living that has continued to grow.

Saba is in the Netherlands' Windward Islands at the top of the Lesser Antilles arc. The location is 150 miles east of Puerto Rico and 90 miles east of St. Croix. Most visitors fly over from the Dutch-held section of St. Maarten (Saba is 28 miles to the south).

Columbus is credited with sighting Saba in 1493. Before it became permanently Dutch, it was passed back and forth among its European masters a total of 12 times. At one time it was English, then French, then Spanish, and so forth.

Sabans have been known in days of yore to take advantage of their special topography—that is, they pelted invaders from above with rocks and boulders. Because of the influence of English missionaries and Scottish seamen from the remote Shetland Islands who settled on the island, Saba has always been English speaking. The official language, however, is Dutch.

Because of those early settlers from Europe, 60% of the population is white. Don't be surprised to run into natives with red hair and freckled fair skin.

On Saba, tidy white houses cling to the mountainside, and small family cemeteries adjoin each dwelling. Lace-curtained gingerbread-trimmed cottages give a Disneyland aura.

The first Jeep arrived on Saba in 1947. Before that, Sabans went about on foot, climbing from village to village. Hundreds of steps had been chiseled out of rock by the early Dutch settlers in 1640.

Engineers told them it was impossible, but Sabans built a single cross-island road by hand. It's filled with hairpin turns, zigzagging from Fort Bay, where a deep-water pier accommodates large tenders from cruise ships, to a height of 1,600 feet. Along the way it has fortress-like supporting walls.

Past storybook villages, the road goes over the crest to **The Bottom.** Derived from the Dutch word *botte,* which means bowl-shaped, this village is nestled on a plateau and surrounded by rocky volcanic domes. It occupies about the only bit of ground, 800 feet above the sea. It's also the official capital of Saba, a Dutch village of charm, with chimneys, gabled roofs, and gardens.

From the Bottom you can take a taxi up the hill to the mountain village of **Windwardside,** perched on the crest of two ravines at about 1,500 feet above sea level. This village of red-roofed houses, the second most important in Saba, is the site of the two biggest inns and most of the shops. From Windwardside, you can climb steep steps cut in the rock to yet another village, **Hell's Gate,** teetering on the edge of a mountain. Only the most athletic go from here to the lip of the volcanic crater.

In Windwardside, the **Harry L. Johnson Memorial Museum** is in an old sea captain's home, with antique furnishings, evoking an 1890s aura. Filled with family memorabilia, the house can be visited throughout the day, and admission is $1. The surprise visit of Jacqueline Kennedy Onassis is still vividly recalled. It is open from 10 a.m. to noon and 1 to 3:30 p.m. Monday to Friday.

GETTING THERE: You can leave New York's JFK Airport in the morning and be at Captain's Quarters in Saba for dinner that night. To do that, you can take a direct flight on any of several major carriers from JFK to St. Maarten. From Juliana Airport there, you can fly to Saba on **Winair.**

Many guests at hotels on St. Maarten fly over to Saba on the morning flight, spend the day sightseeing, then return to St. Maarten on the afternoon flight. Air connections can also be made in Saba to St. Kitts and Statia.

If you're returning to St. Maarten or flying over to Statia, you don't have to pay a departure tax. However, if you're going elsewhere, such as to St. Kitts, a $5 departure tax will be imposed on you.

Arriving by air from St. Maarten, the traveler steps from Windward Island Airways' 20-passenger STOL (short takeoff and landing) plane onto the tarmac runway of the Juancho Yrausquin Airport. The airstrip stretches 1,312 feet along the aptly named Flat Point, one of the few level areas on the island. From there the road rises in 20 serpentine curves to the village of Hell's Gate which, despite its name, nestles in the shadow of the island's largest church.

Saba is now more accessible than ever, with day trips from St. Maarten aboard the *Alisur Amarillo* **ferry,** transporting visitors in just one hour to Saba on Wednesday, and every other Sunday. The modern, air-conditioned ferry leaves St. Maarten from Great Bay Marina at 9 a.m., returning at 4:30 p.m. Round-trip fare is $40 for adults; children under 12, half price. Bus service from many of St. Maarten's hotels to and from Great Bay Marina is offered for $5. For reservations and information, get in touch with **Alisur Caribe, Ltd.,** General Agents, St. Maarten Port Service N.V., Point Blanche (tel. 22304).

GETTING AROUND: Transport is mostly on foot, but taxis and five rental cars are available. In the unlikely event you should dare want to drive a car on Saba, your hotel can make arrangements for you at a cost of about $30 a day. Again, I don't recommend this.

Taxis

Taxis meet every flight, and you can use one to take you to your hotel or to make a sightseeing tour. The cost of a two-hour tour is $6 per person if there are more than four passengers making the trip. One person alone pays $25.

Hitchhiking

Now frowned upon in much of the world, hitchhiking has long been an acceptable means of transport in Saba, where everybody seemingly knows everybody else. On my latest rounds, my taxi rushed a sick child to the plane and picked up an old man to take him up the hill because he'd fallen and hurt himself—all on my sightseeing tour! I welcomed this friendly and cooperative spirit. At least by hitchhiking, you'll get to know everybody else.

Walking

The oldest and most traditional means of getting around on Saba is still much in evidence. But I suggest that only the sturdy in heart and limb walk from the Bottom up to Windwardside. Many do, but you'd better have some shoes that grip the ground, particularly after a recent rain.

PRACTICAL FACTS: The Netherlands Antilles guilder (NAf 1.92 to $1 U.S.) is the official unit of **currency,** but U.S. dollars are accepted by almost everybody here.

Arrival is at **Juancho Yrausquin Airport** at Flat Point where there is no Customs, as this is a free port. Once off the plane, you encounter a temperature of 78° to 82°F (the annual rainfall is 42 inches). The government does require that all U.S. and Canadian citizens show **proof of citizenship,** such as a passport or voter registration card. An ongoing ticket must also be produced.

The **time** is Eastern Daylight Time, and the **electricity** is 110 volts AC, 60 cycles, so most U.S.-made appliances do not need converters.

Licensed physicians practice at the **Princess Irene Hospital,** St. John's (tel. 42232).

The only bank on the island is **Barclays,** at Windwardside, and it's open from 8:30 a.m. to 12:30 p.m. Monday to Friday.

Cables and international **telephone calls** can be placed at the Cable and Wireless office in Windwardside.

Most restaurants and hotels add a 10% or 15% **service charge** to cover tipping. The government imposes a 5% **tax** on hotel rooms.

Whatever your problems, you can take them to Glenn C. Holm, who is the chairman of the Saba Tourist Board. He operates out of a small office, the **Tourist Bureau** (tel. 42231), next door to the post office in Windwardside. Hours are weekdays only from 8 a.m. to noon and 1 to 5 p.m.

WHERE TO STAY: The island has a few inns of character, extremely limited in accommodations, yet special and charming for that reason. If you check into an address here, you could safely say you're "hiding out."

Captain's Quarters, Windwardside (tel. 42201), is a restored 19th-century sea captain's house converted into a guesthouse where many visitors spend secluded holidays. Just off the village center of Windwardside, it's a complex of several wood-frame guesthouses and a long clapboard motel-like annex surrounding the main house with its traditional verandas and covered porches. You make your way here by going down a narrow, steep lane. Thrust out toward the water, almost as if ready to tumble down to the sea, is a freshwater swimming pool surrounded by a terrace where you can sunbathe or order refreshments from an open-air bar. The manager, Steve Hassell (everybody on Saba seems to be named Hassell), and his wife, Cathy, handle the inn with style, and they're rightly proud of the chef, well known in the islands as "Sugar." You'll find the cool and refreshing dining room nestled behind the main house amid a screen of plants. Service is polite and attractively formal; candlelit dinners are romantic.

The main house was built by a Saban sea captain and serves as office, library, sitting room, and kitchen on the first floor, with two private accommodations above (one is a honeymoon suite). The house is furnished with antiques gathered from many ports of the world. About half of the ten bedrooms contain four-poster beds, and each is complete with a private bath and balcony overlooking the sea and Mount Scenery. Well-designed and cozy studio rooms stand in the garden. Everything seems a quaint reminder of New England. The hotel, open all year (except in September), *charges $55 in a single in summer, $70 in a double, and a third or fourth person sharing a room is assessed another $20.* In winter, the single tariff is $65, going up to $80 in a double. These are tariffs for rooms only. For breakfast and dinner, add another $25 per person daily. Modern comfort and infinite charm combine to form a tasteful, distinctive Saban atmosphere.

Scout's Place, Windwardside (tel. 42205), right in the center of the village, is hidden from the street. It's set on the ledge of a hill, giving every table a view of the sea. This old guesthouse was transformed by Ohio-born Scout Thirkield into an inn of atmosphere. He still comes around, but the place is now owned by Diana Medero, who has added ten rooms to the original five. It is sheltered in an old house, with a large covered but open-walled dining room. It's an informal-type place, with a highly individualistic decor that might include everything from Surinam hand-carvings to peacock chairs in red-and-black wicker to silver samovars. Don't be surprised either if you see a plastic chair or two. Rooms open onto an interior courtyard filled with flowers, and each unit has a view of the sea. Furnishings are fairly coordinated, unpretentious, and very informal. Most of the rooms have private baths; others must share. Rates are the same all year—$50 daily for two persons with private bath, $35 per single. These tariffs include breakfast and dinner, plus service. Diana Medero makes guests feel right at home.

Cranston's Antique Inn, The Bottom (tel. 43203), is a frame inn standing near the village roadway, with a front terrace where everyone congregates for rum drinks and gossip. It's an old-fashioned house, more than 100 years old at least, and every bedroom has antique four-poster beds. Mr. Cranston, the owner, will gladly rent you the same room where Queen Juliana once spent a holiday. It's on the second floor, on your left, facing the rear garden. Aside from the impressive wooden beds, the furnishings are mostly hit or miss. Rates, in effect all year, are $32 daily in a single, rising to $48 in a double, including breakfast. Local dishes are offered, such as roast pork from island pigs, red snapper, and broiled grouper. Mr. Cranston has a good island cook, who makes use of locally grown spices. Meals are served on a covered terrace in the garden. The house is within walking distance of Ladder Bay.

Cottages and Apartments. Cottage rentals are becoming more and more popular on Saba, and most are quite economical. Also, a few efficiency apartments are available.

Cottages range in size from one to three bedrooms, and most have ocean views. Some are typical Saban style, while others are of cement construction. Rentals by the week go from $150 to $300, the latter price for a large, newly remodeled house adjacent to the Captain's Quarters hotel.

Apartments accommodating two persons range in price from $125 to $175 per week.

For information and reservations, phone the **Tourist Bureau.** To dial direct from the U.S., the number is 011-599-4-2231.

WHERE TO EAT: For visitors over for the day, **Scout's Place,** Windwardside (tel. 42205), is a favorite dining spot, but you should have your driver stop by early and make a reservation for lunch for you. Food at Scout's is simple and good, rewarding and filling, and the price is low too, about $12 for lunch. Dinner is more elaborate, and because of the limited staff reservations are definitely necessary. For your evening meal, expect to pay about $18. Tables are placed on an open-side terrace, the ideal spot for a Heineken at sundown. Local vegetables, homemade bread, and fruit are served. Lunch is at one sitting, 12:30 p.m., and dinner is also at one sitting, 7:30 p.m.

Captain's Quarters, Windwardside (tel. 42201), is an alternative choice for dinner, and again you must reserve a table. Dining is al fresco; however, if it rains, don't worry—they have a roof. Large, hearty appetites are catered to here, at a cost averaging around $18 for dinner. Perhaps you'll be there on the night they have fresh grouper. It's one of the best selections in the Caribbean. Soups are homemade and often quite good. Because of the limited supplies on Saba, vegetables are often frozen. Likewise, the wine list is very limited. Lunch will cost much less, about $10, and you can also stop in here for a very filling breakfast at around $6. The dining room is open every day of the year except during the June closing. Lunch is at one sitting: 12:30 p.m. daily. Likewise there is one sitting for dinner, at 7:30 p.m.

Saba Chinese Restaurant (Moo Goo Gai Pan), Windwardside (tel. 42268), occupies a house lying amid a cluster of residential buildings on a hillside above Windwardside. Operated by a family from Hong Kong, it offers the largest menu on Saba, an unpretentious decor of plastic tablecloths and folding chairs, and a style of cookery so popular that many residents claim this to be their most frequented restaurant. Full meals cost from 30 NAf ($15.60) and include an array of Cantonese and Indonesian specialties. These include lobster Cantonese, Chinese chicken with mushrooms, sweet-and-sour fish, chicken with cashew nuts, conch chop suey, several curry dishes, roast duck, and nasi goreng. The establishment is open daily except Monday from 11 a.m. to 10 p.m.

Guido's, Windwardside (tel. 42230). The Guido family, formerly from Massachusetts, operates this open-air establishment which serves the only pizza on the island. Specializing in fast food, hamburgers, hot dogs, and light meals, it offers a place for people to drink and chat. A whole pizza, suitable for four persons, runs $9. Light meals cost from $6. You pass through a small bar area to a cement-sided pavilion which at night becomes a disco. This place has no pretensions of glamor of any kind. It is open from 11 a.m. to 11 p.m. Monday through Thursday. On Friday and Saturday it stays open to 2 a.m. There is no cover charge, and the establishment is closed on Sunday.

SHOPPING: After lunch you can go for a stroll in Windwardside, stopping at the boutiques, which often look like someone's living room (sometimes they are). Most stores are open from 9 a.m. to noon and 2 to around 5:30 p.m.

Stitched by Saban wives when their fishermen husbands were off to sea, the traditional drawn threadwork of the island is famous. You don't even have to go to a shop to find it. Chances are, your driver will stop along the road as women, mostly descendants of Europeans, crowd around. You'll find out later that the shy woman selling the drawn threadwork is the sister of your taxi driver.

Sometimes this work, introduced by a local woman named Gertrude Johnson in the 1870s, is called Spanish work, because it was believed to have been perfected by nuns in Caracas. Selected threads are drawn and tied in a piece of linen to produce an ornamental pattern. It can be expensive if a quality linen has been used, not to mention the amount of painstaking human detail that went into its creation.

The **Island Craft Shop,** Windwardside (no phone), has a good selection of drawn threadwork if you didn't buy some along the road. Owned by Bob and Ruth Beebee, it also sells items in linens, and you can purchase many souvenirs as well as black coral jewelry.

The **Saba Artisan Foundation,** The Bottom (tel. 43260), in recent years has made a name for itself in the world of fashion with hand-screened resort fashions. The clothes are casual and colorful. Among the items sold are men's bush jacket shirts, numerous styles of dresses and skirts, napkins, and placemats, as well as yard goods. Island motifs are used in many designs, and you might like a fern or casava-leaf print. Also popular are the famous Saba drawn lace patterns. The fashions are designed, printed, sewn, and marketed by Sabans. Mail-order as well as wholesale distributorship inquiries are invited.

As a final shopping note, try to come home with some "Saba Spice," an aromatic blend of 150-proof cask rum, with such spices as fennel seed, cinnamon, cloves, and nutmeg, straight from someone's home brew. It's not for everyone (too sweet), but will make an exotic bottle to show off at home.

THE SPORTING LIFE: Don't come here for beaches. Saba has only one sand beach, and it's about 20 feet long. Sports here are mostly do-it-yourself. John F. Kennedy, Jr., likes to visit Saba to enjoy the underwater scenery and dark, volcanic sands and coral formations.

Saba, according to some divers, is said to offer "some of the most spectacular diving in the Caribbean." **Saba Deep** (tel. 43347) operates out of Captain's Quarters (see my hotel recommendation). The diving operation is small, and the operators are concerned with individual attention. In spite of the size of the island, they have at their disposal a minimum of two dozen dive sites, ranging from shallow-water caves to spectacular dropoffs.

Sea Saba Dive Center, Windwardside (tel. 42246), is where Joan and Lou Bourque share with clients their knowledge of the underwater elkhorn forests and giant boulder gardens that make Saba "the unspoiled queen of the Caribbean," with regard to the sea world. The Bourques offer packages covering a variety of interests, including underwater photography, slide shows, marine biology seminars, and all PADI certification and resort courses.

Tennis buffs will find a public court in the Bottom. It's a cement court and doesn't charge players.

Mountain walking is actually the major sport, and the top of **Mount Scenery** is a wildlife reserve, the goal of eager bands of hikers. Allow more than a day and take your time climbing the 1,064 concrete steps up to the cloud-reefed mountain. One of the inns will pack you a picnic lunch. The higher you climb, the cooler it grows, about a drop of 1° Fahrenheit every 328 feet. On a hot day this can be an incentive. The peak is 2,855 feet high.

Others not so athletic may settle for a hike up Bobby Hills, 66 terraced steps leading to a peak of 1,500 feet. Beautiful views unfold in every direction.

NIGHTLIFE: Believe it or not, there is some. On weekends, **Guido's** restaurant (see my previous recommendation) becomes a nightclub. It's the most popular disco on the island.

Chapter XI

JAMAICA

**1. Kingston
2. Port Antonio
3. Ocho Rios
4. Montego Bay
5. Negril
6. Mandeville**

JAMAICA, 90 MILES south of Cuba, is the third largest of the Caribbean islands, with some 4,400 square miles of predominantly green land, a mountain ridge peaking at 7,400 feet above sea level, and on the north coast, many beautiful white sand beaches with clear blue sea.

First populated in A.D. 700 by Arawak Indians, gentle people from South America who named the island "Xaymaca," Jamaica was first discovered by Christopher Columbus, who called it "the fairest isle eyes have seen" in 1494—Jamaicans will tell you that he was their first tourist and was a repeat visitor. Spain settled the island in 1509. In due course, Africans were imported by the Spanish as slaves to supplement the Indian labor force, which was gradually depleted by European disease and overwork. By 1655, when the English captured the island, there were no Arawaks left.

Until 1962 Jamaica was a Crown Colony of Great Britain but has now achieved full independence within the Commonwealth. The island's motto is, appropriately, "Out of Many, One People." The islanders are mostly of African or Afro-European descent, with a minority of British, Chinese, Indians, Portuguese, Germans, and people from other West Indian islands, all intermarried to create one people. The government is similar to that of Great Britain, the queen being represented by a governor-general appointed on the advice of the prime minister of Jamaica, who is elected. English is the official language, but with delightful adaptations, and you'll probably hear "Jamaica talk" when you take your *bankra* (basket) and *dunny* (money) to the market or have a meal of fish tea, rundown, and skyjuice.

Tourism has become the biggest industry in Jamaica, surpassing the traditional leaders, bauxite and aluminum.

The average Jamaican is friendly, and responds to a smile and a cheerful hello with kindness. Of course, there are rogues in every country, and common sense has to prevail when you travel.

In general, if you like people, you will like the Jamaicans. Don't call them natives, however. They feel it's insulting, and they are proud of just being called Jamaicans.

GETTING THERE: The most popular routings to Jamaica are from New York or Miami. **Eastern** flies several times a day from Miami to both Kingston and Montego

Bay (Eastern, of course, has many connections throughout the U.S. via Miami). **Air Jamaica**, the national carrier, flies to Jamaica from Atlanta, Memphis, Los Angeles, Toronto, New York, Philadelphia, and Baltimore. **Air Canada** flies three times a week in high season to both Montego Bay and Kingston from Toronto, with connecting service from Montréal.

The single most popular routing is the **American Airlines** connection from New York, which departs daily to both Montego Bay and Kingston. American's flight leaves early enough to allow passengers a late-afternoon sunbath once they reach Jamaica, but late enough for passengers from cities throughout the Northeast to make convenient connections through New York. The aircraft is usually a wide-bodied Airbus, which makes a brief stopover in Montego Bay before continuing to Kingston. Later in the day, the same aircraft reverses its path, returning to New York's JFK via Montego Bay.

A wide array of fares is available. The cheapest ones are contingent on the availability for the particular day of travel of whatever block of seats American has set aside for its promotional fares. Currently, round-trip high-season fares from New York to Kingston were as low as $222 for weekday travel (Monday through Thursday), or $279 at other times (Friday through Sunday). A limited number of these rock-bottom fares are available to the public only if reservations are made in advance and if the return half of the round-trip ticket is used within 3 to 21 days of the original departure date.

If American's quota of inexpensive seats to Jamaica is filled by the time of your hoped-for departure date, it might be necessary to book a regular excursion ticket for which no advance reservations are necessary. From New York to Kingston in high season, the regular round-trip coach-class fare reaches a high of $584, but because of a complicated series of price reductions that are granted to travelers who reserve far enough in advance, it's possible, based on the availability of your seats on the day of your departure, to pay less. The prices of regularly scheduled excursion tickets in low season are substantially less.

So many ticket options are available that only a call to an American Airlines ticketing agent (or else your travel agent) will clarify the exact price at the time of your intended departure.

It's important to remember that American, like most of the other major carriers, maintains a tour desk which can often arrange hotel accommodations for your trip as well as your flight. Because the major carriers book in such volume, you might save money this way than if you book hotels on your own at what is called "the rack rate."

GETTING AROUND: Many people like to see more of Jamaica than just their resort
hotel. If so, I have the following suggestions for seeing the countryside:

By Air

The bulk of travelers to Jamaica, particularly tourists, enter Jamaica via Montego Bay. The island service is by **Trans-Jamaican Airlines Ltd.** (tel. 993-267 in Port Antonio, 923-9498 in Kingston, and 952-5403 in Montego Bay). The international **Air Jamaica** handles sales and provides information overseas. Trans-Jamaican flies between the major towns of the island. Fares are reduced slightly in low season. Incidentally, there are two Kingston airports, which are connected by taxi. One is for domestic flights, the other for international. Car-rental facilities are only available at the international airport.

By Car

Jamaica is big enough and public transportation is unreliable enough that a car is not really a luxury but is almost a necessity if you plan to do any sightseeing beyond the confines of your hotel. Over the years, I have tried and recommended all the major car-rental firms. On my most recent trip, I used the **Budget Rent-a-Car** subsidiary at the Montego Bay airport. Budget maintains three locations in Jamaica—one at the Kingston International airport, one at Montego Bay airport, and one in downtown Ocho Rios.

Renting a car in Jamaica is easy, but there are several things you should be aware of before starting out. Drivers must be between the ages of 25 and 70 and must present their driver's license and a credit card when filling out the forms. Travelers without a credit card must pay a deposit of $700 in cash at the time of rental.

Budget's insurance policies declare that any driver is responsible for the first $500 of damage to the car, regardless of whether he or she has signed a collision damage waiver. (The potential liability is even greater with several other car-rental companies.) If a driver decides to purchase such a waiver, costing $6 per day, his or her eventual liability in the event of an accident will be limited to the first $500 damage. If the driver forgoes the waiver, the responsibility is limited to the first $2,500 worth of damage.

Budget offers a wide variety of vehicles, mainly Japanese. Any rental is cheaper by the week, although daily rentals are also possible. The following prices apply to vehicles reserved at least two full business days in advance through Budget's toll-free reservation system. A Nissan Sunny, with manual transmission and a seating capacity of four, costs $216 per week, with each additional day costing an extra $31. Daily rentals of less than a week cost $41 per day. Unlimited mileage is included in all rates, but a 10% government tax is added. Automatic-transmission cars are also available: a Sunny costs $227 per week with this equipment, and extra days cost an additional $32. Daily rentals of less than a week cost $49 per day. An air-conditioned car with manual transmission costs $268 per week, with each extra day costing $38. Per-day rentals of less than a week are $55.

A clerk at Budget's toll-free reservations center will be glad to explain the rates to you in greater detail. The extended-hour toll-free number is 800/527-0700. Budget's rates for both rentals and insurance in Jamaica are substantially cheaper than those at Avis or Hertz. To compare prices before you start your trip, you can call **Hertz** toll free at 800/654-3131 or **Avis** toll free at 800/331-1212.

By Train

A leisurely sort of travel, but a marvelous way to see the country, is by rail. At each station, peddlers leap onto the train to sell their wares, jumping off at the last possible second as the train leaves the station. Expect to pay about J$10 ($1.90) per mile for second-class rail travel, nearly J$20 ($3.80) per mile for first-class travel. The journey from Kingston to Montego Bay takes about 4½ hours, and there are two departures a day. Check at local stations to see when trains are expected to run.

By Taxi

Kingston has taxis with meters, but not many of them work so agree on a price before you get in. In Kingston and the rest of the island, taxis are operated by JUTA, Jamaican Union of Travellers Association, and have the union's emblem on the side of the vehicle. All prices are controlled, and any local JUTA office will supply a list of rates. JUTA drivers do all the touring and guiding on the island. I've found them a pleasant, friendly, and, in the main, knowledgeable group of people, and good drivers. Most of the cabs are of U.S. origin, but they are old.

Bike, Moped, and Honda Rentals

These can be rented in Montego Bay, and you'll need a valid driver's license for anything mechanized. **Montego Bike Rentals**, 21 Gloucester Ave. (tel. 952-4984), rents Hondas for $14 to $27 per day, requiring a $100 deposit. Ten-speed bicycles cost only $8 per day. Deposits are refundable if vehicles are returned in good shape.

PRACTICAL FACTS: To ease your orientation to an often bewildering island, I have some important information you should know in advance of your arrival:

On departure, you will be charged J$40 ($7.60) **tax** at the airport. All air flights must be reconfirmed no later than 72 hours before departure.

Banks are open from 9 a.m. to 2 p.m. Monday through Thursday, 9 a.m. to noon and 2:30 to 5 p.m. on Friday. In rural towns there is a slight difference in closing times, but you are safe between 9 a.m. and noon.

Expect **temperatures** around 80° to 90° Fahrenheit on the coast. Winter is a little cooler. In the mountains, it can get as low as 40°. There is generally a breeze, which in winter is noticeably cool. The rainy periods are October to early November, and May to early June. Normally rain comes in short, sharp showers; then the sun shines.

As in other British-influenced countries, **driving** is *on the left.* Speed limits in town are 30 miles per hour; elsewhere, 50 mph. Gas costs J$10.90 ($2.05) per imperial gallon, payable only in Jamaican dollars—no credit cards are accepted. (The cost of gasoline may be higher by the time you visit.) Your own driver's license is acceptable.

Hard **drugs** and *ganja* (marijuana) are illegal and imprisonment is the penalty for violation. Prescriptions are accepted only if issued by a Jamaican doctor. Hotels have doctors on call. If you need any particular medicine or treatment, bring evidence, such as a letter from your own doctor.

Most places have the standard **electrical voltage** of 110, as in the U.S. However, some establishments operate on 220 volts, 50 cycles. If your hotel is on a different current from your U.S.-made appliance, ask for a converter.

You can get a **marriage** license after 48 hours' residence on the island, and then marry as soon as it can be arranged. You will need your birth certificates, and where applicable, divorce documents. Apply to the Ministry of Justice, Kingston, and then many Jamaican hotels will arrange the rest.

Nude bathing is allowed at a number of hotels, clubs, and beaches, especially in Negril, which are signposted "Swimsuits Optional." Elsewhere, the law will not even allow topless sunbathing.

U.S. and Canadian residents do not need passports but must hold a return or on-going ticket and **proof of citizenship.** Other visitors need passports, for a maximum stay of six months.

The government imposes a **room tax,** ranging from $4 to $8 in small hotels. This goes up to $8 to $16 in larger establishments, the higher price being for deluxe and first-class accommodations. Some hotels charge an energy tax.

Store hours vary widely, but as a general rule most business establishments open at 8:30 a.m., closing at 5 p.m. (or in some places, earlier at 4:30 p.m.). Some shops are open on Saturday until noon.

Some Jamaicans don't like having their pictures taken, for various reasons. Ask permission first.

All overseas **telephone** calls outside your hotel incur a government tax of 50% over what the hotel will charge!

In winter, Jamaica is on **Eastern Standard Time.** However, when the U.S. is on Daylight Saving Time, when it's 6 a.m. in Miami it's 5 a.m. in Kingston.

Tipping is customary. A general 10% or 15% is expected in hotels and restaurants on occasions where you would normally tip. Some places add a service charge to the bill.

It's safe to drink **water** from the tap at your hotel, as it is piped, filtered, and chlorinated.

MONEY: Be careful! There are Jamaican dollars and there are U.S. dollars. Unless it is clearly stated, either in shops or when agreeing to a rate with a taxi driver or in a restaurant, always insist on knowing which dollar they are quoting. Actually, tourists are required to pay their bills in Jamaican dollars, written J$. However, shopkeepers and hotel owners still, in many cases, quote tourists prices in U.S. dollars. Jamaica adopted the policy of excluding U.S. currency from circulation so that the impact of two recent devaluations could be reflected in the economy of the island. For purposes of clarification, in this book prices quoted in Jamaican dollars will be given as J$, with the U.S. conversion in parentheses after that quotation. Otherwise, the dollar figures given are in U.S. currency. As of this writing, the Jamaican dollar is still fluctuating. Any comment made by me will likely be out of date by the time you actually reach Jamaica. At the time of research for this edition, a visitor could get about J$5.26 to $1 U.S. (J$1 equals about 19¢). But that rate has fluctuated greatly, and is certainly likely to continue upward or downward during the lifetime of this edition. However, to give you a rough idea of what certain services will cost, I will convert at the prevailing rate at the time of research. But remember to check with your bank or a Jamaican tourist office to find what the prevailing rate of exchange will be during your visit.

You should use your immigration card when making bank transactions and also when converting Jamaican dollars back into U.S. dollars.

Jamaican currency comes in different sizes: J$1, J$2, J$5, J$10, and J$20. Coins are 1¢, 10¢, 20¢, 25¢, and 50¢. There is no limit to the amount of foreign currency you can bring in, but it is illegal to import or export Jamaican currency. Duty-free shops, banks, and hotels change money. But wherever you change money, get a currency receipt—you must present it when changing your surplus Jamaican dollars at the end of your stay. Both international airports have banks.

MEET THE PEOPLE: Throughout the island, the Jamaican Tourist Offices in the various towns can arrange for visitors to be hosted by Jamaican families. More than 650 families are registered in the scheme with the Tourist Board, which keeps a list of their interests and hobbies. All you have to do is give the board a rough idea of your own interests and they will arrange for you to spend the day with a similar family.

Once with them, you just go along with whatever they plan to do, sharing their life, eating at their table, joining them at a dinner party. You may end up at a beach barbecue, afternoon tea with the neighbors, or selling fruit at the roadside, working quietly in the garden, or just sitting and expounding theories, arguing, and talking far into the night.

If you have a particular interest—birds, butterflies, music, ham radio, stamp collecting, or spelunking (there are many caves to explore)—the Tourist Board will find you a fellow enthusiast. Many lasting friendships have been developed because of this unique opportunity to meet the people.

It is important to know that this service is entirely free. You need not even take your hostess a gift, but she will certainly appreciate a bunch of flowers after your visit.

In Jamaica, apply at any of the tourist boards: 79-81 Knutsford Blvd., New Kingston (tel. 929-8070); Cornwall Beach, Montego Bay (tel. 952-4425); Visitor's Service Bureau in Negril (tel. 957-4243); Ocean Village Shopping Centre in Ocho Rios (tel. 974-2570); or at the City Centre Plaza in Port Antonio (tel. 993-3051).

FOOD AND DRINK: Because this is an island, there is great emphasis on seafood. Rock lobster is a regular dish on every menu, appearing grilled, Thermidor, cold, hot. Codfish and akee is the national dish, a concoction of salt fish and a brightly colored vegetable that tastes something like scrambled eggs. Escaveche (marinated fish) is usually fried and then simmered in vinegar with onions and peppers. Curried mutton and goat are popular, as is pepperpot stew, all highly seasoned and guaranteed to reduce your body temperature.

Jerk pork is peculiar to country areas, where it is barbecued slowly over wood fires until crisp and brown. Apart from rice and peas (which are really red beans), usually served as a sort of risotto with added onions, spices, and salt pork, vegetables are exotic: breadfruit, imported by Captain Bligh in 1723 when he arrived aboard H.M.S. *Bounty;* callaloo, rather like spinach, used in pepperpot soup (not to be confused with the stew of the same name); cho-cho, served boiled and buttered or stuffed; and green bananas and plantains, fried or boiled and served with almost everything. Then there is pumpkin, which goes into a soup or is served on the side, boiled and mashed with butter.

Coconut water is a refreshing drink, especially when you stop by the roadside to have a local vendor chop the top from a fresh nut straight from the tree. Sweet potatoes appear with main courses, but there is also a sweet potato pudding made with sugar and coconut milk, flavored with cinnamon, nutmeg, and vanilla. You'll meet the intriguing *stamp and go,* salt fish cakes to eat as an appetizer; *fall back,* salty stew with bananas and dumplings; and *rundown,* mackerel cooked in coconut milk, often eaten for breakfast. For the really adventurous, *mannish water,* a soup made from goat offal and tripe, is said to increase virility. Patties—the best in the island are at Montego Bay—are another staple snack. Pastry filled with highly seasoned meat and breadcrumbs, to be eaten at any time of the day or night, is sold with boiled corn, roast yams, and roast salt fish at roadside stands, gas stations, and snack counters.

Rum punches are everywhere, and the local beer is Red Stripe. The island produces many liqueurs, the most famous being Tía Maria, made from coffee beans. Rumona is another good one to take home with you. Bellywash, the local name for lemonade, will supply the extra liquid you may need to counteract the heat of the tropics. Blue Mountain coffee is the best, but tea, cocoa, and milk are usually available to round off a meal.

REGGAE FESTIVAL: The annual Reggae Festival, usually held the second week in August, also in Montego Bay, features Jamaican artists. Arrangements to attend can be made by May of every year. Many local hotels are fully booked for the festival, so advance reservations are necessary. The Jamaican Tourist Boards can give information (see above) about tour packages and group rates for the festival.

THE SPORTING LIFE: If sports are important to your vacation, you may want to review the offerings of Jamaica before deciding on a particular resort. Sports are so spread out, and Jamaica so large, that it isn't feasible to go on a long day's excursion just to play golf, for example. The cost of most activities is generally the same throughout the island, except for golf, which is more expensive in Kingston.

Golf

In all the West Indies, Jamaica has the best courses. Montego Bay alone has four championship courses. Space does not permit a description of all these courses, but one in particular, the one at **Wyndham Rose Hall Beach Hotel and Country Club** (tel. 953-2650), has been called "one of the top five courses in the world." This seaside and mountain course is unusual and challenging. Built on the shores of the Caribbean, its eighth hole skirts the ocean, then doglegs onto a promontory and a green thrusting 200 yards into the sea. The back nine is the most scenic and interesting, rising into steep slopes and deep ravines on Mount Zion. The tenth fairway abuts the family burial grounds of the Barretts of Wimpole Street, and the 14th passes the vacation home of singer Johnny Cash. The 300-foot-high 13th tee offers a rare panoramic view of the sea and the roof of the hotel, and the 15th green is next to a 40-foot waterfall, once featured in a James Bond movie. A fully stocked pro shop, a clubhouse, and a professional staff are among the amenities.

Others include the challenging **Tryall** (tel. 952-5110), in Hanover, 12 miles from town, the Robert Trent Jones–designed **Half Moon** (tel. 953-2560), and the **Ironside Golf Club** (tel. 953-2800).

On the north coast, **Jamaica, Jamaica** (tel. 973-3435) has another 18-hole course. There is also the **Upton Country Club,** above Ocho Rios (tel. 974-2528).

In Kingston, check out **Constant Spring Club** (tel. 924-1610), an 18-hole course in the foothills of the Blue Mountains, and **Caymanas Country Club** (no phone), in the midst of sugarcane fields.

In Mandeville, there's the 9-hole **Manchester Golf Club** (tel. 962-2403).

Water Sports

Water options for the sports lover proliferate throughout Jamaica, with many activities offered as part of all-inclusive packages by the island's major hotels. However, there are other well-maintained facilities for water sports not connected to the hotel offerings.

Jamaica has some of the finest diving waters in the world. The average diving depth ranges from 35 to 95 feet. Visibility is usually from 60 to 120 feet. Most of the diving is done on coral reefs, which are protected by underwater parks where fish, shells, coral, and sponges are plentiful. Experienced divers can also see wrecks, hedges, caves, dropoffs, and tunnels.

Tojo Water Sports, at the Trelawny Beach Hotel in Falmouth (tel. 954-2450), offers scuba-diving programs to the offshore coral reefs that are considered some of the most spectacular of the Caribbean. There are seven A.C.U.C.- certified dive guides, three dive boats, and all the necessary equipment for either inexperienced or already-certified divers. Guests of the Trelawny benefit from free introductory lessons and the availability of a free daily dive. Diving is conducted partly offshore of the hotel and partly near the reefs at Ocho Rios. Night dives are also offered, and transportation is provided to all dive sites. Trelawny Beach also offers free snorkeling, Sunfish sailing, windsurfing, glass-bottom-boat rides, and tennis.

Seaworld Resorts, Ltd., Montego Bay (tel. 953-2180), has facilities at Rose Hall and Cariblue Beach for visitors interested in scuba-diving, either on a beginner basis or as an experienced diver. Snorkeling and other water sports, including waterskiing, are offered. Cruises aboard the M/V *Princess* are available for those who don't want to work too hard, although you can snorkel, swim, waterski, and parasail during the cruise if you wish. Trips to Negril and a dinner cruise are on the program.

The **Negril Scuba Centre,** at the Negril Beach Club Hotel (tel. 957-4220), is operated by a U.S. midwesterner, Karen McCarthy, whose staff of licensed instructors and divemasters teach and supervise.

The **Sans Souci Hotel & Club,** Ocho Rios (tel. 974-2353), has an active program of scuba-diving, snorkeling, paddleboating, waterskiing, sailing, and windsurfing, with jet-skiing and parasailing added if you wish.

Many hotels offer some of the water sports cited above free to their guests. In general, prices are as listed below.

Waterskiing: It costs about $12 for a 20-minute ski run, and many hotels have training facilities. Apply locally.

A Sunfish: Many hotels and some public beaches have Sunfish sailboats for rent at about $10 per hour. Hotels with their own fleets will charge less.

Snorkeling: Equipment is available in many places, for $8 to $12 per day.

Windsurfing: Some hotels have boards for windsurfing available. Expect to pay about $35 for a day, including a basic lesson on the spot.

Horseback Riding

The best riding is in Ocho Rios, where **Prospect Plantation** (tel. 974-2058) provides horses and guides. Montego Bay has a number of stables in the area: the **Good Hope** (tel. 954-2289), inland from Falmouth at Trelawny, is the best.

Also good is the program at **Rocky Point Stables,** Half Moon Club, Montego Bay (tel. 952-1526), offering trail rides and riding lessons.

An international show-jumping champion, **Mrs. Goodwin,** lives at Godfrey Lands, close to Mandeville, where horseback riding and instruction can be arranged. For information, ask Westway Enterprises Ltd., 62 Ward Ave. (P.O. Box 60), Mandeville (tel. 962-3265).

Tennis

Most hotels have their own courts, many floodlit for night games. If your hotel does not have a court, expect to pay about $6 to $8 per hour at the local country club.

All-Jamaica Hardcourt Championships are played in August at the **Manchester Club,** 1 Caledonia Rd., Mandeville (tel. 962-2403). The courts are open for other play the rest of the year. Overseas membership costs $50 per year, November 1 to October 31.

Deep-Sea Fishing

North Jamaica waters are world-renowned for their gamefish, including dolphin, wahoo, blue and white marlin, sailfish, tarpon, Allison tuna, barracuda, and bonito. The Jamaica International Fishing Tournament and Jamaica International Blue Marlin Team Tournaments run concurrently at Port Antonio every September or October. Most major hotels from Port Antonio to Montego Bay have deep-sea fishing facilities, and there are many charter boats.

At Port Antonio, **Coral Baby** (tel. 993-3086) takes out up to six persons for $160 per half day, $300 per day.

Seaworld Resorts Ltd., in Montego Bay (tel. 953-2180), operates flying-bridge cruisers, with deck lines and outriggers, for fishing expeditions. A half-day fishing trip costs $260.

At Ocho Rios, the **Sans Souci Hotel & Club** (tel. 974-2353) offers deep-sea fishing for $250 for six persons.

1. Kingston

Kingston, the largest English-speaking city in the Caribbean, is the capital of Jamaica, with a population of some 587,000 people living on the plains between Blue Mountain and the sea.

The buildings are a mixture of very modern, graceful old, and plain ramshackle. It's a busy city, as you might expect, with a natural harbor which is the seventh largest in the world. The University of the West Indies has its campus on the edge of the city. The cultural center of Jamaica is here, along with industry, finance, and government. Now covering some 40 square miles, the city was founded by the survivors of the 1692 Port Royal earthquake, and in 1872 it became the capital, superseding Spanish Town.

WHERE TO STAY: Kingston has accommodations in all price ranges, but I'll begin with—

The Leading Hotels

Security-conscious Kingston now provides all leading hotels with guards, not unlike the deluxe apartments in New York.

Wyndham Hotel New Kingston, 85 Knutsford Blvd., P.O. Box 112 (tel. 926-5430, or toll free 800/822-4200, 800/631-4200 in Canada), rises in an imposing mass of pink-colored stucco pierced with oversize sheets of tinted glass. Each unit has a white metal balcony, emphasizing to viewers the distinctive rose tint (the designers call it "Wyndham Red Rock") that is the trademark of the Wyndham hotel chain. The $8-million property renovation added scores of improvements. The first thing guests are likely to notice in the reception area, aside from the white marble floors, is the oak paneling and the most beautiful jungle mural in the country, set above the computerized desk where a staff of well-trained, uniformed clerks made check-in easy. On the premises is a gathering place called the Rendezvous Bar where live entertainment is presented in a setting of live plants and soft lights, and a disco called the Jonkanoo Lounge (see "Kingston After Dark," below). The designers of the hotel included lots of extras. The engineers have added an on-site generator, activated during the occasional city power failure. The hotel contains around 400 rooms, three restaurants, four bars, an Olympic-size swimming pool, floodlit tennis courts, a fully equipped health club, and all the amenities to make what was a commercial hotel into an inner-city resort. Each of the bedrooms and suites contains cable TV. Units capable of accommodating from one to two persons are priced from $145 and $170 daily, while suites usually begin at $200 per night. An additional person can stay in any double room for an extra $25 per night, while children under 18 stay free in their parents' room. MAP can be arranged for an additional $30 per person per day. Use of the tennis courts is free daily until 4 p.m., after which they rent for $12 per hour.

The **Jamaica Pegasus,** 81 Knutsford Blvd. (tel. 926-3690, 212/541-4400 in New York City, or toll free 800/223-5672 in the U.S. and Toronto), a Trusthouse Forte hotel, is a favorite with commercial travelers, lying in the banking and a fine residential area of Kingston. After its major renovation it is better than ever, and is the site of many conventions and social events. It competes with panache with any other hotel in town, combining English style with Jamaican warmth. Its 4 p.m. tea service at the Pavilion Restaurant is considered a bit of a social event among some residents. The hotel was built in an international style of milk-white walls, soaring heights, and repetitive balconies exposed on two sides to the sea and land. The latest incarnation of its frequently refurbished lobby is a mixture of colonial Victorian, ethnic Jamaican, and Moorish.

The hotel also makes an effort to provide vacation-related activities which in theory exist only in a resort. A jogging track, health club, tennis courts, an outdoor pool, and a staff willing to arrange water sports and sightseeing help the hotel compete for the vacationers' business. Each of its 350 well-furnished bedrooms is air-conditioned, containing satellite-connected color TV, coffee-making equipment, phone, radio, and private bath. Year-round rates for single or double occupancy cost $140 to $165 daily, plus tax and service. Several floors of luxuriously appointed suites from the Knutsford Club, with special executive services. The Talk of the Town restaurant on the 17th floor is one of the most dramatic in town, and for a change of pace, the Surrey Tavern serves pub lunches and good beer.

Hotel Oceana, corner of King Street and Ocean Boulevard, P.O. Box 986, (tel. 922-0920, or toll free 800/526-2422). Traditionally considered a well-managed commercial hotel, the Oceana has competed for the resort market since its lavish refurbishment in 1986. It occupies an oceanfront neighborhood filled with prominent business and government buildings, a few steps from the cruise-ship piers in Kingston's harbor.

Rising 12 imposing stories, the hotel offers an array of vacation-oriented facilities in spite of its location in the center of town. It has a ten-sided freshwater swimming pool ringed with modern verandas and shingle-capped pavilions, a health club popular with the capital's weightlifters, and a staff who organize water sports, golfing, and tennis. Laundry, Telex services, newsstands, a hairdresser and barbershop, and an in-house drugstore provide big-city-hotel type services. The stylish and popular Fort Charles restaurant is reviewed separately. A lobby-level bar, which converts to an evening disco, combines navy-blue murals of 18th-century Jamaican life with cool jazz and tall drinks. The hotel is physically connected to Jamaica's largest and most modern conference center, and consequently houses delegates from the frequent international meetings conducted next door. Year-round rates range from $80 to $100 per night, single or double. Each of the comfortable air-conditioned bedrooms is freshly painted in shades of peach and pink.

The Courtleigh, 31 Trafalgar Rd. (tel. 926-8174), one of my favorite hotels in Kingston, is housed in a symmetrical, white-painted, two-story building that sprawls amid a flowering garden set back from the busy street. Jamaican owned, the establishment contains a covered reception area with no exterior walls, a plantation-inspired series of verandas and gardens, and extended balconied wings containing the pleasant, simple accommodations. The central core of all this is the flower-bordered pool area, sheltered from the suburbs outside by the hotel as well as by shrubs and trees which a team of gardeners works hard to maintain. Being here strongly evokes plantation living in the middle of Kingston. The polite and charming staff, dressed in red waistcoats, black bow ties, and black trousers, will usher you down open-air hallways to your comfortable room, opening in most cases onto a view of the flowering patio, the pool area, and the bar and restaurant. On the premises is a popular disco, Mingles (see "Kingston After Dark," below), and the recommended Plantation Restaurant (see "Where to Dine"). The price year round for the pleasant rooms, each of which has a modern veranda or balcony of its own, a private bath, air conditioning, and a phone, is $65 for a single or double.

Small Budget Hotels

Terra Nova Hotel, 17 Waterloo Rd. (tel. 926-2211), is a gem among small, independently run hotels. Built in 1924 as a wedding present for a young bride, the house has had a varied career. It was once the family seat of the Myers rum dynasty, and the birthplace and home of Christopher Blackwell, promoter of many Jamaican singers and musical groups, among which were Bob Marley and the Wailers and Millie Small. In 1959 the house was converted into a hotel, and, set in 2½ acres of well-kept gardens with a backdrop of greenery and mountains, is now considered one of the best small Jamaican hotels. There is a swimming pool behind the hotel. You arrive at the colonial-style house by following a sweeping driveway, to be greeted in the cool reception area and led to your well-equipped, simply furnished, air-conditioned bedroom. Most of the 33 bedrooms are in a new wing. All have balconies or patios looking out onto the gardens. Year-round tariffs are the same in a single or double, ranging from $75 to $90 daily, plus service and tax. Your à la carte breakfast is served on the balcony or in the dining room. Above the portico is a balcony roof bar. The Spanish-style dining room, a fairly recent addition to the old building, with a stone floor, wide windows, and spotless linens, offers some of the best international food on the island (see "Where to Dine").

The **Indies Hotel,** 5 Holborn Rd. (tel. 926-2952), is set in one of the small side streets of New Kingston opening onto a flower garden. The pleasant, half-timbered building with double gables has a small reception area decorated with potted plants, a lounge, and a TV lounge. The bedrooms, restaurant, and bar are grouped around a cool patio, all spotless. The 16 rooms go year round for $20 to $35 daily in a single, $33 to $42 in a double. All have shower and toilet and are air-conditioned. Breakfast is

$3.50. Ike Shaw, a Canadian, and his wife, Jean, a Jamaican, have operated the hotel for some 20 years. They have built up a reputation among the locals for friendly atmosphere and good-quality, budget meals. Their fish and chips is renowned, although Jean claims that their specialty is pizza. They also serve steak with all the trimmings, and when they get fancy, prepare lobster Thermidor.

Hotel Four Seasons, 18 Ruthven Rd. (tel. 926-8805), is a nice old house with a colonial-style veranda along the front, looking onto mango trees and a pleasant wooded garden through which you drive. There is good car parking, and you enter through the columns of the veranda to the reception and dining areas of this friendly hotel. The rooms are simple and air-conditioned, each having a phone, color TV, and a private bath or shower. Year round they rent for $37 to $45 daily for a single, $45 to $50 for a double, EP. All meals are served to both hotel guests and outsiders, either on the terrace or in the formal dining room. Monday to Friday, a buffet lunch has an interesting selection of hot dishes, vegetable salads, and desserts. The hotel has two bars (one inside, one out). There is an arrangement for swimming at one of the large hotels nearby.

A Hostel on the Outskirts

Up Blue Mountain, for back-to-nature buffs and backpackers, is **Whitfield Hall,** a hostel and coffee property about six miles from Mavis Bank. Usually people drive to Mahogany Vale, leave their cars in the field of a friendly farmer, and walk or use a Land Rover for J$80 ($15.20) each way. The last four miles are rough and steep. Whitfield Hall is an old coffee plantation house, and is the last inhabited house before the peak, some 4,000 feet above sea level. It's a hostel, providing accommodations for some 30 persons, in rooms containing two or more beds. Blankets and linen are provided, but no personal items such as towels, soap, or food. There is a deep-freeze and a refrigerator as well as good cooking facilities, crockery, and cutlery. All water comes from a freshwater spring, and all lighting is by kerosene pressure lamps (called Tilleys). Wood fires warm the hostel and its guests, for it gets cold in the mountains at night. The charge per night is $6 per person all year. You bring your own food and share the communal kitchen. You can stay here for one night, one week, or if you really want to get away from it all, for longer.

Most visitors tend to aim for seeing the sunrise from the summit of Blue Mountain, which means getting up at around 2 to 3 a.m. to walk the additional 3,402 feet to the summit along bridle paths through the forest. The route is clearly marked, and all you really need is a good flashlight and warm clothing to go with your hiking boots or strong shoes. It's a three-hour walk each way. It is possible to hire a mule or horse to make the jaunt, accompanied by a guide, for approximately J$60 ($11.40) round trip for the 13-mile journey. It is quite possible to spend a week or more in the mountains, just walking to see the vast variety of flowers and trees, the largest number of different varieties of ferns in the world, to listen to the crickets, and to watch the birds. There are many trails, and the hostel has information on various routes to take. However, for those who are apprehensive (people have been lost in these mountains), it is possible to arrange for a guide, negotiable locally.

For reservations at the hostel, information, or a brochure, write or phone John Allgrove, 8 Armon Jones Crescent, Kingston 6 (tel. 922-4759, office; 927-0986, home).

Staying at Port Royal

Morgan's Harbour Hotel, Beach Club, and Marina, Port Royal (tel. 924-8464). Near the end of a long sandpit sheltering the harbor of Kingston, this low-slung resort lies within a five-minute walk of the ramshackle town of Port Royal. To reach it, you can take a sometimes-reliable ferryboat from Victoria Pier at Ocean Boulevard in Kingston or a taxi past the airport and along a narrow peninsula between the bay and open sea. Guests register in a colonial-inspired lobby filled with carved reproductions of mahogany settees and ornate brass chandeliers. The establishment's 18 accommodations encircle a flowering courtyard whose edge abuts the sea. Each unit contains two double beds, a private bath, a ceiling fan, air conditioning, and mahogany furniture in a wide range of styles. In winter, singles cost $60 to $70 daily; doubles, $75 to $85. *In summer, singles go for $48 to $55 daily; doubles, $60 to $70*. MAP can be arranged for another $25 per person daily, and children under 12 stay free when sharing a room with an adult.

Swimmers bathe within the shelter of a stone-and-concrete jetty, which calms the waves surging in from the bay. The hotel offers marina facilities which were upgraded in 1983, a waterside open-air bar shaped like an octagonal cabaña, and a wood-lined restaurant. The hotel is best known by music lovers for its regular concerts which it hosts from a bandstand on the grounds. When this occurs (at regular and widely publicized intervals), as many as 2,000 show up. On other occasions, musical entertainment is provided for guests in the evening. During the day, guests can rent Sunfish or go on scuba and snorkeling trips from the hotel's pier.

WHERE TO DINE: Kingston has a good range of places to eat, whether you're seeking stately meals in plantation houses, hotel buffets, or fast-food shops.

Blue Mountain Inn (tel. 927-3606) is about a 20-minute drive from downtown Kingston, an 18th-century coffee plantation house set on the slopes of Blue Mountain, surrounded by trees and flowers on the bank of the Mammee River. At night, fireflies add their lights to the stars while you relax on the verandas overlooking the river below and the floodlit forest beyond. The house is furnished with fine antiques, set off by the plain white walls. On cold nights, log fires blaze, and the dining room gleams with silver and sparkling glass under the discreet table lights. The inn is one of Jamaica's most famous restaurants, not only for food but for atmosphere and service. Men are required to wear jackets (ties are optional), but the effort is worth it and the cool night air justifies it. Women are advised to take a wrap. Menus change monthly and feature dishes of the Caribbean, fresh seafood, and U.S. steaks. All are served with a selection of fresh vegetables. Top off your meal with tropical fruit salad and cream, Tía Maria parfait, baked Alaska, or a more ambitious banana or pineapple flambé. The wine list includes European varieties together with local beverages. A complete meal costs about $35. Reservations are essential, as it is popular all year. Go between 7 and 9 p.m.

In Devon House, 26 Hope Rd., is the National Picture Gallery. Beside the lovely old house is the restaurant, the **Port Royal Grogg Shoppe** (tel. 926-3580), with its weathered swinging sign, open for lunch, dinner, morning coffee, and snacks. You can eat on patios under the trees, in sight of the royal palms and the fountain in front of the main building. The terraces are called either "mango" or "mahogany." Your meal will have a traditional Jamaican character, and the bar serves 11 different rum punches and 10 fruit punches, such as a tamarind fizz or a papaya (paw-paw) punch. Snacks include coffee and sandwiches. Lunch, from noon to 3 p.m., offers appetizers, among them a "tidbit" of jerk pork or a bowl of soup (perhaps Jamaican red pea—really bean—or pumpkin soup). The cost of the meal, ranging from J$40 ($7.60) to J$75 ($14.25), will depend on your selection, either a sandwich and soup or a complete hot meal. Main dishes include offerings such as Jamaican akee and salt fish, barbecued chicken, or steamed snapper. Also tasty are their unusual homemade ice creams made of local fruits such as soursop. Blue Mountain tea or coffee is also served, and a 10% service charge is added to all bills. The waiters, who are dressed like pirates, serve daily except Sunday from 9 a.m. to midnight.

Restaurant d'Amore, Hotel Wyndham New Kingston (tel. 926-5430). Set beneath the soaring ceiling of the hotel's 17th floor, the restaurant's huge windows encompass a sweeping view of Kingston. The plush interior includes many of the colonial trappings of Old Jamaica, including a polite staff in uniforms and white gloves, a discreet pianist, copies of French armchairs, and polished crystal. You can enjoy drinks at the horseshoe-shaped bar before heading to your table, where menu specialties include an array of Italian and international dishes. Your meal might begin with one of the establishment's more imaginative pastas, such as spaghetti with sautéed chicken breast, three colors of pasta with crabmeat, or pasta shells with squid and tomato sauce. Other items include risotto with chicken breast, filet of beef with oysters, medallions of pork with river shrimp in an exotic sauce, broiled kebab of jumbo shrimp, fricassée of dover sole with fresh mushrooms, stuffed crab with a frozen lime mousse, and desserts from the trolley. Full meals cost from J$150 ($28.50) and are served at dinner only, between 7 p.m. and 1 a.m. nightly except Monday. Reservations are suggested, as well as jackets for men.

Norma, 8 Belmont Rd. (tel. 929-4966), has a sophisticated cuisine and an open-air setting. It was established by Norma Shirley after a return to her native Jamaica from a 20-year residency in the Massachusetts Berkshires. The cuisine is an imaginative collection of creative recipes accumulated from throughout the world, each of which is strongly influenced by nouvelle cuisine. She holds forth in the rear garden of an unpretentious private house in Kew Kingston, about a five-minute drive from the Pegasus Hotel. Acrylic stripes of electric blue and gray wrap themselves around a veranda, where immaculate napery is complemented with bouquets of seasonal flowers. The parsley, thyme, and oregano used in many dishes was cultivated in a garden behind a screen of ficus. Assisted by a trio of friends, Ms. Shirley serves only lunch, between noon and 3 p.m. except Sunday. (The only dinner served is on the last Friday of each month when a classical guitarist is present.) Full meals cost from J$120 ($22.80) to J$175 ($33.25), consisting of menu items written on a blackboard. They might include fettuccine with chicken and shrimp, broccoli bisque, avocado stuffed with tuna, grilled baby lamb chops, and a fresh salad of the day. Reservations are suggested, because the place seems to be one of the preferred luncheon stopovers for a community of artists and gallery owners.

Terra Nova Hotel Restaurant, 17 Waterloo Rd. (tel. 926-9334), in one of the choice small hotels of Kingston, welcomes an enthusiastic crowd of local business people and other dignitaries at mealtimes into a formal dining room. It's owned by Jamaican brothers, Peter and Pat Rousseau, who refurbished the restaurant's Hepplewhite chairs, terracotta walls, high ceilings, and lattice-bordered windows. The palatial dining room was at one time the family headquarters of a large private home. The grounds once included stables, but acres of land and buildings have gradually been sold off to accommodate the encroaching sprawl of Kingston. Today the grandeur of the portico, the elaborate moldings of the hotel reception area, and the restaurant are souvenirs of the affluent one-time owners. The dining room serves a combination of international and Jamaican specialties, with emphasis on fish and shellfish dishes. These include mixed grill, pepper steak, lobster Thermidor, West Indian fish chowder, seafood platters, and baked crab. The chef is also noted for his flambé dishes and his fondues. Complete lunches cost from around J$65 ($12.35), while dinners average J$125 ($23.75) per person.

The **Plantation Terrace,** in the Courtleigh Hotel, 31 Trafalgar Rd. (tel. 926-8174), is a pleasant place to dine and escape from the traffic of Kingston. Meals are served under a covered parapet lined with tropical plants near an outdoor cabaña-style poolside bar. Seated on iron armchairs you'll enjoy à la carte breakfasts, Sunday-night barbecues, Wednesday Jamaican evenings, and popular lunches and dinners. The other guests may include a scattering of business people as well as the employees of the American and Australian consulates nearby. The uniformed staff will serve such specialties as pepperpot soup, lobster Thermidor, shrimp sauté, filet of fish including red snapper and grouper, chicken suprême, chicken gumbo, pork piccata, surf and turf, chicken Cordon Bleu, baked crab backs, and many other dishes which vary according to the culinary culture being emphasized on a particular evening. There's even an occasional Chinese specialty, as well as Jamaican dishes of akee and codfish, hog's tail, and stewed beef served on Wednesday. Complete dinners begin at J$65 ($12.35), while lunches are slightly less expensive. Full Jamaican breakfasts are served even to nonresidents for J$15 ($2.85). The restaurant, which sometimes has live music in the evening, is open seven days a week: 7 to 10 a.m., noon to 3 p.m., and 7 to 11 p.m.

The **Jamaica Pegasus Hotel,** 81 Knutsford Blvd. (tel. 926-3690), offers gourmet dining in its rooftop Talk of the Town restaurant from an à la carte menu which features an excellent four-course meal at about J$125 ($23.75). Discreet, attentive service is provided. Main dishes include red snapper in lime butter or grilled lobster in garlic butter, preceded by smoked salmon or pepperpot soup. It is open from 7 p.m. to 1 a.m. nightly, providing entertainment. Le Pavillon features nouvelle cuisine and is open Monday to Friday from 12:30 to 3 p.m. (on Saturday from noon to 6 p.m.). For snacks, high tea, cakes, or pastries, the Café Orangerie at the Pavillon is open Monday to Friday from 11 a.m. to 8 p.m. In short, there's something to suit everyone's taste.

The **Surrey Tavern,** beside and part of the Jamaica Pegasus (tel. 926-3690), with its own entrance, is a pub-style place with wooden tables and chairs, low lighting, and a long, wood-paneled bar in the English tradition. At lunchtime noon to 3 p.m., a cold pub buffet is served, featuring a daily hot special. Meals cost from J$10 ($1.90). Enjoy a long glass of cold draft beer while tapping to a jazz beat. The pub is closed on Sunday.

Fort Charles Restaurant, in the Oceana Hotel (tel. 922-0920), is open seven days a week from 7 a.m. until 11 p.m. You can use it as a coffeeshop-style place for a quick snack or else as a more formal restaurant. Lunches cost from J$50 ($9.50). You can order a cold roast beef open-face sandwich. There is also barbecued chicken, and the more exotic lobster Thermidor, seafood Newburg, or rock lobster. From 7 p.m., the dinner menu includes a variety of appetizers, soups, steaks, and other meat dishes in addition to the daytime menu. Oceana seafood lasagne is a specialty, and you can also order such dishes as steamed filet of snapper in coconut milk and pork piccata. Their steaks are called the juiciest in town. Depending on your selection of a main course, dinner prices will begin at J$80 ($15.20) and range upward.

Pirate's Cove, Victoria Pier, Ocean Boulevard (tel. 922-3129). Originally built as a private club, this second-story restaurant sits near in the ocean in a cement-sided pavilion accented with swashbuckling murals. Polite waiters wearing red cummerbunds, black trousers, and white shirts serve satisfying seafood meals daily from noon to 4 p.m. and 5 to 9 p.m. Lunches cost from J$75 ($14.25); dinners, from J$100 ($19). Specialties include lobster Thermidor, catch of the day "anyway," stuffed baked crab, conch fritters, and chicken simmered in pineapple sauce. The place is especially well known for its daiquiris, either frozen or plain, concocted from such tropical fruits as lime, papaya, bananas, and strawberries. The location is in a greenbelt near the Oceana Hotel.

The **Indies Pub and Grill,** 8 Holborn Rd. (tel. 926-2952), was designed around a garden terrace, which on hot nights is the best place to sit. Of course, you can always go into the inner rooms, which are haphazardly but pleasantly decorated with caribou horns, tortoise shells, half-timbered walls, an aquarium sometimes stocked with baby sharks, and even a Canadian moosehead. The establishment offers a full sandwich menu at lunchtime. In the evening you can enjoy grilled lobster, fish and chips, barbecued quail, chicken Kiev, or roast beef. You can eat here for about J$45 ($8.50) and up every day of the week from 11 a.m. to 1 a.m.

The **Hot Pot,** 2 Altamont Ave. (tel. 929-3906). Concealed behind a group of large apartment buildings in a residential section of Kingston, this place appears like little more than a simple concrete-sided house. Actually, it's known for its authentic Jamaican food, served in copious quantities in aggressively simple surroundings. Raymond Malcolm, the cooperative manager, serves breakfast and lunch daily except

Sunday from 8 a.m. to 6 p.m. Your meal might include akee with saltfish, callaloo with saltfish, fried cow's liver, oxtail, cow's foot, stewed pork, pork chops, pepperpot soup, chicken soup, and well-prepared versions of the catch of the day. Expect to pay J$75 ($14.25) for a meal.

Chelsea Jerk Centre, Chelsea Avenue (tel. 926-6322). You might at first think this is only an industrial building, set noncommitally between the New Kingston Shopping Centre and the Wyndham New Kingston Hotel. What you'll discover, however, is the city's most popular provider of the Jamaican delicacy known as jerk pork and jerk chicken. Don't expect formality, or even a traditional dining room. There are, it's true, a handful of rustic picnic tables on the asphalt parking lot, but most clients order their food to take away and eat elsewhere, often on the beach. The place is open daily except Sunday from 11:30 a.m. to 2 a.m. A half pound of jerk pork or chicken costs from J$13 ($2.45). You might also order a side portion of what the scrawled blackboard refers to as "Festival," which is fried corn-meal dumplings.

WHAT TO SEE: Even if you're staying at one of the resorts, such as Montego Bay or Ocho Rios, you may want to come into Kingston for sightseeing, and for visits to nearby Port Royal and Spanish Town.

Devon House, 26 Hope Rd., was built in 1881 by George Stiebel, a Jamaican who, after mining in South America, became one of the first black millionaires in the Caribbean. A striking building of classical style, the house has been restored to its original beauty by the Jamaican National Trust. The grounds contain craft shops, boutiques, and a museum of African art and history. The main house also displays furniture of various periods and styles. The former coach house is now the Port Royal Grogg Shoppe (described earlier). Admission to Devon House is J$5 (95¢). The house is open daily from 10 a.m. to 5 p.m., except Sunday.

Almost next door to Devon House are the sentried gates of **Jamaica House,** residence of the prime minister, a fine, white-columned building set well back from the road.

Continuing along Hope Road, at the crossroads of Lady Musgrave Road and King's House Road, turn left and you'll see a gate on the left with its own personal traffic light. This leads to **King's House,** the official residence of the governor-general of Jamaica, the queen's representative on the island. The gracious residence, set in 200 acres of well-tended parkland, is open to view from 10 a.m. to 5 p.m. Monday to Friday. The secretarial offices are housed next door in an old wooden building set on brick arches. In front of the house is a gigantic banyan tree in whose roots, legend says, *duppies* (as ghosts are called in Jamaica) take refuge when they are not living in the cotton trees.

On Old Hope Road, behind the Colleges of Arts, Science, and Technology, are the **Hope Botanical Gardens** (tel. 927-1257), occupying 60 acres on the grounds of the Hope Sugar Estate. It was one of the three largest estates in this area. The others are King's House and the University of the West Indies. The aqueduct constructed in 1759 still brings water to the gardens and augments the city's supply. The pride of the gardens is the fine orchid house containing specimens of some 200 native Jamaican species. There are a cactus garden and more than 600 different types of trees, including an impressive palm avenue, flowering trees, fruit trees, and creepers. For those interested in the plants, a guide is available to escort you and answer your questions. The guide's services are free, as is admission to the gardens, but it is the practice to tip. A quick tour will take about an hour. You may find that you prefer to wander along the tree-lined paths among the flowers and listen to the incessant chirping of the birds hidden in the leaves. A fountain was constructed just to the front of the Palm Avenue, and several picnic structures were set up. The gardens are open from 8:30 a.m. to 6:30 p.m.

Coconut Park Funland (tel. 927-1076) is in Hope Gardens and next to the zoo. The establishment is owned and operated by the Polio Foundation and the Jamaica

Association for Mentally Handicapped Children. The frontal canteen and the land on which the other buildings stand, as well as the zoo, belong to the Ministry of Agriculture. The two charities lease the funland and buildings, while the ministry owns and operates the zoo. Admission to Funland is J$1 (20¢) for adults, J$.50 (10¢) for children, and eight rides cost J$1.50 (30¢). The canteen is open from 10 a.m. to 5 p.m. daily. The gates to the rides open at noon and close at 5 p.m.

Between Old Hope Road and Mona Road, a short distance from the Botanic Gardens, is the **University of the West Indies,** built in 1948 on the Mona Sugar Estate, the third of the large estates in this area. Ruins of old mills, storehouses, and aqueducts are jostled by the modern buildings on what must be the most beautifully situated campus in the world. The chapel, an old sugar factory building, was transported stone by stone from Trelawny and rebuilt on the campus close to the old sugar factory, the remains of which are well preserved and give a good idea of how sugar was made in slave days.

The **National Stadium,** Briggs Park, of which Jamaica is justly proud, has an aluminum statue of Arthur Wint, national athlete, at the entrance. The stadium is used for such activities as soccer, field sports, and cycling, and in 1966 was the site of the Commonwealth Games. Beside the stadium is the **National Arena,** used for indoor sports, exhibitions, and concerts, and there is an Olympic-size pool. Admission prices vary according to activities.

In downtown Kingston, if you go north on King Street, you come to Upper King Street and **National Heroes Park,** formerly known as George VI Memorial Park. This was the old Kingston race course. An assortment of large office blocks, including the offices of the prime minister and various ministries, overlooks the park and the statues of Simón Bolívar, and of George Gordon and Paul Bogle, martyrs of the Morant Bay revolt. Sir Donald Sangster, Norman Manley, and Alexander Bustamante, national heroes of Jamaica, are buried here.

Just north of Heroes Park, on Marescaux Road, is **Mico College** (tel. 929-5260), for "lady" training. Lacy Mico, a rich London widow, left her fortune to a favorite nephew on the condition that he marry one of her six nieces. He did not, and the inheritance was invested, the interest being used to ransom victims of the Barbary pirates. With the end of piracy in the early 19th century, it was decided that the capital would be devoted to founding schools for newly emancipated slaves, and, among others, Mico College was established.

The central administrative offices of the **Institute of Jamaica,** founded in 1879, are between 12 and 16 East St. (tel. 922-0620), in close proximity to the harbor. Open from 8:30 a.m. to 5 p.m. Monday to Thursday, to 4 p.m. on Friday, the institute fosters and encourages the development of culture, science, and history in the national interest. The institute has responsibility for the following divisions and organizations, only some of which are at the East Street headquarters: a Junior Centre, the Natural History Division (which is the repository of the national collection of flora and fauna), and the National Library. Those located elsewhere are the Cultural Training Centre, 1 Arthur Wint Dr., with schools of music, dance, art, and drama; the African-Caribbean Institute, 12 Ocean Blvd.; which conducts research on cultural heritage; the Museums Division, with sites in Port Royal and Spanish Town, which have the responsibility for the display of artifacts of relevance to the history of Jamaica; the National Gallery, 12 Ocean Blvd.; and the Institute of Jamaica Publications Ltd., 2A Suthermere Rd., which publishes a quarterly, the *Jamaica Journal,* as well as other works of educational and cultural merit.

The **National Library of Jamaica** (formerly the West India Reference Library), Institute of Jamaica, 12-16 East St. (tel. 922-0620), a storehouse of the history, culture, and traditions of Jamaica and the Caribbean, is the finest working library for West Indian studies in the world. It has the most comprehensive, up-to-date, and balanced collection of materials, including books, photographs, maps, and prints, to be found anywhere in the Caribbean. Of special interest to visitors are the regular exhibitions which attractively and professionally highlight different aspects of Jamaica and West Indian life. It is open Monday to Friday from 9 a.m. to 4:30 p.m.

Tuff Gong, 56 Hope Rd. (tel. 927-9152), is said to be the most-visited sight in Kingston, although unless you're a Bob Marley fan, it may not mean much to you. The clapboard house with its garden and high surrounding wall was Marley's home and recording studio until his death. Since then, its function has changed several times. It contains rehearsal space for local musicians trying to develop the musical ideas Marley made famous to reggae lovers around the world. If you want a glimpse of the house, you pass through a heavily guarded iron gate where you describe your purpose in coming. Admission is J$7 ($1.35) for adults, J$5 (95¢) for children. It's open daily from 9 a.m. to 5 p.m.

SHOPPING: Downtown Kingston, the old part of the town, is centered around Victoria Park, a walled, nondescript park of little interest, overpowered by the bustling main shopping area of **King Street** and by the heavy, fast-moving traffic on all four sides. King Street runs north from the harbor.

Here you will find covered walkways, with peddlers at small stands selling anything from cooked shrimp and melon slices to cool drinks, cigarettes, chocolates, fruit, matches, and anything else they can find a buyer for. The sidewalks are shaded from the sun by light roofs from which hang a variety of intriguingly worded advertisements and swinging signs: Hanna's Hub, Ready-Made Dresses; Golly Trotters, and Garment People; Buzzers Impossible, Closing-Down Sale (which has been going on for years); Cosmetologist Hair-Stylist; Men's Shop 79½.

Cool arcades lead off from the main street, but everywhere there is a teeming mass of people going about their business. There are some beggars and the inevitable salesmen who sidle up and offer "hot stuff, man," frequently highly polished brass lightly dipped in gold and offered at high prices as real gold. The hucksters do accept a polite but firm "no," but don't let them keep you talking or you'll end up buying. They are very persuasive!

On this street are the General Post Office, the Law Courts, and the bus terminal.

New Kingston Shopping Centre, New Kingston, is one of the most modern shopping centers in Jamaica, known more for its assemblage of merchandise than for any particular merchant. Sleek, contemporary, and stylish, it offers boutiques centered around a Mayan-style pyramid, down the sides of which cascades of water irrigate trailing bougainvillea. Fast-food stores, ice-cream stands, whatever, are also found here.

Sangster's Old Jamaica Spirits, 17 Holborn Rd. (tel. 926-8888), has a full array of unusual rum-based liqueurs available in this well-scrubbed factory outlet on a side street off the modern uptown New Kingston business area. The entrance isn't well marked, but once you enter the showroom, you know from the hundreds of bottles on display that you're in a rum lovers' mecca. The prices vary, based on the quality and size of the container, not on the contents. You can pay from J$26 ($4.95) to J$76 ($14.45) for such tempting flavors as coconut rum (my personal favorite); coffee-orange, wild orange, ortanique, pimento dram, and Blue Mountain coffee liqueurs; 100% rum; and their latest product, Gold Rum Cream. The store is open Monday to Friday from 8:30 a.m. to 4:30 p.m. There's a large trolley filled with samples of the various rums and liqueurs which you can sample from small cups before you buy.

Kingston Crafts Market, at the west end of Harbour Street, is a large, covered area of small stalls individually owned, reached through such thoroughfares as Straw Avenue, Drummer's Lane, and Cheapside. All kinds of island crafts products are on sale: wooden plates and bowls, trays, ashtrays, and pepperpots made from mahoe, the national wood of the island. Straw hats, mats, baskets are also on display. Batik shirts and cotton shirts with gaudy designs are sold. Banners for wall decoration are inscribed with the Jamaican coat-of-arms, and wood masks often have elaborately

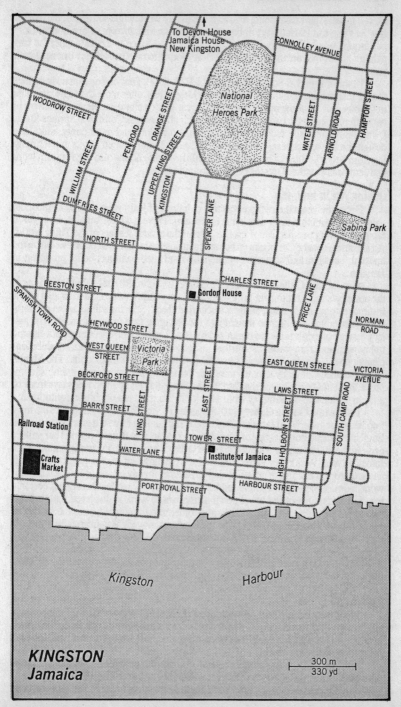

To Devon House
Jamaica House
New Kingston

CONNOLLEY AVENUE

National
Heroes Park

WOODROW STREET

WILLIAM STREET

PEN ROAD

ORANGE STREET

UPPER KING STREET

KINGSTON

DUMFRIES STREET

NORTH STREET

SPENCER LANE

WATER STREET

ARNOLD ROAD

HAMPTON STREET

Sabina Park

BEESTON STREET

SPANISH TOWN ROAD

CHARLES STREET

■ Gordon House

PRICE LANE

NORMAN
ROAD

HEYWOOD STREET

WEST QUEEN
STREET

Victoria
Park

BECKFORD STREET

EAST QUEEN STREET

VICTORIA
AVENUE

BARRY STREET

KING STREET

EAST STREET

LAWS STREET

HIGH HOLBORN STREET

SOUTH CAMP ROAD

■
Railroad Station

■
Crafts
Market

WATER LANE

TOWER STREET

■ Institute of Jamaica

PORT ROYAL STREET

HARBOUR STREET

Kingston   *Harbour*

KINGSTON
Jamaica

300 m
330 yd

carved faces. Apart from being a good place to buy worthwhile souvenirs, the market is where you can learn the art of bargaining and ask for a *brawta,* a free bonus. Only pay around one-half to two-thirds of the asking price, since to the stallholder the bargaining is half the fun and is expected. Don't forget to take your *dunny* (money) with you.

Fashion Whirl, 3 Southdale Plaza (tel. 929-4202). Drawing on Jamaican themes for her inspiration, fashion designer Elaine Dreyer has, after more than a dozen years in the business, become one of the island's best-known clothiers. Her shops are set in two different shopping centers which face each other across Constance Springs Road. Using Jamaican-made fabrics, such as linen and cotton (and more rarely, silk), she designs dressy sportswear, formal wear, and a handful of women's suits in sizes ranging from 8 to 16. Much of her selection is off-the-rack, and she also does custom work and Jamaican couture. Dresses begin at around $50.

Buying Art in Jamaica

For many years the richly evocative paintings of Haiti were viewed as the most valuable contribution to the arts in the Caribbean. There is within Jamaica, however, a rapidly growing perspective of itself as one of the artistic leaders of the Third World. An articulate core of Caribbean critics are focusing the attention of the art world on the unusual, eclectic, and sometimes politically motivated paintings being produced in Jamaica.

Mutual Life Gallery, Mutual Life Centre, 2 Oxford Rd. (tel. 926-9025). One of the country's most prominent art galleries is in the corporate headquarters of a major insurance company. After you pass a security check, you can climb to the corporation's mezzanine level for an insight into the changing face of Jamaican art. The gallery's array of exhibitions are organized by Pat Ramsey, who encourages developing unknowns and showcases established artists with panache and flair. Exhibitions change once a month, but there is usually a stable of long-term exhibits. The Mutual Life Insurance Company donates the space for free as part of its own attempts to improve the status of the arts in the Caribbean. The gallery is open on weekdays from 10 a.m. to 6 p.m. and on Saturday from 11 a.m. to 3 p.m. It is a nonprofit institution.

The **Frame Centre Gallery,** 10 Tangerine Pl. (tel. 926-4644), is one of the most important art galleries in Jamaica. Its founder and guiding force is a graciously elegant English-educated connoisseur of Caribbean art. Margaret Burnall opened her gallery early in the 1970s, and is widely respected today as an honest, nurturing patron of the Jamaican arts. Within her gallery, among the changing array of some 300 paintings and sculpture, a handful of artists go daily to ask her for advice and guidance with their work. Some works can be purchased for J$180 ($34.25), while others could cost into the thousands. One of the best-known artists whose work is displayed here is Edna Manley ("the Jamaican Chagall"), whose other important role was as the mother of prime minister Norman Manley. The gallery is open weekdays from 8:30 a.m. to 5 p.m., and from 9:30 a.m. to 1 p.m. on weekends.

SIGHTS IN THE ENVIRONS: Not far from Kingston are two centers for sightseeing worth a visit—Port Royal and Spanish Town.

Port Royal

From West Beach Dock, Kingston, a J$1 (20¢) ferry ride of 20 to 30 minutes will take you to Port Royal, or you can drive west along the Palisadoes from Kingston's international airport for 13 miles between sea-pounded white beaches and saltwater mangrove swamps.

Port Royal, once the island's capital, conjures up pictures of swashbuckling pirates led by Henry Morgan, swilling grog in harbor taverns. This was once one of the largest trading centers of the New World, with a reputation of being the wickedest city on earth (Blackbeard stopped here regularly on his Caribbean trips). But the whole thing came to an end at 11:43 a.m. on June 7, 1692, when a third of the town disappeared under water as the result of a devastating earthquake. Nowadays, Port Royal, with its memories of the past, has been designated by the government for redevelopment as a tourist destination.

As you drive along the Palisadoes, you arrive first at **St. Peter's Church.** It's usually closed, but you may persuade the caretaker, who lives opposite, to open it if you want to see the silver plate, said to be spoils captured by Henry Morgan from the cathedral in Panama. In the ill-kept graveyard is the tomb of one Lewis Galdy, a Frenchman swallowed up and subsequently regurgitated by the 1692 earthquake.

You next arrive at the gates of the **Police Training Depot,** where the constable on duty will record your name and purpose. When passage is permitted, you follow the road across the edge of the parade ground to the entrance to **Fort Charles,** the only remaining one of Port Royal's six forts. It has withstood attack, earthquake, fire, and hurricane. Built in 1656 and later strengthened by Morgan for his own purposes, the fort was expanded and further armed in the 1700s, until its firepower boasted more than 100 cannons, covering both the land and the sea approaches. After subsequent earthquakes and tremors, the fort ceased to be at the water's edge and is now well inland. For a few short weeks in 1779 Horatio Nelson was commander of the fort and trod the wooden walkway inside the western parapet as he kept watch for the French invasion fleet.

Fort Charles Maritime Museum is in the former British naval headquarters where Nelson served. Scale models of the fort and ships of past eras are to be seen in the small museum. It's open from 10 a.m. to 4 p.m. Monday to Friday, to 5 p.m. on weekends. Admission is J$1 (20¢) for adults (children, free).

Giddy House, once the Royal Artillery storehouse, is another example of what earth movements can do. Walking across the tilted floor is an eerie and disturbing experience.

On the land side of the fort is the **Old Naval Hospital,** which now houses the **Archaeological Museum and Research Centre.** This building was completed in 1818 and is the oldest cast-iron prefabricated building in the western hemisphere. It contains many artifacts unearthed from digs and underwater searches around Port Royal, including a watch which had stopped at the moment of the 1692 earthquake, now in pieces, but totally authentic; a Chinese porcelain madonna, of which only three exist in the world, recovered from the sea; Spanish armor; slave shackles; and much weaponry, together with models and descriptive tableaux of the Port Royal of the past. Admission to the upstairs museum is gained by ringing the 19th-century bell for the guide. You can see such things as Prince Henry's Polygon Battery, the Old Coaling Wharf, the Jail House, and the Victoria and Albert Battery complex, not to mention the Chocolata Hole. The museum is open daily from 10 a.m. to 5 p.m. Admission is J$.50 (10¢).

Spanish Town

From 1662 to 1872 Spanish Town was the capital of the island. Originally founded by the Spaniards as Villa de la Vega, it was sacked by Cromwell's men in 1655 and all traces of papism were obliterated. The English cathedral, surprisingly retaining a Spanish name, **St. Jago de la Vega,** was built in 1666 and rebuilt after being destroyed by a hurricane in 1712. As you drive into the town from Kingston, the new cathedral, built in 1714, catches your eye, with its brick tower and two-tiered wooden steeple, which was not added until 1831. As the cathedral was built on the foundation and remains of the old Spanish church, it is half-English, half-Spanish, showing two definite styles, one Romanesque, the other Gothic.

Of cruciform design and built mostly of brick, the cathedral is historically one of the most interesting buildings on the island. The black and white marble stones of the aisles are interspersed with ancient tombstones, and the walls are heavy with marble memorials that are almost a chronicle of Jamaica's history, dating back as far as 1662. Episcopalian services are held regularly on Sunday at 7 and 10:30 a.m. and at 6:30 p.m., sometimes conducted by the bishop of Jamaica, whose see this is.

Beyond the cathedral, turn right and two blocks along you will reach Constitution Street and the **Town Square.** This delightful little square is surrounded by towering royal palms.

On the west side is **King's House,** gutted by fire in 1925 and not as yet restored because no plans, drawings, or designs of the original have been found. This was the residence of the governor-general, and many celebrated guests, among them Lord Nelson, Admiral Rodney, Captain Bligh of H.M.S. *Bounty* fame, and King William IV, have stayed here.

Behind the house is the **Jamaica People's Museum of Craft and Technology** (tel. 922-0620), open daily from 10 a.m. to 5 p.m. The garden contains examples of old farm machinery, an old water mill wheel, a hand-turned sugar mill, a coffee pulper, an old hearse, and a fire engine. An outbuilding contains a museum of crafts and technology, together with a number of smaller agricultural implements. In the small archeological museum are old prints, models (including one of King's House based on a written description), and maps of the town's grid layout from the 1700s.

On the north side of the square is the **Rodney Memorial,** perhaps the most dramatic of the buildings on the square, commissioned by a grateful assembly to commemorate the victory in 1782 of Baron George Rodney, English admiral, over the French fleet, which saved the island from invasion.

Opposite the Rodney Memorial is the **Court House,** the most recent of the four buildings. The court occupies the ground floor, and when in session, overflows onto the pavement and road, an animated throng of court attendants, defendants, witnesses, and spectators, all apparently accompanied by relatives and friends.

The final side of the square, the east, contains the most attractive building, the **House of Assembly,** with a shady brick colonnade running the length of the ground floor and above it a wooden pillared balcony. This was the stormy center of the bitter debates for Jamaica's governing body. Now the ground floor is the parish library, and council officers occupy the upper floor, along with the Mayor's Parlour.

The streets around the old Town Square contain many fine Georgian town houses intermixed with tin-roofed shacks. Nearby is the **market,** so busy in the morning you will find it difficult, almost dangerous, to drive through. It provides, however, a colorful and bustling scene of Jamaican life.

Driving to Spanish Town from Kingston on the A1 (Washington Boulevard), at Central Village you come to the **Arawak Museum,** on the right. The entrance appears to lead to a quarry, but don't be put off. Drive down to the museum, a hexagonal building on the site of one of the largest Arawak settlements on the island. It is open Monday to Friday from 10 a.m. to 5 p.m. The small, well-planned museum contains drawings, pictures, and diagrams of Arawak life, plus old flints and other artifacts which help you to understand the early history or prehistoric period of Jamaica. Smoking of tobacco seems to have been a habit even in 1518, when Arawaks were recorded as lighting hollow tubes at one end and sucking the other. The visitor can also see signs of an original Arawak settlement at White Marl, around the museum building.

KINGSTON AFTER DARK: There are safer places to be. Use caution when going out.

Nightspots

The **Red Hills Strip** in downtown Kingston has a number of nightclubs, all of which I make it a point to avoid.

Illusions, 2-4 South Ave., Lane Plaza (tel. 926-7419), is one of the most popular discos in Kingston, in spite of its unchic location in a shopping center. It has a gray-and pastel-colored decor, cast-iron Corinthian columns, mirrors, and many hi-tech accessories, along with spinning ceiling fans and Caribbean planting. It also opens for a good-value lunch on weekdays from noon to 3 p.m., costing from J$40 ($7.60) and including an array of sandwiches, salads, and barbecued pork, chicken, or beef. After a two-hour siesta, the bar reopens at 5 p.m. on weekdays, at 6 p.m. on Saturday and Sunday, remaining so until the wee hours. At night, visitors pay a cover of J$35 ($6.65) for men, J$25 ($4.75) for women. In the course of the evening the crowd changes from office workers celebrating to a late-night crowd eager to mingle, mix, and mate.

The **Jonkanoo Lounge,** Wyndham Hotel New Kingston, 77 Knutsford Blvd. (tel. 926-5430), is within the walls of one of Kingston's recently upgraded hotels. This glamorous disco thrives on the friendly rivalry between the batteries of synchronized lights and the rhythms from recently released music. Entrance is free during the happy hour, lasting from 5 to 7 p.m. After that, there's a cover charge of J$12 ($2.30) for singles and J$18 ($3.40) for couples on weeknights, when recorded disco is *de rigueur*. On Thursday, when the music is live, singles are charged J$18 ($3.40) and couples pay J$24 ($4.55).

Mingles Disco, Courtleigh Hotel, 31 Trafalgar Rd. (tel. 926-8174), is set into the innards of the hotel at the far end of the reception area. This popular disco is furnished with a simple dark-grained decor of movable tables, parquet floors, and large expanses of both bar space and dancing areas. Residents of Kingston sometimes pour in here for the live concerts that are held every weekend. On other evenings, disco is featured; there's no cover charge. Red Stripe beer costs around J$12 ($2.30). There's a J$30 ($5.70) cover charge for live concerts. On weekdays the disco and bar are open from 5 p.m. to 2 a.m. and on Saturday from 8 p.m. to 2 a.m. It's closed Sunday.

Scruplez Disco, 19 Cliveden Ave. (tel. 927-9918), attracts a middle-class Jamaican clientele to its second-story interior. To get there, you pass through the garden-style Tropical Inn Hotel. Disco lovers can select a place at the long curving bar or on one of the beige naugahyde banquettes which are clustered tightly together around the room. A J$12 ($2.30) cover charge applies only to people who enter after 9 p.m. except on Saturday when the charge is levied all night long. A Red Stripe beer costs around J$5 (95¢). This disco opened in 1984.

Live Theater

Kingston is called the cultural heart of the West Indies. There are several theaters presenting live performances: **Ward Theatre** on North Parade (tel. 922-0318), **Little Theatre** on Tom Redcam Drive near the National Stadium (tel. 926-6129), and the **Creative Arts Centre** at the University of the West Indies (tel. 927-7546 or 927-0746). Most tickets cost J$15 ($2.85). All stage local or imported plays and musicals, light opera, and revues. You may be fortunate enough to catch a performance by the Jamaica National Dance Theatre or the Jamaica Folk Singers, whose vivid and spontaneous performances show the true Jamaican folk culture.

Most entertainment of this sort is listed in the daily press, along with one-time attractions and sporting activities.

2. Port Antonio

Port Antonio is a seaport on the northeast coast of Jamaica, 63 miles from Kingston, where Brooke Shields filmed *The Blue Lagoon*. It has been called the Jamaica of 100 years ago. In past seasons, Port Antonio has drawn the titled and the wealthy, those European royalty with titles of duchesses and barons, along with such film stars as Bette Davis and Ginger Rogers. Nowadays you are more likely to encounter Raquel Welch or Tommy Tune.

To reach it from the capital, you have a choice between taking the A4 road through Port Morant and up the east coast, or driving north on the A3 through Castleton and approaching along the north coast, where Jamaica's tourist industry started. In other days, visitors arrived by banana boat and stayed at the Titchfield Hotel (which burned down) in a lush, tropical part of the island unspoiled by gimmicks. The small, bustling town of Port Antonio is like many on the island: both clean and untidy, with sidewalks around a market filled with vendors; tin-roofed shacks competing with old Georgian and modern brick and concrete buildings; lots of people busy shopping, talking, laughing, and some just loafing, others sitting and playing Dominoes, loudly banging the pieces down on the table, which is very much part of the game.

The market is a place to browse among local craftwork, spices, and fruits. Captain Bligh landed here in 1793 with the first breadfruit plants, and Port Antonio claims that the ones grown in this area are the best on the island. Visitors still arrive by water, but now it's in cruise ships which moor close to Navy Island, and the passengers come ashore just for the day.

Navy Island and the long-gone Titchfield Hotel were owned for a short time by film star Errol Flynn. The story is that after suffering damage to his yacht, he put into Kingston for repairs, visited Port Antonio by motorbike, fell in love with the area, and in due course acquired Navy Island, some say in a gambling game. Later, he either lost or sold it and bought a nearby plantation, Comfort Castle, still owned by his widow, Patrice Wymore, who spends most of her time there and hopes to open a museum honoring Flynn (refer to "What to See," below). He was much loved and admired by the Jamaicans and was totally integrated into the community. They still talk of him in Port Antonio, especially the men, who refer to his womanizing and drinking skills in reverent tones.

WHERE TO STAY: About 2½ miles east along the coast toward Frenchman's Cove stands **Trident Villas and Hotel,** P.O. Box 119 (tel. 993-2602). This interesting hotel complex, rebuilt after hurricane damage, is a good all-year bet for those who want a quiet, relaxing Jamaican holiday, away from the more publicized tourist areas of the north and northwest coasts. The complex sits above jagged coral cliffs above a seaside panorama. The jagged rocks make the immaculate gardens seem even more civilized. The main building is furnished with many antique reproductions, indigenous flowers decorate the cool lobby, and there is a small boutique owned, incidentally, by Patrice Wymore Flynn.

After checking in, you will be conducted to your room by a cheerful uniformed porter, through gardens with mature and verdant topiary, bright with flowers and filled with the screech of peacocks—which fly up and roost on the roofs, pick their way among the parked cars, and are so tame they come and demand food. Your room will be in a studio cottage reached by a pathway through the tidy gardens. You have your own cottage key. A large bedroom with ample sitting area opens onto a private patio with nothing between you and the sea except grass and a low stone wall. All cottages have their own bathrooms with tub, shower, and toilet. There is plenty of storage space. Jugs of ice and water are constantly replenished, and fresh Jamaican flowers grace the dressing table. The high-peaked wooden roof is fitted with a ceiling fan which produces a highly satisfactory form of air conditioning. Most of the furnishings are made of local materials. Chaises longues provide sunbathing on the patio. Studios, naturally, are cheaper than the one-bedroom villas. *In summer, the single rate begins at $160, the double at $230, both MAP tariffs.* In winter, MAP singles range from $245 to $430 daily, while doubles go for $150 to $240 per person.

There's a small private sand beach, and the gray-green foliage of the immaculate gardens embraces a sapphire-blue pool and a lacy gingerbread gazebo. Lounges, tables, chairs, and bar service add to your pleasure. If you want a sandwich or a drink at lunchtime, you can adjourn to the main building where there are two patios, one covered. Breakfast is served either on the public patio or on your own private patio by your personal butler at no extra charge. He'll soon know your preferences, and you have the advantage of personal service. At dinner, men are required to wear jackets and ties. That meal is served in one wing of the main block. Silver service, crystal, and Port Royal pewter sparkle on the tables. Dinner is a many-course set meal, and for those who are concerned with diets and phobias, it is advisable that requirements be made known early so that alternative food can be served. This is essentially a relaxing place. Tennis, horseback riding, and such water sports as sailing and snorkeling are included in the tariffs.

Fern Hill Club, P.O. Box 100 (tel. 993-3222 or 416/231-2401 in the U.S.). Attractive, airy, and panoramic, this resort occupies 25 lushly forested acres high above the coastline of Port Antonio. Originally built as a private home, it was expanded in 1980 by Canadian entrepreneur Bill Brennan, who "made a killing" in pest control. Today it comprises a glistening colonial-style clubhouse and five outlying villas, plus a comfortable annex at the bottom of the hill. From a seat on the clubhouse terrace, you enjoy a sweeping view over a pair of distant coves, scattered houses belonging to wealthy investors, and a thickly forested peninsula jutting into the sea. On the premises is an 85-foot tennis court; a well-maintained bar, the Blue Mahjoe (named after the wood that sheathes it); a dining patio; and a collection of intensely private air-conditioned accommodations capable of lodging up to 50 guests at a time. Most of these are rented by the week, costing from $799 to $885 per double accommodation in winter, *dropping to $650 weekly for a couple in summer*. A shuttle bus makes infrequent trips down the steep hillside to one of a pair of beaches, Frenchman's Cove, and a wilder, less populated beach called San San. The resort is technically classified as a time-share property, but its accommodations are rented to one-time vacationers by a management company when investors are away.

Jamaica Villas at San San, Goblin Hill (tel. 993-3286, 212/689-3048 in New York City, or toll free 800/235-3505). The verdant and sun-washed hillside it occupies was once reputed to shelter goblins that might carry you off to hell. Today its 14 manicured acres are among the most beautiful on the coast. Its green-and-white lattice-fringed reception area evokes a gracious colonial ambience. The swimming pool is surrounded by a vine-laced arbor, which lies just a stone's throw from an almost-impenetrable forest. On the premises are a pair of illuminated Laykold courts and a long flight of steps leading down to the crescent-shaped sands of San San beach. The resort contains almost 30 stucco-sided villas, each of which is set town-house style against its neighbors. Units contain air conditioning, a ceiling fan, and a four-poster bed. Each is staffed with a personal maid and butler who prepare and serve meals, clean house, and attend to chores. A market on the hotel grounds provides ingredients for any meals which your staff will prepare, within reason, any way you prefer. In winter a one-bedroom villa, suitable for two persons, costs $175 per day, *but only $150 in summer*. A two-bedroom villa, for up to six persons, goes for $265 in winter, *$225 in summer*.

Bonnie View Hotel, P.O. Box 82 (tel. 993-2752), a hillside hugger, opens onto Port Antonio, Navy Island in the middle of the harbor, and the Caribbean. Take "Mango Walk" to the pool and gardens of one of the oldest continuously operated hotels in the Caribbean, in business for more than four decades. The early patrons were passengers from banana boats from England during the 1940s and 1950s. The balcony of Bonnie View is famous. At the hotel's rear is a banana plantation and the cloud-shrouded peaks of the Blue Mountains. The bedrooms are simply but adequately furnished, with private bathrooms. There is no air conditioning, as the hotel has the advantage of the mountain breezes which lower the temperature by some ten degrees. There are 27 rooms and two cottages. All year, rates are $45.30 in a single, $50 in a double. Add $20 per person per day for breakfast and a set dinner. All rooms have balconies, some toward the sea, others toward the mountains. The lounge patio and the veranda are pleasant places to sit and drink a rum punch or nibble a lunchtime snack.

Breakfast is served either in your room or in the dining room set back from the patio. At both lunch and dinner, a mixture of tasty Jamaican and international dishes is offered. At night during the season, a calypso band provides music for dancing after dinner. The pool has a bar and a large lounging area where you can relax under the sun with the mountains for company. Hotel guests can use the free staff bus down to Port Antonio and back at scheduled times. There are tennis courts, and most other sporting activities can be arranged for you. Bunches of bananas hang in the entrance and guests can help themselves to a quick snack at will. You drive up a bumpy road for a sundowner in the Lookout Point Bar.

De Montevin Lodge Private Hotel, 21 Fort George St. (tel. 993-2604), is probably the most ornate and best-maintained version of a gingerbread house in town. It stands on a narrow back street whose edges are lined with architectural reminders (some of them not well preserved) of the colonial days. Originally built as a sea captain's house in 1881, the hotel is really worth a photograph. Cast-iron accents and elongated red and beige balconies set a tone for the charm you find inside: cedar doors, art deco cupboards, a ceiling embellished with lacy plaster designs, and the most elaborate cove moldings in town. Near the entrance, an old enlarged photograph of a young Queen Elizabeth as an equestrienne is proudly displayed. Don't expect modern amenities here: your room might be a study of another, not-yet-renovated era. In any season, a room with a shared bath costs J$85 ($16.15) in a single, J$115 ($21.85) in a double, and J$135 ($20.25) in a triple. Units with bath cost J$10 ($19) more. Mr. Mullings, a prominent local citizen and justice of the peace, is the owner of this 13-room hotel.

Friends, P.O. Box 225 (tel. 925-6738). Its mountaintop setting, coupled with the concerned attentions of its charming owner, create an aura more like a private home than a hotel. This is the panoramic eyrie of one of Port Antonio's most cultivated citizens, the articulate and elfin Ben Ramsay. After living in Barcelona, New York, and Singapore, he returned to his native Jamaica to find a private retreat all his own. This he discovered about a mile and a half west of Port Antonio, amid a thickly forested hillside whose view encompasses the multiple headlands and seacoasts of north Jamaica. Don't expect an easy arrival if you decide to stay here. Its one-lane access road is almost impassable, filled with potholes, and at times seems to fade into brush. Take courage in the belief that at the top a clearing will open to reveal twin chalets and a filling meal prepared by a cooperative employee. Mr. Ramsay constructed parts of the chalets himself. Rooms flow into one another around a central supporting column, and the villas are outfitted with Jamaican paintings and photographs. Year round, a one-bedroom chalet for two persons rents for $60, while a two-bedroom chalet for up to four persons goes for $95 daily.

WHERE TO DINE: A surprising array of atmospheric choices awaits you. All hotels welcome outside guests for dinner, but reservations are required. Check with the hotel.

Trident Hotel Restaurant (tel. 993-2602) has for a long time been frequented by those seeking gourmet cuisine. Part of the main hotel building, the restaurant has an air of elegance. The high-pitched wooden roof set on white stone walls holds several ceiling fans which gently stir the air. The antique tables for two, four, or more are set with old china, English silver, and Port Royal pewter. Warm place settings and candles complete the picture. Dinner is served at 8 o'clock, and men are required to wear jackets and ties. A butler shows you to your table, where warm bread, cold butter, and ice water await. A waiter, resplendent in uniform and white starched shirt, and, to complete the picture, pristine white cotton gloves, will help you choose your wine. The waiter whispers the name of each course as he serves it: Jamaican salad; coconut soup; dolphin with mayonnaise and mustard sauce; French salad with wine vinaigrette; steak with broccoli and sautéed potatoes; peach Melba and Blue Mountain coffee with Wild Orange, a Jamaican liqueur. "More coffee, sir, and more—as much as you want." The cost of the meal is $40 per person. Tip at your discretion. Wine is extra. The six-course menu varies each day, but there is no à la carte service. The meal is expertly cooked and beautifully served. Reservations are required. After dinner, join the crowd around the bar, where a small combo plays tunes on request.

The Rafters' Restaurant (tel. 993-2778). It romantically lies at the edge of the river at the point where still waters provided a convenient resting point for the commercial raft operators who used to float goods downstream. Jamaican entrepreneurs Jean McGill and Beverley Dixon are the graciously softspoken owners of this establishment, where a flautist provides musical diversion throughout the day. The neoclassical pavilion housing the establishment was built in 1954 by a local architect. Today from 9 a.m. to 10 p.m. seven days a week, you can order lunches for J$20 ($3.80), and dinners for J$40 ($7.60). The house drink is the Rio Grande special, which combines four kinds of rum with fresh fruit juice. Other items include open-face sandwiches, burgers, an array of salads, curried goat or chicken, and grilled lobster. The turnoff leading to this place lies about five miles west of Port Antonio.

The **De Montevin Lodge Restaurant,** 21 Fort George St. (tel. 993-2604), is *the* place for a true Jamaican dinner. Start with pepperpot or pumpkin soup, then cod with akee. Follow these with curried lobster and chicken Jamaican style with local vegetables. Top the meal off with coconut or banana cream pie, washed down with coffee, a meal fit for a good trencherman or woman, for J$80 ($15.20) and up. An ice-cold Red Stripe beer goes well with such a meal. The menu changes according to the availability of fresh supplies, but the standard of cooking and the full Jamaican character of the meal are constant. The friendly staff will explain the intricacies of any particular dish that takes your fancy. Always call the day before to let them know you're coming. Mrs. Mullings is considered the best cook in Port Antonio. She was Errol Flynn's cook, incidentally. Meals are served from 12:30 to 2 p.m. and 6:30 to 11 p.m.

Huntress Marina Club, 16 West St. (tel. 993-3318). Set beneath a thatch-covered roof at the end of a somewhat grubby industrial pier, this deliberately raffish bar and restaurant is a favorite of the expatriate yachting set. Many of the ultra-expensive yachts whose crews have dined here have pinned their ensigns on the roughly textured planks and posts. Patrick Knight (who happens to own the adjacent marina as well) is the guiding force of this open-air watering hole. It opens for breakfast at 7 a.m. and remains in business through the day until at least 10 p.m., and often much later. A filling American-style breakfast costs J$15 ($2.85), lunch is from J$20 ($3.80), and a full dinner runs from J$35 ($6.65). Menu items include the usual array of tropical drinks, sandwiches, red snapper, roast chicken, burgers, seafood ceviche, liver with bananas, and akee with saltfish.

WHAT TO DO: For the experience of a lifetime, most guests follow the lead of a legendary film star and go—

Rafting on the Rio Grande

Rafting started on the Rio Grande and on the Martha Brae River as a means of transporting bananas from the plantations to the waiting freighters. In 1871 a Yankee skipper, Lorenzo Dow Baker, decided that a seat on one of the rafts was better than walking, but it was not until Errol Flynn arrived that the rafts became popular as a tourist attraction. Flynn used to hire the craft for his friends and encouraged the drivers to race down the Rio Grande, spurred on by bets on the winner. Now that the bananas are transported by road, the raft skippers make one or maybe two trips a day down the waterway.

The rafts are some 33 feet long and only about 3 feet wide, propelled by stout bamboo poles. There is a raised double seat about two-thirds of the way back for the two passengers. The skipper stands in the front, trousers rolled up to his knees, the water washing his feet, and guides the lively craft down the river, about eight miles between steep hills covered with coconut palms, banana plantations, and flowers, through limestone rock cliffs pitted with caves, through the Tunnel of Love, a narrow cleft in the rocks, then on to wider, gentler water. The whole trip takes about two or three hours, but there may be stops for chats with bankside residents whom the rafters know well. You can disembark and get a drink at a small shop on the way.

The day starts at Rafter's Rest, a few miles west of Port Antonio at Burlington on St. Margaret's Bay. Trips last 2½ hours, and they're available from 8:30 a.m. to 5 p.m. daily, at a cost of $28 per raft. Leave your valuables in the specially provided lockers. A driver will take you to the starting point and pick you up again in your rental car. He is fully insured to do so. If you feel like it, take a picnic lunch. Bring enough for your skipper too, and he will find a peaceful spot for your meal and perhaps a swim, regaling you with lively stories of the river, laughing, and talking—a good companion for an exciting trip. For more information, call Miss Jean McGill, Rio Grande Attraction Ltd., Port Antonio (tel. 993-2778).

A Trip to the Blue Lagoon

About five miles east of Port Antonio, at the end of a winding, gravel-colored road, lie some of the most iridescently turquoise-colored waters in all of Jamaica. The Blue Lagoon, known simply as the "blue hole," is one of the most photographed sights on the island. Driving, you follow the signs off the main road past Frenchman's Cove Hotel down to the beach. Believed to be a function of a shallow bottom, intense sunlight, and the effects of a freshwater tributary which makes the waters even bluer, the place has a parking lot ringed with an animated community of vendors. You can go for a look at the waters, perhaps negotiate with a salesperson over a local handcraft, or even indulge in a scuba or snorkeling exploration of the lagoon's bottom.

Many visitors, however, make a meal at the veranda-style **Blue Lagoon Restaurant,** San San (tel. 993-2495), the focal point of their afternoon. Open for drinks throughout the day and most of the evening, it serves buffet meals whose ingredients are sometimes grilled or charcoaled. Breakfast is from 8 to 11 a.m., costing from J$30 ($5.70), and lunch, at J$50 ($9.50), is from noon to 3 p.m. Dinner is especially romantic because of the water lapping at the piers on which you sit. Served from 7 to 10 p.m. and costing from J$80 ($15.25), it offers lobster, crab backs, oysters, burgers, steaks, chicken wings, and jerk pork or chicken. The restaurant's dangling fish nets and parasols are set up to receive visitors seven days a week.

If you're interested in scuba, and you're a PADI- or NAUI-certified diver, a one-tank dive costs J$150 ($28.50). A shallow-water lesson for beginners is J$150 ($28.50). A half-hour glass-bottom-boat ride goes for J$30 ($5.70), and three big loops around the outlying reef on waterskis is possible for J$60 ($11.40). Snorkeling equipment can be rented for an entire day for J$30 ($5.70).

On Sunday and Tuesday, a Blue Lagoon Celebrity Voyage and Beach Party is held from 1:30 to 3:30 p.m. You sail in flat-bottom boats to the Blue Lagoon, with an informed commentary on 21 points of historic interest and houses of celebrities seen from the sea. There is a cultural show on the beach to follow. On Tuesday, when the charge is $12.50, there is music, dancing, and unlimited rum punch and fruit drinks. A buffet lunch is added on Sunday, when the cost is $16.50. For more information, get in touch with Verne Pettingill, Huntress Marina (tel. 993-3318).

Boat Cruises

Also sailing from Huntress Marina (tel. 993-3318) is a two-hour **historical tour cruise** aboard the *Lady Jamaica.* The cruise takes you to Port Antonio's twin harbors with narration on the town's history and 21 points of interest. The *Lady Jamaica* has a small glass viewing panel in its bottom. The tour, offered daily from 10 a.m. to noon, costs $5 per person.

The *Lady Jamaica* also makes **sunset cruises** on Thursday from 5 to 7 p.m., costing $12.50, with unlimited cocktails, disco, and snacks.

Beaches

Port Antonio has several white sand beaches open to the public, some free and some for a charge for use of facilities. **Boston Beach** is free, and often has light surfing, and there are picnic tables as well as a restaurant and snackbar. Also free is **Fairy Hill Beach** (Winnifred), with changing rooms and showers.

San San Beach, with changing rooms, showers, lounge chairs, a lifeguard, a bar, and a snackbar, plus water-sports equipment, is in the center of the San San residential area. There is a charge for visitors. **Frenchman's Cove Beach** attracts a chic crowd to its white sand beach combined with a freshwater stream. Nonhotel guests are charged a fee.

Navy Island, once Errol Flynn's personal hideaway, is a fine choice for swimming and snorkeling. Take the boat from the Navy Island dock on West Street across from the Esso station. It's a seven-minute ride to the island, a round-trip costing J$19 ($1.90). The ferry runs 24 hours a day.

WHAT TO SEE: Continuing our energetic activities, I have the following suggestions:

Somerset Falls is ten miles west of Port Antonio, just past Hope Bay on the A4. The waters of the Daniels River pour down a deep gorge through the rain forest, with waterfalls and foaming cascades. There are picnic spots, and you can swim in the deep rock pools. You can buy sandwiches, light meals, beer, soft drinks, and even liquor at the snackbar. Admission to the falls is J$2 (40¢) for adults, J$1 (20¢) for children. Hours are 10 a.m. to 5 p.m. Phone 926-2952 for information.

The **Caves of Nonsuch** and the **Gardens of Athenry** are east from Port Antonio past the Blue Lagoon. Turn right, and follow the signs about six miles up into the hills through small villages to the caves. It's an easy drive and an easy walk to see the stalagmites, fossilized marine remains, evidence of Arawak civilization, and signs of volcanic activity, adding up to 1½ million years of life on earth.

From the Gardens of Athenry there are panoramic views over the island and the sea. The gardens are filled with coconut palms, flowers, and trees.

Admission to the caves and gardens is $3.75 per person. The facilities are open seven days a week, and complete guided tours are given from 9 a.m. to 5:30 p.m. Rates include a guide for both the caves and gardens. Refreshments are available at the Athenry Pavilion, and one beverage is included in the tour.

The **Folly Great House** (tel. 993-3740) lies on the outskirts of Port Antonio. The remains of the two-story mansion can be visited free. It was built, it is said, in 1905 by Arthur Mitchell, an American millionaire, for his wife, Annie, daughter of Charles Tiffany, founder of the famous New York store. Sea water was used in the construction, and the house collapsed shortly after they moved in.

Because of the beautiful location, it is easy to see what a fine great house it must have been, but the years and vandals have not added to its attractiveness. Decay and graffiti mar the ruins.

Someone once said, "Anything is possible in Jamaica." Although I can't promise it, it is sometimes possible to arrange a trip to the **Errol Flynn Plantation** (phone 993-3294 for information). Of course, the more in your party, the better your chances of getting to see the land so beloved by the film star and author of the autobiography *My*

Wicked, Wicked Ways. The widow of the film star, Patrice Wymore Flynn (you may remember her from several films she made in the '50s), is now the owner of the working plantation which lies in the area of Priestman's River, 13 miles east of Port Antonio. Sometimes she personally shows visitors about the property where coconut and pimiento are grown. You can also visit a wicker factory—not a large operation—and see how coconut is processed into copra.

If you can't visit the plantation, you may want to visit **Patrice Wymore Flynn's Designer's Gallery,** Trident Villas (tel. 993-3294), owned (but not always attended) by Flynn's soft-spoken widow. This carefully stocked boutique operates out of a two-room headquarters to the side of the previously recommended Trident Villas. Almost everything inside is made in Jamaica, including weavings, cigars, woodcarvings, and clothing. A carefully polished collection of very expensive English silver, some of it antique, is also for sale. The boutique is open daily except Sunday from 9 a.m. to 5 p.m.

3. Ocho Rios

A north-coast resort some two hours by road from Montego Bay, Ocho Rios was once a small banana and fishing port, but in recent years tourism has become the leading industry. The bay is dominated on one side by a bauxite loading terminal and on the other by a range of hotels with sandy beaches fringed by palm trees. Runaway Bay, once only a satellite of Ocho Rios but now a resort area in its own right, is presented at the end of this section.

Many readers of this guide have expressed strong objections to a holiday in Ocho Rios. Culled from several reports, here are the main problems. The rainy months are in May and October. The town is so commercial you won't find the real Jamaica there. Three cruise ships arrive every week (four every other week). The young men on the streets are very aggressive toward selling you any kind of drugs and worthless souvenirs. Therefore it's hard to just walk around the town to see the sights and eat in the local restaurants. Nevertheless, it remains one of the major attractions of Jamaica, and it also offers some of the finest resort living.

WHERE TO STAY: The area of Ocho Rios is a formidable rival of Montego Bay. Some inns of character remain, holding out against the newer developments that may sweep away what is left of the former colonial life of the resort.

The Luxury Leaders

Sans Souci Hotel and Club, P.O. Box 103 (tel. 974-2353; for reservations and information, call Elegant Resorts of Jamaica, 666-3566 in Miami, or toll free 800/237-3237). The fortunate beneficiary of a recent $4-million renovation, this is the most luxurious and tasteful hotel in Ocho Rios. It's set four miles east of town on a forested plot of land whose rocky border abuts the sea. The site it occupies was valued for medicinal qualities of its sulfur-rich mineral springs in the 1930s. Erected, demolished, and erected again, the resort witnessed the visits of some gilt-edged titles of Britain in the 1960s when the premises were leased as private apartments. In 1984, after a financial shuffle, it reopened as a richly deluxe hotel with Ken Kennedy, one of the Caribbean's most experienced hoteliers, as its manager. The rosy interior of a conch shell was the inspiration for the color that is the the theme of the hotel. This, coupled with a subtle tone of yellow, fills bedrooms, public areas, and even sheathes the exterior of the scattered annexes. The resort is terraced into a steeply lush hillside whose manicured pathways and steps traverse a richly flourishing jungle. A skillfully designed cliffside elevator brings guests to a secluded outdoor bar whose perimeter includes rocks and an edging of greenery. There's a freshwater pool, plus a frothy and bubbling mineral bath big enough for an elephant, and a labyrinth of catwalks and bridges stretching over rocky chasms filled with surging water. Each of the 72 air-conditioned accommodations has its own veranda or patio, elegant copies of Chippen-dale furniture, plush upholstery, and a subdued kind of colonial elegance. In winter, EP singles cost $180 to $230 daily; doubles, $200 to $250. *In summer, a single goes for $120 to $160 daily; doubles, $140 to $180.* For a full American breakfast and a five-course à la carte dinner the cost is another $45 per person daily, plus a 10% service charge. Sports lovers appreciate the resort's pair of Laykold-covered tennis courts, the array of water sports that can be arranged at the hotel's private beach, and the golf course nearby.

Jamaica Inn, off Rte. 4 (tel. 974-2514), is a long, low, U-shaped building set close to the sea, surrounded by grass and palm trees with oleander and bougainvillea. The cool, comfortable lounge with books, and the games room with cards and jigsaw puzzles, will provide you with something to do in case of rain, but it's the outdoor attractions that bring people to the inn. Lovely patios open onto the lawns, and the bedrooms, which face the sea, are reached along garden paths. Winter rates, including three meals a day and tea, are $225 in a single (not ocean view), rising to $260 to $310 in a double. *Summer tariffs cost from $145 daily in a single and from $185 to $195 in a double.* The expensive White Suite here was a favorite of Winston Churchill. There is a small pool almost at the water's edge, where a wide, white sand beach invites you to swim or lounge. Arthur, the boatman, will arrange sailing trips. The sea close in is almost too clear to make snorkeling an adventure, but farther out it is rewarding. For the nonaquatic there is tennis, with golf close by at the Upton Country Club.

The inn is proud of its cuisine. The chef was trained in Europe and lends his expertise to the production of dishes both international and Jamaican. You can have breakfast served in your room, selecting from kippers, an omelet, or pancakes with maple syrup, or you can enjoy it in the dining room. Lunch is a pleasant à la carte affair, with a wide menu choice. Dinner, for a set charge of $24, may start with mango nectar, caviar on toast, or stuffed sweet peppers, followed by soup. For the main course, there may be lobster Thermidor, broiled tenderloin with béarnaise sauce or fried chicken. You can finish with a dessert or cheese, and Blue Mountain coffee. The management requires men to wear a jacket and tie at night. (One New Jersey man didn't bring a tie and had to spend one whole day in search of one, finally finding the item in a small native drygoods store.)

Plantation Inn (tel. 974-2501) is a magnificent hotel evoking a southern antebel-lum mansion, reached by a sweeping driveway and entered through a colonnaded por-tico, set above the beach in pleasant gardens. All bedrooms open off balconies and have their own patios overlooking the sea. The rooms are attractively decorated with chintz and comfortable furnishings, and are air cooled by revolving fans. On the MAP, two persons can stay here in winter at prices ranging from $270 to $315 daily, the latter for occupancy of a junior suite. *In summer, prices are reduced: the same MAP is offered for $185 to $215 for two persons.* For single occupancy in either sea-son, deduct $40 per night. Apart from the regular hotel, there are two units that provide living. Plantana Cottage above the east beach sleeps two to six persons. The Family House with a garden view sleeps up to five persons. These, naturally, are far more expensive than the regular rates.

There is an inside dining room, but most of the action takes place under the tropi-cal sky. English tea is served on the terrace every afternoon from 4 to 5:30 p.m. You can have breakfast on your patio. Lunch is served outdoors, with a choice of chilled native nectars of mango, pineapple, guava, or tomato to start, followed by a sandwich, or perhaps you'll enjoy a chicken and onion omelet. In winter, men are required to wear jackets at dinner (and jackets *and* ties, on Friday and Saturday night). In summer the dress code is more relaxed. Men are required to wear jackets only for dinner on Friday and Saturday night. The menu comes at a set price of $30 for five courses and coffee, plus 10% service. On Thursday a Jamaica night buffet is offered, and you can feast, enjoy a local show, and dance to calypso music. The beach is 50 steps down from the garden, and seats on the way provide resting spots. Water sports are available: skindiving, Sunfish sailing, and windsurfing. There is a glass-bottom boat on one of the two private beaches, or you can just take it easy and get a tan while doing nothing at all.

All-Inclusive Resorts

Couples, P.O. Box 330, Tower Isle Post Office, St. Mary (tel. 974-4271). Don't come here alone—you won't get in! You're asked to bring a "little love here," and that means your lover. The management defines couples here as "any man and woman in love." Everything is in couplets, even the double chairs by the moon-drenched beach. Once you've paid the initial fee, you have free use of all facilities—there will be no more bills. It's a taboo subject. Even the cigarettes and whisky are free. You get three meals a day too, including all the wine you want. And tips are not permitted. Every bedroom has either a king-size bed or two doubles, and furnishings are pleasantly traditional. Breakfasts are bountiful. Every room has a patio fronting either the sea or the beach; if not that, then gardens or the mountains. The hotel accepts bookings for eight, nine, and ten days, including seven, eight, or nine nights on a Friday-to-Monday basis. Ten different rate structures are offered, depending on the time of year. The highest winter tab is an ocean-view room at $2,200 per week per couple. *Summer prices are reduced to from $870 upward per person per week.*

Dinners are four courses, and afterward there is dancing on the terrace every evening, with a different kind of entertainment. The piano bar opens at 7 p.m., and stays that way until the last guest retires (this is sometimes at 7 a.m.). You can play tennis on one of the five world-class courts, three of which are lit, or else cycle, go horseback riding, sailing, scuba-diving, or snorkeling. Or you may want to slip away to their private island where you can bask in the buff. The only criticism I have of the resort is that it does away with the mating game, unless you cast a roving eye on someone else's other half.

Eden II, P.O. Box 51, Mammee Bay (tel. 972-2382), knew life as the Jamaica Hilton before becoming an all-inclusive couples resort. It is set on the seafront between Ocho Rios and St. Ann's Bay, facing Mammee Bay in 22 acres of landscaped gardens, reached along an avenue of royal palms. The resort is very sports oriented, with, among other facilities, a Nautilus Fitness Centre that features a hot tub and aerobic exercise classes. Tennis is played both day and night, and other activities include dance lessons, volleyball, and backgammon. You can go horseback riding about 2,000 feet above sea level, jog along a marked trail, and partake of such water sports as skiing, windsurfing, scuba-diving, snorkeling, and sailboat racing.

Rooms are attractively furnished, each with a private balcony if overhead or a patio if on ground level. As in most couples-only resorts in Jamaica, a client gets the works: that is, three meals a day, along with "happy hour" hors d'oeuvres, Sunday champagne brunches, and all bar drinks (even cigarettes). A choice of four wines is available at lunch and dinner. Transfers are arranged between the airport and the hotel. Most guests book in here on the seven-night plan, and during certain peak periods they must arrive on Friday, Saturday, or Sunday only. In winter, a minimum of three nights is accepted for a booking. For the all-inclusive privilege, couples pay $925 to $1,152. However, most couples prefer to stay seven nights for anywhere from $1,665 to $2,130. *In the off-season, two persons can stay here three nights for $765 to $900, or seven nights for $1,500 to $1,750.* The least expensive rooms are called lanai. The second most expensive category is labeled mountain-view, and the ocean-view rooms carry the highest price tags.

First Class

Americana Ocho Rios, P.O. Box 100 (tel. 974-2151), is a 325-room citadel opening onto a long, sandy beach. Its next-door neighbor is the Ocho Rios Sheraton, and guests often wander back and forth between the two hotels, checking out the action. Once they were linked almost like Siamese twins when they were run under the same banner and known then as the Intercontinental Ocho Rios and the Mallards Beach-Hyatt. Many returning guests still remember them under their old names. The Americana is a modern, high-rise building, with air-conditioned units, a large cool lobby, and a shopping arcade which is handy if you don't want to walk to nearby Ocho Rios and the Ocean Village Shopping Centre. *Guests check in here in summer for $65 to $85 daily, EP, in a single, $75 to $95 in a double*. In winter, the EP rate for a single or a double is $119 to $135.

There is a coffeeshop as well on the premises, but most meals are taken on the terrace amid tropical plants. The Victoria Restaurant is the finest dining room of the hotel, offering meals for $30, including such elegant continental fare as veal à la fran-çaise, filet romano with lobster asparagus and béarnaise, and pepper steak. Soups might feature a conch chowder or a cream of pumpkin. Adjoining a wine cellar, the restaurant opens for business at 6 every evening. The setting is Victorian, fitting the name, with soft lights. Air conditioning adds to the comfort of guests. After dark, a disco might (maybe not) hum with life, and native floor shows and calypso music on some occasions could add to your entertainment. Two tennis courts, horseback riding, and golf are available at the Upton Country Club. Waterskiing, fishing, and scuba-diving can be arranged for a small cost.

The **Ocho Rios Sheraton,** P.O. Box 245 (tel. 974-2201), which as mentioned was known as the Mallards Beach-Hyatt in a former lifetime, is a similar high-rise on the beach like its neighbor, the Americana. The upper lobby and reception area of the Sheraton is graced by a fountain and pool. The decor is tropical, and maximum use is made of bamboo, rattan, and batik. A shopping arcade, three bars, and three restaurants are part of the hotel. Waterskiing, snorkeling, sailing, jet-skiing, windsurfing, deep-sea fishing, and tennis are available at the hotel, and golf can be played a couple of miles away. *In the off-season, singles or doubles cost $85 to $100 daily*. In winter, either single or double occupancy goes for $140 to $160 daily.

Less Expensive Choices

Shaw Park Beach Hotel, P.O. Box 17, Cutlass Bay (tel. 974-2552), is an elegant Jamaica Georgian property with all rooms directly on the beach, facing the ocean. It has three bars, two inside and the Beach Bar on the Caribbean Terrace under the sky. The reception area looks like a colonial version of a Georgian living room, and the terrace one floor below is built right up to the crashing waves. All rooms are air-conditioned and comfortably furnished. Most have full bathrooms, but some in the east wing have showers. There is a swimming pool, and ocean water sports—sailing, fishing, windsurfing, waterskiing, snorkeling—are available from the beach at nominal charges. The hotel has its own tennis courts and reciprocity with Upton Golf Club. A resident band plays for dancing nightly. Floor shows are arranged most nights. The nightclub, Silks, vibrates to disco music and has an intimate Jockey Bar. *In summer, singles range in price from $79 to $91 daily; doubles, $90 to $104. Four persons can occupy a deluxe two-bedroom apartment suite for about $250*. Winter rates rise to $134 to $143 daily in a single, $146 to $155 in a double, with a two-bedroom apartment suite costing four persons about $355 daily. One reader, Gregory Speck of New York City, noted that Bergen Davis, the chef here, "prepares just about the best lobster I've ever encountered, and has a degree from the University of Miami in culinary arts." Shaw Park Gardens (described under "Boonoonoonoos") are owned and operated by the hotel and provide a pleasant afternoon's sightseeing.

Hibiscus Lodge Hotel, P.O. Box 52 (tel. 974-2676), is an intimate, friendly little inn in the hills for those who enjoy the character of old architecture surrounded by abundant greenery. You get atmosphere at low prices—from $52 daily in a double in winter and $72 in a triple. *Off-season, reductions are granted: $40 daily in a double* *and $55 in a triple.* No single rates are quoted. The lodge is an old building with wide verandas onto which the brightly furnished bedrooms open. Units are in natural wood with reed trim. All the accommodations contain ceiling fans and private baths. Every kind of island tree and flowering vine seems to grow in the three-acre compound. Within walking distance is a wide sandy beach, and the lodge has a large sundeck. The Almond Tree Restaurant at the lodge is previewed below. Alfred Doswald and Richard Powell run both the restaurant and hotel.

Inn on the Beach, P.O. Box 342, St. Ann (tel. 974-2782), just behind the sprawling Ocean Village Shopping Centre, is an attractively decorated, Jamaican-run inn at the edge of a public beach in the center of town. Its accommodations are as comfortable as those in larger, more expensive resort hotels nearby. If you don't mind the absence of the varied on-the-premises entertainment facilities of the larger hotels, this may be the place for you. Open-air hallways lead to the pleasantly sunny bedrooms, each of which has two double beds, large windows, a terrace, air conditioning, a tile bath, and attractive furnishings, some upholstered in springtime colors. There's no elevator, no bar, and no restaurant in the hotel, but you'll find a number of watering spots within walking distance, and two restaurants, under different management, are connected architecturally with the rear side of the inn. In winter, the 46 accommodations rent for $72 daily in a single, $80 in a double, $95 in a triple, and $105 in a quad. *In summer, rates go down to $48 in a single, $58 in a double, $68 in a triple, and $82 in a quad.*

WHERE TO DINE: One of the most captivating eating places anywhere in Jamaica is **Ruins Restaurant,** on DaCosta Drive on Turtle River (tel. 974-2442). You dine in a spot at the foot of a series of waterfalls that can be considered a tourist attraction in their own right. In 1831 a British entrepreneur constructed a sugar mill on the site, using the powerful stream to drive his water wheels. Today, all that remains is a jumble of ruins, hence the restaurant's name.

After you cross a covered bridge, perhaps stopping off for a drink at the bar in the outbuilding first, you find yourself in a fairyland where the only sounds come from the tree frogs, the falling water from about a dozen cascades, and the discreet clink of silver and china. Tables are set on a wooden deck leading all the way up to the pool at the foot of the falls, where moss and other vegetation line the stones at the base. As part of the evening's enjoyment you may want to climb a flight of stairs to the top of the falls, where bobbing lanterns and the illuminated waters below afford one of the most delightful experiences on the island.

Reservations are important, since in season this restaurant draws crowds. Menu items, since the place was taken over by Messrs. HoSang and Hugh Lee in 1982, include a wide range of Chinese food, such as sweet-and-sour pork or chicken, several kinds of chow mein or chop suey, chicken and pineapple, beef in oyster sauce, and a house specialty—lobster sautéed in a special sauce. International dishes include lamb or pork chops, chicken Kiev, surf and turf, two kinds of steak, and an array of fish. Full meals range from J$45 ($8.55) to J$98 ($18.60). Lunch is served daily except Sunday from noon to 2:30 p.m., and dinner is offered seven days a week from 6 to 9:30 p.m.

The **Almond Tree Restaurant** (tel. 974-2813), at the Hibiscus Lodge Hotel, is run by the lodge owners, Richard (Dick) Powell from England and Alfred (Freddie) Doswald. Dick was originally catering manager for one of England's finest hotels, and Freddie, trained in Switzerland, was executive chef at Couples and also owns and runs a pâtisserie and bread shop in Ocean Village. The Almond Tree patio, with trees growing up through the roof, overlooks the Caribbean over floodlit trees at night. Lunch is served from noon to 3 p.m., offering several possibilities from a limited menu; a meal averages around $12. For breakfast and lunch, you can have tropical fruits in their season. Dinner is served from 7 p.m., with a wide choice of appetizers, including fish cakes, native style. For a soup, you might try pepperpot or pumpkin. Almond Tree specialties include a wide range of continental dishes. I prefer the seafood dishes from the Caribbean, including bouillabaisse (not only pieces of conch, but lobster) and broiled red snapper with a Créole sauce. The chef also prepares a Caribbean seafood fondue. Lobster is the most expensive item on the menu. Expect to spend from $20 for dinner. The wine list offers a variety of vintages, including Spanish and Jamaican wines. Have an apértif in the unique "swinging bar" (swinging chairs, that is) beside the hotel before dinner.

Moxons of Boscobel, St. Mary (tel. 974-3234), is open seven nights a week. This enchanting place, six miles out of Ocho Rios on the A3 going east, is so popular that a reservation is imperative. It was opened about 15 years ago by Oliver and Benita Moxon, when they came to Jamaica from England in search of what they describe as "a middle-age challenge." They arrived on the island, found their cliff-edge site, literally built their restaurant, and trained their staff from waiter to chef. The Moxons built a school in the village, and are totally integrated into the life of the island. Noted diners at their restaurant have included famous authors and politicians, including Alex Haley, Pierre Trudeau, George McGovern, and Dr. Henry Kissinger, and the Moxons claim that in high season they turn down business rather than hurry their guests.

Enter through the stout wooden doors and have a before-dinner drink in the white, tree-covered patio; then dine on the terrace with a fantastic view over the lagoon. The tables are candlelit and adorned with fresh flowers. The musical background complements the scenery. For an appetizer, try liver pâté or oeuf Florentine. There is fresh fish and a variety of lobster dishes served with rice and salad. The steaks are good, but a particular delicacy that is often available is poussin français (the Moxons even taught a farmer how to fatten the chicks). French-fried, creamed, or steamed potatoes come with the meal. The chef's selections are shown daily on a menu board. Homemade desserts are excellent. Count on parting with at least $30 per person.

The Casanova, Sans Souci Hotel and Club (tel. 974-2353), in the main building of this previously recommended hotel, is one of the most elegant dining enclaves along the north coast of Jamaica. Its tables span a plant-fringed swath stretching from inside the high-ceilinged dining room to a raised balcony above the pool. In the late 1960s Harry Cipriani (of Harry's Bar fame in Venice) taught the staff some of his culinary techniques. The pasta is still made fresh daily along with many of the other staples. Jazz from a lattice-roofed gazebo might accompany your meal, served daily from noon to 3 p.m. and 7 to 9:30 p.m. Lunches cost from $20 each, with dinners in the $25 to $50 range. Specialties, served by polite, formally dressed waiters, include smoked marlin, lobster bisque, kingfish en papillotte, lobster Thermidor, ravioli stuffed with lobster, veal Oskar, stuffed pork chops served with a coconut-curry sauce, and chicken suprême flambéed with whisky. Desserts are sumptuous, and might be followed by one of the house's four special coffees. Reservations are suggested.

Carib Inn Restaurant, on Main Street (tel. 974-2445), within walking distance of most hotels, is nestled among crotons and coconut palms on 17 acres of streams and manicured lawns. To enter, you walk over a footbridge to the open-air restaurant, a cluster of six hexagons with teepee-shaped roofs. The glassed-in air-conditioned bar is at the far end and one of the hexagonal structures beside it provides a relaxing atmosphere. You can sit and enjoy a Carib Special, laced with Jamaican rum, or a piña colada. To begin your meal, you might order akee on toast, baked West Indian crab, stuffed avocado, or a seafood crêpe. Soup, a grill, seafood, or a flambé specialty can follow. For dessert, try a Tía Maria parfait (baked banana with coconut cream) or Irish coffee, made with Jamaican coffee. For lunch, I suggest a club sandwich, a lobster salad, or one of the daily specials such as curried goat and white rice, stewed beef, or akee and codfish. A full dinner costs from J$75 ($14.25); lunch goes for J$15 ($2.85) and up. It's open daily: try to go between noon and 2 p.m. and 7 and 9 p.m. Bring your camera and swimwear and get tanned on a private beach or dive into the water of the sea or the Olympic-size freshwater swimming pool.

Dick Turpin, Coconut Grove Shopping Centre (tel. 974-2717), is an English pub and restaurant in this shopping center. Decorated with the newspapers of London as its theme, it has an active, friendly pub, a favorite rendezvous point for both visitors and locals. Lunch, costing around J$50 ($9.50), is served daily from noon to 3:30 p.m. and includes some Chinese dishes; dinner for around $25, is offered from 6:30 to 10:30 p.m. On Sunday, hours are 6 p.m. to midnight. Appetizers are enticing, including stuffed crab back, Jamaican patties, and smoked marlin. A host of main dishes are offered, featuring curried lobster, barbecued spareribs, and steak and shrimp fondue. Roast prime rib of beef is the specialty. Fresh homemade desserts are a regular feature, along with Dick Turpin's "grog mug." Dinner is by candlelight. The host is Bill Letchford, from Wiltshire, England, who likes to see that his produce, meats, and seafood are fresh. Try also his homemade breads.

The Little Pub Restaurant, 59 Main St. (tel. 974-2324), is in a tropical patio surrounded by souvenir shops bordered with gingerbread fretwork. This indoor-outdoor pub's inner rooms focus on a small stage area for native bands. No one will mind if you just enjoy a drink while you sit in one of the pub's barrel chairs, but if you want dinner, you can proceed to one of the linen-covered tables capped with cut flowers and candlelight. Menu items include lobster Thermidor, lobster Créole, a shrimp-filled pineapple boat, barbecued chicken, grilled steaks, grilled kingfish, brown fish stew with peppery brown gravy (a Jamaican specialty), and banana flambé. Dinners cost J$125 ($23.75) and up. Breakfast is from 8 to 11 a.m.; lunch, from 11 a.m. to 4:30 p.m.; and dinner, from 6 p.m. to midnight.

To add to the ambience of this already-colorful spot, live music is offered during dinner, as well as a live show at 10 p.m. during high season. During the show, limbo and cabaret acts are featured. Many guests find that the live music is better than that offered in similar places around town. The pub is immediately west of the Ocho Rios roundabout behind a crumbled fortification and lots of verdant shrubs. Keith Foote is the owner/manager.

Parkway Restaurant, 60 DaCosta Dr. (tel. 974-2667). This popular establishment in the commercial center of town couldn't have a much plainer façade. Inside it continues to be unpretentious, but many local families and members of the business community know you can get some of the best-tasting and least expensive local dishes here of any place in Ocho Rios. On clean napery, amid a serviceable decor, hungry diners are fed from 7:30 a.m. to 11 p.m. Full meals, costing from J$60 ($11.40), include Jamaican-style chicken, tripe and beans, "cowheels," cold lobster plates, curried goat, sandwiches, filet of red snapper, and to top it off, banana cream pie.

WHAT TO DO: A pleasant drive out of Ocho Rios along the A3 will take you inland through **Fern Gully.** This was originally a riverbed, but now the main road winds up some 700 feet between a profusion of wild ferns, a tall rain forest, hardwood trees, and lianas. For the botanist, there are hundreds of varieties of ferns, and for the less plant-minded, roadside stands offer fruit and vegetables, carved wood souvenirs, and basketwork. The road runs for about four miles, sometimes with a large pool of sunlight, sometimes fingers of light just penetrating the overhanging vegetation. Then at the top of the hill, you come to a right-hand turn, onto a narrow road leading to Golden Grove.

You pass Lydford with the remains of **Edinburgh Castle,** built in 1763, the lair of one of Jamaica's most infamous murderers, a Scot named Lewis Hutchinson who used to shoot passersby and toss their bodies into a deep pit built for the purpose. The authorities got wind of his activities, and although he tried to escape by canoe, he was captured by the navy under the command of Admiral Rodney and was hanged. Rather proud of his achievements (evidence of at least 43 murders was found), he left £100 and instructions for a memorial to be built. It never was, but the castle ruins remain.

Continue down the A1 to **St. Ann's Bay,** the site of the first Spanish settlement on the island, where you can see the **Statue of Christopher Columbus,** cast in his hometown of Genoa, erected near St. Ann's Hospital on the west side of town, close to the coast road. There are a number of Georgian buildings in the town. The **Court House** near the parish church, built in 1866, is most interesting.

Follow the A3 back toward Ocho Rios and you will pass **Dunn's River Falls.** There is plenty of parking space, and for a charge of J$3 (55¢) you can relax on the beach or else climb with a guide to the top of the 600-foot falls. Dressing rooms are available. You can splash in the waters at the bottom of the falls or drop into the cool pools higher up between the cascades of water. The beach restaurant provides snacks and refreshing drinks. You can visit from 8 a.m. to 5 p.m. If you're visiting the falls, wear old tennis shoes, whatever, anything to protect your feet from the sharp rocks and to prevent slipping.

The **Green Grotto Caves** are at Runaway Bay, 40 minutes west from Ocho Rios on the A1 past St. Ann's Bay. In 1658 the Spanish governor is said to have hidden here from the English before escaping through an underground passage on to Cuba. Tours of the caves take about 45 minutes. You descend some 395 feet underground, and your guide, flashlight in hand, will show such natural rock formations as the Madonna and Child, with a draping like jeweled lace, or the Spanish conquistador, so lifelike that one is almost convinced he was carved by human hand. At the bottom is the Green Grotto Lake, across which you will take a boat to the bar for a free cool drink. With luck, your guide will play the Arawak piano, which sounds a little like the chimes of Big Ben, before you return to the surface. The caves are open from 9 a.m. to 5 p.m. daily. Admission is J$12 ($2.25) for adults.

Prospect Plantation (tel. 974-2373), 4½ miles east of Ocho Rios, is a working property. A visit to this plantation combines the opportunity to take an educational, relaxing, and enjoyable tour. On your leisurely ride by covered jitney through the scenic beauty of Prospect, you'll readily see why this section of Jamaica is called "the garden parish of the island." You can view the many trees planted by such visitors as Sir Winston Churchill, Dr. Henry Kissinger, Charlie Chaplin, Pierre Trudeau, Sir Noël Coward, and many others. You will learn about and see growing pimento (allspice), bananas, cassava, sugarcane, coffee, cocoa, coconut, pineapple, and the famous leucaena "Tree of Life." You'll see Jamaica's first hydroelectric plant and Jamaica red poll cattle at the feedlot, and sample some of the exotic fruit and drinks. Your guide will be a cadet from **Prospect Training College,** founded more than 27 years ago by Col. Sir Harold Mitchell, Bt.

Horseback riding is available on three scenic trails at Prospect. The rides vary from 1 to 2¼ hours. Advance booking of one hour is necessary to reserve horses.

Tours, costing from $7.50, depart Monday through Saturday at 10:30 a.m. and at 2 and 3:30 p.m., and on Sunday at 11 a.m. and 1:30 and 3 p.m. Children under 12 go free.

Brimmer Hall Estate (tel. 994-2309) is farther east from Ochos Rios in the hills two miles from Port Maria, an ideal place to spend a day, where you can relax beside the pool and sample a wide variety of brews and concoctions, including an interestingly different one called "Wow!" The Plantation Tour Eating House offers typical Jamaican dishes for lunch, and there is a souvenir shop with a good selection of ceramics, art, straw goods, woodcarvings, rums, liqueurs, and cigars. All this is on a working plantation where you are driven around in a tractor-drawn jitney to see the tropical fruit trees and coffee plants, and learn from the knowledgeable guides about the various processes necessary to produce the fine fruits of the island. The plantation tours are at 11 a.m. and 1:30 and 3:30 p.m. daily. The cost is $10.

Firefly, 20 miles east of Ocho Rios above Oracabessa, was the home of Sir Noël Coward and his longtime companion, Graham Payn, who, as executor of Coward's estate, donated it to the Jamaica National Trust. Now open Monday to Saturday from 10 a.m. to 4 p.m. for an admission of J$5 (95¢) the house has been kept exactly as it was on the day Sir Noël died in 1973, even to the clothes, including Hawaiian print shirts, hanging in the closet in his austere bedroom with its heavy mahogany four-poster. The library contains his large collection of books, and the living room is warm and comfortable with big armchairs and two grand pianos where he composed several famous tunes. Here the English Queen Mother was entertained. When the lobster mousse he was serving her melted, Coward opened a can of pea soup. Guests—Coward's "bloody loved ones"—who spent a night or more were housed in Blue Harbour, a villa nearer to Port Maria, where Sir Noël lived before building Firefly. Celebrated guests included Evelyn Waugh, Winston Churchill, Errol Flynn and his wife, Patrice Wymore, Laurence Olivier and Vivien Leigh, and such theatrical and cinema greats as Claudette Colbert, Katharine Hepburn, and Mary Martin. Paintings by the noted playwright, actor, author, and composer adorn the walls. An open patio looks out over the pool and the sea, and across the lawn, on his simple, flat white marble grave is inscribed simply: "Sir Noël Coward, born December 16, 1899, died March 26, 1973."

Coward was a frequent guest of Ian Fleming at **Goldeneye,** on the north shore, made fashionable in the 1950s. It was here that the most famous secret agent in the world, 007, was born in 1952. Fleming built the house in 1946, and wrote each of the 13 original Bond thrillers in it. The island permeates many of the Bond thrillers. Through the large gates, with bronze pineapples on the top, came a host of international celebrities: Evelyn Waugh, Truman Capote, Graham Greene. The house was closed and dilapidated for some time after the writer's death. However, its present owner, Christopher Blackwell, the British music publisher, has restored the property. It is furnished with "just the basics," the way Fleming wanted it, and the beachfront house can be rented (at a rate to be negotiated). Otherwise, unless you're a guest of the tenant, you aren't allowed to visit as it is private property. However, all 007 fans in this part of the world like to go by, hoping for a look. If you're interested in a rental and are prepared to pay at least $2,800 a week, get in touch with Seekers/Finders by calling the company in New York City (tel. 212/535-4515).

Harmony Hall (tel. 974-4233) was built near the end of the 19th century as another one of the "great houses" of Jamaica, this one connected with a pimento estate. Today, after a restoration, it's a center for a gallery selling paintings and other works by Jamaican artists. Arts and crafts are also sold, and some very good ones at that, not the usual junky assortment you often find on the beach. A bar in mahogany paneling has a collection of Victorian memorabilia. The gallery is open from 10 a.m. to 6 p.m., and the pub and restaurant from 11 a.m. to midnight. If you're at Harmony Hall for lunch, you can enjoy a British-style restaurant, the King's Arms, serving such dishes as fish and chips, steak-and-kidney pie, and shepherd's pie, a light luncheon costing around $10 per person. To reach it, you drive about four miles east of Ocho Rios on the main road to Oracabessa. Or else call and inquire about their free shuttle service.

Columbus Park Museum is a large, open area between the main coast road and the sea at Discovery Bay. Admission is free, and hours are 9 a.m. to 5 p.m. daily. You just pull off the road and then walk among the fantastic collection of exhibits, which range from a canoe made of a solid piece of cottonwood in the same way the Arawaks did it more than five centuries ago, to a stone cross, a monument originally placed on the Barrett estate at Retreat by Edward Barrett, whose sister, Elizabeth, became the wife of the poet Robert Browning. You'll see a tally, used to count bananas carried on men's heads from plantation to ship, as well as a planter's strongbox with a weighted lead base to prevent its theft. Also among the exhibits are 18th-century cannons used in the French and Spanish hostilities and during the American Revolution, and a Spanish water cooler and calcifier, a fish pot made from bamboo, a corn husker, a manual grass chopper, and a waterwheel of the type used on the sugar estates in the mid-19th century for all motive power. You can follow the history of sugar since its introduction in 1495 by Columbus, who brought canes from Gomera in the Canary Islands, and see how Khus Khus, a Jamaican perfume, is made from the roots of a plant, and how black dye is extracted from logwood. Pimento trees, from which allspice, used for curing meat, is produced, dominate the park. There is a large mural by Eugene S. Hyde, depicting the first landing of Columbus at Puerto Bueno (Discovery Bay) on May 4, 1494. The museum is well worth a visit to learn of the varied cultures that have influenced the development of Jamaica.

To see a model Jamaican small farm, visitors can go to **Circle B Farm,** Liberty District, near Priory, St. Ann, between Runaway Bay and Ocho Rios. Hilma and Bob Miller open their property to walking guided tours, costing $12 per person, including a welcome rum or fruit punch, fruits in season, and a native buffet lunch. To look at the diversified farm operation and enjoy the Millers' hospitality takes about two hours. The farm is open to visitors from 10 a.m. to 5 p.m. daily.

Another farm tour, visiting **Friendship Farm,** Walkers Wood, St. Ann, is offered daily from 9 a.m. to 4 p.m., lasting about an hour and costing $7 per person. You're taken aboard a jitney through the 530-acre working property where Jack Wilmot, the owner, raises diverse products: citrus, otaheti apples, Jamaican cherries, custard apples, root crops, spices, uncommon species of goats, sheep, rabbits, and ducks among them. There's a hilltop pool for swimming, and you can picnic in the area.

Gallery Joe James, Rio Bueno, Trelawny (no phone), is halfway between Ocho Rios and Montego Bay, 30 miles each way. Joe is one of those rare, gentle men in whose company you could happily spend a day or a year, listening to his talk about art, his life in England and Jamaica, his enthusiasm for painting and carving, and his hopes for the future development of art in Jamaica. He says he owes much of his success as an artist to the years he spent in flat, monochromatic Suffolk, England, but his pictures by contrast capture with ease the color and gaiety of the Jamaicans, their character, and their island. After a prior visit, James returned to Jamaica in 1966 and opened a gallery at Runaway Bay, moving to this site in 1968 where he built the present gallery and restaurant with his own bare hands—including putting in the plumbing and making most of the furnishings. He now employs a staff of 25 in the woodcraft workshop, where he personally supervises production of the delicately carved sculptures and woodcarvings which, with his own striking paintings, fill the gallery.

Enter the gallery from the parking lot. It is brilliant with portraits, landscapes, color, and life. Indigenous woods are used to create carvings of heads, small birds, or bowls. A carved crocodile, a crab, a turtle, or a turtle-shaped ashtray are among the interesting souvenirs.

At the **Lobster Bowl Restaurant,** early visitors can have breakfast for J$15 ($2.85). Lunch, noon to 3 p.m., is served inside or on the patio with the water almost lapping your feet. For dinner, 5 to 10 p.m., the cost of the main dish includes soup, salad, dessert, coffee, and a Tía Maria, plus a main course of grilled fish, broiled lobster, or sirloin steak. The wine list includes a wide variety, or you can order Red Stripe beer. The menu is kept small so that the quality of each dish is high. Lunch costs from $12.50; dinner, from $18.

Warning: Don't try to bargain for the items on sale here. Joe will voluntarily offer a discount if you buy a number of objects of reasonable value. Otherwise, the prices are as marked.

Boonoonoonoos

Boonoonoonoos is Jamaican for "very nice" or "super," and also stands for a "happening" in Jamaica.

At **Shaw Park Gardens,** you can stroll through the magnificent gardens to Lookout Point, where a 17th-century cannon points you to a view over Ocho Rios and Turtle Bay. Other paths lead past rushing waterfalls and babbling streams, and a flight of 100 steps takes you up or down, through the trees and bushes that are a sanctuary for a rich variety of bird life. There is a saying about this path, that those who walk together here will never forget the experience. Don't forget your camera. Hours are 9 a.m. to 5 p.m., and admission is $1. On most Tuesdays, a Boonoonoonoos Tea is served, along with a fashion show, followed by a band concert.

A **Reggae Party** at Coconut Grove Great House is a Jamaican experience you can enjoy Monday and Thursday from 7 to 11 p.m. Reggae music, a native floor show, an open Jamaican bar, and dinner are all part of the package, costing $25 for adults, $12.50 for children. For information, call Carl Young (tel. 974-2619).

All year on Sunday and Tuesday at 7 p.m. you can enjoy a **Jamaican Night on the White River,** a few miles to the east of Ocho Rios. The boat trip takes you up the torchlit river for a picnic supper on the banks. There is an open bar for as much as you can drink. A native folklore show precedes dancing under the stars. Telephone 974-2619 for reservations. The cost is $28.

SHOPPING: There are three main shopping plazas—Ocean Village, Pineapple Place, and Coconut Grove—all open daily except Sunday from 9 a.m. to 5 p.m. Almost everything is offered, including food, clothing, and souvenirs.

At **Ocean Village Shopping Centre,** a self-service laundromat offers ten-hour-a-day service. On Sunday it's only open until 2 p.m. Other facilities include Art Mart, Fantasia Boutique, Pretty Feet Shoeshop, and the Honey Bee Pastry Shop. The Pharmacy (tel. 974-2041) sells most proprietary brands, perfumes, plasters for sore heels, and suntan lotions, among its many wares. The Swiss Stores offer silver and gold charms with a general Jamaican theme. In addition, there are a commercial bank, Family Foods supermarket, a souvenir stand, a boutique for "ladies and gents," and shops selling in-bond perfumes, liquors, and crystal.

Pineapple Place Shopping Centre, just east of Ocho Rios, is a pleasant collection of cedar-shingle-roofed cottages set amid tropical flowers. Many shops are represented, including **Ruth Clarage** (tel. 974-2658), who specializes in beautifully colored hand-silkscreened prints. Many are embroidered by hand in her Montego Bay workshops, and if you wish, you can buy ready-made dresses, evening wear, and sports clothes. Tasteful matching ceramic jewelry can be bought also.

El Dorado (no phone) is a mass of jewelry and souvenirs including pendants of black and pink coral, silver rings with black coral, earrings, linen bags, and liquor. Paintings by local artists are also sold.

Ocho Rios Craft Park is a complex of some 150 stalls through which to browse. At the stalls, an eager seller will weave you a hat or a basket while you wait, or you can buy from the mixture of ready-made hats, hampers, handbags, placemats, and lampshades. Other stands stock hand-embroidered goods and will make up small items while you wait. Alongside all this activity, woodcarvers work on bowls, ashtrays, native heads, and statues chipped from lignum vitae, and make cups from local bamboo. Even if you don't want to buy, the park is worth a visit for it is lively and colorful.

The **Coconut Grove Shopping Plaza** is a collection of low-lying shops linked by walkways and shrubs. The merchandise consists mainly of local craft items. Many of your fellow shoppers may be cruise-ship passengers looking for something to buy.

You can see and purchase work by Jamaican artists at the **Frame Centre Gallery,** above the Little Pub on Main Street (tel. 974-2374). Work of established painters and up-and-coming talent can be seen here.

AFTER DARK: Hotels often provide live entertainment to which nonresidents are invited. Ask at your hotel desk where "the action" is on any given night. Otherwise, you may want to patronize the club previewed below.

Silk's Nightclub, Shaw's Park Hotel, Cutglass Bay (tel. 974-2552). There are slot machines in one corner, well-upholstered banquettes, a smallish dance floor, and a green-and-red decor whose contrasting tones seem to add energy to the sometimes-animated crowd of drinkers and dancers. Nonresidents of this well-known hotel can enter for J$15 ($2.85) each. The club is open nightly from 10 p.m. until very early the next morning, depending on the crowd (or lack of one).

RUNAWAY BAY:
Once this resort was a mere satellite of Ocho Rios. However, with the opening of some large resort hotels, plus a colony of smaller hostelries, Runaway Bay is now a destination in its own right. The place was named for escaped slaves who hid out in local caves.

Jack Tar Village, P.O. Box 112, Runaway Bay (tel. 973-3504), is a restored original plantation hall that has been turned into an all-inclusive package-deal resort similar to the chain's operation in Montego Bay. The brick foundation walls are probably those of an English fort dating from the 17th or 18th century. A subterranean passage, now bricked up, leads from the living room to the coral cliffs behind the house. The hall is named for Timothy Eaton, a Canadian who bought the house in the late 19th century.

The property is a successful coordination of the old blended with newer rooms added in wings that maintain the same architectural tradition. There are suites containing carved mahogany four-poster beds and other furnishings of the 18th-century period. Some of the bedrooms of the great house open onto an arched portico, and four units in the main house front the sea. On each side of the hall are bedroom wings with ocean views. These are furnished in a more restrained way, but with good judgment, utilizing tropical fabric designs and older mahogany pieces. Directly on the beach are the villas, with four bedrooms. Your veranda here will extend out over a rocky ledge, and the water is six feet below you. The mahogany trim used in parts of the hotel is beautiful. In the winter season, the inclusive rate in a single is $160 daily, dropping to $145 per person based on double occupancy. A third person sharing a double room is charged another $80 per night. *In summer, tariffs are reduced to $150 a night in a single, from $135 per person based on double occupancy.* Suites cost extra, of course. Children under 17 are not accepted.

Massages are free, and drinks, including wine at lunch and dinner, are also included in the package deal. There is no scuba-diving, but other water sports are free. Each week a barbecue is offered, along with midnight snacks. Once a week there is a Jamaican buffet with a show; otherwise, the piano bar provides nightly entertainment. The resident band plays six nights a week. The ambience of the great house and its surrounding garden is memorable. The entry lounge has smart styling, with old beams, an open fireplace, traditional wing chairs, and mahogany reproductions. The dining room is dignified yet warm as you sit on carved high-backed chairs. After your meal, you can walk to an adjoining lounge and terrace for a nightcap, watching the flickering lights from the swimming pool. On the grounds is a tennis court.

Jamaica, Jamaica, P.O. Box 58, Runaway Bay (tel. 973-2436, 516/868-6924 in New York, or toll free 800/858-8009), is probably the most interesting all-inclusive resort in the region. A stylish incarnation of a resort which has known several identities since it was built, it operates on a price plan including three meals a day, all drinks, free cigarettes, and a galaxy of other benefits. Its long, low-lying clubhouse is approached by passing through a park filled with tropical trees and shrubbery. Inside the lobby is the best re-creation of the South Seas in Jamaica, with hanging wicker chairs and totemic columns. Live music emanates from a stylish bar every evening at 6:30 p.m., reggae exercise classes are held twice daily, and there's an open-air gym filled with Nautilus equipment. Around one fountain winds a circular staircase whose centerpiece is a seashell-encrusted replica of a mermaid with a parasol. A nightclub offers live shows five nights a week at 10:30 p.m. Near the wide sandy beach, there's even a mini-jungle, with dangling hammocks. The nearby swimming pool is traversed by a wooden footbridge, and at a beachside restaurant and sports center, a complete list of sports-related activities are presented. There's even a nearby nude beach. Each of the 152 rooms has a view of a well-landscaped courtyard. Windows are angled toward the light, and each unit is air-conditioned with a private balcony overlooking the sea. Rates are based on double occupancy for a week. Winter rates range from $1,000 to $1,100 per person weekly, *dropping in the off-season to $900 to $1,000 per person, all inclusive for the week*. Single guests are accepted, but usually placed in a double room with a same-sex stranger. The resort does not accept children under the age of 16.

Caribbean Isle Hotel, P.O. Box 119, Runaway Bay (tel. 973-2364), is a small place with an informal atmosphere, a TV in the bar-lounge, and a dining room leading onto a sea-view patio where budget meals are served throughout the day by the swimming pool. Food service is from 8 a.m. to 9 p.m. The 11 rooms overlook the small beach and ocean, and are tastefully furnished, with private bath and shower and air conditioning. The hotel offers excellent value for your money, with a friendly atmosphere and good food. Dinner includes lobster and shrimp, fish, steak, pork chops, and chicken, all with a choice of french fries or creamed potato. A service charge is added. *In summer, room rates are $50 daily in a double, $40 in a single*. Daily winter rates are $52 in a double, $37 in a single, plus tax.

Ambiance Jamaica, P.O. Box 20, Runaway Bay (tel. 973-2066, or toll free 800/523-6504, 800/331-1262 in Florida). Scattered between its east and west wings, this establishment offers 74 accommodations encircling a garden courtyard with an above-ground swimming pool and nearly two acres of beachfront property. Each has an oceanfront view, air conditioning, and wicker furniture. In winter, a single or double costs from $100 daily. *In summer, a single goes for $50 daily and a double runs $60, plus service and taxes*. On the premises is a big-windowed bar filled with English-style dark paneling and leather-covered chairs. A turquoise-and-white dining room is an attractive setting for MAP, which costs $30 per person daily in any season.

4. Montego Bay

Montego Bay first attracted tourists in the 1940s when Doctor's Cave Beach was popular with the wealthy who bathed in the warm water fed by mineral springs. The town, now Jamaica's second-largest city, is on the northwest coast of the island. In spite of the large influx of visitors, it still retains its own identity with a thriving business and commercial center, and functions as the market town for most of western Jamaica. The history of Mo Bay, as the islanders call it, goes back to 1494 when it was discovered as an Arawak settlement.

As Montego Bay has its own international airport, those who vacation here have little need to visit Kingston, the island's capital, unless they are seeking the cultural pleasures of museums and galleries. Otherwise, you have everything in Mo Bay, the most cosmopolitan of Jamaica's resorts.

WHERE TO STAY: Montego Bay offers accommodations in all brackets, from the luxurious Round Hill to guesthouses. I'll begin with—

The Luxury Leaders

Round Hill (tel. 952-5150) is one of the most distinguished hotels in the Caribbean, a gathering place of the elite. It stands on a 98-acre peninsula, once part of Lord Monson's sugar plantation, lying eight miles west of Montego Bay. Everybody from the Kennedys to Sir Noël Coward to Cole Porter has driven up the casuarina-lined, curving driveway. Perhaps as they got out of the car, they'd hear Irving Berlin trying out one of his new pieces. As a watering spot for the rich and famous, Round Hill helped make Mo Bay a well-known resort when it opened its doors in 1954. Surrounded by gardens, Round Hill accommodates 200 well-heeled guests, who enjoy the private beach, the view of Jamaica's north shore, the vista of the mountains, and those ever-present hummingbirds. On handsome grounds, accommodations are in the Pineapple House's 36 handsome hotel rooms, with large folding windows giving onto views of the sea and coastline, or in shingle-roofed villas scattered over the hillside, some of which have their own pools. Some of the more than two dozen villas are privately owned (rented when the landlords are away). Many of these owners have stylish furnishings, including one-of-a-kind antiques and brass beds with pineapple-topped finials. In winter, room rates range from $300 to $310 daily, double occupancy, AP; and villa suites go for anywhere from $330 to $435 daily, double occupancy, also AP. *Even though the hotel is closed in summer, villas are available on a weekly rental basis, ranging from $1,500 for a two-bedroom selection all the way to $2,500 weekly for the deluxe choice, a four-bedroom honey with a private pool.* Tariffs include maid, cook, and gardener. Michael J. Kemp is the friendly, helpful, and considerate managing director.

At the little sandy bay is an intimate straw hut and an open terrace where guests congregate for informal luncheons. At the core of the building you'll find the celebrated piano bar which used to be familiar to Rodgers and Hammerstein. Dining is on a candlelit terrace beneath a giant banyan tree, or else you'll be served in the roofed-over Georgian colonial room overlooking the sea. The cuisine is a mixture of Jamaican and continental dishes. At times the finest buffet meals in Jamaica are set out here. Guests still dress for dinner, and black tie is more or less the rule on Saturday night. The place is sedate, and entertainment is varied—a bonfire beach picnic on Monday, a calypso barbecue on Wednesday, and dancing nightly. A program of water sports is offered, and guests can play tennis on the hotel's five all-weather courts.

Tryall Golf and Beach Club, in Hanover Parish (tel. 952-5110), is a complex of elegant villas and a stately stone and glass great house built in 1834 and vastly restored. The location is on a 2,200-acre sugarcane plantation, about 14 miles from the airport at Montego Bay and some 12 miles from the heart of the resort itself, a pleasant 20-minute drive. It has been called one of the grande dames of Jamaican resorts, and it is. For my money it's one of the most beautifully decorated resorts on the island, almost a cliché of Caribbean charm, with much use of chintz and vivid floral patterns, everything harmoniously color coordinated in sea blue and canary yellow.

A total of 44 recently refurbished units, all air-conditioned, are rented. The hotel offers large handsomely furnished guest rooms with picture windows and in some cases four-posters. The most expensive rentals are the 50 luxuriously furnished villas, set in lush tropical foliage, and designed and placed on the grounds for privacy. Villas come with full-time staff, including a cook, maid, laundress, and gardener. It's the ultimate in luxury for the island, and very expensive. The regular guest accommodations in winter range from $260 to $310 daily for two persons on the MAP. A two-bedroom villa rents from $2,600 per week, EP. However, there is a shoulder season between the first of November and mid-December and for the last two weeks in April when great house accommodations are reduced. At those times, two persons can stay in the great house at prices ranging from $170 to $210 daily, MAP. *In summer, regular accommodations range from $150 to $190, and a two-bedroom villa rents for $1,500 weekly, a three-bedroom villa for $1,800 weekly, both EP.*

The pride of the estate is the fairways of the 18-hole golf course, a 6,680-yard, par-71 course. Six Laykold tennis courts, two lit for night games, are also offered. Horseback rides along century-old trails can also be arranged. The pool has a swim-up bar. If you want to go on a tour, ask Vincent, the concierge. He seemingly knows everything about Jamaica.

For reservations and more information, get in touch with a travel agent or Tryall Golf and Beach Club, P.O. Box 3492, Alexandria, VA 22303 (tel. 703/370-8377, or toll free 800/336-4571).

The **Half Moon Club** (tel. 953-2211) lies about eight miles from Montego Bay and some six miles from the international airport. Set in a 400-acre estate alongside one of the finest white sandy beaches in Jamaica, it's better than ever, having undergone a much-needed $3-million refurbishing. Its managing director, Heinz E. W. Simonitsch, was awarded the "Golden Conch" as the most outstanding hotelier in the West Indies. Set in pleasant gardens, the resort complex consists of hotel rooms, cottages, apartments, and golf villas. Over the years it has attracted many a distinguished guest, including Vice-President George Bush. *In summer, singles range in price from $110 to $210, the latter for a deluxe suite. Comparable doubles cost $130 to $230. Two persons can rent a one-bedroom deluxe villa with living room, terraces, kitchen, and personal maid/cook for $190 daily.* In winter, the single rate ranges from $180 to $410 daily; doubles, $200 to $430. A one-bedroom villa for two persons costs from $360 daily.

The clubhouse grill has a personal touch, set as it is beside a working water wheel from a bygone sugar estate. For my comments on the cuisine served here, refer to the restaurant section. Connected to the main building, the Seagrape Terrace is also a choice place to dine. Meals are served on an outdoor terrace under the spreading branches of an 80-year-old sea grape tree. A lattice-trimmed gazebo adds decoration, while a covered veranda offers shelter in case of rain. The club has a calypso group, a resident band, and nightly shows, or you can taxi into Montego Bay to sample the nightlife there. The Half Moon also has a shopping arcade with a pharmacy and boutiques, plus a beauty salon, as well as a sauna and massage facilities. From the west side of the property, which offers a mile of swimming beach, a guest can sail, windsurf, or snorkel, and from the east side it's possible to go scuba-diving or deep-sea fishing. One can swim in the club's two major freshwater pools or play tennis on one of the club's 13 courts (four of which are floodlit at night). There are also four lit squash courts (British tradition lives on), and of course the 18-hole Robert Trent Jones–designed golf course is another lure.

All-Inclusive Resorts

Sandals Royal Caribbean Hotel, P.O. Box 167 (tel. 953-2231), was, in 1966, the choice of Queen Elizabeth II and Prince Philip when they visited the island. The building lies on its own private beach, and all its ground-floor rooms and public areas are paved with marble. There are three bars. The air-conditioned rooms with a choice of twin or king-size beds contain radios, phones, and hair dryers, and tariffs include all meals, anytime snacks at the Beach Bar and Grill, unlimited drinks at any of the bars, a continental breakfast you can have served in bed if you prefer, and afternoon tea. In high season, all-inclusive room rates are quoted for seven nights and eight days. Per-person tariffs, based on double occupancy, range from a low of $815 for standard rooms to a high of $1,085, the latter for a junior suite. *In summer, the seven-night/ eight-day package, all inclusive, ranges from a low $680 per person based on double occupancy to a high of $835.* Single guests have two booking options. They may book a room at the listed per-person rate and the resort will match another guest of the same sex as a roommate, or else the single guest may opt for an exclusive (no-share) single room at the listed per-person prices plus 50%.

Activities include day and night tennis, snorkeling, Sunfish sailing, and windsurfing, all free. If you require lessons, there is a charge of $5 per half hour. Also available are scuba-diving, $15 per half hour, and deep-sea fishing, $187.50 per half day and $300 per full day. A full entertainment program is offered year round, and for the young at heart the hotel has added a late-night disco. Sandals Royal Caribbean has undergone considerable refurbishment to enhance its "Old Jamaican" atmosphere.

Sandals Resort Beach Club, P.O. Box 100 (tel. 952-5510), is a couples-only resort, a spin-off of the famous Couples in Ocho Rios. Accommodations are either in villas spread along 1,700 feet of white sand beach or in the main house where house where all bedrooms face the sea and have private balconies. All are air-conditioned and well furnished. Sandals quotes one price for two guests. In winter, the all-inclusive rate for seven nights and eight days ranges from a low of $1,550 for standard rooms to a high of $2,400 for the beach suites. *In summer, the all-inclusive tariff for two persons for seven nights and eight days runs from a low of $1,495 to a high of $1,950.* You can have a drink at the large indoor bar or at the one by the pool. Most meals are served in the open air, or if you prefer, there's a delightful dining room. The Olympic-size pool supplements sea bathing, and the beach is dotted with thatched roofs under which loungers beckon. The resort has its own tennis courts, a croquet lawn, and a sauna. Water sports are provided at the beach. Sandals is one of the most romantic hideaways in Mo Bay. Incidentally, you don't have to be married: all you need do is check in here as a male-female couple. Naturally, children are not welcome.

Jack Tar Village, P.O. Box 144 (tel. 952-4340, or toll free 800/527-9299), is called simply "The Village" in Mo Bay. Like its sister hotels in Puerto Plata, Runaway Bay, and Grand Bahama, it offers one of those "all-inclusive" package deals, including, while you're here: all meals; unlimited wine with lunch and dinner; unlimited beer, wine, and liquor both day and night; daytime tennis; golf greens fees; water sports such as windsurfing, waterskiing, snorkeling, and sailing; nightly entertainment; sauna and massages; free use of the tennis clinic; and even reggae dance lessons. Its policy, as of this writing, is to require no minimum stay. That means a rate in winter of $180 daily in a single, $140 per person in a double. Children under 12 sharing a full double with their parents are charged $50 year round. *Rates go down in summer to $160 daily in a single, $120 per person in a double.* Private balconies open directly onto Montego Bay, and guests practically live in their swimsuits (and skimpy ones at that). A few steps from your private room lead directly to the beach. Lunch is served at beachside or in the main dining room.

Club Paradise, Chatham Beach (tel. 952-4780, or toll free 800/526-2422), about a mile and a half east of Montego Bay, near some of the most popular public beaches, reopened after a facelift in 1986. It stands amid manicured gardens across the street from the sea. Designed in a British colonial style of neo-Victorian gingerbread, tall columns, and white lattices, it is airy, comfortable, and stylish. On the premises are antique cannons, flower-draped arbors, Chippendale-style crisscrossed balustrades, gazebos, and three-tiered fountains where water splashes from one level to another. A dining room is under a high arched ceiling sheathed in mahogany whose view opens onto a flagstone-covered courtyard. The 100 accommodations lie in sprawling motel-like units around the pool in back. Each unit is air-conditioned, containing a private balcony or patio, private bath, and simple mahogany furniture. Prices include three meals a day, all drinks, cigarettes, transfers from the airport, free tennis on a pair of illuminated courts, tax, and gratuities. Depending on the accommodation, winter rates for a seven-night stay range from $900 to $1,050 per person in a double, $1,250 to $1,450 in a single. *In summer, a seven-night sojourn costs between $750 and $900 per person in a double and from $1,000 to $1,300 in a single.*

Lady Diane's Seawatch, 5 Kent Ave. (tel. 952-4415). Its motivating health-conscious philosophy makes guests think they've registered in a yoga and meditation retreat instead of a conventional hotel. It was established in 1983 when Richard and Beva Cherkiss quit their jobs in New York's garment district to return to Beva's native Jamaica. They quickly found, purchased, and redecorated a low-slung, U-shaped villa whose wings encompassed a palm-studded lawn and a formal swimming pool. In its center they built the most charming plank-covered terrace in Montego Bay. From its surface you can enjoy a view of the sea and a popular beach just across the street. The hotel contains 14 stylishly antique bedrooms, dozens of pieces of wicker furniture, lattices, and alluring shades of pink, green, and blue. The kitchens are the only place I know of in Jamaica that have insistently adapted Jamaican ingredients to the rigors of a macrobiotic diet. All meals are "natural," served family style. Ingredients include only organic grains, beans, and flours, these ingredients concocted into all-vegetarian meals which the clientele appreciates. Year-round prices are almost always quoted on a weekly basis: $800 in a single, $1,350 in a double, with meals, snacks, shiatsu massages, taxes, service, and airport transfers included. Call collect for reservations or information.

First-Class Choices

Wyndham Rose Hall Beach Hotel and Country Club, P.O. 999 (tel. 953-2650, or toll free 800/822-4200), is a 500-room hotel on a former sugar plantation that once covered 7,000 acres. The hotel abuts the 200-year-old home of the legendary "White Witch of Rose Hall," now a historic site. Just nine miles east of the Montego Bay Airport, Wyndham Rose Hall is at the bottom of a rolling 30-acre site along the north-coast highway. The hotel is constructed of several ochre-colored rectangular cubes set amid flowering gardens with palms, shrubs, fountains, and winding access roads. Although it's popular as a convention site, the hotel also caters to a family-oriented market where children are considered an important part of the clientele. Behind the reception area at the bottom of a flight of stairs there are three pools—one for wading, one for swimming, and a third for diving. It's never more than a short walk to one of the many bars scattered around the hotel property, and a sandy beach, rental sailboats, and a top-rated golf course meandering over a part of the hotel grounds are here for the enjoyment of the guests. You'll also find three restaurants and a busy staff of social organizers. A seven-court lit tennis complex is headed by world-class professionals who offer a complete tennis program. The all-weather Laykold courts are at the side door of the hotel and within view of the ocean.

The seven-story, H-shaped structure ensures that nearly every room has a view of the sea. Most units have two oversize double beds. Singles are furnished with a Chesterfield that can convert to a double bed. All rooms have private balconies. The charges are $130 to $150 daily in high season for a single or double room. MAP costs another $40 or $50 per person. *Off-season, singles or doubles range in price from $85 to $115 daily.*

Trelawny Beach Hotel (tel. 954-2450) is a 350-room, self-contained resort in Falmouth, about half an hour's drive from Sangster International Airport in Montego Bay, under Warwick International Hotels. It recently underwent a $2-million renovation program. The end result is an open-air, tropical feeling. Locally made materials, in keeping with the policy of the "New Jamaica," were used when possible, including wicker furniture along with Jamaican floral fabrics. The focal point of Trelawny is the circular lobby. The 1,400-foot beach area was achieved with the leasing of 1,100 feet of adjacent frontage. Bohíos were built around the pool area, and many new trees and flowers have been planted in the gardens to give everything a lusher look.

In winter, the daily MAP rates per person are $118 in a single, $93 in a double, and $83 in a triple. Children 14 and under may share a room with an adult at $20, MAP. Accommodations are in air-conditioned rooms with private balconies and an ocean or mountain view. *Daily MAP rates in summer are $92 in a single, $68 per person in a double, and $60 per person in a triple.* There is a maximum of three persons to a room. Lunch is an extra $9 for adults, $5 for children, daily if desired. Taxes and service are extra. A honeymoon package is available. Rates include complimentary tennis, water sports, live entertainment nightly, shuttle-bus service to Mo Bay, and parties. Free lessons are given in scuba-diving, snorkeling, Sunfish sailing, windsurfing, and waterskiing, even reggae dancing. The resort has four lit Laykold tennis courts, plus a swimming pool. Your best bet for lunch or dinner is the Palm Terrace, where an à la carte selection is offered at midday. Dinner is also served in the Jamaican Room, although it's open only depending on occupancy of the hotel and never on barbecue nights. The Jamaican Room is an indoor, air-conditioned facility with wicker chairs, cedar tables, and carpeting. You can order snacks and drinks at the Almond Tree coffeeshop, adjacent to the Palm Terrace, and at poolside.

Holiday Inn, P.O. Box 480 (tel. 953-2485), is an oceanside hotel whose stone façade is separated from the busy street outside by a screen of palm trees. The hotel assures its guests' privacy by having a guard at the entrance to screen persons coming in. Inside you find numerous amenities, including a free-form pool whose narrowest section is spanned by an arched footbridge. A sandy beach, a variety of water sports (glass-bottom boats, sailboats, and scuba- and skindiving), a disco, a Jamaica-style nightclub with limbo dancers and fire-eating entertainers, and tennis courts are also available for the patrons' enjoyment. Other facilities are a children's playground and a choice of five bars—one in an inner atrium—plus four restaurants. In winter, singles range from $102 to $135 daily. Doubles go for $106 to $142. *In summer, singles are priced from $67 to $86 while doubles cost $73 to $89.* Taxes and service are added to the bill. MAP is available for $42 more per adult, $33 per child under 12.

Less Expensive Choices

Winged Victory Hotel, 5 Queen's Dr. (tel. 952-3891). Glistening, tall, and modern, this hotel delays revealing its true beauty until you pass through its comfortable public rooms into a Mediterranean-style courtyard in back. There, urn-shaped balustrades enclose a charming terraced garden, a sapphire-blue pool, fringes of plants, trees, and flowering shrubs, along with a veranda looking over the faraway crescent of Montego Bay. The veranda's best feature is the Calabash Restaurant, reviewed separately. The dignified owner, Roma Chin Sue, added about two dozen additional rooms to her already well-known restaurant in 1985. All but five have a private balcony or veranda, along with an attractively eclectic decor that is part Chinese, part colonial, and part Iberian. In winter, singles cost $55 to $95 daily; doubles, $65 to $115. *In summer, single or double rooms rent for $50 to $85 daily.* MAP can be arranged for another $35 per person daily. By far the most luxurious accommodation is the four-bedroom penthouse. Designed as a duplex, it offers two levels of panoramic balconies, a view of the sun-flooded landscape, an industrial kitchen capable of serving a banquet, and a fine collection of Chinese art and furniture. Each bedroom, suitable for two persons, rents in high season for $170 daily, *dropping to $150 per bedroom in low season.*

Wexford Court Hotel, Gloucester Avenue, P.O. Box 239 (tel. 952-2854), is on the main road about ten minutes to downtown Mo Bay and close to Doctor's Cave Beach. The small hotel has a pleasant pool and a patio where in season calypso is enjoyed. The rooms are air-conditioned, and some have nice living/dining areas, bathrooms, and kitchenettes, if you wish to cook for yourself. All rooms have patios shaded by gables and Swiss chalet-style roofs. *In summer, singles range in price from $50 to $60 daily, and doubles go for $60 to $70. Triple rooms are also available, costing from $70 to $80.* In winter, rates go up: from $60 to $75 daily in a single, from $70 to $85 in a double, and from $80 to $95 in a triple. For breakfast and dinner, add another $24 per person daily. The Wexford Grill includes a good selection of Jamaican dishes, such as chicken deep fried with honey. Guests can enjoy drinks in the Wayside Pub. The hotel is owned and operated by Godfrey G. Dyer, who has led an interesting life, being a former policeman, detective, and taxi business entrepreneur. When he felt his other ventures were getting too demanding, he settled for just running the hotel.

Royal Court Hotel, Sewell Avenue (tel. 952-4531), is a budget accommodation set on the hillside overlooking Montego Bay, with a swimming pool. The rooms are furnished with bright, tasteful colors. All have air conditioning, private bathrooms, and patios. The larger ones have fully equipped kitchenettes. *The charge in summer for a single is $35 to $62; for a double, $45 to $62.* In winter, a single costs $50 to $74; a double $60 to $85, all EP, plus tax. Meals are served in the Grotto Bar, and dinner is a set meal. On Sunday evening, a Jamaican buffet is served around the pool. Nightly, a resident band plays soft music on the patio under the stars, for dancing or listening. Free transportation is provided to the town, the beach, and the golf course and tennis club, where special rates can be arranged for hotel guests. This hotel is spotlessly clean, attractive, has a charming atmosphere, and is good value.

Carlyle Beach Hotel, P.O. Box 412 (tel. 952-4140), is an excellent choice for a budget stay. Separated from the sea by the main road, the hotel is built around the large pool and patio, but you can walk over to the beach if you prefer to swim in the sea. All 52 rooms are air-conditioned and have large, cool balconies with a view of the Caribbean. The lobby is cheerful and spacious, and there is a quiet lounge with comfortable chairs. The Pub Bar and Restaurant is decorated in a British old-world style. For lunch, you can select cold salads, sandwiches, or something from the grill. Dinner might begin with a seafood cocktail and follow with lobster, steak, or fresh fish. Freshly cooked vegetables are served with all main courses. Desserts, cheeses, and excellent coffee will add the finishing touches to your meal. The hotel has a pleasant atmosphere and offers good value. It's on Kent Avenue and is within walking distance of Montego Bay's best shopping area. *In summer, a single costs $46 to $54; a double, $58 to $65; and a triple, $68 to $74.* In winter, costs will rise: $70 to $85 in a single, $80 to $95 in a double, and $90 to $105 in a triple. Children under 12 stay free in a room with adults. For MAP, *add $20 to all rates in summer,* $22 in winter. All three meals cost an additional *$26 in summer,* $30 in winter.

Ocean View Guest House, Sunset Avenue, P.O. Box 210 (tel. 952-2662), is half a mile from the airport and the same distance from the public beach. Buses pass the door for the ride down into Mo Bay, and the owner runs his own bus to and from the airport. There is a small library and TV room. Nightly video movies are shown free, and satellite reception is also available. You can use a stock of Jamaican music tapes to provide background, or you might want to hurl a few darts. All the rooms are either air-conditioned or have fans. Each has hot and cold running water, and most open onto a veranda or the spacious front porch. It's quietest at the back. *In the off-season, room rates are $15 in a single, $12 per person in a double.* In winter, the costs rise to $20 in a single, $18 per person in a double. Breakfast at $3 and dinner from $4 are offered. The owner will arrange for you to play tennis or golf, and water sports can also be arranged.

Toby Inn, P.O. Box 467 (tel. 952-4370), is another budget accommodation. It's not on the sea, but the famous Doctor's Cave Beach is a short walk away. There is a pool, and the Cozy Tree Bay will cater to your immediate needs if you don't want to go into town. In season, live entertainment is presented most nights of the week, but things are quiet off-season. All rooms are air-conditioned and have bathrooms. In winter, singles on the EP range from $70 daily and doubles run $80 and up, all EP. Room tax is extra. *In the off-season, prices drop to $55 daily in a single, $60 in a double.* You'll be served a good breakfast and a pleasant dinner, including Jamaican dishes, in the air-conditioned dining room or on the patio. There is also a Chinese-Polynesian restaurant, the Pagoda Kai.

Doctor's Cave Beach Hotel, P.O. Box 94 (tel. 952-4355), across the highway from the famous beach, is backed by lush vegetation and has a small garden patio among the trees, with a dance floor. There's a pool and a game room for wet days. Meals are taken on the terrace surrounded by trees, which are floodlit at night. In the Cascade bar, with stone walls and wooden roof, you can listen to music. *EP singles in the off-season rent from $55 daily; doubles, from $75, EP.* In winter, tariffs in a single increase to $65 daily; in a double, from $85. For breakfast and dinner, add $25 per person per day extra to the charges quoted. Along one of the passages are pictures of all the national figures from Admirals Rodney and Nelson to the present prime minister.

Richmond Hill, Union Street, P.O. Box 362 (tel. 952-3859), is visited primarily by diners (see my recommendations to follow), but it's also an inn, a remodeled historic manor house built in the 1700s. The property was owned by the Dewars, a Scottish clan from which the famous whisky takes its name. Units are scattered in a series of outbuildings surrounding the pool. The bedrooms aren't spacious, but are in keeping with the character of the old house. A few of the accommodations have kitchens and air conditioning, and all open onto verandas. In winter, singles pay $50 daily; doubles, $68. *In summer, rates are lowered: singles cost from $45; doubles, $55.*

FOOD IN MO BAY: The resort has some of the finest—and most expensive—dining on the island. But if you're watching your wallet, you'll find that food is often sold right on the street. For example, on Kent Avenue you might try jerk pork, a delicacy peculiar to Jamaica. Seasoned spareribs are also grilled over charcoal fires and sold with extra-hot sauce. Naturally, you order a Red Stripe beer to go with it.

Cooked shrimp are also sold on the streets of Mo Bay. They don't look it, but they're very hotly spiced, so be warned. If you have an efficiency unit with a kitchenette, you might also want to buy fresh lobster or the "catch of the day" from Mo Bay fishermen. It's easily and readily available.

Now, my more formal dining selections below.

Brigadoon Restaurant, 2 Sewell Ave., off Queen's Drive (tel. 952-1723), offers free limousine service from and to your Mo Bay hotel. The restaurant is open from 5 p.m. to midnight. The pleasant entrance leads to the bar, where you can sit on a comfortable stool and try a Veta's Special before dinner. There is an inside dining room in case of bad weather, but most of the time you eat on the wide, half-covered patio between the tropical forest and the sea, with candles on the tables and wicker-shaded lights flickering among the trees. A friendly staff knows what good service is and makes sure you enjoy your meal. From the menu of interesting dishes, why not try a Brigadoon conch maska of shellfish with a rum and garlic sauce? You might like the smoked dolphin with lemon sauce or escargots bourguignonnes before embarking on the main meal, which includes soup, hot bread and butter, salad, and fresh vegetables in the price of the main course. Among the main dishes, fresh fish, especially red snapper and kingfish, are the big drawing cards. You can also order U.S. T-bone steaks and prime sirloin. One specialty is labeled simply "Jamaican National Dish," and the chef asks you to trust him! Among the desserts, try the Jamaican banana flambé, followed by coffee from the Blue Mountain. My last dining tab here came to $30. Dress at the Brigadoon is informal, and you can dance after dinner or just listen to calypso music or the latest reggae. There is no cover and no minimum.

The **Diplomat,** 9 Queen's Dr. (tel. 952-3353), offers a delightful, informal yet elegant evening. Hidden behind a long white wall, gates lead to a sweeping driveway through clipped lawns, old trees, and colorful flower beds to a gracious house, not as old as its columned style would suggest. The marble-floored entrance with an Italianate water garden leads into the hall where there's a small bar, and down two steps into the tastefully simple drawing room and lounge. Comfortable sofas and armchairs are gathered around coffee tables. A grand piano in the corner is played softly by a Jamaican, Crawford, who seems to know every tune ever written. The bar waiter takes your drink order, and you will probably be greeted by the manager, Georg Kahl, who has spent more than 30 years in the restaurant business. He was born in Poland of German parents, and has traveled widely. The restaurant does not require ties and jackets for men, but shorts and T-shirts are frowned on. Georg will call the maître d' to take your order from the well-balanced menu.

Guests dine on the terrace overlooking a floodlit ornamental pool with fountains playing and trees silhouetted with lights leading down toward the sea. The calm efficiency of the waiters completes a pleasant evening. Liqueurs are served at your table or in the drawing room. Expect to spend $25 per person. The restaurant is open only for dinner, which it serves year round from 6:30 to 10:30 p.m. except on Sunday. Georg is in partnership with Ralph Chapman, a retired English businessman who built the house as his private home. This is a good place from which to watch Mo Bay's famous sunsets.

The **Club House Restaurant,** Half Moon Golf Course (tel. 953-2314). After a drive through a rolling landscape, you arrive at a stone ruin of what used to be a water wheel for a sugar plantation. Today the site is the center of the sophisticated nouvelle cuisine of its Swiss-born operator, Hans Schenk. The comfortable, breeze-filled building containing the restaurant was constructed in the 1940s as the vacation retreat of a well-known publisher. Guests dine on an open terrace, in a veranda setting of pink napery, candlelight, and a view of water and greenery. The restaurant is open daily from noon to 2 p.m. and 7 to 10 p.m. Full meals cost from $20 at lunch, from $40 at dinner. The creative combinations of Jamaican food have won Mr. Schenk favorable publicity in gastronomic circles of two continents. Specialties include akee with smoked marlin, a fisherman's salad served warm with vinaigrette, Jamaican bouillabaisse, lobster-and-papaya mousse, and a dish called "Best of Jamaica," combining curried goat, akee, shrimp, lobster, fish, and smoked marlin. Flambéed lobster calypso style, with aged rum and a spicy sauce, is a particular favorite. The dessert specialty is orange crêpes, flambéed in brown-sugar brandy and served with oranges, orange liqueur, and ice cream. Reservations are needed, and a mini-van will be sent to most hotels to pick you up.

Julia's, Julia's Estate, Bogue Hill (tel. 952-1772). The winding jungle road you take to reach this place is part of the evening's before-dinner entertainment. After a jolting ride to a site high above the city and its bay, you pass through a walled-in park which long ago was the site of a private home. Today the building that is the land's focal point is a long, low-slung modern house whose fresh decor encompasses sweeping views. Go between 7 and 9:30 p.m., and don't forget to make a reservation (a van will come to your hotel and pick you up). Raimondo and Julia Meglio, drawing on the cuisine of their native Italy, prepare chicken cacciatore, breaded milanese cutlet with tomato sauce and mozzarella cheese, filet of fresh fish with lime juice and butter, and seven different kinds of pasta, among other dishes. Meals cost from $35 per person.

Restaurant Ambrosia, Wyndham Rose Hall (tel. 953-2650). The cuisine it serves stresses northern Italian recipes. It sits across the highway from one of the largest hotels in Montego Bay, a few miles from the center. Its cedar-shingled design and its trio of steeply pointed roofs give the impression that the place is a clubhouse for some neocolonial country club. Once you enter the courtyard, complete with a set of cannons, you find yourself in one of the loveliest restaurants in the area. You'll enjoy a sweeping view over the rolling lawns leading past the hotel and down to the sea, interrupted only by buff-colored Doric columns. Only dinner is served, and it's offered nightly except Wednesday from 6:30 to 9:30 p.m. Full meals, costing from $45 per person, might include zampone (stuffed pig's foot), osso bucco, saltimbocca, veal piccata, manicotti with seafood, zuppa pavese, and an amaretto tart.

Marguerite's by the Sea, Gloucester Avenue (tel. 952-4777), is a well-known Mo Bay eatery, which, as its name implies, overlooks the sea. You can dine on a terrace overlooking the water, enjoying the fresh food which is usually well prepared and served by a friendly staff, along with a tasteful atmosphere. Lobster salad and smoked marlin are popular for lunch. The menu changes, depending on the availability of fresh produce. You can, however, generally count on getting lobster or a grilled New York sirloin. Invariably there is a "catch of the day," and you can ask the chef to steam it in coconut milk if you prefer. International dishes include the likes of chicken chasseur or a seafood crêpe. For a complete dinner with wine, the tab is likely to be $30. It's best to call for a reservation. You may not need it, but why take a chance? The place is open nightly from 6 to 10:30 p.m.

Richmond Hill Inn, Union Street (tel. 952-3859), is an old plantation house above the bustle of the bay area. The restaurant overlooks, and is part of, a large patio with a swimming pool and romanesque statues on low plinths beside it. A stone balustrade runs around the patio, which has views over the town and the bay. Music is muted and classical in the early evening, but calypso is introduced later on. You might begin your repast with a shrimp-and-lobster cocktail, which for many years I have found their best appetizer. Dolphin (the fish, that is) is regularly featured among the "catch of the day." I generally skip over surf and turf to order their well-prepared wienerschnitzel. If you're traditional, try the sirloin or lamb chops, and don't plan to escape for less than $35 for dinner, served from 7 to 9:30 p.m.

The **Calabash Restaurant,** 5 Queen's Dr. (tel. 952-3891). Perched 500 feet above the distant sea, this well-established restaurant has amused and entertained such luminaries as Peter O'Toole, Robert McNamara, Leonard Bernstein, Francis Ford Coppola, and Roger Moore. It was originally built as a private villa by a doctor in the 1920s. About 20 years ago Roma Chin Sue, its owner, established its Mediterranean-style courtyard and its elegantly simple eagle's-nest patio as a well-managed restaurant. Full meals cost from $35, featuring seafood, Jamaican classics, and international favorites. These include curried goat, surf and turf, the house specialty of mixed seafood en coquille (served with a cheese-and-brandy sauce), filet mignon with mushrooms and a Créole sauce, sautéed veal with a sherry sauce, spicy pork in ginger sauce, and a year-round version of a Jamaican Christmas cake. Meals are served daily from noon to 2 p.m. and 6 p.m. "until." Reservations are necessary. The previously recommended Winged Victory Hotel is the mother of this restaurant.

The **Cascade Room** at the Pelican, Gloucester Avenue (tel. 952-3171), in an intimate setting and relaxing atmosphere, is one of Montego Bay's finest seafood restaurants. Rushing waterfalls and cool tropical foliage blend with the natural cedar of the interior to make dining an enjoyable experience. Excellent service combines with the finest of seafood, such as lobster Thermidor, shrimp stuffed with crabmeat, filet of red snapper, and conch chowder, to name a few. There is bar service and an adequate choice of wines. Dinner costs $15 to $25 per person. The restaurant is open from 6 p.m.

The **Town House,** 16 Church St. (tel. 952-2660), is a lovely old, red-brick house built in 1765. The restaurant has recommendations from, among others, *Gourmet* magazine. You find the bar and restaurant around at the back of the house in what used to be the cellars, now air-conditioned with tables set around the walls. Old ship lanterns give a warm light, and pictures of bygone days and of soldiers of the past adorn the walls. Straight-back chairs with cane seats surround tables on which lamps flicker. Flagstones lead from the bar to the restaurant, and you sip your apéritif while choosing your meal. Orders are individually prepared by the chef, James H. Snead. The place is a tranquil, cool luncheon choice, if you want to dine lightly, enjoying sandwiches and salads—or more elaborate fare if you're hungry—far removed from the noonday glare of Mo Bay. If you return for dinner, it becomes more atmospheric, and you're faced with a wide and good selection of main courses. Everybody seemingly talks favorably of red snapper en papillotte, that is, baked in a paper bag. You might also try stuffed lobster. I'm fond of the chef's large rack of barbecued spareribs with the owner's special Tennessee sauce. Another specialty is "surf and turf kebabs." You'll easily spend from $25 for dinner and about $15 for lunch, which is not served on Sunday. Otherwise, it's best to go from noon to 2:30 p.m. and 7 to 9:30 p.m.

House of Lords Supper Club and Seafood Palace, in W. G. Hilcram's entertainment complex, Holiday Village, Rose Hall (tel. 953-2113), is set back from the traffic of the north-coast highway across from the Holiday Inn. This Jamaican-owned restaurant is on the upper floor of a concrete-and-glass building whose lower level contains a popular disco and a snackbar. To go to the dining room, you climb a winding, red-carpeted stairway to reach the slightly faded red-and-white supper club. Here you'll be treated to such specialties as lobster or shrimp cocktail, conch or fish chowder, Jamaican pepperpot soup, three kinds of lobster, a selection of fish, chicken Créole or Cordon Bleu, or sirloin steak. The waiters are formally dressed and usually quite courteous. Full dinners begin at around J$110 ($21). The restaurant is open only for dinner seven days a week, but if you're in the neighborhood at lunchtime, the snackbar on the ground floor is open 24 hours every day. Many dinner guests end their evening with a stop at the ground-floor Disco Inferno (see "After Dark," below).

Dolphin Grill, Holiday Village (tel. 953-2676), is a well-planned complex of eating facilities clustered around a kidney-shaped pool where many guests choose to spend at least part of the afternoon. Near the Holiday Inn, the Jamaican-owned establishment features the pool surrounded with tables, and the Quarterdeck bar's raised and covered platform just a few steps away. If you wish, you can have your meal in the main dining room.

The Gold Unicorn, 7 Queen's Dr. (tel. 952-0884), was established in 1986 and quickly caught on as an excellent restaurant. It lies inside the glistening walls of a private villa in a residential section of town. Its crusty but kindly chef and owner is Bill McCabe, formerly from Delaware. Guests dine amid white lattices around a boomerang-shaped pool, near copses of sea grape and views of the faraway ocean. Lunches, costing from J$25 ($4.75), are served from 11:30 a.m. to 2:30 p.m. daily except Sunday. Dinners, from J$90 ($13.50), are offered daily except Sunday from 7 to 10 p.m. On Sunday a buffet dinner is on from 5:30 to 9:30 p.m. Specialties include well-prepared versions of lobster imperial, pâté with cognac and fresh cream, veal and U.S. prime beef, smoked marlin with capers, lobster bisque with sherry and cognac, fisherman's stew, the catch of the day, and a red pea purée with chopped onion, egg yolk, and sour cream. Dinner reservations are a good idea, especially on weekends in high season.

Dining in Falmouth

Glistening Waters Inn and Marina, Falmouth (tel. 954-3229). Residents of Montego Bay sometimes make the 22-mile drive out here just to sample an ambience of the almost-forgotten Jamaica of another era. The restaurant is housed in what was originally a private clubhouse of the aristocrats of nearby Trelawny. About eight years ago Pat and Patricia Hastings transformed the wood-frame building into a neighborhood restaurant, where one of the few decisions that patrons need to make is whether to sit behind the screens of the wood-walled plantation-style interior or on the outside veranda overlooking the quiet lagoon. The furniture here may remind you of a stage set for *Night of the Iguana.* Wicker chairs alternate with simple wicker tables.

Menu items may include many local fish dishes such as snapper or kingfish, often marinated in a vinegar sauce (with onions, carrots, pimento, peppers, and allspice), served with bammy (a form of cassava bread). Other specialties are three different lobster dishes, three different preparations of shrimp, three different conch viands, fried rice, and pork served as chops or in a stew. Lunches begin at J$50 ($9.50); dinners at J$75 ($14.25). Hours are 9 a.m. to 9 p.m. daily. Many guests look forward to coming here because the waters of the lagoon are memorable. They contain a rare form of phosphorescent microbes which, when the waters are agitated, glow in the dark. Boat cruises, costing J$40 ($7.60), go out between 6 and 7 p.m. and again between 7 and 8 p.m. on Monday, Tuesday, Wednesday, Friday, and Saturday.

WHAT TO DO: Rafting on the Martha Brae is an exciting adventure. To reach the starting point, drive east to Falmouth and turn approximately three miles inland to **Martha Brae's Rafters Village.** The rafts are similar to those on the Rio Grande, and charge about $26 per raft, with only two persons allowed on a raft, plus a small child if accompanied by an adult. The raft trips, lasting about an hour, operate seven days a week from 9 a.m. to 4 p.m. You sit on a raised dais on bamboo logs. The rafters supplement their incomes by selling carved gourds. Along the way you can stop and order cool drinks or beer along the banks of the river. There is a bar, a restaurant, and a souvenir shop in the village. Later you get a souvenir rafting certificate.

Cornwall Beach, opposite the Club Casa Montego, is Jamaica's finest underwater marine park and fun complex, a long stretch of white sand beach with dressing cabañas. Water sports, scuba-diving, and snorkeling are available. Admission to the beach is J$2 (40¢) per adult, J$1 (20¢) for children, for the entire day. A bar and cafeteria offer refreshment. Hours are 9 a.m. to 5 p.m. daily.

Doctor's Cave Beach, across from the Montego Bay Club, helped launch Mo Bay as a resort in the 1940s. Admission to the beach is J$2 (40¢) for adults, J$1 (20¢) for children. You can participate in water sports here. Dressing rooms, chairs, umbrellas, and rafts are available from 9 a.m. to 5 p.m. daily.

For a plantation tour and even a hot-air balloon ride to get a bird's-eye view of the countryside, go on a **Hilton High Day Tour** (tel. 952-3343), with an office on Beach View Plaza. Round-trip transportation on a scenic drive through historic plantation areas is included. Your day starts at the plantation, with the balloon ride if you choose, the next thing being a continental breakfast at the old plantation house on a patio overlooking the fields and hills. You can roam around the 100 acres of the plantation and visit the German village of Seaford Town or St. Leonards village nearby. A Jamaican lunch of roast suckling pig with rum punch is served at 1 p.m. Horseback riding is available for $6 extra per half hour. The charge for the day is $48 per person with the balloon ride included, $36 per person just for the plantation tour, breakfast, lunch, and transportation.

Jamaica Safari Village, outside Falmouth, is open from 8:30 a.m. to 5:30 p.m. daily, with continual conducted tours. The trek leads through a petting zoo area and breeding centers, and alongside crocodile ponds. These reptiles are of special interest —a 750-pound adult is able to move at 40 miles per hour. You may get to hear the crocodile love call, which is original to say the least. Safari Village served as a film set for the James Bond thriller, *Live and Let Die*. Tours cost J$20 ($3.80) for adults, J$10 ($1.90) for children. Reservations can be made by calling 952-4415 or JADCO at 952-4425.

Rocklands Feeding Station, Anchovy (tel. 952-2009), otherwise called Rocklands Bird Sanctuary, was established by Lisa Salmon, known as the Bird Lady of Anchovy, attracting nature lovers and birdwatchers. It's a unique experience to have a Jamaican doctor bird perch on your finger to drink syrup, and to feed small doves and finches millet from your hand, plus watching dozens of other birds flying in for their evening meal. The feeding station is open every afternoon throughout the year from 3:15 until half an hour before sundown (varying with the time of year). Admission is $4. Do not take children age 5 and under, as they tend to worry the birds. Smoking and playing transistor radios are forbidden. Rocklands is about a mile outside Anchovy on the road from Montego Bay.

Montego Bay's most famous trip is the **Governor's Coach Tour,** a railway tour in a coach, which is a second-class European version and not air-conditioned. The trip takes you some 40 miles into the heartland, through banana and coconut groves and coffee plantations, stopping frequently at little villages. At one such stop, Catadupa, you can order men's Jamaican shirts and women's dresses made to measure in the style and material you select. You collect your garments on the return journey.

The tour visits the Appleton Estate Rum Distillery, where you can drink a complimentary rum punch. You also pass Anchovy and Cambridge; and at Ipswich, a visit is made to the famous caves to see the fascinating rock formations. The tour, operated Tuesday to Friday, takes all day, from 9:30 a.m. until 5 p.m. The cost is $35 per person, which includes a picnic lunch with rum punch. Telephone 952-1398 for reservations.

The **Mandeville Rail Tour,** operated by Premier Tours Ltd., The Cage, Sam Sharp Square, Montego Bay (tel. 953-2859), goes from the Montego Bay railway station to Mandeville, stopping at Balaclava for shopping. You transfer at Williamsfield and tour Mandeville, visit a Jamaican home for snacks, tour a private garden, have lunch at the Astra Hotel, and take a train back to Montego Bay. On the run to Mandeville, a continental breakfast is served, with fruits in season and complimentary drinks. A calypso band plays for the trip. The tour runs on Thursday from 7:45 a.m. to 5:30 p.m. and costs $45 per person.

A picnic on Tuesday and Thursday can be a highlight of your visit. The **Miskito Cove Beach Picnic,** which takes place at the cove of that name, leaves at 10 a.m., returning at 3 p.m., with pickups at Tryall and Round Hill. For $35 per person, you can enjoy an open Jamaican bar, buffet lunch, calypso band, sailing on a 40-foot boat (guide and equipment provided for snorkeling), a glass-bottom-boat ride, a raft ride, and water sports including sailing, pedal-boating, and windsurfing. The picnic is arranged by Aqua Cove Centre, Montego Bay (tel. 952-1387).

A **Mountain Valley Rafting and Plantation Tour** is operated at Lethe Property, about ten miles from Montego Bay, daily from 9 a.m. to 6 p.m. For $24, two persons can go rafting, and there are donkey rides and a farm tour. Horseback riding is also offered for $10 per hour. The raft trip takes about an hour, 1½ hours with the tour added. The Montego Bay office for the tour is at 3 Strand St. (tel. 952-0527).

Touring the Great Houses

Occupied by plantation owners, the great houses of Jamaica were always built on high ground so that they overlooked the plantation itself and could see the next house in the distance. It was the custom for the owners to offer hospitality to travelers crossing the island by road. They were spotted by the lookout, who noted the rising dust. Bed and food were then made ready for the traveler's arrival.

The most famous great house in Jamaica is the legendary **Rose Hall** (tel. 953-2323), a nine-mile jaunt east from Montego Bay along the coast road. The subject of at least a dozen Gothic novels, Rose Hall was immortalized in the H. G. deLisser book *White Witch of Rosehall*. The house was built about two centuries ago by a John Palmer. However, it was Annie Palmer, wife of the builder's grandnephew, who became the focal point of fiction and fact. Called "Infamous Annie," she was said to have dabbled in witchcraft. She took slaves as lovers, killing them off when they bored her. Those servants called her "the Obeah woman" (Jamaican for voodoo). Annie was said to have murdered several of her coterie of husbands while they slept, and eventually suffered the same fate herself in a kind of poetic justice. Long in ruins, the house has now been restored and can be visited by the public at a cost of $5. Hours are daily from 9 a.m. to 5 p.m.

Greenwood (no phone) is even more interesting to some house tourers than Rose Hall. On its hillside perch, it lies 14 miles to the east of Montego Bay and 7 miles west of Falmouth. Hours are 9 a.m. to 6 p.m. daily, and admission is J$15 ($2.85) for adults. Erected in the early 19th century, the Georgian-style building was once the residence of Richard Barrett between 1780 and 1800. He was of the same family as Elizabeth Barrett Browning. On display are the original library of the Barrett family, with rare books dating from 1697, along with oil paintings of the Barrett family, china made by Wedgwood for the family, and a rare exhibition of musical instruments in working order, plus a fine collection of antique furniture. The house today is privately owned by Bob and Ann Betton, who have decided to open it to the public.

Chester Castle Great House, about 14 miles west of Montego Bay, in Hanover, is a small example of a great house, built of stone and Jamaican cement (molasses and animal manure) on a 200-acre estate. On display are interesting Arawak artifacts, antique furniture, equipment formerly used to manufacture indigo dye, and many flowering plants. The house tour, lasting about 1½ hours, is conducted Monday to Saturday. For information, get in touch with Ian H. Cooke, c/o Montego Yacht Club (tel. 952-3028).

About five miles from Falmouth, you can take the **Good Hope Plantation and Great House** tour daily (appointments are necessary to tour the house). The house tour, costing J$20 ($3.80), is worthwhile, as you see the interior of the Palladian great house, built in 1755—antique furniture, carpets, paintings, and collectors' items of all sorts. The riding tour, costing an additional J$55 ($10.50), takes you along trails leading to Jamaica's most impressive remains of an 18th-century sugar plantation. You'll see the slave hospital, two overseers' cottages, a storehouse, shop, and assistant manager's house. The 2,000-acre plantation is now a working beef, coconut, and aloe vera farm. For information about the tour, get in touch with Patrick Thompson, owner, Good Hope, Falmouth (tel. 954-3289).

Boat Cruises

Fun cruises are offered aboard the *Mary Ann* (tel. 952-5505) from 10 a.m. to 3 p.m. At the sound of the conch trumpet, played by a quartet blowing conch shells, you set out aboard the 57-foot sailboat on a scenic cruise across the bay, with a stop where you can see colorful coral and reef fish in marine gardens, swim, snorkel, and collect shells. You have lunch ashore in a fishing village in the ship's special picnic grounds. The cruise costs $30 per person.

The *Mary Ann* also makes a sunset dinner cruise, leaving at 5 p.m. You sail around the bay, sip drinks, and enjoy dinner under the stars by candlelight at the Almond Terrace Restaurant by the sea. The dinner cruise costs $35 per person. For both of these jaunts aboard the *Mary Ann,* free pickup and return service is provided.

Another sunset party cruise is offered aboard the *Reggae Queen,* a 100-foot party boat at Montego Freeport. The ship leaves at 7 p.m. and takes you to spots where you see the sunset, the rolling hills of St. James, and the lights of Montego Bay. This cruise includes an open Jamaican bar, a light meal from the grill on board, dancing in the ship's discothèque, and relaxing at the upper-deck bar, sipping Jamaican cocktails. You'll be back ashore about 10 p.m. Free transportation to and from your hotel is included in the rate of $20 per person. The *Reggae Queen* also makes a sunset cruise from 4 to 6 p.m., costing $10 per person. It includes hors d'oeuvres, cocktails, dancing in the disco, and free transportation. The ship is operated by Twin Screw Jamaica Ltd., 14 Market St. (tel. 952-2988).

MONTEGO BAY SHOPPING: The main shopping areas are the **City Centre** (where most of the in-bond shops are, aside from at the large hotels), **Overton Plaza, Holiday Village Shopping Centre,** and **Westgate Shopping Centre.**

Blue Mountain Gems Workshop (tel. 953-2338), at the Holiday Village Shopping Centre, offers a tour of the workshops to see the process from raw stone to the finished product you can buy later.

Throughout the island, Appleton's overproof, special, and punch rums are excellent value. Tía Maria and Rumona (the one coffee-, the other rum-flavored) are the best liqueurs. Khus Khus is the local perfume.

Caribatik Island Fabrics, at Rock Wharf on the Luminous Lagoon (tel. 954-2314), is two miles east of Falmouth on the north-coast road. You'll recognize the place easily, as it has a huge sign painted across the building's side. This is the private living and work domain of Muriel and Keith Chandler, who escaped the snows of Chicago years ago to introduce a batik studio and clothing factory to Jamaica as a pioneer industry in 1970. Today the batiks of Muriel Chandler are viewed as stylish and sensual garments by chic boutiques from Padre Island, Texas, to fashion enclaves in the American Northeast.

There is also a full range of scarves and wall hangings, some patterned after themes such as a parade of the endangered animal species of the world, as well as abstract patterns reminiscent of a painting by Jackson Pollack. Original batik paintings are also sold. The shop, which contains a factory in back where either Muriel or Keith will describe the intricate process of batiking, is open daily except Sunday and Monday from 10 a.m. to 3 p.m.

At the **crafts market** near Harbour Street in downtown Montego Bay you can find a wide selection of handmade souvenirs of Jamaica, including straw hats and bags, wooden platters, straw baskets, musical instruments, beads, carved objects, and toys. That "jippa jappa" hat is important if you're going to be out in the island sun.

Neville Budhai Paintings, Reading Main Road (no phone), lies five miles west of Montego Bay, along the side of the road leading to Negril. This well-known gallery sells original paintings by Jamaican and Puerto Rican artists. Woodcuts, batiks, and lithographs are also sold. The gallery is open daily from 8:30 a.m. until some time in the early evening.

AFTER DARK: There are a lot more activities to pursue in Montego Bay in the evenings than going to the discos, but the resort certainly has those too.

Evita's Bamboo Bar and Nightclub (tel. 952-2301), which draws the chic expatriate community that lives in the hills around Montego Bay, lies six miles west of Montego Bay on the road to Negril. It occupies the sunny end of a rocky peninsula jutting into the bay downhill from the Round Hill Hotel. Guests enter a circular, voodoo-inspired building with a thatch roof and stout vertical columns. The only hi-tech hint in an otherwise charmingly natural decor is a well-equipped stage, where local calypso musicians alternate at night with emissions from MTV and video movies. The special appeal of the place is its creator, Evita, who "speaks 4½ languages." Born in the German-speaking section of northern Italy, she lived for many years in Venice, and today entertains guests from around the world with a flair much like she'd emit in her private home. Evita's special rum, a version of planter's punch, costs J$15 ($2.85). There's disco music for dancing, and on Tuesday and Saturday night, a floor show. Complete dinners cost from J$70 ($13.30). Meals include a well-prepared array of such dishes as red snapper en papillotte in a lobster- and cheese-flavored wine sauce, U.S. steaks, barbecued spareribs, chicken, and, for dessert, an English sherry trifle. The establishment is open every evening in high season, but closed Monday off-season. Reservations are suggested if you want dinner.

Currently, the hottest disco action in Mo Bay is at the **Disco Inferno,** W. G. Hilcram's entertainment complex, Holiday Village, Rose Hall (tel. 953-2113). On the ground floor of the same building that contains both the House of Lords restaurant and a 24-hour snackbar, this spacious gathering place is furnished in a vaguely Spanish style of somber wood and flashing lights. Disco alternates here with live reggae bands, sometimes two per night, each playing to the enthusiastic response of the Jamaican crowds which pour in. Concerts usually are from 10 p.m. to midnight, after which disco music takes over. Women are invited free to this nightclub/disco on Monday and Thursday. Otherwise the entrance fee is J$6 ($1.15). There's a long bar serving rum punch for J$12 ($2.30) and beer for J$7 ($1.35). The Inferno is across from the Holiday Inn on the north-coast highway.

Witch's Hideaway at the Holiday Inn (tel. 953-2485) is for those on a macabre after-dark circuit. You can in fact disco-hop throughout most of the evening, if that is your somewhat dated desire. Entrance is J$15 ($2.85), and drinks begin at $3. Sometimes instead of recorded music you get live entertainment here. One night I saw a fire-eater; on another occasion it might be a limbo dancer or calypso singer. One always hopes (so far in vain) to hear another Jamaican, the equal of Harry Belafonte, "tally me banana." The Holiday Inn has more recently opened the **Thriller Disco** in the nightclub. It is free to hotel guests, and it's open seven days a week at 10 p.m. Video is shown. Entrance is also J$15 ($2.85).

The **Junkanoo Club,** at the Wyndham Rose Hall Beach Club (tel. 953-2650), is one of the liveliest spots in the Mo Bay area. The recently improved 180-seat club has an inviting atmosphere and one of the best sound systems in Jamaica. There is no admission or cover charge, and drinks begin at $1.75. It opens nightly at 8:30 p.m.

For some "life-seeing" adventures, I have the following recommendations:

Every Sunday, Tuesday, and Thursday, there's an **Evening on the Great River,** during which you ride in a fishing canoe up the river ten miles west of Montego Bay. A torchlit path leads to a re-created Arawak Indian village, where you eat, drink as much as you like at the open bar, and watch a floor show. The Country Store offers jackass rope (tobacco by the yard), nutmeg, cinnamon, brown sugar, and all sorts of country items for sale. The cost, with transportation, is $32 per person. The operator is Hartley Morris, Great River Productions, 29 Gloucester Ave., Reading, St. James (tel. 952-5047).

For an interesting Jamaican experience, take a **Jamaica Night to Rahtid,** at Lollypop on the beach, Sandy Bay, Hanover (tel. 952-1202), half a mile west of Tryall, held every Wednesday from 7:30 to 11 p.m. (on Saturday also if the demand is heavy). Your $35 includes round-trip transport to the beach from Mo Bay hotels, a glass-bottom-boat ride with a calypso band, dinner of seafood and jerk meats, and traditional dance groups performing cumina, reggae, the basket dance, the bamboo dance, the limbo, and dancing on the beach. Mrs. Yvonne Clarke manages the festivities for Sunmar Enterprise Ltd., Montego Bay (tel. 952-4121).

Boonoonoonoos Beach Party is held on Friday from 7 to 11 p.m. on Walter Fletcher Beach, Montego Bay, costing $25 (not recommended for children). A live band, three-course Jamaican dinner, open Jamaican bar, and a native floor show make for a festive evening. For information, call the Coconut Grove Great House (no phone).

5. Negril

Jamaica's newest resort, on the western tip of the island, is famed for its seven-mile beach, the pride of the area. A place of legend, Negril recalls Buccaneer Calico Jack (his name derived from his fondness for calico undershorts) and his carousings with his infamous women pirates, Mary Read and Ann Bonney.

Emerging Negril is 50 miles and about a two-hour drive from Montego Bay's airport along a bad road, past ruins of sugar estates and great houses. From Kingston, it's about a four-hour drive, a distance of 150 miles.

This once-sleepy village has turned into a tourist mecca, visitors drawn to its beaches along three well-protected bays—Long Bay, Bloody Bay, and Orange Bay. Negril became famous in the late 1960s when it attracted laid-back American and Canadian youth, who liked the idea of a place with no phones, no electricity. They rented modest digs in little houses where the local people extended their hospitality.

At some point you'll want to explore Booby Cay, a tiny islet off the Negril Coast. Once it was featured in the Walt Disney film *20,000 Leagues Under the Sea,* but now it's rampant with nudists from Hedonism II.

Chances are, however, you'll stake out your own favorite spot along Negril's own seven-mile beach. You don't need to get up for anything, as somebody will be along to serve you. Perhaps it'll be the "banana lady," with a basket of fruit perched on her head. Maybe the "ice cream man" will set up a stand right under a coconut palm. Surely the "beer lady" will find you as she strolls along the beach, a carton of Jamaican beer on her head, a bucket of ice in her hand, and hordes of young men will seek you out peddling illegal "ganja" whether you smoke it or not. Negril has the dubious distinction of being called the marijuana resort of the Caribbean.

WHERE TO STAY: Devoted to the pursuit of pleasure, **Hedonism II,** P.O. Box 25 (tel. 957-4200), is called the "home of hedonism." It includes "the works" in a one-package deal, except at Hedonism they even give you all the booze you want to drink. Some abuse the privilege, but most guests seemingly drink in moderation. The resort is closed to the general public. There is no tender of any sort, and tipping is not permitted. In two-story clusters, 280 rooms are stacked, dotted around a gently sloping 22-acre site. You enter under a cedar-roofed portico to find a miniature "city," totally equipped with everything and a staff usually willing to serve your needs. There is a large covered area filled with rest tables, bars, and at the end, a swimming pool. Most of the guests, who must be above 16 years of age, are Americans, with a significant number of Canadians, some Europeans, and a few South Americans. A minimum stay of one week is required. Rates given below are per person weekly, based on double occupancy. This is not a "couples-only" resort. Singles are accepted, but the rooms are doubles. Therefore you are likely to be assigned a same-sex roommate if you should arrive alone. Arrivals are on Friday, Saturday, Sunday, or Monday. Weekly tariffs in winter range from a low of $890 to a high of $990 and up. *In summer, you get a major reduction, paying from $740 to $810 per person weekly, all inclusive.* In the open-sided dining room, Jamaican and international buffets are served.

If your pursuit of pleasure covers sports activities, you can enjoy the use of all sports facilities, equipment, and instruction, including sailing, snorkeling, water-skiing, scuba-diving, windsurfing, embarking on the underwater vision boat, using the Jacuzzi, and swimming in the hotel pool. There are six tournament-class tennis courts (lit at night) and two badminton courts, and if you prefer, you can play basketball, squash, volleyball, or Ping-Pong. Hedonism has Nautilus and free-weight gyms, areas for aerobics, and an indoor games room. If you want to get out and about, you can go bicycling or horseback riding. If all that activity—or even a portion of it—leaves you any energy, nightly entertainment is presented, along with a live band, show disco, and piano bar. On one section of the beach "clothing is optional," as the management states. Some women prefer to go merely topless. On some nights guests dress up in sheets which they like to think of as Roman togas. Provocative beauty contests are staged as well, including one with wet T-shirts. The resort also has a secluded beach on nearby Booby Key (originally cay) where guests are taken twice a week for a picnic.

Poinciana Beach Villas, Norman Manley Boulevard (tel. 957-4256, or toll free 800/468-6728), is set amid verdant landscaping in its own gardens, beside a broad boulevard leading into town from Montego Bay. The resort contains 16 functionally modern, two-story villas, any of which can be rented as an entire unit. If you're interested in less expansive living, each villa has a labyrinth of halls, doors, kitchens, and baths, so that sections or rooms within the villas can be rented as relatively modest lodgings. Opened in 1983, the resort offers a beachfront bar, a restaurant, a watersports kiosk, and a Thursday-night tradition of live reggae and calypso music. Most, but not all, accommodations have private baths and air conditioning, and a few of the more expensive ones contain kitchens or refrigerators. In winter, a room rents for $80 daily in a single, $90 in a double; after that, units are priced according to their amenities, costing from $95 to $140 for double occupancy. *In summer, a simple room rents for $65 daily in a single, $70 in a double, or from $75 to $115 for two persons in one of the more elaborate accommodations, plus a 10% service charge.* Children under 12 who share a room with an adult stay free.

Sundowner Hotel, P.O. Box 5 (tel. 957-4225), is the traditional beachside favorite—in fact, some say it "invented" Negril as a resort. It was once the secret hideaway of the *Saturday Evening Post* cover artist, Norman Rockwell. The crowd is (usually) convivial, decidedly informal, and often young. At a point north of Negril, Rita Hojan opened this place to an uncertain future. Over the years it's grown steadily, increasing in popularity with a beach-oriented crowd who like the sleepy lifestyle here. Ms. Hojan's staff is most loyal, and many members have been with her almost from the beginning. A family atmosphere prevails. The Sundowner is a two-story motel-like structure, and rooms are simple, but comfortable enough. Bedrooms are nicely coordinated, with one-color themes plus fine fruitwood furnishings, and each unit has a private terrace where you can enjoy breakfast overlooking the sea. All rooms have small refrigerators, ceiling fans, and air conditioning. In winter, two persons can stay here on the MAP at rates ranging from $155 daily, a single person paying from $130. *In summer, two persons are charged from $115, and one person pays $72, all MAP tariffs.*

The cook's creativity reaches its peak at the Wednesday and Saturday buffets when a live calypso band comes in to entertain guests. Meals are served under a spreading breadfruit tree right at the water's edge. Before dining, you can perch at a bar table made from seashell-filled barrels. The main house is the core of the original inn, which has been turned into public rooms. The beach is enough for most people, and you can also partake of water sports at the Negril Beach Village nearby. The Sundowner is a great getaway place.

Rockhouse (for reservations, write to P.O. Box 78, Park Ridge, IL 60068; tel. 312/296-1894) looks, as you approach it, like a remote African village ready to be photographed for *National Geographic*. It lies on the lighthouse road, just south of Negril. Frankly, this place isn't for everyone. It caters to surf lovers who like its lack of phones. Kerosene lamps used to be the only form of illumination at night, but now that the place has electricity, ceiling fans, refrigerators, and hotplates, the old lamps are only used for romantic interludes. The thatched rondavels, rustic style, with their peaked roofs, cling to the trees and cliffs above coves and pools. On the water doesn't mean on the beach. You go swimming "off the rocks." Walls are built of woven split bamboo, but glass doors, big ones, let in the view. Your particular hut might be perched on a rock formation just ten feet above the water. A lot of divers like to lodge here, exploring the crystal-blue coves.

The cottages may look primitive from the outside, but actually they have the desired amenities tucked away. There are studios and villas for two guests, with a sleeping loft for additional beds. The beach house has two bedrooms, a living and a dining room, plus a bath and a kitchen with a two-burner gas plate. There's a private shower with palm trees and sky for a ceiling. This is primarily an adult retreat, but children over 12 are welcomed. In winter, two persons pay from $90 daily in a studio, $120 in a villa. *In the off-season, two persons are charged from $70 to $90 daily*. For the beach house, meals are prepared in your room, or else you can go over to Rick's on the beach. If you'd like to have supper at the complex, ask the management, giving them a 24-hour notice. On my most recent visit, a Jamaican cook taught me how to prepare curried god-a-mi, a shiny black fish from the nearby Cabaritta River.

Charela Inn, P.O. Box 33 (tel. 957-4277), is a seafront inn reminiscent of a Spanish country-style hacienda. It's not the place for social types on the see-and-be-seen circuit, but for those wanting genuine hospitality where they're treated like one of the family. The warmth of the place stems from your hosts, Daniel and Sylvia Grizzle, who personally run and supervise everything. Homey meals and an informal atmosphere attract a loyal following to this site, on the A1, north of Negril. The main house and its addition have a row of arches with air-conditioned bedrooms, all with a tropical architecture and decorative details. In winter, singles can stay here on half-board terms ranging from $120 daily; doubles (also half-board) cost from $80 to $95 per person. *In summer, MAP singles range from $85 to $100 daily, doubles costing from $60 to $65 per person*. The graciously appointed dining room with its high-backed colonial chairs carries out the Spanish theme, and overlooks a garden as well. At sunset most guests gather at the fountain terrace to sample the various rum drinks. At this time your hosts like to introduce fellow guests. Ask about snorkeling, waterskiing, fishing, boating, tennis, golf, horseback riding, and sightseeing.

Negril Gardens, P.O. Westmoreland (tel. 957-4408, or toll free 800/243-9420). Set across the road from the beach, along the wide boulevard leading into the heart of the resort, this is one of the newest and best hotels in Negril. Its 16 units are scattered among a quartet of pink-sided two-story buildings, each of which is accented with Chippendale-style crosshatched balconies. Each accommodation has mahogany furniture, air conditioning, and its own private bathroom, and a five-sided front veranda or balcony with a view over the well-groomed lawns and crotons. John Sinclair, the owner, maintains a pleasant indoor/outdoor restaurant near the reception area, and plans exist for the construction of additional units. In winter, single or double rooms cost from $85 to $90 daily. *In summer, singles or doubles rent for $65 to $70 daily*. MAP is another $20 per person daily, plus 10% service.

Negril Beach Club Hotel, P.O. Box 7 (tel. 957-4220), is a casual, informal resort designed around a series of white stucco cubes adorned with exterior stairways and terraces. The entire complex is clustered like a horseshoe around a rectangular garden whose end abuts a sandy beach. There's ample parking on the premises and easy access to a full range of sporting facilities including snorkeling, a pool, volleyball, table tennis, and windsurfing. Other activities can be organized nearby, and beach barbecues and buffet breakfasts are ample and frequent. This place has been compared to Aggie Grey's old place in Samoa, especially since there's a kind of communal feeling among the residents of the angular "smörgåsbord" of accommodations, which range from simply furnished units to one-bedroom suites with kitchens. *In summer, singles range from $35 to $50; doubles, from $40 to $60; and triples, from $55 to $70.* In winter, singles go for $70 to $85, doubles cost $100, and triples run $85 to $100. MAP can be arranged for $25 per person per day. The Seething Cauldron on the beach serves barbecues, seafood, and such Jamaican specialties as roast suckling pig and akee and codfish.

WHERE TO DINE: Many visitors eat at their hotels. However, there are several other most atmospheric and intriguing possibilities.

Whether you have a meal or not, everybody in Negril at sundown seems to head for **Rick's Café** (tel. 957-4335), the name inspired by the old watering hole of Bogie's *Casablanca.* The "Rick" in this case is owner Carl Newman. Here the sunset is said to be the most glorious at the resort, and after a few fresh-fruit daiquiris (pineapple, banana, or papaya) you'll give whoever's claiming that no argument. I recently drank the night away with a group of divers staying at Rockhouse, a stroll down the road. At this cliffside proximity to nature, "casual" is the word in dress. The location where you order your eggs Benedict, Jamaican style, or fresh lobster is right on the westernmost promontory. Ham omelets are good here, and there are lots of Stateside specialties. The fish is always fresh, and you might have red snapper or grouper. Try the chef's Jamaican fish chowder. Expect to pay from $12 to $25 for dinner. You can also buy plastic bar tokens at the door, which you can use instead of money à la Club Med. Open noon to 9 p.m. daily.

Mariners Inn and Restaurant, West End (no phone). The main reason most guests come here is for the boat-shaped bar and the adjoining restaurant whose access is through a tropical garden which eventually slopes down to the beach. As you drink or dine, the breezes will waft in under the most pleasant and relaxed experiences in Negril. You can lunch here for around $8, although if you want a conch steak or a portion of red snapper, it may cost you twice as much. Lobster, chicken, and tuna salads are also available, as are cheese omelets, club sandwiches, homemade pâté, and—if you really want to dine properly—lobster Thermidor. Manley Wallace is the Jamaican owner who, with his attractive staff, works seven days a week from 8:30 a.m. till very late at night.

Negril Sands (no phone) is a large-scale cabaña where the owner may greet you in a Dorothy Lamour sarong as you disembark from your car near the sandy frontyard between the roadside trees and the water. This is the kind of place where you can arrive sometime in the morning and spend a carefree day on the immaculate beach of this establishment, the first of its kind ever to be built on the sands of Negril. The owner is the cultivated and humorous Elinor Gubler, a Jamaican who married a Swiss expatriate named Hans years ago. You're likely to see a score of well-proportioned Germans and Swedes basking in the tropical sun along with friendly Jamaicans (often artists and diplomats) and a goodly number of North American refugees.

The headquarters and base from which all of the beach action (or non-action, as you prefer) emanates is an octagonal thatch-roofed cabaña where the convivial bar is open all day and where luncheon buffets are served daily from 12:30 to 3 p.m. A full buffet, which sometimes includes half a grilled lobster, costs $12 per person. À la carte items are hamburgers, barbecued chicken and pork chops, and fish of the day with herbs and garlic sauce. You'll always be welcome to stay through dinner, since the bar is open daily until midnight. Live music is featured from 8 p.m. on Saturday and from noon to 4 p.m. on Sunday.

If you're in Negril on a Wednesday night in high season, head over to the **Sundowner** (tel. 957-4225; see my hotel recommendations). There you can sample fine cookery at a West Indian buffet, featuring Jamaican specialties. The evening will cost you about $20, and it's well worth it. At beachside, you dine under a thatched roof, watching the sun set. In fact, you spend a lot of time in Negril watching sunsets. To top your meal, you can order Jamaican coffee. Try to arrive by 7 p.m.

Café au Lait, Lighthouse Road, West End (tel. 957-4277). Both the furniture and the building here were made as a learning project by the students at a nearby technical school. You'll quickly learn, however, that there's nothing experimental about the well-prepared French and Jamaican cuisine served here, where the walls are open to the breezes coming through from the surrounding forest. Daniel and Sylvia Grizzle are the Jamaican/French couple who prepare the cuisine served by a charming staff participating in the well-organized teamwork of this place. Menu items include quiches, escargots, lobster prepared several ways (including in salads and bisques), and an unusual crêpe made with cheese and callaloo. There are four kinds of pizza (one with lobster) and several kinds of salad, one made with fish. The menu also features roast lamb, pork, and chicken, as well as a wine list stressing French products. Dessert may be lime tart with ice cream, concluding a full meal which costs from J$100 ($19). This restaurant is open only for dinner, beginning at 5 p.m. every evening.

Kaiser's Café, West End (no phone). The place is so laid-back that you might end up spending an entire afternoon under its thatch-roofed bar and restaurant. Platters of ham and eggs, sandwiches, and salads are offered in simple surroundings near a rocky beach. You can order food from a service window at one end of the terrace or dine inside under the high rafters of a room where live Jamaican music is sometimes featured. In the event there's entertainment, you pay a cover charge of J$25 ($4.75). The café is open daily from 5 p.m. Swing time usually stretches from 10 p.m. until after midnight.

The most economical way to dine in Negril is to walk along the lighthouse road, where you'll see a string of about ten or so good little restaurants. Ignore their "plain Jane" entrances and think instead of the good food served.

I've found that **Chicken Lavish,** West End (tel. 957-4410), whose name I love, is the best of the lot. Just show up on the doorstep and see what's cooking. Curried goat is a specialty, as is fresh fried fish. Fresh Caribbean lobster is prepared to perfection here, as is the red snapper caught in local waters. But the main reason I've recommended the joint is because of the namesake. Ask the chef to make his special Jamaican chicken. He'll tell you, and you may agree, that it's the best on the island. Along with a salad and dessert, expect to spend around $15 for a complete meal. Dinner is from 7 to 10 p.m. The location is south of the town. What to wear here? Dress as you would to clean up your backyard on a hot August day.

6. Mandeville

The "English Town" Mandeville lies on a plateau more than 2,000 feet above the sea in the tropical highlands. The commercial part of the town is small, surrounded by a sprawling residential area popular with the large North American expatriate population mostly involved with the bauxite-mining industry. Much cooler than the coastal resorts, it's a possible center from which to explore the entire land.

Shopping in the town is a pleasure, whether in the old center or in one of the modern shopping complexes such as Grove Court. The market in the center of town teems with life, particularly on weekends when the country folk bus into town for their weekly visit. The town has several interesting old buildings. The square-towered church built in 1820 has fine stained glass, and the little churchyard tells an interesting story of past inhabitants of Mandeville. The Court House was built in 1816, a fine old Georgian stone-and-wood building with a pillared portico reached by a steep, sweeping double staircase.

Among the interesting attractions, **Marshall's Pen** (tel. 962-2260) is one of the great houses, an old coffee plantation home some 200 years old and filled with antique furniture, fine grandfather clocks, beautiful carpets, and valuable rugs. The house is a history lesson in itself, as it was once owned by the Earl of Balcaris, the island's governor. In 1939 Arthur Sutton, who traces his family back to the old Dutch colony of New Amsterdam, acquired the property. Now, with his son, Robert, he farms the 300 acres, breeding mainly Jamaican red poll cattle. The Suttons have a large collection of seashells, some fine Arawak relics, and a large general stamp collection.

Arthur Sutton, with charm and wit, will entertain you with the history of his home and the island and with anecdotes of the origin of local words. This is very much a private home, and should be treated as such. Reservations to view it are usually made by applying to the Hotel Astra, P.O. Box 60 in Mandeville (tel. 962-3265 for further information). Admission is J$20 ($3.80).

WHERE TO STAY: My top choice for a stay in this area is the **Hotel Astra,** 62 Ward Ave. (tel. 962-3265). It's a family-run hotel, the home of the McIntyres, who do all they can to ensure that visitors and local people alike are satisfied. Diana McIntyre-Pike, known to her family and friends as Thunderbird (she is always coming to the rescue of guests), happily picks up people in her own car, taking them around to see the sights and organizing introductions to people of the island. The hotel has 20 double rooms and two suites, mainly in two buildings reached along open walkways. The tariff all year is J$165 ($31.25) to J$350 ($66.50). No meals are included in the rates.

The Zodiac Room, entered from the lounge area, offers excellent meals served by friendly staff members. Lunch or dinner is a choice of chilled juice, beef-and-vegetable soup, or pumpkin soup; followed by shrimp rice, meatballs Italiano, or braised steak. All main dishes are served with a selection of rice, buttered cho-cho, scalloped potatoes, and other vegetables. A large salad bowl is also included at dinner. The kitchen is under the personal control of Diana, who is always collecting awards in Jamaican culinary competitions, and someone is on hand to explain to you the niceties of any particular Jamaican dish. A complete meal costs J$30 ($5.70) to J$55 ($10.50). Dinner is from 6:30 to 9:30 p.m. Friday night is barbecue night, when guests and townfolk gather around the pool to dine. Spareribs, chicken, and steak are delectable.

The Revival Room is the name of the bar, where everything including the bar stools is made from rum-soaked barrels. Try the family's own homemade liqueur and "reviver," a pick-me-up concocted from Guinness, rum, egg, condensed milk, and nutmeg—guaranteed not to fail. There is a dart board for a game, if the locals haven't beaten you to it. English pub hours are kept, from 11 a.m. to 3 p.m. and from 4 to 11 p.m. Bar snacks, including pizzas, are served if you don't want a full meal. In addition to the pool, there is a sauna, or you can spend the afternoon at the Manchester Country Club, where tennis and golf are available. Horses can be provided for cross-country treks.

Mandeville Hotel, 4 Hotel St. (tel. 962-2138), is a modern place but lacks the intimate atmosphere of the Astra. It has a large indoor bar and a spacious lounge where daily papers and weekly magazines are laid out on a large round table. Activity at the hotel centers mainly around the pool and the coffeeshop, where substantial meals are served at moderate prices and at rates good all year. Room rates range from $20 to $40 single and $25 to $45 double, no meals included, plus the usual taxes. There are attractive gardens with many fine old trees and lovely roses, and golf and tennis at the Manchester Country Club. Horseback riding can also be arranged.

WHERE TO EAT: Bill Laurie's Steak House, Bloomfield Gardens (tel. 962-3116), 100 feet above Mandeville, a long, two-story wooden house with a veranda stretching the length of the upper floor. Outside you are likely to find 14½ cars, none less than 30 years old, including an old London taxi which used to take customers home after a heavy meal. The front end of an old Wolseley makes up the total count. Going upstairs to the bar and restaurant, you meet even more examples of Bill's squirrel-like habits— more than 500 vehicle license plates decorate the walls, pictures of cars fill all available extra space, along with visiting cards by the thousand, beer mats, and model cars vying for space among pewter tankards left there permanently by regulars who are set in their ways. "Play it if you like," says Bill of the old piano. You can even try the old Western Electric telephone to see whether the operator will respond to a turn of the crank. In the lounge beside the restaurant is a wireless with knobs and fabric-covered loudspeaker. The kitchen still has a wood-burning stove in excellent condition, carefully blacked but no longer used. Bill came from Scotland 32 years ago and loves his island highland home in the sun, where he can indulge his love of old cars and collecting things.

The food consists of appetizers such as fruit punch or mango nectar, soups, and steaks varying in size and cut. Ground beef steak, mixed grill, and lamb chops are among the main-dish offerings. All meals are cooked to order and come with french fries, salad, and vegetables. You'll spend about $20. Try to dine between 7 and 9 p.m.

The **Mandeville Hotel,** 4 Hotel St. (tel. 962-2460), is close to the city center and popular with local business people who use the coffeeshop by the pool for a quick, appetizing luncheon stop. A wide selection of sandwiches is available. You can order milkshakes, tea, or coffee. In the hotel restaurant, open for lunch (you must reserve for dinner but not necessarily for lunch), the à la carte menu offers such foods as Jamaican pepperpot soup, lobster Thermidor, fresh snapper, and kingfish. Potatoes and vegetables in season are included in the main-dish prices. A complete meal can cost from $18. If you happen to be there at breakfast, a full Jamaican meal costs from $6. Hours are 7 to 10 a.m., noon to 2 p.m., and 7 to 9 p.m.

WHAT TO SEE AND DO: Mandeville is the sort of place where you can become well acquainted with the people and feel like part of the community.

For the Speleologist

One of the largest and driest caves on the island is at Oxford, about nine miles northwest of Mandeville. Signs direct you to it after you leave Mile Gully, a village dominated by St. George's Church, some 175 years old.

Birdwatching

Marshall's Pen estate boasts 23 endemic species of bird, as well as many winter and summer migrants, mainly warblers from North America which seek shelter among the shrubs and unusual plants in the wildlife reserve. Small parties of six can be taken on early-morning guided tours at prices to be negotiated.

Day tours are also arranged to the Cockpit Country, where if you're lucky you can see a golden swallow.

For further information, get in touch with **Robert L. Sutton,** P.O. Box 58, Mandeville (tel. 962-2260).

Taking the Waters

Milk River Mineral Bath, Milk River, P.O. Clarendon (tel. 924-9544), lies nine miles south of the Kingston–Mandeville highway. It boasts the world's most radioactive mineral waters, recommended for the treatment of arthritis, rheumatism, lumbago, neuralgia, sciatica, and liver disorders. These mineral-laden waters are available to guests of the hotel as well as casual visitors to the enclosed baths or the mineral swimming pool. The restaurant offers fine Jamaican cuisine, health drinks, and special diets in an old-world atmosphere of relaxation. The nearby Milk River affords boating and fishing. Accommodations are available at year-round MAP rates, ranging from J$106 ($20.25) to J$131 ($25) in a single, J$191 ($36.25) to J$221 ($42) in a double, per night.

Huntingdon Summit Tour

On Knockpatrick Road, 1½ miles from Mandeville, you can visit the octagonal, hilltop home of Mr. Cecil Charlton (tel. 962-2432), daily except Wednesday and Saturday from 10 a.m. to 6 p.m. Mr. Charlton also has a collection of rare birds. There is no admission charge, but visitors may tip guides or give donations to charity.

Chapter XII

FRENCH WEST INDIES

1. Martinique
2. Guadeloupe
3. St. Martin
4. St. Barthélemy

FRENCH CHARM and tropical beauty combine in the great curve of the Lesser Antilles. A long way from Europe, France's western border is composed mainly of Guadeloupe and Martinique, with a scattering of tiny offshore dependencies, such as the six little clustered Îles des Saintes.

Almond-shaped Martinique is the northernmost of the Windwards, while butterfly-shaped Guadeloupe is near the southern stretch of the Leewards. These are not colonies, as many visitors wrongly assume, but the westernmost *départements* of France, meaning that these *citoyens* are full-fledged citizens of la belle France.

Other satellites of the French West Indies include St. Martin (which shares an island with the Dutch-held St. Maarten; see Chapter X), St. Barthélemy, Marie-Galante, and Désirade, a former leper colony.

Unlike Barbados and Jamaica, the French West Indies are Johnny-come-latelies to tourism. Although cruise-ship passengers had arrived long before, mass tourism began in these islands only in the 1970s. Before that, Jacques Cousteau or David Rockefeller could retreat here, enjoying a hideaway, but that soon may no longer be possible, as Martinique and Guadeloupe move up as vacation targets. Créole customs make these islands unique in the Caribbean. The inhabitants also serve some of the best food. Don't be afraid if I've sent you to a dilapidated wooden shack. You may find the *New York Times* food editor there too, sampling a sumptuous meal.

Traveler's Advisory: As of this writing, U.S. and Canadian citizens can visit the French West Indies without a visa, even though Martinique and Guadeloupe are part of France which does demand a visa. But in a fast-changing world, policies can change overnight, and prospective visitors should check with tourist boards or airlines flying to a particular destination to determine the latest information. Without cost, a "control visa" is presently being issued. This visa is routinely issued—that is, without investigation except in the most suspicious of cases, and it's good for a visit of three months. However, a visa issued for Martinique is good only for that island. A control visa issued for Guadeloupe is also valid for St. Barts and the French side of St. Martin. That's because the latter two islands are "dependencies" of Guadeloupe. St. Martin is a special case anyway. Most visitors don't need a visa to enter the French side if they've landed on the Dutch side (the border is unguarded). However, those arriving in French St. Martin, at the airport or by boat, will have to clear French Customs. For more information, get in touch with the French West Indies Tourist Board, 610 Fifth Ave., New York, NY 10020 (tel. 212/757-1125).

1. Martinique

France's anchor in the Caribbean world, Martinique is the land of the Empress Josephine. In her youth, Madame de Maintenon, mistress of Louis XIV, also lived here in the small fishing village of Precheur.

Martinique still has remarkable women, considered the most beautiful in the West Indies. A mingling of African and French blood has produced a classic Créole beauty. In days gone by, she was famous for her *madras et foulard* costume, a dress reserved now more for special occasions. Presumably, the flair of the knots of the madras reveals whether the girl is engaged, married, or available (or any combination of the above).

Columbus discovered Martinique, and the French settled the island when the king's gentleman, Belain d'Esnambuc, took possession in the name of Louis XIII. The year was 1635. In spite of some intrusions by British forces, the French have remained in Martinique ever since. Immigration from France produced sugarcane plantations and rum distilleries.

Early in the beginning of their colonization, the French imported black slaves from Africa to work the plantations, but at the time of the French Revolution, slavery began to decline on Martinique. But it wasn't until the mid-19th century that its abolition was obtained by Victor Schoelcher, a Paris-born deputy from Alsace. Since 1946 Martinique has been a part of France.

Martinique is part of the Lesser Antilles and lies in the semitropical zone, its western shore facing the Caribbean, its eastern shore the livelier Atlantic. It is some 4,340 miles from France, 2,000 miles from New York, 2,300 miles from Montréal, and 1,450 miles from Miami.

The surface of the island is only 420 square miles—50 miles at its longest dimension, 21 miles at its widest point.

The ground is mountainous, especially in the rain-forested northern part where Mount Pelée, a volcano, rises to a height of 4,656 feet. In the center of the island the mountains are smaller, Carbet Peak reaching a 3,960-foot summit. The high hills rising among the peaks or mountains are called "Morne." The southern part of Martinique has only big hills, reaching peaks of 1,500 feet at Vauclin, 1,400 feet at Diamant. The irregular coastline of the island provides five bays, dozens of coves, and miles of sandy beaches.

The climate is relatively mild, and the heat is rarely uncomfortable, the average temperature in the 75° to 85° Fahrenheit range. At higher elevations it's considerably cooler. The island is cooled by a wind the French called *alizé,* and rain is frequent but doesn't last very long. From late August to November might be called the rainy season. April to September are the hottest months.

The early Carib Indians, who gave Columbus such a hostile reception, called Martinique "the island of flowers," and indeed it has remained so. The vegetation is lush, including hibiscus, poinsettias, bougainvillea, everything enhanced by such trees as the flamboyant, the royal palm, coconut, giant bamboo, mango, orange, and the locust tree. Almost any fruit that can grow in the ground sprouts out of Martinique's soil—pineapples, avocados, bananas, papayas, and custard apples.

Birdwatchers are often pleased at the number of hummingbirds, while spotting the mountain whistler and blackbird as well. The mongoose is common, and multicolored butterflies add to the panorama of nature. After sunset, there's a permanent concert of grasshoppers, frogs, and crickets.

GETTING THERE: Most airlines route North American passengers to the French departments of Martinique and Guadeloupe in roughly the same patterns. Therefore much of what you read here about getting to Martinique applies equally to its sister island.

Most vacationers in the New York and New Jersey area select a daily flight from JFK, requiring a change of aircraft in San Juan or Miami. Of all the carriers on the route, **American Airlines** offers the most efficient transfer because of its glistening new hub in San Juan. Continuing service on American's partner, **American Eagle,** carries travelers through to Guadeloupe or Martinique in a well-timed sequence. Passengers coming from other parts of North America find that some of the airline industry's best service to San Juan from many parts of the continent is on one of American's aircraft. Because of American's frequency of flights to San Juan (around four a day from New York and many others from throughout North America), it's possible to check your baggage through on American and continue on an American Eagle flight directly through to Martinique or Guadeloupe.

A phone call to a package-tour operator is always a good idea before booking your reservations. A good one is connected to the American Airlines phone reservations desk. Often, reductions are awarded to passengers who book their air fare and hotel reservations at the same time. When they're purchased independently of hotel accommodations, American's least expensive fare requires no advance purchase and a stopover of between 3 and 21 days.

Another possibility is **Eastern,** which funnels all of its flights to Martinique or Guadeloupe through Miami. Flights depart from Miami on Monday, Wednesday, Friday, and Saturday, requiring a change of aircraft in San Juan. Flights leaving from Miami on Tuesday, Thursday, or Sunday require a brief touchdown in Dutch St. Maarten before continuing on to the French islands. Some of Eastern's least expensive fares require a 30-day advance purchase, and a wait of at least one Saturday night before using the return half of the ticket. Any alteration of flight dates or routings requires a forfeiture of 50% of the value of the ticket.

Service is also available on **Air France.** Flights leave Miami every Saturday, heading first to Guadeloupe, then Martinique. Every Tuesday, Wednesday, and Friday, a flight leaves San Juan for Guadeloupe, continuing on to Martinique.

These schedules could—and probably will—change by the time of your departure for the islands. For more information, call the airlines directly or your travel agent.

GETTING AROUND: Travel by **taxi** is the most popular method, and rates are expensive. Most of the cabs aren't metered, and you'll have to agree on the price of the ride before getting in. Most visitors arriving at Lamentin Airport head for one of the resorts along the peninsula of Pointe du Bout. To do so costs about 136F ($20.40) during the day, about 190F ($28.50) for two in the evening. Night fares are in effect from 8 p.m. to 6 a.m.

If you want to rent a taxi for the day, it's better to have a party of at least three or four persons to keep costs low. Depending on the size of the car, expect to pay from 475F ($71.25) for a five-hour trip. Only a few of the drivers will be able to speak English, however.

Ferry

The least expensive way to go between Fort-de-France and Pointe du Bout is by ferry, costing 9F ($1.35) per passenger. However, service is not as frequent as it should be, so check departure points and times before relying on this means of transport.

Buses

There is no railway system in Martinique, but buses are operated from Fort-de-France, linking every single village on the island. Depending on the distance, fares run

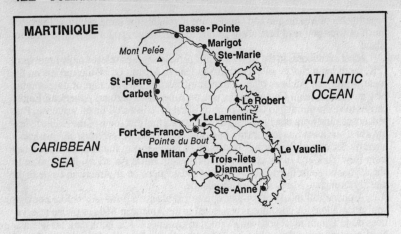

from 50¢ to $3. However, for those taking this local means of transport, I must point out that mama, her kids, or even a chicken may ride on your lap.

"**Taxis collectifs**" are preferred. These are usually limos or vans holding from about eight to ten passengers, charging fares in the 5F (75¢) to 20F ($3) range, depending on where you're going. They are faster than the buses and much less crowded. In Fort-de-France, the departure point for these CTs is at Pointe Simon on the harborfront.

Car Rentals

If you rent a car in Martinique, you must be at least 21 or 25 years old, depending on the company. Driving is on the right. Maintain a slow but average speed, because of the island's zigzagging and narrow secondary roads. Most roads are in fair condition, and the major highways are excellent. Drive defensively, and take out the extra insurance.

Most North American visitors fly into Lamentin Airport, where an array of worldwide and local car-rental companies maintain kiosks. **Hertz, Avis,** and **Budget** are all represented, offering well-maintained cars. Of the three, Budget has the least expensive no-frills vehicle, costing $176 per week, as opposed to $238 for a similar car at Avis and $272 at Hertz. However, if you want to make this savings on your rental, you'll have to call Budget in Martinique directly (tel. 71-69-68), as it is not tied in to the company's worldwide reservations system. If you have the time, you can also write and reserve a car; address your request to Mme Nicole Malidor, P.O. Box 1006, 8 rue Felix-Éboué, 97208 Fort-de-France, Martinique.

On the other hand, your most favorable rate with Avis or Hertz is dependent on two- and three-day advance reservations which you can make by calling Avis toll free at 800/331-2112 or Hertz at 800/654-3131.

Scooter Rentals

"**Funny**" (tel. 63-33-05), with four agencies in Martinique, offers a variety of motorcycles and motor scooters for rent. For a Peugeot 50, Peugeot 80, or Vespa 80, the charge per day is 79F ($11.85). A Vespa 125 costs 83F ($12.45). The rent for a Yamaha 125 or a Honda 125 is 115F ($17.25), while the larger Yamaha 250 or Honda 250 goes for 187F ($28) per day. Rates are for unlimited mileage, and tax is included. A 1,000F ($150) minimum deposit is required unless you pay by a major credit card.

Call the number given above to find out the "Funny" location nearest to you and to reserve the vehicle you wish.

PRACTICAL FACTS: French is the official **language,** spoken by almost everyone. The local Créole patois uses words borrowed from France, England, Spain, and Africa. In the wake of increased tourism, English is occasionally spoken in the major hotels and restaurants. But don't count on driving around the countryside and asking for directions in English. The Martiniquais aren't that bilingual yet.

The **French franc** is legal tender here. You should exchange your money at banks as they give much better rates than the hotels. Currency quotations in this chapter are both in U.S. dollars and French francs, as hotels often publish their rates in American dollars to visitors from North America. Of course, exchange rates are subject to dollar fluctuations. Exchange rates quoted are only for your general guidance, and may not actually be in effect at the time of your visit. One franc is presently exchanged for 15¢ U.S. (6.67 francs equal $1 U.S.).

U.S. and Canadian citizens need **proof of identity** for stays of less than 21 days. After that, a valid passport is required. A return or ongoing ticket is also necessary.

Potable **water** is found throughout the island. **Electric current** is 220 volts, 50 cycles. You'll need a converter or adapter.

Health services and medical equipment are both modern and comprehensive (there are some 18 hospitals and clinics). In an emergency, your hotel can put you in touch with the nearest one.

The **U.S. Consulate** is at 14 rue Blénac (tel. 71-93-01), in Fort-de-France.

Time in Martinique is one hour later than Eastern Standard Time.

A helpful address on the island: **Office Départemental du Tourisme** (Tourist Office), Boulevard Alfassa (Bord de Mer), B.P. 520, 97206 Fort-de-France (tel. 63-79-60).

CARNIVAL: If you like masquerades and dancing in the streets, you should attend carnival, or "Vaval" as it is known here. The event of the year, carnival begins right after the New Year, as each village prepares costumes and floats. Weekend after weekend, frenzied celebrations take place, reaching fever pitch just before Lent.

Fort-de-France is the focal point, and the spirit of the carnival envelops the island, as narrow streets are jammed with floats. On Ash Wednesday the streets of Fort-de-France are filled with *diablesses,* or she-devils (including members of both sexes). They are costumed in black and white, crowding the streets to form King Carnival's funeral procession. As devils cavort about and the rum flows, a funeral pyre is built at La Savane. When it is set on fire, the dancing of those "she-devils" becomes frantic (many are thoroughly drunk at this point).

Long past dusk, the cortège takes the coffin to its burial, ending carnival until another year.

FORT-DE-FRANCE: A mélange of New Orleans and Menton (French Riviera), Fort-de-France is the main town of Martinique, lying at the end of a large bay, surrounded by evergreen hills. Iron-grillwork balconies overflowing with flowers are commonplace here.

The people of Martinique are even more fascinating than the town. Today the Créole beauties are likely to be seen in jeans instead of their traditional turbans and Empress Josephine–style gowns, but they still have the same walk. Heads held high, shoulders up, they have a jaunty spring. They're a proud, sprightly people, and I miss their massive earrings that used to jounce and sway as they sauntered along.

Narrow streets climb up the steep hills on which houses have been built to catch the overflow of the capital's more than 100,000 inhabitants.

At the center of the town lies a broad garden planted with many palms and mangoes, **La Savane,** a handsome savannah with shops and cafés lining its sides. In the middle of this grand place stands a statue of Josephine, "Napoleon's little Créole," made of white marble, the work of Vital Debray. With the grace of a Greek goddess, she poses in a Regency gown. She looks toward Trois-Îlets where she was born.

After viewing her, you can head for the **St. Louis Roman Catholic Cathedral,** built in 1875. It's an extraordinary iron building, which someone once likened to "a sort of Catholic railway station."

There's another statue of the island's second main historical figure, Victor Schoelcher (you'll see his name a lot in Martinique). As mentioned, he worked to free the slaves more than a century ago. This statue stands in front of the Palais de Justice.

The **Library Schoelcher** also honors this popular hero. It was first displayed at the Paris Exposition of 1889. However, the Romanesque portal, in red and blue, the Egyptian lotus-petal columns, even the turquoise tiles, were imported piece by piece from Paris, reassembled finally in this West Indian setting of royal palms and tamarinds.

Guarding the port is **Fort St-Louis,** built in the Vauban style on a rocky promontory. In addition, **Fort Tartenson** and **Fort Desaix** stand on hills overlooking the port.

The **Musée Départemental de la Martinique** (tel. 71-57-05) is the one bastion on Martinique that preserves its pre-Columbian past, the relics left from the early settlers, the peaceful Arawaks and the cannibalistic Caribs. Exhibits depict in artifacts and garments the life of these Indians. The location is along the rue de la Liberté, at the same location as the government-sponsored Caribbean Art Center, facing the Savane. The museum is open Monday to Friday from 8 a.m. to noon and 3 to 6 p.m. (from 8 a.m. to noon on Saturday), charging a 5F (75¢) admission.

Finally, **Sacré-Coeur de Balata Cathedral,** also overlooking Fort-de-France, is a copy of the one looking down upon Montmartre in Paris—and this one is just as incongruous, maybe more so.

Hotels in and Around Fort-de-France

Hotel La Batelière, Schoelcher (tel. 71-90-41), stands on the west coast. The 18-acre estate lies in La Batelière, a residential suburb about a mile from Fort-de-France. This waterside French-modern hotel is a 200-room, air-conditioned white stucco structure, set back in a garden from its wide private beach. The hotel lacks super-glamor but serves successfully as a center of many water sports, social activities, dining choices, and nightlife activities with its casino and disco action.

Furnishings are conservative, brightened considerably by the use of fabrics against a backdrop of white walls. Each unit contains a tile bath, but best of all are the room-wide glass doors opening onto your own water-view terrace. In winter, you can stay here (with a continental breakfast included) in a single for 750F ($112.50) to 1,386F ($208) daily, for 924F ($138.50) to 1,560F ($234) in a double. *Off-season, singles are accepted for 625F ($93.75) to 1,155F ($173.25) daily and doubles for 770F ($115.50) to 1,300F ($195).* For dinner, add 180F ($27) per person to the prices quoted. In the Lafitte dining room, French, international, and Créole cuisine is served, and there's a pizzeria near the swimming pool. You may enjoy a span of dredged sand or the round swimming pool. You can order a drink under the canopied bar as you sit comfortably on cushions. Sports such as scuba-diving, snorkeling, windsurfing, sailing, and waterskiing are available at rates which depend on the season and duration. Tennis is free, however, except at night when there's a surcharge. On the premises are a beauty salon and barbershop, and a sauna.

Hôtel l'Impératrice, Place de la Savane, rue de la Liberté (tel. 63-06-82), favored by business people, faces a landscaped mall. Named for Josephine, it's a 1950s "layer-cake" stucco hotel, with encircling balconies overlooking the traffic at the west side of the Savane. The lounge has large, white wickerwork chairs. Adjoining is a bar

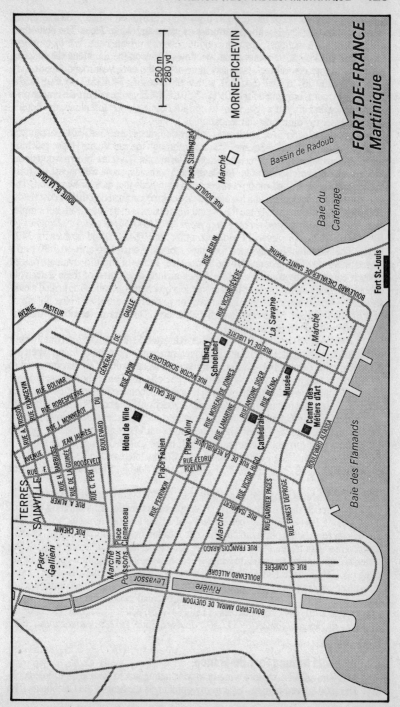

FORT-DE-FRANCE
Martinique

MORNE-PICHEVIN

Bassin de Radoub

Baie du Carénage

La Savane

Fort St-Louis

Baie des Flamands

250 m
280 yd

ROUTE DE LA FOUR

RUE BOUILLÉ

Place Stalingrad

Marché

RUE BERLIN

RUE VICTOR-SÉVÈRE

AVENUE PASTEUR

BOULEVARD CHEVALIER DE SAINTE-MARTHE

RUE DE GAULLE

GÉNÉRAL DU

RUE PAPIN

RUE GALLIENI

RUE VICTOR SCHOELCHER

Library
Schoelcher

RUE DE LA LIBERTÉ

Marché

RUE MOREAU-DE-JONNES

RUE LAMARTINE

RUE ANTOINE SIGER

RUE BLÉNAC

Musée

Cathédrale

Centre des
Métiers d'Art

BOULEVARD ALFASSA

RUE A. TISSOT

RUE PLANGEVIN

RUE BOLIVAR

RUE ROBESPIERRE

RUE J. MONNEROT

AVENUE

JEAN JAURÈS

RUE F.

RUE H. BARBUSSE

RUE DE LA GUINÉE

ROOSEVELT

RUE G. PÉRI

BOULEVARD DU

Hôtel de Ville

RUE A. ALIKER

RUE CHEMIN

TERRES SAINVILLE

Parc Gallieni

Marché aux Poissons

Place Clemenceau

Levassor

RUE PERRINON

Place Volny

Place Fabien

RUE LEDRU ROLLIN

RUE DE LA RÉPUBLIQUE

RUE VICTOR HUGO

RUE ISAMBERT

Marché

RUE GARNIER PAGÈS

RUE ERNEST DEFROGE

RUE FRANÇOIS ARAGO

RUE S. COMPÈRE

BOULEVARD ALLÈGRE

Rivière

BOULEVARD AMIRAL DE GUEYDON

with white furniture set on its tile floor. If you don't like to perch there, you may prefer the bar on the next level, with its harmonious green-and-white decor. The bedrooms are modern and functional, each air-conditioned with private bath. The front rooms tend to be noisy; yet, to compensate, windows overlook the life along the Savane. Since this is not a resort hotel, rates stay more or less the same year round. Singles pay from 265F ($39.75) to 305F ($45.75), with doubles costing 340F ($51) to 380F ($57). Some triple rooms are rented for 450F ($67.50) daily. If you're in Fort-de-France on a shopping excursion, you might want to consider dining at Le Joséphine, the hotel's restaurant (see my dining recommendations).

Le Lafayette, 5 rue de la Liberté, in Fort-de-France (tel. 73-80-50), is a modern 23-room hotel right on La Savane. You enter through the rue Victor-Hugo, reaching the reception hall after climbing a few steps of terracotta. The dark-brown wood doors are offset by the soft beige walls. Inside the bedrooms, Japanese wall tapestries form the decorative motif, and most rooms contain twin beds in a dark-brown wood. The windows have small panes, and the curtains are color coordinated with the bedspreads. Bathrooms are in pure white, and the overall impression is of a neat, clean, but simple, hostelry. *In the off-season, rooms range from 290F ($43.50) in a single. Doubles go for 315F ($47.25).* In winter, EP singles rent for 305F ($45.75) and doubles for 340F ($51). The restaurant is only open for lunch, served from 11:30 a.m. to 2:30 p.m., closed on Sunday. It is decorated in the bistro style. Tables of hors d'oeuvres are placed in each corner of the room. All main dishes include a selection of these delectable appetizers. For a main course, I'd recommend a brochette of scallops or grilled steak. Broiled lobster, when available, is featured, or you may be attracted to the full rib of beef in a butter sauce. Meat is grilled on the charcoal. Desserts are tempting. An average repast will cost from 120F ($18).

Le Bristol, .20 km. rue Martin-Luther-King (tel. 71-31-80), was originally built on a hillside as the center of a plantation which surrounded it in 1890. Later, when the encroaching suburbs of Fort-de-France threatened its agriculture, it was converted in 1925 into the first hotel in town. Today Philippe Solis, the French-born owner, offers doses of Gallic charm along with frothy drinks at his accommodating bar. He also does a thriving restaurant business (refer to the dining section). The hotel's ornate gables are seen at the top of a steep road about a five-minute drive from the center of town, within its own ten-acre garden. The ten simple bedrooms each have air conditioning, private bath, and a kind of roguish charm. With half board included, singles rent for 265F ($39.75), and doubles go for 415F ($62.25). Clients interested in bed and breakfast pay only 200F ($30) in a single, 275F ($41.25) in a double. Prices are in effect year round.

Hôtel Victoria, Rond Point de Didier (tel. 60-56-78). Its central core was built in 1888 by a French slave owner. Today it occupies a residential neighborhood north of the center of Fort-de-France, behind rows of seven-foot-tall hibiscus hedges. The place is far from being plush, and the hillside location may be difficult to find, but still its accommodations are clean and simple. Motel-like units huddle into a sprawling series of outbuildings and satellite wings whose focal point is a sapphire-colored swimming pool. From its terrace and from the windows of some (but not all) of the rooms, you can enjoy a sweeping view over the city to the sea. Each of the 30 accommodations has its own tile bath, big window, and relatively banal modern furniture. In winter, singles cost 275F ($41.25); doubles, 315F ($47.25); and triples, 390F ($52.50). *In summer, singles rent for 250F ($37.50); doubles, 350F ($52.50); and triples, 375F ($56.25).*

Dining in and Around Fort-de-France

Many travel-wise visitors wing in to Martinique just to sample its Créole cookery. The food served here, at least in my opinion, is the best in the Caribbean. The island's chefs and Créole mamas have been called "seasoned sorcerers." They took not only their native talent for good cooking, but have borrowed freely from Spain and Africa. They've even thrown in a bit of Hindu and a touch of Asian cuisine.

In honor of its African roots, Créole cooking is based on seafood, often bought by the chef "fresh from the Caribbean Sea." Out in the country, every cook has his or her own herb garden, as the Martinique cuisine is highly seasoned with herbs and spices. Except in the major hotels, most restaurants are family run, offering real homemade cooking. Best of all, you usually get to dine al fresco.

Stuffed, stewed, skewered, or broiled langoustes, turtles, clams, conchs, oysters, and octopuses are presented to you with French taste and subtlety but with Martiniquais skill and invention. Every good chef knows how to make *colombo*, a spicy rich stew of pork (or beef), served with rice, herbs, sauces, and a variety of seeds. Another Créole favorite is *calalou* (callaloo in English), a soup flavored with savory herbs.

Incidentally, watch those Sunday closings.

Tiffany, La Croix Bellevue, route de Bellevue (tel. 71-33-82), is an elegant little restaurant that's my personal favorite. It may be the best table on the island, and there are those who suggest that it's one of the best restaurants in all the Caribbean. Four miles north of town, it faces the Institut Vivioz. Its owner, Claude Pradines, who also owns an antique shop in Paris, has created an enticing atmosphere in which to serve his exquisite French specialties. It's an old pink-and-white gingerbread house. Louvered windows let in the sea breezes, which are then whirled about by the ceiling fans. He took over an old colonial mansion once owned by Victor Severe, a famous Martiniquais. Monsieur Pradines brought his knowledge of antiques and their use into play here. For example, an old chest he found in the mansion is now used as a server in the dining room. In the hallway is a large shell once used in a church to hold holy water. The walls are bright with watercolors and flamboyant Haitian primitives which are in contrast to the dark-wood furniture.

I suggest you let Monsieur Pradines propose a dinner for you. It might be baby pullet in a tarragon or a Créole sauce, perhaps duck magret with raspberry vinegar. He might suggest a fish filet with green peppercorns or red snapper filets with delicate sauces. The choice depends on what fresh produce was imported from France. I recently dined on filet mignon with a buttery roquefort sauce. That was preceded by asparagus in puff pastry with a herb cream sauce. A menu is offered including three appetizers, filet mignon, fish, veal, and dessert. The finish came with velvety chocolate cake and a Martinique coffee. To improve his culinary skills, he journeys to France every year to learn "what's cooking." Dining here as well as speaking to him is a pleasure, especially if you're sipping his first-class wine. In the garden are lime trees, banana, and papaya loaded with fruit, and darting trips are made there to gather produce for some of the dishes served. When Monsieur Pradines is in a good mood, he'll entertain guests with magic and card tricks. The typical price of an à la carte menu is 270F ($40.50). It is open for lunch from noon to 3 p.m. and for dinner from 7:30 to 10 p.m. It is closed on Saturday for lunch and all day Sunday.

La Grand'Voile, Pointe Simon (tel. 70-29-29). Set near the water at the geographical center of town, this second-story restaurant sits like an oasis of calm, slightly apart from the hectic activity of Fort-de-France's outdoor vegetable markets and the bus station. It occupies the second story of an angular concrete building whose interior is freshly painted in tones of blue and white. Its centerpiece is a thick pole—a bit like the mast of a schooner—from the top of which radiates a fretwork of stout beams. Many guests prefer a seat outdoors on the veranda with a view of the water. Dominique Laval and Muriel Palandri, both from Toulouse, are the owners. Full meals cost from 150F ($22.50) for a fixed-price repast with wine, or from 175F ($26.25) à la carte. The cookery style is nouvelle cuisine, and specialties include young rabbit with juniper berries, roast veal rib with onion purée, salmon with a leek fondue, loup de mer (seabass) with fresh pasta, sole in champagne sauce, sliced filet of warm duck with foie gras and apples, and salmon ravioli. Meals are served daily from 12:30 to 2 p.m. and 7:30 to 10 p.m., and reservations are needed.

La Belle Époque, 2.5 km. route de Didier (tel. 64-01-09). Some of the best-known chefs in Martinique have collaborated in the establishment of this restaurant. It occupies a graciously proportioned neo-Grecian villa, whose creamy walls and ornate balustrades were erected around 1880. It was originally opened by the French-born chef Robert Provost, who still returns from his more famous restaurant in Caracas. In his absence, his charming aunt, Montserrat Fito, instructs a crew of employees in the preparation of the recipes which her nephew learned during his apprenticeship at many of the very best restaurants of Europe. Yves Coyac, the Martinique-born chef, carries on the tradition inherited from Bocuse, Troisgros, and Imbert. Beneath high ceilings, with a view of a lush garden, you can enjoy such specialties as terrine maison, beefsteak with capers, a casserole of chicken with morels, duck filet with mango sauce, slices of venison in pepper sauce, veal kidneys with mustard, hot spinach mousse, shrimp in passion fruit juice, tropical sorbets, and a smooth version of lime mousse. Full meals cost from 175F ($26.25) and are served daily except Sunday and Monday from noon to 2:30 p.m. and 7:30 to 10 p.m. Reservations are suggested.

D'Esnambuc, rue de la Liberté (tel. 71-46-51), is small, select, and elegant, the domain of Josette Kleinpeter since 1981. Stylish in decor and clientele, it overlooks the harbor near La Savane. You climb to the third floor, enjoying not only good food but a view of the bay and a refreshing atmosphere. The staircase foreshadows the abundance of green plants and vines in the dining room. The cool rectangular room is spotlessly white, the basketware chairs also white, with green cushions. The cuisine here is imaginatively French, with hints of West Indian spices added in. A noonday fixed-price lunch costs 80F ($12), and at least three other fixed-price meals are more expensive. If you order à la carte the tab could run to as much as 200F ($30). The list of French and Créole specialties includes fish soup, smoked salmon, sea urchin quiche, coquille de poisson, sole Colbert or meunière, three different preparations of crayfish, red snapper with crème fraîche, octopus with red beans, rabbit chasseur (with red wine and mushrooms), and a colombo of chicken. Lunch is served daily from noon to 3 p.m.; dinner, 7 to 10:30 p.m.

El Raco, 23 rue Lazare-Carnot (tel. 73-29-16), lies in a city residential neighborhood that seems to have changed very little since 1945. Designed after Spanish models, it has plaster interior walls and a cave-like ambience pierced with rounded arches like an Iberian bodega. Despite his origins in France, owner Hughes Balcaen serves a carefully researched medley of Spanish food from regions that include Catalonia, Valencia, and Andalusia. Full meals cost from 150F ($22.50) and might include gazpacho, veal kidneys with sherry, paella, grilled lobster, roquefort salad, and Catalán-style spinach. Dinner is served nightly except Sunday from 7:30 to 10 p.m.; lunch is offered only Tuesday through Friday from noon to 2 p.m. Because of its small size, reservations are important.

L'Escalier, 18 rue de la République (tel. 70-25-22), established in 1986, evokes a turn-of-the-century Parisian bistro. The situation is at the top of a steep flight of stairs on a downtown commercial street. Guests try for a table on the long balcony, but often settle for a seat in the deliberately old-fashioned interior. Jean-Philippe Crampont, the Paris-trained chef de cuisine, prepares full nouvelle cuisine–inspired meals at 190F ($28.50). These are served daily, except Saturday at lunch and all day Sunday, from noon to 2:30 p.m. and 7:30 to 10:30 p.m. Reservations are important. Specialties include rack of lamb roasted with fennel, veal kidneys, deviled fish filet with sea urchins and fumet de champagne, goujonnettes of sarde with a caviar confit and eggplant, crayfish ravioli, délices of potatoes with lime and a brunoise of raw tomatoes, and shrimp with a warm spinach salad, lime juice, and olive oil.

La Biguine, 11 route de la Folie (tel. 70-12-52), has been rated by some food critics as one of the finest restaurants in Martinique. It's the personal statement of a master chef, Gérard Padra, who for a long time was associated with the Bakoua. Wanting to leave the hotel trade and branch out on his own, he found this clapboard colonial-style house in teeming Fort-de-France. In it he installed a restaurant, bar, and tea salon (dining is on the second floor). Few who try his gastronomic menu are disappointed. It is a showcase for the many fine dishes for which he is known, including a Créole mutton soup, shrimp fricassée, broiled lobster, veal cooked with vermouth, a blaff of fish, coq au vin, and shark in tomato sauce. For a perfect ending to one of his repasts, try one of his sorbets (sherbet) made with local fruits. Because he has very few tables but a big reputation as a chef, reservations are essential. Meals are served from noon to 2 p.m. and 7 to 11 p.m. He is closed on Saturday for lunch and all day Sunday. Meals cost from 200F ($30).

Le Coq Hardi, 0.6 km. rue Martin-Luther-King (tel. 71-59-64). If the chef/proprietor isn't too busy, he might take time out to tell you about his days of serving in the French Foreign Legion in Algeria and Indochina. Le Coq Hardi is a steakhouse, known for its meats grilled over a wood fire. You'll find it beside a steeply inclined traffic artery which crisscrosses a residential hillside just outside the center of town. A symmetrical pyramid-shaped staircase prefaces the façade, which sports a bold and vibrant color scheme of forest green and fire-engine red. This is a place for hearty eaters who don't mind spending about $22 for a worthy dinner. In some ways Le Coq Hardi is the type of bistro that the famous food critic Waverley Root was always discovering in some working-class arrondissement of Paris. It is open every day except Wednesday from noon to 1:45 p.m. and 7:15 to 10:45 p.m.

Typic Bellevue, 83 Boul. de la Marne (tel. 71-68-87), a few minutes from the center of town, is a rustic rural house, with eye-catching blue walls and light-brown shutters. Operated by Bruno Raphael-Amanrich, it's frequented by local residents because of its well-prepared Créole dishes, which are served at reasonable prices. As you dine on the terrace, you'll get the feeling of stopping over at a roadside inn. Among the specialties are seafood such as lobster and local shrimp, fricassée of goat, fish soup, turtle steak, steamed baby shark, and frogs' legs. A meal of Créole specialties will lead to a tab in the neighborhood of 130F ($19.50) to 185F ($27.75). It shuts down on Saturday afternoon and Sunday. Otherwise, meals are served from noon to 3 p.m. and 7:30 to 10 p.m.

Shopping in Fort-de-France

Your best buys in Martinique are French luxury imports, such as perfumes, fashions, Vuitton luggage, Lalique crystal, or Limoges dinnerware. Sometimes (but don't count on it) prices are as much as 30% to 40% below Stateside levels.

A cautious reader who is nobody's fool sounds a warning to all readers. He points out that if you pay in dollars, store owners supposedly will give you a 20% discount, which is the "Value Added Tax" imposed on countries of Europe that are members of the Common Market. He proposes a hypothetical example. That is, a shopper will make a purchase for 1,000F. Less 20%, that becomes 800F. However, when you pay in dollars the rates vary considerably from store to store, and almost invariably they are far lower than that proposed at one of the local banks. He writes: "The net result is that you received a 20% discount, but then they take away from 9% to 15% on the dollar exchange, giving you a net savings of only 5% to 11%—not 20%." He further notes, "Actually, you're probably better off shopping in the smaller stores where prices are 8% to 12% less on comparable items and paying in francs that you have exchanged at a local bank."

The main shopping street is rue Victor-Hugo. The other two leading shopping streets are the rues Schoelcher and St-Louis.

Facing the tourist office and alongside Quai Desnambuc is an open market where you can purchase local handcrafts and souvenirs. Many of these are tacky, however.

Far more interesting is the display of vegetables and fruit, quite a show, at the open-air stalls along rue Isambert. Don't miss it for its local ambience, and you can't help but smell the fish market alongside the Levassor River.

Try to postpone your shopping trip if a cruise ship is in town.

Hours at most shops are weekdays from 7:30 a.m. to 12:30 p.m. and 2:30 to 5:30 p.m., on Saturday from 8 a.m. to noon; closed Sunday.

Roger Albert, 7 rue Victor-Hugo (tel. 71-71-71), offers most of the Paris articles of fashion, with all the big names in design, as well as crystal from Daum and Lalique, French perfumes, and chinaware from Limoges. The location is just off the Savane. The merchandise is definitely of high quality, and it's the finest selection on Martinique. Long established, this is the best-known store in Martinique.

Au Printemps, 10 rue Schoelcher, near the cathedral (tel. 71-30-92), is one of the finest department stores in the Caribbean. French fashions are sold, along with china, crystal, and Baccarat, and such famous names in perfume as Lanvin, Chanel, Jean Patou, and Guerlain.

The best place to go for handcrafts and souvenirs is the **Caribbean Art Center,** rue Ernest-Deproge (tel. 70-25-01), facing the Savane, next to the tourist office and Air France. Everything here is handmade. All the craftwork of the island is represented here, particularly basketwork and clay crafts. You'll find madras, napkins, and table settings; bags in coconut husks, moon fishes, and boubous (large multicolored gowns), the latter at much lower prices than in the hotel shops. Look also for the Martiniquais doll in her *madras et foulard.*

For the ubiquitous local fabric, madras, there are shops on every street with bolts and bolts of it, all colorful and inexpensive. So-called haute couture and resortwear are sold in many boutiques dotting downtown Fort-de-France.

Some boutiques, such as **Olympe,** 20-24 rue Lamartine (tel. 71-38-48), are long established *pret-à-porter* (ready-to-wear) shops carrying jeans, slacks, and sports wear from Paris and Côte d'Azur designers.

Young Martinique designers also present their own collections, usually showing on Thursday in their respective shops. A new crop of boutiques seems to blossom each season, although some, such as **Gisele,** 14 rue Victor-Hugo (tel. 71-38-67), have been around a while.

Gigi Shop, 21 rue Moreau-de-Jonnes (tel. 71-36-52). Women find the clothing here risqué, revealing, and racy. Several French designers are represented within the confines of the store, each seemingly revealing more décolletage than his competitors. If you're looking for clothes with casual style, and often humor, along with a barrage of fake jewelry to go with them, this is a likely address.

Crazy Boutique, 17 rue Victor-Hugo (tel. 73-26-68), likes to set a mood that it calls très parisienne. I'd call it the most outrageous fashion in Fort-de-France. The boutique certainly lives up to its name.

Cadet-Daniel, 72 rue Antoine-Siger (tel. 71-41-48), which opened in 1840, sells Christofle silver, Limoges china, and crystal from Daum, Baccarat, Lalique, and Sèvres. Like some nearby stores, it also sells island-made 18-karat gold baubles, including the beaded *collier chou,* or "darling's necklace," long a required ornament for a Créole costume.

Before leaving Martinique, you may want to purchase some rum, considered by aficionados to be one of the world's finest distilled drinks. Hemingway in *A Moveable Feast* lauded it as the perfect antidote to a rainy day. I suggest you try Vieux Acajou, a dark, mellow Old Mahogany, or else a blood-red brown liqueur-like rum bottled by Bally. The best place for browsing is **La Case à Rhum,** Galerie Marchande, 5 rue de la Liberté (tel. 73-73-20).

Gourmet chefs will find all sorts of spices in the open-air markets of the capital, or such goodies as tinned pâté or canned quail in the local *supermarchés*.

Shopping Elsewhere on the Island

If you're staying at one of the hotels on the peninsula of Pointe du Bout, you'll find that the Marina complex there has a number of interesting boutiques. Several sell handcrafts and curios from Martinique. They are of good quality, and are quite expensive, regrettably, particularly if you purchase some of their batiks of natural silk and their enameled jewel boxes.

North of the capital in the village of Bezaudin near Ste-Marie, Madame Nogard's little *boutique gourmande,* **Ella** (tel. 75-30-75), specializes in exotic home-grown spices, homemade preserves of island fruits, and original syrups.

There are the sturdy, attractive straw food baskets in the shops of nearby Morne-des-Esses, the *vannerie* (basket-making) capital of Martinique.

Another homemade delicacy that makes a distinctive gift is rillette Landaise au foie gras, prepared and put up in glass jars by Mme Laurent de Meillac at her 1,500 duck farm, **Habitation Durocher** (tel. 51-13-60), near Lamentin. At Christmas, her specialty is a terrine of foie gras made with armagnac and presented in a lovely crock made by the **Poterie de Trois-Îlets** (tel. 76-03-44), an excellent place on Martinique to buy ceramics.

A Side Trip to Trois-Îlets

Marie-Josephe Rose Tasher de la Pagerié was born here in 1763. As Josephine, she was to become the wife of Napoléon I and empress of France from 1804 to 1809. She'd been married before to Alexandre de Beauharnais, who'd actually wanted to wed either of her two more attractive sisters, taking her as a consolation prize. Six years older than Napoleon, she pretended she'd lost her birth certificate so he wouldn't find out her true age. Although some historians call her ruthless and selfish (certainly unfaithful), she is still revered by some in Martinique as an uncommonly gracious lady. Others have less kind words for her, because Napoleon is said by some historians to have "reinvented" slavery. Some see the influence of Josephine in that hideous practice.

After 20 miles of driving from Fort-de-France, you reach Trois-Îlets, a charming little village. One mile outside the hamlet, you turn left to **La Pagerié,** where a small museum of mementos relating to Josephine has been installed in the former estate kitchen. Along with her childhood bed in the kitchen, you'll see a smouldering letter from Napoleon. The collection was compiled by Dr. Robert Rose-Rosette. Here Josephine gossiped with her slaves and played the guitar.

Still remaining are the partially restored ruins of the Pagerié sugar mill and the church (in the village itself) where she was christened in 1763. The plantation was destroyed in the 1766 hurricane. The museum is open daily, except Monday, from 9 a.m. to 5:30 p.m., charging 8F ($1 20) for admission.

A botanical garden, **Parc des Floralies,** is adjacent to the Golf de l'Impératrice Joséphine, as is the museum devoted to Josephine described above.

POINTE DU BOUT: Pointe du Bout is a narrow, irregularly shaped peninsula across the bay from Fort-de-France. Over the past few years it's become the major resort area of Martinique. This is because of four major hotels—the Frantel, de la Marina, Bakoua, and the Méridien.

In addition to the hotels, you'll find a Robert Trent Jones–designed golf course, a dozen tennis courts, several restaurants, a marina, a gambling casino, discos, swimming pools, facilities for horseback riding, waterskiing, scuba-diving, snorkeling, and volleyball courts.

To drive there from Fort-de-France, leave by Rte. 1, which takes you for a few minutes along the autoroute. You cross the plain of Lamentin, the industrial area of Fort-de-France and the site of the international airport. Very frequently the air is filled with the fragrance of caramel because of the large sugarcane factories in the area.

After 20 miles of driving, you reach Trois-Îlets, Josephine's hometown. Three miles farther on your right, take the D38 to Pointe du Bout.

For those who want to reach Pointe du Bout by sea, there's a ferry service as mentioned, running all day long (until midnight) from Fort-de-France for a 9F ($1.35) fare.

The Resort Hotels

Bakoua Beach Hotel, Pointe du Bout (tel. 66-02-02), has buildings that are not overpowering, allowing the natural beauty of the landscape to survive. The 90-room hotel consists of two hillside buildings in the center of the garden of frangipani and coconut palms, plus another building, a bungalow type, right on the beach. The hotel often draws a list of celebrities, including Jean-Paul Belmondo, Paul McCartney, and Mike Douglas. Of course, they book the imperial suite, with its green marble sunken bathtub and yellow four-poster bed. The style of the rooms is more or less colonial, not really typical of the West Indies. All the units, however, are comfortable, with a refined polish. In the high season, a double, including a full American breakfast, rents for $165 to $185, with singles going for $130 to $145. *In summer, tariffs are lowered to $99 to $110 in a double, from $72 to $83 in a single.* Dinner is from 7 to 10 p.m.

The bar welcomes you to its circular site, dominating an oval-shaped swimming pool right over the beach. The bar, La Rotonde, has a ceiling which is partly in bamboo, partly in striped linen. If you want a snack, you can eat right on the beach, but for an elegant repast I'd suggest Le Chateaubriand with its award-winning French chef. Sports are free here, including tennis, volleyball, snorkeling, and sailing. The hotel closes in September. In high season it provides dancing every night (only four times a week in the off-season). The Ballets Martiniquais usually show up every Friday night.

Hôtel Méridien Trois-Îlets (tel. 66-00-00, 212/956-4390 in New York City, 416/598-3838 in Toronto, or toll free 800/543-4300 in the U.S. and Canada), is actually a miniature village, a dramatically designed Air France property offering first-class accommodations in 300 rooms. It has excellent facilities, including a dramatically designed reception area open to the palm-fringed swimming pool and the waters of the bay. Among the restaurants and bars of this hostelry, the Casa Créole offers gourmet meals served by Créole waitresses dressed in native costume. The Vonvon disco features electronic rhythms for the international crowd, while the casino provides glitter. The hotel is slightly angled to follow the line of the shore. Because of that, all units benefit from a view of either the Caribbean or the bay, at the far end of which you'll be able to see the lights of Fort-de-France. Around the huge block of rooms are a waterside garden, a 100-foot marina, and a cabaña-style bar near the swimming pool.

The bedrooms provide much comfort, with luxurious baths, private balconies, and attractively modern furnishings. Room service is available 24 hours a day. In winter, singles range from $100 to $200, doubles run $120 to $200, and triples cost $174 to $250. *In summer, singles cost $70 to $85; doubles, $85 to $105; and triples, $115 to $135.* Children under 12 stay free in their parents' room. Fixed-price meals are available for around $9 at the buffet breakfast, $21 at lunch, and $23 at dinner. On certain nights of the week the hotel hosts the vibrantly colorful Ballets Martiniquais near the pool. A Créole buffet supper followed by the folkloric show costs 165F ($24.75) for residents of the hotel, 200F ($30) for nonresidents. Farther out on the point is an old fort where you can walk at night, breathing air filled with tropical fragrance.

PLM Azur Carayou (formerly the Frantel Martinique), Pointe du Bout (tel. 66-04-04). One of the advantages of staying here is that you don't realize you're entering a hotel. Rather, you think you've come for a walk in a tropical garden. It's easy to forget that behind the scenes are 200 bedrooms. The buildings are encircled by large lawns planted with coconut or palm trees and many flowering bushes. The rooms are in two-story bungalows, each having a balcony. The view from your abode will be of gardens, a marina, or the bay of Fort-de-France. In the center of everything is a circular swimming pool, also with a view of the bay. The curving beach provides safe swimming as well. Also taking advantage of that bay view, La Paillote, a bar, is nicely decorated and lit by original cord lamps. Rates include free use of the sports equipment, except for waterskiing. However, you're admitted free to the hotel's disco, Vesou. The bedrooms are handsomely coordinated, with white walls and beamed ceilings. The draperies and bedcovers match. The furnishings are in a contemporary style, with wickerwork. On the EP in winter, singles range in price from $80 daily, with doubles going for $98. *Tariffs drop in summer: from $58 daily in a single and from $76 in a double.*

In the Café Créole, you can order a quick snack lunch, without interference with your suntanning schedule. It connects the beach to the pool and acts as an open passage. On the buffet, you'll have a choice of salads and desserts and can select the plat du jour. The café is also open for dinner. It serves some of the best food on Pointe du Bout, tasty and attractively presented. La Boucau is the principal restaurant, created with an island atmosphere of white ceilings and wooden beams. The view over the bay is dramatic at night. In the background is a stage where a local combo plays during dinner. While the atmosphere is quite exotic, the restaurant may also be noisy at times. Fish is the specialty, and Créole cookery is done with flair here. Main dishes include red snapper, stuffed crabs, conch ragoût, or a blaff (stew) of sea urchin. The cuisine is first class, the portions rather generous.

PLM Azur La Pagerié, Pointe du Bout (tel. 66-05-30), gives you a chance to have the independence of your own personal apartment. In neat, efficient, streamlined designs, the club offers 98 air-conditioned rooms, some with kitchenettes and balconies opening onto a view of the bay. The location is across the road from the action swirling around the Bakoua. Units are not only comfortable but attractive, with tile floors and white walls, in contrast to the bright pastel draperies and bedspreads. Furnishings are in a clean-cut contemporary style. In winter, EP rates are 451F ($67.75) to 521F ($78.25) daily in a single, 548F ($82.25) to 618F ($92.75) in a double, with full hotel services. *In summer, prices are 250F ($37.50) daily in a single, 296F ($44.50) in a double.* If you don't want to cook, you can order a meal at one of several restaurants at your doorstep. There is also a large swimming pool.

Small Inns (Budget to Moderate)

Madinina Sidonie, Marina Pointe du Bout (tel. 66-00-54), is an appealing 15-room hotel, directly on the marina. The clean-cut rooms are modern, with built-in headboards and your own bath. Units are air-conditioned, with streamlined furniture and bright colors used in the draperies and spreads. In season, prices are 192F ($28.75) daily in a single, 296F ($44.50) in a double. *In the off-season, the double rate is 212F ($31.75) daily; the single tariff, 147F ($22).* The rooms, however, are not the main reason to stay here. Its owner, Mme Sidonie Pamphile, is a famous woman cook, serving some of the island's best Créole dishes (see my dining recommendations).

Auberge de l'Anse Mitan, Anse-Mitan (tel. 66-00-98). Many of its guests prefer its location at the isolated end of a road whose more commercial side is laden with restaurants and a bustling nighttime parade. Many of the residents of Fort-de-France, 20 minutes away by hourly launch, come here for a weekend retreat at a beach frequented by Martiniquais. The hotel was originally built in 1930, but it's been renovated several times since then by the genteel and hospitable Athanase family. What you see today is a three-story concrete-box-type structure with 16 rooms, plus four other accommodations strung along the beach in one-bedroom cottages. Each unit is air-conditioned and has a private bath. In winter, singles cost 275F ($41.25); doubles,

330F ($49.50). *In summer, singles go for 220F ($33), and doubles run 275F ($41.25), plus 10% service.* For an additional 50F ($6.50) per person, half board can be arranged. Outsiders are welcome to have a fixed-price meal costing 65F ($9.75) if they phone ahead. Dinner is served every night from 7:30 to 9 p.m. The hotel also has a cozy bar, with pine sheathing, dim lighting, and oversize maps of the continents.

Le Matador, Anse Mitan (tel. 66-05-36), is a simple inn where you might spend most of your vacation in your bikini. That bikini is likely to be even snugger after a stay here at this inn. It was launched by François, the former Bakoua chef, and Raymonde Crico. They rent out 11 pleasant rooms, which are comfortable in spite of their simplicity. In season, a single, with breakfast included, ranges from 300F ($45) daily, a double going from 410F ($61.50). *Off-season, tariffs are lowered to 230F ($34.50) in a single, 310F ($46.50) in a double.* The food served here is among the best on the island (see my dining recommendations).

Le Caraibe Auberge, Anse Mitan (tel. 66-03-19), is run by a friendly manager, Louis Yang Ting. The auberge is not antique; rather, it is a contemporary structure at beachside, with blond furniture. The bar on a terrace opens onto a good view of the bay of Fort-de-France. French-speaking visitors will fit in better here. The rooms have functional, clean-cut pieces, and are equipped with showers, private toilets, and air conditioning. For a single in high season, you pay from 360F ($54), the price increasing to 410F ($61.50) in a double, these tariffs including a continental breakfast. *In summer, the single rate is 240F ($36), going up to 290F ($43.50) in a double, a real bargain.* The food is good, with many Créole specialties featured. Expect to pay from 150F ($22.50) for a three-course meal.

Dining Outside "The Big Four"

Chez Sidonie, in the Hotel Madinina, Marina Pointe du Bout (tel. 66-00-54), is the best restaurant on the peninsula for true Créole cookery (see my previous recommendation of the hotel). Its charming owner, who is reputed to be the queen of the Créole cuisine, Mme Sidonie Pamphile, is also known as the island's most attractive patronne. There are two dining rooms, and most guests favor the one at the edge of the marina. If you want your dinner really fresh, you can make your selections from a large aquarium. The second floor is more secluded, with a view of the harbor.

Mme Pamphile knows a lot of Créole secrets, and she uses her knowledge expertly in her dishes. Her fish soup is one of the finest, and she also does another well-known Martinique specialty, pâté en pot. Some of her favorite dishes include crab en fricassée, Créole pudding, crayfish in the style of Mme Pamphile, and squid, also prepared Créole style. You might also try her grilled fish in a Créole sauce or her colombo of curried mutton. She also serves such exotica as beef testicles on a spit. For desserts, I'd suggest bananas Juanita. Of course, the kitchen also knows how to turn out a traditional French cuisine as well—veal scallops, chateaubriand au poivre vert, and crêpes suzette. You'll easily spend 200F ($30) per person here. Service is from noon to 3 p.m. and 7 to 11 p.m. daily except Monday.

La Villa Créole, Anse Mitan (tel. 60-05-03). Even with a reservation, in high season you'll sometimes be requested to wait in the bar for up to an hour before a table becomes available. Events like this are evidence of the vast popularity of what's probably the most original and lighthearted restaurant in Martinique. The entertainment that keeps the guests coming back is produced by the owner himself, Guy Bruere-Dawson. Gifted as a pop musician, he designed his restaurant with an L-shaped rear veranda whose arms encompass a thatch-roofed bandshell-cum-gazebo. From its gingerbread-laden confines, he sings and plays the guitar, often between taking orders for the well-prepared Créole dishes emerging steaming from the kitchen. Guy's wife, Ghislaine, supervises the food, which includes such specialties as salade de morne Créole (codfish with avocado, tomato, and cucumbers), a three-meat colombo, a blaff of sea urchins, grilled beef in a béarnaise sauce, Créole fish soup, Caribbean chicken, fricassée of conch, and for dessert, chocolate mousse and banana flambé. Full meals, costing from 150F ($22.50), definitely require a reservation; no matter how late it is eventually honored. The establishment is open for lunch daily except Sunday and Monday from noon to 2 p.m., and for dinner any night except Sunday from 7 to 10 p.m. The restaurant stands in a cluster of less popular places in a cozy West Indian home.

Au Regal de la Mer, Anse Mitan, Trois-Îlets (tel. 66-04-00), sits in a cluster of competing restaurants on a quiet lane which looks a bit like a raffish version of St. Tropez. Beneath a canopy of woven straw it has an open-air terrace decorated with lace-trimmed napery and flickering lanterns. Créole waitresses in traditional costume serve full meals beginning at 120F ($18). A specialty is a seafood platter, where a tangle of seaweed shelters a selection of rock lobster, oysters, soft-shell crabs, freshwater crayfish, and shrimp. Many French diners adore this. If you're in the mood for something less briny, you can order a rock fish soup, stuffed crabs, gourmet veal tidbits in pastry, several different preparations of lobster, conch in Créole sauce, kingfish filet with a crab and tomato sauce, filet of Caribbean salmon with a mussel-flavored cream sauce, a curried mutton-and-chicken stew, filet of duckling with a sauce concocted from a local liqueur, and an array of desserts. Alain Bourgogne and his partner, Gerard Bobeau, both well-trained French chefs, are the owners. The establishment prefers reservations. Meals are served daily except Monday from noon to 2 p.m. and 7 to 10:30 p.m.

L'Amphore, Anse Mitan (tel. 66-03-09), lies at the end of a bumpy road which begins near the outermost gates of the Bakoua Hotel. The restaurant specializes in seafood, and its ambience is a bit Tahitian, a bit Polynesian, and intimate. Horizontal wooden louvers partially conceal a view of palms and flowering shrubs. It was designed around one of the most exotic-looking lobster tanks on the island: a saltwater aquarium likely to contain whatever you order for supper. Lobster is the most visible ingredient on the menu, and it's offered in many different varieties. You can also order conch stew, octopus stew, seafood spaghetti, stuffed crab, seafood shells, onion soup, and a savory version of a three-meat curry stew. Desserts are light, including an exotic version of fruit soup. Full meals, costing from 150F ($22.50), require a reservation. The restaurant is open daily except Monday from noon to 2 p.m. and 7 to 11 p.m. No lunch is served on Tuesday.

La Mouïna, route de Jeanne d'Arc—Voie 1, Lamentin (tel. 50-47-50). Named after a Créole word for a house of reunion, this isolated restaurant offers one of the finest luncheon stopovers on the island. It occupies a low-slung, tile-roofed building originally intended as a private house. It was converted into a restaurant by Swiss-born Magdeleine Karchesz and her French-born husband, Guy. They carry an aura of European grace which they mix with Créole spice for a memorable collection of specialties. Guests dine on the marble tiles of a long and narrow veranda where a hedge of hibiscus filters the breeze from the garden outside. Lunch is served daily from 12:30 to 4 p.m., and dinners are offered only on Thursday and Friday night from 8 p.m. to midnight. Your meal might include red snapper in a coconut sauce, roast squab, T-bone steak, stuffed crab, Portuguese oysters, veal escalope in cream sauce with mushrooms, tête (head) of veal, filet bordelaise, and veal liver. To top it off, you can try one of the luscious desserts, such as raspberry cake. Full meals cost from 150F ($22.50). The restaurant is favored by many of the island's leading journalists and politicians, so always reserve a table. Ask at your hotel for good directions before setting out, because it's a bit hard to find.

Le Cantonnais, Pointe du Bout la Marina (tel. 66-02-33), is decorated in the classic Chinese fashion of red and gold. Your host, a Martiniquais, Tien-You Guy, offers not only excellent change-of-pace fare, but his tariffs are also kept low. For example, I'd suggest broiled shark fin (I'm perfectly serious). His sliced duckling with black-bean sauce and green pepper is excellent too. You might also prefer the fried crab claw, the lemon chicken, barbecued pork Chinese style, and fish with fresh mushrooms. Soups include braised bird's nest with minced chicken. A simple set meal is offered daily for 65F ($9.75); otherwise, count on spending from 150F ($22.50). Either meal is a fine bargain. The restaurant is open from 6:30 to 11 p.m. seven days a week. Lunch is served only on Sunday from noon to 2 p.m. Closed in August.

Le Matador, Anse Mitan (tel. 66-05-36), has long enjoyed a position as one of the best Créole restaurants in Martinique, and I want only to add to that well-deserved reputation. François and Raymond Crico, your friendly, sophisticated hosts, will present you a selection of such savory dishes as crabes farcis (this is a land crab which has been deviled and flavored with a hot seasoning and tossed in breadcrumbs, then baked in its own shell). Some of the most exotic sea denizens in the Caribbean come out of the kitchen, including octopi, conch, and sea urchins; however, I always gravitate to their classic red snapper, which they simmer in a well-flavored court bouillon. For a main course, the most obvious choice is a colombo of mutton, which is a Créole version of curry. The Martiniquais who dine here often say the Americans make a wrong decision in sticking to the hotel dining rooms instead of venturing out on the island to sample the locally run inns, which offer the best food. Le Matador lies across the bay from Fort-de-France near the hotels of Pointe du Bout which include the Bakoua Beach and the PLM Azur Carayou. The Cricos like to take Tuesday off, but are there every other night, serving you a fine repast for around $20 to $25. Hours are noon to 2:30 p.m. and 7:30 to 10 p.m.

Incidentally, the matador in the title has caused some to believe this might be a Spanish restaurant. Actually, the name is Créole for "arrogant woman in full dress."

THE SOUTH LOOP: We now leave Pointe du Bout, heading south for more sun and beaches. Centers here include Le Diamant, Sainte-Anne, and Le François.

From Trois-Îlets, you can follow a small curved road which brings you to Anse-à-l'Âne, Grande Anse, and Anse d'Arlet. At any of these places are small beaches, quite safe and usually not crowded.

At Anse d'Arlet, for example, the scenery is beautiful. Fishing boats draw up on the beach, the men drying their nets in the sun.

From Anse d'Arlet, two winding roads may be chosen to take you to Diamant. One follows the coastline, the other forcing its way through the hills. Both of them offer pleasant scenery.

Anse-à-l'Âne

Reflet de la Mer, Trois-Îlets (tel. 76-32-14). A ferryboat from Fort-de-France lands every hour at a spot a few steps away from a simple cement building at the edge of the beach housing this restaurant and small hotel. Menu items include blaff of fish and conch, blaff of sea urchin, conch fricassée, colombo of chicken and mutton, stuffed crabs, and fish soup. Full meals are served at lunch and dinner daily except Monday. If you want to make a day of it, you can bring your beach clothes for an after-lunch swim. The owners also rent six very simple rooms which, with half board included, cost 210F ($31.50) in a single, 330F ($49.50) for a double. The rooms contain sinks, showers, and toilets as part of the bedroom, not set off in a separate bathroom.

Grande Anse

Le Tamarin Plage, Anse d'Arlet (tel. 68-65-31), is a place little changed since the time when Paul Gauguin visited this part of Martinique. Sugarcane leaves cover the ceiling, and a rough-textured veranda overlooks the beach. Don't be put off by its rustic appearance. You come here for the food, not for deluxe accouterments. Locals sit at the bar most of the day, while Mr. Perronette, the owner, mixes drinks. Set meals cost 75F ($11.25), with service included. À la carte meals are from 135F ($20.25). Menu items include several kinds of accras, fish soup, stuffed crab, chicken fricassée, sea crab fricassée, and grilled lobster. This restaurant opens every day at 6 a.m., remaining in business until after the last diner has gone home.

Anse d'Arlet

La Case à Cha-Cha (tel. 76-42-28) is an intensely local kind of restaurant which developed when Ginette Adé, her husband, André, and their five children expanded their bakery to include an adjacent eating place. Today the bakery is still in business, yet the main focus of the family's energy is the restaurant's kitchen. Frankly, the building is a makeshift affair filled with the simplest of accessories. Your fellow diners are likely to be Martiniquais rather than tourists. You reach the dining room by going through a corridor bar. Menu choices usually include pig with pineapple, coconut and pumpkin flan, soup z'habitant, seafood tart, boudin, fish blaff, grilled fish, goat colombo, grilled lobster, and conch fricassée. Full meals cost from 130F ($19.50). You'll find this place near the center of town. It's open daily except Monday from noon to 2:30 p.m. and 6 to 9 p.m.

Le Diamant

Here is a village with quite a good beach open to the winds from the south. **Diamond Rock** juts from the sea rising to a height of 573 feet. In a daring maneuver in 1804, the British carried ammunition and 110 sailors to the top. There, in spite of French coastal artillery bombardment, they held out for 18 months, commanding the passage between the rock and Martinique. You can visit it, but the access by small boat is considered risky.

Diamond Beach is excellent, with surf and bathing possibilities. It's lined with the familiar groves of swaying palms.

In the area, **Hôtel Diamant les Bains** (tel. 76-40-14) is a small, beachfront, family-style hotel, with a cluster of cottages. Close to the water, everything rests under palm trees. The cultivated gardens surrounding the bungalows have lounge chairs, where you can sit and enjoy the view of Diamond Rock. Hubert Andrieu is a thoughtful, concerned host. When his father founded the hotel in 1954, it was one of the first to open on the island. The main building, with its upper-deck bedrooms, houses the restaurant where you can dine on the terrace with a view of the sea. The cuisine is mostly Créole, with some French dishes. The chef pays liberal attention to locally caught fish. A special menu is offered at 175F ($26.25). You can sample classic Créole specialties, such as stuffed sand or sea crabs, spicy black pudding, shrimp fritters, Créole steak, a boiled fish blaff, conch in tomato sauce, fricassée of squid, finishing with a coconut flan. However, if you're touring the island, you should note that the restaurant is closed on Wednesday. The air-conditioned beachside bungalows have red-tile floors, light beamed ceilings, and built-in fruitwood headboards, set on a raised level. Baths have tiles and French showers. In high season, a single can stay here, with breakfast and dinner included, for 320F ($52.50) daily; two persons pay 490F ($73.50). *In the off-season, half-board rates are 250F ($37.50) in a single, 335F ($50.25) in a double*.

Novotel Le Diamant (tel. 76-42-42) stands about two miles outside the village on a half island. Architecturally, it's an esthetic success. The reception, opening onto a large pool is decorated in honey brown and sunflower yellow. You cross the pool on a Chinese-style wooden bridge to connect with the buildings where the rooms are located. The bedroom units face either the pool or the coast with its expansive view of the famous Diamond Rock. The furniture in the bedrooms is typically functional and neutral in styling. *The prices off-season are 450F ($67.50) in a single, 550F ($82.50) in a double, both on the EP*. In winter, the EP rates are 600F ($90) for a single, 780F ($117) in a double. Lunch and dinner cost from 150F ($22.50). Half board must be taken from December 20 to January 4, meals costing 150F ($22.50) per person per day extra. Outside of the hotel, the neighboring beaches aren't too crowded, and the view of the Caribbean is splendid in most directions. If you don't want to leave the hotel, you can of course relax around the pool, sipping your rum punch at the bar. Lawns and gardens, as well as tennis courts, surround the hotel. Water sports and many divertissements are also offered by management. The trip from the airport to the hotel in a taxi will take half an hour.

As you follow the road south to Trois Rivières you'll come to **Sainte-Luce,** perhaps one of the island's most charming villages. Beautiful beaches surround the town, and it's the site of the Forest Montravail. Continuing, you'll reach Rivière Pilote, quite a large town, and Le Marin, at the bottom of a bay of the same name. From Le Marin, a five-mile drive brings you to—

Sainte-Anne

At the extreme southern tip of Martinique, this is a sleepy little village, with white sand beaches. It opens onto views of the Sainte Lucia Canal, and nearby is the site of the Petrified Savannah Forest. The French call it **Savane des Pétrifications.** It's a field of petrified volcanic boulders in the shape of logs. The eerie, desert-like site, no man's land, is studded with cacti. The region is so barren you'll not want to linger long.

Before reaching Sainte-Anne, on your right as you head south is the route des Boucaniers which brings you to the **Club Méditerranée,** at Buccaneer's Creek (tel. 76-72-72). Nestled on a peaceful cove, designed like a Créole village, the club is set on the 48-acre site of a former pirate's hideaway. It stands in a forest of coconut palms. In the typical Club Med style, it features around-the-clock activities. Sports such as sailing, waterskiing, and snorkeling are provided for the overall package cost. In a domed two-level building in the heart of the resort, you'll find the dining places, an amusement center, a theater, dance floor, and bar. On one part of the white sandy beach you can go in the buff. A walk along rue du Port (the main street of Club Med) leads to a conically roofed circular Café du Port, the main restaurant, which overlooks the sailboat fleet anchored in the marina.

Accommodations are in comfortable, air-conditioned bungalows which are booked for double occupancy, each with twin beds and private shower baths. *In summer and fall, one-week land rates with everything included run from about $550 per person.* Winter and spring land rates range from around $750 to $1,000 per person weekly (it's most expensive at Christmas, of course). Activities include day-long picnics, dance classes, boat rides, a language lab, and disco dancing at the opposite end of the village.

Nonguests on a tour of Martinique are welcome to stop in here for a meal, enjoying a large buffet for 200F ($30), with Créole specialties where you help yourself to all you want. Every Tuesday night the club throws an Antilles folklore evening, also costing 200F ($30) per person, including food and entertainment. Other facilities include the Café du Port, a small café for afternoon drinks and leisure talk, and the Maison Créole, a restaurant annex opening every night with a different theme, such as Russian, Créole, or Italian.

Hôtel Caritan, also known as Caritan Beach Village (tel. 76-74-12), is a comfortably modern collection of yellow and beige Mediterranean-style villas set side by side on a gently graded hillside. In the center are a swimming pool, a pleasant restaurant, and a bar. Separated from the resort's central core by a green-tree buffer is a wide sandy beach. Each accommodation has its own kitchenette and a terrace set up for family dining. In winter, singles rent for 395F ($59.25), doubles run 590F ($88.50), and triples cost 675F ($101.25). *Summer charges are 280F ($42) in a single, 325F ($48.75) in a double, and 405F ($60.75) in a triple.* All charges are subject to government tax. Some of the public areas are accented with vividly colored murals, including the breezy and very pleasant dining room, where fixed-price meals cost from 93F ($14). Occasionally a limbo artist and an orchestra will entertain guests in the evening. A full range of water sports can be organized on request. This establishment is about five minutes along the coast from the center of town. In many ways, it is a self-contained community.

If you want to stay in Sainte-Anne, I recommend **La Dunette** (tel. 76-73-90), a motel-like structure on the water. It's near the Club Med and the white sandy beaches of the Salines as well. It has only 18 rooms, all of which are air-conditioned. Most of them have large flower-filled balconies which open onto views of the Caribbean. The seaside inn is protected by a garden filled with flowers and tropical plants. Mme Marie-Louise Kambona is the owner. In winter, a single ranges in price from 295F ($44.25), with doubles going for 410F ($61.50). *In summer, singles cost 265F ($39.75) and doubles run from 330F ($49.50).* The furnishings are in casual modern, and some of the units are quite small. In the evening guests gather for drinks in the bar, La Galiote. Sports and excursions can be arranged for you, even a jaunt to watch a mongoose fight a snake.

Aux Filets Bleus (tel. 76-73-42), set on a flat area close to the beach, is a family-run restaurant flanked by a pair of blue canopies and separated from the road by a hedge. Once you've entered, the seaside exposure of the al fresco dining room and its terrace make you feel like you're in an isolated tropical retreat, where the only sound is the splash of waves and the tinkling of ice in glasses. What you think is a glass-covered reflecting pool set into the floor is actually a lobster tank. From it come many specialties, which include several preparations of lobster. Also featured are stuffed crab, turtle soup, fried sea urchins, and many kinds of grilled fish. Meals begin at 100F ($15). The Anglio family, the owners, serve lunch from 12:30 to 3 p.m. and dinner from 7:30 to 10 p.m. The place is closed Monday in low season.

At the end of the main street of Sainte-Anne, turn on your left and head for the **Manoir de Beauregard** (tel. 76-73-40), an 18th-century manor house where Madame Marcelle Saint-Cyr, the owner, has brought a tasteful, personalized touch. The present relais was built somewhere between 1700 and 1720, and the name probably comes from one of its early owners, a settler named d'Orient, whose daughter married a knight called "de la Touche de Beauregard." Madame Saint-Cyr draws many distinguished guests, including Prince Napoléon, a charming French aristocrat, who is descended from Napoléon III.

While its location is near some of the most beautiful beaches on the island, most guests seem to prefer to splash around the swimming pool in the briefest of bikinis. The manoir is a white building under a tile roof, its arches evoking Spain. The interior has been adapted to make it a comfortable place for paying guests, yet the old architectural features have been respected. The hallway has bronze candelabra and a clock on a 19th-century console. The lounge hall is not grand—rather, it's furnished in a Créole style, with pieces handmade by local artisans from island-grown timber. The floors are black-and-white checkerboard tiles, and the ceiling is beamed. Ornate wrought-iron reredos rescued from a cathedral at Fort-de-France serve as room dividers. The stair rail was once the communion rail.

Your bedroom will probably have a four-poster bed made from island trees. Fabrics for windows, beds, and chairs are often in flowering chintz. Each room is air-conditioned, containing a private bath (each one individually decorated). In high season, two persons pay 550F ($82.50) for bed and breakfast; singles go for 390F ($58.50). *Off-season, these same rates are reduced to 235F ($35.25) in a single and 275F ($41.25) in a double.* The main dining room is an enclosure of a long terrace with simple handmade chairs. Another room is used mainly for informal breakfasts, although most guests prefer the terrace. Even if you don't stay here, know that many guests make a reservation for meals just to sample the Créole cookery. A table d'hôte luncheon or dinner costs from 90F ($13.50), rising to 110F ($16.50) à la carte.

After passing Le Marin, you reach **Vauclin,** a fishing port and market town that is pre-Columbian. If you have time, stop in at the Chapel of the Holy Virgin, dating from the 18th century. Visitors like to make an excursion to **Mount Vauclin,** the highest point in southern Martinique. There they are rewarded with one of the most panoramic views in the West Indies.

After that, continuing on Rte. N6, you reach—

Le François

This town is known for its sailing competitions when owners of yawls compete. It also enjoys a reputation for cookery, which is best at **Club Nautique,** Pointe Bateau (tel. 54-31-00). Every morning you can see the owner, Georges Amalis, out checking over the early-morning catch. His keen eye selects only the best. To get to his club, you cross the main street, heading for the sea. Stay along the shoreline until you reach Nautique. Only lunch is served, seven days a week from noon to 4 p.m.

Before you order, you can sample various rum punches at a bar on the terrace. You might begin with a *décollage,* which translates into "takeoff" as in jet, but here means a potent rum drink aged with herbs until it turns green. The less heady *planteur* is concocted of local rums and fruit juices. Then you descend a few steps to the simple but scrubbed-clean dining room. Don't be discouraged by the almost-desolate look of the place, or the bleak furnishings and surroundings. The food is very fresh, the kitchen clean. You can even dip your feet in water if you've just emerged from the sands. A set menu is offered for 175F ($26.25), which includes such delectable items as sea urchin fritters, sweet clams, shellfish, lobster, or broiled fish, perhaps turtle steak along with flambé bananas and aromatic coffee. He also makes a good-tasting fish soup. You can ask for fish in court-bouillon. Lobster is prepared any style, especially charcoal-broiled. A taste sensation is the butter-yellow urchin roe.

Lunch might be preceded by a boat trip to the nearby coral reefs where Josephine used to bathe. Boat excursions leave every day at 10 a.m.

After dining in Le François, you can easily return to Fort-de-France by passing through Le Lamentin, or you can go to the Pointe du Bout route through Ducos and Rivière Salée.

THE NORTH LOOP: As we swing north from Fort-de-France, our main targets are Le Carbet, St-Pierre, Montagne Pelée, and Leyritz. However, I'll sandwich in many fascinating stopovers along the way.

From Fort-de-France there are three ways to head north to the Montagne Pelée. The first way is to follow Rte. N4 up to St-Joseph. There you take the left fork for three miles after St-Joseph, turning onto the D15 toward Marigot.

At Morne des Esses, you might want to stop for lunch at **Le Colibri** (The Hummingbird; tel. 69-32-19), which is the private Créole home of Madame Clotilde Paladino and her daughters. She has been called a sorceress in the kitchen. Here you'll get some of the finest West Indian cookery on the island. Tables are set up in a small dining room on a terrace with black-and-white tile floor. The furnishings are island-made wood pieces. If the terrace fills up with weekenders from Fort-de-France, you'll be seated on another smaller veranda where you can survey the cooking. You'll seem close enough to the church steeple to touch it, or else to reach out and grab a coconut tree. The place is decidedly informal, and it exudes the warmth of madame. The typically Créole cookery is first class. For example, you might begin with a calalou soup with crab or a sea urchin tart. Try also calalou aux crabes or the avocado salade aux crabes. Among the dishes I recommend are a buisson d'ecrevisses (crayfish), stuffed pigeon, chicken with coconut, and roast suckling pig. For dessert, try a coconut flan. The tab comes to about 100F ($15) for a complete meal. The French wines are inexpensively priced. Hours are noon to 3 p.m. and 7 to 11 p.m. seven days a week.

Alternative Routes

Another way to Montagne Pelée is to take the N3 through the vegetation-rich Mornes until you reach Le Morne Rouge. This road is known as "Route de la Trace," and is now the center of the Parc Naturel de la Martinique.

A different way to reach Montagne Pelée is to follow Rte. N2 along the coast. Close to Fort-de-France, the first town you reach is **Schoelcher.**

Farther along Rte. N2 you reach Case Pilote, and then Bellefontaine. This portion, along the most frequented tourist route in Martinique—that is, Fort-de-France to St-Pierre—will remind many a traveler of the French Riviera. Bellefontaine is a small fishing village, with boats stretched along the beach. As an architectural curiosity, note the many houses also built in the shape of boats.

Leaving Bellefontaine, a five-mile drive north will deliver you to—

Le Carbet

Columbus landed here in 1502 and the first French settlers arrived in 1635. In 1887 Gauguin lived here for four months before going on to Tahiti. You can stop for a swim at an Olympic-size pool set into the hills, or else look upon flocks of native women scrubbing clothes in a stream.

The **Musée Paul Gauguin** (tel. 77-22-66) is at Anse Turin, near Carbet. This small building commemorates the French artist's stay in Martinique in 1887, with books, prints, letters, and other memorabilia. There are also paintings by René Corail, sculpture by Hector Charpentier, and examples of the artwork of Zaffannella. Of special interest are faïence mosaics made of once-white pieces which were turned pink, maroon, blue, and black in 1902 when the fires of Montagne Pelée devastated St-Pierre. There are also changing exhibits of works by local artists. The museum is open daily from 10 a.m. to 5 p.m., charging an admission of 6F (90¢).

If you'd like to have lunch here, try **L'Imprévu,** Grande Anse (tel. 78-08-01). It would be difficult to find a less formal restaurant than this, although it's a preferred stopover for many residents who return to it every time they're in the area. Vertical sections of bamboo support the palm-frond roof, below which groups of friends play an unusual form of tarot. Unlike many card players, they're usually happy to decipher the symbols for visitors. Everard Miré is the friendly owner. You can order a drink at the stand-up bar or choose a table under the sunshield overlooking the beach. The house specialty is a libation called golden apple *(prune de cythère)* juice. Menu items include accras made with codfish, titiris (a small river fish), crayfish, stuffed crab, fish soup, calalou with crab, blaff, grilled conch, and pigeon with sauce Imprévu. Several dishes require a 24-hour advance notice. Full meals range from around 150F ($22.50). Open daily from 10 a.m. to 4 p.m. and 7 p.m. to midnight.

St-Pierre

At the beginning of this century St-Pierre was known as the "Little Paris of the West Indies." Home to 30,000 inhabitants, it was the cultural and economic capital of Martinique. On May 7, 1902, the citizens read in their daily newspaper that "Montagne Pelée does not present any more risk to the population than Vesuvius does to the Neapolitans."

However, on May 8, at 8 a.m., the southwest side of Montagne Pelée exploded, raining down fire and lava. At 8:02 a.m. all 30,000 inhabitants were dead—that is, all except one. A black convict in his underground cell was spared, saved by the thickness of the wall. When islanders reached the site, the convict was paroled, leaving Martinique to tour in Barnum and Bailey's circus.

St-Pierre never recovered its past splendor. Now it could be called the Pompeii of the West Indies. Ruins of the church, the theater, and some other buildings can be seen along the coast.

The **Musée Volcanologique** (tel. 77-15-16) was created by an American volcanologist Franck Alvard Perret, who turned the museum over to the city in 1933. Here in pictures and relics dug from the debris you can trace the story of what happened to St-Pierre. Dug from the lava is a clock that stopped at the exact moment the volcano erupted. The museum is open from 9 a.m. to noon and 3 to 5 p.m., charging an entrance fee of 5F (75¢).

La Factorerie, Centre de Formation Rurale (tel. 77-12-53). Many patrons of this restaurant, which was built by a young people's co-op, make it a point to stop in the stone church a few paces away either before or after a meal. Both buildings are set near the top of a steep hill high above the town, with a view that sweeps out over a well-kept lawn, a forest, and the sea. In an al fresco setting under a beamed ceiling, you'll be able to choose Créole specialties such as grilled fish with spicy sauce, fish soup, brochette of conch, grilled lobster, accras of shrimp, and the local recipes for blaff and chicken colombo. Set meals are offered for 80F ($12) and up. The restaurant is open for lunch daily from noon to 2:30 p.m. Tuesday and Thursday are the only nights on which you can order dinner (anytime between 7 and 10 p.m.). Dinners cost from 120F ($18).

From St-Pierre, you can climb to—

Montagne Pelée

A spectacular and winding road takes you through a tropical rain forest. The curves are of the hairpin variety, and the road is twisty and not always kept in good shape. However, you're rewarded with tropical flowers, baby ferns, plumed bamboo, and valleys so deep green you'll think you're wearing cheap sunglasses.

You reach the village of Morne Rouge, right at the foot of Montagne Pelée, a popular vacation spot for Martiniquais. From there on, a narrow and unreliable road brings you to a level of 2,500 feet above sea level, 1,600 feet under the round summit of the volcano that destroyed St-Pierre. Montagne Pelée itself rises 4,656 feet above sea level.

If you're a trained mountain climber, you can scale the peak, reaching Grand Rivière—that is, if you don't mind four or five hours of hiking. Realize that this is a mountain, that rain is frequent, and that temperatures drop very low. Tropical growth often hides deep crevices in the earth, and there are other dangers. That's why if you're really serious about this climb, you should hire an experienced guide. As for the volcano, its death-dealing rain in 1902 apparently satisfied it, at least for the time being!

Upon your descent from Montagne Pelée, you can drive down to Ajoupa Bouillon and Basse-Pointe. A mile before reaching the latter town, you turn on your left and follow a road that goes deeply into sugarcane country to—

Leyritz

Here you can explore the best restored plantation in Martinique, perhaps stopping by for lunch.

Hôtel Plantation de Leyritz, Basse-Pointe (tel. 75-53-92), the pride of Martinique, was built around 1700 by a plantation owner, Bordeaux-born Michel de Leyritz. It was the site of the "swimming pool summit meeting" in 1974 between Presidents Gerald Ford and Valéry Giscard d'Estaing. It's still a working banana plantation which (since 1970) has been restored by Charles and Yveline de Lucy de Fossarieu to its original and authentic character. You can live here in style and elegance, surrounded by an atmosphere of long ago. There are 16 acres of tropical gardens through which guests ride on horseback, and at the core is an 18th-century stone great house. From the grounds, the view sweeps across the Atlantic taking in fearsome Montagne Pelée.

The owners have kept the best of the old, such as the rugged stone walls (20 inches thick), the beamed ceilings, and the tile and flagstone floors. They have created a cozy setting of mahogany tables, overstuffed sofas, and gilt mirrors. A few of the outbuildings, former slave quarters with bamboo roofs and stone walls, now house guests, and new ones have been added. I prefer the units—ten in all—in the manor, because they are probably the most attractive, certainly the most authentic. You can also stay in the carriage house across the lawn. Don't expect luxury—that's not the style here. In winter, guests can stay here on the continental plan, paying 480F ($72) to 800F ($120) in a single and 600F ($90) to 900F ($135) in a double. *In the off-season, with breakfast included, singles run 280F ($42) to 480F ($72) daily, and doubles cost 324F ($48.60) to 560F ($84).*

The proprietors have installed a fully equipped two-story spa center. The spa's ground floor includes three massage rooms, two Jacuzzis, salons for facial and body care, and a lounge for yoga and gymnastics. On the upper level is an open-air terrace with a Jacuzzi and solarium. In residence are a medical doctor, esthetician, yoga instructor, masseur, and a hairdresser. Twenty-one spa rooms have also been built. They are air-conditioned and furnished in antiques. A covered path links them with the spa center. The swimming pool is at the edge of the compound, with grassy lawns and parasol tables where you can order *un punch vieux*, the traditional French plantation owner's libation. Bring your tennis raquet, as there is always someone to join you in a set. A horse can be brought for a ride through the woods.

The dining room is in a rum distillery, incorporating the fresh spring water running down from the hillside. Eating here is dramatic at night, and the cuisine is of a high level, authentically Créole. Afternoon tea or apéritifs are served in the salon, with flickering lights from a 19th-century bronze and globed chandelier. You sit on Martinique-style rockers. On the surrounding walls are gilt-framed family portraits, plus scenic views of the island and Paris. Tour bus crowds predominate at lunch. Most guests visit just for lunch, heading south for the night. If that's the case with you, expect to pay from 65F ($9.75) to have lunch here. On my most recent rounds, I enjoyed a first-class Créole lunch, which was really like a dinner. The main course was grilled chicken covered in coconut milk sauce, along with *oussous,* a freshwater crayfish which came in a herb sauce. Vegetables consisted of sautéed breadfruit and sautéed bananas. Dinners go for 110F ($16.50) and up. Lunch is served from 12:30 to 2 p.m., and dinner, from 7:30 to 8:30 p.m., seven days a week. Dinner is more elaborate, with both French and Créole dishes, including duck with pineapple, chicken with coconut, a colombo of lamb, and boudin (blood pudding) Créole.

Basse-Pointe

At the northernmost point on the island, Basse-Pointe is a land of pineapple and banana plantation fields, covering the Atlantic-side slopes of Mount Pelée volcano.

Chez Mally Edjam (tel. 75-51-18) is a local legend. Many visitors prefer to drive all the way from Pointe du Bout to dine with her instead of at the Leyritz Plantation. Of course, never arrive without calling for a reservation—it's like visiting a private home, which is what it is. You sit out on one of a handful of tables on her side porch. You can also eat in the main dining room. Grandmotherly Mally Edjam is busy in the kitchen, turning out her Créole delicacies. She knows how to do all the dishes for which the island is known: stuffed land crab with a hot seasoning, small pieces of conch in a tart shell, langouste, sea urchins (which are made surprisingly tasty), and a classic colombo de porc, the Créole version of pork curry. She is known also for her lobster vinaigrette, her papaya soufflé (which must be ordered in advance), and her highly original confitures, which are tiny portions of fresh island fruits, such as pineapple and guava, that have been preserved in a vanilla syrup. Expect to spend from 100F ($15) for lunch, which is generally served from noon to 3 p.m. in July. It is open seven days a week.

Grand Rivière

After Basse-Pointe, the town you reach on your northward trek is Grand Rivière. From there, you must turn back. Before doing so, you may want to stop at **Chez Vava** (tel. 75-52-81), a good restaurant right at the entrance to the town. With its bright-orange tiling, it's easy to spot. You'll also find plenty of space to park your car. The style is like a simple country inn. It is actually the *maison privé* of Laurence Viellot. For 100F ($15) you can order a tomato salad, broiled fish with rice, and a dessert. À la carte menu items include Créole soup, a blaff of sea urchins, lobster, and various colombos. An old rum punch, a specialty of the house, is also offered. If you order the most elaborate items on the menu, your tab could climb to 175F ($26.25). Hours are 7 a.m. to 6 p.m.

Lorrain

Even though Lorrain is called the "kingdom of bananas," you might pass through this charming hamlet on the northeastern coast in short time. That is, unless you knew about the restaurant recommended below.

Relais des Îles, rue Chaumereau-Lamotte (tel. 53-43-85), is one of the least known restaurants on the island. Its lack of fame is undeserved, since its Créole food is among the best in Martinique. It's as if it's just awaiting discovery by the major food magazines. It's housed in an old Martiniquais house with shutters, clapboard siding, gingerbread fretwork, and a large veranda looking down on a curve in the road near the center of town. Antoine and Gabrielle Duventru are the hospitable owners of this refreshingly simple place, where specialties vary with the availability of ingredients and where much of the art depends on the inspiration Mme Duventru might feel at the moment. Since she was born within a few miles of this spot, she's been able to pick up many gems of culinary lore.

Your meal might include pâté en pot (which, despite its name, is a kind of lamb soup), soup with crabs, Caribbean lobster, Créole shrimp, six kinds of soufflé including varieties with conch and crayfish, a particularly tasty fish soup, eggplant or codfish fritters, stuffed eggplant, and a unique and original recipe of stuffed cucumbers and onions. Other possibilities are four kinds of tarts (made with sea urchins, onions, crayfish, or conch), stuffed crab, colombo of chicken, a flan of christophine au gratin, and a soupe d'habitants made with such vegetables as cabbage, leeks, onions, celery, and locally grown leaves. Set meals cost from 65F ($9.75), while à la carte menus cost from 140F ($21). The restaurant is open every day from 6 a.m. till after dinner. Reservations are a good idea.

Sainte-Marie

Heading south along the coastal road, you bypass Marigot, coming to a sightseeing stop in the little town of Sainte-Marie where you can visit the attraction previewed below.

The **Rum Museum,** at the Saint James Distillery (tel. 75-30-02), displays engravings, antique tools and machines, and other exhibits tracing the history of sugarcane and rum from 1765 to the present. Guided tours of the museum also include a visit to the distillery and storage area, and a session of rum tasting. Hours are 9 a.m. to 1 p.m. and 2 to 4:30 p.m. Monday to Friday, to 1 p.m. on Saturday, and to noon on Sunday.

Trinité

If you head back south along the coastal route, you'll pass through the small village of Trinité on the Atlantic side of Martinique. It would hardly merit a stopover were it not for the following hotel.

Saint-Aubin Hôtel at Trinité (tel. 69-34-77) is one of the loveliest inns in the Caribbean basin. A former restaurant owner, Normandy-born Guy Forêt has sunk his fortune into restoring this three-story Victorian-style house and turning it into a three-star hostelry. In pink beige with fancy gingerbread, it was once a plantation house, sitting on a hillside above sugarcane fields and Trinité's bay. A long excursion from Pointe du Bout or Fort-de-France, it would make the perfect luncheon stopover or the ideal retreat for a vacation in Martinique. The location is 14½ miles from the airport, 19 miles from Fort-de-France, and 2 miles from the seaside village of Trinité itself. There are 800 yards of private beach as a further enticement, plus a swimming pool on the grounds. All rooms are air-conditioned, with wall-to-wall carpeting and modern (not antique) furniture. There are some family rooms as well. After dinner you can sit on the veranda on the first and second floors, enjoying life as lived long ago. Rooms have a view of either the garden or the sea. In winter, two persons can stay here on the MAP at a rate of 570F ($85.50) daily, while singles pay from 365F ($54.75). *In summer, guests on the MAP pay 345F ($51.75) in a single, 540F ($81) in a double*. The restaurant and bar are reserved for use of hotel guests.

THE SPORTING LIFE: The Martiniquais often don't work at their sports as hard as many North Americans do. Yet they have an active sports program.

Scuba-diving, snorkeling, fishing, and waterskiing can be enjoyed all along the coastline. Golf clubs are at your disposal in all the first-class hotels, where prices are obtainable (tariffs vary considerably, depending on the duration and season).

Tennis

This game is widely played on the island, and each large hotel has courts. Residents play free during the day, and night games usually require a 40F ($6) surcharge for lighting for 30 minutes. Nonguests are faced with a playing-time charge that could range from $8 to $10 per half hour.

Your best bet is to play at one of the three courts on the grounds of **Golf de l'Impératrice Josephine** at Trois-Îlets (tel. 76-32-81), a five-minute drive from one of the major hotels at Pointe du Bout. The setting here is one of the most beautiful in Martinique.

Scuba-Diving and Snorkeling

Scuba-divers come here to explore the St-Pierre shipwrecks sunk in the 1902 volcano eruption and the Diamond Rock caves and walls. Small scuba centers operate at many of the hotels.

Snorkeling equipment is usually available free to hotel guests, who quickly learn that coral, fish, and ferns abound in the waters around the Pointe du Bout hotels.

The Latitude, at Carbet, about a half-hour drive north of Fort-de-France, is tucked neatly into a U-shaped lagoon. Its **Latitude Scuba Club** (tel. 73-69-89) is headed by Michel Metery and has an impressive stock of equipment, including double and single tanks, adaptors, wet suits, and Spirotechnique regulators. Dives of all types can be made from nearby coves and beaches or from sites as far away as an hour by boat. One sample of the latter is the offshore landmark, Îlet la Perle, whose backdrop is the lush, mountainous northern part of Martinique.

From Latitude, waterborne excursions can be made to St-Pierre where shipwrecks from the 1902 volcanic eruption of Montagne Pelée can be seen and explored. The most prominent, filmed for TV by Jacques Cousteau, is the metal-hulled *Roraimi*, which rests on a slant in 150 to 200 feet of water. It takes several dives to cover the entire hulk.

Other special trips, such as the all-day Pique-Nique Nautique, can be arranged by the Latitude Scuba Club. Two or three times a week a boat—minimum ten passengers —departs at 9 a.m. for an hour-long voyage to an offshore fishermen's island. Guests swim and dive among angelfish, batfish, butterfish, grouper, needlefish, rock beauties, soldierfish, trumpetfish, and a long black-and-white fish locally called "Monsieur l'Abbé." After a meal of freshly caught and cooked fish, the boat returns to the hotel at around 5:30 p.m.

To the south, **Bathy's Club** in the Hôtel Méridien (tel. 66-00-00), is the scuba center for Pointe du Bout, serving neighboring hotels Bakoua and Azur Carayou. Jean-Marc and Bertrand Sailly operate the club and, with an assistant, escort daily dive trips on the 37-foot *Egg Harbor* which leaves from the Méridien pier. Prices include equipment rental, transportation, guide, and drinks on board. Dives are conducted twice daily, from 9 a.m. to noon and 3 to 6 p.m., and full-day charters can be arranged. The dive shop on Méridien's beach stocks everything from weight belts and tanks to partial wetsuits and underwater cameras.

Buccaneer's Creek/Club Med (tel. 76-72-72) has long made scuba a part of its weekly packages, costing from $550 to $1,200, depending on the week. The dive school goes to the reefs around Ste-Anne at the southern tip of Martinique, where the club is situated.

Two other Martinique hotels also have scuba centers. La Batalière (tel. 71-90-41) houses the **Tropicasud International Diving Center,** headed by Dominique Temple, a fully licensed and certified divemaster. The boat leaves directly from the hotel.

Facing historic Diamond Rock off the southwestern coast is Diamant-Novotel (tel. 76-42-42), which boasts scuba facilities at its **Caraibe Coltri-Sub Club** and a prime diving location. The crystal-clear underwater world here is challenging to the diver but presents such rewards as coral formations, multicolored fish, sponges, and a cannon or two. Inquire at the hotel about excursions, rates, and the type of scuba instruction.

Windsurfing

This is the most popular sport in the French West Indies. Equipment and lessons are available at all hotel water-sports operators, especially the **Hôtel Méridien** (tel. 66-00-00), where the cost is 50F ($7.50) for a one-hour rental.

Waterskiing

This is available at every beach near the large hotels, the cost about $10 for 10- to 15-minute rides.

The Beaches

The beaches south of Fort-de-France are white while the northern strands are composed mostly of gray sand. Outstanding in the south is the **Plage des Salines,** near Ste-Anne, with palm trees and miles of white sand, and **Diamant,** with the landmark Diamond Rock offshore. Swimming on the Atlantic coast is for experts only, except at **Cap Chevalier** and **Presqu'île de la Caravelle Nature Preserve.** Public beaches do not as a rule have changing cabins or showers. Some hotels charge nonguests for the use of changing and beach facilities, and request a deposit for rental of towels.

Hiking

Inexpensive and guided excursions in which tourists can participate are organized by the personnel of the Parc Régional de la Martinique year round. Special excursions can be organized on request of small groups by getting in touch with the **Parc Naturel Régional de la Martinique,** Caserne Bouillé, Fort-de-France (tel. 73-19-30). A folder is available at the Martinique Tourist Office.

The Presqu'île de la Caravelle Nature Preserve, a well-protected peninsula jutting into the Atlantic Ocean, has safe beaches and well-marked trails to the ruins of historic Château Debuc and through tropical wetlands.

Serious hiking excursions to climb Montagne Pelée and explore the Gorges de la Falaise or the thick coastal rain forest between Grand'Rivière and Precheur are organized with local guides at certain times of the year by the park staff.

Camping

Camping is permitted in some places, including in the mountains and forests and on many beaches. It is advisable to check with the local mayor's office or property owner before setting up camp. Campsites are usually basic, although comfortable camps with cold showers and toilets are on the southeast coast at Macabou; at Ste-Luce, Le Marin, and Ste-Anne on the south coast; and Anse-à-l'Âne near Trois-Îlets. One of the best spots is **Courbaril Camping** at Trois-Îlets (tel. 76-32-30), where the double rate is 135F ($20.25), rising to 156F ($23.40) in a triple.

Horseback Riding

Ranch Jack (tel. 68-63-97) offers daily horseback rides for both experienced and novice riders, at a cost of 270F ($40.50) per half day. This is an ideal way to discover both botanical and geographical Martinique. They'll arrange for you to be picked up at your hotel and delivered back after your outing. Créole horses are used for the rides.

A new horseback riding center, **La Cavale,** directed by Christian and Armelle Sueur, is near the Diamant-Novotel (tel. 76-42-42). It boasts 12 horses and offers a wide range of activities, including introductory lessons, manège riding, walks, and games for beginners and children. Experienced riders can try the obstacle course, cross-country riding, and horseback sightseeing excursions, for periods ranging from an hour to a full day.

Golf

The famous golf course designer, Robert Trent Jones, visited Martinique and left behind the 18-hole **Golf de l'Impératrice Josephine** at Trois-Îlets (tel. 76-32-81), a five-minute, one-mile drive from the leading resort area of Pointe du Bout and about 18 miles from Fort-de-France. The course unfolds its greens from the birthplace of Empress Josephine for whom it is named, across rolling hills with scenic vistas down to the sea. Under Philippe Rosier, full-time president of the club, amenities include a pro shop, a bar, and a restaurant. Jeannine Starek is the hospitable director, and the pro is Raymond Bedard.

Sailing

This is a big pastime in Martinique. It's also a big cost unless there are enough in your party. Only a select few can afford yacht charters, either crewed or bareboat. If you want to see the waters around Martinique, it's better to go on one of the sailboat excursions in the bay of Fort-de-France and the southeast coast of the island.

A 79-foot ketch, *Captain Cap,* sails regularly from the Méridien Hôtel at Pointe du Bout. Reservations can be made by calling 66-02-52. A full-day excursion with lunch is offered, and no more than 60 passengers go out at a time. Also, sunset cruises are offered as well. The day excursion is on Wednesday and Friday, with a 9 a.m. departure, returning at 5 p.m. The cost is 300F ($45) per person. The sunset cruise, with music and rum punch, is on Friday at 5 p.m., returning at 7:30 p.m., at a cost of 50F ($22.50) per person.

A Look at Marine Life

L'Aquascope, at the Marina at Pointe du Bout (tel. 76-36-09), offers visitors a skindiver's view of marine life at a cost of 75F ($11.25). Reservations can be made at the boat dock for the trip, which lasts less than an hour. In a genuine helicopter cockpit, one is taken along the ocean floor for a view of coral colonies, starfish schools, sponges, and sea urchins. You ride in armchair comfort while a fantastic underwater world unfolds around you. *L'Aquascope* is one of the few vessels of its kind in the world.

Sea Fishing

You can make arrangements at the **Hôtel Méridien Trois-Îlets,** Pointe du Bout (tel. 66-00-00). Equipment and a motorboat leader are provided, with departures every day at 6 a.m. and again at 9:30 a.m., at a cost of 1,000F ($150) for a minimum of six people.

The Mongoose vs. the Snake

Some people say you've not really seen Martinique until you've attended a match between a mongoose and a snake. Said to have been imported by East Indian workers, this is a to-the-death struggle. If you attend such an event, you're to remain deadly still. Even lighting a cigarette is supposed to break the concentration of the combatants. Incidentally, the mongoose almost always wins. Some taxi drivers or small innkeepers on the island will tell you where to go to watch this "sport." Frankly, I think you can skip it.

AFTER DARK: Everybody who goes to Martinique wants to see the show performed by **Les Ballets Martiniquais,** a bouncy group of about two dozen dancers, along with musicians, singers, and choreographers. Many members of the troupe look no more than 17 years old. Launched in the early '60s, this group performs the traditional dances of Martinique and has been acclaimed in both Europe and the States.

The other folk ballet troupe is called **Les Grands Ballets de la Martinique.** With a swoosh of gaily striped skirts, a gentle swaying of hips, and clever acting, youthful dancers capture all the exuberance of the island's soul.

The groups have toured abroad with great success, but they perform best on home ground. Dressed in traditional costumes—madras headdresses, gold earrings, lace blouses, silk scarves, billowing skirts, and crisply starched petticoats—the island girls are led by their young men through such dances as the spirited mazurka, which was brought from the ballrooms of Europe, and the exotic beguine. The newer Grands Ballets, with 25 young performers, is considered one of the best ensembles in the Caribbean.

Cole Porter, incidentally, did not invent the beguine. It's a Martinique dance—some would call it a way of life. Instead of having me try to explain it, it's best to see it. Or dance it, if you think you can.

Both groups present tableaux that tell of jealous brides and faithless husbands, demanding overseers and toiling cane cutters. There's a dreamy "Créole Waltz" and an erotic "Calenda," danced to the beat of an African drum. The "Parasol Dance" and "Carnival" add sparkle to the performance, and the show may end with the last mentioned dance or with "Adieu Foulard, Adieu Madras," a tale of a Créole girl's hopeless love for a French naval officer who must leave her.

Les Grands Ballets perform Monday at the Hôtel Diamant-Novotel, Wednesday at the PLM Azur Carayou, and Friday at the Bakoua Beach, but this can vary so check locally. In addition, the troupe gives mini-performances aboard visiting cruise ships. The Ballets Martiniquais can be seen Thursday at the Méridien Trois-Îlets and Saturday at the Hôtel La Batelière. To enjoy a buffet dinner and a ballet show at one of the hotels costs from 200F ($30).

There's also a lot of nightlife revolving around the four major hotels at Pointe du Bout—**Bakoua Beach, PLM Azur Carayou, Méridien Trois-Îlets,** and **PLM Azur La Pagerié.** As mentioned, on certain nights you can watch Les Ballets Martiniquais. In addition, musicians, some of them quite young, play nightly in the larger hotels.

Hotel guests are allowed in free at three of the nightclubs, **Vesou** in the PLM Azur Carayou, **Vonvon** in the Méridien Trois-Îlets, and **Hutte** in Bakoua. If you're not a resident of one of the hotels, you'll be charged an entrance fee of around 80F ($12), including your first drink. Most of these clubs are open nightly except Sunday from 10:30 p.m. It's hard to say which club is the best, as a mainly young crowd wanders from one to the other on a warm night. My preference, however, is for **Vesou.**

Club 21 at the Hôtel La Batelière, Schoelcher (tel. 61-49-49), about a mile from Fort-de-France, swings into action every night at 10, except Monday. Rumor has it that the best-looking people on Martinique are likely to be found here on any given night. The special attraction of the place is a covered terrace hanging over the sea. The entrance fee is 65F ($9.75) per person. Closed Sunday and Monday.

The **Casino Trois-Îlets,** on the premises of the Méridien Trois-Îlets, Pointe du Bout (tel. 66-00-30) is open every night from 9 a.m. to 3 a.m. Here you can try to win the cost of your vacation by playing roulette, blackjack, or chemin-de-fer. Some form of identification with picture is required at the entrance. You present it along with 57F ($8.50).

You might also try your luck at the **Hôtel La Batelière Casino** (tel. 61-49-49), Schoelcher, outside Fort-de-France. Not as glamorous as Las Vegas, it attracts a leisure crowd who play roulette, French chemin-de-fer, craps, or blackjack. An identity card such as a passport is required. The entrance fee is 50F ($7.50), and hours are 9 p.m. to 3 a.m.

I'd advise you to spend your nights in the big hotel clubs. There are other native clubs frequented by the Martiniquais. However, some "incidents" have been reported when tourists strayed in. If you insist on going to one of these clubs "to see the real beguine," I suggest you go there with some local friends, if you've made any, who know the island.

2. Guadeloupe

"The time is near, I believe, when thousands of American tourists will come to spend the winter among the beautiful countryside and friendly people of Guadeloupe." Or so Theodore Roosevelt accurately predicted on February 21, 1916. Guadeloupe isn't the same place it was when the Rough Rider himself rode through, but the natural beauty he witnessed, and certainly the people, are still there to be enjoyed.

Guadeloupe is part of the Lesser Antilles, lying about 200 miles north of Martinique, closer to the United States than its sister island. In addition to tourism, sugar production and rum beef up the local economy. The total surface of Guadeloupe and its satellite islands is close to 700 square miles. There is a lot of similarity in climate, animals, and vegetation between Martinique and Guadeloupe. So no one is surprised coming from one island to the other.

Guadeloupe is, in fact, formed by two different islands, separated by a narrow seawater channel, known as Rivière Salée. **Grande Terre,** the eastern island, is typical of charm of the Antilles, with its rolling hills and sugar plantations.

On the other hand, **Basse Terre,** to the west, is a rugged mountainous island, dominated by the 4,800-foot volcano La Soufrière, which is still alive. Its mountains are covered with tropical forests, impenetrable in many places. Bananas grown on plantations are the main crop. The island is ringed by beautiful beaches which have attracted much tourism, especially in the '70s and '80s.

Among the celebrities from the island, Saint-John Perse (alias Alexis Saint-Leger) was born in St. Leger des Feuilles, a small islet in Pointe-à-Pitre bay, in 1887. The French diplomat was better known as a poet, the Nobel Prize winner in 1960. During all his life he wrote a constant song to the beauty of his island.

Guadeloupe was first called Karukera by the Arawaks, meaning "the island of the beautiful waters." On November 3, 1493, Columbus landed, naming the island Santa Maria de Guadelupe de Estramaduros, which in time became Guadeloupe. The island's modern history is very much related to that of Martinique. Guadeloupe was settled by Sir Lienard de l'Olive and Sir Duplessis d'Ossonville, who were detached from Martinique by its commander, Belain d'Esnambuc. These men arrived with a group of some 500 settlers on June 28, 1635.

The British seized the island in 1759. They gave it back, but took it once more in 1794. A mulatto, Victor Hugues, attacked them with his revolutionary army of blacks and whites, but he faded after Napoleon came to power, allowing the British to move in again in 1810. The island returned to French hands in 1815.

For 100 years Guadeloupe was a dependency of Martinique. In 1946 Guadeloupe became a full-fledged French *département* (the French equivalent of an American state), and its people are citizens of France with all the privileges that that implies.

GETTING THERE: Information on getting to Guadeloupe is the same as for getting to Martinique. See the "Getting There" section on Martinique, earlier in this chapter.

GETTING AROUND: You'll find **taxis** when you arrive at the airport but no limousines or buses waiting to serve you. After 9 p.m., until 7 a.m., cabbies are legally entitled to charge you 40% more. In practice, either day or night, the taxi drivers charge you whatever they think the market will bear. Always agree on the price before getting in.

Buses

As in Martinique, there is no rail service. But buses link almost every hamlet to Pointe-à-Pitre. However, you may need to know some high school French to use the system. From Pointe-à-Pitre you can catch one of these jitney vans, either at the Gare Routière de Bergevin if you're going to Basse Terre, or the Gare Routière de Mortenol

GUADELOUPE

if Grande Terre is your destination. The cost, for example, from Pointe-à-Pitre to Basse-Terre is only 25F ($3.75).

Car Rentals

Your access to a car enables you to circumnavigate Basse Terre, which many aficionados claim is one of the loveliest drives in the Caribbean. Car-rental kiosks at the airport are usually open to meet international flights. Rental rates at local companies might appear less expensive, depending on the agency, but several readers have complained of mechanical problems and bill irregularities. If you want to be sure to get a car when you arrive, it's often best to reserve one in advance through the nationwide toll-free numbers of North America's largest car-rental companies: **Hertz, Avis,** and **Budget,** each of which is represented on the island.

Budget is consistently the least expensive. The cheapest rates at all three companies are awarded to renters who reserve their cars at least two business days before pickup. Budget's least expensive vehicle, a four-passenger Toyota Starlet with manual transmission and without air conditioning, costs $188 per week, plus a whopping 14% tax imposed by the French government. Avis and Hertz charge $219 and $215 for similar cars, plus tax. If you require air conditioning, Budget again offers the best rental. Its cheapest car is $235 per week, as opposed to $307 at Hertz and $315 at Avis. If you want a car with automatic transmission, the cost is $267 per week at Budget and $276 at Avis (none available at Hertz). Younger drivers, however, need be only 21 before renting from Hertz, whereas they must be 22 at Budget and an aging 25 at Avis.

All three companies offer additional insurance. Budget, for example, charges an extra $4.70 per day, but you're protected in case you have an accident. For more information, call Budget toll free at 800/527-0700, Hertz at 800/654-3131, and Avis at 800/331-2112. Drive on the right, and drive defensively.

Taxi Tours

If you're traveling with people or imaginative in putting a party together, it's best to sightsee by taxi. Usually the concierge at your hotel will help you make this arrangement. Depending on the size of car you order, you can expect to pay from 635F ($95.25) a day for this service. Split four ways, the tab is much easier to handle, of course.

PRACTICAL FACTS: The official **language** is French, and Créole is the unofficial second language. As in Martinique, English is spoken only in the major tourist centers, rarely in the countryside. The official **currency** is the French franc, and some shops will take U.S. dollars. For stays of less than 21 days, **proof of identity** is needed, plus a return or ongoing plane ticket. For a longer stay, a valid passport is required and perhaps a visa (see the traveler's advisory in the introduction to this chapter).

Guadeloupe **time** is one hour later than Eastern Standard Time (when it's 6 a.m. in New York, it's 7 a.m. in Guadeloupe). When Eastern Daylight Saving Time is in effect, Guadeloupe and New York keep the same clocks.

The local **electricity** is 220 volts AC, 50 cycles, which means you'll need an adapter. Some of the big resorts lend these to guests, but don't count on it. One hotel I know had only six in stock, and a long, long waiting list (and of the six, two were broken!). Clients should take their own.

Driving is on the right side, and there are several gas stations along the main routes.

The **pharmacies** carry French medicines, and most over-the-counter American drugs have French equivalents. Prescribed medicines can be filled if the traveler has a prescription.

As an important note, it must be remembered that the people of Guadeloupe do not like to be photographed unless they are camera-ready in their best clothes. Tourists should always ask permission before photographing anybody, and don't be surprised if the answer is a flat and resounding no.

Customs allows items for personal use, "in limited quantities," to be brought in tax free.

On scheduled flights, the **departure tax** is included in the fares.

Hotels and restaurants usually add a 10% to 15% **service charge,** and most taxi drivers who own their own cars do not expect a **tip.** Surprisingly, neither do hotel porters.

American tobacco and cigarettes are available at hotel shops, and Guadeloupe also has some **café-tabacs,** selling foreign cigarettes.

If you have a **police emergency,** call 82-00-05 in Pointe-à-Pitre or 81-11-55 in Basse-Terre.

There are five modern **hospitals** in Guadeloupe, plus 23 clinics. Hotels and the Guadeloupe tourist office can assist in locating English-speaking doctors.

The major tourist office in Guadeloupe is called the **Office Départemental du Tourisme,** corner of rue Schoelcher and Délgrés, in Pointe-à-Pitre (tel. 82-09-30).

POINTE-À-PITRE: The port and chief city of Guadeloupe, Pointe-à-Pitre lies on Grande Terre. Unfortunately, it doesn't have the old-world charm of Fort-de-France in Martinique. What beauty it does possess is often hidden behind closed doors.

Having been burned and rebuilt so many times, the port has emerged as a town lacking in character, with modern apartments and condominiums forming a high-rise backdrop over jerry-built shacks and industrial suburbs. The rather narrow streets are jammed during the day with a colorful crowd creating a permanent traffic tie-up. However, at sunset the town becomes quiet again and almost deserted.

The real point of interest in Pointe-à-Pitre is shopping. It's best to visit the town in the morning—you can easily cover it in a half day—taking in the waterfront and outdoor market (the latter is livelier in the early hours).

Open-air stalls surround the **covered market** at the corner of rue Frébault and rue Thiers. Here you can discover the many fruits, spices, and vegetables which are enjoyable just to view if not to taste. A deep fragrance of a Créole market permeates the place. In madras turbans local Créole women make deals over their strings of fire-red pimientos. The bright, colorful fabrics they wear compete with the rich tones of oranges, papayas, bananas, mangoes, and pineapples. The sounds of an African-accented French fill the air.

The town center is the Place de la Victoire, a park shaded by palm trees and poincianas. Here you'll see some old sandbox trees said to have been planted by Victor Hugues, the mulatto who organized a revolutionary army of both whites and blacks to establish a dictatorship. In this square he kept a guillotine busy, and the death-dealing instrument still stood there (but not in use) until modern times.

Sloops that travel through the islands, as well as fishing schooners, tie up at the old port, La Darse. Farther out, Caribbean cruise ships drop anchor to allow their passengers to go on shopping expeditions. We might as well follow suit.

Shopping

Frankly, if you're going on to Fort-de-France in Martinique, I suggest you skip a shopping tour of Pointe-à-Pitre, as you'll find far more merchandise there, and perhaps friendlier service. However, if you're not, I'd recommend the following shops, some of which line the rue Frébault.

Of course, your best buys will be anything French—perfumes from Chanel, silk scarves from Hermès, cosmetics from Dior, crystal from Lalique and Baccarat. I've found (but not often) some of these items discounted as much as 30% lower than Stateside or Canadian prices.

Shops, which accept U.S. dollars, give these discounts only to purchases made by traveler's check. Purchases are duty free if brought directly from store to airplane. In addition to the places below, there are also duty-free shops at Raizet Airport, selling liquor, rums, perfumes, crystal, and cigarettes.

Most shops open at 9 a.m., closing at 1 p.m., then reopening between 3 and 6 p.m. They are closed on Saturday afternoon, Sunday, and holidays. When the cruise ships are in port, many eager shopkeepers naturally change these hours, stretching them out, even on weekends, much to the regret of the clerks.

One of the best places to buy French perfumes, at prices often lower than those charged in Paris, is **Phoenicia,** at several locations: 8 rue Frébault (tel. 83-50-36); 121 rue Frébault (tel. 82-25-75), 93 rue de Nozières (tel. 82-71-93) and Fifth Avenue, 2 rue Frébault, at Pointe-à-Pitre (tel. 82-17-66).

Rosébleu, 5 rue Frébault (tel. 82-93-44), has one of the biggest stocks in Pointe-à-Pitre of jewelry, crystal, perfumes, gifts, and fashion accessories. If you pay with traveler's checks, you'll get discounts of 10% to 20%.

Vendôme, 8–10 rue Frébault (tel. 83-42-84), has imported fashions for both men and women, most of them quite stylish, as well as a large selection of gifts and perfumes, including the big names. Usually you can find someone who speaks English to sell you a Cardin watch.

Boutique Tim-Tim, 15 rue Jean-Jaurès (tel. 83-48-71). There's probably no other store in the French West Indies with as elegant a stock of 19th-century Antillean antiques. However, this is no place for a bargain, as its prices are high. Still, if you yearn for a "plantation antique," you might want to look in. The establishment is closed on Saturday afternoon and Sunday. Its owner, Mme Simone Schwarz-Bart, is a novelist known in local literary circles.

Actually, if you're adventurous you may want to seek out some native goods found in little shops along the back streets of Pointe-à-Pitre. Considered collector's items are the straw hats or salacos made in Les Saintes islands. They look distinctly related to Chinese coolie hats and are usually well designed, often made of split bamboo. Native doudou dolls are also popular gift items.

Where to Stay

For convenience to terminals, if you'd like to seek lodgings in Pointe-à-Pitre, I have the following suggestion:

Hôtel Bougainvillée, Angle des rues Delgrès et Frébault (tel. 82-07-56), is a concrete-walled, unfrilly, but clean and serviceable hotel whose location on a busy street corner guarantees a regular clientele of commercial travelers. Guests register in a wood-trimmed, renovated lobby before taking a cramped elevator to one of the 36 bedrooms. The units are well maintained, with white walls and heavy dark furniture, like something you'd find in Iberia. Each contains air conditioning, a private bath and shower, and a phone. Year round, singles cost 320F ($48) to 370F ($55.50) daily; doubles, 390F ($58.50) to 500F ($75).

Where to Dine

La Canne à Sucre, 17 rue Jean-Jaurès (tel. 83-58-48), is one "sugarcane" that has created a local sensation, and in spite of its youth has already become the most select rendezvous for a superbly prepared Guadeloupean cuisine in Pointe-à-Pitre. Gérard Virginius, along with his wife, Marie, have restored this pink-and-white colonial house, with a kitchen from which emerge all the tempting dishes of the Créole cuisine. You dine in a parlor setting with a choice of two rooms.

For an appetizer, try one of their fritters made with malange, which tastes like sweet potatoes to me, and another with a vegetable known as giraumon, a squash-like pumpkin. Their stuffed land crabs (called crabes farcis here) are among the best sampled on the island. Conch is queen around here, and it's likely to be served in a variety of ways, put in everything from a tart to soup. I consider it best here when it's cooked with eggplant. For a main course, try leg of lamb stuffed with local mint, pigs' feet Antillean style, or tournedos Canne à Sucre. Fresh fish is served in papillotte, and occasionally they have turtle steak. Desserts are lavish and sinful: a soursop sherbet or a coupe Canne à Sucre (a rondelle with old rum, coconut sherbet, whipped cream, banana, caramel, and a touch of cinnamon). It's traditional to begin your meal with a small rum punch. The restaurant is closed on Saturday for lunch and all day Sunday, but open otherwise for those who make a reservation. Hours are noon to 2 p.m. and 7:30 to 10 p.m. Expect to spend from $35 per person for dinner.

Saint-John Perse once wrote about the fine oldtime sailors had when they arrived in Pointe-à-Pitre when it was used as a stopover anchorage on the famous Route du Rhum. But since that day is long gone, you may not want to linger; you can take a different route instead, this one to the "South Riviera," from Pointe-à-Pitre to Pointe de Châteaux.

LE BAS DU FORT: The first tourist complex, lying just two miles from Pointe-à-Pitre, is called Le Bas du Fort, in the vicinity of Gosier.

Where to Stay

PLM Azur Marissol, Le Bas du Fort, Gosier (tel. 83-64-44), is a secluded bungalow colony of two- and three-story structures, set away from the main road, occupying grounds from a secondary route to the shoreline. In a setting of banana trees and lawns, it offers first-class comfort in 200 air-conditioned rooms, either in bungalows or in the two wings, which open onto a view of the park-like grounds or the water. The furnishings are in "sober modern," and the floors are tiled, the baths having a separate toilet. In high season, a single room rents for 595F ($89.25) to 905F ($135.75) daily, *dropping to 400F ($60) to 580F ($87) in low season.* Two persons in a double pay 786F ($117.90) to 1,110F ($166.50) in high season, *570F ($85.50) to 760F ($114) in the off-season.* All units have either twin or double beds.

The beach is small, but you'll have the use of a large swimming pool. The hotel is a complete resort with lots of sports activities. Next to the pool is a circular bar, Le Wahoo. The hotel's deluxe restaurant, Le Grand Baie, opens onto a terrace where you can order both local Créole specialties and the traditional French cuisine. The set menu of four courses costs from 120F ($18). Sicali is an open grill lying halfway between the beach and the pool, providing simple but savory meals, with grilled meat or fish, as well as a serve-yourself salad bar and a dessert buffet. The hut-shaped restaurant enjoys much favor from guests.

Fleur d'Épée Novotel, Le Bas du Fort, Gosier (tel. 83-49-49), is a sister resort to its neighbor, the Azur Marissol. Both share the same beach facilities, and guests mingle freely. The Novotel is a string of connected modular units, 186 in all, with diamond-shaped roofs. At its center is a larger white-roofed restaurant where you can order authentic French dinners, with West Indian overtones. There are plenty of grounds for relaxation, as well as a generous-size pool where guests sometimes remove *le minimum.* Groupings of parasols, with low white lounges, make it a popular spot.

The accommodations offer much comfort, although they are in a simple modern with a few island touches such as bamboo chairs. There are private, angular balconies. The cost is 600F ($90) daily in a single in high season. In a double you pay 780F ($117) in high season. These tariffs rise from December 20 to January 4. *In summer, a single* *rents for 450F ($67.50) daily, and a double goes for 550F ($82.50).* Included in the tariffs quoted are free use of pedalboats, sailboats, and snorkeling equipment, along with Sunfish, Ping-Pong, tennis, and volleyball. Those chaises longues at the swimming pool and beach are given out free to the hotel's guests. Half of the rooms come with an ocean view, and there is usually entertainment offered at dinner, including perhaps a local band or a folkloric group. Children up to 12 years are housed free if they share a room with their parents.

Village Viva, Digue de Bas-du-Fort (tel. 90-87-66). Built in 1984, this is an isolated artificial village set on a flat and sandy peninsula whose rocky edges jut into the bay. Across the water, the hotels and moored boats of a marina offer a distant panorama such as you might find in a heavily developed area of the Côte d'Azur. Deliberately trendy, very French, and sometimes excessively family-oriented, it offers squash, tennis, volleyball, and a large curved-sided swimming pool. Its social center lies in a buffet-style restaurant beneath an overhanging roof, where guests congregate for extended lunches. The in-house formal restaurant may or may not be in business at the time of your visit. A total of 32 accommodations lie in eight one-story bungalows ringing the perimeter of the property. Each bungalow is pleasingly designed in a neo-colonial style of pastel-colored trim with a black roof and a border of crotons. In winter, singles cost 600F ($90) daily; doubles, 720F ($108). An additional guest is 175F ($26.25). *In summer, singles rent for 410F ($61.50), doubles run 530F ($79.50), and an extra person pays 120F ($18).* Children under 12 stay free in their parents' rooms. Over the Christmas holidays each guest pays a 120F ($18) daily supplement.

Where to Dine

La Plantation, Bas du Fort, in the Port de Plaisance shopping center (tel. 90-84-83). Never judge a restaurant by its location. This shopping center, at a marina complex, could easily be on Long Island. The food at this stylish pink-and-green confection is not ordinary in any sense, which is in fact one of the finest dining establishments on the island, serving dinner only, for which it is most important that you reserve a table. In an intimate and modern setting (also air-conditioned), a French and nouvelle cuisine is presented nightly except Sunday. Monsieur François Delage of Bordeaux is the chef de cuisine, and he's one of Guadeloupe's hottest kitchen properties, who knows all about raspberry vinegar. His array of delicate new dishes brings a creative touch to the cookery of Guadeloupe. For a beginning, try either the pumpkin soup, or if featured, a superb hors d'oeuvre of gésier d'oie, a goose giblet salad with a warm vinaigrette, served with walnuts and crisp croûtons. You'll also find staples from the classic repertoire of cooks in France, including a côte de boeuf rôtie with sauce moëlle. You might also be served duck breast with pears, perhaps red snapper in a cream sauce flavored with small baby clams and saffron. Many of his other dishes are outstanding, and he does wonders with crayfish, called ouassous, which he serves with a creamy dressing tinged with carapace and wine. It's easy to spend from $35 for dinner, including wine, served from 7 to 10 p.m.

L'Albatros, Bas du Fort (tel. 82-52-64), is the challenger. It has a far more romantic location, as it opens onto the water near the already-recommended Azur Marissol. In season, diners wanting to escape the confines of either the Marissol or the Fleur d'Épée are likely to fill up all 24 tables, so reservations are important. The most in-the-know diners ask for a table on a big veranda. Only dinner is served, offered nightly from 7 to 10 p.m. The service is elegant, and the cuisine of a high quality. You will find such sophisticated fare as a mousseline of fish in a sorrel sauce, lobster Thermidor, onglet with roquefort, scallops with saffron, a crayfish casserole with fresh mushrooms, and trout with a shrimp mousse. Various set menus are offered, beginning at 65F ($9.75); however, if you order à la carte expect to spend from 150F ($22.50).

Escale à Saigon, route des Fleurs d'Épées, Bas du Fort (tel. 90-86-22), is one of the most pleasant Oriental restaurants in Guadeloupe with a polite staff and a terrace setting designed to evoke a sense of peacefulness. Its only drawback is its location at the top of a long, steep, one-lane driveway where you might have to jockey for position with an advancing car. Full meals, costing from 175F ($26.25), are served daily except Monday from noon to 2 p.m. and 5 to 10:30 p.m. The Vietnamese and Chinese specialties include the fish of the day with ginger sauce, Vietnamese pâté with crabmeat, shrimp-and-chicken Saigon soup, asparagus-and-crabmeat soup, beef sautéed with onions, and several versions of duck (including one with "five perfumes"), along with grilled sea urchins with curry and coconut.

GOSIER: Some of the biggest and most important hotels of Guadeloupe are found at this holiday center, with its nearly five miles of beach, stretching east from Pointe-à-Pitre.

For an excursion, you can climb to **Fort Fleur d'Épée,** dating from the 18th century. Its dungeons and battlements are testaments remaining of the ferocious fighting between the French and British armies in 1794 seeking to control the island. The well-preserved ruins command the crown of a hill. From there you'll have good views over the bay of Pointe-à-Pitre, and on a clear day you can see the neighboring offshore islands of Marie-Galante and Îles des Saintes.

Where to Stay

Ecotel Guadeloupe, Gosier (tel. 84-15-66), is a restful retreat surrounded by gardens. Within an eight-minute drive of the capital and ten minutes from the airport, the hotel is maintained by students from the local hotel school. One part of the building is constructed in the shape of an H, with flower-bordered walkways connecting the segments. It was designed by Gilbert Corbin, who also conceived the Raizet Airport. It's modern in styling, yet its restaurant, bar, and bedrooms are West Indian in feeling. Each of the accommodations, 44 in all, opens onto a view of the pool, the gardens, or the adjoining forest. The units contain many built-in pieces, as well as white molded furniture. The air conditioning is occasionally not strong enough for some guests, but it is silent. Breakfast is served on an al fresco extension of the comfortably furnished reception area. To stay here costs 350F ($58.50) daily in a single in high season, 550F ($82.50) in a double, breakfast included. *These prices drop to 240F ($36) daily in a single off-season, 310F ($46.50) in a double.* With dinner included, add 120F ($18) per person per day to the tariffs quoted.

At the restaurant, Le Galion, serving dinner only, you get not only student waiters but also student cooks, the latter under the tutelage of a trained chef from France. Among the specialties is a filet de machoiran, a fleshy fish shipped in from Guyana. Also try their local red snapper done in a variety of ways. They also do a gâteau de langouste (spiny lobster) with whisky. Snails come with Pernod and walnuts. In winter, the director, Monsieur Castell, presents two gastronomic evenings each with the best chefs of France. Similar evenings are held with the best Créole cooks on Guadeloupe. Expect to pay around $25 for a meal. If you choose, you can dine on lighter fare alongside the swimming pool at Pap-Pap. Here a meal will average 95F ($15.20).

Another quarter of a mile farther on, you come to the tourist complex of—
PLM Azur Callinago Beach Hotel and Village, Gosier (tel. 84-25-25), named after a Carib Indian hero. Built along the Gosier beachfront, the hotel, a PLM operation, lies between the Auberge de la Vieille Tour and the Salako. It's run like a small resort inn along the Mediterranean, and the host, Jacques Savariau, has a friendly, helpful staff. In buildings of white stucco, some 41 rooms, with private baths, air conditioning, and private balconies, are rented. In high season, the cost is 495F ($74.25) daily in a single, rising to 650F ($97.50) in a double, EP. *In the off-season, the single tariff is 280F ($42) daily, and the double, 380F ($57).*

In the residential village complex, next to the hotel, the management offers 96 studios and 22 duplex apartments. The studios, for example, are spacious, with a combination living room and bedroom furnished in Nordic modern, with complete kitchens and baths. A sliding glass wall opens onto a small private balcony overlooking Gosier Bay. The duplexes, of course, are larger. You ascend a spiral staircase to your upstairs bedroom, with a private bath and another small terrace. On the premises is a little, well-stocked market if you'd like to do light housekeeping. In winter, rates are 445F ($66.75) for a studio single, 566F ($84.90) for a studio double, and 932F ($139.80) for a duplex suitable for three or four people. *In summer, one person pays 235F ($35.25), two pay 290F ($43.50), and a duplex for three or four costs 500F ($75).* The prices are for rooms only. If you want to dine out, you can eat in the hotel's restaurant, offering both French and Créole foods, a good meal costing 120F ($18) and up.

The hotel opens onto a white sand beach, and on the grounds is a freshwater pool. Such sports as waterskiing, sailing, snorkeling, pedalboating, windsurfing, and rides on a 36-foot sailing boat are available as well, but you'll pay extra for these. There are two tennis courts as well.

La Créole Beach Hotel, Pointe de la Verdure, Gosier (tel. 84-26-26), has the nicest hotel design of any of the Gosier establishments. Half New Orleans, half colonial, the hotel stands alongside two beaches in a setting of lawns and trees, as well as hibiscus and bougainvillea. The bedrooms, 156 regular ones plus six duplexes, are traditional in tone, with dark wood pieces, carpeted floors, direct phones, TVs, minibars, and individually controlled air conditioning. Your balcony will be large enough to be your breakfast spot or a perch for your sundowner. High-season rates, including a full American breakfast, are $112 daily in a single, $148 in a double, plus another $22-per-person supplement for MAP. *In summer, the cost of a double is 450F ($67.50) daily, with a single going for 338F ($50.70).*

The gourmet restaurant is called Sainte-Anne, and it is attractively decorated with plants. Many local specials are served here, along with a more familiar international cuisine. During the day guests enjoy drinks at the poolside bar, St. Tropez, or a lunch at the beach snackbar named Beethoven. The restaurant Les Alizés stands on an airy terrace near the pool and is full of handsome greenery. Its kitchen is run by an expert French chef, Eugène Zita. Many water sports as well as tennis are provided.

Auberge de la Vieille Tour, Gosier (tel. 84-23-23), is a harmonious combination of the old and the practical new, where you get vintage charm and an authentic Créole quality. Directed by the Frantel interests, the complex encircles an 1835 sugar mill whose thick-walled tower (which looks like a lighthouse) is the reception area. To that original structure, 82 rooms of first-class standard, with balconies overlooking the gardens and a small private beach, have been added. As you enter the driveway, you pass old mechanical parts of the former mill—dented wheels, the furnace, whatever. The modern bedroom extensions flow out into the tropical garden. For those who want even more privacy than that provided by the regular units, there are three intimate bungalows. If you want to stay here, figure on spending 870F ($130.50) to 995F ($149.25) daily in a single and 1,170F ($175.50) to 1,340F ($201) in a double in high season. *These rates drop to 720F ($115.50) to 845F ($126.75) in a single and 1,020F ($153) to 1,190F ($178.50) in a double in low season.* For 180F ($27) in addition to the room tariff, you can have breakfast and dinner.

The waterfront garden is the social center, with its large swimming pool. If you'd like to eat at the hotel, refer to the recommendations in "Dining at Gosier." At the Ajoupa Club beach grill you can dance for free if you're a hotel guest, enjoying the sounds of a local steel band almost every night in season. Sometimes limbo dancers are brought in, and buffets and barbecues are planned. Most sports are available at the hotel, and on the premises is a shop providing local handcrafts at reasonable tariffs. The hotel has a freshwater pool. Tennis is played on three composition courts, which are floodlit for night play.

Serge's Guest House, Perinette Gosier (tel. 84-10-25), right in the middle of town, gives you a chance to live in a Créole family house with an encircling garden awash with tropical flowers and vegetation. Each of the 25 modestly furnished rooms in this Logis de France contains air conditioning and a private bath, while several of the units have verandas and kitchenettes. A swimming pool is set amid the greenery. Meals are consumed in a sunny room whose glass louvers open onto a view of the lush garden. There, an octagonal gazebo serves as a daytime bar and a nighttime rendezvous for occasional live entertainment. Serge Helene is the helpful owner. Year-round rates in rooms without kitchenettes range from 140F ($21) to 190F ($28.50) daily in a single, from 170F ($25.50) to 220F ($33) in a double, including a continental breakfast. Studios with kitchenettes cost 180F ($27) to 210F ($31.50) for two people, without breakfast. The white concrete structure lies just over a mile from the nearest beach, and there's a tennis court on the grounds.

Dining at Gosier

In addition to the hotels, many small restaurants are found in Gosier and the vicinity. At some of these places you'll get Créole cookery with a relaxed atmosphere, and often relaxed service too. Many of these places you may discover on your own. I'll suggest the following. First, I'll document the best in-hotel dining, then the independent places.

Auberge de la Vieille Tour, Gosier (tel. 84-23-23), is one of the finest restaurants on the island. The main dining room is decorated in the French country style, with beamed ceilings, paneled walls, and chandeliers. The service from a staff hired by the Frantel chain in France is among the best on the island. Waitresses, many of them trained at hotel schools, are clad in their Guadeloupe madras Créole garb. The menu will probably change many times during the lifetime of this edition, but you'll get, in whatever form, French nouvelle cuisine here. The fish soup with fennel will get you going, then you are likely to be faced with such temptations as veal sweetbreads delicately braised with honey or roast lamb with a saffron sabayon. The locally caught red snapper is likely to be accompanied by cucumber balls and mango butter (yes, mango butter). My most recent guinea fowl was perfectly cooked and served with fresh cabbage leaves, a garlic cream sauce, and giraumon, the local pumpkin. The price is high, about $35 per head, but it's worth it. Dinner is nightly from 7 to 10 p.m.

Balata, route de Morne Labrousse (tel. 82-85-29). From the gastronomic capital of France (Lyon) to a panoramic site in Grande-Terre, Pierre Cecillon has come a long way. But so far he, along with his wife, Marie, are having much success with their charming little restaurant which combines the classic Lyonnaise cuisine with Créole cookery, and does so exceedingly well. Those who reserve early enough get a table on the terrace, which is reached by going up a steep road. Waitresses in *madras et foulard* dress bring out an array of tempting fare which might include a fish mousse with lobster sauce, perhaps chicken liver in aspic as an appetizer. On the Créole side, raw conch is often marinated in lime juice and olive oil, and blood pudding is invariably featured. The fish of the day might be served simply with parsley and butter, or with chive-flecked butter and tangy capers. A table d'hôte meal is offered for 150F ($22.50), and you'll spend far more, from 200F ($30), ordering à la carte. A choice of desserts from the trolley is offered. The restaurant serves lunch and dinner except on Sunday and Wednesday. Hours are noon to 3 p.m. and 7:30 p.m. to midnight.

Chez Violetta (tel. 84-10-34) stands at the far eastern end of Gosier Village, en route to Ste-Anne. Of all the Créole restaurants on the island, this is the most formally decorated. It has Louis XIII–style velvet-covered chairs, striped wallpaper in rich but somber colors, and a decor which looks as if it were transported from Burgundy. In spite of its neocolonial trappings, this is the domain of the high priestess of Créole cookery, who, though aged, still presides in the kitchen. Her name is Violetta Chaville, and her skill has become almost a legend on the island. Assisted by her brother, Joseph Galaya, along with a battalion of assistant chefs, she serves lunch from noon to

3 p.m. and dinner from 7 to 10:30 p.m. every day of the year. On the à la carte menu, try her stuffed crabs, her blaff of seafood, her fresh fish of the day (perhaps red snapper), and her turtle ragoût. For an appetizer, you might ask for cod fritters or beignets called "accra." The classic blood sausage, boudin, is also served here. In addition to the turtle ragoût, she does a fine conch ragoût, superb in texture and flavor. It's best when served with hot chilis grown on Guadeloupe. On occasion she'll even prepare a brochette of shark, if available. Fresh pineapple makes an ideal dessert, or you can try her banana cake. The restaurant serves seven days a week, both lunch and dinner. For a really fine meal on the à la carte menu, expect to pay from 175F ($26.25). Waitresses here dress in *madras et foulard*.

Chez Rosette, route de Gosier (tel. 84-11-32), is centered near many of the previously recommended hotels whose guests, even though on the half-board plan, come here for dinner. They know they'll get Créole cookery that is zesty and beautifully flavored with spices and herbs. Chez Rosette is one of the largest Créole places in Guadeloupe. It grew from a "front porch" restaurant made famous by Madame Rosette, whose successors carry on today. The restaurant has grown over the years, keeping up to the size of the kindly and vivacious family who own it. The guiding force is a gracious Créole matron, Marie-Louise Limol, whose pretty daughters help keep the kitchens running smoothly. The location is in a sprawling wood-sided building with several wings, a handful of dining rooms, and a sheltered garden of Norfolk Island pines and palms. Lunch is daily from noon to 3:30 p.m., and dinner from 6:30 to 11:30 p.m.

Known for its fish platters, which are often stewed or curried, the restaurant also serves such dishes as seafood stew, grilled fish, octopus, lobster, and colombos of goat, chicken, or conch. A fixed-price meal is popular at 90F ($13.50), while à la carte dinners cost from 150F ($22.50). Service is performed by a bevy of Guadeloupiennes dressed in the traditional *madras et foulard*. If you're interested in renting one of the comfortable, clean bedrooms upstairs, in winter singles cost 250F ($37.50) daily; doubles, 300F ($45). *Tariffs are reduced 30% in summer*. Each unit is recently constructed, containing air conditioning and a private bath.

La Chaubette, route de la Riviera (tel. 84-14-29). Begin with a rum punch, made with white rum and served with a lime wedge and sugar. But don't order too much—it's lethal, and you won't be able to get through the rest of dinner. This is a "front porch" Créole restaurant with lots of local color. About a 12-minute run from Pointe-à-Pitre, it's big and immaculately kept, almost like the Guadeloupe version of a roadside inn, with its red-checked tablecloths and curtains made of bamboo. Mme Gitane Chavalin is in charge, and she's known in the area for her Créole recipes, using, whenever possible, the fish and produce of her island. She gets the name of her restaurant from a small clam that lives in the Caribbean basin, and she makes a broth with these clams to honor the namesake. When it's available, her langouste is peerless, as is her hog's-head cheese with a minced-onion vinaigrette. Of course she knows how to pound and season conch to perfection, and often she'll prepare turtle steak when she can get it. Her ragoût of chatrou (a tiny octopus) is served in a tomato sauce, and I heartily endorse it for those seeking real local cookery. She's closed Sunday, but otherwise will top off a fine meal for you by serving either coconut ice cream or a banana flaming with rum. For her trouble, expect a bill around $25 per person for a complete meal. Service is until 11 p.m.

ST-FÉLIX:
At a distance of some two miles from Gosier, on the road to Ste-Anne, I suggest a stopover in the hamlet of St-Félix. Right in the middle of the fields, past running chickens and jumping kids, you'll come across **Chez Lydie** (tel. 84-13-63), in a kind of building that might be used for Saturday-night grange dances. A handful of friendly neighbors are likely to be seen gossiping on the front porch, but the real heart and soul of the place lies in back, where the Créole owner, Lydie, prepares spicy ver-

sions of island cuisine. Guests sit at five-and-dime-store tables and chairs, and everything is clean, well scrubbed, and decorated with madras tablecloths. Full meals are a bargain at 85F ($12.75), and might include versions of conch, goat, a toutfait (fricassée) of shark, Créole blood sausage, accras, stuffed crab, christophine stuffed with sausage, a gratin of fish, oysters à la nage, a brochette of fish, and different preparations of octopus. Meals are served daily except Monday from noon to 3 p.m. and 8 p.m. to midnight.

PETIT HAVRE: This sleepy hamlet lies between Gosier and Ste-Anne, and is just starting to emerge as a tourist destination. I'll offer both an accommodation and a topnotch restaurant here.

Hôtel Cap Sud Caraïbes, Chemin de la Plage, Petit Havre (tel. 88-96-02). Newly constructed, this friendly, intimate hotel resembles a pink-walled inn in the south of France. Designed in an octagonal shape which effectively shows off its pleasant swimming pool, walled garden, and planting, it offers a dozen rooms to guests who want to avoid the larger and more impersonal hotels. Each of the accommodations has air conditioning, lots of sun-flooded space, Mediterranean-style contrasts of white plaster with dark wood, and a tile bathroom. In winter, with breakfast included, singles rent for 450F ($67.50); doubles, 600F ($90). *In summer, the cost in a double is 400F ($60), dropping to 350F ($52.50) in a single.* Breakfast and light meals are served in a Tahitian-style cabaña bar a few steps from the swimming pool. A mini-forest of banana plants separates guests from the gates, which lie about a five-minute walk from the beach. The Sitbon family, assisted by one of the most genuinely accommodating hoteliers on the island, Mr. Sam, are the owners.

Bistrot, Petit Havre (tel. 88-91-52), took a quantum leap forward as soon as Eric Cesarion took over. The restaurant stands at the bottom of a sloping pathway leading past tall trees from the main road to Petit Havre. Surrounded by walls of coral rock on one side, and a superb view of the jutting peninsulas of the coastline on the other, it's a civilized version of a Tahitian bungalow, with only a roof on stilts above. Born in Guadeloupe, Monsieur Cesarion worked for several years as a pastry chef at a prestigious hotel in Lausanne, Switzerland. His desserts are appropriately sumptuous, making use of luscious island fruits. Some of his award-winning concoctions might include a charlotte of local star fruit or a petit bistro (praline-flavored ice cream with chocolate sauce, rum, and raisins). Other food isn't neglected either, and is often prepared to perfection, as reflected by a pungent version of fish soup, rillettes of rabbit, seafood au gratin, tomato sorbet, gigot of shark with fresh noodles, and stingray with a black-butter sauce. Full meals cost from 200F ($30) and require a reservation. Food is served from 11:30 a.m. to 2:30 p.m. and 7 to 11 p.m. The restaurant is closed Sunday evening, all day Monday, and for a few weeks in July.

STE-ANNE: About nine miles from Gosier, little Ste-Anne is a sugar town and a small resort, offering many fine beaches and lodging facilities. In many ways it's the most charming of the villages of Guadeloupe, with its town hall in pastel colors, its church, and its principal square, Place de la Victoire, where a statue of Schoelcher commemorates the abolition of slavery in 1848.

Where to Stay

Its best-known resort is **Club Med–Caravelle** (tel. 84-12-00, or toll free 800/CLUB-MED) covering 45 acres along a cape covered with palm trees. Its beach is one of the finest in the French West Indies. Beads are legal tender here. Club Med vacations are open to members only, but membership is available. An all-inclusive vacation package is offered, with one price, which depends on the time of year and the city from which you depart. It includes air fare, transfers, all-you-can-eat meals daily, with unlimited wine at lunch and dinner, plus use of all sports facilities, with expert instruction and equipment. The Med-Caravelle accommodates its guests in air-conditioned double-occupancy rooms with private baths. The weekly rate not including air fare is *$600 per person in summer,* from $800 to $1,000 in winter and spring (highest at Christmas).

Food is a specialty at the resort, the breakfast and lunch buffet tables groaning with French, continental, and Créole delicacies. Dinner is served in the main dining room, which has been enlarged and remodeled into a series of small, comfortable sections, or in the new La Maison Créole annex restaurant. At the north end of the beach, this jewel-like dining spot is set above the sand and decorated with bright, white gingerbread trim. You'll be welcomed at the pleasant bar and covered open-air dining area overlooking the sea. There's a weekly folklore night when the dinner features specialties of the region, along with a performance by the Guadeloupe folklore ballet. Also in the evening, guests gather around the bar and dance floor, which becomes the theater for nightly entertainment. Afterward you can dance at the midnight disco. The center of daytime activities is the wide stretch of beach. Windsurfing, sailing, and sunbathing have many devotees, and snorkeling trips leave daily from the dock. There are also sea excursions to explore the island's coastline. Other sports include tennis (six courts), archery, calisthenics, volleyball, basketball, and Ping-Pong. The Med-Caravelle offers a complete line of programs in its computer workshop, with 25 computers available. A special beginners course is available.

Hôtel La Toubana (tel. 88-25-57) is a hostelry centered around a low-lying stone building on a cliff overlooking the bay. Many guests come here just for the view, which on a clear day encompasses Marie-Galante, Dominica, La Désirade, and the Îles des Saintes, but you'll quickly learn that there's far more to this charming place than just a panorama. After parking, you walk into a circular forecourt whose side is flanked with a reflecting pool which doubles as a lobster tank. Registration takes place at an al fresco countertop away from the main building. You'll be shown to one of the 32 rooms or 32 red-roofed bungalows that lie scattered among the tropical shrubs along the adjacent hillsides. *Toubana* is the Arawak word for "small house." In high season, two people are lodged at prices beginning at 500F ($75) and going up to 1,200F ($180), the latter tariff charged only over the Christmas holidays. *In summer, two people pay 340F ($51) to 420F ($63).* A third bed for a child under 12 can be set up in any accommodation, although the hotel doesn't allow more than two adults per room.

The manager of this resort is Patrick Vial-Collet, who studied innkeeping in Switzerland and trained in London. His ideas contributed to the designer's inspiration of lining the dining room walls with illuminated aquariums from which schools of fish and crayfish stare back at curious visitors. The dining room, painted in shades of aqua and white, decked out at dinnertime with immaculate napery, offers both indoor and al fresco dining stretching right up to the edge of the pool. The beach is only a five-minute walk from any lodging, while tennis courts are on the premises. Deep-sea fishing and other water sports can be arranged.

Incongruously named, the ten-room **Hôtel Le Grand Large** (tel. 88-20-06), at the edge of town, is close to the municipal beach. It's nestled in the midst of tropical greenery, including coconut palms, on a two-acre site. Life here is informal and casual, everything beach oriented. The hostess is the charming Mme Georges Damico, and English for her is definitely not even a second language. Accommodations are white bungalows with twin beds and private baths, all air-conditioned. That may not really be necessary as they're exposed to the trade winds. Guests can stay here in winter for a charge of 415F ($62.25) in a single, 590F ($88.50) in a double. *Summer prices are 275F ($41.25) in a single, 415F ($62.25) in a double.* You can usually get salads, sandwiches, and light snacks throughout the day. Mme Damica's daughter, Micheline, is the chef in the in-house restaurant.

Le Relais du Moulin, Châteaubrun, Ste-Anne (tel. 88-13-78). The 19th-century stone tower that gives this place its name juts boldly above the hilly countryside. It required the entrepreneurial skill of two energetic sisters, Patricia and Florence Marie, to transform it into the centerpiece of their well-landscaped hotel. After passing between huge hedges of crimson poinsettia, guests register in the circular confines of the tower. Later they are ushered to one of the hotel's 40 accommodations, about half of which are contained in private red-roofed bungalows. The others are clustered into quartets whose sides are covered with trumpet vines and bougainvillea. Each of the units is air-conditioned and has a private bathroom, terrace with a hammock, and refrigerator. With breakfast included, winter rates are 400F ($60) in a single, from 530F ($79.50) to 650F ($97.50) in a double, depending on the size. *In summer, with breakfast included, singles go for 250F ($37.50); doubles, 325F ($48.75).* Guests congregate at the elegantly breeze-filled bar whose stout timbers overlook the rectangular sapphire of the swimming pool. Free bicycles are available, and facilities for archery are on the premises. A few guests check into this hotel primarily for its horseback riding. For a recommendation of its restaurant, Tap-Tap, see below.

Where to Dine

Tap-Tap, Le Relais du Moulin, Châteaubrun, Ste-Anne (tel. 88-13-78). An excursion to this restaurant gives visitors a chance to see the rolling horse country nearby. You dine in the shadow of a soaring mill, originally built in 1848, beneath a ceiling crisscrossed with heavy beams. Oversize windows flood the interior with sunlight at lunch from 12:30 to 2 p.m. At night, the flickering candles give the room the aura of a Norman farm at dinners served from 7:30 to 9:30 p.m. seven days a week. The kitchen turns out a blend of Antillean-inspired French food. This includes seafood bisque with rondelles of crayfish, a cassolette of conch and crayfish, a pâté of duckling, a refreshing salad of chicken livers soused with raspberry vinegar, seabass and crayfish in puff pastry, a ragoût of octopus with red wine, veal kidneys and sweetbreads in madeira sauce, filet of beef with three kinds of pepper, and crème caramel in a coconut sauce to finish. Full meals cost from 150F ($22.50) and should be reserved in advance.

L'Amour en Fleurs, Ste-Anne (tel. 88-23-72). If anyone can lure guests from the groaning buffet tables at the nearby Club Med, it's Mme Trésor Amanthe, who is considered a "sorceress" of Créole cookery. Assisted in her advanced years by her charming daughter, Maggie, this Créole mama has attracted a surprising amount of attention over the years from some of the most discerning visitors to Guadeloupe. The building is little more than a blue-painted concrete shell, open to the echoes of the whizzing traffic outside, with dime-store chairs, scarred wooden tables, and strings of paper lanterns and streamers. Guests receive a warm-hearted welcome and are served well-prepared Créole food seven days a week from 11 a.m. to 11 p.m. Full meals, costing from 100F ($15), include copious portions of accras, blood pudding, blaff, court bouillon, ragoûts of goat, pork, or chicken, and spicy colombos. Dessert might be a portion of coconut ice cream.

ST-FRANÇOIS: Continuing east from Ste-Anne, you'll notice many old round towers named for Father Labat, the Dominican founder of the sugarcane industry. These towers were once used as mills to grind the cane. St-François, 25 miles east of Pointe-à-Pitre, used to be a sleepy fishing village, known for its native Créole restaurants. Then Air France discovered it and opened a Méridien hotel with a casino. That was followed by the promotional activities of J. F. Rozan, a native, who has invested heavily to make St-François a jet-set resort. Now the once-sleepy village possesses first-class accommodations, as well as an airport available to private jets, a golf course, and a marina.

Where to Stay

In hotels, **Méridien St-François** (tel. 88-51-00) is one of the first Méridien hotels built for Air France, standing alongside one of the best beaches in Guadeloupe on 150 acres of land. The climate, quite dry here, is refreshed by trade winds. A four-star hotel, it offers 272 rooms either overlooking the sea or the Robert Trent Jones–designed golf course. The rooms are fully equipped with many amenities to add to your comfort, and furnishings are in a modern style combined with Créole overtones. The hotel was refurbished in 1984. *In low season, a single pays $76 to $85 daily; a double, $90 to $105*. However, in high season, prices go up to $100 to $115 daily in a single, $120 to $135 in a double. Included in the tariffs are use of the swimming pool, tennis courts, and windsurfers. St-Charles, which offers only an à la carte menu, is in the style of a deluxe restaurant, charging from 250F ($37.50) for a good meal, either from the French cuisine or the Créole repertoire. Or perhaps you'll prefer Balaou, a terraced restaurant in a more relaxed and exotic mood, where your dinner will cost from 125F ($18.50). In addition, the hotel has a grill and barbecue snackbar, Le Casa Zomar, right on the beach, where the prices are quite high, especially if you order lobster. Alongside the swimming pool, the Lele is a tropical bar serving punches and other drinks. At night you can dance at Le Bête à Feu, the hotel's disco.

For people who care for more independence, I suggest a bungalow at Guadeloupe's poshest property, **Hamak** (tel. 88-59-99), founded by J. F. Rozan, the French entrepreneur, who built it right alongside the 600-acre lagoon, a quarter of a mile from the Méridien. Its sandy beach along the lagoon and its proximity to golf and a tiny airport make it popular with jet-setters from Europe and the U.S., or perhaps "the divine friends" of nightclub impresario Régine. "Les amis" like to be elegant, but informally so. It was the site of the 1979 international summit that brought President Carter, among others, here. Spread on a 250-acre estate, accommodations are in villas (each with two individual tropical suites with twin beds opening onto a walled garden patio where you can sunbathe au naturel). Each bungalow houses one to four guests. In peak season, a single ranges in price from $200 to $210 daily, and a double goes for $250 to $270, with an American breakfast. *In the off-season, charges are $125 to $160 daily in a single, $155 to $200 in a double*. These prices include the suite, water sports, greens fees, tennis, taxes, and service. A nearby supermarket provides the supplies you'll need if you're housekeeping. Otherwise, you may take your meals in a popular tavern setting where you can enjoy seafood hors d'oeuvres, fish platters, and bouillabaisse for two. They say this place is the "poor rich man's restaurant."

Trois Mats Hôtel (Three Masts; tel. 88-59-99) is only about a mile from the center of town, although many of its occupants never leave the area surrounding its marina. The hotel is a trio of modern buildings that sit directly on the water a short walk from the Hôtel Méridien. Each of the 36 accommodations has its own kitchen, although cooking facilities are on either a balcony or a large terrace. In midwinter, studio apartments cost $65 to $75 for a single, $85 to $105 for a double. *In summer, tariffs are $50 in a single, $65 in a double*. Taxes and service are included in the rates. Beaches, tennis courts, golf, discos, and restaurants are all easily accessible.

Where to Dine

L'Auberge de Saint-François, 24 Allée Seze (tel. 88-51-71). Isolated, peaceful, and elegant, this very French restaurant is set behind a hedge of flowering shrubs and a spacious garden. A pair of porcelain Foo dogs flank the entrance of this sunny place, where terracotta floors, exposed beams, and a breeze-filled pair of patios evoke life in the south of France. It opened in 1986 under the guidance of a former dealer in fine crystal and porcelain, Claude Simon. Consequently, the Royal Doulton table service is an appropriate foil for fine food which will invariably be served with a Gallic flourish. Full meals begin at 280F ($42) for a menu touristique, but could easily climb to 380F ($57) on the à la carte menu. Specialties include nine different preparations of freshwater crayfish, a cassolette of conch with a suprême sauce, mousseline of wahoo in a lobster cream sauce, a brochette of smoked shark with a pepper sauce, a gigot of chicken with a fiery sauce nicknamed "sauce of the gates of hell," and selections from a dessert trolley. Reservations are important; lunch is from noon to 3:30 p.m. and dinner is served from 7:45 to 11 p.m. No meals are served on Sunday.

Restaurant Les Oiseaux, Anse des Rochers (tel. 88-56-92), is probably the best imitation of a Provençale farmhouse on the entire island. It stands on a seaside road about 3½ miles west of St-François on a scrub-covered landscape whose focal point is the sea and the island of Marie-Galante. Its walled-in front garden frames a stone-sided, low-slung building which produces the perfumes of a southern French and Antillean cuisine worth the detour. This is the domain of Arthur Rolle and his wife, Claudette, who charge from 150F ($22.50) for full meals. These repasts include a fish mousse, a sea-urchin tart, a brochette of seafood, a platter of shellfish nestled in a bed of seaweed, gratin of lobster, tuna with coconut, Créole-style beef, and a filet en croûte with red wine sauce. Dessert might be a composite of four exotic sherbets or a crêpe. Full meals are served from noon to 3 p.m. and 7 to 10:30 p.m. No meals are served on Thursday, and no evening meal is served on Sunday. Reservations in advance are necessary.

La Louisiane, Quartier Ste-Marthe, outside St-François (tel. 88-44-34). The century-old plantation house that encloses this restaurant is sheltered from the road by trees and shrubbery. The French owners, Daniel and Muriel Hugon, painted its trim a vivid combination of green and white, adding lattices and pastel-colored napery to its simple and airy interior. The couple brought with them when they migrated from Europe some of the best parts of the cuisine of their native regions, Provence and the Vosges. Full meals cost from 150F ($22.50) and might include a filet of turbot with passion fruit garnish, duck slices with lychees (flambéed in old rum), fricassée of sweetbreads, fish soup with rouille, a gratin of lobster, scallops with lime and ginger, veal escalope with shrimp, and scallops with ginger and lemon butter. The restaurant is open daily in high season but closed every Monday the rest of the year. Lunch is served from noon to 2 p.m.; dinner, from 7 to 10 p.m. Reservations are needed.

Madame Jerco/Chez Nise, rue Égalité (tel. 88-40-19). Its decor is strictly from the five-and-dime, and your meal might be punctuated with customers buying supplies at the tiny deli that occupies one end of the room. Nonetheless, some of the most prestigious visitors in the French-speaking world have darkened the door of this aggressively simple Créole restaurant in the heart of town. Madame Jerco, its founder and a noted local matriarch, is to an increasing degree assisted by her charming and capable daughter, Madame Cassilingon (her friends, and you too, usually call her Nise after a satisfying and spicy meal). Assisted by her husband, Hector, she prepares fixed-price meals costing from 90F ($13.50) for six courses, plus dessert, coffee, and a shot of a local herb-flavored liqueur which the menu lists as chroub. À la carte meals are a bit more expensive, costing from 110F ($16.50). Food, served on battered metallic chairs and tables with character, is offered from noon to 3 p.m. and 7 to 10 p.m. No meals are served on Sunday night and Monday at lunch. Specialties include stuffed christophine, grilled crayfish, oysters, blood sausage, accras of codfish, blaff of fish, a colombo of chicken or goat, and a calalou of crabmeat. A selection from a simple wine list might accompany your meal.

La Pecherie, rue de la République (tel. 84-48-94), is a tasteful restaurant set in a 200-year-old stone warehouse with a veranda overlooking the water. Owner Harry Parole offers an array of freshly caught seafood, which usually seems to taste better because of the salt breezes that waft over you while you dine. You're served on rustic wooden tables—nothing elaborate or pretentious—daily except Monday from noon to 2:30 p.m. and 7 to 11:30 p.m. Full Créole-inspired meals begin at 135F ($20.25) and include a blaff of fresh fish, a blaff of crayfish, colombo of chicken, a ragoût of seafood or conch, crayfish bisque, accras, a gratin of seafood, and stuffed crayfish.

POINTE DES CHÂTEAUX: Seven miles from St-François is Pointe des Châteaux, the easternmost tip of Grand Terre, at the point where the Atlantic meets the Caribbean. Here, where crashing waves sound around you, you'll see a cliff sculptured by the sea into castle-like formations, the erosion typical of France's Brittany coast. The view from here is splendid. At the top is an old cross put there in the 19th century.

If you wish, you can walk to the Pointe des Colibris, the extreme end of Guadeloupe. From there you'll have a view of the northeastern sector of the island, and to the east a look at La Désirade, another island which has the appearance of a huge vessel anchored far away. Among the coved beaches found around here, Pointe Tarare is the *au naturel* one.

Restaurant La Mouette, Pointe des Châteaux (tel. 84-40-57). Set near the end of a sand-bordered road stretching to Pointe des Châteaux, this veranda restaurant is built like an enlarged version of a Victorian gazebo. Amid turquoise-colored walls and gracefully turned balustrades, you can enjoy fresh seafood from the kitchen of Jacques Nainan. Full meals cost from 130F ($19.50) and are served daily from noon to 3 p.m. and 7:15 to 10:30 p.m. No food is served on Sunday night and all day Tuesday. Your dinner might include a ragoût of conch or fish, grilled lobster, a savory colombo of goat, lamb chops, a blaff of fish, accras, or shellfish.

To go back to Pointe-à-Pitre from Pointe des Châteaux, you can use an alternative route, the N5 from St-François. After a nine-mile drive, you reach the village of—

LE MOULE: Founded at the end of the 17th century, Le Moule was known long before Pointe-à-Pitre. It used to be a major shipping port for sugar. Now a tiny coastal fishing village, it never regained its importance after it was devastated in the hurricane of 1928, like so many other villages of Grand Terre. Because of its more than ten-mile-long crescent-shaped beach, it is developing as a holiday center. Modern hotels, built along the beaches, have opened to accommodate visitors.

Nearby the sea unearthed skulls, grim reminders of the fierce battles fought among the Caribs and the French and English. It's called "The Beach of Skulls and Bones."

The **Edgar Clerc Archeological Museum** (tel. 23-57-57) shows a collection of both Carib and Arawak Indian artifacts gathered from various islands of the Lesser Antilles. The admission-free museum is open Monday, Tuesday, Thursday, and Friday from 9:30 a.m. to 12:30 p.m. and 2:30 to 5:30 p.m.

Restaurants here are simple but good, and also surprisingly inexpensive. **Chez Lucile,** 3 rue St-Jean (tel. 84-51-63), is a very basic, tin-roofed structure whose kitchen—and whose owner—is famed for *spécialités Antillaises*. Lucile Lubin is the Créole chef who learned many of her recipes from her mother. Full meals, costing from 90F ($13.50), include a colombo of rabbit, fricassée of conch, both red and white rice, and fresh sugarcane juice extracted only a few moments before. Meals are served daily from noon to 11:30 p.m. This little restaurant with its oilcloth-covered tables lies at the northern edge of town. Don't overlook the possibility of a seat on the veranda, within view of the vegetable market.

To return to Pointe-à-Pitre, I suggest you use the D3 toward Abymes. The road winds around as you plunge deeply into Grand Terre. As a curiosity, about halfway along the way, a road will bring you to **Jabrun du Nord** and **Jabrun du Sud.** These two villages are inhabited by white peasants with blond hair. They are said to be survivors of aristocrats slaughtered during the Revolution. Those members of their families who escaped found safety by hiding out in Les Grands Fonds. The most important family here is named Matignon, giving its name to the colony known as "les Blancs Matignon." These aristocratic peasants are said to be related to Prince Rainier of Monaco.

Pointe-à-Pitre lies only ten miles from Les Grand Fonds.

THE ROAD NORTH: From Pointe-à-Pitre, head northeast toward Abymes, passing next through Moren à l'Eau, reaching **Petit Canal** after 13 miles. This is Guadeloupe's sugarcane country, and a sweet smell fills the air. It is worth stopping over in the charming but sleepy town of Petit Canal to sample the following restaurant.

Restaurant Le Barbaroc, rue Schoelcher, Petit Canal (tel. 84-72-71). One of the most dedicated cooks in Guadeloupe is Mme Félicité Doloir. In the 1983 edition of the *Annual Book of Cooks* by H. J. Heinz, she was featured as "one of the ten outstanding cooks in the world." She has researched local recipes since her youth and has made trips to such cities as New York to teach her lore to audiences of enthusiastic students. Her restaurant, not far from her birthplace, lies on the main street of town in an unpretentious concrete building whose terrace is reached by climbing a flight of stairs. The daily specials are written on a chalkboard hanging over the street. One of Madame Doloir's goals, which she describes fervently, is the promotion of locally produced ingredients in their most flavorful combinations. Her unique recipes are served in an upstairs room whose decor includes country-French furniture, flowers, wooden balustrades, and large, prominently displayed slogans advocating the dignity of mankind with special stress on the rights of women. Go here as much for an experience as for a good meal.

The restaurant is open every day for lunch and dinner from noon to 3 p.m. and 7 to 10 p.m., serving such dishes as codfish accras (whose pastry shell is made from carrots, eggplant, pumpkins, wheat flour, and breadfruit), burgots (sea snails) gratinée, purée of breadfruit, crab pâté, poulet du pays cuit fumé (smoked chicken), and sweet potato noodles. Even homemade beer is served here, as well as a house drink, maby, made from ingredients which include tree bark and which tastes a little like absinthe. Meals cost from $22 up.

Continuing northwest along the coast from Petit Canal, you come to **Port Louis,** well known for its beautiful beach, La Plage du Souffleur, which I find best in the spring. Then the brilliant white sand is effectively shown off against a contrast of the flaming red poinciana. During the week, the beach is an especially quiet spot. The little port town is asleep under a heavy sun, and it has some good restaurants.

Le Poisson d'Or, rue Sadi-Carnot, Port Louis (tel. 84-90-22), is a little Antillean house, entered by going down a narrow corridor, emerging into a rustic room. You can climb the steps to the second floor, an open terrace overlooking the sea and the fishing boats gently swaying in the water. It's run by Mme Eleanore Boulate. In spite of its simple setting, the food is excellent. Try, for example, the stuffed crabs, the court-bouillon, topped off by coconut ice cream, which is homemade and tastes it. With a bottle of good wine, your bill will come to about $18. The place is a fine choice for an experience with Créole cookery. Meals are served from noon to 3 p.m. and 7 to 10 p.m.

Also in Port Louis, you may want to patronize **Chez Odette,** rue Gambette (tel. 84-90-16). On a weekend, residents of Guadeloupe are likely to drive all the way from Basse Terre to sample the Créole viands offered by Rose Mozar, the *cuisinière patronne,* the daughter of founding mother, Odette. The accras (fritters) here are not made with just saltcod, but also from giraumon, the local pumpkin. They're a savory treat. Her colombos, made with either curried local goat or chicken, are among the best in this part of Guadeloupe. She also stuffs and seasons crabs to perfection. Among the local vegetables served is a delectable christophine (a chayote) gratinée. The dining room is exposed to the trade winds, if there are any, and the place is aggressively simple—and that's how the local diners like it. Meals cost around $18 and are served from noon to 3 p.m. and 7 to 10 p.m.

About five miles from Port Louis lies **Anse Bertrand,** the northernmost village of Guadeloupe. What is now a fishing village was the last refuge of the Carib tribes, and a reserve was once created here. Everything now, however, is lazy and sleepy.

Folie Plage (also known as Chez Prudence; tel. 22-11-17) lies directly north of Anse Bertrand at Anse Laborde. Its owner, Prudence Marcelin, is another *cuisinière patronne,* who enjoys much local acclaim for her Créole cookery. She too draws people from all over the island, especially on Sunday when this place is its most crowded. Island children frolic in the pool, and in between courses, diners can shop for handcrafts, clothes, and souvenirs sold locally. On weekends there is disco action. But at this popular rendezvous the food is still the attraction. Her court-bouillon is excellent, as is either her goat or chicken (curried) colombo. The way she handles palourdes (clams) also attests to her imagination. She also knows how to make a zesty sauce to serve with fish. Her crabes farcis are done to perfection as well. The place is relaxed and casual, and the bill rarely comes to more than $15. Service is from noon to 3 p.m. and 7 to 10 p.m.

From Anse Bertrand, you can drive along a graveled road heading for **Pointe de la Grande Vigie,** the northernmost tip of the island, which you reach after four miles of what I hope will be cautious driving. Park your car and walk carefully along a narrow lane which will bring you to the northernmost rock of Guadeloupe. The view of the sweeping Atlantic from the top of rocky cliffs is remarkable—you stand at a distance of about 280 feet above the sea. If the day is clear, you can see the island of Antigua, about 35 miles away.

Afterward, a four-mile drive south on quite a good road will bring you to the **Porte d'Enfer** or "gateway to hell." Once there, you'll find that the sea comes violently against two narrow cliffs.

After this kind of awesome experience in the remote part of the island, you can head back, going either to Morne à l'Eau or Le Moule before connecting to the road taking you in to Pointe-à-Pitre.

A BASSE TERRE ROUND-UP: Leaving Pointe-à-Pitre by Rte. N1, you can explore the lesser windward coast. After a mile and a half, you cross the Rivière Salée at Pont de la Gabarre. This narrow strait separates the two islands that form Guadeloupe. For the next four miles, the road runs straight through sugarcane fields.

At the sign, on a main crossing, turn right on the N2 toward **Baie Mahault.** Leaving that town on the right, head for **Lamentin.** This village was settled by corsairs at the beginning of the 18th century. Scattered about are some old colonial mansions.

If you should be in the area for lunch, try **Ravine Chaude,** Baie Mahaut (tel. 25-60-53). The hot springs around here attracted so many visitors that this little bistro was opened to satisfy a demand. It's a relaxed, casual place, attracting mainly French-speaking diners who enjoy the local crayfish prepared in a variety of ways. If you're up for it, one of the specialties is a blood pudding omelet (it's called boudin on the menu). Should that not interest you, perhaps the spiny lobster or the lamb brochette will. Meals cost from $15.

Ste-Rose

From Lamentin, you can drive for 6½ miles to **Ste-Rose,** where you'll find several good beaches. On your left, a small road leads to Sofaia, from which you'll have a splendid view over the coast and forest preserve. The natives claim that a sulfur spring here has curative powers.

Chez Clara (tel. 28-72-79) is the culinary statement of Clara Lesueur and her talented and charming mother, Justine. Clara, her hair tightly braided with flashing gold thread, has the manner and appearance of a chic Parisienne, a role she filled when she lived in the French capital and appeared as a model in fashion layouts in *France-Soir*. She said good-bye to that life, however, when she returned to Guadeloupe, her home, and set up her breeze-cooled restaurant. Try for a table on the open patio, where young palm trees complement the color scheme. Clara and Justine artfully meld the French style of fine dining with authentic, spicy Créole cookery. Specialties listed on the blackboard menu may include crayfish, curried skate, lobster, clams, boudin (blood pudding), ouassous (local crayfish), brochette of swordfish, palourdes (small clams), even crabes farcis (red-orange crabs with a spicy filling). The *sauce chien* served with many of the dishes is a blend of hot peppers, garlic, lime juice, and "secret things" that go well with the house drink, made with six local fruits and ample quantities of rum. To further cool your palate, your dessert might be a choice of sherbets such as guava, soursop, or passionfruit. Full meals cost around 100F ($15) and are served daily except Sunday night and all day Wednesday. Hours are noon to 2:30 p.m. and 8 to 10 p.m. The place is closed in October.

At Deshaies/Grand Anse

A few miles farther along, you reach Pointe Allegre, the northernmost point of Basse Terre. At Clugny Beach, you'll be at the site where the first settler landed in Guadeloupe.

A couple of miles farther will bring you to **Grand Anse,** one of the best beaches in Guadeloupe. It's very large and still secluded, sheltered by many tropical trees.

Next to the beach is a good restaurant, **Le Karacoli** (tel. 28-41-17). To get here, you turn off the main highway onto a secondary road leading to the tree-shaded beach. The restaurant stands behind a wall and a large parking lot. There's a pleasant high-ceilinged dining room, but my preferred spot is on the jungle-like terrace. There, dozens of tropical trees almost erupt out of holes in the concrete, allowing shafts of sunlight to dapple the napery of the tables.

This is the domain of Mme Lucienne Salcède, a beautiful Créole woman, one of the most celebrated chefs on the island. Born in Guadeloupe, she was taught to cook by her mother, using, on occasion, 200-year-old recipes. Her accras (saltcod fritters) are considered some of the best on the island. She's also known for her fish, crab, or squid tarts, spiny lobster, small clams (palourdes), and her superb version of curried chicken colombo. A specialty is called simply La Créole, consisting of farina dumplings, crayfish, shrimp, conch, and ten different spices. The place is open from noon to 4 p.m. daily except Friday. Fixed-price lunches cost 85F ($12.75); à la carte meals, from 135F ($20.25). No dinner is served. In winter, an adjacent disco attracts local residents at night. Le Karacoli shuts down in October.

Les Mouillages, Des Haies Bourg (tel. 28-41-12). For many, many years, its location in a Créole house, and its cuisine by a village matron, made it a sought-after but relatively secret address frequented by the yachting crowd. In 1986 it moved into a modern, large, and open-ended room which is reached by passing through a delicatessen on the main street of town. Once seated, diners enjoy a view of the harbor and the hills ringing it. The culinary legend, Mme Cléis Racine, is assisted more and more these days by her son, Fred, and her daughter-in-law, Hélène. If you're not in the mood for an afternoon spent at table, it's best to phone at least 40 minutes in advance of your arrival. In theory, meals are served daily from noon to 3 p.m. and 6 to 9 p.m. Actual service hours vary if they exist at all. Fixed-price meals cost from 110F ($16.50).

At Deshaies, snorkeling and fishing are popular pastimes. The narrow road winds up and down and has a corniche look to it, with the blue sea underneath, the view of green mountains studded with colorful hamlets.

Nine miles from Deshaies, **Pointe Noire** comes into view. Its name comes from black volcanic rocks. Look for the odd polychrome cenotaph in town.

Route de la Traversée

Four miles from Pointe Noire, you reach Mahaut. On your left begins the Route de la Traversée, the Transcoastal Hwy. This is the best way to explore the scenic wonders of **Parc Naturel de Guadeloupe** when traveling between the capital, Basse-Terre, and Pointe-à-Pitre. I recommend going this way, as you pass through a tropical forest.

To preserve the Parc Naturel, Guadeloupe has set aside 74,100 acres or about one-fifth of its entire terrain. Reached by modern roads, this is a huge tract of mountains, tropical forests, and magnificent scenery.

The park is home to a variety of tame animals, including Titi (a raccoon adopted as its official mascot), and such birds as the wood pigeon, turtledove, and thrush. Small exhibition huts, devoted to the volcano, the forest, or to coffee, sugarcane, and rum, are scattered throughout the park.

The Parc Naturel has no gates, no opening or closing hours, and no admission fee.

From Mahaut you climb slowly in a setting of giant ferns and luxuriant vegetation. Four miles after the fork, you reach **Les Deux Mamelles** (The Two Breasts), where you can park your car and go for a hike. Some of the trails are for experts only; others, such as the Pigeon Trail, will bring you to a summit of about 2,600 feet where the view is impressive. Expect to spend at least three hours going each way. Halfway along the trail you can stop at Forest House. From that point, many lanes, all signposted, branch off on trails that will last anywhere from 20 minutes to two hours. Try to find the **Chute de l'Écrevisse,** the "Crayfish Waterfall," a little pond of very cold water which you'll discover after a quarter of a mile. Male hikers are likely to encounter some local beauties swimming here. If so, you can join them for a cooling dip.

After the hike, the main road descends toward Versailles, a hamlet about five miles from Pointe-à-Pitre.

Chez Vaneau (tel. 98-01-71) offers a wide, breeze-filled veranda overlooking a gully, the sight of local neighbors playing cards, and steaming Créole specialties coming from the kitchen. This is the unquestioned domain of Vaneau Desbonnes, who is assisted in the many culinary tasks by his wife, Marie-Gracieuse. Depending on business, meals are served from noon to midnight daily, with an early closing on Sunday. Fixed-price meals begin at 65F ($9.75), and à la carte dinners at 90F ($13.50). Specialties include oysters with a piquant sauce, crayfish bisque, ragoût of goat, different preparations of octopus, and roast pork.

From Mahaut, you reach the village of **Bouillante,** which is exciting for only one reason: you might encounter Brigitte Bardot, as she's a part-time resident.

Try not to miss seeing the small island called **Îlet à Goyave** or **Îlet du Pigeon.** Jacques Cousteau often explores its silent depths.

Facing the islet is the best choice for a luncheon on the whole island:

La Touna, Malendure (tel. 98-70-10), is built on a narrow strip of sand between the road and the sea, its foundation almost touching the water. This gives patrons of this charming restaurant a marine panorama which complements the seafood specialties that Francis and Françoise Ricart and their son, Emmanuel, concoct so skillfully in the kitchen. Most of the dining tables are in a side veranda whose ceiling is covered with palm fronds. Despite its allure, many of the guests delay a meal until after a drink in the sunken bar whose encircling banquettes give the impression of the cabin of a ship. One of the most appealing rituals in Guadeloupe has become a habit here: you are brought a tray on which are seven or eight carafes, each filled with a rum-soaked tropical fruit such as guava, maracoja, pineapple, and passion fruit. You select the ingredients you prefer and mix your own drink. This you can savor as you observe your fellow diners or look out at the glittering waves. Of course if you prefer the house specialty, you'll have a combination of fruit with or without rum, one of the most refreshing drinks on the island.

Menu items make use of the freshest ingredients, many of them brought in daily by the Ricarts' deep-sea fishing business (see my discussion of Sporting Club Antilles in "The Sporting Life," below). Full meals cost from around 140F ($21) and might include a mousse of smoked swordfish, calamari provençale, avocado stuffed with crayfish, stuffed crabs, stuffed sea urchins, kingfish steak, kingfish au poivre, cassoulette of shark with cream sauce, and stingray with black-butter sauce. Lunch, the only meal served, is offered from noon to 3 p.m. daily. Reservations are important on Sunday.

After a meal at La Touna, you can explore around the village of Bouillante, the country known for its thermal springs. In some places if you scratch the ground for only a few inches you'll feel the heat.

Another good choice for lunch is **Chez Loulouse** (tel. 98-70-34), at Malendure Plage, also opposite Pigeon Island. Many guests prefer their rum punches on the panoramic veranda, overlooking a scene of loaded boats preparing to depart and merchants hawking their wares. A quieter oasis is the equally colorful dining room inside, just past the bar. There, beneath a ceiling of palm fronds, is a wrap-around series of Créole murals which seem to go well with the reggae music emanating loudly from the bar. This is the creation of one of the most visible and charming Créole matrons in this end of the island, Madame Loulouse Paisley-Carbon. Assisted by her children, she offers fixed-price meals for 125F ($18.75) when her langouste Loulouse or house-style Caribbean lobster is the main course. Without lobster, full meals cost from 75F ($11.25). Food is served from noon to 3:30 p.m. and 7 to 10 p.m. Specialties in addition to lobster include spicy versions of fish, conch, octopus, accras, grating of christohine (squash), and savory colombos of chicken or pork.

Vieux Habitants

The winding coast road brings you to Vieux Habitants (Old Settlers), one of the oldest villages on the island, founded back in 1636. The name comes from the people who settled it. After serving in the employment of the West Indies Company, they retired here. But they preferred to call themselves inhabitants, so as not to be confused with slaves.

Basse-Terre

Another ten miles of winding roads bring you to Basse-Terre, the seat of the government of Guadeloupe, lying between the water and La Soufrière, the volcano. Founded in 1634, it's the oldest town on the island, and still has a lot of charm, its market squares shaded by tamarind and palm trees.

The town suffered heavy destruction at the hands of British troops in 1691 and again in 1702. It was also the center of fierce fighting during the Revolution. The story of Colonel Delgres blowing himself up in 1802, along with his troops, is like a Guadeloupe Fort Alamo.

In spite of its history, there isn't much to see except for a 17th-century cathedral and Fort St-Charles, which has guarded the city (not always well) since it was established.

Le Clos d'Arbaud, 40 rue de la République (tel. 81-28-10), is the newest, most stylish, and most imaginative restaurant in town. At waterside, on the ground floor of a modern office building, it is graced with its own walled-in garden and sea-view terrace, along with a pink-and-white neo-Victorian decor loaded with wicker and antiques. Its location in the administrative heart of Basse-Terre, near government offices, makes it popular with journalists and politicians. Full meals cost from 225F ($33.75) and are served from noon to 3 p.m. and 6:30 to 11 p.m. daily except Saturday lunch and all day Sunday. Elizabeth, the owner and chef, offers such specialties as a scallop of red snapper with a fondue of leeks, a purée of local root vegetables, crabmeat and fresh seafood with lemon butter in puff pastry, leeks in aspic with chicken livers and essence of sweet peppers, filet of veal with crayfish and a julienne of vegetables, a charlotte of corossol (star fruit) with its own essence, and a prune flan with passion fruit and honey ice cream. Because of its small size, it's important to reserve a table.

Le Houëlmont, 34 rue de la République (tel. 81-35-96), is set in the monumental heart of town, across a boulevard from a massive government building, the Conseil General. After climbing a flight of stairs to the paneled second story, diners enjoy a sweeping view over the hillside, sloping down to the sea one block away. Mme Boulon, the owner, offers fixed-price meals beginning at 100F ($15) or à la carte dinners at 125F ($18.75). Food is served from noon to 3 p.m. and 7 to 10:30 p.m. Specialties include a medley of Créole food such as accras, court-bouillon of fish, grilled fish, steaks, shellfish, and blood sausage.

La Soufrière

The big attraction of Basse Terre is the famous, sulfur-puffing Soufrière volcano, which is still alive, but dormant—for the moment at least. Rising to a height of some 4,800 feet, it is flanked by banana plantations and lush foliage.

After leaving the capital at Basse-Terre, you can drive to **St-Claude,** a wealthy suburb, four miles up the mountainside to a distance of 1,900 feet. It has an elegant reputation for its perfect climate and luxurious tropical gardens.

Instead of going to St-Claude, you can head for **Matouba,** in a country of clear mountain spring water. The only sound you're likely to hear at this idyllically quiet place is of birds and the running water of thousands of springs. The village was settled long ago by Hindus.

You'll find good food at **Chez Paul de Matouba** (tel. 80-01-77), on the banks of the small Rivière Rouge (Red River). The dining room on the second floor is enclosed by windows, allowing you to drink in the surrounding dark-green foliage of the mountains. The cookery is Créole, and crayfish dishes are the specialty. However, because of the influence of the early settlers, Hindu meals are also available. By all means, drink the mineral or spring water of Matouba. Expect to pay around 110F ($16.50) for what one diner called ''an honest meal.'' Specialties include stuffed crab, rabbit in a marengo sauce, colombo (curried) chicken, as well as an array of both French, Créole, and Hindu specialties. It is open only for lunch from noon to 4 p.m., but not on Monday. Regrettably, if you're an independent traveler, you're likely to find the place overcrowded in the winter season with the tour-bus crowd.

Back in St-Claude, you can now begin the climb up the narrow, winding road the Guadeloupeans say leads to hell—that is, **La Soufrière.** The road ends at a car park at La Savane à Mulets, at an altitude of 3,300 feet. That is the ultimate point to be reached by car. Hikers are able to climb right to the mouth of the volcano. However, in 1975, ashes, mud, billowing smoke, and earthquake-like tremors proved that the old beast was still alive.

In the resettlement process, 75,000 inhabitants were relocated to Grande Terre. However, no deaths were reported. But the inhabitants in Basse Terre still keep a watchful eye on the smoking giant.

Even in the parking lot, you can feel the heat of the volcano merely by touching ground. Steam emerges from fumaroles and sulfurous fumes from the volcano's ''burps.'' Of course, fumes come from its pit and mud cauldrons as well.

The Windward Coast

From Basse Terre to Pointe-à-Pitre, the road follows the east coast, called the Windward Coast. The country here is richer and greener than any I've seen so far on the island.

To reach **Trois Rivières** you have a choice of two routes. One goes along the coastline, coming eventually to Vieux Fort, from which you can see Les Saintes archipelago. The other heads across the hills, Monts Caraïbes.

Near the pier in Trois Rivières you'll see some pre-Columbian petroglyphs carved by the original inhabitants, the Arawaks. They are called merely ''Roches Gravées,'' or carved rocks. In this archeological park, the rock engravings are of animal and human figures, dating most likely from A.D. 300 or 400. You'll also see specimens of plants, including the calabash, cassava, cocoa, pimento, and banana, that the Arawaks cultivated long before the Europeans set foot on Guadeloupe. From Trois Rivières, you can take boats to Les Saintes.

After leaving Trois Rivières, you continue on Rte. 1. Passing through the village of Banaier, you turn on your left at Anse Saint-Sauveur to reach the famous **Chutes du Carbet**, a trio of waterfalls. The road to two of them is a narrow, winding one, along many steep hills, passing through banana plantations as you move deeper into a tropical forest.

After three miles, a lane, suitable only for hikers, brings you to Zombie Pool. Half a mile farther along, a fork to the left takes you to Grand Etang, or large pool. At a point six miles from the main road, a parking area is available and you'll have to walk the rest of the way on an uneasy trail toward the second fall, Le Carbet. Expect to spend around 20 to 30 minutes, depending on how slippery the lane is. Then you'll be at the foot of this second fall where the water drops from 230 feet. The waters here aren't too cold, averaging 70° Fahrenheit, which is pretty warm for a mountain spring.

The first fall is the most impressive, but it takes two hours of rough hiking to get there. The third fall is reached from Capesterre on the main road by climbing to Routhiers. This fall is less impressive in height, only 70 feet. When the Carbet water runs out of Soufrière, it is almost boiling.

After Capesterre, you can go along for 4½ miles to see the statue of the first tourist who landed in Guadeloupe. It stands in the town square of Ste-Marie. The tourist was Christopher Columbus, who anchored a quarter of a mile from Ste-Marie on November 4, 1493. In the journal of his second voyage he wrote, "We arrived, seeing ahead of us a large mountain which seemed to want to rise up to the sky, in the middle of which was a peak higher than all the rest of the mountains from which flowed a living stream."

However, when Caribs started shooting arrows at him, he left quickly, heading for new adventures.

If you want to lunch in the area, try **Le Crépuscule** (Chez Dollin), in the village of Habituée, en route to Carbet Falls (tel. 86-34-56). It features the Créole cookery of a native Guadeloupien, Serge Dollin, who is assisted by a staff whose members live, for the most part, within a few steps of the restaurant's front veranda. The building lies about two miles east of the waterfall in a simple concrete building flanked by hibiscus hedges. You can dine well for around 85F ($12.75) from noon to 4 p.m.

After Ste-Marie, you pass through Goyave, then Petit Bourg, seeing on your left the Route de la Traversée before reaching Pointe-à-Pitre. You will have just completed the most fascinating scenic tour Guadeloupe has to offer.

THE SPORTING LIFE: Most visitors come to Guadeloupe for swimming and sunning. There are many well-sheltered beaches where you can enjoy not only this, but fishing, skindiving, and waterskiing. Chances are, your hotel will be built right on a beach, or else will lie no more than 20 minutes from a good one. There is a plentitude of natural beaches dotting the island from the surf-brushed dark strands of western Basse Terre to the long stretches of white sand encircling Grande Terre. Public beaches are generally free, but some charge for parking. Unlike hotel beaches, they have few facilities. Hotels welcome nonguests, but charge for changing facilities, beach chairs, and towels.

Sunday is family day at the beach. You'll see how the local folk enjoy their day off. Topless sunbathing is common at hotels, less so on village beaches.

Golf

The **Golf de St-François** (tel. 88-41-87) is at St-François, about 22 miles east of Raizet Airport. The golf course runs alongside an 800-acre lagoon where windsurfing, waterskiing, and sailing prevail. The course, designed by Robert Trent Jones, is a 6,755-yard, par-71 course, which presents many challenges to the golfer, with water traps on 6 of the 18 holes, massive bunkers, prevailing trade winds, and a particularly fiendish 400-yard par-4 ninth hole. The par-5 sixth is the toughest hole on the course. Its 450 yards must be negotiated into the constant easterly winds.

Scuba and Snorkeling

Hot on the trail of Jacques Cousteau, who has spent much time in local waters, scuba-divers are drawn to Guadeloupe. Cousteau described Guadeloupe's Pigeon Island as "one of the world's ten best diving spots." During a typical dive, sergeant majors become visible at 30 feet, spiny sea urchins and dazzling green parrotfish at 60 feet, and magnificent finger, black, brain, and star coral come into view at 80 feet.

Other dive sites are Mouton Vert, Mouchoir Carré, and Cay Ismini. They are close by the major hotels, in the bay of Petit Cul-de-Sac Marin, south of Rivière Salée, the river separating the two halves of Guadeloupe. North of the Salée is another bay, grand Cul-de-Sac Marin, where the small islets of Fajou and Caret also boast fine diving.

The scuba schools at Guadeloupe's hotels all offer similar arrangements at comparable prices. Every day around noon there is a free trial in the hotel pool. Sea dives in the area around the major hotels of Gosier cost about 175F ($26.25), individually. Excursions to Pigeon Island usually include a glass-bottom-boat ride in addition to the dives, and prices per dive are 300F ($45).

A leading proponent of the sport is divemaster Alain Verdonck whose **Aqua-Feri Club** is based at La Créole Beach Hotel in Gosier (tel. 84-26-26), 15 miles east of Pointe-à-Pitre. Verdonck's underwater journeys explore the remains of two sunken ships, Pointe-à-Pitre Bay, coral reefs, and Pigeon Island.

A second dive center is **Karuketa Plongee** at Hôtel PLM Callinago (tel. 84-25-25), also in Gosier. Five French-licensed instructors under the direction of Stephane Bailly run full-day dive trips to Les Saintes twice a week, as well as offering half-day dives.

The **Nautilus Club,** facing Pigeon Island from the beach at Malendure (tel. 98-70-34), supervised by divemaster Philippe Masson, has four boats for divers. Two dives a day are offered from the beach: at 9:45 a.m. and 2:45 p.m.

Another diving facility at Malendure is **Chez Guy** (tel. 98-81-72). Guy Genin has three boats, and regular dives are at 9:45 a.m. and 2:45 p.m., with a 12:30 p.m. dive available on request. Guy also has a diving center on Les Saintes. Both centers are open all year.

Les Heures Saintes (tel. 90-82-72) operates from the 30-foot boat *Le Yaisa*, moored in the Bassin Pentagonal at the Bas-du-Fort Marina.

Sailing

Sailboats of varying sizes, crewed or bareboat, are plentiful. Information can be secured at any hotel desk. Sunfish sailing can be done at almost every beachfront hotel.

Yachting

Yachting is a challenging sport in Guadeloupe. Facilities are available at Pointe-à-Pitre's **Carénage** and at **Deshaies,** a village on northeastern Basse Terre, as well as at three fairly recently opened marinas. They are **Bas du Fort Port de Plaisance** (tel. 82-54-85), ten minutes from Raizet Airport, five minutes from Pointe-à-Pitre and the same distance from Gosier; **Marina de St-François** (tel. 84-47-48) in the St-François resort area; and **Marina de Rivière-Sens** (tel. 81-77-61), at Gourbeyre, a five-minute drive from the capital of Basse-Terre.

Deep-Sea Fishing

The season for barracuda and kingfish is January to May. For tuna, dolphin, and bonito, it's December to March.

Fishing Club Antilles, Section Poirier-Pigeon (tel. 98-73-77), at Bouillante, isn't a club in the usual sense, more like a deep-sea fishing company. Some avid sport fishermen rent one of the establishment's bungalows so they can be at the pier when the first boat leaves at 5 a.m. Bungalows rent throughout the year for 380F ($57) in a single, 530F ($79.50) in a double. A six-hour boat rental, with equipment and crew, costs 2,700F ($405) from 5 to 11 a.m. An afternoon expedition from 3 to 7 p.m. goes for 2,100F ($315). Francis Ricart and his wife, Françoise, are the French-born owners.

Waterskiing

Most seaside hotels can arrange this at a cost of $13 for 30 minutes' boating time.

Windsurfing

This is the hottest sport in Guadeloupe today, and it's available with lessons at all the major beach hotels.

Tennis

All the large resort hotels have tennis courts, many of which they light at night for games. The noonday sun is often too hot for most players. If you're a guest, tennis is free at most of these hotels. But you will be charged for night play. If your hotel doesn't have a court, you can play at the **Club of St-François** (tel. 84-40-01).

Also you might consider an outing to **Le Relais du Moulin,** Châteaubrun, near Ste-Anne (tel. 88-23-96). There you can play tennis at 40F ($6) per hour.

Horseback Riding

The **Relais du Moulin Hôtel,** at Châteaubrun, near Ste-Anne (tel. 88-23-96), has six English thoroughbred horses which it rents on accompanied tours through sugarcane fields and the local countryside.

Hiking

The **Parc Naturel de Guadeloupe** is the best hiking grounds in the Caribbean, in my opinion (please refer to the touring notes on Route de la Traversée). Marked trails cut through the deep foliage of rain forests until you come upon a waterfall or perhaps a cool mountain pool. The big excursion country, of course, is around the volcano, La Soufrière. However, because of the dangers involved, I recommend that you go out only with a guide. Hiking brochures are available from the tourist office, and guided excursions are arranged by the **Association des Amis du Parc Naturel,** Parc Naturel, Basse Terre (tel. 81-17-20). Guided hiking tours, such as a four-hour scale of La Soufrière, cost about 300F ($45).

Camping

Campsites are basic, except at **Les Sables d'Or** (tel. 81-39-10), Grande Anse Beach near Deshaies, which has good facilities and rents tents. Camping areas separated by trees have water, shaded eating places, toilets, bathrooms, and kitchens. Rates for a camper with its own tent for one person are 35F ($5.25) per day; for two persons, 60F ($9). To rent a camp area and a tent costs 45F ($6.75) for one person, 70F ($10.50) for a two-person tent. Bungalows are also available, costing 60F ($9) for one renter, 80F ($12) for two.

AFTER DARK: Guadeloupeans claim that the beguine was invented here, not on Martinique. Regardless, the people dance the beguine as if they truly did own it. Of course, calypso, the merengue, whatever, moves rhythmically along, as the people of the island are known for their dancing.

Ask at your hotel where the folkloric **Ballets Guadeloupeans** will be appearing. This troupe makes frequent appearances at the big hotels, although they don't enjoy the fame of the Ballets Martiniquais, the troupe already described on the sister island.

Le Foufou is a disco on the grounds of the Hôtel PLM Azur Marissol, Le Bas du Fort, Gosier (tel. 82-64-44), two miles from Pointe-à-Pitre. It's open only from Tuesday to Saturday, and the action begins at 11 p.m. You're charged an entrance fee of 50F ($7.50) which entitles you to your first drink. After that, drinks cost from 35F ($5.25).

Guests from surrounding hotels often head for the **Hôtel Salako**, Pointe de la Verdure (tel. 84-14-90). The after-dark attraction is the Club Caraïbe, a disco nightclub. If the crowd is right, the place can be fun. For your first drink you pay 50F ($7.50), which includes the price of your entrance fee.

The **Casino de la Marina** (tel. 84-41-31) stands near the Hôtel Méridien St-François. It is open from 9 p.m. to 3 a.m. to persons over 21, providing they have proof of identity in the form of a driver's license with a photo (or else a valid passport). The entrance fee is 60F ($9), and once inside, you can play American roulette, chemin-de-fer, and blackjack. Dress is casual. The nightclub in the open garden offers dancing under the stars to a live band or disco. A free buffet is spread Saturday night.

Another casino is **Gosier-les-Bains**, on the grounds of the Hôtel Arawak (tel. 84-24-24) in Gosier. Entrance fee is 60F ($9). Coat and tie are not required, but dress tends to be casually elegant. An identity card with photo is required for admission. It opens at 9 p.m., and the most popular games are blackjack, roulette, and chemin-defer. There is not only a restaurant, but a disco.

ÎLES DES SAINTES:
A cluster of eight islands off the southern coast of Guadeloupe, the Îles des Saintes are certainly off the beaten track. The two main islands and six rocks are Terre-de-Haut, Terre-de-Bas, Îlet-à-Cabrit, La Coche, Les Augustins, Grand Îlet, Le Redonde, and Le Pâté. Of all those Saints, only Terre-de-Haut (''land of high'') and to a lesser extent Terre-de-Bas, (''land below'') attract visitors, mostly Guadeloupeans wanting an escape.

If you're planning a visit, Terre-de-Haut is the most interesting Saint to call upon. It's the only one with facilities for overnight guests.

Some claim Les Saintes has one of the nicest bays in the world, a lilliput Rio de Janeiro with a sugarloaf. The isles, just six miles from the main island, were discovered by Columbus (who else?) on November 4, 1493, who named them ''Los Santos.''

The history of Les Saintes is very much the history of Guadeloupe itself. In years past the islands have been heavily fortified, as they were considered Guadeloupe's Gibraltar. The climate is very dry, and until the desalinization plant opened, water was often rationed.

The population of Terre-de-Haut is mainly white, all fishermen or sailors and their families who descended from Breton corsairs. The fishermen are very skilled sailors, maneuvering large boats called ''saintois.'' They wear coolie-like headgear called a salaco, which is shallow and white with sun shades covered in cloth built on radiating ribs of thick bamboo. Frankly, they look like small parasols. Of course, all visitors want to photograph these sailors, and they seem to resent that. If you can't resist taking a picture, please make a polite request (in French, no less; otherwise they won't know what you're talking about). Women like to buy these hats (if they can find them) for use as beach wear. They are often likened to inverted saucers.

Terre-de-Haut is a place for discovery and lovers of nature, many of whom stake out their exhibitionistic space on the nude beach at Anse Crawen.

Part of the fun of Les Saintes is in getting there. From Pointe-à-Pitre you can drive to Trois Rivières in about an hour. From there, a boat to Les Saintes leaves twice a day, at 8:30 a.m. and 4 p.m., Monday to Saturday. On Sunday, sailing time is 8:30 a.m. Les Saintes can also be reached from the capital, Basse-Terre, a schooner leaving every day at 6 a.m., if anyone wants to get up for that. The ride is over choppy seas, and the round-trip fare is 46F ($6.90). Flights from Pointe-à-Pitre on Air Guadeloupe take just 15 minutes, and depart daily.

At Terre-de-Haut, you'll find the main settlement at **Bourg**, a single street which follows the curve of the fishing harbor. A charming hamlet, it has little houses with red or blue doorways, balconies, and Victorian gingerbread gewgaws. Donkeys are the beasts of burden, and everywhere you look are fish nets drying in the brilliant sunshine. You can also explore the ruins of Fort Napoléon, which is left over from those 17th-century wars, including the famous naval encounter known in European history books as "The Battle of the Saints." You can see the barracks and prison cells, as well as the drawbridge and art museum. Occasionally you'll spot an iguana scurrying up the ramparts. Directly across the bay, atop Îlet-à-Cabrit, sits the fort named in honor of the Empress Josephine.

You might also get a Breton sailor to take you on his boat to the other main island, Terre-de-Bas, which has no accommodations, incidentally. Or you can stay in Terre-de-Haut and go on a hike to Le Grand Souffleur with its beautiful cliffs, and to Le Chameau, the highest point on the island, rising to a peak of 1,000 feet.

Scuba-diving centers are not limited to mainland Guadeloupe. The underwater world off Les Saintes has attracted deep-sea divers as renowned as Jacques Cousteau, but even the less experienced may explore its challenging depths and multicolored reefs. Intriguing underwater grottoes found near Fort Napoléon on Terre-de-Haut are also explored.

There are no roads and no more than a dozen or so cars.

Where to Stay

The best place to stay at Terre de Haut is **Frantel Los Santos** (tel. 99-50-40), a resort operated by this popular hotel chain at the foot of Fort Napoléon. It's the newest and biggest hotel on the island, at least as of this writing. You don't get luxury here, but the rooms are comfortable and well maintained, 54 in all, each with private shower. Accommodations are in bungalows, about half of which are air-conditioned (these are naturally grabbed up first). You can also get a unit with kitchenette, as 16 are equipped with them. Try for an accommodation with a balcony overlooking the sea. *In summer, many guests stay here on the MAP, paying 480F ($72) in a single, 730F ($109.50) in a double. You can also stay here on the continental plan in summer for 360F ($54) in a single, 470F ($70.50) in a double.* However, in winter, this same continental plan is 645F ($96.75) a day in a single, 850F ($127.50) in a double. The hotel has a good restaurant and the most complete resort amenities of any establishment on the island. It also attracts those interested in water sports and underwater photography à la Cousteau.

Hôtel La Saintoise, Terre-de-Haut (tel. 99-52-50), is a modern, two-story building across from the principal plaza, with its almond trees and widespread poinciana. As in a small French village, the inn places tables and chairs on the sidewalk, where you can sit out and observe what action there is. The owner will welcome you, showing you through his uncluttered lobby to one of his modest bedrooms, of which he has only ten, each outfitted with a tile bath. Eight are air-conditioned. They are on the second floor, and the furnishings are admittedly modest. Everything is kept immaculately clean. In winter or summer, the single MAP rate is 350F ($52.50), going up to 460F ($69) in a double. If you're over just for the day, you'll find the hotel perched at water's edge, near where the boat from Trois Rivières on Basse Terre comes in. You can make arrangements to have lunch here, costing from 65F ($9.75) per person, plus 10% service. The restaurant at La Saintoise serves a Créole cuisine on an open-air terrace at the water's edge.

Bois Joli, Terre-de-Haut (tel. 99-50-38), lies in the western part of the islands, overlooking a fine beach. In confectionery white, the stucco block sits on a palm-studded rise of a slope, the home of Monsieur and Madame Philippe Blandin. Accommodations are spread between the main house and in some cottages on the hillside. Bold patterned fabrics are used on the beds, and the rooms are furnished in basic modern. About half the units are air-conditioned, with various combinations of shower bath arrangements. The inn offers 21 rooms in all. *In summer, the single MAP rate in a bathless single is 316F ($47.50), going up to 418F ($62.75) in a unit with bath. Likewise, doubles on the MAP cost from 412F ($61.75) to 526F ($79).* In winter, the single MAP rate ranges from 435F ($78.25) to 495F ($89), and doubles cost 550F ($82.50) to 610F ($91.50). Dinner is another 110F ($16.50) per person, but tax, service, and a continental breakfast are included in the rates quoted. Her food is good Créole-style cooking. Mr. Blandin can arrange for waterskiing, sailing, boat trips to some of the islets or rocks that form Les Saintes, and snorkeling. The place is for those who like their Caribbean holidays remote.

Jeanne d'Arc, Fond du Curé (tel. 99-50-41), lies on a beach in a village, less than a mile from the airport. This ten-room, two-story concrete building lies at the edge of the water. Units are modest in style, but they compensate with private showers (likely to be cold) and views of the water. English is spoken, and pedalboats and windsurfing on the beach can be arranged. Two persons can stay here at a half-board bargain rate of about $40 per person daily, a remarkable bargain for the Caribbean. Fresh fish and other seafood and Créole dishes are served on the simple seaside terrace restaurant.

Kanaoa, Terre-de-Haut (tel. 99-51-36), is a modern structure, utterly plain, that was erected on a little beach at Pointe Coquelet. Théo Giorgi owns this 14-room inn, including five units with views of the sea and Anse Mire Cove. All accommodations contain private showers, and a limited amount of English is spoken. The location is 1¼ miles from the airport, or about five minutes on foot from town. If the furnishings are spartan, so is the tariff: two persons can take one of the doubles at a cost of about $40 nightly. A good Créole meal for 75F ($11.25) is served in the open-air restaurant at the water's edge.

Where to Eat

Many French-speaking guests used to come to Terre-de-Haut to eat roast iguana, the giant, ferocious, but harmless lizard found on many of these islands. It was quite a tasty treat, somewhat like chicken. But now that the species is endangered, it is no longer recommended that this dish be consumed. Instead, you'll find lots of conch (called lambi), Caribbean lobster, and fresh fish. Prices are surprisingly reasonable, among the least expensive meals of any place in France. For your dessert, you can sample the savory island specialty, *tourment d'amour* (agony of love), a coconut pastry available in the restaurants but best sampled from the barefoot children who sell the delicacy near the boat dock. The restaurants below serve meals from noon to 2 p.m. and 7 to 9 p.m. (sometimes later, depending on business).

La Redonde (tel. 99-51-10) is one of the best places to go for a Créole-style paella. The owner of the establishment, "Chicken" Georges, calls his popular dish, "La Redonde," named after the restaurant. It's made with the best of the local catch every day, including conch, clams, and crayfish. Only two persons can order it, paying 145F ($26.75) for the privilege. Grilled crayfish is the other most popular dish. Service is informal and friendly. The restaurant serves daily except Friday.

Les Amandiers, Place de la Mairie (tel. 99-50-06), is perhaps the most traditional bistro setting of any restaurant at Terre-de-Haut. You can order a set menu for only 60F ($9). Conch (called lambi here) is prepared to perfection whether in a fricassée or a colombo, a savory, spicy stew. The cook knows how to prepare an excellent court-bouillon of fish, and you can always count on grilled crayfish, a staple of the island. The catch of the day is also grilled the way you like it (rarely allowed to dry out on the grill). In addition to fish stews, banana stew (yes, that's right) and christophine (chayote, to many readers) stew are also served. A knowledge of French would be helpful around here. It's open daily.

Chez Jeannine (tel. 99-53-37), in Terre-de-Haut, has one of the most ambitious menus on the island. For example, often you have a choice of nearly a dozen appetizers, ranging from avocado stuffed with crabmeat to a gâteau de poissons (literally "fish cake"). The main courses are often adventurous, including goat stew. Crayfish and grilled fish (the ubiquitous catch of the day) appear daily on the menu. Local vegetables are used. Therefore you're likely to see papaya au gratin on the listings, perhaps a purée of pumpkin that's eaten like squash. Expect to pay around 60F ($9) for a meal. The ambience is that of a Créole bistro—in other words, a hut with nautical trappings and bright tablecloths. It is open daily.

MARIE-GALANTE: The island, an offshore dependency of Guadeloupe, is an almost-perfect circle of about 60 square miles. Possessing much rustic charm, it lies 20 miles to the south of Guadeloupe's Grand Terre.

Columbus noticed it before he did Guadeloupe, discovering it on November 3, 1493. He named it for his own vessel, but didn't land there. In fact for the next 150 years no European set foot on its shoreline.

The first French governor of the island was Constant d'Aubigne, father of the Marquise de Maintenon. Several captains from the West Indies Company attempted settlement, but none of them succeeded. In 1674 Marie-Galante was given to the Crown, and from that point on its history was closely linked to that of Guadeloupe.

However, since 1816 the island settled down to a quiet slumber. You could hear the sugarcane growing on the plantations, and that was about it. Many windmills have been built to crush the cane, and lots of tropical fruits are grown here.

Now, some 30,000 inhabitants live here, making their living from sugar and rum, the latter said to be the best in the Caribbean. The island's climate is rather dry, and there are many good beaches. One of these stretches of sand covers at least five miles —brilliantly white, a real paradise. Swimming can be dangerous in some places. The best beach is at Petite Anse, 6½ miles from Grand-Bourg.

Air Guadeloupe will bring you to the island in just 20 minutes from Pointe-à-Pitre.

Les Basse airport on Marie-Galante lies about two miles from **Grand-Bourg,** the main town with an 1845 baroque church. The 18th-century Grand Anse rum distillery can be visited, as can the historic fishing hamlet of Vieux Fort. The island is almost exclusively French speaking.

You can also go over by boat, as there is daily service on *Le Madras,* connecting Grand-Bourg to Pointe-à-Pitre. The round-trip fare is 120F ($18). Call 83-12-45 for departure times.

A limited number of taxis are available at the airport, and prices are to be negotiated.

Food and Lodging

There are only a few little accommodations on the island, which, even if they aren't very up-to-date in amenities, are clean and hearty. At least the greetings are friendly. They may also be bewildering if you speak no French.

I prefer the **Auberge de Soledad** (tel. 97-92-24), which lies about two miles from the airport on the outskirts of Grand-Bourg. In a setting of sugarcane fields, it rents out 20 simply furnished, air-conditioned rooms, each with private shower. Rooms are also equipped with refrigerators and TV sets (the latter of little use to most English guests). The hotel also rents bicycles and small motorcycles to guests. On the grounds are tennis courts and a woman's hairdressing salon. Mme Emma Avril prefers her guests to stay at least a week, but if you're rushed, she'll probably charge by the day. Either single or double occupancy will cost from 200F ($30) to 250F ($37.50) daily. Meals are extra in her Créole restaurant.

LA DÉSIRADE: The ubiquious Columbus spotted this terre désirée or "sought-after land" after his Atlantic crossing in 1493. Named La Désirade, the island, which is less than seven miles long and more than 1½ miles wide, lies just five miles off the eastern tip of Guadeloupe. This former leper colony is often visited on a day's excursion (Club Med types like it a lot).

The island has fewer than 2,000 inhabitants, including the descendants of Europeans exiled here by royal command. Tourism has hardly touched the place, if you can forget about those "day trippers," and there are almost no facilities for overnighting, with an exception or two.

The main hamlet is **Grande Anse,** which has a lovely small church with a presbytery and flower garden, and the homes of the local inhabitants. Le Souffleur is a village where boats are constructed; and at Baie Mahault are the ruins of an old leper colony from the early 18th century.

From Pointe-à-Pitre, Air Guadeloupe flies to Désirade three times daily on a 20-minute flight. The airstrip on Désirade accommodates up to 19-seat aircraft. Should you ever go by sea, the crossing is likely to be rough. A ferry leaves from La Darse in Pointe-à-Pitre, the crossing taking 1½ hours and costing 120F ($18) for a round-trip ticket. Telephone 83-12-45 for departure times.

On Désirade, three minibuses run between the airport and the towns. To get around, you might negotiate with a local driver. Bicycles are also available.

The best beaches are Souffleur, a peaceful and tranquil oasis near the boat-building hamlet, and Baie Mahault, a small beach that is a Caribbean cliché with white sand and palm trees.

For food and lodging, go to **La Guitoune,** near the sea in Grande Anse (tel. 20-01-22), where Mme Jeanville will welcome you to her native-style hotel. She rents out five modest rooms with private cold-water showers (toilets in the hallway) for around $25 per night. Her local restaurant is good, serving Créole meals for about 75F ($11.25), with the emphasis on fresh fish. It is 7½ miles from the airport and is exceptionally basic, but it's all that's available here.

3. St. Martin

Partitioned between the Netherlands and France, the divided island of St. Martin (Sint or St. Maarten in Dutch) has a split personality. The 37-square-mile island is shaped like a lazy triangle. The northern part of the island, a land area of about 21 square miles, belong to France, the southern part to the Netherlands.

The island has two jurisdictions, but there is complete freedom of movement between the two sectors. If you arrive on the Dutch side and clear Customs there, you need not worry anymore with red-tape formalities when crossing over to the French side—either for shopping, perhaps a hotel, and certainly for eating, as it has the best food (with some notable exceptions).

French St. Martin is governed from Guadeloupe and has direct representation in the government in Paris. Lying between Guadeloupe and Puerto Rico, the tiny island has been half French, half Dutch since 1648.

The principal town on the French side is **Marigot,** the seat of the subperfect and municipal council. Visitors come here not only for shopping, as the island is a free port, but also to enjoy the excellent cookery in the Créole bistros.

Marigot is not quite the same size as its counterpart, Philipsburg, in the Dutch sector. It has none of the frenzied pace of Philipsburg, which is often overrun with cruise-ship passengers. In fact, Marigot looks like a tiny French village transplanted to the West Indies. The policeman on the beat is a gendarme. If you climb the hill over this tiny port, you'll be rewarded with a view from the old fort there.

About 20 minutes by car beyond Marigot takes you to **Grand Case**, a small fishing village, an outpost of French civilization that has some very good local Créole restaurants and a few places to stay.

St. Martin hardly has the attractions of St. Thomas, Puerto Rico, Jamaica, or whatever. You may ask, "Why come here?" There are no dazzling sights, no spectacular nightlife. Even the sports program on St. Martin isn't as organized as it is on most Caribbean islands, although the Dutch side has golf and other diversions.

Most people come to St. Martin just to relax. They can do that on the island's many fine beaches. In spite of its many drawbacks, the island has become such a popular tourist destination in the past few years that it's practically impossible to get a room in winter without reserving in advance.

Not just the beaches, but the hospitality of St. Martin is important too. This is a friendly island whose local population welcomes visitors. Some 70% of the residents work in the tourist business. In spite of its lack of great scenic beauty, the island has been called "civilized."

Its major "archeological site" is actually of recent vintage. It's the ruins of La Belle Créole at Pointe du Bluff. This was the resort that never was. A multi-million-dollar dream, it was conceived by Claude Philippe, the erstwhile maître d' at the Waldorf in New York. But sieges of bankruptcy and legal tangles left a group of half-finished Mediterranean-style units unoccupied. It's a grandiose ghost town slowly being eaten away by the natural elements of the Caribbean.

GETTING THERE: Chances are, you will set down on the Dutch side (St. Maarten)

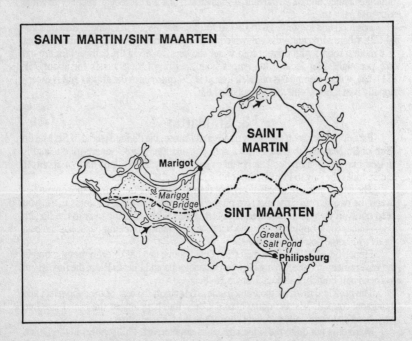

at the Queen Juliana Airport. For a more detailed description of transportation to the island, refer to the "Getting There" section of St. Maarten in Chapter X.

To sum up, however, **American Airlines** serves St. Maarten from New York and Dallas/Fort Worth. **Pan American** flies in from New York, and **Eastern** earns its wings from Miami.

Air Guadeloupe also flies in daily to and from Guadeloupe, and **LIAT, Windward Islands Airways** (Winair), and **Air Martinique** have regularly scheduled inter-island service. All these airlines use the Juliana International Airport on the Dutch side, where there is a $5 airport departure tax.

For its daily ten-minute flights to St. Barts (coming up), Air Guadeloupe uses the Espérance Airport, a small domestic airport near Grand Case on the French side.

PRACTICAL FACTS: English is widely spoken in St. Martin, although it is a French possession. A patois is spoken only by a small segment of the local populace.

The **currency,** officially at least, is the French franc, yet U.S. dollars seem to be preferred wherever you go and are favored over francs. Canadians should convert their money into U.S. dollars and not into francs.

French St. Martin is linked to the Guadeloupe **telephone system,** which can place calls to and from the U.S. To call Dutch St. Maarten from the French side, dial 93 plus the four digits of the St. Maarten number. To call from the Dutch side to the French side, dial 06, then the six-digit French number.

Most arrivals are at the Dutch-controlled **Juliana International Airport;** however, French St. Martin has **Espérance Airport** at Grand Case (tel. 87-51-21), where Air Guadeloupe flies in. The departure tax of 10F ($1.50) at Espérance Airport is now included in the published fare.

U.S. and Canadian citizens should have either a passport, voter registration card, or a birth certificate, plus an ongoing or a return ticket.

The island is on **Atlantic Standard Time,** which means that the only time the U.S. East Coast and St. Martin are in step is during the Daylight Saving Time of summer.

Banks generally are open from 8:30 a.m. to 1 p.m. Monday to Thursday. On Friday they're open during the day but also from 4 to 5 p.m.

The **electric current** is 220 volts, 50 cycles, which of course will necessitate a converter or adapter if you plan to use your appliances such as a hair dryer.

The **water** is safe to drink, and most hotels serve desalinated water. That same hotel is likely to add a 10% to 15% **service charge** to your bill to cover tipping. Likewise, most restaurants include the service charge on your bill.

GETTING AROUND: For visitors, the most common means of transport is the taxi. A **Taxi Service & Information Center** operates at the port of Marigot (tel. 87-56-54), headed by Raymond Helligar. Always agree on the rate before getting into an unmetered cab. Here are some sample fares, subject to change: for one or two persons in a taxi from the center of Marigot to Espérance Airport or the Grand Case Beach Club, $7; to La Samanna Hotel, $8; and to Orient Bay or Le Galion Beach, $12. These fares are in effect from 7 a.m. to 9 p.m. After that, they go up by 25% until midnight, rising by 50% after midnight.

You can also book 2½-hour sightseeing trips around the island, either through the organization listed above or at any hotel desk. The cost is $25 for one or two passengers, plus $10 for each additional guest.

It's much cheaper to go by one of the island's **buses,** running from 6 a.m. until midnight. For example, one departs from Grand Case to Marigot every 20 minutes. There's a departure every hour from Marigot to the Dutch side. The one-way fare from Marigot to Philipsburg on the Dutch side is only 85¢, increasing to $1.50 from Grand Case.

Several **car-rental companies** operate on the island, but vehicles can't be picked up at the Dutch Juliana Airport and have to be delivered free to your hotel. Chances are, you'll make your car-rental arrangements at Juliana Airport before going over to your hotel by taxi on the French side. If so, you may want to refer to the transportation section for St. Maarten in Chapter X. **Budget, Avis, Hertz**—all the big names—are represented in the Dutch side.

Most hotels will reserve a car for guests in advance, and this is highly recommended in winter, when there is often a shortage of rental cars. Most companies insist that drivers be at least 23 to 25 years old. All foreign driver's licenses are honored. One tank of gas should last a week.

There is a **hospital** in Marigot (tel. 87-50-07), and hotels will help visitors in contacting English-speaking doctors.

The **tourist board,** called Syndicat d' Initiative, is at Mairie de Saint-Martin at Marigot (tel. 87-50-04).

WHERE TO STAY: Most of the hotels are on the Dutch side. The French side seems to specialize in efficiency apartments with kitchenettes, and the hotels that do exist are more continental in flavor than some of the beachside hostelries bordering the sands outside of Philipsburg in St. Maarten.

At a few of the St. Martin inns, guests are likely to be French speaking—so be duly warned if you fear a language problem.

The Luxury Leaders

La Samanna, Baie Longue (tel. 87-51-22), admits it's "not for everyone." However, if you're Mick Jagger, or just a person devoted to good, whole-hearted, unabashed sybaritism—and have lots of money—you should fit in beautifully here. Set on a landscaped 55-acre piece of choice property, the confectionery La Samanna opens onto a mile and a half of white sandy beach, filled with some of the best-stuffed bikinis you're likely to see this side of St. Tropez. In fact, the resort, like so many places in St. Martin, is more evocative of the Côte d'Azur or Morocco than the Caribbean.

The place is what the French call *intime, tranquille, et informal.* Yes, *informal,* like *le weekend,* is creeping in to bastardize the French language. Around the blue-green waters of the Moorish-style pool you are likely to see some chic guests.

The hotel is a curious mélange of styles. At one minute you'll think you're in Fez, yet another look convinces you you're in a setting typical of Arizona (even Beverly Hills), and still another glance makes you think you've stopped off at a hotel somewhere in the Aegean Sea. Arches and balconies in pure "Greek fishing village white" are set off effectively by the use of stunning royal-blue doors and umbrellas. Splashes of bold fabrics are used on the puffy cushions on the Haitian furniture which is mostly in wicker and rattan. The colors are like a flamboyant flower garden. The choice of rooms is complicated. In the main building you'll find more than a dozen twin-bedded rooms. These have balconies and are screened from the terrace by a thatched ramada roof. Otherwise, you can ask for one of the two dozen one-bedroom apartments, one of the 16 two-bedroom units, or one of the six villas with three bedrooms each—each with fully equipped kitchens, living rooms, dining areas, and large patios. People often speak in awe of the rates charged here. On the EP in winter, La Samanna charges $400 to $520 daily, either single or double occupancy, and $840 to $1,200 daily in one of the two- or three-bedroom villas. *Two persons can stay here in summer in a twin-bedroom unit, paying from $280 to $380 daily or from $560 daily in a two-bedroom villa.* The hotel is closed in October.

Before dinner, enjoy an apéritif in the bar, where an Indian wedding robe serves as the colorful ceiling. Dining is al fresco with a French and Créole cuisine prepared by some of the best chefs on the island. You eat out on a candlelit terrace overlooking Baie Longue. After dinner, the bar becomes a disco. Down below at the beach, snorkeling, waterskiing, sailing, and island exploring can be arranged. Scuba-diving and other sports are always available, as is tennis.

Happy Bay Hotel, Baie Heureuse (tel. 87-55-20), is a 60-unit complex set on a luxuriantly verdant 35-acre tract of land along the beach. The owners did everything they could to seclude each villa as thoroughly as possible from its neighbors. Each of the handsome accommodations is constructed on the side of the hill, offering views down to the waters off the white sand beach. Efforts have been made to establish this as one of the most exclusive properties on St. Martin. Each cottage contains an all-marble private bath, color TV, phone, and a terrace facing the tropical garden. In winter, the cost is $400 daily in a single, $480 in a double, with a full American breakfast included. *Summer rates are about 20% lower.* Water sports can be arranged, as well as the rental of yachts, aircraft, or cars. Secretarial or translation services are also available on request. Guests have use of a private beach with deck chairs and chaises longues, two tennis courts, an oval freshwater pool, and an excellent restaurant.

L'Habitation, P.O. Box 230, Marcel Cove (tel. 87-59-28, 212/757-0225 in New York City, or toll free 800/847-4249). Owned and developed by a consortium of French insurance companies, this is ambitious real estate. Its isolated location was considered almost inaccessible until a crew of engineers cut a two-mile road through some of the most rugged terrain on the island. It stands on a flat and sandy patch of palm-dotted land between a saltwater pond and the beach, about 11 miles from Marigot. You park near the security-conscious entrance, then take a shuttle bus to the soaring reception area. This might be the single most appealing room at the resort. Flooded with sunlight which glistens off a sheathing pink-and-white marble, it combines design elements from Pharaonic Egypt, the era of art deco, and the colonial tropics.

Accommodations are contained beneath the cedar-covered roofs of the deliberately overscale neo-Victorian buildings ringed with lattices, elaborate gingerbread, and shaded verandas. Each of the more than 250 accommodations has its own kitchenette, soundproofing, air conditioning, balcony, two-sink bathroom, phone, radio, color TV, internal video system, and stylish decor of tropical furniture. In winter, singles cost $230 to $250 daily; doubles, $250 to $280. *In summer, singles rent for $135 daily; doubles, $160.* On the premises is a swimming pool whose twin circles appear like the interconnected petals of an expanding lotus. Near it, a pool bar resembles a tile-sheathed gazebo on stilts at the edge of the water. A full gym and bodybuilding club, a disco, a quartet of restaurants, six tennis courts, a pair of squash courts, archery facilities, and more than a dozen boutiques offer many distractions.

First Class

Le Grand St. Martin, P.O. 99, Marigot (tel. 87-57-91). In 1983 the developers of this comfortable property transformed an already-existing hotel into a tastefully splashy oasis of style and calm. To reach it, you have to negotiate a confusing labyrinth of back streets at the edge of town. Sunk into flat but lush acreage, the hotel has a rectangular pool, considered large by St. Martin's standards, a wrap-around terracotta terrace, and access to a wide sandy beach. The 46 bedrooms are contained in a duet of elongated hip-roofed buildings whose verandas are accented with fretwork. Each accommodation contains air conditioning, a kitchenette, a veranda or balcony, cable color TV, a private bathroom, and tropical furniture. In winter, singles or doubles range from $220. *In summer, a single or double pays from $120.* The in-house restaurants are large, spacious, and appealing, especially the Château Charron, whose tile floor, massive mahogany armchairs, and colorful napery are appropriate foils for the open-air view of the nearby sea.

Grand Case Beach Club (tel. 87-51-87) is a beachfront condominium hotel, run by the Acciani family from New York City and lying within walking distance of Grand

Case. The two-story buildings are elongated, and most units open onto ocean-view terraces. You have a choice of several studios, one-bedroom apartments, and two-bedroom town houses and duplexes. Each apartment contains a fully equipped kitchen and a private bathroom. Units are airy, with tile floors, air conditioning, rattan furnishings, and daily maid service. Accommodations, from studios to two-bedroom duplexes, *range off-season from $87 to $162 for one or two persons daily, all inclusive*. In winter, the rates go from $170 to $285 for two persons, similarly inclusive. Gratuities are optional. There are two beaches and water-sports facilities including scuba-diving, snorkeling, and a 40-foot catamaran, plus the first artificial grass tennis court in the Caribbean. The Waves Restaurant (see "Where to Dine," below), an architectural gem, extends out on a bluff overlooking Grand Case. The ambience at the hotel is informal. This is the type of place where you make friends with other guests and plan to see them the "same time next year."

The Moderate Range

La Résidence, Avenue du Général-de-Gaulle (tel. 87-70-37), in the commercial center of town, has a concrete façade enlivened with a neo-Victorian fretwork of gingerbread. Each of the rooms is arranged around a landscaped central courtyard, where a fish-shaped fountain splashes water into a bowl. A bar with a soaring tent, inspired by a Napoleonic campaign, serves drinks to clients relaxing on wicker and bentwood furniture. Each of the 22 bedrooms is air-conditioned, containing a minimalist decor, a TV, a mini-bar, and phone. All but a few have sleeping lofts and a duplex design of mahogany-trimmed stairs and balustrades. In winter, singles cost 550F ($82.50) to 900F ($135); doubles, 700F ($105) to 1,000F ($150). Breakfast is included. An extra bed can be set up in any unit for another 225F ($33.75) per person. *Expect prices of about 30% less in summer*.

Le Royale Louisiana, Avenue du Général-de-Gaulle (tel. 90-81-49, or toll free 800/982-1255). One of the newest hotels on the French side of the island, this 75-room hotel occupies a prominent position in the center of Marigot. It's designed in a hip-roofed French-colonial style whose rambling balconies are graced with geometrically ornate balustrades. Each accommodation contains air conditioning, TV hookup, bathroom, big sunny windows, a phone, and modern furniture. Suitable for those who like to be in the center of the action, the hotel has a pair of restaurants and a cozy bar. It charges winter rates of $85 daily in a single, $105 in a double, and $155 in a duplex. *In summer, tariffs are reduced by 30%*.

Best for the Budget

Palm Plaza Hotel, rue de la République (tel. 87-51-96), occupies a two-tone pink building whose gabled façade has cross-hatched balustrades and big ground-floor arches. In the center of town, its 21 balconies are outfitted in a modern design of pink tones, sharp angles, and comfortable lines. Each is air-conditioned, and three contain kitchenettes. In winter, singles cost $70 daily; doubles, $80; and a suite for two, $110. *In summer, singles go for $40 daily; doubles, $50; and a suite for two, $72.* A few of the units overlook the partially ruined fort of Marigot. Built in the early 1970s, the hotel has a particularly attractive feature in its center. A palm-shaded courtyard offers a cool tropical bar with a raffishly colonial aura.

Chez Martine, Grand Case (tel. 87-51-59), offers relaxed informality in a small white villa on a sand beach. Rooms downstairs with twin beds rent for $75 in the high season and upstairs with a double bed and terrace for $100 to $150 a day, both with a continental breakfast included. *Off-season, the rates are lowered to $55 downstairs and $70 to $100 upstairs, including a continental breakfast*. This modern two-story building contains only eight rooms at the water's edge. All units are air-conditioned with a private shower, tile floor, and hammock. There's an extra charge for air conditioning. The place is young and friendly. The hotel also offers an excellent open-air French restaurant overlooking the beach, serving lunch and dinner daily (see below).

Bertine's, La Savana, Grand Case (tel. 87-58-39). A description of this place appears in the dining section of Grand Case. In addition to its dining facilities, it offers a quintet of comfortable but simple accommodations whose ambience is a lot like that of a lighthearted private home. Guests are given the use of a residents' lounge filled with wall-mounted fans and louvered windows. The location is isolated, the rooms not glamorous, and you'll need a car to get to the beach, but some guests return year after year. Rooms, single or double occupancy, rent for $60 daily in high season, *dropping to only $35 for two in summer*. An apartment is available for $20 additional per day. The little hotel is closed in October.

WHERE TO DINE: The classic French haute cuisine, with a big touch of the West Indies, is waiting to greet your taste buds. St. Martin has some of the finest food in the Caribbean.

Baie Longue

Even though you may not be staying at **La Samanna,** you might want to make a reservation to enjoy a meal on the resort's dining terrace. Sitting a few feet above the white sands of the glistening beach, it contains dining alcoves where the only sound may be the discreet tinkling of crystal and china and the lapping of the waves. Your fellow diners come here for the well-prepared specialties of the Lyon-born chef. Critics of this cuisine, created by Jean-Pierre Jury and his assistant, Bernard Malanesset, have declared it among the best in the Caribbean. The high prices reflect its image. Your meal could include à la carte specialties such as roast pigeon with puréed green cabbage, red snapper with mint and lemon preserves, fresh foie gras of duckling, lobster with sweetbreads, curry, and squash, and desserts such as pear soufflé. Full dinners, served from 7 to 9:30 p.m., cost from $40 per person. Lunches, where a theatrically prepared steak tartare is a favorite, are less expensive. Reservations are almost essential at any time. Call 87-51-22.

In and Around Marigot

Le Nadaillac, Galerie Périgourdine, rue d'Anguille (tel. 87-53-77). On the waterfront side of this gallery, a little terrace restaurant is like a transplanted pocket of France in the Caribbean. The chef-owner, Fernand Malard, a native of the Périgord region of France (which is famous for its truffles and foie gras), operates a splendid but expensive restaurant, with meals costing from $35. His skilled touch is seen in such dishes as giblet salad (it appears as salade de gésiers aux lardons) and in his preserved goose, or confit d'oie. Portions of goose are cooked in goose fat and preserved in stoneware pots. He gets many of his products from France, but also has imaginative touches with what emerges from local waters, such as red snapper. The service is polite and often quite stylish. Dinner is served nightly (it's best to go between 7 and 9 p.m.) except Sunday, and reservations are recommended. In high season, the restaurant is open for lunch as well, serving from noon to 2:30 p.m. A recently sampled 110F ($16.50) meal included a choice of omelets, soups (both hot and cold), and four different fresh salads, along with daily specials such as duck with small turnips.

La Calanque, Boulevard de France, along the Baie de Marigot (tel. 87-50-82), has a devoted clientele, some of whom acclaim it as the finest French restaurant on the island. Dispensing the haute cuisine with West Indian overtones, this bistro primarily features the cookery of Provence, with nouvelle cuisine variations. Calanque is "Mediterranean French" for "the bay." The decor is Marseille style, and specialties include snails in the style of Bourgogne and a tasty onion soup, followed by frogs' legs provençale. My recent meal, and a splendid one it was, included crêpes stuffed with tender lobster, plus duck in an imaginative banana sauce. For dessert, ask for "the crazy pineapple." However, expect to pay for what you get. A special luncheon menu, at $35, is served from noon to 2 p.m. daily. Dinner, costing from $45, is offered from 7 p.m.

L'Aventure (tel. 87-53-58) is in a high-ceilinged building which was once a movie theater on the harbor. The owners have covered the ceiling with palm fronds to give the interior a tropical note to complement the mainland France touches. There's an airy bar area, accented with blue and white tiles and cooled with ceiling fans. The real soul of the restaurant, however, is on the narrow second-floor veranda overlooking the market and the yachts in the harbor. About 70% of the establishment's tables are there.

The house salad is made of avocado, shrimp, artichoke hearts, and marinated salmon. A fish terrine is filled with pieces of salmon and yellowtail. Shellfish lovers might order the lobster rolls in cabbage leaves, served with a fricassée of sweet red peppers. Other specialties include cream of crayfish soup, filet of sole on a bed of snowpeas baked in puff pastry with truffles, scallop mousse with whole scallops and dill, a pasta lobster turnover in a creamy zucchini sauce, scallops in lime sauce served on a bed of frayed endive, and poached filet of yellowtail with a broccoli mousse. To top it off, your dessert could include a fruit or tea-flavored sherbet, iced pear soufflé with passionfruit sauce, or warm chocolate puff pastry with cold cacáo sauce. Lunch, costing from $40, is served from noon to 2 p.m., and dinner from $50, is presented from 6 to 10 p.m. The restaurant is open seven days a week.

Mini Club, rue de la Liberté, Marigot (tel. 87-50-69). After parking, you'll pass behind the building, climb a gently sloped flight of wooden stairs, and find yourself in an environment once described as a treehouse built among coconut palms. Suspended on a wooden deck above the sands of the beach, this establishment is filled with such accessories as Haitian-style murals, grass carpeting, and immaculate napery. You might begin your meal with a glass of kir royale, made with a healthy dose of champagne. The French and Créole specialties include lobster soufflé (made for two or four persons), an array of fish and vegetable terrines, stuffed land crab, conch stew, several kinds of poached or broiled fish, including red snapper with Créole sauce, sweetbreads in puff pastry, and many kinds of salad, including one with fresh hearts of palm. Dessert might consist of bananas flambéed with cognac. Dinner is served nightly, while lunch is offered every day except Sunday. The owners of the Mini are Claude and Pierre du Plessis, who hold lavish buffets every Wednesday and Saturday night, with unlimited wine included, for $35 per person. À la carte lunches cost around $12, while dinners go for $22 on the fixed-price offering. An à la carte dinner costs from $45. Lunch hours are noon to 3 p.m.; dinner, from 7 to 11 p.m.

La Vie en Rose, Boulevard France (tel. 87-54-42), is a balconied second-floor restaurant whose cozy dining room, with ceiling fans and candlelight, evokes for many observers the nostalgia of the 1920s. If you don't like the parlor, you can gravitate to one of the tables on a little veranda overlooking the harbor, providing you requested one when you made a reservation. A French gourmet rendezvous, the restaurant offers dinner costing from $45 per person. Red snapper is bedded in a spinach mousse. The soupe de poisson is served with a rouille sauce and garlicky croûtons. In the nouvelle cuisine tradition, the duck breast is served rare on a bed of spinach and mushrooms. Try also lobster casserole and sautéed scallops with an orange sauce. The desserts are some of the best made on the island. La Vie en Rose serves lunch (from noon to 2:30 p.m.) and dinner (from 7 to 9:30 p.m.) seven days a week in high season, but is closed on Sunday in the off-season.

Le Boucanier, rue de la Liberté (tel. 87-59-83), is a terraced seaside restaurant reached through an alleyway just opposite the post office. The owner is Michael Newman, whose tropical courtyard establishment features innovative French dishes prepared by original Caribbean methods of smoking, roasting, and grilling. The finest products of meats and game are brought in from France and cooked over aromatic vines and fruit- and nutwood. Great emphasis is given to fresh seafood from nearby waters and prize varieties flown in from Europe. This is one of the best restaurants in town and has been enjoyed by island residents and visitors since its opening more than a decade ago. Specialty island drinks are available all day in lush tropical surroundings. Open from 10 a.m. to midnight, it serves lunches for $10 up and dinners costing from $25.

La Maison sur le Port (tel. 87-56-38) attracts many guests at sundown to watch the yachts bobbing in the harbor and the building's aubergine-colored trim as they catch the fiery rays of the setting sun. Lunch is a refreshing indoor/outdoor experience, where you are seated at tables placed between crisscross balustrades of the covered terrace. Christian Verdeau and his attractive staff also welcome people to dinner in a relaxing and refined atmosphere and elegant surroundings, with a view of the harbor and a waterfall in the garden, with spotlights showing the flowers and plants around the restaurant. The tables are handsomely dressed with snowy tablecloths and Limoges china.

For lunch, which is more simple than dinner, you can choose from a number of salads as well as fish and meat courses. The cost is around $20. A fixed-price dinner menu, costing $37, gives a choice of an appetizer, a main dish, and a dessert. Among the menu choices, you may be offered fresh fish such as snapper, salmon, or lobster; homemade pâté foie gras; and filet of lamb, veal, or steak, each with a light sauce. Duck has always been a specialty of La Maison. You can order from a wine list with an extensive selection of imported French products at moderate prices or you may want to try the house cocktail, made with blanc de blanc wine, fresh orange juice, Grand Marnier, and a splash of lemon juice. The establishment is open for lunch from 11:40 a.m. to 3 p.m. and for dinner from 6 to 10:30 p.m. Reservations are necessary.

Davids, rue de la Liberté in Marigot (tel. 87-51-58), is run by two Englishmen, both of whom used to be at sea, hence the attraction for visiting yachting people to its casual expatriate ambience. A red, white, and blue spinnaker hangs from the rafters. Appetizers include everything from conch fritters to potato skins, and good soups are served too, especially fish chowder and baked onion. Fresh dorado is prepared four different ways, and local lobster is done by the chef any way you want it. The specialty of the house is beef Wellington, served with a red wine sauce. Chicken banzai, marinated in Indonesian soy sauce, is a more recent addition, as is the jumbo shrimp kebab with spicy garlic butter. The steaks are prime quality and can be served with dijonnaise or black pepper sauce. Your final bill will probably run from $25 per person. Light lunch is served from 11:30 a.m. to 4 p.m. and dinner from 6 to 10:30 p.m. The bar is open until midnight seven days a week.

Native food? Try **Cas' Anny** (tel. 87-53-38), which used to be known as Chez Lolotte. It's on the rue de la Liberté in Marigot. The chef has shown expertise in turning out a French Antillean cuisine. If you break bread here, you sit in a garden planted with lush foliage. Mme Anne-Marie Boissard came from Martinique to open this restaurant, which serves both lunch and dinner, costing around $25 and up. Here you can order such local dishes as boudin Créole, a Créole blood sausage. When available, turtle steak is featured. You might also try her conch in the style of Provence (it appears on the menu as lambi), and crabe farci or stuffed crab backs. Even if that weren't reason enough to recommend the place, it's possible to ask for more traditional dishes from the French repertoire, such as soupe de poisson. Desserts are also good. It is open daily for lunch and dinner from 11:30 a.m. to 3 p.m. and 6:30 to 11 p.m.

In and Around Grand Case

This beach town, a scant mile-long brush stroke, has probably the greatest concentration of fine dining spots in the Caribbean. On the town's one and only street there are more than 18 restaurants, serving the cuisines of half a dozen cultures.

The **Ritz Café,** Grand Case (tel. 87-81-58). Its humorously irreverent owner, born of French parents in Vietnam, is perhaps the quintessential French colonial and an astute businessman. With his English-born wife, Sonya, Joel Morand established this, his seventh restaurant, amid one of the most stylish decors on the island. Originally built as a private house, it is now encased in a motif of black, gold, and salmon, with tasteful accents of art deco, along with ornate balustrades, a scattering of antiques, and a neo-Grecian arbor facing the sea. A place like this is so sophisticated that it can be all things to many people. It is open daily between 11 a.m. and 11:30 p.m., during which it is a lunch and dinner restaurant, an afternoon tea house, a bar and meeting place, and a late-night piano bar.

The maître d' and part owner, Christopher Terrasse, ushered movie stars into Ma Maison in Los Angeles before coming to St. Martin. The staff wears formal whites during the day and formal blacks at night. Menu items combine French and Créole nouvelle cuisine for full dinners costing from $45 and served nightly between 6:30 and 11:30 p.m. Lunches, from 11:30 a.m. to 2:30 p.m., cost a bit less. A fixed-price Sunday brunch at $30 includes a half bottle of champagne and is offered from 11:30 a.m. to 4:30 p.m. Menu specialties include oysters Rockefeller, a cassoulet of escargots, lobster bisque with Armagnac, dorade (whitefish) cooked in salt for two, salmon marinated in lime juice, a crêpe Ritz (which Mr. Terrasse invented and served several years ago to Henry Kissinger in Washington), and pastries. Reservations are suggested.

La Nacelle, Grand Case (tel. 87-53-63), has an elegant atmosphere with a whimsical pink trim and a selective menu, which was created by Charles Chevillot of New York's celebrated La Petite Ferme. He has handsomely restored a *gendarmerie* built at the turn of the century, across from the pier. Lying about a ten-minute ride from Marigot, La Nacelle is expensive but worth it. At dinner here, your leek bisque, followed by lobster Caribbean style, is served under an almond tree in a beautiful, flower-filled garden. Outside the courtyard, shaded by palm fronds, is a bright mural of a balloonist (a *nacelle* is the basket of a hot-air balloon). You can also dine inside, enjoying the immaculate service and fine napery and tableware. Dinner, from 6:30 to 9 p.m., is likely to cost around $45. A winter-only restaurant, La Nacelle wisely employs masters of the French cuisine. For dessert, try, if featured, a sherbet made with guava. It's necessary to make a reservation.

L'Auberge-Gourmande, Grand Case (tel. 87-55-45), has generated a lot of local excitement, and deservedly so. You have to go to a bit of trouble to dine here, but it's worth it. The chef-owner, Burgundy-born Daniel Passerie, has opened this small, romantic dining room that is like a little country inn, perhaps somewhere in the heartland of France. Both classic French dishes, plus some with a touch of Burgundy, are served in this old Antillean home. Begin with a duck pâté with walnuts. The salads are well made here, using crisp fresh greens, often mixed with bits of ham, cheese, and walnuts. For a main course, the langouste is the most preferred and expensive selection, and the red snapper is equally as good. Filet of beef is served with morels, which are probably flown in from France. You might also try poultry breast with red wine sauce, sweetbreads with mushrooms, frogs' legs with mustard sauce, or scallops and shrimp with a fresh herb sauce. For dessert, try apple crêpe drenched in Calvados. For a complete meal, expect to spend from $30. The restaurant serves dinner six nights a week, closing Wednesday. Hours are 6:30 to 10 p.m. Trade winds cool the place in lieu of air conditioning.

Chez Martine, Grand Case (tel. 87-51-59), was recommended as a good little budget hotel. Diners sit at a well-set table on a gingerbread terrace overlooking the sea. This is a very French Antillean place, and the staff has been well selected, giving friendly, capable service. You get a number of dazzling choices in cuisine. To begin your meal, you're faced with such appetizers as uncooked salmon (marinated in a sauce of fresh herbs), a savory fish soup, garlicky frogs' legs in a fluffy puff pastry case, snails in garlic butter, or foie gras in a jellied turnip concoction. The most tempting part of the menu is that listed under "les poissons." My favorite is a pot-au-feu de la mer, which they translate here as "homemade sea stew." You can also order lobster in a number of ways, as well as scallops on a bed of endive. Duck filet is given a nouvelle cuisine touch with raspberry vinegar, and the lamb chops are flavored with saffron. Meals cost around $30. For dessert, try a French pastry. Lunch at Chez Martine is served daily from noon to 3 p.m.; dinner, from 6:30 to 10 p.m.

Hévéa, Grand Case (tel. 87-56-85), is a small and intimate restaurant, with only ten tables, whose owner is Jacqueline Dalbera. Here, you can enjoy French cookery in pleasant and surprisingly formal surroundings of pink napery, mulberry-colored carpeting, French furniture, and avant-garde paintings. A pianist adds the final touch to a successful dinner, the only meal served (from 7 to 10 p.m.). Full meals, for which reservations are necessary, cost from $40, and might include a millefeuille of crayfish, lobster bisque, beef tenderloin in crayfish sauce, sliced veal stuffed with mushrooms and chive sauce, rack of lamb with tarragon, filet of pork with venison sauce, and a dessert specialty of iced banana soufflé.

L'Escapade (tel. 87-75-04). Many diners from the capital combine a weekend excursion to the beach with a meal at this restored house on the main street of town. Although the village of Grand Case surrounds you here, you'd never know it because of the masses of plants which the owners cultivate in the garden. You dine on the roofed, perhaps moonlit, terrace overlooking Grand Case Bay. Before- and after-dinner drinks can be enjoyed at the inside bar. The menu might include such specialties as watercress soup with lettuce and boned frogs' legs, local lobster with fresh tomato and basil in a cream sauce, fresh salmon filet with sorrel, veal sweetbreads with morels, duck breast with a raspberry vinegar sauce, and tempting desserts (try their strawberry charlotte topped with a raspberry sauce). Full meals cost $35 per person and up. Dinner is served from 6:30 to 9:30 p.m. Closed Sunday.

Rainbow (tel. 87-55-80) is a popular restaurant created through the professional cooperation of Dutch-born Fleur Raad and American-born David Hendrich. Together, they've taken French St. Martin by storm, serving some of the most original and excellent dishes on the island. Since there are only a few tables, reservations are important for the only meal, dinner, served from 7 to 9:30 p.m. Views from the elegantly casual beachside dining room encompass Grand Case Bay. The chef has imagination, cooking a varied menu that changes night after night. Specialties such as mousse of duckling, salmon, or chicken are often served, as are such delicacies as grilled snapper with fennel, medallions of veal in a special sauce, steak au poivre, roast duckling with brandied cherries, several kinds of fresh pasta, and scallop chowder. The restaurant is closed from June to October. The rest of the year, full meals cost from $50 each.

Hoa-Maï, Grand Case (tel. 87-59-69), is a family-run Vietnamese eating place on the lagoon side of the main street of Grand Case. Near the Grand Case Beach Club, Hoa-Maï is a surprising choice for the Caribbean, which is not known for its Vietnamese restaurants. The fare is superb, and spicy. Try, for example, crisp shrimp fritters in a sauce that's not too sweet, not too sour; or beef cooked with vegetables that have been seasoned with herbs (perhaps cardamom). I personally prefer the hot chili sauce a lot, but those without an asbestos palate may order sesame seed or soy sauce. The chicken with peanuts is another favorite. Only dinner is served, and it's likely to cost from $22 per person. Hours are daily except Monday from 6 to 10 p.m.

Mark's Place, Cul de Sac (no phone). To reach this place, you have to traverse a pot-holed and badly maintained road between Orléans and Grand Case. From the outside it appears like a cozy red-and-white cottage flanked with shrubbery. Inside you find a well-scrubbed and well-lit ambience of trestle tables, Haitian metal sculpture, tortoise shells, wide-plank floors crafted from Guyanese cedar, and a high ceiling. This is the isolated domain of Mark van Dam, who left his native Holland to marry his Guadeloupian wife, Ninotte, and establish this comfortably raffish restaurant. Lunch is served from 12:30 to 2:30 p.m., and dinner from 7:30 to 9:30 p.m. daily except Monday. You can enjoy a glass of kir, kir royale, or a pastel-colored but potent drink

called a sternwheeler before your meal. After that, you might try such Créole specialties as stuffed crab, boudin (blood sausage), colombo de cabri (goat stew), accras
(spicy shrimp fritters), conch or octopus stew, grilled lobster, and strawberry Melba.
There's a small list of international specialties, even hamburgers and snacks. The food
is well prepared.

Bertine's, La Savana, Grand Case (tel. 87-58-39), was previously recommended
for its simple accommodations, but it's better known as an unusual and pleasant restaurant. It's contained in an angular concrete building atop a steep hill 1½ miles from
Grand Case. Its two separate sections are joined by a wide veranda whose hardwood
sheathing is kept spotlessly polished by Bernard and Christine Piticha. Born in Chicago, they moved to a warmer climate, took up cooking, and today are known for their
copious portions, good humor, and charm. The restaurant is open nightly (except in
October) at sunset and remains so until the last client is satisfied. Bernie does the cooking, while Christine serves and creates an ambience like a private dinner party. Between courses, guests watch the sunset glimmering over the sea between two hills. Full
dinners, costing from $25, might include fish Créole, scampi New Orleans style,
conch stew, crab au gratin, hickory-smoked pork ribs Chicago style (with Bernie's
special sauce), a house salad of lettuce, red cabbage, carrots, and gouda cheese, and a
homemade chocolate mousse pie. No reservations are necessary, but it's always wise
to call in advance. The location near the farming hamlet of La Savana is at the top of a
steep driveway.

Inland to Colombier

Minutes from Marigot, in the tiny hamlet of Colombier, is one of the best Créole
restaurants on St. Martin, **La Rhumerie** (tel. 87-56-98). Owners Yannick Le Moine
from Brittany and his West Indian wife, Francillette, serve with finesse dishes that
have influenced many residents on the island to declare this their favorite restaurant.
For years, I recommended their Chez Lolotte when they were in business in Marigot.
There, as here, Yannick's experience in the dining rooms of the Lasserre and Ledoyen
in Paris has enabled his island restaurants to become well known. In this country setting, the Le Moines have taken a private home and turned it into a charming Créole
restaurant which also serves traditional French dishes. These include stuffed crab
back, escargots, and onion soup gratinée. Despite their skill at mainland dishes, they
are best known for Créole cuisine, offering such dishes as curried goat, a salad of cof-
fre (a local fish), conch in fresh herbs, and poulet boucanne Créole (home-smoked
chicken served with baked green papayas and christophine au gratin). There are two
servings every day at dinner, one at 7 and another at 9 p.m. Full meals cost $35 and up
per person.

THE SPORTING LIFE: The island as a whole has 32 perfect white sandy beaches.
The hotels, for the most part, have grabbed up the choicest sands, and usually for a fee
of $3 nonguests can use their beach and changing facilities. Topless sunbathing is prac-
ticed commonly at the beaches on the French side. Club Orient Hôtel (see below) has
the only nudist beach on the island, but nude or mono-kini (as opposed to bikini) is
relatively common, even though total nudity is not officially endorsed. **Îlet Pinel,** a
tiny island off St. Martin, is perfect for beach recluses. Le Galion Beach Hôtel (tel.
87-51-77) will take visitors over to Pinel on request. The trip can also be made by
negotiating with a passing fisherman to provide transport back and forth.

Scuba-Diving

Scuba is excellent around St. Martin. The types of diving are reef, wreck, night,
cave, and drift, and the depth of dives is from 40 to 50 feet. Off the northeast coast on
the French side, dive sites include Îlet Pinel for shallow diving, Green Key, a barrier
reef; Flat Island for sheltered coves and geologic faults; and Tintamarre, known for its

shipwreck. To the north, Anse Marcel and neighboring Anguilla are good choices. Wilson McQueen, a certified divemaster, works out of **Grand Case Beach Club** (tel. 87-51-87) and **Le Galion Beach Hôtel** (tel. 87-51-77). Most hotels will arrange for scuba excursions on request.

Snorkeling

The calm waters ringing the shallow reefs and tiny coves found throughout the island make it a snorkeler's heaven. Equipment is readily available at almost any hotel.

At **Grand Case Beach Club** (tel. 87-51-87), a one-hour snorkeling trip costs $10 to $15 per person, depending on the destination.

Tennis

If tennis is your game, Le Galion and Happy Bay have two courts, and PLM St-Tropez has one. La Samanna has three courts (but these are reserved for guests only). Grand Case Beach Club has installed the first artificial grass tennis surface in the Caribbean (lit for night play) called Omnicourt. If you're not a guest of one of these hotels, fees can range from $8 per hour for daytime play, $10 per hour at night. The Habitation has four courts, all of which are lit for night play.

Waterskiing

This activity can be organized at Grand Case Beach Club (in season only), at La Samanna, at Galion, and at PLM St-Tropez. The cost can range from $15 for ten minutes.

Windsurfing

Almost every beachfront hotel has facilities for this sport, and many offer instructions for beginners.

Golf

An 18-hole golf course is at Mullet Bay on the Dutch side. See Chapter X.

Deep-Sea Fishing

A number of good fishing boats are available for charter by the half day, the day, or the week. Charters usually include tackle, bait, food, and drink. The average cost is $300 for a half day, $550 for a full day. Check the activities desk at any hotel for information. The season for dolphin, kingfish, and barracuda is December to April; for tuna, year round.

SHOPPING: Many day-trippers come over to Marigot from the Dutch side just to look at the collection of boutiques from here. Marigot's streets, lined with neat little boutiques and shopping arcades, invite you to walk and browse.

It is a duty-free port, and because of that you'll find some of the best shopping in the Caribbean. There is a wide selection of French goods, including crystal, perfumes, jewelry, and fashions at 25% to 50% less than in the U.S. and Canada. There are also fine liqueurs, cognacs, and cigars. If you're seeking anything from jewelry to perfume to St. Tropez bikinis, you'll find most of the boutiques, often in mellow old buildings, along the rue de la République and rue de la Liberté in Marigot.

Most of the boutiques on the French side are open from 9 a.m. to noon or 12:30 p.m. and from 2 to 6 p.m., Monday to Saturday. When cruise ships are in on Sunday and holidays, some of the larger shops open again.

Prices are often quoted in U.S. dollars, and salespeople frequently speak English. Credit cards and traveler's checks are generally accepted.

Look especially for French luxury items, such as Lalique crystal, Vuitton bags, and Chanel perfume.

At Marigot

At harborside in Marigot, there is a frisky morning market with vendors selling spices, fruit, shells, and local handcrafts.

At **Port La Royale,** the bustling center of everything, mornings are even more alive: schooners unloading produce from the neighboring islands; boats boarding guests for picinics on deserted beaches; a brigantine setting out on a sightseeing sail. And throughout the handsome complex, the owners of a dozen different little dining spots are setting the stage for the daily ritual of a leisurely lunch. This is the *French* Caribbean, so meals are very important.

La Romana, rue de la République (tel. 87-73-69), in the heart of Marigot, occupies a handsome landmark building transformed into a showcase for the French fashion and jewelry designers represented by La Romana International Boutiques. Customers can also enjoy champagne cocktails offered by the shop at the clients-only café on the overhanging balcony, which provides an unobstructed view of the area. The shop is open from 9 a.m. to 6 p.m.

The largest shopping arcade in St. Martin, Port La Royale has many boutiques, some of which come and go with great rapidity. Try **Lipstick** for cosmetics and beauty preparations by such name designers as Dior and Yves St. Laurent (you can also get facial cleaning and massages here). **Havane** (tel. 87-70-39), also in Port La Royale, offers exclusive collections of French clothing, both in sports and high-fashion designs for men and women.

Should the heat of the day get to you, stop in at **Etna Ice Cream Per Dolce Vita,** Kennedy Avenue (tel. 87-72-72), in Port La Royale. Here, Paolo and Betty Smiroldo operate a gelateria-pasticciere, with many homemade ice creams created from fresh fruit, their specialties costing from $1.25 to $3. You get such delights as a tartufo as good as the one served on the Piazza Navona in Rome, as well as spumoni, cassata, espresso, along with French croissants and mouthwatering pastries. A fresh-fruit drink, Frullato, is prepared in front of you so you can see what goes into it. The ''sweet life'' holds forth here from 9 a.m. to midnight in season. In the off-season it's open from 9 a.m. to 7 p.m. daily (on Sunday from noon to 6 p.m.).

If you opt for a housekeeping holiday in St. Martin, know that the best food is at **K'Dis** in Marigot (tel. 87-52-23). This is a French *supermarché* where you can order pâté, elegant mustards (especially from Dijon), fine French cheese and wine, and all sorts of fresh and canned goodies.

At another shopping complex, the **Galerie Périgourdine,** facing the post office, you'll find another cluster of boutiques. Here you might pick up some designer wear for both men and women, including items from the collection of Ted Lapidus. If you're interested in dining here, the Malards own the waterfront terrace restaurant, Le Nadaillac, part of the complex, which has been previously recommended.

Sandrine Boutique, rue de la Liberté (tel. 87-53-77), across from the post office in Galerie Périgourdine, features the latest fashions for men, women, and children, as well as exclusive beachwear. A wide gift selection is also offered.

Maneks, rue de la République (tel. 87-54-91), is worth a stopover, as it has a little bit of everything: hand-carved figurines, tobacco products, liquors, gifts, souvenirs, cameras, radio cassettes, Kodak film, and swimming wear and T-shirts.

Little Switzerland (tel. 87-50-03), also in Marigot, has a better-known branch in Philipsburg on the Dutch side. But the shop here is a fine one too. In fact it's one of the best places in the country if you're seeking European imports at prices lower than Stateside. You get not only name china and crystal, but Swiss precision watches. There is also a large selection of jewelry. The jewelry collection in both the Dutch and French stores is perhaps the biggest in the West Indies. There are many gift items as well, and you can pick up your favorite fragrance.

Spritzer & Fuhrmann (tel. 87-59-62), the famous jewelry chain, has a branch in Marigot on the rue de la République, just off the bay. It offers a wide range of merchandise. Included in its collection are crystal, china, clocks, and a superb array of 14- and 18-karat gold jewelry.

Oro de Sol, whose branch in St. Maarten was already reviewed, also operates out of Marigot (tel. 87-57-02). Here you'll find a wide selection of perfumes, Italian and French linens, Cuban cigars, crystal, china, silver, fine jewelry, and watches (Patek Philippe, Cartier, and Ebel).

Grand Case

Pierre Lapin (tel. 87-52-10) is a *tiny* store selling original T-shirts made from hand-printed fabrics, paintings, books, and gifts. It's well known and *intime*.

Orléans

Local artist **Roland Richardson,** who lives in Orléans, welcomes visitors into his house to view and purchase his original watercolors and prints of island vistas. It's open Monday through Friday from 9:30 a.m. to 1 p.m.

NIGHTLIFE: Some French St. Martin hotels have dinner-dancing, cocktail-lounge music, and even disco dancing, but the most popular after-dark pastime is leisurely dining. The **Jardin Bresilien** on the rue de la République in Marigot presents live music, often from South America, in season. The club is usually open from 7 p.m. to 4 a.m. A disco, **Night Fever,** is in Colombier, outside Marigot. It's open Wednesday through Sunday from 10 p.m. "until." Since these places don't have phones, you have to show up, hoping they'll be in action. There is casino gambling on the Dutch side (refer to Chapter X).

4. St. Barthélemy

Friends call it "St. Barts" (also St. Barths). That's short for St. Barthélemy—named by its discoverer Columbus in 1493 and pronounced "San Bar-te-le*mee*." The uppermost corner of the French West Indies, it is the only Caribbean island with a touch of Sweden in its personality.

French adventurers first occupied it, selling out to the Knights of Malta in 1651. When the Caribs pushed the knights out in 1656, France regained control, eventually ceding her rights to Sweden, which ruled from 1784 to 1877.

Louis XVI had traded the island and its people to Sweden in exchange for trading rights in Hothenburg.

Once, in the 19th century, Britain also held control. However, in 1878 a plebiscite returned permanent control to France, and today St. Barts is a dependency of Guadeloupe.

For a long time the island was a paradise for a few millionaires such as David Rockefeller who has a magnificent parabolic-roofed hideaway on the northwest shore, or Edmond de Rothschild who occupies some fabulous acres at the "other end" of the island. The Biddles of Philadelphia are in the middle. Nowadays, however, St. Barts is developing a broader base of tourism, as it opens more hotels.

For the most part, St. Bartians are descendants of Breton and Norman fisher folk. The mostly white population is small, about 3,500 living in some eight square miles, 15 miles southeast of St. Martin and 140 miles north of Guadeloupe.

Occasionally you'll see St. Bartians dressed in the provincial costumes of Normandy, and when you hear them speak Norman French, you'll think you're back in the old country—until you feel the temperature. In little Corossol more than anywhere else you can see the following of traditions brought from 17th-century France. Here, if you are near the church before or after early-morning mass, you can probably see the barefoot elderly women who wear the starched white bonnets known as *quichenottes* or the *calèche*. This special headgear, brought from Brittany, was called *quichenotte*, a corruption of "kiss-me-not," and may well have served as protection from the close attentions of Englishmen or Swedes on the island. The bonneted women, who usually stay close to their homes, can also be seen at local celebrations, particularly on August 25, St. Louis' Day. The old women of Corossol are camera-shy, but they offer their homemade baskets for sale to tourists.

Many of the people of St. Barts are long-limbed and attractive, of French and Swedish ancestry, the latter showing in their fair skin, blonde hair, and blue eyes.

The island's capital town is **Gustavia,** named after a Swedish king. In fact, Gustavia is St. Barts' only town and seaport. It's a landlocked, hurricane-proof harbor, looking like a little dollhouse-scale port.

GETTING THERE: From the U.S., the principal gateways are St. Maarten (see Chapter X), St. Thomas (see Chapter V), and Guadeloupe (included in this chapter). At either of these islands, connections to St. Barts can be made on inter-island carriers.

It is just a ten-minute flight from Juliana Airport on Dutch-held St. Maarten. **Air St. Barthélemy** (tel. 27-61-20) combines with **Windward Islands Airways** flights to provide up to 16 round-trip shuttle trips between St. Martin and St. Barts daily. The fare each way is $26. You can also come from Guadeloupe on **Air Guadeloupe,** a one-hour flight.

Many jokes have been made about the makeshift landing strip at St. Barts. It's short to begin with, accommodating small craft. The biggest plane it can land is a 19-seat STOL (short takeoff and landing craft). As a chilling sight, a cemetery adjoins the strip! Natives pray to the white cross that stands between two hills flanking the field. Your plane has to make a curving swoop through a hilltop pass. Others suggest that a good belt of scotch should be downed before takeoff. No matter, everybody seems to arrive in one piece.

If you're flying in, you'll need to present your return or ongoing ticket. A valid passport is needed, or else a photo identification. If you're planning a longer stay, say, three months, check with the French West Indies Tourist Board at 610 Fifth Ave., New York, NY 10020 (tel. 212/757-1125), about visa requirements. In such cities as Beverly Hills, Chicago, Dallas, Montréal, San Francisco, and Toronto, you can check about any special visa requirements with the French Government Tourist Offices.

The **official monetary unit** is the French franc, but most stores and restaurants prefer payment in U.S. dollars. Most hotels also quote their rates in American currency at a discount from the rates as quoted in francs.

GETTING AROUND: The principal means are taxis, car rentals, sightseeing tours, even bikes, all of which are outlined below.

Taxis
They meet all flights. Once you've gone through the minor check at Customs, you can take one of these cabs to your St. Jean Bay hotel or go into Gustavia. Taxis are not very expensive, mostly because no one destination is all that far from any other. There are more than two dozen taxi operators on St. Barts.

Car Rentals
The hilly terrain, and perhaps the sense of adventure of the residents, combine to form a car-rental situation unique in the Caribbean. Never have I seen as many open-sided Mini-Mokes as I have in St. Barts. Painted in vivid primary colors, and designed along lines midway between those of a miniature tank and a World War II Jeep, they're fast, fun, and very windy. You can easily get into the swing of driving one if you're handy with a stick shift and don't care at all about your coiffure.

Budget Rent-a-Car offers them as their least expensive model, dispensing them out of offices at the airport and in Gustavia (tel. 27-67-43). The cheapest rate is awarded to clients who reserve at least two business days before their arrival and who plan to keep their car for at least five days. With unlimited mileage included, this car rents for $222 weekly. You can also rent a more conventional Pony with automatic transmission for $240 weekly (with air conditioning, $270 weekly).

It's a good idea to buy additional insurance for $5 per day regardless of the model rented. Otherwise, you'll be responsible for the first $1,000 of damage to the car (with the insurance you're liable for only $100 of damage). For reservations and information in the U.S., call Budget toll free at 800/527-0700.

Budget's most aggressive competition, **Hertz,** operates in St. Barts through a local dealership, Henry's Car Rentals. With branches at the airport and in St-Jean (tel. 27-60-21), it offers VW Beetles and open-sided Mini-Mokes for prices roughly comparable to those at Budget. Reservations and information are available by calling toll-free in North America at 800/654-3001.

Avis is also represented on the island, but you'll need a reservation a full month in advance in high season, a requirement many visitors find cumbersome. Even with a month's advance reservation, its Mini-Mokes and Beetles cost $20 more per week than the cars at Budget or Hertz. However, this could have changed by the time of your visit. For reservations and information, dial toll-free 800/331-2112.

Regardless of which you select as your agency, remember that no one will mind if you honk your horn furiously while going around the island's blind corners, a practice that avoids many sideswiped fenders. Drive slowly, carefully, and with consideration.

Gas is extra. Tanks hold enough to get you to a gas station, of which there are three; but only one, the Shell station at the airport, is open on Sunday, and then only from 8 to 11 a.m. All valid foreign driver's licenses are honored.

Sightseeing Tours

Group tours are scaled to the island's size: eight passengers per minibus, with a charge of about $6 per person. In a private taxi, two persons can tour for 165F ($24.75). Operators include **René Bernier** (tel. 27-61-24), **Claude Lédée** (tel. 27-60-54), and Hugo Cagan's **St. Barth Tours** (tel. 27-61-28).

Motorbikes

These are plentiful, with Yamahas renting for about $15 per day. A driver's license is required. Call 27-66-16 if you're interested in this means of transport.

Boat Service to St. Martin

There is a variety of service between St. Barts and St. Martin, but schedules vary with the season, so it's best to check on the spot. For **catamarans,** call 27-66-30 or contact the skippers of the *White Octopus, Maho,* or *El Tigre,* who arrive in St. Barts around noon after a one-hour crossing from St. Martin. They depart late the same afternoon.

PRACTICAL FACTS: There are two **banks** on the island, both in Gustavia. The Banque Française Commerciale, rue du Général-de-Gaulle (tel. 27-62-62), is open from 8 a.m. to noon and 2 to 3:30 p.m. The Banque Nationale de Paris, rue du Bord-de-Mer (tel. 27-63-70), is open from 8:15 a.m. to noon and 2 to 4 p.m.

The **climate** of St. Barts is ideal: it's dry with an average temperature of 72° to 86° Fahrenheit.

In **government,** St. Barts, as mentioned, is a dependency of Guadeloupe, which in turn is an overseas *département* of France. As such, the citizens of St. Barts are allowed to participate in French elections. It has its own mayor (elected every seven years), a town constable, and a security force of six policemen and fewer than a dozen gendarmes.

French is the official **language,** and the type spoken by St. Bartians is a quaint Norman dialect. Some of the populace speak English, however, and there is seldom a language problem at major hotels, restaurants, and shops.

St. Barts' **Customs** allows you to bring in items for personal use, including tobacco, cameras, and film.

In **electric current,** voltage is 200 AC, 50 cycles; therefore, American-made appliances require French plugs, converters, and transformers.

In **medical facilities,** Gustavia has one clinic, five doctors, and three dentists. Your hotel reception desk will put you in touch with one if the need should arise.

An airport **departure tax** of $3 is assessed.

For information while on the island, go to the **Office du Tourisme,** Mairie de St-Barth, rue August-Nyman, in Gustavia (tel. 27-60-08).

There is one-hour **time** difference between St. Barts and the East Coast of the U.S. when Standard Time is in effect in the U.S. and Canada. Thus, when it's 7 p.m. in St. Barts, it is only 6 p.m. in New York or Toronto. The island tells time the French way: 1 p.m., for example, is 13 hours; midnight is 24 hours.

To make a direct **telephone call** from the U.S., dial 011-596 plus the St. Barts number for station-to-station calls; dial 01-596 plus the St. Barts number for person-to-person calls.

WHERE TO STAY: With the exception of such places as Les Castelets, most places here are homey, comfortable, and casual. Everything is small, as tiny St. Barts is hardly in the mainstream of tourism. Some furnished hillside and beach cottages are rented out by the week or month. In March it's often hard to get in here unless you've made reservations far in advance. Rates throughout the island, with some exceptions, tend to be expensive.

Les Castelets, Morne Lurin (tel. 27-61-73), is a luxurious private retreat perched on a hillside commanding spectacular views of Gustavia harbor and the offshore islands. Originally built as a private house in the Provençale style, it is exclusive, exceptional, and graciously conscious of its status as the most durably chic resort on the island, lying a steep 1.7 miles from the airport, about three-quarters of a mile from Gustavia. It's owned by financier Justin Colin, a board member of the American Ballet Theater. Because of the owner's theater connections and friendships, you're likely to encounter such illustrious fellow guests as Mikhail Barishnikov. The former president of France, Valéry Giscard d'Estaing, has also stayed here. Mrs. Geneviève Jouany is the capable manager, a most cordial and gracious hostess. Do not expect a beach and the seaside at your doorstep. However, you'll find a small triangular swimming pool with a view on the grounds. The beach at St-Jean is a five-minute drive down the steep hill to the sea.

A fashionable hideaway, this retreat of quiet comfort and relaxed luxury houses its guests in a number of different accommodations, including two small bedrooms in the main building. Villas have two bedrooms, a gracious two-story living room with a marble floor, complete kitchens, carpeted bathrooms (with bidets), and a wide private terrace for that view. Each villa has a tapedeck. The price of this style comes high. *Single or double occupancy of its rooms costs $100 to $130 daily, and villas for one or two persons rent for $120 to $295 from October 8 to mid-December (the hotel is closed from early May to October 8).* In high season, single or double occupancy of rooms costs $130 to $170 daily; villas for two people range in price from $140 to $450.

Even if you're not staying here, you might try to nail down a reservation for dinner, as the place serves the finest food on St. Barts (see my dining recommendations to follow).

For reservations or information, call or write to Jane Martin, Castelets, 717 Fifth Ave., 13th Floor, New York, NY 10022 (tel. 212/319-7488).

Hotel Manapany Cottages, P.O. Box 114, Anse des Cayes (tel. 27-66-55, 212/

757-0225 in New York City, or toll free 800/847-4249). Climbing a steep, well-landscaped hillside on the northwest side of the island, this is one of the most luxurious and stylish hotels in the Caribbean. It offers a cluster of 20 cottages on the hillside and a dozen or so along the water. Each is lavishly ornamented with patterns of gingerbread, and has a red roof and a rambling veranda open to a view of the sea. Wicker furniture combines tropical comfort with Gallic style. Behind sliding glass doors, either one or two air-conditioned bedrooms has a phone connection to a hard-working concierge, a large-screen TV with in-house video movies, ceiling fan, and tile bath. Each unit also has a kitchenette. In peak season, doubles begin at $330 daily, with one-bedroom suites costing $470. *Summer rates for one or two people go for $175 to $200 daily; one-bedroom suites run $262.*

You register in a villa at the base of a hill. Meals are served in an elegant raftered dining room, the Ballahou, which is recommended separately. Owned by Frenchman Guy Roy, the resort is capably directed by its resident manager, Danielle Paris de Boullardière. The name of the hotel, translated from Malagese, means "small paradise." The swimming pool is a perfect oval. Room service arrives on Mini-Mokes, and the sound of the surf is never far away.

Hotel Guanahani, Anse du Grand Cul-de-Sac (tel. 27-66-60, 212/308-3330 in New York City, or toll free 800/235-3505), one of the newest hotels on the island, opened with Gallic fanfare in 1987. It occupies a beachfront site flooded with sunlight, containing 80 stylish accommodations clustered in individual cottages. Units range from deluxe rooms to lavish two-bedroom suites, all of which have private balconies or patios with sea views. Each room or suite has individually controlled air conditioning as well as ceiling fans, and most of them offer kitchens. *Prices in low season begin at around $300 double occupancy.* In high season, two people pay $350, including breakfast, and MAP can be arranged for another $50 per person daily. Expensive, exclusive, and very, very French, the hotel offers fine dining in two restaurants. It also has two tennis courts covered with artificial grass (illuminated for night games), and a refreshing set of water sports available at additional cost to residents.

Filao Beach, St-Jean (tel. 27-64-84), is a crescent-shaped, 30-unit, white stucco bungalow-style hotel, where each room is named after a château in France. This is the only Relais et Château on the island, although, if rumor is correct, some other properties may receive that designation during the life of this edition. This exceptional holiday choice is run by Albert Veille, the former manager of the Bakoua Hotel in Martinique. Right on the beach, it stands across the road from the Village St-Jean and next to the Eden Rock. Try to get Bungalow 40, near the beach. Regardless of which room you get, each is modern (elegantly simple, depending on your point of view), plushly carpeted, and well upholstered. Each contains an old-fashioned engraving of the château for which it was named, plus mahogany closets, air conditioning, phone, radio, TV, and a sun-flooded terrace big enough to enjoy a leisurely breakfast. Winter rates range from 1,900F ($285) to 2,200F ($337.50) for a double and from 1,500F ($225) to 2,100F ($315) for a single, depending on the season. *Summer rates are 1,100F ($165) in a double, 700F ($105) in a single.* The establishment is closed between September 1 and mid-October. The light meals served here at lunch are superb, including French omelets, stuffed land crabs, select cold cuts, and fresh, crisp salads. They're served either at the café-bar or around the freshwater swimming pool.

The Upper Bracket

El Sereno Beach Hotel, Grand Cul-de-Sac (tel. 27-64-80). Four miles from Gustavia, its low-slung blue-and-white façade and its isolated location create the aura of St. Tropez in the Antilles. A lot of the Riviera crowd is attracted to it, partly because of its Lyon-born owner, Marc Llepez, and his wife, Christine. A total of 20 accommodations are scattered over a carefully landscaped interior. On the premises are 17 bungalows with garden views, plus a trio of units overlooking the sea. In winter, singles cost $150 to $190 daily; doubles, $185 to $235. *In summer, depending on the view, singles rent for $100 to $120 daily, and doubles run $120 to $150, including breakfast.* Each unit contains two beds, an individual safe, a refrigerator, air conditioning, and color TV with video movies. The garden has a freshwater pool, in the center of which is a verdant island. The feeling is a bit like a private compound, whose social center is an open-air bar and poolside restaurant, La Toque Lyonnaise. There, full meals cost 300F ($45) and are served from 11:30 a.m. to 2 p.m. and 7 to 9 p.m. seven days a week.

L'Hibiscus, rue Thiers (tel. 27-64-82), is dramatically terraced into one of Gustavia's steep hillsides, a fact which gives visitors the lordly feeling of surveying the entire town from a private panoramic terrace. Its social center is in an imaginatively rambling modern building whose floor space was extended by a hardwood deck surrounding a circular and deep swimming pool. The adjacent bar is an open-air breezy kind of place, encompassing lattices, greenery, and that view of the port. This lovely place and its 11 cottages stand immediately beneath a 200-year-old clock tower in the uppermost region of town. Set amid a labyrinth of terracotta walkways on steeply sloping ground, each cottage has its own veranda, kitchenette, living room, TV with video, and tasteful accessories. Owned by a trio of local entrepreneurs, *the bungalows rent for 900F ($135) in summer for two people,* 1,500F ($225) in winter.

Club La Banane, l'Orient (tel. 27-60-80), about a mile from the airport on the outskirts of the village of l'Orient, is a four-room hotel—small, intimate, well furnished, and filled with some of the most stylish antiques on the island. The complex is ringed by a fence whose boundaries lie within a three-minute walk from the beach. My favorite accommodation contains a large mahogany four-poster bed, whose trim was made from a little-known Central American wood called angelique. It has an almost Japanese type of simplicity, partially created by the wide expanses of carefully crafted Mexican tiles. The trio of other units are less spacious, but each has a TV with video, some Haitian art, a mixture of antique and modern designs, a refrigerator, a private terrace, and louvered windows overlooking the garden. The owner is Jean-Marie Rivière, formerly a cabaret producer at the Alcázar in Paris. Gerard Joffes, the resident manager, charges $260 to $350 daily, single or double occupancy, in high season. *In low season, charges are reduced by 50%.* The establishment is closed in May and June and September and October.

The Moderate Range

PLM Hôtel Jean Bart, St. Jean Bay (tel. 87-63-27). Set a two-minute walk from the beach, on a forested hillside above the bay, this 50-unit hotel is owned and operated by the large French hotel chain PLM. Friendly and well maintained, the hotel offers its own many-sided swimming pool, whose hibiscus-bordered terrace overlooks the sea and a labyrinth of well-landscaped walkways meandering among stone retaining walls. Launched in 1976, the hotel has comfortably modern accommodations contained in seven tile-roofed, vaguely Iberian buildings. Each rental unit has air conditioning, a spacious balcony or terrace (but not necessarily with a sea view), phone, terracotta floors, and thick plaster walls. Twenty of the units offer self-contained kitchenettes. In winter, singles cost $115 to $150 daily, and doubles run $140 to $205, depending on the accommodation. *In summer, singles rent for $60 to $70 daily, and doubles cost $75 to $95, with a continental breakfast included.*

Tropical Hotel, P.O. Box 147, St-Jean (tel. 27-64-87), is a little picture-postcard-type inn, trimmed in gingerbread, offering an intimate and restful atmosphere under the hospitality umbrella of its manager, Alain Jeanney. It's perched on a hillside spot, about 50 yards above St. Jean Beach (a mile from the airport and a mile and a half from Gustavia). The hotel (almost a bungalow inn) rents out some 20 air-conditioned, twin-bedded units, each with private shower, tile floor, color-coordinated schemes, plus a phone and a refrigerator to cool your tropical drinks. Nine of the units come with a sea view and balcony, and 11 contain a porch opening onto a garden which is so lush it looks like a miniature jungle. There's a hospitality center, where guests read, listen to music, or order drinks at a carefully paneled, inviting bar ringed with antiques. The freshwater swimming pool is small, but water sports are available on the beach. Breakfast is served at the poolside terrace. In season, a minimum stay of four days is required. For that privilege, guests pay $110 to $155 daily in a single, $130 to $155 in a double. *In summer, tariffs range from $50 daily in a single and from $65 in a double.*

Eden Rock, St-Jean (tel. 27-60-01). When the rock it sits on was purchased many years ago by the island's former mayor, Remy de Haenen, the seller was an old woman who laughed at him for paying too many francs for it. Today it's part of the lore of the island, offering some of the best panoramas. The building capping its pinnacle looks like an idealized version of a Provence farmhouse. It's surrounded on three sides by the waters of St. Jean Bay. I prefer the terracotta terrace, especially in the glare of noon, when the vista includes bird's-eyes views of frigates wheeling and diving for fish in the turquoise waters. Inside the stone walls is a collection of French antiques and paintings, including a few drawings by Monsieur de Haenen's father, a well-known turn-of-the-century illustrator. The de Haenen family prefers not to accept outside dining guests anymore. However, they still rent six rooms in the main house, along with a trio of red-roofed outbuildings scattered amid the cactus of a rocky garden. Each unit contains a sea view, refrigerator, air conditioning or ceiling fan, and plenty of unfussy, severely decorated charm. In winter, depending on the accommodation, rooms cost $120 to $170, single or double. *In summer, a single or double ranges from $85 to $95, plus service but including a continental breakfast.*

Autour du Rocher, l'Orient (tel. 27-60-73). Named after the gigantic boulders around which it was built, this renovated eagle's nest is sheltered behind a screen of oleander and hibiscus. Inconvenienced only by its limited number of rooms, it is really more like a private villa where three accommodations are rented to paying guests. If you don't want to be on the sands of a beach, this is one of the two or three best-positioned hotels on the island, rising dramatically over a panoramic view. Your charming hosts are a team of entrepreneurs from France and Scotland. Bruno DeBenedictus and David Henderson created much of the well-finished paneling and trim for the in-house restaurant and nightclub, whose merits are recommended separately. Accommodations cost $180 per night, single or double occupancy, in winter, *50% less in summer.* A sun-washed breakfast on the terrace, where St. Martin is visible across the sea, is included in the price. The location is on the north coast, about two miles from Gustavia.

Hostellerie des 3 Forces, Vitet (tel. 27-61-25). Its cedar-sided accommodations are scattered over a dry and sandy slope whose panorama encompasses rolling hills near the village of Vitet, three miles from Gustavia. Only eight bungalows have been built, each graced with the name of one of the signs of the zodiac (as money becomes available, four more will be erected). Each is ringed with neo-Victorian gingerbread, containing a consciously simple decor of exposed wood and roughly textured fabrics, big windows, and private bathrooms. Most units have terraces and air conditioning, and all guests benefit from the gracious attention of the owner and resident astrologist, Hubert de la Mott. With breakfast included, cottages rent for $140 to $175 daily single, $160 to $190 double, in winter. *In summer, a single is $90 daily; a double, $110.* On the premises is a swimming pool. The establishment closes in June and in October. Its restaurant is recommended separately.

WHERE TO DINE: For the most part, you're served an essentially French cuisine with local adaptations, reflecting the island's unusual mixed European heritage. I've found few truly local dishes. However, at a private home I was once served "Madame Jackass," a red fish dish with hot peppers. As a warning, I'd like to note that many of

these restaurants shut down on a whim if there's no business. This is true particularly in the autumn.

Most guests will want to swim and have lunch at one of the clubs right on the beach. See my recommendation of Chez Francine, below, as an example. Most of these clubs are rustic lean-tos, built of wood, more Tahiti in style than St. Barts. From tiny cooking galleys, battle-trained chefs often turn out an amazingly good cuisine, and not just hamburgers either. You might get breast of duck or charcoal-grilled lobster. A favorite specialty of mine is the puffy fritters of salt cod.

In Gustavia

Le Brigantin, rue Jeanne-d'Arc (tel. 27-60-89). Habitués of St. Barts never visit the island without a meal at one of the most cosmopolitan restaurants in Gustavia. Frenchman Dantes Magras and his Swedish wife, Maria, restored the stone and brick walls of what had been the island's yacht club into a historically accurate copy of the original 19th-century design. It's also a lot of fun, according to the clients who line up near the plank-covered bar that at one time sheathed the hull of a sailing ship. There's likely to be live jazz presented in the evening. The attractively decorated restaurant is upstairs. Specialties include a full range of delectable seafood. The restaurant has developed a good wine list, bringing wines directly from France in special containers, kept at the right temperatures. Reservations are often needed well in advance, especially in high season. Full meals, costing 300F ($45), are served from 7 to 10 p.m. daily except Wednesday.

L'Ananas, rue Courbet (tel. 27-63-77) in Gustavia. In 1980 what was originally built as a low-slung private house was gutted and converted into one of the most elegant restaurants on the island. It sits near the historic clock tower above the town on the side of a steeply sloping hill which permits sweeping views over the bay. Refreshingly modern, glossy, and tasteful, it incorporates about a dozen 19th-century paintings of clipper ships with sophisticated lighting and wide planks of a beautifully striated Brazilian hardwood, angélique. Luc Blanchard, born in La Rochelle, France, is the chef and owner. He was a skipper on a chartered yacht before realizing that running a restaurant pleased him more. Guests usually enjoy a drink near the thick mahogany surface of the bar before heading to one of the embroidery-covered tables. Full meals cost from 200F ($30) and are served only at dinner, between 7 and 10 p.m. No meals are offered on Tuesday off-season, and reservations are suggested. Specialties include fresh salmon, seabass, grouper in Pouilly, slices of salmon and monkfish in saffron sauce, roast duck with brandy sauce, carpaccio, lobster salad with mango, followed by lemon pie. Often, the jazz played here draws a music-loving crowd (more about this later).

Au Port, rue Sadi-Carnot (tel. 27-62-36). From the outside it looks like a consciously raffish harborfront building, with a narrow veranda jutting above the bumpy road outside. You climb a steep and tiled flight of stairs to reach its second-floor dining room, where a simple decor of blue-and-white walls and neocolonial charm act as the appropriate foil for the cuisine of Breton-born chef Jean-Pierre Delage. With the restaurant's owner, Gérard Balageas, he prepares a satisfying classic French cuisine. No lunch is served, and dinner is offered throughout the winter from 6:30 to 10:15 p.m. every night of the week. The establishment is closed from June 1 until early November. Full meals cost from 250F ($37.50) and might include filet of lamb in a garlic cream sauce, filet of poached salmon with sage sauce, homemade foie gras, crayfish with fresh noodles, breast of duckling with orange sauce, and a refreshing dessert of fresh seasonal fruits au gratin with coconut. Reservations are suggested, especially if you want one of the tables on the narrow veranda.

La Crémaillère, rue du Général-de-Gaulle (tel. 27-63-89), is easily one of the island's finest restaurants in all respects—service, the menu (in the classic French tradition), carefully selected ingredients, and a fine wine list. It's in a 200-year-old Swedish house which the French-born owner, Michel Brunet, transformed into a chic, elegant country hideaway with an undeniable tropical flair. The heart and soul of the place is prefaced with a cheerfully illuminated courtyard whose centerpiece is a giant sugar apple tree. You can dine on an eyrie-style balcony, but my favorite corner is inside the air-conditioned inner room. There, massive stone walls, ceiling beams, and a large fireplace evoke a country inn in Brittany. To reinforce the image, rows of Quimper porcelain are proudly displayed near the smoke-blackened chimney. Don't overlook, near the open-air bar, the series of medals which an agrarian forebear of Mr. Brunet won in the 1930s for livestock. The cuisine benefits from the education Mr. Brunet received during his career at Maxim's in Paris. Queen Elizabeth II was his most prestigious diner. Dinners at his place cost 300F ($45); lunches, about half that much. Specialties include crayfish bisque, lobster Thermidor, steak Diana, gratin of fish, rillettes maison, steak au poivre, and house-style lobster, with chocolate cake for dessert. Lunch is served only in high season, from noon to 3 p.m.; otherwise, dinner is from 6:30 to midnight seven days a week.

Restaurant aux Trois Gourmands, La Pointe, Gustavia (no phone), sits on the less congested side of the harbor behind a gingerbread-laden façade whose pink and white awnings flutter at boats moored nearby. Diners enjoy a drink on the wicker sofas near the bar, where each of the framed prints seems to evoke the same tropical theme. Open on two ends, the dining room is filled with pink napery, white lattices, and bentwood or wicker chairs. Christophe Gasnier, a much experienced chef de cuisine, serves lunch daily except Sunday from noon to 2 p.m. and dinner every evening between 7 and 10 p.m. No meals are served from mid-August to the end of September. Lunches, costing from 150F ($22.50), include fish soup, filet of red snapper, lobster salad, and faux filet with mustard sauce. Dinners, at 275F ($41.25), might include mussel soup with saffron, fish pâté in a tarragon sauce, homemade pasta with fresh foie gras, breast of duck with a cassis sauce, sliced lobster in a tomato sauce, and filet of yellowtail snapper in a pink peppercorn sauce.

Rôtisserie Bertrand, rue Lafayette and rue du Roi-Oscar-II (tel. 27-63-13), right in the heart of Gustavia, has been called "the best take-out service in the western hemisphere." The much-overworked owners, a young French couple, are Pierre-Marie L'Hermite and his wife, Evelyne. If you don't want to cook, they'll prepare dinner for you. Order it in the morning, give them time to cook it, then pick it up later in the day. They turn out everything from French pizzas to many types of tarts (such as onion), to langouste mayonnaise, to pâté de campagne, to canard à l'orange. If you're here during the Yule season, you can enjoy oysters flown in from Brittany and fresh foie gras. It's no ordinary "deli." It's favored by locals (read that "well-heeled" locals), and it's the best place in St. Barts to pick up items if you're planning a picnic or a boat excursion to a neighboring island. Their casseroles to go include beef bourguignonne. Cooked platters cost between $4 and $7. The place is open from 8 a.m. to 1 p.m. daily and from 4 to 7 p.m. daily except Sunday.

La Langouste, rue du Roi-Oscar-II (tel. 27-66-40), used to be known as "Annie's." Annie, of the island family of Ange, is still around, but she prefers to name her place in honor of the clawless Caribbean lobster instead of herself. In a century-old building, erected during the Swedish domain over the island, her zesty little restaurant is near the Gendarmerie. You get down-to-earth Créole cookery here, and that means stuffed land crabs, conch ragoût, cod fritters (called accra de morue), the namesake langouste, always fresh fish, and curried chicken. Expect to spend about 150F ($22.50) for a filling repast. Lunches are light, but dinner is a Créole delight. Hours are noon to 2 p.m. and 7 to 10 p.m. daily except Thursday.

Anse des Cayes

Restaurant Ballahou, Hôtel Manapany Cottages, Anse des Cayes (tel. 27-66-55). Named after a small variety of swordfish, this is one of the best and most elegant restaurants on the island. To reach its sun-flooded pink-and-white interior, you pass beneath a portal dripping in fanciful Caribbean gingerbread. Dining is under a high ceiling whose rafters curve around the perimeter of an oval swimming pool. Dominique Allègre, the chef, once worked as a private chef in Giscard d'Estaing's private country house. Today he prepares full meals costing from 250F ($37.50) at lunch and 350F ($52.50) at dinner. Lunch, served beside the pool in less formal circumstances, lasts from 12:30 to 3 p.m., and includes salads, stuffed land crabs prepared Créole style, air-dried alpine beef with lentils, and many variations of crayfish. Dinners, from 7:30 to 10 p.m., are served by candlelight inside and are attractively elaborate. They require an advance reservation for nonresidents. Meals, which are accompanied by live music, include such specialties as salmon in puff pastry with a cream sauce, a salad of smoked fish, crayfish in puff pastry in a tomato cream sauce, filet of turbot, a cassoulette of crayfish in a lobster sauce, filet of beef with cognac, and an iced soufflé with old dark rum sauce.

In the St. Jean Beach Area

Le Pelican, Plage de St-Jean (tel. 27-64-64). The ambience and cuisine are so different here during the day and night that you'd almost think you were in two different restaurants. Lunch is served outdoors in the shade of an elongated parasol, within earshot of the nearby surf. From 11:30 a.m. to 3:30 p.m. it features full meals costing from 175F ($26.25). While sipping French wine in the Antillean sunshine, you can enjoy such specialties as fish soup, lobster bisque, specialty salads, grilled steak, and a generously portioned Créole platter laden with accras, shellfish, blood pudding, and grilled fish. Dinners are more elaborate, more expensive, and more formal. Full meals cost from 300F ($45) and are a showcase for the culinary specialties of Gilbert and Martine Molina. From 7 to 10 p.m., they might include a ravioli of sweetbreads, poached chicken with a leek mousseline sauce, braised filet of yellowtail and mussels with endive, a soup of frogs' legs, steamed turbot with lobster butter and caviar, filet of duck with apples and cider, and medallions of fresh lobster with morels. The setting incorporates a trio of high-ceilinged dining rooms with pastel colors, a view of the sea, and candlelight. Evening reservations are suggested.

Chez Francine stands right on St. Jean Beach (tel. 27-60-49). Your host, Alain Van den Haute, maintains a delightfully informal atmosphere. The ladies at an adjoining table are likely to be dining topless. Checking out the action in winter, Sylvester Stallone, Alain Delon, or Lino Ventura might give them an eye. That is, until Lee Radziwill arrives to capture the most attention. People from all over the island come here, mingling with the tourists over a casual lunch, served from 11:30 a.m. to 3:30 p.m. The place is really little more than a boardwalk terrace built on top of the sand a few feet from the beach. Its overhead awnings and blackboard menu encourage an attire of bathing suits, at best, and no one even attempts to be formal. Typical meals, often preceded by a frothy piña colada, usually cost around $18 per person. They might include chilled lobster, grilled chicken or fish, grilled steak, fresh vegetable salad, a selection of wine or beer, and a choice of homemade tortes and cakes. The establishment is a busy focal point of beach life daily except for a two-week vacation sometime in midsummer.

Morne Lurin

Les Castelets, Morne Lurin (tel. 27-61-73), was already previewed as the chicest place to stay in St. Barts. Likewise, this eagle's-nest retreat is the most elegant dining choice. The elite meet in luxury, as celebrities from both sides of the Atlantic enjoy their apéritif on the terrace, said to have the best view on the island. The dining room turns out a classic French and nouvelle cuisine, and the food is backed up by a fine wine cellar, considered one of the finest in the Caribbean. The chef, Michel Viali, was born in Marseilles, but he has long gone beyond the cookery of Provence. An artist of considerable skill, his cookery is not only beautifully prepared (he makes his own pasta and smokes his own fish), it is also well served. In a setting of French provincial antiques, the well-chosen napery and glassware add to the dignity of the occasion.

Guest Jessica Lange, the actress, preferred a salad named for Aphrodite (cubed lobster with mayonnaise and peach bits), while the late Tennessee Williams found a local yellowtail snapper (baked en papillote) his favorite. It's served with a shrimp and lobster sauce. I personally gravitate to a warm salad of walnut-flecked goose giblets. Main courses are likely to include a seafood cassoulet, lobster with fresh pasta, a scallop fricassée flavored with passion fruit, beef tenderloin with pears in a burgundy wine sauce, roast crisp duck à l'orange, and braised sweetbreads with pasta. Whatever you select, it will usually be superb, especially the tarte maison, often presented with homemade ice cream. Castelets is closed all day Tuesday and for lunch on Wednesday. It is imperative to telephone for a reservation, and for the privilege of dining here, expect to pay from $50 per person. Dining hours are noon to either 2 or 2:30 p.m. and 7 to 10 p.m. If you're in the area late in the day, head up to the **Santa Fé Bar Restaurant** (tel. 27-61-04), which lies high up beyond Castelets. Here you'll get the best American-style hamburgers on the island, juicy ones at that. You can take in the view for free. Most checks are under $10 unless you have a lot to drink. Hours are 5:30 to 10 p.m. daily.

Anse du Grand Cul-de-Sac

Bartolomeo, Hôtel Guanahani, Anse du Grand Cul-de-Sac (tel. 27-66-60), is the deluxe dining choice for one of the most exclusive and expensive hotels on the island. It serves dinner only every night from 7 to 11 p.m. Nonresidents of the hotel are welcome if they phone ahead for a reservation. The menu specialties, which are orchestrated by French chefs from Paris, cost from 350F ($52.50) for full meals. The menu frequently changes, but elegant dishes might include shrimp with herb-flavored oils, crayfish salad Guanahani, ravioli stuffed with lobster, medallions of veal in a sweet-and-sour sauce, crabmeat in puff pastry with a sweet-pepper sauce, climaxed by mille-feuilles of pineapple and passion fruit.

L'Orient Bay

Autour de Rocher (tel. 27-60-73) was previously suggested as a small hotel. However, it's also one of the best-known and most frequented restaurants on the island, seemingly holding its own against the onslaught of new restaurants popping up at about the rate of one a month (don't hold me to that!). David Henderson and Bruno de Benedictus operate this first-rate establishment somewhat like a private club. It's worth it almost for the view. But the owners don't rely just on that. Most diners prefer to go there deep in the night, ordering such well-prepared and tasty classic French dishes as bouillabaisse. It may not taste exactly as it does on the Mediterranean, but the version here is special and different, well worth trying. Try to reserve, and anticipate a check ranging from $30 per person. Dinner only is served from 7 p.m. It's closed Monday in low season.

Grande Saline

The favored place in the sun is **Le Tamarin** (no phone), which picks up the beach traffic—many in stunningly revealing bikinis—from the nearby Plage de Saline. It's isolated amid rocky hills and forests, in a low-slung cottage whose eaves are lined with gingerbread. Inside, you'll see Haitian paintings, exotic hardwoods, and wicker armchairs. If you'd like either lunch or dinner on the beach, paying $20 to $30 for the privilege, join the hungry diners at Le Tamarin. I've never seen more than two dozen guests here at the same time, each eagerly reading the blackboard menu for the chef's suggestions. If you have to wait, diners can order an apéritif in one of the lazy hammocks stretched under a tamarind tree (hence the name of the restaurant). Fresh fish is invariably featured, but meat dishes and poultry also are cooked well. Service can be hectic, but if you're in a rush you shouldn't be here. It's for a lazy afternoon on the beach or a relaxed dinner under the stars. Meals are served from 12:30 to 3 p.m. and 7 to 9:30 p.m.

Grand Cul-de-Sac

Restaurant Flamboyant, Grand Cul-de-Sac (tel. 29-64-09). On the western edge of the island lies what many residents consider the best restaurant on the island. It's on the veranda level of the isolated home of Albert Balayn, a young and energetic chef who studied cuisine in France before returning to his native island. The preferred seating is on the panoramic terrace, where the hillside location contributes to a view over fields, forest, and sea. Only dinner is served, every night except Monday from 6:30 to 10 p.m. Full meals without wine cost from 250F ($37.50) and might include a succulent version of French onion soup, christophine (a kind of squash) stuffed with crayfish, a creamy version of fish and lobster soup, crayfish in puff pastry, a salad of filet of duck breast with foie gras, a cassolette of crayfish, a filet of red snapper with a tomato- and rosemary-flavored cream sauce, filet of chicken with aged rum, and scallops with curry sauce. Dessert is appropriately elaborate, perhaps a savarin with rum and chantilly cream. Reservations are strongly suggested.

Club Lafayette (tel. 27-62-51), near the Sereno Beach Hôtel, lies at a cove on the eastern end of the island. Lunching here from noon to 3 p.m. is like taking a meal at your own private beach club. After a dip in the ocean or a pool, you can order a *planteur* in the shade of a sea grape, and later proceed to lunch itself: a roquefort-and-walnut salad, a Créole version of boudin noir (black sausage), charcoaled langouste, grilled fresh fish, and breast of duck. In other words, this is no hamburger fast-food beach joint. Afterward, have a refreshing citrus-flavored sherbet. Prices begin at $25 for a good and satisfying meal. It's open daily.

Vitet

Hostellerie des 3 Forces, Vitet (tel. 27-61-25), has a resident astrologist, a French provincial decor, well-scrubbed surfaces, and food with a genuine allure. The food is well prepared and beautifully served, and for dessert you get an astrological forecast thrown in. The heart and soul of the place is Hubert de la Mott, who arrived from Brittany with his wife and sister to create a hotel (recommended separately) where happiness, good food, comfort, and conversation could be a way of life. Even if you don't stay here, many diners drive out for a meal, enjoying it on a sun-washed, scrub-covered landscape. Food is offered from noon to 3 p.m. and 7:30 to 9:45 p.m. Evening meals are more formal, although each repast costs about 200F ($30) per person. Menu items depend on the availability of ingredients. However, the bill of fare might include salade niçoise, fish pâté, beef shish kebab with curry sauce, grilled fresh lobster, veal kidneys flambé with cognac, chicken livers fried with parsley and garlic, a cassolette of snails, filet of beef with béarnaise sauce, and such succulent desserts as crêpes suzette flambé. "Each dish takes time," in the words of the owner, because it's prepared fresh. Count on a leisurely meal and relax with the flow of the experience.

THE SPORTING LIFE: Unlike the other French islands in the West Indies, total nudism is illegal on St. Barts. However, women can bathe topless in most places. Bikinied casualness seems to be the rule. The most popular beach is St-Jean, which has some waterfront cafés where you can get drinks and light meals. Grand Cul-de-Sac, with its

St. Barths Beach Hôtel, and Anse des Flamands are other attractive beaches. (Golfers please note: There are no golf courses on the island.)

Water Sports

Marine Service, Quai du Yacht Club (tel. 27-64-50). There aren't many watersports facilities in St. Bart's, but of them all, this is the most complete. It operates from a one-story building set directly on the water at the edge of a marina, on the opposite side of the harbor from the more congested part of Gustavia. Sailboat charters cost $70 per person daily, with lunch and open bar included. A Boston whaler is around $200 a day, and scuba, with equipment included, is $40 per dive, regardless of the level of competency. Waterskiing and sports fishing are also offered, depending on the availability of equipment.

People who like **fishing** are fond of the waters of St. Barts. March through July they catch dolphin; in September, wahoo. Atlantic bonito, barracuda, and marlin also turn up with great frequency. I suggest you ask at your hotel to help arrange a trip out with one of the local fishermen, who prefer the handline, incidentally. It's best to bring your own speargun or rod and reel.

In addition, good charter boats are available each season. Names are posted on the pier at Marine Service, Quai du Yacht Club.

Sailing jaunts also can be arranged at many of the hotels, parties booked for trips to neighboring islands. Sometimes these are combined with fishing trips. Some of the hotels, such as Baie des Flamands, have Sunfish craft which they offer free to guests. Yachting isn't organized, however. Yet, in winter, anything's negotiable when stray yachts sail into Gustavia harbor.

Île Fourchue (Forked Island) is a popular rendezvous point for boats. Named for its configuration, with rocky peaks separated by valleys, Île Fourchue is horseshoe-shaped, with a protected anchorage. Its only permanent residents are goats, but a few ruins bear witness to the fact that it was once the home of a Breton who lived a Robinson Crusoe–style life here for many years. A charter to Île Fourchue and other nearby places can be had on the *Zavijava,* from Quai du Yacht Club. You can swim and snorkel, have lunch, and return to Gustavia at 5 p.m., all for a cost of 450F ($67.50) per person. You can make reservations by calling **Le Calèche Yacht Charter Agency** (tel. 27-62-38) in Gustavia from 9 a.m. to noon and 2:30 to 5:30 p.m. Monday to Saturday.

Waterskiing is authorized between 9 a.m. and 1 p.m. and again from 4:40 p.m. to sundown. Because of the shape of the coastline, skiers must remain 80 yards from shore on the windward side of the island and 110 yards off on the leeward side.

Windsurfing is one of the most popular sports practiced on St. Barts. Try **St. Barth Wind School** at the Tom Beach Hôtel on Pelican Beach near Chez Francine. It's open from 9 a.m. to 5 p.m. daily. Windsurfing costs $12 per hour. You can also rent Hobie Cats for one hour for $43 and Sunfish for one hour for $17. Professional instructors are on hand.

Tennis

It's mainly for hotel guests. There's a court at the **St. Barths Beach Hôtel,** Grand Cul-de-Sac (tel. 27-62-73).

One of the best courts is at the **Hôtel Manapany** (tel. 27-66-55), previously recommended. Use of the court is free to residents both day and night. Nonresidents pay 100F ($15) per hour during daylight, 150F ($22.50) for nighttime illumination.

SHOPPING: You don't pay any duty in St. Barts. Everything is out-of-bond. The island, then, is a good place to buy liquor and French perfumes, among the lowest priced in the West Indies. Perfume, for example, is cheaper in St. Barts than it is in France itself. Champagne is cheaper than in Epernay, France. St. Barts is the only completely free-trading port in the world, with the exception of French St. Martin and Dutch St. Maarten.

Only trouble is, selections are limited. However, you'll find good buys in sportswear, crystal, porcelain, watches, and other luxuries.

If you're in the market for some island crafts, try to find those convertible-brim, fine straw hats St. Bartians like to wear. *Vogue* once featured this high-crown headwear in its fashion pages. While I've seen some interesting block-printed resort clothes in cotton, St. Barts, admittedly, isn't a leader in this field.

La Romana, the famous international boutique chain representing renowned Italian and French designers of fashions and jewelry, has two shops in St. Barts: at the Hibiscus Hôtel (tel. 27-64-82), open from 10 a.m. to noon and 5 to 11 p.m.; and at La Villa Créole, where hours are 9 a.m. to 1 p.m. and 3 to 7 p.m. The shop at La Villa Créole offers a sportswear collection for women and men, while the one at the Hibiscus shows fashionable evening wear and designer jewelry.

The **Atelier** (tel. 27-61-72) at Colombier, two miles north of Gustavia, is Jean-Yves Froment's shop and studio, recently completely redecorated and reorganized. Visitors can watch the hand-dyed and block-printed decorations and tropical fashion prints being made.

La Calèche boutique, rue du Général-de-Gaulle (tel. 27-62-38), is an attractive place to purchase bathing suits, shoes, hats, St. Barts T-shirts, jewelry, and gifts. It serves such shoppers as Barbara Goldsmith, author of *Little Gloria . . . Happy at Last*.

Art and Carmen Hansen operate the **Shell Shop,** on rue du Général-de-Gaulle (no phone). It's a small shop, but you can find many interesting shells and coral from all over the world, as well as local handcrafts and exotic jewelry made from coral and shells, some hand-carved. In his diving days Art brought many of the items stocked in the shop up from the ocean. He'll be happy to talk with you about those days and about the objects you'll see in the shop. Art is from the U.S., and Carmen came from Santo Domingo.

Smoke and Booze, rue du Général-de-Gaulle (tel. 87-60-24), is where to go for wine, liquor, liqueurs, and tobacco, as well as for toys and souvenirs. They'll package your beverage purchases for you to take home.

La Fonda Hermès, rue de la République (tel. 27-66-15), is the only outlet in the Caribbean of the famous Parisian haberdasher. It stands, basking in a pool of self-generated chic, across the street from the port. Be warned, you'll pay dearly for some French allure: a beach towel signed with the exalted Hermès name costs around $150, for example.

Little Switzerland, rue de la France (tel. 27-64-66). Behind glistening arrays of glass-frosted cases is an array of untaxed crystal, jewelry, and luxurious frill merchandise.

Boutiques Chamade, rue de la République (tel. 27-62-21). Its interior glistens with the reflection from dozens of Lalique vases, arrays of crystal, bottles of perfume, and a selection of wristwatches. Both the merchandise and the attitude are very French.

Water Sports, rue du Roi-Oscar-II (tel. 27-66-16). Its owners, Jean-Claude and Chantal Varin, manage the single biggest inventory of sports equipment and sports clothing on the island. The place is ideal if you've forgotten some essential item from your wardrobe, or if you want to surround yourself with a wealth of play-related equipment. The merchandise is crammed into two floors of a 150-year-old Swedish house set above the harbor.

Loulou's Marine, rue de la République (tel. 27-62-74). Some of its merchandise could come from any general store in France and some of it is so specialized that only a yacht owner could appreciate it. This is possibly the most gregarious rendezvous point in town, and amid pulleys, coils of rope, and folded sailcloth, you'll find T-shirts and unusual hardware.

NIGHTLIFE: Most guests consider a French Créole dinner under the open stars near the sea (or with a view of the twinkling stars) enough of a noctural adventure. After that, there isn't a lot of excitement.

In Gustavia, the most popular gathering place is the **Select Café** (no phone), apparently named after its more famous granddaddy in the Montparnasse section of Paris. It's utterly simple, and a game of Dominoes might be under way as you walk in. In the open-air café garden, near the port, tables are placed outside on the gravel. The outdoor grill promises a "cheeseburger in Paradise." Beer costs $1.50. The locals like it a lot, and outsiders are welcomed but not necessarily embraced until they get to know you a bit. If you want to spread a rumor and have it travel fast across the island, start it here. In an adjoining garden the talk is of the sea.

Also in Gustavia, overlooking the harbor, is the **Hôtel Hibiscus,** rue Thiers (tel. 27-64-62), popular with visiting yachting people.

Autour du Rocher, l'Orient (tel. 27-60-73), has one of the best-known and most sophisticated nightclubs on the island. A visit here requires a meandering expedition to the island's north coast, about two miles from Gustavia. Its bar opens at 7 p.m. every night, but the nocturnal activities are more likely to get going after 10 p.m. A weekend cover charge of $5 includes the first drink; after that, libations go for $4 each. This seems to be one of the island's more durable discos. Bruno DeBenedictus and David Henderson serve light meals throughout the evening for $20 each, including such menu items as steak sandwiches, cheeseburgers, and the best egg creams this side of Brooklyn. The club is closed in September and for most of October.

L'Ananas Jazz Bar, rue Courbet (tel. 27-63-77) in Gustavia is on the ground floor of the previously recommended L'Ananas restaurant. Drinks are expensive, from $7 per libation, but that gives you the right to listen to some of the best live music played on the island. Music begins at 8:30 p.m., lasting until midnight. In high season there is music every night, at least in theory. In the off-season, no entertainment is offered on Tuesday.

Chapter XIII

THE BRITISH WINDWARDS

1. Dominica
2. St. Lucia
3. St. Vincent
4. The Grenadines
5. Grenada

THESE WINDWARD ISLANDS lie in the direct path of the trade winds, which swoop down from the northeast. British affiliated (now mainly independent), they are Gallic in manner, West Indian in outlook.

French habits often persist because of early Gallic invaders, as the islands changed hands many times before coming into Britain's orbit. On such islands as St. Lucia, and especially Dominica, you'll hear a Créole patois. English, however, is commonly spoken.

The British Windwards are made up of four main islands—St. Lucia, St. Vincent, Grenada, and Dominica—along with a scattering of isles or spits of land known as the Grenadines. Truly far-out islands, the Grenadines are a chain stretching from St. Vincent to Grenada. Some people group Barbados and Trinidad and Tobago in the British Windwards, but I have preferred, for convenience's sake, to treat these independent island nations separately in the following chapters.

Topped by mountains, bursting with greenery, the British Windwards in this chapter are still far enough off the mainline tourist circuit to make a visit to them something of an adventure. At some of the more remote oases, you'll have the sand crabs, iguanas, and sea birds to enjoy all by yourself.

For the most part the islands are small, volcanic in origin. They have no glittering casinos and dazzling resort hotels, but you'll not have a dull time, at least visually.

The islands use the same currency, the Eastern Caribbean dollar, worth about 37¢ U.S. *Note:* Prices in this chapter are given in U.S. dollars unless otherwise indicated. Most of the inhabitants live on their crops. There's little or no industry, and tourism is not overly developed, especially in Dominica.

1. Dominica

It has been called "the most original island in the Caribbean." Covered by a dense tropical rain forest that blankets its mountain slopes, including cloud-wreathed Morne Diablotin at 4,747 feet, it has vegetation unique in the West Indies. Untamed, unspoiled Dominica (pronounced Dom-in-*ee*-ka) is known for its crystal-clear rivers and waterfalls, its hot springs and boiling lakes. According to myth, it has 365 "rivers," one for each day of the year.

Nature lovers and adventurers are attracted to the almond-shaped island, seeking such endangered species as the sisserou and the imperial parrot. Dominica, not to be confused with the Dominican Republic, is also the last reservation of the once-fierce, cannibalistic Carib Indians, who managed to hold out against Europe's two grand armies of the 18th century.

SOME BACKGROUND: Largest of the British Windwards, Dominica (or Sunday Island) was discovered by Columbus in November of 1493. For centuries British and French troops fought each other for its domination. The deadly game eventually turned in Britain's favor, and it had to pay a ransom of $65,000 to France to get that country to leave. In 1805 Britain assumed control, yet it still had to deal with Carib uprisings, including an Indian war which broke out as late as 1930.

On March 1, 1967, Dominica got a new constitution and was declared a state in association with Britain. On November 3, 1978, it became independent.

Dominica, with a population of some 80,000 souls, lies in the eastern Caribbean, between Guadeloupe to the north and Martinique to the south. English is the official language, but a French patois is widely spoken.

The mountainous island is 29 miles long and 15 miles wide, with a total land area of 290 square miles, many of which have never been seen by explorers other than, presumably, the Carib Indians.

Most Dominicans earn their living from agriculture. In the past the government has made a strong bid for tourism, but not the type who would expect miles of white sandy beaches which the island doesn't have. Rather, Dominica is known for its river swimming. Because of the many shipwrecks around the island, scuba-diving is popular, particularly off the west coast.

Rainfall varies from a dryness along the coast to a tropical rain forest downpour in the mountainous interior.

Clothing is casual, including light summer wear most of the year; however, take along a sweater for those trips into the mountains. Bikinis and swimwear should not be worn in the capital city, Roseau, or in the villages.

To sum up, go here for the beauties of nature more than *la dolce vita*.

Portrait of a Great Lady

One of Dominica's most valuable assets is its very human and intelligent prime minister, Miss **Eugenia Charles.** She's credited almost single-handedly with focusing world resolve on the U.S. military action that prevented Grenada from being taken over by Cuba in 1985. Her articulation of the danger of Soviet influence in the Caribbean has placed her near the top of the region's leaders, and probably the most beloved by the media. Firmly allied with the U.S., and a personal friend of Ronald Reagan and Margaret Thatcher, she is known for her ability to listen creatively to the complaints and suggestions of her compatriots.

Once a week she returns to her private offices which she used during her long career as a lawyer and leader of the opposition. A discreet plaque on the door reads simply, "Eugenia Charles, Barrister at Law and Solicitor." Inside you are likely to see as many as 50 people, each with a cause to plead before the island's social and political grande dame.

Born of a prominent Dominican family, and educated in Canada and Britain, she is the island's ambassador to the world at large, and its most articulate spokesperson.

When faced with the myriad possibilities of how to spend development money from the E.E.C. and the U.S., she insisted that the island's notoriously pot-holed roads be widened into the smooth thoroughfares that crisscross the island today. Her rationale was to improve transportation infrastructures so that industries besides tourism could develop in Dominica's lush interior.

As for tourism, Miss Charles foresees that because of the frequent rainfall over Dominica, the island will never have the kind of "fun in the sun" holidays that other neighboring islands have fostered more or less successfully. Rather, she envisions the development of a series of spas in the jungle-covered interior, profiting from the profusion of mineral and hot springs.

Her birthday, May 15, is somewhat of a national event, at least observed by her political allies. One coup which Miss Charles is said to have engineered happened in 1985, when the island's hundreds of government employees went on strike for more pay. She went on the radio to announce in clear, articulate, and rational terms that the government simply had no additional money to pay for salary increases and that such an expenditure could bankrupt the country. Everyone returned to work without incident.

Gracious, hard-driving, and relentlessly realistic, she is indeed a Lady with a capital L, and the most memorable democratic leader of the entire Caribbean.

GETTING THERE: There are two airports in Dominica, neither of which is large enough to handle a jetliner. Therefore there are no direct flights from North America (there wouldn't be a large demand even if there were). The **Melville Hall Airport** is on the northeast coast of the island, almost diagonally across the island from its capital, Roseau. Should you land at Melville Hall, you are faced with a 1½-hour taxi ride. The fare from Melville Hall to Roseau is EC$33 ($12.20) per person, and the driver has the right to assemble at least four passengers in his cab. If a person wants to travel in the taxi alone, there is a minimum charge of EC$60 ($22.20). Therefore, try to avoid booking a flight that might land you at this airport if you have a choice.

It's much better to land at the newer **Canefield Airport,** an airstrip about a ten-minute taxi ride to the north of Roseau. This airfield takes smaller planes than those that can land at Melville Hall.

For many North Americans, the easiest way to reach Dominica is to take a flight to Antigua (see "Getting There" in Chapter IX). From there, you can take a LIAT flight to Dominica—but even though it's scheduled, don't expect it to be on time.

It's also possible to fly from New York to Guadeloupe (see "Getting There" in

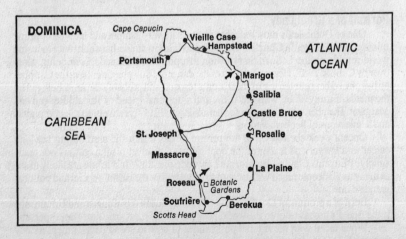

Chapter XII). Once in Guadeloupe, you can make a connection on Air Guadeloupe to Dominica. Air Martinique also flies in from Fort-de-France.

GETTING AROUND: Roseau is the capital, and most of the places to stay are found there.

At either airport, you can rent a **taxi,** and prices are controlled by the government.

If you rent a car, you'll have to pay EC$20 ($7.40) to the government to obtain a driver's license. I've found roads impassible in many parts of the island, except with a four-wheel drive. *Driving is officially on the left.* The two **car-rental establishments** on Dominica are **Valley Rent-a-Car,** Goodwill Road (tel. 448-3233) in Roseau, and at Portsmouth (tel. 445-5252); and **Wide Range,** 81 Bath Rd., Roseau (tel. 448-2198). Rates range from $25 to $35 daily, and $160 to $220 weekly. Drivers must be between 25 and 65 years of age, and a deposit of $100 is required, as well as comprehensive insurance with a $300 deductible clause. Collision damage waivers are available.

There is no public transportation to speak of, except some private **minibus** service between Roseau and the rest of Dominica. These minibuses are filled mainly with schoolchildren, workers, and country people who need to come into the city to buy supplies. They are definitely not recommended to visitors, who should, as mentioned, stick to the taxis as a far more reliable means of transport.

Dominica Tours, Anchorage Hotel, Castle Comfort (tel. 449-2638), run by Carl and Janice Armour, offer the best tours on the island, including hiking and photo safaris. The most popular tour is to the Carib Reservation and to Emerald Pool, a grotto in the heart of the rain forest. With lunch included, the six-hour safari costs $25. The two-hour tour to Sulfur Springs, and a visit to the Botanical Gardens, goes for $10. I'd also recommend a combined tour of Trafalgar Triple Waterfalls, Sulfur Springs (via the Morne and Botanical Gardens), and Freshwater Lake, including a picnic lunch and rum punch, lasting six hours and going for $25.

Otherwise you can negotiate your own terms with the taxi drivers eagerly awaiting your business at the airport when the plane lands. Rates are about $15 per person for each hour of touring. As many as four passengers can go along at the same time.

PRACTICAL FACTS: To enter, U.S. and Canadian residents need **proof of citizenship** such as a passport, voter registration card, or a birth certificate. In addition, an ongoing (or return) ticket must be produced.

Customs is lenient, allowing you personal and household effects, plus 200 cigarettes, 50 cigars, and 40 ounces of liquor or wine.

Dominica maintains **phone,** telegraph, teletype, and Telex services with the rest of the world, but don't count on getting calls through right away. To dial Dominica, the area code is 809, as it is for most of the Caribbean. However, on Dominica, only five digits are required to call anywhere on the island. From overseas, you'll need seven digits (besides the area code), the first two being 44, followed by the five-digit number. To call Marigot, Wesley, and Portsmouth, your first three digits are 445; Roseau, 448; and Canefield, St. Joseph, and Cane Bay, 449.

Its **currency,** is the Eastern Caribbean, or "Bee Wee," dollar.

For U.S.-made appliances, take along an adapter. The **electrical current** is 220 to 240 volts AC, 50 cycles. The **time** is also different, except in the summer when the U.S. goes on Daylight Saving Time. Then Roseau and Miami (or New York) keep the same clocks. But in winter Dominica is one hour ahead of Miami and New York.

Most hotels and restaurants add a 10% **service charge** to bills. The real local island joints do not. In them, **tipping** is up to you. In addition, a 10% government **room tax** is added to every hotel accommodation bill, plus a 10% tax on the sale of alcohol in hotels. Anyone who remains in Dominica for 24 hours must pay a $6 (U.S.) **embarkation tax** (it may have risen by the time of your visit).

Regular **business hours** are 8 a.m. to 4 p.m. daily except on Saturday (from 8 a.m. to 1 p.m.) Lunch break is from 1 to 2 p.m. **Banks** are open Monday to Friday from 8 a.m. to noon. They reopen on Friday from 3 to 5 p.m. to handle last-minute transactions for the weekend.

Water is drinkable from the taps or in the high mountains (pollution is hardly a problem here).

In **climate,** daytime temperatures average between 70° and 85° Fahrenheit. Nights, however, are much cooler, especially in the mountains. The rainy season is from June to October, when there can be warnings of hurricane activity.

Remember to take a flashlight to Dominica.

The **Dominica Tourist Information office** is at 37 Cork St., Roseau (tel. 448-2186). Hours are Monday to Friday from 8 a.m. to 1 p.m. and 2 to 4 p.m.

HOTELS IN DOMINICA: There are several places to stay, but none of them is very large. Only small groups of people or individual travelers can be accommodated at one time. Air conditioning may be found in some hotels, but most establishments on Dominica are a far cry from luxury. As a compensation, the cost of living is low, and tariffs throughout the island entice the bargain seeker.

In Roseau and Castle Comfort

Reigate Hall Hotel, Reigate (tel. 445-4031). Remotely lying on a steep hillside about a mile from Roseau, it was originally built in the 18th century as a plantation house. Some parts of the original structure are left, but the hotel has been substantially altered. Most of the old has been replaced with a comfortably airy design of hardwood floors and exposed stone. The establishment contains 17 rooms curving around the sides of a rectangular swimming pool. Each has a private bath, air conditioning, and phone. Year round, with a full breakfast included, singles cost from $50 daily; doubles, $80; and suites, $125. Tax and service are extra. The hotel has a sauna, an outdoor tennis court, a gym, and a good restaurant (recommended separately).

Anchorage Hotel, P.O. Box 34 (tel. 449-2638), is skillfully terraced so that its true beauty is only visible once you're inside. Lying at Castle Comfort, half a mile south of Roseau, the hotel is an EC$5 ($1.85) ride into town. Carl and Janice Armour provide 36 air-conditioned rooms, each with two double beds, all with shower or bath, plus a balcony overlooking their private pool. Mr. and Mrs. Armour are the most helpful hosts I've encountered on the island. For a peaceful holiday hideaway, year round the Anchorage rents a single for $40 nightly, a double going for $50, both EP. For breakfast and dinner, a supplement of $20 per person is tacked on. Children under 12 are granted reductions of 50%. In the bedrooms, draperies and bedspreads are often in florid prints.

In spite of its location on shore, there is little or no beach available, so guests spend their days around the plant-ringed rectangular pool. However, the hotel does have its own jetty and a pebble beach for saltwater bathing. If you own a yacht, you can moor it here or use the dinghy to come over for a meal at the roof restaurant, with its view of the sea and Roseau Harbor. The hotel also has a squash court. They keep a fresh supply of ginger lilies and anthurium daily in the public rooms. The hotel's French and Caribbean cuisine is the best on the island. The food is simple but good, with an emphasis on fresh fish and vegetables. A table d'hôte luncheon or dinner costs $15. But you can dine much lighter, perhaps ordering only fish, a salad, and rice for $5. Nonresidents aren't allowed to use the swimming pool, but they can drop in for meals. A West Indian band plays music twice a week for dancing.

Excelsior Hotel, P.O. Box 413, Canefield (tel. 449-1501), is one of the newest, best-managed, and most popular hotels in Dominica. Lying about two miles from the center of Roseau, but only a two-minute drive from the airport, it was built and designed by a handsome Dominican entrepreneur, Anthony Williams. Returning to

Dominica after many years in London, he built the white-walled hotel on family-owned land a short distance from a beach. The hotel contains only 14 well-scrubbed bedrooms, each with private bath, comfortable furniture, and access to a veranda. This is the only hotel in Dominica with its own specially designed conference room, making it the center of the island's business and commercial life. Guests are usually met at the airport, then redeposited there at the end of their visit. Even the clean and bright in-house restaurant is worth a special visit. Mr. Williams and his gracious staff charge year-round prices of $50 daily in a single, $65 in a double, with MAP included. He is assisted by his charming aunt, Mrs. May Thompson, and his well-educated wife, Frances.

Standing next to the Anchorage, **Sisserou Hotel,** P.O. Box 134, Castle Comfort (tel. 445-3111), is named after the island bird that is on the endangered-species list. It offers about the same class and comfort of accommodations as the Anchorage. The friendly management lodges guests in one of 20 rooms, each with private bath, air conditioning, and a balcony overlooking the sea. The hotel stands right on the shoreline, but instead of swimming there, most guests dive into the hotel's pool. There's also a breeze-filled wooden bar sitting beneath a sun screen beside the pool. The hotel has a good in-house restaurant. The public area are mostly sheathed in two full-grained tropical hardwoods known as samaan and gommier. Year-round rates are $43 daily in a single, $54 in a double, breakfast included. An excursion tour group, Robinson Crusoe Safaris, works out of the Sisserou, charging the same tariffs as those proposed by the tours at the Anchorage.

Evergreen Hotel, P.O. Box 309, Castle Comfort (tel. 448-3288). Built in 1986, this pleasant family-run hotel looks a bit from the outside like a Swiss chalet. It contains only ten rooms, a few of which have access to wrap-around tile-floored verandas. It sits amid a cluster of other hotels about a mile south of Roseau. A stony beach is visible a few steps beyond the garden. Inside and out, the airy, spacious, comfortably modern place was trimmed with a richly textured local wood called gommier. Mena Winston, the Dominican-born owner, assists in the preparation of each of the well-flavored meals. With MAP included, singles year round cost $55 daily, and doubles run $80, plus service and tax. Each room has stone accents, air conditioning, and a private bath. Laundry service and scuba-diving can be arranged.

A Beachfront Resort

The **Castaways Beach Hotel,** P.O. Box 5, Roseau (tel. 445-6244), is the island's first major resort along the coast north of Roseau, some 13 miles from the capital. Nestled between the tropical forest and a mile-long black sand beach and ringed on the inland side with huge tamarind trees, the hotel has 27 concrete-walled rooms shaded by tall coconut palms. Each accommodation has a private bath and is spacious, well ventilated, and filled with simple contemporary furniture. Linda Harris, the managing director, charges from $90 daily for doubles in winter and $70 for singles. *In summer, prices are $60 in a double, $40 in a single.* Between the hotel units and the sea is an open-air bar built in a fashion similar to the *chikees* of the Seminole Indians in the Florida Everglades, thatched with palmetto fronds. Water sports can be arranged through the reception desk, as can guided excursions to the island's principal sights. The hotel dining room serves some of the best food I've found on Dominica (see my recommendation below).

Rain Forest Retreats

Springfield Plantation, P.O. Box 41, Roseau (tel. 449-1401). It doesn't sit on any beach, and its access roads are winding and bumpy. Still, it's one of the most unusual and raffishly charming hotels in Dominica. Set in a rain forest about seven miles north of Roseau, it occupies a wood-framed plantation house whose U-shaped design embraces a poinsettia-ringed front courtyard. Its dignified premises includes a richly gabled annex and the imposing private house of the estate's absentee owner, John Archibald, who is descended from the original chairman of Standard Oil. Now a resident of Upperville, Virginia, he visited Dominica in 1935, long before the advent of modern tourism, and bought huge parcels of jungle-covered land. At the time only a tiny wood-sided hut was there, but over the years Mr. Archibald added the vaguely neoclassical white-sided colonial compound which you see today. In its heyday a battalion of workers and resident agronomists were employed to supervise orange and grapefruit crops. When the industry declined, the compound with its 250 remaining acres was transformed into a casually managed hotel.

It contains only six rooms and four apartments, each of which has a kitchen. None needs air conditioning because of the constant mountainside breezes. Year round, with MAP included, singles cost $75 daily; doubles, $110. The establishment's social center is a panoramic veranda, from which you can see the sea between the cleft of two mountains. Furnishings throughout are an eclectic mix of 1950s tropical with a few antiques. Mostly, the place offers a simple, unpretentious, slightly eccentric oasis. If you want to go swimming, the Anthurium River, 200 feet from the hotel, offers a safe cold-water river pool secluded from prying eyes by the overhang of nearby trees. Luncheon visitors are welcome to the plantation, but only if they phone in advance. Mountain chicken is a specialty, as is crayfish from the river. Lunches for nonresidents cost EC$50 ($18.50). The gentlemanly manager, Tommy Coulthard, and his wife, Jane, are gracious and charming people.

Emerald Pool Hotel (mailing address: 109 Bathroad, Roseau (tel. 445-8095). Surrounded by a high-altitude jungle wilderness about a mile from Emerald Pool, this isolated guesthouse lies about 24 miles northeast of Roseau and about 5 miles from the Atlantic beaches. It was built in 1979 by Swiss-born Gina Stähli, then rebuilt in 1980 after it was demolished by a hurricane. The in-house bar and restaurant are in a well-maintained clubhouse filled with louvered windows and functional but well-chosen furniture. There's no phone anywhere on the eight acres (reservations are received via an employee in Roseau). Likewise, there's no TV—electricity is supplied by a small generator for no more than four hours every evening. Créole and European food are served in the dining room at prearranged hours to residents of the eight A-frame bungalows. These occupy a sunny clearing about a two-minute walk from the main house. A small above-ground swimming pool is on the premises. The place is so isolated that it's perhaps the most peaceful on the island, with absolutely nothing to do but escape. With MAP included, accommodations rent for $60 to $90 daily, double occupancy, and $40 to $60 single, throughout the year.

Papillote Wilderness Retreat, P.O. Box 67 (tel. 445-2287), is a hotel and restaurant run by the Jean-Baptistes—Dominican-born Cuthbert, who handles the restaurant, and his wife, Florida-born Anne Grey, a marine scientist. Their place, four miles to the east of Roseau, stands right in the middle of Papillote Forest, at the foothills of Morne Macaque. In this remote setting they have created a unique rain-forest resort that is somewhat primitive. You can spend an Adam and Eve life here, surrounded by exotic fruits, flowers, and herb gardens. In a wood-sided outbuilding, eight simple bedrooms share four bathrooms. With MAP included, year-round rates are $65 daily in a single, $100 in a double, plus service and taxes.

Don't expect constantly sunny weather, since this part of the jungle is known for its downpours. Their effect, however, keeps the orchids which line the paths, begonias, and brilliantly colored bromeliads lush. The 12 acres of sloping and forested land are pierced with a labyrinth of masonry walls and trails, beside which flows a network of freshwater streams, a few of which flow from hot sulfur springs. Natural hot mineral baths are available, and you'll be directed to a secluded waterfall where you can swim in the river. The Jean-Baptistes also run a boutique in which they sell Dominican products, including appliquéed quilts, made by local artisans. Even if you don't stay here, it's an experience to dine on the thatch-roofed terrace (see "Where to Dine," below).

WHERE TO DINE: The local delicacy is the fine flesh of the crapaud (a frog) called "mountain chicken." Freshwater crayfish is another specialty, as is *tee-tee-ree*, fried cakes made from tiny fish. Stuffed crab back is usually a delight. The backs of red and black land crabs are stuffed with delicate crabmeat and Créole seasonings. The fresh fruit juices of the island are divine nectar, and no true Dominican spends the day without at least one rum punch.

La Robe Créole, 3 Victoria St. (tel. 448-2896), is considered the most important independent restaurant in the capital. It's contained inside the masonry walls of a low-slung colonial house, sitting beside a sunny plaza on a slope above the sea, behind a façade draped with flowering vines. Waitresses dressed in madras Créole costumes serve full meals costing from EC$65 ($24). In a long and narrow dining room capped with heavy beams and filled with nostalgia-laden reminders of the 19th century, you can enjoy pumpkin pimiento soup, callaloo with cream of coconut soup, crab back, pizzas, several kinds of kebabs, four different preparations of steak (including barbecued), mountain chicken in beer batter, and shrimp in coconut with garlic sauce. For dessert, you can try banana or coconut cake or ice cream. The establishment and its bar are open daily except Sunday from 9 a.m. to 11 p.m. The number of tables is limited, so reserve.

Also at 3 Victoria St. is **The Mouse Hole** (no phone), a good place for food on the run. From its take-out service, you can enjoy freshly made sandwiches and salads. Light meals cost $5. They make good Trinidad-inspired rôtis here. This is burrito-type food, a wheat pancake wrapping beef, chicken, or vegetables. In Dominica, these rôtis are most often flavored with curry.

The **Orchard Restaurant,** 31 King George V St. (tel. 448-3051). Late in 1986 this restaurant opened in its new home, a clean, wood-lined oasis of calm on a busy, centrally located street of the capital. There's a bar, as well as a large dining room and a lattice-covered courtyard to one side for outdoor dining. You can order take-out food here, but most clients come for the bar and the sit-down meals. Lunch is served daily except Sunday from 11:30 a.m. to 4 p.m., and dinner is nightly except Saturday and Sunday from 7 to 9 p.m. Full meals, costing from EC$45 ($16.65), include mountain chicken, callaloo soup with crabmeat, fish court-bouillon, coconut shrimp, black pudding, blood sausage, goat water, several pumpkin dishes, and breadfruit puffs. Friday night features barbecued meat dishes.

Reigate Hall Restaurant, Reigate Hall Hotel (tel. 445-4031), lies only a mile from the center of Roseau, but it seems so much longer because of the tortuous road leading up to it. Contained on the second story of this previously recommended hotel, the restaurant is an intimately lit enclave of such polished tropical hardwoods as greenheart along with exposed stone. A masonry spillway splashing water onto the paddles of a water wheel adds an old-fashioned accent. Lunch is from 1 to 3 p.m., and dinner is served from 7 to 10 p.m. daily. Menu items are derived from both French and Créole recipes, costing from EC$70 ($26) for a full meal. On any given night the bill of fare might include fish soup, beef curry, coq au vin, prawns in garlic sauce, seafood au gratin, and "mountain chicken" in a champagne sauce. Reservations are suggested if you're not a resident of the hotel.

The restaurant at the **Excelsior Hotel,** Canefield (tel. 449-1501), on the ground floor of one of the newest hotels of Dominica, serves well-prepared food at reasonable prices. Guests dine in a clean, inviting room with white walls and straw-bottomed chairs of island cedar. Meals are served without a break from 7 a.m. to 11 p.m. A polite employee will offer you a glass of soursop juice before you order, unless you prefer something stronger from the bar. Lunch costs from EC$30 ($11); dinner, from EC$65 ($24). The bill of fare might include opossum (manicou), delectable preparations of mountain chicken, T-bone steak, fresh crayfish from one of the island's hundreds of freshwater streams, and fish "any style." Anthony Williams is the restaurant's manager.

The World of Food Restaurant and Bar, Vena's Hotel, 48 Cork St. (tel. 445-3286). In the 1930s the garden containing this pleasant restaurant belonged to a well-known novelist, Jean Rhys. Today it's the patio for one of the most charming Créole restaurants in Roseau. Some say that its owner, Vena McDougal, is the best Créole cook in town. You can have a drink at the stone-walled building at the far end of the garden if you want, but many guests select one of the rickety tables in the shadow of a large mango tree. Open from 7:30 a.m. to 10 p.m., seven days a week, the World of Food serves a fixed-price meal costing from EC$11 ($4) to EC$15 ($5.50). Specialties include steamed fish or fish steak, curried goat, chicken-filled rôti, black pudding, mountain chicken, breadfruit puffs, callaloo and watercress soup, crab backs, conch, and tee-tee-ree (fried fish cakes). She's said to make the best rum punches on the island as well—they're a concoction of rich fruits blended with local rums. The restaurant is attached to Vena's Hotel (really a guesthouse). If you want to reach the restaurant without passing through Vena's, its entrance is on Field's Lane.

Guiyave, 15 Cork St. (tel. 448-2930). Near the office of the prime minister, this pleasantly airy restaurant occupies the second floor of a wood-framed West Indian house. Rows of tables almost completely fill the narrow balcony overlooking the street outside. You can enjoy a drink at the stand-up bar on the second floor. At night the third-floor dining room, slightly more formal than its downstairs counterpart, is used. Every Monday, Tuesday, and Wednesday, the establishment is open only for breakfast and lunch from 8 a.m. to 5 p.m. Every Thursday, Friday, and Saturday, the restaurant is open from 8 a.m. till very late at night, with only a one-hour closing between 5 and 6 p.m. for a cleanup (closed all day Sunday). Full meals cost from $8 at lunch, $14 at dinner, and specialties include different preparations of conch and rabbit, octopus and lobster, spareribs, chicken, Saturday-only rôtis, crab backs, mountain chicken, goat stew, and an array of sandwiches. The place is known for its juices, including refreshingly tropical glasses of soursop, tamarind, sorrel, cherry, and strawberry.

Papillote Wilderness Retreat (tel. 445-2287), previously recommended for its lodgings, is also one of the most alluringly located restaurants in Dominica. Even if you're not staying there, call for a reservation, negotiate with a taxi driver, and ask to be taken there for lunch. Amid nature trails rife with exotic flowers, century-old trees, and filtered sunlight, you dine on a masonry terrace a few steps from a sociable bar topped with a slab of samaan wood. The owners are Dominica-born Cuthbert Jean-Baptiste and his wife, Florida-born Anne Grey. The array of health-conscious food includes flying fish, river shrimp, mountain chicken, dolphin, kingfish, dasheen puffs, breadfruit puffs, and a tempting array of tropical salads. Lunch and soothing drinks are served daily except Sunday from 10 a.m. to 6 p.m., costing from EC$35 ($13) for a full meal. Don't forget to bring sturdy walking shoes and a bathing suit. Near the dining terrace, Cuthbert built a Jacuzzi-size masonry basin which is constantly filled with the mineral-rich waters of a hot spring.

If you're touring north along the coast, consider stopping in for a meal at the already-recommended **Castaways Beach Hotel,** P.O. Box 5 (tel. 445-6244), 13 miles north of Roseau. In this resort setting, the managing director, Linda Harris, welcomes nonguests to her hotel dining room with its waterfront setting. Guests dress in casual resortwear and dine informally, enjoying the warm hospitality of the staff. Here you get the cuisine for which Dominica is known, including the crapaud or mountain chicken. Prepared in a number of ways, it is almost always delicious. They have a delicacy most often compared to quail. You can also get lambi (conch), as well as island crab mixed with a savory Créole stuffing. All dishes are garnished with the fruits and vegetables of Dominica's rich soil. For example, you might have glazed ham with passion fruit. Count on spending around $20 for dinner, less for lunch. Before dining, try a rum punch in the lounge or beach bar. Go from noon to 2 p.m. or 7 to 9 p.m.

TOURING THE ISLAND: Those making day trips to Dominica from other islands will want to see the **Carib Indian Reservation,** in the northeast. In 1903 Britain got the Caribs to agree to accept boundaries on 3,700 acres of land set aside for them. Hence, this is the last remaining domain of this once-hostile tribe (now subdued) who gave their name to the archipelago—Caribbean.

Their look is Mongolian, and they are no longer "pure-blooded." Blacks and others have married into the tribe. Today they survive by fishing, growing food, and weaving baskets and vertivert grass mats which they sell to the outside world. They still make dugout canoes too.

It's like going back in time when you explore **Morne Trois Pitons National Park,** a primordial rain forest, "me Tarzan, you Jane" country. Mists rise gently over lush, dark-green growth, drifting up to blue-green peaks that have earned for Dominica the title of "Switzerland of the Caribbean." Framed by banks of giant ferns, rivers rush and tumble. Trees sprout orchids, and everything seems blanketed with some type of parasitic growth. Green sunlight filters down through timeless trees, and the roar of a waterfall creates a blue mist.

Exploring this green heart of Dominica is for serious botanists and only the most skilled hikers, who should never penetrate unmarked trails without a very experienced guide.

Deep in the park is the **Emerald Pool Trail,** a half-mile nature trail that forms a circuit loop on a footpath passing through the forest to a pool with a beautiful waterfall. Downpours are frequent in the rain forest, and at high elevations cold winds blow.

Five miles up from the **Roseau River Valley,** in the south-central sector of Dominica, **Trafalgar Falls** can be reached after your vehicle passes through the village of Trafalgar. There, however, you have to approach by foot, as the slopes are too steep for vehicles. After a 20-minute walk, you arrive at the base of the falls. A trio of falls converge into a rock-strewn pool. Boulders sprout vegetation, and tree ferns encircle the flowing water. On the way there you pass growths of ginger plants or vanilla orchids.

The **Sulfur Springs** are evidence of the island's volcanic past. Jeeps or Land Rovers get quite near. Not only Sulfur Springs but **Boiling Lake** are bubbling evidence of underground volcanic activity, which can be seen near Trafalgar Falls, north and east of Roseau. It's like a bubbling pool of gray mud. Sometimes you hear a belch of smelly sulfurous fumes—the odor is like a rotten egg. Only the very fit should attempt to go to Boiling Lake. Some Dominicans fear that volcanic activity will erupt again. Freshwater Lake lies at the foot of Mount Macaque.

On the northwest coast, **Portsmouth** is Dominica's second-largest settlement. Once there, you can row up the Indian River in native canoes to visit the ruins of old Fort Shirley and bathe at Sandy Beach on Douglas Bay.

The **Cabrits National Park** on the northwest coast of Dominica (tel. 449-2733), is a 650-acre protected site containing mountain scenery, tropical forests, swampland, volcanic sand beaches, coral reefs, and the ruins of a fortified 18th-century garrison of British, then French construction. The Cabrits Park's land area is a spectacular promontory formed by twin peaks of extinct volcanoes, overlooking fine beaches, with Douglas Bay on one side and Prince Rupert's Bay across the headland. Part of Douglas Bay forms the marine section of the park. Fort Shirley, the large garrison last used as a military post in 1854, is being wrested from encroaching vegetation. A small museum highlights the natural and historic aspects of the park. The name Cabrits comes from the Spanish-Portuguese-French word for goat, because of the animals left there by early sailors to provide fresh meat on future visits.

THE SPORTING LIFE: Serious hikers find Dominica a major challenge. Guides should be used for all unmarked trails. You can reach one by going to the office of the **Dominica National Park** in the Botanical Gardens in Roseau (tel. 448-2732).

As for **beaches,** there are good beaches in the northwest of the island around

Portsmouth, the second town. There are also secluded beaches in the northeast, along with spectacular coastal scenery. But all of these are hard to reach, and you might settle instead for a freshwater swimming pool or river swimming.

The best water-sports center is **Dive Dominica,** Castle Comfort Guest House (tel. 449-2188). Introduction to scuba-diving (resort course) costs $50, with all equipment provided. Open-water certification (NAUI) instruction is given. Snorkeling is also possible, with equipment for rent.

Dive Dominica also offers **boat charters,** with a 24-foot Aquasport taking a maximum of ten persons for $60 per hour. Trips are made to such destinations as Douglas Bay, Rodney's Rock, Soufrière, and Portsmouth, with prices depending on the distance traveled and the time consumed.

SHOPPING: In Roseau, **Tropicrafts Ltd.,** at Queen Mary Street and Turkey Lane (tel. 448-2747), offers the well-known grass rugs handmade and woven in several intricate patterns at Tropicrafts' factory. They also have for sale handmade bags, shopping bags, and placemats, all appliquéed by hand. The handmade dolls are popular with doll collectors. The Dominican vertivert-grass mats are known throughout the world.

Caribana Handicrafts, 31 Cork St. (tel. 448-2761). Some island residents claim that the entire straw-weaving industry on Dominica was established by the store's dignified owner, Iris Joseph. You'll be able to see a few of the products being crafted at wooden tables. Near the front, stacks of a lengthy array of baskets in all sizes and shapes are stocked. Mrs. Joseph is usually pleased to explain the dying processes which turn the straw into one of three different earth-related tones. When straw is buried in the earth, it turns black; when it's soaked in saffron, it turns yellow; and when it's boiled with the bark of a tang tree, it turns purple. A selection of other goods, including Bello Hot Pepper (said to be the finest by island connoisseurs), is available.

NIGHTLIFE: It's not very sophisticated, but there is some. A couple of the major hotels, such as Castaways (tel. 445-6244), have entertainment on weekends, usually a combo playing for dancing until midnight.

The **Anchorage Hotel** at Castle Comfort (tel. 449-2638) also has live entertainment and a good buffet at least one night a week.

If you're in Dominica at the right time, don't miss the **Korné Korn-La,** a street party usually held on the second Saturday of the month at Soufrière or Scotts Head Village. The name of the celebration means "blow the conch shell," a traditional sound that summoned plantation workers to the fields or home, announced the return of fishermen to shore with their catch, and signaled village get-togethers. Today's festivities include a row of candlelit stalls placed along the shore, where you can buy freshly barbecued lamb chops and grouper steaks for about $1.30 each and tasty little hotcakes for less than 10¢. There's recorded popular music blaring out, but my favorite is the live melodies of an accordion, a tambou, a boom-boom, a shack-shack, and a gwage. A small entrance fee is charged to pay for cleaning up the village.

2. St. Lucia

Second largest of the Windward Islands, St. Lucia (pronounced *Loo*-sha) is a checkerboard of green-mantled mountains, gentle valleys, wide beaches, banana plantations, a bubbling volcano, giant tree ferns, wild orchids, and fishing villages. There's a smell of the South Pacific about it. With its mixed French and British heritage, it has year-round temperatures of 70° to 90° Fahrenheit.

The actual discovery of this football-shaped island is shrouded in conjecture, some maintaining that Columbus landed on December 13, 1502. However, this widely held opinion is considered a total myth. Records reveal that the explorer was far from St. Lucia on that date. It is often conceded that Spanish seamen discovered the island in some unknown year.

St. Lucia lies some 20 miles from Martinique. An English party coming from St. Kitts settled here in 1605, but the island was to change hands a total of 14 times, as the French and English fought intermittently for its control, their battles lasting for more than a century. Slaughter parties led by cannibalistic Caribs often deterred permanent settlements for years.

The island was a British colony from 1803 to 1967, when it became an associated state within the Commonwealth. St. Lucia arrived at its full sovereignty on February 22, 1979, and in spite of protests, became an independent country and a full-fledged sister in the British Commonwealth of nations.

A mountainous island of some 240 square miles, St. Lucia counts some 120,000 inhabitants. The capital, **Castries,** is built on the southern shore of a large, almost landlocked harbor—a "reliable shelter for ships"—surrounded by hills. The approach to the airport is almost a path between hills, and it's very impressive.

The capital was named for an 18th-century French secretary of state to the foreign colonies, Marshal de Castries. Fires have swept over the town many times, destroying its wooden buildings. The last catastrophe occurred in 1948. As a result, don't expect too many vintage structures.

GETTING THERE:
Getting to Lucia has become easier in recent years, but airline routings from many North American cities require at least a touchdown in one or another Caribbean island before continuing to St. Lucia. Of all the airlines, **BWIA** offers a wider variety of takeoff points (Boston, Baltimore, New York's Kennedy, Toronto, and Miami) than any other airline. A few of their flights, especially in high season, are nonstop, while others require a change on the island of Barbados. **Pan American** offers daily service to Barbados from New York and Miami, after which passengers connect with a smaller aircraft flown by **LIAT. Eastern** offers a connection three days a week from New York via San Juan and service via Miami every five to seven days per week, depending on the season. Finally, **American,** through its hub in San Juan, flies nonstop from both of New York's Kennedy and Newark, as well as from Miami, with a subsequent relatively convenient connection to St. Lucia.

GETTING AROUND:
A good way to travel on St. Lucia is by **taxis,** which are ubiquitous on the island, and most drivers are friendly and eager to please. The drivers have to be quite experienced to cope with the narrow, hilly, switchback roads outside the capital. Special programs have trained them to serve as guides. Their cars are unmetered, but tariffs for all standard trips are fixed by the government.

In asking the fare for a ride, make sure you determine if the driver is quoting a rate in U.S. dollars or the "Bee Wee." Leisure drives cost about EC$40 ($14.75) per hour. For example, one of the most popular runs—from Castries to Marigot Bay—goes for EC$40 ($14.75).

Car Rentals
First, remember to *drive on the left*. The price of a small car ranges from $31 to $40 per day, depending on the type of vehicle, plus 35¢ per mile. You are given the first 45 miles free. National, Europcar, and Tilden are represented by **St. Lucia Car Rental Services,** P.O. Box 542, Castries, with locations at Hewanorra International Airport (tel. 454-6699), Vigie Airport (tel. 452-3050), Elliott Shell Servicentre at Gros Islet (tel. 452-8721), the Cariblue Hotel (tel. 452-8551), Club Méditerranée (tel. 45-46547), Hurricane Hole (tel. 453-4230), and Pointe Seraphine, Cruise Ship Dock.

Also represented is **Budget Rent-a-Car,** which operates from an office in Cul-de-Sac (tel. 452-6445). A representative will arrange to meet your incoming plane if you inform Budget of the details within two business days of your arrival. This two-day advance warning also qualifies you for the cheapest available rate, which is $170 a week with unlimited mileage for a Mazda station wagon without air conditioning and with manual transmission. Air conditioning is another $30 per week.

Avis is the island's most visible car-rental company, with no fewer than eight locations, many in the large hotels. From a headquarters known as Sundrive Rentals, 26 Brazil St. (tel. 452-2202), in Castries, it delivers cars to the airports. However, its cheapest car, a Honda Civic, with manual transmission and no air conditioning, is $258 a week with unlimited mileage. If you don't intend to do a lot of driving, the same car can be rented for 180 miles.

Each company offers an optional collision damage waiver, which negates your financial responsibility in case of an accident. Without it, you'll pay at least the first $1,000 worth of damage. At Budget the cost is around $7 a day.

For toll-free information about the services offered, call Budget at 800/527-0700 or Avis at 800/331-2112.

You will need a St. Lucia's driver's license. This can most easily be obtained at either airport upon arrival or at car-rental locations. Present your valid home license to the immigration officer and pay a fee of EC$30 ($11.10).

Local Buses

Wooden omnibuses, with names like "Lucian Love," and jitneys connect Castries with such main towns as Soufrière and Vieux Fort. They are generally overcrowded and often filled with produce on the way to market. Schedules are also unreliable. However, since taxis are expensive, it might be a reliable means of transport. At least it's cheap, usually from EC$1 (37¢) to EC$5 ($1.85) per ride. Buses for Cap Estate, the northern part of the island, leave from Jeremy Street in Castries, near the market. Buses going to Vieux Fort, Soufrière, leave from Bridge Street in front of the department store.

Sightseeing Bus Tours

Most hotel front desks will make arrangements for excursions, taking in all the major sights of St. Lucia. For example, **St. Lucia Representative Services,** 32 Micoud St., Castries (tel. 452-3762), offers an island tour, taking visitors to the top of Morne Fortune. That's followed by a visit to a rum distillery and on through the banana plantations and the pretty little fishing villages. The most spectacular stop for a view is to look at the Pitons. The tour stops at a restaurant for lunch and then a swim before returning to Castries. The cost is about $35.

Sea Excursions

This type of tour can usually be arranged at your hotel's activities desk. One of the most popular tours, costing EC$100 ($37) per person, is aboard the *Brig Unicorn,* which takes you on a day's sail to Soufrière and the Pitons. The *Unicorn* starred as the slave ship in the TV series "Roots," among other movie roles. Built in 1948, it is a 140-foot vessel with 16 square-rigged sails, carrying a crew of 13. You sail southward from Coal Pot, near Castries, at 9 a.m., heading for Soufrière's Sulfur Springs. On the return voyage you're served a lunch aboard. Later, you swim at Anse Cochon and sail into Marigot Bay. You're back at dock at 4 p.m., where coaches await to return you to your hotel. To make reservations on your own, call 452-5643.

PRACTICAL FACTS: The official **currency** is the Eastern Caribbean dollar, or EC$. It's about 37¢ in U.S. currency. However, most of the quotations will be in American dollars, as they are accepted by nearly all hotels, restaurants, and shops.

English is the official **language,** but St. Lucians may not speak it as you do. Islanders also speak a French-Créole patois, similar to that heard in Martinique.

St. Lucia has two **airports.** Most international flights land at Hewanorra Airport in the south, 45 miles from Castries. If you fly in here and you're booked into a hotel in the north, you'll have to spend up to about an hour and a half going along the pot-holed East Coast Hwy. The average taxi cost is $50. Once this airport was known as "Beane Field," when Roosevelt and Churchill agreed to construct a big air base there.

However, inter-island flights land at Vigie Airport in the northeast, which is much more convenient as it brings you down just outside Castries. LIAT Airways with its small prop planes flies into Vigie.

Customs at either airport should be no major hassle. U.S. or Canadian citizens need **proof of citizenship,** such as a passport, voter registration card, or birth certificate, plus an ongoing or return ticket.

In winter, watch your clock. St. Lucia is on **Atlantic Standard Time,** placing it one hour ahead of New York or Miami. However, during Daylight Saving Time it matches the clocks of the U.S. East Coast.

Electricity is a problem. Bring a converter, as St. Lucia has 220 to 230 volts, 50 cycles, AC.

Shopping hours are 8 a.m. to 4 p.m. in general, but watch those early closings on Wednesday.

Major **banks** in Castries include Chase Manhattan, and they close early, at noon, and even earlier on Saturday, at 11 a.m.

Cable & Wireless provides international telecommunications and also operates a dial **phone system** throughout the island. Cables may be handed in at hotel desks or at the offices of Cable & Wireless in the George Gordon Buildings on Bridge Street in Castries.

You'll find a **tourist information bureau** on the Queen Elizabeth II dock in Castries. For advance information, the **St. Lucia Tourist Board** is at P.O. Box 221 in Castries (tel. 452-5968). In the United States, the office is at 41 E. 42nd St. (Suite 315), New York, NY 10017 (tel. 212/867-2950).

The **General Post Office** is on Bridge Street in Castries. It's open Monday to Friday from 8:30 a.m. to 4 p.m.

Most hotels add a 10% **service charge,** and restaurants do likewise.

The government imposes an 8% **occupancy tax** on hotel room rentals.

If you're flying to one of the islands in the Caribbean Commonwealth (English-speaking islands), you must pay a **departure tax** of EC$10 ($3.70). That is true also for the French West Indies and the U.S. Virgin Islands. However, if you're returning to the U.S. mainland or going elsewhere, the airport tax is EC$20 ($7.40). This tax must be paid in EC dollars.

WHERE TO STAY: Most of the lead hotels on this island are in the same price range. You have to seek out the bargains (begin at the bottom of my list). Once you reach your hotel, chances are you'll feel pretty isolated, but that's what many guests want. Many St. Lucian hostelries have kitchenettes where you can prepare simple meals. Prices are quoted in U.S. dollars.

Couples, P.O. Box 190, Malabar Beach (tel. 452-4211), is, in my opinion, the best place to stay in St. Lucia. The logo—a silhouette of two lions coupling—is a provocative and sophisticated symbol of this unusual hotel, where all meals, drinks, cigarettes, entertainment, and most incidental expenses are included in the initial price. The center of the complex is under a gridwork of peaked roofs floored with tasteful terracotta tiles. Set on the edge of a beach bordered with palm trees, the hotel has a sprawling garden centered around a 150-year-old saman tree. A freshwater swimming pool is graced with a lattice-sheltered bar area. This is a resort for couples only, with no children allowed. (A couple, according to the sophisticated owner, Craig, and his beautiful wife, Penny, can be any two mutually interested persons.) Singles and triples are not accepted, which contributes to the relaxed ambience of lovers enjoying each other, making friends with other couples, and celebrating the beautiful physical plant as well as their relationships.

A member of the staff will meet your plane at the airport with a chest of cold beer and rum punches when you arrive. The bar opens early and closes late, acting as a precursor to the fine cuisine arranged by an expatriate Scotsman named Nigel. Most of the lunches are buffet style, and there's even a cold-cut buffet offered every evening after the end of the dinner hour. Evening action is fun, including a weekly pajama party the likes of which you may always have wanted to attend but never had the chance. All of this goes for a reasonable *$1,600 per couple per week in summer,* $2,000 per couple per week from December till April. The location is at the end of the Vigie runway, near Castries.

Cunard Hotel La Toc and La Toc Suites, P.O. Box 399 (tel. 452-3081), some 2½ miles south of Castries, bills itself as tropical, tranquil, and luxurious, and here's one place that delivers what it promises. The site, about a ten-minute drive from the capital on half a mile of curved beach, was purchased some 20 years ago when a Cunard executive spotted it and quickly decided that it would be ideal for a deluxe hotel. The resort hosts frequent luncheons and beach stopovers for the passengers of the Cunard vessels when they stop in St. Lucia. On 100 secluded acres at the edge of the island, the complex consists of both the hotel which has 200 handsomely furnished rooms, and La Toc Suites with 54 one- and two-bedroom, beautifully appointed units. The privately owned villas are rented as a whole or in sections. The hotel rooms and suites are colorfully accented with a tropical-motif decor. Each accommodation includes a private bath, air conditioning, plus balconies or patios offering views of the ocean or the exotic gardens, planted with red ixora and pink-purple eranthemum. *In summer, twins range in price from $95 to $125 daily; singles cost $75.* In winter, two people pay $120 to $160 daily; one person is charged $110 to $150. For breakfast and dinner, add another $36 per person. Le Toc Suites are like little dollhouses in pastel colors. *Town and Country* called this "one of the ten most luxurious villa complexes in the Caribbean." Set apart, each of the villas nestled against the mountainside facing the sea. They are connected by frequent shuttle service to the main building. In winter, a superior two-bedroom villa costs $250 daily, rising to $300 in a deluxe two-bedroom villa with a private plunge pool. *In summer, these same villas cost $190 to $230 daily.*

All guests have a choice of two swimming pools, one so big it has its own palm-studded island. Among the shops you'll find a beauty salon, souvenir shop, boutique, duty-free shop, and a drugstore. Dining is at the Terrace Restaurant, the casual entertainment center; at Les Pitons Restaurant, which has some of the best food on the island; or at the Quarter Deck, which has classic grills and operates only in the winter season. On the grounds is a manicured nine-hole golf course with a resident pro. Tennis buffs enjoy any of La Toc's three Har-tru courts (lit for night games) or the two hard-surface courts with a resident tennis pro. The front-desk personnel can arrange for you to go fishing for dorado (dolphin), swordfish, cavalle, or barracuda. Water sports include Sunfish sailing, windsurfing, snorkeling, and waterskiing, all free to La Toc guests. The private 120-foot brig, the *Unicorn,* sails twice weekly. There is live entertainment nightly, plus two floor shows a week.

Steigenberger Cariblue, P.O. Box 437, Cap Estate (tel. 452-8551), is a citadel of first-class resort living, on a 1,500-acre estate at the northernmost tip of the island. The famous German hotel chain has staked out this Anse du Cap entry in the Caribbean, within walking distance of the nine-hole golf course at Cap Estate. It is housed in a yellow colonial-style complex with white balconies and seemingly endless covered breezeways. For a unique St. Lucian holiday, this place is number one for many Europeans, and Americans seem to like it equally well. Informality and elegance go hand in hand here. Of course, you're an eight-mile run from Castries, but guests seem to prefer this isolation. Besides, if you want to go shopping, it's only a taxi ride across halfway passable roads. In addition, the hotel bus runs in three days a week for a shopping trip.

Guests are housed in one of 102 individually air-conditioned rooms with their own private balconies overlooking those sunsets which, even though a cliché, still cause a thrill when everybody takes on a cantaloupe glow. You might be reading the *New York Times* and the reader in the next room the *Frankfurter Allgemein,* but you'll share the same facilities—the Caribbean-style bamboo and rattan furnishings, the wall-to-wall carpeting, the polished oak. Most of the units are in the duo of four-story buildings, but I prefer the two-story beachfront wing. With a buffet breakfast, singles in winter range in price from $100 to $150; doubles, $135 to $185. *In summer,* a single on the EP rents for $50 to $90 daily, and a double costs $70 to $110. The grounds open onto a light-colored sandy beach. Covered walkways protect you from the sun's rays, but no one seems to need this shield, as they come here for the sun. Beside the beach stands an open-air dining pavilion with a bar. The hotel is a complete resort, offering not only golf, but a swimming pool (as would be expected), and tennis, golf, water sports such as scuba-diving, even a riding stable which allows you to go horseback riding. Snorkeling can be arranged, as can Laser and Sailfish sailing, windsurfing, and waterskiing.

Club Med (tel. 454-6547, or toll free 800/CLUB-MED) has opened a new village in St. Lucia, which was formerly the Halcyon Days Hotel, set on a 90-acre resort. As Club Med, the project is more successful than it was as a hotel. The carefree lifestyle holds forth on the southernmost tip of St. Lucia, opening onto Savannes Bay, just five minutes from the international airport. Completely refurbished, the club offers eight tennis courts, much beachside living, and free horseback riding. The usual array of Club Med's sports is featured, including volleyball, archery, soccer, basketball, calisthenics, and softball. In addition, the Club's Sailing Center, near the main building, offers two large sail boats, which takes about two dozen sailors on full-day or overnight sailing trips. There is also a well-equipped Workout Center.

Land rates in summer range from $490 to $580 per person, based on double occupancy, with all activities and meals included. In winter, the cost is generally $635 per person for land rates for one week, but between Christmas and New Year's it rises to $1,025 per person for the week. Each unit is air-conditioned, with a private balcony overlooking the sea. Some 512 members are accommodated in four-story, cream-colored buildings which are set in a coconut grove. The twin-bedded rooms offer double occupancy, each with a private shower. In the heart of the complex is an open-air bar, a freshwater swimming pool, and a dance and theater area. At meals, served in the second-floor dining room with a panoramic view, guests enjoy unlimited wine at lunch and dinner.

Membership, costing $25 for a one-time initiation plus $25 for adults and $10 for children in annual dues, is open to all. For more information, call the club's toll-free number, Monday to Saturday, or in New York City you can visit their sales and information office at 3 E. 54th St. (tel. 212/750-1670).

Marigot Bay Resort, at Marigot Bay (tel. 453-4256), is a blanket name to cover a complex of inns, cottages, restaurants, bars, boutiques, and yachting berths lying about a 45-minute drive along the west coast. Much favored by the yachting set, the lagoon setting was described by author James Michener as "the most beautiful bay in the Caribbean." On a low-lying spit of the palm-dotted island, the complex, part of which is reached only by ferry service, is the most idyllic spot on St. Lucia. A cluster of colonial-style cottages is called Marigot des Roseaux, and they are spread along a hillside. Some are privately owned, others controlled by the hotel. Most are one- or two-bedroom buildings, attractively making use of both their indoor and outdoor areas. In winter, a one-bedroom cottage or a studio apartment rents for $140 a day, and a two-bedroom cottage costs $180. However, *in summer, a studio or one-bedroom cottage costs only $80 to $90 daily.*

The yachting set often stays at the Marigot Inn, which is decorated in the West Indian style. The double rooms here are comfortable and attractive, opening onto verandas where the occupants can look at their yachts. There's also a Hurricane Hole, a cottage hotel on the southeastern shore. It offers the only swimming pool in the complex, with a shark painted amusingly onto its cement bottom. In season, hotel rooms cost $105 daily in a single, going up to $135 in a double. *In summer, hotel rooms go for $80 in a double, $60 in a single*. Tax and service are extra. The most popular restaurant is Doolittle's, built out over the water on stilts (it is recommended separately in the dining section). Across the way, the Hurricane Hole's restaurant is the Rusty Anchor, where barbecues are offered on Friday, a traditional English roast beef on Sunday. On Friday and Saturday nights guests or visitors can attend a "jump-up."

Halcyon Beach Club, P.O. Box 388, Choc Bay (tel. 452-5331), a four-mile drive outside Castries, is almost the classic concept of a modern Caribbean hotel today. With 94 of the 140 rooms on the beach and the remaining 46 set in tropical gardens, this hotel offers the perfect vacation for the entire family. In winter, singles range in price from $100 to $130 daily, with twins costing $120 to $150. *In summer, a single costs $50 to $80 daily, and twins are priced from $80 to $100*. On the grounds you can see caged parrots and iguanas, for which St. Lucia is well known. Water sports and sailing are free, as are tennis, volleyball, shuffleboard, and a host of indoor games. There is also a children's playground.

You have a choice of two restaurants for dining, one of which, the Chanteclear à la carte restaurant on Fisherman's Wharf, is built sea style over the ocean for cool evening enjoyment. Danish manager Peter Kouly, who trained at the leading hotel in Copenhagen and then owned a disco and restaurant on Jutland, offers one of the most copious kitchen outputs on the island. The evening menu is filled with an international cuisine, including Danish and French specialties. A barbecue, bar, and disco with the latest sound equipment extends on a platform out into the sea, creating a kind of man-made island. There is also a piano bar.

The **St. Lucian Hotel,** P.O. Box 512 (tel. 452-8351), 6½ miles from Castries, is a well-designed, 192-room hotel complex centered around the open-air restaurant and the oceanside pool. It has lots of flowering shrubs, swaying palms, and latticed breezeways connecting the outlying buildings which once formed two hotels. Accommodations face a sandy beach, where you can participate in such water sports as windsurfing, waterskiing, and sailing. Two tennis courts are lit at night. An in-house disco, Lucifer's, is a popular island nightspot. *Summer rates range from $70 to $80 daily in a single, from $90 to $100 in a double*. In winter, the prices go up to $130 to $150 in a single, and $150 to $170 in a double. MAP supplement is $30 extra per person per day. The rooms are comfortable and the food good.

Smugglers Village, Cap Estate (tel. 452-0551), is a resort built on a flat, sandy area near the Steigenberger Cariblue Hotel. Its bungalow accommodations are scattered over the surrounding landscape. The resort's core is a wooden building with decks from which you can look down on a free-form pool and the curved bay where smugglers used to bring in brandies, cognacs, and cigars from Martinique. A hexagonal wooden canopy covers the open-air bar which becomes a social center early in the day. The manager encourages tranquility and quiet, which is what the tile- and wood-accented bungalows offer in abundance. Each contains a kitchen, which residents can stock from the nearby mini-market. In winter, two persons pay $90 to $160. *In summer, the price is $60 to $85 for two persons*. A regular shuttle bus carries adventure-seeking guests to Rodney Bay and Reduit Beach.

Anse Chastanet, P.O. Box 216, Soufrière (tel. 454-7355), is a beachside hotel scattered along a hill site, above palm-fringed, lava-ash Anse Chastanet Beach, some two miles outside Soufrière. General manager Peter N. Pietruszka provides 37 rooms, including 12 new suites on the beach. The new rooms are designed in the style of old West Indian plantation villas, with four rooms to a villa, two up and two down. All the new lower rooms have plunge pools. Some units overlook the sea and the Pitons, those twin cones that soar abruptly from the sea. The core of the house is a small main building, with a bar and dining room, but there's also a beachside bar and restaurant as well. The latter comes in very handy, as it's 109 steps down to the sands. The climb back is Everest-like. When the sun grows too fierce there, you can always retreat under thatched bohíos. The place keeps you jogger-fit climbing up and down. You can dine or drink on windswept terraces built along the hillside over the beach. Here the owner has provided tropical landscaping, with much use made of flowering bougainvillea, hibiscus, and allamander.

When a quartet of Canadians dropped anchor here many years ago and decided to build a hotel on the hillside-hugging site, many St. Lucians told them it couldn't be done. However, they succeeded, thanks to the poor laborers who had to lug up all that heavy material which had been dumped on the beach. Even if not elaborately decorated, some units have individuality. Cooling is by overhead fans or those sea breezes. Besides the rooms in the villas, others are in the original octagonal gazebos, although one room, described as "dark and jungle-like," sans view, has drawn complaints from at least two readers, so avoid it. In winter, prices in a single range from $84 to $132 daily, depending on the quality of the accommodation. Doubles cost $96 to $144, and triples go for $108 to $165. *Summer rates are $60 to $90 single, $72 to $108 double, and $90 to $120 triple.* All prices quoted are EP. If you want to stay here on the MAP, add $28 per person per day. To reach the hotel requires some doing. It's about an hour and a half from the airport, a $35 taxi ride.

The **Islander,** P.O. Box 907, Rodney Bay (tel. 452-0255, 212/840-6636 in New York City), is near Pat's Pub, the St. Lucian Hotel, and Reduit Beach. This well-recommended hotel has an entrance whose walls are festooned with hanging flowers. Botany-minded guests will appreciate the plaques attached to plants throughout the property, giving the names of the various species that grow here in abundance. Many of the accommodations were completed in 1984, making them among the more up-to-date facilities on the island. All of this was open savanna before it became the ever-expanding hotel. A brightly painted fishing boat serves as a buffet table near the pool, and there's a spacious covered bar area perfect for socializing with the owner, Greg Glacé. Mr. Glacé built this attractive property and serves as restaurateur and manager, using experience he gained during sojourns in Rochester, Los Angeles, New York, and Miami, before returning to St. Lucia.

Units are named after different Caribbean islands. Of the 44 accommodations, 20 are self-contained, with kitchenettes and private baths/showers, while 24 have private showers and small bars with mini-refrigerators. Guests walk a few hundred feet to the beach and to shop in nearby markets if their lodgings are equipped for cooking and entertaining. In winter, apartments cost $80 for single occupancy and $90 for two persons, while rooms go for $70 single, $80 double. *Summer prices drop to $45 for single occupancy of an apartment, $55 double. Rooms are $40 single, $45 double.* Children under 12 stay in their parents' room free. Taxes and service are extra. Accommodations look over a grassy courtyard sheltered with vines and flowers, with a network of walkways leading to the convivial restaurant. There, the Friday-night barbecue is popular, costing EC$40 ($26) per person for grilled fish, steak, pork, and chicken. Other evenings, the Caribbean pepperpot dinners cost EC$30 ($11) per person, drawing an enthusiastic crowd of local residents as well as the hotel guests.

The **Green Parrot Hotel,** Red Tape Lane, Morne Fortune (Good Luck Hill; tel. 452-3167). Connected to the Green Parrot restaurant, this hillside series of balconied accommodations winds sinuously up the side of one of the steepest slopes in Castries. Flanking both sides of the pathways are masses of flowering shrubs and vines, as well as a menagerie of monkeys in chicken-wire cages. (Be careful—they bite!) Near the top of the complex, the landscape architects designed a terraced swimming pool, where guests lounge in comfortable chairs with views of the harbor far below. A courtesy bus makes runs to the beach daily except Saturday. A sunken bar is set into the floor of the Pool Room restaurant, where no one minds if patrons show up in their bathing suits. The 27 accommodations include a handful of apartments with kitchens. All of them are reached via brick-lined hallways whose sides are pierced with breezeway arches that open onto a view of the forest. In winter, singles cost $60 to $72, while doubles go for $75 to $90. *In summer, singles are $40, and doubles, $65.* MAP supplements can be arranged for an extra $22. These prices do not include service and tax.

WHERE TO DINE: If possible, try to break free of your resort hotel and dine in one of St. Lucia's little character-loaded restaurants. The local food is excellent, including such West Indian specialties as pumpkin soup, fried flying fish, stuffed crab back, and stuffed breadfruit, as well as the inevitable callaloo soup.

In Castries

San Antoine, Morne Fortune (tel. 452-4660). Pat and Nick Bowden have created what many consider the finest restaurant in St. Lucia. Open every night from 5:30 p.m., it enjoys a historical setting. It was constructed in the 19th century as a great house, lying up the Morne, offering superb vistas over the capital and the water. Some time in the 1920s it was turned into the first hotel in St. Lucia by Aubrey Davidson-Houston, the British portrait painter whose subjects have included W. Somerset Maugham. However, in 1970 it was destroyed by fire. When it was restored in 1984, whatever could be retained, including the original stonework, was given a new lease on life, cleaned, and repaired. The owners wanted to make the place look as authentic as possible. Candles and oil lamps provide the illumination.

You might begin with a cheese-and-shellfish soufflé, and follow with one of the excellently prepared main dishes such as a crayfish-stuffed filet mignon or veal scaloppine with a parsley-laced béarnaise sauce. The fresh fish is caught locally. The wines are reasonable in price. Meals cost EC$50 ($17.50) to EC$90 ($33.50). The restaurant is set in a 12-acre nature reserve. After dinner you can take a stroll through the lushness, because a pathway is illuminated. Go early and enjoy a sundowner in the attractive bar with a view.

The **Green Parrot,** Red Tape Lane at Morne Fortune (Good Luck Hill; tel. 452-3167), about a mile and a half from the center, overlooks Castries harbor. Your ascent from downtown will take about 12 minutes. Once you get there, the effort will have been worth it as this is an elegant choice for dining. It's the home of its chef, Harry, who got his long years of training in prestigious restaurants and hotels in London, including Claridges. Guests take their time and make an evening of it. Many enjoy a before-dinner drink in the Victorian-style salon near a talkative green cockatoo (caged) which Harry claims has been here almost as long as he has. The price of a meal in the English-style dining room includes entertainment: Harry can not only cook, he is also an entertainer of some note. Show nights are Wednesday and Saturday, beginning at around 10:30 p.m. They feature limbo dancers and fire-eaters, followed by music for dancing. Another special night is Monday—ladies' night. A woman who wears a flower in her hair, when accompanied by a man in a coat and tie, receives a free dinner. Everybody can listen to the music of the Shac-Shac band.

All of this may sound gimmicky, but the food doesn't suffer because of all the activity. There's an emphasis on St. Lucian specialties, using home-grown produce when it's available. The countertop of a stone platform in the dining room usually overflows with almost a week's supply, decoratively displayed like a Renaissance still-life. Try the christophine au gratin (a Caribbean squash with cheese) or the Créole soup made with callaloo and pumpkin. There are also five kinds of curry with chutney as well as a selection of omelets and sandwiches at lunchtime. Some of the American guests seem to go for the steaks or the daily specials. Full meals cost around $25 and up. Try to go between noon and 2 p.m. or 8 and 10 p.m. It's open daily. To precede your meal you might enjoy a house special, the Grass Parrot (made from coconut cream, crème de menthe, bananas, white rum, and sugar). If you choose it instead of a more conservative drink, you'll be in good company, since it's rumored to have been sampled by Michael Caine, Princess Margaret, and many of the prime ministers of the Caribbean islands.

Rain, Columbus Square (tel. 452-3022), has a touch of nostalgia: it's named for that old Somerset Maugham story made into a film where Joan Crawford with her alarmingly enlarged lips did away forever with the rosebud mouth. Going behind its palm green and white façade and under its tin roof, you expect any of the actresses who played Sadie suddenly to come through the door—Gloria Swanson, June Havoc, Jeanne Eagles, Tallulah Bankhead, Rita Hayworth. The inspired creation was the idea of Al Haman, a former advertising man. "Under one roof" he installed a bar, restaurant, and boutique, the latter selling batiks, sarongs, custom-designed bikinis, whatever. A popular rendezvous point, particularly with expatriates on the island. Rain keeps to the Maugham decor of ceiling fans, louvered doors, peacock chairs, and oil lamps. Try to head for the second-floor balcony—a gingerbread-frilled upper gallery—if you're dining. There you can not only order food, but can enjoy a view over the town square and its famous spreading saman tree. One day some lucky guests were treated to the sight of lovely Sophia Loren shopping in the ground-floor boutique while on the island for the filming of *Fire Power*. Rain catered for the crew, including such co-stars as James Coburn, O.J. Simpson, George Grizzard, and Anthony Franciosa.

Menus are chalked up on blackboards, and you read them when not looking at faded posters of *Mommie Dearest*. If you don't dine on the candlelit upper floor, you might prefer a nook in the garden courtyard, where an array of pizzas, burgers, and local foods are available in casually informal surroundings at bargain prices. A nightly feature is "the Champagne Banquet of 1885," a re-creation of the seven-course, four-wine dinner served on Columbus Square the year Rain's landmark house was built. Good cooks turn out a repertoire of other home-cooking in the evening that includes not only Stateside dishes, but West Indian specialties such as dolphin St-Jacques, pepperpot, stuffed crab, beef curries, and shrimp Créole. The salads are crisp and fresh with tangy dressing. The homemade ice creams are mouthwatering, especially soursop which is featured in season. Aside from wine, expect to pay about $25 per person for dinner. Lunches cost from $8. Among drinks, I recommend such rum refreshers as Sadie's Sin and the Reverend's Downfall! Rain is closed Sunday and holidays but open from noon to 11 p.m. otherwise.

Coal Pot, Gantner's Bay (tel. 452-5643), enjoys a waterside perch at historic Vigie Marina, and from that position attracts the yachting set or any stray boaters in the area. Set on its own wharf, the Coal Pot opens onto harbor views. Nautical touches abound, as in the fishnet-draped bar. The Cordon Bleu and Créole menu leans, naturally, to fresh seafood dishes, which are generally well prepared here, depending on what's available from the local catch. Lobster and flying fish are traditionally featured. Ask the owners, Michael and Allison, about the wine list, reputed to be the best on St. Lucia. You might begin your meal by ordering the bartender's special, a Naked Virgin, made with a blend of orange juice, rum, Galliano, and cream of coconut. One, I assure you, is enough. Expect to pay from $22 per person for dinner. Meals are served between noon and 2 p.m. and 7 and 10 p.m. Closed Sunday.

Le Boucan, Columbus Square (tel. 452-2415), is a local restaurant and bar, with a sidewalk café that is a casual rendezvous point for morning shoppers in Castries. If you come just for a drink, make it soursop, golden apple, or passion-fruit juice or any of the delicious local fruit drink specials. If you stick around for a full lunch, snack, or dinner, that's possible too, and the price is right: about $12 more or less for a meal, depending on your selection. The food is simple and good, with emphasis on fresh local flavor as reflected by the curried shrimp, very fresh fish, Créole lobster, and juicy steaks. Chicken Boucan is a specialty. It's open Monday to Saturday from 10 a.m. to 2 p.m. and 6 to 10 p.m. Thursday night is folk-food night.

Capone's, Reduit (tel. 452-0284). In vivid pink and green, this place could have been inspired by the old Billy Wilder film *Some Like It Hot,* with Marilyn Monroe. Actually, it's supposed to be an art deco rendition of a speakeasy along Miami Beach in the 1930s. Near the lagoon, it's brightly lit at night. To get in, rap on the door once or twice and say "Al sent me." That's a reference to Al Haman, a former advertising man who created the equally successful Rain, already recommended. Snacks are for sale in the Pizza Parlour, along with burgers, well-stuffed pita-bread sandwiches, and pizzas. Inside, barmen dressed like gangsters with shoulder holsters will offer you a "Prohibition Punch" or a "St. Valentine's Day Massacre." Stick around till 11 p.m. when drinks are reduced at "happy hour." The cuisine is Italian, and it's well prepared, the service friendly. Count on spending from EC$30 ($11) to EC$75 ($27.75). The pastas are fresh and well flavored, or you may prefer one of the meat dishes such as that favorite of the Milanese kitchen, osso bucco. Service is from 5 p.m. to midnight; closed Monday.

Pisces Restaurant, Choc Bay (tel. 452-5898), serves some of the best food on the island, in an unlikely location at the top of a forbiddingly steep flight of steps from the road just opposite the Halcyon Beach Club. Tables are set on a terraced balcony of a stucco building high above the graveled parking lot near the sea. Opened in 1980 by Eden Elius Xavier ("Eddie," to his friends), who was born under the sign of Pisces, assisted by Lawrence Hilton, also a Pisces, the establishment produces food that includes the best crab backs on the island, savory lobster in season, a shrimp Créole worth writing home about, and my favorite island drink, a White Pigeon, made with vodka, white crème de menthe, milk, and bananas. Many of the accoutrements here are shaped like fish. All of the produce and practically everything except the shrimp (from Guyana) and the sirloin is locally produced. Full meals cost from EC$60 ($22.25) up, although snacks and sandwiches can come to EC$15 ($5.50) for a filling holdover. It's open every day, and you get two drinks for the price of one at happy hour from 5:30 to 6:30 p.m. If you're dining, try to show up from noon to 2 p.m. or 7:30 to 10 p.m.

In Soufrière

The Still (tel. 454-7224) is the first thing you'll see as you drive up the hill from the harbor of Soufrière. It's a very old rum distillery set on a platform of thick timbers. The front garden blossoms with avocado pears, and a mahogany forest is a few steps away. All of this contributes to the country ambience of this stone-walled restaurant where Michael and Monica Du Boulay serve their freshly cooked specialties. The bar near the front veranda is furnished with glossy tables cut from cross sections of tropical tree trunks. A more formal and very spacious dining room is nearby. A three-course lunch costs around EC$25 ($9.25) and might include chicken, pepperpot, pork chops, or fish. A buffet, when available, costs EC$20 ($7.40) per person. Lunch is served daily from noon to 3 p.m., but if you're coming with a big party, it's wise to phone ahead. Dinner, however, is by appointment only.

The Hummingbird (tel. 454-7232) was named for the tiny, darting birds that fly around this restaurant and its adjoining boutique, which sells merchandise carefully handmade by owner Joan Alexander. An outdoor pool is free for use by persons who drop into the restaurant for a meal or just a drink. Patrons have included everyone from Mick Jagger to Christina Onassis. The ceiling is covered with seafan coral. A few larger-than-life wooden status of mermaids support the thatch roof in back, and near the entrance is a rock garden with a woodcarving made from the stump of a poinciana tree that was removed when its roots started interfering with the foundations of the building. The wide-ranging menu features many tempting drinks (for example, a Hummingbird Hangover made of sambuca, golden rum, orange juice, and bitters) as well as such international food specialties as curry, English, Indian, or West Indian dishes including seafood crêpes, ceviche (raw marinated fish), beef Stroganoff, steak Diane, and chateaubriand. Full meals cost around EC$60 ($22.25). Try to show up between noon and 2 p.m. for lunch, 7 and 10 p.m. for dinner. It's open daily.

The Hummingbird has two guest rooms, doubles, for which the charge year round is $35 or $40 per night. Meals are extra. A service charge is added to bills for meals and drinks, not for rooms.

The boutique, selling hand-painted batiks and silkscreen fabrics by Joan, is one of the best stores on the island for creations of women's clothes, wall hangings, and table services of a rare beauty.

Rodney Bay

The **Pub and the French Restaurant** (tel. 452-8314) wouldn't exactly pass for a pub in the English Midlands, what with its native island music, the masses of bougainvillea, the open-air architecture, and the suntanned yacht enthusiasts. This sophisticated ambience draws upon the past experience of Elizabeth Dawson as the owner of a yacht charter service in Jamaica and a former English resident of West Africa. In the Pub, you can order such familiar food as cottage pie, steak-and-kidney pie, and ploughman's lunch—all typical "pub grub" in England—but they also serve homemade pâté, crab farci Créole, and Indian chicken curry, among other selections. Pub meals cost around $25 ($9.25). For à la carte haute cuisine, try the restaurant, choosing from such dishes as French Créole chicken and beef pepperpot; lobster prepared French Créole style; prime filet in crushed peppercorns, cream, and brandy; steak Diane; and escargots in mushroom heads and garlic butter. Desserts include a chocolate rum gâteau and bananas flambé Martinique. Lunch is best from noon to 2 p.m. and dinner from 7 to 10 p.m.

Reservations are preferred for dinner, although no one minds if you drop into the bar area to mingle with the informal mariners waiting for the three-times-weekly evening music to begin. Guitarist Boo Hinkson is reputed to be the best in the Windward Islands, and Ms. Dawson sometimes joins in the singing. The establishment is open daily except Monday.

The **Charthouse,** Rodney Bay (tel. 452-8115), is set in a large grange-like building with a skylit ceiling, thick teak tables, and blue and white upholstery. It's built several feet above the bobbing yachts of Rodney Bay, without walls, to allow an optimum view of the water. Its exterior is crafted from weathered planking into a series of pleasingly soft angles whose corners are masked with masses of hanging plants. Nautical charts of the region adorn the walls, reflecting the marine interests of Nick Ashworth, the Irish-born owner. Full meals, costing from EC$60 ($22.25), might include callaloo soup, St. Lucian crab backs, surf and turf, shrimp créole, local lobster (in season), a choice of local fish, and well-prepared steaks. The restaurant is open daily except Sunday. Try to go from noon to 2:30 p.m. and 7 to 10:30 p.m.

The **Mortar & Pestle,** part of the Harmony Apartel complex on Rodney Bay Lagoon (tel. 452-8756), mixes superb Caribbean cuisine with a fine view of the marina. The menu features more than 30 à la carte gourmet specialties such as baked Antigua clams, Guyana casareep pepperpot, crayfish Dominica, lobster Créole Guadeloupe, and lambi St. Lucia. The specialty of the house is red snapper Martinique, filets of red snapper sautéed in garlic butter with onions and mushrooms, simmered in a white wine cream sauce. It's served with breadfruit balls and christophene au gratin. If you're not in the mood for "haute cuisine des Caraïbes," they also have a European, a Chinese, and an Indian menu. A good selection of wines from Germany, France, Portugal, and California is offered. A complete meal will cost EC$22 ($8.15) to EC$48 ($17.75). The restaurant is open Monday to Saturday for breakfast from 7:30 to 10:30 a.m., for lunch from noon to 2:30 p.m., and for dinner from 7 to 10:30 p.m. Reservations are advised in the evening.

Marigot Bay

Dolittle's, Marigot Bay (tel. 452-4246), was named for the Rex Harrison movie which created a lot of local excitement but didn't generate that much interest from worldwide audiences. But it's a name that still means a lot around here. This popular restaurant, rated among the top three in St. Lucia, is right on the beach. You reach it by a miniature ferryboat which leaves every 20 minutes from the Marigot jetty. If it doesn't, sound your horn three times. That's the signal for the ferry to come over and pick you up. Once at Dolittle's, you can also swim or snorkel before lunch or dinner. Before your meal, try their local bartender's specialty, called a "Love Bird." This is a mixture of fresh "paw-paw" (papaya to us), Sabra orange liqueur, cream, Cherry Heering, and a local rum. A yachting crowd drops in here, and the place has a congenial atmosphere. Perhaps you'll be there for one of their Caribbean evenings. On one night steaming callaloo soup was served in a big pot. Guests helped themselves. Some of the St. Lucian specialties served include marinated red snapper, and you're given skewers of shrimp and beef which you cook yourselves over hot coals in the shishkebab fashion. Locally grown vegetables such as christophine (a Caribbean squash) are also served, followed by homemade ice creams in unusual flavors. Expect to spend at least EC$60 ($22.25), maybe more, for a complete meal. Try to go from noon to 2 p.m. or 7 to 10 p.m.

WHAT TO SEE: Towns, beaches, bays, bananas—even a volcano is here to visit.

Castries

The capital city has grown up around its harbor which occupies the crater of an extinct volcano. Charter captains and the yachting set drift in here, and large cruise-ship wharfs welcome vessels from around the world. Because of those devastating fires mentioned earlier, the town today has a fresh, new look, its sterile glass-and-concrete (or steel) buildings replacing the French colonial or Victorian look typical of many West Indian capitals.

The **Saturday-morning market** in the old tin-roofed building on Jeremy Street in Castries is my favorite "people-watching" site on the island. Country women dress up in their traditional garb of cotton headdress and come into town for the occasion, which makes it all seem carnival-festive. The number of knotted points on top reveals their marital status (ask one of the locals to explain it to you). The luscious fresh fruits and vegetables of St. Lucia are sold, as again, weather-beaten men sit close by playing warrie, which is a fast pre-video game of pebbles on a carved board. You can also pick up St. Lucia handcrafts, such as baskets and unglazed pottery.

Government House is a charming late Victorian building. A Roman Catholic cathedral stands on Columbus Square, which has a few restored buildings.

Beyond Government House lies **Morne Fortune,** the name meaning "Hill of Good Luck." No one had much luck here, certainly not the battling French and British fighting for Fort Charlotte. The barracks and guard rooms changed nationalities many times. You can visit the 18th-century barracks complete with a military cemetery, a small museum, the Old Powder Magazine, and the "Four Apostles Battery" (the apostles being a quartet of grim muzzle-loading cannons). The view of the harbor of Castries is spectacular. You can see north to Pigeon Island or south to the Pitons.

Pigeon Point

This island is connected to the mainland of St. Lucia by a man-made causeway off Gros Islet Bay, on the west coast. Pirates such as "Old Wooden Leg" used it as a retreat, as did Admiral Rodney's British fleet much later. It was from here that Rodney sailed to defeat De Grasse at the Battle of the Saints. Historic ruins of forts can still be seen. The island is called pigeon in honor of Rodney's hobby of breeding the birds here. There are also remnants of the Arawak Indians on the island. It's a perfect place for a picnic, after which you can go for a swim from its white sandy beaches.

Marigot Bay

Movie companies such as those for Rex Harrison's *Dr. Doolittle* or Sophia Loren's *Fire Power* like to use this bay, one of the most beautiful in the Caribbean, for background shots. It's narrow yet navigable by yachts of any size. Here Admiral Rodney camouflaged his ships with palm leaves while lying in wait for French frigates. The shore, lined with palm trees, remains relatively unspoiled, but some building sites have been sold. Again, it's a delightful spot for a picnic if you didn't take your food basket to Pigeon Island.

Soufrière

This little fishing port, St. Lucia's second-largest settlement, is dominated by two pointed hills called **Petit Piton** and **Gros Piton.** These two hills, "The Pitons," have become the very symbol of St. Lucia. They are two volcanic cones rising to 2,460 and 2,619 feet. Once actively volcanic, they are now clothed in green vegetation. Their rise sheer from the sea makes them a spectacular landmark visible for miles around. Formed of lava and rock, they are the remains of St. Lucia's once-active volcanos. Waves crash around their bases.

In the vicinity of Soufrière lies the famous "drive-in" volcano. Called **Mount Soufrière,** it's a rocky lunar landscape of bubbling mud and craters seething with fuming sulfur. You literally drive your car into an old (millions of years) crater, parking the vehicle and walking between the sulfur springs and pools of hissing steam. A local guide is usually waiting beside them shrouded with sulfurous fumes that are said to have medicinal properties. For a small fee, he'll point out the blackened waters, among the few of their kind in the Caribbean.

Nearby are the **Diamond Mineral Baths,** surrounded by a tropical arboretum. Constructed on orders of Louis XVI in 1784, whose doctors told him that these waters were similar in mineral content to the waters at Aix-les-Bains, they were intended for recuperative effects for French soldiers fighting in the West Indies. Later destroyed, they were rebuilt after World War II. They have an average temperature of 106° and lie near one of the geological attractions of the island, a waterfall which changes colors (from yellow to black to green to gray) several times a day. For EC$5 ($1.85), you can bathe and benefit from the recuperative effects. This boiling caldron has not rained down any catastrophes to date, unlike its neighbors in St. Vincent and Martinique.

From Soufrière in the southwest, the road winds toward Fond St. Jacques where you'll have a good view of mountains and villages as you cut through St. Lucia's **Moule-à-Chique** tropical rain forest. You'll see the Barre de l'Isle divide.

Moule-à-Chique

At the southern tip of the island, Moule-à-Chique is where the Caribbean Sea merges with the Atlantic. This is the southernmost tip of St. Lucia, and the town of Vieux Fort can be seen, as can the neighboring island of St. Vincent, 26 miles away.

Banana Plantations

Bananas are the island's leading export. As you're being hauled around the island by a taxi driver, ask him to take you to one of these huge plantations which allow visitors to come on the grounds. I suggest a sightseeing look at one of the trio of big ones—the Cul-de-Sac, just north of Marigot Bay; La Caya, in Dennery on the East Coast; and the Roseau Estate, south of Marigot Bay.

THE SPORTING LIFE: Since most of the island hotels are built right on the beach, you won't have far to go for swimming. I prefer the beaches along the western coast.

On the windward side, a rough surf makes swimming at least potentially dangerous. Pigeon Island, off the north shore, is a fine beach, as is Vigie, just north of the harbor of Castries. For a novelty, you might try the black volcanic sand at Soufrière. The beach there is called **La Toc.**

Snorkeling and Scuba

Arrangements for most water sports are made at your hotel. **La Toc, Club Med, Steigenberger Cariblue,** and **St. Lucian** are particularly well equipped for these sports.

Dive St. Lucia, P.O. Box 412, Vigie, Castries (tel. 452-4127), is a top-quality independent operator. Equipment is supplied by the dive company. Accommodation and dive packages can also be arranged. In addition, snorkeling trips with all equipment can be provided for $18.

In Soufrière, the **Anse Chastenet Hotel,** P.O. Box 216 (tel. 454-7354), employs three professional PADI instructors who offer dive programs two or three times a day. Some of the most spectacular coral reefs in St. Lucia—many only 10 to 20 feet below the surface of the water—lie a short distance from the hotel's beach. Photographic equipment is available for rent (film can be processed on the premises), and instruction is offered in picture taking in price ranges depending on the time and equipment involved. Experienced divers can rent the equipment they need on a per-item basis. The packages include tanks, backpacks, and weightbelts. Through participation in the establishment's "specialty" courses, divers can obtain PADI certification.

Horseback Riding

You can hire a horse at **Cas-en-bas and Cap Estate Stables.** To make arrangements, call René Trim at 452-8273. The cost is EC$33 ($12.25) per 1½ hours. As an added feature, you can ask about a picnic trip to the Atlantic, with a barbecue lunch and drink included. Departures are at 10:15 a.m. on horseback, the return at 3:30 p.m. Nonriders can be included too, as they are transported to the site in a van. Riders pay EC$75 ($27.75) per person; nonriders, EC$50 ($18.50).

Tennis

Most of the big hotels have their own courts. If yours doesn't, ask at the front desk for the nearest one. Some of the courts on St. Lucia are lit for night games for those who'd like to avoid the midday sun.

Golf

St. Lucia has two golf courses. A nine-hole one is at the **Cap Estate Golf Club** (tel. 452-8317) at the northern end of the island, and the larger one is at **Hotel La Toc** (tel. 452-3081).

Deep-Sea Fishing

The waters around St. Lucia are known for their gamefish, including blue marlin, sailfish, mako sharks, and barracuda, with tuna and kingfish among the edible catches. Most hotels can make arrangements for you to go on a fishing expedition, or you might prefer to make your own plans with **Mako Water Sports** (tel. 452-0412) or **Michael Hackshaw** (tel. 452-0216), whose family has been boating and fishing for generations. Most sports-fishing boats charge around $150 for up to four persons for a half day's fishing. The price usually includes liquid refreshments.

SHOPPING: Stores are generally open from 8 a.m. to 4 p.m., except Sunday. Most of the shopping is in Castries, where the principal streets are William Peter Boulevard and Bridge Street. Many stores will sell you goods at duty-free prices (providing you don't take the merchandise with you but have it delivered instead to the airport). There are some good buys—not remarkable—in bone china, jewelry, perfume, watches, liquor, and crystal. Souvenir items include bags and mats, local pottery, and straw hats, again nothing remarkable.

The **West Indian Sea Island Cotton Shop,** Bridge Street (tel. 452-3674), designs and creates original batik artwork entirely by hand. Wall hangings and clothing are among their merchandise which is exclusively available in the West Indies. They also stock a full range of Kokonuts designer T-shirts; Sunny Caribbee herbs, spices, and perfume products; hand-painted jewelry; and St. Lucia souvenirs.

Bagshaws, just outside Castries, at La Toc (tel. 452-2139), are the leading hand-print silkscreeners. An American, Sydney Bagshaw, and family have devoted their considerable skills to turning out a line of fabric that is as colorful as the Caribbean. The birds and flowers of St. Lucia are incorporated into their designs. Linen place-mats, men's shirts, women's skirts, wall hangings, and dress kits are good buys. Each creation is an original Bagshaw design.

Rain Boutique, Columbus Square (tel. 452-3022; see my restaurant recommendation), is fashionable and petit. In the corner of this virtual landmark restaurant, the boutique promises that you can "sip and sup while you shop." Chicly styled cotton clothing is offered. Even Sophia Loren bought some of her clothes here, and O.J. Simpson dropped in for some resortwear.

Y. de Lima's, William Peter Boulevard (tel. 452-2898), has a good range of jewelry in gold and silver, as well as an array of Swiss watches, cameras, and binoculars, all at duty-free prices.

Noah's Arkade, Post Office Lane, Bridge Street (tel. 452-2523), has an array of Caribbean handcrafts and gifts. Many of these are routine tourist items, yet you'll often find something interesting if you browse enough—local straw placemats and rugs, wall hangings, sandals, maracas, steel drums, shell necklaces, and warri boards. Many of the hotels have branches of this emporium.

St. Lucia Perfumes, Red Tape Lane, Morne Fortune (tel. 452-3890), part of the Green Parrot Restaurant complex, manufactures its own fragrances using local spices and flowers—cinnamon, clove, citrus, frangipani, y-lang y-lang, and many more. Merchandise includes perfumes, colognes, and toilet water, and men's colognes, body splashes, and aftershaves. Crystal, porcelain, and local batik and clothing for women of silkscreen fabrics are sold in an adjacent room. Open weekdays from 8:30 a.m. to 4:30 p.m., it closes at 1:30 p.m. on Saturday and all day Sunday.

Eudovic Art Studio, Goodlands, Morne Fortune (tel. 452-2747). Eudovic is a local artist and woodcarver whose sculptures have been exhibited in the O.A.S. headquarters in Washington, D.C., and have gained an increasing island fame. He usually carves his imaginative free-form sculptures from local tree roots, such as cobary, mahogany, and red cedar, and follows the natural pattern, sanding the grain until it's of almost satin smoothness. The studio is open seven days a week.

NIGHTLIFE: There isn't much except the entertainment offered by hotels. If your hotel is silent and you're in the mood for action, ask at your front desk what other hotel might be planning entertainment that evening. In the winter months, at least one hotel offers a steel band, calypso music, whatever, at least every night of the week. Otherwise, check to see what's happening at **Rain** (tel. 452-3022), **Capone's** (tel. 452-0284), and the **Green Parrot** (tel. 452-3167)—see my restaurant recommendations.

Lucifer's, St. Lucian Hotel (tel. 452-8351), one of the best discos on the island, has a decor like a simulated version of the infernos of hell. Banquettes and love seats are cozily strewn amid roughly textured cave rocks, while stalactites hang from the ceiling, whose crevices glow with eerie red lights. This place can get crowded around 11 every evening, when guests from the Steigenberger Cariblue and Couples drop in for disco, calypso, or reggae. The house special is a St. Lucian Hurricane (grenadine, lime juice, sugar syrup, Cointreau, and rum) or a Pigeon Island Drum (lime juice, syrup, orange juice, brandy, white rum, bitters, and grenadine). There's a cover charge of EC$6 ($2.25) on Tuesday, Wednesday, and Thursday, and EC$12 ($4.45) on Friday and Saturday. Guests of the St. Lucian Hotel enter free. You get two drinks for the price of one during happy hour, from midnight to 1 a.m. daily. The disco opens every Tuesday through Saturday at 9 p.m.

3. St. Vincent

An emerald island 18 miles long and 12 miles wide, St. Vincent was discovered by Columbus in 1498 on his third voyage. If the explorer had gone on a field expedition, and assuming he hadn't been devoured by the cannibalistic Caribs, he would have discovered an island of natural beauty.

Amazing for such a small area, St. Vincent has fertile valleys, rich forests, lush jungles, rugged peaks, waterfalls, foam-whitened beaches, outstanding coral reefs (with what experts say is some of the world's clearest water), a volcano nestled in the sky and usually capped by its own private cloud, and 4,000 feet up, Crater Lake.

Fierce, aggressive, warlike, the Caribs held out longer on St. Vincent against the tide of European colonization than they did almost anywhere else. However, in a 1763 treaty the British won the right to possess the island. In 1779 French troups invaded. At the Treaty of Versailles in 1783 they gave it back to His Majesty's colonists.

A few years later Captain Bligh set off on the *Bounty* from England, going to Tahiti. There he loaded his vessel with breadfruit seedlings. Faced with mutiny, and after great difficulties (described in many historical novels), the captain in 1793 reached St. Vincent with his seedlings. The breadfruit trees took fantastically to St. Vincentian soil, earning for the island the title of "the Tahiti of the Caribbean."

In 1795, during the French Revolution, St. Vincent suffered yet another invasion. French revolutionaries, allied with the Caribs, burned British plantations and made a

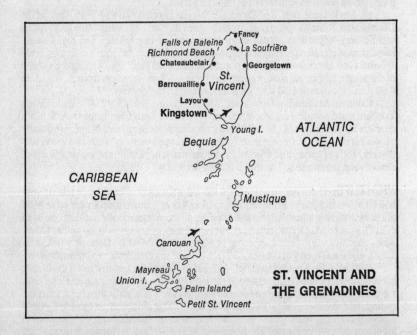

fierce war, only to be defeated by British forces the following year. The Caribs were rounded up and shipped off to British Honduras in Central America, where their descendants live to this day. The British decided St. Vincent was too small for both planters and Indians.

The island remained under "Rule Britannia" from that day until 1979, when it achieved independent statehood within the Commonwealth. The governor-general is appointed by the Crown on the advice of the prime minister. Parliament is comprised of a House of Assembly elected every five years. The state of St. Vincent and the Grenadines has a population of about 120,000, descended mainly from African, East Indian, Portuguese, Carib, and European ancestors.

One of the major Windward Islands, St. Vincent is only now awakening to tourism, which hasn't yet reached massive dimensions. Sailors and the yachting set have long known of St. Vincent and its satellite bays and beaches in the Grenadines.

Much of its interior is inhabited and cultivated with coconut and banana groves. Arrowroot, often used as a thickening in baby foods, grows in abundance.

Unspoiled by the worst fallout which mass tourism sometimes brings, the people are very friendly and actually treat visitors like people, providing that courtesy is returned.

GETTING THERE: In the Eastern Caribbean, St. Vincent—the "gateway to the Grenadines" (see the next section)—lies 100 miles west of Barbados, where most visitors from North America fly first, making connections that will take them on to St. Vincent and the Grenadines. For transportation from North America to Barbados, refer to the "Getting There" section of the next chapter.

From Barbados, you can connect with a **LIAT** flight to St. Vincent. The flight from Barbados takes just 40 minutes, and at least two of them go out daily. LIAT also flies in from Trinidad, St. Lucia, and Martinique.

There is an airport, of course, at St. Vincent, but also small ones at Mustique, Union Island, and Canouan.

Connecting flights to St. Vincent and the Grenadines are also available at the gateways of St. Lucia (Hewannora), Martinique, and Trinidad.

WINLINK provides both scheduled and charter service between St. Lucia, St. Vincent, and Union Island. **Inter Island Air Services** (IAS) offers scheduled service between St. Lucia, St. Vincent, and the Grenadines. **Air Martinique** runs service between Martinique, St. Lucia, St. Vincent, Mustique, and Union Island.

Increasing numbers of visitors to St. Vincent prefer the dependable service of one of the best-managed small airlines in the Caribbean, **Mustique Airways.** Local restrictions prohibit this fine company from offering regularly scheduled service; however, many visitors find that those restrictions can work to their advantage. With advance warning, Mustique Airways will arrange a specially chartered (and reasonably priced) transport for you and your party to many of the surrounding islands. In fact, it's usually easier to make efficient connections through the Grenadines when an airline will work with you and personalize your itinerary. The price of these chartered transfers is less than you might expect. For example, round-trip transport from Barbados to St. Vincent is $120 per person; from Barbados to Mustique, $140; and from Barbados to Union Island, $200.

Currently the airline owns four nine-passenger Islanders and one five-passenger Barons. Jonathon Palmer, the company's dynamic owner, can be reached through the touring company run by his wife, Marnie. For reservations, information, and up-to-the-minute prices, contact the **Grenadine Travel Company,** P.O. Box 1098, St. Vincent (tel. 458-4818). Their office in Mustique is at the airport (tel. 458-4621, ext. 422).

GETTING AROUND: The government sets the rates for fares, but **taxis** are unmetered. The wise passenger, however, will always ask the fare and agree upon the charge before getting in. Figure on spending about EC$15 ($5.50) to go from the St. Vincent Arnos Vale Airport to your hotel, maybe more. Of course, you should tip about 12% of the fare.

If you don't want to drive yourself, you can also hire taxis to take you to the island's major attractions. Most drivers seem to be well-informed guides (it doesn't take long to learn everything you need to know about St. Vincent). You'll spend about EC$30 ($11) per hour for a car holding two to four passengers.

Buses

Flamboyantly painted "al fresco" buses also travel the principal arteries of St. Vincent, linking the major towns and villages. The price is really low, depending on where you're going, and the experience will connect you with the people of the island. At least you'll get to see a preview of what's being taken to market, perhaps a burlap bag of arrowroot. The central departure point is Market Square. Fares range from EC$1 (37¢) to EC$4 ($1.50).

Car Rentals

Rentals can be arranged. However, driving on St. Vincent is a bit of an adventure because of the narrow, twisting roads and the *drive-on-the-left-requirement*. To go motoring like a Vincentian, you'll soon learn to sound your horn a lot as you make the sharp curves and turns. If you present your valid U.S. or Canadian driver's license at the police department, and pay a EC$10 ($3.70) fee, you'll obtain a temporary permit to drive. Go to the police station on Bay Street in Kingstown.

Among the many leasing agents, **Car Rentals Ltd.,** on Halifax Street in Kingstown (tel. 456-1862), rents Mazdas and Fiat 125s. Try also **Star Garage,** Grenville Street (tel. 456-1743), the local representative for Hertz. Avis is represented by **Johnson's U-Drive Rental** (tel. 458-4864). The cost is about $40 per day, but you usually get the first 50 miles free.

PRACTICAL FACTS: British customs are predominant, but with a distinct West Indian flair. Those invading French troops also left their legacy, and Gallic cultural influences remain as delightful traces. English is the official **language,** of course, yet there's a French patois spoken on a number of the Grenadines, including St. Vincent.

Visitors arriving should have **proof of identity** and a return or ongoing ticket, providing they are either Canadian or U.S. citizens. The official **currency** of St. Vincent is the Eastern Caribbean dollar, worth about 37¢ in U.S. terms. *Note:* Most of the quotations in this chapter appear in U.S. dollars. Most restaurants, shops, and hotels will accept payment in U.S. dollars or traveler's checks.

The **climate** of St. Vincent is pleasantly cooled by the trade winds all year. The tropical temperature is in the 78° to 82° Fahrenheit range. The rainy season is May to November.

The **General Post Office** on Halifax Street in Kingstown is open from 8:30 a.m. to 3 p.m. Monday to Friday, from 8:30 to 11:30 a.m. on Saturday. There are sub post offices in all towns and villages.

If you're looking for a **pharmacy,** try Crichton Drug Store, Middle Street in Kingstown (tel. 456-1319).

Electric current is 220 volts, 50 cycles, AC, so you'll need an adapter. Some hotels have voltage converters, but it's best to bring your own.

Both St. Vincent and the Grenadines operate on **Atlantic Standard Time:** when it's 6 a.m. in St. Vincent, it's 5 a.m. in Miami. During Daylight Saving Time, St. Vincent keeps the same time as the U.S. East Coast.

Banks are open from 8 a.m. to noon Monday to Thursday and from 8 a.m. to noon and 3 to 5 p.m. on Friday (always check, as each bank may vary these hours slightly).

There is a general **hospital** in Kingstown and a smaller hospital in Georgetown on the Windward Coast. The Kingstown Hospital is fully equipped with an operating room, X-ray department, dental and eye clinics.

The government imposes an airport **departure tax** of EC$10 ($3.70) per person. A 5% government **occupancy tax** is charged for all hotel accommodations; and in addition to that, most hotels as well as restaurants add a 10% or 15% **service charge.**

Special events include the week-long Carnival in early July, one of the largest in the eastern Caribbean, with steel band and calypso competitions, along with the crowning of the king and queen of carnival.

The local **Tourist Board** is on Halifax Street in Kingstown (tel. 457-1502). Inquiries in the U.S. can be made to the **St. Vincent and Grenadines Tourist Office,** 801 Second Ave., 21st Floor, New York, NY 10017 (tel. 212/687-4490).

WHERE TO STAY: Accommodations range from tropical villas on their own private island to a guesthouse built back in the plantation era serving Créole cookery. Don't expect massive high-rise resorts here, as everything is kept small, and many Vincentians hope it will always be this way. The West Indian lifestyle prevails here. The places are comfortable, not fancy, and you usually get a lot of personal attention from the staffs.

The Leading Resort

Young Island, P.O. Box 211, Young Island (tel. 458-4826), is a 25-acre resort that might have attracted Gauguin. Instead of that artist, it was supposed to be where a Carib Indian chieftain kept his harem. A paradise island promising barefoot happiness, it lies just 200 yards off the south shore of St. Vincent, to which it is linked by a ferry to the mainland from the pier right on Villa Beach, a five-minute ride. Tropical villas—25 deluxe, two luxury, and three suites—are set in a tropical garden of hibiscus, crotons, ferns, and white ginger, as well as giant almond, breadfruit, nutmeg, and mango trees. The beach, however, is of a brilliant white sand. Hammocks are hung under thatched roofs if you want to rest. Carib canoes and Sailfish await your use at the beach's edge. Island specials are served at the Coconut Bar, a thatched bohío on stilts which actually serves many of its drinks in fresh coconuts. The free-form pool, modeled on a tropical lagoon, is set into landscaped grounds. The hotel has one tennis court, which is lit for night games. All water sports, such as scuba-diving and waterskiing, are available. At the far end of the beach there's a saltwater lagoon-like pool where you can hear parrots and macaws chattering.

You're housed in Tahitian cottages with a bamboo decor and outdoor showers. Floors are of seashells and terrazzo, covered by rush rugs. *In low season, single guests on half-board arrangements pay $135 to $185 daily, the cost going up to $210 to $235 daily in a double.* In high season, half board is required. At that time a single person pays from $300 to $360 a day, the cost rising to $350 to $410 in a double. Ask about package rates for lovers, under the categories of "young lovers" and "lucky lovers." These are exceptional bargain deals offered during the off-season periods. The food is well prepared, with an emphasis on lots of fresh fish and lobster and plenty of island-grown vegetables. Dining is by candlelight, and dress is informal. On some nights the hotel transports guests over to the rock on its other island, Fort Duvernette, for a cocktail party. There hors d'oeuvres are cooked over charcoal pits, and a local band plays under torchlight. Sometimes a steel band plays for dancing after dinner, and you're serenaded by strolling singers.

The Upper Bracket

Grand View Beach Hotel, P.O. Box 173, Villa Point (tel. 458-4811). The owner-manager, F. A. ("Tony") Sardine, named this place well. The "grand view" promised is of islets, bays, yachts, Young Island, headlands, lagoons, and sailing craft. Villa Point lies just five minutes from the airport and ten minutes from Kingstown. On well-manicured grounds, it is set on eight acres of tropical gardens, with bougainvillea and frangipani. Tennis and squash courts and a swimming pool are available. A converted private home, the hotel is a large, white, two-story mansion which has a dozen rooms with private baths to rent. Some of these are air-conditioned. Units are simply furnished, with flowery spreads and wood floors. Everything is maintained spotlessly, however. *In the off-season, singles rent for $48 daily; doubles, $66.* In winter, rates go up to $72 daily in a single, $94 in a double. For breakfast and dinner, add another $30 per person to the tariff quoted. For that you get a table d'hôte menu which changes every day. Most of the meals are based on fresh fish and island-grown vegetables. The cuisine is served in bountiful portions. The cookery is sometimes like a West Indian nouvelle cuisine style. The house is not on the beach, but sits on a hill. You have to go down to the shore for a swim. With a name like Sardine, you might suspect that the owners came from Portugal, but that was so far back no one much remembers when.

The Moderate Range

Sunset Shores Beach Hotel, P.O. Box 849, Villa (tel. 458-4411), about four miles from Kingstown, is an attractively landscaped cluster of vacation accommodations set on terraces that descend to a sandy beach (the pleasant beach is fenced off from the lawn). An oblong swimming pool, flanked by a covered bar, is set just below the low-lying bedrooms. These contain comfortable beds, sliding glass doors, hanging wicker lamps, private baths, and air conditioning, and entrances are ringed with yellow-flowered trumpet vines. In winter, singles cost $75 to $90 daily; doubles, $94 to $107. *In summer, singles range from $45 to $56 daily; doubles, from $55 to $66.* All tariffs quoted are EP.

The **Last Resort Hotel** (formerly the Coconut Beach), P.O. Box 355 (tel. 458-4231), five minutes from the airport and 15 minutes from Kingstown, was purchased in 1986 by Joyce Anderson and Sissy George, transplanted Texans, who have established an atmosphere that's friendly, relaxed, and informal, with everyone on a first-name basis. Extensive remodeling has been done. The seaside setting is ideal for swimming, sunbathing, and watching the sunset from comfortable deck chairs on the large stone patio. Island tours, sailing through the Grenadines, diving and snorkeling, mountain climbing, and deep-sea fishing can be arranged for you by the hotel staff. Each of the spacious rooms is clean and tastefully furnished, freshly decorated in tropical colors. Each unit has its own bath and ceiling fans. Air conditioning is available in four of the rooms. From mid-December to mid-April, singles cost $45; doubles, $50; and triples, $55. *The remainder of the year, rates are $35 in a single, $40 in a double, and $45 in a triple.* Add $5 per day for air conditioning. Meal plans and discounts for stays of more than seven days are offered. Banana daiquiris, rum punch, and piña coladas are a few of the tropical drinks available in the beach bar just a few steps from the water's edge. The open-air restaurant features West Indian and Vincentian cooking prepared from local foods brought fresh each morning at the local market. Fish right from the sea, stuffed breadfruit, callaloo and pumpkin soup, as well as mango and coconut crème pies, are a few of the menu selections awaiting your taste.

Villa Lodge Hotel, P.O. Box 222, Indian Bay Beach (tel. 458-4641). Set at the side of a residential hillside a few minutes from the center of Kingstown, this is a favorite of visiting business people from the other islands. Because of its access to the beach and its well-mannered staff, it should be better known to tourists. Originally built as a white-sided private home, it still evokes in residents the feeling of being lodged in a well-proportioned, conservatively modern villa. It's ringed with plants growing in the gardens, which also contain a swimming pool. There's a pleasant wood-sheathed bar on the second floor, and a street-level dining room where good food is served, usually from a table d'hôte menu. Each of the air-conditioned rooms has a ceiling fan, a private bathroom, and a comfortable collection of simple furniture. In winter, MAP costs $115 daily in a single, $165 in a double. *In the off-season, MAP goes for $90 daily in a single, $135 in a double,* plus service and tax. Near the bar is a spacious TV lounge.

Mariner's Inn, P.O. Box 868, Villa Beach (tel. 458-4287). Its core is an old clapboard-sided West Indian house with an accommodating and well-used ring-around veranda. Most of its 20 accommodations are contained in two-story motel-like units which abut the edge of the channel. Protecting moored yachts by its bulk, Young Island rises a few hundred yards offshore. Pleasant, informal, and slightly raffish, the hotel is unpretentious and perhaps a bit tatty, but with a West Indian kind of flair. There are lots of interesting touches, including an outdoor bar crafted from the hull of an old schooner, masonry walls flanked with croton, and an airy kind of indoor/outdoor living. With MAP included, singles cost $60 daily in winter, *$40 in low season.* Doubles on the MAP rent for $80 to $92 daily in winter, *$55 to $70 in the off-season.* Service and tax are extra.

CSY Hotel & Marina, Blue Lagoon (tel. 458-4308), is a two-story grouping of rambling modern buildings crafted from local wood and stone. It's intricately connected to one of the best-known yacht-chartering businesses in the Caribbean, CSY, whose offices lie beneath the hotel's second-story reception area. There's a pleasantly breezy bar, with open walls and lots of exposed planking. As you relax, you'll overlook a moored armada of boats tied up at a nearby marina. A two-tiered swimming pool, terraced into a nearby hillside, offers two lagoon-shaped places to swim. Snorkeling, windsurfing, and daily departures on sailboats to Mustique and Bequia can be arranged through the hotel. Each of the 19 high-ceilinged accommodations has a balcony or patio, as well as a private bath. Clients pay from EC$200 ($74), plus tax and service, for single or double accommodations in all seasons.

Rawacou, Stubbs (tel. 458-4459). When they first moved to St. Vincent from their native Montréal and Cleveland, Peter and Nan Mickles found the perfect 15-acre plot of land along the island's windswept eastern coast. They quickly christened their new property with an obsolete name used on 18th-century naval charters for the rocky headland which jutted from their beach out into the Atlantic. Today the property blossoms with the thousands of trees, bushes, and shrubs they've planted over the years. Because of his dedication to forestry, only two or three persons in the Grenadines can compete with Peter's title as one of the "Johnny Appleseeds" of the islands.

Years ago, the rolling acreage was the site of a peanut and arrowroot plantation. Today ten modern cottages are scattered over the beachfront. Each contains a kitchenette, comfortable furniture, a sleeping loft, and big glass doors opening onto a view of the pounding surf. On any particular morning, a contented cow or one of the hotel's horses might graze near your bedroom window. With MAP included, *singles cost $90 a day in low season,* rising to $110 in high season. On the same plan, *doubles rent for $115 in low season,* $150 in high season. An apartment without meal service is $80 per day single, $106 double, in any season. Meals are served beneath a thatch sun screen near a swimming pool. Seagrape jam and guava jelly from trees on the property are likely to be served at breakfast, along with golden apple and mango chutney. Two-fisted drinks and access to the well-stocked personal library are always available.

Best for the Budget

The **Cobblestone Inn,** P.O. Box 867, Kingstown (tel. 456-1937). Originally built as a warehouse for sugar and arrowroot in 1814, the core of this historic hotel is made of stone and brick. Today it's one of the most famous hotels of St. Vincent, known for its labyrinth of passages, arches, and upper hallways. To reach its high-ceilinged reception area, you pass from the waterfront through a stone-sided tunnel into a chiseled courtyard. At the top of a massive sloping stone staircase you are shown to one of the simply decorated, slightly old-fashioned bedrooms. Each unit has air conditioning and walls covered with wide planks. Bathrooms were added long after the structure was built, so some of these units have regally proportioned windows opening over the rooftops of town. Year round, the 19 bedrooms cost from EC$115 ($42.50) in a single, from EC$150 ($55.50) to EC$175 ($64.75) in a double, with breakfast included, plus tax and service. Meals are served on a third-floor eagle's eyrie high above the hotel's central courtyard. Rows of glass windows and thick mahogany tables in its adjacent bar create one of the most unusual hideaways in town. The hotel is convenient for town; however, you'll have to drive about three miles to the nearest beach.

    Heron Hotel, P.O. Box 226, Kingstown (tel. 457-1631), is one of those enduring favorites of people who like a guesthouse with a lot of West Indian flavor. In a bustling location in town, it's contained in a wood-framed warehouse which a century ago used to store vast quantities of copra (dried coconut) before it was shipped to Europe. Today its well-ventilated, big-windowed premises is a 15-room hotel that's more like a guesthouse. Mrs. Doreen McKenzie is the dignified owner and manager (you'll meet her at the second-story reception area). You can always read quietly in an elegantly sparse living room whose high wood-framed ceiling evokes life of a century ago. Meals are served beneath the soaring ceiling of a room whose view encompasses a private courtyard encircled by some of the simple but comfortable accommodations. Each of these is air-conditioned, containing a private bathroom and simple pinewood furniture. Room 15, my favorite, is particularly spacious. With MAP included, singles cost $37 daily, and doubles run $70, year round, plus tax and service.

WHERE TO DINE: Most guests eat at their hotels on the Modified American Plan. Unlike the situation on many Caribbean islands, many Vincentian hostelries serve an authentic West Indian cuisine. There are also a few independent eateries as well, but not many.

    French Restaurant, Villa Beach (tel. 458-4972). Set in a clapboard house near the pier where the ferryboat from Young Island docks, this is one of the most consistently good restaurants on the island. It offers a long, semi-shadowed bar which you pass on your way to the rear veranda. There, overlooking the moored yachts off the coast of Young Island, you can enjoy well-seasoned, Gallic-inspired food. Surrounded with vine-laced lattices, you pay from EC$65 ($24) for full dinners, served daily from 7 to 9 p.m. Menu suggestions include grilled Cornish game hen, curried conch, seafood cassoulette, fish and shrimp kebab, stuffed crab back, lobster crêpes, onion soup, followed by homemade ice cream or chocolate mousse. Lunch, from noon to 2 p.m. daily, is simpler, costing from EC$30 ($11). Its bill of fare includes quiche Lorraine, omelets, tunafish salads, and cheesecake. The establishment is closed for about two weeks every August.

    The Dolphin, P.O. Box 651, Villa Beach (tel. 458-4238). Its waterside location, wide veranda, neo-Victorian gingerbread, and rambling front lawn make this unusual restaurant popular with the yachting crowd. Inspired by the culinary tradition of their native Scandinavia, co-owners Bjorn Banke and Pertti Makkonen (from Denmark and Finland, respectively) offer Danish and Caribbean specialties. Served in a casual European style beneath the shadow of a huge tamarind tree at outdoor tables, the food appears on platters which often combine smoked herring, lobster, cheese, shrimp, pâté, Danish meatballs, and a small filet steak. Caribbean salmon is smoked in the Danish tradition right on the property. Depending on their size, platters cost EC$25 ($9.25) to EC$30 ($11). A salad bar is available, and a selection of rôtis and an array of pizzas (a favorite is the one studded with lobster) are also available. Open daily, the restaurant serves lunch from 11 a.m. to 3:30 p.m. and dinner from 6 to 10:30 p.m.

    Basil's Bar & Restaurant, Bay Street (tel. 457-2713). This brick-lined enclave is a newer and less famous annex of the legendary Basil's Beach Bar in Mustique. It lies in the early 19th-century walls of an old sugar warehouse, on the waterfront in

Kingstown beneath the previously recommended Cobblestone Inn. The air-conditioned interior is accented with exposed stone and brick, soaring arches, and a rambling mahogany bar where you are likely to meet just about anyone. A daily luncheon buffet costs from EC$25 ($9.25), with an à la carte meal going for EC$35 ($13). The bill of fare could include lobster salad, shrimp in garlic butter, sandwiches, hamburgers, and barbecued chicken. Dinners, from EC$70 ($26), feature grilled lobster, escargots, shrimp cocktail, grilled red snapper, and grilled filet mignon. The Friday-night seafood buffet goes for EC$50 ($18.50), plus service. Lunch is from noon to 2 p.m., and dinner is on from 7 to 9:30 p.m., daily except Sunday. The bar remains open throughout the day, and on Sunday the place opens at 5 p.m., staying so "until very late."

Bounty, Back Street (tel. 456-1776), lies opposite Barclay's Bank in the center of Kingstown behind a green-and-white façade. The color scheme is repeated inside, with a raftered ceiling, clean napery, and large deli-style display case. Friendly faces help create a satisfying restaurant experience. Local people who work in the shops nearby come in for a typical British breakfast, costing from EC$7 ($2.60). Later the place jumps with business at lunch, when hamburgers and snack food are the most frequently ordered items. A snack costs from $4.50 (U.S.); a full meal, from $10. Everything is pleasantly casual, and it's open weekdays from 8:30 a.m. to 4:45 p.m., on Saturday to 1:30 p.m.; closed Sunday.

Juliette's, Middle Street (tel. 457-1645). The alleyway that stretches from Middle Street to this restaurant is so narrow you might miss it. It will lead to a concealed courtyard and a flight of exterior steps which climb to a second-floor dining room. This is the domain of Juliette Campbell and her genteel staff. It's a clean, respectable West Indian dining room where only platters of food are served in place of more traditional three-course meals. Breakfast is from 8 to 10:30 a.m., and lunch is served from 10:30 a.m. to 2 p.m. The restaurant closes promptly at 4:30 p.m. after a busy day of feeding the office workers of Kingstown. A platter of food costs EC$14 ($5.20) to EC$20 ($7.40). The menu consists of such island specialties as curried mutton, an array of fish, stewed chicken, and stewed beef. Many of the platters are garnished with fried plantain and rice. Closed Sunday.

WHAT TO SEE: In the capital, Kingstown, you can still meet oldtime beachcombers if you stroll on Upper Bay Street. White haired and bearded, they can be seen loading their boats with produce grown on the mountain, before heading to some secluded beach in the Grenadines. This is a chief port and gateway to the Grenadines, and you can also view the small boats, dinghies, and yachts that have dropped anchor here. The place is a magnet for charter sailors.

Kingstown

Lushly tropical and solidly British, the capital isn't as architecturally fascinating as St. George's in Grenada. Some English-style houses do exist, many of them looking as if they belonged in Penzance, Cornwall, instead of the West Indies.

At the top of a winding road on the north side of Kingstown, **Fort Charlotte** was built on Johnson Point, enclosing one side of the bay. Constructed about the time of the American Revolution, it was named after Queen Charlotte, the German consort of George III. The ruins aren't much to inspect. Instead, the reason to go here is for the view. The fort sits atop a steep promontory some 640 feet above the sea. From its citadel, you'll have a commanding sweep of the leeward shores to the north, Kingstown to the south, and the Grenadines beyond. A trio of cannons used to fight off French troops are still in place. Admission is 60¢, and for that you'll see a series of oil murals depicting the history of black Caribs.

The second major sight is the **Botanic Gardens,** on the north side of Kingstown, about a mile from the center. Founded in 1765 by Gov. George Melville, they are the oldest botanic gardens in the West Indies. In this Windward Eden, you'll see 20 acres of such tropical exotics as teak, almond, cinnamon, nutmeg, cannonball trees, and mahogany. Some of the trees are more than two centuries old. One of the breadfruit trees, reputedly, was among those original seedlings brought to this island by Captain Bligh in 1793. There is also a large *Spachea perforata* (the Soufrière tree), a species believed to be unique to St. Vincent and not found in the wild since 1812. The gardens are open daily from 6 a.m. to 6 p.m. No admission is charged.

The **Archeological Museum,** in the Botanic Gardens, houses a good collection of stone tools and other artifacts in both stone and pottery. In front of it are shrubs which might have been found in the compound of an early Indian home.

In the heart of town, you might pay a visit to **St. Mary's Catholic Church,** on Grenville Street, with its curious mélange of architecture. Fancifully flawed, it was built in 1935 by a Belgian monk, Dom Carlos Verbeke. He incorporated Romanesque arches, Gothic spires, and almost Moorish embellishments. The result—a maze of balconies, turrets, battlements, and courtyards—creates a bizarre effect.

St. George's Cathedral has some beautiful stained-glass windows: the three on the east are by Kempe and the large one on the south is of Munich glass. The nave and lower part of the tower date from 1820, and the galleried interior is of late Georgian architecture.

After Kingstown, the following targets might intrigue you.

The Leeward Highway

The leeward or west side of the island has the most dramatic scenery. North from Kingstown, you rise into lofty terrain before descending to the water again. There are views in all directions. On your right you'll pass the closed-down Aqueduct Golf Course before reaching Layou. Here you can see the massive **Carib Rock,** with a human face carving dating back to A.D. 600. This is considered one of the finest petroglyphs in the Caribbean.

Continuing north you reach **Barrouallie,** where there is another Carib stone altar. Even if you're not a fisherman, you might want to spend some time in this whaling village where men still set out in brightly painted boats armed with harpoons, *Moby Dick*-style, to seek the elusive whale. However, "Save the Whale" devotees need not harpoon their way here in anger. Barrouallie may be one of the last few outposts in the world where such whale-hunting is carried on, but St. Vincentians point out that it does not endanger an already endangered species since so few are caught each year. If one is caught, it's an occasion for festivities and a lot of blubber.

The leeward highway continues to Chateaubelair, the end of the line. There you can swim at the attractive **Richmond Beach** before heading back to Kingstown. In the distance, the volcano, La Soufrière, looms menacingly in the mountains.

The adventurous set out from here to see the **Falls of Baleine,** 7½ miles north of Richmond Beach on the northern tip of the island, accessible only by boat. Coming from a stream in the volcanic hills, Baleine is a dramatic freshwater fall. If you're interested in making the trip, check with the tourist office in Kingstown about a tour there.

The Windward Highway

This road runs along the eastern Atlantic coast from Kingstown. Waves pound the surf, and all along the rocky shores are splendid seascapes. If you want to go swimming along this often-dangerous coast, stick to the sandy spots, as they offer safer shores. Along this road you'll pass coconut and banana plantations and fields of arrowroot, a crop that St. Vincent seems to monopolize.

North of Georgetown lies the **Rabacca Dry River,** which was the flow of lava from the volcano at its eruption at the beginning of the 20th century. The journey from Kingstown to here is only 24 miles, but it will seem like much longer. For those who want to go the final 11 miles along a rugged road to **Fancy,** the northern tip of the island, a Land Rover, Jeep, or Moke will be needed.

La Soufrière

A safari to St. Vincent's hot volcano is possible. As you travel the island, you can't miss its cloud-capped splendor. On some occasions this volcano has captured the attention of the world.

The most recent eruption was in 1979, when the volcano threw ashes and spit lava and hot mud, covering the vegetation that grew on its slopes and sending thousands of Vincentians fleeing its fury. Without warning, belched-out rock and black curling smoke filled the blue Caribbean sky. Jets of steam spouted 20,000 feet into the air. About 17,000 persons were evacuated from a ten-mile ring around the volcano.

Fortunately, the eruption was in the sparsely settled northern part of the island. The volcano lies away from most of the tourism and commercial centers of St. Vincent, and even if it should erupt again, volcanologists do not consider it a danger to visitors lodged at beachside hotels along the leeward coast. The last major eruption of the volcano occurred in 1902, when 2,000 people were killed. Until its 1979 eruption, the volcano had been quiet since 1972. The activity that year produced a 324-foot-long island of lava rock called Crater Lake.

Even if you're an experienced hiker, don't attempt to explore this volcano without an experienced local guide, many of whom will charge around $40 and up for the trip. Also, wear suitable hiking clothes and know that you're in the best of health before making such an arduous journey.

A guide will direct you in your car through a rich countryside of coconut and banana trees, coming to a clearing at the foot of the mountain. After you get there, you go on foot through a rain forest, following the trail that will eventually lead to the crater rim of La Soufrière. Allow at least three hours, unless you're an Olympic athlete.

At the rim of the crater you'll be rewarded with one of the most panoramic views in the Caribbean. That is, if the wind doesn't blow too hard and make you topple over into the crater itself! Extreme caution is emphasized. Inside, you can see the steam rising from the crater.

The trail back down is much easier, I assure you.

Marriqua Valley

Sometimes known as the Mesopotamia Valley, this land is considered one of the most lushly cultivated valleys in the eastern Caribbean. Surrounded by mountain ridges, the drive takes you through a dramatic landscape richly planted with nutmeg, cocoa, coconut, breadfruit, and bananas. The road begins at Vigie Hwy., to the east of the Arnos Vale Airport runway. At the town of Montréal you'll come upon natural mineral springs. Only rugged vehicles should make this trip.

Around Kingstown, you can also enjoy the **Queen's Drive,** a dramatically scenic loop into the high hills to the east of the capital. From there, the view is magnificent over Kingstown and its yacht-clogged harbor to the Grenadines in the distance.

THE SPORTING LIFE: In St. Vincent you skindive, fish, swim, or snorkel, and of course go sailing, mainly to the Grenadines.

All **beaches** on St. Vincent are public, and many of the best ones border hotel properties which you can patronize for drinks or luncheons. Most of the resorts are in the south, where the beaches have white or golden-yellow sand. However, many of the beaches in the north have sands that look like lava ash in color. The safest swimming is on the leeward beaches, as the windward beaches can be dangerous.

Tennis

Short-term visitors to St. Vincent can play at the **Kingstown Tennis Club,** Murray Road. Guests are charged a subscription of $10 per court per hour. You're asked to provide your own tennis balls and racquets and make arrangements through the chief steward in advance. Telephone 456-1288 for more information. Short-term visitors are allowed to play between 8:30 a.m. and noon.

Young Island and the **Grand View Beach** hotels (both previously recommended) also have tennis courts.

Snorkeling and Scuba-Diving

The best area for snorkeling and scuba-diving is the Villa/Young Island section on the southern end of the island. **Mariners Scuba Shop,** P.O. Box 639 (tel. 458-4228), is run by Susan and Earl Halbich, directly across from Young Island. They offer full diving service; and you can rent equipment here, going on guided reef trips in the warm, fantastically clear waters.

Fishing

It's best to go to a native fisherman for advice if you're interested in this sport, which your hotel will usually arrange for you. The government of St. Vincent doesn't require visitors to take out a license. If you arrange things in time, it's sometimes possible to accompany the local fishermen on one of their trips, perhaps four or five miles from shore. A modest fee should suffice. The fishing fleet leaves from the leeward coast at Barrouallie. They've been known to return to shore with everything from a six-inch redfish to a 20-foot pilot whale.

Sailing and Yachting

St. Vincent and the Grenadines are one of the great sailing centers of the West Indies. Here you can obtain yachts that are fully provisioned if you want to go bareboating, or else, if you're a well-heeled novice, you can hire a captain and a crew.

You can rent boats from **Caribbean Sailing Yachts (CSY),** at P.O. Box 491, Tenafly, NJ 07670 (tel. 201/568-0390), or in St. Vincent at its offices at the Blue Lagoon (tel. 458-4308). This company is in the full-service charter business. The cost of your craft will depend on the season. You'll be asked to prove what kind of sailor you are.

Yacht charters are also offered by **Mariners Scuba Shop,** P.O. Box 639 (tel. 458-4228). You can choose a 35-foot Freedom, a 45-foot Vanderstadt, or a 43-foot Gulfstar.

WHERE TO SHOP: You don't come to St. Vincent to shop, but once there, you might pick up some items in the sea island cotton fabrics and clothing that are specialties here. In addition, Vincentian artisans make pottery, jewelry, and baskets that have souvenir value at least.

Since the capital, Kingstown, consists of about 12 small blocks, you can walk and browse and see about everything in a morning's shopping jaunt. Try to be in town for the colorful, noisy **Friday-morning market.** You might not purchase anything. After all, you don't plan to bring fruit, fish, and poultry back on the plane with you, but you'll surely enjoy the riot of color.

Most shops are open Monday to Friday from 8 a.m. to 4 p.m. Stores generally close from noon to 1 p.m. for lunch. Saturday hours are 8 a.m. to noon.

In the **St. Vincent Handicraft Centre** (tel. 457-1288), up the road from the wharf in Kingstown, you'll see a large display of the handcrafts of the island. On the site of an old cotton gin, this shop offers you a chance to see craftspeople at work, perhaps on macramé or metal-work jewelry.

Batik Caribe, Bay Street, Kingstown (tel. 456-1666), contains some of the most unusual batiks in the Caribbean. This charming establishment justifiably considers its products more as artwork than as garments. This is the headquarters of a Caribbean-wide chain of high-quality shops making brightly colored cloth tinted in an Indonesian technique of lost-wax dye resistance, an item of high fashion. Marnie Palmer is the Canadian-born entrepreneur who pours her artistic input into the skillfully executed patterns. Designs are priced based on the number of colors (and consequently the amount of time) that go into their production. Many of the brightly colored scenes, like paintings, are suitable for framing. Others are better worn as scarves, shawls, or dresses. Sundresses, jumpers, and shirts for both men and women are sold, as well as amusing hats and children's clothing. Often one of the polite sales staff will unfold some of the original bolts of cloth like an Oriental rug. A bikini costs from $20; a gaily painted handkerchief, around $6; the most elaborate design, suitable for framing, goes for $95.

Norma's, on Egmont Street (tel. 457-1207), is one of the leading boutiques of St. Vincent. On the second floor of a Kingstown building, the shop prices its dresses reasonably.

Stechers Jewellery Ltd., Lot 19, Lane Bay Street in Kingstown (tel. 457-1142), offers a good selection of crystal, quality watches, china, porcelain, and jewelry.

The familiar **Y. de Lima Ltd.** (tel. 457-1681) also has a branch in Kingstown, well stocked with cameras, stereo equipment, clocks, binoculars, and jewelry. Its entrance is through the courtyard of the Cobblestone Inn.

Noah's Arkade (tel. 457-1513) is a little shop on Bay Street in Kingstown, selling handcrafts from the West Indies, including woodcarvings. It also offers locally made clothing. Noah's has shops at the Frangipani Hotel, Bequia, St. Vincent, and the Grenadines.

Stamp enthusiasts can visit **St. Vincent Philatelic Services Ltd.,** in the Singer Building (tel. 457-1911), where they can see a full range of the island's colorful postage stamps on display and also make purchases. The stamp themes depict fish, corals, birds, and animals, as well as international themes such as occasions involving royalty.

Finally, as you're leaving you'll be able to purchase duty-free liquors and cigarettes at **Gonsalves Liquors** (tel. 458-4753) at Arnos Vale Airport.

NIGHTLIFE: The focus is mainly on the hotels, and activities are likely to include nighttime barbecues and dancing to steel bands. In season, at least one hotel seems to have something planned every night during a week.

One of the liveliest spots is the **Mariner's Inn,** at Villa Beach (tel. 458-4287). Island calypso and steel-drum music are the featured attractions here, and local people show up to dance to good music. Nonresidents pay an entrance fee of $3, which includes their first drink.

The only casino on the island lies amid a lushly isolated landscape whose rolling hills and surging freshwater streams evoke a tropical version of Scotland. Set in a glen, cradled by the surrounding hills, the **Emerald Valley Casino,** Penniston Valley (tel. 458-7421), is at the end of a rutted dirt road, about 45 minutes from Kingstown. Its stone-sided modern premises contain an array of gaming tables, slot machines, a duet of bars, a swimming pool, and landscaped lawns. The casino is open every night except Monday from 8 to 3 a.m. The entrance fee is EC$5 ($1.85).

Next to the Young Island landing pier, the best-known spot for entertainment remains the **Aquatic Club** (tel. 458-4205), which "jumps up" with action, usually on Friday and Saturday nights. Guests from all the hotels come here to enjoy the music and sing-alongs. Drinks range in price from $3 and up.

4. The Grenadines

South of St. Vincent, which administers them, this small chain of islands extends for more than 40 miles, offering the finest yachting area in the eastern Caribbean. They're strung like a necklace of precious stones, and have such wonderful names as Bequia, Mustique, Canouan, and Petit St. Vincent.

A few of the islands have accommodations, which we'll explore, but many are so small and so completely undeveloped and unspoiled that they attract only beachcombers and stray boating people in the area.

Populated by the descendants of African slaves, the Grenadines collectively add up to a land mass of only 30 square miles.

The islands are called the Grenadines because they lead to Grenada. These bits of land, often dots on nautical charts, may lack natural resources, yet they're blessed with white sandy beaches, coral reefs, and their own kind of sleepy beauty. If you're not spending the night in the Grenadines, you may at least go over for the day to visit one of them, enjoying a picnic lunch (which your hotel will pack for you) on one of the long stretches of beach.

GETTING THERE: The ideal way to go, of course, is to rent your own yacht, and many wealthy visitors do just that. If you'd like to consider that, refer to "The Sporting Life" in the previous section on St. Vincent. The least expensive method of going is on a mail, cargo, and passenger boat. However, to do this, you should be a free-wheeling person with lots of time and patience.

It's a unique experience for adventuresome travelers and for those who've never been on this type of vessel. You should carry along a raincoat to protect you from those quick Caribbean showers or that occasional big wave. Price and times might fluctuate, so you should check at the tourist office in Kingstown, St. Vincent.

The **government mail boat** leaves St. Vincent on Monday and Thursday at 9 a.m., arriving at Bequia at 10 a.m., stopping at Canouan and Mayreau, and arriving at Union Island at 3:30 p.m. On Tuesday and Friday it leaves Union Island at 6:30 a.m., stops at Mayreau and Canouan, reaching Bequia at 10:30 a.m., and making port at St. Vincent at noon. One-way fares from St. Vincent are: to Bequia, EC$5 ($1.85); to Canouan, EC$10 ($3.70); to Mayreau, EC$12 ($4.40); to Union Island, EC$15 ($5.50).

M.V. *Grenadines Star* travels to and from St. Vincent and Bequia, Canouan, Mayreau, and Union Island on Monday, Tuesday, Thursday, and Friday, and only to and from Bequia on Saturday. These are all daytime trips, lasting from 7 a.m. to 3:05 p.m. Fares are the same as those given for the mail boat.

For information on other vessels making the sea trips, inquire at the tourist office in Kingstown or on the island you are visiting.

BEQUIA: Only seven square miles of land, Bequia (pronounced "Beck-wee") is the largest of St. Vincent's Grenadines. It's the northernmost island in the Grenadines, offering quiet lagoons, reefs, and long stretches of nearly deserted beaches. Descended from seafarers and other early adventurers, its population of some 6,000 Bequians will probably give you a friendly greeting if you pass them along the road. Of the inhabitants, 10% are white, of Scottish ancestry, who live mostly in the Mount Pleasant region. A feeling of relaxation and informality prevails in Bequia.

The island lies nine miles south of St. Vincent. There is no airport, but you can travel here by government mail boat (see introduction to this section), by motor vessel, or by a three-masted island schooner, the *Friendship Rose*. This sailing vessel makes trips Monday to Friday, leaving Bequia at 6:30 a.m., arriving at St. Vincent at 7:45 a.m. It departs St. Vincent at 12:30 p.m. on the return, reaching Bequia at 1:45 p.m. M.V. *Grenadines Star* comes to Bequia on Monday, Tuesday, Thursday, Friday, and Saturday.

Its main harbor village, **Port Elizabeth,** is known for its safe anchorage, Admiralty Bay. The bay was a haven in the 17th century for the British, French, and Spanish navies as well as for pirates. Descendants of Captain Kydd (a.k.a. Kidd), still live on the island. Today the yachting set "from anywhere" puts in here, often bringing a kind of dazzling excitement to the locals.

No rental cars are available in the port, but you can hire a taxi at the dock to take you around or to your hotel if you're spending the night. Taxis are reasonably priced, but an even better bet are the so-called "dollar cabs," which take you anywhere on the island for EC$1 (37¢). They don't seem to have a regular schedule. You just flag one down. Before going to your hotel, drop in at the circular Tourist Information Centre. You'll see it right on the beach. There you can ask for a driver who is familiar with the attractions of the island (nearly all of them are). You should negotiate the fare in advance. A three-hour tour with three or four passengers can probably be arranged for about $15 per hour.

If you want to see boats, just walk along the beach. There, craftsmen can be seen constructing vessels by hand, a method they learned from their fathers who learned it from their ancestors. Whalers sometimes still set out from here in wooden boats with hand harpoons, just as they do from a port village on St. Vincent.

Frankly, after you leave Port Elizabeth there aren't many sights, and you'll probably have your driver, booked for the day, drop you off for a long, leisurely lunch and some time on a beach. However, you'll pass a fort with a harbor view, driving on to Industry Estates which has a Beach House restaurant serving a fair lunch. At Paget Farm, you can wander into a village of whalers, and maybe inspect a few jawbones left over from catches of yesterday.

At Moonhole, there's a vacation and retirement community built into the cliffs, really free-form sculpture. These are private homes of course, and you're not to enter without permission. For a final look at Bequia, head up an 800-foot hill which the local people call "The Mountain." From that perch, you'll have a 360° view of St. Vincent and the Grenadines to the south.

Where to Stay

Friendship Bay Hotel (tel. 458-3222, or toll free 800/223-6764) is a beachfront resort offering 27 well-decorated rooms with private verandas nestled in 12 acres of tropical gardens. It sits on a sloping hillside with well-tended vegetation. The entire resort complex stands above a snow-white crescent of one of the best beaches on the island. Guests have a sweeping view of the sea and neighboring islands. The owners are Eduardo and Joanne Guadagnino. Eduardo moved from his homeland, Argentina, a number of years ago, going to California, where he went into the restaurant business and married native Californian Joanne. Joanne has seen to redecorating the hotel, using brightly colored curtains, bedspreads, and handmade wall hangings telling a picture story of life in Bequia, as well as new grass rugs in the rooms, which are cooled by the trade winds. In winter, the MAP rate in a single is $85 to $135, rising to $150 to $200 in a double. *Summer MAP prices are $75 to $85 in a single, $100 to $150 in a double,* all plus service and tax.

The Guadaginos have added a beach bar in Caribbean style. They offer Saturday-night barbecues on the beach, with music provided by the hotel band, Exotica, a popular island combo. The food is good too, with many island specialties on the menu, along with Italian and Argentine cuisine. You can enjoy water sports and tennis here, or take an excursion aboard the hotel's classic yacht, built in 1920 in Cardiff,

Wales, and completely restored by Mr. Guadagnino. The yacht makes trips to and from Mustique and St. Vincent, lavishing guests with refreshments, for about $55 per person round trip.

Sunny Caribee, P.O. Box 16, Admiralty Bay (tel. 458-3425), was completely restored after its purchase by a British concern. Accommodations consist of 17 West Indian cabañas painted in shades of pink and aqua, each with its own private terrace, plus eight rooms in the old colonial-style wood-frame house. The property fronts a 700-foot white sandy beach, with a seafront bar and a kidney-shaped beachside pool. The resort overlooks Admiralty Bay, and its 11 acres of grounds are planted with flowering trees and shrubs. In winter, a hotel room rents for $36 a day for two, a detached cabaña for $80. *In summer, these tariffs drop to $24 in a double room, $60 daily in a cabaña.* The hotel rooms don't have showers en suite, and the cabañas have twin beds, a small sitting area, a shower room, and a terrace (a few come with kitchenettes). Extra beds are available at $10 per person daily, and for breakfast and dinner add another $15 per person daily. A wide-open veranda extends around three sides of the building, and people sit here with absolutely nothing to do but unwind or have another beer, or both. You can also swim, snorkel, sail, waterski, or fish. There's also a tennis court if anybody has that much energy.

Spring on Bequia (tel. 458-3414). In the late 1960s the avant-garde design of this hotel won an award from the American Institute of Architects. Fashioned from beautifully textured honey-colored stone, it combines design elements from both Japan and Scandinavia. However, its flattened hip roof was inspired by the old plantation houses of Martinique. Constructed on the 18th-century foundations of a West Indian homestead, it sits in the middle of 28 acres of hillside orchards, producing oranges, grapefruit, bananas, breadfruit, plums, and mangoes. Because of the almost-constant blossoming of one crop or another, you get the feeling of springtime (hence the name of the establishment). Leslie Candy, the Minnesota-born owner, will welcome you and check you in. From the main building's stone-sided bar and open-air dining room, you might hear the bellowing of a herd of cows. On the premises is a swimming pool, along with a tennis court. There is access to a sandy beach at the bottom of a steep hill. Each of the dozen units is ringed with stone and contains Japanese-style screens to filter the sun. *In the off-season, which is only from November to mid-December, one person pays $65 daily, and two people pay $100, both MAP rates.* In winter, MAP singles cost $100 daily, $140 for two, plus tax and service. The hotel's reservation office can be called in Minneapolis at 612/823-1202.

Julie's and Isola's Guest House, Port Elizabeth (tel. 458-3304). Charming, West Indian, and friendly, these twin establishments are owned by two of the most kind-hearted hoteliers on the island. Julie and Isola McIntosh are almost always on the premises, preparing meals or building extensions onto their family hotels. Julie, a mason, laid many of the bricks for both hotels, which lie across the street from one another about a block from the water. Isola's Guest House is the more modern and attractive, containing a total of 15 rooms, each with private bath. Julie's is slightly older. With MAP included, year-round rates at Julie's are $50 daily in a single, $100 in a double. Rates at Isola's, also with MAP, are $65 daily in a single, $115 in a double. Good West Indian food is served in the dining room which is a bougainvillea-covered veranda. The bill of fare is likely to include pumpkin fritters, very fresh fish, and curry dishes.

Where to Dine

The food is good and healthful here—lobster, chicken, and steaks from fish such as dolphin, kingfish, and grouper, plus tropical fruits, fried plantain, and coconut and guava puddings fresh daily. Even the beach bars are kept spotless.

Friendship Bay Resort (tel. 458-3222) is contained in the stylish and welcoming precincts of the island's finest hotel, Friendship Bay. Guests dine in a candlelit room high above a sweeping expanse of seafront on a hillside rich with the scent of bougainvillea and hibiscus. Argentine-born Eduardo Guadagnino and his California wife, Joanne, prepare a tempting array of locally inspired dishes served by polite, uniformed employees. Lunch is served from noon to 3 p.m., costing from EC$15 ($5.50). Dinner, offered from 6:30 to 9 p.m., is more elaborate, costing from EC$65 ($24) and including such dishes as curried beef, grilled or broiled fish (served Créole style with a spicy sauce), shrimp curry, charcoal-grilled steak flambé, and roast lamb. An island highlight is the Saturday-night jump-up and barbecue. Phone in advance if you're coming for dinner.

Frangipani (tel. 458-3255), the waterside dining room of this previously recommended hotel, is one of the best restaurants on the island. Part of the dining room juts out onto a terraced wharf, whose foundations are sunk on piers into the harbor. Between the tables are clusters of tropical shrubs and a thatch-covered indoor/outdoor bar. With the exception of the juicy steaks imported for barbecues, only local food is used in the succulent specialties. Breakfast begins at 7:30 a.m., and lunches, served throughout the day until 6 p.m., cost from EC$20 ($7.40) and include sandwiches, salads, and seafood platters. Dinner, from 7:30 to 9:30 p.m., is by reservation. Specialties include baked chicken with rice and coconut stuffing, lobster, conch chowder, and an array of fresh fish. A fixed-price menu goes for EC$35 ($13), an à la carte meal costing from EC$45 ($16.75). A Thursday-night barbecue is an island event, costing EC$50 ($18.50) and including live entertainment.

In Port Elizabeth, the **Whaleboner Inn** (tel. 458-3233), has been an enduring favorite. It's still going strong in its new location next to the Hotel Frangipani. Inside, the bar is carved from the jawbone of a giant whale, and the bar stools are made from the vertebrae. It's open seven days a week, serving breakfast at 8 a.m. and offering food throughout the day until either 10 p.m. or midnight, depending on the crowd. Albert C. Hinkson, the owner, offers the best pizza on the island, along with a selection of fish and chips or well-made sandwiches for lunch. At night you may want one of the wholesome dinners prepared by a West Indian cook and including a choice of lobster, fish, chicken, or steak. Meals cost from EC$25 ($9.25) to EC$39 ($14.50). Favored by the yachting set, the restaurant has full bar service. The Whaleboner Boutique adjoins the restaurant, and you may want to check out its merchandise.

Shopping

This is not a valid reason to come to Bequia, but there is some. At shops scattered along the water you can buy hand-screened cotton made by Bequians. The best of these is **The Crab Hole** (tel. 458-3290), run by Carolyn and George Porter. Next door to the Sunny Caribee, they invite guests to visit their silkscreen factory in back. Later you can make purchases at their shop in front.

Noah's Arkade, Belmont (tel. 458-3424), owned and operated by island entrepreneur Lavinia Gunn, sells St. Vincentian and Bequian batiks, scarves, hats, T-shirts, dresses, and a scattering of pottery. There are also dolls, placemats, baskets, and homemade jellies concocted from grapefruit, mango, and guava. This place stands a few steps from the drinking terrace of the Frangipani Hotel.

Anyone on the island can show you the way to the workshops of **Sargeant's Model Boatshop Bequia** (tel. 458-3344). The place is the best known of its kind in the Caribbean, sought out by yacht owners looking for a scale-model reproduction of their favorite vessel. Mr. Lawson Sargeant is the self-taught woodcarver who established this business. Models are carved from a soft local wood called gumwood, then painted in brilliant colors of red, green, gray, or blue, whatever your fancy dictates. When a scale model of the royal family's yacht, *Britannia,* was commissioned in 1985, local newspapers photographed Queen Elizabeth II receiving the boat crafted in this studio. It required five weeks of work, meticulous blueprints, and cost $10,000. You can pick up a model of a Bequia whaling boat for $70. The Sargeant family usually keeps 100 model boats in inventory, and they come in many shapes and sizes. At least five workmen can be seen chiseling out the bodies of more in the backyard.

Water Sports
Dive Bequia, P.O. Box 16 (tel. 458-3425), specializes in diving, snorkeling, windsurfing, and waterskiing. Scuba dives cost $35 for one, $55 for two in the same day, $150 for a five-dive package, and $250 for a ten-dive package. Prices include all the necessary equipment. Introductory lessons cost $15 each per person, a basic two-dive course going for $200 and a five-dive open-water trip for $250. A snorkeling trip is $10 per person. Windsurfing is available at $20 for half a day, $35 per day, and $125 per week.

Boat Charters
No holiday in the Grenadines is complete without at least one outing on a glamorous yacht. A vessel that more than adequately suits this need is the *Sally Ann*. It was built in Cardiff, Wales, in 1920 for a wealthy industrialist. Its all-teak and brass interior, fashioned along pure art deco lines, is considered worth a photograph. Its gentlemanly skipper, Don Young, is an educated and charming expert on the local lore of the Grenadines. Unless someone has engaged her, the boat overnights at harbor in Bequia.

Passage between Mustique and Bequia in either direction costs about $35 per person, A $110 package is offered, including air charter from Barbados to Mustique, a taxi from the airport to the harbor, and then a transit on *Sally Ann* from Mustique to Bequia.

For information and reservations, call toll free 800/223-1108 in North America (in New York, dial 212/628-8149).

MUSTIQUE: This island, 15 miles south of St. Vincent, is so remote and small it almost deserves to be unknown, and it would be if it weren't for the escapades of Princess Margaret (called "Yvonne" here by her intimates). The princess has a cottage on this island of luxury villas which someone once called "Georgian West Indian."

The island is privately owned by a consortium of businessmen. When splashed on front pages in London, describing Princess Margaret's retreat, it was then owned by beer baron Colin Tennant, a millionaire Scottish nobleman, now Lord Glen Conner. An eccentric dandy, he was often photographed in silk scarfs and Panama hats. On the trail of Margaret, and her cousin the Earl of Lichfield, came a host of celebrities, including Truman Capote, Paul Newman, Mick Jagger, Raquel Welch, and Richard Avedon.

Attracting the elite, the island is only three miles long and one mile wide, and it has only one major hotel (see below). The best way to go to Mustique is by air charter on **Mustique Airways.** For a description of how to do that, refer to the "Getting There" section on St. Vincent. Chartered planes arrive on the small airstrip in the middle of the bird sanctuary. The airport closes at dusk, because there are no landing lights. Once there, you'll find no taxis. But chances are, someone at Cotton House will already have seen you land. After settling in, you'll find many good white sandy beaches against a backdrop of luxuriant foliage. My favorite is Macaroni Beach, where the water is like turquoise.

On the northern reef of Mustique you'll find the wreck of the French liner *Antilles*, which went aground on the Pillories in 1971. Today its massive hulk, now gutted, can be seen cracked and rusting a few yards offshore, an eerie sight.

If you wish to tour the small island, you can rent a Mini-Moke to see some of the most elegant homes in the Caribbean. You can even rent Les Jolies Eaux (Pretty Waters), that is if you can afford it. Designed by Oliver Messel, her uncle by marriage, this is the Caribbean home of Princess Margaret. A five-bedroom/five-bath house, it has a large swimming pool, naturally. Accommodating ten well-heeled guests, it is available only when HRH is not in residence. If you rent it, the princess will require references.

Where to Stay

The **Cotton House** (tel. 456-4777), owned by Guy de la Houssaye, is an exclusive hotel, once operating as a private club, a place casually elegant, as is its clientele. The main house is an 18th-century structure, built of coral and stone. The house was painstakingly restored, rebuilt, and redecorated by Oliver Messel. The architecture of the hotel, decor, and amenities suggest the graciousness of the plantation era (that is, providing you weren't a slave). The design of the hotel is characterized by arched louvered doors and cedar shutters. The antique loggia sets the style—everything from Lady Bateman's steamer trunks to a scallop-shell fountain on a quartz base. Guests sit here enjoying their sundowners. Perhaps earlier they played a game on the tennis court or had a swim at the pool surrounded by Messel's "Roman ruins" after a buffet lunch by the pool. Some of the rooms were also designed by Messel. Units are in two fully restored Georgian houses, a trio of cottages, a newer block of eight rooms, or a three-room beach house, all of which open onto windswept balconies or patios. Of course, you pay for all this—$384 daily in a double in winter, from $278 in a single, including full board and tea. *Off-season, the half-board tariffs are $242 daily in a double, $178 in a single.* The hotel enjoys an outstanding reputation for its food and service. The cuisine has a West Indian flavor. Nonresidents are allowed to dine here, but they must make reservations. Lunch ranges from $18, and dinner costs about $27 a head, plus wines.

Charlie's Guest House (tel. 458-4621) is the bargain of Mustique, perhaps the only bargain on the island. Its flamboyant and colorful owner, Virginia Royston, is a personal friend of Princess Margaret and moves freely among the island's legendary inhabitants. Her guest accommodations, six in all, lie adjacent to her low-slung private house on a hillside above the landing strip of the island's airport. The smallish and simply furnished accommodations are usually booked weeks in advance. Year round, two people pay $175 to $195 per week, or $35 a night. Lady Royston runs a decidedly informal place.

Where to Dine

Nobody ever goes to this island of indigenous farmers and fisherfolk without spending a night drinking at **Basil's Beach Bar** (tel. 458-4621). A "South Seas island"–type establishment, it is more authentic than any reproduction in an old Dorothy Lamour flick. The gathering place for yachting people, as well as owners of those luxurious villas, the bar, but mainly its owner, has received a lot of newspaper publicity. Its greeter, Basil, is a six-foot four-inch, heavily muscled charmer whom *Esquire* magazine called "the island's most famous product after its sandy beaches." Some people come here to drink and watch a beautiful view, but Basil's is also, by reputation, one of the finest seafood restaurants in the Caribbean. Both lunch and dinner are served daily at this establishment built on piers above the sea. You can dine under the open-air sun screens or with the sun blazing down on you. Expect to spend about $30 for a meal here, and a good one at that. On Wednesday night you can "jump-up" at a barbecue, and on Friday night there's limbo dancing, fire-eating, and folk dancing. Basil's is open daily from 9 a.m. until very late. There is also a boutique on the premises.

Water Sports

Dive St. Vincent in Mustique offers scuba-diving, ranging from an introductory course for $25 to a one-tank dive at $45 to a two-tank dive at $70. For information, contact Basil's Beach Bar (tel. 458-4621).

CANOUAN: In the shape of a half circle, Canouan is surrounded by coral reefs and dramatic blue lagoons, a virgin paradise, almost totally unspoiled. The island is only 3½ miles by 1½ miles in size, and is visited mainly by those who want to enjoy its splendid long beaches. Canouan has a population of less than 1,000 people, many of whom fish for a living.

You reach Canouan by first taking an international flight to Barbados. It's then 50 minutes by charter flight to Canouan. Alternatively, you can fly to St. Vincent on LIAT. There you'll be able to fly direct to Canouan on Inter-Island Air Services. There are also flights from Grenada.

Charters are also available from a three-seater plane in St. Vincent which can fly to Canouan any day.

The cost of travel from St. Vincent to Canouan by the ferryboat M.V. *Grenadines Star* is usually EC$10 ($3.70).

The mother island, St. Vincent, lies 14 miles to the north and Grenada 20 miles to the south. Canouan rises from its sandy beaches to the 800-foot-high peak of Mount Royal in the north. There you'll find unspoiled forests of white cedar.

Food and Lodging

Canouan Beach Hotel (tel. 458-4413, 212/832-2277 in New York City, or toll free 800/223-5077) is by far the best place to stay on Canouan. Opened in 1984, it offers attractive accommodations on its seven acres of beachfront. The location is about an eighth of a mile from the dirt landing strip of the hotel island's airport on a periwinkle-studded peninsula jutting out between the Atlantic and the Caribbean. Much of the hotel's style comes from the dedicated efforts of its charming French-born managers, Arnaud le Mintier and Emilie von Schmucker. The resort's social center lies beneath the sun screen of a mahogany-trussed parapet whose sides are open to a water view. A pair of lush but uninhabited islands lie offshore. Snorkeling, windsurfing, small sailboats, and a catamaran are available without charge to guests. All water sports, buffet lunches, barbecued suppers, and drinks are included in a weekly price. Depending on the accommodation, guests pay from $650 to $900, double occupancy, per week in high season, but *between $500 and $700 per week in low season*. Single occupants face a 75% surcharge. Each of the stone-sided accommodations is air-conditioned, with sliding glass doors, private baths, and comfortable furnishings.

UNION ISLAND: Midway between Grenada and St. Vincent, Union Island is the most southern of the Grenadines. It's known for its dramatic 900-foot peak, Mount Parnassus, which is seen by yachting people for miles away. If you're cruising in the area, Union is the port of entry for St. Vincent. Yachters are required to check with Customs upon entry.

Perhaps you'll sail into Union on a night when the locals are having a "big drum" dance. Costumed islanders dance and chant to the beat of drums made of goatskin.

The island is reached either by chartered or scheduled aircraft, by cargo boat, by private yacht, or by mail boat (see information under "Getting There" at the beginning of this section). M.V. *Grenadines Star* stops at Union Island, arriving at 3:05 p.m. on Monday and Thursday, departing at 7 a.m. on Tuesday and Friday, on a voyage to and from St. Vincent, with stops at Bequia, Canouan, and Mayreau. The fare on both the motor vessel and the mail boat to and from St. Vincent is EC$15 ($5.50) per person each way. On Monday and Thursday, M.V. *Obedient* goes from Union Island to Carriacou, leaving at 7:45 a.m. and arriving at 1 p.m. Fare for this trip is EC$10 ($3.70) each way.

On a shopping note, check out **Chic/Unique Boutique,** a gift and souvenir shop 50 yards from the airstrip. Even if you don't find something here, you'll have to love its name!

Where to Stay

Accommodations are very limited and simple.

Anchorage Yacht Club (tel. 458-4848). Built in the early 1970s and radically renovated in 1986, this is the leading hotel on the island, occupying a prestige position a few steps from the bumpy landing strip near a cluster of boutiques and shops. It combines a threefold function as a 15-room hotel, a pleasant restaurant and bar, and a marine service facility. Charlotte Hannart, the French-born manager, adds a Gallic flair to the Caribbean specialties served in the wood-and-stone bar. There you can order lunches for EC$30 ($11), and dinners for EC$40 ($14.75) and up. The bill of fare is likely to include fish soup, a wide array of fresh fish, and Créole versions of lamb, pork, and beef. Try the mango daiquiri at the long wooden bar. The bar is open all day and into the night, but meals are served only from 7:30 a.m. to noon for breakfast, noon to 2:30 p.m. for lunch, and 7 to 9:30 p.m. for dinner.

Each of the pleasantly ventilated bedrooms has a pinewood ceiling, white tile floors, and a location midway between a pair of airy verandas. Units are furnished with modern pieces, and each is air-conditioned, with a private bath. In high season, singles or doubles cost $120 per night, *dropping to $90 per night in low season* with breakfast included. A two-bedroom villa, suitable for up to four persons, rents for $195 in high season, *dropping to $145 in low season.*

PALM ISLAND: Is this island a resort or is the resort the island? Casual elegance and privacy prevail on these 100 acres in the southern Grenadines. Surrounded by five white sand beaches, the island is sometimes called "Prune," so one can easily understand the more appealing name change.

A little islet in the sun, it offers complete peace and quiet with plenty of sea, sand, sun, and sailing. To reach the place, it's best to take a share-charter direct to Union Island (operated November through May), one mile west of Palm, where a launch will be waiting.

If you're visiting in summer, you can book a charter plane on your own; or first overnight in Barbados, then fly the next morning to St. Vincent with LIAT. There you can connect with Inter-Island Air Services' scheduled flight to Union Island, where you take the launch over to Palm Island.

Most people don't come to Palm Island to shop, but once there, you might see what's available at **La Boutique,** which has a collection of jewelry, local handcrafts, gifts, swimwear, plus other casual resort attire for both men and women.

Palm Island Beach Club (tel. 458-4804) is the fulfillment of a long-cherished wish held by the Caldwells, John and his gracious, soft-spoken wife, Mary, to establish a hotel on an idyllic and isolated island. John is nicknamed "Coconut Johnny," because of his reforestation hobby of planting palms. At Prune Island, he planted hundreds upon hundreds of trees until its name was changed to Palm Island. An adventurer, this Texan once set out to sail by himself across the Pacific, coming to rest off the coast of Fiji. He made it to Australia, where he constructed his own ketch, loaded his family aboard, and took off again. Eventually he made it to the Grenadines, where he operated a charter business. His exploits, including getting embroiled in a hurricane, were documented in the autobiographical book *Desperate Voyage,* an account of his 106-day, 8,500-mile journey at sea. After that exploit, he operated a charter business in the Grenadines, often taking guests to Palm (then Prune) Island. As his clients would swim or lie on the beach, he'd plant coconut palms.

Just right for the Grenadine frame of mind, he eventually built this cottage colony with enough room for 50 guests spaced under palms on the white sandy beach. Accommodations are in the Beach Club duplex cabañas or in one of the villas, which are equipped for housekeeping. Bungalows are built of stone and wood, with louvered walls as well as sliding glass doors that open onto terraces. The furniture was built by the Caldwells. All rooms are superior, with ceiling fans, window screens, and lots of exposed wood. All have private baths, refrigerators, and outdoor walled patios on the oceanfront. In winter, a single with all meals rents for $165, a double costs $244, and a third person in a double is charged $80. *Summer prices for rooms with all meals are $125 in a single, $175 in a double, and $50 for a third person.* Rates include afternoon tea served on the patio. Be warned that at night this island's legendary mosquitos may prove irritating despite the bug spray and mosquito-chasing incense the management provides. However, the resort's expanse of brilliant white sand and the view of other Grenadines nearby more than makes up for the temporary inconvenience. Dining is in a "South Seas island"–style pavilion where the food is good and plentiful. Nautically oriented guests like to have tall drinks at the circular beach bar.

The Caldwells also maintain a small charter fleet of yachts for day sails, with one of their amiable West Indian crewmen aboard to assist. These natives are experts on local history, customs, and tall tales.

PETIT ST. VINCENT: A private island four miles from Union, in the southern Grenadines, this speck of island is rimmed with white sandy beaches. On 113 acres, it's an out-of-this-world corner of the Caribbean that is only for self-sufficient types, who want to be away from just about everything.

To reach it, fly to Barbados, with luck arriving there before 4 p.m. If so, you can be on "PSV," as it is affectionately called, the same day. Passengers fly a charter or scheduled service. A common departure time will be scheduled for guests arriving that afternoon in Barbados for the 45-minute flight direct to Union Island. At Union Island, the PSV boat will meet you and take you on a half-hour ride to PSV. Connections can also be made through Martinique.

However, in such an offbeat oasis there exists **Petit St. Vincent Resort** (tel. 45-84801), which has a kind of nautical chic. The resort was conceived by Haze Richardson, who had to do everything from planting trees to laying cables. The property was once owned by the archbishop of Trinidad. Open to the trade winds, this self-contained cottage colony was designed by a Swedish architect, Arne Hasselquist, who used purpleheart wood and the local stone, called blue bitch (yes, that's right) for the walls. This is the only place to stay on the island, and if you don't like it and want to check out, you'd better have a yacht waiting. But chances are, you'll be pleased.

Cottages are built on a hillside or set close to the beach, in a 113-acre setting. Units open onto big outdoor patios, all with views. Winter AP rates, charged from mid-December to mid-April, range from $315 to $370 for one person, $410 to $480 for two. *In the off-season, November 1 to mid-December and mid-April to the end of August, AP tariffs drop to $215 daily in a single and $280 in a double.* The place is closed in September and October. Wicker and rattan along with khus-khus rugs set the Caribbean tone of the place. The units have no phones. When you need something, write out your request, place it in a slot in a bamboo flagpole, and run up the yellow flag. One of the waiters will arrive on a motorized cart to collect your order.

To make reservations, write to Petit St. Vincent, P.O. Box 12506, Cincinnati, OH 45212 (tel. 513/242-1333).

MAYREAU: A tiny cay, 1½ square miles of land in the Grenadines, Mayreau is a privately owned island shared by a hotel and a little hilltop village of about 170 inhabitants. It's on the route of the mailboat and M.V. *Grenadines Star,* which ply the seas to and from St. Vincent, visiting also Canouan and Union Island.

Food and Lodging
Saltwhistle Bay Club (tel. toll free 800/387-1752 in the U.S.) is a last frontier for people seeking a tropical island paradise. A young Canadian-German couple, Tom and Undine Potter, who for several years operated a beachside restaurant here catering to yachting visitors, have expanded their operation to a 20-room hotel complex, with

six bedrooms, four one-bedroom suites, and ten deluxe duplex cottages sharing a rooftop gallery with tables, chairs, and hammocks. All the units contain private bath. They were built by local craftsmen using the stone of the island, floor tiles, and purple and green heartwood. They are all cooled by ceiling fans. In winter, single bedrooms rent for $100 to $160 daily, single deluxe units go for $130 to $220, and suites for singles cost $150 to $250. Prices for doubles in winter are $140 to $210 in standard rooms, $170 to $280 in deluxe units, and $200 to $320 in suites. *Summer rates (deluxe rooms and suites only) are $130 and $150 single, $170 and $200 double.* All rates are subject to tax and service, and all these quotations are for MAP.

The dining room at the hotel is made up of circular stone booths topped by thatch canopies, and you can enjoy seafood fresh from the waters around Mayreau—lobster, curried conch, turtle steaks, and grouper. Guests can get acquainted at the bar. By day you can go snorkeling, fishing, windsurfing, cruising on a yacht, or just lolling in one of the hammocks strung among the trees in the 16-acre tropical garden, perhaps taking a swim along the expanse of white sand beach curving along the windward side of the island. One of the enjoyable excursions arranged by the Potters is a "Robinson Crusoe" picnic on a little uninhabited island nearby. Scuba-divers will be glad to know that there's a shipwreck to explore, a 1912 gunboat lying in 40 feet of water half a mile offshore.

5. Grenada

The "Spice Island," Grenada is an independent three-island nation which includes Carriacou, the largest of the Grenadines, and Petit Martinique. The air in Grenada is full of the fragrance of spice and exotic fruits. The island has more spices per square mile than any other place in the world—cloves, cinnamon, mace, cocoa, tonka beans, ginger, and a third of the world's supply of nutmeg. "Drop a few seeds anywhere," the natives will tell you, "and you have an instant garden." The central area is like a jungle of palms, oleander, bougainvillea, purple and red hibiscus, crimson anthurium, bananas, breadfruit, birdsong, ferns, and palms.

Southernmost island of the Windward Antilles, Grenada (pronounced Gre-*nay*-dah) lies 60 miles southwest of St. Vincent and about 90 miles north of Trinidad. An oval-shaped island, it is 21 miles long and about 12 miles wide. Volcanic in origin, the island has an average yearly temperature of 83° Fahrenheit. Because of the constant trade winds, there is little humidity.

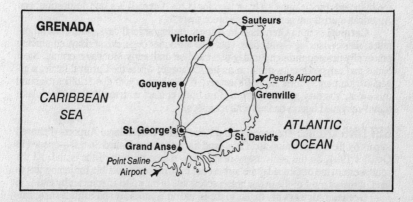

Like most of the Caribbean islands, it was discovered by Columbus, who sailed by it in 1498. Whether he landed or not is the subject of conjecture. Grenada was inhabited by the warmongering, cannibalistic Carib Indians. The first Europeans who visited Grenada were probably London seafaring merchants, who ended up, no doubt, in the Carib stewing pot.

The French in 1650 were the first to establish relations with the Caribs, buying their favors for two bottles of brandy and some baubles. But those peaceful relations didn't last too long when the Indians tired of their trinkets. The conflict ended in 1691 at **Morne du Sauteur** (Jumper Hill), as the last band of Caribs tossed their women and children into the sea, then in a suicide leap, plunged to their own deaths rather than submit to European domination.

After the inevitable British-French disputes and bloody wars for domination, Grenada settled down to British rule in 1783. In 1967 it became an associated state within the Commonwealth. Before it achieved independence in early 1974, political squabbles virtually shut down the island, bringing havoc to the tourist season in late 1973 and early 1974. A general strike shut down the port, as electricity and water were turned off.

Grenada was dominated by a volatile black leader, Eric Gairy, who had been considered a practitioner of black magic and a UFO believer, performing voodoo-like rituals to keep himself in power. On three separate occasions he proposed before a stunned United Nations that it undertake a study of UFOs.

For 12 years he oppressively ruled over the island until he was overthrown in the spring of 1979. The revolution cost only three lives, and boatloads of tourists, including a Soviet cruise ship, hardly noticed they were in the middle of a revolution.

The man who ousted Gairy was Maurice Bishop, along with his radical New Jewel Movement. Bishop launched what is still a controversial 4½-year "revolution," cementing ties with the Soviet Union and Cuba. Dramatically, in 1983 Bishop was placed under house arrest. Later he was executed along with several key supporters. An even more radical Marxist-Leninist faction took over the government and installed a revolutionary military council.

President Reagan, however, looked upon these new leaders as "thugs." In October of that year, the U.S.—backed by other Caribbean countries— launched a successful invasion of Grenada, routing the military council and rounding up Cubans building the controversial Point Saline Airport.

Beefed up by financial aid from the U.S., Grenada has revived a sagging tourist industry. The anti-American slogans have long been down. Instead you are likely to see billboards proclaiming "Thank God for U.S." Grenada is a safe destination, and American tourists are genuinely welcomed there.

Carnival time in Grenada is in August, lasting several days, with colorful parades, music, dancing—what have you. The festivities begin on a Friday, continuing practically nonstop through Sunday night and on until early Monday morning. Steel bands and calypso groups perform on the Carenage, where the Carnival finale, a gigantic "jump-up," takes place. *Be warned:* if you dress in your good clothes to attend this event, you may get sticky from close body contact with the Djab Djab Molassi (devil-costumed figures daubed with molasses).

GETTING THERE: The controversial Point Saline International Airport—financed in part by the Soviet Union and Cuba (and finished by the United States)—opened in October 1984, on the anniversary of the U.S. rescue mission of the island. At the southwestern toe of Grenada, the airport not only makes it possible for jumbo jets to land, it makes most of the major hotels accessible in only 5 to 15 minutes by taxi.

Grenada Airways has flights to the island on Wednesday and Saturday originating at New York's JFK Airport, stopping in Miami, and then continuing nonstop to Grenada's international airport. Grenada Airways has a ticket office at 180 S.E. Third

Ave., Miami (tel. 305/579-9722), and a North American marketing office at 1000 Ponce de Leon Blvd., Coral Gables (tel. 305/441-1265).

BWIA also flies from Grenada to New York and Miami, and both BWIA and LIAT connect with international airlines, including British Airways, Air Canada, Caribbean Airways, Eastern Airlines, American Airlines, Pan Am, and Air France, in Barbados, St. Lucia, Trinidad, Martinique, and Antigua. There is a Grenada Inter-Island Information Desk in the arrival section of the Grantley Adams International Airport in Barbados.

GETTING AROUND: You'll have to establish the price of a **taxi** before getting in. Most arriving visitors take a cab at the Point Saline Airport to one of the hotels near St. George's, at a cost of about EC$25 ($9.25).

You can also use most taxi drivers as a guide for a day's sightseeing, and the cost can be divided among three to four passengers. If so, count on about $150 (U.S.) per day. Again, this figure is to be negotiated.

Car Rentals

The rates are fairly modest if you want this often-difficult means of transport through the length and width of Grenada. First, you must remember to *drive on the left*. A U.S. or Canadian driver's license is valid in Grenada, so you don't have to obtain another permit from the police as you do on most Windward Islands.

A word of warning about local drivers: There's such a thing as a Grenadian driving machismo where the drivers take blind corners with abandon. An extraordinary number of accidents are reported in the lively local paper.

Royston's Rent-a-Car, at Blue Horizons (tel. 4316), rents Daihatsus, Mazdas, and Charmants, among other vehicles. Rental fees, which include 50 free miles a day, are about $40 per day. Unlimited mileage is offered with a full week's rental, and American Express cards are accepted.

Buses

There are two types. The most colorful and traditional ones are painted in red, blue, gold, whatever, and are just as crazy as their names (one, for example, is called "Oo-la-la"). On plank seats, you're bounced until you're squealing just as much as the live pig with which you're likely to be sharing the ride! Most of these buses depart from Market Square in St. George's.

Minibuses have been introduced as well, taking you on most short rides for EC$1 (37¢). They're not as colorful but are more comfortable.

Local Air Services

Many visitors like to fly over to Grenada's satellite island, Carriacou, for the day. LIAT makes the short takeoff and landing (STOL) flight in about ten minutes at a round-trip cost of EC$122 ($45) per person. To book a ticket, the LIAT telephone number is 2796. There are about three flights a day.

PRACTICAL FACTS: **English** is commonly spoken on this island of 90,000 people, because of the long years of British domination. **Proof of citizenship** is needed to enter the country. A passport is preferred, but a birth certificate or voter registration card will do. An ongoing or return ticket must be produced as well.

Grenada has two distinct seasons, dry and rainy. The dry season is from January through May; the rest of the year is the rainy season, although rainfall is not of long duration. The average **temperature** is 80° Fahrenheit.

The official **currency** is the Eastern Caribbean dollar. Always determine which dollars—EC or U.S.—you're talking about when someone on Grenada quotes you a price. In St. George's, the capital, you'll find such **banks** operating as Barclays,

Church and Halifax Street, St. George's (tel. 3232); Scotiabank, Halifax Street, St. George's (tel. 3274); and the National Commercial Bank (NCB), at the corner of Halifax and Hillsborough Streets, St. George's (tel. 3566). There are branches of Barclays at Grenville, St. Andrew's; and on Carriacou. NCB has branches at Grenville, St. Andrew's; Gouyave; Thebaide Junction, St. David's; and Carriacou.

The local **telephone system** maintains 24-hour daily service with the rest of the world. **Cable & Wireless Ltd.,** The Carenage (tel. 2200), offers a telegraphic service in St. George's from 7 a.m. to 7 p.m. daily (on Sunday and holidays from 7 a.m. to 10 a.m. and 4 to 8 p.m.).

The **General Post Office** in St. George's is open Monday through Thursday from 8 a.m. to 4 p.m., with a lunch break from 11:45 a.m. to 1 p.m. On Friday hours are 8 a.m. to 5 p.m. It's closed on weekends.

Radio Grenada, owned and operated by the government, broadcasts the news, and a lot of American pop and disco music.

Customs places no restrictions on the amount of money brought into the island.

Electricity, not always reliable, is supplied on the island by Grenada Electricity Services, and the current is 220/240 volts, 50 cycles, AC.

Grenada celebrates the usual **holidays.**

There is a **general hospital** in St. George's, with an X-ray department and operating theater. Private doctors and nurses are available on call.

For your drugstore needs, try **Benoit Pharmacy,** The Carenage, St. George's (tel. 3174).

Among newspapers, the *Grenadian Voice* is published weekly. You'll also find *Time* or *Newsweek*.

To most restaurant and hotel bills you are presented on the island, a 10% **service charge** will be added. A 20% **VAT** (value added tax) is imposed on food and beverages.

Upon leaving Grenada, you must fill out an immigration card and pay a **departure tax** of EC$25 ($9.25).

For information, go to the **Grenada Tourist Department,** on the Carenage in St. George's (tel. 2001). It's open Monday to Thursday from 8 a.m. to 4 p.m., and on Friday to 5 p.m. Maps, guides, and general information are available. In the U.S., the **Grenada Tourist Office** is at 820 Second Ave., Suite 1100, New York, NY 10017 (tel. 212/687-9554).

WHERE TO STAY: Many of Grenada's hostelries evoke the Mediterranean more than the Caribbean in their architecture, perhaps in deference to the island's Spanish name. Innkeepers think small here. The Ramada Renaissance Hotel, scheduled to open by the time of your visit, is the biggest place at which you can overnight, and nearly everything else is tiny, usually containing no more than a dozen rooms.

The **Ramada Renaissance Hotel,** Grand Anse Beach (tel. 4371, or toll free 800/2-RAMADA), housed the personnel of the American Expeditionary Force that ejected the Cubans from Grenada in 1983. By 1986, however, it had been radically renovated and reopened as the most glamorous, tastefully executed, and stylish hotel on the island. It stands on a desirable stretch of beachfront, behind a cedar-shingle façade whose design might have been inspired by an 18th-century plantation house. Any comparison with another century, however, ends when visitors see the glistening interior. Guests register beneath the soaring octagonal roof of the entrance hall, then are ushered between a pair of manicured formal gardens to their rooms. Each of these is furnished with a formal blend of English reproduction pieces, thick carpeting, air conditioning, tile bath, phone, and radio/alarm. Each has a balcony or veranda, some of which open onto sun-flooded views of the beach. Depending on the exposure, high-season prices are $145 to $170 daily in a single, $10 more per room for double occupancy. *Low-season charges range from $100 to $120 in a single and around $10 more* *per room for double occupancy. Suites for two begin at $275 in low season,* and $350 in high season. MAP can be arranged for *$30 per person in the off-season,* $35 in winter. The hotel has two stylish restaurants, plus a lattice-encased gazebo for dancing the night away when there's live entertainment. On the premises is a swimming pool as well as a water-sports kiosk for the rental of sailboats, windsurfers, and snorkeling equipment.

Secret Harbour, P.O. Box 11, St. George's (tel. 4548), is an elegant site, five miles from the capital on the island's south coast. It's the creation of an English lady, expatriate Barbara Stevens. In her own country she'd been an accountant, but apparently that got to be too much for her one day. Along with her first husband, she sailed across the Atlantic in a ketch, eventually settling in Grenada, where she decided to build this hotel. Seen from the water of Mount Hartman Bay, Secret Harbour reminds one of a Mediterranean complex on Spain's Costa del Sol—a tasteful one, that is, with white stucco arches, red tile roofs, and wrought-iron light fixtures. The design also has a Moorish touch in the tiles and terraces. Some of the decoration is opulent, including stained glass, hand-hewn beams, and two large mahogany four-poster beds in each room. From all over Grenada, including some island plantation homes, antiques were purchased, restored, and installed here. The bathrooms are also luxurious, with sunken tubs lined with color-rich Italian tiles, the lighting from unglazed medallion windows.

Each of Mrs. Stevens's 20 suites has a dressing room, living area, and patio overlooking the water. Steps lead down to the beach, as you pass among lime and papaya trees, palms, frangipani. Pathways take you to the tennis court, the free-form swimming pool, and the main building. Winter EP rates are $115 to $135 daily in a double, $95 to $115 in a single. *In summer, guests are quoted an EP rate of $65 to $85 daily in a double, $55 to $75 in a single.* In the dining room, decorated with style, a chef provides sumptuous meals. Arrangements can be made at the desk for car rentals, island tours, sports fishing, and golf.

Calabash, P.O. Box 382 (tel. 4234, 212/840-6636 in New York City), built in the early 1960s, is today the best-established resort, and perhaps the most venerated hotel, on Grenada. It occupies a lushly landscaped eight-acre beach plot along an isolated section of Prickly Bay (L'Anse aux Épines). Many of the shrubs on the grounds, tiny when they were planted, make some of the stone outbuildings look diminutive. Foremost among the plants are the scores of beautiful calabashes (gourds) for which the resort was named. The social center of the place is a low-slung, rambling building whose walls are chiseled from blocks of dark gray stone. Above the bar, a massive beam of an almost-indestructible tropical hardwood called greenheart serves as a support for the masonry above. Two of the 22 hotel units have private swimming pools and entrances nearly concealed by the thunbergia (trailing orchid) vines. Rates in high season are $200 for a single, $240 for a double. *Off-season, charges are $100 in a single, $135 in a double.* All tariffs are for MAP. Rentals of sailboats and equipment for most other water-related activities are arranged by the friendly staff.

Horse Shoe Beach Hotel, P.O. Box 174, St. George's (tel. 4410), is a little dream with vintage charm. Set on a hilltop, it is built in the Mediterranean style, a total of 18 cozily furnished terracotta cottages—each with a canopied four-poster bed—all with private balconies and air conditioning. Breathing in the fragrant shrubs, you stroll leisurely down the hill to the beach and sea. Constructed on a small promontory, the complex manages to capture the sea breezes at night, and you'll hear the rustling sound of wind blowing through acres of tropical gardens, filled with hibiscus and bougainvillea. Guests are so well coddled here that they keep returning year after year, enjoying the appealingly furnished rooms. Many of the furnishings came from buying up antiques from old island family houses. The doorway to the Spanish stucco building is almost hidden by the foliage, including a towering banyan tree. You enter the Grenadian-Iberian dining pavilion and red-tile lounge, with its cozy nooks and original oil paintings. The dining room frames views of the beach and swimming pool, as well as of the gardens. A double costs $95 daily, and a single goes for $85. *In the off-season, it's possible to stay here at $85 daily in a double, $75 in a single.* All prices are for MAP. Snorkeling and Sunfish sails are yours for the asking, or else you can just lie back and enjoy the bucolic serenity.

Spice Island Inn, P.O. Box 6, St. George's (tel. 4258), is on an estate overlooking the Caribbean and built along 1,200 feet of Grand Anse beach. The main house, reserved for dining and dancing, has a tropical aura and lots of nice touches, showing that taste and concern went into the design of the place. Twenty air-conditioned beach suites are offered, plus ten pool suites, all pleasantly contemporary, stretched along the white sands. About ten of them are set back a bit and have their own private plunge pools, surrounded by high walls where guests can skinny-dip. In high season, the MAP rate runs $165 to $190 a day in a single, $185 to $220 for two persons sharing a double. *In low season, you can stay here on half-board terms at rates ranging from $112 to $130 daily in a single, from $130 to $150 in a double.* Furnishings in the rooms are not elaborate, with outdoor-type pieces such as wicker chairs. The waiter will arrive with your breakfast (a just-plucked red hibiscus resting on the tray), and you'll enjoy it (and, hopefully, who you're with) on a shaded patio, your very own. The place is known for its Sunday buffet, and the cooks do not only a good Grenadian cuisine, but also deftly turn out an international cuisine, including soursop ice cream (nutmeg is also a specialty), breadfruit vichyssoise, green turtle soup, and Caribbean lobster. Sometimes a combo plays for dancing.

Cinnamon Hill and Beach Club, P.O. Box 292, St. George's (tel. 4301), was created by English expatriate Richard Gray, an actor, writer, producer, and architect. Cooperatively owned, Cinnamon Hill is a cluster of luxurious villas, like a Mediterranean-inspired village, surrounded by tropical gardens. Some 20 hacienda-style suites are clustered on the hillside overlooking Grand Anse beach, each fully air-conditioned, with a living room, terrace, fully equipped kitchenette, one or two bedrooms, private bath, and balcony opening onto the sea. *In the off-season, two people can rent either a one- or two-bedroom villa for anywhere from $77 to $114 daily.* In the high season, two guests are accepted for from $121 in a double with one-bedroom, from $153 daily in a two-bedroom villa; each additional person pays $17. A one-bedroom villa or suite can sleep four persons, and a two-bedroom unit can shelter six guests. Breakfast is cooked right in your own villa.

The Cinnamon Restaurant of the hotel specializes in the fresh seafood of Grenada. It serves breakfast from 8 to 10 a.m. and dinner from 7 to 10:30 p.m. No lunch is served. The tiles, stonework, and woodwork of the hotel come from Mr. Gray's own designing factory. A splash of red-tile roofs, white stucco arches, hand-hewn beams— everything is in keeping with the Spanish-Mediterranean theme. Sailing, snorkeling, waterskiing, skindiving, and fishing are arranged at the front desk. Guests can use the big health and fitness center.

Twelve Degrees North, P.O. Box 241, St. George's (tel. 4580), is operated by Joseph Gaylord, a former commercial real estate broker from New York, who greets visitors with a wide smile and an outstretched hand in front of a large flame tree on his front lawn. He owns this cluster of spotlessly clean efficiency apartments, not far from the airport at Point Saline. Many of the staff members have been with Mr. Gaylord since he opened the place many years ago, and are highly trustworthy. They'll cook breakfast, prepare lunch (perhaps pumpkin soup and the flying fish of Barbados), do the cleaning and laundry, go food shopping, and fix regional specialties for dinner (which you heat up for yourself later). The resort has its own tennis court, and a Sunfish and two sailing dinghies are provided for a small fee. A grass-roofed beach bar faces the water, and guests use it on the honor system.

Each unit (two with two bedrooms and six with one bedroom) comes with an individual uniformed attendant, who arrives at 8 o'clock each morning to perform the thousand small kindnesses that make Twelve Degrees North a favorite lair for returning guests from America and Europe. Each unit is equipped with an efficiency kitchen with a 12-cubic-foot refrigerator, large enough to prevent the need for food shopping daily. The large beds can be separated or pushed together, depending on the mood of the guests. The owner prefers to rent by the week, because, as he says, "a few days aren't enough to get to know Grenada." In winter, a two-bedroom apartment, suitable for four, costs from $155 daily, a one-bedroom unit for two persons goes for $95 a day, and each additional person pays another $60. *In summer, four people in a two-bedroom apartment pay $145 per day, and two people in a one-bedroom unit pay $75.*

Blue Horizons Cottage Hotel, P.O. Box 41, Grand Anse (tel. 4316), was purchased by co-owners Royston and Arnold Hopkin from a bankrupt estate. Sons of the famous Grenadian hotelkeepers Audrey and Curtis Hopkin (now retired), they transformed the neglected property into one of the finest on the island, with an occupancy rate second only to that of Spice Island. The 28 suites and four studios are spread throughout a lush and flowering garden of 6¼ acres. Each bungalow has an efficiency kitchen and comfortable furniture. Children are welcomed, and they can watch the 21 varieties of native birds said to inhabit the grounds. High-season rates depend on the category of the cottage: standard, superior, or deluxe. On the EP, doubles in high season cost $80 to $85 daily, singles go for $75 to $90 and an extra person pays $15. *In summer, rates are slashed to $60 to $75 daily in a double, EP, and $55 to $70 in a single.* Guests who prefer to cook in their rooms can buy supplies from a Food Fair at Grand Anse, a ten-minute walk away. Most important, Grand Anse beach is only five minutes away by foot. On the grounds is one of the best restaurants on the island, La Belle Créole (see my dining recommendations). Lunch is served around a pool bar.

WHERE TO DINE: You may eat in all the restaurants of the hotels previously described, but you should call first to make a reservation, as food supplies are often limited if the chef doesn't know to expect you. I've found hotel food better in Grenada than in the other British Windward Islands. Many of the chefs are European or European-an trained, and native cooks are also on hand to prepare Grenadian specialties such as conch (called lambi here), lobster, callaloo soup (with greens and crab), conch-and-onion pie, turtle steaks, and soursop or avocado ice cream.

It is estimated that some 22 kinds of fish, including fresh tuna, dolphin, and barracuda, are caught off the island's shores. Most are good for eating. Naturally, the spices of the island, such as nutmeg, are used plentifully. The cookery is often served family style in an open-air setting, opening onto a vista of the sea.

La Belle Créole, on the grounds at Blue Horizons, Grand Anse beach (tel. 4316), is one of the best restaurants in Grenada. Arnold and Royston Hopkin, who run it, are sons of "Mama" Audrey Hopkin, long considered the best cook on the island if you're seeking West Indian specialties. Archways frame views of the mountains and the beach. Lunch is served from noon to 2 p.m. every day, featuring such summertime snacks as soups, chicken, fish, or lobster salads, plus a variety of sandwiches and omelets. Lunch can be taken poolside. Dinner is table d'hôte, with a variety of choices featuring continental recipes with West Indian substitutions for foods not available on the island. A typical dinner might begin with dolphin (fish) mousse with callaloo, then conch chowder, followed by a main course such as Créole veal roll stuffed with ham, chicken livers, onions, and seasonings, baked in a wine sauce, and served with local vegetables such as a dasheen soufflé and christophines, along with candied plantain. This, plus a dessert of mango delight, would cost around $25. The walls and ceilings are covered with a type of island reed called roseau, which, strangely enough, must be cut only during a certain phase of the moon to provide a durable, long-lasting building surface. If cut at any other time of the month, experience has taught that the covering disintegrates into a powder within six months. Dinner begins promptly at 7 p.m. until the last order is accepted at 8:30. Each of the items on the table d'hôte is priced separately, to allow a guest to order only an entree with coffee, for example.

Spice Island Inn, Grand Anse beach (tel. 4258). A favorite way to enjoy a meal in Grenada is on an uncrowded beachfront in the full outdoors, with only a well-designed parapet over your head to protect you from sudden tropical showers. At this inn, the view is of one of the best beaches in the Caribbean, miles of white sands, sprouting an occasional grove of sea grape or almond trees. The parapet looks like a Le Corbusier rooftop, built of imported pine and cedar, covering suntanned diners at immaculately table clothed place settings. An à la carte lunch, which you can eat in a swimsuit if you elect, costs from $12. Dinner menus change frequently and can be cooked to your specifications. They are usually table d'hôte, costing about $25 each and offering enough selections to make everyone happy. Meals are served seven days a week from 7:30 to 10 a.m., 12:30 to 2:30 p.m., and 7:30 to 9 p.m. Every Friday night there's a barbecue, costing EC$55 ($20.25), when a steel band is brought in. On Wednesday night, a buffet also costs EC$55.

Delicious Landing, The Carenage, St. George's (tel. 3948), is a popular restaurant at the entrance to the harbor, built on piers. Guests sit at tables supported by a mesh of beams, under a parapet of palm fronds. The setting is raffishly rickety and loaded with West Indian style. Some regular visitors argue that it offers yachting people one of the best views of whatever boat has just wandered into the harbor. The establishment is known for its soups, made with such fresh ingredients as callaloo, pumpkin, conch, and pigeon peas. You can select from the seafood salads and seafood dinners made of ocean denizens that are probably only hours away from the fishing vessel. The restaurant is known for its conch steaks, cinnamon-fried chicken, sirloin sukiyaki, and fish pando simmered in local herbs and spices. One of the side dishes is a cheese-laden vegetable specialty called Grumby. My favorite drink is a cinnamon daiquiri, although many former servicemen still celebrate the expulsion of the Cubans with a potent concoction called the U.S. Bomber. The place is open for food and drinks daily from 9:30 a.m. to midnight. Lunch is from 10:30 a.m. to 2 p.m., and dinner from 6:30 to 11:30 p.m. A three-course meal costs EC$30 ($11).

Rudolf's stands on the Carenage (tel. 2241), a deep, U-shaped inner harbor lined with commercial establishments in St. George's. Some people claim this is the best place for dining on the entire island. You might call it "tropical Swiss." The restaurant is open for both lunch and dinner from 10 a.m. to midnight daily except Sunday. On the north corner of the Carenage, it's also a great spot for drinks in the late afternoon if you want to join the yachting machismo set. If you stick around for dinner, you'll find that the food is well prepared, with more choices offered on the menu than in most places at Grenada. About 13 different steak dishes are offered, and if you're dining lighter, you're faced with a selection of some eight different omelets. Soups are both hot and cold, ranging from French onion to gazpacho. The owner is Austrian, Rudolf Hoschtaleik, and his menu reflects many Central European dishes. Try, for example, the specialty, cevapcici, minced beef with parsley potatoes and a salad. Specials are posted daily. Dinners begin at EC$25 ($9.25), but will range much higher if you order either steak or lobster as a main course.

The Nutmeg, also at the Carenage (tel. 2539), is right on the harbor, over the Sea Change Shop where you can pick up paperbacks and souvenirs. It's another rendezvous point for the yachting set and a favorite with just about everybody, both expatriates living on the island and visitors. It is suitable for a snack or a full-fledged dinner, from 11:30 a.m. to 11:30 p.m. Its drinks are very good. Try one of the Grenadian rum punches made with Angostura bitters, grated nutmeg, rum, lime juice, and syrup. An informal friendliness prevails, as you're served your filet of fish with potato croquettes and string beans. There's always fresh fish, and usually callaloo soup, maybe lobster too, on most days. Lambi (that ubiquitous conch) is also done very well here. It can be so disguised you don't know what you're tasting. Lobster Thermidor is the most expensive food item on the menu. Meals cost from EC$25 ($9.25). There's a small wine list with some California, German, and Italian selections. The sea view is good from the second-floor precincts, and you can drop in for just a glass of beer, staying as long as you wish. Sometimes, however, you'll be asked to share a table, but that's a great way to strike up a conversation. It is said that eventually, if you sit here long enough, everybody in Grenada will show up.

Coconut's Beach French Restaurant, Grande Anse beach (no phone), at the bottom of a bumpy, sloping road, is actually more accessible by water than by land. Many of the guests come from yachts moored offshore. The restaurant occupies a ramshackle house with pink clapboard siding and a green roof. Set directly on the beach, it lies about half a mile north of St. George's. In the aquamarine-and-gray dining room you can watch the chefs prepare the French and Créole specialties in the exposed kitchen. The owners, Michel and Brigitte, open the place for bar service from 10 a.m. to 10 p.m. daily except Monday in low season. Meals are served from 10 a.m. to 3 p.m. and 7 to 10 p.m. This is probably the closest thing to Martinique you'll find on Grenada, although unlike Martinique, the lack of a phone makes advance reservations impossible. Full meals cost from EC$50 ($18.50) and might include Tahitian-style fish, the catch of the day with a variety of sauces, curried conch with bananas, several barbecue dishes, T-bone steak, grilled lobster, pizzas, turtle steak, lobster gratin, fisherman's platter, and gratin of conch. Every Wednesday and Sunday afternoon and on Friday evening, a live band performs.

Ristorante Italia, the Harbour, St. George's (tel. 3986), is a pleasant restaurant on the second floor of a waterfront building in the geographical center of town. The somewhat spartan decor relies for its visual distraction on movie posters of Sophia Loren, art posters of Botticelli's *Venus,* and action-packed photographs of speeding Ferraris. Wide, tall shutters open on a sweeping view of the Carenage. The menu lists 15 varieties of pizza, priced beginning at EC$6 ($2.25) each. Other offerings include five types of spaghetti, three kinds of fettuccine, eggplant parmigiana, Provençale shrimp, zuppa di pesce, and Italian versions of beef and veal. Full meals cost from EC$35 ($13), although no one will mind if you just order a pizza or a bowl of pasta. Lunch is served only on weekdays from noon to 2:30 p.m. Dinner is every evening from 6 to 11 p.m. The establishment's owner, whom everyone on the island knows as Ido, moved to Grenada from Sicily in 1983.

St. James Hotel, Grand Etang Road, in St. George's (tel. 2041), is a big, generously proportioned, old-fashioned, white-painted hotel on a hilltop overlooking the activity of St. George's. It caters to many local business people who consider it the best luncheon bargain in town. A fixed-price midday meal is offered every day except Sunday for EC$25 ($9.25), in an airy, light-filled dining room with immaculate tablecloths and good service. Dinner costs EC$35 ($13) and includes an extra fish course not offered at the table d'hôte luncheon. Your meal might begin with an aromatic vegetable-and-chicken soup, then follow with a salad, along with conch casserole with tomatoes or a pungent beef stew with lots of hot peppers. An island dessert often featured is sopadilla delight. Lunch is from noon to 2 p.m. and dinner from 7 to 9 p.m. The 14-room hotel has some of the bargain rooms of the island for those devotees of little West Indian inns that rarely attract the beach-seeking tourist. Year-round rates EP are $29 in a single, $44 in a double.

Mama's (tel. 1459) lies on the road leading to Grenada Yacht Services. Every trip to the Caribbean should include a visit to an establishment like Mama's. Mama (alias Inslay Wardally), judging from her size, likes her own cookery, and serves copious meals out of her private home to brawny local mechanics playing friendly games of dominoes, quietly drunk fishermen stranded from nearby islands, Austrian yachtsmen escorting braless nymphets from California, and groups of initially bewildered foreign tourists. She became particularly famous during the U.S. intervention in Grenada, as U.S. servicemen adopted her as their own island mama. Everyone goes to Mama's, to sit either on rickety chairs on the covered veranda or beside the bar in modest quarters that in the off-hours is Mama's living room.

Mama herself is as generous as her meals, which I am told come in two sizes: "the usual" and "the special." I telephoned ahead to order "the special," which, Mama eventually told me, was really the same as "the usual." It included such dishes as callaloo soup with coconut cream, shredded cold crab with lime juice, freshwater crayfish, fried conch, fried dolphin, breaded turtle served in its own shell, curried chicken with yellow chickpea sauce, mashed tannia root (deep fried in coconut oil), breadfruit salad flavored with three kinds of thyme, and a casserole of cooked bananas, yams, and dasheen, along with ripe baked plantain, and tortillas made of curry and yellow chickpeas, followed by sugar apple ice cream. I failed to try her rich, gamy opossum or her stewed armadillo. The specialty drink of the house is rum punch with cream, the ingredients of which are known only to Mama. Dinner here must be reserved in advance, and it costs EC$36 ($13.30) per person, drinks extra. She is open seven nights a week, serving dinner from 7:30 p.m. to midnight.

For change-of-pace dining, I suggest the **Bird's Nest,** also known as Yin Wo Restaurant, in its own building with three palm trees at the entrance, opposite the Ramada Renaissance (tel. 4264). This simple green-and-white restaurant is run by a Trinidadian-Grenadian couple, Derick and Lucy Steele, who give you a warm welcome. Their family business offers typical Chinese food, mainly Cantonese. The most expensive main courses, of course, are those with a lobster base. You'll see the familiar shrimp eggrolls along with eight different chow meins. Sweet-and-sour fish is a favorite, and daily specials are posted. A take-out service is available. Expect to spend from $18 for a meal, served Monday through Saturday from 11 a.m. to 11 p.m. and on Sunday from 6 p.m. to 11 p.m.

Elsewhere on the island, I'd suggest the **Red Crab,** at L'Anse aux Épines (tel. 4424), which is popular with many Americans. It's a favorite Grenadian luncheon spot, set out under the trees. However, I always like to approach it in the evening, as your vehicle hurtles through an inky night. It's like an English pub in the mock Tudor style, and is in fact run by an Englishman, Reg Blamphin. Before taking your order, one of the waiters will bring you a draft beer, and you can settle back to enjoy the classic fish and chips prepared here. The chef also does some of the best stuffed crab backs on the island. You can also order a savory seafood chowder, fried shrimp, or steamed turtle. Naturally, they offer callaloo soup. Dessert may perhaps be, say, blueberry pie à la mode. Your meal is likely to cost from EC$35 ($13). The pub is open daily from 11 a.m. to 2 p.m. and 6 to 11 p.m. It is closed on Saturday and Sunday for lunch.

Some of the best native food on the island is found at the **Ocean View Guest House** (tel. 6346), recently opened by Dorothy Japal in connection with her restaurant in the village of Crochu. It's far off the beaten track, but reached by either taxi or minibus, available at the airport. Mrs. Japal, a remarkable woman of East Indian descent, quietly established a reputation in Grenada as a superlative native cook, preparing tasty meals for parties who telephone far enough in advance. Her specialty is curried goat, although her curried chicken is also talked about. A woman of great dignity, she will not cook for anyone or everybody, and sometimes is reluctant to quote prices over the phone. You'll probably end up paying about $22 per person, $38 per couple, for a gargantuan repast, including not only the curried goat and curried chicken, but pigeon peas, fried plantains, boiled green bananas (called "figs"), and sweet potatoes with island thyme.

The food is cooked in a 20-gallon iron pot, except for bread, pastries, cakes, roast chicken, and other items which are baked in a 45-gallon steel drum using coconut shells and sugarcane stalks for fuel. The whole experience encompasses far more than good food—it's likely to be one of your most memorable experiences of Grenada. There are no set dining hours. If you're coming for a meal, always agree beforehand with Mrs. Japal on the time of your arrival. Be sure to clarify in advance what drinks are to be provided, and make every effort to be on time. If you'd like to stay over, the

Ocean View Guest House has accommodations for 25 people. Singles rent for $25 and doubles for $45, the prices including two meals. Lunch is available by request only. The place is open year round.

A Special Place

As you're touring north from the beach at Grand Anse and the capital at St. George's, one place is outstanding. It's Betty Mascoll's **Morne Fendue,** in St. Patrick's (tel. 9330). This 1912 plantation house constructed the year she was born, is her ancestral home. It was built of carefully chiseled river rocks held together with a mixture of lime and molasses, as was the custom in that day. Mrs. Mascoll and her loyal staff, two of whom have been with her for many, many years, always need time to prepare for the arrival of guests in advance, so it's imperative to call ahead. If the lady of the house is so inclined, she might rent you lodgings, with MAP, for $65 to $80 daily for a double room. A small single room costs $30 per day. Children, depending on their age, stay in a room with two adults for $10 to $15 each, also with MAP. Lunch, if available, costs from EC$30 ($11) for nonresidents. The noonday repast is likely to include such local delights as yam and sweet potato casserole, curried port with lots of hot spices, and a hotpot of pork and oxtail. Because this is very much a private home, tipping should be performed with the greatest tact. Nonetheless, the hard-working cook and maid seem genuinely appreciative of a friendly gratuity.

Mrs. Mascoll has always lived in the house, except for a wartime stint in England. Her spacious living room is decorated with family portraits and heirlooms, including a patterned rug and heavily carved mahogany furniture. A collection of blue willow antique plates is displayed below the elaborate ceiling moldings. Mrs. Mascoll is known for introducing her house guests to her friends and neighbors on the long verandas beneath the hanging vines of her house. Her garden is host to several varieties of hummingbirds.

WHAT TO SEE: The capital city of Grenada, St. George's, is considered one of the most attractive ports, the picture-postcard variety, in the West Indies. Its landlocked inner harbor is actually the deep crater of a long-dead volcano, or so one is told.

In the town you'll see some of the most charming Georgian colonial buildings to be found in the Caribbean, in spite of a devastating 1955 hurricane. The streets are mostly steep and narrow, and somehow this seems to enhance the attractiveness of the mellowed ballast bricks, wrought-iron balconies, the red tiles of the sloping roofs. Many of the pastel warehouses date back to the 18th century. Frangipani and flamboyant trees add to the palette of color.

The port, which some have compared to Portofino, is flanked by old forts and bold headlands. Among the town's attractions is an 18th-century pink-painted Anglican church, on Church Street, and a Market Square where colorfully attired farm women offer even more colorful produce for sale.

Fort George, built by the French, stands at the entrance to the bay, with subterranean passageways and old guardrooms and cells. It is now the headquarters of the Grenada police force.

Everybody strolls along the waterfront, called the **Carenage,** where bustling activity is connected with the loading and unloading of schooners and the coming and going of the people in their little dinghies from moored yachts. The Carenage is best viewed on Tuesday afternoon when crates and bags of fruit and vegetables are loaded and bound for Trinidad.

On this side of town, the **Grenada National Museum** is set in the foundations of an old French army barrack and prison built in 1704. Small but interesting, it houses finds from archeological digs, including the petroglyphs (the most recent found in the autumn of 1980), native fauna, the first telegraph installed on the island, a rum still, and memorabilia depicting Grenada's colorful history. The most comprehensive exhibit traces the Indian culture of Grenada. One of the exhibits shows two bathtubs—the wooden barrel used by the fort's prisoners and the carved marble tub used by Josephine Bonaparte during her adolescence on Martinique. Hours are 9 a.m. to 3 p.m. Monday to Friday. Admission is 50¢ for adults, 10¢ for children.

The Outer Harbour is also called the **Esplanade.** It's connected to the Carenage by the Sendall Tunnel which is cut through the promontory known as St. George's Point, dividing the two bodies of water.

At the southern edge of town is the **Botanical Garden,** with a wide variety of tropical trees and flowers labeled so that you can identify them. Rare Caribbean animals and birds are kept in an adjoining zoo.

You can also take a drive up to Richmond Hill where **Fort Frederick** stands. The French built this fort in 1779, but before they could finish it, British troops had moved in. The English completed the structure in 1783. From its battlements, you'll have a superb view of the harbor and of the yacht marina.

An afternoon tour of St. George's and its environs should take you into the mountains northeast of the capital. There you'll find **Annandale Falls,** a tropical wonderland, where a cascade about 50 feet high falls into a basin. The overall beauty is almost Tahitian, and you can have a picnic surrounded by liana vines, elephant ears, and exotic tropical flora.

A few miles away is a lake called **Grand Etang,** at a height of 1,800 feet. It's like the mirror of a dead volcano, lying in the midst of a forest preserve and bird sanctuary. Covering 13 acres, the water is a cobalt blue.

Nature enthusiasts may visit a recently opened center for visitors at Grand Etang, in Grenada's interior. The center is in a rain forest near a lake in an extinct volcano crater and some of the Caribbean's most exotic vegetation, birds, monkeys, and armadillos. At present the center has exhibits of the area's flora and fauna. An audio-visual room, snackbar, and handcrafts center as well as facilities for small-scale lake yachting and scenic trails for nature hikes may have been opened to the public by the time you visit.

The next day you can head north out of St. George's along the western coast, taking in beaches, spice plantations, and the fishing villages that are so typical of Grenada.

You pass through **Gouyave,** a spice town, the center of the nutmeg and mace industry. Both spices are produced from a single fruit. Before reaching the village you can stop at the Dougaldston Estate where you'll witness the processing of nutmeg and mace.

At the **Grenada Cooperative Nutmeg Association,** huge quantities of the spice are aged, graded, and processed. Most of the work is done within the ocher walls of the factory, which sprouts such slogans as "Bring God's peace inside and leave the Devil's noise outside." Women sit on stools in the natural light from the open windows of the aging factory, laboriously sorting the raw nutmeg and its by-product, mace, into different baskets for grinding, peeling, and aging.

Proceeding along the coast, you reach **Sauteurs,** at the northern tip of Grenada. This is the third-largest town on the island. It was from this great cliff that the Caribs leaped to their deaths instead of facing enslavement by the French.

To the east of Sauteurs is the palm-lined **Levera Beach,** an idyll of sand where the Atlantic meets the Caribbean. This is a great spot for a picnic lunch, but swimming can sometimes be dangerous. On the distant horizon you'll see some of the Grenadines.

The **River Antoine Rum Distillery** is where you can get an insight into the conditions under which "demon rum" was made 300 years ago. At the site, a series of hand-operated sluice gates set a water-operated sugarcane pulverizer into motion. At first glance the process is shockingly unsanitary (remember, this was the way it was done hundreds of years ago), but the finished product is distilled to a crystal clearness. It's reputed to be one of the best rums produced in the Caribbean. Don't be alarmed by the bats living in the top of the distillery's roof—they only attack insects. It might be advisable to contribute to the "retirement fund" of the employees after touring the premises.

Heading down the east coast of Grenada, you reach **Grenville,** the island's second city. If possible, pass through here on a Sunday morning when you'll enjoy the hubbub of the native fruit and vegetable market. There is also a fish market along the waterfront. A nutmeg factory here welcomes visitors.

From Grenville, you can cut inland into the heart of Grenada. Here you're in a world of luxuriant foliage, passing along nutmeg, banana, and cocoa plantations up to Grand Etang, previously mentioned. Your driver will then begin his descent from the mountains. Along the way you'll pass hanging carpets of mountain ferns. Going through the tiny hamlets of Snug Corner and Beaulieu, you eventually come back to the capital.

On yet another day, you can drive south from St. George's to the beaches and resorts spread along the already much-mentioned **Grand Anse,** which many people consider one of the most beautiful beaches in the West Indies. Water-taxis take you from the Carenage in St. George's to Grand Anse for a fare starting at EC$5 ($1.85). **Point Saline,** now the airport, is at the southwestern tip of Grenada. From the lighthouse, you'll have panoramic views in every direction. This tour of beaches and resorts is often called the "Royal Drive," named in honor of the route Queen Elizabeth II took on her visit to the island. Point Saline, as mentioned in the introduction, is the site of the international airport of Grenada. Along with the beaches, it too is a sightseeing attraction.

Along the way you'll pass through the village of **Woburn,** which was featured in the film *Island in the Sun,* and go through the sugar belt of **Woodlands,** with its tiny sugarcane factory.

THE SPORTING LIFE: The Spice Island can offer the kinds of diversions that urbanites yearn for, ranging from a few relaxing hours on a Sailfish cruising near the island's verdant coastline to a luxuriously catered week on a yacht. It could also include an afternoon in a small boat angling for the perfect dolphin, or a fiercely sunny day in search of that record-breaking big-game fish. Below the water's surface, other distractions appeal to sports lovers. Hundreds of varieties of fish and dozens of species of coral and sponges await your perusal, sometimes with underwater visibility stretching to 120 feet.

Beaches

Swimmers who simply enjoy the white sands of an almost-perfect island might want to spend their days at one of the best beaches in the Caribbean, **Grand Anse,** three miles of sugar-white sands extending into deep waters far offshore. Grenada, by the way, has a strictly enforced policy of public ownership of all beaches. Most of Grenada's best hotels are within walking distance of Grand Anse. In the unlikely event that you get bored there, you can take off and discover dozens more beaches on your own.

Snorkeling and Scuba

Grenada offers the diver an underwater world, rich in submarine gardens, exotic fish, and coral formations. Off the coast is the wreck of the ocean liner *Bianca C,* which is nearly 600 feet long. Novice divers might want to stick to the west coast of Grenada, while more experienced divers might search out the sights along the rougher Atlantic side. Divers should know that Grenada doesn't have a decompression chamber for the relief of bends. Should this happen to you, it would require an excruciatingly painful air trip to Trinidad.

Mosden Cumberbatch at **Grenada Yacht Services,** P.O. Box 168 St. George's (tel. 2508), will arrange scuba-diving and snorkeling expeditions for beginners and intermediates. Resort-course dive packages are available. You can rent equipment also, although it's supplied for some activities. The company also offers windsurfing, waterskiing, yacht charters, offshore fishing, and speedboat cruises.

If you'd rather strike out on your own, take a drive to Woburn and negotiate with a fisherman for a ride to Glovers Island, an old whaling station, and snorkel away.

Golf

At the **Grenada Golf Course and Country Club,** you'll find a nine-hole course, charging greens fees of $8 a day. The course is open Monday to Saturday from 8 a.m. till sunset (on Sunday from 8 a.m. till noon). From the course you'll have a view of both the Caribbean Sea and the Atlantic. Telephone 4554 for information.

Water Sports

Water-sports fans gravitate to the beach near Spice Island Inn, where a collection of agencies rent boating equipment from 9 a.m. to 6 p.m. daily, including catamarans at $15 per hour, jet-skis at $12 per hour, and windsurfers at $12 per hour. It's possible to take speedboat trips at $35 per hour. Many of the island's hotels have Sunfish craft for the use of their guests. The swimming, as mentioned, is particularly good off Grand Anse beach.

Deep-Sea Fishing

Fishermen come here from November to March in pursuit of both blue and white marlin, yellowfin tuna, wahoo, sailfish, and other catches. Most of the bigger hotels have a sports desk which will arrange fishing trips for you.

Tennis

Tennis, like cricket and football, is a popular everyday sport in Grenada. Guests at the Secret Harbour, Calabash Hotel, and Twelve Degrees North can avail themselves of those well-kept courts. Otherwise, the **Richmond Hill Tennis Club** (no phone), which has two hard courts, will arrange a temporary membership for $15. Or as a nonmember you can play for $3 per person hourly. In addition, the **Tanteen Tennis Club** will grant you a membership for $15. Nonmembers pay $3 per hour per person.

Boat Excursions

In St. George's, **The Loafer,** at the Carenage (tel. 2371), an ocean-racing catamaran, is available for sunset and moonlight cruises weaving in and out of the coves and secret harbors of Grenada's coast. The 70-by-30-foot vessel also makes snorkeling trips. Charges are $20 per person per day or $10 per person for a half-day cocktail cruise. *The Loafer* was built in England by Captain De Roche.

The **Rhum Runner,** a metal-hulled catamaran with a parapet, moored at St. George's harbor, takes passengers on water tours for reef viewing, harbor trips, cocktail cruises, barbecue evenings, cruises up Grenada's coast, and all-you-can-drink punch cruises. Live, electronic, or steel-band music is offered. The cost is $20 per person. Telephone 4233 for reservations.

At the **Grenada Sailing School,** P.O. Box 220, St. George's (tel. 4458), you can charter the racer-cruiser *Damosel,* a 43-foot vessel, or the cutter ketch *Samantha II,* a 42-footer. The rate for a semi-bareboat charter aboard the *Damosel* is $255 per day in winter, *$155 per day in summer*. The charge for a semi-bareboat charter aboard *Samantha II* is $317 per day in winter, *$200 per day in summer*. Provisions, either winter or summer, cost $16 per person per day. The maximum number of persons allowed on the semi-bareboat is six, and the maximum on the fully provisioned charter is four.

Carin Travel at Grand Anse (tel. 4363) offers day charters at $20 per person and sunset cocktail cruises on Friday for $12.50 per person. A minimum of five persons is required.

Other charters can be arranged by getting in touch with **Grenada Yacht Services,** P.O. Box 183, St. George's (tel. 2508). They'll arrange a charter on a 45-foot vessel between 9:30 a.m. and 4 p.m. on Saturday or Sunday, with rum punch and juice supplied. However, you're to bring your own lunch. The cost is $25 per person.

Hog Island is a convenient destination for anyone who presents a letter from his yacht club and can afford the daily rental fee for a 40-foot Hughes II sailboat which is rented by **Spice Island Charters,** Prickly Bay, L'Anse aux Épines (P.O. Box 449, St. George's; tel. 4342). They operate out of what has been called "the prettiest boatyard in the Caribbean." Bring a jug of the island's incomparable rum punch with you to really keep your party flowing. An even more exotic destination would be to the so-called Bird Island, an unmarked and unnamed rocky island off the south shore of Grenada. There, thousands of white egrets nest each evening at dusk, flying away in one white mass at daybreak. Yachts can be reserved in advance and sailed without supervision upon the presentation of documentation from a client's local yacht club. Face-masks are provided with the boats free, and scuba equipment can be rented too, but only if you have a PADI certification. Both bareboat and crewed charters are available at Spice Island, along with skippered day charters. Day trips cost $160 per day for up to six people and $25 for each additional person up to ten. Windsurfers and Sunfish are also available to rent hourly or daily.

A cheaper way to visit these islands is through **Woburn Tours** (tel. 5393 between 9 a.m. and 3 p.m.). They go to the uninhabited Calivigny and Hot islands just off the east coast of L'Anse aux Épines. You can enjoy the privacy of the beaches, plus going on a "marine safari."

Air Tours

Seen from the air, Grenada is striking, with harbors, volcanic mountains, and on the south, a jagged pattern of peninsulas with lush, forested hills. **Grenada Tours & Travel,** Young Street, St. George's (tel. 3316), offers two tours on Piper Seneca II aircraft, each accommodating six people. One is a 30-minute Round Grenada flight, costing $29 per person, with a minimum of six passengers. The other is an hour's flight over the nearby Grenadines at $50 per person, based on a minimum of six.

SHOPPING: The one item everybody who visits Grenada comes home with is a basket of spices, better than any you're likely to find in your local supermarket. These hand-woven panniers of palm leaf or straw are full of items grown on the island, including the inevitable nutmeg, as well as mace, cloves, cinnamon, bay leaf, vanilla, and ginger. The local stores also sell a lot of luxury-item imports, mainly from England, at prices that are almost (not quite) duty free.

Store hours, in general, are 8 to 11:45 a.m. and 1 to 3:45 p.m. Monday to Saturday.

For your introduction to shopping on the island, head to **Grencraft,** Melville Street in St. George's (tel. 2655), which is the national outlet for all handcrafts made on the island. You'll find selections of straw, sisal, and khus-khus mats, along with the baskets, rugs, and hats for which Grenada is known. A fine selection of island-grown spices is sold, along with such condiments as nutmeg jam and jelly, hot sauce, and spice baskets. Many of the spices come in gift boxes. There are woodcarvings and utilitarian mahogany items, along with coral and coconut flex jewelry, plus calico dolls with spices inside. The shop enjoys a favorable waterside location which is reached by passing through Sendall Tunnel between the Carenage and the Esplanade, and there is a branch at the international airport.

One of the most interesting shops in St. George's is **Spice Island Perfumes Ltd.,** on the Carenage (tel. 2006). This small store and workshop is open from 8:30 a.m. to 4:30 p.m. Monday through Friday, and from 9 a.m. to noon on Saturday. It produces and sells perfumes, potpourri, and teas made from the locally grown flowers and spices. If you desire, they'll spray you with a number of desired scents, helping you choose among such temptations as island flower, spice, frangipani, jasmine, patchou- li, and wild orchid. The store also serves as the outlet for Spice Island cosmetics prod- ucts, a range of high-quality Grenadian shampoos, conditioners, lotions, and other toiletries. It's also the exclusive distributor in Grenada for Caribelle Batik items and Kokonuts T-shirts. The shop stands near the harbor entrance, close to the Tourist Board, post office, public library, and Grencraft Handicraft Centre.

Veronica's Tropical Fashion, Grand Anse (tel. 4210), near the Grand Anse shopping Centre, is one of the more fashionable clothing outlets on the island.

Straw Mart, on Granby Street (tel. 2341), fronting Market Square, has beautiful hand-plaited and embroidered straw work. The spice dolls, woodcarvings, and sun hats you may find no less enticing.

The most interesting shop for souvenirs and artistic items is **Yellow Poui Art Gallery,** Canash Hill, St. George's, in the next building after Barclays Bank. Here you can see oil paintings and watercolors, sculpture, prints, rare antique maps, engravings, and woodcuts, with prices beginning at $10 and going up. There is also a comprehen- sive display of newly acquired works from Grenada, the Caribbean area, and other sources, shown in four rooms, plus a continuous photography exhibition. You can enjoy chilled local fruit drinks in the courtyard garden. The gallery is open from 8:30 a.m. to 4 p.m. Monday to Friday and from 9 a.m. to noon on Saturday. After hours, on weekends, and on holidays, phone 3001 or 2121 for an appointment.

Noah's Arkade, Cross Street, St. George's (tel. 2482), in the center of town a block from the water, is a branch of the well-known chain of Caribbean gift shops. It sells handcrafts, hammocks, woven straw articles, jewelry, pottery, and terracotta.

Tikal, Young Street (tel. 2310), is behind a narrow sidewalk at the side of a busy commercial street in an old-fashioned brick building. Inside is a collection of batik, terracotta, woodcarvings, wickerware, napery, and carved coconut shells.

NIGHTLIFE: For those seeking culture, the 200-seat **Marryshow Folk Theatre,** Ty- rell Street near Bain Alley, St. George's (tel. 2451), offers performances of Grenadi- an, American, and European folk music and West Indian interpretative folk dance. The theater is the home of the Tamarind Dance Troupe. Check with Marryshow House or the tourist office to see what's on.

Perhaps the best action spot in Grenada at the time of this writing is **The Bou- gainvillaea,** L'Anse aux Épines (tel. 4159). There's a large wooden dance floor with special lighting, where you can dance to a variety of music including disco, funk, soka, reggae, calypso, new wave, and rock. The place is air-conditioned, and you can dine on the veranda from 6 to 9 p.m. Disco starts at 10 p.m. The place is jumping until 1 a.m. on Tuesday and Thursday, until 3 a.m. on Monday, Wednesday, Friday, and Saturday.

The **Sugar Mill,** Grand Anse (tel. 4401), is open only on Wednesday and Satur- day nights. This former rum distillery was built in 1750 and is both a disco and night- club. It's usually much busier on Saturday than on Wednesday. Drinks cost EC$5 ($1.85). Sometimes it gets hot on Saturday night, when guests listen or dance to the sounds of reggae.

CARRIACOU: Largest of the Grenadines, Carriacou, "land of many reefs," is popu- lated by about 8,000 inhabitants, mainly of African descent, who are scattered over its 13 square miles of mountains, plains, and white sand beaches. There's also a Scottish colony, and you'll see names like MacFarland. In the small hamlet of Windward, on the east coast, villagers of mixed Scottish descent carry on the tradition of building wooden schooners. Large skeletons of boats in various stages of readiness line the beach where workmen labor with the most rudimentary of tools, building the West Indian trade schooner fleet. If you stop for a visit, a master boatsman will let you climb the ladder and peer inside the shell, and will explain which wood came from which island, and why he designed his boat in its particular way. The island's two peaks shoot skyward to almost 1,000 feet. Much of the population, according to reputation, is involved in smuggling. Otherwise, they are sailors, fishermen, shipwrights, and farmers.

The best time to visit Carriacou is in August in time for its **Regatta,** which was begun by J. Linton Rigg in 1965. It was started for work boats and schooners, for which the Grenadines are famous. Now work boats, three-masted schooners, and miniature "sailboats" propelled by hand join the festivities. Banana boats docking at the pier are filled with people rather than bananas, and sailors from Bequia and Union Island camp on tiny Jack-a-Dan and Sandy Isle, only 20 minutes away by outboard motor from Hillsborough. The people of the Grenadines try their luck at the greased pole, foot races, and of course the sailing races. Music fills the air day and night, and impromptu parties are held. At the three-day celebration, Big Drum dancers perform in the Market Square, as the sound of conga drums fills the air.

The **Big Drum dance** is part of the heritage of Carriacou brought from Africa and nurtured here more purely than perhaps on any other Caribbean island. The "Go Tambo," or Big Drum, is an integral part of such traditional events as stone feasts (marking the setting of a tombstone) and the accompanying rites. The feast, called saraca, and setting of the tombstone may be as long as 20 years after a death, marking the time when the grave is entombed, or formally marked with a gravestone. Another event involving the Big Drum and saracas is the maroon. This can involve a dream interpretation, but it seems actually to be just a regular festivity, held in various places during the dry season, with dancing and feasting. Boat launching may also be accompanied by the Big Drum and the saraca and usually draws crowds of participants.

Hillsborough is the chief port and administrative center, handling the commerce of the little island which is based mainly on growing limes and cotton. The capital bustles on Monday when the produce arrives, then settles down again until "mail day" on Saturday. The capital is nestled in a mile-long crescent of white sand.

The **Carriacou Museum** has a carefully selected display of Amerindian artifacts, European china and glass shards, and exhibits of African culture. In two small rooms it preserves Carriacou's history, which parallels that of its sister island, Grenada.

Also in Carriacou is the **Sea Life Centre,** created by the North American Environmental Research Products organization and designed to educate both the islanders and visitors about sea life, especially the lambi (conch) and turtle. It features native paintings of fishermen at work, drawings of the life cycles of the sea's inhabitants, and microscopes and incubators set up for visitors to view the baby lambi and turtles that the center breeds.

The island attracts escapists, a sports-oriented crowd who spend their time fishing, snorkeling, waterskiing, and sailing. Of course, you can just go beachcombing.

Getting There and Getting Around

Visitors arrive on the twice-weekly produce and mail **boats** from Grenada, the trip taking five hours. A far faster method of transport is on a nine-seat **plane,** which takes just 25 minutes from the Point Saline International Airport in Grenada. A terminal building opened officially in 1984 at Carriacou's Lauriston Airport. For information on air service between Carriacou and Grenada, see "Local Air Services" in the Grenada section, above. Boat service, other than the mail boat described in the section entitled "The Grenadines," is provided by the *Alexia II* and the *Adelaide B,* which leave Grenada on Wednesday and Saturday at 10 a.m., arriving at Carriacou at 2 p.m.

The Carriacou-to-Grenada voyage leaves at 1 p.m. on Monday and Thursday, reaching Grenada at 5 p.m. The fare is EC$30 ($11) per person each way. The M.V. *Obedient* links Carriacou and Union Island, making trips on Monday and Thursday, leaving Union Island at 7:45 a.m. and reaching Carriacou at 1 p.m. The fare is EC$10 ($3.70) each way.

You can take a **taxi** from the airport, if you've flown in. The fare from the airport to Hillsborough is EC$10 ($3.70); from the airport to Windward, EC$20 ($7.40).

For those wanting a taste of Carriacou but having limited time, **day tours** are available by taxi costing about EC$100 ($37) to EC$140 ($52).

From Grenada, a Carriacou day tour is offered, including lunch and snorkeling off Sandy's Island, costing $105.

Food and Lodging

Prospect Lodge (tel. 7380), on the tranquil leeward side of Carriacou, is three-quarters of a mile from Bogles Village and two miles north of Hillsborough. Guests at this comfortable lodge can engage in hiking, snorkeling, fishing, boating, or just lounging around. Lee and Ann Katzenbach, the owners, have pleasant rooms, a library guests can use, and the requisite binoculars, snorkel gear, small boats, helpful advice, and local guides to take you on expeditions. Lee is a painter and sculptor, and Ann's a photographer and writer. Both are knowledgeable about the activities possible on the island. In winter, prices for accommodations run from $190 for two adults to $250 for four in Orchard Cottage, which has two bedrooms, a kitchen, and a bath. Two cots are available for children for $20 each. *Summer rates in the cottage are $140 to $200, depending on the number of occupants, with cots costing $18 each.* In Prospect House, a two-story building with a common kitchen in which you make your own breakfast and a library, several types of accommodations are offered. Winter prices are $40 single, $60 double in an apartment with two bedrooms, a shared bath, and a shared kitchen. A bedroom, bath, and shared kitchen rents for $50 single, $80 double; and a self-contained one-bedroom apartment with porch rents for $90 single, $120 double. *Summer prices for these lodgings are $30 single, $50 double, in the two-bedroom apartment; $35 single, $65 double, in the bedroom; and $65 single, $95 double, in the one-bedroom apartment.* All prices include a bag lunch and a full-course dinner.

Silver Beach Resort, Beauséjour Bay (tel. 443-7337), is a small hotel lying about a five-minute walk north of Hillsborough on a mile-long white sand beach. Accommodations comprise eight villas, each spacious with both a bedroom, a living room, a private bath, a fully equipped kitchenette, and a patio; and there are also ten bedrooms, each with a sea view from its own patio. In winter, the double EP rate is $50 to $55 daily, dropping to $40 to $45 in a single. *In summer, the double EP rate is $40 to $45 daily, going down to $35 to $40 in a single.* Self-sufficient types are quoted special housekeeping rates of $275 double and $250 single per week in winter, *lowered to $210 double and $190 single in the off-season.* The charges include gas, electricity, linen, cutlery, and crockery. The bar and dining pavilion is found between the cottages and the beach. At dinner you can sample some good local dishes prepared by native cooks and including lobster, conch, and fresh fish. Locally grown vegetables and fruits are served. Fishing, snorkeling, scuba-diving, windsurfing, and boating to nearby islands can be arranged, including trips to World's End Reef in the Tobago Cays. Tennis is also available.

PETIT MARTINIQUE: The only inhabited one of Carriacou's offshore islands and also the largest is 486-acre Petit (pronounced Pitty) Martinique, with a population of about 600. The chief occupation is listed as building and sailing fishing boats, but it's also famous as the center of the smuggling trade among the islands. Cigarettes and liquor from St. Barts' and St. Maarten's duty-free ports are popular smuggled goods.

Chapter XIV

BARBADOS

IN THE 19TH CENTURY Barbados became famous as "the sanatorium of the West Indies," attracting mainly British guests suffering from the vapors who came here for the perfect climate and the relaxed, unhurried life.

In 1751 Maj. George Washington visited Barbados with his half brother Maj. Lawrence Washington, who had developed tuberculosis. Regrettably, the future American president contracted smallpox there which left him marked for life. Thus Barbados is said to have been the only place outside the United States that George Washington ever visited.

That danger long gone, Barbados still remains a salubrious island to visit, with its mixture of coral and lush green vegetation, along with seemingly endless miles of pink and white sandy beaches.

The most easterly of the long chain of Caribbean islands, it still retains its old-world charm, an imprint of grace and courtesy left over from 300 years of British tradition.

Barbados is renowned for the friendliness of its hospitable people and for having the oldest parliament in the western hemisphere, with a British heritage unbroken since the first landing by Englishmen in 1625 until its independence in 1966. Barbados is one Caribbean island *not* discovered by Columbus.

In a way, Barbados is like England in the tropics, with its bandbox cottages with neat little gardens, its centuries-old parish churches, and a scenic, hilly district in the north known as "Little Scotland" where a mist rises in the morning. Narrow roads ramble through green sugarcane fields trimmed in hedgerows. Sugar is king, and rum is its queen.

Once Barbados was the most heavily defended fortress island in the Caribbean, as 26 forts ran along its 21 miles of sheltered coast. Perhaps for that reason, the island was never invaded. Slavery was abolished in 1834, and independence within the Commonwealth was obtained in 1966.

Long before that, the first known inhabitants of Barbados were the Arawak Indians, who came over from South America. But they were gone by the time of the first British expedition in 1625. Two years later Capt. John Powell returned to colonize the island with 80 settlers who arrived at Jamestown (later renamed Holetown).

A thriving colony of Europeans and black slaves turned Barbados into a prosperous land, based on trading in tobacco and cotton, and by 1640, sugarcane. More and more slaves were imported to work these sugar plantations.

Many English families settled here in the 18th and 19th centuries, in spite of the usual plagues such as yellow fever or the intermittent wars. Because of the early importation of so many slaves, Barbados is the most densely populated of the West Indian islands, numbering some 258,000 souls.

A coral island, Barbados is flat compared to the wild, volcanic terrain of the Antilles, previewed in Chapter XIII on the British Windwards. It is 21 miles long and 14 miles wide. Most of its hotels are on the western side, a sandy shoreline. The eastern side, fronting the Atlantic, is a breezy coastline with white-capped rollers. Experienced surfers like it, but it's not safe for amateur swimmers.

It's a land of hills and dales, limousines (carrying such residents as Claudette Colbert) and donkey carts. You'll find hills, but not mountains. The highest point is Mount Hillaby at 1,115 feet. The island is shaped like a shoulder of lamb.

Barbados lies 200 miles from Trinidad and only 4½ jet hours from New York.

GETTING THERE: In the past, I've flown and recommended many airlines to and from Barbados, but on my most recent research trip, I chose the services of **Pan Am,** one of the most experienced airlines in the world. Pan Am offers nonstop daily service to Barbados' Grantley Adams Airport from New York's JFK and from Miami. Easy connections are available on Pan Am through New York from Boston, Washington, Philadelphia, most of upstate New York, and Detroit, while travelers from Tampa, Orlando, New Orleans, Detroit, and Houston can be routed through Miami. Luggage is always sent directly through to a passenger's final destination, to make inter-airport connections even easier.

All of Pan Am's flights into Barbados are on wide-bodied Airbuses. These frequently refurbished aircraft provide smooth, well-scheduled flights whose attentive in-flight service helps get a vacation off to a good start.

Pan Am's cheapest high-season ticket is almost always accompanied by a simultaneous hotel booking through a tour operator. Any of the phone reservations clerks at Pan Am can advise you on this procedure. Many of the hotels that are potentially available using this system are described in the pages of this guide.

Barring this, Pan Am's least expensive high-season ticket is called an excursion fare and requires an advance purchase of at least 7 days and a delay of between 6 and 21 days before returning to your point of origin.

Transportation can also be arranged to Barbados through such airlines as **American,** which flies there daily from New York. **Air Canada** operates nonstop service from Toronto every Friday and Saturday during high season, with easy connections on those same days from Montreal. Through flights via Miami, **Eastern** services many cities throughout North America.

GETTING AROUND: You're faced with a number of options: You can rent a taxi (expensive), rent a bike or scooter (inexpensive), take a bus (very inexpensive), rent a car (expensive), or walk around this island in the sun (very, very inexpensive).

Taxis

Typical of this part of the world, taxis aren't metered, yet their rates are fixed by the government. Taxis on the island are identified by the letter "Z." One to five passengers are transported at the same time, and they can share the fare among themselves. Overcharging is infrequent, as most of the drivers have a reputation for courtesy and honesty. Taxis are plentiful, and most drivers will produce a list of standard rates, outlining fares between Grantley Adams International Airport and the major hotels. For example, it costs $18 BDS ($8.80) to be taken from the airport to

Crane Beach. From most west coast hotels to the airport costs $27 BDS ($13.25) to $42 BDS ($20.60).

Buses

Unlike most of the British Windwards, Barbados has a reliable bus system. Haitian buses may be more colorful, but Bajan buses have springs and fan out from Bridgetown to almost every part of the island. On most of the major routes there are buses running every 15 minutes or so. Bus fares are 75¢ BDS (37¢) wherever you go. Exact change is required.

Car Rentals

If you don't mind *driving on the left*, as you'll have to do in all the British Windward Islands, you may find a self-drive car ideal for a Bajan holiday. A temporary permit is needed if you don't have an International Driver's License. Go to the police desk upon your arrival at the airport. You're charged a registration fee of $30 BDS ($14.75), and you must have your own license. The speed limit is 20 miles per hour within the city limits, 30 mph elsewhere on the island. The main police station is at Bridgetown (tel. 436-6600).

Sunset Crest Rent-a-Car, Sunset Crest, St. James (tel. 432-1482), has the largest fleet of Mini-Mokes on the island. They rent for about $300 BDS ($147) per week.

Scooters and Bicycles

To rent a motor scooter—they call it "to hire" here—you must be 21 years of age and in possession of a valid motorcycle license or automobile driver's license with a motorcycle endorsement.

Mrs. Wells at **Jumbo Rentals** can rent you one for $200 BDS ($98) per week, with a $100 BDS ($49) deposit. You'll be supplied free with a helmet, compulsory by law.

Bicycles rent for about $50 BDS ($24.50) per week. You can get one at **Rent-a-Bike Rodney Roach** (tel. 422-5398). If you don't have a credit card, a deposit of $50 (U.S.) is required.

Sightseeing Taxi Tours

Nearly all Bajan taxi drivers are familiar with the entire island, and usually like to show it off to visitors. If you can afford it, touring by taxi is far more relaxed than, and preferable to, taking one of the standardized bus tours. A five-hour tour of the island costs about $150 BDS ($73.50) for a party of up to five persons.

Sightseeing Bus Tours

One of the leading minibus tour operators is **United Taxi Owners Association,** High Street, St. Michael (tel. 426-0284). Almost any type of land tour can be organized and negotiated with these people. A five-hour island tour is likely to cost from $20 BDS ($9.80) per person on a minibus.

PRACTICAL FACTS: The Barbadians, or Bajans as they are called, speak English of course, but with their own island lilt. They live on an island where daytime temperatures are in the 75° to 85° Fahrenheit range throughout the year.

The Barbados dollar (BDS) is the official **currency,** available in $100, $20, $10, $5, and $1 notes, as well as $1, 25¢, and 10¢ silver coins, plus 5¢ and 1¢ copper coins. The Bajan dollar is worth 49¢ in U.S. currency. Currency translations given in this chapter are only for the reader's convenience, and are subject to change. *Note:* Unless otherwise specified, currency quotations are in U.S. dollars. Most stores take traveler's checks or U.S. dollars. However, it's best to convert your money at banks and pay your bills in Bajan dollars.

Citizens of the U.S. or Canada who embark in their own country and hold valid return tickets do not need a passport to enter the country for stays lasting not more than six months.

When you leave, you'll have to pay a $16 BDS ($7.85) **departure tax.** Not only that, but when you go to pay your hotel bill, you'll find you've been charged an 8% government **sales tax.** And while I'm on the subject, most hotels and restaurants add at least a 10% **service charge** to your bill.

The **electricity** is 110 volts, 50 cycles, AC, so at most establishments recommended you can use your U.S.-made appliances.

Most **banks** in Barbados are open from 8 a.m. to 3 p.m. Monday through Thursday and from 8 a.m. to 1 p.m. on Friday (later reopening from 3 to 5:30 p.m.).

You should have no trouble with telecommunications out of Barbados. Telegrams may be sent at your hotel front desk or at the **Barbados External Telecommunications Ltd.,** offices on Lower Broad Street in Bridgetown, which is open from 9 a.m. to 5 p.m. weekdays and 8 a.m. to 1 p.m. on Saturday. Telex and data-access services are also available.

Most hotel desks can attend to your mailing; otherwise, the **Main Post Office** is in the Public Buildings of Bridgetown.

Barbados has a pure **water** supply. It's pumped from underground sources in the coral rock which covers six-sevenths of the island, and it's safe to drink.

In **medical facilities,** a 600-bed hospital, the Queen Elizabeth (tel. 436-6450), is in Bridgetown. There are as well several private clinics, including the 135-bed St. Joseph Hospital (tel. 422-2232), operated by a Roman Catholic order in St. Peter Parish.

Public **holidays** are January 1, Good Friday, Easter Monday, May Day (May 1), Whit Monday, Kadoment Day (a variable holiday), United Nations Day (first Monday in October), Independence Day (November 30), Christmas Day, and Boxing Day (December 26).

1. Hotels of the Island

Per square inch, Barbados has the best hotels in the West Indies. Here you get elegant comfort, the atmosphere often that of an English house party. Most of the hotels are small and personally run, with a quiet, restrained dignity.

Most of my recommendations are sited on St. James Beach, the fashionable sector. However, you'll have to head south from Bridgetown to such places as Hastings and Worthing for the best bargains, often in self-contained efficiencies or studio apartments where you can do your own cooking.

So as not to paint too rosy a picture, I'll give the bad news. Because of Barbados's long and continuing popularity, nowadays with back-to-back charter groups, the tariffs charged in these hotels often are, in my opinion, outrageous in high season. Many hotels will also insist that you take two meals at their establishments if you're there in the winter.

Know also that Barbados has some very good bargains as well, and I've surveyed the best of these too, on my most recent hotel hop around the island (see the end of this section).

Prices cited in this section, unless otherwise indicated, are in U.S. dollars.

THE TOP RESORTS: Barbados Hilton, P.O. Box 510, on Needham's Point, St. Michael (tel. 426-0200), is a self-contained resort, built on a rugged peninsula around an old stone fort, surrounded on three sides by beaches, with more than 14 acres of landscaped gardens. On the heavily populated south edge of Bridgetown, it nevertheless has a remoteness that is appealing. The architecture of the building is among the most stunning of any Hilton worldwide. It's erected around a New Orleans–style cen-

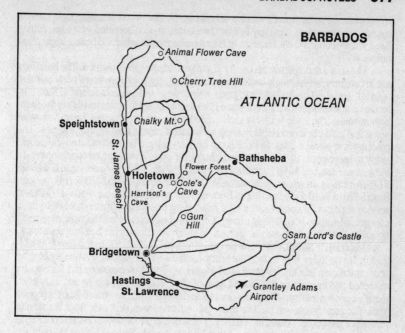

BARBADOS

ATLANTIC OCEAN

○ Animal Flower Cave

○ Cherry Tree Hill

Speightstown ●   ○ Chalky Mt. ○

St. James Beach

● Bathsheba

Flower Forest ○

● Holetown   ○ Cole's

○   Cave

Harrison's

Cave

○ Gun
Hill

○ Sam Lord's Castle

Bridgetown ●

Hastings
St. Lawrence   ✈ Grantley Adams
Airport

tral courtyard full of tropical gardens. Four floors of bedrooms with alcove terracing
open toward the sea, and are reached via a glass elevator. A multitude of hanging baskets are suspended from the encircling inner balconies, and on the lower level is a
circular staircase that takes you through palm trees and ferns. The hotel opened in
1966, at the birth of the island's independence. Its outer silhouette is unpainted, a series of rooftop arches made of locally cut coral. The bedchambers are centrally air
cooled and balconied, opening onto Carlisle Bay on the north side and the Atlantic on
the south.

Singles in summer on the EP pay $85 to $104 daily; doubles $94 to $112. In
winter, tariffs on the EP range from $145 to $190 daily in a single, from $166 to $206
in a double. Opening off the inner core garden room is the Fort Charles Grill (see my
dining recommendations). On the same level is a bar lounge with clusters of rattan
chairs and sofas. Guests can also order meals in the Terrace Café and Grill, later dancing at the Flambeau Bar. Bajan nights here are popular, and barbecues and calypso
shows are staged, along with movies and an international buffet. The beach area,
which adjoins the dining and swimming pool terraces, is secluded, with a stone barrier
to break the force of the waves. You might enjoy a game of tennis on one of the courts,
go horseback riding, or participate in water sports. You can go sailing, rent a boat,
whatever. There's also a sauna, and a masseur who can be summoned for tired mus-
cles.

Sandy Lane, St. James (tel. 432-1311), is a great house–style Trust House Forte
Hotel. Ever since the days of the late Ronald Tree, it has been a deluxe winter haven for
such well-heeled Englishmen as Sir Anthony Eden. Nowadays, however, it draws a
broad base of tourism, especially from Americans. In winter, you are likely to mingle
with royalty and movie stars. The place represents luxury on a small scale, with beautiful suites and rooms, a private beach on one side, an 18-hole golf course on the other.

In between are some fine all-weather tennis courts. The two swimming pools are surrounded by Italianate gardens, Roman fountains, and colonnaded verandas. Sandy Lane was built on 380 choice acres of Bajan real estate on what had been a sugar plantation.

The suites and apartments are set in gardens extravagantly planted. The buildings are in cut coral, with shingle roofs, baronial arches, high ceilings, and a porte cochère —in all, grand-estate-like with tall gates, a driveway, and ornamental steps. Rare butterflies and singing birds flit from water lilies to frangipani to bougainvillea to the flamboyant trees. The style is chicly casual. Bedrooms are traditionally furnished, with white and gold chests and tables, along with Italian bronze wall lighting fixtures. The coloring is in pastel shades. Service is top-drawer, as there is a staff of some 400 people ready to serve you. All 112 rooms and suites have private bath and air conditioning. *In the summer season, MAP guests are charged $260 daily for two persons in a double, $175 in a single.* In winter, these same MAP tariffs rise to $420 to $465 for two people, from $370 to $430 daily in a single. Even more expensive suites are available. Tax and service are extra. You can order a cool salad at the pool at lunchtime, later enjoying a continental-inspired candlelight dinner. Groaning buffet tables are frequent, as is regular native entertainment such as calypso. You can also dine in the Seashell restaurant.

Marriott's Sam Lord's Castle, St. Philip (tel. 423-7350, or toll free 800/228-9290). If you lodge here in the "Regency Rascal's" main house, it's like seeking an accommodation in a kind of Barbadian Mount Vernon. You can sleep in a four-poster canopied bed upstairs on the second floor of the crenellated manor house. However, there's a constant stream of visitors during the day exploring the ground-floor reception area. The great house was built in 1820 and craftsmen were sent over from England to reproduce the queen's castle at Windsor. These ceilings look down on the art of Reynolds, Raeburn, and Chippendale. According to legend, Samuel Hall Lord built the estate on money earned by piracy. A landlubber, Sam is reputed to have lured ships onto the rocks of Cobbler's Reef by placing lanterns in the trees on his estate. He then piled up a fortune by looting wrecked ships.

Set on 72 imaginatively landscaped acres with rare flowering trees, the estate has a wide, lengthy private sandy beach edged by tall coconut trees, as well as seven professional tennis courts which are lit at night. The location is about 14 miles out of Bridgetown, heading east beyond the airport. Depending on traffic, count on anywhere from a 30- to 45-minute drive. You can swim in any of three pools which are built free form to look like small ponds or lakes. There are also a hydrotherapy pool and a children's pool. Other facilities include a games room, exercise room, shuffleboard, table tennis, library, beauty shop, and barbershop. Golf, sailing, horseback riding, snorkeling, waterskiing, fishing, luncheon and nighttime cruises, and other outside activities are available on the island and can be arranged by the activities director.

There are 256 guest rooms including 16 suites. All accommodations are air-conditioned with private bathrooms. There is a service charge and government tax added to all bills. In winter, rates range from $170 to $210 daily. Suites and cottages are more expensive. *Off-season, the tariff runs from $95 to $125 daily.* For breakfast and dinner, add another $40 per person daily to the room tariffs. There is a whole list of dining and entertainment places, including the gourmet Cobbler's Reef Restaurant, open for dinner only. The Garden Restaurant, open for lunch and dinner, is more for family-style dining, featuring a full luncheon buffet. Breakfast and dinner are also served in the Wanderer Restaurant, and you can order a hamburger at Sam's Place, right on the beach. There are many bars as well. A Bajan Fiesta night in the hotel's Bajan Village is offered once a week, as is a shipwreck barbecue and beach party with a steel drum band, a limbo show, and fire-eaters on South Beach. Slot machines are available for play every day, and goat races are held on the beach every Saturday.

Coconut Creek Club, St. James (tel. 420-4952), is an informal celebrity retreat on the fashionable coastline of Barbados. Rooms are snugly perched in a tropical garden overlooking two intimate sandy coves. Many of the bedrooms are built on the low cliff edge, overlooking the ocean. Others open onto the pool. The theme is Caribbean, with cut-out wooden balconies. Bedrooms are simple and uncluttered, with white walls, orange ceramic floors, and splashes of tropical colors on the beds. Each has a private bath, and a veranda or balcony where your breakfast is brought to you. There are some deluxe poolside apartments with small kitchenettes. Rooms come in four different classifications, the cheapest being labeled "moderate." From that, you rise to apartment suites at poolside and superior and deluxe on the oceanfront. *In summer, two persons pay $80 to $115 for a room; a single, from $60 to $80*. For breakfast and dinner, add another $20 per person year round. In winter, doubles cost $150 to $195; singles $130 to $175. Resident manager Patrick D. Porter has created an outpost of Britannic nostalgia in the English pub, the Cricketers. Bajan buffets and barbecues are served on a vine-covered open pergola, overlooking the gardens and the sea. In the inn's cozy restaurant, the food has been praised by *Gourmet* magazine. Architecturally, the room has upside-down stucco arches and rough beamed dividers. There's dancing to West Indian calypso and steel bands. Swimming is in the bay or the freshwater pool, and complimentary water sports include waterskiing, windsurfing, and use of Hobie Cats.

Colony Club, St. James Beach (tel. 422-2335). The entrance to this topnotch resort hotel is impressive, lined with Australian pines. This Bajan "residential club" lies about eight miles from Bridgetown on this well-known beach. An elegant feeling still prevails, even though the Colony has grown from a small "house party"–type establishment to a complex of some 75 rooms which look out on shaded verandas and handsomely landscaped grounds. Twenty-eight of the Colony's rooms are built directly on the beach, and all units have private patios and air conditioning. Accommodations are clustered in two- and three-story Mediterranean-style bungalows with red-tile roofs. The main building is the oldest, reflecting its serenity and Barbadian architecture. White walls and pitched beam ceilings are the perfect foil for the traditional wood furnishings. Sliding glass doors open onto sun terraces. Some units are so close to the pool you can almost dive in. *In summer, singles range from $80 to $130 daily, and doubles go for $100 to $150*. In winter, singles are priced from $175 to $230, while doubles pay $195 to $250. For MAP, add another $20 per person daily. Tax and services are extra. Both a continental cuisine and West Indian specialties are served on a covered terrace, a gracious setting for dining. The beach barbecues are well known here, and deservedly so. Entertainment, such as calypso, limbo, and dancing to a combo, is occasionally provided.

Glitter Bay, St. James (tel. 422-4111), places its emphasis on luxury. Of the 46 available Moorish-style units, 7 are three-bedroom penthouses, 29 are two-bedroom suites, which will convert into one-bedroom suites with kitchen, and the final 10 are one-bedroom suites. Each of the elegantly furnished accommodations has a private bath with double vanity, tub, and shower, as well as a fully carpeted and air-conditioned bedroom with a large private terrace. Suites feature fully equipped kitchens. The resort lies on a ten-acre site. All its units are on a series of descending terraces, giving guests a view from either patio or balcony. The site was once owned by the Cunards, the aristocratic British family of shipping fame. From their elegant grand house and Venetian-style beach house, Glitter Bay was developed. In winter, a single rents for $175 daily, a twin for $225. Twin occupancy of a one-bedroom suite costs $275. *In summer, a single rents for only $96, a twin going for $124, and a one-bedroom suite for two, from $165*. The MAP supplement is $55 per person daily.

The circular eatery here is Piperade, named after the Basque omelet so popular in Biarritz. It offers both classical and nouvelle cuisine, along with West Indian specialties. On Monday, a gala Bajan buffet is presented, and Friday is barbecue night. The Sunset Beach Bar is a popular rendezvous spot for a sundowner. Guests can dance under the stars and enjoy local entertainment such as a steel band or calypso. Water cascades from a children's pool into the main pool spanned by a pine bridge. There is a full range of water sports provided on a complimentary basis, including waterskiing, windsurfing, snorkeling, and catamaran sailing. Many other activities, such as golf and horseback riding, can be arranged. Two tennis courts are lit at night.

Heywoods, St. Peter (tel. 422-4900), one of the island's newest resorts, is a government-built collection of colonial-style buildings set amid recently planted palm trees. The complex stands on a 31-acre flat area near a mile-long sandy beach, a long haul north of Bridgetown. It cost $30 million to build, and when it was completed in 1983 it represented one of the most ambitious resort development projects ever undertaken in Barbados. Although owned by the Barbados Tourism Corporation, the resort is managed by an independent company. On the premises are more than 300 rooms, clustered into seven architecturally different groupings, which contributes to a village-style ambience within each cluster. In winter, singles range from $175 to $210, while doubles cost from $190 to $210. A third person in any double pays an additional $40 per day. Use of a kitchenette is optional, costing in any season an extra $30 per day. *In summer, singles range from $85 to $125, while doubles go for $100 to $155*. MAP can be arranged for a $38 supplement per day per person, year round. Taxes and a service charge are added. Children under 12 sharing a room with their parents stay free.

The complex contains five floodlit tennis courts, a nine-hole golf course, squash courts, a collection of meeting rooms for the conventions sometimes held here, and an assortment of boutiques. It also has a coffeeshop, an outdoor restaurant, a formal dining room, a seafood restaurant, and two bars. The resort's disco, the Club Miliki, is open Tuesday through Saturday from 9 p.m. to 3 a.m. (see my nightlife suggestions). There is also a wide selection of planned activities for guests and their children.

Grand Barbados Beach Resort, P.O. Box 639, Bridgetown (tel. 426-0890). Lavishly renovated to the tune of $3 million, with an eager-to-please staff, this hotel was originally built as a Holiday Inn. After its recent upgrading by local investors, it ranks with some of the most desirable hotels on the island. The location on the outskirts of town is not far from its more famous neighbor, the Hilton, on a flat and sandy plot of beachfront ringed with trees. Each of the more than 130 rooms has its own balcony, mini-bar, satellite-connected TV, and free in-house movies, radio, and hair dryer. In high season, singles range from $180 to $220 daily, doubles run $200 to $240, and suites for two begin at $400. *Off-season, singles cost $110 to $130; doubles, $120 to $150; and suites for two, $210*. MAP can be arranged for another $50 per person daily. There's no charge for teenagers under 18 sharing a room with two adults.

The hotel maintains its own 35-foot trimaran for ocean-going lunches and sunset cruises, and provides an array of water sports. Perhaps best of all, the hotel has a rambling pier jutting out into the sea, at the end of which is a pleasant seafood restaurant, the Schooner, known for its buffets. As you promenade to the restaurant, dozens of glistening chairs and intimate corners invite you to enjoy a view of the surf. Two other restaurants provide a range of menus, including the Golden Shell, the most elegant and relatively formal dining room, and a coffeeshop, the Boardwalk Café on the pier. A cocktail lounge, the Coral Garden, offers nightly entertainment.

Cobblers Cove Hotel, Cobblers Cove (tel. 422-2291), on the northwest coast, grew out of a beachfront mansion built like a false fort with crenellations, which appealed to someone's fantasy. The home was erected over the site of a former British fort which used to protect His Majesty's vessels going into Speightstown, a mile away. Today, after its remake, the hotel is a favorite honeymoon retreat, offering 38 first-class suites in a phalanx of ten Iberian-style villas, each with air conditioning. Overlooking a white sand beach, each unit has a spacious living room, private balcony or patio, and a kitchenette. A full American breakfast appears daily in your suite, and late in the afternoon another waiter returns to take your dinner order. Beachfront units cost more than garden-view apartments. In winter, MAP twins range in price from $270 to $360 daily; singles on the same arrangement go for $199 to $249. *MAP couples in summer pay $140 to $184 daily, and a single pays $96 to $131, also MAP*.

There are many acres of well-developed tropical gardens and lawns, including coconut palms and flowering shrubbery. A beach bar serves tropical drinks, which are more potent than you think at first. The suites have been wisely placed throughout the gardens in horseshoe patterns, each making use of natural woods. The open-air, shingle-roofed dining room overlooks the sea and is held up by huge posts. White tables and chairs give it an elegant touch. The loggia living room reflects the taste of Richard and Jan Williams, who have owned and managed the property for many years, making use of well-selected antiques and country house chintz-covered sofas.

Crane Beach Hotel, Crane Beach, St. Philip (tel. 423-6220), is the most dramatic resort in Barbados. Its remote location on the southeast coast is on the edge of a rugged cliff, overlooking Cobblers Reef and its miles of unspoiled beach, yet it lies only two miles from Sam Lord's Castle and 12 wiggly miles from the capital, Bridgetown. Its core is an 18th-century mansion built of blocks of white coral. All has been carefully remodeled in the "estate mansion." The newer addition, 250 yards from the main hotel, is called the Crane Bank House, and these units are far, far cheaper than in the main house, but they have none of the style and glamor of the estate. Therefore, they are recommended only for serious economizers who plan to spend little time in their rooms and most of the day (or night) enjoying outside activities. One of Barbados's oldest hostelries, Crane has been known to generations upon generations of honeymooners from around the world. Once it was considered *the* resort on the island, lying on more than a dozen acres of sea-bordering land. Both the hotel and the Crane Beach Club overlook a coconut grove, with a 1,000-foot ocean frontage on a white beach of coral sand. Sometimes young Bajans dive from this cliff as Mexican boys do in Acapulco.

Crane gives guests a choice of comfortably furnished rooms, well-equipped apartments, or else individually decorated, large-size deluxe suites, furnished in part with antiques, including half-tester beds with canopy crowns, old paintings, chairs, and chests brought from England, Spain, and France. Each suite is different, with a special character. In winter, EP rates for two people range from $165 to $230 daily, the latter for a one-bedroom suite. A single stays here for $140 daily. In the Crane Bank House, two pay $70 to $90; one person, $60. *In summer, EP doubles range from $105 to $140 in the Estate Mansion, and a single goes for $95. In the bank house, two people are charged $55 to $65; one person, $45*. The MAP supplement year round is $35 per person. All units have balconies, terraces, or sundecks, as well as private baths and phones. There are two swimming pools, the main one of Roman design, with a marble balustrade along the cliffside and rows of white marble fluted Greek columns standing in silhouette against the sea. A brick terrace for sunbathing has large white urns of flowers, and on the beach level is yet another pool. There are two refreshment bars, one dramatically cantilevered 60 feet above the beach.

Barbados Divi St. James Beach Resort, St. Lawrence (tel. 428-7178, or toll free 800/367-DIVI). Included within the embrace of the well-managed Divi chain, this pleasant hotel occupies a 20-acre plot beside the sea in St. Lawrence. Guests register in a round reception area lined with pine and native stone. The accommodations lie in three-story verandaed outbuildings ringing a lagoon-shaped pool. There, shaded by coconut palms, quiet drinking alternates with games of volleyball. The centerpiece is a stylish and airy restaurant and bar capped with a quartet of high cedar-shingled roofs. On the beach, flanking one end of the property, the array of free water sports includes waterskiing, snorkeling, Sunfish rentals, windsurfing, and Hobie Cats. Big signs warn swimmers to enter the water away from the patches of coral which sometimes come close to the water's surface. Each of the units contains air conditioning, a balcony, and tropical furniture. In winter, depending on the exposure, rooms rent for $165 to $175 daily in a single, $170 to $185 in a double. Suites are more expensive. *In summer, singles cost $75 to $85 daily; doubles, $80 to $90.*

Coral Reef Club, St. James Beach (tel. 422-2372). Private cottages surround a main building, which is the lobby and reading room, with some guest rooms on the second floor. The cottages, with names such as "Guava" and "Frangipani," are scattered over about a dozen handsomely landscaped acres with manchineels and casuarinas, fronting a long strip of pure white sandy beach, ideal for swimming. Some furnishings have aesthetic appeal, others are in utilitarian modern. Whatever, there's maximum emphasis on beachside comfort. Rooms are air-conditioned and open onto private patios. Naturally, there's a bath with each unit, and some of the rooms have separate dressing rooms as well. Lacy straw carpets evoke the West Indian touch. *In summer, MAP singles range from a low of $85 daily to a high of $125; doubles $140 to $230.* In winter, the single full-board rate begins at $170, climbing to $230. A twin or double, also AP, starts at $250 daily, working up to $390. When not on the sands, you can go for a dip in the pool before taking lunch in an open-air area, sharing your meal with the sugar birds. Dining and wining in the evening is most gracious, in an attractive room overlooking the ocean. A first-class continental chef is in the kitchen. There's a weekly folklore show and barbecue, and a Bajan buffet on Sunday evening.

Ginger Bay Beach Club, St. Philip (tel. 423-5810), contains a total of 16 suites, painted coral pink. They're built on top of low, rocky cliffs extending into the sand-bottomed waters of the Atlantic. From your comfortable perch at poolside, you'd never guess how dramatic the setting really is. A walk onto the nearby cliffs will reveal exotic grottoes carved by the action of the waves. The focal point of the resort is the thatch-roofed restaurant called Giner's, built inside the shelter of the pool area. Its decor includes a happy combination of tropical lattices set under a peaked roof whose open supports permit a free flow of air even when the ceiling fans are off. In formal contrast to the soft colors and tropical setting, the designer used scores of carved mahogany Chippendale-style armchairs, each crafted in Barbados, copied from 18th-century models. Many people, however, prefer to dine in the Booty Grotto, a unique restaurant in a natural coral cave in which, legend says, the notorious landlubber pirate, Sam Lord, used to store guns and booty from wrecked ships. Inside the 30-foot cavern walls, you can dine on seafood and steak.

Although the villas seem to huddle close to one another, the façades are staggered to permit a feeling of privacy on each accommodation's veranda. Each contains its own hammock, which visitors may soon discover is the perfect place for a midafternoon piña colada. MAP rates in winter, mid-December to mid-April, are $285 in a single, $320 in a double, and $370 in a triple. From mid-April to the end of May and November 1 to mid-Demceber, the price in a single is $225; in a double, $260; and in a triple, $310. *In summer, June 1 to the end of October, you pay $195 in a single, $230 in a double, and $280 in a triple.* Children under 12 sharing their parents' room are charged $30 each.

Discovery Bay Inn, St. James (tel. 432-1301), is a first-class beachfront hotel on 4½ acres of tropical gardens. The main entrance is plantation style. The inn grew out of what had been a private beachside mansion built of coral stone. However, it's now firmly entrenched as a hotel on the casuarina-lined beach. Guest rooms are contained in a stetched-out, two-story wing that was built along the garden. If you don't want to be inspected by passersby, select a second-story perch with raftered ceilings. A more recently built block containing three floors of rooms fronts the sandy beach, with its cluster of thatch shade huts. All rooms have radios and air conditioning, and some contain ceiling fans. The refurbished upstairs lounge has TV and video. Of the 85 rooms, 55 are rated "superior" with a garden or pool view, 21 are deluxe oceanfront units, and 9 are junior suites. Prices in winter for a single on the EP range from $175 to $205 to $225, depending on the rating of your accommodation. Doubles cost $175,

$205, and $235, while triple units go for $215, $255, and $295. *In summer, the tariffs are $80, $95, and $105 in singles; $90, $110, and $130 in doubles; and $115, $135, and $170 in triples*. The MAP supplement, both summer and winter, is $30, and children under 12 can occupy their parents' rooms free. In the center of the complex is a swimming pool, and adjoining are two well-tended tennis courts lit for night play. Free windsurfing, Sunfish sailing, and snorkeling are available for hotel guests, and complimentary transportation is provided to and from Bridgetown. In the entertainment area, a local combo often plays for dancing, and buffets are frequently spread under a covered portico.

Sandpiper Inn, Holetown, St. James (tel. 422-2251), has more of a South Seas look than most of the hotels of Barbados. Affiliated with the also-recommended Coral Reef, it is a self-contained, intimate resort on the waterside, lying along the fashionable west coast. Avoiding sterile modern, it is Bajan in flavor, standing in a small grove of coconut palms and flowering trees. This cluster of rustic-chic rooms and suites surrounds the swimming pool, and some have a fine sea view. Seductive bamboo chairs and overscale drinks make it a pleasant oasis. The hotel is right on the beach, and you can jog along the water's edge. The rooms—11 doubles and 11 ocean-view suites—open onto little terraces that stretch along the second story. Here you can order drinks or have breakfast. Villa rooms have a bamboo Caribbean motif and terracotta tile floors, with room-wide glass doors opening onto terraces or verandas. Bright bedcovers and matching lamps and pillows give the place a holiday resort look. In winter, a MAP single ranges from $192 to $204 daily; a double or twin, from $225 to $300. *On the same MAP, a single in summer costs from $90 daily; a double or twin, from $120 to $202.* Ask about special rates for three to four people in one of the ocean-view suites. Dining is under a wooden ceiling, and the cuisine is both continental and West Indian. Sometimes big buffets are spread out for you, with white-capped chefs in attendance.

Best Western Sandy Beach, Worthing, Christ Church (tel. 428-9033), is an 88-suite Bajan resort on the south shore of Barbados four miles from Bridgetown. It offers one- and two-bedroom suites, and features 16 honeymoon suites with queen-size beds and completely private patios for sunning or whatever. You may be impressed with the tastefully decorated and spacious accommodations, the living and dining areas in the suites in harmonious blues and bronzes. All units also have fully equipped kitchenettes, bathrooms, and private balconies or patios, and all the furniture at this informal place is locally made. *In summer, a one-bedroom suite costs from $115 for two people, and four people are sheltered in a two-bedroom suite for $160*. In winter, one-bedroom suites rent at $175 for two people, two-bedroom suites for two to four people at $260. Facilities for the handicapped are provided in four of the ground-floor suites. The MAP supplement of $45 allows guests unlimited choice from the breakfast and dinner à la carte menus in the Green House Restaurant and also offers a dine and cruise-around special which includes *Jolly Roger* evening cruises, *1627 and All That Sort of Thing* folklore show, and *Barbados! Barbados!*, a comedy play (see the nightlife section). Transportation, unlimited drinks, and dinners are all included in the specials.

The Green House Restaurant, specializing in seafood and steaks, is under a wood-shingled palapa and opens out to the beach and swimming pool. The open-air design and use of wood, hanging plants, browns in the tablecloths, and long skirts of the waitresses give the restaurant a natural look by day that becomes romantic by candlelight at night. Every Friday the resort sponsors a Bajan Cohoblopot buffet for $20, when outsiders are welcome. Caribbean specialties such as flying fish, cou-cou, curries, plantains, and pepperpot are served under the stars. Tuesday is barbecue night (also $20). Another restaurant, the Ocean Terrace, is a casual, open-air facility overlooking the beach, serving lighter, less expensive meals than the Green House. You have a choice of chicken, salads, flying-fish sandwiches, hamburgers, quiche, or omelets. The Ocean Terrace is a casual, open-air facility overlooking the beach, serving lighter, less expensive meals than the Green House. You have a choice of chicken, salads, flying-fish sandwiches, hamburgers, quiche, or omelets. The Ocean Terrace is open five nights a week from 6:30 to 10:30 p.m., but not during the Tuesday barbecue or the Friday Bajan buffet.

Water sports, which cost extra, include three-hour snorkeling trips, windsurfing, paddleboats, Sailfish, scuba lessons, air mattresses, snorkels, fins, and masks.

Tamarind Cove, St. James Beach (tel. 432-1332). Lord Beaverbrook's daughter, the Hon. Janet Kidd, selected the site for this Mediterranean-style hotel of red-tile roofs and wrought iron right on a beach alongside Buccaneer Bay. You get some style and luxury here, but informally so. Guests can enjoy the white sandy beach at their doorstep, or else lounge around the palm-shaded pool. In a setting of tropical gardens, the modern hacienda-style units are comfortable, with balconies overlooking the ocean. In all, there are 74 rooms, plus 12 suites. Standard and superior accommodations enjoy a pool view, and the deluxe and luxury units open onto the sea. *In summer, singles cost $115 to $155 daily, and doubles go for $155 to $195 on the MAP.* In winter, charges in a single range from $155 to $235 daily, while doubles cost $195 to $275, on the MAP. Taxes and service are extra. The food enjoys a good reputation.

The social center is the teepee-shaped bar, whose raftered roof rises above a terracotta floor and the dramatically gnarled trunk of an ancient tree. Water sports such as skindiving, sailing, and waterskiing can easily be arranged, and golf, tennis, horseback riding, and polo are available nearby. Free transportation is provided for a shopping jaunt into Bridgetown, seven miles away.

Divi Southwinds Beach Hotel, St. Lawrence, Christ Church (tel. 428-7181). Repeat visitors to this two-part resort tend to have strong preferences for either its new or its old section, separated from one another by a busy road. The older section lies on the beachfront and consists of a collection of buildings surrounded by palms and sea breezes. The real showplace of the resort, however, is the newer building. It lies just behind what may be the most beautiful bearded fig trees in Barbados (the tree that inspired Portuguese sailors in discovery days to give this island the name it bears). This section looks like a tastefully interconnected series of urban town houses, with prominent wooden balconies and views of a large swimming pool. When you're not enjoying your room, you can appreciate a tropical drink in the cedar-shingled bar, where the roofline looks vaguely Chinese and the terrace is partially cantilevered above the pool. The recently renovated older section has the advantage of opening directly onto a wide and sandy expanse of beach. It also has an oval pool of its own, and visitors need only cross through two groves of palm trees and a little-used street to reach the resort's newer, more stylish twin.

Belonging to the Caribbean-wide Divi hotel chain, the hotel charges $155 to $260 in a single, $160 to $260 in a double in winter. Suites run $290 to $330 for two to four people. *Summer rates in hotel rooms range from $65 to $120 in a single, from $70 to $130 in a double. A two-bedroom suite for two to four people costs $170 to $190.* MAP can be arranged for an additional $32 per day, year round. In the newer section, only suites are available.

Southern Palms, St. Lawrence (tel. 428-7171), is a seafront club with a distinct personality, lying on the Pink Beach of Barbados, midway between the airport and Bridgetown. The core of the resort is an old pink-and-white manor house, built in the Dutch style with a garden-level colonnade of arches. Spread along the sands are multitiarched two- and three-story buildings, on grounds planted with such foliage as oleander, bougainvillea, and hibiscus. Italian fountains and statues add to the Mediterranean feeling, which was the inspiration of Lord Thompson, the Canadian-born British press boss. In its more modern block, an eclectic mixture of rooms includes some with kitchenettes, some facing the ocean, others opening onto the garden, and some with penthouse luxury. On the EP, twin-bedded rooms in winter rent for $145 to $185 daily, and suites are more expensive, of course. *In summer, EP rates are $95 to $107 daily in a double*. For MAP, add another $35 per person daily. Linking the accommodations is a cluster of straw-roofed buildings, including the Khus-Khus Bar and Restaurant, serving both a West Indian and a continental cuisine. A native orchestra often entertains here, and you can dance the merengue to the music of a steel band. There's a terrace for sunning before you take a dip in the beachside freshwater swimming pool.

Cunard Paradise Beach Hotel, Black Rock, St. Michael (tel. 429-7151, 212/661-7036 in New York City, or toll free 800/5-CUNARD). Built and operated by Cunard, this is one of the most sports-oriented resorts in Barbados. It sits on a hillside above a glistening white beach 2½ miles northwest of Bridgetown. Its clubhouse is attractively composed of lattices and chiseled stone in a sun-flooded position overlooking the sea. Within its elegant premises is a gazebo for dancing, an alluring indoor/outdoor restaurant, and two rounded swimming pools. In the Rattan Bar, hanging wicker chairs are a comfortable alternative to bar stools. Its impressively detailed water-sports program, Willie's Water Sports, is covered later. Horseback riding, golf, sightseeing, and shopping trips to Bridgetown can be arranged by the staff. On the premises are a pair of Har-tru tennis courts under the supervision of a pro. Accommodations are scattered among lattice-covered motel-like units rising amid a tropical collection of gardens and forests at the base of a steep hill. One even arches above a sometimes dried-out gulch. Each is air-conditioned, with a modern design of big windows and comfortable furniture. Depending on the exposure, singles rent for $120 to $160 daily in winter, *$80 to $100 in summer*. Doubles cost $145 to $200 daily in winter, *$100 to $125 in summer,* plus tax and service. Children under 12 stay free in a room with adults. MAP is an extra $40 per person.

Casuarina Beach Club, St. Lawrence Gap, Christ Church (tel. 428-3600). You'll approach this resort through a forest of palm trees which sway gracefully above a well-maintained lawn. The main building has a series of arched windows leading onto verandas, although to get to your accommodation, you pass through the outlying reception building and beside the pair of swimming pools. These are separated from the wide sandy beach by a lawn area dotted with casuarina and bougainvillea. On the premises is an octagonal roofed open-air bar and restaurant, as well as tennis and squash facilities. The front desk can arrange most seaside activities through outside agencies. Each of the 64 accommodations is air-conditioned and has a ceiling fan, a kitchenette, and wicker furniture. In winter, two persons are charged $95 to $115 daily. *In summer, two guests are housed for $60 to $70.* Extra people (more than two) staying in any unit pay $12 each per night, and children under 12 are accommodated free in their parents' room.

Settlers Beach, St. James (tel. 422-3052), is a seaside collection of well-appointed villas placed on four acres of beachfront property. Each air-conditioned apartment is self-contained, having two bedrooms with private bath, a spacious tile-floor lounge and dining room, plus a fully equipped kitchen. *In the shoulder and low season, an apartment for two begins at $110, going up to $120 daily.* For breakfast and dinner, add a supplement of $30 per person daily. In high season, two persons stay here for $225 daily; three people, $280. Tariffs go even higher at Christmas. The apartments have sunny colors, and the rates quoted include the services of a maid. Adjoining the buildings is a swimming pool surrounded by palms and lawn. The square-roofed dining room and lounge bar serves good food and drink, and at dinner you can select a table in the moonlight.

Ocean View, Hastings (tel. 427-7821), is an oldtimer that seems just as good as ever, maybe better. It's the oldest hotel in Barbados, founded in 1901. It still maintains some vintage niceties too. For example, your bed is turned down at night. Shoes left outside the door are waiting there polished the next morning. At dinner, vegetables are served from silver dishes. Built between the busy road and the beach, the pink-and-white Ocean View has some of the graciousness of a colonial English house, with

Queen Anne mahogany side tables, chintz-covered armchairs, an open staircase with an old balustrade, a drawing room richly furnished, and a seaside porch that's good for lounging. The location is on the south coast in Christ Church, with Bridgetown about 5 minutes away; the international airport, 15 minutes. The staff of 57 has an average length of service of 17 years, and the two Bajan head cooks have been here for more than a quarter of a century. The bedrooms are not decorated in the usual automatic style. Rather, every chamber is different—some large, some small and cozy—and an attractive use has been made of island antiques. In winter, singles range in price from $45 to $61 daily, a double costing from $64 to $74, all EP. *In summer, you pay $26 to $35 daily in a single, $45 to $55 in a double, EP.* Tax and service are added. For dining here, refer to "Barbados Cookery," below.

THE MIDDLE BRACKET: Bagshot House, St. Lawrence, Christ Church (tel. 428-8125), was built about a quarter of a century ago by a charming Trinidadian, Mrs. Eileen Robinson. She has glamorized her house with flowering vines tumbling over the railing of the balconies. In front of the inn, the beach stretches out before you. Some of the well-kept, simply furnished units have views of the water. All rentals, however, contain private baths. Twins cost $125 daily in winter, and singles run $79, including breakfast and dinner. *In the off-season, these same twins go for $112 daily, singles for $64, both rates including half board as well.* A front sunbathing deck is perched right at the edge of a lagoon. This is actually the living room, but there is a deckside lounge decorated with paintings by local artists. Bridgetown is about a 15-minute drive to the west.

The **Tides Inn,** Gibbes, St. Peter (tel. 422-2403), is a quiet retreat that appeals particularly to those who enjoy a small, friendly hotel with a relaxed, informal atmosphere. Lying on the St. Peter coast in the northern part of Barbados where the sea is calm, it has no swimming pool, but Gibbes Bay, with its clear, warm water, is only a short walk away. The area has been called by some visitors one of the three most beautiful beaches in the world. The Tides is away from the rumble of main-road traffic and enjoys almost constant breezes. Guests are warmly welcomed with a complimentary rum punch, and there is no charge for use of beach and snorkeling equipment, personal laundry, daily newspaper, and room service. It offers a cozy bar near the main dining room which is outfitted in tropical decor of rattan furniture and colorful table linens, overlooking the garden. The varied menu includes West Indian and continental specialties. The accommodations are in three separate buildings, each with veranda. All rooms are on the ground floor, with private bath and shower, and ceiling fans circulate the air. *In summer, two persons pay from $90 daily, MAP (or, for room only, $50).* MAP rates in winter for two persons are from $110. All units are completely screened. The Tides is a good bargain in the Caribbean.

Sichris Apartment Hotel, 2 Worthing, Christ Church (tel. 427-5930, 212/355-6605 in New York City, or toll free 800/221-4588), is shielded from the street by a row of shrubbery and a high wall. It contains a sheltered pool area, 24 one-bedroom apartments, and a friendly and attractive staff directed by David and Anne Walker. When they opened the hotel in 1978, the Walkers named it after their children, Simon and Christopher. Each of the pleasant accommodations contains air conditioning, direct-dial phone, a kitchenette, and a veranda with louvered doors. Beach lovers will find the ocean a short walk away, and visitors who prefer to cook in their own units can shop at supermarkets close by. The in-house restaurant is a pleasantly informal place with an adjoining cabaña bar and a series of scheduled barbecues and buffets with live music. *Summer rates in accommodations suitable for one or two people range from $60 to $70,* while winter prices go from $110 to $125, depending on whether your view is over the pool or over the road. The establishment charges an additional $15 for a third and fourth person in any apartment. Children under 12 stay free. MAP is available for a $48 supplement per person per day.

GOOD FOR THE BUDGET: The **Island Inn,** Garrison, St. Michael (tel. 426-0057), is an old-style compound with bungalows placed in a maze of tropical trees and shrubbery, across the street from the Grand Bay Hotel and down from the Hilton. On this site a British army regiment in 1750 constructed an armory as part of the fort built to protect the harbor. The present unit, unfortunately, stands near a large Mobil refinery (but everyone assures me the wind doesn't blow in the direction of the Island Inn). The inn has a loyal staff who run this place in a home-like way, housing you in one of their 27 air-conditioned garden cottages, each with a covered front veranda. Dollarwise travelers seem to like it here, especially the prices. In winter, the single rate is $34 daily, rising to $46 in a double, with a third person paying another $9. *EP singles in summer cost $24 daily, rising to $34 in a double, plus tax and service.* Dark-wood floors, scatter rugs, louvered shutters, and straw mats set the style tone.

The location is on Needham's Point, about a ten-minute ride south of Bridgetown. At the edge of the patio garden is one of the finest restaurants on the island, Brown Sugar (see my dining recommendations). However, guests can also enjoy breakfast and perhaps a meal in Peter's Patio, the al fresco dining room for guests, with its vines clambering over an old English trellis. Perhaps they'll have a drink first in the informal lounge bar under a large tree. There's a mixture of antiques and simple modern in the public areas. Every Monday night the staff has an "Action at the Inn," with a full Caribbean buffet and native floor show.

Fairholme, Maxwell, Christ Church (tel. 428-9425), is a converted plantation house, once part of the Old Maxwell Plantation, lying five miles from the Grantley Adams Airport and six miles from Bridgetown. The main house with its original gardens is just off a major road, a five-minute walk to the beach, and across from its sister hotel the Sherringham Beach, with its waterfront café and bar which Fairholme guests are allowed to use. The older part has 11 double rooms with private baths, a living room area, and a patio overlooking an orchard and swimming pool. Beside the pool is a grassy lawn for sunbathing and a bar for island beverages. More recently added are 20 Spanish-style studio apartments, all with balcony or patio, built within the walls of the old plantation, with high cathedral ceilings, dark beams, and traditional furnishings. *In summer, rooms rent for $30 daily in double occupancy, $22 in a single, with apartments going for $40 daily for two persons.* In winter, rooms are $36 in a double, $24 in a single, with apartments costing $53 daily, double occupancy. Breakfast and dinner cost an additional $18 per person. The restaurant has a reputation for home-cooking—good, wholesome, nothing fancy, but the ingredients are fresh.

Barbados Windsurfing Club Hotel, Benston Beach, Maxwell, Christ Church (tel. 428-9095), attracts many of its guests just because it's one of the most fun places in town. If you're an avid windsurfer, this could be the perfect place for you, also. Set between the road and the sea, the accommodations at this young-at-heart resort are in a brightly painted three-story rectangular building with angled balconies. The 15 units are spacious and simple, including basic kitchens and simple bathrooms. Phones are in the hallways (one per floor), and the reception area is sunny but spartan. In winter, doubles go for $70 per day, EP. *In summer, rates go down to $40 in a double.* There are no singles. Tax and service are added to all bills. The bedrooms are comfortable, but no one comes here for the decor. It's the youthful ambience and the camaraderie that makes this place noteworthy. Experts say that the windsurfing just off the hotel's sea wall is as good as that in Hawaii, which appeals to nearly fanatical followers of the sport who come from all over the western hemisphere. On a sunny day when the wind is right, observers on the hotel's grassy terrace can see flotillas of sailboards riding the waves, heading either out into the Atlantic or back to shore. For rates and details, see "The Sporting Life," below.

An informal restaurant on the premises serves simple lunches (sandwiches and hamburgers) during the day, while more complete evening dinners, with such main dishes as steak, chicken, and dolphin, cost about $20 BDS ($9.80). Several musical evenings are usually planned per week, drawing an energetic crowd of fun-loving participants. For information about the week's entertainment, call the hotel.

Atlantis Hotel, Bathsheba (tel. 433-9445), is housed in a slightly dilapidated, green-roofed villa built by a wealthy planter in 1882. In the unpretentious hostelry, set directly on the seacoast, simple bedrooms all have private baths and toilets, and the more expensive units have balconies. *Full-board rates range from $22 to $25 in a single in summer, $40 to $50 in a double.* In winter, the full-board tariffs go from $25 to $30 in a single, $45 to $55 in a double, which makes the Atlantis one of the best bargains along the Atlantic coast of Barbados. Aside from inexpensive accommodations, this is the most popular luncheon spot on the east side of the island. Every day around noon, you're likely to see three or four tour buses and a fleet of private cars depositing crowds who flock into the sunny, breeze-filled interior. There, with a sweeping view of the ocean, Enid I. Maxwell will be seated in a small booth, welcoming visitors into her restaurant. She bought the establishment in 1945, and ever since has served copious buffet lunches every Thursday and Sunday to just about everybody in Barbados. On those days, for around $31 BDS ($15.25) per person, patrons feast from an L-shaped table laden with buffet items that are replaced as quickly as they're emptied. On days when buffets are not scheduled, Mrs. Maxwell directs a handful of waitresses who take meal orders at your cloth-covered table. Main courses usually include fish and chicken, accompanied by pumpkin fritters and vegetables. Full meals cost from $25 BDS ($12.25). Dinners are also served from 7 p.m. every day of the week.

YOUR OWN APARTMENT: Travelers' Palm, 265 Palm Ave., Sunset Crest, St.
James (tel. 432-6428), is designed for those who want to be independent, a choice collection of 16 well-furnished apartments with fully equipped kitchens and air conditioning. Attracting a friendly young crowd, the apartments are filled with bright, resort-type colors and handcrafted furniture. They open onto a well-kept lawn with a swimming pool. Serviced by maids, apartments can house one to three people. The rate for one of these apartments runs from $45 daily in winter, *dropping to just $20 in summer*. Apartments also have a large living and dining room area, and a patio where you can have your breakfast or a candlelit dinner which you've prepared yourself.

Inn on the Beach, Holetown, St. James (tel. 432-0385), is an intimate, compact, miniature resort built as a suntrap directly on the beach. Its four floors of well-styled modern apartments give each occupant a protected private balcony which extends the size of the living rooms. Vaguely Aztec in design, it is white, in contrast to the sky blue of the swimming pool and the deep greens of the palms and fir trees. The pool area becomes a communal living room. Before dinner, you'll surely have made friends at the loggia bar, with its tile floors, copper lanterns, and large colored rope and string hangings. Each of the 20 air-conditioned self-contained studios holds a kitchenette where you can prepare your own meals, or you can dine at a poolside restaurant. Nearby is a shopping plaza where you can pick up supplies. *In summer, a single costs $50 daily, a double going for $60. The penthouse suite with a private balcony and a large sundeck rents for $90 daily for three people.* In winter, the single tariff rises to $90 daily, a double going for $105, and the penthouse suites costing $150.

Sherringham Beach Apartments, Christ Church (tel. 428-9339), is a gracious waterfront home, the core of which is a century-old estate of one of Barbados's plantation owners. With its sea-view verandas, it sits under a sloping red roof. To the vintage structure a block of 18 modern, self-contained air-conditioned apartments has been added. Some have balcony perches for a look out at Oistin Bay. The apartments are neat and simple, furnished in the typical Caribbean beachfront style, and all are air-conditioned. The more expensive units open onto the sea. *In summer, two persons can stay here for only $55 per day in a superior unit.* These tariffs range from $65 to $70 daily in winter. In the plantation house, you can take your meals in its restaurant if you don't want to cook yourself. Bajan specialties, among other dishes, are served. Guests can also use the facilities of its sister hotel nearby, the Fairholme, which has a swimming pool, bar, and a more formal restaurant.

2. Barbados Cookery

The famous flying fish jumps up on every menu, and when prepared right it's a delicacy, moist and succulent, nutlike in flavor, approaching the subtlety of brook trout. Bajans boil it, steam it, bake it, stew it, fry it, stuff it, or whatever.

Try also the sea urchin, or oursin, which you may have already sampled in Martinique and Guadeloupe. Bajans often call these urchins "sea eggs." Crab-in-the-back is another specialty, as is langouste, the Barbadian lobster. Dolphin and salt fish cakes are other popular items on the menu.

Such vegetables typical of the Caribbean as yams, sweet potatoes, and eddoes are grown. And Barbadian fruits are luscious, including papaya, passion fruit, and mangos.

If you hear that any hotel or restaurant, such as Sandy Beach, is having a "Cohoblopot," call for a reservation. This is a Barbadian term which means to "cook up," and it inevitably will produce a host of Bajan specialties.

Bajan dishes are a blend of cookery styles: the British, and most definitely the East Indian and African. These recipes have been adapted to include the local meats, fruits, and vegetables. Pepperpot, stews, and curries are made with local chicken, pork, beef, and fish. The secret of the flavorful dishes, as any Bajan cook will tell you, is in the "seasoning up." It is said that seasoning techniques have changed little since the 16th century.

At Christmas, when many U.S. visitors come to Barbados, roast ham or turkey is served with jug-jug, a rich casserole of Scottish derivation that includes salt beef, ground corn flour, green pigeon peas, and spices. Cou-cou, a side dish made from okra and cornmeal, accompanies fish, especially the "flying fish" of Barbados.

If possible, escape the dining requirements of your hotel and eat around, sampling the island's varied cuisine, which is interesting but not spicy exotic.

Note that most of the prices I'll cite are in U.S. dollars.

Bagatelle Restaurant, Hwy. 2A (tel. 425-0666), three miles from Sunset Crest, St. Thomas, is housed in the gubernatorial residence of Lord Willoughby of Parham, a plantation-style house dating back to 1645. The secluded, remote, sylvan retreat lies in the hills in the center of the island, retaining the aura of colonial days. It has been transformed into one of the island's finest and most elegant choices for dining, a sophisticated, popular rendezvous. Cooled by overhead fans, you can dine in rambling cellars, with candles and lanterns illuminating the menu as well as the white coral walls and the old archways. Furnishings are mostly in a heavy black wood, adding a stately serenity and dignity to the place. Service is very gracious, among the best I found on Barbados. You proceed first to a charming little bar where menu selections are made. Later you can select a cozy corner or dine outside, listening to the crickets. For $80 BDS ($39.25), you can select from the set menu, ordering perhaps salmon mousse or a chicken liver pâté, going on to the callaloo soup or a fish chowder made mainly of flying fish, eddoes, and shrimp. For a main course, you might enjoy superbly cooked rack of lamb or a "sort of beef Wellington." Desserts are such luscious concoctions as key lime pie, chocolate mousse, or crème brûlée. Hours are 7 p.m. to midnight, seven days a week.

Reid's, St. James (tel. 432-7623), is one of the island's most fashionable dining spots. It occupies a green-and-white Bajan house whose front veranda overlooks the façade of the Coconut Creek Hotel, just across the street. You might be tempted to order a drink in the darkly intimate brick-floored bar area before dinner. The dining room is in the breeze-filled extension of the main house under a raftered ceiling jutting out toward a sloping English garden. Only dinner is served here, every night except

Monday from 6:30 to 11 p.m. Reservations are essential, especially on weekends. Full meals cost from $60 BDS ($29.50) and might include garlic-flavored shrimp, veal Cordon Bleu, pork en croûte, mixed seafood casserole, lobster tails, seafood crêpe, and beef kebabs.

Restaurant Flamboyant, Hastings Main Road, Christ Church (tel. 427-5588). If you dine here, you'll enter what used to be a private home, considerably simplified since it became a restaurant, with many of the interior walls removed. Still, the tapering columns of the veranda remain in place, and the view still encompasses a large flamboyant (poinciana) tree, which you may be lucky enough to see in full bloom, depending on the time of year of your visit to Barbados. Mr. and Mrs. Brian Cheeseman, the owners, direct a kitchen where, because everything is prepared to order, the food may take a while to be served. While you're waiting, you can enjoy drinks from the long wooden bar while studying the paintings of the whitewashed interior. Menu items include pumpkin and potato soup, a seafood crêpe Flamboyant, wienerschnitzel, a half chicken stuffed Bajan style, shrimp in dill sauce, and apple pie à la mode. Full meals range upward from $60 BDS ($29.50) per person. Reservations are important, especially in high season. Hours are 6 to 9 p.m.; closed Sunday.

Fort Charles Grill, Barbados Hilton, Needham's Point, St. Michael (tel. 426-0200), is an elegant setting for both a continental and a Bajan cuisine. Reservations are recommended, however, as most of the tables, particularly in season, could be booked by the hotel's own guests. For an opener, I suggest the Barbados pepperpot. It's a spicy gumbo with beef, chicken, pork, and duck, or you might prefer sunset soup. I found the most interesting hors d'oeuvre is lobster Silver Sands. Fish from the island is the chef's specialty: red snapper Consett Bay, the chef's own recipe for flying fish, and tropical lobster served in a pineapple. From the rôtisserie, you can order succulent sirloin steaks and lamb chops. Desserts tend to be spectacular. Try the pineapple mulatto with Barbados brown-sugar sauce. You have a choice of ordering à la carte or from the table d'hôte menu (the latter usually includes three main dishes, including roast prime rib of U.S. beef). From the set menu, expect to spend from $25 up, including an appetizer, soup, main course, the vegetable of the day, and a tempting dessert such as guava cheesecake, followed by American brewed coffee. On the à la carte menu you are likely to spend from $40. Hours are 6 to 11 p.m. You can dine and dance every Friday and Saturday night, and there is live entertainment nightly.

La Piperade, Glitter Bay, St. James (tel. 422-4111). Set at the back of the Glitter Bay Hotel, between a freshwater pool and a sandy beach, this restaurant is surrounded with lush and colorful vegetation. The building looks like a low-lying collection of whitewashed domes surrounded with Mediterranean-style terracotta roofs. Newcomers might compare its design to a village church in Greece, although that impression will quickly change at the hedonistic visual pleasure that this restaurant and the resort offer. The restaurant is set in a series of contoured terraces leading on one side to the edge of the free-form pool. At lunchtime, the sun lovers from the hotel's beach may join you inside the Victorian-style interior, where ornate lattices and lathe-turned columns support the sparkling white ceilings. Meals are served on pink tablecloths by a battery of uniformed waiters. They may include such specialties as tournedos Piperade, lobster bisque with brandy, the chef's own chicken-liver pâté, whole Cornish game hen stuffed with wild rice and served with Périgueux sauce, a fresh fish of the day, and desserts such as key lime pie. In addition, the chef prepares daily special dishes which vary with the season. Full meals cost from $70 BDS ($34.25). Reservations are a good idea at this excellent restaurant. Meals are served from 11:30 a.m. to 2:30 p.m. and 7 to 9:45 p.m. daily. The Sunday brunch, costing $20 BDS ($9.80), served from 11:30 a.m. to 4 p.m., features such succulent dishes as crêpes and omelets along with such main dishes as linguine with shrimp sauce.

Restaurant Château Créole, Porters, St. James (tel. 422-4116). In a spot near Glitter Bay, this stucco-and-tile house is set in a pleasant tropical garden dotted with statues of cherubs carrying lambs. After passing under a verdant arbor, you'll be invited to order a drink, served on one of the flowered banquettes filling various parts of the house. Meals are taken on the rear terrace, al fresco style, by candlelight. Barbara and Larry Tatem, formerly of Montréal, are the owners who welcome guests and direct the kitchens. Menu specialties include Créole dishes, which often make use of ample amounts of crabmeat, such as crab diablo and crabmeat au gratin. Perhaps you'd prefer shrimp rémoulade, Créole red-bean soup, New Orleans seafood gumbo, or chicken Pontalba. The establishment makes its own ice cream with local fruits several times a week. Full dinners, served every evening except Sunday, range from $45 BDS ($22) to $75 BDS ($36.75). The restaurant doesn't serve lunch. Dinner reservations are a good idea, especially in high season. Hours are 7 to 9:30 p.m.

da Luciano, "Staten," Hastings, Hwy. 7, Christ Church (tel. 427-5518), is a lovely setting—in a Barbados National Trust–designated building of architectural interest—for a classical Italian cuisine. They offer some of the finest Italian dining in the southern Caribbean. The restaurant has gained in popularity with some of the island's outstanding residents who know they can get good service, top-quality ingredients, and skill and care reflected in what they order. I recommend such specialties as cozze alla marinara (mussels in their shells sautéed in butter and parsley, with white wine and a lot of garlic). Try also the filetto battuto alla Luciano (flattened filet of beef flambéed in brandy, sautéed in butter, served with mustard, fresh cream, and mushrooms). I'm also fond of spaghetti de cecco alla puttanesca (spaghetti sautéed with fresh tomato sauce, sliced olives, capers, anchovies, basil, and black pepper). The pièce de résistance is the quaglia nel nido alla wolfe (charcoal-broiled filet of beef topped with croutons of garlic bread, roast quail, and natural juice). For dessert, you can (in season) order fresh strawberries, finishing with an espresso. Your final bill will be from $30. Hours are 6:30 to 10:30 p.m. Closed Sunday.

Brown Sugar, off Aquatic Gap next to the Island Inn in St. Michael (tel. 426-7684), is a beautiful al fresco dining room whose chefs prepare some of the tastiest Bajan specialties on the island. A friendly staff serves you. The island house is hidden behind lush foliage. The ceiling is latticed, with slow-turning ceiling fans. Two walls open onto a lower garden dining room, with white plastic molded chairs set under parasols. The other walls are in stained pine, and there's an open veranda for dining in a setting of profuse hanging plants. You eat by candlelight.

For an unusual and imaginative opening, try Salomon Grundy, a spicy-hot Jamaican favorite—a pâté of smoked herring, allspice, wine vinegar, onion, chives, and hot bonnie peppers, served with Jamaican water crackers. You might also prefer Bol Jol, a Trinidadian special of salted codfish, seasoned and served with pickled cucumber and lime tips. Among the soups, I suggest hot gungo-pea soup (pigeon peas cooked in chicken broth and zested with fresh coconut milk, herbs, and a touch of white wine). The price of the main course includes one of these appetizers, plus soup, vegetables, dessert, and coffee. Among the most recommendable main course, tandoori chicken is that North Indian classic which is equally popular in the southern Caribbean. Or perhaps you'd like crabmeat Carlisle, a mélange of flaked crabmeat, heavy cream, bread crumbs, local herbs and spices, heightened with a touch of brandy. A selection of locally grown fresh vegetables is offered nightly from the hot trolley, and you'll also be served a tossed green salad with a choice of dressing. For desserts, called confections here, I recommend the coconut cream mousse, which is smooth. You're faced with a $50 BDS ($24.50) or more dinner tab. Dining hours are 7 to 9:30 p.m. The restaurant is also known for it superb luncheon buffet, costing from $30 BDS ($14.75) per person and served Monday to Friday from noon to 2:30 p.m. Add another 18% for tax and service.

The **Witch Doctor,** St. Lawrence Gap, Christ Church (tel. 428-7856), hides behind a screen of thick foliage, across from another popular Barbadian eatery, the Pisces. There's a series of small dining rooms which open onto each other, with rustic wooden poles and shingled walls. Everything is decorated with African and island woodcarvings of witch doctors, in honor of its namesake. The place purveys a fascinating African and Bajan cuisine with some unusual concoctions which, even if unfamiliar, are very tasty and well prepared, a big change from a lot of the bland hotel fare. For an appetizer, try the split-pea and pumpkin soup. You'll also be offered kingfish shango (cold, soused in lime). All main dishes are served with rice. Chef's specialties include shrimp Créole, beef in wine, flying fish, lamb curry, kingfish, and chicken piri-piri (from Mozambique). Dinner, the only meal served here, should run about $30 BDS ($14.75). Hours are 6:15 to 10 p.m. every night.

Pisces, St. Lawrence Gap, Christ Church (tel. 428-6558), is a private cottage, painted olive green, right on the waterfront. The front garden is dominated by coconut trees, and the dining rooms extend along the water's edge. Cooled by sea breezes, you can enjoy fish and seafood in a setting that is rustic yet has a subdued Caribbean elegance. With a name like Pisces, you expect and get well-prepared Neptunian dishes, including the famous flying fish of Barbados, served here stuffed with herbs. I'm very fond of the chef's blackened dolphin, curried kingfish, and his lobster chasseur. Try also the grilled shrimp kebab, which on my latest rounds was flavored to perfection. The pepper chicken and deviled crab are also good. For dessert, I'd endorse the gooseberry coconut pie. Expect to spend around $50 BDS ($24.50) for a complete meal. Go for dinner only, between 6:30 and 9:30 p.m., and be sure to make a reservation.

Restaurant Germania, St. Lawrence Main Road, Christ Church (tel. 428-4537). Sitting on the rear veranda of this charming restaurant is somehow reminiscent of looking out from a balcony in Venice. A well-maintained West Indian clapboard house (which used to house the Bajan telephone exchange), the building is painted lime with cream trim. It's owned by a German/Bajan couple, Clyde and Helga Cox. They met in London years ago, then moved to Helga's hometown of Essen, Germany, before coming to Barbados to follow the career they both like best—running a restaurant. If you order a drink at the large curved bar in the front, Clyde won't stint on the whisky. The libation he'll set on the pine boards will be a stiff one, guaranteed to please even the most hardfisted drinker. However, it's after a visitor moves to one of the nine tables on the back veranda that the Coxes' skill as restauranteurs shows itself. Specialties range from German traditional dishes to Bajan seafood and include fish soup, goulash soup, wienerschnitzel, filet of dolphin, sirloin steak, and a savory pepperpot, served with rice and a salad. The restaurant is open for dinner from 6 to 11 p.m. daily except Sunday. Full meals cost from $50 BDS ($24.50) up. In high season it serves lunch, from 11:30 a.m. to 3 p.m.

La Cage aux Folles, Paynes Bay, St. James (tel. 432-1203), is the venture of Nick Hudson, who earned his fame when he worked at the popular Nick's Diner in London before coming to Barbados, where he was associated for a time with the Bagatelle Restaurant. In a "fit of madness," he decided to open this eatery, which takes its name from the noted French play and movie, later a successful Broadway musical, about two aging homosexuals on the Riviera. However, don't get the wrong idea. The place is aggressively straight, as a perusal of its wine list (with X-rated pictures) will reveal. The menu, with dinners costing from $75 BDS ($36.75), is a surprising combination of the French and Chinese cuisines. You may want to compose your meal from the repertoire of both those celebrated kitchens. I like the idea, having for years considered the Chinese and the French to be the finest cooks on earth. Perhaps you'll choose the sesame prawn pâté, breast of duck with Chinese spices, sweet-and-sour shrimp, or Créole fish soup. Other courses include a fresh fish of the day, Malaysian beef satay, and crêpes with seafood. Hours are 7 to 10 p.m. daily except Sunday.

The Virginian Restaurant, Hastings Main Road, Christ Church (tel. 427-7963), is known for its good home-cookery served in a restored manor house dating from the 18th century. It had deteriorated into a ruin before its owners rebuilt it along its original Georgian lines. Guests climb a flight of exterior stone steps to reach the high-ceilinged dining room where medallions in acanthus-leaved patterns look down on a wide-planked floor of tropical greenheart. Only dinner is served, nightly from 6 to 11 p.m., costing $30 per person, and reservations are suggested. Meals might include tenderloin steak pie, shrimp curry, fried flying fish, ragoût of beef, and house-style chicken.

During the day, if you're in the area you can have lunch at the **Tamarind Tree Club,** which adjoins the Virginian. Every day a luncheon special is featured for $15 BDS ($7.25), including soup, a main course, vegetable, and dessert or coffee. An à la carte menu is available as well. Service is from noon to 3 p.m.

The Ocean View, Hastings (tel. 427-7821), Barbados's oldest hostelry (previously recommended), also serves good food. The location is about a 5-minute drive from Bridgetown and some 15 minutes from the international airport. You will be shown to a table overlooking the sea on the south coast of the island. You can help yourself at the well-known Sunday planters' brunch, featuring, as was done in the olden days, a big spread with authentic Bajan specialties. Ernest Hemingway used to fill his plate high with flying fish and pepperpot, after having a big bowl of callaloo soup. The two Bajan head cooks have been at the hotel for some 30 years. Lunches are likely to cost from $20 BDS ($9.75) to $30 BDS ($14.75), and dinners go for about $55 BDS ($27), plus tax and service. Most recently my party of four enjoyed such dishes as roast chicken with a savory stuffing and fish fondue. There is always a changing list of daily specialties. Perhaps you'll begin with a chilled shrimp soup, finishing off your repast with a moist coconut cake. Breakfast is from 7 to 9 a.m.; lunch, from 12:30 to 2 p.m.; and dinner, from 7:15 to 9 p.m.

The **Captain's Carvery,** the Ship Inn, St. Lawrence Gap, Christ Church (tel. 428-9605). In a wing of my favorite pub in Barbados, this paneled restaurant is one of the most richly atmospheric of any place on the island. It's in a square, high-ceilinged room with an unused wooden balcony. The ambience is Old English, with lots of antique prints, thick paneling, and subdued lighting. Against one wall stands a uniformed carver who serves generous portions of meat and fowl to guests who line up for the heavily laden buffet table in the evening. Dinners go for a fixed price of $36 BDS ($17.75) and are served every day. You select from such specialties as pepperpot or a soup of the day, hot roasts with an array of sauces, a selection of cold cuts with homemade piccalilli, baked potatoes, a full range of green and vegetable salads, and several kinds of dessert. Lunch is less expensive, costing around $15 BDS ($7.25) for access to the buffet table. There is no uniformed carver, and the buffet selection is simpler. Still, at the price, it represents one of the best bargains in Barbados. Lunch is served from noon to 3 p.m. Monday to Saturday, and dinner is on from 6 p.m. to 2 a.m. daily.

Luigi's Restaurant, Dover Woods, St. Lawrence Gap (tel. 428-9218), is an open-air Italian trattoria with a Caribbean flavor. Since 1963 it has been operated in a well-maintained green-and-white house on a quiet road in the middle of a forest, making getting here somewhat of an expedition. Sue Chapman is the manager. From the rafters of this place are clustered hundreds of empty chianti bottles which, when a breeze blows, tinkle gently against one another like wind chimes. The dining areas include a shrub-lined veranda and several inside rooms, one of which prominently displays a map of Italy. Meals are prepared to order and may require as much as a 30-minute wait, but if at any time the conversation lags, you can always study the dozens of travel posters set edge to edge on many of the interior walls. This restaurant serves only dinner, opening its doors between 6 and 9:45 p.m. daily except Tuesday. Three fixed-price meals are offered, at $25 BDS ($12.25) per person. If ordering à la carte, count on spending from $50 BDS ($24.50). Both the fixed-price meals and the à la carte menus include such specialties as lasagne, spaghetti, shrimp cocktail, filet mignon, steak, chicken or shrimp cacciatora on rice, seafood casserole, grilled scampi with spaghetti, stuffed peppers and manicotti, and veal, chicken, and cheese cannelloni.

Waterfront Café, Cavans Lane, on the wharf of the Careenage, Bridgetown (tel. 427-0093), is an indoor/outdoor café, one of the best places to eat in town, set into a row of old warehouses on the harbor near the oldest bridge in town. Its long bar holds jars filled with pickled lemons, which everyone should try at least once. The clientele may include anyone from a Swedish yachtsman to a Jamaican Rasta. Nightly, local musicians play here, the music starting at 8 p.m. No one will mind if you occupy one of the iron chairs while you have a drink or two. Menu choices include curry, seafood, sesame chicken wings, pâté, flying fish, ceviche, gazpacho, and many local specialties. Dinners start at $15 BDS ($7.25) and lunches begin at $8 BDS ($4). The dining room is open from 8 a.m. to 11 p.m.

Peter the Fisherman, the Island Inn, Garrison, St. Michael (tel. 426-0057). Nestled between the reception area and a spacious bar room of this unpretentious hotel, you'll find a lattice-bordered restaurant whose tables are covered in immaculate napery. There's even a small reflecting pool at one end, near the tables crowded gregariously together. The menus here represent good value on an expensive island. À la carte dinners go for $35 BDS ($17.25), with simple but savory dishes—filet of red snapper Bajan style, steak platters, and roast chicken. Dinner is served from 6:30 to 10 p.m. seven days a week. One of the establishment's most popular events is the Monday-night Bajan buffet and cabaret, which costs $35 BDS ($17.25) per person. Music is played for dancing from 9 to 10:30 p.m., and a typical Bajan floor show is offered between 10:30 p.m. and midnight. If you attend only for the show, the charge is $10 BDS ($5), plus the cost of your drinks. The restaurant is on the road leading to the Barbados Hilton, across from the Grand Bay.

T.G.I. Boomers, St. Lawrence Gap (tel. 428-8439), offers some of the best bargain meals on the island. An American/Bajan operation, it stands across from the Maresol Apartment Hotel and has the largest and busiest lounge in Barbados, where music is presented in season during the happy hour. The cook prepares a special catch of the day, and the fish is served with soup or salad, rice or baked potato, and a vegetable. You can always count on seafood, steaks, and hamburgers. A two-egg breakfast with bacon, toast, and coffee costs $6.95 BDS ($3.50). For lunch, you might have a daily Bajan special or perhaps burgers, steak, shrimp, flying fish, or a jumbo sandwich. Expect to pay from $9 BDS ($4.50) to $10 BDS ($5). Dinners, depending on what you order, go for $19 BDS ($9.25) to $29 BDS ($14.25). Be sure to try one of the 16-ounce daiquiris, which come in six flavors. Breakfast is served daily except Saturday from 8 to 11 a.m.; lunch, from 11:30 a.m. to 3 p.m.; and dinner, from 6 to 9:30 p.m.

The Steak House, St. Lawrence Gap (tel. 428-7152), occupies a long-slung Antillean house whose encircling veranda is perfect for passing the afternoon in a rocking chair. Inside is a decor of exposed brick, russet colors, and armchairs covered in leather. The establishment is open only for dinner, every night from 5:30 to 10 p.m. A variety of U.S.-bred steaks are available, weighing between 10 and 16 ounces. Meals cost from $60 BDS ($29.50) and might include rib steak, strip loin, T-bone steak, filet mignon, and a handful of seafood dishes such as broiled lobster tail. The house offers a big salad bowl as well. Many diners start with onion soup, finishing with the chef's dessert specialty, a rum omelet.

3. Touring the Island

Barbados is worth exploring, either in your own car or else with a taxidriver guide. Unlike so many islands of the Caribbean, the roads are fair and quite passable. Usually they're well marked with crossroad signs. If you get lost, the people in the countryside are generally friendly and speak English.

Often hot and traffic clogged, the capital, **Bridgetown,** merits no more than a morning's shopping jaunt. An architectural hodgepodge, it was founded by 64 settlers sent out by the Earl of Carlisle in 1628.

You might begin your tour at the **Careenage,** from the French word meaning to turn vessels over on their side for cleaning. This was a haven for the clipper ship, and even though today it doesn't have its yesteryear color, it's still worth exploring. Maybe you'll see a "mauby woman" making her rounds. In colorful dress, she wends her way among the harbor traffic with her bittersweet brew called mauby. With one raised hand, she turns the tap from which the frothy liquid pours into a glass held in the other hand. Perhaps she no longer calls out "Get your mauby, sweet sweet mauby," as was done in the donkey and horse-drawn cart period. To make the drink, dried bark is imported from neighboring islands. The bark is boiled until the water is dark brown and very bitter. This is called bitters and is the base of the drink to which sweetening, essences, and spices are added.

Perhaps you'll also see a Bajan harbor policeman in his Nelsonian sailor suit, with a wide-brimmed straw hat and a blue-collared middy.

At **Trafalgar Square** the long tradition of British colonization is perhaps immortalized forever. The monument here, honoring Lord Nelson, was executed by Sir Richard Westmacott and erected in 1813. The **Public Buildings** on the square are of the great, gray Victorian Gothic variety that you might expect to find in South Kensington, London. The east wing contains the meeting halls of the Senate and the House of Assembly, with some stained-glass windows representing the sovereigns of England from James I to Queen Victoria. Look for the Great Protector himself, Oliver Cromwell.

Behind the Financial Building, **St. Michael's Cathedral** is the symbol of the Church of England transplanted. This Anglican church was built in 1655, but was completely destroyed in a 1780 hurricane. Reconstructed in 1789, it was also damaged by a hurricane in 1831, but was not completely demolished as before. George Washington is said to have worshipped here on his ill-fated Barbados visit.

Some guides will tell you that the 18th-century "George Washington House" on Upper Bay Street is the spot where the future American president stayed during his Barbados journey. Historians doubt this claim.

At this point you can hail a taxi and visit **Garrison Savannah,** just south of the capital. Cricket matches and other games are played in this open-air space of some 50 acres. Horse races are also held at certain times of the year.

The **Barbados Museum** (tel. 427-0201), housed in a former military prison, has extensive and varied collections including decorative and fine arts and natural history. The prehistory and history of the island are displayed in the remodeled Jubilee Gallery, while a fine collection of historic maps of the island, the earliest dating from 1657, can also be seen. The museum shop sells a variety of quality publications and handcrafts. The museum can be visited from 9 a.m. to 6 p.m. Monday to Saturday. It charges adults $4 BDS ($1.95); children, $1 BDS (50¢).

Nearby, the russet-red **St. Ann's Fort,** on the fringe of the Savannah, garrisoned British soldiers in 1694. The fort wasn't completed until 1703. The Clock House survived the hurricane of 1831.

After Bridgetown, you pass through the middle-class resorts of Hastings-,Rockley, Worthing, and St. Lawrence before arriving at **Oistin,** a former shipping port that today is a fishing village. Here the Charter of Barbados was signed at The Mermaid in 1652, as the island surrendered to Commonwealth forces. The inn, incidentally, was owned by a cousin of the John Turner who built the House of the Seven Gables in Salem, Massachusetts.

From here you can head on to **Sam Lord's Castle** (see my previous hotel recommendation). Although this is a hotel, it is also one of the major sightseeing attractions of Barbados. If you're not a guest, you'll have to pay $3 BDS ($1.50) to be admitted to the grounds. Built by slaves in 1820 and furnished with elegant Regency pieces, the house is like a Georgian plantation mansion. At the desk, you sign in and are then allowed to wander on your own, inspecting the paintings, silver, china, and antiques. Take note of the ornate ceilings, said to be the finest example of stucco work in the western hemisphere. At the entrance to the hotel are shops selling handcrafts and souvenirs.

In the neighboring section, you can visit **Ragged Point Lighthouse,** built in 1885 on a rugged cliff. Since then the beacon has gone out as a warning to ships approaching the dangerous reef, called "The Cobblers." The view from here is spectacular.

Continuing north along the jagged Atlantic coast, you reach **Codrington College,** which opened in 1745. A cabbage-palm-lined avenue leads to old coral block buildings, and on the grounds you can enjoy a picnic lunch. Today the gray stone buildings are the home of the teaching Order of the Resurrection.

Before getting back on the coast road, ask in the neighborhood for directions to **St. John's Church,** perched on the edge of a cliff opening on the east coast, some 825 feet above sea level. The church dates from 1836 and in its graveyard rests a descendant of Emperor Constantine the Great, whose family was driven from the throne in Constantinople (Istanbul) by the Turks. He died in Barbados in 1678.

While in the area, you can go to **Villa Nova** (tel. 433-1524), built in 1834, a fine sugar plantation great house, furnished with period antiques in Barbadian mahogany and set in six acres of beautifully landscaped gardens, featuring wild orchids, flowering shrubs, and tropical fruit trees. It's open from 10 a.m. to 4 p.m. Monday to Friday, charging $5 BDS ($2.45) for admission. The house was once owned by Sir Anthony Eden, Earl of Avon, the former prime minister of Great Britain. The earl and his countess had as their guests in 1966 Queen Elizabeth and Prince Philip, who planted two portlandias which still grow in the gardens. To reach the place, take Hwy. 3B toward St. John's Church, but turn left by the fire station at Four Cross Roads, toward Mt. Tabor Church. Go less than a mile before turning left again. Almost immediately turn right, and up the hill you'll see the entrance.

Before the day is over, if you move fast enough, you can also visit **Andromeda Gardens** (tel. 433-9454). On a cliff overlooking Bathsheba on the rugged east coast, limestone boulders make for a natural eight-acre rock-garden setting, where thousands of orchids are in bloom in the open air every day of the year along with hundreds of hibiscus and heliconia. Other plants are more seasonal, including the flamboyant and frangipani, jade vine and bougainvillea, lipstick tree, candlestick tree, mammee apple, and many more. My favorite is a rare jade vine from the Philippines with its blue-green flowers. Many varieties of ferns, bromeliads, and other species that are house plants in temperate climates grow here in splendid profusion. A section is a palm garden, with more than 100 species. A simple guide helps visitors to identify many of the plants. The garden was started in 1954 by the present owner, Mrs. Iris Bannochie, on land that had belonged to her family for more than 200 years. On the grounds you'll occasionally see frogs, herons, guppies, and sometimes a mongoose or a monkey. Charging $4 BDS ($1.95) for admission, the gardens are open daily.

From the gardens, you can drive to the **Cotton Tower,** one of a chain of old landmark signal stations. English soldiers used these towers to warn when enemy ships were sighted along the coast. As the top of the tower is 1,000 feet above sea level, you'll have a panoramic view of the eastern sector of Barbados. Admission is $2 BDS ($1). It's open seven days a week from 9 a.m. to 5 p.m.

In the same area, **Hackleton's Cliff** also rises to a height of 1,000 feet, giving you another view of the rugged Atlantic coast. The attraction and the view were described in the book *Cradle of the Deep* by Sir Frederick Treves.

Finally, you reach **Bathsheba,** the leading town along the east coast, where ocean rollers break, forming cascades of white foam. The same Sir Frederick compared this place to a "Cornwall in miniature." Today the old fishing village is a favorite resort among Bajans.

For the best dining choice in the area, refer to the previously recommended Atlantic Hotel.

The trail north from Bathsheba takes in the **East Coast Road** which runs for many miles with views of the Atlantic. Chalky Mount rises from the beach to 500 feet, forming a trio of peaks, and a little to the south, Barclays Park is a 15-acre natural wonder presented as a gift to the country by the banking people. There's a snackbar and picnic place here.

Stopping on the western side of Chalky Mount, you can visit Chalky Mount School, going out to see the **Potteries,** where potters turn out different products, some based on designs centuries old.

Back on the north trail, you can see and perhaps take a picture of **Morgan Lewis Mill,** the only windmill remaining in Barbados with its arms and wheelhouses intact. The sight may remind you of the countryside of Holland. You can go inside for $2 BDS ($1). It's open seven days a week from 9 a.m. to 5 p.m.

The view from the top of **Cherry Tree Hill,** on Hwy. 1, is the finest in Barbados. You can look right down the eastern shore past Bathsheba to the lighthouse at Ragged Point, already described. The place is about 850 feet above sea level, and from its precincts you'll see out over "Little Scotland." The cherry trees from which the hill got its name no longer stand there, having given way to mahogany.

Most visitors to the area have come to go through **Farley Hill National Park,** which was used in the filming of *Island in the Sun.* The movie is now largely forgotten by the world, but it is still talked about a lot in Barbados. Paying $2 BDS ($1) per car to enter the park, you can explore the grounds and gracious ruins from 8:30 a.m. to 6 p.m. seven days a week. The filmmakers partially restored the shell of this once great house, but another fire destroyed the Hollywood remake. The older section of the estate dates from 1818. Queen Elizabeth opened it as a national park in 1966.

The **Barbados Wildlife Refuge,** a project operated by the Primate Research Center in Bethesda, is in a lush mahogany forest across the road from Farley Hill National Park. From 10 a.m. to 5 p.m. daily, for an admission charge of $5 BDS ($2.45) for adults (half price for children under 12), you can stroll freely through what is primarily a monkey sanctuary. You can watch the uncaged monkeys of Barbados in their natural setting. Visitors can also see other Barbadian fauna on their home grounds, including wild hares, deer, tortoises, caymans, and a variety of tropical birds. For information, call 422-8826.

From Farley Hill you can head due west to **Speightstown,** which was founded around 1635 and for a time was a whaling port. The "second city" of Barbados, the town has some colonial buildings constructed after the devastating hurricane of 1831. The parish church, rebuilt in a half-Grecian style after the hurricane, is one of the places of interest. Its chancel rail is of carved mahogany.

South from Speightstown is what is known as the **Platinum Coast,** the protected western shoreline which opens onto the gentler Caribbean. Along the shoreline of the parishes of St. James and St. Peter are found the island's plushest hotels, which I've already previewed. Assorted British peers and an occasional movie actress live in mansions along the coast with its excellent white and pink sandy beaches.

Holetown is the center of the coast, taking its name from the town of Hole on the Thames River. Here the first English settlers landed in the winter of 1627. An obelisk marks the spot where the *Olive Blossom* landed the first Europeans. The monument, for some reason, lists the date erroneously as 1605.

Nearby **St. James Church** is Anglican, rebuilt in 1872 on the site of the early settlers' church of 1660. In the southern porch is an old bell, bearing the inscription "God Bless King William, 1696."

Take Hwy. 2 from Bridgetown and follow it to **Welchman Hall Gully,** in St. Thomas, a lush tropical garden owned by the Barbados National Trust. Here are to be found some specimens of plants that were here when the English settlers landed in 1647. Many of the plants are labeled—clove, nutmeg, tree fern, and cocoa among others—and occasionally you'll spot a wild monkey. Here you'll see a ravine and limestone stalactites and stalagmites, as well as breadfruit trees which are claimed to be descended from the seedlings brought ashore by Captain Bligh of the *Bounty*. Admission is $4 BDS ($1.95). It's open seven days a week from 9 a.m. to 5 p.m.

I also suggest a visit to **St. Nicholas Abbey** (tel. 422-8725), the Jacobean plantation great house and sugarcane fields which have been around since 1640. It was never an abbey. An ambitious owner in about 1820 simply christened it as such. More than 200 acres are still cultivated each year. In the parish of St. Peter, the structure—at least the ground floor—is open to the public Monday through Friday from 10 a.m. to 3:30 p.m., charging an admission of $5 BDS ($2.45) per person. The house is believed to be one of three Jacobean houses in the western hemisphere, and it's characterized by curved gables. Lt.-Col. Stephen Cave, the owner, is descended from the family who purchased the sugar plantation and great house in 1810. A movie made in 1934 with scenes of Barbados is shown at 11:30 a.m. and at 2:30 p.m. daily. Light refreshments are offered for sale.

Harrison's Cave at Welchman Hall in the parish of St. Thomas is the number one tourist attraction in Barbados, offering visitors a chance to view this beautiful natural underground world from aboard an electric tram and trailer. Before the tour, a color slide show of the cave is given in the presentation hall. During the tour, visitors see bubbling streams, tumbling cascades, and deep pools which are subtly lit, while all around stalactites hang overhead like icicles and stalagmites rise from the floor. Tours are daily from 9 a.m. to 4 p.m. except on Christmas, Good Friday, and Easter Sunday. You should book in advance by calling 432-6640. Admission is $10 BDS ($4.90).

The **Flower Forest,** St. Thomas (tel. 433-8152), at Richmond Plantation, a mile from Harrison's Cave, is a recently established, 50-acre area dedicated to preserving and encouraging growth of the flowering shrubs, ferns, and trees native to the tropics, together with plantation crops on which the island's economy was once based. Richmond is an old sugar plantation with magnificent views of the Atlantic. The ruins are a relic of sugar cultivation. Local handcrafts and fresh fruit are available, as well as light refreshments. Hours are 9 a.m. to 5 p.m., and you can stay as long as you like. Admission is $6 BDS ($2.95).

Scattered attractions on the island include the following:

Morgan Lewis Sugar Windmill and Museum, St. Andrew, is typical of the wind-driven mills that crushed the juice from the sugarcane in the 17th to the 19th centuries, producing sugar that made Barbados Britain's most valuable possession in the Americas. It was from the Barbados sugarcane that rum was first produced. To reach the mill on the northeast coast of the island, follow Hwy. 1 past Farley Hill National Park to Hwy. 2. The mill and museum are open Monday through Saturday from 9 a.m. to 5 p.m. Admission is $2 for adults, $1 for children under 14.

The 300-year-old **Sunbury House,** on Hwy. 5, has been turned by its owners, Mr. and Mrs. Keith Melville, into a museum showing how a family home looked in other days, with many Barbadian antiques in their collection. A feature also is a collection of old horse-drawn vehicles used in daily living in a bygone era. You may visit it from 10 a.m. to 4 p.m. Monday to Friday. Admission is $6 BDS ($2.95) per person. The Melvilles are also horse lovers, and visitors are invited to see the ponies in the stable yard.

Gun Hill Signal Station, one of two such stations owned and operated by the Barbados National Trust, is strategically placed on the highland of St. George. It commands a magnificent view from the east to the west. Built in 1818, it was the finest of a chain of signal stations and was also used as an outpost for the British army stationed here at the time. Take Hwy. 3 from Bridgetown and then go inland from Hwy. 4 toward St. George Church. Open Monday through Friday from 9 a.m. to 5 p.m., it can be visited by adults for $2, and children under 14 pay $1.

Ronald Tree House, 2 Tenth Ave., Belleville, is the headquarters of the Barbados National Trust. Built in 1893, it's an example of a typical Victorian Barbadian house. It is decorated with authentic furniture and objets d'art of that period and is open to the public one afternoon a week. Hostesses dressed in Victorian costume will show you around. Check the day of opening during your visit in the local press. Hours are 2:30 to 5:30 p.m. Admission is $4.

4. Where to Shop

Barbados merchants can sometimes treat you to duty-free merchandise at prices 20% to 40% lower than in the United States and Canada. Duty-free shops have two prices listed on items of merchandise, the local retail price and the local retail price less the government-imposed tax.

Some of the best duty-free buys include cameras (such as Leica, Rolex, and Fiji), watches (names like Omega, Piaget, Seiko), beautiful crystal (such as Waterford and Lalique), gold (especially jewelry), bone china (such names as Wedgwood and Royal Doulton), cosmetics and perfumes, and liquor (including Barbados rum and liqueurs), along with tobacco products and cashmere sweaters, tweeds, and sportswear from Britain.

The outstanding item in Barbados handcrafts is black coral jewelry made into attractive earrings, pendants, and rings. Clay pottery is another Bajan craft. In the touring section I recommend a visit to Chalky Mount and the Potteries, where this special craft originated. In Barbados you'll find a selection of locally made vases, pots, pottery mugs, glazed plates, and ornaments.

From local grasses and dried flowers, beautiful wall hangings are made, and the island craftspeople also turn out straw mats, baskets, and bags with raffia embroidery. Still in its infant stage, leatherwork is also found now in Barbados, particularly items such as handbags, belts, and sandals.

Shopping hours, in general are 8 a.m. to 4 p.m. Monday to Friday and 8 a.m. to noon on Saturday.

The best place to shop for duty-free items is **Cave Shepherd,** Broad Street in Bridgetown (tel. 426-3451), with branches at Sunset Crest, Speightstown, Hastings, and the Grantley Adams Airport. This is the largest department store in Barbados. One of the most modern such stores in the Caribbean, it was established back in 1906. After it was demolished in 1969, it went public in 1971. Up to then the Cave family had completely owned it, but was finally joined by the financial assistance of more than 2,000 Bajans. The department store offers visitors the widest selection in Barbados of duty-free merchandise from all over the world, including select perfumes and cosmetics, liquor from more than 70 famous names, Swiss watches, gold and silver jewelry, Pringle woolens, Daks slacks, and Caribbean-made dashikis, plus an extensive range of Japanese cameras and photographic equipment. In addition, it has a handcraft department, with Barbados-made items in straw, black coral, or white coral.

While in Bridgetown, go down to the **Pelican Village** on Princess Alice Hwy., leading down to the city's Deep Water Harbour. A collection of island-made crafts and souvenirs is sold here in a tiny colony of thatch-roofed shops, and you can wander from one to the other. Sometimes you can see craftspeople at work. Some of the shops to be found here are gimmicky and repetitive, although interesting items can be found.

Batik Caribe sells original hand-dyed batik in a number of outlets—at Gulf House on Broad Street in Bridgetown, at the Hilton Arcade, and at Marriott's Sam Lord's Castle. You are also welcome to visit their studio at the Colleton Estate in St. John where you can see craftspeople working at this ancient art. Original scarfs, wall hangings, Pareos dresses, jumpsuits, bikinis, and shirts are sold, among other items.

Bridgetown's newest shopping area, **Mall 34,** on Broad Street, offers duty-free shopping in air-conditioned comfort. You can find watches, clocks, china, jewelry, crystal, linens, sweaters, and liquor, together with souvenir items and tropical fashions. A restaurant is on the top floor of the building, and shoppers can stop for a cool drink and a snack at the little café downstairs.

For a fine selection of Caribbean items, go to **Caribbean Creations,** Bridge

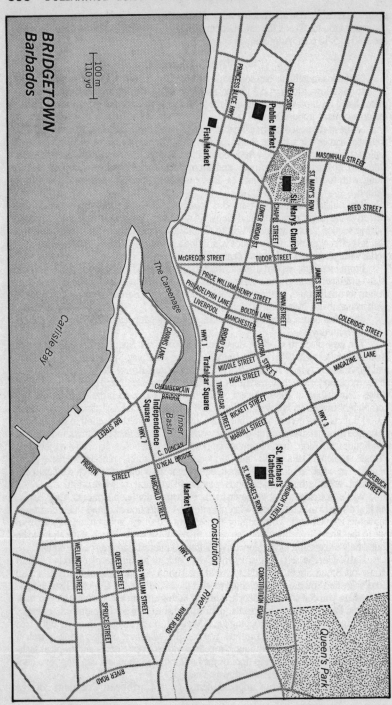

BRIDGETOWN
Barbados

100 m
110 yd

Carlisle Bay

The Careenage

Fish Market

Public Market

PRINCESS ALICE HWY.

CHEAPSIDE

MASONHALL STREET

ST. MARY'S ROW

St. Mary's Church

REED STREET

LOWER BROAD ST.

CHAPEL STREET

McGREGOR STREET

TUDOR STREET

JAMES STREET

COLERIDGE STREET

PRICE WILLIAM HENRY STREET

PHILADELPHIA LANE

LIVERPOOL

BOLTON LANE

MANCHESTER

SWAN STREET

VICTORIA STREET

MAGAZINE LANE

BROAD ST.

HWY 1

MIDDLE STREET

HIGH STREET

Trafalgar Square

TRAFALGAR STREET

CAWINS LANE

CHAMBERLAIN BRIDGE

Independence Square

Inner Basin

RICKETT STREET

MARHILL STREET

HWY 3

BAY STREET

HWY 7

C. DUNCAN

O'NEAL BRIDGE

PROBIN STREET

FAIRCHILD STREET

Market

St. Michael's Cathedral

ST. MICHAEL'S ROW

CHURCH STREET

ROEBUCK STREET

Constitution River

WELLINGTON STREET

QUEEN STREET

KING WILLIAM STREET

SPRUCE STREET

HWY 6

RIVER ROAD

CONSTITUTION ROAD

Queen's Park

RIVER ROAD

House, Careenage, Bridgetown (tel. 427-0611). You'll find baskets, mahogany carvings, mats, bags, and other souvenirs.

Antiquaria, St. Michael's Row, Bridgetown (tel. 426-0635), is a shop I often visit for the collection of maps and prints of the West Indies. However, they also specialize in china, brass, glassware, old bottles and boxes, and some choice English antiques, including furniture, plus Barbadian furnishings and furniture. They also ship.

Harrison's, whose main shop is at 1 Broad St., Bridgetown (tel. 426-0720), has a wide variety of duty-free merchandise, including china, crystal, jewelry, luggage, fashions, perfumes—what have you. They've been in business since the 19th century.

Sea Nymph Dress Shoppe, at the Skyway Shopping Plaza in Hastings, South Coast (tel. 429-4242), specializes in swimwear (if you forgot your bathing suit), hostess gowns, blouses, shorts, slacks, and dresses made to order.

The Loomhouse, Skyway Plaza, Hastings, Christ Church (tel. 426-0442), is one of the showcases for the hand-weaving work of Roslyn of Barbados, a talented Barbadian artist and designer. On the outskirts of Bridgetown, this craft boutique displays work by Roslyn Watson. The government of Barbados has selected some of her pieces to present to such dignitaries as the former Canadian prime minister, Pierre Trudeau. Works by other craftspeople are displayed, in mahogany, clay, and straw. There is also a collection of coral.

Artemis, the Green Chattel House, corner of St. Matthias and Hastings Main Road, Christ Church (tel. 436-3216), has a pleasing selection of hand-painted and hand-dyed designs, local art and antiques, ceramics, shell jewelry, and souvenirs.

At **Da Costas,** Sunset Crest, St. James (tel. 432-1600), you'll find fine china, Waterford crystal, and Lladró and Capodimonte figurines at duty-free prices. The range of merchandise also includes French fragrances, cashmere, merino, and lamb's wool items, as well as local mahogany sculpture.

Best of Barbados, Southern Palms Hotel, St. Lawrence Gap (tel. 428-7171), is perhaps the most attractive of an islandwide chain of stores selling only products crafted in Barbados. It was established in 1975 by an English-born painter, Jill Walker, and her husband, Jimmy. Today the day-to-day administration of the boutiques is handled by their daughter, Sarah, an accountant. They sell articles celebrating aspects of island life, including needlepoint pillows, blackface dolls, coasters and placemats with scenes of Bajan life, steel-band recordings, calendars, and recipe books. This tasteful place is in a pink-and-white building around the corner from the entrance to the Southern Palms Hotel. It's open daily from 9 a.m. to 3 p.m.

5. The Sporting Life

The principal activity is swimming and sunning, which, as has been discussed, is far preferable on the western coast in the clear, buoyant waters, yet you may also want to visit the surf-pounded east. These Atlantic waters, however, might be better for viewing than swimming, because, as I've pointed out, they can be dangerous.

BEACHES: Barbadians will tell you that their island has a beach for every day in the year, and if you're there long enough you may be able to seek them out. If you're only visiting for a shorter time, however, you'll probably be happy with the ones that are easy to find. They're all open to the public, even those in front of the big resort hotels and private homes. The government requires that there be access to all beaches, via roads along the property line or through the hotel entrance. The beaches on the west, the so-called **Platinum Coast,** are the most popular. These include Paradise Beach, Paynes Bay and Sandy Lane Bay, Treasure Beach, Gibbs Bay, Heywoods Beach, Rockley, and Benson Beach. To reach the ones on the east, drive through the cane fields to **North Point, Cove Bay,** or **Archer's Bay,** or head down to the beautiful but more perilous one at **Bathsheba.** Crane Bay, Tent Bay, Long Bay—I could go on and on, but perhaps you'll try them all and then find your own.

SNORKELING AND SCUBA: The clear waters off Barbados have a visibility of more than 100 feet most of the year. More than 50 varieties of fish are found on the shallow inside reefs. On night dives, sleeping fish, night anemones, lobsters, moray eels, and octopi can be seen. On a mile-long coral reef two minutes by boat from **Sandy Beach,** sea fans, corals, gorgonias, and reef fish are plentiful. *J.R.,* a dredge barge sunk as an artificial reef in 1983, is popular with beginners for its coral, fish life, and 20-foot depth. The *Berwyn,* a coral-encrusted tugboat that sank in Carlisle Bay in 1916, attracts photographers because of its variety of reef fish, shallow depth, good light, and visibility.

The **Asta Reef,** with a drop of 80 feet, has coral, sea fans, and reef fish in abundance. It's the site of a Barbados wreck sunk in 1986 as an artificial reef. **Dottins,** the most beautiful reef on the west coast, stretches five miles from Holetown to Bridgetown and has numerous dive sites at an average depth of 40 feet and dropoffs of 100 feet. The S.S. *Stavronika,* a Greek freighter, is a popular dive site for advanced divers. Crippled by fire in 1976, the 360-foot freighter was sunk a quarter-mile off the west coast to become an artificial reef in **Folkstone Underwater Park.** The mast is at 40 feet, the deck at 80 feet, and the keel at 140 feet. It's starting to become encrusted with coral.

The Dive Shop, Pebbles Beach, Aquatic Gap, Bay Street, St. Michael (tel. 426-9947), offers some of the best scuba-diving in Barbados (costing about $33 each). Each day two dive trips go out to the nearby reefs and wrecks. In addition, snorkeling trips and equipment rentals are possible. A one-hour trip to a shipwreck with equipment goes for $8.

Willie's Water Sports, Paradise Beach Hotel (tel. 425-1060), operates out of a wooden building near the beach. Open seven days a week, it offers a wide array of water-related activities that are free to residents of the Paradise Beach Hotel.

Sandy Beach Water Sports, Worthing, Christ Church (tel. 428-9033, ext. 270), takes guests, both resident and nonresident, on scuba-diving trips to reef and wrecks in both shallow and deep water.

Peter Hughes Underwater Barbados, St. Lawrence Gap (tel. 428-3504), is a branch in the wide-flung diving empire of Scottish entrepreneur Peter Hughes. In a wood-sided shed across the street from a sheltered bay, it is said to be the largest scuba facility on the island.

WINDSURFING: Experts say that the windsurfing off Bentson Beach is as good as any this side of Hawaii. Judging from the crowds of 20- to 35-year-olds who flock here, it's probably true. An establishment set up especially to handle the demand is the **Barbados Windsurfing Club,** Bentson Beach, Maxwell, Christ Church (tel. 428-9095). It rents boards and gives lessons to learners. Club Mistral, a company run by Mistral A.G. of Switzerland, manufacturer of the finest windsurfing boards in the world, provides the rental fleet for the Barbados facility. This fleet consists of up to 75 boards, all current models with a selection of 200 sails.

PARASAILING: The excitement of parasailing is offered by **Jolly Roger Watersports,** St. James Beach, Sunset Crest, for $40 BDS ($19.50) per person per sail. With parachute in place, you're lifted into the air from a takeoff raft and pulled through the air at about 80 to 100 feet high by a fast boat. Your sail ends as you are lowered (usually gently) back onto the raft.

GOLF: Your best bet is the **Sandy Lane Hotel Golf Club,** St. James, on the west coast (tel. 432-1311).

A nine-hole executive course is at the **Rockley Resort Hotel,** Golf Club Road, Worthing, Christ Church (tel. 427-5896).

At the **Heywoods Resort,** St. Peter (tel. 422-4900), there is a popular nine-hole golf course.

TENNIS: Most of the major hotels have their own tennis courts, some of which are lit for night games. Generally, if you're not a guest, these hotels charge anywhere from $12BDS ($5.85) to $16 BDS ($7.85) per hour of court time.

At **Rockley Resort,** Christ Church (tel. 427-5890), courts are open from 8 a.m. to 10 p.m.

At **Heywoods Resort,** St. Peter (tel. 422-4900), the courts are in play from 7 a.m. to 11 p.m.

You can play at the **Sunset Crest Club,** St. James (tel. 432-1309), from 8 a.m. to 11 p.m.

HORSEBACK RIDING: A different view of Barbados is offered by **Valley Hill Riding Stables,** Woodbourne, Christ Church (tel. 423-0033). Trail riding in the countryside provides an hour's trip through plantations escorted by experienced guides, followed by relaxation over a cool drink in the clubroom. Experienced riders can follow more varied trails. Instruction is given to newcomers. The price, including transportation to and from your hotel and a complimentary drink, is $40 BDS ($19.50).

DEEP-SEA FISHING: The fishing is first-rate in the waters around Barbados, where fishermen pursue dolphin, marlin, wahoo, barracuda, and sailfish, to name only the most popular catches. There's also an occasional cobia.

The Dive Shop, Pebbles Beach, Aquatic Gap, Bay Street, St. Michael (tel. 426-9947), can arrange half-day charters for one to six persons (all equipment and drinks included), costing $180 per boat. Under the same arrangement, the whole-day jaunt goes for $360. In other words, no discount.

Sandy Beach, Worthing, Christ Church (tel. 428-9033), offers deep-sea fishing on either *Jolly Jumper* or *Jolly Mariner,* two luxury-class cabin cruisers. You can fish for wahoo, dolphin, marlin, sailfish, yellow-fin tuna, barracuda, and bonito. Rates are $35 per person for party fishing, $400 BDS ($196) for private bookings, per half day. All charters have a maximum of six people per trip, and the rates include ground transportation, soft drinks, rum, and beer. A sandwich lunch is provided on full-day charters.

BOAT TRIPS: For cruising fun in Barbados, the *Bajan Queen* (tel. 436-2149), offers daytime trips and sunset voyages. For the water fun cruise on Tuesday and Thursday, leaving at 10:30 a.m. and returning at 3 p.m., free water sports, including snorkeling, swimming, diving, and rope swinging into the water are on the program. Optional waterskiing, jet-skiing, Hobie Cat sailing, and parasailing can also be engaged in. A lunch of barbecued steak, chicken, or fresh local fish and a free bar are included in the cost of $55 BDS ($27) per person. Calypso music is played on this and the sunset cruise, leaving at 5 p.m. and returning at 9 p.m. on Wednesday and Saturday, costing $60 BDS ($29.50). Besides the same feast as on the daytime trip, guests can participate in a calypso dancing contest under the stars.

Another popular cruise is aboard the *Jolly Roger,* a full-size replica of a fighting ship. Aboard the vessel, you can enjoy drinks from an open bar, a full steak barbecue lunch, and nonstop music for dancing on the spacious sundeck. Later the boat stops at a sheltered cove where passengers can put on their bathing suits and go for a swim. Lunch cruises are from 10 a.m. to 2 p.m. Tuesday to Friday. At night passengers cruise and dance to the sounds of top local singing groups (in season only). The cost is $65 BDS ($31.75) for the day cruise, $75 BDS ($36.75) at night, both prices including meals. Night cruises are Thursday and Saturday from 6 to 10 p.m. For information, telephone 436-6424, or visit the berth at Cavans Lane in Bridgetown.

In addition, most of the big hotels have Sunfish and Hobie Cat craft for rent, costing $30 BDS ($14.75) to $50 BDS ($24.50) per hour for one or two passengers.

6. After Dark in Barbados

Most of the big resort hotels feature entertainment nightly, often dancing to steel bands and occasional native floor shows. Sometimes beach barbecues are staged. Otherwise, here's the lineup.

The best place to head if you're in Barbados on a Thursday or Sunday is **1627 And All That Sort of Thing** at the Barbados Museum in St. Michael's Parish (tel. 435-6900 for reservations). The shows, at 7:30 and 10:30 p.m., are a historical celebration of Barbadian culture. At the museum, once a British military prison, the evening features a traditional Bajan buffet dinner, with a liqueur, followed by a folk-dance extravaganza by the Barbados Dance Theatre Company. For the price of $65 BDS ($32), tax included, you are transported to and from the museum and are allowed to tour the exhibits. The drinks and hors d'oeuvres are complimentary as well. For your money, this is one of the best after-dark bargains in town, and you'll learn a lot as well as have fun.

The best dinner show on the island is **Barbados! Barbados!,** a two-act musical comedy based on the life of one of the island's most colorful characters, Rachel Pringle. She was a sort of Bajan Polly Adler. This spectacular is staged every Tuesday in the Barbados Horticultural Society, original Boiling House at Balls Estate, Christ Church (tel. 435-6900 for reservations). The price of $65 BDS ($32) includes transportation to and from your hotel, hors d'oeuvres, complimentary drinks all evening, government tax, the show, and dinner. Hours are 6:30 and 10 p.m.

The **Plantation Restaurant,** Hwy. 7, St. Lawrence (tel. 428-5048), stages two of the most popular dinner shows on the island. Every Tuesday the internationally known Merrymen perform their latest hits, and you can also see a Barbadian floor show featuring one of the island's top steel bands together with limbo dancing and fire-eating. The buffet dinner starts at 7 p.m. and show time is 8:30 p.m. On nights when shows are staged, the cost, including dinner, is $65 BDS ($32). On Wednesday and Saturday, the **Plantation Tropical Spectacular** is staged, a colorful cabaret dinner show with a cast of 30 dancers in scenes from the old marketplace, the mysteries of voodoo, and the splendor and excitement of carnival. A steel band provides dinner music. The dinner show, costing $32.50 (U.S.), is from 6 to 9:30 p.m. A Monday-night dinner show, **Barbados by Night,** features a group called Spice, with pop, reggae, and calypso music, plus costume dancers, limbo, and fire-eating. The price of the show, which starts at 7 p.m., is $27.50 (U.S.), including dinner, the show, drinks, and tax.

The **Flambeau Bar,** at the Barbados Hilton on Needham's Point, St. Michael (tel. 462-0200), is an indoor-outdoor place where you can enjoy your drinks under the stars, at tables around the dance floor, in intimate nooks, or at the large bar that extends to the outdoor terrace. The bar is open from 5 p.m. to 1 a.m. daily, and happy hour, with free appetizers, is from 5:30 to 7 p.m. Live music is presented nightly, varying from small groups to solo entertainers.

The **Odyssey** nightclub, Palmetto Square (tel. 436-7455), offers entertainment for its customers on weekends, with a DJ in charge except when there's a live performance. On Thursday, at $5 per person, music starts at 9 p.m. Friday at 9 p.m. a live combo is the attraction, and admission is $10. Saturday hours are 10 p.m. to 5 a.m., $10 admission; and on Sunday, you can enter at 7 p.m. for $5. There's a dress code: no hats, shorts, armholes (men), slippers, sneakers, or track shoes.

For late wining, dining, dancing, and entertainment, try **Night Club Xanadu,** Ocean View Hotel, Hastings, Christ Church (tel. 427-7821). Downstairs at the hotel, you can enjoy watching a repertory company of some of the top cabaret performers of Barbados while you dine in an old-world atmosphere or just sip drinks. Admission is

$6, with a $12 cover charge for the show. The club is open from Wednesday to Saturday, with a seafood buffet served Thursday night. Dinner is from 8 to 10:30 p.m., and the club closes at 1 a.m. Reservations are recommended.

Club Miliki, Heywoods, St. Peter (tel. 422-4900), plays disco music every evening except Sunday and Monday. There's a $12 BDS ($5.85) entrance charge, after which a beer costs $3 BDS ($1.50). The disco is in one of the many buildings (just follow the trail markers) at the government's Heywoods Resort, covered separately in the hotels section of this chapter.

The **Apple Experience,** Hastings Main Road, Christ Church (tel. 436-7604), is open Thursday to Sunday, featuring calypso, disco, golden oldies, what have you. Admission is free for women; Men pay $5 on Thursday and Sunday and until 11:30 p.m. on Friday and Saturday. A barbecue plus entertainment is a popular attraction from 1 to 5 p.m. on Sunday. Closing is according to the crowd.

Belair Jazz Club, Bay Street, Bridgetown (tel. 436-1664), is reputed to have been the leading jazz club in Barbados for the past 30 years, but it's so unpretentious in appearance from the street that you can miss it if you're not careful. It's inside a frame house near the center of town and affords some of the best listening on the island. Since it was remodeled in 1984 many Bajans claim the interior has lost its allure, but you'd never know it by the crowds of people who still come here. Sunday is steel-band night, but the rest of the week, beginning at 10 p.m. daily, the place welcomes both local and imported jazz talent. Beer costs $3 BDS ($1.50). It's a difficult place to park anywhere near. Closed Monday.

If you're in Barbados on a Thursday night, one of the most enjoyable evenings is to go to the **Barbados Hilton,** on Needham's Point, St. Michael (tel. 426-0200). There, a "night of the buccaneers" is staged at the old fort. Dinner is at 7 p.m., a floor show at 8:30 p.m. The Bajan cuisine features roast suckling pig, barbecued spareribs, and grilled fish. The show that follows is lively. The cost is most reasonable as well: $56 BDS ($27.50) for adults, $30 BDS ($14.75) for children.

A PUB CRAWL: A favorite of mine is **The Coach House,** Paynes Bay, St. James (tel. 432-1163). Fittingly, there are two antique coaches sitting on the lawn of this ochre-colored house which the owners say is 200 years old. Looking at it from the outside, it's difficult to guess the building's age because of its recently added veranda. However, once you're inside under the ceiling beams, the atmosphere is very much that of an English pub. Business people and habitués of the nearby beaches enjoy this establishment's buffet lunches, where Bajan food is served daily except Saturday from noon to 3 p.m. The price is $14 BDS ($6.75) per person for an all-you-can-eat assortment of chicken, baked fish, salads, and local vegetables. If you drop in between 6 and 11 p.m., you can accompany your drinks with bar meals such as flying fish and chips or chicken in a basket plus a fresh salad for a top $15 BDS ($7.25) per person. There's also a more formal evening dining room on a lower floor, where fixed-price meals, excluding service and drinks, cost $38 BDS ($18.50). Menu specialties include pâté with brandy, homemade soup, beef braised in beer, fish Créole, and chicken béchamel. Even if you don't want to eat, you can enjoy drinks here. Live music is presented almost every night, featuring everything from steel bands to country to calypso. The pub is on the main Bridgetown–Holetown road just south of Sandy Lane.

The **Ship Inn,** St. Lawrence Gap, Christ Church (tel. 428-9605), contains an attractive rough decor of dark ceiling beams, ship engravings, scattered banquettes accented with touches of gilt, and muted ship lanterns casting soft shadows. The large curved bar is peopled with handsome yacht owners and crews, local teenagers, and foreign trendsetters. Many guests come for the darts, others for the drinks, and still others for meeting friends and/or enjoying the live music on Wednesday, Friday, and Saturday night. On weekends and late on weeknights the place is sometimes packed with diplomats and other VIPs (including the Bajan prime minister), as well as visiting sailors from the various navies that come into port here. The inn is both a pub and a restaurant, serving such food as steak-and-kidney pie, "bangers and mash," shepherd's pie, and flying fish and chips, brought to you by youthful bar helpers wearing shirts emblazoned with the word "crew." Full meals cost from $12. More substantial meals are served in the Captain's Carvery, reached through a passageway. The inn is open from 6 p.m. to 2 a.m.

Chapter XV

TRINIDAD AND TOBAGO

1. Hotels of Port-of-Spain
2. Food in Trinidad
3. Exploring Trinidad
4. Sports, Shops, Nightlife
5. A Side Trip to Tobago

DISCOVERED BY COLUMBUS on his third voyage in 1498, Trinidad has since then been peopled by immigrants from almost every corner of the world—Africa, the Middle East, Europe, India, China, and the Americas. It is against such a background that the island has become the fascinating mixture of cultures, races, and creeds that it is today.

Trinidad, which is about the size of Delaware, and its sister island, tiny Tobago, 20 miles to the northeast, together form a nation. The islands of the new country are the southernmost outposts of the West Indies. Trinidad lies only ten miles from the Paria Peninsula in Venezuela, to which in unrecorded times it was once connected.

Trinidad is completely different from the other islands of the Caribbean, and that forms part of its charm and appeal. Visitors in increasing numbers are drawn to this island of many rhythms, where the great swinging sounds of calypso, limbo, and steeldrum bands all began.

The people are part of the attraction, the most cosmopolitan island in the Caribbean. Its polyglot population includes Syrians, Chinese, Americans, Europeans, East Indians, Parsees, Madrasis, Venezuelans, and the last of the original Amerindians, the early Indian settlers of the island. You'll also find Hindustanis, Javanese, Lebanese, slave descendants, and Créole mixtures. The main religions are Christian, Hindu, and Muslim.

In all there are a million-plus inhabitants, who speak a strange argot, Trinibagianese, but English is spoken almost everywhere as well.

Port-of-Spain, in the northwest corner of the island, is the capital, with the largest concentration of the population, about 120,000. Every costume and fabric is worn on the streets of this city.

One of the most industrialized nations in the Caribbean, and the third-largest exporter of oil in the western hemisphere, Trinidad, measuring 50 by 38 miles, is also blessed with a huge 114-acre Pitch Lake from which comes most of the world's asphalt. Further, it's also the home of Angostura Bitters, the recipe for which is a guarded secret.

The Spanish settled the island which the Indians had called Iere, or "land of the hummingbird.'' The Spaniards made their first permanent settlement in 1592 and held onto it longer than they did any of their other real estate in the Caribbean. The English captured Trinidad in 1797, and it remained British until the two-island nation declared its independence in 1962.

GETTING THERE: Even if you've never considered a holiday in South America, the **Pan American** daily service to Trinidad makes a stopover in Venezuela so inexpensive that most vacationers find it hard to ignore. Departing daily from New York's JFK Airport, Pan Am's wide-bodied Airbus flies nonstop to Caracas, then continues after a brief unloading to Trinidad. Its 6 p.m. departure from New York is late enough to allow connections in New York from the dozens of cities Pan Am services. Arrival in Caracas is around midnight, when plenty of taxis are still available. Passengers bound for Trinidad continue in the same aircraft after a brief delay. The flight's only disadvantage is its late arrival time in Port-of-Spain. However, if you're on vacation, you've probably planned to sleep late the following day. There are also plenty of taxis at that hour to take you into Port-of-Spain.

Pan Am's cheapest fares apply when a passenger books a hotel reservation simultaneously with his or her air fare. (Many of the hotels Pan Am's agent will suggest are reviewed in this guide.) Currently, midweek round-trip fares which include a free stopover in Caracas are as low as $401 in low season, $441 in high season. Passengers who prefer to book their hotel accommodations separately from their air fare are still allowed to stop over in Caracas without predetermining the dates of their ongoing flights. The least expensive of these tickets needs no advance purchase but requires a delay of between 3 and 30 days before returning to the passenger's point of origin.

Pan Am's service is supplemented by that of **American Airlines.** A wide-bodied airplane departs daily from JFK at 8 a.m., making a stop in Barbados before continuing to Trinidad. **BWIA** offers daily service from New York, with touchdowns in either Barbados or Grenada along the way.

From Miami, Pan Am offers a daily early-afternoon flight to Trinidad which stops off briefly in Barbados. BWIA's flights from Miami stop between one and three times each before arriving in Trinidad. **Eastern** also flies in from Miami.

GETTING AROUND: Taxis, which line up at the airport, are unmetered in Trinidad. When inquiring about the fare, ask if the rates quoted are in U.S. dollars or Trinidadian dollars. It makes quite a big difference. A taxi ride from the airport into Port-of-Spain generally costs about $50 TT ($14) during the day, $75 TT ($21) at night. Most drivers also serve as guides. Their rates, however, are based on route distances, so get an overall quotation and agree on the actual fare before setting off.

The Route Taxi

Trinidadians sometimes call these "pirate taxis." Launched in World War II, a route taxi is like a bus, stopping and taking on passengers or letting them off as they proceed through Port-of-Spain and its environs. Drivers take a maximum of five passengers. Fares vary depending on the route, of course. A typical ride in a pirate taxi costs only $2 TT (58¢).

Buses

All the cities of Trinidad are linked by regular bus service from Port-of-Spain. Fares are inexpensive, costing from 50¢ TT (15¢) for runs within the capital. However, buses are likely to be very overcrowded. Always try to avoid them at rush hours.

Car Rentals

You have to drive on the left-hand side of the road, even though your rented car will probably have a right-hand-mounted wheel. Trinidad has some 4,500 miles of

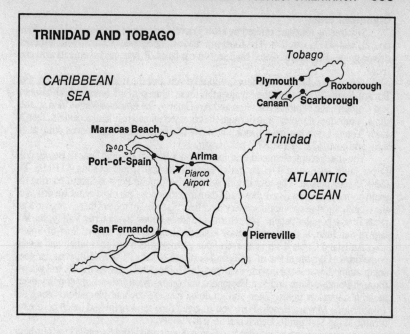

good roads, so touring is easy once you escape the fierce traffic jams of Port-of-Spain. That is, if you know where you're going. There are very few road signs, and good maps are practically nonexistent.

Unfortunately, it's next to impossible to rent a car for a short time in Port-of-Spain. Even people who have reserved in advance often run into trouble getting one. The reason for this is that so many business people tie up all available cars that it becomes difficult for the tourist to rent one. Many local companies require a minimum of four days on all their vehicles. Many readers have expressed their disappointment at not getting to drive, say, to Pitch Lake. Of course, one can take a taxi, but for many they are far, far too expensive.

As a final rub, Trinidad requires prospective drivers to have an international driver's license.

Renting a car in Trinidad can cost far more than on other islands in the Caribbean. Rates are sometimes more than twice as much as, for example, in Curaçaco, and the selection is often limited to one category.

Budget Rent-a-Car has rental facilities at Piarco Airport and in downtown Port-of-Spain, 34 Edward St. (tel. 623-3478). Its cars are well maintained, but there isn't a wide selection. It's imperative that you reserve as far in advance as possible. A Datsun Sunny with automatic transmission rents for $280 a week, with unlimited mileage included. Budget requires drivers to be at least 25 years old before entering into a rental agreement.

The only other U.S.-based car-rental company in Trinidad is **Hertz.** Its rental cost is similar to that charged at Budget, although its collision damage waiver is more and air conditioning is not included in its standard rentals.

For toll-free information and reservations, call the international departments of Budget at 800/527-0700 or Hertz at 800/654-3001.

Organized Tours

Sightseeing tours are offered by **Hub Travel Ltd.**, Suite 27, Bel Air Hotel, Piarco (tel. 664-4771, ext. 27). The tours are made in late-model sedans, with a trained driver-guide. Prices are quoted on a seat-in-car basis. Private arrangements will cost more.

A city tour, lasting two hours, will take you past the main points of interest of Port-of-Spain: White Hall, the President's House, Queen's Park Savannah, the Botanical Gardens, the National Museum and Art Gallery, the Emperor Valley Zoo, cathedrals, a mosque, temples, and through the commercial and residential centers, then to Lady Young Look-out for a panoramic view of the city. This trip leaves daily at 10 a.m. and costs $71 TT ($19.75) per person.

You'll see tropical splendor at its best on a Port-of-Spain/Maracas Bay/Saddle Drive jaunt leaving at 1 p.m. daily, lasting 3½ hours, and costing $110.05 TT ($30.75) per person. The tour begins with a drive around Port-of-Spain, passing the main points of interest listed above and then making one of the most beautiful drives of the island, through mountain scenery over the "Saddle" of the northern range to Maracas Bay, a popular beach. You return via Saddle Drive, Santa Cruz Valley, the village of San Juan, and the Lady Young Road for the panoramic view of Port-of-Spain.

An Island Circle Tour is a seven-hour journey which includes lunch and a welcome drink. Leaving at 9 a.m. daily and costing $266.25 TT ($74.50), your car goes south along the west coast with a view of the Gulf of Paria, across the central plains, through Pointe-à-Pitre and San Fernando, and on eastward into rolling country overlooking sugarcane fields. Then you go down into the coconut plantations along the 14-mile-long Mayaro Beach. Here you're given time for a swim and lunch before returning along Manzanilla Beach and back to the city.

An especially interesting trip is to Caroni Swamp and Bird Sanctuary, a four-hour trek by car and boat into the sanctuary where you'll see rich Trinidad bird life, with vast flocks of exotic and colorful winged creatures gathering to feed (they nest here, also). Among the birds you can see the scarlet ibis, egrets, blue and white herons, roseate spoonbills, kingfisher, and other swamp birds. The tour leaves daily at 3 p.m. and costs $131.35 TT ($36.75).

PRACTICAL FACTS: Trinidad has a tropical **climate** all year, with constant trade winds maintaining mean temperatures of 84° Fahrenheit during the day, 74° at night. The rainy season runs from May to November, but that fact shouldn't deter a visit at that time. The rain usually lasts no more than two hours before the sun comes out again.

Trinidad and Tobago dollars are pegged to the U.S. dollar at an exchange rate of $1 U.S. to $3.60 TT. Ask what **currency** is being referred to when rates are quoted to you. I've used a combination of both in this chapter, depending on the establishment. U.S. and Canadian dollars are accepted in exchange for payment, particularly in places in Port-of-Spain, less so outside the capital. However, you'll do better by converting your Canadian or U.S. dollars into local currency.

Note: Unless otherwise specified, dollar quotations appearing in this chapter are in U.S. currency.

Visitors arriving in Trinidad and Tobago should have a valid **passport** and an ongoing or return ticket from their point of embarkation. You'll be asked to fill out an immigration card upon your arrival. The carbon copy of this should be saved, as it must be returned to immigration officials when you depart.

Going through **Customs** in Trinidad is one of the worst procedures in the West Indies. Officials almost deliberately move at a snail's pace, causing endless delays, and local arriving families seem to transport entire households of goods, of which officials insist on examining every parcel. Even if you have nothing to declare and go through the green sign, you're still likely to be endlessly detained and questioned, often with hostility. Everybody seemingly knows about this situation, but nothing is done about it.

The **electric current** is 115 or 230 volts, 60 cycles, AC—so check before plugging in appliances. U.S.-made appliances will need a converter.

Banks stay open from 9 a.m. to 2 p.m. Monday to Thursday, and from 9 a.m. to 1 p.m. and 3 to 5 p.m. on Friday.

Trinidad and Tobago **time** is the same as the U.S. East Coast, except when the States go to Daylight Saving Time. Trinidad does not, so when it's 6 a.m. in Miami, it's still 5 a.m. in Trinidad.

As to the **climate,** Trinidad has a temperature range which varies between 70° and 90° Fahrenheit.

The big hotels and restaurants add at least a 10% to 15% **service charge** to your final tab; if not, you should **tip** from 12% to 15%. In addition, the government also imposes a 3% **occupancy tax** on room rates. It also imposes a **departure tax** of $20 TT ($5.60) on every passenger more than 5 years old.

The **main post office** is on Wrightson Road, Port-of-Spain, and is open from 7 a.m. to 5 p.m. Monday to Friday. **Cables** may be handed in at the Tourist Bureau, Piarco Airport, at a hotel desk, or at the offices of Textel, 1 Edward St., Port-of-Spain.

The **Tourist Bureau,** 122-124 Frederick St., Port-of-Spain (tel. 623-1932), provides information.

CARNIVAL AND CALYPSO: Called "the world's most colorful festival," the Carnival of Trinidad is a spectacle of dazzling costumes and gaiety. Hundreds of bands of masqueraders parade through the cities on the Monday and Tuesday preceding Ash Wednesday. Traffic, except the human variety, comes to a standstill. The island seems to explode with music, fun-making, and dancing. It's been called a 48-hour orgy!

Hotel accommodations are booked months in advance, and all inns raise their prices by at least 40% at the time.

Some of the carnival costumes cost hundreds of dollars, and their owners spend all year making them, getting ready for next year's big event. For example, "bands" might depict the birds of Trinidad such as the scarlet ibis and the keskidee; or they might be a bevy of women in every shade from sapodilla to brown sugar, coming out in the streets dressed as pussy cats. Others are dragons, devils, and demons. Costumes are also satirical and comical.

The top calypsonian is proclaimed king. On one occasion, the King of Carnival appeared dressed as a "Devil Ray" with a gigantic "delta wing," his eyes glinting behind a black mask, his body bound in black leather studded with silver.

Trinidad, of course, is the land of calypso, which grew out of the folksong of the Afro-West Indian. The lyrics command the greatest attention, as they are rich in satire and innuendo. The calypsonian is considered a poet-musician, and lines have often been considered libelous and obscene, capable of toppling politicians from office as they have in the past. In banter and bravado, the calypsonian reveals and gives voice to the sufferings, hopes, and aspirations of his people. At carnival time the artist sings his compositions to spectators in places called by the traditional name of "tents." There are five or six shows a night at the calypso tents around town, from 8 p.m. to midnight. Tickets for these are sold in the afternoon at most record shops.

Carnival parties, or fêtes, with three or four orchestras at each one, are public and are advertised in the newspapers. Tickets for these events, which go on for several weeks before carnival ends on Shrove Tuesday, cost $50 to $60. For a really wild time, attend a party on Sunday night before Carnival Monday.

You can attend rehearsals of steel bands at their headquarters, called panyards, beginning about 7 p.m. Preliminary band competitions are held at the grandstand of the Queen's Park Savannah in Port-of-Spain and at Skinners Park in San Fernando, beginning some three weeks before carnival.

The Tourist Board publishes a booklet, *Carnival in Trinidad & Tobago*. You can receive this guide and a calendar of carnival events from the **Trinidad & Tobago Tourist Board,** Suite 712-14, 400 Madison Ave., New York, NY 10017 (tel. 212/838-7750).

1. Hotels of Port-of-Spain

The number of hotels is extremely limited. Almost every hotel in Trinidad has a completely different personality, ranging from such posh hillside hostelries as the Hilton to a turn-of-the-century nature preserve center up in the mountains.

But don't check into any Port-of-Spain hotel expecting your room to open directly on a white sandy beach. The nearest beach is a long, costly taxi ride away.

Trinidad Hilton, P.O. Box 442, Port-of-Spain (tel. 624-3211). On a hilltop, Trinidad's most distinguished hotel is called upside-down because the lobby is at the top and the rooms are staggered down below. You press the down button if you want to go to the tenth floor. Because of its location just above Queen's Park Savannah, most of its rooms have a view of the sea and mountains. You get a wide range of accommodations here, everything from a simple single to a suite with connecting doors. Rates, in effect all year, are $105 to $142 daily in a single, from $120 to $156 in a double. All rooms are air-conditioned and have balconies. Most of the guests spend their time at the large tropical swimming pool, with its vast sunning areas and refreshment bar at the Gazebo where you can order the famous "rum and Coca-Cola."

The main dining room is La Boucan, recommended separately, or you can congregate at the Pool Terrace, a tropical dining room with a two-story-high metal sculpture and lighting chandelier. Wicker chairs are set out for breakfast and lunch, with ceiling-high glass walls. Music is played for dancing in the Carnival Bar until 2 a.m. Some of Trinidad's best native entertainment is booked by the Hilton management. There's always plenty of activity around here, with pool barbecues featuring roast suckling pig, weekly fiestas, steel bands, limbo contests, whatever. The two all-weather tennis courts are lit for night games. Several shops, some offering handcrafts, are placed in the two-level arcade of the hotel. For the business traveler, the Hilton is the best choice of the island. Of particular interest are the 24-hour Telex and cable facilities, a worldwide courière service for documents, and secretarial and translation services.

Holiday Inn, Wrightson Road (P.O. Box 1017), Port-of-Spain (tel. 625-3361), was wisely enough placed at the edge of the commercial area of the city, a skillful combination of a business person's hotel yet with resort "trimmings." It stands in gleaming white, a streamlined block topped by La Ronde, its revolving 14th-floor restaurant where diners have a view of the coastline of Venezuela, nine miles across the sea. An international menu is offered. Adjoining the entrance lobby is a cloverleaf-shaped swimming pool, surrounded by Japanese sun parasols and a thatched poolside bar. You forget, at least for a while, the traffic of the city. The pool has some submerged bar stools for those who want to drink while they swim. The Calypso Lounge on the 12th floor is considered the most sophisticated nightspot in Port-of-Spain, with music for dancing nightly. Carnival costumes form part of the decoration.

Most of the hotel bedrooms, 235 in all, have a freshness to them, with colored fabrics on the beds and at the windows. The suites are more romantic, often with a decor inspired by the great house plantation style. Except for carnival, the year-round charge is $88 in a single, $92 in a double, but these are EP rates (no meals). Rooms have private balconies, two double beds, phones, radios, and individually controlled air conditioning.

Chaconia Inn, 106 Saddle Rd., Maraval (tel. 628-8603), named for the country's scarlet national flower, is a miniature self-contained resort just north of Port-of-Spain in the cool mountain residential valley of Maraval. Its buildings are in simple style, and its furnishings in a contemporary motel idiom. Ken E. Duval, the managing director, runs one of Trinidad's finest small hotels, and does so with some flair. Personal hospitality is emphasized here by everybody from the management on down. You'll be housed in one of the following categories of rooms: 13 two-bedroom apartment suites, 18 superior rooms with kitchenettes, and nine standard rooms. All are equipped with private bath, air conditioning, phone, TV, and radio, and are tastefully decorated. All year, tariffs are the same except during Carnival. Singles range in price from $55 to $65; doubles and twins, from $65 to $75; and triples, from $75 to $85. Two-bedroom suites cost $100 to $140. All tariffs are EP and subject to tax and service charge. For MAP, add $25 per person daily, plus service. In addition to the dining room/lounge, there is a roof garden where barbecue dinners are served on Wednesday, Friday, and Saturday. The lounge is open from 10 a.m. to 3 a.m. with DJ music for nightly dancing and live entertainment on Friday and Saturday from 10 p.m. to 3 a.m. The inn has a swimming pool.

Hotel Normandie, 10 Nook Ave. (P.O. Box 851), Port-of-Spain (tel. 622-2639), originally built in the 1920s, was already a well-established hotel when its owners drastically modernized it in 1986. It sports a new and stylish façade. The two-story hotel rises around a banyan- and banana-filled courtyard in the center of which is a cool swimming pool accented with a jet of water. Inside, the 60 air-conditioned rooms each have a balcony or patio, parquet floors, and TV. Year-round prices for a single range from $60 to $70 daily, rising to $70 to $80 in a double. More elaborate accommodations, such as loft studios and suites, begin at $85 daily. Calm and cosmopolitan, the hotel sits next to one of the best art galleries in Trinidad, a skylit-covered shopping center, an attractive restaurant, and the botanical gardens of Port-of-Spain.

Kapok Hotel and Restaurant, 16-18 Cotton Hill, St. Clair (tel. 622-6441), is a nine-floor modern little hotel at the corner of Queen's Park Savannah. From its lounge, you have not only a panoramic view of the park but of the Gulf of Paria. The lounge has been redecorated in pleasing, harmonious tones. Many guests who shun the Hilton seem to feel at home here, liking the slick neatness, the handsomely appointed bedrooms, and the rooftop restaurant serving Polynesian food. On the ground floor of the hotel is the Café Savanna, one of the finest restaurants in Trinidad. The location, in St. Clair, is in a pleasant and quiet residential area. They rent 71 well-furnished rooms, each with private bath, phone service, color TV, and air conditioning. The rooms have been refurnished with wicker, adding a tropical warmth to the spacious accommodations. Year-round rates (except during Carnival when they're higher) are $55 daily in a single, from $68 in a double, all EP. In the back is a small pool with a sunning area.

Moniques, 114 Saddle Rd., Maraval (tel. 628-3334), is a bungalow in the lush Maraval Valley, about eight minutes from the downtown sector of Port-of-Spain. It's the home of Mr. and Mrs. Charbonne. He has been the public relations head of the Angostura Bitters factory in Port-of-Spain. They have an informal, freshly decorated, and most comfortable home where they have set aside seven rooms for paying guests. All units are air-conditioned, and each has its own bath. Singles range from $22 daily; doubles, $28; and triples, $35. These tariffs are in effect all year. Fellow guests like to gather on the tiny front lawn to exchange travel tips, and there is also a TV room. Arrangements are made for guests to go to a nearby swimming pool.

Zollna House, 12 Ramlogan Development, La Selva, Maraval (tel. 628-3731), is on a hillside in the Maraval Valley with a view of Port-of-Spain and the Gulf of Paria, two miles from the capital and a quarter of a mile off the Saddle Road. The two-story building has seven bedrooms and four spacious baths. Year-round rates are $22 for a single, $14 per person in a double, and $12 per person in a triple, EP. Tariffs go up by $8 per person during Carnival and $17 per person year round if breakfast and dinner are included. The house has two large porches, two indoor lounges, a beverage bar and games room, and dining areas on two floors, as well as a patio/barbecue setup outdoors. The garden is lush with flowering shrubs and fruit trees, home to a variety of birds. The house, white with black trim, is almost obscured by trees, but you can find it by going along the Saddle Road, turning into La Seiva Road, and going uphill for about a quarter of a mile. Owners are Gottfried Franz and Barbara Zollna, who also operate the Blue Waters Inn on Tobago.

Mount St. Benedict Guest House, Tunapuna (tel. 662-4084), is a friendly, well-run guesthouse occupying a substantial building nestled on the ledge of a hill halfway between the airport and Port-of-Spain. It's really like a spiritual retreat and was once used as such for Catholic Dutch fathers. Capping the hillside are a church, monastery, and school, although the guesthouse is nonsectarian. Nine miles east of Port-of-Spain, this hilltop hostelry charges from $45 per person daily for a room and three meals. The neat, clean, uncluttered rooms have twin beds with cold water. Guests use the corridor baths, which have hot water. The food is above average, with an emphasis on local specialties. The dining room is spacious with two walls of windows providing a view of the valley. Long tables are covered in oilcloth, and meals are served family style. Against one wall is an ornate Victorian sideboard, and on yet another wall is a painting of the pink guesthouse as it once was. The reception and living room has a few comfortable chairs, and there's also a wide front veranda from which you can look out onto vistas of hibiscus, bougainvillea, and poinsettia. Bus transport is possible, but of course it's better to have your own wheels.

Asa Wright Nature Center, Spring Hill Estate (P.O. Box 10), Arima (no phone). There really isn't anything like it in the Caribbean. Known by birdwatchers throughout the world, it sits on 190 acres of protected land near uplands where hummingbirds and rare varieties of toucans flourish. It was established in the 19th century as a coffee plantation. Asa Wright, its most memorable owner, bought it in the 1930s, working the fields herself until her death in the late 1960s. Before her, Charles William Meyer (1875–1948) built the estate's green-and-white frame house for his bride in 1907 (they reared 11 children here). Today the acreage is a national trust managed by seven Trinidadian board members and run by an attractive manager, Rita Iton, who used to work in London as an investment banker. Trinidadian families sometimes arrive en masse for picnics, and it's a favorite outing for school groups.

Devoted nature lovers can rent one of its 18 simple accommodations. Nine units are in the original Edwardian house, with another nine in wood-frame outbuildings. Amenities are aggressively simple, the visual stimuli coming from the flocks of birds at the feeding stations. *The daily rate is $45 per person, double occupancy, from May to the end of November.* From December 1 to April 30, the price is $60 per person, also double occupancy. The tariffs include three meals a day, afternoon tea, and a complimentary rum punch each evening. A service charge of 10% is added to the rates.

Visiting hours for nonresidents are 9 a.m. to 5 p.m., for an entrance fee of $5 TT ($1.40). The grounds contain dozens of carefully marked nature trails. The area has witnessed the arrival of 240 of the 660 species of butterflies known in Trinidad, and of more than 183 of the 418 species of native birds. Tours for birdwatchers, ecologists, botanists, ornithologists, entomologists, and photographers are arranged.

You can make toll-free reservations by calling 800/426-7781 (in New York, call 800/327-2753). Otherwise, write to Caligo Ventures, 387 Main St., Armonk, NY 10504.

2. Food in Trinidad

The food in Trinidad is as varied and cosmopolitan as the islanders themselves. It was a British colony for years, yet the cookery of olde England never made much impression on Trinidadians. Red-hot curries remind one of the island's strong Indian influence, and some Chinese dishes are about as good here as any you'd find in Hong Kong. Créole and Spanish fare, as well as French, are also to be enjoyed.

A typical savory offering is a rôti, a king-size crêpe, highly spiced, and rolled around a filling of chicken, shellfish, or meat. Of course, you may prefer to skip such local delicacies as opossum stew and fried armadillo! Naturally, your fresh rum punch will have a dash of Angostura bitters.

La Boucan, Trinidad Hilton (tel. 624-3211). Considered the finest restaurant in Trinidad, this establishment satisfies the eye as well as the palate. Against one of its longest walls stretches a graceful mural by Geoffrey Holder, the most famous (and most expensive) artist who came out of the Caribbean. Born in Trinidad, though living in New York most of his life, he painted this mural to honor the social gatherings which used to take place in Port-of-Spain's central park, the Savannah. The mural, along with this fine restaurant, are in the previously recommended Hilton. Staffed by a battalion of polite waiters, it serves its sophisticated cuisine amid a decor of Empire sconces, pink napery, burning candles, and an airy kind of spaciousness. Lunch is served on weekdays only, from noon to 2:30 p.m.; dinner is offered every evening except Sunday and Monday from 7 to 10:30 p.m. Full meals cost from $160 TT ($44.75), slightly less at lunch, and require a reservation. Menu specialties include smoked breast of duckling with seasonal fruits, thinly sliced filet of shark (smoked on the premises over coals of guava wood), stuffed crab back, mushroom crêpes, West Indian curried boneless breast of chicken, flambéed pepper steak with Madagascar pepper, grilled kingfish steak with Créole sauce, Colorado-bred lamb chops, and succulently smoked pork, beef, duck, and lamb dishes. Desserts are sumptuous. As you dine, live music from a lacquered piano on a central dais provides digestible entertainment.

La Ronda, Holiday Inn, Wrightson Road (tel. 625-3361), offers not only a well-prepared cuisine, but because of its 14th-floor perch, provides a dazzling view of the coastline. Contained in a glass-sided circular tower atop the Holiday Inn, the restaurant spins slowly on its axis, permitting guests a 360° panorama and might make two complete revolutions by the time a dinner is over. If you tire of the view, a quartet of the most elaborate carnival costumes in Trinidad stand at the four corners of the compass. Covered with sequins and flamboyant yards of glistening fabric, they are accompanied by plaques explaining the legendary spirits they represent. Meals are served daily from noon to 2:30 p.m. and 7 to 11 p.m. Lunch, costing from $40 TT ($11.25), and dinner from $80 TT ($22.50), are likely to include Tobago flying fish, U.S.-bred sirloin, New Zealand baby lamb, gazpacho, and curried dishes.

Café Savanna, Kapok Hotel, 16-18 Cotton Hill, St. Clair (tel. 622-6441), on the ground floor of a previously recommended hotel, serves an excellent continental cuisine. You get refined service in a sophisticated and romantic setting. A complete dinner ranges from $20 to $30. Many of the specialties are prepared with flair, but they change seasonally so I can't recommend any particular dishes. There are always sizzling steaks, of course, and lobster when available. The café serves both lunch and dinner. Also in the same hotel is the equally popular Tiki Village (see below). The café is open Monday to Saturday. Lunch is Monday to Friday from noon to 2 p.m. and dinner from 7 to 10 p.m. On Saturday, only dinner is served.

The Waterfront, West Mall Shopping Center, Westmoorings (tel. 632-0834), is the showcase restaurant of the biggest shopping center in Port-of-Spain, lying about five miles west of the Savannah. Built without windows, it's modeled after the 19th-century wharves which once made Trinidad a commercial center of the West Indies. Barrel-shaped chairs pull up to a darkly illuminated bar, and barricades of rope as thick as a man's wrist separate the dining from the drinking areas. As you dine, a low-volume recording of splashing surf subliminally evokes memories of the sea. The establishment is open daily except Sunday from 10 a.m. to 11 p.m. You might begin with one of the specially concocted and nautically inspired drinks, such as a fogcutter. Lunches cost from $20 TT ($5.60) and dinners from $70 TT ($19.50), but tabs could go higher if you order lobster or shellfish. Specialties include Caribbean fish fingers, coconut-flavored shrimp, lobster Thermidor, stuffed filet of flounder, shrimp and mussel bisque, grilled kingfish with a watercress-flavored butter sauce, stuffed squid with spinach, crabmeat quiche, and at lunchtime, sandwiches and salads.

La Fantasie, 10 Nook Ave., St. Ann's Village (tel. 624-1181), named after an 18th-century plantation which once stood here, is loaded with style and features a tempting version of nouvelle Créole cuisine. Alternating shades of pastel were used to paint the lofty ceiling panels a playful array of carnival colors, while soaring fan-topped windows bring in the daylight. Open daily from noon to 2 p.m. and 7 to 10 p.m., it charges around $35 TT ($9.75) for lunch, from $75 TT ($21) for dinner. On any particular day the changing menu might include chicken cocotte in a rich Créole sauce with herb dumplings, tournedos deluxe with wedges of apple and onion rings, stuffed crab back, lettuce soup, lamb with rosemary and garlic, chicken breast with papaya and banana, and shrimp in a black-bean-and-ginger sauce, followed with a Trinidadian fruitcake with a rum-flavored custard.

Restaurant Singho, Long Circular Mall (tel. 628-2077). Lined with planks of cedar, this restaurant contains an almost mystically illuminated bar and aquarium. After a drink, you proceed into a large dining room whose darkly intimate lighting complements the Chinese cuisine. The restaurant is on the second floor of one of the capital's largest shopping malls. Open daily from 10 a.m. to 11 p.m., it's owned and operated by Roma Kim Sabeeney, who for several years organized a series of beauty contests. Most guests order a fixed-price six-course meal, plus soup and one drink, for $60 TT ($16.75). À la carte dishes include shrimp with oyster sauce, shark-fin soup, stewed or curried beef, almond pork, and spareribs with black-bean sauce.

Tiki Village, Kapok Hotel, 16-18 Cotton Hill, St. Clair (tel. 622-6441), perches on the top floor of this hotel, offering a panoramic view at night. Polynesian creations with a Chinese flair are presented nightly, except Monday, from 5:30 to 10:30 p.m. You can also have lunch here, from 11:30 a.m. to 2:30 p.m. In the evening you should make a reservation. To get started, try the Polynesian delight, a combination of hors d'oeuvres. The eggroll is among the best I've ever ordered in the West Indies. Among the main courses, I'd recommend the Hawaiian luau fish. This is a whole fish coated with water-chestnut flour and fried crisply before it's engulfed in a sweet-and-pungent sauce. The Tiki pork, which has been sautéed with plum sauce and garnished with shredded onion and sweet pepper, is superb. Chicken provincial is boneless cubes sautéed in a black-bean sauce. Desserts include an icebox cake, followed by Chinese tea, and then a bill of, say, $25. The village is open seven days a week, serving meals from 11:45 a.m. to 10:15 p.m.

Chaconia Inn, 106 Saddle Rd., Maraval (tel. 629-2101), recommended previously as a hotel, serves some of the best food of any hotel in Trinidad. Ken E. Duval, the managing director, has a good wine list and lots of continental specialties as well as Trinidadian dishes. The staff is helpful, and the service quite good. The dining choice is between the main dining room, noted for steaks, and the Roof Garden Restaurant. The main dining room is open daily from 6:30 a.m. for breakfast and 11:30 a.m. for lunch. Dinner is served à la carte Sunday through Thursday from 6:30 to 10:30 p.m. Breakfast ranges from $5 to $9; lunch, from $20 to $35; and dinner, from $20 to $40. There is a large selection of appetizers, steaks, seafood, and poultry, as well as salads, desserts, and sandwiches. The Roof Garden Restaurant serves barbecue dinners on Friday and Saturday from 7 to 10:30 p.m. The cost for dinner here, including salad and dessert, is from $25. Reservations are recommended.

Veni Mangé, 13 Lucknow St. (no phone), built in the 1950s of ochre stucco, lies on a tranquil street of private residences right off Western Main Road. If you can find this tiny home, you'll get a fine welcome from Allyson Hennessy and her sister, Rosemary Hezekiah. Considered a local media personality, Allyson runs a daily television talk show broadcast throughout much of Trinidad. Best described as articulate examples of a new generation of Créole mammas, Allyson and Rosemary dress in lavish neo-Victorian costumes, never without several pounds of fake amethysts, oversize rhinestones, and jangling bracelets. Their conversational banter and tactfully exaggerated sense of theatricality have established this restaurant's lunch hour as the most interesting, lighthearted, and fun place to dine in all of Port-of-Spain. Because of local zoning laws, only lunch is served. Open weekdays from 11:30 a.m. to 2:30 p.m., on Friday, they remain open until 9 p.m. as a bar and rendezvous point. No meals are served on weekends. The walls are decorated with the works of home-grown artists, and the tables are pleasant and inviting.

Start with their bartender's special, which is a coral-colored fruit punch, a rich, luscious mixture that combines the golden papaya with a banana whose skin is allowed to turn black so that its taste is most flavorsome. On some days they do an authentic callaloo soup, which, according to Trinidadian legend, can make a man propose marriage, even if the idea hadn't occurred to him before. If not callaloo, then one of their other rich-tasting broths, such as pumpkin or red bean, will be served. Whatever, you'll get a kettle of hearty, provincial fare. Save room for one of the main courses, such as curried crab or West Indian hot pot (a variety of meat cooked Créole style), perhaps a vegetable lentil loaf. The helpings are large, and if you still have room, order their pineapple upside-down cake, unless you prefer fresh fruit or homemade ice cream with such tropical flavors as guava, mango, and coconut. For all this, you'll pay $22 or more for a fine meal and an example of local hospitality.

Villa Créole, 133 Western Main St., at Mathura Street (tel. 622-1518), is a second-floor restaurant with high-ceilinged dining rooms. Ringed by a veranda, it's in a commercial neighborhood, about a mile east of the Savannah. This sociable enclave is the creation of its owner, Helen Apparicio. After an education in London, she returned to her native country to set up this restaurant as a "Créole home away from home." The handwritten menu is prepared fresh daily. Based on the availability of ingredients, menu items might include a whole redfish (red snapper) baked in garlic sauce, stewed filet of kingfish with "steamed down" breadfruit and callaloo, Créole-style shrimp, cowheel and oxtail soup, crab backs, baked pork chops with mushroom sauce and pumpkin pie, pepperpot stuffed with dumplings and "provisions," stewed oxtail, and Créole steak. For the adventurous, the restaurant sometimes offers armadillo with rice (the menu might list it as wildmeat or tattoo). Full meals cost from $50 TT ($14), and lunch is every weekday from 11 a.m. to 5 p.m. Dinner, drinks, and light entertainment are provided on Wednesday from 5 to 11:30 p.m. and Friday from 5 p.m. to 2:30 a.m.

Sam's, 67 Western Main Rd., St. James (no phone), is probably the dining bargain of Port-of-Spain. Its ambience is very much like that of a Formica-covered West Indian version of a fast-food emporium. The specialty (and the only food offered) is an array of rôtis. Defined as an unsweetened pastry envelope stuffed with filling, it more often appears on a paper plate like a taco with the stuffing placed beside it. Rôtis cost from $10 TT ($2.80), including a variety of fillings, the most basic of which is dhal purée (a mash of boiled green peas). If you're adventurous, you can order such fillings as gizzard or goat, but most North Americans stick to shrimp, chicken (the deboned version), beef, liver, or vegetarian. The establishment is open daily from 10 a.m. to midnight. There's another branch at 47 Richmond St.

3. Exploring Trinidad

AROUND THE CAPITAL: One of the busiest harbors in the Caribbean, Trinidad's capital, Port-of-Spain, can be explored on foot. Most tours begin at **Queen's Park Savannah,** on the northern edge of the city. Called "The Savannah," it consists of 199 acres, complete with a race course, cricket fields, and vendors hawking coconut water. What is now the park was once a sugar plantation until it was swept by a fire in 1808 which destroyed hundreds of homes.

Among the Savannah's outstanding buildings is the pink-and-blue Queen's Royal College, containing a clock tower with Westminister chimes. Today a school for boys, it stands on Maraval Road at the corner of St. Clair Avenue. On the same road, the family home of the Roodal clan is affectionately called "the gingerbread house" by Trinidadians. It was built in the baroque style of the French Second Empire.

In contrast, the family residence of the Stollmeyers was built in 1905 and is a copy of a German Rhenish castle. Nearby stands Whitehall, which was once a private mansion but today has been turned into the office of the prime minister of Trinidad and Tobago. In the Moorish style, it was erected in 1905 and served as the U.S. Army headquarters in World War II.

These houses, including Hayes Court, the residence of the Anglican bishop of Trinidad, and others form what is known as "the magnificent seven" big mansions standing in a row.

On the south side of the park stands the **National Museum and Art Gallery,** 117 Frederick St. (tel. 623-6419). It's open from 10 a.m. to 6 p.m. daily, except Monday, charging no admission. On the ground floor you'll see some Amerindian artifacts, traces of Trinidad's early Indian settlers.

At the southern end of Frederick Street, the main artery of Port-of-Spain's shopping district, stands **Woodford Square.** The gaudy **Red House** seen there is a large neo-Renaissance building built in 1906. It is the seat of the government of Trinidad and Tobago. Nearby stands **Holy Trinity Cathedral,** whose Gothic look may remind you of the churches of England. Inside, look for the marble monument to Sir Ralph Woodford made by the sculptor of Chantry.

Another of the town's important squares is called **Independence Square,** dating from Spanish days. Now mainly a car park, it stretches across the southern part of the capital from the **Cathedral of the Immaculate Conception** to Wrightson Road. The Roman Catholic church was built in 1815 in the neo-Gothic style and consecrated in 1832.

The cathedral has an outlet that leads to the **Central Market** on Beetham Hwy., on the outskirts of Port-of-Spain. Here you can see all the spices and fruits for which Trinidad is known. It's one of the island's most colorful sights, made all the more so by the wide diversity of people who sell their wares here.

At the north of the Savannah, the **Botanical Gardens** cover 70 acres. Once part of a sugar plantation, the park is filled with flowering plants, shrubs, and rare and beautiful trees, including an orchid house. The cocaine bushes planted here always seem to intrigue visitors. Seek out also the raw beef tree—an incision made in its bark is said to resemble rare, bleeding roast beef. Licensed guides will take you through and explain the luxuriant foliage to you. In the garden is the President's House, the official residence of the president of Trinidad and Tobago. Victorian in style, it was built in 1875.

One part of the gardens is the **Emperor Valley Zoo,** which shows a good selection of the fauna of Trinidad as well as some of the usual exotic animals. The star attractions are a family of mandrills, a reptile house, and open bird parks. You can take shady jungle walks through tropical vegetation. Adults pay $2 TT (55¢); children, $1 TT (30¢). Hours are 9 a.m. to 5 p.m.

OUTSIDE PORT-OF-SPAIN: In the environs of Port-of-Spain, you may want to seek out the following sights. For one of the most popular attractions in the area, the Asa Wright Nature Center, refer to my hotel recommendations.

Fort George

On a peak 1,100 feet above Port-of-Spain, this fort was built by Gov. Sir Thomas Hislop in 1804 as a signal station in the days of the sailing ships. Once it could be reached only by hikers, but today it's accessible by an asphalt road. From its citadel you can see the mountains of Venezuela. The drive is only ten miles, but to play it safe, allow about two hours for the excursion.

Caroni Bird Sanctuary

At sundown, clouds of scarlet ibis, the national bird of Trinidad and Tobago, fly in from their feeding grounds to roost here. The 450-acre sanctuary couldn't be more idyllic, with blue, mauve, and white lilies, oysters growing on mangrove roots, and caimans resting on mudbanks. The sanctuary lies about a half hour's drive (actually seven miles) south of Port-of-Spain. Admission is $12 TT ($3.35) for adults, $6 TT ($1.70) for children.

Blue Basin

This dell lies at the head of the Diego Martin Valley, a freshwater pool fed by a waterfall. The location is about 18 miles outside Port-of-Spain (the tour takes about 2½ hours). You can park your car less than a mile from the pool. From the car park you have to proceed by a footpath that is often steep in places. Once there you can take a dip in this pool. From the car park you have to proceed by a footpath that is often steep in places. Once there you can take a dip in this pool. Regrettably, this once-enchanted place, widely touted in the tourist literature of Trinidad, is being allowed to serve in places as somewhat of a garbage dump. To reach the basin, the route begins on Western Main Road, goes through Four Roads and Diego Martin, and then passes through the government-owned River Estate. Don't get lost. Make sure you know where you're going if you succumb to the bait in the tourist pamphlets. It's hard to find, and what signs there are are inadequate.

Pitch Lake

One of the wonders of the world, its surface like elephant skin, the lake is 300 feet deep at its center. It's possible to walk on its rough hide, but I don't recommend that you proceed far. Legend has it that the lake devoured a tribe of Chayma Indians, punishing them for eating hummingbirds in which the souls of their ancestors reposed. The bitumen mined here has been used for paving highways throughout the world. This lake was formed millions of years ago, and it is believed that at one time it was a huge mud volcano into which mud asphaltic oil seeped. Churned up and down by underground gases, the oil and mud eventually formed asphalt. Sir Walter Raleigh, according to legend, discovered the lake in 1595, using the asphalt to caulk his ships. However, don't believe those legends that no matter how much is dug out the lake is fully replenished in a day. Actually, the level of the lake drops at the rate of about six inches a year. Only problem is, to visit the lake is a tour of 120 miles, lasting ten hours.

The Saddle

This is a humped pass on a ridge dividing the Maraval Valley and the Santa Cruz Valley. Along this circular run you'll see the luxuriant growth of the island, as reflected by grapefruit, papaya, cassava, and cocoa. You leave Port-of-Spain by Saddle Road, going past the Trinidad Country Club. You pass through Maraval Village with its St. Andrew's Golf Course. About a quarter of a mile from Perseverance Estate there's a sharp turn. The road rises to cross the ridge at the spot from which "The Saddle" gets its name. After going over the hump, you descend through Santa Cruz Valley, rich with giant bamboo, into San Juan and back to the capital along Eastern Main Road or via Beetham Hwy. You'll see splendid views in every direction. The tour recommended takes about two hours, covering 18 miles.

The North Coast Road

Nearly all cruise-ship passengers are hauled along Trinidad's "Skyline Highway" which opened in 1944. Starting at "The Saddle," previously recommended, it wends for seven miles across the Northern Range, and down to Maracas Bay. At one point, 100 feet above the Caribbean, you'll see on a clear day as far away as Venezuela in the west or Tobago in the east, a sweep of some 100 miles.

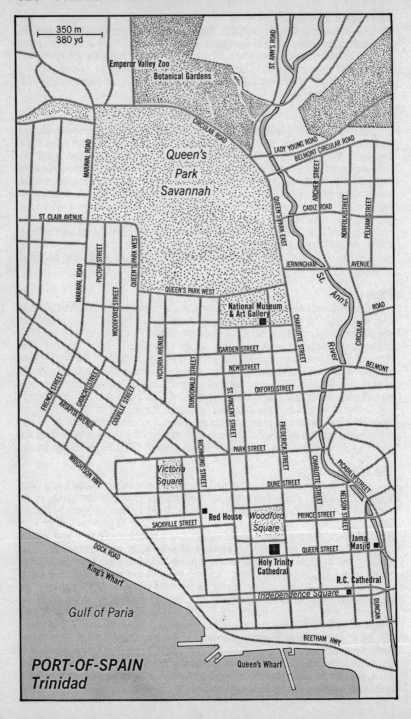

350 m
380 yd

Emperor Valley Zoo
Botanical Gardens

ST. ANN'S ROAD

CIRCULAR ROAD

LADY YOUNG ROAD

BELMONT CIRCULAR ROAD

MARAVAL ROAD

Queen's
Park
Savannah

QUEEN'S PARK EAST

ARCHER STREET

CADIZ ROAD

NORFOLK STREET

PELHAM STREET

ST. CLAIR AVENUE

PICTON STREET

QUEEN'S PARK WEST

JERNINGHAM AVENUE

St. Ann's River

CIRCULAR ROAD

MARAVAL ROAD

WOODFORD STREET

QUEEN'S PARK WEST

National Museum
& Art Gallery

CHARLOTTE STREET

BELMONT

VICTORIA AVENUE

GARDEN STREET

NEW STREET

OXFORD STREET

DUNDONALD STREET

ST. VINCENT STREET

FREDERICK STREET

FRENCH STREET

CADIZ-PESTREET

ARAPITA AVENUE

COUVILLE STREET

PARK STREET

RICHMOND STREET

WRIGHTSON HWY.

Victoria
Square

DUKE STREET

CHARLOTTE STREET

PICADILLY STREET

SACKVILLE STREET

Red House

Woodford
Square

PRINCE STREET

NELSON STREET

DOCK ROAD

King's Wharf

QUEEN STREET

Jama
Masjid

Holy Trinity
Cathedral

R.C. Cathedral

DUNCAN

Gulf of Paria

Independence Square

BEETHAM HWY.

PORT-OF-SPAIN
Trinidad

Queen's Wharf

Most visitors take this route to **Maracas Beach,** one of the most splendid in Trinidad. Enclosed by mountains, it has the cliché charm of a Caribbean fantasy—white sands, swaying coconut palms, and crystal-clear water.

4. Sports, Shops, Nightlife

In Trinidad, you'll find much to see and do in the capital itself, beginning with your morning shopping tour of the Port-of-Spain bazaars, going on to water sports, ending with some calypso entertainment in the evening.

THE SPORTING LIFE: Whatever your sporting pleasure—hunting an alligator or playing a simple game of tennis—Trinidad has many possibilities for athletic activities. However, no one surely ever arrived in Port-of-Spain seeking these endeavors alone. In Trinidad, sports are integrated into daily life, and for golf and tennis holidays one should read some of the previous chapters where much more emphasis is placed on such pursuits.

Beaches

Trinidad isn't thought of as beach country, yet surprisingly it has more beach frontage than any other island in the West Indies. The only problem is that most of its beaches are undeveloped and found in distant, remote places, far removed from Port-of-Spain. The closest of the better beaches, Maracas, is a full 18 miles from Port-of-Spain. (For lovely, inviting, and more accessible beaches, see the section immediately following, on Tobago.)

Tennis

The **Hilton** (tel. 624-3111) has the best courts, and you can also play at the **Trinidad Country Club** (tel. 622-3470) as well. On the grounds of the Prince's building, there are public courts in Port-of-Spain (ask at your hotel for directions to these).

Fishing

All year long good catches are possible either in the deep sea or in inland Trinidadian waters. In the waters of the Gulf of Paria and on the north shore, you can pursue salmon, snapper, and grouper, or troll for Spanish mackerel, kingfish, wahoo, dolphin, or bonita. **Hub Travel,** 68-78 Maraval Rd., Port-of-Spain (tel. 622-0936), can arrange fishing trips.

Hunting

Hunters bag everything from an armadillo to an alligator in Trinidad, and there's wild game in the forest too, including agouti, wild hog (called quenk), or deer. Ask at the Trinidad Tourist Bureau for particulars about hunting licenses.

Golf

The oldest golf club on the island, **Moka** (tel. 629-2314), is in Maraval, about two miles from Port-of-Spain. This 18-hole course has a clubhouse that offers every facility to all visitors, and the course has been internationally acclaimed since it was the setting for the 1976 Hoerman Cup Golf Tournament.

WHERE TO SHOP: One of the large bazaars of the Caribbean, Port-of-Spain has luxury items from all over the globe, including Irish linens, English china, Scandinavian crystal, French perfumes, and of course, Swiss watches and Japanese cameras.

More interesting than these usual items are the Oriental bazaars where you can pick up items in ivory or brass, perhaps a carved chest. It takes only a day or two for a Hong Kong tailor to make you a suit or dress.

Reflecting the island's culture are calypso shirts (or dresses), sisal goods, woodwork, cascadura bracelets, silver jewelry in local motifs, and saris. For souvenir items, visitors often like to bring back figurines of limbo dancers, carnival masqueraders, calypso singers, or sari-draped Hindu lovelies.

Most stores are open from 8 a.m. to 4 p.m. Monday to Friday (some shops remain open until 5 p.m.). Liquor and food stores close at noon on Thursday, and nearly all shops, except liquor and food, close at noon on Saturday.

For those luxury items mentioned, I suggest you pay a call at **Stecher's,** 27 Frederick St. (tel. 623-5912), which sells crystal, watches, jewelry, perfumes, Georg Jensen silver, handbags, Royal Copenhagen china, and other in-bond items which can be delivered to Piarco International Airport upon your departure. If you don't want to go downtown, there's a branch at the Hilton. Among the famous names represented here are Patek-Phillippe, Piaget, Girard Pérregaux, Royal Crown Derby, Bing & Grondahl, Belleek, Rosenthal, Lalique, Baccarat, and Swarovski. If you miss both shops, you can always pay a last-minute call at their tax-free airport branch, where they sell perfume, Cartier lighters, pens, leather goods, Hummel figurines, Swarovski crystal, local ceramics, other gift items, cigarettes, and cigars.

Y. de Lima, 23A Frederick St. (tel. 623-1364), is another good store for duty-free cameras, watches, and local jewelry. Its third-floor workroom will make what you want in goldwork, be it charms, brooches, pins, earrings, whatever. You may emerge with everything from steel-drum earrings to a hibiscus blossom brooch.

Lakhan's Bazaar, 32 W. Main Rd. (tel. 622-4688), has an interesting selection of Indian merchandise, including beautifully designed saris, rugs, embroidered purses, as well as sandals. Go here also for ivory figurines, silk scarfs, and brass and copper ware.

Art Creators and Suppliers, Apt. 402, Aldegonda Park, 7 St. Ann's Rd., St. Ann's (tel. 624-4369). It's in a relatively banal concrete-sided apartment complex, but the paintings sold inside are among the finest in the Caribbean. Clara Rosa de Lima is the creative force behind the gallery. Recognized as an authority on Trinidadian art, she spends a good portion of her time evaluating, encouraging, and educating emerging artists. The works sold here, however, are fairly priced examples of the very best of Trinidad. Among the artistic giants represented are the Holder brothers, both Geoffrey and Boscoe, along with Robert Mackie and Noël Vaucrosson. Ms. de Lima is usually candid about the relative merits of artists she represents, and maintains dialogues with a handful of artists in Brazil and Guyana as well. Paintings begin at $400 TT ($112), but could stretch up into the thousands of U.S. dollars. The gallery is open weekdays from 10 a.m. to 1 p.m. and on Saturday from 10 a.m. to noon. It is closed on Sunday.

Gallery 1-2-3-4, St. Ann's Village (tel. 627-1673). Probably more iconoclastic and less conservative than any other gallery on the island, this art center displays its paintings in a space of minimalist walls and careful lighting. Marie Henderson, the Marseille-born director, uses her soft-spoken charm to encourage local artists in their endeavors. The gallery opened in 1985, and since then has attracted the attention of the art world. Its hours on weekdays are 10 a.m. to 6:30 p.m., on Saturday from 11 a.m. to 4 p.m., and on Sunday a variable schedule depending on a particular exhibit on display.

Meiling's, Marli Street, at the corner of Woodford (tel. 622-2987), is the island's only outlet for the creations of one of Trinidad's most famous designers, Meiling Esau. The free-flowing women's clothing is usually made from cotton, cotton jersey, or cotton voile (often with sequins and sometimes in batik). Dresses are appropriate for sports or evening wear and are priced from $110 TT ($30.75) to $800 TT ($224). Meiling's is located in the same Edwardian house as the previously recommended Veranda Restaurant.

St. Ann's Village, Nook Avenue (tel. 624-1181), is one of the most fashionable shopping complexes in Trinidad, containing (perhaps at the time of your visit) 27 boutiques. Its client list includes some of the best jewelers, designers, and art dealers in

Trinidad. Some of these shops come and go, so I won't recommend any one specifically. It's more a place for window-shopping and browsing at leisure. The complex forms an interconnected bride among three previously recommended establishments, the Hotel Normandie, the Restaurant Fantasie, and a top-notch art emporium, the Gallery.

The **Trinidad and Tobago Blind Welfare Association,** 118 Duke St. (tel. 624-4659), makes everything from furniture to shopping baskets with rattan peel, rattan core, and sea grass. If you make a purchase here, you'll also be helping a sightless worker who is trying to help himself or herself.

The **Trinidad and Tobago Handicraft Cooperative** has its main shop at the Trinidad Hilton (tel. 624-3111). Here they offer items in fiber, straw, and wood, and they also sell small steel drums known locally as "ping pongs." Many other local products are sold, including everything from hammocks to salad bowls in purple heart.

AFTER DARK: At night in Port-of-Spain you'll hear the sounds of calypso and steel bands. Or hopefully you will.

Unfortunately, some of the best calypso is not in the capital, but at places such as **Sparrow's Hideaway** (no phone), my personal favorite. It costs only $40 TT ($11.25) to enter, but it's a nine-mile taxi ride from the center of Port-of-Spain. Go only on a Saturday night. I recently asked three taxi drivers what it would cost to take me there and each one came up with a different figure, so I don't know what the going rate will be at the time of your visit. Of course, all collectors of calypso records know that "The Sparrow" is one of Trinidad's most famous singers. He is in fact known as the "calypso king of the world." If you're devotee enough to go, don't expect to see any fellow tourists. It's strictly a local crowd. Ask at your hotel reception desk for directions on how to get there. The club lies in Petit Valley at Diego Martin.

If you like your calypso in tamer surroundings than the famous but dangerous Independence Square, try the **Calypso Lounge** at the Holiday Inn, Wrightson Road (tel. 625-3361), in Port-of-Spain. A local combo plays for dancing and some of the best calypsonians are brought in to entertain guests, especially in the winter months. Special shows are staged on Friday and Saturday when the minimum charge is $10 TT ($2.75).

Chaconia Inn, 106 Saddle Rd., Maraval (tel. 629-2101), becomes a "hot spot" on Friday and Saturday night when a Trinidadian band is brought in between 11 p.m. and 1 a.m. The charge is $15 TT ($4.25) for a couple, $10 TT ($2.75) for a single.

At **Jay Bee's** in the Valpark Plaza (tel. 662-5837), the restaurant offers fine steaks and seafood, and is open weekdays for lunch and Monday to Saturday for dinner, costing from $25. The disco is open Wednesday to Saturday from 9 p.m. You should dress up a bit, as a dress code is strictly enforced. No reservations are necessary.

Finally, you may want to attend the **Hilton Poolside Fiesta** at the already-recommended Trinidad Hilton, Port-of-Spain (tel. 624-3211). For about $85 TT ($23.75) per person, every Monday night at 10 the Hilton presents a traditional native show with limbo dancers and a steel band. A barbecue at 7 p.m. precedes the entertainment.

5. A Side Trip to Tobago

Unlike bustling Trinidad, its sister island of Tobago is sleepy. Trinidadians go there, especially on weekends, to enjoy its wide sandy beaches. The legendary home of Robinson Crusoe, Tobago is only 27 miles long and 7½ miles wide. The people are quiet and friendly, and their villages are so tiny they seem to blend with the landscape.

Fish-shaped Tobago was probably sighted by Columbus in 1498 when he discovered Trinidad, but the island was so tiny he paid no attention to it in his log. For the next 100 years it lay almost unexplored. In 1628 when Charles I of England gave it to one of his nobles, the Earl of Pembroke, the maritime countries of Europe suddenly showed a belated interest. From then on, Tobago was fought over no fewer than 31 times by the Spanish, French, Dutch, and English, as well as marauding pirates and privateers.

After 1803 the island settled down to enjoy a sugar monopoly unbroken for decades. Great houses were built, and in London it used to be said of a wealthy man that he was "as rich as a Tobago planter." The island's economy collapsed in 1884 and Tobago entered an acute depression. The ruling monopoly, Gillespie Brothers, declared itself bankrupt and went out of business. The British government made Tobago a ward of Trinidad in 1889, and sugar was never revived.

Tobago lies 20 miles to the northeast of Trinidad, from which it is reached by frequent flights. It has long been known as a honeymooner's paradise. The physical beauty of Tobago is stunning, with its forests of breadfruit, mango, cocoa, and citrus, through which a chartreuse-colored iguana will suddenly dart. Jungle brooks dance over rocks.

The island's village-like capital is **Scarborough**, which is also the main port. Most of the shops are clustered in streets around the market. From Scarborough one can either go cross-country toward Plymouth or head toward the southwest part of Tobago.

For "Practical Facts," refer to Trinidad. Essentially the same customs apply.

The **Tobago Tourist Bureau**, Administration Building, Scarborough (tel. 639-2125), provides general information about the island.

Nearly all passengers arrive from Trinidad, where they have already cleared Customs.

GETTING THERE: First, you go to Trinidad (see "Getting There" in the preceding section). Between Trinidad and Tobago, **BWIA** links the two sister islands with about 14 flights a day (sometimes they are impossibly overbooked). The first flight for Tobago leaves Trinidad at 6:20 a.m., and the last flight back to Trinidad departs Tobago at 8:45 p.m. You're airborne only 20 minutes. Inter-island flights tend to be crowded on weekends when Trinidadians themselves head to Tobago and its beaches. On certain flights to Trinidad, the side trip to Tobago can be included for no extra charge (ask a travel agent before flying to Trinidad how this works).

If you want to go to Tobago by boat, the *Getling,* a coastal ferry with a bar and a trio of restaurants, makes the trip in about five hours. Tourist class is only $13 TT ($3.64) one way.

Tobago's small airport is at its southwestern tip, Crown Point.

GETTING AROUND: From the airport to your hotel, take an unmetered taxi. The taxi fare from say, Crown Point Airport to the Arnos Vale Hotel is $45 TT ($12.50). You can also arrange (or have your hotel do it for you) a sightseeing tour by taxi. Rates have to be negotiated on an individual basis. For example, five passengers can take a four-hour tour going all the way to Charlotteville and back for a cost of $225 TT ($63).

For car rentals, get in touch with **Tobago Travel**, Milford Road, Store Bay (tel. 639-8778), where the average cost of a small vehicle is about $45 to $50 per day, unlimited mileage. Gas, as of this writing, is $4.50 TT ($1.25) per liter. An international driver's license, if valid, entitles you to drive on Tobago's often bad roads. *Don't forget that you must drive on the left.*

If you prefer to get around by motor scooter, **Banana Rentals,** Banana House, Kariwak Village, Scarborough (tel. 639-8441), offers Honda vehicles that are economical to operate. You can rent a scooter for as little as $12.

Public buses are sometimes modern and always very inexpensive. Buses travel from one end of the island to the other several times a day. Of course, expect an unscheduled stop at any passenger's doorstep, and never, but never, be in a hurry.

HOTELS OF TOBAGO: Quiet, tranquil oases, the hotels of Tobago are more for retreats, attracting those visitors who seek hideaways instead of action at high-rise resorts. Many of the hotels recommended below have been handsomely landscaped to blend into the natural terrain. Because of the shortage of restaurants on the island, it's best to take the MAP (breakfast and dinner) when booking a room.

Mount Irvine Bay Hotel, P.O. Box 222, Scarborough (tel. 639-8871), is Tobago's most expensive spa, built around an old sugar mill and bordering one of the finest golf courses in the Caribbean. On the north shore of the island, about a 20-minute drive from the airport, it brings to mind one of those luxurious country clubs, San Clemente style. The setting is on 150 acres of spread-out lawns, tropical gardens, areas for tennis, and an angular, free-form swimming pool with a swim-in bar and its surrounding terrace. It's like a resort community. Built L-shaped around the pool, a two-story hacienda wing of guest rooms is all air-conditioned, each with a private bath and its own terrace or balcony. These units open toward the green lawns with their brilliantly colored blossoms on flowery shrubbery. The rest of the cottages are in small square houses covered with such planting as beliconia. Each of these cottages has two rooms which are rented separately, each with a private bath and patio and a view of the fairways or the water. In winter, single rates in the main building range from $175 to $190 daily, with doubles costing $205 to $220, all half-board terms. Cottages cost $205 daily if occupied by one person, $235 if by two, both half-board rates. *In the off-season, it becomes cheaper, from $95 to $110 daily in a single, from $135 to $145 in a double, all MAP terms. Cottages cost a peak $125 daily in a single, from $160 in a double, again MAP*.

The most impressive place to dine is the Sugar Mill Restaurant, built around the 200-year-old circular stone mill, under a shingled, raftered conical roof. While enjoying the smell of jasmine, you dine at a candlelit table. The cuisine is of an acceptable international standard. You can order drinks in the Cocrico Lounge, named after the national bird of Tobago. There's dancing almost every evening on the Sugar Mill Patio. Calypso singers are brought in, barbecues are held, and limbo dancers and occasional shows entertain you, particularly in season. Guests of the hotel also become temporary members of the golf club (see "The Sporting Life," below).

Arnos Vale, P.O. Box 208 (tel. 639-2881), was once a sugar plantation, but you wouldn't know that now. On the north coast about a mile from Plymouth, Arnos Vale is one of the oldest hotels on Tobago, an unusual retreat tucked away on 400 tropical acres opening directly on Arnos Vale Bay. A former English owner was a lover of nature, and he planted the place like a botanical garden, with frangipani and oleander predominating. In days of yore you might have run into one of the Beatles sneaking through the lush foliage, or perhaps a married movie star with a wife not his own. A Mediterranean aura prevails, but the bananaquits and mot-mots keep it definitely in the Caribbean. Its red-tile-roofed main house stands at the top of the hill. You can enjoy good drinks in the bar or on the al fresco patio, then go across to the dining room to be served one of the best meals on the island. Both an English fare and a Tobago cuisine are served, including such island dishes as callaloo soup, souse, and pelau. From this main house, you'll have a magnificent panorama out over a secluded crescent bay to the sea. Part of Arnos Vale's historical legacy can be seen in the dining room—an original grand piano built by Playel for the Paris Exhibition in 1851. The piano is completely hand-painted.

Rooms come in many different styles and shapes, ranging from the Jacamar just off the beach to the Coral Cottage with an aerial view of the bay. Most of the furniture is custom made of local cedar. In winter, a single on the half-board arrangement rents for $135 daily, going up to $180 to $175 in a twin. *In summer, these rates are lowered to $100 daily in a single, from $120 to $140 in a twin*. All tariffs include breakfast, dinner, and afternoon tea. On the richly planted grounds is a freshwater swimming pool. Peace and tranquility are stressed, but occasionally native steel bands are brought in to play, and there are beach barbecues. In addition, you'll find a tennis court.

Turtle Beach, P.O. Box 201 (tel. 639-2851), stands directly on one mile of sandy beach opening on Great Courtland Bay, on the leeward shore in the midst of a 600-acre coconut plantation. Housed in two-story units, all rooms are oceanfront and air-conditioned, with private baths containing both tub and shower, patio or balcony, and almost direct access to the beach. The location is just eight miles from the airport, from which taxi transfers are available. The inn is also five miles from Scarborough. The entrance loggia is the longest covered terrace on the island, where a slow pace sets the tempo of the relaxed, casual lifestyle of the hotel. While seated on sofas and in armchairs, you can enjoy tall fruit-and-rum drinks. Lunches are served around the garden pool or at the beach. Three times a week calypso music can be heard in the evening. Perhaps a steel band will be brought in. If you don't want the beach, you can swim in a freshwater pool. Bedroom accommodations lie in an interconnected series of white bungalows with V-shaped roofs, between beds of hibiscus and oleander. Units have individual air conditioning and smartly tailored furnishings. Rooms on the second floor have sloped open-beamed ceilings, with white walls and shuttered doors that can be pushed back to enlarge the living areas. EP rates are $112 in a single, $120 in a double in winter, *dropping to $120 in a single and $75 in a double in summer*. Fishing trips can be arranged, as can snorkeling at Buccoo Reef. A dive and water-sports shop is on the hotel premises.

Kariwak Village, P.O. Box 27, Scarborough (tel. 639-8545), is a self-contained cluster of cottages that evoke the South Pacific in style. The location of this 18-room cluster is about a six-minute walk from the beach and only ten minutes from the airport. The hotel's name was formed by combining Carib with Arawak, the original inhabitants of the Caribbeans. The builders turned to the original elements of Tobago in their construction, making much use of palm fronds, raw teak, coral stone, and bamboo. EP singles in high season rent for $60 daily; couples pay $76. *In the low season, EP singles cost $36; doubles, $50*. Breakfast and dinner are about another $15 per person daily. Each well-furnished unit has air conditioning and a private bathroom. Live entertainment, at least in season, is provided on weekends. The food served in the main restaurant is among the best on the island, and you may want to come here for a meal even if you aren't staying here.

Crown Reef Hotel, P.O. Box 45, Storebay (tel. 639-8571), is handsomely modern, standing on landscaped grounds with much tropical greenery and flowers. It also opens onto its own coral reef and an excellent, uncrowded beach. Don't come here seeking local island color. However, if you want some of the finest contemporary facilities Tobago has to offer, then you're at the right place, and can select from among 115 well-furnished suites and bedrooms, each with a private balcony or patio. In winter, a single rents for $130 daily, and a double goes for $130 to $150 on the EP, plus tax and service. *In the off-season, EP terms in a single are $70 daily, going up to $80 to $96 in a double*. The dining room is approached from the lobby by a circular, open staircase, extending on rocks over water. The terrazzo lounge has white deck chairs with pillows covered in flamboyant fabric. The menu has both Stateside and continental dishes, along with some Trinidadian specialties. Perched on a coral rock at water's edge is a thatched beach bar. Sometimes native dancers and steel bands are brought in. A freshwater swimming pool is set in the midst of the lush gardens. Most water sports are offered, including scuba-diving and snorkeling, and you can play tennis on the hotel's courts. An 18-hole golf course is nearby.

Sandy Point Beach Club, Crown Point (tel. 639-8533), is a winning miniature vacation village built in 1977 somewhat in the style of a Riviera condominium. Each apartment has a kitchenette, allowing guests to be independent. It's just a three-minute run from the airport, but its shoreside position makes it seem remote. The little village of peaked and gabled roofs is landscaped all the way down to the sandy beach, where there's a rustic Steak Hut which serves meals throughout the day and evening. The units, consisting of 20 suites and 22 studio apartments, are air-conditioned and fully equipped, each opening onto a patio, toward the sea, or onto a covered loggia. The rental units contain living and dining areas with pine trestle tables, plus a color TV. In some of the apartments is a rustic open stairway leading to a loft room with bunk beds, although there is a twin-bedded room on the lower level as well. *Double occupancy costs $42 to $50 daily in the off-season, EP*, and $70 to $80 daily in winter. Service and tax are extra. The hotel has a sauna, and you can emerge from its intense heat to the shade of a banyan tree beside a swimming pool. To avoid overcrowding, the hotel has added another swimming pool as well.

The **Della Mira Guest House,** Windward Road, Scarborough (tel. 639-2531), is a simple West Indian guesthouse where the warm hospitality of Neville Miranda and his wife, Angela, is extended. The place is modest and intimate—in reality a small inn where there's an open living room area with pleasantly provincial furnishings. In an adjoining dining room Angela serves authentic island dishes. Tobagoans are fond of coming here, as it has a real atmosphere which most of the other hotels lack. The location is on a cool, airy site overlooking the sea, about half a mile from stores and churches and some 50 yards from the beach. You can also swim in a pool set in the lawn of the garden, around which a terrace has been built for sunning. The bedrooms overlook the garden and the pool, but some cheaper units look out onto the hills. The bedrooms, 14 in all, have a basic simplicity, nothing fancy, yet everything is clean and comfortable. All the rooms come with private bath, and about half of them are air-conditioned as well. Rates, in effect all year, range from $18 to $20 daily in a single, from $25 to $29 in a double. Some triples are rented for only $40 a day. Lunches or dinners range from $12 to $15. On the premises is one of Tobago's leading nightclubs, La Tropicale, plus a beauty salon. Mrs. Miranda, incidentally, is one of two licensed barbers on the island.

Man-o-War Bay Cottages, Charlotteville (tel. 639-4327). If you're seeking a Caribbean hideaway—that is, a cluster of beach cottages—then the Man-o-War might be for you. The cottages are a part of Charlotteville Estate, a working 1,000-acre cocoa plantation. The entire estate is open to visitors, who may wander through at will. Pat and Charles Turpin rent out four bungalows near a two-mile-long white sandy beach. Each unit comes complete with two bedrooms, a kitchen, a spacious living and dining room, a private bath, and a porch opening onto the sea. Year round you can rent a cottage at $60 daily or a large four-bedroom bungalow (big enough to sleep ten) for only $100 a day. A maid and or cook can be hired for very little extra. Near the colony is a coral reef that is an ideal ground for snorkelers. The couple will also arrange a boat rental if you want to explore Lovers' Beach. Many birdwatchers looking for rare species often book one of these bungalows.

Man-o-War Cottages are 36 miles from the bustle of the airport. The ride follows a bumpy coastal road offering views over the sea and passing through many small villages en route.

Blue Waters Inn, Batteaux Bay, Speyside (tel. 639-4341), is a little inn run by Barbara and Fred Zollna. They are to be applauded for charging the same rates for foreign visitors as they do to local residents (unlike many, many places in the Caribbean which have two sets of tariffs). The remotely perched inn lies on the northeast coast of Tobago, about 24 miles from the airport and 20 miles from Scarborough. Figure either by private car or taxi that it's a 1½-hour drive along narrow, winding country roads. They rent out 17 rooms and cabañas, each unit with private shower and toilet. On the EP, rates in winter are $34 daily in a single, $52 in a double. *Summer prices are $25 in a single, $45 in a double.* The MAP supplement is $21. Meals are served in their casual restaurant, and there's also a bar dispensing tropical libations. This is an extremely informal place, so leave your fancy resortwear at home. Fishing, tennis, shuffleboard, scuba, and skindiving can be arranged, as well as boat trips to Little Tobago. The property is a veritable bird sanctuary, a boon for nature lovers and bird-watchers.

Holiday Homes

There are 15 attractive, almost luxurious, privately owned holiday houses which can be rented throughout the year in Tobago. These rental units are among the most inexpensive ways of living well in the West Indies. Private owners have built and completely furnished these retreats for their own holidays. However, to cut back on expenses they rent these houses out to visitors, either weekly or monthly. When shared by a group of four to six persons, they become very cheap. Most houses accommodate at least six guests. In winter, villas rent for $120 to $165, *The rates dropping to $110 to $150 in summer*. Houses vary greatly in shape, price, and size, but all of them have tile baths, comfortable twin-bedded rooms, living rooms, fully equipped kitchens, patios, terraces, gardens, and private swimming pools. Half-day maid service is included, except on Sunday. Some of the houses have panoramic views of the coastline and the Buccoo Reef, and some are on a rise overlooking the 18-hole Mount Irvine Golf Course. All are close to fine beaches. For further information, write to **Tobago Villas Agency**, P.O. Box 301, Scarborough, Tobago, W.I. (tel. 639-8737).

WHERE TO EAT: Most guests eat at their hotels, which seem to have a monopoly on the best chefs. However, increasingly there are some good independent restaurants.

Sugar Mill Restaurant, Mount Irvine Bay Hotel (tel. 639-8871). Its core is a 200-year-old sugar mill whose walls were fashioned from chiseled blocks of coral. Out of it radiate the spidery arms of a beamed ceiling, the shingles of which protect the dozens of manicured tables from the direct sunlight. Open-air, breezy, and casually elegant, this is probably the best restaurant in Tobago. Nonresidents are welcome, but only if they phone for a reservation. Breakfast costs from $15 TT ($4.25) and is served from 7 to 10 a.m. Lunch, depending on how formal you want to be, goes for $20 TT ($5.50) to $60 TT ($16.75) and includes everything from salads and sandwiches to lamb chops provençale or sirloin steak. Dinner, from 7 to 10 p.m., includes a fixed-price menu at $80 TT ($22.50). On any given night the chef might prepare lobster bisque, a carbonade of beef, shrimp Newburg with rice pilaf, and filet of dolphin. Meals are usually accompanied by live music and entertainment, at least in season.

Turtle Beach Hotel Restaurant, Turtle Beach Hotel (tel. 639-2851). Informally casual, its tables sit on an outdoor veranda whose edges overlook a tropical garden and the sea. On certain nights, limbo dancers and Tobagoan musicians provide live entertainment. Lunch is served daily from 1 to 2:30 p.m.; dinner, from 8 to 9:30 p.m. Cuisine minceur is available as a calorie-conscious alternative to the other specialties. These include lobster Thermidor, breast of chicken with paprika sauce, fish filet in cider, pan-fried kingfish, callaloo, and stuffed Plymouth crab back. Full dinners cost from $75 TT ($21), with less elaborate lunches going for $45 TT ($12.50). Reservations are suggested for nonresidents.

Old Donkey Cart House, Bacolet Street, Scarborough (tel. 639-3551). An unusual and noteworthy restaurant, it occupies a green-and-white Edwardian house about half a mile south of Scarborough. Its entrepreneurial owner, Gloria Jones Schoen, capitalized on her exotic beauty by working as a fashion model in West Germany. She still makes occasional forays into the Teutonic world of couture, but most of her time is spent directing her polite staff. "Born, bred, and dragged up" in Tobago, she is today the island's leading authority on German wines, which she buys directly from well-established German vineyards and sells in her restaurant as appropriate complements to her Caribbean and Germanic cuisine. She's open from noon to 2 a.m. daily except Sunday when she opens at 6:30 p.m. Slide shows and sometimes performances of live music add to the Sunday-evening allure. When Gloria is away, her competent daughter, Samantha Mackey, replaces her. Full meals cost from $60 TT ($16.75). These might include stuffed crab back, shrimp and crabmeat cocktail, beef Stroganoff, omelets, and a succulent collection of shrimp, crabmeat, and fresh fish. When Ms. Schoen established her business in 1978, "sheep and goats scampered through the living room.'' Today you can dine behind a screen of bamboo and palmetto in the front garden or head for one of the plank-topped tables inside.

The Steak Hut, Sandy Point Beach Club, Crown Point (tel. 639-8533), serves the best meat on the island, specializing in U.S. sirloin, T-bone, porterhouse, and tenderloin. The location near the beach and swimming pool of this previously recommended hotel is ideal, especially in the evening. The seafront restaurant also features local fish steaks from shark, flying fish, grouper, dolphin, barracuda, and kingfish. A regular à la carte dinner costs $75 TT ($21). However, specials are staged many times. For example, every Friday night a three-course fish dinner costs $40 TT ($11.25), and a steak dinner goes for $50 TT ($14), with all the rum you can drink. A steel band plays most Friday nights. Every Wednesday a complete Indian curry dinner with a choice of curry shrimp or chicken or beef is available, costing $35 TT ($9.75). Daily hours are 7:30 a.m. to 10 a.m. if you want breakfast, noon to 3 p.m. for lunch, and 7 to 9 p.m. for dinner.

The Blue Crab, corner of Fort and Main Streets, Scarborough (tel. 639-2737). One of my favorite restaurants in the capital, this family-run establishment occupies an Edwardian-era house with an oversize veranda. This is the domain of the Sardinha family, who returned to their native country after a sojourn in New York. Keeping their establishment together with ''spit and love'' after setting it up in 1984, they learned to make the most of local ingredients and local spices. Lunch is daily from 11 a.m. to 2:30 p.m., costing from $22 TT ($6.25). Dinners, however, require an advance reservation and might not always be available. When they are served, the menu will be dictated by whatever was available that day in the market place. The cost is likely to be from $35 TT ($9.75) unless lobster is served. If so, meals are about twice that much. Menu items include fresh seafood, shrimp, an array of Créole-style meat dishes grilled over coconut husks, flying fish in a mild curry-flavored batter, shrimp with garlic butter or cream, and a vegetable-laced rice dish of the day.

WHAT TO SEE: In Tobago's capital, **Scarborough,** you can enjoy a native market every morning except Sunday, listening to the sounds of a Créole patois.

The village-like place need claim your attention very little before you climb up the hill to **Fort King George,** about 430 feet above the town. Built by the English in 1779, it was later captured by the French. After that it jockeyed back and forth between various conquerors until nature decided to end it all in 1847, blowing off the roofs of its buildings. Sunset over Tobago is spectacular. The cannons still mounted had a three-mile range, and one is believed to have come from one of the ships of Sir Francis Drake (you can still see a replica of the Tudor rose). One building used to house a powder magazine, and you can see the ruins of a military hospital. Artifacts are displayed in a gallery on the grounds.

From Scarborough you can drive northwest to **Plymouth,** Tobago's other town. In the graveyard of the little church is a tombstone dating from 1783 with a mysterious inscription: ''She was a mother without knowing it, and a wife, without letting her husband know it, except by her kind indulgences to him.''

Perched on a point at Plymouth is **Fort James,** which dates from 1768 when built by the British as a barracks. It is now mainly in ruins.

From Speyside you can make arrangements with some local fisherman to go to **Little Tobago,** an offshore 450-acre island where a bird sanctuary attracts ornithologists. Threatened with extinction in New Guinea, many birds, perhaps 50 species in all, were brought over to this little island in the early part of this century.

Off Pigeon Point lies **Buccoo Reef** (see the ''Sporting Life'' section) where sea gardens of coral and hundreds of colorful fish can be seen in waist-deep water. This is the natural aquarium of Tobago. Nearly all the major hotels arrange boat trips here to these acres of submarine gardens which offer the best scuba-diving and snorkeling. You can get right in among the various types of tropical fish and other marine creatures. Even nonswimmers can wade knee-deep in the crystal-clear waters. Remember to protect your head and body from the tropical heat and to guard your feet against the sharp coral. A broad-brimmed hat plus an old shirt are necessary, as are canvas shoes.

After about half an hour at the reef, passengers reboard their boats and go over to Nylon Pool, with its crystal-clear waters. There in this white sand bottom, about a mile offshore, you can enjoy water only three to four feet deep. After a swim, the boatman returns you to Buccoo Village jetty in time for a goat and crab race.

At the **Museum of Tobago History,** on the grounds of the Mount Irvine Bay Hotel (tel. 639-8871), you'll find artifacts, implements, and pottery of the Caribs and Arawaks who used to inhabit Tobago. Tobago's archeological and historic past comes alive. The museum is open from 5:30 to 8:30 p.m. on Tuesday and Thursday, from 4:30 to 7:30 p.m. on Sunday. Admission is $2 TT (55¢) for adults, 25¢ TT (7¢) for children.

SHOPPING: Scarborough's stores have a limited range of merchandise, more to tempt the browser than the serious shopper.

Stecher's, Main Street (tel. 639-2377), has a more famous and better branch in Trinidad. However, this store stocks a limited range of merchandise, including crystal, pipes from Scotland, Seiko watches, and gold jewelry.

Y. de Lima, Burnett Street (tel. 639-2464), has a small outlet in Scarborough (a much bigger supply is in Trinidad). Here you'll find a small range of merchandise, including jewelry and cameras. It's not duty free, however.

THE SPORTING LIFE: If beach-fringed Tobago wasn't in fact the alleged locale of Daniel Defoe's immortal story, the visitors who enjoy its superb beaches hardly seem to care. On Tobago sands you can still feel like Robinson Crusoe in a solitary cove, at least for most of the week before the Trinidadians fly over to sample the sands on a Saturday.

A good beach, **Back Bay,** is within an eight-minute walk of the Mount Irvine Bay Hotel. Along the way you'll pass a coconut plantation and an old cannon emplacement. Sometimes there can be dangerous currents here. But you can always enjoy exploring Rocky Point with its brilliantly colored parrot fish.

Try also **Man O'War Bay,** one of the finest natural harbors in the West Indies, at the opposite end of the island. Once there, you'll find a long sandy beach, and you can also enjoy a picnic at a government-run rest house.

The finest for last, **Pigeon Point** on the island's northwest coast is the best-known bathing area with a long coral beach. You'll find thatched shelters for changing into bathing attire, as well as tables and benches for picnics.

Golf

Tobago is the proud possessor of an 18-hole, 6,800-yard golf course at Mount Irvine. Called the **Tobago Golf Club** (tel. 639-8871), it covers 150 acres of breeze-swept courses and was featured in the "Wonderful World of Golf" TV series. The course—and even beginners agree—is considered "friendly" to golfers. As a guest of the Mount Irvine Bay Hotel you are granted temporary membership and use of the clubhouse and facilities. Resident hotel guests are entitled to discounts. All serious golfers should stay at the Mount Irvine.

Tennis

The Crown Reef (tel. 639-8571) and **Turtle Beach Hotels** (tel. 639-2851) have courts. The best courts, however, are at the **Mount Irvine Bay Hotel** (tel. 639-8871), where two good courts are available free to guests. There is a $3 surcharge for night games.

Scuba-Diving and Snorkeling

Unspoiled reefs off Tobago teem with a great variety of marine life. Colorful sponges and fish can be seen against a background of gorgonians and coral formations ranging from the tiniest spines to giant brain coral. Divers can swim through rocky canyons 60 to 130 feet deep, and underwater photographers can shoot pictures they won't find anywhere else. Snorkeling over the celebrated Buccoo Reef is one of the specialties of Tobago. Hotels arrange for their guests to visit this underwater wonderland.

The **Turtle Beach Hotel,** Great Courtland Bay (tel. 639-2851), is the best equipped for water sports. Scuba-diving is offered at prices covering equipment rental or for use of your own gear.

Dive Tobago Ltd., P.O. Box 53, Pigeon Point (tel. 639-2266), offers dives at prices which vary according to whether the diver has his or her own equipment.

Tobago Scuba Ltd., Speyside (tel. 639-4360), offers scuba-dives, snorkeling, and windsurfing, as well as boat trips and fishing excursions. Prices of scuba-dives depend on whether you have your own equipment (must include mask, snorkel, fins, B.C., and regulator) or rent it from the shop.

Windsurfing

Instruction as well as rental of gear for experienced windsurfers, is offered at the **Turtle Beach Hotel,** Great Courtland Bay (tel. 639-2851).

Boating

The **Turtle Beach Hotel,** Great Courtland Bay (tel. 639-2851), also rents Sunfish for $50 TT ($14) per hour and paddleboats at $15 TT ($4.25) for half an hour or $25 TT ($7) per hour.

Deep-Sea Fishing

Stanley Dillon, Milford Bay (tel. 639-8765), takes anglers out on his 31-foot twin outboard with outriggers and fighting chairs. The boat holds a maximum of four persons. The price is to be negotiated with Captain Dillon.

Field Trips

Ten different field trips offer closeup views of Tobago's exotic and often rare tropical birds, as well as a range of other island wildlife. Two renowned naturalists of the Trinidad-Tobago area guide these excursions. They are David Rooks, four-time president of the Field Naturalist Club of Trinidad and Tobago, and Renson Jack, a game warden for the Forestry Division of the islands. The trips lead you to forest trails, coconut plantations, along rivers, and past waterfalls. Each trip lasts about two to three hours so you can take at least two per day if you like. One excursion goes to two nearby islands.

The price per trip is $15 per person. For details, get in touch with **Pat Turpin,** Man-O-War Bay Cottages, Charlotteville, Tobago (tel. 639-4327).

NIGHTLIFE: Hotels with nightlife, luring the well-heeled visitor, include **Mount Irvine Bay Hotel** (tel. 639-8871) and **Turtle Beach Hotel** (tel. 639-2851), both previously recommended. The Turtle Beach has a popular barbecue on Saturday night from 8 to 9:30 p.m., with poolside dancing to a steel band continuing until late.

For the best island nightclub entertainment on the "big" Saturday night, head for **Club La Tropicale,** at the Della Mira Guest House, Windward Road, Scarborough (tel. 639-2239). In a tropical breeze-swept setting, it offers floor shows, steel bands, and calypso. The cover charge is $10 TT ($2.75), and hours are 8 p.m. to 1 or 2 a.m.

Chapter XVI

THE DUTCH LEEWARDS

1. Aruba
2. Bonaire
3. Curaçao

AS DUTCH AS a wooden shoe, the so-called ABC group of islands—Aruba, Bonaire, and Curaçao—lie just off the northern coast of Venezuela. The islands cover only 363 square miles, with a widely diversified population of some 225,000 people, many of whom speak Papiamento, a patois language, although Dutch is the official tongue.

Duty-free shopping and gambling are promoted by the government in all three islands. Curaçao has the most Dutch atmosphere, with a number of 18th-century buildings. Curaçao, along with Aruba, also has the most developed tourist centers, with Bonaire attracting the most dedicated scuba-divers. Someone once said that there are more flamingos than people in Bonaire. Aruba has the best beaches and the most hotel accommodations.

These spotless islands still retain old-world charm and are clean and prosperous.

The canny Dutch emerged from the European power struggle in the West Indies with these tiny specks of land, arid and for all appearances inconsequential. But they proceeded to turn these ugly-duckling properties into some of the most valuable real estate in the Caribbean. In January of 1986, Aruba broke away from its sister islands and plans full independence by 1996.

Other Dutch-held islands in the Caribbean, including Saba, St. Eustatius (Statia), and St. Maarten, have already been previewed in Chapter X, "Dutch Windwards in the Leewards."

1. Aruba

At first you'll think you're on a movie set for a Hollywood western, the terrain is so similar. But instead of cowboys you'll meet a friendly people, many of whom speak Papiamento, a mélange of Spanish, Portuguese, Dutch, and some Indian words.

Forget lush vegetation and palm-framed vistas in Aruba. That's impossible with only 17 inches of rainfall annually. Aruba is dry and sunny year round, its clean, exhilarating air desert-like. However, trade winds keep the island from becoming uncomfortably hot. At least you can be sure of the sun every day of your vacation in Aruba.

Cactus fences surround pastel-washed houses, divi-divi trees with their wind-blown look stud the barren countryside, free-form boulders are scattered about, and on occasion you'll come across an abandoned gold mine.

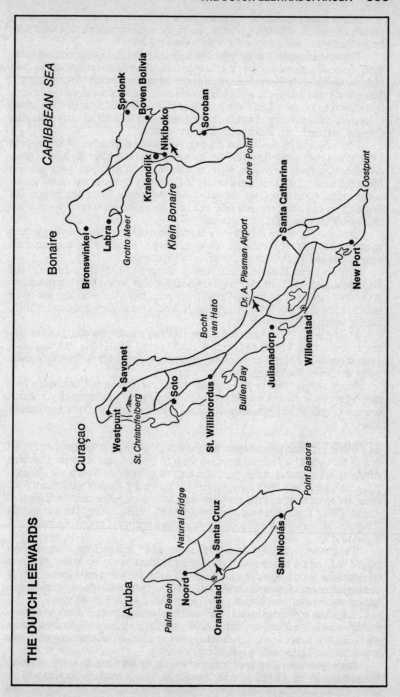

THE DUTCH LEEWARDS

CARIBBEAN SEA

Bonaire

Spelonk
Boven Bolivia
Soroban
Nikiboko
Kralendijk
Klein Bonaire
Labra
Grotto Meer
Bronswinkel
Lacre Point

Curaçao

Santa Catharina
Dr. A. Plesman Airport
New Port
Oostpunt
Willemstad
Bocht van Hato
Julianadorp
Bullen Bay
Savonet
Soto
St. Willibrordus
Westpunt
St. Christoffelberg

Aruba

Point Basora
Natural Bridge
Santa Cruz
San Nicolás
Noord
Palm Beach
Oranjestad

Aruba stands outside the hurricane path. Its coastline on the leeward side is smooth and serene, with sandy beaches; but on the eastern coast, the windward side, the look is rugged and wild, typical of the windswept Atlantic.

The westernmost of the Netherlands Antilles, Aruba lies 15 miles north of Venezuela. Some 40 nationalities live peacefully on the island, which is an autonomous part of the Kingdom of the Netherlands, with a political structure called "Status Aparte." This gives Aruba the right to administer its own internal affairs, while the Netherlands is responsible for the island's foreign affairs and defense. Aruba also has strong economic, cultural, and political ties to Holland and to its sister islands of Bonaire, Curaçao, and the Dutch Windwards in the Leewards.

First inhabited by the Arawak Indians, Aruba was discovered by Spaniards in 1494. It was claimed for Spain in 1499 by Alonso de Ojeda, although Madrid never considered Aruba of any value. Near the culmination of the 80-year war between Spain and Holland, the Dutch took over in 1643. Pieter Stuyvesant was named governor of Aruba, a post he held for four years before going on to Nieuw Amsterdam. The English were in control between 1805 and 1816 during the Napoleonic Wars. When the English departed, the Dutch returned.

Gold was discovered in 1825 and was mined up until 1916 when the yield became so meager it ceased to be profitable. However, every now and then someone uncovers a big nugget and the excitement is generated all over again.

Aruba's rather bleak economic outlook changed in 1929 when Lago Oil and Transport Company, a subsidiary of Standard Oil of New Jersey, built a large refinery at the southeast tip of the island. Dating from those days, Aruba became one of the most prosperous islands in the West Indies. However, the refinery shut down in 1985, causing widespread unemployment.

Mainly in the 1970s Aruba entered the Caribbean resort sweepstakes when visitors discovered that it has one of the finest beaches in the West Indies stretching along its west coast. In addition to the sands, casinos in high-rise hotels draw the crowds today, as tourism has become Aruba's new industry.

Many visitors come to the island for the annual pre-Lenten **Carnaval,** a two-month-long festival with something going on day and night. Music, dancing, parades, costumes, "jump-ups," whatever—Carnaval is the highlight of Aruba's winter season.

GETTING THERE: Several major airlines service the route to and from Aruba, although the easiest connections for many areas of North America are on **American Airlines.** Aruba-bound passengers in the Northeast, including Boston and Philadelphia, can catch a daily flight leaving from New York's JFK Airport at 9:30 a.m. After about 4½ hours of flying time, the plane lands with no stopovers near the beaches of Aruba, giving passengers time for a brief sunbath before dinner. The return flight leaves Aruba every day at 3:45 p.m., touching down briefly at Curaçao before continuing on to JFK.

The least expensive fare is included as part of a "land package," where prearranged and prepaid accommodations at selected hotels (reviewed in this guide) are booked at the same time as the air fare through American's tour department. The options available are too complicated for this brief overview, although an American Airlines phone reservations clerk, or a travel agent, will discuss them with you.

For clients preferring to make their own hotel arrangements, American's cheapest high-season fare from New York to Aruba is $499 on weekends (Saturday and Sunday) and $469 on weekdays. This ticket requires no advance purchase, but you'll have to wait for 3 to 21 days before using the return half.

Passengers from Toronto or Montréal usually fly **Air Canada** to Miami before connecting with the **ALM** 2 p.m. flight to Aruba. This connects in Curaçao with another aircraft, allowing passengers to continue on to Aruba. ALM offers a daily flight to Aruba from New York, but the plane touches down in either Haiti or St. Maarten and then in Curaçao before continuing on to Aruba.

Eastern Airlines also flies from Miami, leaving every day on a nonstop flight, with easy connections from many other cities throughout the U.S.

GETTING AROUND: In Aruba, the **taxis** are unmetered, but rates are fixed, so it's necessary to tell the driver your destination and ask the fare before getting in. A ride from the airport to most of the hotels, including those at Palm Beach, costs $10 to $12 per car, and a maximum of four passengers are allowed to take the journey. Some of the local people don't tip, although it's good to give something extra, especially if the driver has helped you with a lot of luggage. Taxis can be found at the **Dispatch Office, Boulevard Center** in Oranjestad (tel. 22116 or 21604).

Buses

Aruba has a decent bus service. The bus stand for the return to most of the hotels is in Oranjestad, opposite the Tourist Bureau. The fare is 90¢. Your hotel reception desk will know the approximate times the buses pass by where you're staying. There is regular service from 7:40 a.m. to 6:05 p.m.

Car Rentals

Unlike most Caribbean islands, Aruba makes it easy for the independent traveler to rent a car and explore on his or her own. The roads between the major tourist attractions are excellent, and a valid U.S. or Canadian driver's license is accepted by each of the major car-rental companies. Most of the big hotels have desks which will rent cars for you. Always ask them a day in advance and you'll stand a better chance of getting the car you specify.

Three of the nation's major car-rental companies maintain offices in Aruba, usually with both airport branches as well as outlets at some of the major hotels. High-season rates offered by most of the companies are fairly consistent: a peppy two- or four-door car with manual transmission and unlimited mileage costs a minimum of around $150 a week, although an occasional midwinter special might bring the weekly price on a no-frills car down to $110 per week with unlimited mileage. There's no tax imposed on car rentals in Aruba, and few hidden extras other than insurance.

Hertz, Avis, and **Budget Rent-a-Car** offer collision damage waivers to their clients. These policies, which, depending on the value of the car, cost about $5 and $8 a day at all three companies, reduce but do not always eliminate a driver's financial responsibility in the event of an accident. A close look at the fine print is needed.

Budget Rent-a-Car requires that each driver purchase the company's waiver, which then removes *all* financial responsibility from the driver for any collision damage. Although the policies at Hertz and Avis are not mandatory, they are less comprehensive than the one at Budget. Collision damage to cars rented through Hertz and Avis can cost a driver up to $10,000 if the damage is severe enough! Even if a renter opts for the purchase of the waiver, he or she is still responsible for the first $300 and $1,500 worth of damage at Avis and Hertz, respectively.

Currently, the company with the most expensive rentals is Hertz. Budget and Avis offer less expensive rates. With economy in mind, I used a car from Budget and was happy with the service and the vehicle.

In a final comparison, underage or overage drivers might not be qualified for rentals at all three agencies. For insurance reasons, Budget requires that drivers in Aruba be between 23 and 65, Avis will rent only to qualified drivers between the ages of 23 and 60, and Hertz requires only that a qualified driver be older than 21.

For detailed information on rentals at the time of your trip, call the toll-free international departments of Budget (tel. 800/527-0700), Avis (tel. 800/331-2112), or Hertz (tel. 800/654-3131).

Scooters

Aruba Scooters and Mopeds Rentals, 1 Kolibristraat (tel. 28600), offers 50-cc fully automatic Mopeds for $12.50 per day, suitable for one person. An 80-cc scooter, fully automatic, at $22.50 per day, and a 225-cc shift Scramble, at $30, can both be ridden by two persons. The shop is open from 8 a.m. to 6 p.m. Free pickup and delivery are provided. Minimum age for renters is 18, and gasoline is not included in the rates.

Sightseeing Taxi Tours

Taxis with English-speaking drivers are available as guides. Most of them seem well informed about their island and are anxious to share it with you. A one-hour tour (and you don't need much more than that) is offered at a cost of $22 per hour for a maximum of five passengers.

Sightseeing Bus Tours

De Palm Tours, 142 L. G. Smith Blvd. in Oranjestad (tel. 24400 or 24401), has offices at major hotels. Their most popular jaunt is a 2½-hour excursion leaving at 9:30 a.m. and costing $12.50 per person. The tour takes in the island's major attractions, including a haul across the windswept countryside with its divi-divi trees, continuing on to the north coast to see Aruba's Natural Bridge.

PRACTICAL FACTS: Dry and sunny, Aruba has a median temperature of 83° Fahrenheit (trade winds, as mentioned, make it more bearable). To enter, U.S. and Canadian citizens may submit a **passport** or a birth certificate (or for U.S. citizens only, a voter registration card).

In an emergency, for the **police,** dial 110, 24555, or 24000. For a **hospital** emergency, call 24300. The **fire** department emergency number is 115.

At your hotel, you'll find a 10% to 15% **service charge** on room, food, and beverages. **Tipping** (more politely known as a service charge) usually appears on the bill at 10% to 15% extra. Otherwise, it's up to you.

The **water** is pure (it comes from the world's second-largest desalinization plant). The **electrical current** is 110 volts AC, 60 cycles, the same as in the U.S. **Atlantic Standard Time** is observed year round.

The **currency** is the Netherlands Antillean florin or guilder which is divided into 100 cents. The current exchange rate is $1 U.S. to 1.92 NAf. U.S. dollars are accepted throughout the island, but you should carry along some small bills. It is difficult to get even a $10 bill changed outside the casinos. *Note:* Unless otherwise stated, currency quotations in this chapter are in U.S. dollars.

Bank hours are Monday through Friday from 8 a.m. to noon and 1:30 to 4 p.m. In taxes, you're hit with a 5% **room tax,** plus another $9.50 airport **departure tax,** plus 16 NAf ($8.30) in added government tax.

Cables and **Telexes** can be arranged by contacting Landsradio Telecommunicatie Dienst (tel. 21655, ext. 124). Local and international **telephone calls** can be made via hotel operators or from the Government Long Distance Telephone Office, in the Post Office Building in Oranjestad.

In **medical services,** the Horacio Oduber Hospital (tel. 24300) opened in 1976. It's a modern building near Eagle Beach with excellent medical facilities. Hotels also have medical doctors on call, and there are good dental facilities as well (appointments can be made through your hotel).

For information, go to the **Aruba Tourist Bureau,** 2 A. Shuttestraat in Oranjestad (tel. 23777).

The official **language** is Dutch, but don't worry, as nearly everybody speaks English. They also speak Papiamento.

WHERE TO STAY: Most of Aruba's hotels are of the resort variety, bustling and self-contained. There's a tremendous dearth of family hotels or those of the budget variety. Guesthouses are few and tend to be booked up early in winter by faithful returning visitors. In season, it's imperative to make reservations way, way in advance. Don't ever arrive expecting to find a room on the spot. You may end up spending the night under a cactus.

The Resort Hotels

Aruba Concorde Hotel-Casino, Palm Beach (tel. 24466), competes, rather successfully, for the title of "the biggest and the best" along the Palm Beach strip. The 18-story property is the quintessential Las Vegas–style hotel, set on the sands of Aruba. To augment its big-time image, the hotel has associated itself with the Sands hotels of Las Vegas and Atlantic City. It's the most dramatic, high-class, glitzy, and perhaps the most exciting hotel on the island. The reception desk assigns one of the 500 ocean-view rooms, each with private balcony, closed-circuit color TV (movies shown from 11 a.m. to 3 a.m.), and radio with private channel music, as well as refrigerators and a vaguely continental decor. The designer was lavish in his colors, accented in vibrant walls, floors, and fabrics. Expensive suites are available, as you'd expect. Otherwise, single rooms range in price from $140 to $195 daily, with doubles going for $145 to $200, all winter tariffs. *In spring, summer, and fall, the single tariffs range from $85 to $115; the double, from $95 to $120 daily.* For breakfast and dinner, add another $42 per person per day.

The free-form swimming pool is Olympic size, and between the hotel and the sea is a tremendous playtime terrace with sunning areas and a multitude of lounge chairs. The sugar-white beach offers probably the most crowded panorama of bodies of anywhere in the Caribbean. Professional tennis courts are lit for night games. Breakfast, lunch, and dinner are served in the Kadushi Restaurant, with its balloon-like globe lighting and stylized tile cut-out murals on its pillars and walls. Perhaps the best experience is to descend the central cantilevered interior staircase to the lower level. It's a flow of various rooms, Japanese style, all open, with large planters and delicate screens setting off the various sections. Shimmering white floors and walls of glass give a sense of space. Somehow this warmness makes up for the coldness of the ultramodern reception area. In the evening guests dine at La Serre or any of the four other varied restaurants, later playing baccarat or roulette in the casino or enjoying nightclub entertainment in the Arubesque.

Aruba Palm Beach Hotel & Casino, Palm Beach (tel. 23900), is a white palacio with Moorish arches. At this sleek, stylish, high-rise total resort, you are given all the trimmings. Built in 1968, it is placed firmly on a sizable portion of powdery Palm Beach. The glistening lobby is deliberately spartan, and the spaciousness is enhanced by an array of palm trees and other local vegetation. The Dutch Arcade houses a shopping center behind colorfully painted reproductions of Holland-type storefronts. Staggered along its eight stories are 200 guest rooms, including pool-side lanais and oceanfront suites, all modern and first class. Every unit has quality and character, with many amenities, including air conditioning. Bedrooms overlook the swimming pool or the gardens, and all are ocean view. In winter, singles range in price from $135 daily for standard units to $210 for an "ocean room," and doubles in the same category cost the same. For breakfast and dinner, add $37 per person daily to these tariffs. *In summer, May to December, big reductions are granted: a single costs $75 to $95 daily, and a double, $80 to $100.*

This government-financed hotel spared little expense in developing a large sunning and sports area between the hotel and the sea. The Balashi Bar, informal and thatch-roofed, surrounds an overscale freshwater swimming pool, and there's a smaller pool for children. Surrounding gardens are well kept and planted with palms intermixed with more flamboyant varieties of shrubbery and trees. Scuba-diving, tennis, sailing, skindiving, even glass-bottom-boat rides, can easily be arranged at the sports desk. For breakfast, choose from Arawak Coffeehouse, with a decorative theme of primitive hex signs and handsome Delft china, or the outdoor terrace buffet. Dine either in the elegant Rembrandt Room with walls of red velvet displaying many reproductions of the artist's finer works, where a dinner and floor show average $30, or at the outdoor Steak Pub, where the evening breeze carries the aromas of an open hearth cooking steaks, lobsters, and shrimp. For nightly divertissement, the disco Galactica, done in steel gray and red with chrome trim, offers good music. It's open seven days a week from 11 a.m. to 4 a.m. Disco action gets animated around 9 p.m. Of course, the prime nighttime target is the modernized Grand Casino.

Golden Tulip Aruba Caribbean, L. G. Smith Boulevard (tel. 33555, 212/832-2277 in New York City, or toll free 800/223-6510). Its original core was one of the first palace-style hotels in Aruba, and it reopened after massive renovations in 1986. Today it qualifies as one of the most stylish hotels on the island, boasting more than 400 accommodations. These are scattered among a quartet of different buildings sitting on a flat and sandy garden a few steps from one of the best beaches in Aruba. The main building's angular façade rises above a curved driveway whose centerpiece is a splashing fountain, huge weathered rocks, and a cluster of cactus. The lobby incorporates tones of blue and sea-green into many different themes, ranging from traditional to beach resort modern. Don't overlook the massive mural crafted from Delft tiles, depicting the world's first salute to the American flag in 1776. The hotel has a popular swimming pool shaped like a double-headed hatchet, a casino, five attractive restaurants and bars, four tennis courts, and an array of water-sports facilities, a health club, and a nightclub, along with a shopping arcade. Each of the accommodations has air conditioning, a satellite-reception color TV, a mini-bar, sun-flooded windows, a private terrace or veranda, and a stylishly contemporary decor of semitropical motifs. Depending on the accommodation and its exposure, single or double rooms range from $150 to $220 daily in high season. *In low season, single or double rooms cost $110 to $150 daily.*

Americana Aruba, Palm Beach (tel. 24500), is a high-rise giant, boasting 206 double-bedded, air-conditioned, and colorfully decorated rooms. Opened in 1975, it staggers its rooms on ten floors, and all its units have balconies and room phones. The decorative style goes from a Caribbean motif to more traditional designs. *In the off-season, singles range from $85 to $105 daily, and doubles go for $90 to $110.* In winter, tariffs are raised: $145 to $190, single or double occupancy. The hotel rises from a seaside setting. Contemporary paintings and shell wall hangings displayed in the corridors give the public areas a stylish effect. Much space has been devoted to sports and recreational facilities. A row of thatched shade huts was built along the water's edge, and there are two tennis courts. A buffet-style breakfast is served at Las Mananitas Café terrace, and you can order an al fresco luncheon here as well. You can dine in the garden-style Villa Fiorita restaurant while seated in tall white wrought-iron banquettes. Happy hour guests gather in Le Club Lounge. Between 6:30 and 7:30 p.m. this is a popular gathering point for tourists, as drinks are priced at only half price (for example, you can enjoy what is reputedly the best piña colada on the island). The Stellaris Supper Club has a theater-style setting (see my nightlife recommendations).

Holiday Inn Aruba, Palm Beach (tel. 23600), with nearly 400 rooms, is the most action-packed hostelry along the sands of Palm Beach. Private balconies frame vistas of white sands, and each air-conditioned bedroom comes with a TV offering in-house video movies, a private tile bath, and a phone. Bedrooms, furnished to Holiday Inn traditional standards, have color coordination and are well furnished, with wall-to-wall carpeting, two double beds, and large closets. In winter, singles range from $110 to $160 daily, while doubles go for $110 to $175. *In the off-season, terms are lowered to anywhere from $70 to $100 daily in a single, from $76 to $106 in a double.* For breakfast and dinner, add another $32 per person daily. The Olympic-size swimming pool with distilled fresh water seemingly has room for everybody, and it's surrounded by a sun terrace. There's a health club with a sauna, plus four lit tennis courts. The social hostess arranges a full program of water sports.

Musicians serenade you as you dine in Le Salon, with its continental menu and many specialties. In addition, within the hotel precincts is the Grand Holiday Casino. Their Chinese restaurant, the Empress of China, features a fine cuisine, as does the outside dining facility.

Divi-Divi Beach Hotel, Druif Bay Beach (tel. 23300), stands near the largest beach on the island. A rambling, low-rise structure, it has Iberian architectural accents, offering some rooms in the bungalow style, others in two- or three-story buildings or lanais. In all, there are 203 rooms with private baths, all with tub and shower—92 units in the main buildings, 40 casitas, and 20 lanais, all of which have two double beds; plus 50 new luxury rooms and one royal suite. Each accommodation has a private terrace or balcony and is fully air-conditioned. The Wiggins family of Ithaca, New York, have brought their own special touch to Divi-Divi, named after the famous wind-whipped tree, and to its companion accommodation, the nearby Tamarijn Beach Hotel. Casual and comfortable, the Divi-Divi is one of the island's friendliest oases. Each member of the Wiggins family has added judgment, good taste, and a free spirit to this hotel on the outskirts of Oranjestad. Through a buying spree in Mexico, the Wigginses gave the place a real Spanish flavor, with handmade mirrors, leather and dark-wood chairs, terracotta floors, and dark wooden shutters at the windows, along with hand-carved beds. In winter, singles range in price from $175 to $225 daily and doubles run $180 to $230. *However, in the off-season, rates are reduced to $95 to $115 in a single, $100 to $120 in a double.* For breakfast and dinner, add another $34 per person to the daily tariffs.

Meals are served on the casual Pelican Terrace or in the Red Parrot dining room. Sunday brunch is a popular occasion. On the grounds are two freshwater swimming pools and three Jacuzzis, and the hotel has a tennis court. All year, dancing and entertainment are offered nightly. The Alhambra Casino stands across the road from Divi-Divi.

Tamarijn Beach Hotel, Druif Bay Beach (tel. 24150), the center of a trio of properties owned and well managed by the Divi Hotel chain, enjoys one of the longest beachfronts in Aruba. Built in a Dutch style of two-story motel-like units, it resembles a meandering assemblage of interconnected waterfront town houses. The narrow strip of sandy turf between the accommodations and the beach is planted with copses of almonds, palms, and sea grapes. Facilities include two isolated Jacuzzis, a collection of hard-surface tennis courts, and an array of water sports. At one end of the long and narrow property the open-air Bunker Bar is perched, as its name suggests, on stilts above a lopsided fortification remaining intact from World War II. On the premises are several drinking spots and a pair of tropical restaurants along with a rectangular swimming pool. There's also an armada of electric carts which will transport visitors to the Alhambra Casino and the Divi-Divi Beach Hotel. Each of the sun-flooded rooms contains air conditioning, a private bathroom, and big glass doors that slide open to accept the breezes from the beach. *In off-season, singles cost $85 daily; doubles, $90.* In winter, singles go for $165 daily; doubles, $170.

Talk of the Town, Oranjestad (tel. 23380), was created by Mr. and Mrs. Ike Cohen, who'd lived in Jacksonville, Florida, before taking over this property in Aruba. Originally built as an eight-room structure in 1942, the Cohens discovered it in 1964 when it was the offices of a chemical plant. Learning, and occasionally making mistakes along the way, they transformed the moldy, termite-ridden building into a first-class resort hotel, the only one in the capital itself. The hotel is best known for its restaurant, one of the most famous in the Caribbean. In fact, the name of the restaurant, Talk of the Town, eventually replaced the name of the hotel, Coral Strand. Between the hotel and its beachside sister, the Manchebo, there are five different places to eat, including the Moorish-style Surfside, across from the Talk of the Town.

The hotel stands on the coastal road leading to the airport, and its two-floor bedroom units are built motel-like around a large swimming pool. The tiers of arches and rough plaster walls give it a Spanish look. There's also a heated hydrotherapy whirlpool bath. Traditional furnishings and strong colors are used, and all units have TVs and refrigerators, and some have small kitchenettes. In winter, singles range from $83 to $103 daily, and doubles go for $88 to $108. For breakfast and dinner, add another $34 per person daily. *In summer, doubles drop to a low of $65 daily, with singles costing from $60 to $65.* At poolside in a sheltered dining room, three meals are served every day, and a latticed gazebo is the setting for cocktail parties. Musicians entertain every evening.

Manchebo Beach Resort Hotel, Manchebo Beach (tel. 23444), offers spread-out beach-club facilities, in a setting across from the Alhambra Casino. Owned by the Cohens of Talk of the Town (guests have exchange privileges), the Manchebo consists of groups of two-story motel-like air-conditioned bedrooms, with balconies or patios overlooking the Caribbean. Its private-seeming 1,600 feet of beach strip is ideal for suntanning and water sports. Close to the surf line is a large freshwater swimming pool. On the grounds are facilities for volleyball, shuffleboard, and tennis. The 74 bedrooms all have private baths, TVs, refrigerators, and phones, and they are light and airy in feeling, with white walls. Many units have built-ins, and the baths are tile. In winter, singles pay from $83 daily for a room, and doubles cost $88 to $118. Add another $35 for breakfast and dinner. *In summer, the single tariff is $75, and the double rate runs from $80.* A relaxed, informal atmosphere prevails. On the grounds is the French Steak House (see my dining recommendations), plus a patio restaurant specializing in fish dishes.

A Guesthouse

Many travelers prefer to visit Aruba on a much simpler basis than what we've been considering. There are some apartments and a handful of guesthouses overlooking the sea or within walking distance of a beach. Others are on a bus route, and still others require a car. My personal favorite follows:

The Edge's, 458 L. G. Smith Blvd., Malmok-by-the-Sea (tel. 21072), owned by Virginians, is a guest house complex of 11 units 50 yards across from the beach. It's less than a mile from the Holiday Inn Hotel and Casino going toward the lighthouse. A carpeted patio with chaise longues separates two rows of motel-style units, and each apartment has a private entrance and patio with furniture for outdoor dining. These are really efficiency units with kitchenette, refrigerator, dishes, toaster, coffee pot, and all utensils for cooking. All apartments are air-conditioned with large tile baths. Each unit has at least two beds and is pleasantly furnished and clean. There are two deluxe units and a luxury suite with king-size beds, sitting rooms, full kitchens, and private patios with a view of the ocean. You'll receive a welcome from the owner and manager, Elizabeth W. Johnson, or Filomena and Miranda, who smilingly take care of the needs of their guests. To the right of the entrance gate, you can watch sunsets from a whirlpool spa at no charge. The house lies only a 70¢ bus ride from Oranjestad. In winter, occupancy costs $56 to $100 per apartment daily. *In the off-season, tariffs are lowered to $28 to $50 per apartment per day.* An extra $10 is charged for each person over two per apartment.

Time-Share Properties

Time-sharing has become a major vacation investment in Aruba. Even if you're not interested for yourself, you may want to consider renting one temporarily as a one-time vacationer. The most recommendable ones are previewed below.

Dutch Village, 93 L. G. Smith Blvd. (tel. 32300, or toll free 800/367-3484). Its high, angular sides evoke the chimneys of 17th-century Dutch buildings. Within a lush garden, the complex is not set directly on the beach, but the sands are only a short walk away. In the center of the compound, a re-creation of a tropical lagoon splashes water from an artificial grotto. Units contain satellite color TVs, air conditioning, complete kitchens, king-size beds, private Jacuzzis, and patios or verandas. Studios, one-bedroom apartments, and two-bedroom town houses are offered when they're not occupied by their investors. In high season, studios for one or two people rent for $200; one-bedroom apartments for two to four, $260; and two-bedroom units housing two to six people, $400. *Low-season prices are $130 in a studio, $160 in a one-bedroom apartment, and $260 in a two-bedroom unit.* The complex is owned and managed by the Divi Hotel chain.

Playa Linda Beach Resort, P.O. Box 235 (tel. 31000). Designed in a ziggurat shape of receding balconies, the complex sits on a desirable stretch of white sandy beachfront sheathed in a façade of terracotta and cream. Depending on the time of your visit, a trio of lagoon-shaped swimming pools, a mini-village of thatch-covered beach-front cabañas, and tennis courts may (or may not) have been completed. As in any large-scale development project, much of its future depends on financing. The accommodations are stylishly comfortable and outfitted with private kitchens, verandas, air conditioning, and many amenities. In winter, units for up to four guests cost $220 per day, going up to $400 per day for six guests. *In summer, four people can stay here for $115 daily, six persons for $300,* plus service and tax.

Aruba Beach Club / Casa del Mar, P.O. Box 368 (tel. 23000), were two properties built at different times, but now they're connected by a common wing and a shared reception desk. The older and more staid of the properties, the Aruba Beach Club, is a hotel of more than 170 rooms, dating from the late 1970s. Each of its pleasant units contains a kitchenette, air conditioning, cable-connected color TV, and a decor of tropical furniture. Its ochre exterior embraces a rear courtyard, an expanse of seafront, and its own swimming pool. In winter, accommodations for three to five people rent for $150 to $250 per night. *In summer, these same units cost $80 to $120 daily for three to five guests.*

The new time-sharing section, the Casa del Mar, contains tasteful, well-decorated apartments, and plans call for additional units. More expensive than the accommodations at Aruba Beach, they offer some of the most luxurious units in Aruba. These include Jacuzzi tubs, well-equipped kitchens, oak-trimmed furniture, spacious verandas or patios, air conditioning, and sun-flooded views of the sea. In winter, each of the two-bedroom units cost around $280 per night for up to four people. Additional occupants (up to a total of six) pay $10 each. *In summer, each unit costs around $140 for up to four guests. Additional occupants (up to six) pay an extra $10.* Casa del Mar wraps itself around its own stretch of beachfront and a private courtyard fringed with palms and thatch-covered cabañas. In its center, a swimming pool, shaped like a pair of interconnected octagons, provides an alternative to the beach. Across from the Alhambra Casino, both hotels are encircled by urn-shaped balustrades. The establishments share the same tennis courts, bars, and an appealingly rustic restaurant, the Taverna.

ARUBA COOKERY:

A few of Aruba's restaurants serve rijsttafel, the "Asian smörgåsbord," or nasi goreng, a "mini rijsttafel." In addition, a surprising number of Chinese restaurants operate in Oranjestad. Most of the major hotels have several dining options, ranging from fast food in coffeeshops to so-called gourmet restaurants. More and more Aruban specialties are beginning to appear on menus, although Stateside dishes such as hamburgers still predominate. French cuisine is the second major choice of most chefs. Sometimes, at least on off-season package deals, visitors on the MAP (breakfast and dinner) are allowed to dine around on an exchange plan with the other hotels.

La Dolce Vita, 164 Nassaustraat (tel. 25675). Once it was a private home, but since 1980 it has been the most acclaimed restaurant in Aruba, serving, as its name suggests, Italian specialties. It wasn't long before it was discovered by the food and wine critics of such prestigious Stateside magazines as *Gourmet*. Only dinner is served, costing from $25, and it's seven days a week from 6 p.m. to midnight. Because of the popularity of "The Sweet Life," it's best to call and reserve a table, especially in high season, when it can quickly fill up. If you like pasta with salmon and cream (which became the rage in Italy in the 1980s), you'll find it served here. You might begin your repast, however, with a sampling of their antipasti, including fine Italian salami and cheese, along with artichokes and marinated squid. They also do a savory, perfectly flavored "kettle" of fruits de mer. Naturally you get some good veal, along with such familiar Italian standby dishes as baked clams and linguine. An espresso or perhaps some Italian ice cream will finish off your meal nicely.

Papagayo Restaurant, L. G. Smith Boulevard (tel. 24140), is one of the most delightful restaurants in Aruba. It's decorated like a forest, with live birds, trees, and plants, along with a fish pond. In addition to that, it opens onto a view of the harbor. It has steadily grown in popularity ever since it opened in 1983. Managed by Divi Hotels, it offers such tempting fare as linguine with lobster and seafood and chicken Papagayo (one of the chef's many specialties—stuffed breast of chicken). In addition to that, you get excellent prime steaks along with the superb fare of the northern Italian kitchen. Prices are moderate: a typical meal costs $20. Before dinner, you might want to have an apéritif in the lounge. It's open from 11 a.m. to 11 p.m. daily. In addition, you may want to stop at **Tiki-Tiki Café** for tropical drinks and light lunches. Across the harbor, it's open from 10 a.m. to midnight.

Papiamento, 7 Wilhelminastraat (tel. 24544), considered one of the most desirable independent restaurants in Aruba, sits inside the thick stone walls of an old West Indian house in the center of the capital. Transformed into a stylish and intimate hideaway by Arubian entrepreneur Eduardo Ellis, it boasts wide-plank floors, latticework ceilings, a changing exhibition of contemporary paintings (each of which is for sale), and such old-world touches as massive brass chandeliers. It's open daily for dinner from 6:30 p.m. to midnight. A distinguishing culinary feature is the way fresh meat or seafood is served raw on sizzling marble slabs so that your dinner is cooked in front of you the way you like it. Chicken or fish is cooked in an Aruba-made clay pot which is then broken open at your table. Full meals, costing from $40 each, might include fresh lobster, chicken breast, lamb chops, or mixed seafood cooked directly on the stone, selections from a salad bar, grilled veal cutlets, rack of lamb for two, lobster Thermidor, and broiled porterhouse steak. Reservations are suggested, especially on weekends.

Bali Floating Restaurant, off L. G. Smith Boulevard (tel. 22131), is moored in Oranjestad's harbor. The restaurant is housed in an Oriental houseboat decorated with bamboo and Indonesian art. Diners are treated to the popular Indonesian rijsttafel (rice table), a complete meal of rice surrounded by 21 different dishes, served at your table in individual portions. The rijsttafel is not spicy, but the sambal (hot, hot) is served on the side for the more adventurous to try. A mini-version is served for lunch, as well as sandwiches and snacks. Expect to pay from $22 for a full rijsttafel, which may be ordered per person, but try to go with a group if possible since it's a fun meal that everyone will enjoy. Besides the rijsttafel, the menu offers a fine selection of tenderloin steaks and fresh local fish dishes. Hours are noon to midnight daily.

Talk of the Town Restaurant, Airport Road (tel. 23380). As a boy when Ike Cohen was growing up in Rotterdam, he learned the meat business from his father. While still a boy he knew how to purchase meat for the family's wholesale butcher business. When he and his wife, Grete, founded the Talk of the Town Restaurant, Mr. Cohen applied that knowledge to his present business. Today his meat freezer is the best and most fully stocked on the island. A self-taught resort operator, Mr. Cohen now runs one of Aruba's best-known restaurants, lying between the airport and Palm Beach (see my hotel recommendation). From 6:30 p.m. candlelight dining is offered, backed up by a good wine list and live music. Mr. Cohen has always believed in feeding people well, and the portions here are gigantic. The setting could easily be Miami, and there's no view—but people don't come here for that. They want to dine well. You can begin with escargots à la bourguignonne or perhaps vichyssoise. As mentioned, Mr. Cohen specializes in beef, and a favorite order is an ample cut of roast prime ribs of beef. The filet mignon Dutch style is also good. Other specialties include frogs' legs à la bourguignonne and veal Cordon Bleu. He also offers a selection of seafood dishes, including king crab legs and Dover sole meunière. Prices are high, but all items are imported, and you get a lot for your money. A complete meal could cost around $30 per person here. After 11 p.m., there's disco action.

The **Red Parrot,** Divi-Divi Beach Hotel, Druif Bay Beach (tel. 23300), is one of the better hotel restaurants. You dine seated on sturdy Spanish armchairs, and the view is through arched windows framed with vines and plants, opening onto the sea. The Iberian decor is reflected by the rough stone walls and wood paneling, as well as the archways. The menu leads off with an unusual appetizer, tender scallops lightly cooked in saffron. Or you may prefer a rich pea soup, Dutch style, with pigs' feet and geldersewurst. Main-dish specialties include tropical-style chicken filled with kiwi and served with a lemon-butter sauce as well as a local favorite, keshi yena. In addition, the chef prepares good seafood daily, including Alaska king crab leg and fresh snapper. A dessert selection is made from the trolley. Expect to spend from $28 to $35 per person for a complete meal. On Tuesday night a buffet of local dishes is presented, everything enlivened by the Divi-Divi steel band, complete with a parade of award-winning carnival costumes and an island-wear fashion show and water ballet. Open from 6:45 to 10 p.m. daily.

De Olde Molen, Palm Beach (tel. 22060), is housed in a landmark, standing just across the street from the Concorde Hotel. It can be reached on foot from a number of Palm Beach hotels. Originally, the windmill in which the restaurant is housed was built in 1804 in Friesland, Holland, but it was torn down and shipped to Aruba where it was reconstructed piece by piece. Since 1960 it has been a tourist-focused destination for dinner, served nightly except Sunday from 6 p.m. to 11 p.m. Jackets are suggested for men. The chefs seem to change with some frequency here, but all of them know how to prepare an international cuisine with such classic offerings as pepper steak for two persons, veal Cordon Bleu, and shrimp provençale. Try also, if offered, the red snapper amandine. Some guests begin with a shrimp cocktail, although I prefer the thick Dutch split-pea soup. For dessert, I suggest a pineapple mousse or Irish coffee. A complete meal can easily run around $20 to $35 per person. A 15% service charge is added to all bills.

Cattle Baron, 228 L. G. Smith Blvd. (tel. 22977). Its location amid a dry and dusty landscape beside the highway seems appropriate to its western theme. Amid a decor of ruffled gingham curtains, roughly textured planking, and wagon-wheel chandeliers, diners enjoy generous portions of aged U.S.-bred beef, as well as a scattering of seafood. Served by waiters whose costumes enhance the cattle baron theme, the specialties include Dutch steak, porterhouse steak, prime rib, barbecued ribs, and pepper steak. The seafood features red snapper San Francisco style (with crabmeat, mushrooms, and bordelaise sauce), broiled lobster, shrimp bisque, fish Oriental, and snapper arubiano (with Créole sauce, fried plantain, and funghi). Full meals cost from $25 and are served from noon to 3 p.m. every day except Sunday and from 6 to 11 p.m. nightly. Reservations are suggested.

Dragon-Phoenix, 31 Havenstraat (tel. 21928), in downtown Oranjestad, is run by a kindly gentleman who came from Canton province and brought his mild-flavored cuisine to Aruba with him. The setting is interesting, with some furniture made to order in Hong Kong and betasseled Chinatown light fixtures—in all, a soothing atmosphere for dining if you don't mind an occasional dragon. In these cool, comfortable surroundings, you can make selections from a large menu. If you're confused by such a big choice, I'd suggest a special Chinese rice table. Perhaps there will be four or five people in your party. Your party will receive the chef's special eggroll, sharkfin with chicken soup, chow kai kow with vegetables, shrimp in cashew nuts, lobster with oyster sauce, crabmeat with black-bean sauce, special fried rice, plus dessert. At least 18 Cantonese dishes are offered, including lobster chop suey. In addition, the chef has at least 22 other specialties. A complete meal is likely to cost about $20 here. It's open daily from 11:30 a.m. to 11 p.m.

Heidelberg, 136 L. G. Smith Blvd. (tel. 33020). About the last place you'd expect to find a restaurant with a name like Heidelberg is the desert-like island of Aruba. But owner-chef Manfred Hein, along with his wife, Ilona, has brought such a dining room to Aruba, serving dinner nightly, except Wednesday, from 6 to 11 p.m. Established in 1982, it became immediately popular. Arubans even came here to celebrate Christmas by ordering the Heins' fat, juicy Christmas goose. Here you get traditional German fare, including wienerschnitzel and goulash and noodles. In addition to goose, duck is well prepared. But before that, you may want to order the herring hausfrau style. Sauerbraten and good, rich-tasting soups are some of the other dishes served here. For dessert, select something from the trolley. Most diners, however, go for the strudel. Count on paying around $25 for a big, hearty, and altogether satisfying meal.

The **French Steak House,** Manchebo Beach Hotel, Manchebo Beach (tel. 23444), is a beachside bistro where the atmosphere is gracious and the food is good. Guests from the other hotels often come here for the romantic candlelit dining, and no one need worry about putting on a jacket or tie. Service is friendly, and it's easy to make a night of it if you dine here in these relaxed surroundings. The place is owned by Ike and Grete Cohen, who also run the previously recommended Talk of the Town. It's open from 6 to 11 p.m.; closed Monday. If you arrive between 6 and 7 p.m. you can order a five-course set dinner for $10. Or you can order à la carte, enjoying such chef's specialties as red snapper provençale or the classic veal Stroganoff flamed with vodka and madeira. You can also help yourself at a New York–style salad bar. Of course, beef is the big feature here, including either the filet mignon or the New York sirloin, the latter a 14-ounce boneless strip char-broiled to your taste. You can also order either chateaubriand or pepper steak for two people. If you order à la carte, chances are you'll end up paying from $30 per head.

Buccaneer, 11C Gasparito (tel. 26172), is a seafood restaurant with a saltwater aquarium. But you don't go here to watch the fish: you go to eat them. The atmosphere evokes (or means to) that of a ship's cabin. The location is near many of the major hotels, about two miles from Palm Beach (taxis are always waiting outside). The owners, Josef Munzenhofer and Peter Dorer, are also the chefs. For an opener, the pirate's hotpot is a seaworthy choice (a native fish soup that somehow manages to taste different every night). Among the "fruits of the sea," the lobster Thermidor is everybody's favorite. I always ask the waiter for the catch of the day, which he'll prepare with a Créole sauce. Meats are frozen of course, but well prepared, including tournedos in a number of ways. Every main dish is served with the vegetable of the day, along with a stuffed potato and salad on the side. Coup Melba or homemade cheesecake are favored to finish off your meal, which most likely will cost from $20 per person or more. The service is excellent. Open from 7 to 11 p.m.; closed Sunday.

EXPLORING ARUBA: The capital of Aruba, **Oranjestad** attracts mainly shoppers instead of sightseers. The bustling city has a very Caribbean flavor, and it's part Spanish, part Dutch in architecture. Cutting in from the airport, the main thoroughfare, L.

G. Smith Boulevard, goes along the waterfront and on to Palm Beach. But most visitors cross it heading for Nassaustraat or "Nassau Street." Here is where they find the best free-port shopping.

After a shopping trip, you might return to the harbor where fishing boats and schooners, many from Venezuela, are moored. Nearly all newcomers to Aruba like to take a picture of the **Schooner Harbor.** Not only does it have colorful boats docked along the quay, but boatmen display their wares in open stalls. The local patois predominates. A little farther along, at the fish market, fresh fish is sold directly from the boats. Also on the seaside of Oranjestad, **Wilhelmina Park** was named after Queen Wilhelmina of the Netherlands. A tropical garden has been planted along the water, and there's a sculpture of the Queen Mother.

Aside from shopping along Nassaustraat, the major attractions of Aruba are **Eagle Beach** and **Palm Beach,** considered among the finest in the Caribbean. Most of Aruba's hotels are stretched Las Vegas strip style along these pure-white sand stretches on the leeward coast.

Museums of Aruba

I know you didn't come to Aruba to look at museums, but just in case—
Museo Arubano, just off L. G. Smith Boulevard behind the government buildings, in the restored Fort Zoutman, contains material on the culture and history of Aruba, with artifacts dating from the earliest times of the island through colonial days and up to the present. The 18th-century fort, oldest building in Aruba, has at its entrance the King Willem III Tower, which served as a lighthouse for almost 100 years. Museum hours are 9 a.m. to 4 p.m. Monday to Friday, to noon on Saturday. Admission is 1 NAf (50¢). The place is also called the King Willem III Tower and Fort Zoutman Museum.

The **Archeology Museum,** 1 Zoutmanstraat (tel. 28979), is diagonally across the street from the police station. Its two rooms have displays of ancient Indian artifacts found mainly in Cer'i Noka near Santa Cruz. You'll see agricultural and home equipment, even skeletons of people who were buried in big earthenware urns. Open from 8 a.m. to noon and 1:30 to 4:30 p.m., the museum charges no admission.

A privately owned **shell collection** of the Adrian de Man family can be seen at 18 Morgenster (tel. 24246 for an appointment). The permanent collection, which includes a rare murex, is in a room at the rear of the de Mans' home. Shells from all over the world make up the display.

In the **Numismatic Museum,** 2-A Irausquin Plein, in front of the post office and near St. Francis Catholic Church, you can see an outstanding collection of coins and paper currency. The museum, in the Ministry of Culture Building, is open from 9 a.m. to noon and 1:30 to 5:30 p.m. Monday to Friday.

Out in the Country

If you can lift yourselves from the sands for one afternoon, you might like to drive into the **canucu,** which in Papiamento means the countryside. Here Arubans live in very modest but colorful pastel-washed houses. Of course, all visitors venturing into the center of Aruba want to see the strangely shaped divi-divi tree with its trade-wind-blown coiffure. Even though they live in a very dry climate where cactus thrives better than flowers, Arubans like to have bougainvillea, oleander, hibiscus, and other tropical plants around their homes. However, to grow them, they often use expensive desalinated water.

Rocks stud Aruba, and the most impressive ones are those found at **Ayo** and **Casibari,** to the northeast of Hooiberg. These stacks of diorite boulders are the size of buildings. The rocks, weighing several thousand tons, are a puzzle to geologists. On the rocks at Ayo are ancient Indian drawings. At Casibari, you can climb the boulder-strewn terrain to the top for a panoramic view of the island or wander around lower down looking at rocks Mother Nature has carved into seats and likenesses of prehistoric birds and animals. Casibari is open daily from 9 a.m. to 5 p.m. No admission is charged. There is a lodge at Casibari where you can buy souvenirs, snacks, soft drinks, and beer.

If the subject interests you, guides can also point out drawings on the walls and ceiling of the **Caves of Canashito,** south of Hooiberg. While there you may get to see the giant green parakeets.

Hooiberg is affectionately known as "The Haystack." It is Aruba's most outstanding landmark, and anybody with the stamina can take the steps all the way to the top of this 541-foot-high hill. One Aruban jogs up there every morning. From its precincts in the center of the island you can see Venezuela on a clear day.

On the jagged, windswept northern coast, the **Natural Bridge** has been carved out of the coral rock by the relentless surf. In a little café overlooking the coast you can order snacks. There you'll also find a souvenir shop with a large selection of trinkets, T-shirts, and wall hangings, all selling at reasonable prices.

You turn inland for the short trip to **Pirate's Castle** at Bushiribana, which stands on a cliff on the island's windward coast. This is actually a deserted gold mill from the island's now-defunct industry. Another gold mill is in the old ghost town on the west coast, **Balashi.**

You can continue to the village of Noord, known for its **St. Anne's Church** with a hand-carved Dutch altar dating from the 17th century.

East to San Nicolás

Driving along the highway more or less paralleling the south coast of Aruba toward the island's southernmost section, you may want to stop at the **Spanish Lagoon** (Spaans Lagoen), where legend says pirates used to hide out as they waited to plunder rich cargo ships in the Caribbean. Whatever the truth about that, today this is an ideal place for snorkeling, and you can picnic at tables under the mangrove trees.

On to the east, you'll pass an area called **Savaneta,** where some of the most ancient traces of human habitation have been unearthed. You'll see along here the first oil tanks marking the position of the Lago Oil & Transport Company Ltd., the Exxon subsidiary around which the town of San Nicolás developed, although it had been an industrial center since the days of phosphate mining in the late 19th century. A "company town" until the refinery was closed in 1985, San Nicolás, 12 miles from Oranjestad, is called the Aruba Sunrise Side, and tourism has become its main economic factor.

The town has a blend of cultures—customs, style, languages, color, and tastes. In the area are caves with Arawak Indian artwork on the walls and a modern innovation, a PGA-approved golf course with sand "greens" and cactus traps. **Boca Grandi,** on the windward side of the island, is a favorite windsurfing location; or if you prefer quieter waters, you'll find them at **Baby Beach** and **Rodgers Beach,** on Aruba's lee side.

Overlooking the latter two beaches is **Seroe Colorado** (Colorado Point), from which it's possible to see the coastline of Venezuela as well as the pounding surf on the windward side. You can climb down the cliffs, perhaps spotting an iguana here and there. Protected by law, the once-endangered saurians now proliferate in peace.

Other sights in the San Nicolás area are the **Guadarikiri Cave** and **Fontein Cave,** where you can see the Indian wall drawings, plus the **Huliba** and **Tunnel of Love** caves, with guides and refreshment stands. Guadarikiri Cave is a haven for wild parrots.

Brisas del Mar, 222A Saveneta near the police station (tel. 47718), is like a place you might encounter in some outpost in Australia. Here in very simple surroundings, right at water's edge, Lucia Rasmijn opened this little hut with an air-conditioned bar in front at which the locals gather to drink the day away. The place is often jammed on weekends with many of the same local people, who come here to drink and dance. On Friday, Saturday, and Sunday, Mrs. Lucia Rasmijn offers entertainment, with home-grown talent playing everything from the guitar to the harp.

In back the tables are open to the sea breezes, and nearby you can see a fisherman slicing the catch of the day, perhaps wahoo, selling it to local housewives. The cooks try to confine their menu to fish caught in the Caribbean. Perhaps you'll have the pan-broiled fish of the day, prepared Aruban style (with a Créole sauce), or breaded conch cutlet. Try also the baby shark steak or the turtle steak with port wine. The breaded squid cutlet is yet another favorite. For an appetizer, perhaps you'll select the "fisher-man's fish soup." Desserts are simple, including fresh fruit or ice cream. Expect to spend from $20 per person. The restaurant is open daily from noon to 3 p.m. and 6:30 to 10:30 p.m. It's always best to call first for a reservation to avoid making the trip there, only to find the place full. Even with a reservation, you still may have to wait more than an hour or so to get a seat if the place is really jumping. To reach the restau-rant's location at Savaneta, turn off to the right from the main road leading from Oran-jestad to San Nicolas between Anthony Sales and the police station. You'll need a car to get there or else you'll have to take a cab. By bus it's more than an hour's trip.

Marina Pirata, Pos Chiquito (tel. 47150), is probably the most authentically raffish seafood restaurant in Aruba. It lies a 15-minute drive east of Oranjestad, along an isolated section of the coastline known as Pos Chiquito. Its exterior boasts a series of false crenellations, giving it the appearance of a mock fortress. It was built over the water on the rusted hulk of a steel-sided barge which in World War II was a hideout for Allied marines guarding the island's oil refineries. Every afternoon local fishermen deliver directly to the restaurant's pier whatever fresh fish they caught that day. Sea-food is consumed in wind-cooled comfort amid a simple decor of exposed planking, picnic-style tables, and nautical lanterns. Full meals, costing from $20, are served every evening except Tuesday from 6 to 11 p.m. Lunch is served only on Sunday, when the restaurant remains open from noon to 11 p.m. in a continuous party which includes live music between 5 and 7 p.m.

Charlie's Bar, 56 Mainstreet (tel. 45086). Its decor and history, dating from 1941, qualifies it as the most interesting reason to visit San Nicolas. It's the most overly decorated bar in the West Indies, sporting an array of memorabilia and local souvenirs which, when assembled, create a Caribbean version of kitsch. Where roustabouts and roughnecks once brawled, you'll find tables filled with contented tourists admiring thousands of pennants, banners, and trophies dangling from the high ceiling. Two-fisted drinks are still served, but the menu has improved since the good old days when San Nicholas was one of the toughest towns in the Caribbean. Meals are served from noon to 3 p.m. and 6 to 9:30 p.m. daily except Sunday. The bar is open daily except Sunday from 10 a.m. to midnight. Full meals cost 20 NAf ($10.50) and include grilled scampi, freshly made soups of the day, Créole-style squid, beefburgers, and chur-rasco.

THE SPORTING LIFE:
Its western and southern shore, called the **Turquoise Coast,** is what attracts sun seekers to Aruba. Palm Beach and Eagle Beach (the latter closer to Oranjestad) are the best beaches. No hotel along the strip owns the beaches, all of which are open to the public. However, if you use any of the hotel's facilities, you'll be charged, of course. You can also spread your towel on Manchebo or Druif Bay Beach—in fact, anywhere along seven miles of uninterrupted sugar-white sands. In total contrast to the leeward side, the north or windward shore is rugged and wild.

Water Sports
Snorkeling, scuba-diving, windsurfing, waterskiing, and doing your own sailing are all part of the fun offered in the waters around Aruba. You can snorkel in rather

shallow waters, and scuba-divers find stunning marine life with endless varieties of coral as well as tropical fish in infinite hues. At some points visibility is up to 90 feet. The goal of most divers is the German freighter *Antilia*, which was scuttled in the early years of World War II, lying off the northwest tip of Aruba, not too far from Palm Beach.

The best place to book water sports is from **De Palm Tours**, whose main office is at 142 L. G. Smith Blvd. in Oranjestad (tel. 24400), although it also has offices at the major hotels as well. Here a certified teacher will give scuba-diving instruction at a cost of $50 per person. Subsequent dives can be arranged at $40 per person, as can scuba-diving trips for experienced divers. Snorkelers are often taken out on a boat ride to a site, with complete gear furnished, for $15 per person.

Caribbean Sea Adventures (tel. 45804), whose boat, *Sea Trek*, docks across from the mall on L. G. Smith Boulevard in Oranjestad, near the outdoor food market and Bali Pier, caters to scuba and snorkel aficionados. Instruction in scuba-diving costs $60 for four hours, while snorkel instruction, also for four hours, is priced at $40. Rates include Scubapro snorkel or scuba equipment, and you can have snacks aboard the *Sea Trek*, which takes divers to the best sites. Landlubbers can go along just for a cruise. A three-hour Sunset Cruise costs $20, while the Moonlight Voyage goes for $25.

Pleasure Cruises

Visitors interested in combining a pleasant boat ride with a few hours of snorkeling can get in touch with **De Palm Tours.** This company maintains an office in seven of the island's hotels. Its main office is at 142 L. G. Smith Blvd. in Oranjestad (tel. 24400). For $35 per person they'll take you on a "fun cruise" aboard a catamaran. After a windswept sail of 1½ hours, passengers stop for three hours at a coral reef for snorkeling. Lunch and an open bar are included in the price. The tour, if participation warrants it, departs daily between 10 a.m. and 4 p.m.

Pelican Watersports, 1 Rockefellerstraat, Oranjestad (tel. 23888), has some attractive cruises in the daytime, at sunset, and by moonlight. You can sail aboard the *Blue Melody*, a 60-foot catamaran; the 40-foot trimaran, *Octopus;* or the 43-foot sloop, *Tranquilo;* among the company's fleet of boats. They offer morning cruises with brunch and lunch, sunset trips with an open bar, and even combination of those voyages with snorkeling stops. Their 97-foot *Maria Monica* will take you on a luxury sightseeing trip, on a barbecue cruise, a sunset excursion, or a moonlight cruise. Prices range from $15 per person for sunset booze cruises and sailing snorkeling expeditions, to $38 per person for a fun cruise aboard the *Maria Monica*, including dinner at a seaside restaurant. Pelican also offers glass-bottom-boat trips at 10 a.m. and 3 p.m., costing $15 per person.

Deep-Sea Fishing

In the deep waters off the coast of Aruba you can test your skill and wits against the big ones—wahoo, marlin, tuna, bonito, and sailfish. **De Palm Tours**, 142 L. G. Smith Blvd. in Oranjestad (tel. 24400), takes out a maximum of six people (four of whom can fish at the same time) on one of its four boats, which range in length from 27 to 34 feet. Half-day tours, with all equipment included, go for $125 to $160 for two persons, from $135 to $170 for four, and from $190 to $200 for six. The prices are doubled for full-day trips. Boats leave from the docks beside the Bali Floating Restaurant in Oranjestad. De Palm maintains seven branches, most of which lie within the precincts of Aruba's major hotels.

Capt. Hubert Kelkboom (tel. 22756 in the daytime, 28834 in the evening) offers charter fishing trips aboard the **Macabi,** a 33-foot cabin yacht with a spacious fishing cockpit. A half-day charter costs $160, and a full day goes for $300. Captain Kelkboom will arrange, if possible, a party (maximum of six persons) for a charge of $40 per person.

The **Mahi-Mahi** (tel. 34321), a 41-foot Hattaras, makes fishing trips to spots where the fish of the season are usually running. Half-day charters cost $195 per boat. Lunch is included in the full-day trip. For information and reservations, contact John Visser (tel. 29163 for an answering machine). The *Mahi-Mahi* leaves from Bali Pier.

Golf

Visitors can play at the nine-hole **Aruba Golf Club,** 82 Golfweg (tel. 93485), near the oil refineries of San Nicolas at the eastern end of the island. Goats run across the course, and the oiled sand greens add zest to the game. Fast-food items and sandwiches are available at the clubhouse and bar.

Tennis

Most of the island's beachfront hotels have tennis courts, and some have top pros on hand to give instruction. Many of the courts can also be lit for night games (I don't advise playing in Aruba's noonday sun). Usually there's a $4 surcharge at night, although day games are free if you're a guest. Some hotels restrict their courts to use by guests.

Horseback Riding

Rancho El Paso, 44 Washington (tel. 23310), is owned by Aruba's largest tour operator, De Palm. A stable of around 20 horses is maintained for the riding pleasure of visitors. Both beginners and advanced riders are accommodated. All tours are guided, and last between one and two hours. Unless you're accustomed to the saddle you'd better opt for the one-hour tour, costing $12.50. For the rugged, the two-hour tour, taking in both the countryside and beach rides, is $25 per person. Rides are offered daily except Sunday at 9:30 a.m., 2:30 p.m., and 5 p.m.

SHOPPING: Aruba manages to compress six continents into the half-mile-long Nassaustraat, in what is called Mainstreet Shopping Center, in Oranjestad. Not technically a free port, the duty is so low (3.3%) that articles are very attractively priced. Aruba also has no sales tax. You'll find the usual array of Swiss watches, German and Japanese cameras, jewelry, liquor, English bone china and porcelain, Dutch, Swedish, and Danish silver and pewter, French perfume, British woolens, Indonesian specialties, and Madeira embroidery. Delft blue pottery is an especially good buy. You'll find good buys on Holland cheese (Edam and Gouda), as well as Holland chocolate and English cigarettes in the airport departure area.

Store hours in general are Monday through Saturday from 8 a.m. to noon and 2 to 6 p.m. Many stores are also closed on Tuesday afternoon and some seem to keep irregular hours in the off-season, especially in the fall and spring.

The **Alhambra Shopping Bazaar** (tel. 35000), adjacent to the Alhambra Casino, is a blend of international shops, outdoor marketplaces, and cafés and restaurants. Merchandise ranges from fine jewelry, chocolates, and flowers to imported craft items, leather goods, clothing, and lingerie. Like the casino, the shopping bazaar is open seven days a week from early afternoon until early morning hours.

The **Boulevard Shopping Mall,** the only enclosed mall in Aruba, contains more than 60 shops, plus four restaurants, Club Scaramouche, twin movie theaters, and the only McDonald's on the island. The mall is decorated with lush tropical plants and rare birds from South America. It's open Monday through Saturday from 9 a.m. to 6 p.m. daily.

In the heart of Nassaustraat stands the legendary **Spritzer & Fuhrmann's** (tel. 24360), with its main building and the much-photographed carillon chiming "Bon Bini" (welcome). Gold and diamond jewelry and fine watches are sold here, not only for the discriminating taste of the connoisseur but also for the budget buyer seeking good jewelry. S&F also has a collection of fine china, crystal, and flatware, in most of the better-known brands. If you can't make it into town, you'll find branches of the store at the Holiday Inn, the Concorde, and Divi-Divi.

The **Aruba Peasant Shop,** 70 Nassaustraat (tel. 22900), is the island's oldest gift shop and souvenir store. Handcrafts from more than 50 countries include the Delft blue pottery as well as wooden shoes from Holland. Also sold is an extensive variety of exotic clothing and the largest Aruba T-shirt collection, along with exquisite figurines, miniatures, and other gifts at reasonable prices.

Photo El Globo Aruba (tel. 22900) is under one roof with the Aruba Peasant Shop at Nassaustraat. All your needs in photographic, hi-fi, and video equipment can be supplied in the world's best makes at good prices.

Aruba Book and Gift Store (Aruba Boekhandel), 94 Nassaustraat (tel. 21273), started as the island's first bookstore (in 1948) but has added an extensive collection of toys, gifts, and souvenirs.

Kan Jewelers, 47 Nassaustraat (tel. 21192), is famous for its duty-free 14- and 18-karat gold jewelry and watches. These are jewelers from Holland, and they enjoy a good reputation in the Dutch Leewards. They also carry a big variety of Swiss watches such as Rolex, Cartier, and Movado, and many more. Kan has nine locations in Aruba, at most of the large hotels, and one in Curaçao.

New Amsterdam Store, 10 and 50 Nassaustraat (tel. 21152), is best for linens, with its selection of napkins, placemats, and embroidered tablecloths with sources that range all the way from China. It has an extensive line of other merchandise as well, from Delft blue pottery to beachwear and boutique items, along with an exquisite gold collection, gift items under $20, porcelain figures by Lladrò, watches, French and Italian women's wear, and leather bags and shoes.

Directly next door, the **Aruba Trading Company,** 14 Nassaustraat (tel. 22600), offers a complete range of attractive tourist items: perfumes, cosmetics, souvenirs, and gift items of porcelain, Delft, Hummel, and crystal ware, liquor, and cigarettes (the latter purchases can be delivered to your plane).

Casa del Mimbre, 76 Nassaustraat (tel. 27268), specializes in Colombian arts and crafts, including woolen ruanas, which are ponchos popularized by Avianca stewardesses. They also have souvenirs and gifts from Central America and other South American countries. Mayan napkins from Guatemala, woven wall hangings from Mexico, cowhide golf bags from Colombia—the collection is wide ranging and intriguing.

The **Artistic Boutique,** 25 Nassaustraat (tel. 23142), open from 9 a.m. to 6 p.m. with no siesta, stocks fine linens, hand-embroidered madeiras, orangies, and Irish linen articles, such as napkins, place mats, and guest towels. You may be able to find just what you want in the $1 corner. Crystal figurines, Oriental antiques, handmade rugs, paintings, jade and ivory artworks, silks, gold and silver jewelry, and handcrafted articles of the islands and the Orient are among the treasures offered. There is a women's boutique on the second floor. A branch in the Boulevard Shopping Mall is open from 9 a.m. to 5 p.m. (no siesta).

Gandelman Jewelers, at the beginning of Mainstreet and in the Alhambra Shopping Bazaar (tel. 29143), is the exclusive agent for the Gucci accessory collection, Baume and Mercier, Raymond Weil, and Tag-Heuer. A dazzling selection of precious stones, 14- and 18-karat gold jewelry, and famous watches has made them known throughout the Caribbean. The Gucci accessories include wallets, belts, handbags, and other items. Shops handling only the Gucci line are at the Americana Hotel, the Holiday Inn, and in the airport departure hall.

Penha, 11-13 Nassaustraat (tel. 24161), offers a selection of gifts, clothing, and perfumes, all in the top categories. For example, they are exclusive purveyors here of Giorgio, and they also have Estée Lauder, Lancôme, and Clinique cosmetics. Men's clothing includes that of famous designers such as Pierre Cardin, Papillon, Lanvin, and Givenchy, and women can choose garments from Dior, Liz Claiborne, and Castoni. If you're shopping on a smaller scale, you'll find T-shirts and souvenirs here. Penha also has boutiques at the Tamarijn, Divi-Divi, Holiday Inn, and Americana hotels.

Boulevard Book and Drugstore (tel. 27358), in the Boulevard Shopping Mall, has a complete range of goods from books to cosmetics, candies, gifts, and unique souvenirs.

Tamarijn Hotel Giftshop and Minimarket, in the Tamarijn Beach Hotel (tel. 24150), offers a complete selection of gifts, souvenirs, and drugstore items, plus a full range of delicatessen offerings, liquor, and wines.

Divi-Divi Hotel Giftshop and Minimarket, in the Divi-Divi Beach Hotel (tel. 23300), is stocked like the Tamarijn shops, just previewed.

The Wooden Shoe (tel. 35000) in the Alhambra Casino and Bazaar, is a gift and souvenir shop with the biggest selection of Delft blue and other quality gift items.

Philatelists interested in the wealth of colorful and artistic stamps issued in honor of the changed government status of Aruba can purchase a complete assortment, as well as other special issues, at the post office in Oranjestad.

AFTER DARK: The casinos of the big hotels along Palm Beach are the liveliest nighttime destinations. In plush gaming parlors, guests try their luck at roulette, craps, blackjack, and of course the one-armed bandits. The **Americana Aruba** (tel. 24500) opens daily at 1 p.m. for slots, at 3 p.m. for blackjack and roulette, and at 9 p.m. for all games. Early birds go to the **Aruba Concorde** (tel. 24466) at 10 a.m. for slots, 1 p.m. for games. The **Holiday Inn** (tel. 23600) wins the prize for all-around action. Its casino doors are open 22 hours a day, closing only for two hours to clean. The **Aruba Palm Beach** (tel. 23900) opens its gambling tables from 9 p.m. on. The **Golden Tulip Aruba Caribbean** (tel. 33555) has one of the newest casinos on the island.

The busiest casino in Aruba is the **Alhambra,** L. G. Smith Boulevard (tel. 35000). More than just a casino, it offers a collection of restaurants and boutiques, along with an inner courtyard designed like an 18th-century Dutch village. From the outside the complex looks Moorish, with serpentine mahogany columns and repeating arches rising to a pinnacle defined by a duet of sea-green domes. The desert setting of Aruba seems appropriate. A strapping "Moor" greets you at the door, shaking your hand to wish you luck.

Away from the gaming tables, cabaret shows are presented nightly except Sunday at 9 and 11 p.m. at the Aladdin Theater. Entrance to the show, whose stars and format change regularly, is $10 per person. It's best to phone in advance for a reservation (tel. 35000), since many hotels sell tickets to these shows without confirming reservations. Included among the almost 30 different boutiques and a scattering of eating places is a New York–style deli open 24 hours a day (tel. 25434), the Batidos Bar, specializing in frozen fruit cocktails, and the Roseland Disco and nightclub. Owned and operated by the Divi hotel chain, the casino offers free transportation from its front door to each of the three Divi hotels on the island. The casino and its satellites are open daily from 10 a.m. till very late at night.

Nongamblers or those who grow tired of the slots and tables can patronize the hotel's cocktail lounges and supper clubs. You don't have to be a guest of the hotel to visit to see the shows, but you should make a reservation. Tables at the big shows, especially in season, are likely to be booked early in the day. Usually you can go to one of the major hotel supper clubs and only order drinks. Expect to pay from $4 for most libations.

One of the best nightlife options on the island is the **Stellaris Gourmet Dinner Show** at the Americana Aruba (tel. 24500). Amid a dramatically terraced decor of red, black, and silver, guests enjoy cabaret shows at 9:15 p.m. nightly and à la carte dinners from 7 to 11 p.m. Full meals cost $25 to $50 per person, including such elegant dishes as medallions of beef with crabmeat and hollandaise, roast duckling with cherries, chicken Kiev, and a specialty of roast prime rib served in either queen- or king-sized portions. Reservations are necessary.

Also in the Americana Aruba complex is **Le Club Lounge** (tel. 24500). Guests sit either at one of the smallish tables or at a long rectangular bar of burnished mahogany near an array of East Indian wall hangings. An elongated window exposes a view of the palm-fringed pool outside. Live music is presented from the bandstand, and disco music plays before and after the midnight show. There's a two-drink minimum (each drink costs $4). The bar is open nightly from 9 p.m. to 3 a.m.

The **Arabesque Nightclub** is in the Aruba Concorde (tel. 24466), a hotel affiliated with the Sands of Las Vegas. Perhaps inspired by Nevada, this nightclub offers some of the grandest, glitziest, and most stylish acts in Aruba. For example, you're likely to see a bevy of dancers, the Copa Girls, presenting a music and dance extravaganza with artfully undressed costumes. Reservations are necessary, especially in high season, and the entrance price of $15 per person includes the first two drinks. Shows are presented nightly except Monday at 11 p.m.

On the disco circuit, **Club Scaramouche** (tel. 24954), in the penthouse of the Boulevard Shopping Mall in Oranjestad, is clearly the leader. Technically, this is a private membership club, charging dues of $100 per year. Getting in without being a member is not a real problem, however. While residents of the island must be a member of the guest or a member to enter, island visitors may enjoy an evening for a charge of $5, or may obtain one of the VIP passes available in many of the leading hotels and some of the better restaurants. Jeans are not allowed, nor are tennis shoes or T-shirts. Hours are 9 p.m. to 5 a.m. weeknights, with a daily 4 to 7 p.m. cocktail hour. The Scaramouche is a posh and comfortable entertainment establishment, with an inlaid dance floor and Aruba's largest bar. Sumptuous leathers, spacious divans, and sparkling glassware form a backdrop for enjoyment of complimentary hors d'oeuvres and dancing to disco sound. However, there are intimate conversation nooks where the sound is controlled so that you can hear your companions talk.

The other leading disco is the **Contempo** at the Talk of the Town (tel. 21990). After 10:30 p.m. the tables are moved away in a part of this popular restaurant and there's dancing until 3 a.m. There's also a $6 entrance fee, including drinks, and tickets are on sale in the lobby. The management warns that prices are subject to change on special nights. Jackets are required, and no one under 18 is admitted.

Temptations on the Beach (tel. 23380), across from the Talk of the Town Hotel, Oranjestad, is a combination open-air café and cabaret, popular both for its snacks, served *tapas* fashion, and for its entertainment. You may hear classical guitarists, a jazz singer, or just music to dance to. On Tuesday night there's an exhibition of Aruban folkloric dancing with traditional and Carnaval costumes, along with an authentic Aruban buffet with a salad bar. You mix your own drinks from 6 to 10:30 p.m. The price for this special event is $24 per person, including service. Another special night is Thursday, when a beach barbecue is held, with a steel band, dancing, and games. The charge of $23.50 per person covers everything from 6 to 9 p.m. A "Flaming Limbo Show," with audience participation, is presented on Sunday. From 6 to 7 p.m., a frozen piña colada hour is joined by your selection from a salad bar and hot buffet. You can eat and drink what you like from 6 to 10 p.m., all for the $27 charge.

The **Bamboo Bar** (tel. 22131), on the Bali Pier (see my Bali Floating Restaurant recommendation under "Aruba Cookery"), is the home of Aruba's first piano bar. A "Happy Happy Hour" is featured from 6:30 to 7:30 p.m., while the sun sets over the harbor. Come in for drinks or open-air dining (same menu as the Bali Floating Restaurant) and enjoy the scene of boats and yachts bobbing at anchor. Romantic piano and guitar music sets the mood for a relaxing evening. The Bamboo Bar, open daily except Sunday, is one of Aruba's favorite meeting places.

2. Bonaire

Unlike some islands, Bonaire isn't just surrounded by coral reefs. It *is* the reef! And its shores are thick with rainbow-hued fish. Five miles wide and 24 miles long, Bonaire is poised in the Caribbean, close to the Spanish Main. The island attracts those seeking the out-of-the-way spot, the uncrowded shore.

Bonaire is best reached from its sister island of Curaçao, 30 miles to the west. Like Curaçao, it is desert-like, with a dry and brilliant atmosphere. Often it is visited by "day trippers," who rush through here in pursuit of the shy, elusive flamingo, the glamor bird of the Caribbean.

Boomerang-shaped Bonaire comprises about 112 square miles, making it the second largest of the ABC Dutch grouping. Its northern sector is hilly, tapering up to Brandaris Peak, all of 788 feet. However, the southern half, flat as a flapjack, is given over to bays, reefs, beaches, and a salt lake which attracts the flamingos. The island's population is approximately 10,000.

The island has powdery white beaches and turquoise waters, where underwater photographers find a visibility of 100 feet or more. Unspoiled Bonaire is one of the world's best scuba and snorkeling grounds, a beachcomber's retreat, and a birdwatcher's heaven, with 145 different species—not only the graceful flamingo, but the big-billed pelican, as well as bright-green parrots, snipes, terns, parakeets, herons, hummingbirds, and others. Bring a pair of binoculars.

Contrary to a popular misconception often published in travel guides, Bonaire doesn't mean good air. Rather, it comes from the Indian, signifying low country.

Bonaireans zealously want to protect their environment. Even though they eagerly seek tourism, they aren't interested in creating "another Aruba" with its high-rise hotel blocks. Spearfishing isn't allowed in their waters, nor is the taking or destruction of any living animal or coral from the sea.

The island was discovered in 1499 by a party of explorers commanded by Amerigo Vespucci, who lent his name to the New World. Amerigo found some Indians living on the island in Stone Age conditions. After Spanish domination, Bonaire witnessed the arrival of the Dutch in 1634, perhaps seeking to protect Curaçao's flanks, an island they already occupied. Bonaire was assigned the duty of supplying livestock, corn, and salt.

Once the British occupied the island, eventually leasing it to a New York merchant for $2,400 annually, including the services of 300 "salt-mine" slaves.

The Dutch came back in 1816, setting up plantations to grow dyewood, cochenille, and aloes. At the abolition of slavery in 1863, the economy collapsed. Bonaire settled into a long, dreary depression. Relief came in the form of what was known as the "money order economy" era, when Bonaireans migrated to Curaçao and Aruba to work in the oil industry. Automation of that industry in the 1950s caused the loss of many jobs, and Bonaireans returned to their native island. Fortunately, instead of being plunged permanently back into depression, Bonaire was discovered, along with other Caribbean islands, by international tourism, and the economy began to look up. The first hotel opened in 1951. The salt pans were modified to use solar energy and became the most successful base of plants in the world. The island's power facilities were enlarged to assure further development.

The big annual event is the **October Sailing Regatta,** a five-day festival of racing sponsored by the local tourist bureau. Now an international affair, the event attracts sailors and spectators from around the world, as a flotilla of sailboats and yachts anchor in Kralendijk Bay. If you're planning to visit during regatta days, make sure you have an iron-clad hotel reservation.

GETTING THERE: Flights are offered by **American** and **Eastern** from New York to Curaçao with connecting service to Bonaire via **ALM.** Eastern and ALM have service from Miami to Curaçao, with connecting service via ALM. ALM offers direct service from Miami to Bonaire weekly and service from New York via Haiti and Curaçao. ALM also offers direct service to Curaçao from other Caribbean locations, including San Juan, St. Maarten, St. Kitts, and Trinidad.

GETTING AROUND: As per usual, **taxis** are unmetered, but the government has established rates. All licensed taxicabs carry a number plate with the letters "TX." Each driver should have a list of prices to be produced upon request. As many as four passengers can go along for the ride unless they have too much luggage. As examples of what rates to expect, a trip from the airport to the Flamingo Beach Hotel should cost $4; from the Flamingo Beach Hotel to Hotel Bonaire, $5. From 8 p.m. to midnight fares are increased by 25%, and from midnight until 6 a.m. they go up by 50%.

Car Rentals

It's easy to drive in Bonaire, and car rentals are reasonable. I recommend **Budget/Boncar** (tel. 8300, ext. 225 in town; tel. 8315 at the airport). This firm rents Suzuki Frontes, Suzuki Jeeps, Hondas, VW vans, Ford Econovans with 9 to 12 seats), and other vehicles starting at $22 per day with unlimited mileage. Your U.S. or Canadian driver's license, if valid, is acceptable for driving in Bonaire. One- and two-seater scooters are also available for rent. Driving in Bonaire is on the right.

Scooter Rentals

Happy Chappy Rentals, Kaya C. E. B Hellmund (tel. 8761), can supply you with an 80-cc Yamaha on which two persons can ride for a cost of about $15 per day.

Sightseeing Taxi Tours

All taxi drivers are informed about Bonaire's sightseeing attractions, and will reveal them to you (as well as three other passengers) at a cost of about $25 to $30 for a half-day jaunt, which is plenty of time to take in the highlights, both north and south.

Sightseeing Bus Tours

Bonaire Sightseeing Tours (tel. 8300, ext. 225) hauls you on tours of the island, both north and south, taking in the flamingos, slave huts, conch shells, Goto Lake, the Indian inscriptions, and other sights. The northern tour, lasting two hours, costs $9 per person; the southern tour, also lasting two hours, costs the same. You can take a whole-island tour, lasting 3 hours and costing $13 per person, allowing you to see the entire northern section and the southern part as far as the slave huts. A special four-hour tour of Washington National Park can be booked at a cost of $17 per person for a minimum of four. An all-day tour of the national park costs $32 per person.

PRACTICAL FACTS: Bonaire is part of the Netherlands Antilles (an autonomous part of the Netherlands), with its own legislative council, island council, and lieutenant governor.

Bonaire is known for its **climate,** with temperatures hovering at 82° Fahrenheit. The water temperature averages 80°. It's warmest in August and September, coolest in January and February. The average rainfall is 22 inches, December through March being the rainiest months.

Like Aruba and Curaçao, the Netherlands Antillean florin (NAf) or guilder (equal to 52¢ in U.S. dollars) is the coin of the realm. However, U.S. dollars are also accepted.

Upon leaving Bonaire, you'll be charged an airport **departure tax** of $5.75, so don't spend every penny. There is also an inter-island tax of $2.75.

Drinking **water** is safe (it comes from distilled and purified sea water).

To enter Bonaire, all you need is **proof of citizenship** and a return or continuing ticket.

English is widely spoken on the island, but you'll also hear Spanish, Dutch, and Papiamento.

The **electric current,** is 127 volts AC, 50 cycles. Divers with precise equipment should provide their own converters.

For tourist information in Bonaire, go to the **Tourist Office,** Caya Grandi in Kralendjik (tel. 8322 or 8649). Hours are Monday to Friday from 7:30 a.m. to noon and 1:30 to 5:30 p.m.

There is no **Customs** requirement for Bonaire.

The government requires a 5% **room tax** on all hotel rates. Most hotels and guesthouses add a 10% **service charge** in lieu of tipping. Restaurants generally add a service charge of 15% to the bill.

You can **dial direct** to Bonaire numbers. Just call 011-599-7 plus the four-digit number you want to reach. Service for telephone, Telex, telegraph, radio, and TV is available in English.

Banking hours are usually 8:30 a.m. to noon and 2 to 4 p.m. Monday to Friday.

Bonaire operates on **Atlantic Standard Time** all year round.

The island has a hospital, doctors, a dentist, an eye doctor, a visiting orthodontist, and a drugstore. A plane on standby at the airport takes seriously ill patients to Curaçao for treatment.

HOTELS: Hotels are low-key and unhassled, and all of them face the sea. There are no high-rises here, only low-lying, personally run operations where everybody gets to know everybody else rather fast.

The Top Resorts

The **Flamingo Beach Hotel** (tel. 8285) is one of the most personalized and charming hotels in the ABC islands. This complete beachfront resort, with its watersports facilities and stylized bedrooms, is the product of the Wiggins family of Ithaca, New York. They discovered a neglected, gone-to-seed hotel with a cluster of flimsy wooden bungalows that had been used as an internment camp for German prisoners of World War II. With foresight and taste they turned it into a top-notch resort, offering both individual cottages and modern seafront rooms with private balconies resting on piers above the surf, so you can stand out and watch rainbow-hued tropical fish in the water below.

The resort's original 110 rooms were supplemented in 1986 with the addition of 40 stylish time-sharing units, forming Club Flamingo. Each of the units is rentable, when available, by the day or week. Accommodations in both sections are spacious, stylish, and sunny, with air conditioning, ceiling fans, private bathrooms, and a selection of Mexican accessories. The newer units are clustered into a green-and-white neo-Victorian pavilion facing its own curve-sided swimming pool. Each contains a stylish kitchenette with carved cupboards and cabinets of pickled hardwoods. Both sections benefit from the attentions of a pair of social hostesses and the proximity of a good dive operation and a beautiful beach. Units in the still-stylish older section rent in winter for $85 to $165 daily in a single, $95 to $170 in a double. *In summer, singles are $65 to $110; doubles, $70 to $115*. MAP is another $38 per person daily. Units in the newer section rent for $175 daily for two people in high season, *dropping to $125 daily in low season*. Tax and service are extra. On the premises, a pair of individually recommended restaurants include the Chibi-Chibi and the Calabas Terrace, providing a setting for relaxing and satisfying meals.

Bonaire Beach Hotel, P.O. Box 34 (tel. 8448), which was taken over by the government, lies about half a mile north of town on its own beach, Playa Lechi (Milk

Beach). On the premises are two illuminated tennis courts, a casino, and a bar and restaurant featuring specialty evenings. Its headquarters is in a low-slung central building filled with plants. Long covered walkways lead across a sandy terrain through gardens to the comfortable air-conditioned accommodations. These lie in motel-like annexes scattered around a freshwater pool. Some are freshly painted with tasteful accessories, while others are less desirable and less dramatic. In winter, singles cost $100 to $110 daily; doubles, $120 to $130. *Low-season rates range from $45 to $65 daily in a single, from $50 to $70 in a double.*

The Dive Resorts

Captain Don's Habitat (tel. 8290, 802/496-5067 in Vermont, or toll free 800/ BONAIRE) is a unique diving, snorkeling, and nature-oriented community with an air of congenial informality and a philosophy and lifestyle for those whose souls belong to the sea. The establishment is built on a coral bluff overlooking the sea and one of Bonaire's most popular dive sites. Habitat and its accompanying dive shop are the creation of Capt. Don Stewart, Caribbean pioneer and "caretaker of the reefs," a former Californian who sailed his schooner from San Francisco through the Panama Canal, arriving on a reef in Bonaire in 1962—and he's been here ever since. You'll spot him at once, with his one earring and bare feet. Called the "godfather of diving" on the island, Captain Don was instrumental in the formation of the Bonaire Marine Park whereby the entire island became a protected reef. The captain still dives weekly, taking his guests to his favorite diving sites.

Habitat consists of eight new luxury oceanfront villas, nine spacious and airy two-bedroom cottages, four single economy rooms, and six double economy units. Each villa contains three luxury doubles with air-conditioning and hot water. The deluxe villa suite has a full kitchen and seaside veranda. The cottages with kitchens, living rooms, and verandas may be the best value per person. All accommodations are within a minute's walk of the sea. Daily rates in high season, from December 22 to early April, are $25 in a single economy room, $48 double economy, $90 for one to two guests in a cottage, $108 for three in a cottage, and $120 for four. Villa luxury doubles cost $80 to $110, and an entire villa rents for $220 to $225. *In the off-season, mid-April to just before Christmas, rates are $18 for single economy, $34 for double economy, $58 for one to two people in a cottage, $73 for three in a cottage, and $80 in a similar accommodation for four. Luxury doubles in a villa rent for $63 to $92, and entire villas for $160 to $180.*

Among the amenities are an on-site boutique, the Captain's Locker, and the recently renovated, open-air seaside Captain Don's Bar and Restaurant. Great attention has been put into the design of the adjoining terraced loggias and small terraces leading down to the water, providing an informal setting in which to relax, drink, eat, whatever. A meandering terracotta pathway is a seaside promenade linking the new villas with the Habitat Dive Shop and the rest of the Habitat community.

Carib Inn, P.O. Box 68 (tel. 8819). Set directly on the water, and containing only eight rooms, this hotel is occupied by dedicated scuba-divers who purchase accommodations as part of a dive package. It was established by an American, Bruce Bowker. About half of the units ring an oval-shaped swimming pool; others are in separate cottages on the beach, facing the hotel's dock. Depending on the accommodation (about four of them contain kitchens), in winter units rent for $60 to $130 for two people. *In summer they cost between $40 and $105 for two guests.* Each room is air-conditioned with simple tropical furniture and few frills. A six-day dive package with a dozen boat dives, all the air you can use, welts, belt, and tank goes for $220. Unlimited beach diving over a six-day period, with air and all equipment, costs $80. For more details, see "The Sporting Life," below.

DINING OUT: The food is generally acceptable. Nearly everything has to be imported, of course. Your best bet is fresh-caught fish and an occasional rijsttafel, the traditional Indonesian rice table, or try the local dishes. Popular foods are conch cutlet or stew, pickled conch, red snapper, tuna, wahoo, dolphin, fungi (a thick cornmeal pudding), rice, beans, saté (marinated meat with curried mayonnaise), goat stew, and Dutch cheeses.

Chibi-Chibi, Flamingo Beach Hotel (tel. 8285), is my favorite restaurant on the island. Built on piers above the rock-studded sea bottom, it rises in an imposing two-tiered design of exposed planking and wooden balustrades. Schools of fish, the same varieties as might be served on your dinner plate, foam through the illuminated waters to feed on bread diners throw from their breeze-filled perches. Stephen Adams, the Massachusetts-born chef, prepares a delectable seafood menu of fresh local ingredients. Specialties include a seafood crêpe, Antillean onion soup, fettuccine flamingo, keshi yena (chicken, onions, raisins, and olives baked in Dutch Gouda cheese), and a changing array of fish which depends on the catch of the day. Full meals, costing from $35 per person, are served only at dinner from 6 to 10 p.m. Reservations are important, especially if you want a waterside table. The restaurant is named after a species of yellow-breasted local bird.

Calabas Terrace, Flamingo Beach Hotel (tel. 8285). Its veranda setting, a few steps from the sea, is worth a detour. A pleasant staff works hard to ensure satisfaction, and the food is appetizing. The U.S.-born chef, Stephen Adams, supplements the regular à la carte menu with no fewer than four specialty evenings, which draw an enthusiastic crowd from the island's other hotels. A Sunday-night roast beef / roast lamb buffet costs $19 per person, $11 for children. A Monday-night barbecue buffet at the same price is one of the most elaborate in Bonaire. The Tuesday-night Indonesian buffet goes for $18, and Thursday night's seafood buffet at $21 offers samplings of such dishes as wahoo amandine, stewed conch, scallops in white wine, fresh local tuna, and "peel and eat" shrimp. All evening meals are served from 7 to 10:30 p.m. À la carte lunches, from noon to 2:30 p.m., feature hamburgers, salads, and such food as South Philly cheesesteak hoagies along with daily specials. When no buffet is scheduled, à la carte dinners cost $30 each. A Sunday brunch from noon to 2:30 p.m. goes for $14. A 15% service charge is added.

Outside of the hotels, I prefer the **Beefeater,** 12 Kaya Grandi (tel. 8081), in the heart of Kralendijk opposite the tourist office. Here a charming Englishman, Richard Dove, a former inspector for the Michelin guides, has created a handsome restaurant and decorated it with prints and pictures. It is found in an old town house. An apéritif is served in an intimate bar, and you're shown to your table where you'll enjoy excellent personal service in a dignified, somewhat elegant atmosphere. Steaks and seafood are the main feature. The chef prepares an excellent steak au poivre. Before your main course, try his pâté, crêpe, or conch. Expect to pay from 30 NAf ($15.50) to 45 NAf ($23.50) for a three-course meal. The restaurant is open Monday through Saturday for dinner only, from 6:30 to 11 p.m. In season, it's necessary to make a reservation.

Zeezicht, Kaya Corsow (tel. 8434), is the best place in the capital to go for a sundowner. You join the old salts or the people who live on boats to watch the sun go down, hoping to see the "green flash" that Hemingway wrote about. Pronounced "zay-zicht" and meaning sea view, this place has long been popular with fishermen who like the excellent local cookery and the Chinese dishes. Rebuilt into a two-story operation, the restaurant offers an oyster soup that might be the best beginning. Perhaps you'll prefer a conch chop suey, a first for me. A small rijsttafel is also offered. Fried fish is invariably featured, the catch coming from the nearby fish market. Lobster à la Zeezicht is occasionally offered, and there's always the Zeezicht steak. Count on parting with about $22. Zeezicht is open from 8:30 a.m. to 11 p.m.

China Garden, Kaya Grandi (tel. 8480), is housed in a restored Bonairean mansion. Good-tasting Eastern dishes, with some Indonesian specialties, are served to West Indians. Portions are enormous, and prices are low, considering what you get.

The chefs from Hong Kong also cook Chinese, American, and local dishes, and do so daily from 11:30 a.m. to 10 p.m. except Tuesday. A variety of curries ranges from beef to lobster. Seafood dishes, prepared in a variety of styles, including lobster in black-bean sauce, are served. Special culinary features include a Java rijsttafel and the nasi goreng special. The place is air-conditioned, seating 60 guests, and it offers pleasant and courteous service. You can dine here for $20, but a lot of hungry scuba-divers spend a lot more, of course.

Restaurant Lisboa, Kaya Grandi (tel. 8286), in front of the Hotel Rochaline, lies beneath a vine-covered arbor. This pleasant restaurant is one of the best choices for a good meal outside the island's major hotels. Straw-covered bottles of wine dangle above your head as you enjoy a view of the nearby ocean and the little fish market. Breakfast is served daily from 7:30 to 11 a.m., lunch is from noon to 3 p.m., and dinner is on from 6:30 p.m. until the final diner finishes. Angelino Apolinario and his family charge $12 for lunch, from $20 for dinner. Specialties include fresh oysters, fresh fish with fried plaintain, octopus filet, several styles of pizza, grilled shrimp, deep-fried chicken legs, and fish soup.

Den Laman Bar and Restaurant, Gouverneur Debrotweg (tel. 8955), next to the Hotel Bonaire, serves some of the best seafood on Bonaire. The restaurant has a huge 9,000-gallon aquarium, covering two walls. Housed within are such creatures as sharks, along with beautiful and fascinating tropical fish. The fish are not just for viewing, as you'll soon agree after ordering a cocktail as an appetizer (shrimp, lobster, or mixed seafood). Another excellent beginning is the fish soup, the chef's special. The fresh fish of the day depends on what was caught, of course. Perhaps you'll order conch flamingo, a local favorite, or lobster Thermidor. When it's featured, I always go for the turtle steak or the red snapper Créole. It's easy to spend $35 here, but also possible to dine for less. Dinner is served from 6 to 11 p.m. Closed Tuesday.

Bistro des Amis, 1 Kaya L. D. Gerharts (tel. 8003), is one of my favorites. It's intimate, it's friendly, and it serves good food. In the heart of Kralendijk, the bistro is owned by a woman known only as "Lucille." She will tell you her specials of the day, which are likely to include the best onion soup on the island, escargots served piping hot in garlic butter, mousse of smoked eel, pepper steak in cream-cognac sauce, filet of duck in raspberry sauce, lamb cutlets, and scallops swimming in a velvety cream sauce. The wine selection is limited, but among the best on the island. Incidentally, you dine in air-conditioned comfort. Hours are 6:30 to 11 p.m. daily except Sunday, and there is often dancing so you can make a night of it. Count on a bill beginning at $22 for dinner. There's also a large bar if you'd like to drop in for a drink before dinner.

EXPLORING BONAIRE: The capital, Kralendijk, means "coral dike" and is pronounced "Krah-len-dike," although most denizens refer to it as "Playa," Spanish for beach. A dollhouse town of some 2,500 residents, it is small, neat, and pretty, also Dutch clean, and its stucco buildings are painted in pastels of pink and orange, with an occasional lime green. The capital's jetty is lined with island sloops and fishing boats.

Kralendijk nestles in a bay on the west coast, opposite Klein Bonaire or Little Bonaire, an uninhabited, low-lying islet a ten-minute swim from the capital.

The main street of town leads along the beachfront on the harbor. A Protestant church was built in 1834, and St. Bernard's Roman Catholic Church has some lovely stained-glass windows.

At Ford Oranje you'll see a lone cannon dating from the days of Napoleon. If possible, try to get up early to see the Fish Market on the waterfront, looking like a little gold Greek temple. Here you'll see a variety of strange and brilliantly colored fish.

Around town you'll probably see the official tourist guide and welcoming committee of one, Caicai Cecelia. In his sparkling white uniform and with his ever-present smile, he roams the streets, welcoming newcomers and offering advice and assistance. He's also a singer and has made records.

Bonaire Marine Park

To maintain the coral reef ecosystem off Bonaire and to ensure returns from scuba-diving, snorkeling, fishing, and other recreational activities, the Bonaire Marine Park was created, with the help of the International Union for Conservation of Nature and Natural Resources and of the World Wildlife Fund. The park incorporates the entire coastline of Bonaire and neighboring Klein Bonaire, defined as the "seabottom and the overlying waters from the high-water tidemark down to 200 feet." All park activities are controlled by island government legislation and a marine environment management program. The park is policed, and services and facilities are provided for visitors. These include a **Visitor Information Center** at the Karpata Ecological Center, park brochures, lectures, slide presentations, films, and permanent dive-site moorings.

Visitors are asked to respect the marine environment and to engage in no activities that may damage it, such as sitting on corals. All marine life is completely protected. This means no fishing or collecting of fish, shells, or corals, dead or alive. Spearfishing is forbidden. Anchoring is not permitted. All craft must use permanent moorings, except for emergency stops. Boats of less than 12 feet may use a stone anchor. Most recreation activity in the marine park takes place on the island's leeward side and among the reefs surrounding Klein Bonaire, a small uninhabited islet.

The reefs are home to various coral formations that grow at different depths, ranging from the knobby brain coral at three feet to staghorn and elkhorn up to about ten feet deeper, and gorgonians, giant brain; and others all the way to 40 to 83 feet. Many species of fish inhabit the reefs, and the deep reef slope is home to a range of sponges, groupers, and moray eels.

The Tour North

After leaving Kralendijk, and passing the Bonaire Beach Hotel and the desalinization plant, you'll come to **Radio Nederland Wereld Omroep** (Dutch World Radio). It's a 13-tower, 300,000-watter. Opposite the transmitting station is a lovers' promenade, built by nature. It's an ideal spot for a picnic.

The road north is one of the most beautiful stretches in the Antilles, with turquoise waters on your left, coral cliffs on your right. You can stop at several points along this road where you'll find paved paths for strolling or bicycling.

Continuing, you'll pass the storage tanks of the Bonaire Petroleum Corporation, the road heading to **Gotomeer,** the island's loveliest inland sector, with a saltwater lake. Several flamingos prefer this spot to the salt flats in the south.

Down the hill the road leads to a section called **"Dos Pos"** or two wells, which has palm trees and vegetation in contrast to the rest of the island, where only the drought-resistant kibraacha and divi-divi trees, tilted before the constant wind, can grow, along with forests of cacti.

Bonaire's oldest village is **Rincon.** Slaves who used to work in the salt flats in the south once lived here. There are a couple of bars, including the Amstel and the Tropicana, where you can order beer before continuing on your journey. The Rincon Ice Cream Parlour makes homemade ice cream in a variety of interesting flavors. Above the bright roofs of the village is the crest of a hill called Para Mira or "stop and look."

A side path outside of Rincon leads to some Arawak Indian inscriptions supposedly 500 years old. The petroglyph designs are in pink-red dye. At nearby **Boca Onima,** you'll find grotesque grottos of coral.

Before going back to the capital, you might take a short bypass to **Seroe Larguy,** which has a good view of Kralendijk and the sea. Lovers frequent the spot at night.

Washington/Slagbaai National Park

Just as the Bonaire Marine Park is aimed at the conservation of the underwater environment, so Washington/Slagbaai National Park is concerned with the conservation of the island's fauna, flora, geology, and geomorphology. Its landscape is a changing vista highlighting desert-like terrain, secluded beaches, caverns, and a bird sanctuary. Occupying 15,000 acres of Bonaire's northwesternmost territory, the park was once a plantation, producing divi-divi, aloe, charcoal, and goats. It was purchased by the Netherlands Antilles government, and since 1967 part of the land, formerly the Washington plantation, has been a wildlife sanctuary. The southern part of the park, the Slagbaai plantation, was added in 1978.

The park can be seen in a few hours, although it takes days to appreciate it fully. Touring the park is easy, with two routes: a 15-mile "short" route, marked by green arrows, and a 22-mile "long" route, marked by yellow arrows. The roads are well marked and safe, but somewhat rugged, although they are gradually being improved. Tickets cost $2 per person and can be purchased at the gate. A guide booklet, costing $4.15, is available.

Whichever route you take, there are a few important stops you should make. Just past the gate is **Salina Mathijs,** a salt flat that is home to flamingos during the rainy season. Beyond the salt flat on the road to the right is **Boca Chikitu,** a white sand beach and bay. A few miles up the beach lies **Boca Cocolishi,** a two-part black sand beach. Its deep, rough seaward side is separated from the calm, shallow basin by a ridge of coralline algae. Hermit crabs walk the beach and shallow water.

The main road leads to **Boca Bartol,** a bay full of living and dead elkhorn coral, seafans, and reef fish. A popular watering hole good for birdwatching is **Poosdi Mangel. Wajaca** is a remote reef where many sea creatures live, including turtles, octopi, and trigger-fish. Immediately inland towers 746-foot **Mount Brandaris,** Bonaire's highest peak, at whose foot is **Bronswinkel Well,** a watering spot for colorful pigeons and parakeets. Some 130 species of birds live in the park, some with such exotic names as banana quilt and black-faced grassquit. Bonaire has few mammals, but you'll see goats and donkeys, perhaps even a wild bull.

Heading South

Leaving the capital again, you pass the **Trans World Radio** antennas, towering 500 feet in the air, transmitting with 810,000 watts. This is one of the hemisphere's most powerful medium-wave radio stations, the loudest voice in Christendom and the most powerful nongovernment broadcast station in the world. It beeps out interdenominational Gospel messages and hymns in 20 languages to countries as far away as the Iron Curtain and the Middle East.

Later, you come on the salt flats where the brilliantly colored pink **flamingos** live. Bonaire shelters the largest accessible nesting and breeding grounds in the world. The flamingos build high mud mounds to hold their eggs. In the background, mounds of salt look like snow mountains, glistening in the sun. The birds are best viewed in spring when they're usually nesting and tending their young.

The salt flats were once worked by slaves, and the government has rebuilt some primitive stone huts, bare shelters little more than waist high. The slaves slept in these huts, returning to their homes in Rincon in the north on weekends. The centuries-old salt pans have been reactivated by the International Salt Company. Near the salt pans you'll see some 30-foot obelisks in white, blue, and orange. They were built in 1838 to help mariners locate their proper anchorages.

Farther down the coast is the island's oldest lighthouse, Willemstoren, built in 1837. Still farther along, Sorobon Beach and Boca Cai come into view. They're at landlocked **Lac Bay** which is ideal for swimming and snorkeling. Conch shells are stacked up on the beach. The water here is so vivid and clear you can see coral 65 to 120 feet down in the reef-protected waters.

SHOPPING: Kralendijk features an assortment of goods, including precious gemstone jewelry, wood, leather, sterling, ceramics, liquors, and tobacco at 25% to 50% less than in the U.S. and Canada. Prices are often quoted in U.S. dollars, and major credit cards and traveler's checks are usually accepted. Most shops are open from 8 a.m. to noon and 2 to 6 p.m. Walk along Kaya Grandi in Kralendijk to sample the merchandise.

Of course, the famous **Spritzer & Fuhrmann's** (tel. 8455) has a branch on Kaya Grandi, selling elegant Swiss watches, clocks, and jewelry, the largest collection on Bonaire. You can also buy English china and French crystal here.

Fundashon Arte Industria Bonairiano, on J. A. Abraham Boulevard (no phone), is the best shop for handcrafts, including woodcarvings, goatskin leather articles, tortoise-shell jewelry (could be seized by U.S. Customs), and jewelry.

Ki Bo Ke Pakus, at the Flamingo Beach Hotel (tel. 8239), has some of the most imaginative merchandise on the island—Bonaire T-shirts, handbags, dashikis, locally made jewelry, batiks from Indonesia, Delft blue items, and khangas, the African material which can be worn a dozen ways.

Littman Jewelers, 35 Kaya Grandi (tel. 8160), is in an old Bonaire house which Steven D. and Esther Littman have restored to its original state. They sell Rolex and Chronosport watches, plus fine Orbit timepieces. The shop also carries many gift items. Next door, Mr. and Mrs. Littman have a shop called **Aries Cheez and Tee's,** selling T-shirts from standard to hand-painted, plus Dutch cheeses, chocolates, fine wines, imported crackers, and other food items.

Things Bonaire, on Kaya Grandi (tel. 8423), sells Jean Meiss hand-painted T-shirts and terry beachwear, as well as hand-painted pottery souvenirs. They also own the former Boutique Bonaire at the Bonaire Beach Hotel (tel. 8190), which they have expanded to many gift items, including Delft, pewter, beach coral jewelry, locally made ceramics, sunglasses, dresses from Greece and Ecuador, and handmade dough Christmas tree ornaments, plus guayaberas, unisex shirts, and terry beachwear.

THE SPORTING LIFE: The true beauty on Bonaire is under the sea, where visibility is 100 feet 365 days of the year, and the water temperatures range from 78° to 82° Fahrenheit. Many dive sites can be reached directly from the beach, and sailing is another pastime. Birdwatching is among the best in the Caribbean, and for beachcombers there are acres and acres of driftwood, found along the shore from the salt flats to Lac.

Swimming

Bonaire has some of the whitest sand beaches in the West Indies. The major hotels have beaches, but you may want to wander down to the southeast coast for a swim at Sorobon and Boca Cai on Lac Bay. In the north, you may want to swim at Playa Foenchi, on the coastline of the Washington/Slagbaai National Park.

Snorkeling

In an unusual development for snorkelers, an easily accessible trail along Bonaire's shoreline has been identified and marked off in the Marine Park. Here a great many of the hundreds of fish and coral varieties to be found anywhere can be seen within a quarter-mile stretch of shallow water. The area attracts snorkelers from far and wide. While scuba enthusiasts come from all parts of the world to dive at Bonaire's 40-plus designated underwater scenic sites, snorkelers had not heretofore received special attention.

Scuba

One of the richest reef communities in the entire West Indies, Bonaire has plunging walls which descend to a sand bottom at 130 or so feet, abounding with hard corals, numerous seawhips, black coral trees, basket sponges, gorgonia, and swarms of rainbow-hued tropical fish. One magazine said Bonaire had "the lushest, most colorful coral reefs to be found anywhere." Most of the diving is done on the leeward side where the ocean is lake flat. There are more than 40 dive sites on sharply sloping reefs.

The waters off the coast of Bonaire received an additional attraction in 1984. A rust-bottomed general cargo ship, 80 feet long, was confiscated by the police. Its contraband cargo, about 25,000 pounds of marijuana, was discovered hidden between a real and a false bulkhead. Its owners never came forward (obviously) to claim either the ship or cargo, so it remained in lonely disgrace, moored without purpose. Known as *Hilma Hooker* (affectionately dubbed "The Hooker" by everyone on the island), she sank without fanfare one calm day in 90 feet of water. Lying just off the southern shore near the capital, her wreck is now a popular dive site. Divers try to get a look at the massive propeller, whose brass is still visible if you scratch off a layer of the rapidly accumulating coral and algae.

Bonaire has a unique program for divers in that all three major hotels offer personalized, closeup encounters with the island's fish and other marine life. That way, the diver can experience underwater contacts in different dimensions under the expertise of Bonaire's dive guides.

Captain Don's Habitat Dive Shop (tel. 8290) is a PADI five-star training facility. The open-air, full-service dive shop includes a classroom, photo/video lab, equipment repair, and compressor rooms around spacious seafront patios. Habitat's slogan is "Diving Freedom," and divers can take their tanks and dive anywhere any time of day or night, most often along "The Pike," half a mile of protected reef right in front of the shop and hotel. The highly qualified staff is there to assist and advise but not to police or dictate dive plans. Diving packages are based on six days and include unlimited air fills.

One of the island's most complete scuba facilities has two separate outlets on the beachfront of the Flamingo Beach Hotel (tel. 8285). Demand was so great that several years ago, Scotland-born Peter Hughes, its Miami-based owner, split his well-known branch in Bonaire (Dive Bonaire) into **Dive I** and its newer, slightly smaller, **Dive II** subsidiary. Both operate out of well-stocked beachfront buildings at opposite ends of the hotel's waterfront, and both charge the same prices and offer the same type of expeditions. At both branches, diving equipment can be rented.

The **Bonaire Scuba Center** lies on the 600-foot beach of the Bonaire Beach Hotel, where one of Bonaire's most spectacular reefs is located just 50 feet offshore. The center's equipment includes three flat-top boats, two Mako compressors, and diving equipment for 80 divers. The center caters to both novice and experienced divers. It offers resort and certification courses, guided boat and night dives, mini photo courses, and still- and movie-camera rentals. Boats are available to experienced groups for exploration trips. For reservations, get in touch with Bonaire Tours, Inc., P.O. Box 775, Morgan, NJ 08879 (tel. 201/566-8866).

Deep-Sea Fishing

The island's offshore fishing grounds are virtually untouched, making for some of the best deep-sea fishing in the Caribbean. A good day's catch may include mackerel, tuna, wahoo, and swordfish, among the many species out there. If relaxation is what you have in mind, try a full- or half-day sailing charter.

Almost any hotel on the island can arrange this for you, usually through the well-recommended expert, **Chris Morkas.** You can reach him or his wife directly at his house at 69 Kaya Grandi (tel. 8774). A native Bonairean, he has been fishing almost since he was born. He offers two boats for half-day excursions: the larger one, 23½ feet long, costs $250 per half day, with equipment and lunch included in the price; a 14½-foot boat goes for $110 per half day.

Boating

Every visitor to Bonaire wants to take a trip to uninhabited **Klein Bonaire.** The Flamingo Beach and Bonaire Beach hotels offer trips daily. You'll be left in the morning for a day of snorkeling, beachcombing, and picnicking, then picked up later that afternoon. Other hotels will also arrange a trip to the islet for you, perhaps including a barbecue.

For a sailing trip along the coast, **Poseidon Nemrod** (tel. 8761) takes passengers aboard the *Iltshi,* anchoring near a beach where you can swim, skindive, or scuba-dive. A daily trip, lasting from 9:30 a.m. to 3:30 p.m., costs $35 per person, including sandwiches and soft drinks. A sunset trip is also offered, from 5 to 7 p.m. daily, for $15 per person, with rum punch included in the rates.

Most of the major hotels rent Sunfish or windsurfers for $10 per hour (they're free to guests of the Bonaire Beach Hotel). The Bonaire Beach Hotel also offers a sunset cruise to anyone who is interested, requiring a minimum of ten guests. It departs from the hotel every evening at 5 p.m., returning an hour later. You ride on a vessel that resembles a pontoon-supported floating barge. There's a cash bar, but snacks are free. The price is $8 per person, and it's best to reserve a seat 24 hours in advance.

Golf

This is not a serious sport here. There's only a miniature course at the Bonaire Beach Hotel.

Tennis

The **Bonaire Beach Hotel** (tel. 8448) has two good courts, which are illuminated for night play and covered with artificial grass. Use of the courts is free to guests of the hotel, but nonresidents pay $6 per half hour of play. A tennis pro is on the premises, and racquets and balls can be borrowed without charge.

Horseback Riding

Tinis Stables offers 1½-hour guided tours at a cost of $20 per person. Pickup is at the Bonaire Beach Hotel (tel. 8448) at 7:30 a.m., returning at 4 p.m. Make arrangements at the hotel desk.

NIGHTLIFE: Underwater slide shows provide entertainment for both divers and non-divers in the evening. **Capt. Don's Habitat** (tel. 8290) offers two shows weekly. On Monday at 8:45 p.m., Dee Scarr, dive guide, shows *Touch the Sea,* slides about the island's marine life and its interactions. Fish personalities are shown in their individual roles. On Wednesday at 8:45 p.m., Habitat's underwater photographer, André Nahr, shows his slides. For nondivers, Captain Don shows his *Above the Plimsoll Mark,* a view of Bonaire, at 9 p.m. Friday. The Bonaire Beach Hotel (tel. 8448) is the location for a slide show Wednesday at 9:30 p.m. presented by Bonaire Scuba Center. On Sunday at 9:30 p.m., an underwater video, *Discover the Caribbean,* is presented at the Flamingo Beach Hotel (tel. 8285). The shows are free.

Outside of the hotels, check out the action at **"E Wowo"** ("The Eye" in Papiamento), which lies right in the heart of town near the tourist office, at the corner of Kaya Grandi and L. D. Gerharts. It's distinguished by two flashing op art eyes. The club caters to members, but if you ask at your hotel desk you'll usually be granted an admission pass. Hours are Wednesday through Sunday from 9 p.m. until the early hours. The club occupies the second floor of one of the oldest and most colorful Dutch colonial buildings on the island. It is the only nightclub in Bonaire. Admission costs 10 NAf ($5.25).

Upstairs over the already-recommended Zeezicht Bar and Restaurant, Kaya Corsow (tel. 8434), the same manager, Maddy Visser, also operates **Pirate House,** where you can eat and dance after 11 p.m. and occasionally see a show. Otherwise it's disco music. Drinks cost around $3.

As part of the Flamingo Beach Hotel (tel. 8285), a **casino** opened in 1984 in a former residence adjoining the property. It is being promoted as "The World's First Barefoot Casino." Whatever the name, visitors are not allowed inside clad only in swimsuits. The casino is open daily except Monday from 8 p.m. to 4 a.m. Blackjack, roulette, poker, wheel of fortune, video games, and slot machines are available. Gambling on the island is under government regulations.

The **Black Coral Casino** at the Bonaire Beach Hotel (tel. 8448) was taken over by the government, and its policies and hours have fluctuated. Call the hotel before you arrive for a visit. One almost certain bet for a good time, however, is the hotel's Saturday-night buffet and folkloric show, beginning at 7:30 p.m. and lasting until 10:30. The cost is $15 per person. Entertainment usually begins at 9 p.m. Check with the hotel for whatever specialty night (if any) is being held on the night of your intended visit.

Karel's, the Waterfront (no phone). Almost Tahitian in its high-ceilinged, open-walled design, this popular bar is perched above the sea on stilts. You can sit at the long rectangular bar with many of the island's dive and boating professionals or else select a table near the balustrades overlooking the illuminated surf. Drinks cost from 4 NAf ($2.10) each, and are served every evening except Monday from 5 p.m. to 2 a.m.

3. Curaçao

Just 35 miles off the coast of Venezuela, Curaçao, the "C" of the Dutch ABC islands of the Caribbean, is the most populated in the Netherlands Antilles. It attracts visitors because of its friendly people, who extend a big welcome, as well as its almost duty-free shopping, lively casinos, water sports, and international cuisine. Fleets of ocean-going tankers head out from its harbor to bring refined oil to all parts of the world.

A peaceful, self-governing part of the Netherlands, Curaçao has an average temperature of 81° Fahrenheit. Trade winds keep the island fairly cool, and it is flat and arid with an average rainfall of only 22 inches per year, hardly your idea of a lush, palm-studded tropical island.

Curaçao was discovered not by Columbus, but by one of his lieutenants, Alonso de Ojeda, as well as Amerigo Vespucci, in 1499. The Spaniards exterminated all but 75 members of a branch of the peaceful Arawak Indians. However, they in turn were ousted by the Dutch in 1634, who also had to fight off French and English invasions.

The Dutch made the island a tropical Holland in miniature. Pieter Stuyvesant, stomping on his peg, ruled Curaçao in 1644.

The island was turned into a Dutch Gibraltar, bristling with forts. Thick ramparts guarded the harbor's narrow entrance, the hilltop forts (many now converted into restaurants) protected the coastal approaches.

Because of all that early Dutch building, what one finds today is more European flavor than anywhere else in the Caribbean. Curaçao is the most important island architecturally in the entire West Indies.

In this century, it remained sleepy until 1915 when the Royal Dutch/Shell Company built one of the world's largest oil refineries to process crude from Venezuela. Workers from some 50 countries poured into the island, turning Curaçao into a polyglot, cosmopolitan community.

Curaçao is only 37 miles long and 7 miles across at its widest point. After leaving the capital, Willemstad, you plunge into a strange, desert-like countryside that may remind you of the American Southwest. Three-pronged cactus studs the land, as do the spiny-leafed aloes and the weird divi-divi trees, with their coiffures bent by centuries of trade winds. The landscape is an amalgam of browns and russets.

Windmills that evoke Dorothy's in *The Wizard of Oz* are in and around Willemstad and in some parts of the countryside. These standard farm models pump water from wells to irrigate vegetation.

GETTING THERE: The air routes to Curaçao are strongly linked to those leading to and from Aruba, since several airlines combine flights from North America to both destinations.

The **Curaçao International Airport,** Margareth Abraham Plaza (tel. 82288), has an 11,155-foot runway, one of the largest in the Caribbean. It has enough room to land a Boeing 747.

American Airlines operates a daily flight to Curaçao which leaves from New York's JFK Airport at 9:30 a.m., in enough time to connect with incoming flights from many cities of the American Northeast and Middle West. It touches down briefly in Aruba before continuing to Curaçao.

The return flight from Curaçao to JFK is nonstop, landing at the New York airport after 4½ hours of flight time. Round-trip air fare is cheaper when a passenger arranges prepaid hotel accommodations through American's tour desk simultaneously with air transport. However, clients who want to arrange their own transport can opt for a 21-day excursion fare, where no advance booking is needed and where customers must wait for between 3 and 21 days before using the return half of their tickets. Round-trip fares for this kind of ticket are $469 for midweek travel, $499 for weekend flights. However, look for low-season discounted fares if you plan to go in summer.

Eastern Airlines services Curaçao from Miami, combining many of its frequent flights with touchdowns in Aruba. Eastern's connections from many other cities of the U.S. link with its flight leaving from Miami.

Likewise, **ALM** offers a daily afternoon flight to Curaçao from Miami, stopping at Haiti on the way. ALM also offers a daily flight to Curaçao from New York, and the route requires a stop at either Haiti or St. Maarten (depending on the day of the week) before continuing on to Curaçao. For connections to Curaçao from other islands (especially the ABC group), your best bet is usually ALM because of its frequent service in the Caribbean.

GETTING AROUND: Since **taxis** don't have meters, ask your driver to quote you the rate before getting in. Charges go up by 25% after 11 p.m. Drivers are supposed to carry an official tariff sheet which they'll produce upon request. Generally there is no need to tip, unless a driver helped you with your luggage. The cost from the airport to, say, the Las Palmas or Curaçao Caribbean is $10, and the charges can be split among four passengers. If a piece of luggage is so big the trunk lid won't close, you'll be assessed a surcharge of $1. In town, the best place to get a taxi is on the Otrabanda side of the floating bridge.

Buses

Some of the hotels operate a free bus shuttle, taking you from the suburbs to the shopping district of Willemstad. A fleet of DAF yellow buses operate from Wilhelminapleim, near the shopping center, to most parts of Curaçao for an average fare of 40¢. Some limousines function as "C" buses. When you see one listing the destination you're heading for, you can hail it at any of the designated bus stops.

Sightseeing Taxi Tours

A tour by taxi costs about $15 per hour, and up to four passengers can go on the jaunt.

Sightseeing Tours

Tabor Tours, Maduro Plaza, 19 Emancipatie Blvd. (tel. 7-6637), offers several tours, both day and night, to points of interest in and around Curaçao. The east part tour, costing $10 per person for adults, $5 for children under 12, takes you for a drive through Willemstad, to the Curaçao Liqueur distillery, through the residential area and the Bloempot shopping center, and to the Curaçao Museum (admission fee included in the tour price).

Gray Line Sightseeing, 22 Perseusweg (tel. 61-3622), also makes an interesting tour throughout the city and countryside.

Jeep Safari Curaçao (tel. 7-3829) affords visitors a chance to visit such places as the San Pedro plain, a stalactite cave, freshwater wells, St. Christoffel park, Boca Wandomie, and Boca Cortalein, with a possible swimming and snorkeling stop at Boca Santu Pretu and a visit to a plantation house. You can drive your own Jeep if you want to, but strict regulations govern this, and a guide will be along on the trip. Short trips, three hours in duration, cost $13 per person, and seven-hour Jeep jaunts go for $19 per person.

Car Rentals

Since all points of tourist interest are easily accessible by paved roads, you may want to rent a car. U.S. and Canadian citizens can use their own licenses, if valid, and traffic moves on the right. International road signs are observed.

Several car-rental companies are represented in Curaçao, but **Budget Rent-a-Car,** the largest, offers one of the best high-season car-rental arrangements anywhere in the Caribbean. A four-passenger, two-door Daihatsu Charade without air conditioning is rented for an unlimited-mileage rate of $156 per week, $19 for each additional day. This rate requires an advance booking of 36 hours and a minimum rental of five days. Visitors who prefer a car with air conditioning can reserve a manual-transmission four-door Toyota Corolla for a weekly rate of $270.

Purchase of insurance in the form of a collision damage waiver is usually a very good idea. This costs between $8 and $11 per day, depending on the value of the car, and lessens a driver's financial responsibility for collision damage in the event of an accident. If you decide to purchase this optional insurance, you'll pay up to the first $200 in the event of an accident. If you decide not to purchase this insurance, you'll pay up to the first $750 worth of damage in the event of an accident. Insurance benefits are the same for all car-rental companies in Curaçao.

Budget maintains four locations at major hotels throughout the island, as well as a branch at the airport. A phone call from 7 a.m. to 11 p.m. to Budget's island headquarters, 517 F. D. Rooseveltweg (tel. 8-3198), can help to arrange transportation to the nearest outlet. Budget requires that drivers be between the ages of 23 and 65.

Visitors who don't meet these age requirements can try at **Avis,** which is the largest rental company in Curaçao since its minimum age is 21, with no restrictions for drivers over 65. Avis operates completely air-conditioned fleets. A Toyota Starlet at Avis costs $216 per week and requires advance booking of at least two days.

Hertz is also represented in Curaçao. The least expensive high-season rates, $228 for a week's rental of a Nissan with unlimited mileage, are about the same as the prices charged at Avis. Handling Hertz rentals in Curaçao is Ric Car Rental, 22 Perseusweg (tel. 61-3622).

All three companies maintain toll-free numbers for callers. For rates and information while still in the States, call Budget at 800/527-0700, Avis at 800/331-2112, or Hertz at 800/654-3131.

PRACTICAL FACTS: To enter Curaçao, **proof of citizenship,** such as a voter registration card or a passport, is required, along with a return or continuing airline ticket out of the country. No visa or vaccination is required.

The drinking **water** comes from a modern desalinization plant and is safe to drink. The **electrical current** is 110-130 volts AC, 50 cycles, the same as in North

America, although many hotels will have adapters if your appliances happen to be European.

While Canadian and U.S. dollars are accepted for purchases on the island, the official **currency** is the guilder (also called a florin), which is divided into 100 NA (Netherlands Antillean) cents. The exchange rate is $1 U.S. to 1.92 NAf. (Stated another way, 52¢ U.S. equals 1 NAf.)

Banks are open Monday to Friday from 8:30 a.m. till noon and 1:30 till 4:30 p.m. The only exceptions are the Banco Popular and the Bank of America, which remain open during lunch, from 9 a.m. till 3 p.m. Monday through Friday.

Curaçao is on **Atlantic Standard Time,** one hour ahead of Eastern Standard Time and the same as Eastern Daylight Saving Time.

Shops, hotels, and restaurants usually accept most major U.S. and Canadian credit cards.

Dutch, Spanish, and English are spoken in Curaçao, along with Papiamento, a **language** which combines the three major tongues with Indian and African dialects. The largest island in the Netherlands Antilles, Curaçao has 172,000 people representing more than 50 national groups.

A word of caution to swimmers: The sea water remains an almost-constant 76° Fahrenheit year round, with good underwater visibility, but beware of stepping on spines of the sea urchins which sometimes abound in these waters. To give temporary first aid for an imbedded urchin's spine, try the local remedies of vinegar or lime juice, or as the natives advise, a burning match if you are tough. While the urchins are not fatal, they can cause several days of real discomfort.

There is a **departure tax** of $5.75, plus a 5% **room tax** along with 10% added for **service.**

For problems about passports or other matters, telephone the **U.S. Consulate** at 61-3066).

Medical facilities are well equipped, and the 820-bed St. Elisabeth Hospital, 193 Breedestraat (tel. 62-4900), near Otrabanda in Willemstad, is considered one of the most up-to-date facilities in the Caribbean.

For tourist information, go to the **Curaçao Tourist Board,** Plaza Pier (tel. 61-3397).

The **police emergency** number is 4-4444.

The **post office** is on Waaigat (tel. 61-1125).

For **cable** service, call 61-1433 for All America Cables, or 61-3500 for Landsradio. For long-distance **telephone calls,** dial 021.

WHERE TO STAY: Your hotel will be in Willemstad or in one of the suburbs, which lie only 10 to 15 minutes from the shopping center. The bigger hotels often have free shuttle buses running into town, and most of them have their own beaches and pools.

Remember that Curaçao is a bustling commercial center, and the downtown hotels often fill up fast with business travelers and Venezuelans on a shopping holiday. Therefore, reservations are always important.

The Upper Bracket

Curaçao Caribbean Hotel & Casino, P.O. Box 2133, Willemstad (tel. 62-5000), is a distinguished, "honeycomb-on-stilts" high-rise resort on the outskirts of Willemstad, with a free bus service to take you shopping in town. It's a self-contained complex, with a charming little beach and cove set among rocky bluffs where a dive shop offers the best water-sports program on the island, including skindiving, sailing, deep-sea fishing, and sea Jeeps. You have a choice of two Grasstex tennis courts lit for night games. The structure is a block of rooms encased in a concrete façade, its arches not unlike Dutch lace. Most impressive to me is the wide, open lower lounge areas, giving everyone a trade-wind-swept view of Piscadera Bay. Furnished in wicker, the wall-less Pisca Terrace bar and restaurant opens onto an eight-pointed-star-shaped pool and the ruins of a fort two centuries old. You can order breakfast on this terrace. Glass-enclosed elevators built outside on the hotel offer a panoramic view as you're whisked to your room. The bedrooms have much space, immaculate baths with big towels, air conditioning that really works, and traditional furnishings, plus breeze-cooled private balconies, and an ice machine on each floor.

In winter, singles range in price from $145 to $240 daily, the difference based on the view. Doubles go for $150 to $190 daily. For breakfast and dinner, add another $35 per person daily. *In summer, the single tariff ranges from $95 to $115 daily; the twin, from $100 to $120.* Service and tax are added to all bills. The Willemstad is an air-conditioned dining room offering meals from $25. Wednesday is barbecue night. Antillean night with a folkloric show is presented on the terrace on Friday. To the left as you enter the hotel is a well-stocked shopping complex, including a branch of Spritzer & Fuhrmann.

Golden Tulip Las Palmas Hotel and Vacation Village, Piscadera Bay (P.O. Box 2179), Willemstad (tel. 62-5200), across from the Curaçao Caribbean, is ideal for those who seek a moderately priced resort, one of the stated goals of this guide. The atmosphere here is casual and convivial. The location is only two miles from Willemstad, on a breezy hillside a few hundred yards from the sea and its own little beach with water sports. The cacti that used to stud the hillside have now given way to a botanical garden. Accommodations are in a three-story, 100-room main building, or in one of the little casitas with Samoan-style roofs sprinkled through the hillside gardens. Think of a casita as your own self-contained summer house, the kind you might have at a beach resort. The main building has public rooms off the garden-style entry lounge. At its core is a courtyard, with a lily pond, bamboo, and flowering vines. Here you can start your day with a breakfast, later enjoying drinks and entertainment in the evening. Perhaps a family steel band will be brought in, or a fire-eating limbo dancer. Native-style buffet dinners are often hauled out of the kitchen.

Rooms in the main building have contemporary styling with bold colors, and each has a private bath and air conditioning. A single rents for $85 daily in high season, the tariff going up to $103 in a twin-bedded room. For breakfast and dinner on the MAP, expect to pay from $28 per person in addition to the rates quoted. *Rates for the off-season are about $72 daily in a single, going up to about $82 in a twin-bedded room.* The casitas, 94 in all, can accommodate four persons and possibly six (although that would be crowded). Each villa has two well-furnished bedrooms, a living room, a kitchenette, and a porch where you can set up breakfast you prepared yourself after shopping at the grocery mini-market on the grounds. Even in the expensive winter months, these casitas cost $125 daily for two people, *that rate dropping to about $120 in summer,* plus service and tax. The furnishings are in a rustic style, resting under beamed ceilings. The sliding doors enlarge the living room which can spill out onto the terrace.

A fully equipped beach with a snackbar is less than 800 yards away from the entrance to the hotel. On the grounds is a tennis court lit for night games. Slot machines and croupiers are found inside the Las Palmas, although you can also go to the much bigger casino at the Curaçao Caribbean just across the way. Other sporting facilities include two swimming pools—one Olympic size for adults, plus a tiny wading pool for children. In King Arthur's pub and restaurant, you can order Amstel beer, made with desalinated water, and good food, including some Antillean dishes. Every night there's dinner music, except on Saturday when a Caribbean night with a folklore show is presented.

Curaçao Plaza Hotel and Casino, P.O. Box 229, Plaza Piar (tel. 61-2500), stands guard over the Punda side of St. Anna's Bay, as it's nestled in the ramparts of an 18th-century water fort on the eastern tip of the entrance to the harbor. It is in fact one of the harbor's two "lighthouses." Its designer saw fit to leave its ramparts intact, and now they serve as a promenade for guests. Of course, the hotel has to carry marine collision insurance, the only hostelry in the Caribbean with that distinction. The original part of the hotel followed the style of the arcaded fort. However, now there is a tower of rooms stacked 15 stories high. In winter, singles or doubles cost $90 to $135. *From mid-April until mid-December, the charge is lowered to anywhere from $70 to $105 daily in a single or double*. For breakfast and dinner, add another $30 per person daily to the rates quoted. Each of the 245 bedrooms—your own crow's nest—is attractively furnished with a private bath and phone, TV, air conditioning, and a small refrigerator.

The pool is placed inches away from the parapet of the fort. There's also a poolside bar and suntanning area, with a lobby-level bar. Crowning the tower is a rooftop dining room that offers the most spectacular sunset views over Willemstad. It's the Penthouse Cocktail Lounge and Gourmet Room, open from 7 to 11:30 p.m., and featuring not only dining but dancing. In the Waterfort Grill you can order New York–type sirloin steaks either at lunch or dinner. The Kini-Kini bar is an intimate oasis. The Waterfront offers buffet breakfasts and luncheons, and the Terrace Bar, with its view of the sea and the supertankers passing within a few feet, serves light lunches daily. The hotel also stages special events, including Caribbean nights and barbecue fiestas with dancing to local bands. It also has one of the most popular casinos on the island.

Holiday Beach Hotel & Casino, 31 Pater Eeuwensweg (P.O. Box 2178), Willemstad (tel. 62-5400), built about a mile from the capital, opened in 1968 with 200 modern air-conditioned bedrooms. It has all the facilities of a complete resort hotel, erected along a sandy beach dotted with palm trees and a grassy land projection. The main part of the complex houses the Casino Royale, largest casino on the island, and the principal dining spot, the Green Terrace. The sleeping quarters are in two four-story wings, centering around a U-shaped garden with a large freshwater swimming pool. In size and amenities the bedrooms are well furnished, with two double beds in each unit, opening onto private balconies overlooking the water. Wall-to-wall carpeting, big tile baths, and lots of towels are just part of the comforts, along with phones and color TV. *In summer, singles cost $64 to $71 daily; doubles, $75 to $82*. In winter, rates go up to $80 to $90 daily in a single, $95 to $105 in a double, plus government tax, service, and a $3 daily energy surcharge per room. Rates are based on the EP. At the water-sports shop, Sun Dive, all water sports are arranged, and you can also play tennis on the regulation courts. Local entertainment is offered in Le Rouge Nightclub. After dinner, you can enjoy a drink in the Cocolishi Lounge before heading to the Casino Royale.

Princess Beach Hotel, Martin Luther King Boulevard (tel. 61-4944), is a two-story, lanai-style waterfront resort a short drive from the heart of the city, which is reached by frequent shuttle service. From a bird's-eye point of view, it's a huge chunk of sea-bordering property with its own docks for deep-sea fishing. All major water sports are featured, and a nine-hole golf course is nearby. On the grounds is a professional tennis court. A large, elevated saltwater swimming pool is centered between the building blocks housing 140 units, all air-conditioned with private baths. Remodeled in 1986, the rooms are done in subtle shades of green and pink, with plush carpeting and tropical furniture. The better units look out over the beach and contain verandas or loggias attractively shielded by tropical plants. *In the off-season, singles range in price from $55 to $68 daily; doubles, from $65 to $80*. In winter, rates go up to $70 to $76 daily in a single, from $85 to $92 in a double. For breakfast and dinner, add another $30 per person daily to the tariffs quoted. The best spot is the terrace where you can sun and drink. The pool bar is one of the most popular hangouts in Curaçao at happy hour. There is also an octagonal casino painted with vivid accents of magenta and turquoise, which is one of the busiest on the island. The main building housing the casino, supper club, cabaret, and other facilities is a reconstruction, following a fire that gutted the structure in the early 1980s. In one courtyard, a new generation of divi-divi trees is already being twisted by the constant winds, taking on eerie shapes. This hotel lies three miles east of Oranjestad, between the seacoast road and a beach.

The Best Bargains

Avila Beach Hotel, 130-134 Penstraat, P.O. Box 791 (tel. 61-4377), is a beautifully restored 200-year-old mansion standing on the shore road leading eastward out of the city from the shopping center. It's the only beachfront hotel in Willemstad, set on its own small but lovely private beach. The mansion was built by the English governor of Curaçao during the occupation of the island by the British at the time of the Napoleonic Wars. Subsequent governors, including Dutch ones, have used the place as a retreat. Converted into a hotel in 1949, the mansion, now run by F. N. Moller, has added a modern bedroom wing opening toward the sea. It also has an open-air restaurant, Belle Terrace, with split-level dining and a bar area overlooking the beach (see my dining recommendations, below). While the Dutch architecture and colonial style have been preserved on the exterior, the interior of the mansion has been totally rebuilt with a spacious lobby, conference room, offices, and guest rooms. The 45 guest rooms and two suites are all air-conditioned and furnished with Scandinavian modern pieces. In all, it's a comfortable, family-style hotel. In winter, singles range from $60 to $90 daily; twins, from $68 to $98. *Off-season, singles cost $55 to $75; twins, $58 to $78.* MAP is an additional $30 per person. The hotel stands next door to the Octagon Museum, a building where Bolívar the Liberator used to visit his sisters.

Hotel Holland, 524 F. D. Rooseveltweg (tel. 8-1120), is a few minutes' drive from the airport and contains a bar that is a popular gathering place. For a few brief minutes of every day, you can see airplanes landing from your perch at the edge of the poolside terrace, where well-prepared meals are served during good weather (see my dining recommendation). This property is the domain of ex-navy frogman Hans Vroljjk and his wife, Henne. Hans still retains his interest in scuba, arranging dive packages for his guests. Assisted by his daughter, Patricia, he also directs the service at his Dutch-style restaurant, 'T Kokkeltje. The 20 accommodations have baths, air conditioning, TVs and videos, refrigerators, and balconies. Singles rent throughout the year for $33, doubles for $44, and triples for $55. Guests who remain for more than a week receive a free breakfast daily, as well as a slight discount on the room price.

San Marco Hotel, 7 Columbusstraat (tel. 61-2988), is the one acceptable bargain hotel in the downtown area. Its simple interior is facing a floor-by-floor renovation. Much of the lobby level is filled with a vermilion-sided casino whose jangling slot machines attract sidewalk business. Its buff-colored façade rises from a quiet street corner, close to everything, including restaurant and nightlife facilities. Each of the 58 rooms is air-conditioned, with a private bath. Depending on their state of renovation, singles cost $30 to $40 daily, doubles run $43 to $48, and triples are $55 to $60. These tariffs are in effect year round.

CURAÇAO COOKERY: The basic cuisine is Dutch, but there are many specialty items, particularly Latin American and Indonesian. The cuisine strikes many visitors as heavy for the tropics, and you may want to have a light lunch, ordering the more filling concoctions such as rijsttafel in the evening.

Erwtensoep, the well-known Dutch pea soup, is a popular dish, as is keshi yena, Edam cheese stuffed with meat, then baked. Funchi, a Caribbean tortilla, accompanies many local dishes. Sopito, fish soup often made with coconut water, is an especially good local dish, and conch is featured in curries and many other dishes.

Curaçao, the liqueur that made the island famous, is made from oranges.

The settings for dining are often dramatic, either in restored forts or haciendas, maybe al fresco.

De Taveerne, Landhuis Groot Develaar (tel. 7-0669), is a country manor house in a residential section. A red-brick octagonal cupola rises over the roof of the building, and inside where the cows used to be sheltered Holland-born Jerry Wielinga has created a tavern atmosphere with an antique decor. He and his wife, Anna, scoured Curaçao's old homes, finding furnishings for their charming restaurant, bar, and wine cellar. The setting is enhanced by burnished copper, white stucco walls, dark woods, and terracotta tiles. The chef has created a number of specialties, including a steak à escargots. To begin your meal, perhaps he'll have smoked Dutch eel or lobster soup. He also has a winning way with snails bourguignonne. Other recommendable dishes include shrimp Thermidor and sole meunière. The chateaubriand Stroganoff for two persons is yet another specialty. A complete meal will set you back anywhere from $28 to $35. The restaurant is open for lunch from noon to 2 p.m. and for dinner from 7 to 11 p.m. daily except Sunday. You should definitely make a reservation.

Fort Nassau, near Point Juliana (tel. 61-3450), is a restored restaurant and bar built in the ruins of a formidably buttressed fort dating from 1792. From its Battery Terrace a 360° panorama unfolds of the sea, the harbor, and Willemstad, just a five-minute drive away. You'll even see the Shell refinery. A signal tower on the cliff sends out beacons to approaching ships. The inn has retained an 18th-century decor. Before you approach the restaurant, you can enjoy an apéritif in a fashionably decorated bar. Many come up here just to have a drink and watch the sunset. On cruise-ship days, the place overflows. The restaurant serves both lunch and dinner. Smoked salmon with horseradish leads off the list of appetizers, or you may prefer to begin with shrimp soup. From the grill, you can order a 16-ounce T-bone steak, or perhaps you may want to try one of the chef's specialties such as veal with fruit sauce. A limited selection of international desserts such as coffee mousse tops a most recommendable repast. You'll spend from $18 to $30. You can dress casually and enjoy your meal in air-conditioned comfort. Lunch is served from noon to 2 p.m. except on weekends. Dinner is nightly from 6:30 to 11 p.m. There's a cozy disco called Infinity in the lower depths, open from 9 p.m. to 2 a.m. daily. It has an intimate atmosphere, a waterfall wall, and good music.

La Bistroëlle, Astroidenweg/Schottegatweg in the Promenade Shopping Center (tel. 7-6929), is an elegant, family-run restaurant with an international cuisine and a good selection of wines, all served in a cozy, atmospheric place. The decor is one of high-backed red velvet chairs, brick accents, stucco, darkened beams, and rustic chandeliers, like a French country inn. The location is in a residential area east of the harbor, a short drive from the center of Willemstad. The continental cuisine is largely French, beginning with such selections as snails in herb garlic butter. You might prefer instead mussels in a light whisky sauce. A rich fish soup is served and a steaming French onion soup. Some of the chef's specialties include octopus in a vinaigrette sauce, sole Picasso, lobster Thermidor, and chicken saltimbocca. For dessert, you might prefer the crêpes suzette flavored with Curaçao, for two people. A complete meal will run from 70 NAf ($36.50). The place is open daily from noon to 2 p.m. and 7 to 11 p.m.

Rijsttafel Restaurant Indonesia and **Holland Club Bar,** 13 Mercuriusstraat in Cerrito (tel. 61-2606), is the best place to go on the island to sample the Indonesian rijsttafel, the traditional rice table with all the zesty side dishes. You're allowed to season your plate with peppers rated hot, very hot, and palate-melting. You must ask a taxi to take you to this villa in the suburbs. The site is near Salinja. Your host is Johan Dreijerink. The Holland Club bar is only for diners and their guests, who can visit daily from noon to 2 p.m. and 6 to 9:30 p.m. At lunchtime, the selection of dishes is more modest, but for dinner, Javanese cooks prepare the specialty of the house, a rijsttafel consisting of 16, 20, or 25 dishes. Warming trays are placed on your table and the service is buffet style. It's best to go to this place with a party so that all of you can share in the fun and feast. A dinner for two will cost between $25 and $40. Before going you should call to make a reservation.

Bistro Le Clochard, on the Otrabanda side of the pontoon bridge (tel. 62-5666), has been snugly fitted into the grim ramparts of Fort Rif at the gateway to the harbor. Its entrance is marked with a brown canopy, which leads into a series of rooms, each built under the stucco vaulting of the old Dutch fort. Only one table has a view of the water, since the only window is the rectangular opening that was formerly used to receive munitions from the adjacent stone quay. Overall, the colors are warm, reflecting copper utensils and exposed brick. A simulated grape arbor was installed above the bar of the pub area, Le Brick, where a piano sometimes provides live music. The restaurant is open daily except Saturday at lunch and all day Sunday. The place is well run, and the owners seem to anticipate the needs of their patrons. Cuisine is basically French, including a few dishes from the Alps such as raclette and two kinds of fondue. Dishes change every week, but the fare is likely to include roast hare flambéed in Calvados with a cream sauce, medallions of venison with a wild game sauce, guinea fowl with paprika, ham, garlic, and white wine, and wild boar chops in a mushroom-cream sauce. A full dinner will cost from $30. Lunches are less expensive. The Bistro is open from noon to 3 p.m. and 6:30 to 11 p.m.

Wine Cellar, Ooststraat/Concordiastraat (tel. 61-2178), opposite the cathedral, is the domain of Nico Cornelisse, a *chevalier du tastevin,* who has one of the most extensive wine cartes on the island. He welcomes you to air-conditioned comfort in his Victoriana dining room, as you slowly make your wine selection for the evening. Food isn't ignored either. He has good meat dishes, well prepared, and a limited selection of seafood. Count on spending from $25 for a meal, plus the cost of your wine. There are only eight tables, so reservations are essential. Hours are noon to 2 p.m. and 6 p.m. till "whenever."

Le Recif (tel. 62-3824) is lodged under the arches of Fort Rif, near the shuttlebus stops for the Otrabanda hotels and the pontoon bridge. This place used to be a prison, but now it's one of the best places in town for Caribbean seafood. Its interior is festooned with fish nets and nautical implements hanging just below the vaulted ceilings. A terrace in front extends the darkly lit interior out into the sunshine. The owner of Le Recif is Don Llewellyn, a former police officer, who knows how to control any unruly member of his clientele. After 11 p.m. the establishment becomes a disco, and in high season there is striptease Wednesday through Sunday. Full meals range from 60 NAf ($31.25) and might include shrimp Créole, Curaçao fish stew, red snapper Cordon Bleu, conch soup, snails, curried crab, lobster Thermidor, and turtle soup (when available). The ingredients for the seafood come either from neighboring waters, from Haiti, or from the Dominican Republic. Le Recif is open from noon to 2 p.m. and 7 p.m. to 3 a.m. seven days a week.

Belle Terrace, Avila Beach Hotel, 130-134 Penstraat (tel. 61-4377), is an open-air restaurant in a 200-year-old mansion on the beachfront of Willemstad. In a relaxed and informal atmosphere, it offers split-level dining. The Schooner Bar, where you can enjoy a rum punch, is shaped like a weather-beaten ship's prow looking out to sea, with a thatch roof projecting from its mast. The restaurant, sheltered by an arbor of flamboyant branches, features Scandinavian and local cuisine with such special dishes as pickled herring, barracuda, and a Danish lunch platter. Local dishes, such as sopito (fish soup with coconut flavor) and keshi jena (Edam cheese stuffed with chicken, olives, raisins, and sweet peppers), are on the menu for both lunch and dinner. A special three-course meal is served every night except Saturday, in addition to a full à la carte menu. On Saturday night the chef has a beef tenderloin barbecue and a help-yourself salad bar. Fish is always fresh at Belle Terrace, and the chef prepares the catch of the day to perfection: grilled, poached, meunière, or amandine. Desserts include Danish pastry and cakes, as well as a cocoa sherbet served in a coconut shell. Expect to spend $10 to $18 for lunch, $20 to $28 for dinner. The special three-course dinner costs $21. Open from noon to 2 p.m. and 7 to 9:30 p.m.

Bistro Larousse, 5 Penstraat (tel. 65-5418), built in 1742, is a typical little stone and plaster house with ornate edging on its roof. It was recently acquired by Holland-born Nico Cornelisse, who installed a collection of 19th-century artifacts under the original beamed ceiling and extended the dining area onto an alcove-style second floor. Amid Colombian-made copper and iron chandeliers, Victorian etched-globe lighting, and Oriental rugs, visitors are served on flowered china the foods they have chosen from well-prepared specialties. These include cheese fondue for two people, red snapper Curaçao style, a soup made from fresh cherry tomatoes, beef Stroganoff, and several kinds of steaks. A dessert specialty is Dutch egg liqueur and fresh whipped cream laced with vanilla or chocolate fondue according to an old Swiss recipe. Full meals range from 85 NAf ($44.25). The establishment is open only for dinner, from 5 p.m. to midnight.

Fort Waakzaamheid Tavern, Seru di Domi, Otrabanda (tel. 62-3633), was the old fort that Captain Bligh of *Bounty* fame captured in 1804. He laid seige to Willemstad for almost a month. In the fort a stone-and-hardwood tavern and restaurant have been installed, opening onto a view of the Otrabanda and the harbor entrance. The atmosphere is that of a country tavern. On the dinner menu, the fish soup will get you going, and you can follow with curried veal, wienerschnitzel, or garlic shrimp. Lobster is the most expensive item on the menu, and you may settle instead for Curaçao snapper. Each day a fresh fried fish is offered, with a salad. Meals run from $20. The fort is open daily except Tuesday from 7 to 11 p.m. The bar remains open until 1 a.m. (even later on weekends).

Rodeo Ranch Steakhouse, on Van Staverenweg in the suburban section of Cas Cora (tel. 67-0501), is a lot of fun. Stanley Gibbs and his Netherlands-born wife, Kathe, have created a touch of the Old West. There's a replica of a covered wagon set over the entrance, and an interior decor of rough-sawn planking, dark woods, and antique wagon wheels. So many guests of this popular place have attached their business cards to a bulletin board near the kitchen that it reads like a lesson in international geography. A "sheriff" (usually Stanley) greets visitors at the door in an outfit that includes a ten-gallon hat and a silver star. No one will mind if you just stop off for a drink at the dimly lit bar, but if you want one of the most copious dinners in town, you'll be presented with a cowhide-covered menu by a cowgirl/waitress. To the sounds of country and western music, you'll enjoy the specialties of steak, soup from the kettle, a chuckwagon choice of potato specials, roast prime rib, and seafood. All steaks are U.S. prime beef, and are accompanied by as many visits as you want to make to the soup and salad bar. Don't dress up to go here. Casual is the keynote. You'll spend $25 for a full meal, which you can enjoy in air-conditioned comfort. Hot snacks are served at the happy hour between 5 and 7 p.m. Lunch is offered daily from noon to 2 p.m., with the dinner bell ringing between 6 and 11 p.m. The bar remains open till "whenever."

Bellevue Restaurant, Baai Macolaweg, Parera (tel. 65-4291), is in an edifice built in 1942 by the Americans as headquarters for the naval base protecting the island's oil refineries. In the late 1970s it was purchased by the Den Dulk family, whose culinary skills quickly made it one of the leading restaurants on the island. A trio of imitation palm trees decks the sunny interior, which sometimes hosts some of the biggest landowners on the island. It's run by Martin and Curaçao-born Johanna, with their son, Martin Jr. (winner of an island-wide contest to design the Curaçao national flag). They adhere strictly to local culinary lore in the preparation of their specialties. Your meal could begin with a bandera. Loaded with cream, "secret ingredients," and Curaçao rum, it is the first blue drink many visitors have ever tried, and its smooth, not-too-sweet flavor is delicious. This could be followed with oyster soup, turtle soup, cactus soup, iguana soup, stewed goat meat, a tasty okra soup, sauerkraut stew, papaya stew, shark meat, turtle steak, stewed cucumbers, or Edam cheese stuffed with meat and spices. Patrons looking for a cross-sampling of the local dishes might try the funchi table, which includes five local viands on one savory platter. The restaurant is open seven days a week, from noon to 2 p.m. and 7 to 10 p.m. Full meals range upward in price from around 55 NAf ($28.50).

Pisces Seafood, 476 Caracasbaaiweg (tel. 67-2181). This West Indian restaurant may be difficult to find, set as it is on a flat industrial coastline near a marina and an oil refinery, about 20 minutes from the capital. There's been a restaurant here since the 1930s, when sailors and workers from the oil refinery came for home-cooked meals. Today the simple frame building offers seating near the rough-hewn bar or in a breeze-swept inner room whose unglazed, open windows have hinged shutters to seal them off after closing. Pisces serves combinations of seafood that depend on the catch of the local fishermen. Main courses, served with rice, vegetables, and plantains, might include sopi, "seacat" (squid), mula (similar to kingfish), shark meat, red snapper, or any of these served, if you wish, in copious quantities for two or more persons in the Pisces platter. Shrimp and conch are each prepared three different ways: with garlic, with curry, or Créole style. Average meals cost 35 NAf ($18.25). Hours are 11:30 a.m. to 2:30 p.m. for lunch and 6 to 11 p.m. on Monday and Tuesday for dinner, with continual service from noon to midnight the rest of the week.

Golden Star, 2 Socratesstraat (tel. 65-4795), is the best place to go on the island for "criollo" or local food. Inland from the coast road, leading southeast from St. Anna Bay, the air-conditioned restaurant is very simple, evoking a roadside diner. But it has a large menu of native dishes that are very tasty. Such Antillean dishes are featured as carco stoba or conch stew and bestia chiki (goat-meat stew). Try also bakijauw (salted cod) and concomber stoba (stewed meat and marble-size spiny cucumbers). Other specialties include criollo shrimps (kiwa) and soppi carni. Everything is served with a side order of funchi, the cornmeal staple. Meals cost from 30 NAf ($15.50). The place is very friendly, and has a large local following with an occasional tourist dropping in. It's open daily from 11 a.m. till 1 a.m. The location is at the corner of Dr. Hugenholtzweg and Dr. Maalweg.

'T Kokkeltje, Hotel Holland, 524 F. D. Rooseveltweg (tel. 68-1120), is directed by Hans Vrolijk, an ex-frogman with the Dutch navy. This warmly decorated hideaway is especially popular around happy hour after most people finish daily work. You'll find the place on the scrub-bordered road leading to the airport, a few minutes away from the landing strips. If you want to follow your drinks with dinner, full meals cost from 55 NAf ($28.50) and include such specialties as nasi goreng, fresh fish in season, Dutch-style steak, wienerschnitzel, Caribbean-style chicken, and split-pea soup. All dishes are accompanied by fresh vegetables and Dutch-style potatoes. Patrons enjoy their meals around the pool outside or in a paneled and intimately lit room near the bar. Hours are 7 a.m. to 11 p.m. daily.

Playa Forti, in the Westpunt area (tel. 64-0273), is a good address to know if you're touring the island. The restaurant is built on the foundation of a fortress dating from Bonaparte's day. Not only do you get good local food here, but one of the most spectacular sea views on the island. International dishes are presented, but it would be wiser to order some of the Antillean specialties, such as succulent goat stew which tastes a bit like veal. It's called cabrito. Try also keshi yena, a tasty mixture of beef and chicken, which has been pickled and cooked with tomatoes and onions, then wrapped in Edam cheese. Ayaca is a combination of chicken and beef, with olives, raisins, nuts, and spices wrapped in a soft corndough tortilla (it's packed and cooked in banana leaves). The fish soup makes a zesty opening. It's called sopi di plata. Or try the fried red snapper Curaçao style—that is, fried a golden brown, then covered in a sauce of tomatoes, onions, and green peppers. It's served with fried plantains and funchi, the local cornmeal preparation. Expect to pay from 35 NAf ($18.25) for a complete meal. The waters of Westpunt are perfect for snorkeling and scuba-diving if you want to bring your own equipment. In the restaurant food is served from 10 a.m. to 6:30 p.m. except Monday. If you're touring, it's also possible to drop in for drinks in the afternoon.

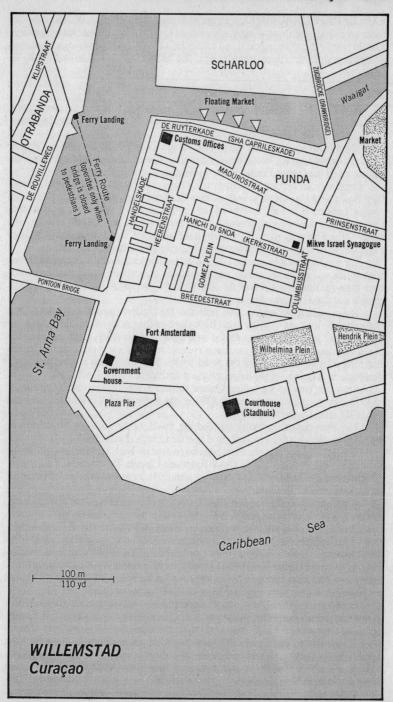

SCHARLOO

ZUGBRÜCKE (DRAWBRIDGE)

Waaigat

Market

Floating Market

Ferry Landing

DE RUYTERKADE

Customs Offices

(SHA CAPRILESKADE)

MADUROSTRAAT

PUNDA

KLIPSTRAAT

OTRABANDA

DE ROUVILLEWEG

Ferry Route
(operates only when
bridge is closed
to pedestrians)

HANDELSKADE

HEERENSTRAAT

HANCHI DI SNOA

(KERKSTRAAT)

PRINSENSTRAAT

Mikve Israel Synagogue

Ferry Landing

GOMEZ PLEIN

COLUMBUSSTRAAT

PONTOON BRIDGE

BREEDESTRAAT

St. Anna Bay

Fort Amsterdam

Wilhelmina Plein

Hendrik Plein

Government
house

Plaza Piar

Courthouse
(Stadhuis)

Caribbean   Sea

100 m
110 yd

WILLEMSTAD
Curaçao

EXPLORING CURAÇAO: Most cruise-ship passengers see only Willemstad—or, more accurately, the shops—but you may want to get out into the cunucu or countryside, exploring the towering cacti and rolling hills topped by landhuizen or plantation houses built more than three centuries ago. The 38-mile-long island is seen in a day or so.

Willemstad

In Willemstad the Dutch found a vast natural harbor, a perfect hideaway along the Spanish Main. Not only is Willemstad the capital of Curaçao, it is also the seat of government for the Netherlands Antilles.

The city grew up on both sides of the canal. Today it is divided into the **Punda** and the **Otrabanda,** the latter literally meaning "the other side." Both sections are connected by the **Queen Emma Pontoon Bridge,** a pedestrian walkway.

Originally, ferryboats linked the two sections of town, since by the mid-19th century Willemstad had spread to both sides of St. Anna Harbor. In 1887 the American consul, Leonard B. Smith, convinced the city fathers that a bridge was a good idea. One year later the swinging pontoon bridge across the harbor opened, and the tolls made Smith a wealthy man. Powered by a diesel engine, it swings open many times every day to let ships from all over the globe pass in and out of the harbor.

The view from the bridge is of the old gabled houses in harmonized pastel shades such as lilac and aquamarine. The bright pastel colors, according to legend, are a holdover from the time when one of the island's early governors is said to have had eye trouble and flat white gave him headaches.

The colonial-style architecture, reflecting the Dutch influence, gives the town a "storybook" look, as is often said. Built three or four stories high, the houses are crowned by "step" gables and roofed with orange Spanish tiles. Hemmed in by the sea, a tiny canal, and an inlet, the streets are narrow, and they're crosshatched by still narrower alleyways. Except for the pastel colors, Willemstad may remind you of old Amsterdam. It has one of the most intriguing townscapes in the Caribbean.

Replacing the pontoon bridge, **Queen Juliana Bridge** opened to vehicular traffic in 1973. Spanning the harbor, it rises 195 feet, the highest bridge in the Caribbean and one of the tallest in the world.

The **Waterfront** originally guarded the mouth of the canal on the eastern or Punda side. Now it's been incorporated into the Curaçao Plaza Hotel.

The task of standing guard has been taken over by **Fort Amsterdam,** site of the Governor's Palace and the 1769 Dutch Reformed Church. The church still has a British cannonball embedded in it. The arches leading to the fort were tunneled under the official residence of the governor.

A corner of the fort stands at the intersection of Breedestraat and Handelskade, the starting point for a plunge into the island's major shopping district.

A few minutes' walk from the pontoon bridge, at the north end of Handelskade, is the **Floating Market,** where scores of schooners tie up alongside the canal, a few yards from the main shopping section. Docked boats arrive from Venezuela and Colombia, as well as other West Indian islands, to sell tropical fruits and vegetables, a little bit of everything in fact. The modern market under its vast cement cap has not replaced this unique shopping expedition which is fun to watch.

Between the I. H. (Sha) Capriles Kade and Fort Amsterdam stands the **Mikve Israel Emanuel Synagogue,** at the corner of Columbusstraat and Kerkstraat. Consecrated on the eve of the Passover in 1732, it antedates the first U.S. synagogue in Newport, Rhode Island, by 31 years. It houses the oldest Jewish congregation in the New World, dating from 1651. One of the oldest synagogue buildings in the western hemisphere, it is a fine example of Dutch colonial architecture, covering about a square block in the heart of Willemstad.

It was built around a Spanish-style walled courtyard, with four large portals.

Sand covers the sanctuary floor following a Portuguese Sephardic custom, representing the desert where Israelis camped when the Jews passed from slavery to freedom. Early settlers, led by Samuel Coheno, were Sephardic refugees from a Portuguese pogrom. Four brass chandeliers hang from the arched ceiling.

The theba (pulpit) is in the center, and the congregation surrounds it. Highlight of the east wall is the Holy Ark, rising 17 feet, and a raised banca, canopied in mahogany, is on the north wall. The synagogue has services every Friday at 6:30 p.m. and Saturday at 10 a.m.; as well as similar holiday service times. Visitors are welcome to all services, with appropriate dress required.

Adjacent to the synagogue courtyard is the **Jewish Cultural Historical Museum,** housed in two buildings dating back to 1728. They were originally the rabbi's residence and the bathhouse. The 2½-centuries-old *mikvah*, or bath for religious purification purposes, was in constant use until around 1850 when this practice was discontinued and the buildings sold. They have recently been reacquired through the Foundation for the Preservation of Historic Monuments and turned into the present museum. On display are a great many ritual, ceremonial, and cultural objects, many of which are still in use by the congregation for holidays and life cycle events. The synagogue and museum are open to visitors Monday to Friday from 9 to 11:45 a.m. and 2:30 to 5 p.m. (on Sunday from 9 a.m. to noon if there is a cruise ship in port). There is a $1.50 entrance fee to the museum. The gift shop is in the synagogue office (tel. 61-1633).

A statue of Pedro Luís Brion dominates the square known as **Brionplein** right at the Otrabanda end of the pontoon bridge. Born in Curaçao in 1782, he became the island's favorite son and best-known war hero. Under Simón Bolívar, he was an admiral of the fleet and fought for the independence of Venezuela and Colombia.

West of Willemstad

The **Curaçao Museum** on Van Leeuwenhoekstraat can be walked to from the pontoon bridge. Built in 1823 as a Seamen's Hospital, it has been carefully restored as a fine example of Dutch architecture. Furnished with paintings, objets d'art, and antiques, it re-creates a colonial atmosphere. A novelty is the polka-dot kitchen. The museum contains some relics of the Caiquetio Indians, the early settlers discovered by Vespucci, who claimed they were seven feet tall. You'll also see the cockpit of the Fokker F-XVIII trimotor which made the first commercial crossing of the southern Atlantic from the Netherlands to Curaçao in 1934. In the gardens are specimens of the island's trees and plants. There is also a reconstruction of a traditional bandstand in the garden where Curaçao musicians give performances on the first Sunday of every month. Hours are 9 a.m. to noon and 2 to 5 p.m. Tuesday to Saturday, 10 a.m. to 4 p.m. on Sunday; closed Monday. Admission is 2 NAf ($1).

The **Curaçao Seaquarium,** off Martin Luther King Boulevard at a site called Bapor Kibrá (tel. 61-6666), has more than 400 species of fish, crabs, anemones, and other invertebrates, sponges, and coral displayed and growing in a natural environment. This effect is achieved by pumping ocean water into the many pools and tanks so that the sea life indigenous to the area thrives. A rustic boardwalk connects the low-lying hexagonal buildings comprising the Seaquarium complex, erected on a point off which the ship, *Oranje Nassau,* broke up on the rocks and sank in 1903. The name of the site, Bapor Kibrá, means sunken ship. Besides the aquarium, there are two wild waterslides for teenagers and adults, plus a smaller one for small children. You can use the beach and water sports facilities or relax in the seaside bar and restaurant. Seaquarium is open daily from 10 a.m. to 10 p.m. Restaurant hours are 10 a.m. to 9 p.m., and the bar is open from 3 to 10 p.m. weekdays, from 11 a.m. to 10 p.m. on Saturday and Sunday. Admission to the Seaquarium is $5 for adults, $2.50 for children under 15 years of age. It's a few minutes' walk along the rocky coast from the Princess Beach Hotel.

The **Curaçao Underwater Park,** established in 1983 with the financial aid of the World Wildlife Fund, stretches from the Princess Beach Hotel to the east point of the island, a strip of about 12½ miles of untouched coral reefs. There are 16 permanent mooring buoys in the park, where dive operators can safely tie up their boats without damage to the coral. Spearfishing, anchoring in the coral, and taking anything from the reefs except photographs are strictly prohibited. For information on snorkeling, scuba-diving, and trips in a glass-bottom boat to view the park, see "The Sporting Life," below.

Traveling northwest along the road, you reach the tip of the island. The **Landhuis Jan Kock,** on the road to Westpunt, is open to the public. Built in 1650, it is probably the oldest building on the island. The owner once stood on its adobe porch to watch slaves gather salt from huge flat fields flooded with sea water left to evaporate in the sun. The house, said to be haunted, was restored as a museum by the late Dr. Jan Diemont in 1960. Inside are many pieces from the 18th and early 19th centuries, including a hurdy-gurdy machine from this century. Daily tours are 9 to 10 a.m. Reserve in advance by phoning 64-8087.

Out toward the western tip of Curaçao, a high wire fence surrounds the entrance to the 4,500-acre **Christoffel National Park,** about a 45-minute drive from the capital. A macadam road gives way to dirt, surrounded on all sides by abundant cactus and in the higher regions by rare orchids. Rising from flat, arid countryside, 1,230-foot-high St. Christoffelberg is the highest point in the Dutch Leewards. Donkeys, wild goats, iguanas, the Curaçao deer, and many species of birds thrive in this preserve, and there are some Arawak Indian paintings on a coral cliff near the two caves. Piedra di Monton is nothing more than a rockheap accumulated by African slaves who worked on the former plantations. A folk legend passed down through the generations said that any worker would be able to climb to the top of the rockpile, jump off, and fly back home across the Atlantic. If, however, the slave had at any time in his life tasted a grain of salt, the magic would not work and he would crash to his death below. The park has 20 miles of one-way driving trails, with lots of flora and fauna along the way. The shortest trail is about 5 miles long, and because of the rough terrain, takes about 40 minutes to drive through. Various walking trails are available also. One of them will take you to the top of St. Christoffelberg in about 1½ hours. (Come early in the morning when it isn't so hot.) The park is open from 8 a.m. to 3 p.m. (open as early as 6 a.m. on Sunday). Admission is 3 NAf ($1.55). Make a phone call in advance to learn if you'll fit into a guided round-trip tour by Jeep (tel. 64-0363). Also en route to Westpunt, you'll come across a dramatic seaside cavern known as **Boca Tabla,** one of many such grottos on this rugged, uninhabited north coast. For information, write to P.O. Box 2090.

Playa Forti is a 45-minute ride from Punda in Willemstad. A stark region, it is characterized by soaring hills and towering cacti, along with 200-year-old Dutch land houses, the former mansions that housed the slaveowner plantation heads. For a dining suggestion, see my recommendation of the Playa Forti Restaurant.

North and East of Willemstad

Just northeast of the capital, **Fort Nassau** was completed in 1797 and christened by the Dutch as Fort Republic. It was built high on a hill, overlooking the harbor entrance to the south and St. Anna Bay to the north. It was fortified as a second line of defense in case Waterfort gave way. When the British invaded in 1807, they renamed it Fort George in honor of their own king. Later, when the Dutch regained control, they renamed it Orange Nassau in honor of the Dutch royal family. Today diners have replaced soldiers (see my restaurant recommendations).

Along the coast to the southeast of the town, the oddly shaped **Octagon House** on Penstraat was where the liberator, Bolívar, used to visit his two sisters during the wars for Venezuelan independence. Now a museum, it has been restored and furnished with antiques. It also contains some of the liberator's memorabilia. Hours are 8 a.m. to noon and 2 to 6 p.m., Monday through Saturday. No admission is charged.

From the house you can head north, going along the eastern side of the water, to the intersection of Rijkseenheid Boulevard and Fokkerweg. There you'll see the **Autonomy Monument,** a vibrant 20th-century sculpture representing the Dutch islands as birds feed from their nest.

In the area, the **Amstel Brewery** allows visitors to tour its plant where Curaçao beer is brewed from desalinated seawater. Hours are Tuesday from 10 a.m. to noon (telephone 61-2944 for more information).

In addition, the **Curaçao Liqueur Distillery** offers free tours and tastes at Chobolobo, the 17th-century landhuis where the famous liqueur is made. Tours are Monday through Friday from 8 a.m. to noon and 1 to 5 p.m. (call 61-3526 for more information). The cordial, named after the region where it originated, is a distillate of dried peel of a particular strain of orange found only in Curaçao. (This strain grows only in Curaçao, where the soil and climate are unique.) Several herbs are added to give it an aromatic bouquet. It's made by a secret formula handed down through generations. One of the rewards of a visit here is a free snifter of the liqueur at the culmination of the tour.

On Schottegatweg West, lying northwest of Willemstad, past the oil refineries, lies the **Beth Haim Cemetery,** oldest Caucasian burial site still in use in the western hemisphere. Meaning "House of Life," the cemetery was consecrated before 1659. On about three acres are some 2,500 graves. The carving on some of the 17th- and 18th-century tombstones is exceptional.

Landhuis Brievengat, 4 Rheastraat (tel. 3-6229), gives visitors a chance to visit a Dutch version of an 18th-century West Indian plantation house. This stately building, set into a scrub-dotted landscape on the eastern side of the island, contains a few antiques, high ceilings, and a frontal gallery facing two entrance towers, said to have been used to imprison slaves and even for romantic trysts. The plantation was originally used for the cultivation of aloe and cattle, but an 1877 hurricane killed more than three-quarters of the livestock and the plantation operation ceased. The building was pulled down and the land purchased by Shell Oil. Around 1925 the remains of the structure were donated to the Society for the Preservation of Monuments, which rebuilt and restored it. Today it receives visitors for $1 daily from 9:30 a.m. to 12:30 p.m. and 3 to 6 p.m. Every Friday night, an exotic Indonesian dinner is served at the landhuis, for about $15. You can dance to local musical groups and experience an authentic island ambience. On the last Sunday of each month an open house is held, with folkloric dances and other activities. Local food specialties are served.

A SHOPPING EXPEDITION: The place is a shopper's paradise. Some 200 shops line the major shopping malls of such wooden-shoe-named streets as Heerenstraat and Breedestraat. Right in the heart of Willemstad, the **Punda** shopping area is a five-block district. Most stores are open Monday through Saturday from 8 a.m. to noon and 2 to 6 p.m. (some from 8 a.m. to 6 p.m.). When cruise ships are in port, stores are also open for a few hours on Sunday and holidays. To avoid the cruise-ship crowds, do your own shopping in the morning.

Look for good buys in French perfumes. Dutch Delft blue souvenirs, finely woven Italian silks, Japanese and German cameras, jewelry, silver, Swiss watches, linens, leather goods, liquor, and island-made rum and liqueurs, especially Curaçao.

Incidentally, Curaçao is not technically a free port, but its prices are low because of its low import duty.

I always head first to the legendary **Spritzer & Fuhrmann** (tel. 61-2600), on a corner of vehicle-free Gomezplein, the leading jewelers of the Netherlands Antilles.

This name stands for great values, service, and integrity, whether you buy a $50,000 diamond ring or a $50 gold chain. The finest Swiss watches are found here. In addition to the main store, there are other S&F specialty stores in the heart of Curaçao, carrying fine china and crystal. You will find names like Waterford, Baccarat, Lalique, Hummel, and Lladró among their stock.

Penha & Sons, 1 Heerenstraat (tel. 61-2266), occupies the oldest building in town, built in 1708. Established in 1865, they're the distributor of such names as Chanel, Jean Patou, Yves Saint Laurent, and other perfumes, and cosmetics of Lancôme, Clinique, Orlane, and Estée Lauder, among others. The collection of merchandise at this prestigious store is quite varied—Hummel figurines, Delft blue souvenirs, leather goods from Italy, even cashmeres from Scotland. The firm has 14 other stores in Curaçao, Aruba, and St. Maarten.

Gandelman Jewelers, 35 Breedestraat (tel. 61-1854), has a large selection of fine jewelry set with diamonds, rubies, sapphires, emeralds, and other stones. Exclusive here is the Gucci line of handbags, wallets, belts, ties, scarves, and many other items. You will also find Swiss timepieces by Baume & Mercier, Raymond Weil, and Heuer, among others. Gandelman Jewelers has six stores in Aruba and Curaçao.

Boolchand's, 4B Heerenstraat, Punda (tel. 61-2798), features Seiko and Citizen watches and a complete line of cameras, photo, and audio-video equipment. A branch store, La Fortunata, has clothing for men, women, and children. Boolchand's has been in business since 1930.

On Gomezplein, you'll find the **New Amsterdam Store** (tel. 61-2437), on the corner of the popular plaza. On the ground floor they offer hand-embroidered wash-and-wear linens at 25% off. There's a wide selection of Swiss watches, including Oris and Seiko, gold and silver jewelry from Italy. In an upstairs sports boutique they stock a complete line of Adidas, Nike, and all kinds of sneakers as well as beachwear.

Kan Jewelers, 44 Breedestraat, Punda (tel. 61-2111), has been in the jewelry business for more than half a century. Its Willemstad store is in an 18th-century gabled building. They feature a superb collection of 14- and 18-karat gold jewelry, as well as famous brand Swiss watches, such as Rolex. They also carry an exclusive line of Rosenthal china, crystal, and flatware.

The **Yellow House (La Casa Amarilla),** on Breedestraat (tel. 61-3222), is housed in a 19th-century yellow-and-white building. It's been operating since 1887, selling an intriguing collection of perfume from all over the world, and is the exclusive distributor of such names as Christian Dior, Guerlain, and Van Cleef & Arpels.

Obra di Man, 57 Bargestraat (tel. 61-2413), is filled with authentic local handcraft items, including printed T-shirts, handmade dolls, hand-screened fabrics, carved driftwood, and filigree jewelery. They also have some merchandise from the Netherlands.

Boutique Gina, in the Curaçao Caribbean Shopping Gallery (tel. 62-5042), has some of the most sophisticated sportswear for women to be found on the island. They offer Triumph, Gottex, and Solar among their swimwear. Handbags, hats, T-shirts, costume jewelry, and batik clothing from Bangkok are also to be found here.

Bert Knubben Black Coral, at the Princess Beach Hotel (tel. 61-4944), is a name synonymous with craftsmanship and quality. Although collection of black coral has been made illegal by the Curaçao government, an exception was made for Bert, a diver who has been harvesting corals from the sea and fashioning them into fine jewelry and objets d'art for more than 30 years.

THE SPORTING LIFE: Its **beaches** are not as good as Aruba's seven-mile strip of sand, but Curaçao does have some 38 beaches, ranging from hotel sands to secluded coves. Thirty minutes from town, in the Willibrordus area on the south side of Curaçao, **Daaibooi** is a good beach. It's free but there are no changing facilities. Two good private beaches on the eastern side of the island are those of **Jan Thiel Bay** and **Santa**

Barbara. Jan Thiel Bay has rest rooms and changing facilities, plus a snackbar. A good place for snorkelers and scuba-divers, this beach is closed on Tuesday. Admission is 5 NAf ($2.75) per person. Santa Barbara Beach, in the island's primary water sports and recreational area known as Spanish Water, is on land owned by a mining company. Almost entirely man-made, the white sand beach is sometimes hard and pebbly, but the water is calm. The mining company maintains rest rooms and changing rooms, a snackbar, and a sundries stand. The cost is 6 NAf ($3) per carload. The beach is open daily from 8 a.m. to 6 p.m. Both these beaches have access to the Curaçao Underwater Park.

Water Sports

Most hotels offer their own programs of water sports. However, if your hotel isn't equipped, I suggest that you head for one of the most complete water-sports facilities in Curaçao, **Piscadera Watersports,** at the Curaçao Caribbean Hotel (tel. 62-5000, ext. 177). Specializing in snorkeling and scuba-diving trips to reefs and underwater wrecks, it operates from a hexagonal kiosk set on stilts above the water, just offshore from the hotel's beach. Eva van Dalen, the Curaçao-born owner, welcomes visitors with a smile, eager to ensure their safety and satisfaction.

Open from 8 a.m. to 5 p.m. seven days a week, the company offers snorkeling excursions for $10 per person, glass-bottom-boat rides for $6, pedalboats for $10 per hour, powerful water scooters for $20 per half hour, waterskiing for $25 per half hour, and windsurfing at $20 per 1½ hours. A Sunfish rents for $20, and an introductory scuba lesson, conducted by a competent diver, goes for $25. Packages of five dives cost $110. Bottom fishing, with all equipment included, aboard a 22-foot Aquasport, is $100 for a half day. One trip enthusiastically endorsed by some readers departs from the hotel at 7 a.m., when participation warrants. The destination is Little Curaçao, midway between Curaçao and Bonaire. Clothes are optional once you get to the sugar-white sands of the island. Fishing, snorkeling, and the acquisition of an "overall tan" are highlights. The price is $40 per person, and the excursion lasts all day. Another possibility is a boat ride to one of Curaçao's more isolated beaches, Santa Barbara Beach. A full day's outing is $30 per person.

Piscadera can also arrange deep-sea fishing for $225 for a half-day tour carrying a maximum of six people, $450 for a full day. Drinks and equipment are included, but you'll have to get your hotel to pack your lunch.

Peter Hughes Underwater Curaçao, adjacent to Curaçao Seaquarium and Curaçao Underwater Park (tel. 61-6666), a Divi Hotels diving operation, has a complete underwater sports program. A fully stocked modern dive shop has retail and rental equipment. Peter Hughes designed the three state-of-the-art dive boats used by the trained staff for instruction and scuba-diving. Individual dives and dive packages are offered, costing $25 for one dive, $120 for a six-dive package. A six-day unlimited package, including one night boat dive, is priced at $225. Complete vacation/dive packages are offered through cooperation of Peter Hughes and Curaçao's top resorts, including Holiday Beach Hotel, Golden Tulip Las Palmas, the Princess Beach Hotel, and Trupial Inn.

Peter Hughes also offers day or night glass-bottom-boat tours in a boat equipped with underwater lights.

Dive Curaçao & Watersports (tel. 61-4944, ext. 20, 1-4944), at the Princess Beach Hotel, offers scuba-diving at $25 for one dive, including tank, backpack, air, and weight, as well as equipment rental and trips to Santa Barbara Beach for reef watching and snorkeling at a wreck. A scuba lesson, including all equipment, is offered for $30. Snorkeling tours, costing $10 per person and lasting 1½ hours, are made at Boka Disorsaka and the Snorkel Trail of the underwater park. Boat and equipment are provided.

Scuba-divers and snorkelers can expect spectacular scenery in waters with visibility often exceeding 100 feet at the **underwater park** off the Princess Beach Hotel. There are steep walls, two shallow wrecks, lush gardens of soft corals, and more than 30 species of hard corals. Although access from shore is possible at Jan Thiel Bay and Santa Barbara Beach, most people visit the park by boat. For easy and safe mooring, the park has 16 mooring buoys, placed at the best dive and snorkel sites. A snorkel trail with underwater interpretive markers is laid out just east of the Princess Beach Hotel and is accessible from shore.

Santa Barbara Beach tours are also offered aboard the glass-bottom boat, costing $15 per person and lasting four hours. A stop is made for snorkeling at *Towboat*, the wreck of a tug in shallow water, with snorkel equipment provided. Snacks and drinks are available at the beach. You can also take a one-hour trip into the Curaçao Underwater Park in the glass-bottom boat for $5 per person.

Dive Curaçao has a cabin cruiser available for half- or full-day deep-sea fishing trips. One to four people can make a half-day excursion for $150, the same number paying $250 for a full day. If you prefer bottom fishing, they'll take you to the best ocean spots, charging $125 for half a day for one to four people. Bait, lines, tackle, and soft drinks are provided.

Golf

Curaçao Golf and Squash Club in Emmastad is open to the general public by arrangement only. Telephone Jan Cramar, the Holland-born golf pro, the day before you wish to play (tel. 7-3590). Greens fees are $10. Equipment can be rented at $3 for clubs, $2 for a pull cart, and $15 for an electric cart. The course is open on Monday from 8 a.m. to noon and 1 to 7 p.m. Other days, it's open from 8 a.m. to noon and 1 to 8 p.m., except that on Saturday and Sunday there's no lunch break.

A Fitness Center

Chirino, a sport and recreation center at 12 Orionweg (tel. 61-3346), has fully equipped studios for bodybuilding, aerobic dancing, fitness training, jazz dancing, massage, and sauna. Programs for youngsters can be found in the kiddies' gym and *arte infantil,* where children learn to dance, act, sing, and play. Chirino is open from 7:30 to 10 a.m. and 4 to 9 p.m.

Boating Tours

Taber Tours, Maduro Plaza, 19 Emancipatie Blvd. (tel. 7-6637), offers trips by sea as well as the sightseeing tours by bus recommended earlier. A combination sea excursion takes you to the Seaquarium, for a swim at Santa Barbara Beach, over the underwater park by glass-bottom boat, and snorkeling at a wreck (snorkeling equipment included). Soft drinks are served on board, and transportation to and from your hotel is provided. The cost is $27.50 per person for adults, $17.50 for children under 12.

A sunset sailing trip, costing $25 for adults, $15 for children, includes two hours of sailing while you feast on cheese, French bread, and wine.

A daytime trip, with lunch included, is the Coral sailing tour. You're picked up at your hotel, taken on a sailing trip to Santa Martha Bay, and served a light lunch at the Coral Cliff Hotel, where you can use all the hotel's facilities, including snorkeling gear. Beer and soft drinks are served during the sail. The cost is $35 for adults, $25 for children.

Tennis

There are courts at the Curaçao Caribbean, Golden Tulip Las Palmas, Princess Beach, and Holiday Beach Hotels. Las Palmas's court is open 24 hours a day.

AFTER DARK: Most of the action spins around six **casinos** at the Curaçao Caribbean, the Holiday Beach, the Princess Beach, the Curaçao Plaza, the Golden Tulip Las Palmas, and the San Marco, all hotels previously recommended. These hotel gaming houses usually start their action at 2 p.m., and some of them remain open until 4 a.m. The Princess Beach serves complimentary drinks.

Sometimes a sailor in port heads for **Campo Alegre,** known as "the compound." Others refer to it as "happy valley." This is the most famous, or notorious, bordello in the Caribbean. In the vicinity of the airport, the bordello is privately run, but under strict government controls. Controls or not, business is way down because of the fear of AIDS.

The **Willemstad Room** at the Curaçao Caribbean (tel. 62-5000) books some of the best acts on the island. There are two dinner seatings, one at 7 p.m. and again at 9 p.m., with meals costing from $25. For current shows, check the bulletin board in the hotel's lobby or else call. Remember to make a reservation in season, as the room can fill up quickly with the hotel's own guests. Live entertainment is offered nightly except Wednesday, with show time at 11 p.m. The minimum consumption is about $10 per person.

Sabine's, Curaçao Plaza Hotel (tel. 61-2500). On the mezzanine level of Willemstad's most prominent hotel, this disco and nightclub has traditionally employed some of the best DJs on the island. Amid a blue-and-red decor dotted with artificial stars are three different bars and an animated crowd. Open seven nights a week from 10 p.m. to very late, the club asks $8.60 per person as a cover on Friday and Saturday. On other nights entrance is free. Live entertainment is sometimes offered between disco sessions.

La Fontaine Discothèque Night Club, 78 Cas Coraweg (tel. 7-8596), about a ten-minute taxi ride from the center of Willemstad, is one of the most sophisticated after-dark spots on the island. It has a modern design and an array of psychedelic lighting. Andy Rhodes and Robby Dos Santos run this friendly disco/nightclub that occasionally has live shows. It's open from 10 p.m. to 4 p.m. Tuesday through Sunday, with drinks costing from $3. There's a $6 cover on weekends.

The **Holiday Beach Hotel and Casino,** 31 Pater Euwensweg (tel. 62-5400), presents some of the splashiest musical comedies and revues in Curaçao. You get the show and dinner for $27.50 per person. Dinner is served between 7 and 8:30 p.m., with show time at 9 p.m. A cocktail show, costing $12 and including two drinks, is at 11 p.m. On Friday and Saturday a Night Owl show, also costing $12 and including two drinks per person, is presented at 1 a.m. Reservations are required.

Studio Club, 2 Ontarioweg, Salinja (tel. 61-2272), is a place to come just for drinks if you wish, but you can also dance as much as you want to from 9 p.m. until 4 a.m., except on Monday when it's closed and on Friday and Saturday when live shows feature local and international artists. On weekends, a cover charge of 15 NAf ($7.75) is levied, and reservations are advisable. The club's owner, E. Graanoogst, gives guests his personal attention.

The **Temple Theater** (tel. 61-3410) is a restored landmark in the heart of Willemstad on the Wilhelminaplein by the Waterfort, built in 1867. A comfortable, air-conditioned, modern, multipurpose theater, it presents movies, plays, concerts, and stage shows.

Date_____

FROMMER BOOKS
PRENTICE HALL PRESS
ONE GULF + WESTERN PLAZA
NEW YORK, NY 10023

Friends:

Please send me the books checked below:

FROMMER'S $-A-DAY GUIDES™

(In-depth guides to sightseeing and low-cost tourist accommodations and facilities.)

☐ Europe on $25 a Day $12.95
☐ Australia on $25 a Day $10.95
☐ Eastern Europe on $25 a Day $10.95
☐ England on $35 a Day.............. $10.95
☐ Greece on $25 a Day................ $10.95
☐ Hawaii on $50 a Day................$10.95
☐ India on $15 & $25 a Day........... $9.95
☐ Ireland on $30 a Day............... $10.95
☐ Israel on $30 & $35 a Day $10.95
☐ Mexico on $20 a Day $10.95

☐ New Zealand on $25 a Day $10.95
☐ New York on $45 a Day............. $9.95
☐ Scandinavia on $50 a Day........... $10.95
☐ Scotland and Wales on $35 a Day..... $10.95
☐ South America on $30 a Day $10.95
☐ Spain and Morocco (plus the Canary Is.) on $40 a Day $10.95
☐ Turkey on $25 a Day............... $10.95
☐ Washington, D.C., on $40 a Day $10.95

FROMMER'S DOLLARWISE GUIDES™

(Guides to sightseeing and tourist accommodations and facilities from budget to deluxe, with emphasis on the medium-priced.)

☐ Alaska............................ $12.95
☐ Austria & Hungary $11.95
☐ Belgium, Holland, Luxembourg $11.95
☐ Egypt............................. $11.95
☐ England & Scotland $11.95
☐ France............................ $11.95
☐ Germany $11.95
☐ Italy............................. $11.95
☐ Japan & Hong Kong $12.95
☐ Portugal (incl. Madeira & the Azores) . $11.95
☐ South Pacific...................... $12.95
☐ Switzerland & Liechtenstein $11.95
☐ Bermuda & The Bahamas........... $10.95
☐ Canada $12.95
☐ Caribbean $12.95

☐ Cruises (incl. Alaska, Carib, Mex, Hawaii, Panama, Canada, & US) $12.95
☐ California & Las Vegas $11.95
☐ Florida............................ $10.95
☐ Mid-Atlantic States $12.95
☐ New England....................... $11.95
☐ New York State $11.95
☐ Northwest......................... $11.95
☐ Skiing in Europe $12.95
☐ Skiing USA—East................... $10.95
☐ Skiing USA—West $10.95
☐ Southeast & New Orleans............ $11.95
☐ Southwest......................... $11.95
☐ Texas............................. $11.95

TURN PAGE FOR ADDITIONAL BOOKS AND ORDER FORM.